For
reference

The GALE ENCYCLOPEDIA of CHILDREN'S HEALTH

INFANCY THROUGH ADOLESCENCE

The GALE ENCYCLOPEDIA *of* CHILDREN'S HEALTH

INFANCY THROUGH ADOLESCENCE

VOLUME

2

D-K

KRISTINE KRAPP AND JEFFREY WILSON, EDITORS

THOMSON

™

GALE

Detroit • New York • San Francisco • San Diego • New Haven, Conn. • Waterville, Maine • London • Munich

THOMSON
GALE

The Gale Encyclopedia of Children's Health: Infancy through Adolescence

Product Manager
Kate Millson

Project Editors
Kristine M. Krapp, Jeffrey J. Wilson

Editorial
Donna Batten, Shirelle Phelps, Erin Watts

Editorial Support Services
Luann Brennan, Andrea Lopeman, Mark Springer

Rights Acquisition Management
Margaret Abendroth, Ann Taylor

Imaging
Randy Bassett, Lezlie Light, Dan Newell, Christine O'Bryan, Robyn Young

Product Design
Michelle DiMercurio, Tracey Rowens

Composition and Electronic Prepress
Evi Seoud, Mary Beth Trimper

Manufacturing
Wendy Blurton, Dorothy Maki

Indexing
Synapse Corp. of Colorado

LIBRARY OF CONGRESS CATALOGING-IN-PUBLICATION DATA

The Gale encyclopedia of children's health : infancy through adolescence / Kristine Krapp and Jeffrey Wilson, editors.
    p. cm.
        Includes bibliographical references and index.
        ISBN 0-7876-9241-7 (set hardcover : alk. paper) –
        ISBN 0-7876-9427-4 (v. 1) – ISBN 0-7876-9428-2 (v. 2) –
        ISBN 0-7876-9429-0 (v. 3) – ISBN 0-7876-9430-4 (v. 4)
        1. Children–Health and hygiene–Encyclopedias.
        2. Children–Diseases–Encyclopedias. 3. Pediatrics–
        Encyclopedias. [DNLM: 1. Pediatrics–Encyclopedias–
        English. 2. Pediatrics–Popular Works. 3. Child
        Welfare–Encyclopedias–English. 4. Child Welfare–
        Popular Works. 5. Infant Welfare–Encyclopedias–English.
        6. Infant Welfare–Popular Works. WS 13 G1515 2005]
        I. Title: Encyclopedia of children's health. II. Krapp,
        Kristine M. III. Wilson, Jeffrey, 1971- IV. Gale Group.

RJ26.G35 2005
618.92'0003–dc22
                                          2005003478

This title is also available as an e-book
ISBN 7876-9425-8 (set)
Contact your Gale sales representative for ordering information.
ISBN 0-7876-9241-7 (set)
0-7876-9427-4 (Vol. 1)
0-7876-9428-2 (Vol. 2)
0-7876-9429-0 (Vol. 3)
0-7876-9430-4 (Vol. 4)
Printed in Canada
10 9 8 7 6 5 4 3 2 1

CONTENTS

LIST OF ENTRIES

A

Abandonment
Abdominal wall defects
Acetaminophen
Acne
Acromegaly and gigantism
Acting out
Adaptive behavior scales for infants and early childhood
Addiction
Adenoid hyperplasia
Adenovirus infections
Adjustment disorders
Adolescence
Adoption
Aggressive behavior
Albinism
Alcoholism
Allergic purpura
Allergic rhinitis
Allergies
Allergy shots
Allergy tests
Allowance and money management
Alopecia
Alpha-fetoprotein test
Alternative school
Amblyopia
Amenorrhea
Amniocentesis
Anabolic steroids
Analgesics
Anaphylaxis
Anatomical age
Anemias

Angelman's syndrome
Animal bite infections
Anorexia nervosa
Antenatal testing
Antepartum testing
Antiacne drugs
Antiasthmatic drugs
Antibiotics
Antibiotics, topical
Antidepressants
Antiepileptics
Antihistamines
Antisocial behavior
Antisocial personality disorder
Antiviral drugs
Anxiety
Apgar testing
Apnea of infancy
Appendicitis
Arteriovenous fistula
Asphyxia neonatorum
Assessment
Asthma
Ataxia telangiectasia/chromosome breakage disorders
Atopic dermatitis
Atrial septal defect
Attachment between infant and caregiver
Attention-deficit/Hyperactivity disorder (AD/HD)
Audiometry
Auditory discrimination test
Autism

B

Babysitters
Battered child syndrome
Bayley Scales of Infant Development
Bed-wetting
Beery-Buktenica test
Bejel
Bell's palsy
Biliary atresia
Bilingualism/Bilingual education
Bilirubin test
Binge eating disorder
Bipolar disorder
Birth order
Birthmarks
Bites and stings
Blood sugar tests
Bonding
Botulism
Brachial plexopathy, obstetric
Breast development
Breath holding spells
Breech birth
Bronchiolitis
Bronchitis
Bruises
Bruton's agammaglobulinemia
Bulimia nervosa
Bullies
Burns

Fear
Febrile seizures
Fetal alcohol syndrome
Fetal hemoglobin test
Fever
Fever of unknown origin
Fifth disease
Fine motor skills
Fingertip injuries
Flu vaccine
Fluoridation
Folic acid
Food allergies and sensitivities
Food poisoning
Foreign objects
Foster care
Fractures
Fragile X syndrome
Friedreich's ataxia
Frostbite and frostnip

G

Galactosemia
Gangs
Gastroenteritis
Gastroesophageal reflux disease
Gender constancy
Gender identity
Gross motor skills
Growth hormone tests

H

Handedness
Hand-eye coordination
Hand-foot-mouth disease
Head injury
Head Start programs
Headache
Hearing impairment
Heart murmurs
Heat disorders
Heavy metal poisoning
Heimlich maneuver

Hemophilia
Hemophilus infections
Hepatitis A
Hepatitis B
Hepatitis B vaccine
Hereditary fructose intolerance
Hereditary hemorrhagic
    telangiectasia
Hernia
Herpes simplex
Hib vaccine
High-risk pregnancy
Hirschsprung's disease
Histiocytosis X
HIV infection and AIDS
Hives
Home schooling
Homosexuality and bisexuality
Hospitalization
Human bite infections
Hydrocephalus
Hyperglycemia
Hyperhidrosis
Hyper-IgM syndrome
Hypertension
Hyperthyroidism
Hypoglycemia
Hypogonadism
Hypospadias
Hypothyroidism
Hypotonia

I

Idiopathic thrombocytopenic
    purpura
Ileus
Immobilization
Immune system development
Immunodeficiency
Immunoglobulin deficiency
    syndromes
Impetigo
Impulse control disorders
Inclusion conjunctivitis
Infant massage

Infant mortality
Infectious mononucleosis
Influenza
Insect sting allergy
Intelligence
Intermittent explosive disorder
Intersex states
Intestinal obstructions
Intrauterine growth retardation
Intravenous rehydration
Iron deficiency anemia
Irritable bowel syndrome
Itching

J

Jaundice
Juvenile arthritis

K

Kawasaki syndrome
Klinefelter syndrome

L

Labyrinthitis
Lactation
Lactose intolerance
Language delay
Language development
Language disorders
Laxatives
Lead poisoning
Learning disorders
Leukemias, acute
Leukemias, chronic
Lice infestation
Lipidoses
Lisping
Listeriosis
Lying
Lyme disease
Lymphadenitis

PLEASE READ—IMPORTANT INFORMATION

The Gale Encyclopedia of Children's Health is a medical reference product designed to inform and educate readers about a wide variety of health issues related to children, ranging from prenatal to adolescence. Thomson Gale believes the product to be comprehensive, but not necessarily definitive. It is intended to supplement, not replace, consultation with a physician or other healthcare practitioner. While Thomson Gale has made substantial efforts to provide information that is accurate, comprehensive, and up-to-date, Thomson Gale makes no representations or warranties of any kind, including without limitation, warranties of merchantability or fitness for a particular purpose, nor does it guarantee the accuracy, comprehensiveness, or timeliness of the information contained in this product. Readers should be aware that the universe of medical knowledge is constantly growing and changing, and that differences of medical opinion exist among authorities. They are also advised to seek professional diagnosis and treatment for any medical condition, and to discuss information obtained from this book with their healthcare provider.

INTRODUCTION

The Gale Encyclopedia of Children's Health: Infancy Through Adolescence (GECH) is a one-stop source for medical information that covers common and rare diseases and medical conditions, immunizations and drugs, procedures, and developmental issues. It particularly addresses parents' concerns about their children's health from before birth through age 18. The book avoids medical jargon, making it easier for the layperson to use. The Gale Encyclopedia of Children's Health presents authoritative, balanced information and is more comprehensive than single-volume family medical guides.

SCOPE

Approximately 600 full-length articles are included in The Gale Encyclopedia of Children's Health. Articles follow a standardized format that provides information at a glance. Rubrics include:

Diseases/Disorders
- Definition
- Description
- Demographics
- Causes and symptoms
- Diagnosis
- Treatment
- Prognosis
- Prevention
- Parental concerns
- Resources
- Key terms

Procedures
- Definition
- Purpose
- Description
- Risks
- Normal results

- Parental concerns
- Resources
- Key terms

Immunizations/Drugs
- Definition
- Description
- General use
- Precautions
- Side effects
- Interactions
- Parental concerns
- Resources
- Key terms

Development
- Definition
- Description
- Common problems
- Parental concerns
- Resources
- Key terms

A preliminary list of diseases, conditions, procedures, drugs, and developmental issues was compiled from a wide variety of sources, including professional medical guides and textbooks, as well as consumer guides and encyclopedias. The advisory board, composed of seven doctors with specialties in pediatric medicine, evaluated the topics and made suggestions for inclusion. Final selection of topics to include was made by the medical advisors in conjunction with Thomson Gale editors.

INCLUSION CRITERIA

A preliminary list of diseases, conditions, procedures, drugs, and developmental issues was compiled from a wide variety of sources, including professional medical guides and textbooks, as well as consumer guides and encyclopedias. The advisory board, composed of seven doctors with specialties in pediatric medicine, evaluated the topics and made suggestions for inclusion. Final selection of topics to include was made by the medical advisors in conjunction with Thomson Gale editors.

ABOUT THE CONTRIBUTORS

The essays were compiled by experienced medical writers, including healthcare practitioners and educators, pharmacists, nurses, and other healthcare professionals. *GECH* medical advisors reviewed all of the completed essays to insure that they are appropriate, up-to-date, and medically accurate.

HOW TO USE THIS BOOK

The Gale Encyclopedia of Children's Health has been designed with ready reference in mind:

- Straight **alphabetical arrangement** allows users to locate information quickly.
- Bold faced terms function as *print hyperlinks* that point the reader to related entries in the encyclopedia.
- A list of **key terms** is provided where appropriate to define unfamiliar words or concepts used within the context of the essay. Additional terms may be found in the **glossary**.

- **Cross-references** placed throughout the encyclopedia direct readers to where information on subjects without their own entries can be found. Synonyms are also cross-referenced.
- A **Resources section** directs users to sources of further medical information.
- An appendix of updated **growth charts** from the U.S. Centers for Disease Control for children from birth through age 20 is included.
- An appendix of **common childhood medications** is arranged alphabetically and includes descriptions of each drug and important information about their uses.
- A comprehensive **general index** allows users to easily target detailed aspects of any topic, including Latin names.

GRAPHICS

The Gale Encyclopedia of Children's Health is enhanced with approximately 300 full-color images, including photos, tables, and customized line drawings.

ADVISORY BOARD

An advisory board made up of prominent individuals from the medical community provided invaluable assistance in the formulation of this encyclopedia. They defined the scope of coverage and reviewed individual entries for accuracy and accessibility. The editors would therefore like to express our appreciation to them.

G. Peter Beardsley, MD
Department of Pediatrics
Yale University School of Medicine
New Haven, CT

Kirsten Bechtel, MD
Asst. Professor of Pediatric Emergency Medicine/Attending Physician
Yale-New Haven Children's Hospital
New Haven, CT

Paul Checchia, MD, FAAP
Director, Pediatric Cardiac Intensive Care Program
St. Louis Children's Hospital
Assistant Professor of Pediatric Critical Care and Cardiology

Washington University School of Medicine
St. Louis, MO

Renuka Gera, MD
Professor and Associate Chair, Pediatrics/Human Development
Michigan State University
Lansing, MI

Elizabeth Secord, MD
Assistant Professor, Dept. of Pediatrics
Wayne State University
Training Program Director, Allergy and Immunology Div.
Children's Hospital of Michigan
Detroit, MI

Jonathan B. Strober, MD
Director, Clinical Services, Division of Child Neurology
Assistant Clinical Professor, Neurology and Pediatrics
University of California at San Francsico, Division of Child Neurology
San Francisco, CA

Rebecca Swan, MD
Interim Chief, Division of General Pediatrics
Pediatric Residency Program Director
Vanderbilt Children's Hospital
Nashville, TN

CONTRIBUTORS

Margaret Alic, PhD
Medical Writer
Eastsound, WA

Kim Saltel Allan, R.D., BHEcol
Clinical Dietitian
Winnipeg, Manitoba, Canada

Linda K. Bennington, MSN, CNS, RNC
Lecturer, School of Nursing
Old Dominion University
Norfolk, VA

Mark A. Best, MD, MBA, MPH
Pathologist
Eastview, KY

Rosalyn Carson-Dewitt, M.D.
Medical Writer
Durham, NC

Angela Costello
Medical Editor
Cleveland, OH

L. Lee Culvert
Medical Writer
Alna, ME

Tish Davidson, MA
Medical Writer
Fremont, CA

L. Fleming Fallon, Jr., MD, DrPH
Professor of Public Health
Bowling Green University
Bowling Green, OH

Paula Ford-Martin, MA
Medical Writer
Warwick, RI

Janie Franz
Medical Writer
Grand Forks, ND

Rebecca J. Frey, PhD
Medical Writer
New Haven, CT

Clare Hanrahan
Medical Writer
Asheville, NC

Crystal H. Kaczkowski, MSc.
Medical Writer
Chicago, IL

Christine Kuehn Kelly
Medical Writer
Havertown, PA

Monique Laberge, Ph.D.
Medical Writer
Philadelphia, PA

Aliene S. Linwood, BSN, DPA, FACHE
Medical and Science Writer
Athens, Ohio

Mark Mitchell, M.D.
Medical Writer
Seattle, WA

Deborah L. Nurmi, M.S.
Medical Writer, Public Health Researcher
Atlanta, GA

Martha Reilly, OD
Clinical Optometrist
Madison, WI

Joan M. Schonbeck, RN
Medical Writer
Marlborough, MA

Stephanie Dionne Sherk
Medical Writer
Ann Arbor, MI

Judith Sims, MS
Science Writer
Logan, UT

Jennifer E. Sisk, M.A.
Medical Writer
Philadelphia, PA

Genevieve Slomski, Ph.D.
Medical Writer
New Britain, CT

Deanna M. Swartout-Corbeil, RN
Medical Writer
Thompsons Station, TN

Samuel Uretsky, PharmD
Medical Writer
Wantagh, NY

Ken R. Wells
Freelance Writer
Laguna Hills, CA

D

Dandruff *see* **Seborrheic dermatitis**

Day care

Definition

Day care refers to the care provided for infants and toddlers, preschoolers, and school-aged children, either in their own homes, in the home of a relative or other caregiver, or in a center-based facility.

Description

The last half of the twentieth century saw a dramatic rise in the numbers of women with young children who worked outside of the home. In 2000, 55 percent of mothers with infants were in the labor force. In 2001, 64 percent of mothers with children under the age of six, and 78 percent of mothers with children ages six to seventeen were in the labor force. These developments led to an increased demand for childcare providers by parents while they are at work.

In 2001, 61 percent of all children participated in some sort of nonparental care. As children grow older, the likelihood they will receive care from someone other than a parent increases.

Types of day care

Center-based care

Center-based care may also be labeled child or daycare centers, nursery schools, or preschools. These facilities care for children in groups. They may have different sponsors, including universities, schools, churches, social service agencies, independent owners or chains, and employers. Many parents choose center-based care because they believe the presence of multiple caregivers, larger groups of children, and state inspections make them both safer and more dependable. Some parents also consider these types of centers a better learning environment for their children.

The National Association for the Education of Young Children (NAEYC) issues recommendations relating to the organization and structure of daycare centers, particularly those that provide care for infants and toddlers. These recommendations are considered to be the minimum standards a daycare center should observe. Their recommendations concerning staff to child ratios are as follows:

- There should be no more than four infants per caregiver, and no more than eight infants per one group of children in center-based care.

- There should be no more than four young toddlers (12–24 months) per caregiver, with a maximum of 12 young toddlers and three caregivers per group. They recommend there be no more than six older toddlers (24–36 months) per caregiver, and a maximum of 12 older toddlers and two caregivers per group.

Some of the advantages of center-based care are:

- The staff are trained and supervised.

- There are more resources and equipment available.

- Care is still available when a staff member is absent.

- The centers are more likely to be licensed and subject to state regulation.

- Children in center-based care demonstrate slightly better **cognitive development** than those cared for in homes, possibly because they have more opportunities to interact with other children and are exposed to more learning materials.

Some of the disadvantages of center-based care are:

- The costs are higher than for other types of care.

- The background of staff can vary greatly, and there is often greater staff turnover.

- Larger groups of children may mean less individual attention for the child.
- There is a greater likelihood of exposure to communicable illnesses.

Family childcare providers

Family childcare providers offer care for children in the provider's home. Requirements differ from state to state. However, the majority of states require that providers be regulated if they are watching more than four children. Many states may have a voluntary regulation process in place for those providers caring for four or fewer children. Regulations usually require providers to meet minimum health, **safety**, and **nutrition** standards. In addition, they are usually required to have a criminal background check. Some states yearly inspect the homes of family childcare providers, and many require ongoing training. Parents often make this childcare choice because they prefer their children to stay in a more home-like environment. This arrangement may be less expensive and more flexible than center-based care. Parents may also believe that their children are better off in smaller groups with a single caregiver.

The American Academy of Pediatrics recommends that family childcare providers should have six children or fewer per one adult caregiver, including the caregiver's own children. The total number should be fewer if infants and toddlers are involved. No caregiver who works alone should be caring for more than two children younger than two years of age.

Some of the advantages of family child care are:

- There are usually fewer children than in center-based care.
- There may be children of different ages.
- The child gets to stay in a home-like environment.

Some of the disadvantages of family child care are:

- Many family childcare providers are not licensed or regulated.
- Resources and equipment may vary widely.
- Family childcare providers normally work alone, which may make it more difficult to judge their work.

In-home caregivers

In-home care occurs in the child's own home. This care includes both live-in and live-out nannies and **babysitters**. Most in-home caregivers are not state-regulated, though many nanny-placement agencies are subject to state regulation. If in-home caregivers receive childcare subsidy payments, they may be required by many states to have a criminal background check done, and a very few states have minimal health and safety training requirements.

The advantages of in-home caregivers are:

- Children receive one-on-one care.
- Children may be safer and feel more secure in their own home.
- Parents may feel they have more control over the type of care their children receive.
- There is the possibility of more flexible scheduling.
- Care will usually be available even if the child is ill.

There are also disadvantages to in-home care. These include:

- It is often the most expensive type of care.
- The parent may bear the burden of obtaining background checks and providing ongoing supervision.

Care provided by relatives, friends, and neighbors

This type of care is often referred to as kith and kin care and may take place either in the child's or the caregiver's home. Some of the advantages of this type of care are:

- Parents may believe their children are receiving more loving, affectionate care and that the child is more secure.
- A relative, friend, or neighbor may be more likely to share the parents' values.
- The child receives one-on-one care.
- There may be a great deal of flexibility in this option.
- Care may be low- or no-cost.

Some of the disadvantages of having friends and relatives caring for children include:

- There is minimal regulation required by most states (though some parents may view this as an advantage).
- There may be a lack of care if the friend or relative is sick or on vacation.

The type of care chosen is related to the child's age. Twenty-three percent of newborn to two-year-olds and 22 percent of three- to six-year-olds are cared for in a home by a relative. Eighteen percent and 14 percent of these same respective ages were cared for by a nonrelative in a home environment. Higher percentages of three- to six-year-olds (56%) participated in center-based programs while only 17 percent of newborn to two-year-olds did. Some children may participate in more than one type of arrangement.

Chidren during play time at a day-care center. *(AP/Wide World Photos.)*

Center care is more common for black and white children with **working mothers** (30% and 24%, respectively) than for Hispanic children (10%). However, relative care is more common for Hispanic children (39%) versus black and white children (27% for blacks; 25% for whites). Use of parent care does not differ depending on racial and ethnic background. Black children with working mothers are more likely to be in care full-time than are white and Hispanic children (58% for black children, 36% for white children, and 34% for Hispanic children).

Choosing and finding high-quality child care is important and may play a key role in a child's health and development. Parents need to consider a variety of factors when deciding who should care for their child. There are several positive factors parents should look for when evaluating child-care options. These include:

• There is adequate supervision and attention to each child. Parents can find out their state's specific daycare regulations by contact their state's department of health and human services.

• Caregivers are well-trained and professional.

• Close attention is paid to health and safety issues. There are proper hand-washing routines, and the facility (or home) is clean. Caregivers have training in first aid and **cardiopulmonary resuscitation**. Safety precautions and accident prevention measures are in place.

• Children are encouraged to explore and are exposed to games, songs, and conversation in order to foster language development.

• There is appropriate and sufficient equipment and play materials.

• Parents are welcomed to make unscheduled visits and are encouraged to voice concerns and suggestions.

• Stability of caregivers is recognized as an important component of quality care. There is a low rate of staff turnover.

The following signs may indicate that there are problems with the child care provider or facility:

- The caregiver or center staff do not answer questions or address parent concerns.
- There is no written copy of center day-care policies.
- There is a high turnover of staff.
- The child indicates he or she is not happy with the day-care experience.
- There are recurring unexplained accidents.
- Parents are discouraged from participating in activities or voicing opinions about policies or practices.
- Other parents report concerns or problems.

Common problems

Parents who are deciding to place their children in some sort of day care should be aware that some problems may occur. A comprehensive study of early child care was started in 1991 by the National Institute of Child Health and Human Development (NICHD), part of the National Institutes of Health. More than 1,300 children were followed from birth to find out how the amount, type, and quality of day care they encounter affected their development. The study found that, at 15 months, child care neither promoted nor negatively affected infants' attachment to their mothers. However, a low-quality child-care environment combined with less sensitive mothering did leave infants less securely attached. The findings from this study also suggest that toddlers who spend long hours in day care display a slightly weaker bond with their mothers.

Child care can influence the behavior of the child, as well. More time spent in day care during the first two years led to more caregiver-reported behavioral problems at age two, although the effect was negated by age three. Higher quality care led to better child compliance and self-control, and children in larger groups (over three) appeared to be more cooperative than those in smaller groups. The biggest indicator of a child's behavior, however, was the family environment, particularly the sensitivity of mothering practices. This also carried over into the area of cognitive development, in which researchers found no benefit for children being raised exclusively by the mother. Those in high-quality care were at an advantage compared to those with exclusive maternal care, while low-quality child care presented a disadvantage. In general, fewer problem behaviors, higher cognitive performance, and better mother-child attachments were noted when children received higher quality care.

An additional concern for parents is that children who attend day care, especially in center-based environments,

are more frequently exposed to communicable diseases and more frequently experience respiratory illnesses, ear infections, and **diarrhea** than children who are cared for primarily at home. The size of the group the child is in seems to play a role. Larger groups have higher incidences than smaller groups. In contrast, however, children who spend more time in day care miss fewer days of school than their peers who were cared for at home. Finally, parents need to consider who will care for their child if the child is ill, since most daycare providers will not accept ill children for **fear** of infecting other children.

Parental concerns

Most parents are concerned about how their child will cope and adapt to being cared for by someone else. Parents can help their child adjust to a new childcare arrangement in several ways. They can arrange a visit to the center or home where they will receive care. Introducing them to the caregiver(s) may make the first days away from their parents easier. Some children like to bring a reminder of home with them when they attend day care. Parents may also choose one of the several books for children about day care and read it to their child.

See also Attachment between infant and caregiver.

Resources

BOOKS

Everstadt, Mary. *Home-Alone America: The Hidden Toll of Day Care, Behavioral Drugs, and Other Parent Substitutes.* East Rutherford, NJ: Penguin Group, 2005.

Jackson, Sonia, et al. *People under Three: Young Children in Day Care.* Florence, KY: Routledge, 2004.

Petrie, Steph, et al. *Respectful Care for Infants in Groups: The RIE Approach to Day Care Practice.* Herndon, VA: Jessica Kingsley Publishers, 2005.

Robertson, Brian C. *Day Care Deception: What the Child Care Establishment Isn't Telling Us.* San Francisco, CA: Encounter Books, 2004.

PERIODICALS

Greenspan, Stanley I. "Child Care Research: A Clinical Perspective." *Child Development* 74 (July-August 2003): 4, 1064–9.

"Questioning Child Care: A Government-funded Study Has Provoked Controversy about the Effects of Day Care on Children." *Harvard Mental Health Letter* 19 (December 2002): 6.

ORGANIZATIONS

National Association of Child Care Resource and Referral Agencies (NACCRRA). 1319 F. Street, NW, Suite 500, Washington, DC 20004–1106. Web site: <www.naccrra.org>.

WEB SITES

Ehrle, Jennifer, et al. "Who's Caring for Our Youngest Children? Child Care Patterns of Infants and Toddlers." *Urban Institute,* January 1, 2001. Available online at <www.urban.org/urlprint.cfm?ID=7495> (accessed January 11, 2005).

Fiene, Richard. "13 Indicators of Quality Child Care: Research Update." *United States Department of Health and Human Services,* 2002. Available online at <http://aspe.hhs.gov/hsp/ccquality-ind02/> (accessed January 11, 2005).

"Indicators of Child, Family, and Community Connections: Family, Work, and Child Care." *United States Department of Health and Human Services,* 2004. Available online at <http://aspe.hhs.gov/hsp/connections-charts04/ch3.htm> (accessed January 11, 2005).

Deanna M. Swartout-Corbeil, RN

Death and mourning

Definition

Mourning is the grieving process an individual experiences in response to the loss (often through death) of someone.

Description

Almost every child or adolescent faces the death of someone close (a relative, friend, or even a pet) at some point in his or her life. In fact, it is estimated that about 6 percent of children under age 15, or about three of every 50 children, will lose a parent. Though this figure is low compared to 25 percent at the turn of the twentieth century, children in the twenty-first century are more likely to experience more types of violent and catastrophic death, such as in wars, natural disasters, and homicides. Children experience deaths of their peers through **suicide**, acts of violence in school or on the street, and in terminal illness.

In 1900, children experienced death firsthand, seeing a loved one die on the farm or in the home. Then, two world wars came and children experienced death in the remote events of far off places. By the 1950s, though some children did experience the death of a loved one in the Korean War, these were few. Death became an abstraction, something children only read about or experienced in a movie or television. The Vietnam War and racial unrest during the civil rights era connected death as reported by newspapers and television to events occurring U.S. city streets. By the last two decades of the twentieth century, death came knocking on the school-house door as children brought weapons and shot other children. Drive-by shootings became more frequent in some neighborhoods. With the September 11, 2001, terrorist attacks on the United States, children began to see widespread death in a very personal way.

Children experience grief or mourning in very different ways than adults do. That is why over 160 bereavement centers have opened across the United States to help children mourn in ways that are appropriate to their age and developmental stage. These centers also allow children to participate in their own mourning rituals, which can be a comfort to children and a healthy way to move on. Unlike in some religious organizations, children are allowed to express anger as well as sadness about the death of their loved ones. They are encouraged to remember and create tangibles, such as paintings, stories, and even quilts, to remind them of the deceased.

Parents, caregivers, and teachers can provide support and minimize **fear** by answering honestly a child's questions about death. Encouraging communication helps the child through the essential grieving period. At one time, well-meaning adults felt that it was in the child's best interests to avoid discussing death. However, research has shown that children cope more successfully with a death if they feel included in the group that has experienced the loss and share in grieving and mourning.

When listening to a child's observations about death, adults must keep an open mind. A child may respond to the death of a grandmother, who used to make cupcakes for her, by observing that there will be no more cupcakes for dessert. This response could be interpreted as selfish, but it is in fact an expression of the child's loss in her own, very personal, terms. When a child learns of the accidental death of a playmate, he may ask to go out to **play**. This too may be an expression of the loss, as the child might want to remember his friend by engaging in the activity the two of them shared. The child's response to loss can be misunderstood by adults, especially by those who are also grieving. By passing judgment on the child's reactions, adults undermine the child's feelings and make the loss even more difficult for the child to handle.

For most people, deeply felt grief and loss are felt for about a week, followed by sorrow which can last two years or longer. In the days, weeks, and months that follow a death, adults should refrain from criticizing or reacting negatively to the child's feelings. When the child seems to repeat the same questions over and over, the same answers, as open and honest as possible, must be repeated patiently. Young children may express concern, either directly or through behavior, about being abandoned or neglected, or they may fear they have in some way caused the death. Changes in appetite, complaints of feeling sick, and changes in activity patterns can be indications that the child is worried or anxious. Adults can help a child deal with these feelings by acknowledging them and by reassuring the child that he will still be cared for and that no one can cause a death by thoughts and feelings.

When a death is unanticipated, as in a case of accident or violence, children may grieve longer and more intensely. Sad feelings may resurface over the years when the child experiences the loss anew, such as on holidays or other occasions. When a parent is deeply affected by the death of a loved person, the child may need the steady support of another adult. Books about illness and death can also be helpful. Adults should review the books in advance or ask a librarian, teacher, or counselor for advice. Issues of concern include age-appropriateness, situation-appropriateness, and religious point of view.

Children mourn a bit at a time, returning to their grief anew at different stages. Understanding a child's developmental stages helps parents, teachers, and caregivers provide appropriate responses and support for the child.

Toddlerhood and preschool age

By the time a child is about two and a half or three, the child is able to acknowledge that a death has occurred but will not really understand the reality of death. The child may echo the parents' words but may also express their lack of understanding. This is less denial than it is the inability to understand the concept of death. If a child has experienced the death of a **family** pet and understands that the dog or cat will not come back, the child is more likely to understand that the person who dies will not come back either.

Children between two and five years of age will often be restless, have **sleep** disturbances, or frightening dreams. They will sometimes revert to behaviors they had at a younger age, such as wetting the bed or **thumb sucking**. Because children of this developmental stage do not fully understand the concept of death, they may blame themselves, thinking that if only they had been good enough, their loved one would not have died.

Parents and other adults need to offer comfort in simple but honest words and in physical contact. They need to make sure the child's routine remains intact to preserve a sense of security in a loving environment.

Caregivers can draw pictures of the loved one or read books about mourning so the child can feel that they are not alone. Even children of this age can participate in funerals or other death rituals.

School age

By the age of six, children begin to understand that death is the cessation of bodily functions and that it is permanent. They show a morbid curiosity about death. They may talk about the details of death repeatedly. They want to know what happens physically and spiritually. Children of this age may also begin to acknowledge the universality of death, that it happens to everyone. But they may find it difficult to believe that it could ever happen to them.

Around this age, children are capable of taking part in rituals of death, such as visits with the deceased's family, the wake, and the funeral or memorial service. Prior to participating in a visit or funeral, it is helpful to prepare the child for the experience by explaining the purpose of the visit, how long it will last, and what the child will experience there. If a child expresses reluctance to participate in any aspect of the rituals of death, adults should accept the child's feelings and not exert pressure. Children look to adults and their peers for role models of how to conduct themselves at these events.

School-aged children can understand what death means, but they may be so overwhelmed that they act as if nothing has happened. Unexpressed feelings may surface as physical symptoms, such as stomachache, **headache**, and unusual complaint of tiredness. Behavior may also change, demonstrated by reluctance to go to school, daydreaming in class, or a decline in academic performance. Children of this age usually need extra time for physical activity. Even a short walk or a turn at the playground can help them work off some of the physical tensions connected with mourning.

Children both grieve alone and share their grief with others. Families can take a number of actions to support emotional healing, such as openly acknowledging the death, letting children participate in the rituals, and maintaining familiar routines such as school and bedtime activities. Parents should also let children witness their own adult grief. Rather than avoiding any mention of the deceased, it may help to display a photograph in a prominent place as a way of letting family members maintain memories. The visual reminder provides a way to help the child understand that it is okay to talk about the person who died.

For some children, the threat of being alone is central. One of their first questions is usually, "Who is going to take care of me?" Caregivers need to reassure the child that he or she is still loved and will be cared for.

Some older children begin to understand that death can happen to anyone, especially if a child their own age dies. The child may also worry that he or she may die at any time. This is especially a problem when the child's peer dies suddenly in an accident or after a long illness. Questions like "Will I die, too?" need reassuring answers.

Adolescence

Teenagers understand more as an adult does, but they may find it even more difficult than younger children to deal with their sorrow. Behavior problems, dropping out of school, physical complaints such as headache or chest **pain**, sexual promiscuity, and even suicide attempts may result from their feelings of pain and loss. Often, teenagers are reluctant to talk to adults who could help them through their grief.

The death of a peer, even someone they hardly knew, affects adolescents differently than the death of an older person. They must cope not only with the shock of life's unpredictability, but their own mortality.

Some adolescents may feel anger and want to rage at the world for letting death take a loved one. Research has shown that in the majority of cases adolescents in juvenile facilities have lost someone close to them.

Adolescents can also feel very vulnerable. Some express the need to feel like a child again, to be taken care of and protected, to feel secure in a safe world.

Common problems

Nighttime is particularly problematic since the child is now able to remember his or her loss without other distractions intervening. The child may also feel abandoned and alone. Many children will want to sleep with a parent or a sibling. Others request that a light be left on, even if they have long since stopped needing a nightlight.

Many children will also revert to a previous developmental stage. Some children will wet the bed. Others will request permission to sleep with a stuffed animal or return to sucking their thumbs. Some of these behaviors are comfort actions. They seek the security of the earlier developmental stage.

Older children and adolescents may express their bottled up anger through aggression toward other children. They may also turn that unresolved anger inward, becoming depressed or adopting a dark, gloomy lifestyle. Some adolescents may participate in risk-taking behaviors or want to do everything because they are worried that they may not have time to do everything before some random act kills them. Other children and adolescents may mutilate themselves or get body piercings or tattoos. (It should be noted that **piercing and tattoos** are

Students at Columbine High School in Littleton, Colorado comfort each other after the death of classmates. *(Photograph by David Zalubowski. AP/Wide World Photos.)*

not necessarily a cry for help; they may simply be acts of self-expression.)

Parental concerns

Parents need to help their children work through their grief, not get around it or avoid it. Parents should never minimize their child's grief. It is as individual as any adult's. Parents and other caregivers need to be available to listen as children express their grief in their own ways. This means that parents should seek counseling themselves if their own grief gets in the way of helping their children move through the grieving process.

Grieving children need their friends' support as much as adults do. Parents should make sure that children are allowed to phone their friends or play with them during the grieving process. Children will often express their sadness to friends much more easily than to their parents or other adults.

In addition, funerals and other death rituals are important to children as well as adults. These gatherings allow

PERIODICALS

Dickinson, Amy. "Kids and Funerals: Rather than Protect Our Children from Grief, We Should Encourage Them to Experience It." *Time* 155 (March 6, 2000): 79.

Kelly, Katy. "After a Loss, Kids Need to Mourn and Be Reassured." *U.S. News & World Report* 130 (January 8, 2001): 51.

Janie Franz

KEY TERMS

Bereavement—The emotional experience of loss after the death of a friend or relative.

Grief reaction—The normal depression felt after a traumatic major life occurrence such as the loss of a loved one.

Mourn—To express grief or sorrow, usually for a death.

---

the bereaved to express their sorrow, remember those they have lost, and receive and offer support from a community of friends and relatives. Death rituals often are the moments when the death of a loved one becomes real and not just tragic news. The bereaved often need to see the body of the deceased or participate in some activity that expresses the letting go of their dead loved one's presence in this life. Some families release balloons after a funeral; others light candles and let them burn down; both activities express the release of the deceased from life to death. Many of these activities coincide with religious beliefs and customs. Children who participate in a funeral by reading a poem or offering a gift are often better able to cope with their loss.

When to call the doctor

About one third of grieving children may need to seek professional counseling or therapy of some kind. This can be in individual sessions or in a group. It can also come from religious sources. Behaviors that warrant grief counseling or therapy are unresolved anger and hostility, not expressing grief at all or minimally, or depression or **anxiety** that interferes with daily activities that lasts for weeks or months.

Resources

BOOKS FOR ADULTS

Ashenburg, Katherine. *The Mourner's Dance: What We Do When People Die.* New York: North Point Press, 2003.

Doka, Kenneth J. *Living with Grief: Children, Adolescents, and Loss.* New York: Brunner-Routledge, 2000.

Huntley, Theresa. *Helping Children Grieve: When Someone They Love Dies.* Minneapolis, MN: Augsburg Fortress Publishers, 2002.

BOOKS FOR CHILDREN

Joosse, Barbara M. *Ghost Wings.* San Francisco, CA: Chronicle Books, 2001.

Parker, Marjorie Blain. *Jasper's Day.* Tonawanda, NY: Kids Can Press, 2002.

▌Decongestants

Definition

Decongestants are medicines used to relieve nasal congestion (stuffy nose).

Description

Decongestant drugs are chemically similar to epinephrine and norepinethrine, which are hormones that cause excitation in the body. These hormones cause constriction of blood vessels. A stuffy nose is caused by dilated blood vessels, which swell the nasal passages and make it harder to breathe.

Because these drugs have actions similar to the natural hormones, they have been used for purposes other than the treatment of nasal congestion. Some of these uses, such as treatment of hypotension, can be very important. Some of these drugs have also been abused because of their stimulant effects.

General use

A congested or stuffy nose is a common symptom of colds and **allergies**. This congestion results when membranes lining the nose become swollen. Decongestants relieve the swelling by narrowing the blood vessels that supply the nose. This narrowing reduces the blood supply to the swollen membranes, causing them to shrink.

These medicines do not cure colds or reverse the effects of histamines, chemicals released as part of the allergic reaction. They will not relieve all of the symptoms associated with colds and allergies, only the stuffiness.

Nasal decongestants may be used in many forms, including tablets, nose drops, and nasal sprays.

Precautions

Because decongestants have the potential for many side effects and adverse effects, they must be dosed carefully.

Side effects

When decongestants are used in the form of nose drops or nasal spray, the following adverse effects are common:

- stinging
- burning
- sneezing
- increased nasal discharge
- altered sense of taste

The following adverse effects are very rare when decongestants are given by drops or spray and also quite rare but possible when given by mouth:

- restlessness
- anxiety
- nervousness
- weakness
- difficulty breathing

Even more severe adverse effects are possible when decongestants are taken in large overdose. These include heart problems and tremors.

Some people complain of rebound congestion, which occurs when, after the decongestant has worn off, the congestion returns even worse than before.

Interactions

Decongestants do not have any interactions with drugs that would be taken by a generally healthy child. Even so, people using decongestants should review their drug therapy with a physician or pharmacist before starting treatment.

Although decongestants have the potential for serious side effects and adverse effects, they are very safe when used properly. However, nasal decongestants should only be used for three days at a time to avoid significant rebound effect. The most severe adverse effects can be avoided by using nose drops and nasal sprays in place of tablets or capsules.

Parental concerns

Parents administering these drugs to their children should use nose drops or nasal spray and avoid tablets or

---

> ## KEY TERMS
>
> **Constricted**—Made smaller or narrower.
>
> **Dilate**—To expand in diameter and size.
>
> **Hypotension**—Low blood pressure.
>
> **Tremor**—Involuntary shakiness or trembling.

---

capsules, which are more likely to cause adverse effects. They should also review the proper administration of nose drops and nasal spray with a physician or nurse.

Decongestants are subject to abuse. Parents should observe the behavior of adolescents and teens who may be purposely overdosing on these drugs.

In the event of severe adverse effects, parents should get medical care immediately for their child.

See also Cough suppressants; Expectorants.

Resources

BOOKS

Beers, Mark H., and Robert Berkow, eds. *The Merck Manual*, 2nd home ed. West Point, PA: Merck & Co., 2004.

Mcevoy, Gerald, et al. *AHFS Drug Information 2004*. Bethesda, MD: American Society of Healthsystems Pharmacists, 2004.

Siberry, George K., and Robert Iannone, eds. *The Harriet Lane Handbook*, 15th ed. Philadelphia: Mosby Publishing, 2000.

PERIODICALS

Daggy, A., et al. "Pediatric Visine (tetrahydrozoline) ingestion: case report and review of imidazoline toxicity." *Veterinary and Human Toxicology* 45, no. 4 (August 2003): 210–2.

Leung, A. K., and J. D. Kellner. "Acute sinusitis in children: diagnosis and management." *Journal of Pediatric Health Care* 18, no. 2 (March-April 2004): 72–6.

Watanabe, H., et al. "Oxymetazoline nasal spray three times daily for four weeks in normal subjects is not associated with rebound congestion or tachyphylaxis." *Rhinology* 41, no. 3 (September 2003): 167–74.

ORGANIZATIONS

American Academy of Emergency Medicine. 555 East Wells Street, Suite 1100, Milwaukee, WI 53202–3823. Web site: <www.aaem.org>.

American Academy of Pediatrics. 141 Northwest Point Boulevard, Elk Grove Village, IL 60007–1098. Web site: <www.aap.org>.

WEB SITES

Allergic Child. Available online at <www.allergicchild.com/> (accessed October 17, 2004.

HealthyMe! Available online at <www.ahealthyme.com/topic/childrens;jsessionid=5KZUMWMWHEM1 2CTYAEOS4EQ> (accessed October 17, 2004.)

Deanna M. Swartout-Corbeil, R.N.
Samuel Uretsky, PharmD

Dehydration

Definition

Dehydration is the loss of water and salts that are essential for normal body function.

Description

Dehydration occurs when the body loses more fluid than it takes in. Dehydration can upset the delicate fluid-salt balance needed to maintain healthy cells and tissues. The human body is generally over 60 percent water. The body works to maintain water balance through mechanisms such as the thirst sensation. When the body requires more water, the brain stimulates nerve centers to encourage a person to drink in order to replenish the water stores. Water intake can vary widely on a daily basis, influenced by such factors as access to water, thirst, habit, and cultural factors.

The kidneys are responsible for maintaining water balance through the elimination of waste products and excess water. Water is primarily absorbed through the gastrointestinal tract and excreted by the kidneys as urine. The variation in water volume ingested is dependent on the ability of kidneys to dilute and concentrate the urine as needed.

Children need more water than adults because they expend more energy, and most children who drink when they are thirsty get as much water as their systems require. Dehydration in children usually results from losing large amounts of fluid and not drinking enough water to replace the loss. This condition generally occurs in children who have a stomach flu characterized by **vomiting** and **diarrhea** or who cannot or will not take enough fluids to compensate for excessive losses associated with **fever** and sweating of acute illness. Dehydration can result from illness; a hot, dry climate; prolonged exposure to sun or high temperatures; not drinking enough water; and overuse of diuretics or other medications that increase urination.

Types of dehydration

Dehydration is classified as mild, moderate, or severe based on how much of the body fluid is lost, estimated by loss in bodyweight. Mild dehydration is the loss of no more than 5 to 6 percent loss of body weight. Loss of 7 to 10 percent is considered moderate dehydration. Severe dehydration (loss of over 10 percent of body weight) is a life-threatening condition that requires immediate medical care.

Complications of dehydration

When the body's fluid supply is severely depleted, hypovolemic shock is likely to occur. This condition, which is also called physical collapse, is characterized by pale, cool, clammy skin; rapid heartbeat; and shallow breathing.

Blood pressure sometimes drops so low it cannot be measured, and skin at the knees and elbows may become blotchy. **Anxiety**, restlessness, and thirst increase. After a child's temperature reaches 107°F (41.7°C) damage to the brain and other vital organs occurs quickly.

Demographics

Dehydration is a major cause of infant illness and death throughout the world. Dehydration is often a result of gastrointestinal disease and diarrhea in children. Among children in the United States, short-term diarrhea results in approximately 200,000 hospitalizations and 300 deaths per year. In developing countries, dehydration from illness is a common cause of death in children under five years of age, accounting for about 2 million deaths per year.

Causes and symptoms

Dehydration is a deficit of body water that results when the output of water exceeds intake. Dehydration stimulates a child's thirst mechanism. Causes of dehydration may include the following:

- decreased water or fluid intake
- diarrhea
- vomiting
- excessive heat
- excessive sweating
- fever
- excessive urination (polyuria)
- diuretics or other medication that increase fluid loss
- caffeine or alcohol consumption

Sweating and the output of urine both decrease during dehydration. If water intake continues to fall short of water loss, dehydration worsens and a child may become critically ill.

Reduced fluid intake may be a result of the following:

- appetite loss associated with acute illness
- nausea
- bacterial or viral infection or inflammation of the pharynx (pharyngitis)
- inflammation of the mouth caused by illness, infection, irritation, **canker sores**, or vitamin deficiency

Other conditions that can lead to dehydration include the following:

- disease of the adrenal glands, which regulate the body's water and salt balance and the function of many organ systems
- diabetes mellitus
- eating disorders
- kidney disease
- chronic lung disease

With mild dehydration, increased thirst and restlessness are usually the only apparent symptoms. In moderately dehydrated children, eyes are somewhat sunken, and the mouth and tongue are dry. Thirst is increased: an older child asks for water, and a younger child drinks eagerly when offered a cup or spoon of water. The skin is less elastic than it should be and is slow to return to its normal position after being pinched. The radial pulse (wrist area) is detectable, but rapid. The soft spot on a baby's head (fontanelle) is somewhat sunken. Two of the following symptoms usually indicate some degree of dehydration: drinks eagerly, thirsty, restless, irritable, sunken eyes, or skin pinch goes back slowly.

Children with severe dehydration are usually lethargic, in a stupor, or even in a coma. Symptoms are even more apparent (deeply sunken eyes without tears, very dry mouth and tongue, rapid and deep breathing). A skin pinch retracts very slowly (over two seconds). Children who are awake are very thirsty, although a child may drink poorly if in a stupor. A child may not have urinated for six hours or longer. When in hypovolemic shock, systolic blood pressure taken in the arm is low or not detectable, the arms and legs are cool, and the nail beds may have a bluish or purplish discoloration. Two of the following symptoms indicate severe dehydration: lethargic or unconscious, very slow skin pinch, sunken eyes, and not able to drink or drinking poorly.

Dehydration can cause confusion, **constipation**, discomfort, drowsiness, and fever. The skin turns pale and cold, the mucous membranes lining the mouth and nose lose their natural moisture. The pulse sometimes races and breathing becomes rapid. Significant fluid loss can cause serious neurological problems or death.

When to call the doctor

A doctor should be notified whenever an infant or child exhibits signs of dehydration or a parent is concerned that a stomach virus or other acute illness may lead to dehydration.

A doctor should also be notified if any of the following is the case:

- Symptoms of dehydration worsen.
- A breast-fed or bottle-fed infant is unable to feed or feeds poorly.
- An infant or child urinates very sparingly or does not urinate at all during a eight-hour period.
- An infant younger than two months of age has diarrhea or is vomiting.
- Dizziness, listlessness, or excessive thirst occurs.
- The child's heart is beating fast.
- The child has dry eyes, sunken eyes, a dry mouth, or is not producing tears.
- There is blood in the stool or vomit.

An infant can become dehydrated within hours after the onset of illness. In general, the smaller the child, the lower the threshold should be for healthcare intervention if dehydration is suspected.

Diagnosis

A child's symptoms and medical history alone usually suggest dehydration. Physical symptoms are usually all that is necessary for diagnosing dehydration, although laboratory tests may be ordered by the physician. Physical examination may reveal shock, rapid heart rate, and/or low blood pressure. Laboratory tests, including blood tests (to check electrolyte levels) and urine tests (e.g. urine specific gravity and creatinine), may be used to evaluate the severity of the problem.

Treatment

Increased fluid intake and replacement of lost electrolytes are extremely important for restoring fluid balances in infants and children who are dehydrated. Treatment is given based on severity of dehydration. Treatment should include two phases: a rehydration phase and a maintenance phase. In the rehydration phase, fluid losses are replaced quickly, within three to four hours until normal hydration is achieved. In the maintenance phase, calories and fluids are given. Rapid refeeding should follow rapid rehydration with the goal of returning the child to an unrestricted, age-appropriate diet including solids. Withholding foods to rest the gut is not recommended. Breastfeeding should be continued at all times through both stages of treatment. Full-strength formula is usually tolerated. Changing formula or diluting to half strength are common practices but are usually unnecessary and may even prolong symptoms and delay nutritional recovery.

To replace calories quickly during acute illness, food should be given as soon as the child will tolerate it. During both rehydration and maintenance phases, fluid losses from vomiting and diarrhea should be replaced continuously. Restricting lactose (milk and milk products) is usually not necessary but may be helpful in a child with a severe intestinal disease or diarrhea in a malnourished child.

Children with minimal dehydration weighing less than 10 kilograms (22 pounds) should be given 60 to 120 mL (2–4 ounces) of an oral rehydration solution (ORS) for each episode of vomiting or diarrheal stool. Those weighing more than 10 kg (22 lbs) should be given 120 to 240 mL (4–8 ounces). Food should not be restricted. Children with mild to moderate dehydration should be given 50 to 100 mL (roughly 2–3.5 ounces) of an ORS per kilogram body weight during two to four hours to replace fluid losses. Additional ORS should be administered to replace ongoing losses from vomiting and diarrhea. In a sick child, a teaspoon, syringe, or medicine dropper can be used to offer a small amount at first with amounts increasing as tolerated. If the child appears to want more, more can be given. Severe dehydration is a medical emergency requiring intravenous fluids immediately.

For moderate or severe dehydration, a child should be treated in a medical facility. Moderate dehydration can be treated orally, but severe dehydration requires the child to take fluids intravenously (IV). When treating dehydration, the underlying cause must also be addressed. For example, if dehydration is caused by vomiting, medications may be prescribed to resolve these symptoms. However, anti-diarrheal medications are not recommended in children. A child who is dehydrated due to diabetes, kidney disease, or adrenal gland disorders must receive treatment for these conditions as well as for the resulting dehydration.

For older children who are mildly dehydrated, just drinking plain water may be all the treatment that is needed. For infants and younger children, especially when ill, drinking a commercial ORS should be encouraged. Parents should follow label instructions when giving children Pedialyte or other commercial products recommended for relieving dehydration. Sports drinks are not recommended as they contain a lot of sugar and may worsen diarrhea.

In order to accurately calculate fluid loss, it is important to chart weight changes every day and keep a record of how many times a child vomits or has diarrhea. Parents should note how many times a baby's diaper must be changed.

Alternative treatment

Gelatin water may be substituted for electrolyte-replacement solutions if an ORS is unavailable. It is made by diluting a 3-oz package in a quart of water or by adding one-fourth teaspoon of salt and a tablespoon of sugar to a pint of water. Receiving the right amount of electrolytes is very important, and thus homemade remedies such as gelatin (or adding salt or sugar to water) are not recommended because of the potential for quantity errors when mixing. However, these may be useful if ORS cannot be obtained in an emergency. Parents should keep a can of ORS on hand for emergencies.

Formulas containing soy fiber have been reported to reduce liquid stools.

Prognosis

Mild dehydration rarely results in complications. If the cause is eliminated and lost fluid is replaced, mild dehydration can usually be cured quickly.

Vomiting and diarrhea that continue for several days without adequate fluid replacement can be fatal. However, dehydration that is rapidly recognized and treated has a good outcome.

Prevention

Ensuring that children always drink adequate fluids during an illness helps to prevent dehydration. Parents can prevent dehydration in infants and children who are vomiting or who have diarrhea by increasing fluids to compensate for losses. Infants and children with diarrhea and vomiting should be given ORS such as Pedialyte immediately to help prevent dehydration.

Children who are not ill can maintain proper fluid balance by drinking water or fluids even before they are thirsty. Children should drink fluids before going outside to **exercise** or **play** (especially on a hot day). Dehydration can usually be prevented by drinking enough fluid for urine to remain the color of pale straw. Water in foods, especially fruits and vegetables, is a great source of fluid. Fruits and vegetables can contain up to 95 percent water, so a well-balanced diet is a good way to stay hydrated.

Parents should know whether any medication their child is taking can cause dehydration and should get

KEY TERMS

Diuretic—A group of drugs that helps remove excess water from the body by increasing the amount lost by urination.

Electrolytes—Salts and minerals that produce electrically charged particles (ions) in body fluids. Common human electrolytes are sodium chloride, potassium, calcium, and sodium bicarbonate. Electrolytes control the fluid balance of the body and are important in muscle contraction, energy generation, and almost all major biochemical reactions in the body.

prompt medical care to correct any underlying condition that increases the risk of dehydration.

Other methods of preventing dehydration and ensuring adequate fluid intake are as follows:

- eating more soup at mealtime
- drinking plenty of water and juice at mealtime and between meals
- keeping a glass of water nearby

Children should not be given coffee or tea, because they increase body temperature and water loss. Avoiding caffeinated soft drinks may also reduce the risk of dehydration. These beverages are all diuretics (substances that increase fluid loss).

Resources

BOOKS

Batmanghelidj, F. *Water: For Health, For Healing, For Life: You're Not Sick, You're Thirsty!* New York: Warner Books, 2003.

Kleinman, Ronald E., and the American Academy of Pediatrics Committee on Nutrition. *Pediatric Nutrition Handbook,* 5th ed. Elk Grove Village, IL: American Academy of Pediatrics, 2003.

Physicians Committee for Responsible Medicine. *Healthy Eating for Life for Children.* Hoboken, NJ: Wiley, 2002.

Speakman, Elizabeth, and Norma Jean Weldy. *Body Fluids and Electrolytes,* 8th ed. London: Mosby Incorporated, 2001.

Willett, Walter C., and P. J. Skerrett. *Eat, Drink, and Be Healthy: The Harvard Medical School Guide to Healthy Eating.* New York: Simon & Schuster Source, 2002.

Workman, M. Linda. *Introduction to Fluids, Electrolytes and Acid-Base Balance.* London: Saunders, 2001.

PERIODICALS

Steiner, M. J., et al. "Is this child dehydrated?" *Journal of the American Medical Association* 291, no. 22 (June 2004): 2746–54.

ORGANIZATIONS

American Academy of Pediatrics. 141 Northwest Point Blvd., Elk Grove Village, IL 60007–1098. Web site: <www.aap.org>.

American College of Emergency Physicians. 1125 Executive Circle, Irving, TX 75038–2522. Web site: <www.acep.org>.

WEB SITES

Rehydration Project. Available online at <www.rehydrate.org> (accessed November 16, 2004).

"Why Is Dehydration so Dangerous?" *Rehydration Project.* Available online at <www.rehydrate.org/dehydration/index.html> (accessed November 16, 2004).

Crystal Heather Kaczkowski, MSc.
Maureen Haggerty

Dental development

Definition

Dental development is the process by which children develop their first and second (permanent) teeth.

Description

A child's first set of 20 teeth are called baby, primary, deciduous, or milk teeth. As these teeth fall out, they are replaced by 32 permanent, adult, or secondary teeth. The entire process of dental development may take more than two decades. Both primary and permanent teeth usually erupt (break through the gum) in a specific order on each side of the upper and lower jaws. However, the timing of both primary and permanent tooth eruption can vary by two or more years.

Both the timing of dental development and tooth size are determined primarily by heredity. Individuals differ greatly in the size of the crown (the part of the tooth above the gum line). Except for the earliest stages of **prenatal development**, and possibly the third permanent molars or wisdom teeth, dental development in girls proceeds ahead of that in boys, often by as much as 6 percent. Girls also have slightly smaller crowns and slightly shorter tooth roots than boys.

Prenatal

Dental development begins at about three weeks of gestation. By six weeks of gestation the tips or cusps of the primary teeth appear. By the fourth month the hard tissues (the enamel and dentin) of the primary teeth have begun to form. The enamel crowns of most primary teeth are fully formed by eight months of gestation. Permanent teeth begin to form shortly before or at birth.

Baby teeth

At birth the developing teeth usually are still embedded in the gums. Occasionally a baby is born with some erupted teeth or teeth that erupt shortly after birth. These natal or neonatal teeth usually are poorly formed and mobile. However in most infants the front teeth begin to peek through the gums between four and eight months. Generally from about six months on, children get four new teeth every four months. By 12 to 15 months all of the baby teeth within the gums have formed crowns. Most children have all 20 baby teeth by the age of two-and-a-half to three years. The permanent teeth continue to develop within the jaw.

Baby teeth erupt in pairs on the right and left of the mouth, alternating between the lower and upper jaws, and proceeding from front to back. The 20 primary teeth usually erupt in the following order:

- four front teeth or central incisors, first in the lower jaw and then in the upper jaw
- four lateral incisors, on each side of the front teeth, uppers before lowers
- four first molars, uppers first
- four canines or cuspids, between the lateral incisors and the first molars, usually uppers before lowers
- four second molars behind the first molars, lowers first

Baby teeth may come in straight or at an angle, appearing crooked, although they eventually straighten out. Once all of the baby teeth have erupted, the tongue adapts to their shape and the child's pre-teeth swallowing pattern switches to an adult pattern.

Children start losing their baby teeth at about age six, after the permanent front teeth are almost formed beneath the gums. The pressure of the developing permanent teeth causes the roots of the baby teeth to dissolve. Without their anchor in the jaw, the baby teeth loosen and eventually fall out. Most children lose their lower front baby teeth first. The earlier that the baby teeth come in, the earlier they will fall out. Most children have lost all of their baby teeth by age 13.

Permanent teeth

Between the ages of two-and-a-half and six, the permanent teeth continue to develop within the jaw. The first permanent teeth, the six-year-molars that become the first permanent molars, erupt behind each of the four second baby molars, usually between the ages of five and six. If the baby teeth are properly positioned and aligned, the six-year-molars usually erupt properly. If the baby teeth are pushed too close together, the six-year-molars will be too far forward, crowding the permanent teeth that erupt in front of them. However if the six-year-molars erupt properly and if the jaw is large enough, the permanent teeth have a good chance of coming in correctly.

By about age eight, enamel has formed on all of the permanent teeth except the wisdom teeth. A permanent tooth comes in completely about two months after the corresponding baby tooth is lost. Between the ages of about six and 12 to 14, as the jaw grows, 28 permanent teeth erupt, replacing the primary teeth, incisor for incisor, canine for canine, premolar or bicuspid for molar. The 32 permanent teeth generally erupt in the following order:

- four six-year or first molars
- four central incisors or front teeth, first in the lower jaw and then in the upper jaw
- four lateral incisors, lowers usually first
- four canine teeth, lowers first
- four first premolars or bicuspids, between the canines and the six-year molars, uppers usually first
- four second premolars or bicuspids, between the first premolars and the six-year or first molars, uppers usually first
- four second molars, behind the first molars, lowers usually first
- four third molars or wisdom teeth at the back, usually between ages 17 and 21

Common problems

Teething

Teething (the eruption of the primary teeth through the gums) may cause discomfort or **pain**, particularly with the large molars. Teething babies may:

- be restless and irritable
- lose their appetites
- sleep poorly
- cry excessively
- have flushed cheeks
- have a slight **fever**
- have congestion
- dribble or drool
- have red, swollen gums at the new teeth sites

- rub their gums
- suck their thumbs
- want something to chew on

For teething symptoms, parents may massage the gums to relieve discomfort and offer teething **toys** to help speed tooth eruption. A frozen teething toy numbs the gums and reduces swelling, although it should not be left on the gum for more than one minute without a break. They may also relieve symptoms by the following:

- massaging the gums, with or without ice
- giving the baby a cold teething ring
- encouraging the baby to chew on cold, wet washcloth or frozen bagel
- administering **acetaminophen** (Tylenol)

Eruptions of the permanent teeth are usually much less distressing, although the eruption of the first four broad permanent molars may cause discomfort. As the permanent molars push through the gums, they often leave a flap of tissue over the tooth. If food becomes trapped under the flap, the gums may become sore, swollen, and painful, infected, or abscessed.

Developmental delay

While dental development may be slightly advanced in obese children, development delay can occur with the emergence of some permanent teeth. Delay can be caused by the following:

- hereditary factors
- chronic **malnutrition**
- developmental disorders
- hyperdontia (extra or supernumerary teeth)
- **Down syndrome**
- radiation or chemotherapy
- cysts or tumors
- the absence of lateral incisors or wisdom teeth

Decay

The enamel on baby teeth is thinner and softer than on permanent teeth and decay can move through it very rapidly. Some children develop decay as soon as a tooth erupts and about 50 percent of two-year-olds have at least one cavity.

Baby bottle **tooth decay** occurs when sugary liquids, including milk, juice, or formula, cling to the baby's teeth, particularly when the child is put to bed with a bottle. The decay occurs most often in the upper front teeth but other teeth also can be affected. If a decayed baby tooth is lost too early, the adjacent teeth may move into the space, causing crooked and over-crowded permanent teeth.

Malocclusion

In a perfect jaw, all of the teeth fit exactly without crowding or spacing. The teeth are not rotated, twisted, or leaning forward or backward. With a perfect bite (occlusion), the teeth of the upper jaw slightly overlap those of the lower jaw. The points of the molars fit into the grooves of the opposing molars.

Few children develop perfect teeth and occlusion. More than 90 percent of children have some degree of **malocclusion** or poor bite. Skeletal malocclusions occur when the upper and lower jaws are not properly aligned with each other and with the skull. Dental malocclusions occur when the teeth are crowded or the upper and lower teeth are not properly aligned with each other. Malocclusions can be caused by the following:

- heredity
- crowded or misaligned baby teeth
- premature loss of baby teeth due to decay or injury, so that the permanent first molars move forward, causing crowding and misalignment of the new front teeth
- loss of permanent tooth structure due to untreated decay in the baby teeth
- a tooth emerging at an angle such that it pushes on and damages an adjacent tooth
- sucking that continues after the permanent teeth erupt
- wisdom teeth that erupt crookedly
- accidental injury

Some children experience mild, temporary symptoms of malocclusion resulting from a growth spurt. Severe malocclusion may require orthodontic intervention to improve appearance or to prevent problems with eating and speaking. Most alignment problems develop gradually, although they may be apparent at eruption. Symptoms of alignment problems include the following:

- lack of space between teeth
- teeth that are out-of-line or abnormally spaced
- front teeth that do not meet
- protruding of the upper or lower jaw
- protruding upper front teeth (overbite)
- protruding lower front teeth (underbite)
- an open bite wherein the upper and lower front teeth do not touch during biting

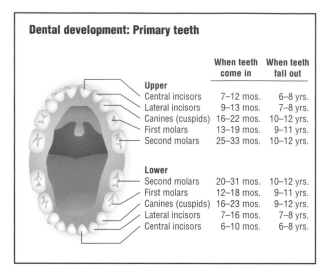

Dental development: Primary teeth

		When teeth come in	When teeth fall out
Upper			
	Central incisors	7–12 mos.	6–8 yrs.
	Lateral incisors	9–13 mos.	7–8 yrs.
	Canines (cuspids)	16–22 mos.	10–12 yrs.
	First molars	13–19 mos.	9–11 yrs.
	Second molars	25–33 mos.	10–12 yrs.
Lower			
	Second molars	20–31 mos.	10–12 yrs.
	First molars	12–18 mos.	9–11 yrs.
	Canines (cuspids)	16–23 mos.	9–12 yrs.
	Lateral incisors	7–16 mos.	7–8 yrs.
	Central incisors	6–10 mos.	6–8 yrs.

Illustration of the eruption of primary, or baby teeth. *(Illustration by GGS Information Services.)*

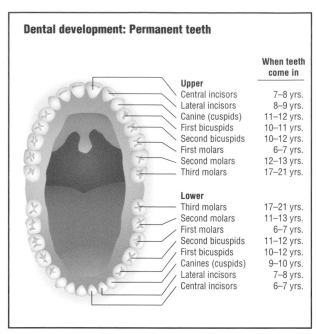

Dental development: Permanent teeth

		When teeth come in
Upper		
	Central incisors	7–8 yrs.
	Lateral incisors	8–9 yrs.
	Canine (cuspids)	11–12 yrs.
	First bicuspids	10–11 yrs.
	Second bicuspids	10–12 yrs.
	First molars	6–7 yrs.
	Second molars	12–13 yrs.
	Third molars	17–21 yrs.
Lower		
	Third molars	17–21 yrs.
	Second molars	11–13 yrs.
	First molars	6–7 yrs.
	Second bicuspids	11–12 yrs.
	First bicuspids	10–12 yrs.
	Canines (cuspids)	9–10 yrs.
	Lateral incisors	7–8 yrs.
	Central incisors	6–7 yrs.

Illustration of the eruption of permanent teeth. *(Illustration by GGS Information Services.)*

Developmental disorders

Dental development disorders may occur as a result of the following:

- numerous inherited syndromes
- improper prenatal development
- endocrine disorders
- environmental factors

Developmental disorders include the following:

- hypodontia, in which one or more permanent teeth, usually the wisdom teeth or the lateral incisors, fail to form and the remaining teeth tend to be smaller
- anodontia, a very rare condition in which many or all of the permanent teeth fail to form
- supernumerary or extra teeth (These are more common in permanent teeth than in baby teeth; extra teeth usually are somewhat shapeless pegs, although occasionally an extra molar develops fully.)

Discolored and misshapen teeth

Disorders that may cause discoloration of the teeth include:

- hypoplasia, in which insufficient or irregular enameling of the teeth caused by the administration of tetracycline to a pregnant or nursing mother or to the infant or young child
- enamel and dentin hypoplasia, in which the enamel and dentin are not calcified (hardened by the depositing of **minerals**) due to **vitamin D deficiency** during tooth development

- hypocalcification, in which the enamel is of poor quality due to genetic factors, extensive plaque deposits, excessive sucking on citrus fruits, or high consumption of very acidic carbonated beverages
- amelogenesis imperfecta, an inherited defect that causes thin and discolored enamel
- dentinogenesis imperfecta, a defect of the dentin that causes discoloration and loss of enamel
- extrinsic enamel coloration due to liquid iron supplements administered for anemia or due to plaque or stains adhering to calculus, hard mineral deposits on the crowns and roots
- intrinsic enamel coloration due to pigments carried in the blood from tetracycline or other drugs or from excessive fluoride

Illness or trauma during infancy or early childhood, including infections, high fever, malnutrition, or disorders such as congenital syphilis or Down syndrome, can cause misshapen or discolored teeth. Both the baby teeth and the permanent teeth are usually affected, particularly the eight front teeth and the six-year or first molars. Crowns may be pitted, grooved, and discolored.

Wisdom teeth

Wisdom teeth frequently have difficulty erupting because the jaw is too small. A wisdom tooth may rotate,

KEY TERMS

Abscess—A localized collection of pus in the skin or other body tissue caused by infection.

Bicuspid—Premolar; the two-cupped tooth between the first molar and the cuspid.

Calcification—A process in which tissue becomes hardened due to calcium deposits.

Calculus—Plural, calculi. Any type of hard concretion (stone) in the body, but usually found in the gallbladder, pancreas, and kidneys. They are formed by the accumulation of excess mineral salts and other organic material such as blood or mucus. Calculi (pl.) can cause problems by lodging in and obstructing the proper flow of fluids, such as bile to the intestines or urine to the bladder. In dentistry, calculus refers to a hardened yellow or brown mineral deposit from unremoved plaque, also called tartar.

Canines—The two sharp teeth located next to the front incisor teeth in mammals that are used to grip and tear. Also called cuspids.

Crown—The natural part of the tooth covered by enamel. A restorative crown is a protective shell that fits over a tooth.

Dentin—The middle layer of a tooth, which makes up most of the tooth's mass.

Enamel—The hard, outermost surface of a tooth.

Eruption—The process of a tooth breaking through the gum tissue to grow into place in the mouth.

Impacted tooth—Any tooth that is prevented from reaching its normal position in the mouth by another tooth, bone, or soft tissue.

Incisor—One of the eight front teeth.

Malocclusion—The misalignment of opposing teeth in the upper and lower jaws.

Molars—The teeth behind the primary canines or the permanent premolars, with large crowns and broad chewing surfaces for grinding food.

Occlusion—The way upper and lower teeth fit together during biting and chewing. Also refers to the blockage of some area or channel of the body.

Plaque—A deposit, usually of fatty material, on the inside wall of a blood vessel. Also refers to a small, round demyelinated area that develops in the brain and spinal cord of an individual with multiple sclerosis.

Premolar—Bicuspid; the two-cupped teeth between the first molars and the cuspids.

Wisdom teeth—The third molars at that back of the mouth.

---

tilt, or be displaced as it attempts to emerge, and it can become impacted (partially buried) in the gums. Impacted wisdom teeth do not always cause problems. However wisdom teeth are always difficult to clean and susceptible to decay and gum disease; thus an impacted wisdom tooth is usually extracted. An impacted tooth can cause:

- bad breath
- an unpleasant taste in the mouth
- gum pain
- recurrent infection of the tooth and surrounding gums

Parental concerns

Some evidence indicates that infants' jaws and teeth develop better and more completely if babies are fed breast milk rather than infant formula. To promote their baby's dental development, pregnant and nursing mothers should do the following:

- practice good nutrition
- refrain from prescription and nonprescription drugs, particularly during the first trimester of pregnancy

- refrain from alcohol, tobacco, and excessive sugar

Parents must clean and care for their children's teeth until children are able to do it themselves. Furthermore, parents are the first to teach their children good dental hygiene. After feeding, a baby's gums should be wiped with clean gauze. Brushing should begin with the first tooth eruption and the remaining gums should be cleaned and massaged. Flossing should begin as soon as all of the baby teeth have erupted.

When to call the dentist

The rapidity with which decay can advance in baby teeth necessitates periodic dental examinations and cleanings. Pediatric dentists often recommend a first dental appointment at 12 to 18 months of age. Some recommend a first appointment at six months. At the very least, a child should see a dentist by age two-and-a-half or when all of the baby teeth have erupted.

Between two-and-a-half and six years of age is a critical period for dental development. Parents should regularly examine a child's teeth for signs of decay, crowdedness, or misalignment. A dentist should be consulted if any of the following occurs:

- A child has an inherited disorder that affects the teeth or jaws, such as a protruding or recessed lower jaw.

- Tooth eruption occurs at least a year sooner or later than normal.

- The baby teeth do not erupt properly or seem crowded.

- A baby tooth becomes loose before the age of four or five years.

- A permanent tooth begins to erupt before the baby tooth that it is replacing has been lost.

- Swelling or infection occurs during eruption of the molars.

- A child has difficulty chewing or closing their jaw.

- A child continues to thumb-suck or suck on a pacifier after all of the baby teeth have erupted.

- A child's diet contains excessive sugar.

- A child has a serious fall or blow to the head.

- A permanent tooth is loosened in an accident.

Parents should pay close attention to the child-dentist relationship and voice any concerns, since it is very important to prevent a child from having an unpleasant dental experience. Many parents choose to take their child to a pediatric dentist. A pediatric dentist has undergone additional training and may be more experienced with dental development in children. Their offices are usually designed specifically to make children feel comfortable.

See also Fluoridation; Orthodontics.

Resources

BOOKS

Keller, Laurie. *Open Wide: Tooth School Inside.* New York: Henry Holt, 2000.

Nanci, Antonio. *Ten Cate's Oral Histology: Development, Structure, and Function.* St. Louis: Mosby, 2003.

Teaford, Mark F., et al., eds. *Development, Function, and Evolution of Teeth.* New York: Cambridge University Press, 2000.

PERIODICALS

Griffen A. L. "Normal Formation and Development Defects of the Human Dentition." *Pediatric Clinics of North America* 47, no. 5 (2000): 975–1000.

Macknin, M. L., et al. "Symptoms Associated with Infant Teething: A Prospective Study." *Pediatrics* 105, no.4 (2000): 747–52.

ORGANIZATIONS

American Academy of Pediatric Dentistry. 211 East Chicago Avenue, Suite 700, Chicago, IL 60611–2663. Web site: <www.aapd.org>.

American Dental Association. 211 East Chicago Avenue, Chicago, IL 60611–2678. Web site: <www.ada.org>.

National Maternal and Child Oral Health Resource Center (OHRC). Georgetown University, Box 571272, Washington, DC 20057–1272. Web site: <www.mchoralhealth.org>.

WEB SITES

"Early Childhood Tooth Decay (Baby Bottle Tooth Decay)." *American Dental Association.* Available online at <www.ada.org/public/topics/decay_childhood_faq.asp> (accessed December 10, 2004).

"A Health Professional's Guide to Pediatric Oral Health Management." *National Maternal and Child Oral Heath Resource Center*, 2004. Available online at <www.mchoralhealth.org/PediatricOH/index.htm>(accessed December 10, 2004).

"Tooth Eruption Charts." *American Dental Association.* Available online at <www.ada.org/public/topics/tooth_eruption.asp> (accessed December 10, 2004).

Margaret Alic, PhD

Dental hygiene *see* **Oral hygiene**

Dental trauma

Definition

Dental trauma is injury to the teeth, gums, and jawbones. The most common dental trauma is a broken or displaced tooth.

Description

Dental trauma may be inflicted in a number of ways: contact **sports**, motor vehicle accidents, fights, falls, eating hard foods, drinking hot liquids, and other such mishaps. Dental trauma includes teeth that are knocked out (dental avulsion), cracked (fractured), forced out of position (dental luxation, lateral displacement, or extrusion), pushed up into the jawbone (dental intrusion), or loosened by impact (subluxation or dental **concussion**). Oral tissues are sensitive, and injuries to the mouth are typically very painful. Dental trauma should receive prompt treatment from a dentist and in some cases is considered a dental emergency.

Demographics

Children between the ages of 1.5 and 3.5 years are most likely to experience dental trauma to their primary (baby) teeth, because this is the age at which they are learning to run. According to the International Association of Dental Traumatology, half of children experience dental injury, with injury occurring most often in children ages eight to 12. Fracture of the tooth crown (the part that is above the gum line) is the most common injury. School-age boys are twice as likely to experience dental trauma as girls.

Causes and symptoms

The cause of dental trauma varies depending on the age of the child. Toddlers are more likely to injure a tooth by falling, while older children are more likely to suffer dental trauma from a sports injury. Teenagers often present with dental trauma as the result of fights. The incisors in the upper jaw are the most commonly injured teeth.

Pain characterizes all dental trauma. The tooth may be knocked out and the socket bleeding, or it may be loose. There may be additional damage to the bones of the jaw and to the soft tissues of the mouth.

When to call the dentist

A permanent tooth that has been knocked out is a dental emergency. The dentist should also be called whenever dental trauma results in pain, dislocation of the tooth, or tooth sensitivity to hot or cold.

Diagnosis

Dental trauma is readily apparent upon examination. Dental **x rays** may be taken to determine the extent of the damage to fractured teeth. More comprehensive x rays are needed to diagnose a broken jaw.

Treatment

There is a possibility that a permanent tooth that has been knocked out can be re-implanted if handled promptly and correctly. If possible, the tooth should be reinserted in the socket and held there until the child sees a dentist or visits the emergency room. If it is not possible to replace the tooth in the socket, the tooth should immediately be placed in milk, saliva, or cool water with a pinch of saline solution (not contact lens solution or plain water). The tooth should be handled only by the crown and never be allowed to dry out. If a dentist can see the child within half an hour and the tooth has been preserved correctly, there is a possibility that it may be successfully re-implanted. Primary teeth are usually not re-implanted.

For lesser dental trauma, soft tissue injuries may require only cold compresses or ice to reduce swelling. Bleeding may be controlled with direct pressure applied with clean gauze. Deep lacerations and punctures may require stitches. Pain may be managed with aspirin or **acetaminophen** (Tylenol, Aspirin Free Excedrin), or ibuprofen (Motrin, Advil).

Treatment of a broken tooth will vary depending on the severity of the fracture. For immediate first aid, the injured tooth and surrounding area should be rinsed gently with warm water to remove dirt, then covered with a cold compress to reduce swelling and ease pain. A dentist should examine the injury as soon as possible. Any pieces from the broken tooth should be saved and taken to the dentist with the child.

If a piece of the outer tooth has chipped off, but the inner core (pulp) is undisturbed, the dentist may simply smooth the rough edges or replace the missing section with a small composite filling. In some cases, a fragment of broken tooth may be bonded back into place. If enough tooth is missing to compromise the entire tooth structure, but the pulp is not permanently damaged, the tooth will require a protective coverage with a gold or porcelain crown. If the pulp has been seriously damaged, the tooth will require root canal treatment before it receives a crown. A tooth that is vertically fractured or fractured below the gum line will require root canal treatment and protective restoration. A tooth that no longer has enough remaining structure to retain a crown may have to be extracted (surgically removed).

A broken jaw must be set back into its proper position and stabilized with wires while it heals. This is usually done by an oral surgeon. Healing may take six weeks or longer, depending on the patient's age and the severity of the fracture.

Alternative treatment

There is no substitute for treatment by a dentist or other medical professional. There are, however, homeopathic remedies and herbs that can be used simultaneously with dental care and throughout the healing process. Homeopathic arnica (*Arnica montana*) should be taken as soon as possible after the injury to help the body deal with the trauma. Repeating a dose several times daily for the duration of healing is also useful. Homeopathic hypericum (*Hypericum perforatum*) can be taken if nerve pain is involved, especially with a tooth extraction or root canal. Homeopathic comfrey (*Symphytum officinale*) may be helpful in treating pain due to broken jaw bones but should only be used after the bones have been reset. Calendula (*Calendula officinalis*) and plantain (*Plantago major*) can be used as a

KEY TERMS

Avulsion—The forcible separation of a piece from the entire structure.

Crown—The natural part of the tooth covered by enamel. A restorative crown is a protective shell that fits over a tooth.

Extraction—The removal of a tooth from its socket in the bone.

Pulp—The soft, innermost layer of a tooth that contains its blood vessels and nerves.

Root canal treatment—The process of removing diseased or damaged pulp from a tooth, then filling and sealing the pulp chamber and root canals.

mouth rinse to enhance tissue healing. These herbs should not be used with deep lacerations that need to heal from the inside first.

Prognosis

When dental trauma receives timely attention and proper treatment, the prognosis for healing is good. As with other types of trauma, infection may be a complication, but treatment with **antibiotics** is generally effective.

Prevention

Most dental trauma is preventable. Car seat belts should always be worn, and young children should be secured in appropriate car seats. Homes should be monitored for potential tripping and slipping hazards. **Childproofing** measures should be taken, especially for toddlers. Parents can place gates across stairs and pad sharp table edges.

Everyone who participates in contact sports should wear a mouth guard to avoid dental trauma. Athletes in football, ice hockey, wrestling, and boxing commonly wear mouth guards. The mandatory use of mouth guards in football prevents about 200,000 oral injuries annually. Mouth guards should also be worn along with helmets in noncontact sports such as skateboarding, in-line skating, and bicycling. An athlete who does not wear a mouth guard is 60 times more likely to sustain dental trauma than one who does. Any activity involving speed, an increased chance of falling, and potential contact with a hard piece of equipment has the likelihood of dental trauma that may be prevented or substantially reduced in severity with the use of mouth guards.

Parental concerns

Parents are sometimes concerned about the appearance of their child after he or she loses a permanent tooth. Cos-

metic dentistry and orthodonture can with time and patience correct almost any problems arising from dental trauma.

Resources

ORGANIZATIONS

American Academy of Pediatric Dentistry. 211 East Chicago Ave., Ste. 700, Chicago, IL 60611–2616. Web site: <www.aapd.org>.

American Association of Endodontists. 211 East Chicago Ave., Ste. 1100, Chicago, IL 60611–2691. Web site: <www.aae.org>.

American Association of Oral and Maxillofacial Surgeons. 9700 West Bryn Mawr Ave., Rosemont, IL 60018–5701. Web site: <www.aaoms.org>.

American Dental Association. 211 E. Chicago Ave., Chicago, IL 60611. Web site: <www.ada.org>.

WEB SITES

Flores, M. T., et al. "Guidelines for the Evaluation and Management of Traumatic Dental Injuries." *International Association of Dental Traumatoloty*, 2000. Available online at <www.iadt-dentaltrauma.org/Trauma/guidelines.htm> (accessed November 29, 2004).

Goss, Lisa A. "Tooth Injuries." *KidsHealth*, May 2004. Available online at <www.kidshealth.org/parent/firstair_safe/emergencies/tooth_injury.html> (accessed November 29, 2004).

Ravel, Daniel. "Management of Dental Trauma in Children." *Pediatric Dental Health*, August 1, 2003. Available online at <http://dentalresource.org/topic50trauma.html> (accessed November 29, 2004).

Tish Davidson, A.M.
Bethany Thivierge

Dependent personality disorder

Definition

Dependent personality disorder is a lack of self-confidence coupled with excessive dependence on others.

Description

Persons affected by dependent personality disorder have a disproportionately low level of confidence in their own **intelligence** and abilities and have difficulty making decisions and undertaking projects on their own. Their pervasive reliance on others, even for minor tasks or decisions, makes them exaggeratedly cooperative out of **fear** of alienating those whose help their need. They are reluctant to express disagreement with others and are often willing to go to abnormal lengths to win the approval of those on whom they rely. Another common feature of the disorder is an exaggerated fear of being left to fend for oneself. Adolescents with dependent personality disorder rely on their parents to make even minor decisions for them, such as what they should wear or how they should spend their free time, as well as major ones, such as what college they should attend or which career they should choose.

It is important to note that in other societies where cultural norms are different, dependent and/or passive traits may be valued, particularly in women. The criteria outlined here for dependent personality disorder is applicable to Americans only, and even then may not apply to all cultural groups within the United States.

Demographics

Dependent personality disorder occurs equally in males and females and usually begins by early adulthood. Overall prevalence is approximately one to two percent of the general population. Because children and adolescents are dependent on adults by necessity, dependent personality disorder is very rarely diagnosed in these age groups.

Causes and symptoms

In the *Diagnostic and Statistical Manual of Mental Disorders, 4th Edition Text Revision (DSM-IV-TR)*, the American Psychiatric Association states that five of the following criteria should be present for a diagnosis of dependent personality disorder:

- difficulty making decisions, even minor ones, without guidance and reassurance from others

- requiring others to take responsibility for major decisions and responsibilities beyond what would be age-appropriate (e.g., letting a parent choose a college without offering any input on the decision)

- difficulty disagreeing with others due to an unreasonable fear of alienation

- unable to initiate or complete projects or tasks due to a belief that he or she is either inept or that the appearance of success would lead a support person(s) to abandon him or her

- takes on unreasonably unpleasant tasks or sacrifices things in order to win the approval of others

- unable to spend time alone due to a lack of self-reliance and an unreasonable fear of being unable to care for oneself

- inability to remain independent of a close relationship as manifested by seeking a substitute support relationship immediately after one ends (e.g., a teenager who feels she must have a boyfriend constantly to validate her self-worth)

- unrealistic preoccupation with the thought of being left to care for oneself

Dependent personality disorder is more common in those who have suffered from chronic illness in childhood. A child may also exhibit dependent behavior in response to a specific stressful life event (such as the death of a caregiver or a **divorce**). However, it should not be considered a potential symptom of dependent personality disorder unless the behavior becomes chronic and significantly interferes with day-to-day functioning and/or causes the child significant distress.

When to call the doctor

It is developmentally suitable for young children to go through "clingy" stages where overt dependent behavior on a parent or caregiver is commonplace. However, if dependency in a child or adolescent starts to interfere with school work, daily living, and the child's sense of **self-esteem** and well-being, parents should seek professional help from their child's doctor. If a child or teen indicates at any time that he/she has had recent thoughts of self-injury, **suicide**, or of inflicting harm on others, professional assistance from a mental health care provider or care facility should be sought immediately.

Diagnosis

Older teens or young adults who have demonstrated at least five of the *DSM-IV-TR* criteria (or symptoms) outlined above are eligible for a diagnosis of dependent personality disorder. In the *DSM-IV-TR*, the APA warns that a diagnosis of dependent personality disorder "should be used with great caution, if at all, in children and adolescents, for whom dependent behavior may be developmentally appropriate." Children are dependent on parents and other adults in their lives for support and physical and emotional **safety** by necessity; it is only when the behaviors are excessive and age inappropriate that a diagnosis of dependent personality disorder can be contemplated.

Treatment

The primary treatment for dependent personality disorder is psychotherapy, with an emphasis on learning to cope with **anxiety**, developing assertiveness, and improving decision-making skills. Group therapy can also be helpful. In cases where parents or other adult caregivers seem to be facilitating the behavior, therapy for them is also appropriate.

Prognosis

Dependent personality disorder frequently occurs in tandem with other personality-based mental illness, such as borderline, histrionic, and avoidant **personality disorders**. It is also believed that those diagnosed with dependent personality disorder are at an increased risk of mood and anxiety disorders.

Prevention

There is no known prevention strategy for dependent personality disorder. However, some tactics that can promote healthy socialization and positive self-esteem from an early age include encouraging healthy peer relationships, investing a child with increasing levels of age-appropriate responsibilities and independence, and offering choices to even the smallest children.

Parental concerns

Dependent personality disorder is an extremely rare diagnosis in children. Parents of children who have been diagnosed with dependent personality disorder may wish to seek a second opinion from a trained psychologist or psychiatrist specializing in pediatric care. **Separation anxiety** shares some common features with dependent

personality disorder, and should be considered as a differential diagnosis.

Resources

BOOKS

Diagnostic and Statistical Manual of Mental Disorders, 4th edition, text revision (DSM-IV-TR). Washington, DC: American Psychiatric Press, Inc., 2000.

PERIODICALS

Grant, BF et al. "Prevalence, correlates, and disability of personality disorders in the United States: results from the national epidemiologic survey on alcohol and related conditions." *Journal of Clinical Psychiatry.* 65, no. 7 (July 2004): 948–58.

ORGANIZATIONS

The American Academy of Child and Adolescent Psychiatry. 3615 Wisconsin Ave., N.W., Washington, D.C. 20016–3007. (202) 966–7300. Web site: <www.aacap.org>.

National Institute of Mental Health. 6001 Executive Boulevard, Rm. 8184, MSC 9663, Bethesda, MD 20892–9663. (301) 443–4513.

Paula Ford-Martin

Depersonalization disorder *see* **Dissociative disorders**

Depression *see* **Depressive disorders**

Depressive disorders

Definition

Depression and depressive disorders (unipolar depression) are mental illnesses characterized by a profound and persistent feeling of sadness or despair and/or a loss of interest in things that once were pleasurable. Disturbance in **sleep**, appetite, and mental processes are common symptoms of depression.

Description

Everyone experiences feelings of unhappiness and sadness occasionally. However, when these depressed feelings start to dominate everyday life and cause physical and mental deterioration, they become what are known as depressive disorders.

There are two main categories of depressive disorders: major depressive disorder and dysthymic disorder.

Major depressive disorder is a moderate to severe episode of depression lasting two or more weeks. Individuals experiencing this major depressive episode may have trouble sleeping, lose interest in activities they once took pleasure in, experience a change in weight, have difficulty concentrating, feel worthless and hopeless, or have a preoccupation with death or **suicide**. In children, the major depression may often appear as irritability.

While major depressive episodes may be acute (intense but short-lived), dysthymic disorder is an ongoing, chronic depression that lasts two or more years (one or more years in children) and has an average duration of 16 years. The mild to moderate depression of dysthymic disorder may rise and fall in intensity, and those afflicted with the disorder may experience some periods of normal, non-depressed mood of up to two months in length. Its onset is gradual, and dysthymic patients may not be able to pinpoint exactly when they started feeling depressed. Individuals with dysthymic disorder may experience a change in sleeping and eating patterns, low **self-esteem**, fatigue, trouble concentrating, and feelings of hopelessness. Parents of children suffering from dysthymic disorder may notice their child experience a fall in grades and a lack of interest in **extracurricular activities** that were once enjoyable.

Depression also can occur in **bipolar disorder**, an affective mental illness that causes radical emotional changes and mood swings, from manic highs to depressive lows. The majority of bipolar individuals experience alternating episodes of mania and depression.

Demographics

The Substance Abuse and Mental Health Services Administration (SAMSHA) estimates that one out of every 33 children may suffer from depression. Among adults 18 and older, depressive disorders affect an estimated 18.8 million Americans each year. Women are twice as likely to suffer from a depressive disorder than men; approximately 12.4 million American women and 6.4 million men deal with depression. The average age a first depressive episode occurs is in the mid-20s, although the disorder strikes all age groups indiscriminately, from children to the elderly.

According to the U.S. Surgeon General, major depression occurs in about 5 percent of children between age nine and 17, and at any one point in time, 10 to 15 percent of U.S. children and adolescents experience some symptoms of depression.

Causes and symptoms

The causes behind depression are complex and as of 2004 not fully understood. While an imbalance of certain neurotransmitters—the chemicals in the brain that transmit messages between nerve cells—is believed to be key to depression, external factors such as upbringing may be as important. For example, it is speculated that, if an individual is abused and neglected throughout childhood and **adolescence**, a pattern of low self-esteem and negative thinking may emerge. From that, a lifelong pattern of depression may follow.

Heredity seems to play a role in who develops depressive disorders. Individuals with major depression in their immediate **family** are up to three times more likely to have the disorder themselves. It would seem that biological and genetic factors may make certain individuals pre-disposed to depressive disorders, but environmental circumstances often may trigger the disorder as well.

External stressors and significant life changes such as chronic medical problems, death of a loved one, or **divorce** or estrangement of parents also can result in a form of depression known as adjustment disorder. Although periods of adjustment disorder usually resolve themselves, occasionally they may evolve into a major depressive disorder.

Common red flags that children may be experiencing a depressive disorder include a sudden decline in grades and/or disinterest in schoolwork, avoidance of friends, loss of interest in extracurricular activities, and withdrawal from family.

Major depressive episode

Individuals experiencing a major depressive episode have a depressed mood and/or a diminished interest or pleasure in activities. Children experiencing a major depressive episode may appear or feel irritable rather than depressed. In addition, five or more of the following symptoms will occur on an almost daily basis for a period of at least two weeks:

- significant change in weight
- insomnia or hypersomnia (excessive sleep)
- psychomotor agitation or retardation
- fatigue or loss of energy
- feelings of worthlessness or inappropriate guilt
- diminished ability to think or to concentrate, or indecisiveness
- recurrent thoughts of death or suicide and/or suicide attempts

Dysthymic disorder

Dysthymia commonly occurs in tandem with other psychiatric and physical conditions. Up to 70 percent of dysthymic patients have both dysthymic disorder and major depressive disorder, known as double depression. Substance abuse, panic disorders, **personality disorders**, social **phobias**, and other psychiatric conditions also are found in many dysthymic patients. Dysthymia is prevalent in patients with certain medical conditions, including multiple sclerosis, **AIDS**, **hypothyroidism**, chronic fatigue syndrome, diabetes, and post-cardiac transplantation. The connection between dysthymic disorder and these medical conditions is unclear, but it may be related to the way the medical condition and/or its pharmacological treatment affects neurotransmitters. Dysthymic disorder can lengthen or complicate the recovery of patients also suffering from medical conditions.

Along with an underlying feeling of depression, people with dysthymic disorder experience two or more of the following symptoms on an almost daily basis for a period for two or more years (most suffer for five years) or one year or more for children:

- under-eating or overeating
- insomnia or hypersomnia
- low energy or fatigue
- low self-esteem
- poor concentration or trouble making decisions
- feelings of hopelessness

When to call the doctor

Just like adults, children have days when they are feeling down. But if those blue or bad moods begin to interfere with schoolwork and daily living and start to increase in frequency, parents or caregivers need to seek help from their child's doctor. If a child or teen reveals at any time that they have had recent thoughts of self-injury or suicide, professional assistance from a mental healthcare provider or care facility should be sought immediately.

Diagnosis

In addition to an interview, a clinical inventory or scale such as the Child Depression Inventory (CDI) or the Child Depression Rating Scale (CDRS) may be used to assess a child's mental status and determine the presence of depressive symptoms. Tests may be administered in an outpatient or hospital setting by a pediatri-cian, general practitioner, social worker, psychiatrist, or psychologist.

Treatment

Major depressive and dysthymic disorders are typically treated with **antidepressants** or psychosocial therapy. Psychosocial therapy focuses on the personal and interpersonal issues behind depression, while antidepressant medication is prescribed to provide more immediate relief for the symptoms of the disorder. When used together correctly, therapy and antidepressants are a powerful treatment plan for the depressed child or adolescent.

Antidepressants

Selective serotonin reuptake inhibitors (SSRIs) such as fluoxetine (Prozac) and sertraline (Zoloft) reduce depression by increasing levels of serotonin, a neuro-transmitter. Some clinicians prefer SSRIs for treatment of dysthymic disorder. **Anxiety**, **diarrhea**, drowsiness, **headache**, sweating, **nausea**, and insomnia all are possible side effects of SSRIs. As of 2004, fluoxetine was the only SSRI (and the only antidepressant drug) approved by the U.S. Food and Drug Administration for use in children and adolescents with major depressive disorder. However, physicians may prescribe other SSRIs in younger patients in an off-label use of these drugs.

In 2004, fluoxetine and nine other antidepressant drugs came under scrutiny when the FDA issued a public health advisory and announced it was requesting the addition of a warning statement in drug labeling that outlined the possibility of worsening depression and increased suicide risk. These developments were the result of several clinical studies that found that some children taking these antidepressants had an increased risk of suicidal thoughts and actions. The FDA announced at the time that the agency would embark on a more extensive analysis of the data from these clinical trials and decide if further regulatory action was necessary.

Older classes of antidepressant drugs—(tricyclic antidepressants (TCAs), heterocyclics, and monoamine oxidase inhibitors (MAOIs)—do not have any substantial demonstrated effectiveness in pediatric populations and have potentially serious side effects that make them undesirable for child and adolescent use.

For severe depression that does not respond well to antidepressant, mood stabilizer drugs (e.g., lithium, carbamazepine, valproic acid) may be recommended.

Depressive disorders

Diagnosis	Symptoms	Treatment
Sadness	Transient, normal depressive response or mood change due to stress.	Emotional support
Bereavement	Sadness related to a major loss that persists for less than two months after the loss. Thoughts of death and morbid preoccupation with worthlessness are also present.	Emotional support; counseling
Sadness problem	Sadness or irritability that begins to resemble major depressive disorder, but lower in severity and more transient.	Support; counseling; medication possible
Adjustment disorder with depressed mood	Symptoms include depressed mood, tearfulness, and hopelessness, and occur within three months of an identifiable stressor. Symptoms resolve in six months.	Psychotherapy; medication
Major depressive disorder	A depressed or irritable mood or diminished pleasure as well as three to seven of the following criteria almost daily for two weeks. The criteria include: recurrent thoughts of death and suicidal ideation; weight loss or gain; fatigue or energy loss; feelings of worthlessness; diminished ability to concentrate; insomnia or hypersomnia; feeling hyper and jittery, or abnormally slow.	Psychotherapy; medication
Dysthymic disorder	Depressed mood for most of the day, for more days than not, for one year, including the presence of two of the following symptoms: poor appetite or overeating; insomnia/hypersomnia; low energy/fatigue; poor concentration; feelings of hopelessness. Symptoms are less severe than those of a major depressive episode but are more persistent.	Psychotherapy; medication
Bipolar I disorder, most recent episode depressed	Current major depressive episode with a history of one manic or mixed episode. (Manic episode is longer than four days and causes significant impairment in normal functioning.) Moods are not accounted for by another psychiatric disorder.	Psychotherapy; medication
Bipolar II disorder, recurrent major depressive episodes with hypomanic episodes	Presence or history of one major depressive episode and one hypomanic episode (similar to manic episode but shorter and less severe). Symptoms are not accounted for by another psychiatric disorder and cause clinically significant impairment in functioning.	Psychotherapy; medication

SOURCE: Academy of American Family Physicians. 2000. http://www.aafp.org.

(Table by GGS Information Services.)

Psychotherapy

Psychotherapy, or talk therapy, involves analyzing a child's life to bring to light possible contributing causes of the present depression. During treatment, the therapist helps the patient to become aware of his or her thinking patterns and how they came to be, and works with them to develop healthy problem solving and copying skills. In very young patients, a therapist may use **toys**, games, and dolls as a vehicle for helping a child express her emotions. This type of therapy, sometimes referred to as play therapy, is useful in children who may not have the developmental capacity or language skills to express the thoughts and feelings behind their depression.

Cognitive-behavioral therapy assumes that the patient's faulty thinking is causing the current depression and focuses on changing the depressed patient's thought patterns and perceptions. The therapist helps the patient identify negative or distorted thought patterns and the emotions and behavior that accompany them and then retrains the depressed individual to recognize the thinking and react differently to it.

Electroconvulsant therapy

Electroconvulsive therapy (ECT) is only considered after all therapy and pharmaceutical treatment options have been unsuccessful, and even then it is a treatment of last resort, typically employed when a patient has become catatonic, suicidal, or psychotic as well as depressed.

The treatment consists of a series of electrical pulses that move into the brain through electrodes on the patient's head. ECT is given under anesthesia, and patients are administered a muscle relaxant to prevent convulsions. Although the exact mechanisms behind the success of ECT therapy are not known, it is believed that the electrical current modifies the electrochemical processes of the brain, consequently relieving depression. Headaches, muscle soreness, nausea, and confusion are possible side effects immediately following an ECT procedure. Memory loss, typically transient, also has been reported in ECT patients.

Alternative treatment

St. John's wort (*Hypericum perforatum*) is used throughout Europe to treat mild depressive symptoms. Unlike traditional prescription antidepressants, this herbal antidepressant has few reported side effects. Despite uncertainty concerning its effectiveness, a 2003 report said acceptance of the treatment continues to increase. A poll showed that about 41 percent of 15,000 science professionals in 62 countries said they would use St. John's wort for mild to moderate depression. The usual adult dose is 300 mg three times daily and may be lowered for children and adolescents.

In several small studies, S-adenosyl-methionine (SAM, SAMe) was shown to be more effective than placebo and equally effective as tricyclic antidepressants in treating depression. In 2003, a U.S. Department of Health and Human Services team reviewed 100 clinical trials on SAMe and concluded that it worked as well as many prescription medications without side effects of stomach upset.

Parents and caregivers of children who suffer from depression should consult their child's physician before administering any herb or dietary supplement. Some supplements can interfere with the action of other prescription and over-the-counter medications. In addition, some supplements may not be appropriate for use in children with certain medical conditions.

A report from Great Britain published in 2003 emphasized that more physicians should encourage alternative treatments such as behavioral and self- help programs, supervised **exercise** programs, and watchful waiting before subscribing antidepressant medications for mild depression.

Nutritional concerns

Poor **nutrition**, especially eating habits that lead to overweight or **obesity** in children, can also contribute to depression. A 2003 study in the journal Pediatrics found that children who are substantially overweight for long periods of time are more likely to suffer from depression. Whether the depression causes the weight problem or the weight issue triggers the depression was not completely clear.

Prognosis

Untreated or improperly treated depression is the number one cause of suicide in the United States. Proper treatment relieves symptoms in 80 to 90 percent of depressed patients. After each major depressive episode,

KEY TERMS

Hypersomnia—An abnormal increase of 25% or more in time spent sleeping. Individuals with hypersomnia usually have excessive daytime sleepiness.

Neurotransmitter—A chemical messenger that transmits an impulse from one nerve cell to the next.

Psychomotor agitation—Disturbed physical and mental processes (e.g., fidgeting, wringing of hands, racing thoughts); a symptom of major depressive disorder.

Psychomotor retardation—Slowed mental and physical processes characteristic of a bipolar depressive episode.

the risk of recurrence climbs significantly: 50 percent after one episode, 70 percent after two episodes, and 90 percent after three episodes. For this reason, patients need to be aware of the symptoms of recurring depression and may require long-term maintenance treatment of antidepressants and/or therapy.

Prevention

Good nutrition, proper sleep, exercise, and family support are all important to a healthy mental state, particularly in children. Extended maintenance treatment with antidepressants may be required in some patients to prevent relapse. Early intervention for children with depression can be effective in avoiding the development of more severe psychological problems later in life.

Parental concerns

Children who are diagnosed with depression should be reassured that the condition is quite common and that it is due to factors beyond their control (i.e., genetics, neurochemical imbalance) rather than any fault of the child. For those children and teens who feel stigmatized or self-conscious about their depression, arranging psychotherapy sessions outside school hours may lessen their burden. Any child prescribed antidepressants should be carefully monitored for any sign of side effects, and these should be reported to their physician when they do occur. A dosage adjustment or medication change may be warranted if side effects are disruptive or potentially dangerous.

See also Bipolar disorder.

Resources

BOOKS

Barnard, Martha Underwood. *Helping Your Depressed Child.* Oakland, CA: New Harbinger Publications, 2003.

Diagnostic and Statistical Manual of Mental Disorders, 4th ed., text revision (DSM-IV-TR). Washington, DC: American Psychiatric Press, 2000.

Shaffer, David, and Bruce Waslick, eds. *The Many Faces of Depression in Children and Adolescents.* Arlington, VA: American Psychiatric Publishing, 2002.

PERIODICALS

"A Natural Mood-Booster that Really Works: A Group of Noted Researchers Found that the Supplement SAMe Works as Well as Antidepressant Drugs." *Natural Health* (July 2003): 22.

"FDA Approves Once-daily Supplement." *Biotech Week* (September 24, 2003): 6.

"Try Alternatives Before Using Antidepressants." *GP* (September 29, 2003): 12.

Vitiello, B., and S. Swedo. "Antidepressant Medications in Children." *New England Journal of Medicine* 350, no. 15 (April 8, 2003): 1489–91.

ORGANIZATIONS

American Psychiatric Association. 1000 Wilson Blvd., Suite 1825, Arlington, VA 22209. Web site: <www.psych.org>.

American Psychological Association (APA). 750 First St. NE, Washington, DC 20002–4242. Web site: <www.apa.org>.

Depression and Bipolar Support Alliance (DBSA). 730 N. Franklin St., Suite 501, Chicago, IL 60610. Web site: <www.dbsalliance.org>.

National Alliance for the Mentally Ill (NAMI). Colonial Place Three, 2107 Wilson Blvd., Ste. 300, Arlington, VA 22201–3042. Web site: <www.nami.org>.

National Institute of Mental Health (NIMH). Office of Communications, 6001 Executive Blvd., Room 8184, MSC 9663, Bethesda, MD 20892–9663. Web site: <www.nimh.nih.gov>.

WEB SITES

Larsen, Willow. "The Obesity-Depression Link." *Psychology Today* (May 30, 2003). Available online at <www.psychologytoday.com/htdocs/prod/ptoarticle/pto-20030527-000010.asp> (accessed December 26, 2004).

U.S. Food and Drug Administration. "Antidepressant [links]." Available online at <www.fda.gov> (accessed December 26, 2004).

Paula Ford-Martin
Teresa Odle

Dermatitis

Definition

Dermatitis is a general term used to describe inflammation of the skin.

Description

Most types of dermatitis are characterized by an itchy pink or red rash.

Contact dermatitis is an allergic reaction to something that irritates the skin and is manifested by one or more lines of red, swollen, blistered skin that may itch or seep. It usually appears within 48 hours after touching or brushing against a substance to which the skin is sensitive. The condition is more common in adults than in children.

Contact dermatitis can occur on any part of the body, but it usually affects the hands, feet, and groin. Contact dermatitis usually does not spread from one person to another, nor does it spread beyond the area exposed to the irritant unless affected skin comes into contact with another part of the body. However, in the case of some irritants, such as **poison ivy**, contact dermatitis can be passed to another person or to another part of the body.

Atopic dermatitis is characterized by **itching**, scaling, swelling, and sometimes blistering. In early childhood it is called infantile eczema and is characterized by redness, oozing, and crusting. It is usually found on the face, inside the elbows, and behind the knees.

Seborrheic dermatitis may be dry or moist and is characterized by greasy scales and yellowish crusts on the scalp, eyelids, face, external surfaces of the ears, underarms, breasts, and groin. In infants it is called cradle cap.

Demographics

Allergic reactions are common. No formal statistics are kept on such attacks.

Causes and symptoms

Allergic reactions are genetically determined, and different substances cause contact dermatitis to develop in different people. A reaction to resin produced by poison ivy, **poison oak**, or **poison sumac** is the most common source of symptoms. It is, in fact, the most common allergy in the United States, affecting one of every two people in the country.

Flowers, herbs, and vegetables can also affect the skin of some people. **Burns** and **sunburn** increase the risk of dermatitis developing. Chemical irritants that can cause the condition include:

- chlorine
- cleansers
- detergents and soaps
- fabric softeners
- glues used on artificial nails
- perfumes
- topical medications

Contact dermatitis can develop when the first contact occurs or after years of use or exposure.

Atopic dermatitis can be caused by **allergies**, **asthma**, or stress, and there seems to be a genetic predisposition for atopic conditions. It is sometimes caused by an allergy to nickel in jewelry.

Seborrheic dermatitis (for which there may also be a genetic predisposition) is usually caused by overproduction of the oil glands. In adults it can be associated with **diabetes mellitus** or gold allergy. In infants and adults it may be caused by a biotin deficiency.

When to call the doctor

A doctor or other healthcare provider should be consulted when **rashes** appear. With some experience, common rashes can be accurately identified by parents. Rashes that cannot be accurately identified should be referred to competent healthcare professional for identification and possible treatment.

Diagnosis

The diagnosis of dermatitis is made on the basis of how the rash looks and its location. The doctor may scrape off a small piece of affected skin for microscopic examination or direct the person to discontinue use of any potential irritant that has recently come into contact with the affected area. Two weeks after the rash disappears, the person may resume use of the substances, one at a time, until the condition recurs. Eliminating the substance most recently added should eliminate the irritation.

If the origin of the irritation has still not been identified, a dermatologist may perform one or more patch tests, which involves dabbing a small amount of a sus-

pected irritant onto skin on the person's back. If no irritation develops within a few days, another patch test is performed. The process continues until the person experiences an allergic reaction at the spot where the irritant was applied.

Treatment

Treating contact dermatitis begins with eliminating or avoiding the source of irritation. Prescription or over-the-counter corticosteroid creams can lessen inflammation and relieve irritation. Creams, lotions, or ointments not specifically formulated for dermatitis can intensify the irritation. Oral **antihistamines** are sometimes recommended to alleviate itching, and **antibiotics** are prescribed if the rash becomes infected. Medications taken by mouth to relieve symptoms of dermatitis can make skin red and scaly and cause hair loss.

People who have a history of dermatitis should remove their rings before washing their hands. They should use bath oils or glycerin-based soaps and bathe in lukewarm saltwater.

Patting rather than rubbing the skin after bathing and thoroughly massaging lubricating lotion or nonprescription cortisone creams into still-damp skin can soothe red, irritated nummular dermatitis. Highly concentrated cortisone preparations should not be applied to the face, armpits, groin, or rectal area. Periodic medical monitoring is necessary to detect side effects in people who use such preparations on rashes covering large areas of the body.

Coal-tar salves can help relieve symptoms of nummular dermatitis that have not responded to other treatments, but these ointments have an unpleasant odor and stain clothing.

Coal-tar shampoos may be used for seborrheic dermatitis that occurs on the scalp. Sun exposure after the use of these shampoos should be avoided because the risk of sunburn of the scalp is increased.

Alternative treatment

Some herbal therapies can be useful for skin conditions. Among the herbs most often recommended are:

- burdock root (*Arctium lappa*)
- calendula (*Calendula officinalis*) ointment
- chamomile (*Matricaria recutita*) ointment
- cleavers (*Galium* ssp.)
- evening primrose oil (*Oenothera biennis*)
- nettles (*Urtica dioica*)

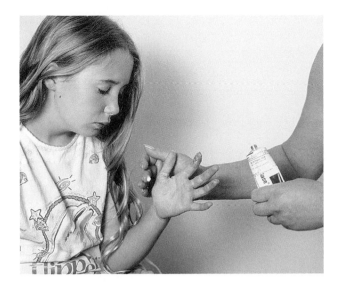

Diprobase cream, an emollient, used to treat contact dermatitis. (© Jim Selby/Photo Researchers, Inc.)

Contact dermatitis can be treated botanically and homeopathically. Grindelia (*Grindelia* spp.) and sassafras (*Sassafras albidum*) can help when applied topically. Determining the source of the problem and eliminating it is essential. Oatmeal baths are very helpful in relieving the itch. Bentonite clay packs or any mudpack draws the fluid out and helps dry up the lesions. Cortisone creams are not recommended.

Selenium-based shampoos, topical applications of flax oil and/or olive oil, and biotin supplementation are among the therapies recommended for seborrheic dermatitis.

Prognosis

Dermatitis is often chronic, but symptoms can generally be controlled.

Prevention

Contact dermatitis can be prevented by avoiding the source of irritation. If the irritant cannot be avoided completely, the person should wear gloves and other protective clothing whenever exposure is likely to occur.

Immediately washing the exposed area with soap and water can stem allergic reactions to poison ivy, poison oak, or poison sumac, but because soaps can dry the skin, people susceptible to dermatitis should use them only on the face, feet, genitals, and underarms.

Clothing should be loose fitting and 100 percent cotton. New clothing should be washed in dye-free, unscented detergent before being worn.

Yoga and other relaxation techniques may help prevent atopic dermatitis caused by stress.

Avoidance of sweating may aid in preventing seborrheic dermatitis.

A person who has dermatitis should also notify a doctor if any of the following occurs:

- fever develops
- skin oozes or other signs of infection appear
- symptoms do not begin to subside after seven days of treatment
- he/she comes into contact with someone who has a wart, **cold sore**, or other viral skin infection

Nutritional concerns

Eating a balanced and adequate diet is generally helpful. People who are susceptible to dermatitis that is linked to particular foods obviously should avoid consuming them.

Parental concerns

Parents should try to monitor new substances and foods when their children encounter them for the first time.

Resources

BOOKS

Bolognia, Jean L., and Irwin M. Braverman. "Skin Manifestations of Internal Disease." In *Harrison's Principles of Internal Medicine*, 15th ed. Edited by Eugene Braunwald et al. New York: McGraw-Hill, 2001, pp. 315–30.

Darmstadt, Gary L., and Robert Sidbury. "Diseases of the Dermis." In *Nelson Textbook of Pediatrics*, 17th ed. Edited by Richard E. Behrman et al. Philadelphia: Saunders, 2003, pp. 2204–9.

———. "Eczematous Disorders." In *Nelson Textbook of Pediatrics*, 17th ed. Edited by Richard E. Behrman et al. Philadelphia: Saunders, 2003, pp. 2188–90.

———. "Nutritional Dermatoses." In *Nelson Textbook of Pediatrics*, 17th ed. Edited by Richard E. Behrman et al. Philadelphia: Saunders, 2003, pp. 2248–50.

Lim, Henry M. "Eczemas, Photodermatoses, Papulosquamous (including Fungal) Diseases, and Figurate Erythemas." In *Cecil Textbook of Medicine*, 22nd ed. Edited by Lee Goldman et al. Philadelphia: Saunders, 2003, pp. 2458–65.

Swerlick, Robert A., and Thomas J. Lawley. "Eczema, Psoriasis, Cutaneous Infections, Acne, and Other Common Skin Disorders." In *Harrison's Principles of Internal Medicine*, 15th ed. Edited by Eugene Braunwald et al. New York: McGraw-Hill, 2001, pp. 309–14.

PERIODICALS

Capon, F., et al. "An update on the genetics of psoriasis." *Dermatologic Clinics* 22, no. 4 (2004): 339–47.

Johnson, S. M., et al. "Topical treatment for atopic dermatitis in the 21st century." *Journal of Arkansas Medical Society* 101, no. 3 (2004): 86–90.

Smith, A. "Contact dermatitis: diagnosis and management." *British Journal of Community Nursing* 9, no. 9 (2004): 365–71.

Ward, S. "The effective management of atopic dermatitis in school-age children." *Nursing Times* 100, no. 32 (2004): 55–6.

ORGANIZATIONS

American Academy of Dermatology. 930 N. Meacham Road, PO Box 4014, Schaumburg, IL 60168–4014. Web site: <www.aad.org/>.

WEB SITES

"Atopic Dermatitis." *National Institute of Arthritis and Musculoskeletal and Skin Diseases*, April 2003. Available online at <www.niams.nih.gov/hi/topics/dermatitis/> (accessed January 5, 2005).

"Atopic Dermatitis (Atopic Eczema)." *National Jewish Research and Medical Center*. Available online at <www.nationaljewish.org/medfacts/atopic.html> (accessed January 5, 2005).

"Dermatitis." *MedlinePlus*. Available online at <www.nlm.nih.gov/medlineplus/dermatitis.html> (accessed January 5, 2005).

"Eczema (Atopic Dermatitis)." *MedlinePlus*. Available online at <www.nlm.nih.gov/medlineplus/ency/article/000853.htm (accessed January 5, 2005).

Seborrheic Dermatitis." *American Academy of Family Practice*, April 2004. Available online at <http://familydoctor.org/157.xml> (accessed January 5, 2005).

L. Fleming Fallon, Jr., MD, DrPH

Dermatomyositis

Definition

Dermatomyositis is one of a group of relatively uncommon diseases known as inflammatory **myopathies**, or inflammatory disorders of the muscles. Dermatomyositis is distinguished from other diseases in this category by the fact that it causes a characteristic skin rash as well as affecting the strength and functioning of the muscles. Dermatomyositis in children and adolescents is called juvenile dermatomyositis (abbreviated JDMS or simply JD) because it is different from the adult form of the disorder in several respects. The most significant differences between JDMS and adult dermatomyositis are as follows:

- Children are more likely than adults to develop calcinosis (calcium deposits in the skin) and gastrointestinal symptoms.
- Children are more likely to develop pains in the joints.
- Adults with dermatomyositis over the age of 50 have a 15 percent risk of developing **cancer**, whereas juvenile dermatomyositis is rarely associated with malignancy.

Description

JDMS is sometimes called childhood idiopathic dermatomyositis. The word *idiopathic* means that the cause of the disease is unknown and that it appears to begin spontaneously. The disorder is also occasionally defined as a systemic vasculopathy, *systemic* meaning that it affects the body as a whole rather than just one part, and *vasculopathy* meaning that it affects the blood vessels.

JDMS usually begins with a reddish or reddish-purple rash, called a heliotrope rash because of its color. In most children the rash first appears on the eyelids or cheekbone area and is often mistaken for an allergy symptom. It may also appear as dry patches of reddened skin on the child's knuckles, knees, elbows, or ankles that are often misdiagnosed as eczema. In a few children, the rash may spread over the entire body. In some children, the rash is made worse by exposure to sunlight.

The heliotrope rash is either accompanied or followed by weakness of the body's central muscles; that is, the muscles on or close to the trunk of the body. These muscles are also called proximal muscles. The child may complain of tiredness and have trouble sitting up, standing, or moving the neck, shoulders, abdomen, back, or hips. The muscular weakness varies in severity; while some children may simply have less energy than usual, others may be literally unable to get out of bed or may have trouble swallowing or breathing. In some cases the child's voice may sound as if he or she is talking through the nose.

The third major symptom of juvenile dermatomyositis is a low-grade **fever** (one or two degrees Fahrenheit above normal).

Transmission

Although fever is one of the most common symptoms of JDMS, the disease cannot be transmitted from one child to another.

Demographics

Juvenile dermatomyositis most commonly affects children between the ages of five and 15 years of age. The ratio of girls to boys is 2:1. The disease is thought to be equally common around the world, affecting about three children per million. It is estimated that 3,000 to 5,000 children in the United States have JDMS as of the early 2000s. The incidence appears to be increasing, however. Although Caucasian children are affected more often than African-American children, the rate is rising faster among African Americans. The reasons for this increase are not known as of 2004.

JDMS has a seasonal pattern in North America, occurring more frequently in the spring and summer months.

Causes and symptoms

Causes

The precise causes of JDMS are not yet fully understood. One theory holds that the disease is an autoimmune reaction caused by the body's abnormal response to a virus. In an autoimmune reaction, the body begins to attack its own tissues after it has successfully eliminated the virus. Some researchers have identified virus-like structures in the muscle cells of patients known to have dermatomyositis, while others have noted that children newly diagnosed with JDMS often have a history of infection with a Coxsackie virus within three months of the first JDMS symptoms.

Genetic factors are also thought to be involved in juvenile dermatomyositis. In 2002 a group of researchers at Northwestern University reported that susceptibility to JDMS is related to a genetic marker known as DQA1*0501. Another team of doctors at the Children's National Medical Center in Washington, DC, has suggested that children with this particular genetic marker develop JDMS when a viral infection triggers an abnormal interaction among the body's immune system, the muscles, and the vascular system. There may also be other genes that increase children's susceptibility to the disease that have not yet been identified.

Symptoms

The major symptoms of juvenile dermatomyositis include a characteristic reddish or purplish rash called a heliotrope rash; weakness or **pain** in the proximal muscles; and a low-grade fever.

Other symptoms that may occur in children with juvenile dermatomyositis include:

- Contractures: A contracture is an abnormal shortening of the muscles near a joint that causes the joint to remain in a bent position. JDMS may lead to contractures for two reasons. The first is that the muscle may form scar tissue during the healing process. The second is that the child may avoid exercising his or her muscles because he or she feels weak. The muscles then gradually lose their ability to hold the joint in its proper position.
- Stunted or slowed growth: The child may grow more slowly than normal during an acute attack of JDMS because some of the medications used to treat the disease slow down the growth of bones. In addition, some

of the body's energy that is ordinarily used for growth is used instead to fight off the disease.

- Sore or swollen joints: About half of all children diagnosed with JDMS have sore or swollen joints, caused by the inflammation of the muscles around the joints. The joint may feel warm to the touch and look reddish as well as swollen.

- Vasculitic ulcers: Vasculitis refers to inflammation of a blood vessel. A vasculitic ulcer is a hole or tear that develops in the tissues around an inflamed blood vessel. In children with JDMS, vasculitic ulcers usually appear either in the skin rash or in the digestive tract. Vasculitic ulcers in the skin look like open sores within the reddish-purple rash; they vary in size from small spots to sores as much as an inch across. Vasculitic ulcers in the digestive tract may lead to perforation of the intestines, which is a medical emergency.

- Calcinosis: Calcinosis is a condition in which small lumps of calcium compounds develop beneath the skin or in the muscles of children with JDMS. They affect between 50 percent and 60 percent of children with the disorder and range in size from less than a millimeter across to lumps the size of small pebbles. Large lumps may interfere with the movement of the muscles, cause pain if they are located close to a joint, or even break through the skin. In most cases, however, the pieces of calcium are reabsorbed by the body during the recovery process.

- Dysphagia: Dysphagia refers to difficulty or discomfort when swallowing. Children whose throat muscles are affected by the disorder may experience difficulty in swallowing food; some lose weight because the dysphagia affects their appetite.

- Abnormal heart rhythms and myocarditis: Myocarditis refers to inflammation of the muscles of the walls of the heart. About 50 percent of children with JDMS develop an abnormal heart rhythm.

When to call the doctor

It is not always easy to tell when a child might have juvenile dermatomyositis. The skin rash associated with JDMS is often mistaken for eczema. In addition, some children may develop a mild form of muscle weakness before the telltale rash appears. While about 50 percent of children diagnosed with JDMS have an acute onset of symptoms, the other 50 percent have what is called a subacute onset, which means that the symptoms are milder and come on more slowly. While most children with acute symptoms are diagnosed within three months, the correct diagnosis of children with subacute symptoms may take a year or even longer.

Children who have developed sudden weakness of the muscles that control breathing or swallowing, or those who have developed vasculitic ulcers in the digestive tract may need to be hospitalized. Parents should call the doctor *at once* if they notice any of the following symptoms:

- choking on food or being unable to swallow
- weak voice or total loss of voice
- severe pain in the abdomen
- coal-black or tarry-looking stools
- change in bowel habits
- passing red blood with stools

Diagnosis

History and physical examination

The first step in diagnosing juvenile dermatomyositis is the taking of a complete history and giving the child a thorough physical examination. The doctor will ask the child and the parents when the symptoms began, what parts of the body are affected, whether the child can keep up his or her normal activities, and (in some cases) whether other **family** members have arthritis or muscle diseases.

During the physical examination, the doctor looks for several specific signs and symptoms, including heliotrope rash on the child's face, knuckles, knees, elbows, or the cuticles of the fingers; swelling around the eyes; a nasal quality to the child's voice; sore or weak muscles; and sore or swollen joints. The doctor will test the strength of the muscles by asking the child to lift his or her head, arms, or legs while the doctor gently pushes or presses downward.

The child's doctor may use a set of criteria first established in 1975 as part of the process of diagnosis. These so-called Bohan-Peter criteria are interpreted as follows: If the child meets the first criterion (the characteristic rash), three of the remaining four criteria must be met to make the diagnosis of juvenile dermatomyositis. The last three criteria listed below require special laboratory tests. If two out of four are met, the child is considered to have "probable" JDMS:

- heliotrope rash
- weakness of the central muscles on both sides of the body
- a higher than normal level of muscle enzymes in the blood
- a specific pattern of changes in the muscle tissue caused by inflammation

- an abnormal pattern of electrical activity in the muscles

Laboratory tests

The doctor will have a sample of the child's blood tested for certain muscle enzymes known as aldolase and CPK. These enzymes are leaked into the blood stream when muscles become inflamed. Abnormally high levels of aldolase and CPK indicate muscle damage. In addition to testing for muscle enzymes, the doctor may also have the blood sample tested for antinuclear antibodies (ANA), which are produced when a person's immune system is producing antibodies against the body's own tissues. Between 60 percent and 80 percent of children with JDMS have elevated levels of ANA.

A muscle biopsy may also be performed. In this test, the doctor removes a small piece of muscle tissue and has it examined under a microscope to see whether the muscle fibers and nearby blood vessels have undergone certain changes that indicate JDMS. Many doctors, however, skip this test if the child has the typical heliotrope rash, shows signs of muscle weakness during the physical examination, and has high muscle enzyme levels in the blood test. A muscle biopsy is necessary, however, if the child has the heliotrope rash but normal enzyme levels.

An electromyogram (EMG) measures electrical activity in the muscles. The doctor pierces the child's skin with a thin needle connected to a wire running to a machine that records the pattern of electrical activity in the muscle tissue. EMGs are not always performed, however, because the test is somewhat painful.

Imaging studies

Some doctors may order a **magnetic resonance imaging** (MRI) test in order to evaluate the presence of inflammation in the muscles of children with normal muscle enzyme levels in their blood. It may also be done in order to identify appropriate muscles for testing when a biopsy is necessary.

Treatment

The treatment of juvenile dermatomyositis involves a combination of approaches. The treatment plan may also have to be changed periodically as the child's symptoms change.

Medications

Medications are the mainstay of treatment for juvenile dermatomyositis. The most common drug used is prednisone, a steroid that is given to reduce pain, control the fever and skin rash, and improve the strength of the child's muscles. Prednisone may be given in pill form or as a weekly intravenous infusion. Unfortunately, prednisone has a number of side effects, ranging from high blood pressure, weight gain, and stretch marks to mood changes and weak or damaged bones. If taken for a long period of time, prednisone may also lead to the development of eye cataracts and slow down the child's growth.

Another drug that is used to treat JDMS is methotrexate, an immunosuppressive drug that may be taken as pills or given as an injection. Methotrexate works by slowing down the immune system. It is usually given together with prednisone. It also has some potentially serious side effects, including **nausea and vomiting**, **diarrhea**, increased susceptibility to infections, skin **rashes**, a decrease in the number of blood cells, and potential liver damage. In some cases, the doctor may recommend another immunosuppressive drug known as cyclosporine to be taken together with methotrexate. If the child's skin rash is unusually severe, the doctor may prescribe hydroxychlorethotrexate (Plaquenil). Methotrexate, cyclosporine, and hydroxychlorethotrexate all belong to a category of medications known as disease-modifying anti-rheumatic drugs, or DMARDs.

Exercise and physical therapy

Exercise and physical therapy are an important part of treatment for JDMS because they help to prevent contractures, keep the child's joints flexible, and strengthen muscles. In most cases, the child will be referred to a physical therapist who can design an exercise program for the specific sets of muscles affected by the disease. The exercise program is modified as the child's strength gradually returns.

Psychotherapy

Because JDMS usually requires two years or even longer of drug treatments, exercise programs, limitations on some activities, and special attention to diet, children often become angry, depressed, or self-pitying. In some cases they may express resentment toward healthy siblings or classmates. The child's doctor may recommend either individual psychotherapy for the affected child or **family therapy** for the family as a whole.

Alternative treatment

Very little has been published regarding complementary and alternative (CAM) treatments for juvenile dermatomyositis, although some practitioners of traditional Chinese medicine (TCM) have reported success in treating the fever and heliotrope rash of JDMS with various Chinese herbal formulae.

Nutritional concerns

Children diagnosed with JDMS must eat a regular balanced diet with generous amounts of protein and calcium. The protein is necessary to repair damaged muscle tissue, and the calcium is needed to keep the child's bones strong. Because of the possible side effects of prednisone, however, the diet must be low in salt and sugar. More specifically, the child should not be allowed to eat take-out or fast foods except on rare occasions as a special treat. Parents should consult a professional dietitian or nutritionist to help plan a diet that is appealing to the child as well as healthful.

Prognosis

The prognosis of juvenile dermatomyositis varies but is usually related to the child's age and the severity of the vasculitis associated with the disease. Younger children generally recover more rapidly than adolescents. Most children with JDMS have active symptoms for about two years, although some may be able to do without medications after the first year and others may need drug treatment and physical therapy for many years. Some children recover without any relapses; however, most children with the disease have periods of remission alternating with recurrences of the symptoms.

Most children eventually recover completely from juvenile dermatomyositis; however, some have lifelong stiffness or muscle weakness from the disease. In a very few cases the child may die from complications related to myocarditis or from bowel perforation or lung disease caused by vasculitic ulcers.

Prevention

Because the causes are still unknown, there is no way to prevent juvenile dermatomyositis as of 2004.

Parental concerns

Although JDMS is rarely fatal, it can lead to medical emergencies if the child develops vasculitic ulcers. More commonly, however, the disease has a severe impact on families because of the length and complexity of treatment as well as the possibility of complications from the disease itself and side effects from the medications. Although two years is the average length of acute symptoms, some children are affected for years, even into adulthood. In addition, the unpredictable nature of

KEY TERMS

Calcinosis—A condition in which calcium salts are deposited in various body tissues. In juvenile dermatomyositis, calcinosis usually takes the form of small lumps of calcium compounds deposited in muscles or under the skin.

Contracture—A tightening or shortening of muscles that prevents normal movement of the associated limb or other body part.

Coxsackie virus—A type of enterovirus that may produce a variety of illnesses, including upper respiratory infections, myocarditis, and pericarditis. Coxsackieviruses resemble the virus that causes polio.

Cutaneous—Pertaining to the skin.

Disease-modifying anti-rheumatic drugs (DMARDs)—A group of medications given to treat severe cases of arthritis, JDMS, and other diseases that affect the joints. All DMARDs work by modifying the immune system.

Dysphagia—Difficulty in swallowing.

Heliotrope—A plant (*Heliotropium arborescens*) related to borage that has lavender or deep violet flowers. The characteristic skin rash of JDMS is sometimes called a heliotrope rash because of its reddish-purple color.

Idiopathic—Refers to a disease or condition of unknown origin.

Myocarditis—Inflammation of the heart muscle (myocardium).

Myopathy—Any abnormal condition or disese of muscle tissue, characterized by muscle weakness and wasting.

Myositis—Inflammation of the muscle.

Proximal muscles—The muscles closest to the center of the body.

Remission—A disappearance of a disease and its symptoms. Complete remission means that all disease is gone. Partial remission means that the disease is significantly improved, but residual traces of the disease are still present. A remission may be due to treatment or may be spontaneous.

Rheumatologist—A doctor who specializes in the diagnosis and treatment of disorders affecting the joints and connective tissues of the body.

Vasculopathy—Any disease or disorder that affects the blood vessels.

remissions and recurrences can be difficult to handle. If the child with JDMS has siblings, the parents must balance the needs of the affected child with the needs of healthy siblings. It is not unusual for either the affected child or other children in the family to develop emotional or behavioral problems. The Myositis Association and the **Muscular Dystrophy** Association, which are listed below under Resources, can help parents find support groups in their area for dealing with family members' emotional reactions to the disease as well as other problems of daily living.

With regard to education, most children with JDMS can continue to attend their regular school although they may need special transportation. They should not be isolated from other children.

See also Juvenile arthritis; Myopathies; Vasculitides.

Resources

BOOKS

Parker, James, et al. *The Official Patient's Sourcebook on Dermatomyositis.* San Diego, CA: Icon Group International, 2002.

"Polymyositis and Dermatomyositis." Section 5, Chapter 50 in *The Merck Manual of Diagnosis and Therapy*, edited by Mark H. Beers and Robert Berkow. Whitehouse Station, NJ: Merck Research Laboratories, 2002.

PERIODICALS

Chari, Geetha, and Teresita A. Laude. "Juvenile Dermatomyositis: An Overview." *International Pediatrics* 15 (January 2000): 21–5.

Duffy, C. M. "Health Outcomes in Pediatric Rheumatic Disease." *Current Opinion in Rheumatology* 16 (March 2004): 102–8.

Koler, Anthony, and Andrew Montemarano. "Dermatomyositis." *American Family Physician* 64 (November 1, 2001): 1565–72.

Pachman, L. M. "Juvenile Dermatomyositis: Immunogenetics, Pathophysiology, and Disease Expression." *Rheumatic Diseases Clinics of North America* 28 (August 2002): 579–602.

Rao, Y. A. "Survey on TCM Treatment of Polymyositis and Dermatomyositis." *Journal of Traditional Chinese Medicine* 23 (September 2003): 230–35.

Tezak, Z., et al. "Gene Expression Profiling in DQA1*0501+ Children with Untreated Dermatomyositis: A Novel Model of Pathogenesis." *Journal of Immunology* 168 (April 15, 2002): 4154–63.

Wedderburn, L. R., and C. K. Li. "Paediatric Idiopathic Inflammatory Muscle Diseases." *Best Practice and Research: Clinical Rheumatology* 18 (June 2004): 345–58.

Zipitis, C. S., et al. "Treatment Approaches to Juvenile Dermatomyositis." *Expert Opinion on Pharmacotherapy* 5 (July 2004): 1509–15.

ORGANIZATIONS

American Academy of Dermatology (AAD). PO Box 4014, Schaumburg, IL 60168–4014. Web site: <www.aad.org>.

Arthritis Foundation. PO Box 7669, Atlanta, GA 30357–0669. Web site: <www.arthritis.org>.

Muscular Dystrophy Association (MDA). 3300 East Sunrise Drive, Tucson, AZ 85718–3208. Web site: <www.mdausa.org>.

Myositis Association. 1233 20th Street NW, Suite 402, Washington, DC 20036. Web site: <www.myositis.org>.

National Institute of Arthritis and Musculoskeletal and Skin Diseases (NIAMS). 1 AMS Circle, Bethesda, MD 20892–3675. Web site: <www.niams.nih.gov>.

National Institute of Neurological Disorders and Stroke (NINDS). National Institutes of Health. 9000 Rockville Pike, Bethesda, MD 20892. Web site: <www.ninds.nih.gov>.

WEB SITES

Callen, Jeffrey P. "Dermatomyositis." *eMedicine*, December 5, 2002. Available online at <www.emedicine.com/derm/topic98.htm> (accessed November 24, 2004).

"Juvenile Dermatomyositis (JDMS)." *Arthritis Foundation.* Available online at <www.arthritis.org/conditions/DiseaseCenter/jdms.asp> (accessed November 24, 2004).

Mayo Clinic Staff. "Dermatomyositis." *MayoClinic.com*, October 15, 2003. Available online at <www.mayoclinic.com/invoke.cfm?id=DS00335> (accessed November 24, 2004).

OTHER

National Institute of Neurological Disorders and Stroke (NINDS). *NINDS Dermatomyositis Information Page.* Bethesda, MD: NINDS, 2003.

Rebecca Frey, PhD

Development tests

Definition

Development tests are tools that are used to help measure a child's developmental progress from infancy through **adolescence**.

Purpose

Every child develops at an individual pace. However, development tests may help to discriminate between normal variations in development among children and early signs of a developmental problem. About 16 percent of children have some form of developmental difficulty or delay, and more than 500,000 American children are assessed for early-intervention programs every year.

Development tests have different purposes depending on the age of the child and may be administered under a variety of circumstances. They are designed according to the expected skills of children at a specific age. The tests range from the passive evaluation of an infant to the complex testing of adolescents.

Development testing begins at birth in order to identify any problems as early as possible and try to correct them. The testing of a newborn can be used to detect neurological problems such as **cerebral palsy**. Testing continues with well-baby visits to the pediatrician. Although there are various schedules for routine well-child visits, the American Academy of Pediatrics recommends visits at the following ages:

• two to four days after birth or discharge from the hospital

• one month

• two months

• four months

• six months

• nine months

• 12 months

• 15 months

• 18 months

• yearly between the ages of two and six

• eight years

• ten years

• yearly until age 21

Many daycare centers and preschools use development tests. Most schools administer school readiness tests before admission. Many states and metropolitan school districts have devised or adapted their own development tests to be administered by schools. Development tests are also used to identify specific social or academic problems.

Developmental assessments usually combine standardized tests and observations to cover all aspects of a child's development, including the following:

• motor skills

• **language development**

• mental development

• social/emotional development

• self-help skills, including dressing and toileting

The types of developmental **assessment** include:

• developmental screening to identify children with special needs or who may be at risk for developmental delays or school difficulty

• diagnostic evaluation, if indicated by the screening, to confirm the presence and extent of a disability

• readiness tests to assess a child's specific skills and information

• observational and performance assessments to provide ongoing information about a child's development

Developmental screening tests usually are brief, general, play-based tests of skills. Screenings include tests administered to the child by an educator or healthcare professional and questionnaires for parents or childcare providers that inquire about developmental milestones. Screening tests only try to identify children who may have one or more problems. A screening test is not a diagnosis. Rather it may indicate that a child should be referred for developmental assessment or evaluation.

Developmental evaluations are lengthy, in-depth assessments of a child's skills. They are administered by trained professionals. They provide a profile of a child's strengths and weaknesses in all developmental areas and may be used to determine if the child is in need of an early-intervention and/or treatment program.

Readiness tests measure the extent to which a child has acquired certain skills for successfully undertaking some new learning activity. Although school-readiness tests may concentrate on academic skills, most of them also evaluate other aspects of development.

Description

A multitude of different development tests address every aspect of development at every age. They vary greatly in their reliability or validity (how consistently the test measures what it purports to measure). Many widely used tests have been administered, analyzed, and revised by professionals over a period of years. These, as well as new development tests, undergo frequent examination and review for reliability and validity. Other tests are devised by individuals and sold to parents over the Internet. Parents administer these tests to their child and return them for evaluation.

Some tests use developmental ages to describe a child's physical, perceptual, social, and emotional maturity. Development tests do not necessarily correlate in any way with **intelligence** tests. A standardized development has the following features or functions:

- attempts to obtain a systematic sample of a child's performance under prescribed conditions

- is scored by defined rules

- enables professionals to compare a child's performance to the performance of every other child who takes the same test

- has defined norms (averages, means, or patterns) that are regarded as typical for the specific population being tested

Some development specialists use a standard battery of tests. Others customize tests for the individual child, choosing the most appropriate. A written evaluation of the child is based on the child's test results. Standardized tests for infants and toddlers may be used to assess social, emotional, and intellectual development. Such tests usually consist of presenting a variety of tasks to the child, from very simple to challenging, in order to assess the child's full range of skills.

Test types

Types of development tests include the following:

- infant development scales

- sensory-motor tests

- speech and hearing tests

- neuropsychological tests that measure neurological functioning

- **preschool** psychoeducational batteries

- early screeners

- developmental surveys or profiles

- early learning profiles

- kindergarten or school readiness tests

- tests of **play** behavior

- social skills and social acceptance tests

Sensory-motor tests include general or specific measures of each of the five senses and **gross motor skills** (large muscle movement and control), **fine motor skills** (hand and finger skills), and **hand-eye coordination**. The development of motor skills generally progresses from head to toe. Thus babies usually gain control of their body parts in the following order:

- head and neck at about two months of age

- arms and hands, with grasping at about three months

- trunk, with sitting well by about eight months

- legs and feet, with most children walking by 14 or 15 months

Sensory-motor tests may include:

- visual acuity

- visual perception and organization

- color discrimination or color blindness

- visual-motor skills

- sensory integration

- perceptual skills

- perceptual-motor skills

- motor development

- movement and posture

- manual dexterity

An audiologist may test an infant or young child for signs of **hearing impairment** or loss, usually by transmitting sounds through earphones. Speech and hearing tests measure the mechanics of speaking and hearing the spoken word. These include tests for the following:

- auditory discrimination and comprehension

- speech perception and discrimination

- articulation

- voice fluency

- hearing loss or impairment

- stuttering

Infant/toddler tests

There are countless development tests designed for children from birth to about seven years of age, as well as tests for assessing development in disabled school-age children. The tests measure various skills, including the following:

- gross motor skills

- fine motor skills

- communication

- memory

- number concepts

- letter recognition

- social competence

Development tests are performed at each well-baby visit to the healthcare provider. Children are weighed and measured for height and head circumference. The results may be plotted on a growth chart that is specific for the child's age and gender (EpicCare Growth Chart) and compares a child's growth to other children of the same age and gender. The pediatrician may check the child's eyesight and hearing and ask various questions about the child's development, including the following areas:

- eating and sleeping patterns
- head control
- alertness
- response to voices
- voice recognition
- eye focusing
- strength and coordination
- posture
- noises
- smiling

THE BRAZELTON TEST In 1973 Harvard University pediatrician T. Berry Brazelton and his colleagues developed the Neonatal Behavioral Assessment Scale (NBAS), commonly known as "the Brazelton." It is based on the assumption that babies are highly capable at birth and communicate through their behavior. Test examiners are trained to support the infant in achieving the best possible scores. The test assumes that infants are born with four major developmental tasks:

- regulation of their autonomic nervous systems, including breathing and temperature regulation
- controlling their motor systems
- controlling their states or levels of consciousness
- social interaction

The NBAS examines a wide range of behaviors in newborns up to two months of age, creating a portrait of the infant's strengths, adaptive responses, possible vulnerabilities, and individuality. It tests 28 behavioral and 18 reflex items, including the following:

- signals that may overtax the infant, such as looking at the mother's face, noise, startles, or color changes
- muscle tone, reflexes, and activity levels
- ability to follow a red ball, a face, or a voice
- ability to control his or her state of consciousness and transitions between states

The examiner tests the infant's response to light, sound, or touch during **sleep** and the infant's ability to block out stimulation during sleep. The states examined are as follows:

- quiet sleep
- active sleep
- drowsy waking
- quiet alert
- fussing
- active crying

CLINICAL NEWBORN BEHAVIORAL ASSESSMENT SCALE (CLNBAS) The Clinical Newborn Behavioral Assessment Scale (CLNBAS), based on the NBAS, was developed in 2004 for use by clinicians. It is conducted in the presence of the parents. It focuses on the baby's individuality and unique adaptive or temperamental style and is designed to develop parent-infant and clinician-family relationships.

Ages and stages questionnaires are used to identify infants and young children who may need further evaluation. These questionnaires are completed by the parent or primary caregiver and are administered at the following ages:

- two-month intervals between the ages of four and 24 months
- three month intervals between the ages of 24 and 36 months
- six-month intervals between the ages of 36 and 60 months

Development tests for infants and toddlers usually include testing for the typical sequence of development that most children go through; for example, most children crawl before they walk and eat with their fingers before using utensils. These tests often are administered by a development assessment specialist, a developmental pediatrician, or an early-childhood special educator. The tests may measure developmental domains that include the following:

- gross motor development
- fine motor development
- language/communication and speech
- relationships to **toys** and other objects, to people, and to the larger world
- emotions
- coping behavior
- self-help skills

ARNOLD L. GESELL TESTS One of the earliest development tests was designed by Arnold L. Gesell, who founded the Clinic of Child Development at Yale University in 1911. By observing and filming infants and young children, and analyzing their functioning by studying the films frame by frame, Gesell delineated 10 normal stages of early childhood development. Gesell's tests include:

- Gesell Developmental Schedules
- Gesell Child Developmental Age Scale (GCDAS)
- Gesell Preschool Test to measure relative maturity in four basic fields of behavior
- Gesell Developmental Observation to assess a child's developmental age for grade placement and the development of instructional programs

NANCY BAYLEY SCALES OF INFANT DEVELOPMENT Developmental psychologist Nancy Bayley authored the **Bayley Scales of Infant Development** in the mid-twentieth century. Her mental scale evaluates various abilities, yielding a normalized standard score called the Mental Development Index. The Bayley Scales of Mental and Motor Development are used worldwide as standardized measures of infant development at eight months of age. The motor scale assesses:

- the degree of body control
- large-muscle coordination
- fine-motor manipulatory skills
- postural imitation
- motor quality

The behavior rating scale consists of 30 items, which measure the following:

- attention
- arousal
- orientation
- engagement
- emotional regulation
- test-taking behaviors

OTHER TESTS Other infant/toddler development tests include:

- Peabody Developmental Gross Motor Scale for infants
- Bury Infant Check to help identify children with special needs
- Infant Monitoring System for children aged four months to 36 months
- Early Coping Inventory of 48 items on sensory-motor organization, reactive behavior, and self-initiated behavior that are used to assess everyday coping strate-

gies in children between the ages of four and 36 months

Preschool tests

Developmental milestones are widely used tests for development in infants and children of all ages. Milestones in preschoolers evaluate the development of the following skills:

- gross motor skills
- fine motor skills
- language and communication
- emotional and social competency
- thinking, reasoning, and problem solving
- reading and writing
- creativity

The milestone test uses collection forms that are completed by a parent, caregiver, or educator on a monthly basis. The forms cover **family**, friends, and milestones corresponding to a specific area of development. They include a photo or anecdote that illustrates the activity corresponding to the milestone. The forms request that the activities be categorized according to the following descriptors:

- child-initiated
- teacher-initiated
- a new task
- a familiar task
- performed independently
- performed with adult guidance
- performed with peers
- one to five minutes in duration
- five to 15 minutes in duration
- more than 15 minutes in duration

Children who are slow to reach developmental milestones in one area may be ahead of their age in other areas. Sometimes developmental milestones are used as part of an assessment method known as minimum adequate surveillance that combines simple testing with the collection of relevant data.

TYPES OF PRESCHOOL TESTS The Assessment, Evaluation, and Programming System (AEPS) for infants and children often is used to test three to six-year-olds. Using activity stations in a school setting, the test measures skills such as balance, mobility, standing, and walking as well as play skills. The AEPS consists of the following:

- a 98-item family report on functional and social skills used in the child's everyday environment

- 87 cognitive items

- 49 social/communicative items

- 33 social items

- 39 adaptive items

- eight gross motor items

- four fine motor items

Other development tests that frequently are administered to preschoolers include the following:

- Griffith's mental development scales, which measure gross motor skills, personal-social development, hand and eye coordination, and performance, providing a general developmental quotient (GDQ) and separate subquotients (DQs) for each area of development

- Mullen Scales of Early Learning (MSEL), a comprehensive assessment of language, motor, and perceptual abilities in children from birth to five years, eight months of age

- Vineland Social-Emotional Early Childhood Scales

Screening tests

The Denver Developmental Screening Test (DDST) is a widely-used test of motor, language, speech, and interpersonal skills for children from birth to six years of age. It is used by physicians in well-baby visits and may include parental questionnaires.

Other screening tests include the following:

- Infant Developmental Screening Scale

- ages and stages questionnaires

- Battelle Developmental Inventory (BDI) screening test for screening, preliminary assessment, and/or initial identification of possible developmental strengths and weaknesses

- Brigance Early Preschool Screen for two-year-old and two-and-a-half-year-old children

- Brigance K and 1 Screen for kindergarten and first-grade children

- Miller FirstSTEP Screening Test for evaluating preschoolers

- Preschool Development Inventory, a brief screening inventory to help identify children with developmental, behavioral, or health problems

- Children at Risk Screener: preschool and kindergarten

- Early Screening Inventory for children aged three to six

- Howell Prekindergarten Screening Test

- Humanics National Child Assessment Form

- Kindergarten Screening Inventory

- Milani-Comparetti Motor Development Screening Test

Readiness tests

Readiness tests include the following:

- ABC Inventory to Determine Kindergarten and School Readiness

- Developmental Tasks for Kindergarten Readiness

- Kindergarten Readiness Test

- Phelps Kindergarten Readiness Scale

- Pediatric Examination of Educational Readiness at Middle Childhood

Communication tests

Communication development tests include the following:

- Sequenced Inventory of Communication Development for testing various early **communication skills** and assigning a communication age

- Assessing Semantic Skills Through Everyday Themes for preschool and early-elementary-aged children

- Expressive One-Word Picture Vocabulary Test to measure a child's ability to verbally label objects and people; a standardized test that yields age equivalents, standard scores, scaled scores, and percentile ranks

- Receptive One-Word Picture Vocabulary Test to provide information about a child's ability to understand language; a standardized test that yields age equivalents, standard scores, scaled scores, and percentile ranks

- Early Language Milestone (ELM) Scale to measure language development in children from birth to three years of age

- Peabody Picture Vocabulary Test, called "the Peabody," a short test that measures vocabulary in two-and-a-half to four-year-olds; sometimes used for screening

Speech and hearing tests include the following:

- Early Speech Perception Test

- Joliet 3-Minute Preschool Speech and Language Screen

- Fluharty Preschool Speech and Language Screening Test to identify preschool children who may warrant a comprehensive communication evaluation

- Assessing Linguistic Behaviors, Assessing Prelinguistic and Early Linguistic Behaviors in Developmentally Young Children

- Assessment of Fluency in School-Age Children

- Children's Articulation Test

- Clinical Evaluation of Language Fundamentals

- Phonological Assessment of Child Speech

Intelligence tests

Intelligence tests attempt to measure a child's ability to learn. Many such tests generally measure what a child has already learned. Results of these tests may be represented on a scale, as a mental age, or as an intelligence quotient (IQ). Some research indicates that IQ tests for children aged 18 to 20 months are not good indicators of future or even current abilities and that they usually measure motor rather than mental skills. However, other research has indicated that IQ tests in children as young as six months are good predictors of school IQ test results years later.

Frequently used intelligence tests include the following:

- Wechsler Preschool and Primary Scale of Intelligence for children aged three to seven years with norms for 17 age groups at three-month intervals

- Wechsler Intelligence Scale for Children

- Differential Ability Scales (DAS), for measuring overall cognitive ability and specific abilities in children aged two years and six months to seventeen years and eleven months

- Stanford-Binet Intelligence Scale for ages two years to adult, for scoring verbal reasoning, abstract and visual reasoning, quantitative reasoning, and short-term memory and yielding a composite score with a mean of 100

The Columbia Mental Maturity Scale (CMMS) does not depend on reading skills. The child makes perceptual discriminations involving color, shape, size, use, number, missing parts, and symbolic material. It appears to measure general reasoning ability, although there is some evidence that it is more a test of the ability to form and use concepts than a test of general intelligence. It provides standard age deviation scores for chronological ages between three years and six months and nine years and eleven months. The Maturity Index indicates the age group of the child in terms of test performance.

The Test of Nonverbal Intelligence is a quick, language-free measure of cognitive ability in children aged five years and older. It contains 55 problem-solving tasks of progressively increasing difficulty. It often is used for assessing children with speech, language, or hearing impairments, academic handicaps, or brain impairments, and for children who do not speak English. The Merrill-Palmer Scale of Mental Tests (MPSMT) is widely used as a nonverbal test for assessing visual-spatial skills in children aged one year and six months to six years.

Precautions

Designing child development tests presents numerous difficulties that may affect the results, including the following:

- motivating the child

- keeping the child's attention

- not discriminating among children

Some healthcare and education professionals are concerned that children are being over-tested, over-screened, and overanalyzed. Some experts question the use of conventional early childhood development tests for the following reasons:

- Young children are inexperienced at test-taking.

- High-stakes tests, such as those that influence major educational decisions, can have long-term negative consequences for children.

- Tests may be too narrow or one-dimensional.

- Teaching and learning may be negatively affected because of a focus on test results.

- There are major differences in the learning opportunities available to children.

- Sometimes tests are used for purposes other than those for which they were designed.

Preparation

The parent, the person who knows the child best, should participate in development tests as much as possible. Tests should be explained to parents who can then explain them to their children in terms that they will understand. The parents' feelings and personal observations should be considered when evaluating a child's development.

Risks

The major risk of development tests is that some children may be labeled in inappropriate ways because of their test results. Development tests are not infallible. Developmental screenings may over- or under-identify children with developmental delays. For example, some children who under-perform on a school readiness test go on to perform very well in school. Development tests may become outdated because of new, improved methods. Other tests may be found to be unreliable. Development tests must keep pace with demographic changes in the United States, in order to meet the needs, for example, of large numbers of young children who speak languages other than English.

Normal results

The range of normal development is very large. No two children develop at exactly the same rate. Children reach developmental milestones on their individual schedules and at their own pace. Some children completely skip developmental milestones such as rolling over or **crawling**. Although some children begin walking at eight months, others do not walk until 18 months; both are within the normal range. Children also may regress periodically. For example, children who sleep through the night may begin waking up often as they learn to talk.

Parental concerns

Although development tests often are used to reassure parents that their child is normal, many parents may feel anxious or defensive when told that their child should be tested. Parents should try to become active participants in their child's testing and understand the testing process and terminology. Increasingly parents and other family members are joining healthcare professionals and educators in administering development tests.

ZERO TO THREE: National Center for Infants, Toddlers, and Families recommends the following:

- Young children should not be separated from their parent or caregiver during testing since separation can cause anxiety.
- Children should not be assessed by a person they have just met for the first time.
- Tests should not be limited to easily measured factors such as motor or cognitive skills.
- Normative tests or milestone scales should not be the major basis for the developmental assessment of infants and young children.

Development tests can provide parents with a better understanding of their child's development and any possible need for intervention. Parents should feel free to disagree with test results and participate in further discussions concerning their child's development.

When to call the doctor

A pediatrician should be consulted if any of the following occurs:

- an infant's growth or development seems abnormal
- an infant or child seems to be losing developmental milestones

Resources

BOOKS

Plake, Barbara S., et al. *Fifteenth Mental Measurements Yearbook.* Lincoln, NE: Buros Institute of Mental Measurements, 2003.

ORGANIZATIONS

American Academy of Pediatrics. 141 Northwest Point Blvd., Elk Grove Village, IL 60007. Web site: <www.aap.org>.

The Brazelton Institute. Children's Hospital Boston, 1295 Boylston Street, Suite 320, Boston, MA 02215. Web site: <www.brazelton-institute.com>.

Buros Center for Testing. University of Nebraska-Lincoln, Lincoln, NE 68588. Web site: <www.unl.edu/buros/index.html>.

Child Development Institute. 3528 E. Ridgeway Road, Orange, CA 92867. Web site: <ww.cdipage.com/index.htm>.

Children's Institute. 27 N. Goodman St., Suite D103, Rochester, NY 14607. Web site: <www.childrensinstitute.net>.

ZERO TO THREE: National Center for Infants, Toddlers and Families. 2000 M Street NW, Suite 200, Washington, DC 20036. Web site: <www.zerotothree.org>.

WEB SITES

"The Clinical Neonatal Behavioral Assessment Scale: What Is It?" *The Brazelton Institute*. Available online at <www.brazelton-institute.com/clnbas.html> (accessed December 10, 2004).

"Diagnostic and Assessment Instruments Appropriate for Use with Children with Autism Spectrum Disorders." Available online at <www.isn.net/~jypsy/tests.htm> (accessed December 10, 2004).

"List of Terms: Terms Frequently Used in Developmental Assessment." *The Zero to Three New Visions for Parents Work Group*. Available online at <www.zerototthree.org/glossary.html>(accessed December 10, 2004).

Meisels, Samuel J. "Screening and Child Assessment." *The National Head Start Child Development Institute*, October 23, 2003. Available online at <http://hsnrc.org/CDI/smeisels1.cfm> (accessed December 10, 2004).

"Questions a Development Specialist Might Ask." *BabyCenter*. Available online at <www.babycenter.com/general/baby/babydevelopment/6598.html> (accessed December 10, 2004).

"Understanding the Baby's Language." *The Brazelton Institute*. Available online at <www.brazelton-institute.com/intro.html> (accessed December 10, 2004).

Margaret Alic, Ph.D.

Developmental delay

Definition

A developmental delay is any significant lag in a child's physical, cognitive, behavioral, emotional, or social development, in comparison with norms.

Description

Developmental delay refers to when a child's development lags behind established normal ranges for his or her age. Sometimes the term is used for **mental retardation**, which is not a delay in development but rather a permanent limitation. If most children crawl by eight months of age and walk by the middle of the second year, then a child five or six months behind schedule in reaching these milestones may be classified as developmentally delayed regarding mobility.

At least 8 percent of all children from birth to six years have developmental problems and delays in one or more areas of development. Some have global delays, which means they lag in all developmental areas.

Doctors try to locate the source of the delay and then design a treatment plan. When the cause of a child's delay is identified, the pediatrician and **family** know better what to expect, and the child can begin to receive appropriate treatment and support. If the problem is a genetic disorder, then parents may seek genetic counseling regarding their decision on having additional children.

The doctor's **assessment** has various components. The following are some of them:

- Developmental assessment: The physician's review of a child's current competencies (including knowledge, skills, and personality), and consideration of the best ways to help the child develop further.

- Family assessment: Interpretation of a child's development from family members, as well as their ideas about priorities and concerns about the child's future development.

- Multidisciplinary assessment: The assessment by a group of professionals who work with the child and family, directly or indirectly. The assessment interprets different phases of a child's development and types of behavior and skills.

- Play-based assessment: This assessment involves observation of the child playing alone, with peers, or with parents or other familiar caregivers, in free **play** or in special games. Play provides a diagnostic framework within which children show abilities, feelings, learning style, and social skills in groups.

Infancy

Infants who have medical problems at birth have an increased chance of developmental difficulties. High-risk infants should be in a follow-up program to track their progress because of an increased likelihood of developmental problems that may appear gradually in the first years of life.

Most children begin to speak their first words before they are 18 months old, and by age three the vast majority of children speak short sentences. Therefore, any child who is not speaking words or sentences by the third birthday may be developmental delayed.

Toddlerhood

Between the ages of 12 and 30 months, a child begins to strike out independently from a secure base of trust set up with the primary caregiver during the first year. As toddlers learn to walk, there is access to new territory. Boundless energy and insatiable curiosity drives the child to explore the environment and master new skills. Increased motor skills, immaturity, and lack of experience also place the toddler at risk for accidental injury. Children with developmental delays may tend to be more reserved and less adventuresome. They may tend not to explore their environment or take risks in it.

The healthy toddler years are characterized by the struggle for autonomy as the child develops a sense of personhood separate from the parent. Toddlers' egocentric and demanding behavior, often marked by temper **tantrums** and negativism, has given this period a negative reputation. However, toddlers who do not evince this challenging behavior may be delayed. Dramatic growth of language and cognitive skills during the second year enables the healthy toddler to think and solve problems for the first time. For the child who is not progressing in language skills, developmental delays are readily identifiable.

Preschool

The **preschool** period, from age three to five years, is a time of relative tranquility after the tumultuous toddler period. The healthy preschooler becomes increasingly independent, mastering many motor skills and developing greater social and emotional maturity. The preschooler is imaginative, creative, and curious. The developmentally delayed preschooler may act more egocentrically and show more signs of demanding behavior.

School age

Children from six to 12 years of age experience slow, steady physical growth and rapid cognitive and social development. The school-age child develops a sense of industry and learns the basic skills needed to be comfortable in society. The child develops appreciation of rules and a conscience that influences compliance and affects disobedience. Cognitively, the child grows from egocentrism in early childhood to more mature thinking. This maturity supports the ability to solve problems and make reasonably independent decisions. Competence and **self-esteem** increase with each academic, social, and athletic achievement. The relative stability and security of the school-age period prepare the child to manage the challenges of **adolescence**. However, the developmentally delayed child might not evince this growing competence.

Common problems

Although there are several areas of developmental areas, this article is restricted to global delay, delay in speech and language, motor and fine motor delays, and personal and social developmental delays.

Global developmental delay

Children with a diagnosis of mental retardation often have mixed or global development delays. However, low IQ may or may not be causally related to the delays. Two to three children out of every 100 have a mental handicap, and those with IQs of 55 or lower may have a physiological reason for their delay. Some children experience global developmental delay due to chromosomal abnormalities such as **Down syndrome** or **fragile X syndrome**. Global delays also are common in children with **fetal alcohol syndrome**.

Speech and language delay

Speech and language developmental delays are often prevalent in children with developmental disabilities. Eleven percent of toddlers have a speech and language problem. Expressive **language delay** is the most common developmental presentation. The social and educational development of children with delayed speech and language may be significantly disruptive (even in mild delays), so early identification and intervention is essential. Clinical diagnosis of delayed speech and language in children also considers hearing loss and **autism**, among other possible causes.

All children with delayed speech and language should have an audiometric assessment. Congenital sensorineural hearing loss (most common birth deficiency, affecting roughly two to four per 1,000 children) may cause delayed speech and language. Hearing problems occur often in newborns and in a higher number of babies who are in a neonatal intensive care unit. Universal newborn hearing screening programs should help in determining hearing acuity.

Hearing loss

Approximately half of all preschool children have varying hearing loss from **otitis media**. Language skills are affected by hearing loss, and more than one third of children with unilateral deafness fail one or more school grades. In general, children with the greatest hearing loss have the greatest language deficits. The earlier the hearing loss is identified, the better the outcome.

Autism

Children with delayed speech and language should be evaluated for cognitive disabilities. There is a close association among social and affective abilities and cognitive, sensory, and **language development**. Children who are unable to communicate effectively may have problems interacting verbally with their peers. Because social and pragmatic deficits are core characteristics of autism, it is important to look for dissociation among language, social adaptive skills, and motor behavior. Autism is a common disorder, occurring once in 500 children. It is one of the most complex neurodevelopment disorders. Children with autism have significant communication impairment.

In order to be eligible for programs and services for autism, a student must have delayed or abnormal functioning in at least one of three areas with onset before the age of three. These children have difficulty communicating and lack the ability to connect with peers. There may be a delay or total lack of language or the use of repetitive and idiosyncratic language. Other behaviors can include preoccupation with parts of objects, hand or finger flapping, and rocking.

Pervasive developmental disorder is two to three times more common than autism but less severe. When behaviors resembling autistic disorders are present with abnormalities of speech and language development, other syndromes and disorders are considered, for example, Asperger disorder, childhood disintegrative disorder, and Rett syndrome.

Musculature dysfunction

Oral motor dysfunction of the speech-producing musculature (in which children have dysarthria, or mechanical difficulties in speaking) is present in children with **cerebral palsy** and other conditions. The dysfunction leads to uncoordinated oral musculature.

Verbal difficulties

Verbal learning disability is often associated with speech and language problems in preschool children. Children with a specific learning disability, like children with severe mental retardation or autism, may present with dissociation in developmental skills. For example, language may be more delayed than motor skills. Also, lack of academic success at school can reflect dissociation between academic achievement and general intellectual abilities. Delays in language and cognitive areas may suggest a neurodevelopment diagnosis that presents as a nonverbal learning disability. In such cases, a child may have impaired visual-spatial perceptual abilities.

It is helpful to consider a child's expressive and receptive language skills. Children with an ability to understand are more likely to improve than children with expressive and receptive delays. Children whose primary difficulty involves receptive language are more likely to have developmental cognitive disability or autism spectrum disorder. Neurological problems may also be present when a child's head circumference is increasing either too fast or too slowly. Although physical and cognitive delays may occur together, one is not necessarily a sign of the other.

Neurological or medical conditions

In developmental language disorder, impaired language cannot be attributed to a neurological or general medical condition. There is a slow rate of language development, in which speech begins late and advances slowly. Children with developmental language disorder have an inconsistency between their cognitive functioning (nonverbal or performance measures) and their language skills. Different patterns of language impairment in developmental **language disorders** have distinct profiles of linguistic strengths and weaknesses. Developmental dysphasia may be the problem with some of these children. There are many reasons for a developmental language disorder, which occurs in about 10 percent of the population.

An unusual cause of acquired language disorder is an epileptic syndrome called Landau-Kleffner syndrome. Children with Landau-Kleffner develop typical language skills, which then deteriorate. The characteristics of this condition may be confused with autism.

Motor delay

Physician referrals of motor delay are most common during the first six to 18 months of a child's life. By evaluating a child's developmental profile, a doctor may develop a differential diagnosis.

Early motor delays are often a sign of neurological dysfunction. When a child has primarily motor delays, conditions such as cerebral palsy, ataxia, **spina bifida**, **spinal muscular atrophy** (withering) and myopathy may be present. If there is no motor delay, a child does not have cerebral palsy. When a motor delay exists with delays in other developmental areas, the child should be examined for visual impairment or mental handicap.

Older children with poor motor skills may have a developmental coordination disorder in which their motor skills are substantially below their cognitive abilities. Their clumsiness may link with a learning disability or attention-deficit hyperactivity disorder. Children with Asperger disorder are often clumsy; their neuropsychological profiles display significantly stronger verbal skills than nonverbal abilities.

HYPOTONIA Hypotonia is the most common symptom of motor dysfunction in newborns and infants. The child's developmental assessment should include the quality of the pregnancy, including the onset and vitality of fetal movements and problems during labor and delivery. The child's presentation in the neonatal period should be described, with special attention to the family history to document the potential for genetic disorder.

The key to diagnosing a hypotonic infant is a neuro-development examination. The challenge in correctly diagnosing a "floppy" child lies in distinguishing between central and neuromuscular hypotonia. A hypotonic infant who is not weak has low tone because of a central nervous disorder. Weakness strongly implies neuromuscular involvement. Normal or increased deep tendon reflexes suggest central hypotonia.

FINE-MOTOR ADAPTIVE DELAY If there is a delay in fine-motor adaptive development combined with delays in other developmental domains, the doctor will consider whether the child is visually impaired or mentally handicapped. It is important to assess the eyes and visual acuity of a child presenting with delayed fine-motor adaptive development.

If the delay occurs mainly in one developmental area, the child may have hemiplegia, a brachial plexus injury, such as Erb's or Klumple's palsy, or a broken clavicle. All symmetries of movement in the first two or three years should be watched.

In older preschool or elementary school children with fine-motor delays, developmental coordination disorder or a disorder of written expression may be causal. Developmental coordination disorder presents in about 6 percent of all children. It is often associated with attention deficit hyperactivity disorder or a learning disability.

PERSONAL AND SOCIAL DELAY When a child presents with personal and social delays, the doctor will consider whether the child has developmental cognitive

---

KEY TERMS

Accommodation—The ability of the lens to change its focus from distant to near objects and vice versa. It is achieved through the action of the ciliary muscles that change the shape of the lens.

Assessment—In the context of psychological assessment (a structured interview), assessment is information-gathering to diagnose a mental disorder.

Child development specialist—A professional who is trained in infant and toddler development and in the tools used to identify developmental delays and disabilities.

Development—The process whereby undifferentiated embryotic cells replicate and differentiate into limbs, organ systems, and other body components of the fetus.

Developmental milestone—The age at which an infant or toddler normally develops a particular skill. For example, by nine months, a child should be able to grasp and toss a bottle.

Disability—An inability to do something others can do; sometimes referred to as handicap or impairment.

Hypotonia—Having reduced or diminished muscle tone or strength.

Motor skills—Controlled movements of muscle groups. Fine motor skills involve tasks that require dexterity of small muscles, such as buttoning a shirt. Tasks such as walking or throwing a ball involve the use of gross motor skills.

---

disability, has autism, or is living in an environment of abuse, neglect, or deprivation.

Parental concerns

Many doctors routinely include developmental screening in physical examinations. Parents concerned about any of their child's development should seek the opinion of their pediatrician.

See also Cognitive development; Emotional development; Fine motor skills.

Resources

BOOKS

Beirne-Smith, Mary R., et al. *Mental Retardation: An Introduction to Intellectual Disability.* Paramus, NJ: Prentice-Hall, 2005.

Bloom, Paul. *Descartes' Baby: How the Science of Child Development Explains What Makes Us Human.* New York: Basic Books, 2005.

Harms, Louise. *Understanding Human Development: A Multidimensional Approach.* Oxford, UK: Oxford University Press, 2004.

Kass, Corrine E., et al. *A Human Development View of Learning Disabilities: From Theory to Practice.* Springfield, IL: Charles C. Thomas Publisher, 2005.

Loraas, O. Ivar. *Teaching Individuals with Developmental Delays: Basics.* Austin, TX: PRO-ED Inc., 2002.

PERIODICALS

Norberg, Shani. "Early Signs of Impaired Motor Development in Infants and Toddlers." *A Pediatric Perspective* 10 (July-August 2001): 1–3, 5.

Tervo, Raymond. "Identifying Patterns of Developmental Delays Can Help Diagnose Neurodevelopment Disorders." *A Pediatric Perspective* 12 (July 2003): 1–5.

WEB SITES

Carter, Sheena. "Developmental Follow-up of Pre-term Infants at High Risk for Delays." *Emory Regional Perinatal Center*, September 20, 2004. Available online at <www.childrensdisabilities.info/prematurity/followup.html> (accessed December 15, 2004).

Aliene S. Linwood, RN, DPA, FACHE

Developmental reading disorder *see*
Dyslexia

Dextromethorphan *see* **Cough suppressants**

▌Diabetes mellitus

Definition

Diabetes mellitus is a chronic disease in which the body is not able to correctly process glucose for cell energy due to either an insufficient amount of the hormone insulin or a physical resistance to the insulin the body does produce. Without proper treatment through medication and/or lifestyle changes, the high blood glucose (or blood sugar) levels caused by diabetes can cause long-term damage to organ systems throughout the body.

Description

There are three types of diabetes mellitus: type 1 (also called juvenile diabetes or insulin-dependent diabetes), type 2 (also called adult-onset diabetes), and gestational diabetes. While type 2 is the most prevalent, consisting of 90 to 95 percent of diabetes patients in the United States, type 1 diabetes is more common in children. Gestational diabetes occurs in pregnancy and resolves at birth.

Every cell in the human body needs energy in order to function. The body's primary energy source is glucose, a simple sugar resulting from the digestion of foods containing carbohydrates (primarily sugars and starches). Glucose from the digested food circulates in the blood as a ready energy source for any cells that need it. However, glucose requires insulin in order to be processed for cellular energy.

Insulin is a hormone or chemical produced by cells in the pancreas, an organ located behind the stomach. Insulin bonds to a receptor site on the outside of a cell. It acts like a key to open a doorway into the cell through which glucose can enter. When there is not enough insulin produced (as is the case with type 1 diabetes) or when the doorway no longer recognizes the insulin key (which happens in type 2 and gestational diabetes), glucose stays in the bloodstream rather entering the cells. The high blood glucose, or blood sugar, levels that result are known as **hyperglycemia**.

Type 1 diabetes

Type 1 diabetes occurs when the beta cells of the pancreas are damaged and stop producing the hormone insulin. While the exact cause of this cell damage is not completely understood, it is thought to be a combination of environmental and autoimmune factors. Despite the name juvenile diabetes, type 1 diabetes can be diagnosed at any stage of life, although diagnosis in childhood through young adulthood is most common.

Children who develop type 1 diabetes must eventually take regular insulin injections to keep blood glucose levels under control and do the job of the pancreas. Regular home testing of blood sugar levels is also important to make sure that the treatment is working effectively and to avoid a diabetic emergency such as **hypoglycemia** (low blood sugar) or hyperglycemia (high blood sugar).

Type 2 diabetes

The hallmark characteristic of type 2 diabetes is insulin resistance. The pancreas typically produces enough insulin (often too much insulin); however, cells are resistant to the insulin and it may not work as effectively. Type 2 is the most common form of diabetes, and most individuals with the disease are adults. However, children and adolescents can develop type 2 diabetes too, particularly if they are overweight and have a history of type 2 diabetes in their **family**.

Type 2 diabetes is treated with diet, **exercise**, and in some cases, oral medication and/or insulin. Self-monitoring of blood glucose levels is also important to assess how well treatment is working.

Demographics

An estimated 18.2 million Americans live with diabetes, and over 5 million of those remain undiagnosed. Up to 95 percent of diabetes patients in the United States have type 2 diabetes; the vast majority of Americans with diabetes are over 20 years of age. Those under 20 represent only 206,000 of the total cases of diabetes in the United States.

While type 2 diabetes is a growing problem among American youth due to climbing **obesity** rates and more sedentary lifestyles, type 1 diabetes is more prevalent in children and adolescents. An estimated one in 400 to 500 children have type 1 diabetes.

The American Diabetes Association reports that in 2002, diabetes cost Americans an estimated $132 billion in direct medical costs and indirect expenses such as lost productivity and disability payments.

Causes and symptoms

The causes of diabetes are not completely understood; however, there seem to be both genetic and environmental factors involved in the development of both type 1 and type 2 diabetes, meaning that a person may have a genetic predisposition to developing diabetes, but it takes an environmental factor such as a viral infection or excessive weight gain to actually make the disease surface.

Research has shown that some people who develop diabetes have common genetic markers. In type 1 diabetes, the immune system, the body's defense system against infection, is believed to be triggered by a virus or another microorganism that causes an autoimmune reaction that eventually destroys the insulin-producing cells (i.e., beta cells) in the pancreas. Up to 90 percent of cases of type 1 diabetes are the autoimmune subtype, sometimes called type 1A or immune-mediated diabetes.

The other subtype of type 1 diabetes is called idiopathic, or type 1B diabetes. People who have idiopathic type 1 diabetes also experience beta cell destruction, but it is due to a chromosomal abnormality or an unknown cause rather than any autoimmune process. Only tests for islet cell antibodies and other autoimmune markers can differentiate between the two subtypes, and because testing can be costly and treatment for both is the same (i.e., insulin), a physician may not necessarily order tests for autoimmunity.

Finally, damage caused by diseases of the pancreas (such as pancreatitis), endocrine disorders (e.g., endocrine tumors), and drugs or toxins can also destroy beta cell function.

In type 2 diabetes, family history, age, weight, activity level, and ethnic background can all play a role in the genesis of the disease. Individuals who are at high risk of developing type 2 diabetes mellitus include the following groups:

- people who are overweight or obese (more than 20 percent above their ideal body weight)
- people who have a parent or sibling with type 2 diabetes
- those who belong to a high-risk ethnic population (African-American, Native American, Asian-American, Hispanic, or Pacific Islander)
- people who live a sedentary lifestyle (i.e., exercise less than three times a week)
- women who have been diagnosed with gestational diabetes or have delivered a baby weighing more than 9 lbs (4 kg)
- people with high blood pressure (140/90 mmHg or above)
- people with high density lipoprotein cholesterol (HDL, or "good" cholesterol) level less than or equal to 35 mg/dl and/or a triglyceride level greater than or equal to 250 mg/dl

Several common medications can cause chronic high blood sugar levels and/or promote insulin resistance. These include atypical antipsychotics, beta blockers, corticosteroids, diuretics, estrogens, lithium, protease inhibitors, niacin, and some thyroid preparations.

Both type 1 and type 2 diabetes share similar symptoms caused by chronically high blood glucose levels.

Symptoms of both type 1 and type 2 diabetes include:

- excessive thirst
- frequent urination
- weight loss
- increased appetite
- unexplained fatigue
- slow healing cuts, **bruises**, and **wounds**

- frequent or lingering infections (e.g., urinary tract infection)
- mood swings and irritability
- blurred vision
- headache
- high blood pressure
- dry and itchy skin
- tingling, **numbness**, or burning in hands or feet

Symptoms of diabetes can develop suddenly (over days or weeks) in previously healthy children or adolescents, or can develop gradually, particularly in the case of type 2 diabetes.

Children and adolescents sometimes develop a condition known as diabetic ketoacidosis (DKA) at the time of their diagnosis. Ketones are acid compounds that form in the blood when the body breaks down fats and proteins for energy. When blood sugars are high (i.e., over 249 mg/dl, or 13.8 mmol/L) for prolonged periods of time, ketones build up in the bloodstream to dangerous levels. Symptoms of DKA include abdominal **pain**, excessive thirst, **nausea and vomiting**, rapid breathing, extreme lethargy, and drowsiness. Patients with ketoacidosis will also have a fruity or sweet breath odor. Left untreated, this condition can lead to coma and has the potential to be fatal. DKA is more common in people with type 1 diabetes, although it can occur in type 2 diabetes as well.

Symptoms of type 2 diabetes can begin so gradually that a person may not know that he or she has it. It is not unusual for type 2 diabetes to be detected while a patient is seeing a doctor about another health concern that is actually being caused by the yet undiagnosed diabetes, such as heart disease, chronic infections (e.g., urinary tract infections, yeast infections), blurred vision, numbness in the feet and legs, or slow-healing wounds.

When to call the doctor

If left untreated, diabetes is a life-threatening condition. Any child displaying symptoms of diabetes should be taken to a doctor or emergency care facility for evaluation immediately.

Diagnosis

Diagnosis of diabetes is suspected based on symptoms and confirmed by blood tests that measure the level of glucose in blood plasma. Dipstick or reagent test strips that measure glucose in the urine can only detect glucose levels above 180 mg/dl and are non-specific, so they are not useful in the diagnosis of diabetes. However, they are a non-invasive way to obtain a fast and simple reading that a physician might use as a basis for ordering further diagnostic blood tests for diabetes, particularly in children.

Blood tests are the gold standard for the diagnosis of both type 1 and type 2 diabetes in children and adults. The American Diabetes Association recommends that a random plasma glucose, fasting plasma glucose, or oral glucose tolerance test (OGTT) be used for diagnosis of diabetes. The OGTT is commonly used as a screening measure for gestational diabetes. Fasting plasma glucose is the test of choice unless a child is exhibiting classic symptoms of diabetes, in which case a random (or casual) plasma glucose test is acceptable.

Unless hyperglycemia is obvious (e.g., blood glucose levels are extremely high or the child experiences DKA), the fasting or random plasma glucose test should be confirmed on a subsequent day with a repeat test.

Fasting plasma glucose test

Blood is drawn from a vein in the child's arm following an eight-hour fast (i.e., no food or drink), usually in the morning before breakfast. The red blood cells are separated from the sample and the amount of glucose is measured in the remaining plasma. A fasting plasma glucose level of 126 mg/dl (7.0 mmol/l) or higher indicates diabetes (with a confirming retest on a subsequent day).

Random plasma glucose test

Blood is drawn at any time of day, regardless of whether the patient has eaten. A random plasma glucose concentration of 200 mg/dl (11.1 mmol/l) or higher in the presence of symptoms indicates diabetes.

Oral glucose tolerance test

Blood samples are taken both before and several times after a patient drinks 75 grams of a glucose-based beverage. If plasma glucose levels taken two hours after the glucose drink is consumed are 200 mg/dl (11.1 mmol/L) or higher, the test is diagnostic of diabetes (and should be confirmed on a subsequent day if possible).

Although the same diagnostic blood tests are used for both types of diabetes, whether a child is diagnosed as type 1 or type 2 can typically be determined based on her personal and medical history. The majority of children diagnosed in childhood are type 1, but if blood test results indicate prediabetes and a child is significantly overweight and has a history of type 2 diabetes in her family, type 2 is a possibility.

Further blood tests can help to differentiate between type 1 and type 2 when the diagnosis is unclear. One of these is an assessment of c-peptide levels, a protein released along with insulin that can help a physician determine whether or not a patient is producing sufficient amounts of insulin. The other is a GAD (Glutamic Acid Decarboxylase) autoantibody test. The presence of GAD autoantibodies may indicate the beginning of the autoimmune process that destroys pancreatic beta cells.

Treatment

Children with type 1 diabetes must take insulin injections or infusions. Their dosage needs may change over time. Sometimes children will experience a decreased need for insulin once blood sugars are brought under control following diagnosis. Their insulin needs may go down, and in some cases, they can stop taking injections for a time. This phenomenon, known as the honeymoon period, can last anywhere from a few days to months.

Children with diabetes and their parents should learn to operate a home blood glucose monitor. Home testing can prevent dangerous highs and lows and help parents and children understand how food and exercise impact blood sugar levels. Blood glucose levels taken before meals are also used to calculate dose size of insulin. A small needle or lancet is used to prick the finger or alternate site and a drop of blood is collected on a test strip that is inserted into a monitor. The monitor then calculates and displays the blood glucose reading on a screen. Although individual blood glucose targets should be determined by a medical professional in light of a child's medical history, the general goal is to keep them as close to normal (i.e., 90 to 130 mg/dl or 5 to 7.2 mmol/L before meals) as possible.

Insulin

Children with type 1 diabetes need daily injections of insulin to help their bodies use glucose. The amount and type of insulin required depends on the height, weight, age, food intake, and activity level of the individual diabetic patient. Some patients with type 2 diabetes may also need to use insulin injections if their diabetes cannot be controlled with diet, exercise, and oral medication. Injections are given subcutaneously, that is, just under the skin, using a small needle and syringe, an insulin pen injector, an insulin infusion pump, or a jet injector device. Injection sites can be anywhere on the body where there is a layer of fat available, including the upper arm, abdomen, or upper thigh.

Insulin may be given as an injection of a single dose of one type of insulin once a day, or different types of insulin can be mixed and given in one dose or split into two or more doses during a day. Patients who require multiple injections over the course of a day may be able to use an insulin pump that administers small doses of insulin on demand. The small battery-operated pump is worn outside the body and is connected to a cannula (a thin, flexible plastic tube) that is inserted into the abdomen called an insertion set. Pumps are programmed to infuse a small, steady infusion of insulin (called a basal dose) throughout the day, and larger doses (called boluses) before meals. Because of the basal infusion, pumps can offer many children much tighter control over their blood glucose levels and more flexibility with their diet than insulin shots afford them.

Regular insulin is fast-acting and starts to work within 15 to 30 minutes, with its peak glucose-lowering effect about two hours after it is injected. Its effects last for about four to six hours. NPH (neutral protamine Hagedorn) and Lente insulin are intermediate-acting, starting to work within one to three hours and lasting up to 18 to 26 hours. Ultra-lente is a long-acting form of insulin that starts to work within four to eight hours and lasts 28 to 36 hours. Peakless, or basal-action insulin (insulin glargine, or Lantus) starts working in 15 minutes and has a duration of between 18 and 26 hours.

Nutritional concerns

Because dietary carbohydrates are the primary source of glucose for the body (the other source being the liver), it is very important that children with diabetes learn to read labels and be aware of the amount of carbohydrates in the foods they eat. Children and their parents are usually advised to consult a registered dietitian (RD) to create an individualized, easy to manage food plan that fits their family's health and lifestyle needs. A well-balanced, nutritious diet provides approximately 50 to 60 percent of calories from carbohydrates, approximately 10 to 20 percent of calories from protein, and less than 30 percent of calories from fat. The number of calories required depends on age, weight, and activity level. An RD can also teach the family how to use either the dietary exchange lists or carbohydrate counting system to monitor food intake.

Each food exchange contains a known amount of calories in the form of protein, fat, or carbohydrate. A patient's diet plan will consist of a certain number of exchanges from each food category (meat or protein, fruits, breads and starches, vegetables, and fats) to be eaten at meal times and as snacks. Patients have flexibility in choosing which foods they eat as long as they stick with the number of exchanges prescribed by their RD based on their caloric requirements.

Carbohydrate counting involves totaling the grams of carbohydrates in the foods your child eats to ensure the child does not exceed her goal for the day. In the simple-carb counting method, one carbohydrate choice or unit equals 15 grams of carbohydrates (which is equivalent to one starch or fruit exchange in the exchange method). The number of carb choices allowed daily is based on caloric requirements.

Children with type 1 diabetes who use fast-acting insulin before meals may find that carb counting gives them tighter control of their blood glucose levels, since they can compute the number of insulin units based on both their carbohydrate intake (called the carbohydrate to insulin ratio) and before-meal blood glucose readings.

Dietary changes and moderate exercise are usually the first treatments implemented in type 2 diabetes. Weight loss may be an important goal in helping overweight children and adolescents control their blood sugar levels. Exercise helps keep blood glucose levels down and has other health benefits, as well.

Oral medications

Children with type 2 diabetes may be prescribed oral medications if they are unable to keep their blood glucose levels under control with dietary and exercise measures. As of 2004, metformin was the only oral medication approved by the U.S. FDA for use in children over age ten. Metformin (trade name Glucophage) is in the biguanide class of drugs and works by reducing the amount of glucose the liver produces and the amount of circulating insulin in the body. Other adult type 2 diabetes medications, such as sulfonylureas and meglitinide drugs, which work by increasing insulin production, may be prescribed off-label for pediatric use.

Transplants

Transplantation of a healthy pancreas into a patient with type 1 diabetes can eliminate the need for insulin injections; however, this transplant is typically done only if a kidney transplant is performed at the same time. Although a pancreas transplant is possible, it is not clear if the potential benefits outweigh the risks of the surgery and life-long drug therapy needed to prevent organ rejection, particularly in the case of children.

A second type of transplant procedure, as of 2004 in experimental clinical trials and not available to children, is an islet cell transplant. In this type of treatment, insulin-producing islet cells are harvested from a donor pancreas and injected into the liver of a recipient, where they attach to new blood vessels and (ideally) begin producing insulin. A lifetime regimen of immunosup-pressive drugs is required to prevent rejection of the transplanted cells.

Prognosis

As of 2004 diabetes is a chronic and incurable disease. While stem cell research holds great promise for future therapies and potential cures, as of the early 2000s the best hope for keeping children well with diabetes and avoiding long-term complications is maintaining good blood glucose control. The landmark Diabetes Control and Complications Trial (DCCT) found that patients with type 1 diabetes who kept their blood sugar levels as close to normal as possible reduced their risk for developing diabetic eye disease by 76 percent, for diabetic kidney disease by 50 percent, and for diabetic neuropathy by 60 percent.

Diabetes and its related complications was the sixth leading cause of death in 2000. According to the National Institutes of Health, cardiovascular, or heart and blood vessel disease, is the leading cause of diabetes-related death. Uncontrolled diabetes is a leading cause of blindness, end-stage renal disease, and limb amputations. Eye problems including cataracts, glaucoma, and diabetic retinopathy also are more common in people with diabetes.

Diabetic neuropathy is the result of nerve damage caused by uncontrolled diabetes. Autonomic neuropathy affects the autonomic nervous system and can cause gastroparesis (nerve damage of the stomach), neurogenic bladder (nerve damage of the urinary bladder), and a host of other problems with involuntary functions of the nervous system.

In peripheral neuropathy (PN), nerve damage in the extremities (e.g., the legs and feet) causes numbness, pain, and burning. Diabetic foot ulcers are a particular problem since frequently the patient does not feel the pain of a blister, callous, or other minor injury. Poor blood circulation in the legs and feet contribute to delayed wound healing. The inability to sense pain along with the complications of delayed wound healing can result in minor injuries, blisters, or calluses becoming infected and difficult to treat. The most serious consequence of this condition is the potential for amputation of toes, feet, or legs due to severe infection.

Diabetic kidney disease is another common complications of diabetes. Long- term complications may include the need for kidney dialysis or a kidney transplant due to kidney failure. Diabetes is the number one cause of chronic kidney failure in America.

Children and adults with the autoimmune form of type 1 diabetes are also at greater risk for other autoimmune disorders, including thyroid disease, celiac sprue (sometimes called gluten intolerance), autoimmune hepatitis, myasthenia gravis, and pernicious anemia.

Prevention

As of 2004 research continues on diabetes prevention and improved detection of those at risk for developing diabetes. While the onset of type 1 diabetes is unpredictable, the risk of developing type 2 diabetes may be reduced by maintaining ideal weight and exercising regularly. Both physical and emotional stress can cause increases in blood glucose levels, so getting regular immunizations and well-child check-ups, practicing good **sleep** and hygiene habits, encouraging emotional and social growth, and maintaining a stress- controlled lifestyle is important for children with type 1 or type 2 diabetes.

Parental concerns

Parents of children with diabetes must work with their child's teachers and school administrators to ensure that their child is able to test her blood sugars regularly, take insulin as needed, and have access to food or drink to treat a low. Someone at school should also be trained in how to administer a glucagon injection, an emergency treatment for a hypoglycemic episode when a child loses consciousness.

Section 504 of the Rehabilitation Act of 1973 enables parents to develop both a Section 504 plan (which describes a child's medical needs) and an individualized education plan (IEP) (which describes what special accommodations a child requires to address those needs). An IEP should cover such issues as blood glucose monitoring, dietary plans, and treating highs and lows. If school staff has little to no experience with diabetes, bringing in a certified diabetes educator (CDE) to offer basic training may be useful.

Children with diabetes can lead an active life and enjoy most of the activities and foods their peers do, with a few precautions to avoid blood sugar highs or lows. A certified diabetes educator that has experience working with children can help them understand the importance of regular testing as well as methods for minimizing discomfort. Diabetes summer camps, where children can learn about diabetes care in the company of peers and counselors who also live with the disease, may be useful from both a health and a social standpoint. In addition, peer support groups can sometimes help children come to terms with their diabetes.

Hypoglycemia, or low blood sugar, can be caused by too much insulin, too little food (or eating too late to

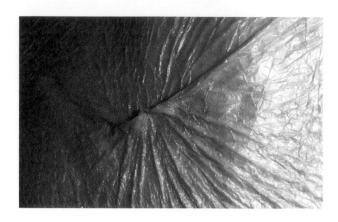

Wrinkled, dehydrated skin of a person in a diabetic coma. Untreated diabetes mellitus results in elevated blood glucose levels, causing a variety of symptoms that can culminate in a diabetic coma. *(© Dr. P. Marazzi/Science Photo Library, National Audubon Society Collection/Photo Researchers, Inc.)*

coincide with the action of the insulin), alcohol consumption, or increased exercise. A child with symptoms of hypoglycemia may be hungry, cranky, confused, and tired. The patient may become sweaty and shaky. Left untreated, a child can lose consciousness or have a seizure. This condition is sometimes called an insulin reaction and should be treated by giving the patient something sweet to eat or drink like candy, juice, glucose gel, or another high sugar snack. A child who loses consciousness due to a low should never be given food or drink due to the risk of **choking**. In these cases, a glucagon injection should be administered and the child should be taken to the nearest emergency care facility.

While exercise can lower blood glucose levels, children with diabetes can and do excel in **sports**. Proper hydration, frequent testing, and a before-game or practice snack can prevent hypoglycemia. Coaches or another onsite adult should be aware of a child's medical condition and be prepared to treat a hypoglycemic attack if necessary.

The other potential danger to a child with diabetes— diabetic ketoacidosis—is uncommon and most likely to occur prior to a diagnosis. It may also happen if insulin is discontinued or if the body is under stress due to illness or injury. Ketones in the urine can be detected using dipstick tests (e.g., Ketostix), or detected using a home ketone blood monitor. Early detection facilitates early treatment and can prevent full-blown DKA.

Because the symptoms of DKA can mimic the flu, and the flu can increase blood sugar levels, a child who comes down with a flu-like illness should be monitored closely and tested regularly. An increase in insulin may also be necessary; parents of children with diabetes

KEY TERMS

Diabetic retinopathy—A condition seen most frequently in individuals with poorly controlled diabetes mellitus where the tiny blood vessels to the retina, the tissues that sense light at the back of the eye, are damaged. This damage causes blurred vision, sudden blindness, or black spots, lines, or flashing light in the field of vision.

Glucagon—A hormone produced in the pancreas that changes glycogen, a carbohydrate stored in muscles and the liver, into glucose. It can be used to relax muscles for a procedure such as duodenography. An injectable form of glucagon is sometimes used to treat insulin shock.

Honeymoon phase—A period of time shortly following diagnosis of type 1 diabetes during which a child's need for insulin may decrease or disappear altogether. The honeymoon phase is transitional, and insulin requirements eventually increases again.

Hyperglycemia—A condition characterized by excessively high levels of glucose in the blood. It occurs when the body does not have enough insulin or cannot use the insulin it does have to turn glucose into energy.

Hypoglycemia—A condition characterized by abnormally low levels of glucose in the blood.

Insulin—A hormone or chemical produced by the pancreas that is needed by cells of the body in order to use glucose (sugar), a major source of energy for the human body.

Ketoacidosis—Usually caused by uncontrolled type I diabetes, when the body isn't able to use glucose for energy. As an alternate source of energy, fat cells are broken down, producing ketones, toxic compounds that make the blood acidic. Symptoms of ketoacidosis include excessive thirst and urination, abdominal pain, vomiting, rapid breathing, extreme tiredness, and drowsiness.

Off-label use—Prescribing a drug for a population (e.g., pediatric) or condition for which it was not originally approved by the U.S. FDA. For example, sulfonylurea drugs are not FDA approved for use in children with type 2 diabetes due to a lack of clinical studies in pediatric populations, but a physician may prescribe them in an off-label use of the drug.

Prediabetes—A precursor condition to type 2 diabetes, sometimes called impaired glucose tolerance or impaired fasting glucose. Prediabetes is clinically defined as individuals who have elevated blood glucose levels that are not diagnostic of type 2 diabetes but are above normal (for the fasting plasma glucose test, this measurement would be 100 to 125 mg/dL (5.6 to 6.9 mmol/L).

should talk with their pediatrician about a sick day plan for their child before they need it.

See also Hypoglycemia.

Resources

BOOKS

The American Diabetes Association Complete Guide to Diabetes, 3rd ed. Alexandria, VA: American Diabetes Association, 2002.

Brackenridge, Betty, and Richard Rubin. *Sweet Kids: How to Balance Diabetes Control and Good Nutrition with Family Peace*, 2nd ed. Alexandria, VA: American Diabetes Association, 2002.

Ford-Martin, Paula, with Ian Blumer. *The Everything Diabetes Book*. Avon, MA: Adams Media, 2004.

ORGANIZATIONS

American Diabetes Association. 1701 North Beauregard St., Alexandria, VA 22311. Web site: <www.diabetes.org>.

American Dietetic Association. 216 W. Jackson Blvd., Chicago, IL 60606–6995. Web site: <www.eatright.org>.

Children with Diabetes. 5689 Chancery Place, Hamilton, OH 45011. Web site: <www.childrenwithdiabetes.org>.

Juvenile Diabetes Research Foundation. 120 Wall St., 19th Floor, New York, NY 10005. Web site: <www.jdrf.org>.

National Diabetes Information Clearinghouse. 1 Information Way, Bethesda, MD 20892–3560. Web site: <www.niddk.nih.gov/health/diabetes/ndic.htm>.

WEB SITES

"2004 Clinical Practice Recommendations." *Diabetes Care*, January, 2004. Available online at <http://care.diabetesjournals.org/content/vol27/suppl_1/> (accessed December 26, 2004).

Ford-Martin, Paula. "About Diabetes" Available online at <http://diabetes.about.com> (accessed December 26, 2004).

Mendosa, David. *David Mendosa's Diabetes Directory.* Available online at <www.mendosa.com/diabetes.htm> (accessed December 26, 2004).

Paula Ford-Martin
Altha Roberts Edgren
Teresa G. Odle

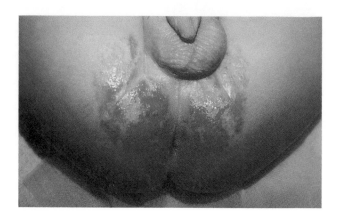

Baby with severe diaper rash. *(© Custom Medical Stock Photo, Inc.)*

Diaper rash

Definition

Dermatitis of the buttocks, genitals, lower abdomen, or thigh folds of an infant or toddler is called diaper rash. The outside layer of skin normally forms a protective barrier that prevents infection; when the barrier fails, the child may develop a rash in the area covered by the diaper. Diaper **rashes** occur equally with cloth diapers and disposable diapers.

Description

Diaper dermatitis results from prolonged contact with irritants such as moisture, chemical substances, and friction. Urine ammonia, formed from the breakdown of urea by fecal bacteria, is irritating to sensitive infant skin. Ammonia by itself does not cause skin breakdown. Only skin damaged by infrequent diaper changes and constant urine and feces contact is prone to damage from ammonia in urine. Inadequate fluid intake, heat, and detergents in diapers aggravate the condition. Bouts of **diarrhea** can quickly cause rashes in most children. Diaper rash begins with erythema in the perianal region. Left untreated, the area can quickly excoriate and progress to macules and papules, which form erosions and crust. Under certain circumstances (in infants under the age of six months, toddlers who have been on **antibiotics**, and immune compromised children) diaper dermatitis may become secondarily infected with Candida ablicans. Sometimes severe diaper dermatitis becomes super-infected with bacteria (streptococci or staphylococci).

Demographics

Diaper rashes occur in the diaper-wearing age group (birth to three years of age). Diaper rash occurs in about 10 percent of infants and is most common between the ages of seven and nine months. Some infants seem predisposed to diaper dermatitis. These infants have such sensitive skin that diaper dermatitis is a problem from the first few days of life.

Causes and symptoms

When parents and caretakers do not change the children's diapers often, feces is in contact with skin and irritation develops in the perianal area. Urine left in diapers too long breaks down into ammonia, a chemical that is irritating to infant skin. Ammonia dermatitis of this type is a problem in the second half of the first year of life when the infant is producing a larger quantity of urine.

When the diaper area has prolonged skin contact with wetness the natural oils are stripped away, the outer layer of skin is damaged, and there is increased susceptibility to infection by bacteria or yeast.

Frequently a flat, red rash resulting from chafing of the diaper against tender skin causes friction rash. This rash is not in the skin folds. It may be more definite around the edges of the diaper, at the waist and leg bands. The baby does not seem to experience much discomfort.

Sometimes chemicals in detergents contribute to **contact dermatitis**. These rashes should clear up as soon as the chemicals are removed. Ignoring the condition may lead to a secondary infection that is more difficult to resolve.

Another infectious cause of diaper rash is **impetigo**. This bacterial infection is characterized by blisters that ooze and crust.

When to call the doctor

Parents should call the child's healthcare provider for the following reason:

- newborn with rash looks or acts sick or has a fever
- rash looks infected (pimples, blisters, boils, weeping sores, yellow crusts, red streaks)

- rash is not better in three days after treatment for yeast
- rash bright red then peeling off in sheets or raw and bleeding
- rash beyond the diaper area
- rash painful and not responding to home care

Diagnosis

Diagnosis is made by examining the diaper area and taking the history of the onset and duration of the lesions.

The presence of skin lesions means the baby has diaper rash. However, there are several types of rash that may need specific treatment to heal. It is useful to be able to distinguish them by their appearance and causes.

A baby with a rash that does not clear up within two to three days or a rash with blisters or bleeding should receive an evaluation and care from a healthcare professional.

Treatment

Antibiotics are prescribed for rashes caused by bacteria and impetigo. This may be a topical or oral formula, depending on the size of the area involved and the severity of the infection.

Over-the-counter antifungal creams are often used to treat a rash resulting from yeast. If topical treatment is not effective, an oral antifungal is prescribed. Treatment of diaper candida in young infants should include oral drops to treat any candida in the mouth and gut to avoid re-infection.

Mild steroid creams, such as 0.5 to 1 percent hydrocortisone, may be used to treat **seborrheic dermatitis** and intertrigo. Prescription strength creams are needed for short-term treatment of stubborn cases. Intertrigo can be treated with a combination of hydrocortisone and anti-fungal creams.

Complication

The main complication is secondary infection by yeast or bacteria.

Home care

Good diaper hygiene prevents or clears up many simple cases of diaper rash. Many rashes can be treated as follows:

- Change diapers frequently.

- Keep the area dry and clean. Check the diaper often, every hour if the baby has a rash and change the diaper as soon as it is wet or soiled. Check at least once during the night. Good air circulation is also important for healthy skin. Babies should have some time without wearing a diaper. A cotton pad can protect the bed while the baby is diaper free.

- Frequent and vigorous washing with soap can strip the baby's tender skin of natural protective barriers. Wash gently but thoroughly, including the skin folds. Plain water may be the best cleaning agent when there is a rash. Using warm water in a spray bottle (or give a quick bath) and then lightly pat the skin dry to avoid irritation.

- Instead of cleaning the baby's bottom with a moist wipe or washcloth, hold the diaper area over the sink and let warm water wash over the inflamed skin. Then dry the area using a blow-dryer set on cool. Washing with plain water and drying with air is soothing to sore skin; it speeds healing by decreasing friction on the area. Some wipes contain alcohol or chemicals that can be irritating and only make diaper rash worse.

- Parents can sit the baby in a basin or tub of lukewarm water for several minutes with each diaper change. This helps clean and may also be comforting. Or they can pour warm water from a pitcher or use a squirt bottle. They should not use soap unless there is sticky stool, then a mild liquid soap in a basin of warm water is effective; wash gently and rinse well. Baby oil on a cotton ball can also remove stool from small areas.

- Leave diaper off for a while.

- Do not use airtight rubber pants over the diaper area. Some cloth-like disposable diapers promote better air circulation than plastic-type diapers. If disposable diapers are used, it helps to punch holes in them to let in air.

- Petroleum jelly provides a protective coating, even on sore, redden skin, and is easy to clean. Parents should not use talcum powder because of the risk of **pneumonia**. However, cornstarch reduces friction and may prevent future rashes.

Nutrition

What the baby eats can make a difference in stool frequency and acidity. Typically, breast-fed babies have fewer problems with rashes. When adding a new food to the diet, the baby should be watched closely to see whether rashes appear around the baby's mouth or anus. If they do, the new food should be avoided temporarily.

Babies who are taking antibiotics are more likely to get rashes because of yeast. To help bring the good bacterial counts back to normal, *Lactobacillus bifidus* can be added to the diet. It is available in powder form from most health food stores.

Herbal treatment

Some herbal preparations can be useful for diaper rash. Calendula reduces inflammation, tightens tissues, and disinfects. It is recommended for seborrheic dermatitis as well as for general inflammation of the skin. The ointment should be applied at each diaper change. Chickweed ointment can also sooth irritated skin when it is applied once or twice daily.

Prognosis

With proper treatment these rashes are usually better in three days if there is no underlying health problem or skin disease. If the rash does not improve with treatment then the child probably has a yeast infection. In that case, the rash becomes bright red and raw, covers a large area, and is surrounded by red dots. For yeast infection, the child needs a special cream.

Prevention

Changing the diaper immediately and good cleaning are the best action a parent can take to prevent diaper rash. Diaper rashes occur equally with cloth diapers and disposable diapers. Some children will get a rash from certain brands of disposable diapers or from sensitivity to some soaps used in cloth diapers. If cloth diapers are used, always wash them separate from other clothing and add bleach to the soap. After washing, the diapers should be rinsed thoroughly.

Parental concerns

Diapering. There are two choices, cloth or disposable. Parents need to decide what works best for their baby and lifestyle.

In the event of suspected yeast, a tablespoon of cider vinegar in a cup of warm water can serve as a diaper area wash. This is diluted enough that it should not burn, but acidifies the skin pH enough to hamper the yeast growth.

Barrier ointments can be valuable to treat rashes. Those that contain zinc oxide are especially effective. These creams and ointments protect already irritated skin. Cornstarch powder is soothing to rashes that are moist, such as impetigo.

KEY TERMS

Dermatitis—Inflammation of the skin.

Diaper dermatitis (diaper rash)—An inflammatory reaction to irritants in the diaper area.

Impetigo—A bacterial infection of the skin characterized by skin blistering.

Lactobacillus bifidus—A property of breast milk that interferes with the growth of pathogenic bacteria in the gastrointestinal tracts of babies, reducing the incidence of diarrhea. Lactobacillus bifidus can be added to infant formulas to help control diarrhea.

Resources

BOOKS

Middlemiss, Prisca. *What's That Rash?: How to Identify and Treat Childhood Rashes.* London: Hamlyn, 2002.

WEB SITES

Kazzi, Amin, and Khoa Nguyen. "Pediatrics: Diaper Rash." *eMedicine.com*, November 1, 2004. Available online at <www.emedicine.com/emerg/topic374.htm> (accessed December 15, 2004).

Aliene S. Linwood, RN, DPA, FACHE

Diarrhea

Definition

To most individuals, diarrhea means an increased frequency or decreased consistency of bowel movements; however, the medical definition is more exact than this. Diarrhea best correlates with an increase in stool weight; this increase is mainly due to excess water, which normally makes up 60 to 85 percent of fecal matter. In this way, true diarrhea is distinguished from diseases that cause only an increase in the number of bowel movements (hyperdefecation) or incontinence (involuntary loss of bowel contents).

Diarrhea is also classified by physicians as acute, which lasts one to two weeks, and as chronic, which continues for longer than two or three weeks. Viral and bacterial infections are the most common causes of acute diarrhea.

Description

In many cases, acute infectious diarrhea is a mild, limited annoyance common to adults and children. Chronic diarrhea, though, can have considerable effect on health and on social and economic well-being. People with **celiac disease**, inflammatory bowel disease, and other prolonged diarrheal illnesses develop nutritional deficiencies that diminish growth and immunity. They affect social interaction and result in the loss of many working hours. Rapid diagnosis and proper treatment can prevent much of the suffering associated with these illnesses.

Demographics

Worldwide, acute infectious diarrhea has a huge impact, causing over 5 million deaths per year. While most deaths are among children under five years of age in developing nations, the impact, even in developed countries, is considerable. For example, over 250,000 individuals are admitted to hospitals in the United States each year because of one of these episodes.

Causes and symptoms

Diarrhea occurs because more fluid passes through the large intestine (colon) than that organ can absorb. As a rule, the colon can absorb several times more fluid than is required on a daily basis. However, when this reserve capacity is overwhelmed, diarrhea occurs.

Diarrhea is caused by infections or illnesses that either lead to excess production of fluids or prevent absorption of fluids. Also, certain substances in the colon, such as fats and bile acids, can interfere with water absorption and cause diarrhea. Rapid passage of material through the colon can also do the same.

Symptoms related to any diarrheal illness are often those associated with any injury to the gastrointestinal tract, such as **fever**, **nausea**, **vomiting**, and abdominal **pain**. All or none of these may be present depending on the disease causing the diarrhea. The number of bowel movements can vary—up to 20 or more per day. In some persons, blood or pus is present in the stool. Bowel movements may be difficult to flush (float) or contain undigested food material.

The most common causes of acute diarrhea are infections (the cause of traveler's diarrhea), **food poisoning**, and medications. Medications are a frequent and often over-looked cause, especially **antibiotics** and antacids. Less often, various sugar-free foods, which sometimes contain poorly absorbable materials, cause diarrhea.

Chronic diarrhea is frequently due to many of the same things that cause the shorter episodes (infections, medications, etc.); however, symptoms last longer. Some infections can become chronic. This occurs mainly with parasitic infections (such as *Giardia*) or when people have altered immunity (such as **AIDS**). In children, more common causes of chronic diarrhea are food allergy and **lactose intolerance**. Toddlers who drink too much juice can have frequent, loose stools.

When to call the doctor

A physician or other healthcare provider should be contacted when the number of bowel movements exceeds three per day for 2 days or more or when fecal material contains blood. A doctor should be called if a person becomes dehydrated. Signs of **dehydration** include decreased urination, lethargy, poor skin tone, and generalized weakness. In very young children, the parents should call a doctor if they observe these symptoms of dehydration:

- dry mouth or tongue
- few or no tears when crying
- no wet diapers for three hours or more
- sunken eyes, cheeks, and fontanel (soft spot on the head of infants)
- irritability and listlessness
- skin that flattens slowly when pinched

Parents should also call the doctor if a child is vomiting so often that he or she cannot keep fluids down, has a high fever, complains of severe abdominal pain, or shows no improvement in symptoms after 24 hours.

Diagnosis

Most cases of acute diarrhea never need diagnosis or treatment, as many are mild and produce few problems. But persons of any age with fever over 102°F (38.9°C), signs of dehydration, bloody bowel movements, severe abdominal pain, known immune disease, or prior use of antibiotics need prompt medical evaluation.

When diagnostic studies are needed, the most useful are stool culture and examination for parasites; however, these are often negative, and a cause cannot be found in a large number of people. The earlier cultures are performed, the greater the chance of obtaining a positive result. For those with a history of antibiotic use in the preceding two months, stool samples need to be examined for the toxins that cause antibiotic-associated colitis. Tests are also available to check stool samples for microscopic amounts of blood and for cells that indicate severe inflammation of the colon. Examination with an endoscope is sometimes helpful in determining severity and extent of inflammation. Tests to check changes in blood chemistry (potassium, magnesium, etc.) and a complete blood count (CBC) are also often performed.

Chronic diarrhea is quite different, and most persons with this condition receive some degree of testing. Many exams are the same as for an acute episode, as some infections and parasites cause both types of diarrhea. A careful history to evaluate medication use, dietary changes, **family** history of illnesses, and other symptoms is necessary. Key points in determining the seriousness of symptoms are weight loss of over 10 lbs (4.5 kg), blood in the stool, and nocturnal diarrhea (symptoms that awaken an individual from **sleep**).

Both prescription and over-the-counter medications can contain additives, such as lactose and sorbitol, that will produce diarrhea in sensitive individuals. Review of **allergies** or skin changes may also point to a cause. Social history may indicate that stress is playing a role or may identify activities which can be associated with diarrhea (for example, diarrhea that occurs in runners).

A combination of stool, blood, and urine tests may be needed in the evaluation of chronic diarrhea; in addition, a number of endoscopic and x-ray studies are frequently required.

Treatment

Treatment is ideally directed toward correcting the cause; however, the first aim should be to prevent or treat dehydration and nutritional deficiencies. The type of fluid and nutrient replacement depends on whether oral feedings can be taken and on the severity of fluid losses. Oral rehydration solution (ORS) or intravenous fluids are the choices; ORS is preferred if possible.

A physician should be notified if a person is dehydrated. If oral replacement is suggested then commercial (Pedialyte and others) or homemade preparations can be used. The World Health Organization (WHO) has provided this easy recipe for home preparation, which can be taken in small frequent sips:

- table salt, 3/4 tsp
- baking powder, 1 tsp
- orange juice, 1 c
- water, 1 qt

When feasible, food intake should be continued even in those people with acute diarrhea. A physician should be consulted regarding what type and how much food is permitted.

Anti-motility agents (loperamide, diphenoxylate) are useful for those with chronic symptoms; their use is limited or even contraindicated in most individuals with acute diarrhea, especially in those with high fever or bloody bowel movements. They should not be taken without the advice of a physician, and should not be used in children.

Other treatments are available, depending on the cause of symptoms. For example, the bulk agent psyllium helps some people by absorbing excess fluid and solidifying stools; cholestyramine, which binds bile acids, is effective in treating bile-salt-induced diarrhea. Low fat diets or more easily digestible fat is useful in some people. Antidiarrheal drugs that decrease excessive secretion of fluid by the intestinal tract is another approach for some diseases. Avoidance of medications or other products that are known to cause diarrhea (such as lactose) is curative in some people but should be discussed with a physician.

Alternative treatment

It is especially important to find the cause of diarrhea, since stopping diarrhea when it is the body's way of eliminating something foreign is not helpful and can be harmful in the long run.

One effective alternative approach to preventing and treating diarrhea involves oral supplementation of aspects of the normal flora in the colon with the yeasts *Lactobacillus acidophilus*, *L. bifidus*, or *Saccharomyces boulardii*. In clinical settings, these "biotherapeutic" agents have repeatedly been helpful in the resolution of diarrhea, especially antibiotic-associated diarrhea.

Nutrient replacement also plays a role in preventing and treating episodes of diarrhea. Zinc especially appears to have an effect on the immune system, and deficiency of this mineral can lead to chronic diarrhea. Also, zinc replacement improves growth in young persons. To prevent dehydration, individuals suffering from diarrhea should take plenty of fluids, especially water. The BRAT diet also can be useful in helping to resolve diarrhea. This diet limits food intake to bananas, rice, applesauce, and toast. These foods provide soluble and insoluble fiber without irritation. If the toast is slightly burnt, the charcoal can help sequester toxins and pull them from the body.

Acute homeopathic remedies can be very effective for treating diarrhea especially in infants and young children.

KEY TERMS

Antimotility drug—A medication, such as loperamide (Imodium), dephenoxylate (Lomotil), or medications containing codeine or narcotics that decrease the ability of the intestine to contract.

Colitis—Inflammation of the colon (large intestine).

Endoscope—A medical instrument that can be passed into an area of the body (the bladder or intestine, for example) to allow visual examination of that area. The endoscope usually has a fiber-optic camera that allows a greatly magnified image to be shown on a television screen viewed by the operator. Many endoscopes also allow the operator to retrieve a small sample (biopsy) of the area being examined, to more closely view the tissue under a microscope.

Endoscopy—Visual examination of an organ or body cavity using an endoscope, a thin, tubular instrument containing a camera and light source. Many endoscopes also allow the retrieval of a small sample (biopsy) of the area being examined, in order to more closely view the tissue under a microscope.

Lactose intolerance—An inability to properly digest the lactose found in milk and dairy products.

Oral rehydration solution (ORS)—A liquid preparation of electrolytes and glucose developed by the World Health Organization that can decrease fluid loss in persons with diarrhea. Originally developed to be prepared with materials available in the home, commercial preparations have recently come into use.

Steatorrhea—An excessive amount of fat in the feces due to poor fat absorption in the gastrointestinal tract.

Prognosis

Prognosis is related to the cause of the diarrhea; for most individuals in developed countries, a bout of acute, infectious diarrhea is at best uncomfortable. However, in both industrialized and developing areas, serious complications and death can occur.

For those with chronic symptoms, an extensive number of tests are usually necessary to make a proper diagnosis and begin treatment; a specific diagnosis is found in 90 percent of people. In some, however, no specific cause is found and only treatment with bulk agents or anti-motility agents is indicated.

Prevention

Proper hygiene and food handling techniques can prevent many cases. Traveler's diarrhea can be avoided by people using products containing bismuth, such as Pepto-Bismol and/or antibiotics. The most important action is to prevent the complications of dehydration.

Nutritional concerns

Replacement of fluids and electrolytes is important for people experiencing diarrhea. These individuals should take in foods that contain salt, potassium, phosphates, and sugar. Most sodas, sport drinks and non-cream soups are good sources of electrolytes.

Parental concerns

Parents should be sure that their children who experience diarrhea drink plenty of fluids and replace electrolytes with an oral rehydration solution. A doctor should be called if the parent suspects a child is becoming dehydrated. Severe dehydration requires intravenous fluid administration in a medical setting. Antidiarrheal medications should be be given only on the advise of a physician.

Resources

BOOKS

Ahlquist, David A., and Michael Camilleri. "Diarrhea and Constipation." In *Harrison's Principles of Internal Medicine*, 15th ed. Edited by Eugene Braunwald et al. New York: McGraw- Hill, 2001, pp. 241–9.

Ghishan, Fayez K. "Chronic Diarrhea." In *Nelson Textbook of Pediatrics*, 17th ed. Edited by Richard E. Behrman et al. Philadelphia: Saunders, 2003, pp. 1276–80.

Greenbaum, Larry A. "Acute Diarrhea and Oral Rehydration." In *Nelson Textbook of Pediatrics*, 17th ed. Edited by Richard E. Behrman et al. Philadelphia: Saunders, 2003, pp. 249–50.

———. "Diarrhea in Chronically Malnourished Children." In *Nelson Textbook of Pediatrics*, 17th ed. Edited by Richard E. Behrman et al. Philadelphia: Saunders, 2003, pp. 2250–1.

Sack, R. Bradley. "The Diarrhea of Travelers." In *Cecil Textbook of Medicine*, 22nd ed. Edited by Lee Goldman et al. Philadelphia: Saunders, 2003, pp. 1864–5.

Semrad, Carol E. and Don W. Powell. "Approach to the Patient with Diarrhea and Malabsorption." In *Cecil Textbook of*

Medicine, 22nd ed. Edited by Lee Goldman et al. Philadelphia: Saunders, 2003, pp. 842–60.

ORGANIZATIONS

American Academy of Pediatrics. 141 Northwest Point Blvd., Elk Grove Village, IL 60007–1098. Web site: <www.aap.org>.

American College of Gastroenterology. 4900 B South 31st Street, Arlington VA 22206. Web site: <www.acg.gi.org/>.

WEB SITES

"Diarrhea." *Centers for Disease Control and Prevention.* Available online at <www.cdc.gov/ncidod/dpd/parasiticpathways/diarrhea.htm> (accessed January 5, 2005).

"Diarrhea." *Merck Manual.* Available online at <www.merck.com/mrkshared/mmanual/section3/chapter27/27b.jsp> (accessed January 5, 2005).

"Diarrhea." *National Digestive Diseases Information Clearinghouse.* Available online at <http://digestive.niddk.nih.gov/ddiseases/pubs/diarrhea/> (accessed January 5, 2005).

"Diarrhea." *MedlinePlus.* Available online at <www.nlm.nih.gov/medlineplus/diarrhea.html> (accessed January 5, 2005).

"Traveler's Diarrhea." *American Academy of Family Practice.* Available online at <http://familydoctor.org/182.xml> (accessed January 5, 2005).

L. Fleming Fallon, Jr., MD, DrPH

DiGeorge syndrome

Definition

DiGeorge syndrome is a rare congenital disease that affects an infant's immune system and that is due to a large deletion from chromosome 22. The syndrome is marked by absence or underdevelopment of the thymus and parathyroid glands. It is named for the pediatrician who first described it in 1965.

Normally the thymus gland is located below the thyroid gland in the neck and front of the chest and is the primary gland of the lymphatic system, which is necessary for normal functioning of the immune system. The parathyroid glands, located on the sides of the thyroid gland, are responsible for maintenance of normal levels of calcium in the blood. In children with DiGeorge syndrome, the thymus and parathyroid glands are missing or undeveloped. The symptoms of this disorder vary, depending on the extent of missing thymus and parathyroid tissue. The primary problem for children who survive with DiGeorge syndrome is repeated infections due to a defective immune system.

DiGeorge syndrome is sometimes described as a "CATCH 22" disorder, so named because of their characteristics—cardiac defects (C), abnormal facial features (A), thymus underdevelopment (T), **cleft palate** (C), and hypocalcemia due to hypoparathyroidism(H)—all resulting from deletion of portions of chromosome 22. Specific facial features associated with DiGeorge syndrome include low-set ears, wide-set eyes, a small jaw, and a short groove in the upper lip.

DiGeorge syndrome is also called congenital thymic hypoplasia, or third and fourth pharyngeal pouch syndrome, because the congenital abnormalities occur in areas known as the third and fourth pharyngeal pouches, which later develop into the thymus and parathyroid glands.

Demographics

The prevalence of DiGeorge syndrome, is debated; estimates have ranged from one in 4,000 to one in 6,395. Because the symptoms caused by the chromosomal abnormality vary somewhat from child to child, the syndrome probably occurs much more often than was previously thought. In the United States, autopsy studies for DiGeorge syndrome accounted for 0.7 percent of 3469 postmortem examinations in the Seattle, Washington, area over a period of 25 years. Internationally, the incidence of DGS was estimated to be one case per 20,000 persons in Germany and one case per 66,000 persons in Australia. However, with the advent of fluorescence in situ hybridization (FISH) techniques to detect monosomy 22 and the inclusion of related syndromes, more recent estimates place the incidence of DiGeorge syndrome in the range of one case per 3,000 persons.

No major difference is noted in the incidence of DiGeorge syndrome between males and females. The syndrome also appears to be equally common in all racial and ethnic groups.

Causes and symptoms

DiGeorge syndrome is caused either by inheritance of a defective chromosome 22 or by a new defect in chromosome 22 in the fetus. The type of defect that is involved is called deletion. A deletion occurs when the genetic material in the chromosomes does not recombine properly during the formation of sperm or egg cells. The deletion means that several genes from chromosome 22 are missing in children with DiGeorge syndrome. According to a 1999 study, 6 percent of children with DiGeorge syndrome inherited the deletion from a parent, while 94 percent had a new deletion.

The loss of the genes in the deleted material means that the baby's third and fourth pharyngeal pouches fail to develop normally during the twelfth week of pregnancy. This developmental failure results in a completely or partially absent thymus gland and parathyroid glands. In addition, 74 percent of fetuses with DiGeorge syndrome have severe heart defects. The child is born with a defective immune system and an abnormally low level of calcium in the blood.

These defects usually become apparent within 48 hours of birth. The infant's heart defects may lead to heart failure, or there may be seizures and other evidence of a low level of calcium in the blood (hypocalcemia).

When to call the doctor

Because the immune system of a child with DiGeorge syndrome is defective, a doctor should be consulted at any signs of illness or disease.

Diagnosis

Diagnosis of DiGeorge syndrome can be made by ultrasound examination around the eighteenth week of pregnancy, when abnormalities in the development of the heart or the palate can be detected. Another technique that is used to diagnose the syndrome before birth is called fluorescence in situ hybridization, or FISH. This technique uses DNA probes from the DiGeorge region on chromosome 22. FISH can be performed on cell samples obtained by **amniocentesis** as early as the fourteenth week of pregnancy. It confirms about 95 percent of cases of DiGeorge syndrome.

If the mother has not had prenatal testing, the diagnosis of DiGeorge syndrome is sometimes suggested by the child's facial features at birth. The child is also born with a defective immune system and an abnormally low level of calcium in the blood. These defects usually become apparent within 48 hours after birth. The infant's heart defects may lead to heart failure, or there may be seizures and other evidence of a low level of calcium in the blood. The doctor may make the diagnosis of DiGeorge syndrome during heart surgery when he or she notices the absence or abnormal location of the thymus gland. The diagnosis can be confirmed by blood tests for calcium, phosphorus, and parathyroid hormone levels and by the sheep cell test for immune function.

Treatment

Hypocalcemia

Hypocalcemia in a child with DiGeorge syndrome is unusually difficult to treat. Infants are usually given calcium and vitamin D by mouth. Severe cases have been treated by transplantation of fetal thymus tissue or bone marrow.

Heart defects

Infants with life-threatening heart defects are treated surgically.

Defective immune function

Children with DiGeorge syndrome should be kept away from crowds or other sources of infection. They should not be immunized with vaccines made from live viruses or given corticosteroids.

Nutritional concerns

Children with DiGeorge syndrome should be kept on low-phosphorus diets.

Prognosis

The prognosis is variable; many infants with DiGeorge syndrome die from overwhelming infection, seizures, or heart failure within the first year. A one-month mortality rate of 55 percent and a six-month mortality rate of 86 percent has been reported due to **congenital heart disease**. Advances in heart surgery indicate that the prognosis is most closely linked to the severity of the heart defects and the partial presence of the thymus gland. In most children who survive, the number of T cells, a type of white blood cell, in the blood rises spontaneously as they mature. Survivors are likely to be mentally retarded, however, with mild to moderate learning disabilities, and to have other developmental difficulties, including short stature as well as psychiatric problems in later life

Prevention

Genetic counseling and testing is recommended for a person with DiGeorge syndrome who becomes pregnant, because the disorder can be detected prior to birth. Although most children with DiGeorge syndrome do not inherit the chromosome deletion from their parents, they have a 50 percent chance of passing the deletion on to their own children. Parents should be screened, however, to see if they are carriers, even though inheritance of DiGeorge syndrome is rare.

KEY TERMS

Amniocentesis—A procedure performed at 16-18 weeks of pregnancy in which a needle is inserted through a woman's abdomen into her uterus to draw out a small sample of the amniotic fluid from around the baby for analysis. Either the fluid itself or cells from the fluid can be used for a variety of tests to obtain information about genetic disorders and other medical conditions in the fetus.

Chromosome—A microscopic thread-like structure found within each cell of the human body and consisting of a complex of proteins and DNA. Humans have 46 chromosomes arranged into 23 pairs. Chromosomes contain the genetic information necessary to direct the development and functioning of all cells and systems in the body. They pass on hereditary traits from parents to child (like eye color) and determine whether the child will be male or female.

Congenital—Present at birth.

Deletion—The absence of genetic material that is normally found in a chromosome. Often, the genetic material is missing due to an error in replication of an egg or sperm cell.

Hypocalcemia—A condition characterized by an abnormally low level of calcium in the blood.

Hypoplasia—An underdeveloped or incomplete tissue or organ usually due to a decrease in the number of cells.

T cell—A type of white blood cell that is produced in the bone marrow and matured in the thymus gland. It helps to regulate the immune system's response to infections or malignancy.

Because of an association between DiGeorge syndrome and **fetal alcohol syndrome**, pregnant women should avoid drinking alcoholic beverages.

Parental concerns

Recurrent infections are a major problem in children with DiGeorge syndrome and an important cause of later mortality. Therefore, prevention of infections must be a high priority.

Resources

BOOKS

Moore, Keith L., et al. *Before We Are Born: Essentials of Embryology and Birth Defects.* Kent, UK: Elsevier—Health Sciences Division, 2002.

PERIODICALS

Schinke, M., and S. Izumo. "Deconstructing DiGeorge Syndrome." *Nature Genet* 27 (2001): 238–240.

ORGANIZATIONS

Chromosome 22 Central. 237 Kent Avenue, Timmins, Ontario. Web site: <www.c22c.org>.

Immune Deficiency Foundation. 40 West Chesapeake Avenue, Towson, MD 21230. Web site: <http://primaryimmune.org>.

WEB SITES

Guduri, Sridhar, et al. "DiGeorge Syndrome." *emedicine*, August 14, 2004. Available online at <www.emedicine.com/med/topic567.htm> (accessed November 17, 2004).

Judith Sims, MS
Rebecca J. Frey PhD

Diphenhydramine *see* **Antihistamines**

Diphtheria

Definition

Diphtheria is a potentially fatal, contagious disease that usually involves the nose, throat, and air passages but may also infect the skin. Its most striking feature is the formation of a grayish membrane covering the tonsils and upper part of the throat.

Description

Like many other upper respiratory diseases, diphtheria is most likely to break out during the winter months. At one time it was a major childhood killer, but in the early 2000s it is rare in developed countries because of widespread immunization.

Persons who have not been immunized may get diphtheria at any age. The disease is spread most often by droplets from the coughing or sneezing of an infected person or carrier. The incubation period is two to seven days, with an average of three days. It is vital to seek medical help at once when diphtheria is suspected, because treatment requires emergency measures for adults as well as children.

Demographics

Diphtheria is a reportable disease in many countries in the world. Since 1988, all confirmed cases in the United States involved visitors or immigrants. In countries that do not have routine immunization against this infection, the mortality rate varies from 1.5 to 25 percent.

Causes and symptoms

The symptoms of diphtheria are caused by toxins produced by the diphtheria bacillus, *Corynebacterium diphtheriae* (from the Greek for "rubber membrane"). In fact, toxin production is related to infections of the bacillus itself with a particular bacteria virus called a phage (from bacteriophage, a virus that infects bacteria). The intoxication destroys healthy tissue in the upper area of the throat around the tonsils or in open **wounds** in the skin. Fluid from the dying cells then coagulates to form the telltale gray or grayish green membrane. Inside the membrane, the bacteria produce an exotoxin, which is a poisonous secretion that causes the life-threatening symptoms of diphtheria. The exotoxin is carried throughout the body in the bloodstream, destroying healthy tissue in other parts of the body.

The most serious complications caused by the exotoxin are inflammations of the heart muscle (myocarditis) and damage to the nervous system. The risk of serious complications is increased as the time between onset of symptoms and the administration of antitoxin increases, and as the size of the membrane formed increases. The myocarditis may cause disturbances in the heart rhythm and may culminate in heart failure. The symptoms of nervous system involvement can include seeing double (diplopia), painful or difficult swallowing, and slurred speech or loss of voice, which are all indications of the exotoxin's effect on nerve functions. The exotoxin may also cause severe swelling in the neck ("bull neck").

The signs and symptoms of diphtheria vary according to the location of the infection.

Nasal

Nasal diphtheria produces few symptoms other than a watery or bloody discharge. On examination, there may be a small visible membrane in the nasal passages. Nasal infection rarely causes complications by itself, but it is a public health problem because it spreads the disease more rapidly than other forms of diphtheria.

Pharyngeal

Pharyngeal diphtheria gets its name from the pharynx, which is the part of the upper throat that connects the mouth and nasal passages with the voice box. This is the most common form of diphtheria, causing the characteristic throat membrane. The membrane often bleeds if it is scraped or cut. It is important not to try to remove the membrane because the trauma may increase the body's absorption of the exotoxin. Other signs and symptoms of pharyngeal diphtheria are mild **sore throat**, **fever** of 101–102°F (38.3–38.9°C), a rapid pulse, and general body weakness.

Laryngeal

Laryngeal diphtheria, which involves the voice box or larynx, is the form most likely to produce serious complications. The fever is usually higher in this form of diphtheria (103–104°F or 39.4–40°C) and the person is very weak. People may have a severe **cough**, have difficulty breathing, or lose their voice completely. The development of a bull neck indicates a high level of exotoxin in the bloodstream. Obstruction of the airway may result in respiratory compromise and death.

Skin

This form of diphtheria, which is sometimes called cutaneous diphtheria, accounts for about 33 percent of all diphtheria cases. It is found chiefly among people with poor hygiene. Any break in the skin can become infected with diphtheria. The infected tissue develops an ulcerated area, and a diphtheria membrane may form over the wound but is not always present. The wound or ulcer is slow to heal and may be numb or insensitive when touched.

When to call the doctor

A doctor should be called whenever a case of diphtheria is suspected.

Diagnosis

Because diphtheria must be treated as quickly as possible, doctors usually make the diagnosis on the basis of the visible symptoms without waiting for test results.

In making the diagnosis, the doctor examines the affected person's eyes, ears, nose, and throat in order to rule out other diseases that may cause fever and sore throat, such as **infectious mononucleosis**, a sinus infection, or **strep throat**. The most important single symptom that suggests diphtheria is the membrane. When a person develops skin infections during an outbreak of diphtheria, the doctor will consider the possibility of cutaneous diphtheria and take a smear to confirm the diagnosis.

Laboratory tests

The diagnosis of diphtheria can be confirmed by the results of a culture obtained from the infected area. Material from the swab is put on a microscope slide and stained using a procedure called Gram's stain. The diphtheria bacillus is Gram-positive which means it holds the dye after the slide is rinsed with alcohol. Under the microscope, diphtheria bacilli look like beaded rod-shaped cells, grouped in patterns that resemble Chinese characters. Another laboratory test involves growing the diphtheria bacillus on a special material called Loeffler's medium.

Treatment

Diphtheria is a serious disease requiring hospital treatment in an intensive care unit if the person has developed respiratory symptoms. Treatment includes a combination of medications and supportive care.

Antitoxin

The most important step is prompt administration of diphtheria antitoxin, without waiting for laboratory results. The antitoxin is made from horse serum and works by neutralizing any circulating exotoxin. The doctor must first test people for sensitivity to animal serum. People who are sensitive (about 10%) must be desensitized with diluted antitoxin, since as of 2004 the antitoxin is the only specific substance that counteracts diphtheria exotoxin. No human antitoxin is available for the treatment of diphtheria.

The dose ranges from 20,000 to 100,000 units, depending on the severity and length of time of symptoms occurring before treatment. Diphtheria antitoxin is usually given intravenously.

Antibiotics

Antibiotics are given to wipe out the bacteria, to prevent the spread of the disease, and to protect people from developing **pneumonia**. They are not a substitute for treatment with antitoxin. Both adults and children may be given penicillin, ampicillin, or erythromycin. Erythromycin appears to be more effective than penicillin in treating people who are carriers because of better penetration into the infected area.

Cutaneous diphtheria is usually treated by cleansing the wound thoroughly with soap and water and giving an individual antibiotics for ten days.

Supportive care

Persons with diphtheria require bed rest with intensive nursing care, including extra fluids, oxygenation, and monitoring for possible heart problems, airway blockage, or involvement of the nervous system. People with laryngeal diphtheria are kept in a **croup** tent or high-humidity environment; they may also need throat suctioning or emergency surgery if their airway is blocked.

People recovering from diphtheria should rest at home for a minimum of two to three weeks, especially if they have heart complications. In addition, persons should be immunized against diphtheria after recovery, because having the disease does not always induce antitoxin formation and protect them from reinfection.

Prevention of complications

People with diphtheria who develop myocarditis may be treated with oxygen and with medications to prevent irregular heart rhythms. An artificial pacemaker may be needed. Persons with difficulty swallowing can be fed through a tube inserted into the stomach through the nose. Persons who cannot breathe are usually put on mechanical respirators.

Prognosis

The prognosis depends on the size and location of the membrane and on early treatment with antitoxin; the longer the delay, the higher the death rate. The most vulnerable persons are children under the age of 15 years and those who develop pneumonia or myocarditis. Nasal and cutaneous diphtheria are rarely fatal.

Prevention

Prevention of diphtheria has four aspects: immunization, isolation of infected persons, identification and treatment of contacts, and reporting cases to health authorities.

Immunization

Universal immunization is the most effective means of preventing diphtheria. The standard course of immunization for healthy children is three doses of DPT (diphtheria-tetanus-pertussis) preparation given between two months and six months of age, with booster doses given at 18 months and at entry into school. Adults should be immunized at ten-year intervals with Td (tetanus-diphtheria) toxoid. (A toxoid is a bacterial toxin that is treated to make it harmless but still can induce immunity to the disease.)

Isolation of affected persons

Individuals with diphtheria must be isolated for one to seven days or until two successive cultures show that the individuals are no longer contagious. Children placed in isolation are usually assigned a primary nurse for emotional support.

Identification and treatment of contacts

Because diphtheria is highly contagious and has a short incubation period, **family** members and other contacts of persons with diphtheria must be watched for symptoms and tested to see if they are carriers. They are usually given antibiotics for seven days and a booster shot of diphtheria/tetanus toxoid.

Reporting cases to public health authorities

Reporting is necessary for tracking potential epidemics, to help doctors identify the specific strain of diphtheria, and to see if resistance to penicillin or erythromycin has developed.

Parental concerns

Parents in the United States should ensure that their children have full immunizations against diphtheria. Completion of the three-shot series initiates lifelong immunity from diphtheria.

Resources

BOOKS

Diphtheria: A Medical Dictionary, Bibliography, and Annotated Research Guide to Internet References. San Diego, CA: ICON Health Publications, 2004.

Holmes, Randall K. "Diphtheria, Corynebacterial Infections and Anthrax." In *Harrison's Principles of Internal Medicine*, 15th ed. Edited by Eugene Braunwald et al. New York: McGraw-Hill, 2001, pp. 909–14.

Long, Sarah S. "Diphtheria (Corynebacterium diphtheriae)." In *Nelson Textbook of Pediatrics*, 17th ed. Edited by Richard E. Behrman et al. Philadelphia: Saunders, 2003, pp. 886–9.

Miller, Debbie S. *Great Serum Race: Blazing the Iditarod Trail.* New York: Walker & Company, 2002.

Salisbury, Gay. *The Cruelest Miles: The Heroic Story of Dogs and Men in a Race against an Epidemic.* New York: Norton, 2003.

PERIODICALS

Bertuccini, L., et al. "Internalization of non-toxigenic Corynebacterium diphtheriae by cultured human respiratory epithelial cells." *Microbial Pathogenesis* 37, no. 3 (2004): 111–8.

Clarke, P., et al. "DTP immunization of steroid treated preterm infants." *Archives of Disease in Childhood: Fetal and Neonatal Edition* 89, no. 5 (2004): F468–9.

Colgrove, J. "The power of persuasion: Diphtheria immunization, advertising, and the rise of health education." *Public Health Rep* 119, no. 5 (2004): 506–9.

Netterlid, E, et al. "Persistent itching nodules after the fourth dose of diphtheria-tetanus toxoid vaccines without evidence of delayed hypersensitivity to aluminium." *Vaccine* 22, no. 27–28 (2004): 3698–706.

ORGANIZATIONS

American Public Health Association. 800 I Street, NW, Washington, DC 20001–3710. Web site: <www.apha.org/>.

Centers for Disease Control and Prevention. 1600 Clifton Road, Atlanta, GA 30333. Web site: <www.cdc.gov>.

Pan American Health Organization. 525 23rd St., NW, Washington, DC 20037. Web site: <www.paho.org>.

World Health Organization, Communicable Diseases. 20 Avenue Appia, 1211 Geneva 27, Switzerland. Web site: <www.who.int/gtb/>.

WEB SITES

"Diphtheria." *MedlinePlus.* Available online at <www.nlm.nih.gov/medlineplus/ency/article/001608.htm> (accessed January 5, 2005).

"Diphtheria." *World Health Organization.* Available online at <www.who.int/topics/diphtheria/en/> (accessed January 5, 2005).

"Diphtheria, Tetanus, and Pertussis." *Centers for Disease Control and Prevention.* Available online at <www.cdc.gov/travel/diseases/dtp.htm> (accessed January 5, 2005).

L. Fleming Fallon, Jr., MD, DrPH

Diphtheria, tetanus, pertussis vaccine *see* DTP vaccine

Discipline

Definition

The term "discipline" comes from the Latin word "disciplinare," which means "to teach." Many people, however, associate the word with punishment, which falls short of the full meaning of the word. Discipline, properly practiced, uses a multifaceted approach, including models, rewards, and punishments that teach and reinforce desired behavior. Through discipline, children are able to learn self-control, self-direction, competence, and a sense of caring.

Description

The American Academy of Pediatrics suggests that an effective discipline system must contain three elements. If these three aspects are all present in a program of discipline, the result generally is improved child behavior. The elements are:

- a learning environment characterized by positive, supportive parent-child relationships
- a proactive strategy for systematic teaching and strengthening of desired behaviors
- a reactive strategy for decreasing or eliminating undesired behaviors

There are several reasons why children may not behave properly, including a lack of effective disciplinary measures. Children also commonly misbehave when they are deprived of adult attention or when they are tired, bored, or hungry. Children from families affected by **divorce** and separation, poverty, substance abuse, and parental depression seem to be at greater risk for behavior problems. There may also be biologic factors such as **attention-deficit/hyperactivity disorder** (ADHD) and certain temperaments that predispose particular children towards misbehavior. There is also research suggesting that harsh disciplinary measures may actually increase poor behavior.

Ideally, discipline is based on appropriate expectations for each child, based on age and stage of development. It should be used to set reasonable limits in a consistent manner while still allowing some choice among acceptable alternatives. Discipline teaches both social and moral standards and should protect children from harm by teaching what is safe. It should also guide children to respect the rights and property of others.

Though there are a variety of ways in which children may be disciplined, there are some guidelines that all parents should follow:

- Discipline must be age appropriate. While reasoning and verbal explanations may be appropriate for the older child, children younger than 18 months are typically unable to comprehend the reasons for punishment.
- Parents should demonstrate a unified front when it comes to discipline. If parents exhibit opposing approaches, children learn to exploit these differences.
- Rules should be few but simple. Punishment should be a logical or natural consequence of the misbehavior.
- Though consistency is important, parents should remember that it is sometimes appropriate to be flexible and allow for some negotiation, especially with

older children. Doing so can teach decision-making, enhance children's moral judgment, and reinforce independence.

Disciplinary techniques that are most effective take place in the context of a loving and secure relationship between parent and child. Parents' responses to a child's behavior, whether approving or disapproving, are likely to have a greater effect in a secure, loving environment, because children long for their parents' approval. As children respond to this positive relationship and consistent discipline, the need for negative interaction decreases.

Positive reinforcement

Positive reinforcement focuses on good behavior rather than on undesirable behavior. Parents should identify appropriate behaviors and give frequent feedback, rewarding good behavior quickly so that the child associates the "prize" with the wanted behavior. A reward can be a word of praise, a special activity, additional privileges, or material items. Many desirable behavioral patterns start to emerge as a part of the child's normal development. The role of parents is to notice these behaviors and provide positive attention to them. Some other desirable behaviors are not part of a child's normal development and need to be modeled and taught by their parents. These behaviors include sharing, good manners, effective study habits, among others. Parents need to identify those skills and behaviors they want their children to demonstrate and then make a concerted effort to teach and strengthen those behaviors. Children who learn through positive reinforcement tend to internalize the newly learned behaviors.

Extinction

Extinction is a type of discipline that seeks to prevent inadvertent positive reinforcement for negative behavior. "Time-out" is one of the most common methods in this category. For younger children, time out usually involves removing parental attention and praise or placing the child a chair or some other place for a specified time with no parental interaction. The environment should be neutral, boring, and safe. Time-out works well for children from 18 months up to five or six years of age and is particularly useful for temper **tantrums**, yelling, whining, and fighting. The session should end only when the child has been calm and quiet for at least 15 seconds. Time out should last for a specified time, usually one minute per year of life (to a maximum of five minutes). Withholding privileges is another form of extinction that is more appropriate for older children and adolescents. This strategy requires the removal

of a valued privilege and works best if it is used infrequently.

Verbal punishment

Parents may express disapproval of a behavior by scolding or yelling. This may be effective if used very sparingly. However, if used too often it can cause **anxiety** in the child and encourage the child to ignore the parent.

Corporal punishment

Corporal punishment involves the application of some sort of physical **pain** in response to a child's undesired behavior. This response can range from a light slapping of a hand to severe beatings that qualify as **child abuse**. Because of this range in form and severity, the use of corporal punishment as a disciplinary method is controversial. In spite of the significant concerns raised by child-care experts, one form of physical punishment—spanking—remains a widely used measure to reduce undesired behavior in children. Over 90 percent of all families report having used spanking at some time as a means of discipline. Despite its common acceptance, research shows that spanking is a less effective form of discipline than others, such as time-out or removal of privileges. Although it may immediately stop a behavior, the effectiveness of spanking tends to decrease with repeated use. The only way to maintain the initial effect of spanking is to increase its intensity, which runs the risk of escalating to abuse. Spanking, at best, is only effective when used in selective, very infrequent situations.

Children who receive corporal punishment tend to grow into angry adults. The use of spanking in older children is associated with higher rates of substance abuse and crime and has been linked to poor **self-esteem**, depression, and poor educational performance.

Infancy

Discipline strategies with infants should be passive. The main goal is for parents to generally structure daily routines but to also demonstrate flexibility in meeting infants' emerging needs. As infants become more mobile, parents need to impose some limitations and structure in order to create a safe environment in which the child can **play** and explore. Parents must protect infants from all potential hazards in the home by instituting **childproofing** practices. If a child does attempt to play with or approach something dangerous or unacceptable, a firm "No" should suffice, along with either removing the child from the area or by distracting the child with an alternative activity. Parents should not expect that reasoning or reprimands will control the behavior of an infant.

Toddlerhood

Toddlers, like infants, still benefit most from passive types of discipline and a toddler-safe environment. Again, saying "No", along with redirecting behavior, is usually effective if the toddler is doing something unacceptable. At this stage, however, children are starting to test the limits of their power over and over again. It is important for parents to consistently set limits and stick to them. Doing so reduces the child's confusion and his or her need to test. This is also the time when time-outs might be introduced, especially when redirecting the child's attention no longer seems to work.

Preschool

Preschoolers are starting to understand the need for rules, and their behavior should be guided by these rules and the associated consequences. It is very important that children understand what is expected of them and why they are punished for a particular behavior. Preschoolers also learn from having their good behaviors rewarded.

School age

If rules for behavior have been consistently modeled and expected by the parents, children should exhibit an increased sense of responsibility and self-control when they become school age. Timeouts and consequences continue to be effective disciplinary measures in this age group. As children continue to mature and desire more responsibility and independence, teaching them to deal with the consequences of their behavior is an effective method of discipline. By the time they have become teenagers, children should know what is expected of them and what the potential consequences of misbehavior are. However, discipline remains just as important for teens as it does for younger children. Teens require boundaries. This structure continues to provide order and a sense of security for children until they reach adulthood. When teens do break rules, taking away some of their privileges seems to be the most effective type of disciplinary measure.

Common problems

One of the most common problems in child discipline is an inconsistent approach between two parents. It may prove helpful for parents to regularly communicate regarding their child's behavior and decide ahead of time what disciplinary methods are to be used.

KEY TERMS

Punishment—The application of a negative stimulus to reduce or eliminate a behavior. The two types typically used with children are verbal reprimands and punishment involving physical pain, as in corporal punishment.

Time-out—A discipline strategy that entails briefly isolating a disruptive child in order to interrupt and avoid reinforcement of negative behavior.

Parental concerns

Parents may be worried that the disciplinary methods they have decided are appropriate for their child may not be respected or followed by teachers and other adult caregivers. If this is a concern, parents should outline exactly what consequences or punishments they feel are appropriate and communicate openly with the other adults who care for their child.

Resources

BOOKS

MacKenzie, Robert J. *Setting Limits with Your Strong-Willed Child: Eliminating Conflict by Establishing Clear, Firm and Respectful Boundaries.* Prima Lifestyles, 2001.

PERIODICALS

Banks, J. Burton. "Childhood Discipline: Challenges for Clinicians and Parents." *American Family Physician* (October 15, 2002).

Regalado, Michael, et al. "Parents' Discipline of Young Children: Results from the National Survey of Early Childhood Health." *Pediatrics* 113 (June 2004): 1952–1958.

Sears, William. "A Beginner's Guide to Discipline: Dr. William Sears Offers Six Strategies to Use Now to Help You Raise a Child Who's a Treat—Not a Terror." *Baby Talk* (September 1, 2003): 52.

ORGANIZATIONS

Center for Effective Discipline. 155 West Main St., Suite 1603, Columbus, OH 43215. Web site: <http://stophitting.com>.

Positive Parenting. 402 West Ojai Avenue, 101–246, Ojai, CA 93023. Web site: <www.positiveparenting.com>.

WEB SITES

"Disciplining Your Child." *KidsHealth*, June 2001. Available online at <www.kidshealth.org/parent/positive/family/discipline.html> (accessed December 27, 2004).

Deanna M. Swartout-Corbeil, RN

Divorce

Definition

Divorce is the legal termination of a marriage.

Description

More than 1 million children each year experience their parents' divorce. Less than 60 percent of American children live with both of their biological parents; about 25 percent live with their biological mother only; and about 4 percent live with their biological father only. The remaining 11 percent live with step-families, adoptive parents, foster homes, or with other relatives.

In 2002 it was estimated that up to 30 percent (19.8 million) of children in the United States, representing 11.9 million families, lived in single-parent households. While the number of single mothers has remained constant through the 1990s and into the early 2000s at 9.9 million, the number of single fathers has grown from 1.7 million in 1995 to 2 million in 2002, according to data from the U.S. Census Bureau. In 2002, 19.8 million children lived with one parent. Of these, 16.5 million lived with their mother and 3.3 million with their father.

In 2002, fewer than half of single-parent children under the age of 18 received any financial support from the non-custodial parent. The income of more than one third of these households fell below the poverty level. The term "deadbeat dads" is often used in discussions about **abandonment** because most of the divorced parents who do not contribute financially to support their offspring are fathers.

Even though divorce rates peaked in 1979–81 and decreased slightly in the years following, half of all first marriages and 60 percent of second marriages end in divorce. The divorce process is often more emotionally traumatic for the children than for the parents, because children are less able to cope with the separation. About half of all children do not see their fathers following a divorce and only a small percentage have spent the night in their fathers' homes in any given month.

Divorce is the termination of the **family** as a unit. The effects of divorce on children can usually be seen long before the divorce itself, when conflict between the parents can cause behavior changes in the children, even in preschoolers. After the divorce, the children's sense of loss often increases, leading to great sadness, depression, and anxieties, especially on special occasions, such as birthdays, holidays, and school events. The children's emotions depend on their age, but common feelings include sadness, anger, and **fear**. Often these feelings are manifested in behavior changes that are also age-related. Children may grieve the loss of the "traditional" family, and they mourn the loss of the noncustodial parent, typically but not always, the father.

Common childhood and adolescent reactions to parental divorce include a continuing desire for the parents to reunite; fears of desertion; feelings of guilt over having been responsible for the divorce; developmental regression; **sleep disorders**; and physical complaints. While researchers have found that some children recover from the trauma of divorce within one to three years, subsequent long-term studies have documented persistent negative effects that can follow a child into **adolescence** and beyond, especially with regard to the formation of intimate relationships later in life. The effects of parental divorce have been linked to phenomena as diverse as emotional and behavioral problems, school dropout rates, crime rates, physical and sexual abuse, and physical health. However, mental health professionals continue to debate whether divorce is more damaging for children than the continuation of a troubled marriage.

Infancy

Infants' reactions to divorce come from interference with the satisfaction of their basic needs. The removal of the noncustodial parent or increased work hours for the custodial parent can cause **separation anxiety**, while the parents' emotional distress tends to be felt by babies, upsetting their own emotional balance. The inability of infants to understand the concept of divorce makes the changes in their situation seem frighteningly unpredictable and confusing. Reactions include irritability, increased crying, fearfulness, separation **anxiety**, and **sleep** problems.

Toddlerhood

Toddlers may revert to an earlier development stage in such areas as eating, sleeping, **toilet training**, motor activity, language, and emotional independence. Other signs of distress include anger, fearfulness, **nightmares**, fantasies, and withdrawal.

Preschool

In preschool-age children, continued self focus, coupled with a more advanced level of **cognitive development**, leads to feelings of guilt as these children may become convinced that they are the reason for their parents' divorce. Children at this age are also prone to powerful fantasies, which can include imagined scenarios involving abandonment or punishment. The disruption that follows divorce, particularly in the relationship with the father, also becomes an important factor for children at this age. Developmental regression may take the form of insisting on sleeping in the same room or bed as the parent; refusing to eat all but a few types of food; **stuttering** or reverting to baby talk; disruptions in toilet training; and developing an excessive emotional dependence on one parent.

School age

By the early elementary grades, children are better able to handle separation from the noncustodial parent. Their greater awareness of the divorce situation, however, may lead to elaborate and frightening fantasies of abandonment or of being replaced in the affections of the noncustodial parent. Typical reactions at this stage include sadness, depression, anger, and general anxiety. Disruption of basic development in such areas as eating, sleeping, and elimination is possible but less frequent than in younger children. Many children this age suffer a sharp decline in academic performance, which often lasts throughout the entire school year in which the divorce takes place.

Children in the upper elementary grades are capable of better understanding of the divorce. At this age, the simple fears and fantasies of the younger child are replaced by more complex internal conflicts, such as the struggle to preserve one's allegiance to both parents. Older children become adept at erecting defense mechanisms to protect themselves against the **pain** they feel over a divorce. Such defenses include denial, displacement of feelings, and physical complaints such as fatigue, headaches, and stomachaches. Children in the upper elementary grades are most likely to become intensely angry at their parents for divorcing. Other common emotions at this stage of development include loneliness, grief, anxiety, and a sense of powerlessness.

For teenagers, divorce is difficult because it is yet another source of upheaval in their lives. Teenage behavior is affected not only by recent divorces but also by those that occurred when the child was much younger.

One especially painful effect of divorce on adolescents is the negative attitude it can produce toward one or both parents, whom they need as role models but are often blamed for disappointing them.

Teens are also prone to internal conflicts over their parents' divorce. They are torn between love for and anger toward their parents and between conflicting loyalties to both parents. Positive feelings toward their parents' new partners come into conflict with anxiety over the intimacy of these relationships, and the teenager's close affiliation with the custodial parent clashes with his or her need for increased social and emotional independence. Although children at all ages are distressed by parental divorce, during the teen years it can result in potentially dangerous behavior, including drug and alcohol abuse, promiscuous sexual activity, violence, and delinquency.

Children ages 12–15 need consistent support from both parents but may not accept equal time-sharing of their living arrangements. They may blame one or both parents and may become controlling by demanding to stay in one place or to switch residences constantly.

Youths ages 15–18 group may become focused on establishing their independence and on social and school activities, and they may become intolerant of their parents' problems. Although teens still needs parental support, they may also tire of worrying about one or both parents. Being able to listen to teens when they are able to talk about their feelings may be helpful. Although teens may want to see their parents happy, they may have mixed feelings about seeing their parents dating other people. They may feel that condoning parental dating would be disloyal to the other parent. Older teens who need help may have behavior problems, exhibit depression, show poor school performance, run away from home, or get into trouble with the law.

Common problems

Not all children react the same way when told their parents are divorcing. Some ask questions, some cry or get angry, and some initially do not react at all. Problems to watch for include trouble sleeping, crying, aggression, deep anger and resentment, feelings of betrayal, difficulty concentrating, chronic fatigue, and problems with friends or at school.

Experts agree that it is important for parents who are divorcing to avoid involving their children in their disputes or forcing them to choose sides, and parents are often advised to avoid criticizing their former mates in front of their children. In order for children to heal from the emotional pain of parental divorce, they need an outlet for open expression of their feelings, whether it is a sibling, friend, adult mentor or counselor, or a divorce support group. Extended families can be a significant source of support for children, providing them with stability and with the reassurance that others care about them. Although parental divorce is undeniably difficult for children of all ages, loving, patient, and enlightened parental support can make a crucial difference in helping children cope with the experience both immediately and over the long term.

Parental concerns

The custodial parent should be aware of the effects of the divorce on the child and above all, should reassure the child that the remaining parent will not abandon them. It is also important to maintain as much normalcy as possible after a divorce by sticking to regular routines, such as meal times, bedtime, rules of behavior, and methods of **discipline**. Relaxing limits during a time of change can make children feel insecure.

When to call the doctor

Medical help may be needed if a child inflicts self-injury. Psychological counseling may also be needed to help the child understand and cope with the divorce. This is especially true if any of the common reactions last for an unusual amount of time, intensify over time, or if the child talks about or threatens **suicide**.

Resources

BOOKS FOR ADULTS

Hannibal, Mary Ellen, and Ina Gyemant. *Good Parenting Through Your Divorce: How to Recognize, Encourage, and Respond to Your Child's Feelings and Help Them Get Through Your Divorce.* New York: Marlowe & Company, 2002.

Samenow, Stanton. *In the Best Interest of the Child: How to Protect Your Child from the Pain of Your Divorce.* New York: Crown Publishers, 2002.

Wallerstein, Judith S., and Sandra Blakeslee. *What About the Kids? Raising Your Children Before, During, and After Divorce.* New York: Hyperion, 2003.

BOOKS FOR CHILDREN AND TEENS

MacGregor, Cynthia. *The Divorce Helpbook for Teens.* Atascadero, CA: Impact Publishers, 2004.

Masurel, Claire, and Kady MacDonald Denton. *Two Homes.* Cambridge, MA: Candlewick Press, 2003.

Reilly, Natalie June, and Brandi J. Pavese. *My Stick Family: Helping Children Cope with Divorce.* Far Hills, NJ: New Horizon Press Publishers, 2002.

> ## KEY TERMS
>
> **Custodial parent**—A parent who has legal custody of their child or children.
>
> **Deadbeat dad**—A father who has abandoned his child or children and does not pay child custody as required by a court.
>
> **Noncustodial parent**—The parent who does not have legal custody of the child and does not live in the same home with the child. The noncustodial parent has financial responsibility for the child and visitation rights.

PERIODICALS

Cohen, George. "Helping Children and Families Deal with Divorce and Separation." *Pediatrics* (November 2002): 1019–23.

"Helping Your Child Through a Divorce." *The Brown University Child and Adolescent Behavior Letter* (December 2002): S1–S2.

"Intervention for Children of Divorce Prevents Future Mental Disorders." *Mental Health Weekly* (October 21, 2002): 3–4.

Martin, Paige D., et al. "Expressed Attitudes of Adolescents Toward Marriage and Family Life." *Adolescence* (Summer 2003): 359–67.

Shansky, Janet. "Negative Effects of Divorce on Child and Adolescent Psychosocial Adjustment." *Journal of Pastoral Counseling* (Annual 2002): 73–87.

Winslow, Emily B. "Preventive Interventions for Children of Divorce." *Psychiatric Times* (February 1, 2004): 45.

ORGANIZATIONS

Kids in the Middle Inc. 121 W. Monroe, St. Louis, MO 63122. Web site: <www.kidsinthemiddle.org>.

National Family Resiliency Center Inc. 2000 Century Plaza, Suite 121, Columbia, MD 21044. Web site: <www.divorceabc.com>.

WEB SITES

"A Kid's Guide to Divorce." *Kids Health*, April 2002. Available online at <www.kidshealth.org/kid/feeling/home_family/divorce.html> (accessed November 24, 2004).

"Promoting Mental Health for Children of Separating Parents." *Canadian Paediatric Society*, January 2004. Available online at <www.cps.ca/english/statements/PP/pp00-01.htm> (accessed November 24, 2004).

Ken R. Wells

Dizziness

Definition

As a disorder, dizziness is classified into three categories: vertigo, syncope, and nonsyncope nonvertigo. Each category has its own set of symptoms, all related to the sense of balance. In general, syncope is defined by a brief loss of consciousness (fainting) or by dimmed vision and feeling uncoordinated, confused, and light-headed. Many people experience a sensation like syncope when they stand up too fast. Vertigo is the feeling that either the individual or the surroundings are spinning. This sensation is like being on a spinning amusement park ride. Individuals with nonsyncope nonvertigo dizziness feel as though they cannot keep their balance. This feeling may become worse with movement.

Description

The brain coordinates information from the eyes, the inner ear, and the body's senses to maintain balance. If any of these information sources is disrupted, the brain may not be able to compensate. For example, people sometimes experience **motion sickness** because the information from their body tells the brain that they are sitting still, but information from the eyes indicates that they are moving. The messages do not correspond and dizziness results.

Vision and the body's senses are the most important systems for maintaining balance, but problems in the inner ear are the most frequent cause of dizziness. The inner ear, also called the vestibular system, contains fluid that helps fine tune the information the brain receives from the eyes and the body. When fluid volume or pressure in one inner ear changes, information about balance is altered. The discrepancy gives conflicting messages to the brain about balance and induces dizziness.

Certain medical conditions can cause dizziness because they affect the systems that maintain balance. For example, the inner ear is very sensitive to changes in blood flow. Because medical conditions such as high blood pressure or low blood sugar can affect blood flow, these conditions are frequently accompanied by dizziness. Circulation disorders are the most common causes of dizziness. Other causes are **head injury**, ear infection, **allergies**, and nervous system disorders.

Dizziness often disappears without treatment or with treatment of the underlying problem, but it can be long term or chronic.

Demographics

According to the National Institutes of Health, 42 percent of Americans seek medical help for dizziness at some point in their lives. The costs may exceed a billion dollars and account for 5 million doctor visits annually. Episodes of dizziness increase with age, and are common among the elderly.

Causes and symptoms

Careful attention to symptoms can help determine the underlying cause of the dizziness. Underlying problems may be benign and easily treated, or they may be dangerous and in need of intensive therapy. Not all cases of dizziness can be linked to a specific cause. More than one type of dizziness can be experienced at the same time, and symptoms may be mixed. Episodes of dizziness may last for a few seconds or for days. The length of an episode is related to the underlying cause.

The symptoms of syncope include dimmed vision, loss of coordination, confusion, lightheadedness, and sweating. These symptoms can lead to a brief loss of consciousness or fainting. They are related to a reduced flow of blood to the brain; they often occur when a person is standing up and can be relieved by sitting or lying down. Vertigo is characterized by a sensation of spinning or turning, accompanied by **nausea**, **vomiting**, ringing in the ears, **headache**, or fatigue. An individual may have trouble walking, remaining coordinated, or keeping balance. Nonsyncope nonvertigo dizziness is characterized by a feeling of being off balance that becomes worse if the individual tries moving or performing detail-intense tasks.

A person may experience dizziness for many reasons. Syncope is associated with low blood pressure, heart problems, and disorders in the autonomic nervous system, the system of involuntary functions such as breathing. Syncope may also arise from emotional distress, **pain**, and other reactions to outside stressors. Nonsyncope nonvertigo dizziness may be caused by rapid breathing, low blood sugar, or migraine headache, or by more serious medical conditions.

Vertigo is often associated with inner ear problems called vestibular disorders. A particularly intense vestibular disorder, Meniere's disease, interferes with the volume of fluid in the inner ear. This disease, which affects approximately one in every 1,000 people, causes intermittent vertigo over the course of weeks, months, or years. Meniere's disease is often accompanied by ringing or buzzing in the ear, hearing loss, and a feeling that the ear is blocked. Damage to the nerve that leads from the ear to the brain can also cause vertigo. Such damage can result from head injury or a tumor. An acoustic neuroma, for example, is a benign tumor that wraps around the nerve. Vertigo can also be caused by disorders of the central nervous system and the circulatory system, such as hardening of the arteries (arteriosclerosis), **stroke**, or multiple sclerosis.

Some medications cause changes in blood pressure or blood flow. These medications can cause dizziness in some people. Prescription medications carry warnings of such side effects, but common drugs, such as **caffeine** or nicotine, can also cause dizziness. Certain **antibiotics** can damage the inner ear and cause hearing loss and dizziness.

Diet may cause dizziness. The role of diet may be direct, as through alcohol intake. It may be also be indirect, as through arteriosclerosis caused by a high-fat diet. Some people experience a slight dip in blood sugar and mild dizziness if they miss a meal, but this condition is rarely dangerous unless the person is diabetic. **Food sensitivities** or allergies can also be a cause of dizziness. Chronic conditions, such as heart disease, and serious acute problems, such as seizures and strokes, can cause dizziness. However, such conditions usually exhibit other characteristic symptoms.

When to call the doctor

A doctor should be called whenever a person experiences dizziness or other unusual state of mental confusion that does not spontaneously resolve within a few minutes.

Diagnosis

During the initial medical examination, an individual with dizziness should provide a detailed description of the type of dizziness experienced, when it occurs, and how often each episode lasts. A diary of symptoms may help track this information. The person should report any symptoms that accompany the dizziness, such as a ringing in the ear or nausea, any recent injury or infection, and any medication taken.

Blood pressure, pulse, respiration, and body temperature are checked, and the ear, nose, and throat are scrutinized. The sense of balance is assessed by moving the individual's head to various positions or by tilt-table testing. (In tilt-table testing, the person lies on a table that can be shifted into different positions and reports any dizziness that occurs.)

Further tests may be indicated by the initial examination. Hearing tests help assess ear damage. **X rays**, **computed tomography** scan (CT scan), and **magnetic resonance imaging** (MRI) can pinpoint evidence of nerve damage, tumor, or other structural problems. If a vestibular disorder is suspected, a technique called electronystagmography (ENG) may be used. ENG measures the electrical impulses generated by eye movements. Blood tests can determine diabetes, **high cholesterol**, and other diseases. In some cases, a heart evaluation may be useful. Despite thorough testing, however, an underlying cause cannot always be determined.

Treatment

Treatment is determined by the underlying cause. If an individual has a cold or **influenza**, a few days of bed rest is usually adequate to resolve dizziness. Other causes of dizziness, such as mild vestibular system damage, may resolve without medical treatment.

If dizziness continues, drug therapy may prove helpful. Because circulatory problems often cause dizziness, medication may be prescribed to control blood pressure or to treat arteriosclerosis. Sedatives may be useful to relieve the tension that can trigger or aggravate dizziness. Low blood sugar associated with diabetes sometimes causes dizziness and is treated by controlling blood sugar levels. An individual may be asked to avoid caffeine, nicotine, alcohol, and those substances that cause allergic reactions. A low-salt diet may also help some people.

When other measures have failed, surgery may be suggested to relieve pressure on the inner ear. If the dizziness is not treatable by drugs, surgery, or other means, physical therapy may be used and the person may be taught coping mechanisms for the problem.

Because dizziness may arise from serious conditions, it is advisable to seek medical treatment. Alternative treatments can often be used alongside conventional medicine without conflict. Relaxation techniques, such as **yoga** and **massage therapy**, that focus on relieving tension are popularly recommended methods for reducing stress. Aroma therapists recommend a warm bath scented with essential oils of lavender, geranium, and sandalwood.

Homeopathic therapies can work very effectively for dizziness and are especially applicable when no organic cause can be identified. An osteopath or chiropractor may suggest adjustments of the head, jaw, neck, and lower back to relieve pressure on the inner ear. Acupuncturists also offer some treatment options for acute and chronic cases of dizziness. Nutritionists may be able to offer advice and guidance in choosing dietary supplements, identifying foods to avoid and balancing nutritional needs.

KEY TERMS

Acoustic neuroma—A benign tumor that grows on the nerve leading from the inner ear to the brain. As the tumor grows, it exerts pressure on the inner ear and causes severe vertigo.

Arteriosclerosis—A chronic condition characterized by thickening, loss of leasticity, and hardening of the arteries and the build-up of plaque on the arterial walls. Arteriosclerosis can slow or impair blood circulation. It includes atherosclerosis, but the two terms are often used synonymously.

Autonomic nervous system—The part of the nervous system that controls so-called involuntary functions, such as heart rate, salivary gland secretion, respiratory function, and pupil dilation.

Computed tomography (CT)—An imaging technique in which cross-sectional x rays of the body are compiled to create a three-dimensional image of the body's internal structures; also called computed axial tomography.

Electronystagmography—A method for measuring the electricity generated by eye movements. Electrodes are placed on the skin around the eye and the individual is subjected to a variety of stimuli so that the quality of eye movements can be assessed.

Magnetic resonance imaging (MRI)—An imaging technique that uses a large circular magnet and radio waves to generate signals from atoms in the body. These signals are used to construct detailed images of internal body structures and organs, including the brain.

Vestibular system—The brain and parts of the inner ear that work together to detect movement and position.

Prognosis

Outcome depends on the cause of dizziness. Controlling or curing the underlying factors usually relieves dizziness. In some cases, dizziness disappears without treatment. In a few cases, dizziness can become a permanent disabling condition and a person's options are limited.

Prevention

Most people learn through experience that certain activities make them dizzy and they learn to avoid them. For example, if reading in a car produces motion sickness, an individual leaves reading materials for after arrival. Changes to the diet can also cut down on episodes of dizziness in susceptible people. Relaxation techniques can help ward off tension and **anxiety** that can cause dizziness.

These techniques can help minimize or even prevent dizziness for people with chronic diseases. For example, persons with Meniere's disease may avoid episodes of vertigo by omitting salt, alcohol, and caffeine from their diets. Reducing blood cholesterol can help diminish arteriosclerosis and indirectly treat dizziness.

Some cases of dizziness cannot be prevented. Acoustic neuromas, for example, were not as of 2004 predictable or preventable. When the underlying cause of dizziness cannot be discovered, it may be difficult to recommend preventive measures. Alternative approaches designed to rebalance the body's energy flow, such as acupuncture and constitutional homeopathy, may be helpful in cases where the cause of dizziness cannot be pinpointed.

Nutritional concerns

Persons who experience dizziness should limit alcohol intake and avoid diets that are high in fat. Persons with diabetes should eat their meals on a regular schedule. People for whom some foods cause allergic reactions or sensitivities or dizziness, should avoid consuming the offending substances.

Parental concerns

Parents should be alert for complaints from their children of dizziness or other states of mental confusion that do not spontaneously resolve within a minute or so.

Resources

BOOKS

Benditt, David G. *Evaluation and Treatment of Syncope: A Handbook for Clinical Practice*. Malden, MA: Blackwell, 2003.

Daroff, Robert B., and Mark D. Carlson. "Faintness, Syncope, Dizziness, and Vertigo." In *Harrison's Principles of Internal Medicine*, 15th ed. Edited by Eugene Braunwald et al., New York: McGraw-Hill, 2001, pp. 111–8.

Grubb, Blair P., and Mary C. McMann. *Fainting Phenomenon: Understanding Why People Faint and What Can Be Done about It*. Malden, MA: Futura Publishing, 2001.

The Official Patient's Sourcebook on Syncope: A Revised and Updated Directory for the Internet Age. San Diego, CA: ICON Health Publications, 2003.

Simon, Roger P. "Syncope." In *Cecil Textbook of Medicine*, 22nd ed. Edited by Lee Goldman et al. Philadelphia: Saunders, 2003, pp. 2268–71.

PERIODICALS

Chamelian, L., and A. Feinstein. "Outcome after mild to moderate traumatic brain injury: The role of dizziness." *Archives of Physical Medicine and Rehabilitation* 85, no. 10 (2004): 1662–6.

Heid, L., et al. "Vertigo, dizziness, and tinnitus after otobasal fractures." *International Tinnitus Journal* 10, no. 1 (2004): 94–100.

ORGANIZATIONS

American Academy of Neurology. 1080 Montreal Avenue, St. Paul, MN 55116. Web site: <www.aan.com/>.

American Academy of Pediatrics. 141 Northwest Point Blvd., Elk Grove Village, IL 60007–1098. Web site: <www.aap.org>.

American Council for Headache Education. 19 Mantua Rd., Mt. Royal, NJ 08061. Web site: <www.achenet.org>.

WEB SITES

"Dizziness." *Mayo Clinic*, August 6, 2004. Available online at <www.mayoclinic.com/invoke.cfm?id=DS00435> (accessed January 5, 2005).

"Dizziness and Motion Sickness." *American Academy of Otolaryngology/Head and Neck Surgery.* Available online at <www.entnet.org/healthinfo/balance/dizziness.cfm> (accessed January 5, 2005).

"Dizziness and Vertigo." *MedlinePlus.* Available online at <www.nlm.nih.gov/medlineplus/dizzinessandvertigo.html> (accessed January 5, 2005).

"Dizziness and Vertigo." *National Multiple Sclerosis Society*, March 2003. Available online at <www.nationalmssociety.org/Sourcebook-Dizziness.asp> (accessed January 5, 2005).

L. Fleming Fallon, Jr., MD, DrPH

Down syndrome

Definition

Down syndrome is the most common cause of **mental retardation** and malformation in a newborn. A genetic disorder, it occurs because of the presence of an extra chromosome.

Description

Chromosomes are units of genetic information that exist within every cell of the body. Twenty-three distinctive pairs, or 46 total chromosomes, are located within the nucleus (central structure) of each cell. When a baby is conceived by combining one sperm cell with one egg cell, the baby receives 23 chromosomes from each parent, for a total of 46 chromosomes. Sometimes, an accident in the production of a sperm or egg cell causes that cell to contain 24 chromosomes. This event is referred to as nondisjunction. When this defective cell is involved in the conception of a baby, that baby will have a total of 47 chromosomes. The extra chromosome in Down syndrome is labeled number 21. For this reason, the existence of three such chromosomes is sometimes referred to as trisomy 21.

In a very rare number of Down syndrome cases (about 1–2%), the original egg and sperm cells are completely normal. The problem occurs sometime shortly after fertilization; during the phase when cells are dividing rapidly. One cell divides abnormally, creating a line of cells with an extra chromosome 21. This form of genetic disorder is called a mosaic. The individual with this type of Down syndrome has two types of cells: those with 46 chromosomes (the normal number) and those with 47 chromosomes (as occurs in Down syndrome). Some researchers have suggested that individuals with this type of mosaic form of Down syndrome have less severe signs and symptoms of the disorder.

Another relatively rare genetic accident which can cause Down syndrome is called translocation. During cell division, the number 21 chromosome somehow breaks. A piece of the number 21 chromosome then becomes attached to another chromosome. Each cell still has 46 chromosomes, but the extra piece of chromosome 21 results in the signs and symptoms of Down syndrome. Translocations occur in about 3–4 percent of cases of Down syndrome.

Demographics

Down syndrome occurs in about one in every 800 to 1,000 births. It affects an equal number of boys and girls. Less than 25 percent of Down syndrome cases occur due to an extra chromosome in the sperm cell. The majority of cases of Down syndrome occur due to an extra chromosome 21 within the egg cell supplied by the mother (nondisjunction). As a woman's age (maternal age) increases, the risk of having a Down syndrome baby increases significantly. For example, at younger ages, the risk is about one in 4,000. By the time the woman is age 35, the risk increases to one in 400; by age 40 the risk increases to one in 110; and by age 45 the risk becomes one in 35. There is no increased risk of either mosaicism or translocation with increased maternal age.

Causes and symptoms

While Down syndrome is a chromosomal disorder, a baby is usually identified at birth through observation of a set of common physical characteristics. Babies with Down syndrome tend to be overly quiet; less responsive; with weak, floppy muscles. Furthermore, a number of physical signs may be present. These include:

- flat appearing face
- small head
- flat bridge of the nose
- smaller than normal, low-set nose
- small mouth, which causes the tongue to stick out and to appear overly large
- upward slanting eyes
- extra folds of skin located at the inside corner of each eye, near the nose (called epicanthal folds)
- rounded cheeks
- small, misshapen ears
- small, wide hands
- an unusual, deep crease across the center of the palm (called a simian crease)
- a malformed fifth finger
- a wide space between the big and the second toes
- unusual creases on the soles of the feet
- overly flexible joints (sometimes referred to as being double-jointed)
- shorter than normal height

Other types of defects often accompany Down syndrome. About 30 to 50 percent of all children with Down syndrome are found to have heart defects. A number of different heart defects are common in Down syndrome, including abnormal openings (holes) in the walls that separate the heart's chambers (**atrial septal defect**, ventricular septal defect). These result in abnormal patterns of blood flow within the heart. The abnormal blood flow often means that less oxygen is sent into circulation throughout the body. Another heart defect that occurs in Down syndrome is called **tetralogy of Fallot**. Tetralogy of Fallot consists of a hole in the heart, along with three other major heart defects.

Malformations of the gastrointestinal tract are present in about 5–7 percent of children with Down syndrome. The most common malformation is a narrowed, obstructed duodenum (the part of the intestine into which the stomach empties). This disorder, called duodenal atresia, interferes with the baby's milk or formula leaving the stomach and entering the intestine for digestion. The baby often vomits forcibly after feeding and cannot gain weight appropriately until the defect is repaired.

Other medical conditions that occur in patients with Down syndrome include an increased chance of developing infections, especially ear infections and **pneumonia**; certain kidney disorders; thyroid disease (especially low or hypothyroid); hearing loss; vision impairment that requires corrective lenses; and a 20-times greater chance of developing leukemia (a blood disorder).

Development in a baby and child with Down syndrome occurs at a much slower than normal rate. Because of weak, floppy muscles (**hypotonia**), babies learn to sit up, crawl, and walk much later than their normal peers. Talking is also quite delayed. The level of mental retardation is considered to be mild-to-moderate in Down syndrome. The actual IQ range of Down syndrome children is quite varied, but the majority of such children are in what is sometimes known as the trainable range. This means that most people with Down syndrome can be trained to do regular self-care tasks, function in a socially appropriate manner in a normal home environment, and even hold simple jobs.

As people with Down syndrome age, they face an increased chance of developing the brain disease called Alzheimer's (sometimes referred to dementia or senility). Most people have a six in 100 risk of developing Alzheimer's, but people with Down syndrome have a one-in-four chance of the disease. Alzheimer's disease causes the brain to shrink and to break down. The number of brain cells decreases, and abnormal deposits and structural arrangements occur. This process results in loss of brain function. People with Alzheimer's have strikingly faulty memories. Over time, people with Alzheimer's disease lapse into an increasingly unresponsive state. Some researchers have shown that even Down syndrome patients who do not appear to have Alzheimer's disease have the same changes occurring to the structures and cells of their brains.

As people with Down syndrome age, they also have an increased chance of developing a number of other medical difficulties, including cataracts, thyroid problems, diabetes, and seizure disorders.

Children with Down syndrome. The disease is caused by trisomy 21, meaning their bodies' cells have an extra chromosome 21. *(© Lester V. Bergman/Corbis.)*

Diagnosis

Diagnosis is usually suspected at birth, when the characteristic physical signs of Down syndrome are noted. Once this suspicion has been raised, genetic testing (chromosome analysis) can be undertaken in order to verify the presence of the disorder. This testing is usually done on a blood sample, although chromosome analysis can also be done on other types of tissue, including skin. The cells to be studied are prepared in a laboratory. Chemical stain is added to make the characteristics of the cells and the chromosomes stand out. Chemicals are added to prompt the cells to go through normal development, up to the point where the chromosomes are most visible, prior to cell division. At this point, they are examined under a microscope and photographed. The photograph is used to sort the different sizes and shapes of chromosomes into pairs. In most cases of Down syndrome, one extra chromosome 21 will be revealed. The final result of such testing, with the photographed chromosomes paired and organized by shape and size, is called the individual's karyotype.

Treatment

As of 2004 no treatment is available to cure Down syndrome. Treatment is directed at addressing the indivi-

dual concerns of a particular patient. For example, heart defects often times require surgical repair, as will duodenal atresia. Many Down syndrome patients need to wear glasses to correct vision. Patients with **hearing impairment** benefit from hearing aids.

In the mid 1900s, all Down syndrome children were quickly placed into institutions for lifelong care. Research shows, however, that the best outlook for children with Down syndrome is **family** life in their own home. This arrangement requires careful support and education of the parents and the siblings. Parents and other siblings face a life-changing event in receiving a new baby who has a permanent condition that will affect essentially all aspects of his or her development. Some community groups are committed to helping families deal with the emotional effects of this new situation. Schools are required to provide services for children with Down syndrome, sometimes in separate **special education** classrooms and sometimes in regular classrooms, a practiced called mainstreaming or inclusion.

Prognosis

The prognosis in Down syndrome is quite variable, depending on the types of complications (heart defects, susceptibility to infections, development of leukemia) of each individual baby. The severity of the retardation can also vary significantly. Without the presence of heart defects, about 90 percent of children with Down syndrome live into their teens. People with Down syndrome appear to go through the normal physical changes of aging more rapidly, however. The average age at death for an individual with Down syndrome is about 50 to 55 years.

Still, in the early 2000s, the prognosis for a baby born with Down syndrome is better than ever before. Because of modern medical treatments, including **antibiotics** to treat infections and surgery to treat heart defects and duodenal atresia, life expectancy has greatly increased. Community and family support allows people with Down syndrome to have rich, meaningful relationships and in some cases to hold jobs.

Men with Down syndrome appear to be uniformly sterile (meaning that they are unable to have offspring). Women with Down syndrome, however, are fully capable of having babies. About 50 percent of these babies, however, will also be born with Down syndrome.

Prevention

Efforts at prevention of Down syndrome are aimed at genetic counseling of couples who are preparing to have babies. A counselor needs to inform a woman that her risk of having a baby with Down syndrome increases with her increasing age. Two types of testing is available during a pregnancy to determine if the baby being carried has Down syndrome.

Screening tests are used to estimate the chance that an individual woman will have a baby with Down syndrome. At 14–17 weeks of pregnancy, measurements of a substance called AFP (alpha-fetoprotein) can be performed. AFP is normally found circulating in the blood of a pregnant woman but may be unusually high or low with certain disorders. Carrying a baby with Down syndrome often causes AFP to be lower than normal. This information alone, or along with measurements of two other hormones, is considered along with the mother's age to calculate the risk of the baby being born with Down syndrome. These results are only predictions and are only correct about 60 percent of the time. Other screening tests measure and compare the levels of other markers present in the mother's blood. A specialized ultrasound exam measures the thickness of the back of the fetus's neck (called nuchal lucency). Thicker measurements correlate with the possibility of Down syndrome or other chromosomal abnormalities.

All of these screening tests are used to decide which mothers will be offered other, more definitive testing to

KEY TERMS

Chromosome—A microscopic thread-like structure found within each cell of the human body and consisting of a complex of proteins and DNA. Humans have 46 chromosomes arranged into 23 pairs. Chromosomes contain the genetic information necessary to direct the development and functioning of all cells and systems in the body. They pass on hereditary traits from parents to child (like eye color) and determine whether the child will be male or female.

Karyotype—A standard arrangement of photographic or computer-generated images of chromosome pairs from a cell in ascending numerical order, from largest to smallest.

Mental retardation—A condition where an individual has a lower-than-normal IQ, and thus is developmentally delayed.

Mosaic—A term referring to a genetic situation in which an individual's cells do not have the exact same composition of chromosomes. In Down syndrome, this may mean that some of the individual's cells have a normal 46 chromosomes, while other cells have an abnormal 47 chromosomes.

Nondisjunction—An event that takes place during cell division in which a chromosome pair does not separate as it should. The result is an abnormal number of chromosmes in the daughter cells produced by that cell division.

Translocation—The transfer of one part of a chromosome to another chromosome during cell division. A balanced translocation occurs when pieces from two different chromosomes exchange places without loss or gain of any chromosome material. An unbalanced translocation involves the unequal loss or gain of genetic information between two chromosomes.

Trisomy—An abnormal condition where three copies of one chromosome are present in the cells of an individual's body instead of two, the normal number.

ascertain whether the baby has Down syndrome. These more definitive tests each carry a risk of miscarriage, which is why screening tests are an important first step. The only way to definitively establish (with about 98–99% accuracy) the presence or absence of Down syndrome in a developing baby is to test tissue from the pregnancy itself. This is usually done either by **amniocentesis** or chorionic villus sampling (CVS). In amniocentesis, a small amount of the fluid in which the baby is floating is withdrawn with a long, thin needle. In chorionic villus sampling, a tiny tube is inserted into the opening of the uterus to retrieve a small sample of the placenta (the organ that attaches the growing baby to the mother via the umbilical cord, and provides oxygen and **nutrition**). Both amniocentesis and CVS allow the baby's own karyotype to be determined. A couple must then decide whether to use this information in order to begin to prepare for the arrival of a baby with Down syndrome or to terminate the pregnancy.

Once a couple has had one baby with Down syndrome, they are often concerned about the likelihood of future offspring also being born with the disorder. Most research indicates that this chance remains the same as for any other woman at a similar age. However, when the baby with Down syndrome has the type that results from a translocation, it is possible that one of the two parents is a carrier of that defect. (A carrier carries the genetic defect but does not actually have the disorder.) When one parent is a carrier of a translocation, the chance of future offspring having Down syndrome is greatly increased. The specific risk will have to be calculated by a genetic counselor.

Parental concerns

Parenting a child with Down syndrome can be both challenging and rewarding. Children with Down syndrome have a wide range of potential outcomes. Early intervention programs have been proven to be of great help in assisting these children in achieving the highest level of functioning possible. There are many support groups available for parents and siblings of Down syndrome children.

Resources

BOOKS

Hall, Judith G. "Chromosomal Clinical Abnormalities." In *Nelson Textbook of Pediatrics.* Edited by Richard E. Behrman et al. Philadelphia: Saunders, 2004.

Simpson, Joe Leigh. "Genetic Counseling and Prenatal Diagnosis." In *Obstetrics: Normal and Problem Pregnancies.* Edited by Steven G. Gabbe. London: Churchill Livingstone, 2002.

Tierney, Lawrence, et al. *Current Medical Diagnosis and Treatment.* Los Altos, CA: Lange Medical Publications, 2001.Periodicals

Canick, J. A. "Prenatal screening for Down syndrome: current and future methods." *Clinical Laboratory Medicine* 86 (June 2003): 395–411.

Roizen, N. J. "Medical care and monitoring for the adolescent with Down syndrome." *Adolescent Medicine* 13 (June 2002): 345–58.

Tyler, C. "Down syndrome, Turner syndrome, and Klinefelter syndrome: primary care throughout the life span." *Primary Care* 31 (September 2004): 627.

ORGANIZATION

National Down Syndrome Congress. 1370 Center Drive, Suite 102 Atlanta, GA 30338 (800) 232-6372. Web site: <www.ndsccenter.org>

National Down Syndrome Society. 666 Broadway, 8th Floor, New York, NY 10012-2317. Web site: <www.ndss.org>.

Kim A. Sharp, M.Ln.
Rosalyn Carson-DeWitt, MD

Doxycycline *see* **Tetracyclines**

Drawings

Definition

Children's drawings are visual representations made with crayons, markers, or pencils that are generated for pleasure but can also be used for therapeutic purposes or developmental **assessment**.

Description

Children's art, especially a drawing, represents one of the delights of childhood. The child's artistic endeavors are mainly produced for pleasure and the exploration of art media. They can also be used for developmental and therapeutic assessment.

Children's drawings obviously show artistic development and expression. In educational and clinical settings, they can be vehicles for assessing a child's personality, intellectual development, **communication skills**, and emotional adjustment. Children's drawings can also aid in helping to diagnose learning disabilities. Law enforcement officers, social workers, and counselors often have children draw traumatic events, especially when they lack the communication skills to explain what they have witnessed or experienced. Children may also feel distanced from the traumatic event by drawing it and talking about what is happening in the picture, as if discussing a character in a book or on television.

Color analysis has often been a means of determining a child's emotional state. A lot of black or red recurring in a child's drawing may be a troublesome sign. Black often is an indication of depression or feeling hopeless or restricted. Red may indicate intense anger. Blues and greens are usually calm colors, and yellows and oranges often indicate cheerfulness. Therapists are not ordinarily concerned if a child does one drawing in one of the troublesome colors, but may want to investigate a series of dark drawings, especially if the content is also frightening or disturbing. Therapists may use the therapeutic session as a means of emotional release and may encourage a child to create drawings that express their deep fears and angers. Drawings in this case are not assessment instruments, but become therapeutic tools.

Stages of creative development

In 1975, Viktor Lowenfeld launched a theory of artistic development based on systematic creative and cognitive stages. Each stage demonstrated specific characteristics and had an age range. He encouraged the use of his artistic development stages in classrooms and as guides for parents.

These stages are as dependent on a child's exposure to art and art media as they are on a child's innate artistic ability or **fine motor skills**. It should be noted that because a child does not seem to go beyond a specific developmental stage, it does not mean that the child has a cognitive or developmental problem. This apparent arrest of development may be due to limited exposure to art, lack of interest, or fine-motor differences. Cultural values can also affect artistic expression and development, influencing content, art media, style, and symbolic meaning as represented in the child's view of the world.

The following stages are generalized from Lowenfeld's work and that of Betty Edwards. Both theories show children moving from scribbling through several stages to realistic art. Children may overlap stages, making drawings with elements of one stage while progressing or regressing to another. Generally, boys and girls will develop similarly in the initial stages. Whether any child progresses to the latter stages usually requires instruction of some kind.

SCRIBBLING STAGE The scribbling stage usually begins around two years old and lasts until the child is about four years of age. In some cases, it can begin as soon as a child can hold a fat crayon and make marks on paper, which is sometimes around 18 months old. At first, the child is interested only in watching the color flow on the paper. Some children are more interested in the marking itself and may even look away while scribbling. What results on the paper is accidental and often delights the child, even though it is indistinguishable to adults.

With about six months of practice, the child will be more deliberate and may start drawing circles. Later, the child will name the drawing, saying, "This is a dog." The child may even look at the drawing of the dog the next day and say, "This is Daddy." The child will also start drawing people that resemble a tadpole or amoeba (a circle with arms and legs, and sometimes eyes).

PRE-SCHEMATIC STAGE The pre-schematic, or pre-symbolic, stage begins around age four; however, it may start earlier or later, depending on the child's cultural and artistic experience. In this stage, the amoeba or tadpole people may have faces, hands, and even toes, but no bodies. These figures face front and often have big smiles. Omission of body details is not a sign that something is developmentally wrong. It just means that other things in the drawing of the person are more important. For example, heads are the first objects drawn and may continue to be bigger than other parts of the body. This is usually done because the child sees the head as being very important. The child eats, speaks, sees, and hears with parts of the head.

Colors are selected on whim and usually have no relationship with what is being drawn. Figures may be scattered all over the page, or the page turned in every direction as the figures fill the paper. Objects and figures may appear to float all over the page because children do not yet know how to express three-dimensional objects on a two-dimensional surface.

The child's self-portrait appears as an amoeba person, but it will usually be the biggest figure, appearing in the center of the page. The child may test different ways to draw a self-portrait before settling on one for a period of time. In this instance, art helps define a child's self image.

SCHEMATIC STAGE The schematic stage usually begins around seven years old and extends through age nine. At this time, the child has developed specific schema, or symbols for people and objects in his or her environment, and will draw them consistently over and over. Human figures have all necessary body parts. Arms and legs also fill out, instead of being stick-like. This is usually due to more body awareness and recognition of what body parts do; e.g. parts of the body help the child run, catch a ball, jump, etc. Adults usually have very long legs because that is how children see them.

Houses and people no longer float on the page. They are grounded by a baseline that acts as a horizon line. As the child continues to draw, there may be two or more baselines to show distance or topography. Children may also draw a series of pictures, like cartoon squares, to show action sequences over time. This seems to reflect a child's desire to tell stories with the drawings. By eight or nine years of age, children will often draw their favorite cartoon characters or superheroes.

REALISTIC OR GANG STAGE The realistic or gang stage begins around nine years old. Here, the child begins to develop more detail in drawing people and in determining perspective (depth or distance) in drawings. Shapes now have form with shadows and shading. The people they draw show varying expressions. Colors are used to accurately depict the environment, and more complex art materials may be introduced.

Children at this stage are eager to conform and are very sensitive to teasing or criticism from classmates. They also are very critical of their work, individually or when it is compared to the work of others. Children at this stage can be easily discouraged about creating art if they are overly criticized, teased by their peers, or become frustrated with art media or problems expressing what they see in their minds. This is the time to begin quality art instruction, where children receive the technical training in mastery of art media, perspective, figure drawing, and rendering (shading).

Somewhere between ages 12 and 16 years, children face a crisis in artistic development. They will either already have enough skill and encouragement to continue a desire to create art, or they will not. If it is only a matter of training, finding appropriate art classes will help the child through this crisis. If the child has been discouraged by criticism or lack of enough art experience or exposure, the child may not continue to draw or participate in visual art activities. Some discouraged children may change to a different art medium. For example, a child may not draw or paint again, but may enjoy making clay pots or welding metal sculptures. Other children will find alternate ways to express their **creativity**. For example, a child may become involved with auto detailing, fly-tying, sewing, or needlework. Still others will never participate in any other kind of artistic activity and may ridicule or disdain those who do.

Common problems

When to call the doctor

Generally, children's drawings are no cause of alarm, despite color choice or content. They are merely artistic expressions and may present a variety of emo-

tions, representations, and themes that are explored and then discarded.

Nevertheless, if a young child is repeatedly drawing violent pictures, there may be reason to seek out a therapist for the child to see if deeper emotional issues exist. For teenagers, especially those who are artistic, entertaining a dark period or even a quasi-violent Goth or vampire series of art work may simply be artistic exploration of darker themes. If this period of art work is coupled with risky behaviors or depression, it may represent a cry for help and therapy may be appropriate.

Other indicators of possible emotional problems may be drawings of a particular object or person much bigger than a drawing the child makes of himself or herself, or a drawing of a human figure in disjointed parts. In these cases, a child should be evaluated by a therapist because drawings of this sort usually indicate being overwhelmed by something or feeling fragmented. Drawings with incomplete or hesitant lines may indicate that a child feels unsure or insecure. Children who make these drawings may just need encouragement. Further evaluation may be necessary if these kinds of drawings continue for a long period of time.

Parental concerns

Since artistic expression and appreciation is an element of a balanced life, encouragement by parents and other adults is essential. Adults can encourage art expression by offering art materials to children at an early age. Even toddlers can make drawings with fat crayons, as crayons are non-toxic. Art materials should be good quality. The materials do not need to be expensive, but they should be good enough so that they perform as they are intended. For example, a child may be given a set of colored markers; but if they do not flow well or are dried up, the child can become discouraged because the tools do not function properly.

Children also enjoy experimenting with a variety of art materials. Using chalks, pastels, charcoal, and pencils of different softness expands the artistic possibilities that crayons and markers begin. This variety allows a child to explore different media and how they behave. No child is expected to become the master of any or all of these media, but the experience with each helps them expand their artistic voice and opens up greater appreciation for artwork by others found in museums or created by their fellow classmates.

Adults can encourage artistic expression by allowing children to use the media they have experimented with in ways that are truly unique. Adults can make sure that children know that drawings are not always

Drawing by a young child depicting a family. *(© Royalty-Free/ Corbis.)*

supposed to look like photographs, but are each person's view of the world. Children's drawings become expressions of how and what each child sees. Adults can help children understand that art is self expression and that there is nothing wrong with what the child chooses to express. Artistic risk taking, experimentation, and the development of meaning are intrinsic to making art, and children can begin to understand these concepts through their own artistic efforts.

Exposure to a variety of visual art at an early age can encourage a child's lifelong appreciation of art. This can be in the form of quality children's picture books that have beautiful illustrations. Trips to art galleries and museums can broaden a child's exposure to a variety of artists, styles, and content. Visiting artists at art shows or art fairs can also be a way to show children how artists work or handle different media. Adults can extend this exposure through discussions about the art works and talking about media or content.

Children's responses to their own drawings and their perception of the level of their competence is often affected by the attitudes of their peers and adults who react to their art work. Direct and indirect criticism of a child's drawings should be avoided. When children are very young, it is sometimes difficult for adults to figure out just what a child's drawing is about. In order to avoid quashing young talent or a child's **self-esteem** by commenting on the beautiful bee the child drew when it really was a dog, adults can praise the child for having made something wonderful and then ask the child to tell about the drawing. From the answer, the adult can then praise the child's work in context. For example, if the child brings a drawing of yellow and blue scribbles, the adult can say, "What beautiful colors! Tell me about your picture." If the child says the drawing is about a flying horse, the adult can respond, "What a graceful flying horse! Does he like to fly?" The adult can continue to engage the child in discussion about the horse, choices of color, reasons for drawing a flying horse that day, or how the child felt doing the drawing.

Criticism can occur constructively when children enroll in technical art classes. There is a context in the art education setting for mastery of art media and technique. The normal **preschool** or elementary classroom is not the place for this kind of critique. Many children have been so severely criticized by teachers that they never pick up art materials again and some are even turned away from appreciating anyone else's art.

See also Cognitive development.

Resources

BOOKS

Gaitskill, C., et al. *Children and Their Art.* New York: Harcourt Brace Jovanovich, 1982.

Golomb, C. *The Child's Creation of a Pictorial World.* Berkeley and Los Angeles: University of California Press, 1992.

Levick, Myra. *See What I'm Saying: What Children Tell Us Through Their Art.* Dr. Myra Levick, 2003.

Malchiodi, Cathy. *Understanding Children's Drawings.* New York: Guilford Press, 1998.

Oster, Gerald. *Using Drawings in Assessment and Therapy: A Guide for Mental Health Professionals.* New York: Brunner/Mazel, 2004.

Rubin, Judith. *Art Therapy.* New York: Brunner/Mazel, 1999.

PERIODICALS

Burkitt, Esther et al. "Children's Colour Choices for Completing Drawings of Affectively Characterised Topics." *Journal of Child Psychology and Psychiatry*(2003): 445.

McDonald, Faith Tibbets. "What Drawings Reveal" *Christian Parenting Today*.14, no. 18 (March/April 2002): 20.

"Scribbles Can Measure Kids' Development." *USA Today*(December 2001).

Janie Franz

Drowning *see* **Near-drowning**

Drug abuse *see* **Substance abuse and dependence**

Drug allergies/sensitivities

Definition

A drug allergy is an adverse reaction to a medication, often an antibiotic, that is mediated by the body's immune system. A drug sensitivity is an unusual reaction to a drug that does not involve the immune system.

Description

Adverse reactions to medication may be allergic reactions involving a child's immune system, individual sensitivities to a drug, or side effects of the drug itself. Some children are allergic or sensitive to drugs that are not harmful for most people. Some drugs, such as aspirin and penicillin or related **antibiotics**, may induce allergic reactions in some children and sensitivities in other children.

Drug allergies

Drug **allergies** account for 5–10 percent of all adverse reactions to medications. They occur when the immune system—designed to protect the body from foreign substances such as bacteria and viruses—recognizes a medication as a harmful substance that must be destroyed. Drugs often induce an immune response; however, the symptoms of an allergic reaction occur in only a small number of children. Although most allergic drug reactions have mild symptoms, on rare occasions they can be life-threatening.

Drug allergies are unpredictable. Most drug allergies develop within days or occasionally weeks of beginning a drug treatment. Although it is very unusual to develop an allergy after months of taking a drug, sometimes children develop a drug allergy after having received multiple doses of the drug.

Unlike other types of adverse drug reactions, the frequency and severity of allergic reactions to drugs usually are independent of the amount of drug that is administered. Even a very small amount of a drug can trigger an allergic reaction.

Many classes of drugs can induce allergic reactions, resulting in a wide variety of symptoms affecting various tissues and organs. The likelihood that a drug will cause an allergic reaction depends in part on the chemical properties of the drug. Larger drug molecules are more likely to cause allergic reactions than smaller drug molecules. Larger drug molecules include the following:

- insulin
- antiserum which contains large immune-system proteins called antibodies
- recombinant proteins produced by genetic engineering

Unlike most other allergens, such as pollen or mold spores, drug molecules often are too small to be detected by the immune system. Smaller drugs such as antibiotics cannot induce an immune response unless they combine with a body cell or a carrier protein in the blood. Furthermore, drug allergies often are caused by the breakdown products or metabolites of the drug rather than by the drug itself. Sometimes the same drug, such as penicillin, can induce different types of allergic reactions.

IGE-MEDIATED ALLERGIES Most allergies, including most drug allergies, occur because of a reaction with an immune system antibody called immunoglobulin E (IgE). The first exposure to the drug sensitizes the child's immune system by inducing specialized white blood cells to produce IgE that recognizes the specific drug. On subsequent exposure to the drug, the drug-specific IgE antibodies bind to the drug on the surfaces of certain cells of the immune system. This binding activates the cells to release histamine and other chemicals that can cause a variety of symptoms. Thus, a child who has no reaction on first exposure to a drug may have a severe reaction with subsequent exposure.

Drug-specific IgE antibodies may cross-react with other drugs that have similar chemical properties, thereby triggering an allergic reaction, as is the case in the penicillin **family**. For example, the antibodies of a child allergic to penicillin may cross-react with the antibiotic amoxicillin or nafcillin.

Insect **stings** and the intravenous injection of certain drugs are the most common causes of

anaphylaxis, the most severe and frightening allergic response. Anaphylaxis involves the entire body. Although it is rare, several hundred Americans die of anaphylaxis every year. Anaphylaxis is most common in children who are allergic to **penicillins** and similar drugs. These drugs cause 97 percent of all deaths from drug allergies.

OTHER TYPES OF DRUG ALLERGIES Some drug allergies occur via immune system components other than IgE. Cytotoxic/cytolytic drug allergies occur when a drug allergen that is associated with a cell membrane, usually a blood cell, interacts with other types of antibodies—called immunoglobulin G (IgG) or immunoglobulin M (IgM)—along with other immune system factors. These interactions damage or destroy body cells.

Immune complex drug allergies occur when a drug combines with antibodies and other immune system components to form complexes in the blood. These complexes can be deposited in blood vessels and on membranes, causing inflammatory reactions that may be either localized or throughout the body. For instance, serum sickness typically causes a rash and joint swelling after the offending drug is administered.

T-cell-mediated allergic drug reactions require immune system cells called T-memory cells that are specific for the drug allergen. When exposed to the allergen, the T-cells are activated and cause an inflammatory response. The most common example of this type of reaction is allergic **contact dermatitis** that causes inflammations of the skin.

Drug sensitivities

Drug sensitivities (also called idiosyncratic reactions or unusual adverse reactions) do not involve the child's immune system or the release of histamine. However, the symptoms of drug sensitivities can be very similar to the symptoms of a drug allergy. Unlike drug allergies, sensitivities often occur upon first exposure to a drug and do not lead to anaphylaxis.

Demographics

Anyone can develop an allergy to any drug at any time. It is not clear why some children develop allergies to drugs that are well tolerated by most people. It is estimated that up to 10 percent of all people develop allergies to penicillin or other antibiotics at some point in their lives. Those taking multiple medications or frequent courses of antibiotics appear to be more at risk for developing drug allergies.

The most common drug sensitivity is to aspirin. Nearly 1 million Americans, primarily adults, are sensitive to aspirin. However, many medications, including aspirin and other non-steroidal anti-inflammatory drugs (NSAIDs) such as ibuprofen (Advil, Motrin, and others), can trigger an **asthma** attack in children. Asthma is a common chronic respiratory condition in children. Attacks occur when the air passages from the lungs to the nose and mouth are narrowed causing difficulty breathing. Aspirin and aspirin-like medications are common triggers for asthma attacks in as many as 30 percent of asthmatic children.

Causes and symptoms

Drug allergies

Any drug (either prescription or over-the-counter) can evoke an allergic reaction; however, antibiotics, especially penicillin and related drugs, are the most common cause of drug allergies. Children also frequently (i.e. to these agents more frequently than to other agents) develop allergies to the following:

- aspirin
- sulfa-based drugs
- barbiturates
- anticonvulsants
- insulin preparations, particularly those from animal sources
- dyes that are injected into blood vessels before taking x rays

The symptoms of a drug allergy vary from quite mild to life-threatening anaphylaxis. Unlike other common allergies, drug allergies often affect the entire body. The most common symptoms of a drug allergy are skin conditions including rash, generalized **itching**, and urticaria (**hives**; a very itchy rash with red swellings affecting only a small area of skin or the entire body; possibly the early symptom of anaphylaxis). The type of rash depends on the type of allergic response.

Less common symptoms of drug allergies include runny nose, sneezing, and congestion.

Uncommon but more serious symptoms of a drug allergy include the following:

- nausea, **vomiting**, diarrhea
- abdominal **pain** or cramps
- **fever**
- low blood cell count
- wheezing and difficulty breathing

- inflammation of the lungs, kidneys, and joints
- angioedema (a sudden swelling of the mucous membranes and tissues under the skin, anywhere on the body but especially on the face, eyes, lips, neck, throat, and genitals)

Angioedema occurs within a few minutes of exposure to the drug, often in conjunction with urticaria. Angioedema often is asymmetrical: for example, only one side of the lip may be affected. Swelling of the tongue, mouth, and airways can cause difficulty speaking, swallowing, or breathing. Angioedema can become life-threatening if the swelling affects the larynx (voice box) and the air passages become blocked. Emergency symptoms of a drug allergy include obstruction of the throat from swelling, severe asthma attack, and anaphylaxis.

Allergic reactions to drugs are the most common cause of an inflammation of the kidneys called tubulointerstitial nephritis. The allergic reaction and development of this acute condition may occur between five days and five weeks after exposure to penicillin, **sulfonamides**, diuretics (drugs to increase urination), and aspirin and other NSAIDs.

IGE-MEDIATED ALLERGIES IgE-mediated allergies can be caused by the following:

- penicillin when the allergic reaction is immediate
- blood factors, including antisera
- hormones
- vaccines (usually an allergic reaction to some component of the vaccine such as egg protein, gelatin, or neomycin, an antibiotic)
- very rarely, local anesthetics such as Novocain

The most common symptom of an IgE-mediated drug allergy is a rash that develops after the child has taken the drug for several days and produced antibodies against it.

ANAPHYLAXIS Anaphylaxis is a violent immune system reaction that can occur when a child who has large amounts of drug-specific IgE antibodies is re-exposed to the drug. The antibodies bind to the drug very rapidly causing an immediate, severe response. Anaphylaxis most often is caused by the following:

- penicillin and related antibiotics
- streptomycin
- tetracycline
- insulin

Anaphylaxis usually begins within one to 15 minutes following exposure to the drug. Only rarely does the reaction begin an hour or more after exposure. Anaphylaxis can progress very rapidly leading to collapse, seizures, and loss of consciousness within one to two minutes. Without treatment, cessation of breathing, anaphylactic shock, and death can occur within 15 minutes. Any drug that has caused anaphylaxis in a child will probably cause it again on subsequent exposure, unless measures are taken to prevent it.

Symptoms of anaphylaxis include:

- urticaria on various parts of the body
- angioedema
- intense itching
- flushing of the skin
- coughing and sneezing
- nausea, vomiting, diarrhea
- abdominal pain or cramping
- tingling sensations
- ear throbbing
- heart palpitations
- uneasiness or sudden extreme **anxiety**
- swollen throat and/or constricted air passages causing a hoarse voice, wheezing, and difficulty breathing, the most characteristic symptom of anaphylaxis

Constriction of the air passages in the bronchial tract and/or throat, accompanied by shock, can cause a drastic drop in blood pressure that may lead to the following:

- rapid pulse
- paleness
- weakness
- dizziness, lightheadedness
- slurred speech
- mental confusion
- unconsciousness

OTHER DRUG ALLERGIES Cytotoxic/cytolytic-type drug allergies can be caused by the following:

- penicillin
- sulfonamides
- quinidine
- methyldopa

Cytotoxic/cytolytic-type of drug allergy can result in the following:

- immune hemolytic anemia due to the destruction of red blood cells

- thrombocytopenia from the reduction in blood platelets

- granulocytopenia from a deficiency of a type of white blood cell called a granular leukocyte

Drugs that can cause immune complex reactions, such as serum sickness or drug-induced lupus syndromes, include:

- hydralazine

- procainamide

- isoniazid

- phenytoin

Serum sickness (a delayed type of drug allergy that may take one to three weeks to develop) can be caused by an allergic reaction to penicillin or related antibiotics. Serum sickness also can be an allergic response to animal proteins present in an injected drug. Serum sickness is characterized by the following:

- fever

- aching joints

- swelling of the lymph nodes

- rash

- general body swelling

- skin lesions

- nephritis (an inflammation of the kidneys)

- hepatitis (an inflammation of the liver)

Some drugs, including penicillins and sulfonamides, can cause delayed dermatologic allergic reactions. These are various types of skin reactions, including eczema, that do not occur immediately upon exposure to the drug. These types of allergies are thought to be caused by metabolites formed from the breakdown or further reaction of the drug.

Drug allergies can result in hypersensitivity reactions, which in turn can result in liver disorders. Such damage can be caused by the following:

- sulfonamides

- phenothiazines

- halothane

- phenytoin

- isoniazid

Pulmonary hypersensitivity allergic reactions that affect the lungs and result in **rashes** and fever may be caused by nitrofurantoin and sulfasalazine.

Drug sensitivities

Children may have drug sensitivities to aspirin; other NSAIDs; opiates such as morphine and codeine; and some antibiotics, including erythromycin and ampicillin.

Symptoms of drug sensitivities often are very similar to those of drug allergies and include rashes, urticaria, and angioedema.

Anaphylactoid drug reactions are similar to anaphylactic reactions. However, they are caused by a drug sensitivity rather than a drug allergy and can occur upon the first exposure to a drug. Anaphylactoid reactions can occur in response to the following:

- opiates

- radiopaque dyes (radiocontrast media) used in x-ray procedures; 2–3% of patients have immediate generalized reactions to these dyes

- aspirin and other NSAIDs in some people, usually adults

- polymyxin

- pentamidine

When to call the doctor

A physician should be consulted whenever a child has an allergic reaction or sensitivity to a drug. The parent or caregiver should seek emergency assistance if a child has a severe or rapidly worsening allergic reaction to a drug that includes wheezing, difficulty breathing, or other symptoms of anaphylaxis.

Diagnosis

It is important to distinguish between an uncomfortable but mild side effect of a drug and an allergic reaction or sensitivity which could be life-threatening. A drug allergy or sensitivity most often is diagnosed by discontinuing the drug and observing whether the symptoms disappear.

Following a drug reaction the parent should describe the exact course of the reaction; the type of symptoms, when they occurred, and how long they lasted; and whether the child had previously been exposed to the drug. A previous allergic-type reaction to the medication usually is considered diagnostic of a drug allergy. A reaction upon a child's first exposure to the drug is probably a drug sensitivity.

Further diagnosis of a drug allergy may depend on the following:

- a complete medical history, including all drugs taken in the past month, when and how the child received certain drugs, and previous drug reactions
- whether the drug is known to cause allergic reactions
- a family history of drug allergies
- the timing of symptom-onset following drug exposure
- the timing of symptom-disappearance after discontinuing the drug
- the type of rash
- involvement of joints, lymph nodes, or liver
- associated viral infections
- other concurrent medications
- the presence of a chronic disease

Allergy tests

Skin prick tests or intra dermal tests to demonstrate IgE allergies are standardized for very few medications. Penicillin testing is standardized and can be used in extreme situations. Incremental drug challenge tests are also available for several drugs. These tests differ from tests for IgE antibodies but are still useful for demonstrating drug sensitivities. They must be done cautiously as patients are likely to have reactions during the challenge.

The allergist injects a tiny amount of the drug under the skin. If the child is allergic to the drug, swelling and itching occur at the site of injection within 15 to 20 minutes. Skin tests can be used to test for only a few drug allergies, for example, for penicillin and closely related antibiotics. Incremental challenge tests are performed for insulin, streptokinase, chymopapain, and antiserum.

Patch tests may be used to test for allergies to drugs that are applied to the skin such as **topical antibiotics**. A patch containing a small amount of the drug is applied to the skin to test for a localized reaction.

Desensitization is a test in which the allergist gives the child a tiny dose of the drug—as little as 0.001 or 0.00001 of the usual dose—in its usual form—orally, topically, or by injection. Gradually the dose is increased, and the child's reaction of observed. This procedure is done only in life-threatening situations, however, and only under close observation.

Treatment

Mild allergies/sensitivities

Drug allergies and sensitivities most often are treated by discontinuing the medication and replacing it with an alternative one. Mild symptoms usually disappear within a few days after discontinuation of the drug. Hives usually disappear within a few hours. Itchy rashes and hives may be treated with over-the-counter products such as oral **antihistamines**. Occasionally topical corticosteroid drugs are applied to the skin. Angioedema can take hours or days to subside; however, the swelling can be reduced with a corticosteroid or antihistamine.

Severe reactions

Severe immediate reactions occurring within one hour of drug administration, accelerated reactions occurring one to 72 hours after drug exposure, and late reactions (including rash, serum sickness, or fever) that develop more than 72 hours after drug exposure are all treated as follows:

- discontinuation of all nonessential suspect drugs
- antihistamines for hives and rashes
- oral corticosteroids for inflammation

Severe angioedema requires an immediate injection of epinephrine (a form of adrenaline) and further observation in a hospital.

Anaphylaxis requires an immediate injection of epinephrine into a thigh muscle. Epinephrine opens the air passageways and improves blood circulation. Intravenous fluids and injections of antihistamines or corticosteroids such as hydrocortisone also are administered. **Cardiopulmonary resuscitation** (CPR) and intubation may be necessary.

An asthma attack that is triggered by aspirin or other medications can be relieved by quick-relief or rescue medications. These include:

- epinephrine
- short-acting bronchodilators such as albuterol, proventil, ventolin, or xopenex
- prednisone for all moderate to severe reactions

Desensitization

Desensitization or immunotherapy sometimes is used by an allergy/immunology specialist to treat drug allergies to insulin, penicillin, or other antibiotics. Small amounts of the drug are injected or swallowed over a period of hours or a few days or in slowly increasing doses, to reduce sensitivity. Once antibiotic desensitization has been achieved, the full course of antibiotic treatment is followed. The procedure must be repeated if the drug has been discontinued for more than 72 hours.

KEY TERMS

Allergen—A foreign substance that provokes an immune reaction or allergic response in some sensitive people but not in most others.

Anaphylactoid—A non-allergic sensitivity response resembling anaphylaxis.

Anaphylaxis—Also called anaphylactic shock; a severe allergic reaction characterized by airway constriction, tissue swelling, and lowered blood pressure.

Angioedema—Patches of circumscribed swelling involving the skin and its subcutaneous layers, the mucous membranes, and sometimes the organs frequently caused by an allergic reaction to drugs or food. Also called angioneurotic edema, giant urticaria, Quincke's disease, or Quincke's edema.

Antibody—A special protein made by the body's immune system as a defense against foreign material (bacteria, viruses, etc.) that enters the body. It is uniquely designed to attack and neutralize the specific antigen that triggered the immune response.

Antihistamine—A drug used to treat allergic conditions that blocks the effects of histamine, a substance in the body that causes itching, vascular changes, and mucus secretion when released by cells.

Antiserum—Human or animal blood serum containing specific antibodies.

Corticosteroids—A group of hormones produced naturally by the adrenal gland or manufactured synthetically. They are often used to treat inflammation. Examples include cortisone and prednisone.

Cytotoxic—The characteristic of being destructive to cells.

Epinephrine—A hormone produced by the adrenal medulla. It is important in the response to stress and partially regulates heart rate and metabolism. It is also called adrenaline.

Histamine—A substance released by immune system cells in response to the presence of an allergen. It stimulates widening of blood vessels and increased porousness of blood vessel walls so that fluid and protein leak out from the blood into the surrounding tissue, causing localised inflammation of the tissue.

Immunoglobulin E (IgE)—A type of protein in blood plasma that acts as an antibody to activate allergic reactions. About 50% of patients with allergic disorders have increased IgE levels in their blood serum.

Radiopaque dyes, radiocontrast media—Injected substances that are used to outline tissues and organs in some x-ray and other radiation procedures.

Urticaria—An itchy rash usually associated with an allergic reaction. Also known as hives.

Sometimes desensitization is used for non-IgE-mediated drug reactions. Desensitization may take up to a month for the following:

- aspirin
- alloprinol
- gold
- sulfamethoxazole
- sulfasalazine

Prognosis

Mild symptoms of a drug allergy usually disappear without treatment within a few days of discontinuing the drug. Although children may lose their sensitivity to penicillin, if the reaction was urticarial or anaphylaxis, they are not re-challenged with the drug for safety reasons (i.e. it is not possible to predict who has lost sensitivity). In rare cases drug allergies may cause severe asthma attacks, anaphylaxis, or death.

Prevention

Drug allergies are unpredictable because they occur after a child has been exposed to the drug one or more times. The major prevention for known drug allergies and sensitivities is to avoid those drugs and to inform all physicians, hospital personnel, and dentists of the allergies or sensitivities before treatment. In the case of a serious drug allergy, the child should wear a medical alert necklace or bracelet or carry a card (Medic-Alert and others) at all times to alert emergency medical personnel.

Children with allergies or sensitivities to aspirin should avoid all aspirin-containing drugs. Such children usually can tolerate **acetaminophen** and non-acetylated salicylates such as sodium salicylate and salsalate.

If a child is allergic to a drug for which there is no substitute, sometimes the dosage can be reduced to prevent an allergic reaction. If the allergy is mild and the drug cannot be discontinued, the physician may decide to pretreat the allergy, with an antihistamine such as diphenhydramine or a corticosteroid such as prednisone, before the drug is administered to reduce or eliminate the allergic reaction. The physician also may "treat through" the allergy by prescribing antihistamines and corticosteroids during drug administration.

Some disorders cannot be diagnosed without the use of radiopaque dyes. Special dyes that reduce the risk of an anaphylactoid reaction can be used. Children at risk for reaction to such dyes may be premedicated with antihistamines and corticosteroids alone or in combination with beta-adrenergic agents before the dye is injected. Premedications include the following:

- prednisone
- diphenhydramine
- ephedrine

Parental concerns

When a child is given a new medication or starts a new course of treatment with a previous medication, parents should watch closely for symptoms of a drug allergy or sensitivity.

If a child suffers a mild to moderate allergic reaction or sensitivity to a drug, the parent should take the following steps:

- stay calm and reassure the child; anxiety can worsen the symptoms
- apply calamine lotion and cold cloths for an itchy rash; do not use medicated lotions
- observe the child for signs of increasing distress

If a child shows signs of a severe allergic reaction or sensitivity, the parent or caregiver should:

- inject allergy medication if it is available
- check the child's air passage, breathing, and circulation
- call 911 or other emergency assistance if the child is having difficulty breathing, becomes very weak, or loses consciousness
- begin rescue breathing or CPR if necessary
- calm and reassure the child

- inject emergency allergy medicine if available; do not give oral medication if the child is having difficulty breathing
- prevent shock by laying the child flat, elevating the feet, and covering the child with a coat or blanket

In the case of a severe allergic reaction, a parent should not:

- assume that any pretreatment with allergy medication will protect the child
- place a pillow under the child's head if the child is having trouble breathing since this could block the air passage
- give the child anything by mouth

Resources

BOOKS

Honsinger, Richard W., and George R. Green. *Handbook of Drug Allergy*. Philadelphia: Lippincott Williams & Wilkins, 2004.

PERIODICALS

Honsinger, Richard W. "Drug Allergy." *Annals of Allergy, Asthma, and Immunology* 93, no. 2 (August 2004): 111.

Roberts, Shauna S. "Drug Allergy FAQ." *Diabetes Forecast* 57, no. 4 (April 2004): 21–2.

ORGANIZATIONS

American Academy of Allergy, Asthma, & Immunology. 555 East Wells Street, Suite 1100, Milwaukee, WI 53202–3823. Web site: <www.aaaai.org>.

American College of Allergy, Asthma & Immunology. 85 West Algonquin Road, Suite 550, Arlington Heights, IL 60005. Web site: <www.acaai.org>.

Asthma and Allergy Foundation of America. 1233 20th Street NW, Suite 402, Washington, D.C. 20036. Web site: <www.aafa.org>.

National Institute of Allergy and Infectious Diseases. 6610 Rockledge Drive, MSC 6612, Bethesda, MD 20892–6612. Web site: <www.niaid.nih.gov>.

WEB SITES

"Drug Reactions." *The Allergy Report.* Available online at <www.aaaai.org/ar/working_vol3/051.asp> (accessed December 27, 2004).

Shepherd, Gillian. "Allergic Reactions to Drugs." *Allergy & Asthma Advocate*, Spring 2001. Available online at <www.aaaai.org/patients/advocate/2001/spring/reactions.stm> (accessed December 27, 2004).

Margaret Alic, Ph.D.

DTP vaccine

Definition

DTP vaccine confers immunity to **diphtheria**, **tetanus**, and pertussis. The vaccine used in the United States is actually multiple diphtheria and tetanus toxoids combined with acellular pertussis (DTaP). The original vaccine, which as of 2004 was still used in other parts of the world, contains whole cells of *Bordatella pertussis*, the organism that causes pertussis, better known as **whooping cough**. The whole cell vaccine is more likely to cause adverse effects and does not provide any greater immunity.

Description

DTP vaccine conveys immunity to three different infectious diseases:

- Diphtheria is a potentially fatal disease that usually involves the nose, throat, and air passages, but may also infect the skin. Its most striking feature is the formation of a grayish membrane covering the tonsils and upper part of the throat. It is caused by *Corynebacterium diphtheriae*. Routine **vaccination** has almost eradicated diphtheria from the United States, but it is still seen in many parts of the world.

- Tetanus, sometimes called lockjaw, is a disease caused by the toxin of *Clostridium tetani*. The disease affects the central nervous system and causes painful muscle contractions. Food is not given by mouth to those with muscle spasm but may be given via nasogastric tube or intravenously. Tetanus is often fatal.

- Pertussis, also called whooping cough, is a respiratory disease caused by *Bordatella pertussis*. The name comes from a typical cough which starts with a deep inhalation, followed by a series of quick, short coughs that continues until the air is expelled from the lungs, and ends with a long shrill, whooping inhalation. Pertussis is very contagious and usually affects young children.

General use

Diphtheria and tetanus toxoids and acellular pertussis, taken together, provides immunity against diphtheria, tetanus, and whooping cough. The vaccine is normally given to children somewhere between the ages of two months and seven years of age (prior to their seventh birthday). Because these diseases can pose a severe problem in early childhood, the shots should be given as early in life as possible.

Precautions

DTP vaccine should not be given to children seven years of age or older. Moreover, children who are allergic to any component of the vaccine should not receive the drug. Because there are several different brands on the market, some children may be allergic to one brand and not to another. Because some of the bacterial cultures are grown in beef broth, the injections may be inadvisable for children who are allergic to beef. Children who have an allergic reaction after the first shot should be referred to an allergist before continuing with the DTP injections. Children who within a week after vaccination develop encephalopathy that cannot be traced to any other cause should not receive further injections. These children may be treated with DT (diphtheria-tetanus) vaccine. Also, DTP vaccine should be used with caution in patients who are receiving anticoagulant therapy. If a patient with a history of fevers and febrile convulsions is to be given DTP, the patient should receive **acetaminophen** at the time of the injection and for the following 24 hours.

Side effects

DPT vaccine has been associated with allergic reactions and with encephalopathy, both of which are rare but severe conditions. Other risks are common but minor:

- redness, irritation, and **itching** at injection site
- fever
- loss of appetite
- drowsiness
- irritability

Interactions

Because DTP vaccine is injected deep into the muscle, it should be given with care to patients receiving anticoagulant therapy. Also, immunosuppressant drugs, including steroids and **cancer** drugs, may reduce the ability of the body to produce antibodies in response to DTP vaccine.

Parental concerns

DTP is given in a series of four doses. Usually, the doses are given at two, four, and six months of age and at 17 to 20 months of age. While the customary age for the first dose is two months, it may be given as early as six weeks of age and up to the seventh birthday. The interval

KEY TERMS

Encephalopathy—Any abnormality in the structure or function of brain tissues.

Larynx—Also known as the voice box, the larynx is the part of the airway that lies between the pharynx and the trachea. It is composed of cartilage that contains the apparatus for voice production–the vocal cords and the muscles and ligaments that move the cords.

Toxin—A poisonous substance usually produced by a microorganism or plant.

between the third and fourth dose should be at least six months.

Although there have been warnings about severe, even fatal reactions to DTP vaccine, these reactions were seen in about one in 140,000 cases with whole cell DTP. The risk with DTaP is considerably lower. Children who had seizures due to the vaccine normally made a full recovery with no neurologic problems afterward. Five well-designed studies failed to show a link between DTP vaccine and any chronic nerve conditions.

The most serious risk of DTaP vaccine is a severe allergic reaction. These reactions, which also occur in response to other vaccines, are potentially fatal. Pre-term infants should be vaccinated according to their chronological age from birth. Interruption of the recommended schedule with a delay between doses should not interfere with the final immunity achieved. There is no need to start the series over again, regardless of the time between doses.

See also Vaccination.

Resources

BOOKS

Behrman, Richard, Robert M. Kliegman, and Hal B. Jenson. *Nelson Textbook of Pediatrics*, 17th ed. Philadelphia: Saunders, 2003.

Mcevoy, Gerald K., et al. *AHFS Drug Information 2004*. Bethesda, MD: American Society of Healthsystems Pharmacists, 2004.

Siberry, George, and Robert Iannone, eds. *The Harriet Lane Handbook*, 15th ed. Philadelphia: Mosby, 2000.

PERIODICALS

Dombkowski K. J., P. M. Lantz, G. L. Freed. "Risk factors for delay in age-appropriate vaccination." *Public Health Report* 119, no. 2 (March-April 2004): 144–155.

Robinson M. J., et al. "Antibody response to diphtheria-tetanus-pertussis immunization in preterm infants who receive dexamethasone for chronic lung disease." *Journal of Pediatrics* 113, no. 4 (April 2004): 733–737.

Jefferson T., M. Rudin, C. Di Pietrantonj. "Adverse events after immunization with aluminum-containing DPT vaccines: systematic review of the evidence." *Lancet Infectious Diseases* 4, no. 2 (February 2004): 84–90.

WEB SITES

"2004 Childhood and Adolescent Immunization Schedule." *Centers for Disease Control and Prevention.* Available online at <www.cdc.gov/nip/recs/child-schedule.htm> (accessed September 28, 2004).

"Pediatric Patient Textbooks." Available online at <www.vh.org/navigation/vch/textbooks/pediatric patient pediatrics.html> (accessed September 28, 2004).

Samuel Uretsky, PharmD

Duodenal obstruction

Definition

Duodenal obstruction is a partial or complete obstruction of the duodenum, the first part of the small intestine. Obstruction prevents food from passing through the digestive tract, interfering with digestion and **nutrition**.

Description

The duodenum is the first part of the small intestine, extending from the valve at the bottom of the stomach that regulates stomach emptying (pylorus valve) to the second part of the small intestine (jejunum). It is a short but often troublesome section of the digestive tract. The stomach, gallbladder, and pancreas each empty their contents into the duodenum in anticipation of digestion. Obstruction prevents the normal passage of stomach contents into the duodenum and keeps the gallbladder and pancreas from draining their secretions. This problem can lead to a number of conditions and complications involving digestion, nutrition, and fluid balance. In infants and children, congenital defects (anomalies) usually cause duodenal obstruction, and symptoms are present at birth or shortly after when the infant attempts to feed.

When obstruction occurs, regardless of cause, food, gas, and secretions from within the intestine will accumulate above the point of obstruction, bloating (distending) the affected portion of intestine. Infection of peritoneal tissue lining the intestines and the abdomen (peritonitis) may result from bacteria growing in the accumulation of undigested material. As the distention increases, fluids continue to increase, and the intestine absorbs less. The fluid accumulation and reduced absorption lead to bilious **vomiting**, which is the vomitus will appear greenish, the classic sign of upper intestinal obstruction. Persistent vomiting or **diarrhea** (which can occur in a partial blockage) can result in **dehydration**. Fluid imbalances upset the balance of specific essential chemicals (electrolytes) in the blood, which can cause complications such as irregular heartbeat and, without correction of the electrolyte imbalance, shock.

In newborns, congenital duodenal obstruction can occur when the duodenal channel (duodenal lumen) is not correctly formed (recanalized) during fetal development. The duodenum may have a membrane reducing the channel size (lumen), or two blind pouches instead of one duodenal channel, or a gap or flap of tissue may be present. In each case, the channel is not be sufficiently developed at birth or sufficiently open to allow the passage of food and liquid, resulting in poor digestion and poor nutrition. This condition is known as duodenal atresia, and it results in duodenal obstruction. About 30 to 50 percent of infants born with duodenal atresia also have **Down syndrome**, and some have cardiac abnormalities as well. Duodenal atresia can occur with other conditions such as a narrowing of the duodenal lumen (duodenal stenosis) or twisting of the duodenum around itself (duodenal volvulus). It may also occur in combination with volvulus in another part of the bowel below the duodenum. Inflammation of the pancreas (pancreatitis) may also accompany duodenal atresia.

Malrotation of the duodenum is a more common cause of duodenal obstruction, typically appearing in the first few weeks of life. In malrotation, the duodenum is usually coiled to the right, causing obstruction of the duodenum and failure of the stomach contents to pass through to the next portion of small intestine. Malrotation may also involve the presence of Ladd's bands, abnormal folds or bands of tissue under tension across the lumen of the duodenum. Malrotation can also occur with duodenal volvulus or volvulus lower in the bowel.

With volvulus, it can result in serious consequences by cutting off the supply of blood to a portion of bowel (strangulation), reducing the flow of oxygen to bowel tissue (ischemia), and leading to tissue death (gangrene) and shock or to rupture (perforation) of the intestine. Surgery is required immediately to correct this type of duodenal obstruction.

Demographics

Duodenal atresia, one of the causes of duodenal obstruction, affects one in 10,000 live births in the United States and is found equally among boys and girls and more often among premature births. Intestinal malrotation is a more common cause, occurring in one in 500 live births, although only a small percentage of these have duodenal malrotation. The male to female ratio is two to one in the first year of life and then becomes equal.

Causes and symptoms

Obstruction of the duodenum occurs in infants as a result of congenital causes. The duodenal channel may be underdeveloped (duodenal hypoplasia), narrowed (duodenal stenosis), or the duodenum channel may not be properly formed (duodenal atresia). Malrotation or coiling of the duodenum can also obstruct the duodenum, sometimes accompanied by volvulus, a twisting of the duodenum around itself. As of 2004 the specific cause of these congenital defects was not known.

Vomiting is the prevailing symptom of duodenal obstruction and may occur in the first day of life. The vomitus will be greenish (bilious) because it contains bile from the gallbladder. An infant will vomit feedings, lose weight, and be restless and irritable. Other symptoms may include difficulty breathing, excessive salivation and drooling, the presence of a palpable mass in the abdomen, yellow-tinted skin (**jaundice**), and failure to respond (lethargy). If the duodenum is twisted as in volvulus, the newborn may have a distended abdomen and bloody diarrhea.

When to call the doctor

Frequent or constant vomiting, unsuccessful feeding, and poor weight gain should be reported to the pediatrician as soon as noted. If an infant in the first few weeks of life pulls the knees up and intermittently cries in **pain** along with frequent vomiting, the pediatrician should be consulted immediately, and examination in the emergency department of the hospital may be necessary.

KEY TERMS

Anastomosis—Surgical reconnection of two ducts, blood vessels, or bowel segments to allow flow between the two.

Anomaly—Something that is different from what is normal or expected. Also an unusual or irregular structure.

Atresia—The congenital absence of a normal body opening or duct.

Bowel—The intestine; a tube-like structure that extends from the stomach to the anus. Some digestive processes are carried out in the bowel before food passes out of the body as waste.

Congenital—Present at birth.

Contrast agent—Also called a contrast medium, this is usually a barium or iodine dye that is injected into the area under investigation. The dye makes the interior body parts more visible on an x-ray film.

Electrolytes—Salts and minerals that produce electrically charged particles (ions) in body fluids. Common human electrolytes are sodium chloride, potassium, calcium, and sodium bicarbonate. Electrolytes control the fluid balance of the body and are important in muscle contraction, energy generation, and almost all major biochemical reactions in the body.

Gangrene—Decay or death of body tissue because the blood supply is cut off. Tissues that have died in this way must be surgically removed.

Hypoplasia—An underdeveloped or incomplete tissue or organ usually due to a decrease in the number of cells.

Ischemia—A decrease in the blood supply to an area of the body caused by obstruction or constriction of blood vessels.

Lumen—The inner cavity or canal of a tube-shaped organ, such as the bowel.

Peritonitis—Inflammation of the peritoneum. It is most often due to bacterial infection, but can also be caused by a chemical irritant (such as spillage of acid from the stomach or bile from the gall bladder).

Shock—A medical emergency in which the organs and tissues of the body are not receiving an adequate flow of blood. This deprives the organs and tissues of oxygen and allows the build-up of waste products. Shock can be caused by certain diseases, serious injury, or blood loss.

Diagnosis

Abdominal **x rays** will be performed and will typically show what is called the characteristic "double bubble," a combination of air bubbles in the stomach and a dilated duodenum. An echocardiogram and chest x rays may be done to evaluate the infant for any other possible abnormalities, including cardiac defects and abnormal development of the pancreas, which is often associated with duodenal obstruction. If malrotation is suspected, contrast-enhanced x rays of the upper intestinal region are usually able to visualize the twisted duodenum. Ultrasound imaging may also be used to evaluate these conditions.

Diagnostic tests performed in the clinical laboratory will include a complete blood count (CBC), electrolytes (sodium, potassium, chloride), blood urea nitrogen (BUN), and other blood chemistries, especially to evaluate kidney and pancreas function. A urinalysis will be performed. Coagulation tests may be performed if the child is going to have surgery.

Treatment

Duodenal obstruction requires surgery, but it is not always urgent. Treatment may be delayed to evaluate or treat other life-threatening congenital anomalies. A nasogastric tube will first be placed through the infant's nose down into the stomach to decompress both the stomach and duodenum. Intravenous fluids may be given to maintain fluid levels and urine output or to correct dehydration that already has occurred. Electrolyte solutions may be given intravenously to restore electrolyte balance. Surgery to correct duodenal atresia is usually duodeno-duodenostomy. It involves opening the duodenum channel along its length from the stomach to the next portion of intestine, correcting the duodenal lumen end to end (gastrojejunal anastomosis) so that it is a fully open channel.

Ladd's procedure is used to surgically correct malrotation. The abdomen is opened and the large intestine is placed to the left side in order for the doctor to perform the surgery. The appendix is usually removed to avoid a later diagnosis of **appendicitis**. The malrotation, stenosis, or membranous bands are corrected surgically so that the duodenum has a normal opening and connects properly to the stomach and jejunum. Broad-spectrum **antibiotics** may be given to help avoid infection.

Prognosis

Prognosis will depend on the type and extent of the obstruction, the infant's age at diagnosis, the infant's overall condition, and the presence and severity of any other congenital anomalies. Survival rates for surgical repair of the duodenum is greater than 90 percent, regardless of the cause. Most children do not have continuing digestive problems. Complications occur in 12 to 15 percent of those undergoing surgery. Complications can include other digestive disorders such as intestinal motility, duodenogastric reflux, gastritis, peptic ulcers, and megaduodenum. If malrotation or duodenal volvulus has caused the blood supply to be cut off in a portion of the intestine before surgery, death of intestinal tissue can result and life-threatening gangrene can develop. Widespread infection (peritonitis) may also develop from bacteria growing in the accumulation of undigested material above the obstruction. Mortality in infants who have gangrene or peritonitis is particularly high in those with other defects.

Prevention

No specific measures are recommended to prevent congenital anomalies that result in duodenal obstruction.

Parental concerns

In most cases, parents do not know before the birth of the child that an intestinal obstruction is present, although sometimes examination of the amniotic fluid during pregnancy (**amniocentesis**) alerts the obstetrician of possible abnormalities and prepares parents for the diagnosis. If obstruction is suspected or diagnosed in the first few days of the child's life, parents may be concerned about the risks associated with surgery and possible complications in infancy or early childhood. Parents can be reassured that newer surgical techniques have constantly improved the outcome of surgeries for intestinal obstruction, including duodenal obstruction. Diagnosed early, intestinal obstruction can be corrected with few complications, and a child who does not have other congenital problems usually is able to resume normal development.

Resources

Allan, W., et al. *Pediatric Gastrointestinal Disease: Pathophysiology, Diagnosis, Management*, 3rd ed. Boston, MA: B. C. Decker, 2000.

"Intestinal Obstruction." *The Merck Manual of Medical Information*, 2nd ed. Edited by Mark H. Beers et al. White House Station, NJ: Merck & Co., 2003.

ORGANIZATIONS

American Association of Family Physicians. 11400 Tomahawk Creek Parkway, Leawood, KS 66211-2672. Web site: <www.aafp.org>.

WEB SITES

"Intestinal Obstruction." *MedlinePlus*, 2004. Available online at <www.nlm.gov./medlineplus/ency/article/000260.htm> (accessed December 21, 2004).

L. Lee Culvert

Dwarfism

Definition

Dwarfism is a term applied broadly to a number of conditions resulting in unusually short stature.

Description

While dwarfism is sometimes used to describe achondroplasia, a condition characterized by short stature and disproportionately short arms and legs, it is also used more broadly to refer to a variety of conditions resulting in unusually short stature in both children and adults. In some cases physical development may be disproportionate, as in achondroplasia, but in others the parts of the body develop proportionately. Short stature may be unaccompanied by other symptoms, or it may occur together with other problems, both physical and mental.

There are many conditions and diseases that can cause short stature. Some of these conditions involve a primary bone disorder, namely that the bones do not grow and develop normally. These conditions are called skeletal dysplasia. Over 500 specific skeletal dysplasias have been identified. Of these, Achondroplasia is the most common, affecting about 80 percent of all little people. An individual with achondroplasia has disproportionate short stature.

The four most common causes of dwarfism in children are achondroplasia, **Turner syndrome**, inadequate pituitary function (**pituitary dwarfism**), and lack of emotional or physical nurturance. Achondroplasia (short-limbed dwarfism) is a genetic disorder that impairs embryonic development, resulting in abnormalities in bone growth and cartilage development. It is one of a class of illnesses called chondrodystrophies, all of which involve cartilage abnormalities and result in short stature. In achondroplasia, the long bones fail to develop normally, making the arms and legs disproportionately short and stubby (and sometimes curved). Overly long fibulae (one of two bones in the lower leg) cause the bowlegs that are characteristic of the condition. In addition, the head is disproportionately large and the bridge of the nose is depressed. Persons with achondroplasia are 3–5 feet (91–152 cm) tall and of normal **intelligence**. Their reproductive development is normal, and they have greater than normal muscular strength. The condition occurs in one out of every 10,000 births, and its prevalence increases with the age of the parents, especially the father. Many infants with the condition are stillborn.

Turner syndrome is a chromosomal abnormality occurring only in females in whom one of the X chromosomes is missing or defective. Girls with Turner syndrome are usually between 4.5 and 5 feet (137–152 cm) tall. Their ovaries are undeveloped, and they do not undergo **puberty**. Besides short stature, other physical characteristics include a stocky build and a webbed neck.

Pituitary dwarfism is a result of growth hormone deficiency. The deficiency may be genetic or the result of a severe brain injury. When untreated, skeletal growth is extremely slow, and puberty may or may not occur. Development can be normalized with the regular administration of synthetic hormones.

Parental neglect and malnourishment can cause a child to fail to grow properly. Infants in particular need physical comfort as well as caloric nourishment in order to thrive.

Demographics

Adult males under 5 feet (1.5 m) tall and females under 4 feet 8 inches (1.4 m) are classified as being short-statured. Children are considered unusually short if they fall below the third percentile of height for their age group. In 2004 there were approximately 5 million people of short stature (for their age) living in the United States, of whom 40 percent were under the age of 21.

Achondroplasia occurs in all races and with equal frequency in males and females and affects about one in every 40,000 children. The prevalence of Turner syndrome is widely reported as being approximately one per 2,500 live female births.

In 2004, more than 20,000 children in United States were receiving supplemental growth hormone (GH) ther-

apy. It is estimated that about one-fourth of them had organic causes of GH deficiencies. There appears to be no racial or ethnic component to pituitary dwarfism, but males seem to be afflicted more often than females.

Causes and symptoms

Some prenatal factors known to contribute to growth retardation include a variety of maternal health problems, including toxemia, kidney and heart disease, infections such as **rubella** and maternal **malnutrition**. Maternal age is also a factor (adolescent mothers are prone to have undersize babies), as is uterine constraint (which occurs when the uterus is too small for the baby). Possible causes that center on the fetus rather than the mother include chromosomal abnormalities, genetic and other syndromes that impair skeletal growth, and defects of the placenta or umbilical cord. Environmental factors that influence intrauterine growth include maternal use of drugs (including alcohol and tobacco). Some infants who are small at birth (especially **twins**) may attain normal stature within the first year of life, while others remain small throughout their lives.

Endocrine and metabolic disorders are another important cause of growth problems. Growth can be impaired by conditions affecting the pituitary, thyroid, parathyroid, and adrenal glands (all part of the endocrine system). Probably the best known of these conditions is growth hormone deficiency, which is associated with the pituitary and hypothalamus glands. If the deficiency begins prenatally, the baby will still be of normal size and weight at birth but will then experience slowed growth. Weight gain still tends to be normal, leading to overweight and a higher than average proportion of body fat. The facial structures of children with this condition are immature, making them look younger than their actual age. Adults in whom growth hormone deficiency has not been treated attain a height of only about 2.5 feet (76 cm). They also have high-pitched voices, high foreheads, and wrinkled skin. Another endocrine disorder that can interfere with growth is **hypothyroidism**, a condition resulting from insufficient activity of the thyroid gland. Affecting one in 4,000 infants born in the United States, it can have a variety of causes, including underdevelopment, absence, or removal of the thyroid gland, lack of an enzyme needed for adequate thyroid function, iodine deficiency, or an under-active pituitary gland. In addition to retarding growth, it can cause **mental retardation** if thyroid hormones are not administered in the first months of an infant's life. If the condition goes untreated, it causes impaired mental development in 50 percent of affected children by the age of six months.

About 15 percent of cases of short stature in children is caused by chronic diseases, of which endocrine disorders are only one type. Many of these conditions do not appear until after the fifth year of life. Children with renal disease often experience growth retardation, especially if the condition is congenital. **Congenital heart disease** can cause slow growth, either directly or through secondary problems. Short stature can also result from a variety of conditions related to inadequate **nutrition**, including malabsorption syndromes (in which the body is lacking a substance—often an enzyme—necessary for proper absorption of an important nutrient), chronic inflammatory bowel disorders, caloric deficiencies, and zinc deficiency. A form of severe malnutrition called marasmus retards growth in all parts of the body, including the head (causing mental retardation as well). Marasmus can be caused by being weaned very early and not adequately fed afterwards; if the intake of calories and protein is limited severely enough, the body wastes away. Although the mental and emotional effects of the condition can be reversed with changes in environment, the growth retardation it causes is permanent. On occasion, growth retardation may also be caused solely by emotional deprivation.

When to call the doctor

Growth problems should be tracked and addressed by a doctor at a child's regular check-ups. If the child is consistently below the fifth percentile on standard growth charts or if a child stops growing at all, the parent(s) should discuss the implications with the child's pediatrician.

Diagnosis

Dwarfism is determined by direct measurement of a person's height. Achondroplasia can be detected through prenatal screening. **X rays** of the long bones may be performed in a newborn. Pituitary dwarfism can be diagnosed with blood tests for growth hormones or MRI of the head.

Treatment

Since growth problems are so varied, there is a wide variety of treatments for them, including nutritional changes, medications to treat underlying conditions, and, where appropriate, hormone replacement therapy. There is no specific treatment for achondroplasia, besides treating any orthopedic problems that may arise.

More than 150,000 children in the United States receive growth hormone therapy to remedy growth retardation caused by endocrine deficiencies. Growth hor-

Young female dwarf standing next to a boy of normal stature. *(Photograph by Dr. Richard Pauli. U. of Wisconsin, Madison, Clinical Genetics Center.)*

mone for therapeutic purposes was originally derived from the pituitary glands of deceased persons. However, natural growth hormone, aside from being prohibitively expensive, posed health hazards due to contamination. In the 1980s, men who had received growth hormone therapy in childhood were found to have developed Kreuzfeldt-Jakob disease, a fatal neurological disorder. Since then, natural growth hormone has been replaced by a biosynthetic hormone that received FDA approval in 1985.

Prognosis

People who are short statured have approximately normal life expectancy. Administration of human growth

KEY TERMS

Achondroplasia—A congenital disturbance of growth plate development in long bones that results in a person having shortened limbs and a normal trunk.

Midget—An individual who is short statured but has normal body proportions. The term is considered to be offensive.

hormone may increase their adult height although they are unlikely to attain normal height. Those with achondroplasia seldom reach 5 feet (1.5 m) in height.

Prevention

There is no known way to prevent dwarfism because it results from genetic causes. Short stature as a result of parental neglect can be prevented. Education of the parents on the needs of the child is necessary, or the child may be removed from parental custody.

Nutritional concerns

Persons who have short stature should eat nutritionally sound, balanced meals. Their caloric requirements are slightly less than those of people who have normal height.

Parental concerns

Parents of children who are short statured should provide the same love and support as they would to any other child. In addition, they should offer counseling to help their children cope with their smaller stature. Adequate medical treatment should be provided to assure the best possible outcome.

See also Pituitary dwarfism; Turner syndrome.

Resources

BOOKS

Adelson, Betty M. *Dwarfism: Medical and Psychological Aspects of Profound Short Stature.* Baltimore, MD: Johns Hopkins University Press, 2005.

Kennedy, Dan. *Little People: Learning to See the World through My Daughter's Eyes.* Emmaus, PA: Rodale Press, 2003.

Parker, James N., and Philip M. Parker. *Dwarfism (3-in-1 Medical Reference): A Medical Dictionary, Bibliography, and Annotated Research Guide to Internet References.* San Diego, CA: Icon Publishers, 2004.

PERIODICALS

Chiavetta, J. B. "Total hip arthroplasty in patients with dwarfism." *Journal of Bone and Joint Surgery: American Volume* 86-A, no. 2 (2004): 298–304.

Faivre, L., et al. "Recurrence of achondrogenesis type II within the same family: evidence for germline mosaicism." *American Journal of Medical Genetics* 126A, no. 3 (2004): 308–12.

Laron, Z. "Laron syndrome (primary growth hormone resistance or insensitivity): the personal experience 1958–2003." *Journal of Clinical Endocrinology and Metabolism* 89, no. 3 (2004): 1031–44.

Pandian, R., and J. M. Nakamoto. "Rational use of the laboratory for childhood and adult growth hormone deficiency." *Clinical Laboratory Medicine* 2224, no. 1 (2004): 141–74.

ORGANIZATIONS

Human Growth Foundation. 7777 Leesburg Pike (PO Box 309), Falls Church, VA 22043. Web site: <www.hgfound.org/>.

Little People of America Inc. PO Box 745, Lubbock, TX 79408. Web site: <www.lpaonline.org/>.

WEB SITES

"Dwarfism." *Dwarfism.org.* Available online at <www.dwarfism.org/> (accessed January 6, 2005).

"Dwarfism." *MedlinePlus.* Available online at <www.nlm.nih.gov/medlineplus/dwarfism.html> (accessed January 6, 2005).

"Dwarfism." *Nemours Foundation.* Available online at <http://kidshealth.org/parent/medical/bones/dwarfism.html> (accessed January 6, 2005).

"Dwarfism." *Short Persons Support.* Available online at <www.shortsupport.org/Health/Dwarfism.html> (accessed January 6, 2005).

"Dwarfism." *University of Kansas Medical Center.* Available online at <www.kumc.edu/gec/support/dwarfism.html> (accessed January 6, 2005).

"Dwarfism: What Is It?" *Little People's Research Fund.* Available online at <www.lprf.org/dwarfism.html> (accessed January 6, 2005).

L. Fleming Fallon, Jr., MD, DrPH

Dyslexia

Definition

Dyslexia is a learning disability characterized by problems in reading, spelling, writing, speaking, or listening. It results from the inability to process graphic symbols. In many cases, dyslexia appears to be inherited.

Description

The word dyslexia is derived from the Greek word, *dys* (meaning poor or inadequate) and the word *lexis* (meaning words or language). Dyslexic children seem to have trouble learning early reading skills, problems hearing individual sounds in words, analyzing whole words in parts, and blending sounds into words. Letters such as "d" and "b" may be confused. Often a child with dyslexia has a problem translating language into thought (such as in listening or reading), or translating thought into language (such as in writing or speaking). Dyslexia is also referred to as developmental reading disorder (DRD).

Dyslexia is a problem involving higher (cortical) processing of symbols in the brain. Most children with dyslexia are of normal **intelligence**; many have above-average intelligence. However, when a child is dyslexic, there is often an unexpected difference between achievement and aptitude. Each child with dyslexia has different strengths and weaknesses, although many have unusual talents in art, athletics, architecture, graphics, drama, music, or engineering. These special talents are often in areas that require the ability to integrate sight, spatial skills, and coordination.

Common characteristics of a child with dyslexia include problems with:

- identifying single words
- understanding sounds in words, sound order, or rhymes
- spelling
- transposing letters in words
- handwriting
- reading comprehension
- the spoken language
- understanding directions
- understanding opposites, such as up/down or early/late

Social and emotional difficulties often accompany this disorder, as children are unable to meet expectations of parents and teachers and feel frustrated at their inability to achieve their goals. They may have a negative self-image and become angry, anxious, and depressed.

Demographics

About 15–20 percent of the population of the United States has a language-based learning disability. Of students with specific learning disabilities receiving **special education** services, 70–80 percent have deficits in reading. With such a high incidence, there is a question as to whether this is really a difference in learning style rather than a true "disability." The condition affects males more than females, and appears in all ages, races, and income levels.

Causes and symptoms

The underlying cause of dyslexia is not known, although research suggests the condition is often inherited. In 1999, The Centre for Reading Research in Norway presented the first research to study the largest **family** with reading problems ever known. By studying the reading and writing abilities of close to 80 family members across four generations, the researchers reported, for the first time, that chromosome 2 can be involved in the inheritability of dyslexia. When a fault occurs on this gene, it leads to difficulties in processing written language. Previous studies have pointed out linkages of other potential dyslexia genes to chromosome 1, chromosome 15 (DYX1 gene), and to chromosome 6 (DYX2 gene). The researchers who pinpointed the localized gene on chromosome 2 (DYX3) hope that this finding will lead to earlier and more precise diagnoses of dyslexia.

Research suggests a possible link with a subtle visual problem that affects the speed with which affected people can read. Anatomical and brain imagery studies show differences in the way the brain of a dyslexic child develops and functions.

Indicators of dyslexia include:

- possible family history of **learning disorders**
- difficulty learning to recognize written words
- difficulty rhyming
- difficulty determining the meaning (idea content) of a single sentence
- writing or arithmetic learning problems

When to call the doctor

The doctor should be called if a child appears to have difficulty learning to read or exhibits any symptoms of dyslexia.

Diagnosis

Anyone who is suspected to have dyslexia should have a comprehensive evaluation, including medical, psychological, behavioral, hearing, vision, and intelligence testing. The test should include all areas of learning and learning processes, not only reading. Other causes of learning disabilities, such as attention deficit hyperactivity disorder (ADHD), affective disorders (e.g. depression or **anxiety**), central auditory processing dysfunction, **pervasive developmental disorders**, and physical or sensory impairments, must be ruled out before the diagnosis of dyslexia can be confirmed. A child of any age may be evaluated for dyslexia using an age-appropriate battery of tests.

Test results are used to determine eligibility for special education services in many states as well as eligibility for programs in colleges and universities. They provide a basis for making educational recommendations, and determine the baseline for evaluation of improvement in the child's performance. In the United States, the Individuals with Disabilities Education Act (IDEA), Section 504 of the Rehabilitation Act of 1973 and the Americans with Disabilities Act (ADA) define the rights of children with dyslexia and other learning disabilities. These children are legally entitled to special services to help them overcome and accommodate their learning problems, including education programs to meet their needs. The Acts also protect people with dyslexia against unfair and illegal discrimination.

As further research pinpoints the genes responsible for some cases of dyslexia, there is a possibility that earlier testing will be established to allow for timely interventions to prevent the onset of the condition and treat it when it does occur. Unfortunately, in many schools, a child is not identified as having dyslexia until after repeated failures.

Treatment

Dyslexia is a life-long condition, but with proper intervention, a child can learn to read and/or write well. When a child is diagnosed with dyslexia, the parents should find out from the school or the diagnostician exactly what the problem is, what method of teaching is recommended, and why a particular method is suggested.

The primary focus of treatment is aimed at solving the specific learning problem of each affected child. Most often, this may include modifying teaching methods and the educational environment, since traditional educational methods will not always be effective with a dyslexic child. An Individual Education Plan (IEP)

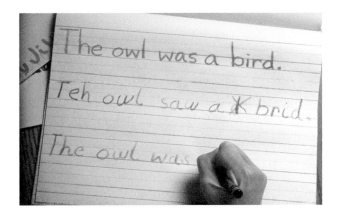

A student with dyslexia has difficulty copying words. (© Will & Deni McIntyre/Science Source, National Audubon Society Collection/Photo Researchers, Inc.)

should be created for each child, reflecting his or her specific requirements. Special education services may include specialist help by an instructor specifically trained to teach dyslexic students through individualized tutoring or special day classes. It is important to teach these students using all the senses—hearing, touching, writing, and speaking—through a multi-sensory program.

People with dyslexia need a structured language program, with direct instruction in the letter-sound system. Teachers must provide the rules governing written language. Most experts agree that the teacher should emphasize the association between simple phonetic units with letters or letter groups, rather than an approach that stresses memorizing whole words.

To assist with associated social and emotional difficulties, teachers must use strategies that will help the child find success in academics and personal relationships. Such strategies include rewarding efforts and not just the results, helping the child set realistic goals, and encouraging the child to do volunteer work that requires empathy and a social conscience (for example, a child with dyslexia who does well in science or math could serve as a peer tutor in those subjects or could tutor a younger child with dyslexia). Psychological counseling may also be helpful.

Prognosis

There is a great deal of variation among different people with dyslexia, producing different symptoms and degrees of severity. The prognosis depends on the severity of the disability, but is usually good if the condition is diagnosed early, the intervention used is effective and appropriate for the specific child, and if the child has a

KEY TERMS

Individualized educational plan (IEP)—A detailed description of the educational goals, assessment methods, behavioral management plan, and educational performance of a student requiring special education services.

Learning disorders—Academic difficulties experienced by children and adults of average to above-average intelligence that involve reading, writing, and/or mathematics, and which significantly interfere with academic achievement or daily living.

Spatial skills—The ability to locate objects in a three-dimensional world using sight or touch.

strong self-image and supportive family, friends, and teachers. However, difficulties with reading may persist throughout adulthood, which may result in occupational problems in certain careers. However, many successful people, such as Erin Brockovich and Whoopi Goldberg, have dyslexia.

Prevention

Since learning disorders often run in families, affected families should try to recognize learning disability problems early. For families without a previous history of learning disabilities, an intervention can begin as early as **preschool** or kindergarten if teachers detect early signs.

Parental concerns

There are many resources available to aid parents in helping their children. For example, the International Dyslexia Association (<http://interdys.org>) provides extensive information for parents, teachers, and children. Parents are encouraged to utilize these resources to ensure their child's success in school and in interactions with their peers and later as working adults. They must also guard against feeling that the child is lazy or not trying hard. Instead, they should provide a supportive and loving environment.

Dyslexia may have an impact upon the child's family. Non-dyslexic siblings may be jealous of the attention, time, and money the dyslexic child receives from the parents. Since dyslexia runs in families, one or both parents may have had similar school problems. The child's problems may bring back feelings of frustration and failure for parents, which may interfere with their parenting skills.

See also Language delay; Language disorders.

Resources

BOOKS

Reid, Gavin. *Dyslexia—A Complete Guide for Parents.* Hoboken, NJ: John Wiley & Sons, 2004.

Shaywitz, Sally. *Overcoming Dyslexia: A New and Complete Science-Based Program for Overcoming Reading Problems at Any Level.* New York: Knopf, 2003.

Stowe, Cynthia. *How to Reach and Teach Children with Dyslexia: A Parent and Teacher Guide to Helping Students of All Ages Academically, Socially, and Emotionally.* San Francisco, CA: Jossey-Bass, 2002.

ORGANIZATIONS

International Dyslexia Association. Suite 382, Chester Bldg., 8600 LaSalle Rd., Ste. 382, Baltimore, MD 21286-2044. (800) ABC-D123 or (410) 296-0232. <http://interdys.org/index.jsp/bibcit.composed>

Learning Disabilities Association. 4156 Library Rd., Pittsburgh, PA 15234-1349. (412) 341-1515; Fax: (412) 344-0224. <www.ldanatl.org>

Judith Sims
Beth A. Kapes

Dysmenorrhea

Definition

Dysmenorrhea refers to the **pain** or discomfort associated with **menstruation**. Although not a serious medical problem, the term describes a woman adolescent girl with menstrual symptoms severe enough to keep her from functioning for a day or two each month.

Description

Menstrual cramps are a common problem for adolescent girls and women. They may be mild, moderate, or severe and are the single most common cause of days missed from school and work. About 10 percent of girls are incapacitated for up to three days each month. Although many teens do not suffer from dysmenorrhea because their uterus is still growing, they may get it several years after their first period begins. The symptoms may begin one to two days before menses, peak on the first day of flow, and subside during that day or over several days.

Causes and symptoms

Primary dysmenorrhea is the more common type of dysmenorrhea and is due to the production of prostaglandins. Prostaglandins are natural substances made by cells in the inner lining of the uterus and other parts of the body. Those made in the uterus make the uterine muscles contract and help the uterus to shed the lining that has built up during the menstrual cycle. It appears, however, that the level of prostaglandins has nothing to do with how strong a woman's cramps are. Some women have high levels of prostaglandins and no cramps, whereas other women with low levels have severe cramps. Thus cramps must also be related to something other than prostaglandins, such as genetics, stress, and different body types. The first year or two of a girl's periods are not usually very painful; however, once ovulation begins, the blood levels of the prostaglandins rise, leading to stronger contractions during menstruation. Prostaglandins can also cause headaches, **nausea**, **vomiting**, and **diarrhea**. The likelihood that a woman will have cramps increases if the following apply to her:

- She has a **family** history of painful periods.
- She leads a stressful life.
- She does not get enough **exercise**.
- She uses **caffeine**.
- She has pelvic inflammatory disease.

Primary dysmenorrhea usually presents during **adolescence**, within three years of menarche. It is unusual for symptoms to start within the first six months after menarche. Affected young women experience sharp, intermittent spasms of pain, usually centered in the suprapubic area. Pain may radiate to the back of the legs or the lower back. Systemic symptoms of nausea, vomiting, diarrhea, fatigue, **fever**, **headache**, or lightheadedness are fairly common. Pain usually develops within hours of the start of menstruation and peaks as the flow becomes heaviest during the first day or two of the cycle. Some women notice that painful periods disappear after having their first child. This could be due to the stretching of the opening of the uterus or the fact that birth improves the uterine blood supply and muscle activity.

Secondary dysmenorrhea is defined as menstrual pain due to pelvic pathology. This condition usually occurs after a woman has had normal menstrual periods for some time. It differs from primary dysmenorrheal in that the pain is caused by an abnormality or disease of the uterus, tubes, or ovaries. The most common causes are:

- pelvic inflammatory disease
- fibroids (intracavitary or intramural)
- intrauterine contraceptive devices
- endometriosis
- inflammation and scarring(adhesions)
- functional ovarian cysts
- benign or malignant tumors of ovary, bowel or bladder, or other site
- inflammatory bowel disease

Diagnosis

A focused history and physical examination are usually sufficient to make the diagnosis of primary dysmenorrhea. The history reveals the typical cramping pain with menstruation, and the physical examination is completely normal. A doctor should perform a thorough pelvic exam and take a patient history to rule out an underlying condition that could cause cramps. It is usually possible to differentiate dysmenorrhea from **premenstrual syndrome** (PMS) based on the patient's history. The pain associated with PMS is generally related to breast tenderness and abdominal bloating, rather than a lower abdominal cramping pain. PMS symptoms begin before the menstrual cycle and resolve shortly after menstrual flow begins.

Circumstances that may indicate secondary dysmenorrheal include the following:

- dysmenorrhea occurring during the first one or two cycles after menarche (congenital outflow obstruction)
- dysmenorrhea beginning after 25 years of age
- late onset of dysmenorrhea after a history without previous pain with menstruation (possibly caused by complications of pregnancy: ectopic or threatened spontaneous abortion)
- pelvic abnormality on physical examination; infertility (possible endometriosis, pelvic inflammatory disease or other causes of scarring); heavy menstrual flow or irregular cycles (consider adenomyosis, fibroids, polyps); dyspareunia
- little or no response to therapy with **nonsteroidal anti-inflammatory drugs**, **oral contraceptives**, or both

Treatment

Secondary dysmenorrhea is controlled by treating the underlying disorder.

The appropriate choice of therapy for most women with primary dysmenorrheal is a nonsteroidal anti-inflammatory drug (NSAIDs), which prevents the forma-

KEY TERMS

Adenomyosis—Uterine thickening caused when endometrial tissue, which normally lines the uterus, extends outward into the fibrous and muscular tissue of the uterus.

Endometriosis—A condition in which the tissue that normally lines the uterus (endometrium) grows in other areas of the body, causing pain, irregular bleeding, and frequently, infertility.

Hormone—A chemical messenger secreted by a gland or organ and released into the bloodstream. It travels via the bloodstream to distant cells where it exerts an effect.

Ovary—One of the two almond-shaped glands in the female reproductive system responsible for producing eggs and the sex hormones estrogen and progesterone.

Ovulation—The monthly process by which an ovarian follicle ruptures releasing a mature egg cell.

Progesterone—The hormone produced by the ovary after ovulation that prepares the uterine lining for a fertilized egg.

Uterus—The female reproductive organ that contains and nourishes a fetus from implantation until birth. Also called the womb.

tion and release of prostaglandins. Aspirin is not used for the treatment of dysmenorrheal because it is not potent enough in the usual dosage. Response to NSAIDs usually occurs within 30 to 60 minutes, but since individual response may vary, it is sometimes necessary to try different NSAIDs if the pain is not relieved with the first drug after one or two menstrual cycles. The NSAIDs include ibuprofen, naproxen (Aleve), and Motrin.

If an NSAID is not available, **acetaminophen** (Tylenol) may help ease the pain. Heat applied to the painful area may bring relief, and a warm bath twice a day also may help. Birth control pills are 90 percent effective in easing the pain of dysmenorrheal. They work by a twofold action: they reduce the menstrual fluid volume and suppress ovulation. They are generally not prescribed initially because it is a daily medication unless the woman also wants a birth control method. They may be chosen as a first line of therapy.

Alternative treatment

Simply changing the position of the body can help ease cramps. The simplest technique is assuming the fetal position, with knees pulled up to the chest while hugging a heat-

ing pad or pillow to the abdomen. Likewise, several **yoga** positions are popular ways to ease menstrual pain. In the "cat stretch," position, the woman rests on her hands and knees, slowly arching the back. The pelvic tilt is another popular yoga position, in which the woman lies on her back with knees bent and then lifts the pelvis and buttocks.

Dietary recommendations to ease cramps include increasing fiber, calcium, and complex carbohydrates, cutting fat, red meat, dairy products, caffeine, salt, and sugar. **Smoking** also has been found to worsen cramps. Some research suggests that vitamin B supplements, primarily vitamin B6 in a complex, magnesium, and fish oil supplements (omega-3 fatty acids) also may help relieve cramps.

Other women find relief through visualization, concentrating on the pain as a particular color, and gaining control of the sensations. Aromatherapy and massage may ease pain for some women. Others find that imagining a white light hovering over the painful area can actually lessen the pain for brief periods.

Exercise may be a way to reduce the pain of menstrual cramps through the brain's production of endorphins, the body's own painkillers. And orgasm can make a woman feel more comfortable by releasing tension in the pelvic muscles.

Acupuncture and Chinese herbs are additional alternative treatments for cramps.

Prognosis

Medication should lessen or eliminate pain by the end of three menstrual cycles. If it does not work, then a re-evaluation is necessary.

Prevention

NSAIDs taken one to two days before a period begins should eliminate cramps for some women.

Resources

BOOKS

Carlson, K. J., et al. *The New Harvard Guide to Women's Health.* Cambridge, MA: Harvard University Press, 2004.

ORGANIZATIONS

National Women's Health Network. 514 10th St. NW, Suite 400, Washington, DC 20004. Web site: <www.womenshealthnetwork.org>.

WEB SITES

Clark, Alan D. "Dysmenorrhea." *eMedicine*, October 12, 2004. Available online at <http://www.emedicine.com/emerg/topic156.htm> (accessed December 21, 2004).

Linda K. Bennington

Dystonia *see* **Spasticity**

E

E. coli infection *see* **Enterobacterial infections**

Ear exam with otoscope

Definition

An otoscope is a hand-held instrument with a tiny light and a cone-shaped attachment called an ear speculum. It is used to examine the ear canal.

Purpose

An ear examination is a normal part of most routine physical examinations by a doctor or nurse. It is also done when an ear infection or other type of ear problem is suspected. An otoscope allows the doctor to look into the ear canal to see the ear drum. Redness or fluid in the eardrum can indicate an ear infection. Some otoscopes (called pneumatic otoscopes) can deliver a small puff of air to the eardrum to see if the eardrum will vibrate (which is normal). An ear examination with an otoscope can also detect a build-up of wax in the ear canal or a rupture or puncture of the eardrum.

Description

An ear examination with an otoscope is usually done by a doctor or a nurse as part of a complete physical examination. The ears may also be examined if an ear infection is suspected due to **fever**, ear **pain**, or hearing loss. The child will often be asked to tip the head slightly toward the shoulder opposite of the ear being examined, so the ear to be examined is pointing up. The doctor or nurse may hold the ear lobe as the speculum is inserted into the ear and may adjust the position of the otoscope to get a better view of the ear canal and eardrum. Both ears are usually examined, even if there seems to be a problem with just one ear.

The ear canal is normally skin-colored and is covered with tiny hairs. It is normal for the ear canal to have some yellowish-brown earwax. The eardrum is typically thin, shiny, and pearly-white to light gray in color. The tiny bones in the middle ear can be seen pushing on the eardrum membrane like tent poles. The light from the otoscope will reflect off of the surface of the ear drum.

An ear infection will cause the eardrum to look red and swollen. In cases where the eardrum has ruptured, there may be fluid draining from the middle ear. A doctor may also see scarring, retraction of the eardrum, or bulging of the eardrum.

Precautions

No precautions are required. However, if an ear infection is present, an ear examination may cause some discomfort or pain. If there is an object lodged in the ear canal, pushing on the otoscope may push the object further into the ear and damage the eardrum.

Preparation

No preparation is required prior to an ear examination with an otoscope. The ear speculum, which is inserted into the ear, is cleaned and sanitized before it is used. Speculums come in various sizes, and the doctor or nurse selects the size that is most comfortable for the child's ear. Sometimes if there is an excessive build up of wax in the ear, the doctor or nurse will remove some of it so that the eardrum can be seen more clearly.

Aftercare

If an ear infection is diagnosed, the patient may require treatment with **antibiotics**. If there is a buildup

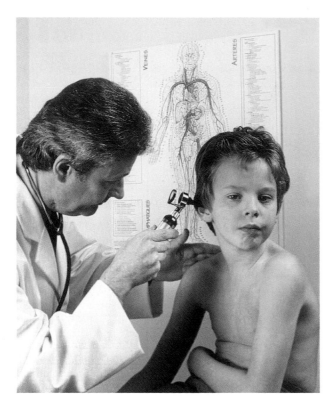

Doctor examining a boy's ear canal with an otoscope, an instrument with a tiny light and cone shaped attachment called an ear speculum. *(Photograph by SPL. Custom Medical Stock Photo, Inc.)*

of wax in the ear canal, it might be rinsed or scraped out.

Risks

This type of ear examination is simple and generally harmless. Caution should always be used any time an object is inserted into the ear. This process can irritate an infected external ear canal and can rupture an eardrum if performed improperly or if the patient moves suddenly. If an object lodged in the ear is what is causing discomfort, pushing in the otoscope without checking first may result in the object being pushed further into the ear, possibly causing damage to the eardrum or further irritating the ear canal.

Parental concerns

An ear exam with an otoscope can occasionally cause some discomfort if there is an ear infection or other ear problem. If a child has frequent ear infections a doctor may recommend getting an otoscope designed for in home use. In this case, the doctor will show the parent how to use it, and the parent is encouraged to

---

practice on healthy adults before attempting to use it on the child.

See also Otitis media.

Resources

PERIODICALS

Jones, Woodson S., and Phillip H. Kaleida. "How Helpful is Pneumatic Otoscopy in Improving Diagnostic Accuracy?" *Pediatrics* 112 (September 2003): 510–14.

ORGANIZATIONS

American Academy of Pediatrics. 141 Northwest Point Boulevard, Elk Grove Village, IL 60007–1098. Web site: <www.aap.org>.

Tish Davidson, A.M.
Altha Roberts Edgren

Ear infection, middle *see* **Otitis media**

Ear infection, outer *see* **Otitis externa**

Ear tubes *see* **Myringotomy and ear tubes**

Ear wax impaction *see* **Cerumen impaction**

Eardrum perforation *see* **Perforated eardrum**

Early childhood education

Definition

Early childhood education consists of activities and/or experiences that are intended to effect developmental

---

changes in children prior to their entry into elementary school.

Description

Early childhood education (ECE) programs include any type of educational program that serves children in the **preschool** years and is designed to improve later school performance. In the second half of the twentieth century, the early education system in the United States grew substantially. This trend allowed the majority of American children to have access to some form of early childhood education.

There are several types of programs that represent early childhood education. They are also known by a variety of names, including preschool and pre-kindergarten (pre-K). One of the first early childhood education initiatives in the United States was the Head Start program, started in 1965. Head Start is a federal government education initiative that has provided children from low-income families free access to early education. It targets children of low socioeconomic status or those who qualify in some at-risk category. **Head Start programs** are funded by the federal Department of Health and Human Services.

Many early childhood education programs operate under the auspices of Title I of the Elementary and Secondary Education Act. Under Title I, local educational agencies apply to state agencies for approval of their program, and when approved, the programs are then funded with federal money. The No Child Left Behind Act (NCLB) of 2001 encourages the use of Title I, Part A funds for preschool programs, recognizing the importance of preparing children for entering school with the language, cognitive, and early reading skills that help them meet later academic challenges. In the school year of 2001–2002 approximately 300,000 children benefiting from Title I services were enrolled in preschool.

Other early childhood education programs may be run by private for-profit companies, churches, or as part of a private school curriculum. These programs are normally tuition-based.

Since the early 1990s, many states have developed options for children from middle- and upper-income families for receiving free preschool education. Georgia introduced the first statewide universal pre-K program, offering free early childhood education to all four-year-old children. New York and Oklahoma have also developed universal pre-K programs, and Florida voters have approved a constitutional amendment for a free preschool program to be available for all four-year-olds by 2005.

Nearly three-fourths of young children in the United States are involved in some sort of early childhood education. Some groups of children have higher rates of participation in early childhood education programs than others. Children living in low-income households are less likely to be enrolled in ECE than those children in families living above the poverty line. Black and white children enroll in these programs in higher numbers than Hispanic American children. Children with better-educated mothers are more likely than other children to participate.

Benefits of early childhood education

Early childhood education can produce significant gains in children's learning and development. High quality early childhood education assists many at-risk children in avoiding poor outcomes, such as dropping out of school. Although the benefits seem to cross all economic and social lines, the most significant gains are almost always noted among children from families with the lowest income levels and the least amount of formal education. However, whether these benefits are long lasting is disputed. Some studies focused on the IQ score gains of disadvantaged children in Head Start programs, but these gains seemed to be short-term. However, studies also indicate that ECE produces persistent gains on achievement test scores, along with fewer occurrences of being held back a grade and being placed in **special education** programs. Other long-term benefits include decreased crime and delinquency rates and increased high school graduation. One extensive study found that people who participated in ECE were less likely to be on welfare as adults compared to those who had not received any early childhood education.

All programs in early childhood education are not equally effective in promoting the learning and development of young children. Long-term benefits are usually seen only in high-quality early childhood education programs. A significant problem with early childhood education is that most programs available cannot be considered high quality. In addition, the most effective ones are unaffordable for most American families. The overall effectiveness of an early childhood program is dependent upon several factors: quality staff, an appropriate environment, proper grouping practices, consistent scheduling, and parental involvement. According to the U.S. Department of Education, some additional characteristics of a high-quality early education program are as follows:

• Children have a safe, nurturing and stimulating environment, with the supervision and guidance of competent, caring adults.

- Teachers plan a balanced schedule in which the children do not feel rushed or fatigued.

- The school provides nutritious meals and snacks.

- The program includes a strong foundation in **language development**, early literacy, and early math.

- The program contains a clear statement of goals and philosophy that is comprehensive and addresses all areas of child development.

- The program engages children in purposeful learning activities and **play**, instructed by teachers who work from lesson and activity plans.

- Balance exists between individual, small-group, and large-group activities.

- Teachers frequently check children's progress.

- The staff regularly communicate with parents and caregivers so that caregivers are active participants in their children's education.

- Preschools that operate for a full day on a year-round basis, thus providing children with two years of preschool, achieve better results than those that offer less intense services.

In high-quality preschool programs, observers should see children working on the following:

- learning the letters of the alphabet

- learning to hear the individual sounds in words

- learning new words and how to use them

- learning early writing skills

- learning about written language by looking at books and by listening to stories

- becoming familiar with math and science

Because of the potential benefits to children, some people support the idea of government-sponsored universal early childhood education programs. Those who support this movement do so for the following reasons:

- The private and social costs of failing children early in their lives can be high. The lifetime social costs associated with one high school dropout may be as high as $350,000. Even modest improvements may justify the costs of ECE.

- Some studies show that for every dollar invested in quality ECE citizens save about $7 or more on investment later on.

- There is a potential for less reliance on welfare and other social services. Government receives more tax revenue because there are more taxpaying adults.

- People should rethink the value of early childhood education because of increasing needs for a more highly educated workforce in the twenty-first century.

- Early intervention may prevent intergenerational poverty.

Opponents of universal government early childhood education give the following reasons for objecting to it:

- Evidence indicates that the positive effects from the fairly expensive and intensive pre-K programs tend to be short-term.

- The public schools are already fraught with problems, and providing a downward extension to three- and four-year-olds is ill conceived.

- Some studies show that premature schooling may potentially slow or reduce a child's overall development by reducing valuable play time.

- Additional studies show that quality early education could as of 2004 cost more than $5,800 per year. The government would be taxing many people who may not wish to pay for preschool for another family's children.

In spite of the controversies, demographic trends in the early 2000s indicate that early childhood education has become, and will continue to be, an important aspect of the U.S. educational system.

Parental concerns

Parents are often understandably concerned about the quality of the early childhood education programs available to them. By taking the time to investigate several schools, most parents find a program with which they and their child are comfortable.

Resources

PERIODICALS

Barnett, W. Steven, and Jason T. Hustedt. "Preschool: The Most Important Grade." *Educational Leadership* 60 (April 2003): 7, 54–57.

Pascopella, Angela. "Universal Early Education: Point/ Counterpoint." *District Administration* (August 2004): 28–31.

WEB SITES

"Enrollment in Early Childhood Education Programs." *National Center for Education Statistics*, 2002. Available online at <http://nces.ed.gov/programs/coe/2002/section1/indicator01.asp> (accessed January 5, 2005).

Deanna M. Swartout-Corbeil, RN

Early puberty *see* **Precocious puberty**

Ecstasy *see* **Stimulant drugs**

Eczema *see* **Dermatitis**

Edwards' syndrome

Definition

Edwards' syndrome is caused by an extra (third) copy of chromosome 18. The extra chromosome is lethal for most babies born with this condition. It causes major physical abnormalities and severe **mental retardation**. Very few children afflicted with this syndrome survive beyond the first year.

Description

Edwards' syndrome is associated with the presence of a third copy of chromosome number 18. Humans normally have 23 pairs of chromosomes. Chromosomes are numbered 1–22, and the 23rd pair is composed of the sex chromosomes, X and Y. A person inherits one set of 23 chromosomes from each parent. Occasionally, a genetic error occurs during egg or sperm cell formation. A child conceived with such an egg or sperm cell may inherit an incorrect number of chromosomes. In the case of Edwards' syndrome, the child inherits three (trisomy), rather than two, copies of chromosome 18. Ninety-five percent of the children are full trisomies, 2 percent are due to translocations, where only part of an extra chromosome is present (this may be hereditary), while 3 percent are mosaic trisomies, where the extra chromosome is present in some but not all of the cells.

Edwards' syndrome is usually fatal, with most babies dying before birth. Of those who do make it to birth, 20–30 percent die within one month. However, a small number of babies (less than 10 percent) live at least one year.

Edwards' syndrome is also referred to as trisomy 18, trisomy E, and trisomy 16–18. It is the second most common trisomy, after trisomy 21 (**Down syndrome**).

Demographics

Edwards' syndrome occurs in approximately one in every 5,000 live births and one in every 5,000 stillborn births; it affects girls more often than boys. Women older than their early thirties have a greater risk of conceiving a child with Edwards' syndrome, but it can also occur with younger mothers.

Causes and symptoms

Most children born with Edwards' syndrome appear weak and fragile, and they are often underweight. The head is unusually small and the back of the head is prominent. The ears are malformed and low-set, and the mouth and jaw are small (micrognathia). The baby may also have a **cleft lip** or **cleft palate**. Frequently, the hands are clenched into fists, and the index finger overlaps the other fingers. The child may have clubfeet, and toes may be webbed or fused.

Numerous problems involving the internal organs may be present. Abnormalities often occur in the lungs and diaphragm (the muscle that controls breathing), and blood vessel malformations are common. Various types of **congenital heart disease**, including ventricular septal defect (VSD), atrial septal defect (ASD), or PDA (**patent ductus arteriosus**), may be present. The child may have an umbilical or inguinal **hernia**, malformed kidneys, and abnormalities of the urogenital system, including undescended testicles in a male child (cryptochordism).

When to call the doctor

A child with Edwards' syndrome is likely to have many medical and development needs. Parents should develop good working relationships with their doctor, other specialists, and therapists, and should consult them as needed.

If a woman gives birth to a child with Edwards' syndrome and plans to have another child, a doctor as well as a genetic counselor should be consulted so that prenatal screening and genetic counseling can be conducted.

Diagnosis

Edwards' syndrome at birth may be diagnosed by the physical abnormalities characteristic to the syndrome. Physical examination of the infant may show arched type finger print patterns, while **x rays** may reveal a short breast bone (sternum). Definitive diagnosis is achieved through karyotyping, which involves drawing the baby's blood for a microscopic examination of the chromosomes. Using special stains and microscopy, individual chromosomes are identified, and the presence of an extra chromosome 18 is revealed.

Edwards' syndrome can be detected before birth. If a pregnant woman is older than 35, has a **family** history of genetic abnormalities, has previously conceived a child with a genetic abnormality, or has suffered earlier miscarriages, she may undergo tests to determine whether her child carries genetic abnormalities. Potential tests include maternal serum alpha-fetal protein analysis or screening, ultrasonography, **amniocentesis**, and chorionic villus sampling.

In addition, a pregnant woman carrying a child with Edwards' syndrome may have an unusually large uterus during pregnancy, due to the presence of extra amniotic fluid (polyhydramnios). An unusually small placenta may be noted during the birth of the child.

Treatment

There is no cure for Edwards' syndrome. Since babies with Edwards' syndrome frequently have major physical abnormalities, doctors and parents face difficult choices regarding treatment. Abnormalities can be treated to a certain degree with surgery, but extreme invasive procedures may not be in the best interests of an infant whose lifespan is measured in days or weeks. Medical therapy often consists of supportive care with the goal of making the infant comfortable, rather than prolonging life.

However, 5–10 percent of children with Edwards' syndrome do survive past the first year of life, and require appropriate treatment for the many chronic effects associated with the syndrome. Problems with muscle tone and nervous system abnormalities will affect the development of motor skills, possibly resulting in **scoliosis** (curvature of the spine) and esotropia (crossed eyes). Surgical interventions may be limited by child's cardiac health.

Constipation due to poor abdominal muscle tone is often a life-long problem for babies and children with Edwards' syndrome, resulting in fretfulness, discomfort, and feeding problems. Anti-gas medication, special milk formulas, stool softener medicines, **laxatives**, and suppositories are all possible treatments that the doctor may recommend to ease the discomfort of gas in the bowels or constipation. An enema should not given to the baby or child because it can deplete electrolytes and alter body fluid composition.

Children with Edwards' syndrome will exhibit severe developmental delays, but with early intervention through **special education** and therapy programs, they can attain some developmental milestones.

Children with Edwards' syndrome appear to have increased risk of developing a **Wilms' tumor**, a **cancer** of the kidney that primarily affects children. Therefore, it is recommended that older infants and children with Edwards' syndrome have a routine ultrasound of the abdominal cavity.

Other illnesses that may affect a child with Edwards' syndrome and that may require treatment include congenital heart disease, pulmonary **hypertension**, elevated blood pressure, apnea episodes, pneumonias, sinus infections, seizures, urinary tract infections, ear infections, and eye infections. Other abnormalities that may require consideration of medical or surgical intervention include club foot, facial clefts, **spina bifida**, and **hydrocephalus**.

Nutritional concerns

Babies with Edwards' syndrome generally have feeding problems related to difficulties in coordination of breathing, sucking, and swallowing. Many have a weak suck and uncoordinated swallow resulting in **choking** and sometimes **vomiting**. **Gastroesophageal reflux disease**, or GERD (the upward movement of small amounts of stomach contents to the esophagus or throat), aspiration (inhalation or trickle of fluids into the lungs), and oral facial clefts may also contribute to feeding difficulties. The baby should be referred to a feeding specialist to help with feeding problems. The specialist can show the parents how to position the baby's head up, in good body alignment, because a baby with Edwards' syndrome may have hyperextension of the head. This is a common condition that occurs before the baby has developed head control. It results in the elongation of throat muscles, making swallowing more difficult. Because of feeding difficulties, many babies with Edwards' syndrome are fed through a tube inserted through the nose or mouth, down through the esophagus, and into the stomach. Some babies eventually progress to bottle or breastfeeding, while others have a gastrostomy (G-tube) placed abdominally to prevent the trauma of tube insertion. Some children are fed both orally and through the tube.

The baby should be fed with pre-softened preemie nipples and given small amounts frequently. To help prevent reflux, the baby's head should be elevated about 30 degrees or more during feeding and for one to two hours after a feeding. If tolerated, high calories formulas or supplements may be fed to help the baby gain weight.

Prognosis

Most children born with Edwards' syndrome die within their first year of life. The average lifespan is less than two months for 50 percent of the children, and 90–

KEY TERMS

Amniocentesis—A procedure performed at 16-18 weeks of pregnancy in which a needle is inserted through a woman's abdomen into her uterus to draw out a small sample of the amniotic fluid from around the baby for analysis. Either the fluid itself or cells from the fluid can be used for a variety of tests to obtain information about genetic disorders and other medical conditions in the fetus.

Atrial septal defect—An opening between the right and left atria (upper chambers) of the heart.

Chorionic villus sampling—A procedure performed at 10 to 12 weeks of pregnancy in which a needle is inserted either through the mother's vagina or abdominal wall into the placenta to withdraw a small amount of chorionic membrane from around the early embryo. The amniotic fluid can be examined for signs of chromosome abnormalities or other genetic diseases.

Chromosome—A microscopic thread-like structure found within each cell of the human body and consisting of a complex of proteins and DNA. Humans have 46 chromosomes arranged into 23 pairs. Chromosomes contain the genetic information necessary to direct the development and functioning of all cells and systems in the body. They pass on hereditary traits from parents to child (like eye color) and determine whether the child will be male or female.

Karyotyping—A laboratory test used to study an individual's chromosome make-up. Chromosomes are separated from cells, stained, and arranged in order from largest to smallest so that their number and structure can be studied under a microscope.

Maternal serum analyte screening—A medical procedure in which a pregnant woman's blood is drawn and analyzed for the levels of certain hormones and proteins. These levels can indicate whether there may be an abnormality in the unborn child. This test is not a definitive indicator of a problem and is followed by more specific testing such as amniocentesis or chorionic villus sampling.

Patent ductus arteriosus—A congenital defect in which the temporary blood vessel connecting the left pulmonary artery to the aorta in the fetus doesn't close after birth.

Trisomy—An abnormal condition where three copies of one chromosome are present in the cells of an individual's body instead of two, the normal number.

Ultrasonography—A medical test in which sound waves are directed against internal structures in the body. As sound waves bounce off the internal structure, they create an image on a video screen. Ultrasonography is often used to diagnose fetal abnormalities, gallstones, heart defects, and tumors. Also called ultrasound imaging.

Ventricular septal defect—An opening between the right and left ventricles of the heart.

95 percent die before their first birthday. The 5–10 percent of children who survive their first year have severe developmental disabilities. They need support to walk, and learning is limited. Verbal communication is also limited, but they can respond to comforting and can learn to recognize, smile, and interact with caregivers and others, and acquire such skills as rolling over and self-feeding. They will have many physical abnormalities that require constant care as doctors and parents work together to prevent and treat various problems.

Prevention

Most cases of Edwards' syndrome are not hereditary and cannot be prevented. However, parents who have had a child with Edwards' syndrome are at increased risk of having another child with the syndrome.

Parental concerns

Following the birth of a child with Edwards' syndrome, families may wish to seek counseling regarding the effects on relationships within the family. Many people respond with guilt, **fear**, or blame when a genetic disorder is manifested within a family. Support groups are good sources of information about Edwards' syndrome and can offer emotional and psychological support.

For those families whose child does survive the first weeks of life, the doctor should review with the parents the expected clinical course of the condition, and prepare a management plan for use when the child goes home. Each case must be considered on an individual basis, and the doctor should acknowledge the personal feelings of the parents, as well as the individual circumstances of each child. The theme of "best interest of the child" helps

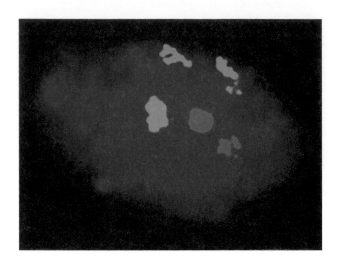

Micrograph showing trisomy 18, three copies of chromosome 18 (green) in cell's nucleus (blue) versus the normal two. The two fuschia spots are the sex chromosomes, XX, a female. *(© Department of Clinical Cytogenetics/Addenbrookes Hospital/Science Photo Library/Photo Researchers, Inc.)*

as a guiding principle in decision-making throughout the life of the child. There will be many challenges associated with the care of a child with Edwards' syndrome. As medical crises occur, parents will face decisions and emotions related to the possibility of the child dying.

See also Atrial septal defect; Congenital heart disease.

Resources

BOOKS

Barnes, Ann M., and John C. Carey. *Care of the Infant and Child with Trisomy 18 and 13: Medical Problems, Reported Treatments, and Milestones.* Omaha, NE: Munroes-Meyer Institute for Genetics and Rehabilitation, 2000.

Stenson, Carol M., et al. *Trisomy 18: A Guidebook for Families.* Omaha, NE: Munroes-Meyer Institute for Genetics and Rehabilitation, 2000.

ORGANIZATIONS

Chromosome 18 Registry & Research Society. 7715 Oakridge Drive, San Antonio, TX 78229. (210) 657-4968. Web site: <www.chromosome18.org>.

Support Organization for Trisomy 18, 13, and Related Disorders (SOFT). 2982 South Union St., Rochester, NY 14624. (800) 716-7638. Web site: <www.trisomy.org>.

WEB SITES

Trisomy 18 Support: Families Caring for Families. Available online at: <www.trisomy18support.org>.

Judith Sims
Julia Barrett

EEG *see* **Electroencephalogram**

Ehlers-Danlos syndrome

Definition

The Ehlers-Danlos syndrome (EDS) refers to a group of inherited disorders that affect collagen structure and function. Genetic abnormalities in the manufacturing of collagen within the body affect connective tissues, causing them to be abnormally weak. Ehlers-Danlos syndrome is also referred to as inherited connective tissue disorder.

Description

Collagen is a strong, fibrous protein that lends strength and elasticity to connective tissues such as the skin, tendons, organ walls, cartilage, and blood vessels. Each of these connective tissues requires collagen tailored to meet its specific purposes. The many roles of collagen are reflected in the number of genes dedicated to its production. There are at least 28 genes in humans that encode at least 19 different types of collagen. Mutations in these genes can affect basic construction as well as the fine-tuned processing of the collagen.

EDS is a group of inherited connective tissue disorders that usually affects the skin, ligaments, joints, and blood vessels. Classification of EDS types was revised in 1997. The new classification involves categorizing the different forms of EDS into six major sub-types, including classical, hypermobility, vascular, kyphoscoliosis, arthrochalasia, and dermatosparaxis, and a collection of rare or poorly defined varieties. This new classification is simpler than the previous classification system and is primarily based on descriptions of the actual symptoms.

Classical type

Under the old classification system, EDS classical type was divided into two separate types: type I and type II. The major symptoms associated with EDS classical type involve the skin and joints. The skin has a smooth, velvety texture, and bruises easily. Affected individuals typically have extensive scarring, particularly at the knees, elbows, forehead, and chin. The joints are hyperextensible, giving a tendency toward dislocation of the hip, shoulder, elbow, knee, or clavicle. Due to decreased muscle tone, affected infants may experience a delay in reaching motor milestones. Children may have a tendency to develop hernias or other organ shifts within the abdomen. **Sprains** and partial or complete joint dislocations are also common. Symptoms can range from mild to severe. EDS classical type is inherited in an autosomal dominant manner.

There are three major clinical diagnostic criteria for EDS classical type: skin hyperextensibility, unusually wide scars, and joint hypermobility. There is no definitive test for the diagnosis of classical EDS. Both DNA and biochemical studies have been used to help identify affected individuals. In some cases, skin biopsy has been found useful in confirming a diagnosis. Unfortunately, these tests are not sensitive enough to identify all individuals with classical EDS. If there are multiple affected individuals in a **family**, it may be possible to perform prenatal diagnosis using a DNA information technique known as a linkage study.

Hypermobility type

Excessively loose joints are the hallmark of this EDS type, formerly known as EDS type III. Both large joints, such as the elbows and knees, and small joints, such as toes and fingers, are affected. Partial and total joint dislocations are common, particularly involving the jaw, knee, and shoulder. Many individuals experience chronic limb and joint **pain**, although **x rays** of these joints appear normal. The skin may also bruise easily. Osteoarthritis is a common occurrence in adults. EDS hypermobility type is inherited in an autosomal dominant manner.

There are two major clinical diagnostic criteria for EDS hypermobility type. These include skin involvement (either hyperextensible skin or smooth and velvety skin) and generalized joint hypermobility. There is no test for this form of EDS.

Vascular type

Formerly called EDS type IV, EDS vascular type is the most severe form. The connective tissue in the intestines, arteries, uterus, and other hollow organs may be unusually weak, leading to organ or blood vessel rupture. Such ruptures most likely occur between ages 20 and 40, although they can occur any time, and may be life-threatening.

There is a classic facial appearance associated with EDS vascular type. Affected individuals tend to have large eyes, a thin pinched nose, thin lips, and a slim body. The skin is thin and translucent, with veins dramatically visible, particularly across the chest.

The large joints have normal stability, but small joints in the hands and feet are loose, showing hyperextensibility. The skin bruises easily. Other complications may include collapsed lungs, premature aging of the skin on the hands and feet, and ruptured arteries and veins. After surgery, there may be poor wound healing, a complication that tends to be frequent and severe. Pregnancy also carries the risk of complications. During and after pregnancy, there is an increased risk of the uterus rupturing and of arterial bleeding. Due to the severe complications associated with EDS type IV, death usually occurs before the fifth decade. A study of 419 individuals with EDS vascular type, completed in 2000, found that the median survival rate was 48 years, with a range of six to 73 years. EDS vascular type is inherited in an autosomal dominant manner.

There are four major clinical diagnostic criteria for EDS vascular type. These include thin translucent skin, arterial/intestinal/uterine fragility or rupture, extensive bruising, and characteristic facial appearance. EDS vascular type is caused by a change in the gene COL3A1, which codes for one of the collagen chains used to build Collagen type III. Laboratory testing is available for this form of EDS. A skin biopsy may be used to demonstrate the structurally abnormal collagen. This type of biochemical test identifies more than 95 percent of individuals with EDS vascular type. Laboratory testing is recommended for individuals with two or more of the major criteria.

DNA analysis may also be used to identify the change within the COL3A1 gene. This information may be helpful for genetic counseling purposes. Prenatal testing is available for pregnancies in which an affected parent has been identified and the DNA mutation is known or the biochemical defect has been demonstrated.

Kyphoscoliosis type

The major symptoms of kyphoscoliosis type, formerly called EDS type VI, are general joint looseness. At birth, the muscle tone is poor, and motor skill development is subsequently delayed. Also, infants with this type of EDS have an abnormal curvature of the spine (**scoliosis**). The scoliosis becomes progressively worse with age; affected individuals are usually unable to walk by age 20. The eyes and skin are fragile and easily damaged, and blood vessel involvement is a possibility. The bones may also be affected as demonstrated by a decrease in bone mass. Kyphoscoliosis type is inherited in an autosomal recessive manner.

There are four major clinical diagnostic criteria for EDS kyphoscoliosis type. These include generally loose joints, low muscle tone at birth, scoliosis at birth (which worsens with age), and a fragility of the eyes, which may give the white area of the eye a blue tint or cause the eye to rupture. This form of EDS is caused by a change in the PLOD gene on chromosome 1, which encodes the enzyme lysyl hydroxylase. A laboratory test is available in which urinary hydroxylysyl pryridinoline is measured. This test, performed on urine, is extremely sensitive and specific for EDS kyphoscolios type. Laboratory testing is recommended for infants with three or more of the major diagnostic criteria.

Prenatal testing is available if a pregnancy is known to be at risk and an identified affected family member has had positive laboratory testing. An **amniocentesis** may be performed in which fetal cells are removed from the amniotic fluid and enzyme activity is measured.

Arthrochalasia type

Dislocation of the hip joint typically accompanies arthrochalasia type EDS, formerly called EDS type VIIB. Other joints are also unusually loose, leading to recurrent partial and total dislocations. The skin has a high degree of stretchability and bruises easily. Individuals with this type of EDS may experience mildly diminished bone mass, scoliosis, and poor muscle tone. Arthrochalasia type is inherited in an autosomal dominant manner.

There are two major clinical diagnostic criteria for EDS arthrochalasia type. These include severe generalized joint hypermobility and bilateral hip dislocation present at birth. This form of EDS is caused by a change in either of two components of Collagen type I, called proa1(I) type A and proa2(I) type B. A skin biopsy may be performed to demonstrate an abnormality in either component. Direct DNA testing is also available.

Dermatosparaxis type

Individuals with this type of EDS, once called type VIIC, have extremely fragile skin that bruises easily but does not scar excessively. The skin is soft and may sag, leading to an aged appearance even in young adults. Individuals may also have hernias. Dermatosparaxis type is inherited in an autosomal recessive manner.

There are two major clinical diagnostic criteria for EDS dematosparaxis type. These include severe skin fragility and sagging or aged-appearing skin. This form of EDS is caused by a change in the enzyme called procollagen I N-terminal peptidase. A skin biopsy may be performed for a definitive diagnosis of dermatosparaxis type.

Other types

There are several other forms of EDS that have not been as clearly defined as the aforementioned types. Symptoms of EDS within this category may include soft, mildly stretchable skin, shortened bones, chronic **diarrhea**, joint hypermobility and dislocation, bladder rupture, or poor wound healing. Inheritance patterns within this group include X-linked recessive, autosomal dominant, and autosomal recessive.

Demographics

EDS was originally described by Dr. Van Meekeren in 1682. Dr. Ehlers and Dr. Danlos further characterized the disease in 1901 and 1908, respectively. According to the Ehlers-Danlos National Foundation, one in 5,000 to one in 10,000 people are affected by some form of EDS.

Causes and symptoms

There are numerous types of EDS, all caused by changes in one of several genes. The manner in which EDS is inherited depends on the specific gene involved. There are three patterns of inheritance for EDS: autosomal dominant, autosomal recessive, and X-linked (extremely rare).

Chromosomes are made up of hundreds of small units known as genes, which contain the genetic material necessary for an individual to develop and function. Humans have 46 chromosomes, which are matched into 23 pairs. Because chromosomes are inherited in pairs, each individual receives two copies of each chromosome and likewise two copies of each gene.

Changes or mutations in genes can cause genetic diseases in several different ways, many of which are represented within the spectrum of EDS. In autosomal dominant EDS, only one copy of a specific gene must be changed for a person to have EDS. In autosomal recessive EDS, both copies of a specific gene must be changed for a person to have EDS. If only one copy of an autosomal recessive EDS gene is changed, the person is referred to as a carrier, meaning he or she does not have any signs or symptoms of the disease itself, but carries the possibility of passing the disorder to a future child. In X-linked EDS, a specific gene on the X chromosome must be changed. However, this affects males and females differently because males and females have a different number of X chromosomes.

The few X-linked forms of EDS fall under the category of X-linked recessive. As with autosomal recessive, this implies that both copies of a specific gene must be changed for a person to be affected. However, because males only have one X-chromosome, they are affected if an X-linked recessive EDS gene is changed on their single X-chromosome. That is, they are affected even though they have only one changed copy. On the other hand, that same gene must be changed on both of the X-chromosomes in a female for her to be affected.

Although there is much information regarding the changes in genes that cause EDS and their various inheritance patterns, the exact gene mutation for all types of EDS is not known.

When to call the doctor

The doctor should be called if a child has symptoms of Ehlers-Danlos syndrome. Medical advice should also be sought if a person has a family history of Ehlers-Danlos syndrome and is planning to conceive a child.

Diagnosis

Clinical symptoms such as extreme joint looseness and unusual skin qualities, along with family history, can lead to a diagnosis of EDS. Specific tests, such as skin biopsies, are available for diagnosis of certain types of EDS, including vascular, arthrochalasia, and dermatosparaxis types. A skin biopsy involves removing a small sample of skin and examining its microscopic structure. A urine test is available for the kyphoscoliosis type.

Treatment

Medical therapy relies on managing symptoms and trying to prevent further complications. There is no cure for EDS.

Braces may be prescribed to stabilize joints, although surgery is sometimes necessary to repair joint damage caused by repeated dislocations. Physical therapy teaches individuals how to strengthen muscles around joints and may help to prevent or limit damage. Elective surgery is discouraged due to the high possibility of complications.

There are anecdotal reports that large daily doses (0.04–0.14 oz, or 1–4 g) of vitamin C may help decrease bruising and aid in wound healing. Constitutional homeopathic treatment may be helpful in maintaining optimal health in persons with a diagnosis of EDS. Before beginning these types of therapies, an individual with EDS should discuss them with his or her doctor. Therapy that does not require medical consultation

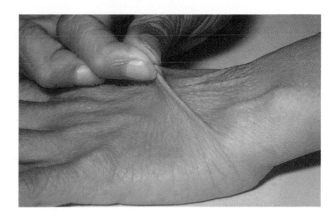

Elasticity of the skin is one characteristic of Ehlers-Danlos syndrome. *(Photo Researchers, Inc.)*

involves protecting the skin with sunscreen and avoiding activities that place stress on the joints. **Wounds** and infections must be treated with care because tissue healing may be poor. Suturing can be difficult, for the skin can be extremely fragile.

Prognosis

The outlook for individuals with EDS depends on the type of EDS with which they have been diagnosed. Symptoms vary in severity, even within one sub-type. Some individuals have negligible symptoms, while others are severely restricted in their daily life. Extreme joint instability and scoliosis may limit a person's mobility. Most individuals will have a normal lifespan. However, those with blood vessel involvement, particularly persons with EDS vascular type, have an increased risk of fatal complications.

EDS is a lifelong condition. Affected individuals may face social obstacles related to their disease on a daily basis. Some individuals with EDS have reported living with fears of significant and painful skin ruptures, becoming pregnant (especially those with EDS vascular type), experiencing worsening of their condition, becoming unemployed due to physical and emotional burdens, and undergoing social stigmatization in general.

Some people with EDS are not diagnosed until well into adulthood and, in the case of EDS vascular type, occasionally not until after death due to complications of the disorder. The diagnosis may be devastating to the individual and, in many cases, to other family members when they learn they are at risk for being affected.

Although children with EDS face significant challenges, it is important to remember that each child is unique with his or her own distinguished qualities and

KEY TERMS

Arthrochalasia—Excessive loosness of the joints.

Blood vessels—General term for arteries, veins, and capillaries that transport blood throughout the body.

Cartilage—A tough, elastic connective tissue found in the joints, outer ear, nose, larynx, and other parts of the body.

Collagen—The main supportive protein of cartilage, connective tissue, tendon, skin, and bone.

Connective tissue—A group of tissues responsible for support throughout the body; includes cartilage, bone, fat, tissue underlying skin, and tissues that support organs, blood vessels, and nerves throughout the body.

Dermatosparaxis—Skin fragility caused by abnormal collagen.

Hernia—A rupture in the wall of a body cavity, through which an organ may protrude.

Homeopathy—A holistic system of treatment developed in the eighteenth century. It is based on the idea that substances that produce symptoms of sickness in healthy people will have a curative effect when given in very dilute quantities to sick people who exhibit those same symptoms. Homeopathic remedies are believed to stimulate the body's own healing processes.

Hyperextensibility—The ability to extend a joint beyond the normal range.

Hypermobility—Unusual flexibility of the joints, allowing them to be bent or moved beyond their normal range of motion.

Joint dislocation—The displacement of a bone from its socket or normal position.

Kyphoscoliosis—Abnormal front-to-back and side-to-side curvature of the spine.

Ligament—A type of tough, fibrous tissue that connects bones or cartilage and provides support and strength to joints.

Osteoarthritis—A noninflammatory type of arthritis, usually occurring in older people, characterized by degeneration of cartilage, enlargement of the margins of the bones, and changes in the membranes in the joints. Also called degenerative arthritis.

Scoliosis—An abnormal, side-to-side curvature of the spine.

Tendon—A tough cord of dense white fibrous connective tissue that connects a muscle with some other part, especially a bone, and transmits the force which the muscle exerts.

Uterus—The female reproductive organ that contains and nourishes a fetus from implantation until birth. Also called the womb.

Vascular—Pertaining to blood vessels.

---

potential. Persons with EDS go on to have families and careers, and to be respected citizens, surmounting the challenges of their disease.

Prevention

If a couple has had a child diagnosed with EDS, the chance that they will have another child with the same disorder depends on the form of EDS the child has and if either parent is affected by the same disease.

In classical autosomal dominant EDS, the risk for recurrence in the parents' other children is one in four.

X-linked recessive EDS is accompanied by a slightly more complicated pattern of inheritance. If a father with an X-linked recessive form of EDS passes a copy of his X chromosome to his children, the sons will be unaffected and the daughters will be carriers. If a mother is a carrier for an X-linked recessive form of

EDS, she may have affected or unaffected sons, or carrier or unaffected daughters, depending on the second sex chromosome inherited from the father.

Prenatal diagnosis is available for specific forms of EDS, including kyphosocliosis type and vascular type. However, prenatal testing is only a possibility in these types if the underlying defect has been found in another family member.

Parental concerns

Constant bruises, skin wounds, and trips to the hospital take their toll on affected children and their parents. Prior to diagnosis, parents of children with EDS have found themselves under suspicion of **child abuse**.

Management of all types of EDS may include genetic counseling to help the affected individual and his or her family understand the disorder and its impact on other family members and future children.

Resources

BOOKS

Icon Health Publications. *Ehlers-Danlos Syndrome: A Medical Dictionary, Bibliography, and Annotated Research Guide to the Internet.* San Diego, CA: Icon Health Publications, 2004.

————. *The Official Patient's Sourcebook on Ehlers-Danlos Syndrome: A Revised and Updated Directory for the Internet Age.* San Diego, CA: Icon Health Publications, 2002.

Massoud, Lindalee. *Ehlers-Danlos Syndrome: Medical and Practical Information.* Flint, MI: SignQuest Publishers, 1997.

PM Medical Health News. *21st Century Complete Guide to Ehlers-Danlos Syndrome (EDS), Connective Tissue Disorders, Hypermobility, Authoritative Government Documents, Clinical References, and Practical Information for Patients and Physicians.* Washington, DC: Progressive Management, 2004.

PERIODICALS

"Living a Restricted Life with Ehlers-Danlos Syndrome." *International Journal of Nursing Studies* 37 (2000): 111–118.

ORGANIZATIONS

Ehlers-Danlos Support Group - UK. P.O. Box 335, Farnham, Surrey, GU10 1XJ. UK. +44 1252 690 940. Web site: <www.ehlers- danlos.org>.

Ehlers-Danlos National Foundation. 6399 Wilshire Blvd., Ste. 203, Los Angeles, CA 90048 (323) 651-3038. Fax: (323) 651-1366. Web site: <www.ednf.org>.

WEB SITES

GeneClinics. Available online at: <www.geneclinics.org>.

Judith Sims
Java O. Solis, M.S.

Elbow injury *see* **Nursemaid's elbow**

Electric shock injuries

Definition

Electric shock injuries are caused by lightning or electric current passing through the body. In infants, electric shock injuries occur most often when they put metal objects in their mouths.

Description

Electric current can be described as the flow of microscopic particles called electrons through wires and electrical appliances. Materials like metal and water through which electric current (electricity) travels easily are called conducting materials or conductors. The body is an excellent conductor, and electric current from any source passing through the body produces electric shock injuries.

The severity of electric shock injuries depends on the current's voltage, the amount of current (amperage), the type of current (direct or alternating), the body's resistance to the current, the current's path through the body, and the length of time the body remains in contact with the current. The interplay of these factors can produce effects ranging from a mild **tingling** to instant death. How electric shocks affect the skin depends on the skin's resistance to current, which in turn depends on the wetness, thickness, and cleanliness of the skin. Thin or wet skin is much less resistant than thick or dry skin. When the skin's resistance to current is low, the current may cause little or no skin damage but severely burn internal organs and tissues. By contrast, high skin resistance can produce severe skin **burns** but prevent the current from entering the body.

The nervous system (brain, spinal cord, and nerves) is very sensitive to electric shock injury, and neurological problems are the most common consequences suffered by electric shock victims. Neurological damage can be minor and clear up on its own or with medical treatment or can be severe and permanent. Damage to the respiratory and cardiovascular systems is highest at time of injury. Electric shocks can paralyze the respiratory system or disrupt heart action, causing instant death. Also at risk are the smaller veins and arteries, which can develop blood clots. Damage to the smaller vessels is often followed by amputation after high-voltage injuries. Many other injuries are possible after an electric shock, including cataracts, kidney failure, and destruction of muscle tissue. The victim may also suffer a fall or an electric arc may set clothing or nearby flammable substances on fire. Strong shocks are often accompanied by violent **muscle spasms** that can break and dislocate bones.

Demographics

Electric shocks are responsible for about 1,000 deaths in the United States each year, or about 1 percent of all accidental deaths. Children are not often seriously injured by electricity, but they are prone to electric shock by the low voltage (110–220 volts) of typical household current. In children aged 12 years and younger, household appliance electrical cords and extension cords are reported to cause more than 63 percent of injuries. Wall outlets are responsible for 15 percent of electric injuries.

Causes and symptoms

Electric shocks are caused by the passage of electric current through the body. They are caused in infants and young children by their playing with electrical appliances or cords and in older children by mischievous exploration of electrical systems or use of faulty electrical appliances or tools.

A child who has suffered an electric shock may have very little external injury or may have obvious severe burns. Burns are usually most severe at the points of contact with the electrical source. The hands, heels, and head are common points of contact. Other injuries are also possible if the child has been thrown clear of the electrical source by forceful muscular contractions. The child may have internal injuries especially if he or she is experiencing any shortness of breath, chest **pain**, or abdominal pain. In children, the typical electrical mouth burn from biting an electric cord appears as a burn on the lip. The area has a red or dark, charred appearance.

When to call the doctor

A person shocked by high voltage (500 volts or more) should be evaluated in the emergency department of a hospital or clinic. Any person present at the scene of the accident should immediately call 911.

Brief low-voltage shocks (110–220 volts or less) that do not result in any symptoms or burns of the skin do not require care. However, following a low-voltage shock, parents should consult their healthcare provider if the child has any noticeable burn to the skin, any **numbness**, tingling, or vision, hearing, or speech problems, no matter how mild. A doctor should also always evaluate electric cord burns to the mouth of a child.

Diagnosis

Diagnosis relies on the information gathered about the circumstances of the electric shock, a thorough physical examination, and monitoring of cardiovascular and kidney activity. The physician's primary concern is to determine if significant unseen injury exists. Injury may occur to muscles, the heart, or the brain from the electricity or to any bones or other organs from being thrown

from the electric source. Tests may include any of the following:

- electrocardiogram (ECG) to check the heart
- complete blood count (CBC)
- urine test for muscle enzymes, to screen for muscle injury
- x rays or **magnetic resonance imaging** (MRI) to look for **fractures** or dislocations, both of which may be caused by electrocution
- CT scan for internal injuries

Treatment

When a severe electric shock injury happens at home, the main power should immediately be shut off. If that cannot be done, and current is still flowing through the child, the alternative is to stand on a dry, nonconducting surface such as a folded newspaper, flattened cardboard carton, or plastic or rubber mat and use a nonconducting object such as a wooden broomstick (never a damp or metallic object) to push the child away from the source of the current. The victim and the source of the current must not be touched while the current is still flowing, for doing so can electrocute the rescuer. Emergency medical help should be summoned as quickly as possible. People who are trained to perform **cardiopulmonary resuscitation** (CPR) should, if appropriate, begin first aid while waiting for emergency medical help to arrive.

At the clinic or hospital, treatment depends on the severity of the burns and/or the nature of other injuries found. Minor burns are usually treated with topical antibiotic ointment and dressings. More severe burns may require surgery to clean the **wounds** or even to perform skin grafting. Severe burns on the arms, legs, or hands may require surgery to remove damaged muscle or even amputation.

Prognosis

Recovery from electric shock depends on the nature and severity of the injuries. The percentage of the body surface area burned is the most important factor affecting prognosis. Electric shocks cause death in 3–15 percent of cases, with infection being the most common cause of death in people hospitalized following electrical injury. Electrical damage to the brain may result in a permanent **seizure disorder**, depression, **anxiety**, or other personality changes. Injuries from household appliances and other low-voltage sources are less likely to produce extreme damage.

KEY TERMS

Computed tomography (CT)—An imaging technique in which cross-sectional x rays of the body are compiled to create a three-dimensional image of the body's internal structures; also called computed axial tomography.

Conducting materials—Materials that conduct electricity, materials through which electric current travels easily. Examples are metals and water.

Electric current—The rate of flow of electric charge, measured in amperes. Electric current can also be described as the flow of microscopic particles called electrons flowing through wires and electronic components and appliances.

Electrical resistance—Resistance to the flow of electrical current.

Magnetic resonance imaging (MRI)—An imaging technique that uses a large circular magnet and radio waves to generate signals from atoms in the body. These signals are used to construct detailed images of internal body structures and organs, including the brain.

Non-conducting materials—Also called insulators, materials through which electric current does not propagate. Examples are ceramics, rubber, wood.

Skin grafting—A surgical procedure by which skin or a skin substitute is placed over a burn or non-healing wound to permanently replace damaged or missing skin or to provide a temporary wound covering.

Prevention

Parents and other adults need to be aware of possible electric dangers in the home. Damaged electric appliances, wiring, cords, and plugs should be repaired, replaced or discarded. Hair dryers, radios, and other electric appliances should never be used in the bathroom or where they may accidentally come in contact with water. Young children need to be kept away from electrical appliances and should be taught about the dangers of electricity as early as possible. They should not be allowed to **play** with any electrical cord. Electric outlets also require **safety** covers in homes with young children. In children older than 12 years, most electrical injuries result from exploring and playing around high-power systems. Teenagers should accordingly be warned not to climb on power towers, play near transformer systems, or explore electrified train rails or other electrical systems.

See also Computed tomography.

Resources

BOOKS

Cadick, John, et al. *Electrical Safety Handbook*, 2nd ed. New York: McGraw-Hill, 2001.

Kovacic, Thomas, M., et al. *An Illustrated Guide to Electrical Safety*. Des Plaines, IL: American Society of Safety Engineers, 2003.

Marne, David. *McGraw-Hill's National Electrical Safety Code Handbook*. New York: McGraw-Hill Professional Publishing, 2002.

PERIODICALS

Koumbourlis, A. C. "Electrical Injuries." *Critical Care in Medicine* 11 Suppl. (November 2002): S424–30.

Marinez, J. A., and T. Nguyen. "Electrical Injuries." *South Medical Journal* 93, no. 12 (December 2000): 1165–68.

ORGANIZATIONS

Home Safety Council. 1725 Eye Street NW, Suite 300, Washington, DC 20006. Web site: <www.homesafetycouncil.org>.

National Center for Injury Prevention and Control (NCIPC). Mailstop K65, 4770 Buford Highway NE, Atlanta, GA 30341–3724. Web site: <www.cdc.gov/ncipc/>

WEB SITES

"First Aid for Electric Shock." *HealthWorld Online*. Available online at <www.healthy.net/scr/article.asp?id=1490> (accessed November 25, 2004).

Price, Timothy G. "Electric Shock." *emedicine.com*, August 10, 2004. Available online at <www.emedicine.com/aaem/topic177.htm> (accessed November 25, 2004).

Monique Laberge, Ph.D.

Electroencephalogram

Definition

An electroencephalogram (EEG), also called a brain wave test, is a diagnostic test which measures the electrical activity of the brain (brain waves) using highly sensitive recording equipment attached to the scalp by fine electrodes.

Purpose

EEG is performed to detect abnormalities in the electrical activity of the brain which may help diagnose the presence and type of various brain disorders, to look for causes of confusion, and to evaluate head injuries, tumors, infections, degenerative diseases, and other disturbances that affect the brain. The test is also used to investigate periods of unconsciousness. EEG may also confirm brain death in someone who is in a coma. EEG cannot be used to measure **intelligence** or diagnose mental illness. Specifically, EEG is used to diagnose the following:

- seizure disorders (such as epilepsy or convulsions)
- structural brain abnormality (such as a brain tumor or brain abscess)
- head injury, **encephalitis** (inflammation of the brain)
- hemorrhage (abnormal bleeding caused by a ruptured blood vessel)
- cerebral infarct (tissue that is dead because of a blockage of the blood supply)
- **sleep** disorders (such as narcolepsy)

Description

Brain cells communicate by producing tiny electrical impulses, also called brain waves. These electrical signals have certain rhythms and shapes, and EEG is a technique that measures, records, and analyzes these signals to help make a diagnosis. Electrodes are used to detect the electrical signals. They come in the shape of small discs that are applied to the head and connected to a recording device. The recording machine then converts the electrical signals into a series of wavy lines that are drawn onto a moving piece of graph paper. An EEG test causes no discomfort. Although having electrodes pasted on the skin may feel strange, they only record activity and do not produce any sensation. The patient needs to lie still with eyes closed because any movement can affect results. The patient may also be asked to do certain things during the EEG recording, such as breathing deeply and rapidly for several minutes or looking at a bright flickering light.

An EEG is performed by an EEG technician in a specially designed room that may be in the doctor's office or at a hospital. The patient is asked to lie on a bed or in a comfortable chair so that a relaxed EEG recording can be done. The technician either measures the scalp and marks the spots where small discs (electrodes) will be placed or fits the head with a special cap containing between 16 and 25 of these discs. The scalp is then rubbed with a mild, scratchy cleanser that may cause mild discomfort for a short while. The discs are attached to the body with a cream or gel. Alternatively, the technician may secure the discs to the skin with an adhesive. The heart may also be monitored during the procedure.

Precautions

Before an EEG, care should be taken to avoid washing hair with an oily scalp product 24 hours before the test. Doctors usually recommend that patients eat a meal or light snack some four hours before the test. Caffeinated drinks should be avoided for eight hours before the test. Sometimes, the EEG gives better results when the patient has had less than the usual amount of sleep. The doctor may ask that the child be kept awake for all or part of the night before the EEG. The healthcare provider may also discontinue some medications before the test.

Preparation

The physical and psychological preparation required for this test depends on the child's age, interests, previous experiences, and level of trust. For older children, research has shown that preparing ahead can reduce crying or resisting the test. In addition, children report less **pain** and show less distress when prepared. Proper preparation for the test can reduce a child's **anxiety**, encourage cooperation, and help develop coping skills.

Some general guidelines for preparing a toddler or preschooler for an EEG include the following:

- Explain the EEG procedure in words that the child understands, avoiding abstract terminology.
- Ensure that the child understands the exact body part involved and that the procedure will be limited to that area.
- Describe how the test is likely to feel.
- Give the child permission to yell, cry, or otherwise express any pain or discomfort verbally.
- Stress the benefits of the EEG procedure and list things that the child may find pleasurable after the test, such as feeling better or going home.

The above guidelines also apply to school age children. Additionally, for older children, parents can try the following:

- Suggest ways to keep calm and reduce anxiety such as counting, deep breathing, or thinking pleasant thoughts.
- Include the child in the decision-making process, such as the time of day where the EEG is performed.

KEY TERMS

Electrode—A medium for conducting an electrical current.

Encephalitis—Inflammation of the brain, usually caused by a virus. The inflammation may interfere with normal brain function and may cause seizures, sleepiness, confusion, personality changes, weakness in one or more parts of the body, and even coma.

Epilepsy—A neurological disorder characterized by recurrent seizures with or without a loss of consciousness.

Hemorrhage—Severe, massive bleeding that is difficult to control. The bleeding may be internal or external.

Hyperventilation—Rapid, deep breathing, possibly exceeding 40 breaths/minute. The most common cause is anxiety, although fever, aspirin overdose, serious infections, stroke, or other diseases of the brain or nervous system. Also refers to a respiratory therapy involving deeper and/or faster breathing to keep the carbon dioxide pressure in the blood below normal.

Narcolepsy—A life-long sleep disorder marked by four symptoms: sudden brief sleep attacks, cataplexy (a sudden loss of muscle tone usually lasting up to 30 minutes), temporary paralysis, and hallucinations. The hallucinations are associated with falling asleep or the transition from sleeping to waking.

Seizure—A sudden attack, spasm, or convulsion.

Sleep disorder—Any condition that interferes with sleep. Sleep disorders are characterized by disturbance in the amount of sleep, in the quality or timing of sleep, or in the behaviors or physiological conditions associated with sleep.

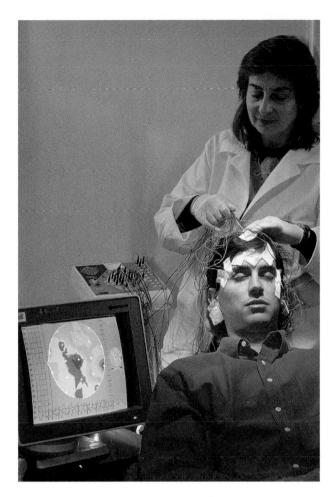

Patient receiving an electroencephalogram, a neurological test to measure and record electrical activity in the brain. (© Richard T. Nowitz/Corbis.)

• Suggest that the child hold the hand of the technician or someone else helping with the procedure.

As for adolescents, detailed information about the EEG should be provided and the reasons for the procedure should be explained in correct medical terminology. When the EEG is required for a **seizure disorder**, there is the potential risk that the test will trigger a seizure. This possibility should be openly discussed. Adolescents commonly have high concerns about risks and the best way to prepare them is to fully inform them. The healthcare provider could also be asked to limit the number of strangers entering and leaving the room during the EEG procedure, since they can raise the patient's anxiety level.

Aftercare

There are no side effects or special procedures required after an EEG. The technician simply removes the gel with water and the adhesive, if used, with a special cleanser. Shampooing will rid the hair of any other material. A few patients are mildly sensitive to the gel or may get irritation from the rubbing of their scalps.

Risks

The EEG test is very safe. However, if a patient has a seizure disorder, a seizure may be triggered by the flashing lights or hyperventilation. The healthcare provider performing the EEG is trained to take care of the patient if this happens.

Normal results

An EEG returns normal results when brain waves have normal frequency and amplitude and other characteristics are typical.

Parental concerns

Before the test, parents should know that the child probably will cry, and restraints may be used. The most important way to help a child through an EEG procedure is by being there and caring. Crying is a normal response to the strange environment, unfamiliar people, restraints, and separation from the parent. Infants and young children will cry more for these reasons than because the test or procedure is uncomfortable. Knowing this from the onset may help parents feel less anxiety about what to expect. Having specific information about the test may further reduce anxiety.

See also Encephalitis; Narcolepsy; Sleep disorders.

Resources

BOOKS

Electroencephalogram: A Medical Dictionary, Bibliography, and Annotated Research Guide to Internet. San Diego, CA: Icon Health Publications, 2004.

Shaw, John C. *The Brain's Alpha Rhythms and the Mind.* New York: Elsevier Science, 2003.

PERIODICALS

Foley, C. M., et al. "Long-term Computer-assisted Outpatient Electroencephalogram Monitoring in Children and Adolescents." *Journal of Child Neurology* 15, no. 1 (January 2000): 49–55.

Jenny, O. G., and M. A. Carskadon. "Spectral Analysis of the Sleep Electroencephalogram during Adolescence." *Sleep* 27, no. 4 (June 2004): 774–83.

Nasr, J. T., et al. "The Electroencephalogram in Children with Developmental Dysphasia." *Epilepsy Behavior* 2, no. 2 (April 2001): 115–18.

Wassmer, E., et al. "Melatonin as a Sleep Inductor for Electroencephalogram Recordings in Children." *Clinical Neurophysiology* 112, no. 4 (April 2001): 683–85.

ORGANIZATIONS

American Academy of Neurology Foundation. 1080 Montreal Avenue, St. Paul, MN 55116. Web site: <www.neurofoundation.com>.

American Society of Neurophysiological Monitoring. PO Box 60487, Chicago, IL 60660–0487. Web site: <www.asnm.org>.

National Institute of Neurological Disorders and Stroke (NINDS). PO Box 5801, Bethesda, MD 20824. Web site: <www.ninds.nih.gov>.

WEB SITES

"EEG." *Medline Plus.* Available online at <www.nlm.nih.gov/medlineplus/ency/article/003931.htm> (accessed November 17, 2004).

"The '10–20 System' of Electrode Placement." Available online at <http://faculty.Washington.edu/chudler/1020.html> (accessed November 17, 2004).

Monique Laberge, Ph.D.

Electronic fetal monitoring

Definition

Electronic fetal monitoring (EFM) involves the use of an electronic fetal heart rate (FHR) monitor to record the baby's heart rate. Elastic belts are used to hold sensors against the pregnant woman's abdomen. The sensors are connected to the monitor and detect the baby's heart rate as well as the uterine contractions. The monitor then records the FHR and the contractions as a pattern on a strip of paper. Electronic fetal monitoring is performed late in pregnancy or continuously during labor to ensure normal delivery of a healthy baby. EFM can be utilized either externally or internally in the womb.

Purpose

All electronic fetal monitors detect the FHR and maternal uterine activity (UA), and both are displayed for interpretation since the pattern of the baby's heartbeat during labor often reflects the baby's condition. During contractions, the normal pattern is for the FHR to slow somewhat, picking up again as the contraction ends. The EFM continuously prints out a record of both the FHR and the duration and frequency of the uterine contractions, so that deviations from normal patterns can be identified. Certain variations in this pattern, such as precipitous drops in the FHR at the end of a contraction can constitute a true life or death situation requiring emergency delivery of the baby. Prior to the use of EFMs, nurses and doctors periodically monitored the baby's heartbeat manually by placing a stethoscope on the mother's abdomen. It is important to note that the EFM is a screening tool and not diagnostic of any particular disorder.

Fetal asphyxia (an impaired exchange of oxygen and carbon dioxide) is recognized as an important cause of stillbirth and neonatal death. Asphyxia has also been implicated as a cause of **cerebral palsy**, although many cases of cerebral palsy have occurred without evidence of birth asphyxia. Most fetuses, however, tolerate intrauterine hypoxia during labor and are delivered without complications. If the interruption to the supply of oxygen is short, the baby may recover without any damage. If the time is longer, there may be some injury that is reversible. If the time period without oxygen is especially long, there may be permanent injury to one or more organs of the body.

Fetal monitoring can be helpful in a variety of different situations. During pregnancy, fetal monitoring can be used as a part of **antepartum testing**. If the practitioner feels that a baby may be at risk for problems during pregnancy, non-stress tests, biophysical profiles, or even contraction stress tests are performed twice a week to monitor fetal well-being. In this test, changes in the baby's heart rate are noted with the fetus's own movements. The heart rate of a healthy baby should go up whenever she or he moves.

Description

Using the external fetal monitor is simple and painless. Two belts are placed around the pregnant woman's abdomen. One is to hold the transducer that picks up the FHR and the other is to hold a tocodynanometer, which picks up uterine activity or contractions. External monitoring of the fetus is accomplished by means of a transducer that emits continuous sound waves (ultrasound). A water-soluble gel is placed on the underside of the transducer to permit the conduction of fetal heart sounds. When the transducer is placed correctly on the maternal abdomen, the sound waves bounce off the fetal heart and are picked up by the electronic monitor. The actual moment-by-moment FHR can be simultaneously viewed on a screen while being printed on graph paper. Incorrect placement of the transducer may detect a pulsating maternal vessel with a resultant swooshing sound (uterine soufflé), and the rate will be the same as the maternal pulse. Maternal uterine activity is noted and recorded when the pressure of a contraction pushes on a sensor, which is on the underside of a tocodynanometer. Once again, incorrect placement may not completely detect contractions. The sensor on the tocodynanometer must be placed on

that part of the uterus that can be palpated easily. If it is too high or too low, the contractions may not be detected.

If it becomes difficult to detect the FHR with the external monitor or if there are subtle signs of a developing problem, the practitioner may recommend the use of an internal monitor. The measurement of fetal heart activity is performed most accurately by attaching an electrode directly to the fetal scalp. This is an invasive procedure that requires the rupture of membranes (amniotomy) and is associated with occasional complications.

An internal monitor may also be used to determine the actual strength of the contraction as well as the resting tone of the uterus. A woman may appear to be having strong contractions but not be progressing in labor. Progress in labor is determined by cervical dilation. The insertion of an intrauterine pressure catheter (IUPC) permits the determination of the strength of the contractions in millimeters of Hg, a measurement used for pressure. A good labor pattern that facilitates cervical dilation can be calculated by taking the difference in pressure between the peak of the contraction and the resting tone and adding them up over a ten-minute period. The unit of measurement for this calculation is called a Montevideo unit, and ideally the sum total of the pressures should be between 150 and 250 Montevideo units to achieve cervical dilation. If the calculation is in this range and the woman's cervix is not changing, then and only then can a diagnosis of failure to progress be made. The IUPC also provides an accurate measurement of the resting tone of the uterus. It is important that the uterus relax between contractions in order for the baby to receive oxygen. If the uterus is not relaxing or if the resting tone is rising, this can be an indication of a placental abruption (the tearing away of the placenta from the wall of the uterus).

Another use of an IUPC is for amnioinfusion. This is a procedure in which a physiologic solution (such as normal saline) is infused into the uterine cavity to replace the amniotic fluid. It is used to relieve cord compression, reduce fetal distress caused by meconium staining, and as a correction of decreased amniotic fluid.

Preparation

There are no special preparations needed for fetal monitoring. An explanation of the procedure and its risks should be provided by the healthcare provider and a consent form may be signed for the procedure.

Risks

Besides the risk of an unnecessary **cesarean section**, other risks posed to the mother by EFM include her **immobilization** in bed. Immobilization simultaneously limits changing positions for comfort and causes changes in blood circulation, which decreases the oxygen supply to the fetus and can lead to abnormal changes in the FHR on the EFM that was applied to detect these changes. Another problem with the use of the EFM is that practitioners have a tendency to focus on it instead of the laboring woman. For these and other reasons, the United States Preventive Services Task Force states that there is some evidence that using EFM on low-risk women in labor might not be indicated. EFM, however, has become an accepted standard of care in many settings in the United States for management of labor. Interestingly, there has not been a reported reduction in perinatal morbidity in the United States with the use of EFM. There is a benefit to using EFM in women with complicated labors, such as those induced or augmented with oxytocin, prolonged labors, vaginal birth after having a cesarean section, abnormal presentation, and twin pregnancy.

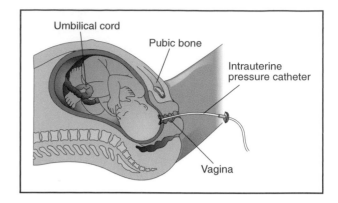

Electronic fetal monitoring (EFM) is performed late in pregnancy or continuously during labor to ensure normal delivery of a healthy baby. EFM can be utilized either externally or internally in the womb. This illustration shows the internal procedure, in which an electrode is attached directly to the baby's scalp to monitor the heart rate. Uterine contractions are recorded using an intrauterine pressure catherter which is inserted through the cervix into the uterus. *(Illustration by Electronic Illustrators Group.)*

Generally the insertion of a fetal scalp electrode is a safe procedure, but it may occasionally cause umbilical cord prolapse or infection due to early amniotomy. Problems could also occur if the electrode or IUPC causes trauma to the eye, fetal vessels, umbilical cord, or placenta. Scalp infections with the herpes virus or group B streptococcus are possible, and concern has been raised regarding the potential for enhancing transmission of the human **immunodeficiency** virus (HIV). As with any procedure, the potential benefit of EFM must be weighed against the potential risks.

Normal results

The average fetal heart rate is in the range of 110 to 160 beats per minute (bpm). A baby who is receiving sufficient oxygen through the placenta moves around and the monitor strip will show the baby's heart rate rising briefly as he or she moves. The monitor strip is considered to be reactive when the baby's heart rate elevates at least 15 bpm above the baseline heart rate for at least 15 seconds twice in a 20-minute period. Other indicators of fetal well-being include short term variability (STV), which constitutes changes in the FHR from one beat to another, and long term variability (LTV), which is changes in the FHR over a long period of time.

If the baby's heart rate drops very low or rises very high, this can signal a serious problem if it occurs for longer than a ten-minute period. During a contraction, the flow of oxygen (from the mother) through the placenta (to the baby) is temporarily blocked. The baby should be capable of withstanding this condition since it

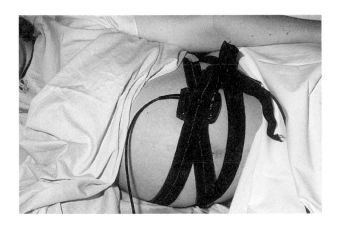

Fetal monitor belt around a pregnant woman's torso to record the heart rate of her baby. (© *Custom Medical Stock Photo, Inc.*)

is receiving sufficient oxygen between contractions. The first sign that a baby is not getting enough oxygen between contractions is often a drop in the baby's heart rate after a contraction, called a late deceleration. The baby's heart rate recovers to a normal level between contractions, only to drop again after the next contraction. This is a more subtle sign of distress. These babies will do fine if they are delivered in a short period of time following the onset of the late decelerations. Sometimes, these signs develop long before delivery is expected. In that case, a c-section may be necessary.

One of the worst indications of fetal distress, however, is a tracing that shows no variability at all. It is a flat tracing and indicates that the baby has sustained a severe assault on its central nervous system. It is not capable of responding to stimuli in its environment. The mother may report that she has experienced decreased fetal movement as the baby has only enough oxygen to keep the heart beating. It is for this reason that all pregnant women should be taught to keep track of fetal movement every day and to report any significant changes.

See also Apgar testing; Cesarean section.

Resources

BOOKS

Freeman, Roger, et al. *Fetal Heart Rate Monitoring*, 3rd ed. Philadelphia: Lippincott Williams & Wilkins, 2003.

Gabbe, Steven. *Obstetrics: Text and Pocket Companion Package.* St. Louis, MO: Harcourt Health Sciences Group, 2003.

Tucker, Susan. *Pocket Guide to Fetal Monitoring and Assessment*, 4th ed. St. Louis, MO: Mosby, 2000.

ORGANIZATIONS

American College of Obstetricians and Gynecologists. 409 12th Street, SW, PO Box 96920, Washington, DC 20090. Web site: <www.acog.org>.

Association of Women's Health, Obstetric, and Neonatal Nursing. 2000 L Street, NW, Suite 740, Washington, DC 20036. Web site: <www.awhonn.org>.

International Childbirth Education Association Inc. (ICEA). PO Box 20048, Minneapolis, MN 55420. Web site: <www.icea.org>.

Linda K. Bennington, BSN, MSN, CNS

Elimination diet

Definition

An elimination diet is the systematic elimination of foods or group of foods from the diet suspected in causing a food allergy. It is used as a means to diagnose an allergic reaction to foods.

Purpose

While people of all ages can develop an allergic sensitivity to certain foods, such **allergies** are especially common among children. In the United States, one child in six develops an allergic reaction to certain substances, and foods are among the prime offenders. (Many **food allergies** are outgrown during adolescence.) Food elimination is considered only when no other cause can be found for the symptoms the child is experiencing. Common symptoms of food allergies include **hives**, angioedema (swelling), **rashes**, respiratory congestion, and gastrointestinal problems such as **constipation**, **diarrhea**, and/or gas. Food allergies are also known to play a secondary role in many chronic conditions, such as **asthma**, **acne**, ear infections, eczema, headaches, and hay fever. The most effective means of treating food allergies is to avoid the foods that produce allergic reactions.

Description

There are two main ways of diagnosing food allergies by the elimination method. A casual approach involves eliminating, one at a time, foods from the diet suspected of causing allergic reactions and observing the person to see if there is a reduction in symptoms in the absence of particular foods. This method is often recommended for children, as it is easier to follow than the standard elimination diet. The more rigorous method (which is a true elimination diet) reverses this strategy by eliminating many foods at the outset and then reintroducing suspected allergens (allergy-producing substances) one at a time. Elimination diets often include a rotation component, by which even the limited foods allowed at the beginning are allocated in such a way that no single food is eaten more than once within a three-day period. This feature has two purposes. First, it alleviates the monotony of a limited diet. Second, it allows for the possibility that some persons may even be allergic to the relatively safe foods allowed initially. If there is an allergic reaction at this stage, rotating foods makes it possible to identify the cause of the problem.

An elimination diet is divided into two parts: the elimination phase and the reintroduction (or food challenge) phase. During the elimination phase, which generally lasts between one and two weeks, as many known allergy-producing foods as possible are eliminated from the diet. Foods commonly known to cause allergies include: citrus fruits, strawberries, corn, peas, tomatoes, peanuts, nuts, legumes, soy products, wheat, oats, chicken, shellfish, eggs, dairy products, cow's milk, vinegar and other products of fermentation, coffee and tea, cane sugar, chocolate, and food additives. The elimination diet can be very strict or more liberalized depending on the severity of the symptoms. It is important to personalize the diet whenever possible.

During the elimination phase of the diet, which clears the body of allergens, ingredient labels for all processed foods should be carefully scrutinized to make sure that none of the proscribed foods makes its way into the diet. Different diets handle the reintroduction phase differently. In some cases, the "test" foods are introduced at three-day intervals while in others, a new food is reintroduced every day for 15 days. Foods should be reintroduced in as pure a form as possible (for example, cream of wheat rather than bread) for maximum certainty that the resulting effects are produced by the substance in question rather than by some other ingredient added during the manufacturing process.

A strict elimination diet should not be undertaken without the supervision of a physician and/or dietitian.

Another way to identify food allergies is to keep a food diary, recording everything eaten for a period of three or four weeks and noting any allergic reactions during that period.

Risks

The elimination phase of the diet should not last more than two weeks, since this restricted regimen will lack some essential nutrients. Also, a child's growth may be affected if placed on an elimination diet for an extended period. For example, a child with a cow's milk allergy must obtain his calcium, vitamin D, and other essential nutrients found in milk from other sources. Children with food allergies need to be followed by a physician and or dietitian to ensure they are not at risk for growth problems or inadequate intake of nutrients.

Normal results

Persons with chronic food allergies should see their symptoms subside during the elimination period. Sometimes they may experience withdrawal, an episode in which symptoms may actually worsen before they subside. These include: bloating, food cravings, **headache**, fatigue, and general aches and pains. This condition may last for a few days. Upon reintroduction of the offending food, these symptoms should return and are often worse than previously reported.

Parental concerns

In order to effectively eliminate the offending foods, a parent should be educated on label reading, cross-contact, and selecting alternate foods for an allergic child.

Resources

BOOKS

Kleinman, Ronald E., and the American Academy of Pediatrics Committee on Nutrition. *Pediatric Nutrition Handbook*, 5th ed. Elk Grove Village, IL: American Academy of Pediatrics, 2003.

Mahan, L. Kathleen, and Sylvia Escott-Stump. *Krause's Food, Nutrition, & Diet Therapy*, 10th ed. Philadelphia: Saunders, 2000.

Physicians Committee for Responsible Medicine. *Healthy Eating for Life for Children*. Hoboken, NJ: Wiley, 2002.

Willett, Walter C., and P. J. Skerrett. *Eat, Drink, and Be Healthy: The Harvard Medical School Guide to Healthy Eating*. New York: Simon & Schuster Source, 2002.

PERIODICALS

Christie, Lynn, et al. "Food Allergies in Children Affect Nutrient Intake and Growth." *Journal of the American Dietetic Association* 102, no. 11 (November 2002): 1648–51.

Mofidi, Shideh. "Nutritional Management of Pediatric Food Hypersensitivity." *Pediatrics* 111, no. 6 (June 2003): 1645–53.

Schiltz, Barbara. "Elimination Diet: Food Challenge Tools for Patients with Allergies." *Journal of the American Dietetic Association* 103, no. 4 (April 2003).

ORGANIZATIONS

American Academy of Pediatrics. 141 Northwest Point Blvd., Elk Grove Village, IL 60007–1098. Web site: <www.aap.org>.

American Dietetic Association. 120 South Riverside Plaza, Suite 2000, Chicago, IL 60606–6995. (Web site: <www.eatright.org>.

Laura Kim Saltel Allan, R.D.

Embryonic development *see* **Prenatal development**

Encephalitis

Definition

Encephalitis is an inflammation of the brain, usually caused by a direct viral infection or a hypersensitivity reaction to a virus or foreign protein. Brain inflammation caused by a bacterial infection is sometimes called cerebritis. When both the brain and spinal cord are involved, the disorder is called encephalomyelitis. An inflammation of the brain's covering, or meninges, is called **meningitis**.

Description

Encephalitis is an inflammation of the brain. The inflammation is a reaction of the body's immune system to infection or invasion. During the inflammation, the brain's tissues become swollen. The combination of the infection and the immune reaction to it can cause **headache** and a **fever**, as well as more severe symptoms in some cases.

The viruses causing primary encephalitis can be epidemic or sporadic. The **polio** virus is an epidemic cause. Arthropod-borne viral encephalitis is responsible for most epidemic viral encephalitis. The viruses live in animal hosts and mosquitoes that transmit the disease. The most common form of non-epidemic or sporadic encephalitis is caused by the **herpes simplex** virus, type 1 (HSV-1) and has a high rate of death. **Mumps** is another example of a sporadic cause.

Demographics

Approximately 2,000 cases of encephalitis are reported to the Centers for Disease Control and Prevention in Atlanta, Georgia, each year. Encephalitis can strike anyone, at any age, although some kinds of encephalitis are more common in children. Other kinds of encephalitis can affect anyone, but may affect children more severely.

Causes and symptoms

There are more than a dozen viruses that can cause encephalitis, spread by either human-to human contact or by animal **bites**. Encephalitis may occur with several common viral infections of childhood. Viruses and viral diseases that may cause encephalitis include:

- **chickenpox**
- **measles**
- mumps
- Epstein-Barr virus (EBV)
- cytomegalovirus infection
- HIV
- herpes simplex
- herpes zoster (shingles)
- herpes B
- polio
- **rabies**
- mosquito-borne viruses (arboviruses)

Primary encephalitis is caused by direct infection by the virus, while secondary encephalitis is due to a post-infectious immune reaction to viral infection elsewhere in the body. Secondary encephalitis may occur with measles, chickenpox, mumps, **rubella**, and EBV. In secondary encephalitis, symptoms usually begin five to ten days after the onset of the disease itself and are related to the breakdown of the myelin sheath that covers nerve fibers.

In rare cases, encephalitis may follow **vaccination** against some of the viral diseases listed above. Creutzfeldt-Jakob disease, a very rare brain disorder caused by an infectious particle called a prion, may also cause encephalitis.

Mosquitoes spread viruses responsible for equine encephalitis (eastern and western types), St. Louis encephalitis, California encephalitis, and Japanese encephalitis. **Lyme disease**, spread by ticks, can cause encephalitis, as can Colorado tick fever. Rabies is most often spread by animal bites from dogs, cats, mice, raccoons, squirrels, and bats and may cause encephalitis.

Equine encephalitis is carried by mosquitoes that do not normally bite humans but do bite horses and birds. It is occasionally picked up from these animals by mosquitoes that do bite humans. Japanese encephalitis and St. Louis encephalitis are also carried by mosquitoes. The risk of contracting a mosquito-borne virus is greatest in mid- to late summer, when mosquitoes are most active, in those rural areas where these viruses are known to exist. Eastern equine encephalitis occurs in eastern and southeastern United States; western equine and California encephalitis occur throughout the West; and St. Louis encephalitis occurs throughout the country. Japanese encephalitis does not occur in the United States but is found throughout much of Asia. The viruses responsible for these diseases are classified as arbovirus, and these diseases are collectively called arbovirus encephalitis.

Herpes simplex encephalitis, the most common form of sporadic encephalitis in western countries, is a disease with significantly high mortality. It occurs in children and adults and both sides of the brain are affected. It is theorized that brain infection is caused by the virus moving from a peripheral location to the brain via two nerves, the olfactory and the trigeminal (largest nerves in the skull).

Herpes simplex encephalitis is responsible for 10 percent of all encephalitis cases and is the main cause of sporadic, fatal encephalitis. In untreated people, the rate of death is 70 percent while the mortality is 15 to 20 percent in persons who have been treated with acyclovir. The symptoms of herpes simplex encephalitis are fever, rapidly disintegrating mental state, headache, and behavioral changes.

The symptoms of encephalitis range from very mild to very severe and may include:

- headache
- fever
- lethargy (sleepiness, decreased alertness, and fatigue)
- malaise
- **nausea and vomiting**
- visual disturbances
- tremor
- decreased consciousness (drowsiness, confusion, delirium, and unconsciousness)
- stiff neck
- seizures

Symptoms may progress rapidly, changing from mild to severe within several days or even several hours.

When to call the doctor

A physician should be called whenever a headache does not respond to medication or when a person experiences a fever over 104°F (40.0°C), **nausea and vomiting**, visual disturbances, a stiff neck, or seizures.

A doctor should be called when an infant's temperature rises above 100°F (37.8°C) and cannot be brought down within a few minutes. Infants whose temperatures exceed 102°F (38.9°C) should be sponge-bathed in cool water while waiting for emergency help to arrive.

Diagnosis

Diagnosis of encephalitis includes careful questioning to determine possible exposure to viral sources. Tests that can help confirm the diagnosis and rule out other disorders include:

- blood tests (to detect antibodies to viral antigens and foreign proteins)
- cerebrospinal fluid analysis, or spinal tap (to detect viral antigens and provide culture specimens for the virus or bacteria that may be present in the cerebrospinal fluid)
- electroencephalogram (EEG)
- CT and MRI scans

A brain biopsy (surgical gathering of a small tissue sample) may be recommended in some cases in which treatment has thus far been ineffective and the cause of the encephalitis is unclear. Definite diagnosis by biopsy may allow specific treatment that would otherwise be too risky.

Treatment

Choice of treatment for encephalitis depends on the cause. Bacterial encephalitis is treated with **antibiotics**. Viral encephalitis is usually treated with **antiviral drugs**, including acyclovir, ganciclovir, foscarnet, ribavirin, and AZT. Viruses that respond to acyclovir include herpes simplex, the most common cause of sporadic (non-epidemic) encephalitis in the United States.

The symptoms of encephalitis may be treated with a number of different drugs. Corticosteroids, including prednisone and dexamethasone, are sometimes prescribed to reduce inflammation and brain swelling. Anticonvulsant drugs, including phenytoin, are used to control seizures. Fever may be reduced with **acetaminophen** or other fever-reducing drugs.

A person with encephalitis must be monitored carefully, since symptoms may change rapidly. Blood tests may be required regularly to track levels of fluids and salts in the blood.

KEY TERMS

Cerebrospinal fluid analysis—A laboratory test, important in diagnosing diseases of the central nervous system, that examines a sample of the fluid surrounding the brain and spinal cord. The fluid is withdrawn through a needle in a procedure called a lumbar puncture.

Computed tomography (CT)—An imaging technique in which cross-sectional x rays of the body are compiled to create a three-dimensional image of the body's internal structures; also called computed axial tomography.

Electroencephalogram (EEG)—A record of the tiny electrical impulses produced by the brain's activity picked up by electrodes placed on the scalp. By measuring characteristic wave patterns, the EEG can help diagnose certain conditions of the brain.

Inflammation—Pain, redness, swelling, and heat that develop in response to tissue irritation or injury. It usually is caused by the immune system's response to the body's contact with a foreign substance, such as an allergen or pathogen.

Magnetic resonance imaging (MRI)—An imaging technique that uses a large circular magnet and radio waves to generate signals from atoms in the body. These signals are used to construct detailed images of internal body structures and organs, including the brain.

Vaccine—A substance prepared from a weakened or killed microorganism which, when injected, helps the body to form antibodies that will prevent infection by the natural microorganism.

Virus—A small infectious agent consisting of a core of genetic material (DNA or RNA) surrounded by a shell of protein. A virus needs a living cell to reproduce.

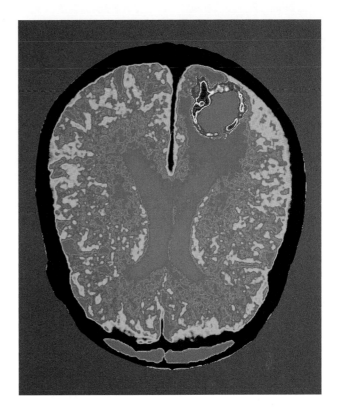

Computed tomography scan (CT scan) of a child with encephalitis. The right side of the brain shows abnormal dilation of the ventricles (orange). *(© Airelle-Joubert/Photo Researchers, Inc.)*

Prognosis

Encephalitis symptoms may last several weeks. Most cases of encephalitis are mild, and recovery is usually quick. Mild encephalitis usually leaves no residual neurological problems. Overall, approximately 10 percent of those with encephalitis die from their infections or complications such as secondary infection. Some forms of encephalitis have more severe courses, including herpes encephalitis, in which mortality is 15 to 20 percent with treatment, and 70 to 80 percent without. Antiviral treatment is ineffective for eastern equine encephalitis, and mortality is approximately 30 percent.

Permanent neurological consequences may follow recovery in some cases. Consequences may include personality changes, memory loss, language difficulties, seizures, and partial paralysis.

Prevention

Because encephalitis is caused by infection, it may be prevented by avoiding the infection. Minimizing contact with others who have any of the viral illnesses listed above may reduce one's chances of becoming infected. Most infections are spread by hand-to-hand or hand-to-mouth contact; frequent hand washing may reduce the likelihood of infection if contact cannot be avoided.

Mosquito-borne viruses may be avoided by preventing mosquito bites. Mosquitoes are most active at dawn and dusk and are most common in moist areas with standing water. Covering skin and using mosquito repellents on exposed skin can reduce the chances of being bitten.

Vaccines are available against some viruses, including polio, herpes B, Japanese encephalitis, and equine encephalitis. **Rabies vaccine** is available for animals; it is also given to people after exposure. Japanese encephalitis vaccine is recommended for those traveling to Asia and staying in affected rural areas during transmission season.

Nutritional concerns

Adequate **nutrition** and fluids improve the chances for a full recovery from encephalitis.

Parental concerns

Parents should carefully monitor their infants and young children for symptoms of fever. Any fever that exceeds 103°F (39.4°C) for more than a few minutes should be promptly treated. Any complaints of a stiff neck, loss of consciousness, unexplained vomiting, or seizure activity should be promptly brought to competent medical attention.

Resources

BOOKS

Halstead, Scott A. "Arbovirus Encephalitis in North America." In *Nelson Textbook of Pediatrics*, 17th ed. Edited by Richard E. Behrman et al. Philadelphia: Saunders, 2003, pp. 1086–8.

Johnston, Michael V. "Encephalopathies." In *Nelson Textbook of Pediatrics*, 17th ed. Edited by Richard E. Behrman et al. Philadelphia: Saunders, 2003, pp. 2023–8.

Nath, Avindra, and Joseph R. Berger. "Acute Viral Meningitis and Encephalitis." In *Cecil Textbook of Medicine*, 22nd ed. Edited by Lee Goldman, et al. Philadelphia: Saunders, 2003, pp. 2232–5.

Tyler, Kenneth L. "Viral Meningitis and Encephalitis." In *Harrison's Principles of Internal Medicine*, 15th ed. Edited by Eugene Braunwald et al. New York: McGraw-Hill, 2001, pp. 2471–80.

PERIODICALS

Arciniegas, D. B., and C. A. Anderson. "Viral encephalitis: neuropsychiatric and neurobehavioral aspects." *Current Psychiatry Reports* 6, no. 5 (2004): 372–9.

Cunha, B. A. "Differential diagnosis of West Nile encephalitis." *Current Opinions in Infectious Disease* 17, no. 5 (2004): 413–20.

Lyle, P., et al. "Evaluation of encephalitis in the toddler: what part of negative don't you understand?" *Current Opinions in Pediatrics* 16, no. 5 (2004): 567–70.

Morgan, R. "West Nile viral encephalitis: a case study." *Journal of Neuroscience of Nursing* 36, no. 4 (2004): 185–8.

Savas, L., et al. "Full recovered meningoencephalomyelitis caused by mumps virus." *European Journal of Neurology* 11, no. 9 (2004): 639–40.

ORGANIZATIONS

American Academy of Neurology. 1080 Montreal Avenue, St. Paul, MN 55116. Web site: <www.aan.com>.

American Academy of Pediatrics. 141 Northwest Point Blvd., Elk Grove Village, IL 60007–1098. Web site: <www.aap.org/>.

American College of Emergency Physicians. PO Box 619911, Dallas, TX 75261-9911. Web site: <www.acep.org/>.

WEB SITES

"Arboviral Encephalitides." *Centers for Disease Control and Prevention.* Available online at <www.cdc.gov/ncidod/dvbid/arbor/> (accessed January 5, 2005).

"Encephalitis." *Mayo Clinic.* Available online at <www.mayoclinic.com/invoke.cfm?id=DS00226> (accessed January 5, 2005).

"Encephalitis." *MedlinePlus.* Available online at <www.nlm.nih.gov/medlineplus/encephalitis.html> (accessed January 5, 2005).

"Encephalitis." *World Health Organization.* Available online at <www.who.int/topics/encephalitis/en/> (accessed January 5, 2005).

Encephalitis Information Resource. Available online at <www.encephalitis.info/> (accessed January 5, 2005).

"NINDS Encephalitis and Meningitis Information Page." *National Institute of Neurological Disorders and Stroke.* Available online at <www.ninds.nih.gov/health_and_medical/disorders/encmenin_doc.htm> (accessed January 5, 2005).

L. Fleming Fallon, Jr., MD, DrPH

Encopresis

Definition

Encopresis is defined as repeated involuntary defecation somewhere other than a toilet by a child age four or older that continues for at least one month.

Description

Soiling, fecal soiling, and fecal incontinence are alternate terms used for this behavior. Whatever the cause, parents should talk openly about the problem with the child. When parents treat a bowel problem as a cause for embarrassment or shame, they may unintentionally aggravate or prolong it.

Demographics

About 1 to 3 percent of children are affected by encopresis. More boys than girls are affected.

Causes and symptoms

Encopresis can be one of two types, nonretentive encopresis and retentive encopresis. About 80 to 95 percent of all cases are retentive encopresis. Children with this disorder have an underlying medical reason for soiling. The remaining cases have no physical condition that bars normal toileting behaviors. This type, nonretentive encopresis, is a behavioral condition in which the child refuses to defecate in a toilet.

Retentive encopresis is most often the result of chronic **constipation** and fecal impaction. In these children, feces have become impacted in the child's colon, causing it to distend. This causes the child to not feel the urge to defecate. The anal sphincter muscle becomes weak and unable to contain the soft stools that pass around the impaction. Despite the constipation, these children actually do have regular, though soft, bowel movements that they are unable to control. The child may not even be aware that he or she has defecated until the fecal matter has already passed. Many children have a history of constipation that extends back as far as five years before the problem is brought to medical attention.

A child may exhibit nonretentive encopresis, or functional encopresis, for several reasons. First, he or she may not be ready for **toilet training**. When a child is learning appropriate toilet habits during toddlerhood and **preschool** years, involuntary or inappropriate bowel movements are common. Second, the child may be afraid of the toilet or of defecating in public places like school. Others may use fecal incontinence to manipulate their parent or other adults. These children often have other serious behavioral problems.

When to call the doctor

A doctor should be called whenever children experience unresolved constipation or difficulty controlling their stools.

Diagnosis

Before beginning treatment for encopresis, the pediatrician first looks for any physical cause for the inappropriate bowel movements. The doctor asks parents about the child's earlier toilet training and typical toileting behaviors and inquires about a history of constipation. The doctor will digitally examine the child's anal area to check the strength of the anal sphincter muscle and look for a fecal impaction. An abdominal x ray may be needed to confirm the size and position of the impaction.

Treatment

If the pediatrician makes a diagnosis of retentive encopresis, the physician may recommend **laxatives**, stool softeners, or an enema to free the impaction. Subsequently, the doctor may make several suggestions for to avoid chronic constipation. Children should eat a high-fiber diet, with lots of fruits, vegetables, and whole grains. They should be encouraged to drink larger amounts of water and get regular **exercise**. Children should be taught to not feel ashamed of toileting behaviors, and psychotherapy may help decrease the sense of shame and guilt that many children feel.

If no fecal impaction is found, the pediatrician works with a counselor or psychiatrist to analyze the variables that characterize the encopresis. If the child is not physically or cognitively ready for toilet training, it should be postponed.

In the remainder of nonretentive encopresis cases, treatment should then center on making sure the child has comfortable bowel movements, since some cases of nonretentive encopresis involve some level of discomfort associated with constipation.

Prognosis

The prognosis for most children with encopresis is good, assuming that all underlying problems are identified and appropriately treated.

Prevention

There is no known way to prevent encopresis. Experienced counselors suggest that early identification of problems and accurate diagnosis are useful in limiting the severity and duration of encopresis.

Nutritional concerns

A high-fiber diet may be recommended for persons with encopresis. Affected persons should consume lots of fruits, vegetables, and whole grains. Adequate to copious intake of fluids are also recommended.

Parental concerns

Parents of a child with a serious behavior disorder like **oppositional defiant disorder** should work with their child's therapist to deal with encopresis in the context of other behavioral problems. Parents should work with their children to establish appropriate stooling behaviors and institute a system of rewards for successful toileting.

Resources

BOOKS

Boris, Neil, and Richard Dalton. "Vegetative Disorders." In *Nelson Textbook of Pediatrics*, 17th ed. Edited by Richard E. Behrman et al. Philadelphia: Saunders, 2003, pp. 73–9.

Brazelton, T. Berry, et al. *Toilet Training: The Brazelton Way.* Cambridge, MA: Perseus Publishing, 2003.

Perkin, Steven R. *Gastrointestinal Health: The Proven Nutritional Program to Prevent, Cure, or Alleviate Irritable Bowel Syndrome (IBS), Ulcers, Gas, Constipation, Heartburn, and Many Other Digestive Disorders.* London: Harper Trade, 2005.

PERIODICALS

De Lorijn, F., et al. "Prognosis of constipation: clinical factors and colonic transit time." *Archives of Disease in Childhood* 89, no. 8 (2004): 723–7.

Loening-Baucke, V. "Functional fecal retention with encopresis in childhood." *Journal of Pediatric Gastroenterology and Nutrition* 38, no. 1 (2004): 79–84.

Schonwald, A., and L. Rappaport. "Consultation with the specialist: encopresis: assessment and management." *Pediatric Reviews* 25, no. 8 (2004): 278–83.

Voskuijl, W. P., et al. "Use of Rome II criteria in childhood defecation disorders: applicability in clinical and research practice." *Journal of Pediatrics* 145, no. 2 (2004): 213–7.

ORGANIZATIONS

American Academy of Pediatrics. 141 Northwest Point Blvd., Elk Grove Village, IL 60007–1098. Web site: <www.aap.org>.

American College of Gastroenterology. 4900 B South 31st St., Arlington VA 22206. Web site: <www.acg.gi.org/>.

WEB SITES

"Encopresis." *eMedicine.* Available online at <www.emedicine.com/ped/topic670.htm> (accessed January 6, 2005).

"Encopresis." *MedlinePlus.* Available online at <www.nlm.nih.gov/medlineplus/ency/article/001570.htm> (accessed January 6, 2005).

"Encopresis." *Merck Manual.* Available online at <www.merck.com/mmhe/sec23/ch269/ch269d.html> (accessed January 6, 2005).

"Stool Soiling and Constipation in Children." *American Academy of Family Physicians.* Available online at <http://familydoctor.org/x1782.xml> (accessed January 6, 2005).

L. Fleming Fallon, Jr., MD, DrPH

Enterobacterial infections

Definition

Enterobacterial infections are disorders of the digestive tract and other organ systems produced by a group of rod-shaped bacteria called Enterobacteriaceae.

Description

Enterobacterial infections can be produced by bacteria that normally live in the human digestive tract without causing serious disease or by bacteria that enter from the outside. The most troublesome organism in this group is *Escherichia coli*. Other examples of enterobacteria are species of *Salmonella*, *Shigella*, *Klebsiella*, *Enterobacter*, *Serratia*, *Proteus*, and *Yersinia*.

Transmission

Enterobacterial infections in the digestive tract typically start when the organisms invade the mucous tissues that line the digestive tract. They may be bacteria that are already present in the stomach and intestines, or they may be transmitted by contaminated food and water. It is also possible for enterobacterial infections to spread by person-to-person contact. In many cases these infections are nosocomial, which means that they can be acquired in the hospital. The usual incubation period is 12 to 72 hours.

Demographics

Diarrhea caused by enterobacteria is a common problem in the United States. It is estimated that each person has an average of 1.5 episodes of diarrhea each year, with higher rates in children, institutionalized people, and Native Americans. This type of enterobacterial infection can range from a minor nuisance to a life-threatening disorder, especially in infants; elderly persons; patients with **immunodeficiency**, including acquired immunodeficiency syndrome (**AIDS**); and malnourished people. Enterobacterial infections are one of the two leading killers of children in developing countries.

Causes and symptoms

E. coli infections cause most of the enterobacterial infections in the United States. The organisms are categorized according to whether they are invasive or noninvasive. Noninvasive types of *E. coli* include what are called enteropathogenic *E. coli* (EPEC), and enterotoxigenic *E. coli* (ETEC). EPEC and ETEC types produce a bacterial poison (toxin) in the stomach that interacts with the digestive juices and causes the patient to lose large amounts of water through the intestines.

The invasive types of *E. coli* are called enterohemorrhagic *E. coli* (EHEC), and enteroinvasive *E. coli,* (EIEC). These subtypes invade the stomach tissues directly, causing tissue destruction and bloody stools. EHEC can produce complications leading to hemolytic-uremic syndrome (HUS), a potentially fatal disorder marked by the destruction of red blood cells and kidney failure. EHEC has become a growing problem in the United States because of outbreaks caused by contaminated food. A particular type of EHEC known as O157:H7 has been identified since 1982 in undercooked hamburgers and unpasteurized milk and apple juice. Between 2 and 7 percent of infections caused by O157:H7 develop into HUS.

Klebsiella and *Proteus* sometimes cause urinary tract infections; **pneumonia** occurs generally in immunocompromised hosts or alcoholics, and ear and sinus infections in immunocompromised hosts. *Enterobacter* and *Serratia* can cause bacterial infection of the blood (bacteremia), particularly in patients with weakened immune systems.

Symptoms

The symptoms of enterobacterial infections are sometimes classified according to the type of diarrhea they produce.

WATERY DIARRHEA Patients infected with ETEC and some types of EPEC develop watery diarrhea. Rarely *Shigella* and *Salmonella* cause watery diarrhea. These infections are located in the small intestine, result from bacterial toxins interacting with digestive juices, do not produce inflammation, and do not usually need treatment with **antibiotics**.

BLOODY DIARRHEA (DYSENTERY) Bloody diarrhea, sometimes called dysentery, is produced by EHEC, EIEC, some types of *Salmonella*, some types of *Shigella*, and *Yersinia*. In dysentery, the infection is located in the colon, cells and tissues are destroyed, inflammation is present, and antibiotic therapy is usually required.

NECROTIZING ENTEROCOLITIS (NEC) **Necrotizing enterocolitis** (NEC) is a disorder that begins in newborn infants shortly after birth. Although NEC was not as of 2004 fully understood, it is thought that it results from a bacterial or viral invasion of damaged intestinal tissues. The disease organisms then cause the death (necrosis) of bowel tissue or gangrene of the bowel. NEC is primarily a disease of **prematurity**; 60–80 percent of cases occur in high-risk preterm infants. NEC is responsible for 2–5 percent of cases in newborn intensive care units (NICU). Enterobacteriaceae that have been identified in infants with NEC include *Salmonella, E. coli, Klebsiella,* and *Enterobacter.*

When to call the doctor

A healthcare professional should be called if an infected child exhibits any of the following symptoms:

- symptoms of **dehydration** such as decreased urination, dry mouth, irritability, and few or no tears when crying
- **vomiting** for more than three days
- **fever** greater than 102.2°F (39°C) in a toddler or older child, or any fever in an infant less than six months old
- fever that cannot be controlled with **acetaminophen** (Tylenol) or ibuprofen (Motrin), or that lasts more than three days
- presence of blood in diarrhea
- hard, swollen belly

Diagnosis

In order to confirm a diagnosis of enterobacterial infection, physicians usually rely on patient history, physical examination, and laboratory tests.

Patient history

The diagnosis of enterobacterial infections is complicated by the fact that viruses, protozoa, and other types of bacteria can also cause diarrhea. In most cases of mild diarrhea, it is not critical to identify the organism because the disorder is self-limiting. Some groups of patients, however, should have stool tests. They include:

- patients with bloody diarrhea
- patients with watery diarrhea who have become dehydrated
- patients with watery diarrhea that has lasted longer than three days without decreasing in amount
- patients with disorders of the immune system

The patient history is useful for public health reasons as well as a help to the doctor in determining what type of enterobacterium may be causing the infection. The doctor will ask about the frequency and appearance of the diarrhea as well as about other digestive symptoms. If the patient is nauseated and vomiting, the infection is more likely to be located in the small intestine. If the patient is running a fever, a diagnosis of dysentery is more likely. The doctor will also ask if anyone else in the patient's **family** or workplace is sick. Some types of enterobacteriaceae are more likely to cause group outbreaks than others. Other questions pertain to the patient's food intake over the previous few days and recent travels to countries with typhoid fever or cholera outbreaks.

Physical examination

The most important parts of the physical examination are checking for signs of severe fluid loss and examining the abdomen. The doctor will look at the inside of the patient's mouth and evaluate the skin for signs of dehydration. The presence of a skin rash and an enlarged spleen suggests typhoid fever rather than a bacterial infection. If the patient's abdomen hurts when the doctor examines it, a diagnosis of dysentery is more likely.

Laboratory tests

The stool test is most commonly used for identifying the cause of diarrhea. Examining a stool sample under a microscope can help to rule out parasitic and protozoal infections. Routine stool cultures, however, cannot be used to identify any of the four types of E. coli that cause intestinal infections. ETEC, EPEC, and EIEC are unusual in the United States and can usually be identified only by specialists in research laboratories. Because of concern about EHEC outbreaks, however, most laboratories in the United States as of 204 screen for O157:H7 with a test that identifies its characteristic toxin. All patients with bloody diarrhea should have a stool sample tested for E. coli O157:H7.

Treatment

The initial treatment of enterobacterial diarrhea is usually empiric. Empiric means that the doctor treats the patient on the basis of the visible symptoms and professional experience in treating infections, without waiting for laboratory test results. In uncomplicated cases, symptoms usually go away within five to ten days without treatment of antibiotics. In other cases, antibiotics may be necessary to overcome the infection. Newborn infants and patients with immune system disorders are given antibiotics once the organism has been identified. Gentamicin, tobramycin, and amikacin are in the early 2000s used more frequently to treat enterobacterial infections because many of the organisms are becoming resistant to ampicillin and cephalosporin antibiotics.

Alternative treatment

Alternative treatments for diarrhea are intended to relieve the discomfort of abdominal cramping. Most alternative practitioners advise consulting a medical doctor if the patient has sunken eyes, dry eyes or mouth, or other signs of dehydration.

HERBAL MEDICINE Herbalists may recommend cloves taken as an infusion or ginger given in drop doses to control intestinal cramps, eliminate gas, and prevent vomiting. Peppermint (*Mentha piperita*) or chamomile (*Matricaria recutita*) tea may also ease cramps and intestinal spasms.

HOMEOPATHY Homeopathic practitioners frequently recommend *Arsenicum album* for diarrhea caused by contaminated food and *Belladonna* for diarrhea that comes on suddenly with mucus in the stools. *Veratrum album* would be given for watery diarrhea, and *Podophyllum* for diarrhea with few other symptoms.

Nutritional concerns

Because of the extensive loss of water through diarrhea, it is important to prevent dehydration. The affected child should be encouraged to drink fluids such as water, breast milk or formula (if applicable), electrolyte replacement drinks, or clear broths. Diluted juice should be avoided because juice can worsen diarrhea. Drinks with **caffeine** should be avoided because of caffeine's diuretic effects (i.e., causes water to be lost through urine).

Prognosis

The prognosis for most enterobacterial infections is good; most patients recover in about a week or ten days without needing antibiotics. HUS, on the other hand, has a mortality rate of 35 percent even with intensive care. About one-third of the survivors have long-term problems with kidney function, and another 8 percent develop high blood pressure, seizure disorders, and blindness.

KEY TERMS

Dysentery—A disease marked by frequent watery bowel movements, often with blood and mucus, and characterized by pain, urgency to have a bowel movement, fever, and dehydration.

Empirical treatment—Medical treatment that is given on the basis of the doctor's observations and experience.

Escherichia coli—A type of enterobacterium that is responsible for most cases of severe bacterial diarrhea in the United States.

Hemolytic-uremic syndrome (HUS)—A potentially fatal complication of *E. coli* infection characterized by kidney failure and destruction of red blood cells.

Necrotizing enterocolitis—A serious bacterial infection of the intestine that occurs primarily in sick or premature newborn infants. It can cause death of intestinal tissue (necrosis) and may progress to blood poisoning (septicemia).

Nosocomial infection—An infection acquired in a hospital setting.

Toxin—A poisonous substance usually produced by a microorganism or plant.

Prevention

The World Health Organization (WHO) offers the following suggestions for preventing enterobacterial infections, including *E. coli* O157:H7 dysentery:

- Cook ground beef or hamburgers until the meat is thoroughly done. Juices from the meat should be completely clear, not pink or red. All parts of the meat should reach a temperature of 158°F (70°C) or higher.

- Do not drink unpasteurized milk or fruit juices or use products made from raw milk.

- Wash hands thoroughly and frequently, especially after using the toilet.

- Wash fruits and vegetables carefully or peel them. Keep all kitchen surfaces and serving utensils clean.

- If drinking water is not known to be safe, boil it or drink bottled water.

- Keep cooked foods separate from raw foods and avoid touching cooked foods with knives or other utensils that have been used with raw meat.

Parental concerns

Because of the extensive media coverage that often follows outbreaks of enterobacterial infections such as *E. coli*, many parents associate such infections with eating undercooked meat such as hamburger. It is important, however, that other modes of transmission be considered, such as poorly or infrequently washed hands. Frequent hand washing is encouraged for caregivers and children alike, particularly in settings such as daycares and schools.

Resources

BOOKS

Eisenstein, Barry I., and Dori F. Zaleznik. "Enterobacteriaeae." In *Principles and Practice of Infectious Diseases*, 5th ed. Edited by Gerald L. Mandell, John E. Bennett, and Raphael Dolin. New York: Churchill Livingstone, 2000.

Rozenberg-Arska, Maja, and Maarten R. Visser. "Enterobacteriaeae." In *Infectious Diseases*. Edited by Jonathan Cohen et al. New York: Mosby, 2004.

ORGANIZATIONS

Centers for Disease Control and Prevention. 1600 Clifton Rd., NE, Atlanta, GA 30333. Web site: <www.cdc.gov>.

WEB SITES

Cuthill, Sara L. "*Escherichia coli* Infections." *eMedicine*, October 16, 2003. Available online at <www.emedicine.com/ped/topic2696.htm> (accessed January 6, 2005).

"*Escherichia coli* O157:H7." *Centers for Disease Control and Prevention*, January 27, 2004. Available online at <www.cdc.gov/ncidod/dbmd/diseaseinfo/escherichiacoli_g.htm> (accessed January 6, 2005).

Rebecca J. Frey, PhD
Stephanie Dionne Sherk

Enuresis *see* **Bed-wetting**

Eosinophilic gastroenteropathies

Definition

Eosinophilic gastroenteropathies are gastrointestinal (GI) diseases (enteropathies) in which one or more layers of the GI tract (most commonly the stomach and small intestine) are selectively infiltrated with a type of white blood cell called eosinophils, as part of an allergic response.

Description

Eosinophilic gastroenteropathies are characterized by the accumulation of an abnormally large number of eosinophils (eosinophilic infiltration) in one or more specific places anywhere in the digestive system and associated lymph nodes resulting in **nausea**, difficulty swallowing, abdominal **pain**, **vomiting** and **diarrhea**, excessive loss of proteins in the GI tract, and **failure to thrive**. All gastroenteropathies are characterized by the presence of abnormal GI symptoms, eosinophilic infiltration in one or more areas of the GI tract, and the absence of an identified cause for the formation of an abnormally large number of eosinophils in the blood (eosinophilia). Some patients also suffer loss of protein from the body that often results in low blood levels of albumin and total protein (protein-losing enteropathy) due to increased GI tract permeability. As the GI tract wall becomes infiltrated with large numbers of eosinophils, its normal architecture is disrupted, and so is its function. Eosinophils are immune system white blood cells that destroy parasitic organisms and play a major role in allergic reactions. For this reason, the gastroenteropathies are often considered as food-related gastrointestinal allergy syndromes.

Eosinophilic gastroenteropathies have a specific name corresponding to the area of the digestive system where the highest numbers of eosinophils are found. They include the following:

- eosinophilic **gastroenteritis** (EG), in which eosinophilic infiltration occurs in one or more layers of the stomach and/or small intestine

- eosinophilic esophagitis (EE), in which eosinophilic infiltration is confined to the muscular tube that carries food from the throat to the stomach (esophagus)

- eosinophilic colitis (EC), in which the infiltration is confined to the large intestine (colon)

- eosinophilic duodenitis (ED), in which the infiltration is confined to the small intestine

Eosinophilic gastroenteritis (EG) is the best characterized gastroenteropathy. It is classified according to the layer of the GI tract involved, and mixed forms also occur. The walls of the GI tract have four layers of tissue, called mucosa, submucosa, muscularis externa, and serosa. The innermost layer is the mucosa, a membrane that forms a continuous lining of the GI tract from the mouth to the anus. In the large bowel, this tissue contains cells that produce mucus to lubricate and protect the smooth inner surface of the bowel wall. Connective tissue and muscle separate the muscosa from the second layer, the submucosa, which contains blood vessels, lymph vessels, nerves, and glands. Next to the submucosa is the muscularis externa, consisting of two layers of muscle fibers, one that runs lengthwise and one that encircles the bowel. The fourth layer, the serosa, is a thin membrane that produces fluid to lubricate the outer surface of the bowel so that it can slide against adjacent organs. The different types of EG are:

- Pattern I eosinophilic gastroenteritis: Children affected with Pattern I EG have extensive infiltration of eosinophils in the area below the submucosa and muscularis layers. It is more commonly seen in the stomach (gastric antrum) but may also affect the small intestine or colon. Patients typically have intestinal obstruction. Cramping and abdominal pain associated with **nausea and vomiting** occur frequently. Food allergy and past history of allergy are less common in these patients than in patients with Pattern II EG.

- Pattern II eosinophilic gastroenteritis: In this the most prevalent form of EG, extensive infiltration of eosinophils occurs in the mucosal and submucosal layers. These patients have colicky abdominal pain, nausea, vomiting, diarrhea, and weight loss. Infants with Pattern II EG also commonly have a history of allergy. The condition may also be associated with protein-losing enteropathy, low levels of iron in the blood serum or in the bone marrow (iron-deficiency anemia), or impaired absorption of nutrients by the intestines (malabsorption). Growth retardation, delayed **puberty**, or abnormal menstruations has also been reported in children and adolescents with Pattern II EG.

- Pattern III eosinophilic gastroenteritis: This least common form of eosinophilic gastroenteropathy involves the serosal layer and the entire GI wall is usually affected. Its inflammation leads to an accumulation of fluid in the abdomen (ascites). This fluid contains many eosinophils and can infiltrate the membrane of the lungs (pleural effusion). A history of allergy also appears to be common in this group. Symptoms may include chest pain, **fever**, shortness of breath, and limited motion of the chest wall.

Eosinophilic esophagitis (EE) is characterized by the abnormal accumulation of eosinophils localized in the esophagus. In EE, high levels of eosinophils are detected in the esophagus but not in any other parts of the digestive tract. The presence of the eosinophils in the esophagus causes inflammation of its walls, which makes digestion extremely painful. Unlike that of normal children, the esophagus of an individual with EE does not have a smooth, uniform pink surface but displays lines (furrowing) and white patches. Children with EE have classic signs of gastroesophageal reflux (abdominal pain, difficulty swallowing, and vomiting) but fail to respond to antireflux medications. The danger of failing to diagnose this disorder is that children may be referred for unnecessary surgery because of their reflux symptoms.

Eosinophilic colitis (EC) is characterized by eosinophilic infiltration localized only in the large bowel, resulting in fever, diarrhea, bloody stools, **constipation**, obstruction/strictures, acute abdominal pain, and tenderness often localized in the right lower abdomen. EC often follows the onset of EG.

Eosinophilic duodenitis (ED) is characterized by eosinophilic inflammation of the small bowel that results in the production of leukotrienes, substances that participate in defense reactions and contribute to hypersensitivity and inflammation. Malabsorption of nutrients always results along with severe cramping, bowel obstruction, and intestinal bleeding with passage of bloody stools.

Related diseases

Other diseases feature enteropathies with symptoms similar to that of eosinophilic gastroenteropathies:

- Whipple's disease: This rare digestive disease of unknown origin affects the lining of the small intestine and results in malabsorption of nutrients. It may also affect other organs of the body.

- **Celiac disease** (celiac sprue): This chronic, hereditary, intestinal malabsorption disorder is caused by an intolerance to gluten, the insoluble component of wheat and other grains. Clinical improvement of symptoms follows withdrawal of gluten-containing grains in the diet.

- Mastocytosis: This genetic disorder is characterized by abnormal accumulations of a type of cell (mast cells) normally found in connective tissue. The liver, spleen, lungs, bone, skin, and sometimes the membrane surrounding the brain and spine (meninges) may be affected.

- Tropical sprue: This disorder unknown cause is characterized by malabsorption, multiple nutritional deficiencies, and abnormalities in the small bowel mucosa. It appears to be acquired and related to environmental and nutritional conditions and is most prevalent in the Caribbean, South India, and Southeast Asia.

- Crohn's disease: Also known as ileitis, regional enteritis, or granulomatous colitis, this disease is a form of inflammatory bowel disease characterized by severe, chronic inflammation of the wall of the GI tract.

- Dietary protein enteropathy: This disease is characterized by persistent diarrhea and vomiting with resulting malabsorption and failure to thrive with onset most commonly in infancy. Protein-losing enteropathy may lead to abnormally large amounts of fluid in the intercellular tissue spaces of the body (edema), abdominal distension, and lack of red blood cells (anemia).

- Dietary protein-induced proctocolitis: In generally healthy infants this disease of unknown origin causes visible specks or streaks of blood mixed with mucus in the stool. Blood loss is usually minimal, and anemia is rare. The disorder appears in the first months of life, with a mean age at diagnosis of two months.

Transmission

Although many factors have been identified as causing eosinophilic gastroenteropathies, some researchers suspect that undiscovered infections may also play a role. Thus, as of 2004, researches also believe an unknown mode of transmission may possibly be involved.

Demographics

In the United States, eosinophilic gastroenteritis is very rare, and the incidence is difficult to estimate. However, since Kaijser's description in 1937, more than 280 cases have been reported in the medical literature. Although cases have also been reported worldwide, the exact incidence is unclear because of a lack of diagnostic precision. Cases of EG are reported mostly in Caucasians, with some cases occurring among Asians. A slight male preponderance has also been documented. People with a history of **allergies**, eczema, and seasonal **asthma** are more likely to have this disease. Eosinophilic esophagitis was long thought to be a variant of stomach reflux disease. It is as of 2004 known to be a distinct disorder predominately occurring in children. A study published in the *New England Journal of Medicine* in 2004 shows that EE rates have risen so dramatically in recent years that they may be at higher levels than that of other inflammatory gastrointestinal disorders. At Cincinnati Children's hospital, cases of EE were examined in patients from Hamilton County. Between 1991 and 2003, 315 cases met diagnostic criteria for EE. Only 2.8 percent of these cases were identified prior to 2000. Of the 315 cases, 103 resided within the county. Incidence rates of EE have not been reported in any other region of the United States, so national incidence rates are impossible to determine. However, if rates were the same as they are in Hamilton County, the annual occurrence of EE would be one in every 10,000 children, or approximately 22,000 children in the United States. The exact incidence and prevalence of EC and ED are not known, but these diseases are occurring or being diagnosed with increasing frequency and are especially prominent in children.

Causes and symptoms

The eosinophil is a component of the immune system and is particularly involved with defense against parasites, but as of 2004 no parasite had been found responsible for any of the eosinophilic gastroenteropathies. The cause or mechanism of eosinophilic infiltration is also unknown, although some scientists suspect that the condition, first identified in Europe in the mid 1940s, is genetic, as it seems that in about 16 percent of known cases, an immediate **family** member is also diagnosed with an eosinophilic GI disorder. Various factors have been shown to trigger eosinophilic infiltration of the GI tract, and it has been shown that this, in turn, causes tissue damage by loss of cell granules (degranulation) and the untimely release of small proteins specialized in cell-to-cell communication (cytokines) that directly damage the GI tract wall. Examples of factors that are believed to have an incriminating role in triggering a flare-up include foods that trigger an allergic reaction (allergens) and **immunodeficiency** disorders caused by very low levels of immunoglobulins that result in an increased susceptibility to infection. Honey intolerance and bee pollen administration have also been suggested as a causative agent for EG. Researchers have confirmed a familial pattern to EE, which suggests either a genetic predisposition or a relationship to an unknown environmental exposure.

Gastroenteropathy symptoms vary depending on where the eosinophils are found and in what layer of the digestive system their numbers are highest. Symptoms therefore tend to be highly specific to each individual case. They may only appear when certain foods are ingested, or only during certain seasons of the year, or every few weeks, or in severe cases, every time any food is eaten. Infants with eosinophilic gastroenteropathies usually have acute reactions after food intake (within minutes to in one to two hours) that generally include nausea, vomiting and severe abdominal pain, later followed by diarrhea. These symptoms may occur alone or as part of a shock reaction. Symptoms vary depending on the type of gastroenteropathy (EG, EE, EC, or ED) and on the precise location of eosinophilic infiltration within the digestive system, as well as which layer or layers of the digestive system wall is infiltrated with eosinophils. Symptoms include, but are not limited to, the following:

- abdominal pain (EG, EE, ED)
- anorexia (EG, EE)
- asthma (EE)
- bloating (EG, ED, EC)
- cramps (EG, EC, ED)
- feeling full before finishing a meal (early satiety) (EG)
- milk/formula regurgitation (EG, EE)
- nausea, vomiting (EG, EE, EC, ED)
- weight loss (EG, EE, EC, ED)
- diarrhea (EG, EC, ED)
- presence of fluid (edema) in ankles (EG, EE)
- choking (EE)
- difficulty swallowing (dysphagia) (EG, EE)
- strictures (EE, EC)
- passage of dark stools (melena) (EG, EC, ED)
- constipation (EC, ED)
- bowel obstruction (EC, ED)
- intestinal bleeding (EC, ED)

When to call the doctor

Parents should call their healthcare provider to test for eosinophilic involvement if their child has recurrent symptoms of gastrointestinal disorder and feeding problems.

Diagnosis

Eosinophilic gastroenteropathies are diseases that can be easily misdiagnosed. EE has long been misdiagnosed as gastroesophageal reflux, another digestive disease in which partially digested food from the stomach regurgitates and backs up (reflux). However, EE differs from esophageal reflux in the large numbers of eosinophils that are present in the GI tract. Diagnosis for eosinophilic gastroenteropathies is therefore only established on microscopic analysis of a tissue specimen (biopsy) revealing eosinophilic infiltration. Additionally, diagnosis is based on the following:

- Complete blood count (CBC): CBC reveals the presence of blood eosinophilia, found in 20 to 80 percent of cases. CBC also appears to differentiate between different types of eosinophilic gastroenteropathies, since they have different total eosinophil counts.

- Mean corpuscular volume test: This test can determine the presence of iron-deficiency anemia and serum albumin levels that vary according to disorder type.

- Fecal protein loss test: This test is used to identify the inability to digest and absorb proteins in the GI tract.

- Imaging tests: Ultrasound and CT scan may show thickened intestinal walls and ascitic fluid in patients with Pattern III EG, as well as the degree of involvement of the different layers.

- Barium studies: In this test, the patient ingests a barium sulfate solution that makes for contrast on **x rays**. Barium studies can reveal mucosal edema and thickening of the small intestinal wall in EC and ED.

- Exploratory abdominal surgery (laparotomy): In some cases, laparotomy may be indicated, especially in patients with Pattern III EG.

Treatment

Treatment of eosinophilic gastroenteropathies is mainly symptomatic and supportive. Surgery may be necessary in severe EC cases in which there is obstruction of the intestines.

As of 2004 there is no known cure for eosinophilic gastroenteropathies, so medications are used to relieve symptoms and prevent full-blown attacks (or flare-ups). The only known medication to successfully stop eosinophilic inflammation is the corticosteroid drug, prednisone. Oral glucocorticosteroids are usually prescribed for those with EC or ED obstructive symptoms. Children with Pattern II EG may benefit from anti-inflammatory medications (for example, oral glucocorticoids or oral cromolyn) and specialized diet therapy, particularly in the case of food intolerance or allergy. Fluticasone propionate (Flonase, Flovent) is reported to be helpful in most cases of EG, if the medicine is swallowed so that it comes directly in contact with the esophageal tissues that are infiltrated by eosinophils. There is also reported success with use of a drug (Montelukast) that stops the production of the inflammatory leukotrienes associated with EC. Elemental formulas are also very effective. Cromolyn sodium (Gastrocrom) has been used with some success but does not work in all cases.

Clinical trials

Parents may consider enrolling their EG diagnosed child or adolescent in a clinical trial sponsored by the National Institute of Allergy and Infectious Diseases (NIAID). For example, in as of 2004 on-going omalizumab clinical study, participants undergo the following procedures:

- Leukapheresis: This procedure is performed to collect quantities of white blood cells to study the effects of the drug omalizumab on eosinophils and other immune system substances. Blood flows from a needle inserted in an arm vein through a catheter (plastic tube) into a machine that separates the blood into its components by centrifugation (spinning). Some of the white cells are removed, and the rest of the blood (red cells, plasma, and platelets) is returned to the body through a needle placed in the other arm.

- Skin testing: Participants are tested for allergies to specific allergens. A small amount of various allergens are placed on the arm. The skin is pricked at the sites of the allergens and the skin reaction after several minutes is observed.

- Upper and lower endoscopy: These procedures are performed so doctors can examine the specific part of the GI tract involved in the disorder. If both endoscopies are required, they are performed at the same time. For the upper endoscopy procedure, the throat is sprayed with an anesthetic (numbin) medicine and a long, flexible tube is passed through the esophagus, stomach, and small intestine. For the lower endoscopy procedure, the tube is passed through the rectum into the large intestine. Subjects are given a medication to cause relaxation through a vein before the procedure. Biopsies are performed during both endoscopies.

- Omalizumab therapy: This procedure is given as an injection under the skin. Following the first injection, subjects stay in the NIH clinical center hospital for 24 hours for **safety** monitoring. The remaining doses are scheduled as outpatient visits. Two weeks after the last dose, patients are admitted to the clinical center for two to three days for repeat endoscopy, leukapheresis, skin testing, and physical examination. Additional follow-up visits are scheduled.

Alternative treatment

As of 2004, a study is being conducted on the effectiveness of the membrane stabilizing drug sodium chromoglycate. More research is required to determine long-term safety and effectiveness of this drug. An experimental steroid called Budesonide may be helpful, but no clinical trials had been performed as of 2004. The severity of EG flare-ups has been reduced in some patients with **antihistamines** (such as Claritin, Allegra, or Zyrtec). A new class of asthma medications called leukotriene inhibitors has shown some mixed results in clinical trials for asthma patients and has been used experimentally in cases of EG but without conclusive results.

Nutritional concerns

It is believed that whole food proteins are the most common triggers of an EG attack. Most infants with this condition are, therefore, put on a restricted diet and

KEY TERMS

Allergic reaction—An immune system reaction to a substance in the environment; symptoms include rash, inflammation, sneezing, itchy watery eyes, and runny nose.

Anemia—A condition in which there is an abnormally low number of red blood cells in the bloodstream. It may be due to loss of blood, an increase in red blood cell destruction, or a decrease in red blood cell production. Major symptoms are paleness, shortness of breath, unusually fast or strong heart beats, and tiredness.

Antibody—A special protein made by the body's immune system as a defense against foreign material (bacteria, viruses, etc.) that enters the body. It is uniquely designed to attack and neutralize the specific antigen that triggered the immune response.

Antigen—A substance (usually a protein) identified as foreign by the body's immune system, triggering the release of antibodies as part of the body's immune response.

Ascites—An abnormal accumulation of fluid within the abdominal cavity.

Biopsy—The surgical removal and microscopic examination of living tissue for diagnostic purposes or to follow the course of a disease. Most commonly the term refers to the collection and analysis of tissue from a suspected tumor to establish malignancy.

Complete blood count (CBC)—A routine analysis performed on a sample of blood taken from the patient's vein with a needle and vacuum tube. The measurements taken in a CBC include a white blood cell count, a red blood cell count, the red cell distribution width, the hematocrit (ratio of the volume of the red blood cells to the blood volume), and the amount of hemoglobin (the blood protein that carries oxygen).

Corticosteroids—A group of hormones produced naturally by the adrenal gland or manufactured synthetically. They are often used to treat inflammation. Examples include cortisone and prednisone.

Cytokines—Chemicals made by the cells that act on other cells to stimulate or inhibit their function. They are important controllers of immune functions.

Dysphagia—Difficulty in swallowing.

Enteropathy—A disease of the intestinal tract.

Eosinophil—A type of white blood cell containing granules that can be stained by eosin (a chemical that produces a red stain). Eosinophils increase in response to parasitic infections and allergic reactions.

Eosinophilia—An abnormal increase in the number of eosinophils, a type of white blood cell.

Gastroesophageal reflux disease (GERD)—A disorder of the lower end of the esophagus in which the lower esophageal sphincter does not open and close normally. As a result the acidic contents of the stomach can flow backward into the esophagus and irritate the tissues.

Gastrointestinal (GI) system—The body system involved in digestion, the breaking down and use of food. It includes the stomach, small intestine, and large intestine. Also known as the gastrointestinal tract.

Gastrostomy tube—A tube that is inserted through a small incision in the abdominal wall and that extends through the stomach wall into the stomach for the purpose of introducing parenteral feedings. Also called a gastric tube, gastrointestinal tube, or stomach tube.

Glucocorticoids—A general class of adrenal cortical hormones that are mainly active in protecting against stress and in protein and carbohydrate metabolism. They are widely used in medicine anti-inflammatories and immunosuppresives.

Immunodeficiency disease—A disease characterized chiefly by an increased susceptibility to infection. It is caused by very low levels of immunoglobulins that result in an impaired immune system. Affected people develop repeated infections.

Immunoglobulin G (IgG)—Immunoglobulin type gamma, the most common type found in the blood and tissue fluids.

Leukotrienes—Substances that are produced by white blood cells in response to antigens and contribute to inflammatory and asthmatic reactions.

Malabsorption—The inability of the digestive tract to absorb all the nutrients from food due to some malfunction or disability.

Melena—The passage of dark stools stained with blood pigments or with altered blood.

Protein-losing enteropathy—Excessive loss of plasma and proteins in the gastrointestinal tract.

Shock—A medical emergency in which the organs and tissues of the body are not receiving an adequate flow of blood. This deprives the organs and tissues of oxygen and allows the build-up of waste products. Shock can be caused by certain diseases, serious injury, or blood loss.

Stricture—An abnormal narrowing or tightening of a body tube or passage.

provided with elemental formulas containing no whole food proteins, such as Neocate or Elecare. For older children, physicians usually start by recommending a trial **elimination diet** that excludes milk, eggs, wheat, gluten, soy, and beef, because a link has been established with food intolerance and food allergy. Most patients improve significantly on diets avoiding foods to which they are allergic. Radioallergosorbent assay test (RAST) or skin testing can identify food hypersensitivity. If an exceptionally high number of food reactions are found, an amino-acid-based diet or elemental diet is often considered. Some patients with EE/EG/EC are even fed elemental formulas via a gastrostomy tube or are limited to TPN (blood-vessel feeding) if the disease is severe with many complications.

Prognosis

As of 2004 there is no cure for eosinophilic gastroenteropathies, and outcomes depend on the specific enteropathy. A small subset of patients are partly or totally disabled by the effects of the disorder, but most can have active and fulfilling lives. Eosinophilic gastroenteropathies are not known to be fatal, but some types cause such severe bleeding or nutritional deficiency that the condition may be life-threatening if not treated with appropriate medications and support measures. Some younger children who have been diagnosed at an early age are known to outgrow the most severe symptoms. Children with EG have a good prognosis. Mild and sporadic symptoms can be managed with observation, and disabling GI flare-ups can be controlled with prednisone. Most patients also respond well to oral glucocorticosteroids.

Prevention

No specific prevention measures can be recommended for eosinophilic gastroenteropathies since their specific cause was unknown as of 2004.

Parental concerns

Because of the high risk of misdiagnosis for eosinophilic gastroenteropathies, parents of infants who have persistent feeding problems and do not respond well to classical digestive disorder medications should request biopsies to test for possible eosinophilic involvement.

When diagnosis is confirmed, certain lifestyle changes are usually required, such as avoidance of certain foods or making sure that medication is taken every day. Parents should also be aware that commonly prescribed corticosteroid medications have side effects that are potentially serious. People who use them tend to become overweight, with swollen faces. Long-term use has also been shown to damage kidneys.

See also Food allergies/sensitivities; Gastroenteritis; Gastroesophageal reflux disease.

Resources

BOOKS

Baehler, P., and E. G. Seidman. "Gastrointestinal manifestations of food-protein-induced hypersensitivity; eosinophilic gastroenteritis." In *Rudolph's Pediatrics*, 21st ed. Edited by C. D. Rudolph, et al. New York: McGraw-Hill, 2002.

Friedman, Scott L., et al. *Current Diagnosis & Treatment in Gastroenterology*, 2nd ed. New York: McGraw-Hill/ Appleton & Lange, 2002.

Lucky, A., and J. Powell. "Cutaneous manifestations of endocrine, metabolic, and nutritional disorders." In *Pediatric Dermatology*, 3rd ed. Edited by L. Schachner and R. Hansen. New York: Harcourt Health Sciences, 2003.

Metcalfe, Dean, et al. *Food Allergy: Adverse Reactions to Food and Food Additives*, 3rd ed. Oxford, UK: Blackwell Publishers, 2003.

PERIODICALS

Amirav. I., et al. "Coexistence of celiac disease and eosinophilic gastroenteropathy." *Journal of Pediatric Gastroenterology & Nutrition* 33, no. 2 (August 2001): 200–01.

Daneshjoo, R., and N. Talley. "Eosinophilic gastroenteritis." *Current Gastroenterology Reports* 4, no. 5 (October 2002): 366–72.

De Augustin, J. C., et al. "Successful medical treatment of two patients with eosinophilic oesophagitis." *Journal of Pediatric Surgery* 37, no. 2 (February 2002): 207–13.

Gokhale, R. "Chronic abdominal pain: inflammatory bowel disease and eosinophilic gastroenteropathy." *Pediatric Annals* 30, no. 1 (January 2001): 49–55.

Kahn, S., and S. R. Orenstein. "Eosinophilic gastroenteritis: epidemiology, diagnosis and management." *Paediatric Drugs* 4, no. 9 (2002): 563–70.

Kweon, M. N., and H. Kiyono. "Eosinophilic gastroenteritis: a problem of the mucosal immune system?" *Current Allergy and Asthma Reports* 3, no. 1 (January 2003): 79–85.

Losanoff, J. E., and J. W. Jones. "Eosinophilic colitis." *ANZ Journal of Surgery* 72, no. 1 (January 2002): 75–9.

Mine, T. "Hypereosinophilic syndrome vs. eosinophilic gastroenteritis." *Internal Medicine* 43, no. 4 (April 2004): 277–78.

Orenstein, Susan R. "The spectrum of pediatric eosinophilic esophagitis beyond infancy: a clinical series of 30 children." *American Journal of Gastroenterology* 95, no. 6 (June 2000): 1422–27.

Rothenberg, M. E. "Eosinophilic gastrointestinal disorders (EGID)." *Journal of Allergy and Clinical Immunology* 113, no. 1 (January 2004): 11–28.

Rothenberg. M. E., et al. "Pathogenesis and clinical features of eosinophilic esophagitis." *Journal of Allergy and Clinical Immunology* 108, no. 6 (December 2001): 891–94.

Vasilopoulos, S., et al. "The small-caliber esophagus: an unappreciated cause of dysphagia for solids in patients with eosinophilic esophagitis." *Gastrointestinal Endoscopy* 55, no. 1 (January 2002): 99–106.

ORGANIZATIONS

American Academy of Pediatrics. 141 Northwest Point Boulevard, Elk Grove Village, IL 60007–1098. Web site: <www.aap.org>.

American College of Gastroenterology. 4900–B South 31st St., Arlington, VA 22206. Web site: <www.acg.gi.org>.

American Gastroenterological Association (AGA). 4930 Del Ray Avenue, Bethesda, MD 20814. Web site: <www.gastro.org>.

Clinical Trials, a service of the National Institutes of Health (NIH). 9000 Rockville Pike, Bethesda, Maryland 20892. Web site: <www.clinicaltrials.gov>.

Digestive Disease National Coalition. 507 Capitol Court, Suite 200, Washington, DC 20002. Web site: <www.ddnc.org>.

NIH/National Digestive Diseases Information Clearinghouse. 2 Information Way, Bethesda, MD 20892-3570. Web site: <www.niddk.nih.gov>.

WEB SITES

"Eosinophilic Disorders Homepage." *Cincinnati Children's Hospital Medical Center.* Available online at <www.cincinnatichildrens.org/svc/prog/eosinophilic/patients.htm> (accessed November 26, 2004).

Rowe, William A. "Inflammatory Bowel Disease." *emedicine.com.* Available online at <www.emedicine.com/med/topic1169.htm> (accessed November 26, 2004).

Monique Laberge, Ph.D.

Epigastric hernia *see* **Abdominal wall defects**

Epiglottitis

Definition

Epiglottitis is an infection of the epiglottis, which can lead to severe airway obstruction.

Description

When air is inhaled (inspired), it passes through the nose and the nasopharynx or through the mouth and the oropharynx. These are both connected to the larynx, a tube made of cartilage. The air continues down the larynx to the trachea. The trachea then splits into two branches, the left and right bronchi (bronchial tubes). These bronchi branch into smaller air tubes that run within the lungs, leading to the small air sacs of the lungs (alveoli).

Either food, liquid, or air may be taken in through the mouth. While air goes into the larynx and the respiratory system, food and liquid are directed into the tube leading to the stomach, the esophagus. Because food or liquid in the bronchial tubes or lungs could cause a blockage or lead to an infection, the airway is protected. The epiglottis is a leaf-like piece of cartilage extending upwards from the larynx. The epiglottis can close down over the larynx when someone is eating or drinking, preventing these food and liquids from entering the airway.

Epiglottitis is an infection and inflammation of the epiglottis. Because the epiglottis may swell considerably, there is a danger that the airway will be blocked off by the very structure designed to protect it. Air is then unable to reach the lungs. Without intervention, epiglottitis has the potential of being fatal. Because epiglottitis involves swelling and infection of tissues, which are all located at or above the level of the epiglottis, it is sometimes referred to as supraglottitis (supra meaning above). About 25 percent of all children with this infection also have **pneumonia**.

Demographics

In the twentieth century, epiglottitis was primarily a disease of two- to seven-year-old children, with boys twice as likely to become ill as girls. In the early 2000s vaccines have greatly reduced the incidence of *Haemophilus influenzae* type b (Hib) epiglottitis, and the disease is more frequently seen in adults. In children, epiglottitis is an incredibly rare disease, thanks to timely Hib **vaccination** in childhood.

KEY TERMS

Epiglottis—A leaf-like piece of cartilage extending upwards from the larynx, which can close like a lid over the trachea to prevent the airway from receiving any food or liquid being swallowed.

Extubation—The removal of a breathing tube.

Intubation—A procedure in which a tube is inserted through the mouth and into the trachea to keep the airway open and to help a patient breathe.

Laryngospasm—Spasmodic closure of the larynx.

Larynx—Also known as the voice box, the larynx is the part of the airway that lies between the pharynx and the trachea. It is composed of cartilage that contains the apparatus for voice production–the vocal cords and the muscles and ligaments that move the cords.

Nasopharynx—One of the three regions of the pharynx, the nasopharynx is the region behind the nasal cavity.

Oropharynx—One of the three regions of the pharynx, the oropharynx is the region behind the mouth.

Supraglottitis—Another term for epiglottitis.

Trachea—The windpipe. A tube composed of cartilage and membrane that extends from below the voice box into the chest where it splits into two branches, the bronchi, that lead to each lung.

Tracheostomy—A procedure in which a small opening is made in the neck and into the trachea or windpipe. A breathing tube is then placed through this opening.

Causes and symptoms

The most common cause of epiglottitis is infection with the bacteria called *Haemophilus influenzae* type b. Other types of bacteria are also occasionally responsible for this infection, including some types of *Streptococcus* bacteria and the bacteria responsible for causing **diphtheria**.

A patient with epiglottitis typically experiences a sudden **fever** and begins having severe throat and neck **pain**. Because the swollen epiglottis interferes significantly with air movement, every breath creates a loud, harsh, high-pitched sound referred to as **stridor**. Because the vocal cords are located in the larynx just below the area of the epiglottis, the swollen epiglottis makes the patient's voice sound muffled and strained. Swallowing becomes difficult, and the patient may drool. The patient often leans forward and juts out his or her jaw, while struggling for breath.

Epiglottitis strikes suddenly and progresses quickly. A child may begin complaining of a **sore throat** and within a few hours be suffering from extremely severe airway obstruction.

Diagnosis

Diagnosis begins with a high level of suspicion that a quickly progressing illness with fever, sore throat, and airway obstruction is very likely to be epiglottitis. If epiglottitis is suspected, no efforts should be made to look at the throat or to swab the throat in order to obtain a culture for identification of the causative organism. These maneuvers may cause the larynx to go into spasm (laryngospasm), completely closing the airway. These procedures should only be performed in a fully equipped operating room, so that if laryngospasm occurs, a breathing tube can be immediately placed in order to keep the airway open.

An instrument called a laryngoscope is often used in the operating room to view the epiglottis, which will appear cherry-red and quite swollen. An x ray picture taken from the side of the neck should also be obtained. The swollen epiglottis has a characteristic appearance, called the "thumb sign."

Treatment

Treatment almost always involves the immediate establishment of an artificial airway: inserting a breathing tube into the throat (intubation) or making a tiny opening toward the base of the neck and putting a breathing tube into the trachea (tracheostomy). Because the patient's apparent level of distress may not match the actual severity of the situation, and because the disease's progression can be quite surprisingly rapid, it is preferable to go ahead and place the artificial airway, rather than adopting a wait-and-see approach.

Because epiglottitis is caused by a bacteria, **antibiotics** such as cefotaxime, ceftriaxone, or ampicillin with sulbactam should be given through a needle placed in a vein (intravenously). This prevents the bacteria that are circulating throughout the bloodstream from causing infection elsewhere in the body.

Prognosis

With treatment (including the establishment of an artificial airway), only about 1 percent of children with epiglottitis die. Without the artificial airway, this figure jumps to 6 percent. Most patients recover from the infection and can have the breathing tube removed (extubation) within a few days.

Prevention

Prevention involves the use of a vaccine against *H. influenzae* type b (called the **Hib vaccine**). It is given to babies at two, four, six, and 15 months. Use of this vaccine has made epiglottitis a very rare occurrence.

Parental concerns

Parents should be aware of the advantages of the Hib vaccine. They should also call the doctor immediately if a child has a sudden, high fever and neck or throat pain.

Resources

BOOKS

Long, Sarah S., et al, eds. *Principles and Practice of Pediatric Infectious Diseases*, 2nd ed. St. Louis, MO: Elsevier, 2003.

Roosevelt, Genie E. "Acute Inflammatory Upper Airway Obstruction." In *Nelson Textbook of Pediatrics*. Edited by Richard E. Behrman et al. Philadelphia: Saunders, 2004.

ORGANIZATIONS

American Academy of Otolaryngology-Head and Neck Surgery Inc. One Prince St., Alexandria VA 22314–3357. Web site: <www.entnet.org>.

Rosalyn Carson-DeWitt, MD

Epilepsy *see* **Seizure disorder**

Erb's palsy *see* **Brachial plexopathy, obstetric**

Erythema *see* **Fifth disease**

Erythroblastosis fetalis

Definition

Erythroblastosis fetalis, also known as hemolytic disease of the newborn or immune hydrops fetalis, is a disease in the fetus or newborn caused by transplacental transmission of maternal antibody, usually resulting from maternal and fetal blood group incompatibility.

Rh incompatibility may develop when a woman with Rh-negative blood becomes pregnant by a man with Rh-positive blood and conceives a fetus with Rh-positive blood. Red blood cells (RBCs) from the fetus leak across the placenta and enter the woman's circulation throughout pregnancy with the greatest transfer occurring at delivery. This transfer stimulates maternal antibody production against the Rh factor, which is called isoimmunization. In succeeding pregnancies, the antibodies reach the fetus via the placenta and destroy (lyse) the fetal RBCs. The resulting anemia may be so profound that the fetus may die in utero. Reacting to the anemia, the fetal bone marrow may release immature RBCs, or erythroblasts, into the fetal peripheral circulation, causing erythroblastosis fetalis. Maternal-fetal incompatibilities of ABO blood types leading to neonatal erythroblastosis are less severe and less common than those of the Rh factor.

Description

Red blood cells (RBCs) carry several types of proteins, called antigens, on their surfaces. The A, B, and O antigens represent the classification of an individual's blood as type A, B, AB, or O. Depending on the genetic predisposition of the parents, an A, B, or O antigen gene can be passed to a child. How the genes are paired determines the person's blood type.

A person who inherits an A antigen gene from each parent has type A blood; receiving two B antigen genes corresponds with type B blood; and inheriting A and B antigen genes means a person has type AB blood. If the O antigen gene is inherited from both parents, the child has type O blood; however, the pairing of A and O antigen genes corresponds with type A blood; and if the B antigen gene is matched with the O antigen gene, the person has type B blood.

Another red blood cell antigen, called the Rh factor, also plays a role in describing a person's blood type. A person with at least one copy of the gene for the Rh factor has Rh-positive blood; if no copies are inherited, the person's blood type is Rh-negative. In blood typing, the presence of A, B, and O antigens plus the presence or absence of the Rh-factor determine a person's specific blood type, such as A-positive, B-negative, and so on.

A person's blood type has no effect on health. However, an individual's immune system considers only that person's specific blood type, or a close match, acceptable. If a radically different blood type is introduced into the bloodstream, the immune system produces antibodies, proteins that specifically attack and destroy any cell carrying the foreign antigen.

Determining a woman's blood type is very important when she becomes pregnant. Blood cells from the unborn baby (fetal red blood cells) can cross over into the mother's bloodstream, and this risk is higher at delivery. If the mother and her baby have compatible blood types, the crossover does not present any danger. However, if the blood types are incompatible, the mother's immune system produces antibodies against the baby's blood.

Usually, this incompatibility is not a factor in a first pregnancy, because few fetal blood cells reach the mother's bloodstream until delivery. The antibodies that form after delivery cannot affect the first child. In subsequent pregnancies, however, the fetus may be at greater risk. The threat arises from the possibility that the mother's antibodies will attack the fetal red blood cells. If this happens, the fetus can suffer severe health effects and may die.

There are two types of incompatibility diseases: Rh incompatibility disease and ABO incompatibility disease. Both diseases have similar symptoms, but Rh disease is much more severe, because anti-Rh antibodies cross over the placenta more readily than anti-A or anti-B antibodies. (The immune system does not form antibodies against the O antigen.) As a result, a greater percentage of the baby's blood cells may be destroyed by Rh disease.

Both incompatibility diseases are uncommon in the United States due to medical advances since the 1950s. Prior to 1946 (when newborn blood transfusions were introduced) 20,000 babies were affected by Rh disease yearly. Further advances, such as suppressing the mother's antibody response, have reduced the incidence of Rh disease to approximately 4,000 cases per year.

Rh disease only occurs if a mother is Rh-negative and her baby is Rh-positive. For this situation to occur, the baby must inherit the Rh factor gene from the father. Most people are Rh-positive. Only 15 to 16 percent of the Caucasian population is Rh-negative, compared to approximately 8 percent of the African-American population and significantly lower in Asian populations. Interestingly, the Basque population of Spain has an incidence of 30 to 32 percent Rh-negativity.

ABO incompatibility disease is almost always limited to babies with A or B antigens whose mothers have type O blood. Approximately one third of these babies show evidence of the mother's antibodies in their bloodstream, but only a small percentage develop symptoms of ABO incompatibility disease.

Cause and symptoms

Rh disease and ABO incompatibility disease are caused when a mother's immune system produces antibodies against the red blood cells of her unborn child. The antibodies cause the baby's red blood cells to be destroyed and the baby develops anemia. The baby's body tries to compensate for the anemia by releasing immature red blood cells, called erythroblasts, from the bone marrow.

The overproduction of erythroblasts can cause the liver and spleen to become enlarged, potentially causing liver damage or a ruptured spleen. The emphasis on erythroblast production is at the cost of producing other types of blood cells, such as platelets and other factors important for blood clotting. Since the blood lacks clotting factors, excessive bleeding can be a complication. If this condition develops in the fetus in utero, the pregnant woman will generally notice a decrease in fetal movement, which should be immediately reported to her clinician.

The destroyed red blood cells release the blood's red pigment (hemoglobin) which degrades into a yellow substance called bilirubin. Bilirubin is normally produced as red blood cells die, but the body is only equipped to handle a certain low level of bilirubin in the bloodstream at one time. Erythroblastosis fetalis overwhelms the removal system, and high levels of bilirubin accumulate, causing hyperbilirubinemia, a condition in which the baby becomes jaundiced. The **jaundice** is apparent from the yellowish tone of the baby's eyes and skin. If hyperbilirubinemia cannot be controlled, the baby develops kernicterus. The term kernicterus means that bilirubin is being deposited in the brain, possibly causing permanent damage.

Other symptoms that may be present include high levels of insulin and low blood sugar, as well as a condition called hydrops fetalis. Hydrops fetalis is characterized by an accumulation of fluids within the baby's body, giving it a swollen appearance. This fluid accumulation inhibits normal breathing, because the lungs cannot expand fully and may contain fluid. If this condition continues for an extended period, it can interfere with lung growth. Hydrops fetalis and anemia can also contribute to heart problems.

Diagnosis

Erythroblastosis fetalis can be predicted before birth by determining the mother's blood type. If she is Rh-negative, the father's blood is tested to determine whether he is Rh-positive. If the father is Rh-positive, an antibody screen is done to determine whether the

Rh-negative woman is sensitized to the Rh antigen (developed isoimmunity). The indirect Coombs test measures the number of antibodies in the maternal blood. If the Rh-negative woman is not isoimmunized, a repeat antibody determination is done around 28 weeks' gestation, and the expectant woman should receive an injection of an anti-Rh (D) gamma globulin called Rhogham.

In cases in which incompatibility is not identified before birth, the baby suffers recognizable characteristic symptoms such as anemia, hyperbilirubinemia, and hydrops fetalis. The blood incompatibility is uncovered through blood tests such as the direct Coombs test, which measures the level of maternal antibodies attached to the baby's red blood cells. Other blood tests reveal anemia, abnormal blood counts, and high levels of bilirubin.

Treatment

Negative antibody titers can consistently identify the fetus that is not at risk; however, the titers cannot reliably point out the fetus which is in danger because the level of titer does not always correlate with the severity of the disease. For example, a severely sensitized woman may have antibody titers that are moderately high and remain at the same level while the fetus is being more and more severely affected. Conversely, a woman sensitized by previous Rh-positive fetuses may have a high antibody titer during her pregnancy while the fetus is Rh-negative.

When a mother has antibodies against her unborn infant's blood, the pregnancy is watched very carefully. Fetal **assessment** includes percutaneous umbilical cord blood sampling (PUBS) (cordocentesis), **amniocentesis**, amniotic fluid analysis, and ultrasound. Ultrasound should be done as early as possible in the first trimester to determine gestational age. Following that, serial ultrasounds and amniotic fluid analysis should be done to follow fetal progress. Complications are indicated by high levels of bilirubin in the amniotic fluid or baby's blood or if the ultrasound reveals hydrops fetalis. If bilirubin levels in amniotic fluid remain normal, the pregnancy can be allowed to continue to term and spontaneous labor. If bilirubin levels are elevated, indicating impending intrauterine death, the fetus can be given intrauterine transfusions at ten-day to two-week intervals, generally until 32 to 34 weeks gestation, when delivery should be performed.

There are two techniques that are used to deliver a blood transfusion to a baby before birth. The original intrauterine fetal transfusion, an intraperitoneal transfusion technique was first performed around 1963. With this method, a needle is inserted through the mother's abdomen and uterus and into the baby's abdomen. Red blood cells injected into the baby's abdominal cavity are absorbed into its bloodstream. In early pregnancy if the baby's bilirubin levels are gravely high, PUBS (cordocentesis) is performed. This procedure involves sliding a very fine needle through the mother's abdomen and, guided by ultrasound, into a vein in the umbilical cord to inject red blood cells directly into the baby's bloodstream.

After birth, the baby's symptoms are assessed. One or more transfusions may be necessary to treat anemia, hyperbilirubinemia, and bleeding. Hyperbilirubinemia is also treated with phototherapy, a treatment in which the baby is placed under a special light. This light causes changes in how the bilirubin molecule is shaped, which makes it easier to excrete. The baby may also receive oxygen and intravenous fluids containing electrolytes or drugs to treat other symptoms.

Prognosis

In many cases of blood type incompatibility, the symptoms of erythroblastosis fetalis are prevented with careful monitoring and blood type screening. Treatment of minor symptoms is typically successful, and the baby does not suffer long-term problems.

Nevertheless, erythroblastosis is a very serious condition for approximately 4,000 babies annually. In about 15 percent of cases, the baby is severely affected and dies before birth. Babies who survive pregnancy may develop kernicterus, which can lead to deafness, speech problems, **cerebral palsy**, or **mental retardation**. Extended hydrops fetalis can inhibit lung growth and contribute to heart failure. These serious complications are life threatening, but with good medical treatment, the fatality rate is very low.

Prevention

With any pregnancy, whether it results in a live birth, miscarriage, stillbirth, or abortion, blood typing is a universal precaution against blood compatibility disease. Blood types cannot be changed, but adequate forewarning allows precautions and treatments that limit the danger to unborn babies.

Parental concerns

If an Rh-negative woman gives birth to an Rh-positive baby, she is given an injection of Rhogam within 72 hours of the birth. This immunoglobulin destroys any

KEY TERMS

Amniocentesis—A procedure performed at 16-18 weeks of pregnancy in which a needle is inserted through a woman's abdomen into her uterus to draw out a small sample of the amniotic fluid from around the baby for analysis. Either the fluid itself or cells from the fluid can be used for a variety of tests to obtain information about genetic disorders and other medical conditions in the fetus.

Amniotic fluid—The liquid in the amniotic sac that cushions the fetus and regulates temperature in the placental environment. Amniotic fluid also contains fetal cells.

Anemia—A condition in which there is an abnormally low number of red blood cells in the bloodstream. It may be due to loss of blood, an increase in red blood cell destruction, or a decrease in red blood cell production. Major symptoms are paleness, shortness of breath, unusually fast or strong heart beats, and tiredness.

Antibody—A special protein made by the body's immune system as a defense against foreign material (bacteria, viruses, etc.) that enters the body. It is uniquely designed to attack and neutralize the specific antigen that triggered the immune response.

Antigen—A substance (usually a protein) identified as foreign by the body's immune system, triggering the release of antibodies as part of the body's immune response.

Bilirubin—A reddish yellow pigment formed from the breakdown of red blood cells, and metabolized by the liver. When levels are abnormally high, it causes the yellowish tint to eyes and skin known as jaundice. Levels of bilirubin in the blood increase in patients with liver disease, blockage of the bile ducts, and other conditions.

Hemoglobin—An iron-containing pigment of red blood cells composed of four amino acid chains (alpha, beta, gamma, delta) that delivers oxygen from the lungs to the cells of the body and carries carbon dioxide from the cells to the lungs.

Hemolysis—The process of breaking down of red blood cells. As the cells are destroyed, hemoglobin, the component of red blood cells which carries the oxygen, is liberated.

Hydrops fetalis—A condition in which a fetus or newborn baby accumulates fluids, causing swollen arms and legs and impaired breathing.

Hyperbilirubinemia—A condition characterized by a high level of bilirubin in the blood. Bilirubin is a natural byproduct of the breakdown of red blood cells, however, a high level of bilirubin may indicate a problem with the liver.

Isoimmunization—The development of antibodies in a species in response to antigens from the same species.

Percutaneous umbilical blood sampling (PUBS)—A technique used to obtain pure fetal blood from the umbilical cord while the fetus is in utero and also called cordocentesis.

Placenta—The organ that provides oxygen and nutrition from the mother to the unborn baby during pregnancy. The placenta is attached to the wall of the uterus and leads to the unborn baby via the umbilical cord.

Platelet—A cell-like particle in the blood that plays an important role in blood clotting. Platelets are activated when an injury causes a blood vessel to break. They change shape from round to spiny, "sticking" to the broken vessel wall and to each other to begin the clotting process. In addition to physically plugging breaks in blood vessel walls, platelets also release chemicals that promote clotting.

Rh factor—An antigen present in the red blood cells of 85% of humans. A person with Rh factor is Rh positive (Rh+); a person without it is Rh negative (Rh-). The Rh factor was first identified in the blood of a rhesus monkey and is also known as the rhesus factor.

Transplacental—Passing through or occurring across the placenta.

fetal blood cells in her bloodstream before her immune system can react to them. In cases where this precaution is not taken, antibodies are created, and future pregnancies may be complicated. Because antibody production does not usually begin in a previously unsensitized

mother until after delivery, erythroblastosis in subsequent children can be prevented by giving the mother an injection of Rhogam within 72 hours of delivery. The preparation must be given after each pregnancy—whether it ends in delivery, ectopic pregnancy,

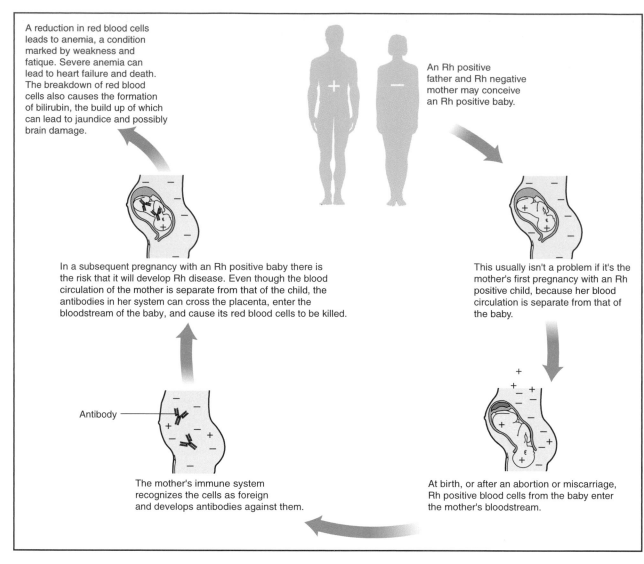

A reduction in red blood cells leads to anemia, a condition marked by weakness and fatigue. Severe anemia can lead to heart failure and death. The breakdown of red blood cells also causes the formation of bilirubin, the build up of which can lead to jaundice and possibly brain damage.

An Rh positive father and Rh negative mother may conceive an Rh positive baby.

In a subsequent pregnancy with an Rh positive baby there is the risk that it will develop Rh disease. Even though the blood circulation of the mother is separate from that of the child, the antibodies in her system can cross the placenta, enter the bloodstream of the baby, and cause its red blood cells to be killed.

This usually isn't a problem if it's the mother's first pregnancy with an Rh positive child, because her blood circulation is separate from that of the baby.

Antibody

The mother's immune system recognizes the cells as foreign and develops antibodies against them.

At birth, or after an abortion or miscarriage, Rh positive blood cells from the baby enter the mother's bloodstream.

Flow chart demonstrating how Rh disease is carried to fetus through mother. *(Illustration by Hans & Cassidy.)*

miscarriage, or abortion. The anti-Rh antibodies from the preparation destroy fetal RBCs in the mother's blood before they can sensitize the maternal immune system. If a massive fetomaternal hemorrhage has occurred, additional injections of the preparation may be necessary. This treatment has a failure rate of about 1–2 percent, apparently due to the mother's sensitization during pregnancy rather than at delivery. Therefore, all mothers who have Rh-negative blood and no apparent sensitization (as indicated by antibody titer) should be treated with a standard 300g dose of Rh(D) immune globulin (Rhogam) at about 28 weeks of gestation. The exogenous antibodies in the mother's circulation are gradually destroyed over the next three to six months, and the mother remains unsensitized. Rhogam should also be given after any episode of bleeding and after amniocentesis or chorionic villus sampling.

Delivery should be as nontraumatic as possible. The placenta should not be removed manually to avoid squeezing fetal cells into the maternal circulation. A newborn born with erythroblastosis should be attended to immediately by a pediatrician who is prepared to perform an exchange transfusion at once if required.

Resources

BOOKS

Kenner, Carole, and Judy Lott. *Comprehensive Neonatal Nursing*. Philadelphia: Saunders, 2002.

Slotnick, Robert N. "Isoimmunization." In *Manual of Obstetrics*. Edited by K. Niswander and A. Evans. Philadelphia: Lippincott, Wilkins & Wilkins, 2000.

ORGANIZATIONS

Association of Women's Health, Obstetric and Neonatal Nursing. 2000 L Street, N.W. Suite 740, Washington, DC 20036. Web site: <www.awhonn.org>.

National Association of Neonatal Nurses. 4700 W. Lake Avenue, Glenview, IL 60025–1485. Web site: <www.naan.org>.

Linda K. Bennington, BSN, MSN, CNS

Erythromycins

Definition

Erythromycins, also called macrolides, are a group of **antibiotics**, medicines that kill bacteria or prevent their growth.

Description

The antibiotics in this group are:

- azithromycin (Zithromax)
- clarithromycin (Biaxin)
- clindamycin (Cleocin)
- erythromycin (EES, Pediazole)
- lincomycin (Lincocin)

These drugs are chemically related and have similar uses, but because they are distributed differently in the body, they may be used for different purposes. There are other, older drugs in this group, but they are no longer in general use.

General use

Erythromycin is similar in use to penicillin and is widely used for patients who are allergic to penicillin. Penicillin has advantages over erythromycin in that it kills bacteria, while erythromycin only stops bacterial growth and relies on the body's immune system to kill bacteria. Also, erythromycin is more likely to cause stomach upset than is penicillin. Sometimes erythromycin may be used to treat a microorganism that is resistant to penicillin.

Azithromycin and clarithromycin both reach the lungs and respiratory tract better than does erythromycin.

These two drugs may be preferred for respiratory tract infections.

Clindamycin and lincomycin are similar to each other and are more effective than erythromycin for treatment of infections caused by anaerobic bacteria. Anaerobic bacteria can grow in the absence of oxygen.

Precautions

Symptoms should begin to improve within a few days of beginning to take this medicine. If they do not, or if they get worse, parents should check with the physician who prescribed the medicine.

Erythromycins may cause mild **diarrhea** that usually goes away during treatment. However, severe diarrhea could be a sign of a very serious side effect. Anyone who develops severe diarrhea while taking erythromycin or related drugs should stop taking the medicine and call a physician immediately.

Side effects

The most common side effects are mild diarrhea, **nausea**, **vomiting**, and stomach or abdominal cramps. These problems usually go away as the body adjusts to the drug and do not require medical treatment. Less common side effects, such as sore mouth or tongue and vaginal **itching** and discharge also may occur and do not need medical attention unless they persist or are bothersome.

More serious side effects are not common but may occur. If any of the following side effects occurs, check with a physician immediately:

- severe stomach **pain**, nausea, vomiting, or diarrhea
- fever
- skin rash, redness, or itching
- unusual tiredness or weakness

Although rare, very serious reactions to azithromycin (Zithromax) are possible, including extreme swelling of the lips, face, and neck, and **anaphylaxis** (a violent allergic reaction which can potentially include shock). If children develop these symptoms after taking azithromycin, they should stop taking the medicine and parents should get them immediate medical help.

Other rare side effects may occur with erythromycins and related drugs.

Interactions

Erythromycins may interact with many other medicines. When interaction happens, the effects of one or both of the drugs may change or the risk of side effects may be greater. Parents of children taking erythromycins should let the physician know all other medicines their children are taking. Among the drugs that may interact with erythromycins are:

- acetaminophen (Tylenol)

- medicine for overactive thyroid

- male hormones (androgens)

- female hormones (estrogens)

- other antibiotics

- blood thinners

- antiseizure medicines such as valproic acid (Depakote, Depakene)

- caffeine

- antihistamine such as astemizole (Hismanal)

- antiviral drugs such as zidovudine (Retrovir)

The list above does not include every drug that may interact with erythromycins. Parents should be sure to check with a physician or pharmacist before combining erythromycins with any other prescription or nonprescription (over-the-counter) medicine.

Some of the stomach upset caused by erythromycin can be minimized by changing the dosage form. Erythromycin is available as enteric-coated tablets, which are released in the intestine rather than the stomach; as a liquid; and as bead-filled capsules. These forms are less likely to cause stomach upset than traditional tablets.

Parental concerns

If a child has had an allergic reaction to erythromycin or any of its related drugs, the prescriber should be notified.

It is very important for patients to take erythromycins for as long as they have been prescribed. Patients must not stop taking the drug just because symptoms begin to improve. This point is important with all types of infections, but it is especially important in strep infections, which can lead to serious heart problems if they are not cleared up completely.

Erythromycins work best when they are at constant levels in the blood. To help keep levels constant, patients should take the medicine in doses spaced evenly through the day and night. No doses should be missed. Some of these medicines are most effective

when taken with a full glass of water on an empty stomach, but they may be taken with food if stomach upset is a problem. Others work equally well when taken with or without food. Check package directions or ask the physician or pharmacist for instructions on how to take the medicine.

Liquid forms of erythromycin should be administered with a medicinal teaspoon or other measuring device. Household teaspoons vary in size and may give either too much or too little of the medication.

Bead-filled capsules may be opened and sprinkled on pudding or applesauce for ease of administration. Enteric-coated tablets should never be split or crushed, since doing so will destroy the effectiveness of the coating.

Parents should never ask physicians to prescribe antibiotics for children's illnesses. Antibiotics are important for appropriate infections but are seriously overprescribed. Overuse leads to needless expense for the parents, some discomfort and risk for the child, and the development of antibiotic-resistant bacteria, which have become a public health problem.

Children have complained about the bitter taste of clarithromycin oral liquid. This factor should not be considered a problem. Liquid medications that taste good may be mistaken for candy or sweets, and children may overdose themselves. All medications should be kept away from children.

See also Pneumonia; Penicillins.

KEY TERMS

Anaphylaxis—Also called anaphylactic shock; a severe allergic reaction characterized by airway constriction, tissue swelling, and lowered blood pressure.

Enteric coating—A coating or shell placed on a tablet that breaks up and releases the medicine into the intestine rather than the stomach.

Microorganism—An organism that is too small to be seen with the naked eye, such as a bacterium, virus, or fungus.

Respiratory system—The organs that are involved in breathing: the nose, the throat, the larynx, the trachea, the bronchi and the lungs. Also called the respiratory tract.

Resources

BOOKS

Behrman Richard, Robert M. Kliegman, and Hal B. Jenson. *Nelson Textbook of Pediatrics*, 17th ed. Philadelphia: Saunders, 2003.

Mcevoy, Gerald K., et al. *AHFS Drug Information 2004*. Bethesda, MD: American Society of Healthsystems Pharmacists, 2004.

Siberry, George, and Robert Iannone, eds. *The Harriet Lane Handbook*, 15th ed. Philadelphia: Mosby, 2000.

PERIODICALS

Cunha, B. A. "Therapeutic implications of antibacterial resistance in community-acquired respiratory tract infections in children." *Infection* 32, no. 2 (April 2004): 98–108.

Gonzalez, B. E., et al. "Azithromycin compared with beta-lactam antibiotic treatment failures in pneumococcal infections of children." *Pediatric Infectious Diseases Journal* 23, no. 5 (May 2004): 399–405.

McIsaac, W. J., and T. To. "Antibiotics for lower respiratory tract infections: Still too frequently prescribed?" *Canadian Family Physician* 50 (April 2004): 569–575.

ORGANIZATIONS

American Academy of Pediatrics. 141 Northwest Point Boulevard, Elk Grove Village, IL 60007–1098. Web site: <www.aap.org>.

Office of Health Communication National Center for Infectious Diseases, Centers for Disease Control and Prevention. Mailstop C-14, 1600 Clifton Road Atlanta, GA 30333. Web site: <www.cdc.gov>.

WEB SITES

"Macrolides." Available online at <www.healthwell.com/healthnotes/healthnotes.cfm?ContentID=1430001> (accessed September 29, 2004.)

Nancy Ross-Flanigan
Samuel Uretsky, PharmD

Esophageal atresia

Definition

Esophageal atresia (EA) is a birth defect (congenital anomaly) in which the esophagus, which connects the mouth to the stomach, is shortened and closed off (dead ended) at some point along its length. This defect almost always occurs in conjunction with **tracheoesophageal fistula** (TEF), a condition in which the esophagus is improperly attached to the trachea, the "windpipe" that carries air into the lungs. It is believed that these defects occur around the fourth week of pregnancy when the digestive tract is forming. There is no known cause for the defects.

Description

Failure of an unborn child (fetus) to develop properly can result in birth defects. These defects typically involve organs whose function is either incidental or not necessary at all before birth, meaning that the defects will not be detected until the baby is born. The digestive tract is unnecessary for fetal growth, since all **nutrition** comes from the mother through the placenta and umbilical cord. During fetal development, the esophagus and trachea arise from the same original tissue, forming into two side-by-side passageways, the esophagus leading from the throat to the stomach and digestive tract, and the trachea leading from the larynx to the lungs and respiratory system. Normally, the two tubes form separately (differentiate); however, in the case of EA/TEF, they do not differentiate, which results in various malformed configurations. There are five configurations, as follows:

- Type A (7.7%): Esophageal atresia in which both segments of the esophagus end in blind pouches. Neither segment is attached to the trachea.

- Type B (0.8%): Esophageal atresia with tracheoesophageal fistula in which the upper segment of the esophagus forms a fistula to the trachea. The lower segment of the esophagus ends in a blind pouch. This condition is very rare.

- Type C (86.5%): Esophageal atresia with tracheoesophageal fistula, in which the upper segment of the esophagus ends in a blind pouch (EA) and the lower segment of the esophagus is attached to the trachea (TEF).

- Type D (0.7%): Esophageal atresia with tracheoesophageal fistula, in which both segments of the esophagus are attached to the trachea. This is the rarest form of EA/TEF.

- Type H (4.2%): Tracheoesophageal fistula in which there is no esophageal atresia because the esophagus is continuous to the stomach. Fistula is present between the esophagus and the trachea.

Normally, the esophagus moves food from the mouth to the stomach. When the esophagus ends in a pouch instead of emptying into the stomach, food, liquids, and saliva cannot pass through. The combination of EA with TEF compromises digestion, nutrition, and respiration (breathing), creating a life-threatening condition that requires immediate medical attention. All babies with EA/TEF require surgical repair to correct the condition and allow proper nutrition and swallowing. Many children have surgeries performed in separate stages over a period of years.

Demographics

Esophageal atresia alone or with tracheoesophageal fistula (EA/TEF) occurs in approximately one in 4,000 live births. Children's hospitals in the United States report from five to 20 babies undergo surgery each year for EA/TEF.

Causes and symptoms

The cause of esophageal atresia, like that of most birth defects, was as of 2004 unknown.

An infant born with EA/TEF may at first appear to swallowing normally. However, the first signs of EA/TEF may be the presence of tiny, white, frothy bubbles of mucous in the infant's mouth and sometimes in the nose as well. When these bubbles are suctioned away, they reappear. This symptom occurs when the blind pouch begins to fill with mucus and saliva that would normally pass through the esophagus into the stomach. Instead these secretions back up into the mouth and nasal area, causing the baby to drool excessively. Although the infant may swallow normally, a rattling sound may be heard in the chest along with coughing and **choking**, especially when the infant tries to nurse. Some infants, depending on the severity of the defect, may appear blue (cyanosis), a sign of insufficient oxygen in the circulatory system. The infant's abdomen may be swollen and firm (distended) because the abnormal trachea allows air to build up in the stomach, filling the abdominal space that holds the surrounding organs. Aspiration **pneumonia**, an infection of the respiratory system caused by inhalation of the contents of the digestive tract, may also develop.

When to call the doctor

EA is suspected when an infant drools excessively, accompanied by choking and sneezing and difficulty feeding. This condition may be detected within the first few days of life while the infant is still in the hospital or birthing center. If a newborn being cared for at home shows excessive drooling or begins to **cough** and struggle when nursing or swallowing, it is essential to contact the pediatrician immediately and to go to an emergency department for immediate care. If respiratory distress develops, it is critical to obtain immediate care to reduce the risk of aspiration of material (saliva or milk) into the trachea and the lungs.

Diagnosis

When a physician suspects esophageal atresia after being presented with the typical symptoms, diagnosis usually begins with gently passing a catheter through the nose and into the esophagus. Esophageal atresia is indicated if the catheter stops at the blind pouch, indicating that it has hit an obstruction. If EA is present, the catheter will typically stop at 4 to 5 inches (10–12 cm) from the nostrils. Barium-enhanced x-ray examination may reveal a dilated esophageal pouch, made larger by the collection of amniotic fluid in the pouch. During fetal development, the enlarged esophagus may also have pressed on and narrowed the trachea, a condition in the fetus that can contribute to fistula development. Air in the stomach may confirm the presence of fistula; gas in the large intestine rules out intestinal (duodenal) atresia. The physician will also perform a comprehensive physical examination, looking for other congenital anomalies that are known to accompany EA/TEF. Chest **x rays** may be taken to look for skeletal and cardiac abnormalities. Abdominal x rays may be taken as well to look for intestinal obstruction and abnormalities. An echocardiogram (ECG) may be performed to evaluate heart function and ultrasound of the kidneys performed to evaluate kidney function.

Treatment

Infants with EA, with or without TEF, are unlikely to survive without surgery to reconnect the esophagus. The procedure is done as soon as possible; however, **prematurity**, the presence of other birth defects, or complications of aspiration pneumonia may delay surgery. Once diagnosed, the baby may be fed intravenously until surgery is performed. Mucus and saliva will also be continuously removed via a catheter. Healthy infants who have no complications, such as heart or lung problems or other types of intestinal malformations, can usually have surgery within the first 24 hours of life. Surgery techniques used to treat the five types of EA/TEF defects are similar.

Surgery is conducted while the infant is under general anesthesia; a tube is placed through the mouth to continuously suction the esophageal pouch during the procedure. An intravenous line (IV tubing into the veins) is established to allow fluids to be administered as needed during surgery. Oxygen therapy is administered if needed. In infants with pulmonary problems, tracheal intubation (an airway placed in the trachea) may be

KEY TERMS

Anastomosis—Surgical reconnection of two ducts, blood vessels, or bowel segments to allow flow between the two.

Anomaly—Something that is different from what is normal or expected. Also an unusual or irregular structure.

Atresia—The congenital absence of a normal body opening or duct.

Congenital—Present at birth.

Esophagus—The muscular tube that leads from the back of the throat to the entrance of the stomach. It is coated with mucus and surrounded by muscles, and pushes food to the stomach by sequential waves of contraction. It functions to transport food from the throat to the stomach and to keep the contents of the stomach in the stomach.

Fetal—Refers to the fetus. In humans, the fetal period extend from the end of the eight week of pregnancy to birth.

Fistula—An abnormal channel that connects two organs or connects an organ to the skin.

Trachea—The windpipe. A tube composed of cartilage and membrane that extends from below the voice box into the chest where it splits into two branches, the bronchi, that lead to each lung.

Tracheoesophageal fistula—An abnormal connection between the trachea and esophagus, frequently associated with the esophagus ending in a blind pouch.

performed. If lung infection is suspected, the infant is given broad-spectrum **antibiotics** intravenously, either pre- or post-operatively.

The surgeon makes an incision in the right chest wall between the ribs, allowing access to the esophagus and the trachea for repair of one or both as needed. If the gap between the two portions of the esophagus is short, the surgeon may join both ends of the esophagus (anastomosis). If the upper portion of the esophagus is short and a long gap exists between upper and lower portions, reconstructive surgery cannot be performed, and the infant must receive nutrition in some way to allow several months of growth. In this case, a gastrostomy (stomach tube) may be surgically placed directly into the stomach for feeding. In the most typical EA/TEF repair, the fistula is first closed off, creating a separate airway.

Then the blind esophageal pouch is opened and connected with suturing (stitching) to the other portion of the esophagus, creating a normal "food pipe" directly into the stomach. The esophagus is separated from the trachea if necessary. If the two ends of the esophagus are too far apart to be reattached, tissue from the large intestine is used to join them.

Nutritional concerns

If an infant is unable to nurse normally before surgery can be performed, nutrition is provided intravenously (parenteral) or directly through a tube into the stomach (gastronomy). After the surgery, infants should be able to swallow normally and resume nursing or feeding.

Prognosis

Surgery to correct esophageal atresia is usually successful, with survival rates close to 100 percent in otherwise healthy infants after the condition is corrected. Postoperative complications may include difficulty swallowing, since the esophagus may not contract efficiently, and gastrointestinal reflux, in which the acidic contents of stomach back up into the lower part of the esophagus, possibly causing ulcers.

Prevention

No preventive measures are recommended because the cause of these birth defects was as of 2004 unknown and their occurrence not predictable.

Parental concerns

Despite a difficult beginning for infants with esophageal atresia with or without TEF, parents can be reassured that the defect can usually be corrected with surgery, allowing normal digestion, nutrition, and breathing to take place in their child. Concerns about complications are well founded, including increased susceptibility to colds and infections, as well as the presence of chronic conditions. Ongoing medical care helps manage these conditions and maintain good health in children who have had EA/TEF. Parents can seek advice about strengthening the child's immune system through appropriate nutrition and supplements.

See also Tracheoesophageal fistula.

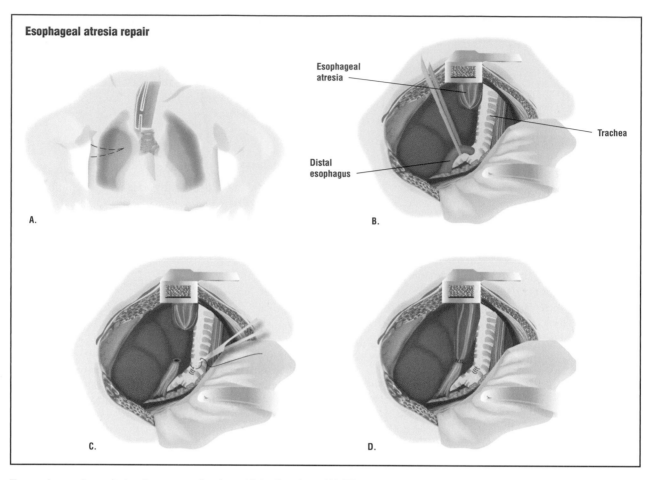

Esophageal atresia repair

Esophageal atresia

Distal esophagus

Trachea

A.

B.

C.

D.

To repair esophageal atresia, an opening is cut into the chest (A). The two parts of the existing esophagus are identified (B). The lower esophagus is detached from the trachea (C) and connected to the upper part of the esophagus (D). *(Illustration by GGS Information Services.)*

Resources

BOOKS

Allan, W., et al. *Pediatric Gastrointestinal Disease: Pathophysiology, Diagnosis, Management*, 3rd ed. Boston, MA: B.C. Decker, 2000.

Stringer, David A., et al. *Pediatric Gastrointestinal Imaging and Intervention*. Boulder, CO: netLibrary, 2000.

ORGANIZATIONS

EA/TEF child and Family Support Connection. 111 West Jackson Blvd., Suite 1145, Chicago, IL 60604. Web site: <www.eatef.org>.

WEB SITES

"Esophageal Artesia." *University of Michigan Section of Pediatric Surgery*. Available online at <http://pediatric.um-surgery.org/new_070198/new/Library/Esophageal%20Artesia.htm> (accessed November 27, 2004).

"Esophageal Atresia and Tracheoesophageal Fistula." *University of Minnesota Medical School*. Available online at <http://www1.umn/edu/eatef/> (accessed November 27, 2004).

"What is esophageal atresia?" *TEF/VATER International*, 2004. Available online at <www.tefvater.org> (accessed November 27, 2004).

L. Lee Culvert
J. Ricker Polsdorfer, MD

Exercise

Definition

Exercise is physical activity that is planned, structured, and repetitive for the purpose of conditioning the body. Exercise consists of cardiovascular conditioning, strength and resistance training, and flexibility.

Purpose

Exercise is essential for improving overall health, maintaining fitness, and helping to prevent the development of **obesity**, **hypertension**, and cardiovascular disease. Surveys conducted by the Centers for Disease Control and Prevention (CDC) indicate that 61.5 percent of children aged nine to 13 years do not participate in any organized physical activity (for example, **sports**, dance classes) and 22.6 percent are not physically active during their free time. According to the American Obesity Association, approximately 30 percent of children and adolescents aged six to 19 years are overweight and 15 percent are obese.

A sedentary lifestyle and excess caloric consumption are the primary causes of this increase in overweight and obesity; regular exercise is considered an important factor in controlling weight. Overweight and obese children and adolescents are at higher risk of developing several medical conditions, including the following:

- **asthma**
- diabetes
- hypertension
- orthopedic complications, such as hip and knee **pain** and limited range of motion
- cardiovascular disease
- high cholesterol
- sleep apnea
- psychosocial disorders, such as depression, negative body image, and eating disorders

Clinical studies have shown that regular exercise has numerous benefits, including the following:

- preventing weight gain and maintaining healthy weight
- reducing blood pressure and cholesterol
- improving coordination
- improving **self-esteem** and self-confidence
- decreasing the risk of developing diabetes, cardiovascular disease, and certain types of cancer
- increased life expectancy

Description

Exercise consists of cardiovascular conditioning, strength and resistance training, and flexibility to improve and maintain the fitness of the body's heart, lungs, and muscles.

Cardiovascular conditioning

Cardiovascular conditioning involves moderate to vigorous physical activity that results in an elevated heart rate for a sustained period of time. Regular cardiovascular exercise improves the efficiency of the functioning of the heart, lungs, and circulatory system. For adults, aerobic exercise within a target heart rate range calculated based on a maximum heart rate by age is recommended. For healthy children, cardiovascular exercise that elevates the heart rate to no greater than a maximum heart rate of 200 beats per minute is recommended.

In general, the American Heart Association recommends at least 60 minutes of moderate to vigorous physical activity every day for children and adolescents. Cardiovascular conditioning activities should be appropriate for the age, gender, and emotional status of the child. Examples of exercise that elevates the heart rate are bicycle riding, running, swimming, jumping rope, brisk walking, dancing, soccer, and basketball.

Strength and resistance training

Strength and resistance training increases muscle strength and mass, bone strength, and the body's metabolism. Strengthening exercises increase muscle strength by putting more strain on a muscle than it is normally accustomed to receiving. Strength training can be performed with or without special equipment. Strength/resistance training equipment includes handheld dumbbells, resistance machines (Nautilus, Cybex), and elastic bands. Strength training can also be performed without equipment; exercises without equipment include push-ups, abdominal crunches, and squats. Children as young as six years can participate in strength training with weights, provided they are supervised by a fitness professional trained in youth strength training. Child-sized resistance machines may be available at some fitness facilities. According to youth strength training guidelines, children and adolescents should perform strength training for approximately 20 minutes two or three times weekly on nonconsecutive days.

Flexibility

Flexibility is important to improve and maintain joint range of motion and reduce the likelihood of muscle **strains**. Most young children are naturally more flexible than older children and adults and will instinctively perform movements that promote flexibility. As children age, they should be encouraged to continue to stretch. Flexibility is especially important for children and adolescents engaged in vigorous exercise (running, competitive sports). Stretching is best performed following a warm-up and/or at the completion of an exercise session or sport. One activity that promotes flexibility that is increasing in popularity for children is **yoga**, in the form of children's yoga classes or exercise videos.

Precautions

Before a child begins any exercise program, he or she should be evaluated by a physician in order to rule out any potential health risks. Children and adolescents with physical restrictions or certain medical conditions may require an exercise program supervised by a health-care professional, such as a physical therapist or exercise physiologist. If **dizziness**, **nausea**, excessive shortness of breath, or chest pain occur during any exercise program, the activity should be stopped, and a physician should be consulted before the child resumes the activity. Children and adolescents who use any type of exercise equipment should be supervised by a knowledgeable fitness professional, such as a personal trainer.

Preparation

A physical examination by a physician is important to determine if strenuous exercise is appropriate or detrimental. Prior to beginning exercise, a proper warm-up is necessary to help prevent the possibility of injury resulting from tight muscles, tendons, ligaments, and joints. Appropriate warm-up exercises include walking, light calisthenics, and stretching.

Aftercare

Proper cool-down after exercise is important and should include a gradual decrease in exercise intensity to slowly bring the heart rate back to the normal range, followed by stretches to increase flexibility and reduce the likelihood of muscle soreness. Following vigorous activities that involve sweating, lost fluids should be replaced by drinking water.

Risks

Improper warm-up and inappropriate use of weights can lead to muscle strains. Overexertion without enough time between exercise sessions to recuperate also can lead to muscle strains, resulting in inactivity due to pain. Some children and adolescents may be susceptible to exercise-induced asthma. For children and adolescents who perform high-impact activities, such as running, stress **fractures** may occur. **Dehydration** is a risk during longer activities that involve sweating; children and adolescents should be supplied with water during and after activity.

KEY TERMS

Aerobic—An organism that grows and thrives only in environments containing oxygen.

Calisthenics—Exercise involving free movement without the aid of equipment.

Normal results

Significant health benefits are obtained by including at least a moderate amount of physical exercise for 30 to 60 minutes daily. Regular physical activity plays a positive role in preventing disease and improving overall health status. For children and adolescents just beginning an exercise program, results (including weight loss, increased muscle strength, and aerobic capacity) will be noticeable in four to six weeks.

Parental concerns

Given the increasing prevalence of overweight and obesity in children and adolescents, it is important for parents to encourage regular exercise and also serve as role models by exercising themselves. Television, computers, and **video games** have replaced physical activity for playtime for the majority of children. Parents should make a commitment to replacing sedentary activities with active indoor and outdoor games. For busy families, exercise can be performed in multiple 10- to 15-minute sessions throughout the day.

For children aged two to five years, physical activities should emphasize basic movement skills, imagination, and **play**. Examples of appropriate activities for this age group include rolling and bouncing a ball, jumping, hopping, skipping, mimicking animal movements, and pedaling a tricycle.

For children aged five to eight years, physical activities should emphasize basic motor skills and more complex movements (eye-hand coordination). Non-competitive group sports or classes are appropriate for this age, and parents should focus on helping their children find an enjoyable physical activity.

For children aged eight to ten years, physical activities should emphasize the benefits of regular exercise. Team sports and group classes are appropriate for this age. Experts have found that physical activity decreases in this age group, so parents should focus on being

---

Mother and daughter practicing yoga. *(© Ariel Skelley/Corbis.)*

supportive and encouraging their children to be physically active.

For children aged 11 to 14 years, physical activities should continue to emphasize the benefits of regular exercise. Participation in team sports, as well as individual activities, such as dance or martial arts, is appropriate for this age. Peer influence and hormonal changes can affect participation in group physical activities, so parents should consider encouraging exercise at home for children reluctant to participate with peers.

Community centers, local YMCAs, health clubs, and other organizations offer age-appropriate exercise programs for children and adolescents led by experienced and knowledgeable instructors. In addition, home exercise videos geared toward children are available in stores and from Web sites.

For children and adolescents with medical conditions that may limit exercise or place them at higher risk for exercise-related complications, supervised exercise programs may be available at hospital-based wellness centers.

Resources

BOOKS

Inspire Kids and Teens to Fitness. San Diego, CA: IDEA Health and Fitness Association, 2003.

LeMay, Michelle. *Essential Stretch.* New York: Berkeley Publishing Group, 2003.

McArdle, William D., Frank I. Katch, and Victor L. Katch. *Exercise Physiology: Energy, Nutrition, and Human Performance*, 5th ed. Philadelphia: Lippincott, 2001.

PERIODICALS

Anderson, Ross E., and John M. Jakicic. "Physical Activity and Weight Management: Building the Case of Exercise." *The Physician and Sports Medicine* 31 (November 2003): 39–45.

Centers for Disease Control and Prevention. "Physical Activity Levels among Children Aged 9–13 Years—United States, 2002." *Morbidity and Mortality Weekly Report* 52 (2003): 785–88.

ORGANIZATIONS

Aerobics and Fitness Association of America. 15250 Ventura Blvd, Suite 200, Sherman Oaks, CA 91403. Web site: <www.afaa.com>.

American College of Sports Medicine. 401 W. Michigan Street, Indianapolis, IN 46202–3233. Web site: <www.acsm.org/>.

American Council on Exercise. 4851 Paramount Drive San Diego, California 92123. Web site: <www.acefitness.org>.

American Heart Association. National Center. 7272 Greenville Ave., Dallas, TX 75231. Web site: <www.americanheart.org>.

WEB SITES

Ekeland, E., et al. "Exercise to Improve Self-Esteem in Children and Young People." *The Cochrane Collaboration*, 2004. Available online at <www.medscape.com/viewarticle/486742> (accessed November 29, 2004).

IDEA Health and Fitness Association. *Fitness for Your Child*.2004. <www.ideafit.com/articles/fitness_child.asp> (accessed November 29, 2004).

"Physical Education for Preschoolers." *KID-FIT*, 2004. Available online at <www.kid-fit.com> (accessed November 29, 2004).

Jennifer E. Sisk, MA

Expectorants

Definition

Expectorants are drugs that loosen and clear mucus and phlegm from the respiratory tract.

Description

There are two drugs that are routinely used to clear mucus from the respiratory tract: guaifenesin and acetylcysteine. Guaifenesin may be taken by mouth and is an ingredient in many over-the-counter **cough** and cold remedies. Although acetylcysteine is by far the more reliable of the two, it must be administered with special inhalation equipment or instilled directly into the trachea.

Other drugs have been used as expectorants, but lack evidence of either efficacy or **safety** or both:

• ammonium chloride

• bromhexine

• ipecacuanha

KEY TERMS

Asthma—A disease in which the air passages of the lungs become inflamed and narrowed, causing wheezing, coughing, and shortness of breath.

Bronchitis—Inflammation of the air passages of the lungs.

Chronic—Refers to a disease or condition that progresses slowly but persists or recurs over time.

Cough suppressant—A medication that stops or prevents coughing.

Emphysema—A chronic respiratory disease that involves the destruction of air sac walls to form abnormally large air sacs that have reduced gas exchange ability and that tend to retain air within the lungs. Symptoms include labored breathing, the inability to forcefully blow air out of the lungs, and an increased susceptibility to respiratory tract infections. Emphysema is usually caused by smoking.

Mucus—The thick fluid produced by the mucous membranes that line many body cavities and structures. It contains mucin, white blood cells, water, inorganic salts, and shed cells, and it serve to lubricate body parts and to trap particles of dirt or other contaminants.

Phlegm—Thick mucus produced in the air passages.

Respiratory system—The organs that are involved in breathing: the nose, the throat, the larynx, the trachea, the bronchi and the lungs. Also called the respiratory tract.

Secretion—A substance, such as saliva or mucus, that is produced and given off by a cell or a gland.

Trachea—The windpipe. A tube composed of cartilage and membrane that extends from below the voice box into the chest where it splits into two branches, the bronchi, that lead to each lung.

• potassium iodide

• wild cherry syrup

These drugs, and others, are not in common use, although wild cherry syrup may be used as a flavoring agent in some liquid cough preparations. Some home remedies, including chicken soup and hot tea, may also be useful in breaking up mucus.

General use

Guaifenesin, the only medicinal product in common use as an expectorant, is an ingredient in many cough medicines, such as Anti-Tuss, Dristan Cold & Cough, Guaifed, GuaiCough, and some Robitussin products. Some products that contain guaifenesin are available only with a physician's prescription; others can be bought without a prescription. They come in several forms: capsules, tablets, and liquids. There is some dispute, even among experts, about whether guaifenesin is an effective expectorant. In some studies, it has been useful, while in others it has not shown any value. Guaifenesin should not be given to children under the age of two years unless directed by a physician.

Precautions

Guaifenesin is not meant to be used for coughs associated with **asthma**, emphysema, chronic **bronchitis**, or **smoking**. It also should not be used for coughs that are producing a large amount of mucus. A lingering cough could be a sign of a serious medical condition. Coughs that last more than seven days or are associated with **fever**, rash, **sore throat**, or lasting **headache** should have medical attention. Parents should call a physician as soon as possible.

Side effects

Side effects are rare but may include **vomiting**, **diarrhea**, stomach upset, headache, skin rash, and **hives**.

Interactions

Guaifenesin is not known to interact with any foods or other drugs. However, cough medicines that contain guaifenesin may contain other ingredients that do interact with foods or drugs. Parents should check with a physician or pharmacist for details about specific products.

Because the value of guaifenesin is uncertain, while the adverse effects have been documented, parents should consider using alternatives to guaifenesin-containing cough remedies for children.

Parental concerns

There is no good evidence either for or against the use of over-the-counter products for treatment of coughs. Parents may wish to avoid using cough remedies for children unless instructed to do so by a physician. Expectorants are for use only in coughs with mucus production, sometimes called productive coughs. They are of no value in coughs without mucus, sometimes called dry coughs or non-productive coughs. The recommended dosage on the product label should not be exceeded. A calibrated medicinal teaspoon, not a household teaspoon, should be used to measure any medication.

See also Cough supressants; Decongestants.

Resources

BOOKS

Mcevoy, Gerald K., et al. *AHFS Drug Information 2004.* Bethesda, MD: American Society of Healthsystems Pharmacists, 2004.

Siberry, George, and Robert Iannone, eds. *The Harriet Lane Handbook*, 15th ed. Philadelphia: Mosby, 2000.

PERIODICALS

Hopkins, Alan B. "Chicken soup cure may not be a myth." *Nurse Practitioner* 28, no. 6 (June 2003): 16–18.

WEB SITES

"Cough Expectorant." *Family Practice Notebook.* Available online at <www.fpnotebook.com/LUN116.htm> (accessed September 29, 2004).

"What's the difference between an expectorant and a cough suppressant?" *Parent Center.* Available online at <http://parentcenter.babycenter.com/expert/71851.html> (accessed September 29, 2004).

Nancy Ross-Flanigan
Samuel Uretsky, PharmD

Extracorporeal membrane oxygenation

Definition

Extracorporeal membrane oxygenation (ECMO) is a procedure that uses an artificial heart-lung machine to take over the work of the lungs (and sometimes the heart). ECMO is used most often in newborns and young children, but it also can be used as a last resort for adults whose heart or lungs are failing.

Purpose

In newborns, ECMO is used to support or replace an infant's undeveloped or failing lungs by providing oxygen and removing carbon dioxide waste products so the lungs can rest. Infants who need ECMO may include those with the following problems:

- Meconium aspiration syndrome: Breathing in of a newborn's first stool by a fetus or newborn, which can block air passages and interfere with lung expansion.

- Persistent pulmonary **hypertension**: A disorder in which the blood pressure in the arteries supplying the lungs is abnormally high.

- Respiratory distress syndrome: A lung disorder usually of premature infants that causes increasing difficulty in breathing, leading to a life-threatening deficiency of oxygen in the blood.

- Congenital diaphragmatic **hernia**: The profusion of part of the stomach and/or intestines through an opening in the diaphragm.

- Pneumonia

- Blood poisoning

- Inborn errors of metabolism: Some genetic diseases.

ECMO is also used to support a child's damaged, infected, or failing lungs for a few hours to allow treatment or healing. It is effective for those children with severe, but reversible, heart or lung problems who have not responded to treatment with a ventilator, drugs, or extra oxygen. Children who need ECMO usually have one of the following problems:

- immature or underdeveloped lungs

- heart failure

- pneumonia

- respiratory failure caused by trauma or severe infection

- status asthmaticus (severe **asthma** attack)

The ECMO procedure can help a patient's lungs and heart rest and recover, but it will not cure the underlying disease. Any patient who requires ECMO is seriously ill and will likely die without the treatment. Because there is some risk involved, this method is used only when other means of support have failed.

Precautions

Typically, ECMO patients have daily chest **x rays** and blood work, and constant vital sign monitoring. They are usually placed on a special rotating bed that is designed to decrease pressure on the skin and help move secretions from the lungs.

After the child is stable on ECMO, the breathing machine settings are lowered to "rest" settings, which allows the lungs to rest without the risk of too much oxygen or pressure from the ventilator.

Description

There are two types of ECMO. Venoarterial (V-A) ECMO supports the heart and lungs and is used for patients with blood pressure or heart functioning problems in addition to respiratory problems. Venovenous (V-V) ECMO supports the lungs only.

V-A ECMO requires the insertion of two tubes, one in the jugular and one in the carotid artery. In the V-V ECMO procedure, the surgeon places a plastic tube into the jugular vein through a small incision in the neck.

Once in place, the tubes are connected to the ECMO circuit, and then the machine is turned on. The child's blood flows out through the tube and may look very dark because it contains very little oxygen. A pump pushes the blood through an artificial membrane lung, where oxygen is added and carbon dioxide is removed. The size of the artificial lung depends on the size of the child. The blood is then warmed and returned to the patient. A steady amount of blood (called the flow rate) is pushed through the ECMO machine every minute. As the patient improves, the flow rate is lowered.

Many patients require heavy sedation while they are on ECMO to lessen the amount of oxygen needed by the muscles.

As the patient improves, the amount of ECMO support is decreased gradually, until the machine is turned off for a brief trial period. If the patient does well without ECMO, the treatment is stopped.

Typically, newborns remain on ECMO for three to seven days, although some babies need more time (especially if they have a diaphragmatic hernia). Once the baby is off ECMO, he or she will still need a ventilator (breathing machine) for a few days or weeks.

Preparation

Before ECMO is begun, the patient receives medication to ease **pain** and restrict movement.

Aftercare

Because infants on ECMO may have been struggling with low oxygen levels before treatment, they may be at higher risk for developmental problems. They will need to be monitored as they grow. Some infants may have difficulty feeding after ECMO treatment.

Risks

Bleeding is the biggest risk for ECMO patients, since blood thinners (most often heparin) are given to guard against blood clots. Bleeding can occur anywhere

KEY TERMS

Carotid artery—One of the major arteries supplying blood to the head and neck.

Congenital diaphragmatic hernia—A profusion of part of the stomach through an opening in the diaphragm that is present at birth.

Meconium aspiration syndrome—Breathing in of meconium (a newborn's first stool) by a fetus or newborn, which can block air passages and interfere with lung expansion.

Membrane oxygenator—The artificial lung that adds oxygen and removes carbon dioxide.

Pulmonary hypertension—A disorder in which the pressure in the blood vessels of the lungs is abnormally high.

Respiratory distress syndrome—A lung disorder usually of premature infants that causes increasing difficulty in breathing, leading to a life-threatening deficiency of oxygen in the blood.

Venoarterial (V-A) bypass—The type of extracorporeal membrane oxygenation that provides both heart and lung support, using two tubes (one in the jugular vein and one in the carotid artery).

Venovenous (V-V) bypass—The type of extracorporeal membrane oxygenation that provides lung support only, using a tube inserted into the jugular vein.

in the body but is most serious when it occurs in the brain. This is why doctors periodically perform ultrasound brain scans of anyone on ECMO. **Stroke**, which may be caused by bleeding or blood clots in the brain, has occurred in some children undergoing ECMO.

If bleeding becomes a problem, the patient may require frequent blood or platelet transfusions or operations to control the bleeding. If the bleeding cannot be stopped, ECMO is withdrawn.

Other risks include infection or vocal cord injury. Some patients develop severe blood infections that cause irreversible damage to vital organs.

There is a small chance that some part of the complex equipment may fail, which could introduce air into the system or affect the patient's blood levels, causing damage or death of vital organs (including the brain). For this reason, the ECMO circuit is constantly monitored by a trained technologist, nurse, or respiratory therapist.

Normal results

Normal results include the lungs and/or heart returning to healthy functioning while on ECMO treatment.

Parental concerns

ECMO is used only for severely ill children. Parents need to talk with the nurse and doctor on a daily basis for updates on the condition of the child. The child may appear slightly swollen.

When to call the doctor

Notify a doctor if the child on ECMO is not behaving as expected (sedated and quiet), appears less pink (or bluer than normal), or is bleeding.

Resources

BOOKS

Cohen, Margaret, et al. *Sent Before My Time: A Child Psychotherapist's View of Life on a Neonatal Intensive Care Unit.* London: Karnac Books, 2003.

ORGANIZATIONS

American Society of Extra-Corporeal Technology. 503 Carlisle Dr., Suite 125, Herndon, VA 20170. Web site: <www.amsect.org>.

ECMO Moms and Dads. Rt. 1, Box 176ΛΛ, Idalou, TX 79329. Web site: <www.medhelp.org/amshc/amshc341.htm>.

Extracorporeal Life Support Organization. 1327 Jones Dr., Ste. 101, Ann Arbor, MI 48105. Web site: <www.elso.med.umich.edu>.

Mark A. Best
Carol A. Turkington

Extracurricular activities

Definition

Extracurricular activities are those sponsored by and usually held at school but that are not part of the academic curriculum. They often involve some time commitment outside of the regular school day.

Description

Extracurricular activities range from **sports** to newspaper editing to music and theater. Many activities, like football and drama, enjoy extreme longevity, serving as a part of their school's program over a number of years. Others, like an ecology club or writers' workshop, may be offered for a shorter time span to reflect a community interest or involvement by a particular sponsoring faculty member or class of students. For many students, extracurricular activities present an opportunity to practice social skills and to experiment in activities that may represent a career interest. For a child who is not gifted academically, the opportunity to excel in the arts or sports may make a big difference in his or her **self-esteem**.

Many extracurricular activities, such as the school newspaper, photography, and drama, can lead to careers. Extracurricular activities also help to form the student's profile for consideration in college admissions. A student's academic record and scores on standardized tests form the core of his or her college application profile. However, admissions officers consider other factors, such as a demonstrated talent in athletics or the arts or leadership in school or extracurricular activities. After-school activities can also include scouting and volunteering, such as working with the Red Cross, a local animal shelter, a homeless shelter, or in a political campaign. Through these diverse activities, students can have fun, build a resume for college, increase **creativity**, improve organizational skills, learn time management, and develop people skills.

A 2001 survey of more than 50,000 high school students in Minnesota published in the March 2003 issue of the *Journal of School Health* found that those who participated in extracurricular activities had higher levels of social, emotional, and healthy behavior than students who did not participate. Students were classified into four groups based on their participation in sports and other activities, such as clubs, volunteer work, band, choir, or music lessons: neither activity, both, other activities only, and sports only. Odds ratios for the group involved in both types of activities were significantly higher than those for all the other groups for all healthy behaviors and measures of connectedness and significantly lower for all but one of the unhealthy behaviors.

Students involved in sports alone or in combination with other activities had significantly higher odds than the other two groups for **exercise**, milk consumption, and healthy self-image, and significantly lower odds for emotional distress, **suicidal behavior**, **family** substance abuse, and physical and sexual abuse victimization. Students involved in other activities alone or in combination with sports had significantly higher odds than the other two groups for doing homework and significantly lower

odds for alcohol consumption, marijuana use, and vandalism.

Among male students in the Minnesota study, 19.1 percent engaged in neither sports nor other activities, 23.4 percent in other activities only, 15.1 percent in sports only, and 42.4 percent in both. Among female students, 12.6 percent were involved in neither, 31.6 percent in other activities only, 7.3 percent in sports only, and 48.6 percent in both. Analyses by race/ethnicity showed that white students were more likely than students of color to be involved in both sports and other activities (48.1% versus 33.6%) and sports only (11.4% versus 9.5%), while students of color were more likely to be involved in other activities only (33.8% versus 26.3%) and neither activity (23.1% versus 14.2%). Combining categories to look specifically at involvement in sports shows, that while participation rates for males (57.5%) and females (55.8%) are similar, a substantially higher proportion of white students participated in sports than students of color (59.5% versus 43.1%), according to the *Journal of School Health* article.

Preschool

Preschoolers are often enrolled in classes or activities outside of **preschool**. These activities include dance, swimming, T-ball, soccer, and gymnastics. Children this age can benefit from these activities, but the number of activities should be limited. Parents or other primary caregivers should consider how much time their children spend on these activities and the impact they have. Before enrolling children in activities outside the home and preschool, they should first attend a session to make sure it is appropriate for the child and that the child will benefit from it. A schedule that is too demanding can be stressful on a child and can lead to behavioral problems. Studies have shown that young children who feel stressed due too many extracurricular activities are more prone to illness.

School age

Studies show that children who participate in one or more after-school activities are less prone to negative **peer pressure** and have higher levels of self-esteem than children who do not participate. Studies have also shown that extracurricular activities can boost a child's academic performance and provide students with a way to feel proud of themselves and their capabilities. They can help a child release pent-up frustration and energy, develop social skills, and discover talents, abilities, and interests.

In the early school age years, it is important for parents to let the child chose the activity or activities.

Parents should not to press the child to win or excel. They should make sure the child does not overdo it, either by taking on an activity he or she cannot handle or by taking on too many activities. Parents need to insure the extracurricular activities do not interfere with school work or time spent with the family.

Once children reach middle or high school, there are usually many extracurricular activities available, including team sports such as soccer, baseball, basketball, and volleyball, and academic interests such as foreign language club, debate team, chess club, student government, student publications, 4-H Club, environmental clubs, choir, band, photography, politics, and business. Students may also have the chance to join clubs made up of students with a similar heritage or culture, including African American, Latino, Jewish, and gay and lesbian, such as the Gay-Straight Student Alliance groups found at some high schools.

Most school teachers, counselors, or principals provide a list of activities for student participation. The lists are often posted on student bulletin boards, and announcements are sometimes made in appropriate classes, such as history teachers promoting the history club or teachers promoting the group that they advise. Information can also be found in the school's student newspaper. Some students like to join clubs that one or more friends are joining while others join clubs to make friends. Students may want to keep in mind the following issues when they consider joining an extracurricular activity:

• Age: Students may have to be a certain age or in a certain grade to participate in an activity.

• Money: Some clubs or activities require students to pay a fee. There may also be costs involved with group outings, uniforms, or other items. Some groups require members to participate in fundraising activities.

• Physical exam: Students who want to join a sports team may be required to take a physical, and some schools require drug tests before students qualify to participate in sports or other extracurricular activities. Students with concerns or specific health problems, such as **asthma** or diabetes, should check with their family doctor before joining a team that requires physical activity, such as a sport or cheerleading.

• Grades: Some clubs, teams, or schools may require a minimum grade point average to join.

• Time: In competitive sports, time must be set aside for practice and competition. Team members are sometimes required to set up a game or help in other ways. Clubs can meet weekly, every other week, or monthly while athletic teams sometimes practice every day after school and on weekends.

Common problems

A common problem for many students involved in extracurricular activities is that they take on too much. Students should make out a schedule in advance of a semester that balances school, work, after-school activities, and home life. Also, activities should be fun rather than stressful for students. School grades should not suffer because of time spent at work or in after-school activities.

In sports, injuries are not uncommon but can sometimes be prevented with proper conditioning. Every child who plans to participate in organized athletic activity should have a pre-season sports physical. This special examination is performed by a pediatrician or family physician who carefully evaluates the site of any previous injury, may recommend special stretching and strengthening exercises to help growing athletes create and preserve proper muscle and joint interaction, and pays special attention to the cardiovascular and skeletal systems.

Telling the physician which sport the athlete plays helps that physician determine which parts of the body will be subjected to the most stress. The physician then is able to suggest steps to take for minimizing the chance of injury. Other injury-reducing game plans include:

• being in shape

• knowing and obeying the rules that regulate the activity

• not playing when tired, ill, or in **pain**

• not using steroids, which can improve athletic performance but cause life-threatening problems

• taking good care of athletic equipment and using it properly

• wearing appropriate protective equipment

Parental concerns

Parents must stay focused and make sure the extracurricular activities do not interfere with their child's schoolwork. If a child is tense, irritable, has difficulty concentrating in class, is often fatigued, or is shirking homework, it may be due to the extracurricular activities taking too much of his or her time. Parents may find it helpful to require a certain realistic level of academic achievement in order for the student to continue participation in extracurricular activities. Parents must also be

KEY TERMS

Cardiovascular—Relating to the heart and blood vessels.

Peer pressure—Social pressure exerted by a group or individual in a group on someone to adopt a particular type of behavior, dress, or attitude in order to be an accepted member of a group or clique.

Primary caregiver—A person who is responsible for the primary care and upbringing of a child.

Self-esteem—A sense of competence, achievement, and self-respect. Maslow felt that the most stable source of self-esteem is genuine accomplishment rather than public acclaim or praise.

Steroids—Hormones, including aldosterone, cortisol, and androgens, that are derived from cholesterol and that share a four-ring structural characteristic.

willing to put in a certain amount of time and effort, such as taking the child to and from after-school activities and events if the student does not drive.

It is important, especially with younger children, that parents check the activities to make sure there is adequate adult supervision for any team or club in which their children participate.

When to call the doctor

Children who refuse to join any extracurricular activities yet appear unhappy or have no friends may be suffering from emotional problems such as depression or low self-esteem. Professional help, such as counseling, may be needed. Sometimes a lack of self-esteem or other problems are too much for a student to handle alone. Parents may need to seek professional psychological help for children suffering from low self-esteem when the child is depressed or shows overly **aggressive behavior**.

When a child is hurt while playing sports, the family physician, pediatrician, or an orthopedic surgeon, should evaluate symptoms that persist, intensify, or reduce the athlete's ability to **play** without pain. Prompt diagnosis often can prevent minor injuries from becoming major problems or causing long-term damage.

Resources

BOOKS

DeBroff, Stacy M. *Sign Me Up! The Parents' Complete Guide to Sports, Activities, Music Lessons, Dance Classes, and Other Extracurriculars*. New York: Free Press, 2003.

Garner, Ruth. *Hanging Out: Community-Based After-School Programs for Children*. Bergen, CT: Bergin & Garvey, 2002.

Mahoney, Joseph L., et al. *Organized Activities as Contexts of Development: Extracurricular Activities, After-School, and Community Programs*. Mahwah, NJ: Lawrence Erlbaum Associates, 2004.

Malina, Robert M., and Michael A. Clark. *Youth Sports: Perspectives for a New Century*. Monterey, CA: Coaches Choice Books, 2003.

PERIODICALS

Eccles, Jacquelynne S., et al. "Extracurricular Activities and Adolescent Development." *Journal of Social Issues* 59 (Winter 2003): 865–89.

Harrison, Patricia A., and Gopalakrishnan Narayan. "Differences in Behavior, Psychological Factors, and Environmental Factors Associated with Participation in School Sports and Other Activities in Adolescence." *Journal of School Health* 73 (March 2003): 113–20.

Huebner, Angela J., and Jay A. Mancini. "Shaping Structured Out-of-School Time Use Among Youth: The Effects of Self, Family, and Friend Systems." *Journal of Youth and Adolescence* 32 (December 2003): 453–63.

Ishee, Jimmy H. "Participation in Extracurricular Physical Activity in Middle Schools." *The Journal of Physical Education, Recreation & Dance* 74 (April 2003): 10.

ORGANIZATIONS

Association for Supervision and Curriculum Development. 1703 Beauregard St., Alexandria, VA 22311. Web site: <www.acsd.org>.

National Institute on Out-Of-School Time. 106 Central St., Wellesley, MA 02481. Web site: <www.niost.org>.

Society for Research in Child Development. University of Michigan, 3131 S. State St., Suite 302, Ann Arbor, MI 48108. Web site: <www.srcd.org>.

WEB SITES

"Extracurricular Excitement." *TeensHealth*, July 2004. Available online at <www.kidshealth.org/teen/school_jobs/school/involved_school.html> (accessed November 27, 2004).

Ken R. Wells

Eye abrasion *see* **Corneal abrasion**

Eye and vision development

Definition

The visual system is the most complex sensory system in the human body. However, it is the least mature system at birth. Though they have the anatomical structures needed for sight, infants have not learned to use them yet. Much of their first weeks and months are spent learning to see. As children grow, more complex skills, like visual perception, develop.

Description

At birth, the sense of hearing is much more dominant than the sense of sight. Normal visual development is the change from just responding to simple brightness or high contrast, toward the organization of details into patterns and the ability to apply meaning to an object or picture.

Infancy

At birth, babies are capable of seeing shapes by following lines where light and dark meet. They can see variations of light and dark and shades of gray. Newborns can only focus between 8–12 inches (20–30 cm), so much of their vision is blurred. Full-term babies should be able to see their mother's facial expressions within a week of birth.

Eye muscle coordination in a newborn is also very immature. Babies' eyes often turn in or out or do not work together, a condition called **strabismus**. Babies initially learn to focus their eyes by looking at faces. They then gradually move out to objects brought close to them. Tracking and eye teaming skills begin to develop when infants start following moving objects. This usually happens by three months of age. Brightly colored moving objects, such as a mobile, can help stimulate visual development. Babies then start to learn how to coordinate their eye movements. At four months of age, babies can see the full range of colors. Between four and six months, the child normally begins batting at or reaching for the mobile or **toys** held in front of him or her.

During the first three to six months, the retina is fairly well-developed, and babies can visualize small objects. Depth perception also develops. By six months of age, the eye has reached about two-thirds of what will be its adult size. At this stage, the two eyes are most likely working together. The result is good binocular, or two-eyed, vision. It is during the first year of life that the eyes' greatest physical development occurs.

As babies start controlling their own physical movements, their eye/body coordination develops. By the fourth or fifth month, babies' brains have finished learning how to blend the images coming in from both their left and right eyes into a single image, with strong depth perception. Spatial and dimensional awareness keep improving as the baby learns to aim accurately when reaching for objects. Babies at this age also learn to change focus quickly and accurately between near and far distances.

A child's clarity of vision (visual acuity) has usually developed to 20/20 by the time the child reaches six months of age. At this time, babies achieve fairly precise eye movement control. At ages eight to 12 months, babies are judging distances well. Their eye/hand/body coordination continues to evolve, allowing them to grasp and throw objects with some accuracy. The integration of their fine motor abilities and their vision permits the child to manipulate smaller objects, and many begin feeding themselves. Once children begin to walk, they learn to use their eyes to guide and manage their bodies' large muscle groups to direct their whole movements.

Infancy

The following timeline discussion highlights some of the developmental milestones of vision development in a child's first year. Between birth and one month, a baby shows preference for familiar faces and objects, pays attention to the human face for short periods of time, has acuity of about 20/400 but can detect a black line on a white background that is only 1/16 of an inch (1.6 mm) wide, and possesses color vision, with the exception of blue.

At two months, a baby will visually lock onto a human face, watches people who are some distance away, is able to alternate his or her gaze between two people or objects, and demonstrates simple visual preferences.

Between four and six months, a baby is enthralled with other baby's faces, and he or she enjoys looking in a mirror. At this age the baby recognizes a person on sight and smiles. The baby also shifts from preferring what is familiar to that which is new, with the exception of people. The child will also look for objects when they fall from view.

From six to 12 months, a baby continues to "see" objects even when they are no longer visible. At this age, the baby also responds to words a parent uses to label familiar objects and people, by gazing in their direction.

Toddlerhood

After the first year, children's eyes and vision continue to develop. Their eye muscles gain strength, and the connections between nerves multiply. This development is aided by providing visual stimulation. Activities such as stacking building blocks, coloring, and cutting all assist in improving eye/hand/body coordination, eye teaming, and depth perception. By age three, most children have developed the necessary language and motor skills that allow them to participate in some traditional vision tests.

Preschool

During the **preschool** years, a child's vision keeps developing. The child develops visually guided eye/hand/body coordination, the **fine motor skills** and visual motor skills required for reading. The following can facilitate a preschooler's visual development:

• reading aloud to the child and letting him or her see what is being read

• providing a chalkboard or finger paints and demonstrating how to use them in play

• allowing time for interacting with other children and for playing alone

School age

It is important that children have a complete eye examination before beginning school. The optometrist or ophthalmologist needs to determine if a child's vision is prepared to handle reading, writing, and other close-up activities. While toddlers use their eyes primarily for distance sight, school requires that the child's eyes focus on very close work for hours every day. This activity occasionally causes eye problems to arise. It is important to note that children rarely report vision problems. They believe their vision is normal and believe others see the way they do. The basic vision skills needed for school work are:

• near vision (the ability to see clearly at 10–13 inches [25-32 cm])

Child being tested for visual acuity. (© Laura Dwight/Corbis.)

• distance vision (the ability to see clearly beyond arm's reach)

• binocular vision (using both eyes together for depth perception)

• focusing skills (the ability to keep both eyes accurately focused at the proper distance)

• eye movement skills (the ability to aim the eyes accurately)

• peripheral awareness (the awareness of objects located to the side while looking straight ahead)

• eye-hand coordination

Common problems

Infants born prematurely have more difficulty integrating and interpreting visual information even when their acuity is normal. In some cases, children develop their visual reflex later than normal. This is called visual maturation delay. A condition, **nystagmus**, which sometimes develops in infancy, causes the eyes to jump, dance, wiggle, or oscillate. Babies with this problem may or may not have normal vision.

Parental concerns

Parents need to assess their child frequently for any signs that the child's visual development is not progressing as expected. Some vision disorders are untreatable at later ages, so it is important to have the child seen by an optometrist or ophthalmologist no later than the age of three.

When to call the doctor

At the first signs of eye and vision problems, parents should consult their pediatrician, optometrist, or ophthalmologist. Some of these signs are:

- an eye that is crossed far into the nasal area

- eyes turned grossly in or out or which do not move normally before the age of three months

- an eye that moves while the other remains still

- an eye that appears considerably different from the other

- the inability at three months of age of an infant to follow a toy passed in front of him from side to side

During the preschool years, parents should continue looking for signs that a vision development problem exists. These signs may include a short attention span for the child's age; difficulty with eye/hand/body coordination; or the avoidance of coloring, puzzles, and other activities.

A child should have his first eye exam by the age of three (or sooner if vision problems run in the **family**), so the practitioner can assess if vision is developing normally. Vision should be checked again when the child enters school.

Some of the signs of visual problems in the school age child are:

- frequently losing his or her place while reading

- frequently avoiding close work

- holding reading material closer than usual

- frequently rubbing the eyes

- complaining of headaches

- turning or tilting the head to use one eye only

Since vision changes may occur without the parents or the child noticing them, a child should visit an eye doctor at least every two years, more frequently if specific problems or risk factors exist.

Resources

BOOKS

Marks, Paul. *Through a Baby's Eyes: An Infant's Humorous Diary on the First Year of Life.* Chula Vista, CA: Black Forest Press, 2004.

ORGANIZATIONS

National Eye Institute. 31 Center Drive MSC 2510 Bethesda, MD 20892–2510. Web site: <www.nei.nih.gov>.

WEB SITES

Glass, Penny. "What Do Babies See?" *Vision Connection*, December 3, 2004. Available online at <www.visionconnection.org/Content/ChildrensVision/AboutChildrensVision/AboutInfantsVision/WhatDoBabiesSee.htm> (accessed January 11, 2005).

Deanna M. Swartout-Corbeil, RN

Eye cancer *see* **Retinoblastoma**

Eyeglasses and contact lenses

Definition

Eyeglasses and contact lenses are devices that correct refractive errors in vision. Eyeglass lenses are mounted in frames that are worn on the face, sitting mostly on the ears and nose, so that the lenses are positioned in front of the eyes. Contact lenses appear to be worn in direct contact with the cornea, but they actually float on a layer of tears that separates them from the cornea.

Purpose

The purpose of eyeglasses and contact lenses is to correct or improve the vision of people with nearsightedness (**myopia**), farsightedness (hyperopia), presbyopia, and astigmatism.

Description

Eyes are examined by optometrists (OD) or by ophthalmologists (MD or DO). Prescriptions, if necessary, are then given to patients for glasses. Eyeglasses are generally made by an optician. A separate contact lens-fitting exam is necessary if an individual wants contact lenses, because an eyeglass prescription can differ from a contact lens prescription.

Eyeglasses

More than 140 million people in the United States wear eyeglasses. People whose eyes have refractive errors do not see clearly without glasses, because the light emitted from the objects they are observing does not come into focus on their retinas. For people who are farsighted, images come into focus behind the retina; for people who are nearsighted, images come into focus in front of the retina. For both, the result is a blurring of vision.

LENSES Lenses work by changing the direction of light so that images come into focus on the retina. The greater the index of refraction of the lens material and the greater the difference in the curvature between the two surfaces of the lens, the greater the change in direction of light that passes through it and the greater the correction.

Lenses can be unifocal, with one correction for all distances, or they can correct for more than one distance (multifocal). One type of multifocal, the bifocal, has an area of the lens (usually at the bottom) that corrects for nearby objects (about 14 in [35 cm] from the eyes); the remainder of the lens corrects for distant objects (about 20 ft [6 m] from the eyes). Another type of multifocal, a trifocal, has an area in-between that corrects for intermediate distances (usually about 28 in [71 cm]) Conventional bifocals and trifocals have visible lines between the areas of different correction; however, lenses in which the correction gradually changes from one area to the other, without visible lines, have been available since the 1970s. Such lenses are sometimes called progressives or no-line bifocals.

To be suitable for eyeglass lenses, a material must be transparent, without bubbles, and have a high index of refraction. The greater the index of refraction, the thinner the lens can be. Lenses are made from either glass or plastic (hard resin). The advantage of plastic is that it is lightweight and more impact-resistant than glass. The advantage of glass is that it is scratch resistant and provides the clearest possible vision.

Glass was the first material to be used for eyeglass lenses and was used for several hundred years before plastic was introduced. The crown glass used for eyeglass lenses has an index of refraction of 1.52.

In the early 2000s eyeglass wearers can choose polycarbonate or polyurethane materials for their lenses. Polycarbonate is the most impact-resistant material available for eyewear, and polyurethane has exceptional optical qualities and an index of refraction of up to 1.66, much higher than the conventional plastics used for lenses and even higher than glass. Parents whose children have high prescriptions should ask about high-index material options for their lenses. Aspheric lenses are also useful for high prescriptions. They are flatter and lighter than conventional lenses.

There are many lenses and lens-coating options for individual needs, including coatings that block the ultraviolet (UV) light and/or blue light which have been found to be harmful to the eyes. Such coatings are not needed on polycarbonate lenses, which already have UV protection. UV coatings are particularly important on sunglasses and ski goggles. Sunglasses, when nonprescription, should be labeled with an indication that they block out 99 to 100 percent of both UV-A and UV-B rays.

There are anti-scratch coatings that increase the surface hardness of lenses (an important feature when using plastic lenses) and anti-reflective (AR) coatings that eliminate almost all glare and allow other people to see the eyes of the wearer. AR coatings may be particularly helpful to people who use computers or who drive at night. Mirror coatings that prevent other people from seeing the wearer's eyes are also available. There is a whole spectrum of tints, from light to dark, used in sunglasses. Tint, however, does not block-out UV rays, so a UV coating is needed. Polaroid lenses that block out much of the reflected light also allow better vision in sunny weather and are helpful for people who enjoy boating. Photosensitive (photochromatic) lenses that darken in the presence of bright light are handy for people who do not want to carry an extra set of glasses. Photochromatic lenses are available in glass and plastic.

FRAMES Frames can be made from metal or plastic, and they can be rimless. There is an almost unlimited variety of shapes, colors, and sizes. The type and degree of refractive correction in the lens determine to some extent the type of frame most suitable. Some lenses are too thick to fit in metal rims, and some large-correction prescriptions are best suited to frames with small-area lenses.

Rimless frames are the least noticeable type, and they are lightweight because the nosepiece and temples are attached directly to the lenses, eliminating the weight of the rims. They tend not to be as sturdy as frames with rims, so they are not a good choice for children, or for people who frequently remove their glasses and put them on again. They are also not very suitable for lenses that correct a high degree of farsightedness, because such lenses are thin at the edges.

Metal frames are less noticeable than plastic, and they are lightweight. They are available in solid gold, gold-filled, anodized aluminum, nickel, silver, stainless steel, and titanium and titanium alloy. Until the late 1980s, when titanium-nickel alloy and titanium frames were introduced, metal frames were, in general, more fragile than plastic frames. Titanium frames, however, are very strong and lightweight. An alloy of titanium and nickel, called Flexon, is strong, lightweight, and returns to its original shape after being twisted or dented. It is not perfect for everyone, though, because some young people are sensitive to its nickel content. Flexon frames are also relatively expensive.

Plastic frames are durable, can accommodate just about any lens prescription, and are available in a wide range of prices. They are also offered in a variety of plastics, including acrylic, epoxy, cellulose acetate, cellulose propionate, polyamide, and nylon, and in different colors, shapes, and levels of resistance to breakage. Epoxy frames are resilient and return to their original shape after being deformed, so they do not need to be adjusted as frequently as other types. Nylon frames are almost unbreakable. They revert to their original shape after extreme trauma and distortion; because of this property, though, they cannot be readjusted after they are manufactured.

FIT An individual should have the distance between the eyes (PD) measured, so that the optical centers of the lenses will be in front of the person's pupils. Bifocal heights also have to be measured with the chosen frame in place and adjusted on the person. Again, this is so that the lenses will be positioned correctly. If not positioned correctly, the individual may experience eyestrain, **headache**, or other problems.

Children may sometimes need a few days to adjust to a new prescription. However, problems should be reported, because the glasses may need to be rechecked.

Contact lenses

Over 32 million people in the United States wear these small lenses that fit on top of the cornea. They provide a field of view unobstructed by eyeglass frames. They do not fog up or get splattered, so it is possible to see well while walking in the rain. They are less noticeable than any style of eyeglass. On the other hand, they take time to get accustomed to; require more measurements for fitting; require many follow-up visits to an eye doctor; can lead to complications such as infections and corneal damage; and may not correct astigmatism as well as eyeglasses, especially if the astigmatism is severe.

Originally, hard contact lenses were made of a material called PMMA. The more common types of contact lenses are listed below:

- Rigid gas-permeable (RGP) daily-wear lenses are made of plastic that does not absorb water but allows oxygen to get from the atmosphere to the cornea. (This is important because the cornea has no blood supply and needs to get its oxygen from the atmosphere through the film of tears that moves beneath the lens.) These lenses must be removed and cleaned each night.

- Rigid gas-permeable (RGP) extended-wear lenses are made from plastic that also does not absorb water but is more permeable to oxygen than the plastic used for daily-wear lenses. They can be worn up to a week.

- Daily wear soft lenses are made of plastic that is permeable to oxygen and absorbs water; therefore, they are soft and flexible. These lenses must be removed and cleaned each night, and they do not correct all vision problems. Soft lenses are easier to get used to than rigid lenses but are more prone to tears and do not last as long.

- Extended-wear soft lenses are highly permeable to oxygen, are flexible by virtue of their ability to absorb water, and can usually be worn for up to one week. They do not correct all vision problems. There is more risk of infection with extended-wear lenses than with daily-wear lenses.

- Extended-wear disposable lenses are soft lenses worn continually for up to six days and then discarded, with no need for cleaning.

- Planned-replacement soft lenses are daily-wear lenses that are replaced on a regular schedule, which is usually every two weeks, monthly, or quarterly. They must also be cleaned.

Soft contact lenses come in a variety of materials. There are also different kinds of RGP and soft multifocal contact lenses available. Monovision, where one contact lens corrects for distance vision while the other corrects for near vision, may be an option for persons with presbyopia. Monovision, however, may affect depth perception and may not be appropriate for everyone. Contact lenses also come in a variety of tints. Soft contacts are available that can change the color of dark-colored eyes. Even though such lenses have no prescription, they must be fitted and checked to make sure that an eye infection does not occur. People should never wear someone else's contact lenses. Doing so can lead to infection or damage to the eye.

Risks

Young people allergic to certain plastics should not wear contact lenses or eyeglass frames or lenses manufactured from that type of plastic. People allergic to nickel should not wear Flexon frames. Children and teens at risk of being in accidents that might shatter glass lenses should wear plastic lenses, preferably polycarbonate. (Lenses made from polycarbonate, the same type of plastic used for the space shuttle windshield, are about 50 times stronger than other lens materials.) Also, young people whose work places them at risk of receiving electric shock should avoid metal frames.

KEY TERMS

Astigmatism—An eye condition in which the cornea doesn't focus light properly on the retina, resulting in a blurred image.

Cornea—The clear, dome-shaped outer covering of the eye that lies in front of the iris and pupil. The cornea lets light into the eye.

Index of refraction—A constant number for any material and any given color of light that is an indicator of the degree of bending of the light caused by that material.

Lens—The transparent, elastic, curved structure behind the iris (colored part of the eye) that helps focus light on the retina. Also refers to any device that bends light waves.

Permeable—A condition in which fluid or certain other substances are allowed to pass through.

Polycarbonate—A very strong type of plastic often used in safety glasses, sport glasses, and children's eyeglasses. Polycarbonate lenses have approximately 50 times the impact resistance of glass lenses.

Presbyopia—A condition affecting people over the age of 40 where the system of accommodation that allows the eyes to focus on near objects fails to work because of age-related hardening of the lens of the eye.

Retina—The inner, light-sensitive layer of the eye containing rods and cones. The retina transforms the image it receives into electrical signals that are sent to the brain via the optic nerve.

Ultraviolet (UV) radiation—A portion of the light spectrum with a wavelength just below that of visible light. UV radiation is damaging to DNA and can destroy microorganisms. It may be responsible for sunburns, skins cancers, and cataracts in humans. Two bands of the UV spectrum, UVA and UVB, are used to treat psoriasis and other skin diseases.

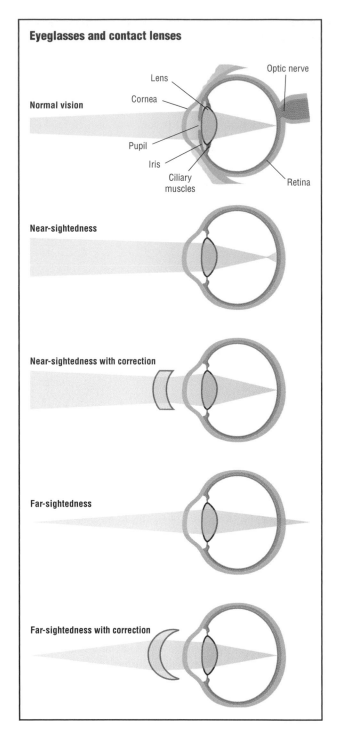

When the eyes function properly, the lens can focus images perfectly on the retina. However, nearsightedness causes the image to focus before it reaches the retina, and far-sightedness causes the image to focus past the retina. In each case, a corrective lens is used to adjust the focus of the image to bring a clear picture to retina, optic nerve, and eventually to the brain. *(Illustration by GGS Information Services.)*

People employed in certain occupations may be prohibited from wearing contact lenses or may be required to wear **safety** eyewear over the contact lenses. Some occupations, such as construction or auto repair, may require safety lenses and safety frames. Physicians and employers should be consulted for recommendations.

Contact lens wearers must be examined periodically by their eye doctors to make sure that the lenses fit properly and that there is no infection. Both infection and lenses that do not fit properly can damage the cornea. People can be allergic to certain solutions that are used to clean or lubricate lenses. For that reason, individuals should not randomly switch products unless they speak with their doctor. Contact lens wearers should seek immediate attention if they experience eye **pain**, a burning sensation, red eyes, intolerable sensitivity to light, cloudy vision, or an inability to keep the eyes open.

To avoid infection, it is important for contact lens wearers to exactly follow their instructions for lens insertion and removal, as well as cleaning. Soft contact lens wearers should never use tap water to rinse their lenses or to make-up solutions. All contact lens wearers should also always have a pair of glasses and a carrying case for their contacts with them, in case the contacts have to be removed due to eye irritation. Wearing contact lenses increases the risk of corneal damage and eye infections.

Normal results

Improved vision is the primary result of corrective lenses. The normal expectation is that people will achieve 20/20 vision while wearing corrective lenses. Contact lenses may contribute to improved cosmetic appearance for some users.

Parental concerns

Parents of young children requiring corrective lenses should be prepared for broken or lost glasses. Parents of adolescents who wear contact lenses should help their children to maintain a regular cleaning schedule. Glasses normally last one to two years. Growing children may require changes of prescription more frequently than people in other age groups.

Resources

BOOKS

Douglas, Lloyd G. *My Eyes*. Bridgeport, CT: Children's Press, 2004.

Milder, Benjamin, and Melvin L. Rubin. *The Fine Art of Prescribing Glasses Without Making a Spectacle of Yourself*, 3rd ed. Gainesville, FL: Triad Publishing, 2004.

Olitsky, Scott, and Leonard B. Nelson. "Disorders of Vision." In *Nelson Textbook of Pediatrics*, 17th ed. Richard E. Behrman et al. Philadelphia: Saunders, 2003, pp. 2087–2089.

Willson, Sarah. *Hocus Focus*. New York: Kane Press, 2004.

PERIODICALS

Glavas, I. P., et al. "Sunglasses- and photochromic lens-wearing patterns in spectacle and/or contact lens-wearing individuals." *Eye and Contact Lens* 30, no. 2 (2004): 81–84.

Kemper, A. R., D. Bruckman, and G. L. Freed. "Prevalence and distribution of corrective lenses among school-age children." *Optometry and Vision Science* 81, no. 1 (2004): 7–10.

Kemper, A. R., L. M. Cohn, and K. J. Dombkowski. "Patterns of vision care among Medicaid-enrolled children." *Journal of Pediatrics* 113, no. 3 pt 1 (2004): e190–e196.

ORGANIZATIONS

American Academy of Ophthalmology. PO Box 7424, San Francisco, CA 94120. Web site: <www.eyenet.org>.

American Optometric Association. 243 North Lindbergh Blvd., St. Louis, MO 63141. Web site: <www.aoanet.org/>.

Contact Lens Society of America. 441 Carlisle Drive, Herndon, VA 20170. Web site: <www.clsa.info/index.shtml>.

Opticians Association of America. 44 Carlisle Drive, Herndon, VA 20170. Web site: <www.oaa.org>.

WEB SITES

"Contact Lenses." *Contact Lens Council*. Available online at <www.coontactlenscouncil.org/> (accessed September 28, 2004).

"Eyeglasses." Available online at <www.allaboutvision.com/eyeglasses/> (accessed September 28, 2004).

"Eyeglass Recycling." Available online at <www.lionsclubs.org/EN/content/vision_eyeglass_recycling.shtml> (accessed September 28, 2004).

"How to Read Your Eyeglasses Prescription." Available online at <www.medem.com/MedLB/article_detaillb.cfm?article_ID=ZZZG178LH4C&sub_cat=2017> (accessed September 28, 2004).

L. Fleming Fallon, Jr., MD, DrPH

F

Fabry's disease *see* **Lipidoses**

Facial nerve palsy *see* **Bell's palsy**

Factor IX deficiency *see* **Hemophilia**

Factor VIII deficiency *see* **Hemophilia**

Failing a grade *see* **Retention in school**

Failure to thrive

Definition

Failure to thrive (FTT) is a term used to describe children whose physical growth over time is inadequate when compared to a standard growth chart.

Description

There is no universally accepted definition of failure to thrive, though it has been recognized as a medical condition since the early 1900s. It describes a condition rather than a specific disease. Children are considered as failing to thrive when their rate of growth does not meet the expected growth rate for a child their age. The difficulty lies in knowing what rate of growth is expected for any individual child, since many factors, including race and genetics, may influence growth.

Recognizing abnormal growth requires an understanding of normal infant growth. Infants normally lose up to 10 percent of their weight in the first few days of life. However, this weight should be regained within two weeks. The average full-term baby doubles its birth weight by six months and has tripled it by one year. Children with failure to thrive are often not meeting those milestones. If a baby continues to lose weight or does not gain weight as expected, he or she is probably not thriving.

Children who fail to thrive are either not receiving or have an inability to take in or retain adequate **nutrition** in order to gain weight and grow. If the condition progresses, the undernourished child may become irritable and/or apathetic and may not reach typical developmental markers such as sitting up, walking, and talking at the usual ages.

Demographics

The incidence of growth failure of American children is difficult to assess. Failure to thrive is believed to affect up to 5 percent of the population but is most common in the first six months of a child's life. It is commonly seen in babies born prematurely. Most diagnoses of failure to thrive are made in infants and toddlers in the first few years of life. An estimated 10 percent of children seen in primary care settings have symptoms of failure to thrive. The condition can appear in all socioeconomic groups, although it is seen more frequently in those families experiencing poverty. There is an increased incidence among children receiving Medicaid, those living in rural areas, and in children who are homeless.

Causes and symptoms

Failure to thrive may have several underlying causes. The causes of failure to thrive are typically differentiated into organic and non-organic. Organic causes are those caused by an underlying medical disorder. Inorganic causes are those caused by a caregiver's actions. However, these definitions are simplified, as both medical and behavioral causes often appear together.

Organic causes of failure to thrive may include:

- premature birth, especially if the fetus had intrauterine growth retardation

- maternal **smoking**, alcohol use, or illicit drugs during pregnancy

- mechanical problems present, resulting from a poor ability to suck or swallow, for example, presence of **cleft lip** and cleft palate

- unexplained poor appetites that are unrelated to mechanical problems or structural abnormalities, for example, breathing difficulties that can result from congestive heart failure (Any difficulty in breathing makes eating more difficult and can result in FTT. Inadequate intake also can result from metabolic abnormalities, excessive **vomiting** caused by obstruction of the gastrointestinal tract, or kidney dysfunction. In addition, gastroesophageal reflux causing regurgitation of formula or refusal of feeding.)

- poor absorption of food, inability of the body to use absorbed nutrients, or increased loss of nutrients

Some examples of non-organic causes of failure to thrive are:

- poor feeding skills on the part of the parent
- dysfunctional **family** interactions
- difficult parent-child interactions
- lack of social support
- lack of parenting preparation
- family dysfunction, such as abuse or divorce
- child neglect
- emotional deprivation

Studies show that only between 5 percent and 26 percent of FTT cases are due to a purely organic cause. Children in abusive or neglectful families are at higher risk of FTT, but these cases make up only a small proportion of the total. The most common cause of failure to thrive is **malnutrition**, either as part of an organic problem or simply because of an energy imbalance.

The following symptoms are possible indications of failure to thrive:

- delayed social and mental skills

- delayed development of secondary sexual traits in adolescents

- height, weight, and head circumference in an infant or young child not progressing as expected on growth charts

- edema (swelling)
- wasting
- enlarged liver
- rashes or changes in the skin
- changes in hair texture

When to call the doctor

Parents should notify their physician if their child does not seem to be developing at a normal pace. If parents notice a drop in weight or if the baby does not want to eat, the doctor should be notified. A major change in eating patterns also warrants contact.

Diagnosis

If a child fails to gain weight for three months in a row during the first year of life, physicians normally become concerned. The most important part of a physician's evaluation is taking a detailed history. Prenatal history is important, and the doctor will want to know if the pregnant mother smoked, consumed alcohol, used any medications, or had any illness during the pregnancy. The doctor will also want a dietary history, to determine if there have been any feeding problems. A history of how formula is mixed is important, because improperly prepared formula can result in failure to thrive. Parents will also be asked about whether the child had any illnesses, as some can cause a problem with the growth potential of children. A family and social history will also be done.

Doctors diagnose failure to thrive by plotting the child's weight, length, and head circumference on standard growth charts. Children who fall below a particular weight range for their age or who dip below two or more percentile curves on the chart over a short period of time will likely have a more thorough evaluation to find out if there is a problem. A complete blood count, various serum chemical and electrolyte tests, and a urinalysis may be helpful in discovering any underlying medical disorders. The doctor will want to determine if the child is receiving enough nourishment. To do this, the parents will be asked to record what the child eats each day, and a subsequent calorie count will be done. The doctor may also talk to the parents to help identify any home problems like financial difficulties, household stress, or neglect.

It is important to remember that some children will normally fall below the standards on growth charts. If children are full of energy, interacting normally with their parents, and show no signs of illness, then they are probably not failing to thrive and are just smaller children.

Once the diagnosis of failure to thrive has been made, the physician will attempt to determine if it is from an organic or non-organic cause.

Treatment

Because there are numerous factors that may contribute to a failure to thrive diagnosis, children diagnosed with the disorder sometimes have an entire medical team working on the case. If there is an underlying physical cause, correcting that problem may reverse the condition. The doctor will recommend high-calorie foods and place the child on a high-density formula like Pediasure. More severe cases may involve tube feedings, which can take place at home. A child with extreme failure to thrive may need **hospitalization**, during which he or she can be fed and monitored continuously. This will give the treatment team an opportunity to also observe the caregiver's interactions with the child.

The duration of treatment will vary from child to child. Weight gain takes time, so several months may go by before a child returns to his normal weight range. Children requiring hospitalization usually stay for approximately two weeks or more to get them out of danger, but many months can pass before the symptoms of malnutrition disappear.

Nutritional concerns

The long-term goal for every child with FTT is to provide adequate energy intake for growth. Therefore, even if no causative factor is uncovered for a child with FTT, aggressive dietary management is the key to successful treatment. Proper feeding can be achieved through infant formulas that are adjusted to meet the child's specific nutrient needs. Infants may be given concentrated formulas, assuming their kidney function is normal. In cases of kidney disorders, increasing the fat content of the formula may be useful as a way of delivering additional calories. Older children with FTT may benefit from adding cheese, sour cream, butter, margarine, or peanut butter to meals. Also, high-calorie shakes can be used to supplement meals. Multivitamin and mineral supplements, including iron and zinc, usually are recommended to all undernourished children. Tube feeding is usually not indicated except for severe cases of malnutrition.

Prognosis

Whether FTT results from organic or non-organic reasons, children with this condition require aggressive calorie supplementation. Some cases may lead to significant developmental delays in children. The cognitive outcome of children who have had FTT is not clear, and this may lead to emotional and behavioral problems later. However, carefully looking for the causes of failure to thrive and implementing calorie supplementation is important for obtaining a positive outcome in these children.

Prevention

Initial failure to thrive caused by physical defects cannot be prevented but can often be corrected before they become a danger to the child. Maternal education as well as emotional and economic support systems may help to prevent failure to thrive in those cases where is no physical deformity.

Parental concerns

Parents who note any of the symptoms of failure to thrive should report them to their child's physician so that treatment can begin.

Resources

BOOKS

Bremmer, J. Gavin, et al. *The Blackwell Handbook of Infant Development*. Oxford, UK: Blackwell Publishing, 2004.

Slater, Alan, et al. *Introduction to Infant Development*. Oxford, UK: Oxford University Press, 2002.

PERIODICALS

"Failure to Thrive." *Update* (June 17, 2004): 567.

Krugman, Scott D., and Howard Dubowitz. "Failure to Thrive." *American Family Physician* 68 (September 1, 2003): 5, 879–84.

WEB SITES

Bassali, Reda W., and John Benjamin. "Failure to Thrive." *Emedicine*, August 11, 2004. Available online at

<www.emedicine.com/ped/topic738.htm> (accessed January 11, 2005).

"Failure to Thrive." *Kidshealth.org*, February 2001. Available online at <www.kidshealth.org/parent/growth/growth/failure_thrive.html> (accessed January 11, 2005).

"Failure to Thrive." *MedlinePlus*, November 3, 2002. Available online at <www.nlm.nih.gov/medlineplus/ency/article/000991.htm> (accessed January 11, 2005).

Deanna M. Swartout-Corbeil, RN

Fallot's tetralogy *see* **Tetralogy of Fallot**

Familial Mediterranean fever

Definition

Familial Mediterranean fever (FMF) is an inherited disorder characterized by an inflammatory response recurring with attacks of fever accompanied by intense **pain** in the abdomen, chest, or joints. Attacks usually last 12–72 hours and can occasionally involve a skin rash. Kidney disease is a serious complication that may develop if the disorder is not treated. FMF is most prevalent in people of Armenian, Sephardic-Jewish, Arabic, and Turkish ancestry. The disorder takes its name from the fact that these ethnic groups live in countries along or near the eastern coast of the Mediterranean Sea.

FMF is sometimes grouped together with other periodic fevers in a category called autoinflammatory disorders. The term was invented to describe illnesses caused by genetic defects in the human immune response. Other disorders in this group are TNF-receptor associated periodic syndrome (TRAPS), hyper-IgD syndrome (HIDS), and familial Hibernian fever.

Description

FMF has been described as a disorder of "inappropriate" inflammation or an autoinflammatory syndrome. That is, an event that causes a mild or unnoticeable inflammation in most people might cause a severe inflammatory response in someone with FMF. Certain areas of the body are at risk for FMF-related symptoms. A serosa is a serous (fluid-producing) membrane that can be found inside the abdominal cavity (peritoneum), around the lungs (pleura), around the heart (pericardium), and inside the joints (synovium). The symptoms of FMF are due to inflammation of one or more of the serosal membranes (serositis). Thus, FMF is sometimes called recurrent polyserositis. Other names for the disorder are periodic peritonitis, periodic fever, periodic disease, familial paroxysmal polyserositis, periodic amyloid syndrome, periodic peritonitis syndrome, Reimann periodic disease, Reimann syndrome, Siegel-Cattan-Mamou syndrome, and Armenian syndrome.

During an attack of FMF, large numbers of neutrophils, a type of white blood cell, move into the affected areas of the body, where they cause painful inflammation and fever. These episodes may be accompanied by a skin rash (erythema) or joint pain. In a few cases, chronic arthritis is a problem. Amyloidosis is a potentially serious condition in which proteins called amyloids are mistakenly produced and deposited in organs and tissues throughout the body. Left untreated, amyloidosis often leads to kidney failure, which is the major long-term health risk in FMF.

In most cases, patients diagnosed with FMF first notice the attacks of fever and pain in childhood or **adolescence**. The intervals between these episodes may extend for days or months and are unpredictable. People with FMF typically lead normal lives during these pain-free intervals. It is not entirely clear what brings on an attack, although people with FMF often report mild physical trauma, physical exertion, or emotional stress just prior to the onset of symptoms. The mainstay of treatment for FMF is an oral medication called colchicine, which is highly effective for the fever and pain that accompany the disorder, as well as for amyloidosis and the kidney disease that can result from it.

Demographics

Estimates of the incidence of FMF in specific eastern Mediterranean populations range from one in 2,000 Arabs to one in 250 Sephardic Jews, one in 500 Armenians, and one in 1,000 Turks. Specific mutations in the MEFV gene are more common in certain ethnic groups and may cause a somewhat different course of the disease. Researchers think that a few mutations in the MEFV gene likely became common in a small population in the eastern Mediterranean several thousand years ago. The mutation was transmitted to later generations because people who carried a single copy of the mutated gene had a modified (but not abnormal) inflammatory response that may have protected them against some infectious agent at that time. Those who carried a single "beneficial" mutation in the MEFV gene were more likely to survive and reproduce, which may explain the high carrier frequency (up to one in five) in some populations. A better understanding and recognition of the symptoms of FMF in the late 1990s and early 2000s has resulted in more reports of the condition in other ethnic groups such as Ashkenazic Jews, Italians, Armenian-Americans, and Japanese. About 50 percent of patients diagnosed with FMF, however, have no **family** history of the disease.

With regard to sex, FMF is more common in men than in women, with a gender ratio of two men for every one woman. In terms of age groups, FMF is more common in younger people. One researcher states that 50–60 percent of patients are younger than 10 years, 80–95 percent are below the age of 20, with the remainder between 20 and 40 years of age. FMF is rare in people older than 40.

Causes and symptoms

Causes

FMF is a genetic condition inherited in an autosomal recessive fashion. Mutations in the MEFV gene (short for Mediterranean fever) on chromosome number 16 are the underlying cause of FMF. Autosomal recessive inheritance means that a person with FMF has mutations in both copies of the MEFV gene. All genes come in pairs, and one copy of each pair is inherited from each parent. If neither parent of a child with FMF has the condition, it means they carry one mutated copy of the MEFV gene, but also one normal copy, which is enough to protect them from disease. If both parents carry the same autosomal recessive gene, there is a one in four chance with each pregnancy that the child will inherit both recessive genes and develop FMF.

The MEFV gene carries the instructions for production of a protein called pyrin, named for pyrexia, a medical term for fever. The research group in France that codiscovered the protein in 1997 named it marenostrin, after *mare nostra*, the Latin words that the ancient Romans used for the Mediterranean Sea. Research has shown that pyrin has some function in controlling neutrophils, which are the white blood cells that move into an area of the body affected by stress or trauma. In a person with a normal immune system, some inflammation may follow stress or trauma, but the pyrin protein is responsible for shutting down the response of neutrophils once they are no longer needed. An abnormal pyrin protein associated with FMF may be partly functional but unstable. In some instances, the abnormal pyrin itself seems to be "stressed", and loses its ability to regulate the inflammatory response to trauma. Without such regulation, a normal inflammatory response spirals out of control. Exactly what causes pyrin in FMF to lose its ability to control neutrophils in some situations is not fully understood as of 2004.

Symptoms

The recurrent acute attacks of FMF typically begin in childhood or adolescence. These acute episodes of fever and painful inflammation usually last 12–72 hours. About 90 percent of people with FMF have their first attack by age 20. The group of symptoms that characterizes FMF includes the following:

- Fever: An FMF attack is nearly always accompanied by a fever, but it may not be noticed in every case. Fevers are typically 100 to 104°F (38–40°C). Some people experience chills prior to the onset of fever.

- Abdominal pain: Nearly all people with FMF experience abdominal pain at one point or another, and for most it is the most common complaint. The pain can range from mild to severe and can be diffuse or localized. It can mimic **appendicitis**, and many people with undiagnosed FMF have had appendectomies or exploratory surgery of the abdomen only to have the fever and abdominal pain return.

- Chest pain (pleuritis): Pleuritis, also called pleurisy, occurs in up to half of the affected individuals in certain ethnic groups. The pain is usually felt on one side of the chest. Pericarditis, an inflammation of the membrane surrounding the heart, would also be felt as chest pain.

- Joint pain: About 50 percent of people with FMF experience joint pain during attacks. The pain is usually confined to one joint at a time, and often involves the hip, knee, or ankle. For some people, however, the recurrent joint pain eventually becomes chronic arthritis.

- Muscle pain (myalgia): Up to 20 percent of individuals with FMF report muscle pain. These episodes typically last less than two days and tend to occur in the evening or after physical exertion. Rare cases of muscle pain and fever lasting as long as one month have been reported.

- Skin rash. A rash described as an erythema (skin reddening) resembling erysipelas accompanies FMF attacks in a minority of people. The rash typically occurs on the front of the lower leg or top of the foot, and appears as a red, warm, swollen area about 4–6 inches (10–15 cm) in diameter.

- Amyloidosis: FMF is associated with high levels in the blood of a protein called serum amyloid A (SAA). Over time, excess SAA tends to be deposited in tissues and organs throughout the body. The presence and deposition of excess SAA is known as amyloidosis. Amyloidosis may affect the gastrointestinal tract, liver, spleen, heart, and (in males) testes, but its effects on the kidneys are of greatest concern. The frequency of amyloidosis varies among the different ethnic groups, and its overall incidence is difficult to determine because of the use of colchicine to avert the problem. Left untreated, however, those individuals who do develop amyloidosis of the kidneys may require a kidney transplant or may even die of renal failure. The frequency and severity of a person's attacks of fever and serositis seem to have no relation to the risk of developing amyloidosis. In fact, a few people with FMF have been described who have had amyloidosis but apparently no other FMF-related symptoms.

- Other symptoms: A small percentage of boys with FMF develop painful inflammation around the testes, while girls may experience episodes of inflammation in the pelvis. In other patients, headaches are a common occurrence during attacks. Lastly, certain types of vasculitis (inflammation of the blood vessels) seem to be more common in people diagnosed with FMF.

When to call the doctor

Parents should consult a doctor for their child if they have Mediterranean ancestry and their child develops recurrent attacks of fever and pain consistent with the symptoms of FMF as described above.

In general, symptoms involving one or more of the following broad groups should lead to suspicion of FMF. Unexplained recurrent fevers, polyserositis, skin rash, and/or joint pain; abnormal blood studies (see below); and kidney or other disease associated with amyloidosis. A family history of FMF or its symptoms would obviously be an important clue, but the recessive nature of FMF means there usually is no family history. The diagnosis may be confirmed when a person with unexplained fever and pain responds to treatment with colchicine, since colchicine is not known to have a beneficial effect on any other condition similar to FMF. Abnormal results on a blood test typically include leukocytosis (elevated number of neutrophils in the blood); an increased erythrocyte sedimentation rate (the rate at which red blood cells form a sediment in a blood sample); and increased levels of proteins associated with inflammation (called acute phase reactants) such as SAA.

Diagnosis

The diagnosis of FMF is often delayed because the symptoms that define the condition are common to many other disorders. Fevers occur for many reasons, and non-specific pains in the abdomen, chest, and joints are also frequent ailments. Several infections can result in symptoms similar to FMF (Mallaret **meningitis**, for instance), and many people with FMF undergo exploratory abdominal surgery and ineffective treatments before they are finally diagnosed. Membership in a less commonly affected ethnic group may also delay or hinder the correct diagnosis. In many cases the doctor is able to diagnose the disorder only by a slow process of eliminating other diagnostic possibilities. He or she may order **x rays** or other imaging studies in order to rule out certain types of arthritis.

Direct analysis of the MEFV gene for FMF mutations is the only method to be certain of the diagnosis. While it was as of 2004 not yet possible to detect all MEFV gene mutations that might cause FMF, successful cloning of the MEFV gene has led to a rapid test that can identify the most common mutations of the gene. Thus, if DNA analysis is negative, clinical methods must be relied upon. If both members of a couple were proven to be FMF carriers through genetic testing, highly accurate prenatal diagnosis would be available in any subsequent pregnancy.

Similar syndromes of periodic fever and inflammation include familial Hibernian fever and hyperimmunoglobulinemia D syndrome, but both are much less common than FMF.

Treatment

Colchicine is an anti-inflammatory chemical compound that can be used as a medication and is frequently prescribed for gout. In the late twentieth century, colchicine was discovered to also be effective in reducing the frequency and severity of attacks in FMF. Treatment for FMF in the early 2000s consists of taking colchicine daily. Studies have shown that about 75 percent of FMF patients achieve complete remission of their symptoms, and about 95 percent show marked improvement when taking colchicine. Compliance with taking colchicine every day may be hampered by its side effects, which include **diarrhea**, **nausea**, abdominal bloating, and gas. Colchicine is also effective in preventing, delaying, or reversing kidney disease associated with amyloidosis.

Other medications may be used as needed to treat the pain and fever associated with FMF attacks. The most common drugs used are narcotics for severe pain and **nonsteroidal anti-inflammatory drugs** (NSAIDs) for arthritis and muscle pain. Dialysis and/or a kidney transplant might become necessary in someone with advanced kidney disease.

KEY TERMS

Acute phase reactants—Blood proteins whose concentrations increase or decrease in reaction to the inflammation process.

Amyloid—A waxy, translucent, starch-like protein that is deposited in tissues during the course of certain chronic diseases such as rheumatoid arthritis and Alzheimer's disease.

Amyloidosis—The accumulation of amyloid deposits in various organs and tissues in the body so that normal functioning is compromised. Primary amyloidosis usually occurs as a complication of multiple myeloma. Secondary amyloidosis occurs in patients suffering from chronic infections or inflammatory diseases such as tuberculosis, rheumatoid arthritis, and Crohn's disease.

Colchicine—A drug used to treat painful flare-ups of gout. It is also effective in reducing the frequency and severity of attacks in familial Mediterranean fever.

Erythema—A diffuse red and inflamed area of the skin.

Leukocyte—A white blood cell that defends the body against invading viruses, bacteria, and cancer cells. There are five types of leukocytes–neutrophils, basophils, eosinophils, lymphocytes, and monocytes.

Leukocytosis—An increased level of white cells in the blood. Leukocytosis is a common reaction to infections.

Neutrophil—The primary type of white blood cell involved in inflammation. Neutrophils are a type of granulocyte, also known as a polymorphonuclear leukocyte. They increase in response to bacterial infection and remove and kill bacteria by phagocytosis.

Pericarditis—Inflammation of the pericardium, the sac that surrounds the heart and the roots of the great blood vessels.

Peritonitis—Inflammation of the peritoneum. It is most often due to bacterial infection, but can also be caused by a chemical irritant (such as spillage of acid from the stomach or bile from the gall bladder).

Pleuritis—Inflammation of the pleura, the membrane surrounding the lungs. Also called pleurisy.

Pyrexia—A medical term meaning fever.

Pyrin—A protein that regulates the body's inflammatory response to stress or trauma. The MEFV gene involved in FMF produces an unstable form of pyrin that fails to adequately control the inflammatory response.

Serositis—Inflammation of a serosal membrane (any membrane that lines a body cavity that does not open to the outside of the body). Polyserositis refers to the inflammation of two or more serosal membranes.

Synovitis—Inflammation of the synovial membrane, the membrane that lines the inside of the articular capsule of a joint.

Alternative treatment

Some researchers have reported on herbal compounds that appear to be useful in managing patients with FMF. One Japanese case report concerned a patient who was helped by Kampo formulations, which are the traditional herbal medicines of Japan. A larger study of 24 Armenian patients diagnosed with FMF reported that the 14 patients who were given ImmunoGuard, a herbal preparation containing licorice root and schisandra along with several other herbs, had fewer and milder attacks of FMF than the 10 patients who were given a placebo.

Prognosis

Children who are diagnosed early enough and take colchicine consistently have an excellent prognosis. Most will have very few, if any, attacks of fever and polyserositis and will likely not develop serious compli-

cations of amyloidosis. Future research should provide doctors with a better understanding of the inflammation process, focusing on how neutrophils are genetically regulated. That information could then be used to develop treatments for FMF with fewer side effects and might also assist in developing therapies for other autoinflammatory diseases.

With regard to long-term effects of FMF, about 5 percent of patients will develop severe arthritis in adult life. Girls with FMF are likely to have fertility problems as adults; about 30 percent will be unable to have children at all, and those who can conceive have a 20 to 30 percent chance of miscarriage.

Prevention

Given the genetic nature of FMF, there is as of 2004 no cure for the disorder. Any couple that has a child diagnosed with FMF or anyone with a family history of the condition (especially those in high-risk ethnic groups) should be offered genetic counseling to obtain the most up-to-date information on FMF and testing options.

Parental concerns

Parental concerns about a child with FMF depend to some extent on the frequency and severity of attacks, as the frequency can range from two episodes per week to one per year. Families whose children have relatively infrequent attacks will be much less affected by the disorder than those whose plans are frequently disrupted by a child's acute attack. In most cases, however, children diagnosed with FMF have excellent health between attacks, can keep up with their schoolwork, participate in **sports**, and enjoy a normal social life. They do not require special diets, educational programs, isolation from other children, or other modifications of the family's routine. One concern that parents may wish to discuss with the doctor, however, is the narcotic medications that are often prescribed to ease the pain that accompanies acute attacks of FMF. Some of these drugs are potentially addictive, and their use should be carefully supervised.

Resources

BOOKS

"Familial Mediterranean Fever." Section 21, Chapter 289 in *The Merck Manual of Diagnosis and Therapy*, edited by Mark H. Beers and Robert Berkow. Whitehouse Station, NJ: Merck Research Laboratories, 2002.

PERIODICALS

Amaryan, G., et al. "Double-Blind, Placebo-Controlled, Randomized, Pilot Clinical Trial of ImmunoGuard: A Standardized Fixed Combination of *Andrographus paniculata Nees*, with *Eleutherococcus senticosus Maxim*, *Schizandra chinensis Bail.*, and *Glycyrrhiza glabra L.* Extracts in Patients with Familial Mediterranean Fever." *Phytomedicine* 10 (May 2003): 271–85.

Komatsu, M., et al. "Familial Mediterranean Fever Medicated with an Herbal Medicine in Japan." *Pediatrics International* 46 (February 2004): 81–4.

Kotone-Miyahara, Y., et al. "E148Q/M6941 Mutation in 3 Japanese Patients with Familial Mediterranean Fever." *International Journal of Hematology* 79 (April 2004): 235–37.

Toitou, I., et al. "Infevers: An Evolving Mutation Database for Auto-Inflammatory Syndromes." *Human Mutation* 24 (September 2004): 194–98.

ORGANIZATIONS

National Institute of Arthritis and Musculoskeletal and Skin Diseases. National Institutes of Health, One AMS Circle, Bethesda, MD 20892. Web site: <www.nih.gov/niams>.

National Organization for Rare Disorders Inc. (NORD). 55 Kenosia Avenue, Danbury, CT 06813–1968. Web site: <www.rarediseases.org>.

National Society of Genetic Counselors. 233 Canterbury Dr., Wallingford, PA 19086–6617. Web site: <www.nsgc.org/GeneticCounselingYou.asp>.

WEB SITES

Meyerhoff, John. "Mediterranean Fever, Familial." *eMedicine*, April 29, 2004. <www.emedicine.com/med/topic1410.htm> (accessed November 27, 2004).

Scott J. Polzin, MS

Family

Definition

A family is a group of two people or more related by marriage, blood relation, or **adoption** and who live together. The immediate family traditionally consists of parents and their offspring.

Description

No other factor influences children as deeply as their families. As a social unit with genetic, emotional, and legal dimensions, the family can foster the child's growth, development, health, and well-being. The family can provide the child with affection, a sense of belonging, and validation. Every area of a child's life is affected by the family.

Family functions

The family has basic functions. In order for the family to meet a child's psychological needs, its members must be nurturing, convey mutual respect, provide for intimacy, and engage in **bonding** and attachment. The family also socializes the child, guiding the child to be members of the society beyond the family. The family conveys religious and cultural beliefs and traditions to the next generation. The family is the child's source of economic resources, which meet the child's various physical needs for food, shelter, and clothing. Then, too, the family sees to it that the child receives health and dental care.

Demographics

Family structure is dynamic. In 1970, traditional nuclear families made up 40 percent of all households, but only 26 percent of all households in 1991. In addition, roles have changed within the nuclear family. The role of provider, once assigned mainly to the father, gradually came in the early 2000s to be shared by both parents, and as of 2004 many fathers are more active in parenting their children than their fathers were in parenting them.

Toward the end of the twentieth century, increasing numbers of families did not fit the nuclear profile. Some families have only one parent; others are combinations based on second marriages; still others are comprised of unmarried couples living with or without children.

The number of **single-parent families** increased from 12.9 percent of all families in 1970 to 29 percent in 1991 and 28 percent (20 million) in 1997. The increases are mostly the result of the increase in the **divorce** rate and the increase in births to single mothers. Many women are single parents and heads of households, and many of these live in poverty.

Common problems

Poverty is the single most powerful risk for families and children and affects families in many ways. Poverty exerts its greatest impact during children's **preschool** years, the age group in which children are most likely to live in poverty. Poor families are less likely or able to provide educational and cultural experiences for their children.

Parents' economic status (education, occupation, and income) controls the parent's ability provide adequate housing, a safe environment, and responsible child care while the parents work. Availability of and quality of social support influence family life and well-being as individuals cope with raising children in poverty.

Unemployment by either or both parents causes financial hardships and social and emotional strain, which can disrupt family life. The quality of the parent's work and the satisfaction the parent gets from it affects the parents and, in turn, their effectiveness in parenting.

Child abuse and neglect is a destructive force in families and results in children's **anxiety**, depression, lowered **self-esteem**, and a decline in school performance. Similarly, children who witness domestic violence suffer some of these same consequences.

KEY TERMS

Coping—In psychology, a term that refers to a person's patterns of response to stress.

Culture—The system of communal beliefs, values behaviors, customs, and materials that members of a society use to understand their world and each other, and which are passed down among suceeding generation.

Custodial parent—A parent who has legal custody of their child or children.

Extended family—Traditionally defined as the biological relatives of a nuclear family (the parents, sisters, and brothers of both members of a married couple); sometimes used to refer to the people living in the household as partners and parents with children.

Noncustodial parent—The parent who does not have legal custody of the child and does not live in the same home with the child. The noncustodial parent has financial responsibility for the child and visitation rights.

Stress—A physical and psychological response that results from being exposed to a demand or pressure.

Parental concerns

Parents are troubled by children who are out of control and have problem behaviors such as **running away**, **truancy**, school failings or suspensions, and delinquency. Youths who are habitually truant may need school counseling. Truancy specialists provide topic-focused workshops and referrals to family counseling; court intervention is sometimes necessary.

The frequency of divorce and remarriage produces **stepfamilies** with their own difficulties and challenges. The new stepfamily members may have no shared family history or common lifestyle, and members may have different beliefs. In addition, children may feel torn between the custodial parent, with whom they live, and the noncustodial parent, with whom they visit.

Economic stress affects the whole family. When financial problems occur, the family may be forced to move for employment. Families have lifestyle commitments and ties to their community. When these ties break-up, children, especially adolescents, are likely to experience a loss of hope. Parental career disappointments can cause anxiety and self-

---

A traditional family of father, mother, daughter, and son. *(© Ariel Skelley/Corbis.)*

doubt in children. Family economic stress may cause parental substance abuse, which can lead to school distraction and declining academic performance in young people.

Finally, children may feel isolated from parents and friends. The most stressful time for a family can be the period preceding a possible foreclosure or business failure. Parents may make desperate attempts to save their source of income. They may also be trying to keep their loss hidden from the rest of the community. Such behaviors can isolate children from parents who are too busy to notice and from neighbors who are not even aware of their trouble.

The long-term effects of continued family stress can cause physical and psychological problems for children. If problems occur often and if several problems appear at the same time, serious attention should be given the child.

When to call the doctor

Parents should call their pediatrician if the child shows unhealthy physical or emotional symptoms that may be in response to family problems or transitions. Physical problems may include weight gain or weight loss, or unexplained stomachaches or headaches. Emotional problems may cause a decline in academic performance, breaking curfews, or getting into trouble in school or with the law.

Resources

BOOKS

Bernstein, Bob. *Families of Value: Intimate Profiles of Pioneering Lesbian and Gay Parents.* New York: Avalon Publishing Group, 2005.

Cunningham-Burley, Sarah, et al. *Families, Relationships, and Boundaries.* Livingston, NJ: Policy Press, 2005.

Evans, Tony. *Divorce and Remarriage.* Chicago, IL: Moody Press, 2003.

Everett, Craig A. *The Consequences of Divorce: Economic and Custodial Impact on Children and Adults.* Binghamton, NY: Haworth Press, 2003.

Forbes, L. S. *A Natural History of Families.* Princeton, NJ: Princeton University Press, 2005.

Hansen, Karen V. *Not-so-Nuclear Families: Class, Gender, and Networks of Care.* Piscataway, NJ: Rutgers University Press, 2005.

Jeynes, William. *Divorce, Family Structure, and the Academic Success of Children.* Binghamton, NY: Haworth Press, 2002.

McKenry, Patrick C., et al. *Families and Change: Coping with Stressful Events and Transitions.* Thousand Oaks, CA: Sage Publications, 2005.

ORGANIZATIONS

American Academy of Child and Adolescent Psychiatry. 3615 Wisconsin Ave., NW, Washington, DC 20016 3007. Web site: <www.aacap.org/>.

Aliene S. Linwood, RN, DPA, FACHE

Family therapy

Definition

Family therapy is a type of psychotherapy that involves all members of a nuclear family or stepfamily and, in some cases, members of the extended family (e.g., grandparents). A therapist or team of therapists conducts multiple sessions to help families deal with important issues that may interfere with the functioning of the family and the home environment.

Purpose

The goal of family therapy is to help family members improve communication, solve family problems, understand and handle special family situations (for example, death, serious physical or mental illness, or child and adolescent issues), and create a better functioning home environment. For families with one member who has a serious physical or mental illness, family therapy can educate families about the illness and work out problems associated with care of the family member. For children and adolescents, family therapy most often is used when the child or adolescent has a personality, **anxiety**, or mood disorder that impairs their family and social functioning, and when a stepfamily is formed or begins having difficulties adjusting to the new family life. Families with members from a mixture of racial, cultural, and religious backgrounds, as well as families made up of same-sex couples who are raising children, may also benefit from family therapy.

Description

Family therapy is generally conducted by a therapist or team of therapists who are trained and experienced in family and group therapy techniques. Therapists may be psychologists, psychiatrists, social workers, or counselors. Family therapy involves multiple therapy sessions, usually lasting at least one hour each, conducted at regular intervals (for example, once weekly) for several months. Typically, family therapy is initiated to address a specific problem, such as an adolescent with a psychological disorder or adjustment to a death in the family. However, frequently, therapy sessions reveal additional problems in the family, such as communication issues. In a therapy session, therapists seek to analyze the process of family interaction and communication as a whole and do not take sides with specific family members. Therapists who work as a team can model new behaviors for the family through their interactions with each other during a session.

Family therapy is based on family systems theory, in which the family is viewed as a living organism rather than just the sum of its individual members. Family therapy uses systems theory to evaluate family members in terms of their position or role within the system as a whole. Problems are treated by changing the way the system works rather than trying to fix a specific member. Family systems theory is based on several major concepts.

Concepts in family therapy

THE IDENTIFIED PATIENT The identified patient (IP) is the family member with the symptom that has brought the family into treatment. Children and adolescents are frequently the IP in family therapy. The concept of the IP is used by family therapists to keep the family from scapegoating the IP or using him or her as a way of avoiding problems in the rest of the system.

HOMEOSTASIS (BALANCE) Homeostasis means that the family system seeks to maintain its customary organization and functioning over time, and it tends to resist change. The family therapist can use the concept of homeostasis to explain why a certain family symptom has surfaced at a given time, why a specific member has become the IP, and what is likely to happen when the family begins to change.

THE EXTENDED FAMILY FIELD The extended family field includes the immediate family and the network of grandparents and other relatives of the family. This concept is used to explain the intergenerational transmission of attitudes, problems, behaviors, and other issues.

Children and adolescents often benefit from family therapy that includes the extended family.

DIFFERENTIATION Differentiation refers to the ability of each family member to maintain his or her own sense of self, while remaining emotionally connected to the family. One mark of a healthy family is its capacity to allow members to differentiate, while family members still feel that they are members in good standing of the family.

TRIANGULAR RELATIONSHIPS Family systems theory maintains that emotional relationships in families are usually triangular. Whenever two members in the family system have problems with each other, they will "triangle in" a third member as a way of stabilizing their own relationship. The triangles in a family system usually interlock in a way that maintains family homeostasis. Common family triangles include a child and his or her parents; two children and one parent; a parent, a child, and a grandparent; three siblings; or, husband, wife, and an in-law.

In the early 2000s, a new systems theory, multisystemic therapy (MST), has been applied to family therapy and is practiced most often in a home-based setting for families of children and adolescents with serious emotional disturbances. MST is frequently referred to as a "family-ecological systems approach" because it views the family's ecology, consisting of the various systems with which the family and child interact (for example, home, school, and community). Several clinical studies have shown that MST has improved family relations, decreased adolescent psychiatric symptoms and substance use, increased school attendance, and decreased re-arrest rates for adolescents in trouble with the law. In addition, MST can reduce out-of-home placement of disturbed adolescents.

Preparation

In some instances the family may have been referred to a specialist in family therapy by their pediatrician or other primary care provider. It is estimated that as many as 50 percent of office visits to pediatricians have to do with developmental problems in children that are affecting their families. Some family doctors use symptom checklists or psychological screeners to assess a family's need for therapy. For children and adolescents with a diagnosed psychological disorder, family therapy may be added to individual therapy if family issues are identified as contributing factors during individual therapy.

Family therapists may be either psychiatrists, clinical psychologists, or other professionals certified by a specialty board in marriage and family therapy. They usually evaluate a family for treatment by scheduling a series of interviews with the members of the immediate family, including young children, and significant or symptomatic members of the extended family. This process allows the therapist(s) to find out how each member of the family sees the problem, as well as to form first impressions of the family's functioning. Family therapists typically look for the level and types of emotions expressed, patterns of dominance and submission, the roles played by family members, communication styles, and the locations of emotional triangles. They also note whether these patterns are rigid or relatively flexible.

Preparation also usually includes drawing a genogram, which is a diagram that depicts significant persons and events in the family's history. Genograms include annotations about the medical history and major personality traits of each member. Genograms help uncover intergenerational patterns of behavior, marriage choices, family alliances and conflicts, the existence of family secrets, and other information that sheds light on the family's present situation.

Precautions

Individual therapy for one or more family members may be recommended to avoid volatile interaction during a family therapy session. Some families are not considered suitable candidates for family therapy. They include:

- families in which one, or both, of the parents is psychotic or has been diagnosed with antisocial or paranoid personality disorder
- families whose cultural or religious values are opposed to, or suspicious of, psychotherapy
- families with members who cannot participate in treatment sessions because of physical illness or similar limitations
- families with members with very rigid personality structures (Here, members might be at risk for an emotional or psychological crisis.)
- families whose members cannot or will not be able to meet regularly for treatment

Risks

The chief risk in family therapy is the possible unsettling of rigid personality defenses in individuals or relationships that had been fragile before the beginning of therapy. Intensive family therapy may also be difficult for family members with diagnosed psychological disorders. Family therapy may be especially difficult and stressful for children and adolescents who may not fully

Blended family—A family formed by the remarriage of a divorced or widowed parent. It includes the new husband and wife, plus some or all of their children from previous marriages.

Differentiation—The ability to retain one's identity within a family system while maintaining emotional connections with the other members.

Extended family field—A person's family of origin plus grandparents, in-laws, and other relatives.

Family systems theory—An approach to treatment that emphasizes the interdependency of family members rather than focusing on individuals in isolation from the family. This theory underlies the most influential forms of contemporary family therapy.

Genogram—A family tree diagram that represents the names, birth order, sex, and relationships of the members of a family. Therapists use genograms to detect recurrent patterns in the family history and to help the family members understand their problem(s).

Homeostasis—The balanced internal environment of the body and the automatic tendency of the body to maintain this internal "steady state." Also refers to the tendency of a family system to maintain internal stability and to resist change.

Identified patient (IP)—The family member in whom the family's symptom has emerged or is most obvious.

Nuclear family—The basic family unit, consisting of a father, a mother, and their biological children.

Stepfamily—A family formed by the marriage or long-term cohabitation of two individuals, where one or both have at least one child from a previous relationship living part-time or full-time in the household. The individual who is not the biological parent of the child or children is referred to as the stepparent.

Triangling—A process in which two family members lower the tension level between them by drawing in a third member.

understand interactions that occur during family therapy. Adding individual therapy to family therapy for children and adolescents with the same therapist (if appropriate) or a therapist who is aware of the family therapy can be helpful.

Normal results

Normal results vary, but in good circumstances, they include greater insight, increased differentiation of individual family members, improved communication within the family, loosening of previously automatic behavior patterns, and resolution of the problem that led the family to seek treatment.

Parental concerns

Stepfamilies, which are increasing in prevalence, are excellent candidates for family therapy. Children and adolescents in stepfamilies often have difficulties adjusting, and participating in family therapy can be beneficial. Stepfamilies, increasingly referred to as "blended families," experience unique pressures within each new family unit. Stepfamily researchers, family therapists, and the Stepfamily Association of America (SAA) view the term as inaccurate because it seems to suggest that members of a stepfamily blend into an entirely new family unit, losing their individuality and attachment to other outside family members. Because other family types (biological, single-parent, foster, adoptive) are defined by the parent-child relationship, the SAA believes that the term "stepfamily" more accurately reflects that relationship and is consistent with other family definitions. Viewing the stepfamily as a blended family can lead to unrealistic expectations, confused and conflicted children, difficult adjustment, and in many cases, failure of the marriage and family. Family therapy can help family members deal with these issues.

Children and adolescents and, in some cases even the parents, may be reluctant to participate in family therapy. Home-based family therapy has in the early 2000s become available as an option for families with severely disturbed adolescents and family members reluctant to see a therapist. In home-based therapy, a therapist or team of therapists comes directly to the family's home and conducts therapy sessions there.

Resources

BOOKS

Barnes, Gill Gorell. *Family Therapy in Changing Times.* Gordonville, VA: Palgrave Macmillan, 2004.

Carlson, Jon, et al. *Family Therapy Techniques: Integrating and Tailoring Treatment.* Florence, KY: Brunner-Routledge, 2005.

Landau, Elaine. *Family Therapy.* Danbury, CT: Scholastic Library Publishing, 2004.

Sells, Scott P. *Treating the Tough Adolescent: A Family-Based, Step-by-Step Guide.* New York: Guilford Publications, 2004.

PERIODICALS

Cortes, Linda. "Home-Based Family Therapy: A Misunderstanding of the Role and a New Challenge for Therapists." *The Family Journal: Counseling and Therapy for Couples and Families* 12 (April 2004): 184– 88.

Heater, Mary Lou. "Ethnocultural Considerations in Family Therapy." *Journal of the American Psychiatric Nurses Association* 9 (April 2003): 46– 54.

Hutton, Deborah. "Filial Therapy: Shifting the Balance." *Clinical Child Psychology and Psychiatry* 9 (April 2004): 261– 70.

Sheidow, Ashli J., and Mark S. Woodford. "Multisystemic Therapy: An Empirically Supported, Home-Based Family Therapy Approach." *The Family Journal: Counseling and Therapy for Couples and Families* 11 (July 2003): 257– 63.

ORGANIZATIONS

American Association for Marriage and Family Therapy. 112 South Alfred St., Alexandria, VA 22314– 3061. Web site: <www.aamft.org/index_nm.asp>.

International Family Therapy Association. Web site: <www.ifta-familytherapy.org/about.htm>.

Stepfamily Association of America. Web site: <www.saafamilies.org>.

Stepfamily Foundation. Web site: <www.stepfamily.org>.

Jennifer E. Sisk, M.A.

FAS *see* **Fetal alcohol syndrome**

Father-child relationships *see* **Parent-child relationships**

Fear

Definition

Fear is an intense aversion to or apprehension of a person, place, activity, event, or object that causes emotional distress and often avoidance behavior. Fears are common in childhood.

Description

More than 50 percent of children experience normal **phobias**, which is the fear of a specific object, or more general worries, called anxieties, before they are 18 years old. For adults it may be helpful to distinguish between rational fears, such as fear of snakes or guns, which are survival mechanisms and serve to protect a person from danger; and irrational fears, or phobias, which cannot be traced to any reasonable cause.

Most children have some fears. Fears are normal, and can be a good thing. For example, children need to know they should not run into a street. They need to know not to **play** with knives. A little fear is good, but too much fear is a problem. So is too little fear. A child with too much fear may not want to leave the house. A child with not enough fear may get into a stranger's car. Children's personalities also will influence their fears. One child may be scared of more things than another child. Some children are braver, while others are more shy and fearful.

Many childhood fears fall somewhere between the rational and irrational, occurring in phases as the child or adolescent is exposed to new experiences and as both cognitive reasoning and the capacity for imagination develop. Whether a child's fear is considered normal generally depends on his or her age, background, and most importantly on how much it interferes with his or her normal daily activities. Fear of water may be considered normal in a child who has never learned how to swim, but it might be considered abnormal in the adolescent son of a coastal fisherman.

The most significant factors in overcoming fear are identifying the fear, developing a sense of control over the feared environment, and envisioning alternatives to the feared negative outcomes. Forcing children to perform activities they are afraid to do destroys, rather than builds, autonomy and self-confidence. If a child refuses to do something or explicitly voices fear, those feelings should be taken seriously and explored through questions and discussion. Parents can ask the child or adolescent what change can be made to accommodate the fear in order to make him or her feel more in control.

Some research suggests that reading scary picture books functions as a courage-building tool for children and helps them face their fears in a controlled environment; they are free to turn the page or to remind themselves that the monster is not real. Horror stories or movies may serve the same purpose for teens but not for children who cannot exercise the same level of choice by leaving the theater and should not be exposed to disturbing movies.

Infancy

Babies fear falling, being dropped, and loud noises. A fear of strangers is also common in infants starting at the age of seven to nine months and lasting until about 18 months, when it begins to decrease. Fear symptoms in infants are primarily crying, stiffening, and sometimes shaking.

Toddlerhood

Fears among toddlers include strangers, animals, bugs, storms, sirens, large objects, dark colors, darkness, people with masks, monsters, and "bad" people, such as burglars. Children at this age also commonly fear being separated from their parents. Fear symptoms in toddlers include crying and avoidance of the feared person or object.

Preschool

Preschoolers fear being separated from parents, being left alone or sleeping alone, and imaginary figures, such as ghosts, monsters, and supernatural beings. Symptoms may be physical, such as a stomachache or **headache**.

School age

In younger school-age children, fears include **separation anxiety**; death; violence, such as in war or murder; kidnapping and physical injury; natural disasters such as floods, earthquakes, and tornados; and **anxiety** about academic achievement and other forms of school performance. Children at age seven often have a fear of not being liked while children ages eight and nine may worry about personal inabilities.

In older adolescents, common fears include anxiety about school achievement, social rejection and related worries, and sexual anxieties, including dating and **sexually transmitted diseases**, especially human **immunodeficiency** virus (HIV).

Symptoms in adolescents and teens include anger, avoidance, and denial of the fear, and panic reactions, such as sweating, trembling, fast heartbeat, and rapid breathing.

Nearly all fears have a scientific name, such as triskaidekaphobia, the fear of the number 13. In the classic Christmas television special, "A Charlie Brown Christmas," Charlie Brown had pantophobia, the fear of everything. Other common fears include:

- ailurophobia (fear of cats)
- didaskaleinophobia (fear of going to school)
- entomophobia (fear of insects)
- glossophobia (fear of speaking)
- myctophobia (fear of darkness)
- ophidiaphobia (fear of snakes)
- xenophobia (fear of strangers or foreigners)
- zoophobia (fear of animals)

Common problems

Research shows that most children report having several fears at any given age. Some research shows that 90 percent of children ages two to 14 have at least one specific fear. If the fear does not interfere with the child's daily life, such as sleeping, going to school, and engaging in social activities, then professional help is generally not needed.

Phobias belong to a large group of mental problems known as anxiety disorders and can be divided into three specific types: specific phobias (formerly called simple phobias), social phobias, and agoraphobia.

A specific phobia is the fear of a particular situation or object, including anything from airplane travel to dentists. Found in one out of every ten Americans, specific phobias seem to run in families and are roughly twice as likely to appear in women. If the person rarely encounters the feared object, the phobia does not cause much harm. However, if the feared object or situation is common, it can seriously disrupt everyday life. Common examples of specific phobias, which can begin at any age, are fear of snakes, flying, dogs, escalators, elevators, high places, or open spaces.

People with social phobia have deep fears of being watched or judged by others and of being embarrassed in public. Common social phobias in children include reading aloud in front of a class; participating in a musical, drama, or athletic event; starting or joining in a conversation; talking to adults; attending social events, such as dances and parties; taking tests; attending physical education class; using school or public bathrooms; and asking a teacher for help.

Social phobia is not the same as **shyness**. Shy people may feel uncomfortable with others, but they do not experience severe anxiety, they do not worry excessively about social situations beforehand, and they do not avoid events that make them feel self-conscious. On the other hand, people with social phobia may not be shy; they may feel perfectly comfortable with people except in a public place. This feeling usually begins about age 15 and affects three times as many women as men.

An episode of spontaneous panic is usually the initial trigger for the development of agoraphobia. After an initial panic attack, the person becomes afraid of experiencing a second one. Patients literally "fear the fear," and worry incessantly about when and where the next attack may occur. As they begin to avoid the places or situations in which the panic attack occurred, their fear generalizes. Eventually the person completely avoids public places. In severe cases, people with agoraphobia can no longer leave their homes for fear of experiencing a panic attack.

Agoraphobia is the intense fear of feeling trapped and having a panic attack in specific situations. Social phobias may be only mildly irritating, or they may significantly interfere with daily life. It is not unusual for people with social phobia to turn down job offers or avoid relationships because of their fears.

Parental concerns

While normal fears tend to be experienced in phases and tend to be outgrown by adulthood, abnormal fears are those that are persistent and recurrent or fears that interfere with daily activities for at least a month. Abnormal fears, including extreme separation anxiety, being afraid to go to school, or extreme social fears, may indicate an anxiety disorder.

When to call the doctor

When children's fears persist beyond the age when they are appropriate, they can begin to interfere with their daily lives. Typically, children who experience this type of irrational fear, or phobia, should get treatment from a psychologist.

The most popular and effective treatment for phobias is behavior therapy, which approaches the phobia as an undesirable behavior to be unlearned. Most often it takes the form of desensitization, a technique by which the fearful person is exposed to the feared stimulus in an extremely mild form and then with gradually increasing degrees of intensity. For example, a child who fears dogs may first be asked to look at pictures of dogs, then perhaps play with a stuffed dog or view a dog from afar, ultimately getting to the point when she is able to pet and play with dogs.

Phobias also respond to treatment by medication, including anti-anxiety drugs such as Xanax and BuSpar and selective serotonin reuptake inhibitors (SSRIs), such as Prozac and Zoloft. Medication is especially helpful for social phobia, where it can help the child overcome her aversion to social interaction sufficiently to work with a therapist. When agoraphobia accompanies panic

---

KEY TERMS

Agoraphobia—Abnormal anxiety regarding public places or situations from which the person may wish to flee or in which he or she would be helpless in the event of a panic attack.

Ailurophobia—Fear of cats.

Cognitive—The ability (or lack of) to think, learn, and memorize.

Didaskaleinophobia—Fear of going to school.

Entomophobia—Fear of insects.

Glossophobia—Fear of speaking.

Myctophobia—Fear of darkness.

Ophidiaphobia—Fear of snakes.

Pantophobia—Fear of everything.

Phobia—An intense and irrational fear of a specific object, activity, or situation that leads to avoidance.

Selective serotonin reuptake inhibitors (SSRIs)—A class of antidepressants that work by blocking the reabsorption of serotonin in the brain, thus raising the levels of serotonin. SSRIs include fluoxetine (Prozac), sertraline (Zoloft), and paroxetine (Paxil).

Triskaidekaphobia—Fear of the number thirteen.

Xenophobia—Fear of strangers or foreigners.

Zoophobia—Fear of animals.

---

attacks, it also responds to cognitive-behavioral treatment for panic disorder, often in conjunction with anti-anxiety and antidepressant medications similar to those prescribed for other phobias.

Before, during, and after exposure to the source of fear, the child can begin to imagine controlling the environment and his own reactions in other ways. Creative visualization, for example, imagining a switch the child can use to control his fear when visiting the doctor or dentist, can sometimes be effective. A comforting ritual, a familiar object, or thoughts of a beloved person can be used as a good luck charm before embarking on a scary trip or performing a task such as speaking in class or sleeping alone. Relaxation techniques can also be taught to older children.

Resources

BOOKS

Chansky, Tamar E. *Freeing Your Child from Anxiety: Powerful, Practical Solutions to Overcome Your Child's*

Fears, Worries, and Phobias. New York: Broadway Books, 2004.

Foxman, Paul. *The Worried Child: Recognizing Anxiety in Children and Helping Them Heal.* Alameda, CA: Hunter House, 2004.

Ollendick, Thomas H., and John S. March. *Phobic and Anxiety Disorders in Children and Adolescents: A Clinician's Guide to Effective Psychosocial and Pharmacological Interventions.* Oxford, UK: Oxford University Press, 2003.

Spencer, Elizabeth DuPont, et al. *The Anxiety Cure for Kids: A Guide for Parents.* Hoboken, NJ: Wiley, 2003.

PERIODICALS

Dragon, Natalie. "Behind the Headlines: Could TB Pill Help Banish Phobias?" *GP* (December 15, 2003): 39.

Epstein, Randi Hutter. "Experts Try Fast-Track Fix for Children with Phobias." *The New York Times* (January 20, 2004): F5.

London, Robert T. "Conquering Phobias." *Clinical Psychiatry News* (May 2004): 43.

Purvis, Patty. "Fear of Talking (Selective Mutism)." *Clinical Reference Systems* (Annual 2002): 1261.

Travis, John. "Fear Not: Scientists Are Learning How People Can Unlearn Fear." *Science News* (January 17, 2004): 42–4.

Tucker, Libby. "Fear Factors: Everyone Reacts to Fear Differently. Scientists Are Beginning to Understand Why." *Science World* (February 7, 2003): 14–15.

ORGANIZATIONS

Anxiety Disorders Association of America. 8730 Georgia Ave., Suite 600, Silver Spring, MD 20910. Web site: <www.adaa.org>.

Mood and Anxiety Disorders Institute. Massachusetts General Hospital, 55 Fruit St., Boston, MA 02114. Web site: <www.mghmadi.org>.

WEB SITES

"The Anxious Child." *American Academy of Child & Adolescent Psychiatry*, December 2000. Available online at <www.aacap.org/publications/factsFam/anxious.htm> (accessed December 10, 2004).

"Helping Your Child Deal with Fears & Phobias." *Child Development Institute*, March 25, 2004. Available online at <www.childdevelopmentinfo.com/disorders/fears.htm> (accessed December 10, 2004).

Ken R. Wells

Febrile seizures

Definition

Febrile seizures are convulsions of sudden onset due to abnormal electrical activity in the brain that is caused by **fever**. Fever is a condition in which body temperature is elevated above normal (generally above 100.4°F [38°C]).

Description

Febrile seizures were first distinguished from epileptic seizures in the twentieth century. The National Institutes of Health defined febrile seizures in 1980 as "an event in infancy or childhood usually occurring between three months and five years of age, associated with fever, but without evidence of intracranial infection or defined cause."

There are three major subtypes of febrile seizures. The simple febrile seizure accounts for 70 to 75 percent of febrile seizures and is one in which the affected child is age six months to five years and has no history or evidence of neurological abnormalities, the seizure is generalized (affects multiple parts of the brain), and lasts less than 15 minutes, and the fever is not caused by brain illness such as **meningitis** or **encephalitis**. The complex febrile seizure shares similar characteristics with the exception that the seizure lasts longer than 15 minutes or is local (affects a localized part of the brain), or multiple seizures take place and accounts for about 20 to 25 percent of all febrile seizures. Lastly, about 5 percent of febrile seizures are diagnosed as symptomatic, in cases in which the child has a history or evidence of neurological abnormality.

The seizure activity itself is generally characterized as clonic (consisting of rhythmic jerking movements of the arms and/or legs), or tonic-clonic (commencing with a stiffening of the body followed by a clonic phase).

Demographics

Fever is the most common cause of seizures in children, occurring in 2 to 5 percent of children from six months to five years of age. First onset usually occurs by two years of age, with the risk decreasing after age three; most children stop having febrile seizures by the age of five or six. Male children have been shown to have a higher incidence of febrile seizures. The majority of children who experience a febrile seizure will only have one in their lifetime; approximately 33 percent will go on to have more than one.

Causes and symptoms

Under normal circumstances, information is transmitted in the brain by means of electrical discharges from brain cells. A seizure occurs when the normal electrical patterns of the brain become disrupted. A febrile seizure is caused by fever, most commonly a high fever that has risen quickly. The average fever temperature in which febrile seizures take place is 104°F (40°C). Conversely, a healthy person's body temperature fluctuates between 97°F (36.1°C) and 100°F (37.8°C).

Fevers are caused in most cases by viral or bacterial infections, such as **otitis media** (ear infection), upper respiratory infection, pharyngitis (throat infection), **pneumonia**, **chickenpox**, and urinary tract infection. Other conditions can induce a fever, including allergic reactions, ingestion of toxins, teething, autoimmune disease, trauma, **cancer**, excessive sun exposure, or certain drugs. In some cases no cause of the fever can be determined.

Febrile seizures generally last between one and ten minutes. A child experiencing a febrile seizure may exhibit some or all of the following behaviors:

- stiff body
- twitching or jerking of the extremities or face
- rolled-back eyes
- unconsciousness
- inability to talk
- problems breathing
- involuntary urination or defecation
- vomiting
- confusion, sleepiness, or irritability after the seizure

Approximately one third of children who have had a febrile seizure will experience recurrent seizures. Several risk factors are associated with recurrent febrile seizures; children who exhibit all four are at a 70 percent chance of developing recurrent seizures, while those who have none of the risk factors have only a 20 percent chance. The risk factors include:

- family history of febrile seizures
- young age of the child (i.e. less than 18 months of age)
- seizure occurs soon after or with onset of fever
- seizure-associated fever is relatively low

When to call the doctor

A healthcare provider should be contacted after a febrile seizure. A visit to the emergency room is warranted if the accompanying fever is greater than 103°F (39.4°C) in a child older than three months or 100.5°F (38°C) in an infant of three months or younger or if the seizure is the child's first. Emergency medical personnel (telephone 911) should be called if a febrile seizure lasts more than five minutes; if the child stops breathing; if the child's skin starts to turn blue; or if the fever is greater than 105.8°F (41°C), a condition called hyperpyrexia.

Diagnosis

A key focus of diagnostic tests will be to determine the underlying cause of the fever. A comprehensive medical history including the fever's duration and course, other symptoms the child is experiencing, prior or current medical conditions, recent vaccinations or exposure to communicable diseases, and the child's current behaviors may point to the fever's origin. A temperature below 100.4°F (38°C) suggests another cause for the seizure. The caregiver who was present with the child while he or she was having the seizure will be asked questions relating to the child's behaviors in an attempt to determine the type of seizure.

Physicians may administer tests to rule out conditions other than fever that could have caused the seizure, such as epilepsy, meningitis, or encephalitis. Children who suffer from recurrent febrile seizures are not diagnosed with epilepsy, a **seizure disorder** that is not caused by fever. In the case of children under 18 months of age, a lumbar puncture (spinal tap) may be recommended to rule out meningitis because symptoms are often lacking or subtle in children of that age. Because of the benign nature of the simple febrile seizure, tests such as **computed tomography** (CT) scans, **magnetic resonance imaging** (MRI), or **electroencephalogram** (EEG) are not usually recommended.

Treatment

During a seizure parents or caregivers need to remain calm and take steps to make sure the child remains safe. During the period after the seizure the child may be disoriented and/or sleepy (called the postictal state), but quick recovery from this state is normal, and medical treatment is not normally needed.

During a seizure

If a parent or caregiver observes a child having a seizure, there are a number of measures that should be taken to ensure the child's **safety**. These include:

- staying calm
- laying the child on his or her side or front to prevent vomited matter from being aspirated into the lungs

- loosening any tight clothing or items that could constrict breathing
- marking the start and end time of the seizure
- clearing the surrounding area of unsafe items
- attending to the child for the duration of the seizure
- clearing the child's airway if it becomes obstructed with vomited material or other objects

Parents or caregivers should not attempt to stop the seizure or slap or shake the child in attempt to wake him/her. The child may move around during the seizure, and parents should not try to hold the child down. If the child vomits, a suction bulb can be used to help clear the airway.

After a seizure

A healthcare professional should be called immediately after the seizure in the event that further treatment or tests are required. **Hospitalization** is not normally required unless the child is suffering from a serious infection or illness or the seizure itself was abnormally long. Parents or caregivers may be instructed to take certain measures at home to reduce the child's fever, such as administering fever-reducing drugs (called antipyretics) such as **acetaminophen** (Tylenol) or ibuprofen (Advil). There is, however, no evidence that shows fever-reducing therapies reduce the risk of another febrile seizure occurring. If the child is suffering from a bacterial infection that is the cause of the fever, he or she may be placed on **antibiotics**.

Treating the fever

The treatment of pediatric fever varies according to the age of the child and the fever's cause, if known. Physicians recommend that newborns less than four weeks of age with fever be admitted to the hospital and administered antibiotics until a complete workup can be done to rule out bacterial infection or other serious illness. The same is recommended for infants ages four to 12 weeks if they appear ill. Infants of this age who otherwise appear well can often be managed on an outpatient basis with antipyretics and antibiotics in the case of bacterial infection.

For children ages three months and older, the course of treatment depends on the extent and cause of the fever. Most fevers and associated conditions can be managed on an outpatient basis. Low-grade fevers often do not need to be treated in otherwise healthy children. Antipyretics may be suggested to lower a fever and make the child more comfortable but will not affect the course of an underlying infectious disease. Aspirin should not be given to a child or adolescent with a fever since this drug has been linked to an increased risk of the serious condition called **Reye's syndrome**. Antibiotics may be administered if the child has a known or suspected bacterial infection.

Alternative treatment

There are some outpatient treatments that parents or caregivers may administer to reduce their febrile child's discomfort, although there is no evidence that indicates such treatments reduce the risk of febrile seizures. These include dressing the child lightly, applying cold washcloths to the face and neck, providing plenty of fluids to avoid **dehydration**, and giving the child a lukewarm bath or sponging the child in lukewarm water.

Prognosis

The risk of complications associated with febrile seizures is very low. Some of the complications that may occur are:

- biting the tongue
- choking on items that were in the mouth at the start of the seizure
- injury from falling down
- aspirating fluid or vomit into the lungs
- developing recurrent febrile seizures
- developing recurrent seizures unrelated to fever (epilepsy)
- complications related the underlying cause of the fever

Children who have had a febrile seizure are at an increased risk of having another; approximately one third of febrile seizure cases become recurrent. The risk of recurrent seizures decreases with age: infants younger than 12 months have a 50 percent chance of having a second seizure, while children over the age of 12 months have a 30 percent chance. The risk of a child going on to develop epilepsy is slightly increased at approximately 2–5 percent, compared to 1 percent for the general population; such a risk is increased in children who have a history of neurological abnormalities such as **cerebral palsy** or developmental delays and in children whose seizures recur or are prolonged. Research has shown that febrile seizures do not affect a child's **intelligence** level or achievement in school.

Prevention

In some cases, a febrile seizure may be the first indication that a child is ill. Prevention is, therefore, not always possible. While the use of anticonvulsants such as Phenobarbital or Valproate has been shown to prevent recurrent febrile seizures, these drugs are associated with significant side effects such as adverse behaviors, allergic reaction, and organ injury, and have not been shown to benefit simple febrile seizures. Only rarely is anticonvulsant therapy recommended for a child with febrile seizures because of the generally benign nature of the seizures and the risk of side effects from the drugs. In some cases oral diazepam (Valium) can be administered at the first sign of fever to reduce the risk of febrile seizures; about two-thirds of children who receive this drug experience side effects such as sleepiness and loss of coordination. The majority of children who have had a febrile seizure do not need drug therapy. Parents may be directed to administer over-the-counter antipyretics at the first sign of fever.

Parental concerns

A febrile seizure can be a frightening experience for both the child and his or her parents. It is important that parents be educated about the low risk of simple febrile seizures and the measures that can be taken to ensure their child's safety during and after a seizure.

Resources

BOOKS

Barkin, Roger M., and D. Demetrios Zukin. "Fever." In *Rosen's Emergency Medicine: Concepts and Clinical Practice*, 5th ed. Edited by John A. Marx. St. Louis, MO: Mosby, 2002.

Powell, Keith R. "Fever." In *Nelson Textbook of Pediatrics*, 17th ed. Edited by Richard E. Behrman, Robert M. Kliegman, and Hal B. Jenson. Philadelphia: Saunders, 2004.

PERIODICALS

Jankowiak, J., and B. Malow. "Seizures in Children with Fever: Generally Good Outcome." *Neurology* 60, no. 2 (January 28, 2003): E1–2.

ORGANIZATIONS

American Academy of Pediatrics. 141 Northwest Point Blvd., Elk Grove Village, IL 60007–1098. Web site: <www.aap.org>.

American College of Emergency Physicians. 1125 Executive Circle, Irving, TX 75038–2522. Web site: <www.acep.org>.

WEB SITES

Baumann, Robert. "Febrile Seizures." *eMedicine*, March 12, 2001. Available online at <www.emedicine.com/neuro/topic134.htm> (accessed November 28, 2004).

"Febrile Seizure Fact Sheet." *National Institute of Neurological Disorders and Stroke*, July 1, 2001. Available online at <www.ninds.nih.gov/health_and_medical/pubs/febrile_seizures.htm> (accessed November 28, 2004).

Zempsky, William T. "Pediatrics, Febrile Seizures." *eMedicine*, October 14, 2004. Available online at <www.emedicine.com/emerg/topic376.htm> (accessed November 28, 2004).

Stephanie Dionne Sherk

Fetal alcohol syndrome

Definition

Fetal alcohol syndrome (FAS) is a set of physical and mental birth defects that can result from a woman drinking alcohol during her pregnancy. The syndrome is characterized by brain damage, facial deformities, and growth deficits. Heart, liver, and kidney defects are also common, as well as vision and hearing problems. These infants generally have difficulties with learning, attention, memory, and problem solving as they get older.

Description

Although there is a wide range of effects that result from in utero alcohol exposure, the diagnosis of FAS is recognized as the most severe birth defect that occurs. Fetal alcohol effect (FAE) is a term used to describe alcohol-exposed individuals whose condition does not meet the full criteria for an FAS diagnosis. The term alcohol-related neurodevelopmental disorders (ARND) is used for individuals with functional or cognitive impairments linked to prenatal alcohol exposure, including decreased head size at birth, structural brain abnormalities, and a pattern of behavioral and mental abnormalities. Alcohol-related birth defects (ARBD) describes the physical defects linked to prenatal alcohol exposure, including heart, skeletal, kidney, ear, and eye malformations.

FAS is the leading known preventable cause of **mental retardation** and birth defects. It affects one in 100 live births or as many as 40,000 infants born each year in the United States, and it is felt that the incidence is significantly under-reported. An individual with FAS can incur a lifetime health cost of over $800,000. In 2003, FAS cost the United States $3.9 billion in direct costs with indirect costs at approximately $1.5 billion. Children do not outgrow FAS. The physical and behavioral problems can last a lifetime. The syndrome is found in all racial and socio-economic groups. It is not a genetic disorder, so women with FAS or affected by FAS have healthy babies if they do not drink alcohol during their pregnancy.

Causes and symptoms

Alcohol is readily absorbed from the gastrointestinal tract into a pregnant woman's bloodstream and circulates to the fetus by crossing the placenta. Here it interferes with the ability of the fetus to receive sufficient oxygen and nourishment for normal cell development in the brain and other organs. The consumption of alcohol directly contributes to **malnutrition** because it contains no **vitamins** or **minerals**, and it uses up what the woman has for metabolism. Studies suggest that drinking a large amount of alcohol at any one time may be more dangerous to the fetus than drinking small amounts more frequently. The fetus is most vulnerable to various types of injuries depending on the stage of development in which alcohol is encountered. During the first eight weeks of pregnancy, organogenesis (the formation of organs) is taking place, which places the embryo at a higher risk of

deformities when exposed to teratogens. Since a safe amount of alcohol intake during pregnancy has not been determined, twenty-first century authorities agree that women should not drink at all during pregnancy. A problem is that many women do not realize they are pregnant until the sixth to eight week. Therefore, women who are anticipating a pregnancy should abstain from all alcoholic beverages.

Unlike many birth defects which are identified at birth and then treated, FAS and FAE are usually overlooked at birth and treated later by mental health specialists, and often unknowingly. Possible FAS symptoms include:

- growth deficiencies: small body size and weight, slower than normal development, and failure to catch up
- skeletal deformities: deformed ribs and sternum; curved spine; hip dislocations; bent, fused, webbed, or missing fingers or toes; limited movement of joints; small head
- facial abnormalities: small eye openings; skin webbing between eyes and base of nose; drooping eyelids; near-sightedness; **strabismus**; failure of eyes to move in same direction; short upturned nose; sunken nasal bridge; flattened or absent groove between nose and upper lip; thin upper lip; **cleft palate** (opening in roof of mouth); small jaw; low-set or poorly formed ears
- organ deformities: heart defects, **heart murmurs**, genital malformations, kidney and urinary defects
- central nervous system handicaps: small brain; faulty arrangement of brain cells and connective tissue; mental retardation (usually mild to moderate but occasionally severe); learning disabilities; short attention span; irritability in infancy; hyperactivity in childhood; poor body, hand, and finger coordination

Since the primary birth defect in FAS and FAE involves central nervous system damage in utero, these newborns may have difficulties with feeding due to a poor suck, have irregular sleep-wake cycles, decreased or increased muscle tone, and seizures or tremors. Delays in achieving developmental milestones such as rolling over, **crawling**, walking, and talking may become apparent in infancy. Behavior and learning difficulties typical in the **preschool** or early school years include poor attention span, hyperactivity, poor motor skills, and slow **language development**. A common diagnosis that is associated with FAS is attention deficit-hyperactivity disorder. Learning disabilities or mental retardation may be diagnosed during this time. Arithmetic is often the most difficult subject for a child with FAS. During middle school and high school years, the behavioral difficulties and learning difficulties can be significant. Memory problems, poor judgment, difficulties with daily living skills, difficulties with abstract reasoning skills, and poor social skills are often apparent by this time. It is important to note that animal and human studies have shown that neurologic and behavioral abnormalities can be present without characteristic facial features. These individuals may not be identified as having FAS but may fulfill criteria for alcohol-related diagnoses, as set forth by the Institute of Medicine.

In 1991, Streissguth and others reported some of the first long-term follow-up studies of adolescents and adults with FAS. In the approximate 60 individuals they studied, the average IQ was 68 (70 is the lower limit of the normal range). However, the range of IQ was quite large, as low as 20 (severely retarded) to as high as 105 (normal). The average achievement levels for reading, spelling, and arithmetic were fourth grade, third grade, and second grade, respectively. The Vineland Adaptive Behavior Scale was used to measure adaptive functioning in these individuals. The composite score for this group showed functioning at the level of a seven-year-old. Daily living skills were at a level of nine years, and social skills were at the level of a six-year-old.

In 1996, Streissguth and others published further data regarding the disabilities in children, adolescents, and adults with FAS. Secondary disabilities (those disabilities not present at birth and that might be preventable with proper diagnosis, treatment, and intervention) were described. These secondary disabilities include: mental health problems; disrupted school experiences; trouble with the law; incarceration for mental health problems, drug abuse, or a crime; inappropriate sexual behavior; alcohol and drug abuse; problems with employment; dependent living; and difficulties parenting their own children. In that study, only seven out of 90 adults were living and working independently and successfully. In addition to the studies by Streissguth, several other authors in different countries have as of the early 2000s reported on long term outcome of individuals diagnosed with FAS. In general, the neurologic, behavioral, and emotional disorders become the most problematic for individuals. The physical features change over time, sometimes making the correct diagnosis more difficult in older individuals, without old photographs and other historical data to review. Mental health problems, including attention deficit, depression, panic attacks, psychosis, **suicide** threats and attempts, were present in over 90 percent of the individuals studied by Streissguth. A 1996 study in Germany reported more than 70 percent of the adolescents they followed had persistent and severe developmental disabilities, and many had psychiatric disorders, the most common of which were emotional disorders, repetitive habits, **speech disorders**, and hyperactivity disorders. (Some of the above information derives from Ann Streissguth's book, *Fetal Alcohol Syndrome: A Guide for Families and Communities*, which appeared in 1997.)

Diagnosis

FAS is a clinical diagnosis, which means that there is no blood test, x ray, or psychological test that can be performed to confirm the suspected diagnosis. The diagnosis is made based on the history of maternal alcohol use and detailed physical examination for the characteristic major and minor birth defects and characteristic facial features. It is often helpful to examine siblings and parents of an individual suspected of having FAS, either in person or by photographs, to determine whether findings on the examination might be familial and if other siblings may also be affected. Individuals with **developmental delay** or birth defects may be referred to a clinical geneticist for genetic testing or to a developmental pediatrician or neurologist for evaluation and diagnosis of FAS. Psychoeducational testing to determine IQ and/or the presence of learning disabilities may also be part of the evaluation process.

Treatment

There is no treatment for FAS that will reverse or change the physical features or brain damage associated with maternal alcohol use during the pregnancy. Most of the physical birth defects associated with prenatal alcohol exposure are correctable with surgery. Children should have psychoeducational evaluation to help plan appropriate educational interventions. Commonly associated diagnoses as attention deficit-hyperactivity disorder, depression, or **anxiety** should be recognized and treated appropriately. The disabilities that present during childhood persist into adult life. However, some of the secondary disabilities already mentioned may be avoided or lessened by early diagnosis and intervention. Streissguth has describe a model in which an individual affected by FAS has one or more advocates to help provide guidance, structure, and support as the individual seeks to become independent, successful in school or employment, and develop satisfying social relationships.

Prognosis

The prognosis for FAS depends on the severity of birth defects and the brain damage present at birth.

Cleft palate—A congenital malformation in which there is an abnormal opening in the roof of the mouth that allows the nasal passages and the mouth to be improperly connected.

Congenital—Present at birth.

Intelligence quotient (IQ)—A measure of somebody's intelligence, obtained through a series of aptitude tests concentrating on different aspects of intellectual functioning.

Microcephaly—An abnormally small head.

Miscarriage—Loss of the embryo or fetus and other products of pregnancy before the twentieth week. Often, early in a pregnancy, if the condition of the baby and/or the mother's uterus are not compatible with sustaining life, the pregnancy stops, and the contents of the uterus are expelled. For this reason, miscarriage is also referred to as spontaneous abortion.

Organogenesis—The formation of organs during development.

Placenta—The organ that provides oxygen and nutrition from the mother to the unborn baby during pregnancy. The placenta is attached to the wall of the uterus and leads to the unborn baby via the umbilical cord.

Strabismus—A disorder in which the eyes do not point in the same direction.

Teratogen—Any drug, chemical, maternal disease, or exposure that can cause physical or functional defects in an exposed embryo or fetus.

A boy with fetal alcohol syndrome, a birth defect caused by his mother consuming alcohol during pregnancy. *(Photograph by David H. Wells. Corbis.)*

Parental concerns

Prevention of FAS is the key. Prevention efforts must include public education efforts aimed at the entire population, not just women of child bearing age, appropriate treatment for women with high-risk drinking habits, and increased recognition and knowledge about FAS by professionals, parents, and caregivers.

Resources

BOOKS

Armstrong, Elizabeth M. *Conceiving Risk, Bearing Responsibility: Fetal Alcohol Syndrome and the Diagnosis of Moral Disorder.* Baltimore, MD: Johns Hopkins University, 2003.

Fetal Alcohol Syndrome No. V: Index to New Information. Washington, DC: A B B E Publishers Association, 2005.

Golden, Janet. *Message in a Bottle: The Making of Fetal Alcohol Syndrome.* Cambridge, MA: Harvard University Press, 2005.

Kleinfeld, Judith, et al. *Fantastic Antone Grows Up: Adolescents and Adults with Fetal Alcohol Syndrome.* Fairbanks, AK: University of Alaska, 2000.

PERIODICALS

Committee of Substance Abuse and Committee on Children with Disabilities. "Fetal Alcohol Syndrome and Alcohol-Related Neurodevelopmental Disorders." *Pediatrics* 106 (August 2000): 358–61.

Miscarriage, stillbirth, or death in the first few weeks of life may be outcomes in very severe cases. Major physical birth defects associated with FAS are usually treatable with surgery. Some of the factors that have been found to reduce the risk of secondary disabilities in FAS individuals include diagnosis before the age of six years, stable and nurturing home environments, never having experienced personal violence, and referral and eligibility for disability services. The long-term data help others understand the difficulties that individuals with FAS encounter throughout their lifetimes and can help families, caregivers, and professionals provide the care, supervision, education, and treatment geared toward their special needs.

Hannigan, J. H., and O. R. Armant. "Alcohol in Pregnancy and Neonatal Outcome." *Seminars in Neonatology* 5 (August 2000): 243–54.

ORGANIZATIONS

Fetal Alcohol Syndrome Family Resource Institute. PO Box 2525, Lynnwood, WA 98036. Web site: <www.fetalalcoholsyndrome.org>.

March of Dimes Birth Defects Foundation. 1275 Mamaroneck Ave., White Plains, NY 10605. Web site: <www.modimes.org>.

National Institute on Alcohol Abuse and Alcoholism. 5635 Fishers Lane, MSC 9304, Bethesda, MD 20892–9304. Web site: <www.niaaa.nih.gov/>.

National Organization on Fetal Alcohol Syndrome (NOFAS). 900 17th Street, NW, Suite 910, Washington, DC 20006. Web site: <www.nofas.org>.

Linda K. Bennington

Fetal hemoglobin test

Definition

A fetal hemoglobin test (Hgb electrophoresis) measures the level of fetal hemoglobin (Hemoglobin F or HbF) in the blood of infants and children. It can also be measured in adults, though is more typically needed for diagnoses of congenital illnesses in children. Fetal hemoglobin, an alkali-resistant form of hemoglobin, is the major hemoglobin component in the bloodstream of the fetus. After birth, it decreases rapidly until only traces are found in healthy children and adults. Fetal hemoglobin is one of six types of hemoglobin measured in the clinical laboratory by a method called hemoglobin electrophoresis.

Purpose

The determination of fetal hemoglobin in the blood of infants and children identifies normal and abnormal levels, defining what percentage of total hemoglobin is made up of fetal hemoglobin. Knowing this level may help doctors evaluate low concentrations of normal hemoglobin in red blood cells (anemia), as well as higher-than-normal levels of fetal hemoglobin or its hereditary persistence. Fetal hemoglobin measurement helps diagnose a group of inherited disorders that affect hemoglobin production, among which are the thalassemias and **sickle cell anemia**. It may also be done to help doctors diagnose acquired illnesses such as acquired hemolytic anemia, leukemia, pernicious anemia, and certain types of **cancer**.

Description

Hemoglobin is the oxygen-carrying protein in red blood cells. It is also the pigment that gives red blood cells their color. Red blood cells deliver hemoglobin throughout the body, ensuring that all body tissues have the oxygen they need for life and proper function. Hemoglobin consists primarily of iron-bearing proteins called heme groups and moiety globin protein, which together give hemoglobin its ability to carry oxygen. The heme groups are molecular chains of different types and actually create six different hemoglobins that vary in their amino acid composition and also in the genes that control them. Among the six types of hemoglobin, HbA is the normal adult hemoglobin, and HbF is the major fetal hemoglobin. Abnormal types of hemoglobin include Hgb S and Hgb C. All types of hemoglobin are electrically charged, which enables them to be identified and quantified in the laboratory by hemoglobin electrophoresis techniques.

During fetal development, fetal hemoglobin composes about 90 percent of total hemoglobin. At birth, the newborn's blood is composed of about 70 percent fetal hemoglobin. As the infant's bone marrow begins to produce new red cells, fetal hemoglobin begins to decrease rapidly. Normally, only 2 percent or less of total hemoglobin is found as fetal hemoglobin after six months and throughout childhood; in adulthood, only traces (0.5% or less) are found in total hemoglobin.

In some diseases associated with abnormal hemoglobin production (hemoglobinopathy), fetal hemoglobin may persist in larger amounts. When this occurs, the increased amounts of fetal hemoglobin raise questions of possible underlying dysfunction or disease. For example, HbF can be found in higher levels in sickle cell anemia and other hereditary **anemias**. It has also been reported to be elevated in some other conditions such as leukemia, pregnancy, diabetes, thyroid disease, and sometimes as a side effect of anticonvulsant therapy. It may also reappear in adults when the bone marrow is overactive, as in disorders such as pernicious anemia, multiple myeloma, and invasive (metastatic) cancer affecting bone marrow. When HbF is elevated after age four, the cause is typically investigated. (Persistence of fetal hemoglobin in inherited hemolytic anemias can be associated with less severe disease symptoms.)

Defects in hemoglobin production may be either genetic or acquired. The genetic defects are subdivided into errors of heme production (porphyria) and those of globin production, known collectively as the hemoglobinopathies. There are two categories of hemoglobinopathy: in one, abnormal globin chains give rise to abnormal hemoglobin molecules; in the other, normal hemoglobin chains are produced but in abnormal amounts. Sickle cell anemia, the inherited condition characterized by curved (sickle-shaped) red blood cells and chronic hemolytic anemia, is an example of the first category. Disorders in the second category are called the thalassemias, which are classified according to which amino acid chain, alpha or beta, is affected, and whether one defective gene (**thalassemia** minor) or two defective genes (thalassemia major) are responsible for the disorder. Testing for levels of fetal hemoglobin and other types of hemoglobin may be a first, important step in the investigation of possible hemoglobinopathies.

Levels of HbF are of interest in diagnosing several hemoglobinopathies, including the following:

- thalassemia minor or thalassemia trait (heterozygous thalassemia), in which HbF does not decrease normally after birth and may remain high in later life

- thalassemia major (homozygous thalassmia or Cooley's anemia), the hereditary persistence of HbF involving larger than normal amounts of HbF

- sickle cell anemia associated with the abnormal Hgb S, which occurs primarily in African-Americans; also Hgb C, another abnormal hemoglobin found in African-Americans, causing hemolytic anemia

- beta-chain hemoglobinopathies with increased HbF during childhood

- disease-related hematologic stress as in hemolytic anemias, leukemia, and aplastic anemia

Precautions

Blood transfusions received prior to testing may alter results.

Preparation

Parents may wish to explain the blood-drawing procedure to older children to help prepare them for the slight discomfort they will experience.

Testing for fetal hemoglobin requires that a blood sample be drawn from the child. No preparation is needed before performing fetal hemoglobin tests, and fasting (nothing to eat or drink for a period of hours before the test) is not required. Proper identification and careful handling of the child are important when a blood sample is being obtained for testing. A site, usually the heel on an infant and a finger on an older child, is chosen

by the phlebotomist who will draw the blood. A baby's foot may be wrapped in a warm cloth for a few minutes to bring blood to the surface and allow it to flow more easily. The baby's heel or child's finger is then wiped with alcohol and/or an antibacterial solution such as betadine to sterilize the surface. Puncture is performed quickly with a lancet, avoiding the center of an infant's heel to prevent inflammation of the bone. The blood sample is drawn into tiny capillary tubes, properly labeled, and taken to the laboratory for testing. In rare instances, a phlebotomist will not be able to draw sufficient blood from an infant's heel puncture, and a physician may draw venous blood from a femoral vein in the groin area, which is larger than veins in an infant's arms. Older children may also have venous blood drawn, particularly if other blood tests are being done.

Aftercare

Pressure is applied to the blood-drawing site for a few minutes to prevent bleeding. The site of heel stick, finger stick, or venipuncture must be kept clean and dry and observed for any undue bleeding or bruising. A small bandage can be used to cover the site. Any unusual conditions or reactions should be reported to the pediatrician.

Risks

Risks for this test are minimal but may include slight bleeding from the blood-drawing site or blood may accumulate under the puncture site (hematoma). Fainting, **nausea**, or feeling lightheaded after venipuncture may occur in some children.

Normal results

Reference values vary from laboratory to laboratory but results of hemoglobin electrophoresis are generally reported within the following ranges:

- Newborn to six months: HbF may be up to 70 percent of total hemoglobin.

- Six months to adult: HbF may be up to 2 percent of total hemoglobin.

Levels of HbF greater than 2 percent of total hemoglobin is abnormal after the age of six months. Some hemoglobinopathies have elevated levels of other types of hemoglobin and normal levels of HbF as shown below.

Typical results for certain hemoglobinopathies include:

KEY TERMS

Anemia—A condition in which there is an abnormally low number of red blood cells in the bloodstream. It may be due to loss of blood, an increase in red blood cell destruction, or a decrease in red blood cell production. Major symptoms are paleness, shortness of breath, unusually fast or strong heart beats, and tiredness.

Hemoglobinopathy—A disorder of hemoglobin, which can be either the presence of abnormal types of hemoglobin or abnormal levels of specific types of hemoglobin.

Hemolytic anemia—A form of anemia characterized by chronic premature destruction of red cells in the bloodstream. Hemolytic anemias are classified as either inherited or acquired.

Heterozygote/Heterozygous—Having two different versions of the same gene.

Homozygote/Homozygous—Having two identical copies of a gene.

Trait—A distinguishing feature of an individual.

- Sickle cell disease: Hemoglobin S 80–100%, Hgb A 0%, HbF 2%.
- Sickle cell trait: Hemoglobin S 20–40%, Hgb A 60–80%, HbF 2%.
- Hgb C disease: Hgb C 90–100%, Hgb A 0%, and Hb F 2%.
- Thalassemia major: HbF 65–100%, Hgb A 5–25%.
- Thalassemia minor: HbF 1–3%, Hgb A 50–90%.

Parental concerns

Children generally respond well to blood-drawing procedures if they are prepared for the slight discomfort. If parents are concerned about the possibility of inherited blood disorders, it may be helpful to remember that abnormal levels of fetal hemoglobin may be caused by a variety of conditions, not all of which are inherited or serious, and early recognition of a blood condition usually leads to early treatment and effective management of the condition.

See also Sickle cell anemia; Thalassemia.

Resources

BOOKS

Chernecky, Cynthia C., et al. *Laboratory Tests and Diagnostic Procedures.* Philadelphia, PA: Elsevier—Health Sciences Division, 2003.

Fischback, Frances Talaska. *Manual of Laboratory and Diagnostic Tests.* Hagerstown, MD: Lippincott Williams & Wilkins, 2004.

Nicoll, Diana, et al. *Pocket Guide to Diagnostic Tests.* Backlick, OH: McGraw-Hill Professional Publishing, 2003.

ORGANIZATIONS

The National Institutes of Health. 9000 Rockville Pike, Bethesda, MD 20892. Web site: <www.nih.gov>.

WEB SITES

"An Introduction to Genetics and Genetic Testing." *Kids Health,* 2004. Available online at <www.kidshealth.org/parent/system/medical/genetics.html> (accessed January 12, 2005).

L. Lee Culvert
Janis O. Flores

Fetal monitoring, electronic *see* **Electronic fetal monitoring**

Fever

Definition

A fever is any body temperature elevation over 100.4°F (38°C).

Description

A healthy person's body temperature fluctuates between 97°F (36.1°C) and 100°F (37.8°C), with the average being 98.6°F (37°C). The body maintains stability within this range by balancing the heat produced by the metabolism with the heat lost to the environment. The "thermostat" that controls this process is located in the hypothalamus, a small structure located deep within the brain. The nervous system constantly relays information about the body's temperature to the thermostat, which in turn activates different physical responses designed to cool or warm the body, depending on the circumstances. These responses include: decreasing or increasing the flow of blood from the body's core, where it is warmed, to the surface, where it is cooled; slowing down or speeding up the rate at which the body turns food into energy (metabolic rate); inducing shivering, which generates heat through muscle contraction; and inducing sweating, which cools the body through evaporation.

A fever occurs when the thermostat resets at a higher temperature, primarily in response to an infection. To reach the higher temperature, the body moves blood to the warmer interior, increases the metabolic rate, and induces shivering. The chills that often accompany a fever are caused by the movement of blood to the body's core, leaving the surface and extremities cold. Once the higher temperature is achieved, the shivering and chills stop. When the infection has been overcome or drugs such as aspirin or **acetaminophen** have been taken, the thermostat resets to normal and the body's cooling mechanisms switch on: the blood moves to the surface and sweating occurs.

Fever is an important component of the immune response, though its role is not completely understood. Physicians believe that an elevated body temperature has several effects. The immune system chemicals that react with the fever-inducing agent and trigger the resetting of the thermostat also increase the production of cells that fight off the invading bacteria or viruses. Higher temperatures also inhibit the growth of some bacteria, while at the same time speeding up the chemical reactions that help the body's cells repair themselves. In addition, the increased heart rate that may accompany the changes in blood circulation also speeds the arrival of white blood cells to the sites of infection.

Demographics

Fevers are components of many disease entities. Virtually all persons experience fevers at some time in their lives. Elevations in temperature are not reportable events. Thus, accurate data regarding the prevalence of fevers are not available.

Causes and symptoms

Fevers are primarily caused by viral or bacterial infections, such as **pneumonia** or **influenza**. However, other conditions can induce a fever, including allergic reactions; autoimmune diseases; trauma, such as breaking a bone; **cancer**; excessive exposure to the sun; intense **exercise**; hormonal imbalances; certain drugs; and damage to the hypothalamus. When an infection occurs, fever-inducing agents called pyrogens are released, either by the body's immune system or by the invading cells themselves that trigger the resetting of the thermostat. In other circumstances, the immune system may overreact (allergic reactions) or become damaged (autoimmune diseases), causing the uncontrolled release of pyrogens. A **stroke** or tumor can damage the hypothalamus, causing the body's thermostat to malfunction. Excessive exposure to the sun or intense exercise in hot weather can result in heat stroke, a condition in which the body's cooling mechanisms fail. Malignant hyperthermia is a rare, inherited condition in which a person develops a very high fever when given certain anesthetics or muscle relaxants in preparation for surgery.

How long a fever lasts and how high it may go depends on several factors, including its cause, the age of the person, and his or her overall health. Most fevers caused by infections are acute, appearing suddenly and then dissipating as the immune system defeats the infectious agent. An infectious fever may also rise and fall throughout the day, reaching its peek in the late afternoon or early evening. A low-grade fever that lasts for several weeks is associated with autoimmune diseases such as lupus or with some cancers, particularly leukemia and lymphoma.

When to call the doctor

A doctor or other healthcare provider should be called when a fever does not resolve after two to three days. Anyone with a fever over 104°F (40.0°C) should seek immediate medical treatment.

A doctor should be called when an infant's temperature rises above 100°F (37.8°C) and cannot be brought down within a few minutes. Infants whose temperatures exceed 102°F (38.9°C) should be immersed in warm or tepid water to help reduce temperature slowly, while waiting for emergency help to arrive.

Diagnosis

A fever is usually diagnosed using a thermometer. A variety of different thermometers are available. Glass thermometer should not be used since they can break and release mercury, which is toxic. Digital thermometers can and should be used in place of glass thermometers rectally, orally, and under the arm in all age groups. Electronic thermometers can be inserted in the ear to quickly register the body's temperature.

As important as registering a person's temperature is determining the underlying cause of the fever. The presence or absence of accompanying symptoms, a person's medical history, and information about what he or she may have ingested, any recent trips taken, or possible exposures to illness all help the physician make a diagnosis. Blood tests can aid in identifying an infectious agent by detecting the presence of antibodies against it or providing samples for growth of the organism in a culture. Blood tests can provide the doctor with white blood cell counts. Ultrasound tests, **magnetic resonance imaging** (MRI) tests, or **computed tomography** (CT) scans may

KEY TERMS

Antipyretic drug—Medications, like aspirin or acetaminophen, that lower fever.

Autoimmune disorder—One of a group of disorders, like rheumatoid arthritis and systemic lupus erythematosus, in which the immune system is overactive and has lost the ability to distinguish between self and non-self. The body's immune cells turn on the body, attacking various tissues and organs.

Febrile seizure—Convulsions brought on by fever.

Hyperthermia—Body temperature that is much higher than normal (i.e. higher than 98.6°F).

Malignant hyperthermia—A type of reaction (probably with a genetic origin) that can occur during general anesthesia and in which the patient experiences a high fever, muscle rigidity, and irregular heart rate and blood pressure.

Meningitis—An infection or inflammation of the membranes that cover the brain and spinal cord. It is usually caused by bacteria or a virus.

Metabolism—The sum of all chemical reactions that occur in the body resulting in growth, transformation of foodstuffs into energy, waste elimination, and other bodily functions. These include processes that break down substances to yield energy and processes that build up other substances necessary for life.

Pyrogen—A chemical circulating in the blood that causes a rise in body temperature.

Reye's syndrome—A serious, life-threatening illness in children, usually developing after a bout of flu or chickenpox, and often associated with the use of aspirin. Symptoms include uncontrollable vomiting, often with lethargy, memory loss, disorientation, or delirium. Swelling of the brain may cause seizures, coma, and in severe cases, death.

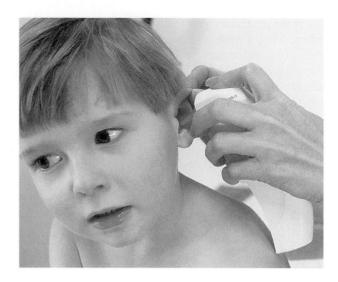

An ear thermometer is used to measure body temperature through the ear canal. (© LWA-Stephen Welstead/Corbis.)

usually should be allowed to run its course. Drugs to lower fever (antipyretics) can be given if a person (particularly a child) is uncomfortable. These include acetaminophen and ibuprofen. Aspirin, however, should not be given to a child or adolescent with a fever since this drug has been linked to an increased risk of **Reye's syndrome**. Bathing a person in tepid water can also help alleviate a high fever.

A fever requires emergency treatment under the following circumstances:

- newborn (three months or younger) with a fever over 100.5°F (38°C)
- infant or child with a fever over 103°F (39.4°C)
- fever accompanied by severe **headache**, neck stiffness, mental confusion, or severe swelling of the throat

A very high fever in a small child can trigger seizures (**febrile seizures**) and, therefore, should be treated immediately. A fever accompanied by the above symptoms can indicate the presence of a serious infection, such as **meningitis**, and should be brought to the immediate attention of a physician.

be ordered if the doctor cannot readily determine the cause of a fever.

Treatment

Physicians agree that the most effective treatment for a fever is to address its underlying cause, such as through the administration of **antibiotics**. Also, because a fever helps the immune system fight infection, it

Prognosis

Most fevers caused by infection end as soon as the immune system rids the body of the pathogen, and these fevers do not produce lasting effects. The prognosis for fevers associated with more chronic conditions, such as autoimmune disease, depends upon the overall outcome of the disorder.

Prevention

Fevers may be prevented by avoiding the various diseases that cause them.

Nutritional concerns

Adequate **nutrition** via a well-balanced diet and sufficient intake of liquid help to reduce many fevers. Adequate intake of electrolytes such as sodium, chloride, potassium, phosphate, and bicarbonate helps to prevent **dehydration** that often accompanies a fever.

Parental concerns

Parents should carefully monitor their infants and young children for symptoms of fever. Any fever that exceeds 103°F (39.4°C) for more than a few minutes should be promptly treated.

Resources

BOOKS

Barlam, Tamar F., and Dennis L. Kasper. "Approach to the Acutely Ill Infected Febrile Patient." In *Harrison's Principles of Internal Medicine*, 15th ed. Edited by Eugene Braunwald et al. New York: McGraw-Hill, 2001, pp. 95–101.

Beutler, Bruce, and Steven M. Beutler. "The Pathogenesis of Fever." In *Cecil Textbook of Medicine*, 22nd ed. Edited by Lee Goldman et al. Philadelphia: Saunders, 2003, pp. 1730–32.

Bisno, Alan L. "Rheumatic Fever." In *Cecil Textbook of Medicine*, 22nd ed. Edited by Lee Goldman et al. Philadelphia: Saunders, 2003, pp. 1788–93.

Dale, David C. "The Febrile Patient." In *Cecil Textbook of Medicine*, 22nd ed. Edited by Lee Goldman et al. Philadelphia: Saunders, 2003, pp. 1729–30.

Dinarello, Charles A., and Jeffrey A. Gelfand. "Fever and Hyperthermia." In *Harrison's Principles of Internal Medicine*, 15th ed. Edited by Eugene Braunwald et al. New York: McGraw-Hill, 2001, pp. 91–4.

Dumler, J. Stephen. "Q Fever (Coxiella burnetii)." In *Nelson Textbook of Pediatrics*, 17th ed. Edited by Richard E. Behrman et al. Philadelphia: Saunders, 2003, pp. 1009–10.

———. "Spotted Fever Group Rickettsioses." In *Nelson Textbook of Pediatrics*, 17th ed. Edited by Richard E. Behrman et al. Philadelphia: Saunders, 2003, pp. 999–1003.

Halstead, Scott B. "Yellow Fever." In *Nelson Textbook of Pediatrics*, 17th ed. Edited by Richard E. Behrman et al. Philadelphia: Saunders, 2003, pp. 1095–6.

———. "Dengue Fever and Dengue Hemorrhagic Fever." In *Nelson Textbook of Pediatrics*, 17th ed. Edited by Richard E. Behrman et al. Philadelphia: Saunders, 2003, pp. 1092–4.

Kaye, Elaine T., and Kenneth M. Kaye. "Fever and Rash." In *Harrison's Principles of Internal Medicine*, 15th ed. Edited by Eugene Braunwald et al. New York: McGraw-Hill, 2001, pp. 95–101.

Powell, Keith R. "Fever without a Focus." In *Nelson Textbook of Pediatrics*, 17th ed. Edited by Richard E. Behrman et al. Philadelphia: Saunders, 2003, pp. 841–5.

———. "Fever." In *Nelson Textbook of Pediatrics*, 17th ed. Edited by Richard E. Behrman et al. Philadelphia: Saunders, 2003, pp. 839–40.

PERIODICALS

Dinarello, C. A. "Infection, fever, and exogenous and endogenous pyrogens: some concepts have changed." *Journal of Endotoxin Research* 10, no. 4 (2004): 201–22.

Galache, C., et al. "Q fever: a new cause of 'doughnut' granulomatous lobular panniculitis." *British Journal of Dermatology* 151, no. 3 (2004): 685–7.

Huang, S. Y., et al. "Effect of Recent Antipyretic Use on Measured Fever in the Pediatric Emergency Department." *Archives of Pediatric and Adolescent Medicone* 158, no. 10 (2004): 972–6.

ORGANIZATIONS

American Academy of Emergency Medicine. 611 East Wells St., Milwaukee, WI 53202. Web site: <www.aaem.org/>.

American Academy of Pediatrics. 141 Northwest Point Boulevard, Elk Grove Village, IL 60007–1098. Web site: <www.aap.org/>.

American Association of Naturopathic Physicians. 8201 Greensboro Drive, Suite 300, McLean, VA 22102. Web site: <naturopathic.org/>.

American Society of Clinical Pathologists. 2100 West Harrison Street, Chicago IL 60612. Web site: <www.ascp.org/index.asp>.

College of American Pathologists. 325 Waukegan Road, Northfield, IL 60093. Web site: <www.cap.org/>.

Meningitis Foundation of America Inc. 7155 Shadeland Station, Suite 190, Indianapolis, IN 46256–3922. Web site: <www.musa.org/default.htm>.

WEB SITES

"Fever." *MedlinePlus.* Available online at <www.nlm.nih.gov/medlineplus/ency/article/003090.htm> (accessed January 6, 2005).

"Typhoid Fever." *Centers for Disease Control and Prevention.* Available online at <www.cdc.gov/ncidod/dbmd/diseaseinfo/typhoidfever_g.htm> (accessed January 6, 2005).

"Yellow Fever." *Centers for Disease Control and Prevention.* Available online at <www.cdc.gov/travel/diseases/yellowfever.htm> (accessed January 6, 2005).

"Yellow Fever." *World Health Organization.* Available online at <www.who.int/csr/disease/yellowfev/en/> (accessed January 6, 2005).

L. Fleming Fallon Jr., MD, DrPH

Fever blister *see* **Cold sore**

Fever of unknown origin

Definition

Fever of unknown origin (FUO) refers to the presence of a documented elevation in body temperature for a specified time, for which a cause has not been found after basic medical evaluation. FUO is categorized as classic, hospital acquired FUO; FUO associated with low white blood cell counts (immunosuppression); and HIV-associated (AIDS-related) FUO.

Description

Fever, an elevation of normal body temperature, is a natural response of the body that helps fight off foreign substances, such as microorganisms (bacteria and viruses), parasites, fungi, and toxins. Body temperature is set by the thermoregulatory center, located in an area in the brain called the hypothalamus. Body temperature is not constant all day, but actually is lowest at 6 a.m. and highest around 4 to 6 p.m. Temperature also varies in different regions of the body; for example, rectal and urine temperatures are about one degree Fahrenheit higher than oral temperature, and rectal temperature is higher than urine. Certain normal conditions can also effect body temperature, such as food ingestion, age, pregnancy, and certain hormonal changes.

Substances that cause fever are known as pyrogens, which can be either exogenous (originate outside the body, such as bacterial toxins) or endogenous (formed by the body's own cells in response to an outside stimulus, such as a bacterial toxin). Researchers have discovered that there are several endogenous pyrogens, each made up of small groups of amino acids, the building blocks of proteins. When these natural pyrogens, called cytokines, are injected into humans, fever and chills develop within an hour. Interferon, tumor necrosis factor, and various interleukins are the major fever-producing cytokines.

In the complex process that produces fever, cytokines cause the thermoregulatory center in the hypothalamus to reset the normal temperature level. The body's initial response is to conserve heat by vasoconstriction, a process in which blood vessels narrow and prevent heat loss from the skin and elsewhere. This process alone raises temperature by two to three degrees. Certain behavioral activities also occur, such as adding more clothes and seeking a warmer environment. If the hypothalamus requires more heat, shivering occurs.

In children, the definition of FUO is applied when fever has been present for 14 days with no apparent cause, even though physical examinations have been made and laboratory tests performed. Doctors pay special attention to the ears, nose, throat, sinuses, and chest as sites of infection, since most childhood infections are respiratory in nature. The majority of children with FUO are eventually found to have one of several infectious diseases or an autoimmune disease. In many cases the disease is common, and in some cases an allergic response is causing the fever. Fever increases the body's metabolic rate and oxygen consumption, which can have a devastating effect on individuals with poor circulation. In addition, fever can lead to seizures in the very young. Some possible infectious causes shown in studies of children with FUO are as follows:

- acute **otitis media** (middle ear infection)
- bacterial meningitis
- blastomycosis
- brucellosis
- cystic fibrosis
- ehrlichiosis
- endocarditis
- enteric infection
- herpes infection
- HIV infection
- infectious mononucleosis
- lower respiratory tract infection
- malaria
- osteomyelitis
- Rocky Mountain spotted fever
- strep infection (streptococcus infection)
- systemic viral syndrome

- tonsillophyaryngitis or tonsillitis
- **tuberculosis**
- tularemia
- urinary tract infection
- viral meningoencephalitis

Transmission

It is possible for a child with FUO to spread infection or illness to other individuals, particularly if an infectious organism is the underlying cause. If a child has FUO, it is best to reduce contact with other young children or immune compromised **family** members until the cause of the fever has been identified.

Demographics

Fever of unknown origin can occur in anyone, male or female, of any age at any time depending upon exposure to infectious organisms such as bacteria or viruses or to other causes of illness such as fungi, parasites, or toxins or to underlying autoimmune or allergic conditions. Because the underlying cause of the fever is usually recorded as the diagnosis, accurate statistics for those presenting with FUO are not available.

Causes and symptoms

There are many possible causes of FUO; generally though, a diagnosis can be found. The most frequent cause of FUO is still infection, though the percentage has decreased in the early 2000s. Tuberculosis remains an important cause, especially when it occurs outside the lungs. The decrease in infections as a cause of FUO is due in part to improved culture techniques that allow more precise identification of organisms and, therefore, more appropriate treatment. In addition, advances in diagnostic technologies have made it easier to identify non-infectious causes. For example, tumors and autoimmune diseases were as of 2004 easier to diagnose. An autoimmune disease is one that arises when the body's immune system attacks its own tissue as if it were foreign. This happens when the immune system does not recognize protein markers (antigens) on its own cells. In some cases, reactions to medications can also cause prolonged fever.

In about 10 percent of cases, no definite cause is found. In another 10 percent, "factitious fevers" (either self induced or no fever at all) are identified.

General constitutional symptoms tend to occur along with fever, including muscle aches and pains (myalgias), chills, and **headache**. Sometimes symptoms such as a rash suggest an allergic reaction.

When to call the doctor

An infant under three months should be seen as soon by a pediatrician as possible if a fever develops. If a toddler or older child has a fever for more than a day or two (48 to 72 hours), with or without other symptoms, the pediatrician should be consulted so that an early diagnosis can be made and treatment begun. It is especially important to watch for signs of **dehydration**, particularly if the child is not drinking liquids or seems too sick to drink. A crying child with fever may have **pain** associated with a specific condition and should be seen by the pediatrician as soon as possible.

Diagnosis

Few symptoms in medicine present such a diagnostic challenge as fever. Nonetheless, if a careful, logical, and thorough evaluation is performed, the underlying cause generally can be diagnosed. The child's medical history is first reviewed along with travel, social, and family history, which can reveal important clues.

The first step medically is to search for an infectious cause. Skin and other screening tests for diseases such as tuberculosis and examination of blood, urine, and stool are generally indicated. Antibodies to a number of infectious agents can be measured; if antibody levels are rising, they may point to an active infection. In some cases, a febrile agglutination test can be performed to detect the presence in blood of certain infectious organisms that may stimulate the immune system to produce antibodies known as febrile agglutinins. The test helps diagnose or confirm certain febrile diseases that are known to be associated with febrile agglutinins. These may include:

- brucellosis, a type of infection caused by bacteria belonging to the genus *Brucella* and characterized by intermittent fever, sweating, chills, aches, and mental depression
- rickettsial infections, a group of diseases caused by the bacteria *Rickettsia*
- salmonellosis, caused by *Salmonella* bacteria and marked by **nausea** and severe diarrhea
- tularemia, also called rabbit fever, a bacterial infection characterized by a high fever and swollen lymph nodes

Various x-ray studies are of value and may be performed, particularly if organisms are identified that may indicate involvement of abdominal organs. Imaging techniques such as ultrasound, **computed tomography** (CT scan), and **magnetic resonance imaging** (MRI) may be performed. These enable physicians to examine areas that were once accessible only through surgery. Furthermore, new studies using radioactive materials (nuclear medicine) can detect areas of infection and inflammation previously almost impossible to find, even with surgery.

The removal and microscopic examination of tiny bits of tissue (biopsy) from any suspicious areas found on an x-ray exam can be performed by either traditional or newer surgical techniques. Material obtained by biopsy is then examined by a pathologist in order to look for clues as to the cause of the fever. Evidence of infection, tumor, or other diseases can be found in this way. Portions of the biopsy are also sent to the laboratory for culture in an attempt to grow and identify an infectious organism.

Fever in an individual with HIV, primary immune deficiency, recent transplant, on **chemotherapy**, or anyone else who is immunocompromised constitutes an especially difficult problem, as these patients often suffer from many unusual infections. HIV itself is a potential cause of fever.

Treatment

Most children who undergo evaluation for FUO do not receive treatment until a clear-cut cause is found. **Antibiotics** or medications designed to suppress a fever such as antipyretics (**acetaminophen**) or non-steroidal anti-inflammatory drugs (NSAIDs) will only hide the true cause. Once physicians are satisfied that there is no infectious cause, they may recommend medications such as acetaminophen, NSAIDs, or corticosteroids to decrease inflammation and reduce constitutional symptoms. Parents are advised not to give children aspirin for fever because of a side effect called Reye syndrome, which may cause liver failure. Fluids are replenished by having the child consume clear liquids. A child too sick to drink may be hospitalized and given intravenous fluids.

The development of FUO in certain settings, such as when it is acquired by patients in the hospital or in immunosuppressed individuals with a low white blood count, often needs rapid treatment to avoid serious complications. Therefore, in these instances antibiotics may be given after a minimal number of diagnostic studies. Once test results are known and causative organisms identified, treatment can be adjusted appropriately.

Alternative treatment

Practitioners of complementary medicine recommend herbs to treat fever. A tea made with catnip, lobe-lia, and dandelion will reduce fever or catnip tea enemas administered daily. Rest is recommended and large quantities of clear liquids to flush out toxins and help prevent dehydration. Some practitioners recommend letting a fever run its course or cooling the body with cool sponge baths.

Supporting the immune system is one way to help avoid infection by exposure to bacteria, viruses, and toxins as a potential source of fever. Green drinks made with young barley are believed to cleanse the blood and supply chlorophyll and nutrients for maintaining healthy tissue. Because stress is known to produce biochemicals that reduce white blood cell functioning, it is important to get sufficient **sleep** and reduce stress to help keep the immune system functioning well. Therapeutic massage, **yoga**, and other types of stress reduction programs are available in most communities.

Prognosis

The outlook for children with FUO depends on the cause of the fever. If the basic illness is easily treatable and can be found rather quickly, the potential for a cure is quite good. Some children may continue to have an elevated temperature steadily or intermittently for six months or more. If no serious disease is found, medications such as NSAIDs are used to decrease the effects of the fever. Careful follow-up and reevaluation is recommended in these cases.

Prevention

Although FUO cannot actually be prevented because the sources are unknown, the immune system can be strengthened to help avoid infection from bacteria, viruses, and toxins. Several nutritional supplements are reported to help build the immune system. These include garlic (contains the essential trace element germanium), essential fatty acids (found in flax seed oil, evening primrose oil, and fish oils), sea vegetables such as kelp, acidophilus to supply natural bacteria in the digestive tract, and **vitamins** A and C, both powerful antioxidants that improve immune function and increase resistance to infection. Zinc is another nutrient essential to immune system functioning.

Nutritional concerns

Immune system function requires ingesting certain essential nutrients and avoiding others that depress immunity. A diet that improves immune system functioning includes fresh fruits and vegetables, as many eaten raw as possible to provide necessary enzymes; whole grain cereals, brown rice, and whole grain pasta

KEY TERMS

Acquired immune deficiency syndrome (AIDS)— A disease associated with infection by the human immunodeficiency virus (HIV) that attacks the immune system.

Antibiotics—Drugs that are designed to kill or inhibit the growth of the bacteria that cause infections.

Antibody—A special protein made by the body's immune system as a defense against foreign material (bacteria, viruses, etc.) that enters the body. It is uniquely designed to attack and neutralize the specific antigen that triggered the immune response.

Antigen—A substance (usually a protein) identified as foreign by the body's immune system, triggering the release of antibodies as part of the body's immune response.

Computed tomography (CT)—An imaging technique in which cross-sectional x rays of the body are compiled to create a three-dimensional image of the body's internal structures; also called computed axial tomography.

Culture—A test in which a sample of body fluid is placed on materials specially formulated to grow microorganisms. A culture is used to learn what type of bacterium is causing infection.

Immunosuppression—Techniques used to prevent transplant graft rejection by the recipient's immune system.

Magnetic resonance imaging (MRI)—An imaging technique that uses a large circular magnet and radio waves to generate signals from atoms in the body. These signals are used to construct detailed images of internal body structures and organs, including the brain.

Nonsteroidal anti-inflammatory drugs (NSAIDs)— A group of drugs, including aspirin, ibuprofen, and naproxen, that are taken to reduce fever and inflammation and to relieve pain. They work primarily by interfering with the formation of prostaglandins, enzymes implicated in pain and inflammation.

Toxin—A poisonous substance usually produced by a microorganism or plant.

Ultrasonography—A medical test in which sound waves are directed against internal structures in the body. As sound waves bounce off the internal structure, they create an image on a video screen. Ultrasonography is often used to diagnose fetal abnormalities, gallstones, heart defects, and tumors. Also called ultrasound imaging.

for essential vitamins, **minerals**, and fiber; and non-meat sources of protein such as nuts, seeds, tofu, legumes (beans), and eggs. Fish, fowl, and lean meats can be consumed in small amounts. Sweets, especially if sweetened with refined sugars, should be reduced or avoided altogether. A diet high in fats and processed foods made with refined flours and sugars can actually suppress the immune system. Alcohol and **caffeine** should be avoided.

Parental concerns

When FUO is present, parents may be concerned that effective treatment will be delayed by waiting for a diagnosis, which may depend on waiting for the results of diagnostic tests. Depending on the extent of the fever, keeping the child quiet and in bed is probably recommended until all results are available and a definitive diagnosis is made. The doctor will undoubtedly recommend giving clear liquids as often as possible to avoid dehydration from the high body temperature. After the tests have been performed, the physician may recommend fever-reducing medications such as acetaminophen or ibuprofen. If the fever is high enough for concern, physicians may prescribe a broad spectrum antibiotic as initial treatment rather than waiting for the results of all diagnostic tests. When results are available, the physician will likely prescribe a new medication most appropriate for the diagnosis.

See also HIV infection and AIDS; Rheumatic fever.

Resources

BOOKS

Hay, William. *Current Pediatric Diagnosis & Treatment.* New York: McGraw Hill, 2002.

Matten, Grace. *Fever of Unknown Origin.* Durham, NC: Oyster River Press, 2001.

ORGANIZATIONS

American Medical Association. 515 N. State St., Chicago, IL 60612. Web site: <www.ama-assn.org>.

Centers for Disease Control and Prevention. 1600 Clifton Rd., NE, Atlanta, GA 30333. Web site: <www.cdc.gov>.

WEB SITES

Chan-Tack, Kirk M., and John Bartlett. "Fever of Unknown Origin." *emedicine*, November 17, 2004. Available online at <www.emedicine.com/med/topic785.htm> (accessed November 18, 2004).

L. Lee Culvert
David Kaminstein, MD

Fever seizures
  see **Febrile seizures**

Fifth disease

Definition

Fifth disease is a mild childhood illness caused by the human parvovirus B19 that causes flu-like symptoms and a rash. It is called fifth disease because it was fifth on a list of common childhood illnesses that are accompanied by a rash, including **measles**, **rubella** (or German measles), **scarlet fever** (or scarlatina), and scarlatinella, a variant of scarlet fever.

Description

The Latin name for fifth disease is *erythema infectiosum*, meaning infectious redness. It is also called the "slapped cheek disease" because, when the bright red rash first appears on the cheeks, it looks as if the face has been slapped. Anyone can get the disease, but it occurs more frequently in school-aged children. The disease is usually mild, and both children and adults usually recover quickly without complications. Some individuals exhibit no symptoms and never even feel ill.

Transmission

The virus that causes fifth disease lives in the nose, mouth, and throat of an infected person; therefore, the virus can be spread through the air by coughing and sneezing. It can also be spread through shared drinking glasses and eating utensils.

Demographics

Fifth disease is very common in children between the ages of five and 15. Studies show that although 40 percent to 60 percent of adults worldwide have laboratory evidence of a past parvovirus B19 infection, most of these adults cannot remember having had symptoms of fifth disease. This fact leads medical experts to believe that most people with parvovirus B19 infection have either very mild symptoms or no symptoms at all.

Fifth disease occurs everywhere in the world. Outbreaks of parvovirus tend to occur in the late winter and early spring, but there may also be sporadic cases of the disease any time throughout the year.

In households where a child has fifth disease, another **family** member who has not previously had fifth disease has about a 50 percent chance of also getting the infection, while classmates of a child with fifth disease have about a 60 percent chance of getting the disease.

Causes and symptoms

Fifth disease is caused by the human parvovirus B19, a member of the Parvoviridae family of viruses, that lives in the nose, mouth, and throat of an infected person. Because the virus needs a rapidly dividing cell in order to multiply, it attacks the red blood cells of the body. Once infected, a person is believed to be immune to reinfection.

Symptoms may appear four to 28 days after being exposed to the virus, with the average time to onset ranging from 16 to 17 days. Initial symptoms are flu-like and include **headache**, stuffy or runny nose, body ache, **sore throat**, a mild fever of 101°F (38.3°C), and chills. It is at this time, prior to the development of the rash, that individuals are contagious. These symptoms last for two to three days. Other symptoms that sometimes occur with fifth disease include swollen glands, red eyes, and **diarrhea**. In older teens and adults, fifth disease may be followed by joint swelling or **pain** in the hands, wrists, knees, and ankles, lasting from a few months to several years.

In children, especially those under the age of ten, a bright red rash that looks like a slap mark develops suddenly on the cheeks a few days after the original symptoms were experienced. The rash may be flat or raised and may or may not be itchy. Sometimes, the rash spreads to the arms, legs, and trunk, where it has a lace-like or net-like appearance as the centers of the blotches fade. By the time the rash appears, individuals are no longer infectious. On average, the rash lasts for ten to 11 days but may last for as long as five to six weeks. The rash may fade away and then reappear upon exposure to sunlight, hot baths, emotional distress, or vigorous **exercise**.

The virus causes the destruction of red blood cells and, therefore, a deficiency in the oxygen-carrying capacity of the blood (anemia) can result. In healthy children, the anemia is mild and only lasts a short while. In children with weakened immune systems, however, either because they have a chronic disease like **AIDS** or **cancer** (immunocompromised) or are receiving medication to suppress the immune system (immunosuppressed), such as organ transplant recipients, this anemia can be severe and last long after the infection has subsided. Symptoms of anemia include fatigue, lack of color, lack of energy,

KEY TERMS

Anemia—A condition in which there is an abnormally low number of red blood cells in the bloodstream. It may be due to loss of blood, an increase in red blood cell destruction, or a decrease in red blood cell production. Major symptoms are paleness, shortness of breath, unusually fast or strong heart beats, and tiredness.

Antibody—A special protein made by the body's immune system as a defense against foreign material (bacteria, viruses, etc.) that enters the body. It is uniquely designed to attack and neutralize the specific antigen that triggered the immune response.

Immunocompromised—A state in which the immune system is suppressed or not functioning properly.

Immunosuppressed—A state in which the immune system is suppressed by medications during the treatment of other disorders, like cancer, or following an organ transplantation.

Reye's syndrome—A serious, life-threatening illness in children, usually developing after a bout of flu or chickenpox, and often associated with the use of aspirin. Symptoms include uncontrollable vomiting, often with lethargy, memory loss, disorientation, or delirium. Swelling of the brain may cause seizures, coma, and in severe cases, death.

Sickle cell anemia—An inherited disorder in which red blood cells contain an abnormal form of hemoglobin, a protein that carries oxygen. The abnormal form of hemoglobin causes the red cells to become sickle-shaped. The misshapen cells may clog blood vessels, preventing oxygen from reaching tissues and leading to pain, blood clots and other problems.

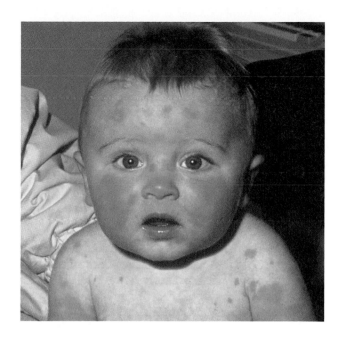

Infant with a rash caused by fifth disease, or erythema infectiosum. *(Custom Medical Stock Photo, Inc.)*

and shortness of breath. Some individuals with **sickle cell anemia**, iron deficiency, a number of different hereditary blood disorders, and those who have received bone marrow transplantations may be susceptible to developing a potentially life-threatening complication called a transient aplastic crisis in which the body is temporarily unable to form new red blood cells.

In very rare instances, the virus can cause inflammation of different areas of the body, including the brain (**encephalitis**), the covering of the brain and spinal cord (**meningitis**), the lungs (pneumonitis), the liver (hepatitis), and the heart muscle (myocarditis). The virus can also aggravate symptoms for people with an autoimmune disease called systemic lupus erythematosus.

Although no association with an increased number of birth defects has been demonstrated, there is concern that infection during the first three months of pregnancy may lead to a slight increase in the number of miscarriages due to the fetus developing severe anemia. There is also some concern that infection later in pregnancy may involve a very small risk of premature delivery or stillbirth. As a result, women who get fifth disease while they are pregnant should be monitored closely by a physician.

When to call the doctor

Parents should call their child's doctor if their child develops a rash, especially if the rash is widespread over the child's body or if the rash is accompanied by other symptoms.

Diagnosis

Fifth disease is usually suspected based on a patient's symptoms, including the typical appearance of the bright red rash on the cheeks, patient history, age, and the time of year. The physician will also exclude other potential causes for the symptoms and rash, including rubella, **infectious mononucleosis**, bacterial infections such as **Lyme disease**, allergic reactions, and lupus.

In addition, there is a blood test for fifth disease, but it is generally used only for pregnant women and for people who have weakened immune systems or who suffer from blood disorders, such as sickle cell anemia. The test involves measuring for a particular antibody or protein that the body produces in response to infection with the human parvovirus B19. The test is 92–97 percent specific for this disease.

Because fifth disease can pose problems for an unborn fetus exposed to the disease through the mother, testing for the disease may be conducted while a fetus is still in the uterus. This test uses fluid collected from the sac around the fetus (amniotic fluid) instead of blood to detect the viral DNA.

Prognosis

Generally, fifth disease is mild, and patients tend to improve without any complications. In cases where the patient is either immunocompromised or immunosuppressed, a life-threatening aplastic crisis can occur. With prompt treatment, however, the prognosis is good. Mothers who develop the infection while pregnant can pass the infection on to their fetus and thus stand an increased risk of miscarriage and stillbirth. There are tests and treatments, however, that can be performed on the fetus while still in the uterus that can reduce the risk of anemia or other complications.

Prevention

As of 2004, there was no vaccine against fifth disease. Avoiding contact with persons who exhibit symptoms of a cold and maintaining good personal hygiene by regularly washing hands may minimize the chances of an infection. Pregnant women should avoid exposure to persons infected with the disease and notify their obstetricians immediately if they are exposed so that they can be tested and monitored closely.

Parental concerns

Generally parents should not be concerned if their child contracts fifth disease. However, if the mother is pregnant, she should contact her doctor.

Resources

BOOKS

Laskey, Elizabeth. *Fifth Disease*. It's Catching Series. Oxford, UK: Heinemann Library, 2003.

PM Medical Health News. *21st Century Complete Medical Guide to Fifth Disease, Parvovirus: Authoritative Government Documents, Clinical References, and Practical Information for Patients and Physicians*. Washington, DC: Progressive Management, 2004.

WEB SITES

Eppes, Stephen. "Fifth Disease." *KidsHealth*, April 2004. Available online at <http://kidshealth.org/parent/infections/bacterial_viral/fifth.html/> (accessed November 18, 2004).

"Fifth Disease." *Centers for Disease Control (CDC)*, September 7, 2004. Available online at <www.cdc.gov/ncidod/diseases/parvovirus/B19.htm> (accessed November 18, 2004).

Judith Sims, MS
Lata Cherath, PhD

Fighting *see* **Aggressive behavior**

Fine motor skills

Definition

Fine motor skills generally refer to the small movements of the hands, wrists, fingers, feet, toes, lips, and tongue.

Description

Motor skills are actions that involve the movement of muscles in the body. They are divided into two groups: **gross motor skills**, which include the larger movements of arms, legs, feet, or the entire body (**crawling**, running, and jumping); and fine motor skills, which are smaller actions, such as grasping an object between the thumb and a finger or using the lips and tongue to taste objects. Both types of motor skills usually develop together, because many activities depend on the coordination of gross and fine motor skills.

Infancy

The hands of newborn infants are closed most of the time and, like the rest of their bodies, they have little control over them. If their palms are touched, they will make a very tight fist, but this is an unconscious reflex action called the Darwinian reflex, and it disappears within two to three months. Similarly, infants will grasp at an object placed in their hands, but without any awareness that they are doing so. At some point their hand muscles relax, and they drop the object, equally unaware that they have let it fall. Babies may begin flailing at objects that interest them by two weeks of age but cannot grasp them. By eight weeks, they begin to discover and **play** with their hands, at first solely by touch, and then, at about three months, by sight as well. At this age, however, the deliberate grasp remains largely undeveloped.

Hand-eye coordination begins to develop between the ages of two and four months, inaugurating a period of trial-and-error practice at sighting objects and grabbing at them. At four or five months, most infants can grasp an object that is within reach, looking only at the object and not at their hands. Referred to as "top-level reaching," this achievement is considered an important milestone in fine motor development. At the age of six months, infants can typically hold on to a small block briefly, and many have started banging objects. Although their grasp is still clumsy, they have acquired a fascination with grabbing small objects and trying to put them in their mouths. At first, babies will indiscriminately try to grasp things that cannot be grasped, such as pictures in a book, as well as those that can, such as a rattle or ball. During the latter half of the first year, they begin exploring and testing objects before grabbing, touching them with an entire hand and, eventually, poking them with an index finger.

One of the most significant fine motor accomplishments is the pincer grip, which typically appears at about 12 months. Initially, infants can only hold an object, such as a rattle, in their palm, wrapping their fingers (including the thumb) around it from one side. This awkward position is called the palmar grasp, which makes it difficult to hold on to and manipulate the object. By the age of eight to 10 months, a finger grasp begins, but objects can only be gripped with all four fingers pushing against the thumb, which still makes it awkward to grab small objects. The development of the pincer grip—the ability to hold objects between the thumb and index finger—gives the infant a more sophisticated ability to grasp and manipulate objects and also to deliberately drop them. By about the age of one, an infant can drop an object into a receptacle, compare objects held in both hands, stack objects, and nest them within each other.

Toddlerhood

Toddlers develop the ability to manipulate objects with increasing sophistication, including using their fingers to twist dials, pull strings, push levers, turn book pages, and use crayons to produce crude scribbles. Dominance of either the right or left hand usually emerges during this period as well. Toddlers also add a new dimension to touching and manipulating objects by simultaneously being able to name them. Instead of only random scribbles, their **drawings** include patterns, such

as circles. Their play with blocks is more elaborate and purposeful than that of infants, and they can stack as many as six blocks. They are also able to fold a sheet of paper in half (with supervision), string large beads, manipulate snap **toys**, play with clay, unwrap small objects, and pound pegs.

Preschool

The more delicate tasks facing **preschool** children, such as handling silverware or tying shoelaces, represent more challenge than most of the gross motor activities learned during this period of development. The central nervous system is still in the process of maturing sufficiently for complex messages from the brain to get to the child's fingers. In addition, small muscles tire more easily than large ones, and the short, stubby fingers of preschoolers make delicate or complicated tasks more difficult. Finally, gross motor skills call for energy, which is boundless in preschoolers, while fine motor skills require patience, which is in shorter supply. Thus, there is considerable variation in fine motor development among this age group.

School age

By the age of five, most children have clearly advanced beyond the fine motor skill development of the preschool age. They can draw recognizably human figures with facial features and legs connected to a distinct trunk. Besides drawing, five-year-olds can also cut, paste, and trace shapes. They can fasten visible buttons (as opposed to those at the back of clothing), and many can tie bows, including shoelace bows. Their right- or left-handedness is well established, and they use the preferred hand for writing and drawing.

School-age children six to 12 years old should have mastered hand and eye coordination. Early school age children should be able to use eating utensils and other tools, be able to help with household chores, such as sweeping, mopping, and dusting; care for pets; draw, paint, and engage in making crafts; and begin developing writing skills. Children will continue to fine-tune their fine motor skills through **adolescence** with such activities as **sports**, crafts, hobbies, learning musical instruments, computer use, and even **video games**.

Helping a child succeed in fine motor tasks requires planning, time, and a variety of play materials. Fine motor development can be encouraged by activities that youngsters enjoy, including crafts, puzzles, and playing with building blocks. Helping parents with everyday domestic activities, such as baking, can be fun for the child in addition to helping the child develop fine motor skills. For example, stirring batter provides a good work-

KEY TERMS

Beery-Buktenica Test—A test that identifies problems with visual perception, fine motor skills (especially hand control), and hand-eye coordination.

Darwinian reflex—An unconscious action in infants in which if a palm is touched, the infant makes a very tight fist. This instinct disappears within two to three months.

Developmental coordination disorder—A disorder of motor skills.

Gross motor skills—The abilities required to control the large muscles of the body for walking, running, sitting, crawling, and other activities. The muscles required to perform gross motor skills are generally found in the arms, legs, back, abdomen, and torso.

Hand-eye coordination—The ability to grasp or touch an object while looking at it.

Lincoln-Oseretsky Motor Development Scale—A test that assesses the development of motor skills.

Palmar grasp—A young infant's primitive ability to hold an object in the palm by wrapping fingers and thumb around it from one side.

Pincer grip—The ability to hold objects between thumb and index finger, which typically develops in infants between 12 and 15 months of age.

Top-level reaching—The ability of an infant to grasp an object that is within reach, looking only at the object and not at the hands. Typically develops between four and five months of age.

Fine motor skills

Age	Skill
One to three months	Reflexively grasps finger or toy placed in hand.
Three months	Grasping reflex gone. Briefly holds small toy voluntarily when it is placed in the hand.
Four months	Holds and shakes rattle. Brings hands together to play with them. Reaches for objects but frequently misses them.
Five months	Grasps objects deliberately. Splashes water. Crumples paper.
Six months	Holds bottle. Grasps at own feet. May bring toes to mouth.
Seven months	Transfers toy from hand to hand. Bangs objects on table. Puts everything into the mouth. Loves playing with paper.
Nine months	Able to grasp small objects between thumb and forefinger.
Ten months	Points at objects with index finger. Lets go of objects deliberately.
Eleven months	Places object into another's hand when requested, but does not release.
Twelve months	Places and releases object into another's hand when requested. Rolls ball on floor. Starts to hold crayon and mark paper with it.
Fifteen months	Builds tower of two blocks. Repeatedly throws objects on floor. Starts to be able to take off clothing, starting with shoes.
Eighteen months	Builds tower of three blocks. Starts to feed self well with spoon. Turns book pages two or three at a time. Scribbles on paper.
Two years	Builds tower of six or seven blocks. Turns book pages one at a time. Turns door knobs and unscrews jar lids. Washes and dries hands. Uses spoon and fork well.
Two and a half years	Builds tower of eight blocks. Holds pencil between fingers instead of grasping with fist.
Three years	Builds tower of nine or ten blocks. Puts on shoes and socks. Can button and unbutton. Carries containers with little spilling or dropping.
Four years	Dresses self except for tying. Cuts with scissors, but not well. Washes and dries face.
Five years	Dresses without help. Ties shoes. Prints simple letters.

SOURCE: *Miller-Keane Encyclopedia and Dictionary of Medicine, Nursing, and Allied Health, 5th ed.* and Child Development Institute, http://www.childdevelopmentinfo.com.

(Table by GGS Information Services.)

out for the hand and arm muscles, and cutting and spooning out cookie dough requires hand-eye coordination. Even a computer keyboard and mouse can provide practice in finger, hand, and hand-eye coordination. Because the development of fine motor skills plays a crucial role in school readiness and **cognitive development**, it is considered an important part of the preschool curriculum.

Common problems

Fine motor skills can become impaired in a variety of ways, including injury, illness, **stroke**, and congenital deformities. An infant or child up to age five who is not developing new fine motor skills for that age may have a developmental disability. These problems can include major health conditions including **cerebral palsy**, **mental retardation**, blindness, deafness, and diabetes. Children with delays in fine motor skills development have difficulty controlling their coordinated body movements, especially with the face, hands, and fingers. Signs of fine motor skills delays include a failure to develop midline

A toddler demonstrates his fine motor skills by grasping and munipulating building blocks. (© S. Villeger/Explorer/ Photo Researchers, Inc.)

orientation by four months, reaching by five months, transferring objects from hand to hand by six months, a raking grasp by eight months, a mature pincer grip by one year, and index finger isolation by one year.

Developmental coordination disorder is a disorder of motor skills. A person with this disorder has a hard time with things like riding a bike, holding a pencil, and throwing a ball. People with this disorder are often called clumsy. Their movements are slow and awkward. People with developmental coordination disorder may also have a hard time completing tasks that involve movement of muscle groups in sequence. For example, such a person might be unable to do the following in order: open a closet door, get out a jacket, and put it on. It is thought that up to 6 percent of children may have developmental coordination disorder, according to the 2002 issue of the annual journal *Clinical Reference Systems*. The symptoms usually go unnoticed until the early years of elementary school. It is usually diagnosed in children who are between five and 11 years old.

Parental concerns

Parents, teachers, and primary caregivers need to have a clear understanding of how young children develop fine motor skills and the timetable for development of the skills.

Fine motor skills development tests

The Lincoln-Oseretsky Motor Development Scale is an individually administered test that assesses the development of motor skills in children and adults. Areas covered include fine and gross motor skills, finger dexterity and speed, and hand-eye coordination. The test consists of 36 tasks arranged in order of increasing difficulty. These include walking backwards, standing on one foot, touching one's nose, jumping over a rope, throwing and catching a ball, putting coins in a box, jumping and clapping, balancing on tiptoe while opening and closing one's hands, and balancing a rod vertically. Norms have been established for each part of the test for children aged six to 14.

The **Beery-Buktenica Test**, also known as VMI or Developmental Test of Visual-Motor Integration, is designed for individuals two years of age through adult. The text identifies problems with visual perception, fine motor skills (especially hand control), and hand-eye coordination. It is usually administered individually but can also be given in groups. The child is given a booklet containing increasingly complex geometric figures and asked to copy them without any erasures and without rotating the booklet in any direction. The test is given in two versions: the Short Test Form, containing 15 figures, is used for ages three through eight; the Long Test Form, with 24 figures, is used for older children, adolescents, and adults with **developmental delay**. A raw score based on the number of correct copies is converted based on norms for each age group, and results are reported as converted scores and percentiles. The test is not timed but usually takes 10 to 15 minutes to administer.

When to call the doctor

Some symptoms of impaired fine motor skills may appear up to age two. These symptoms include having a difficult time sitting up or raising the head, being unable to stand without help or having a very hard time standing without help, being unable to crawl or having a very hard time crawling, and walking very late or having a hard time walking. Other symptoms usually appear during the preschool or grade school years. These may include the child having difficulty holding a pencil or drawing, throwing a ball, riding a bicycle, playing sports, having a hard time with clothes that have buttons or zippers, having poor handwriting, and being clumsy.

Children with any one or combination of these symptoms should be seen by a pediatrician who specializes in motor skills development delays. Children who lose previously acquired motor skills should also be seen by a doctor. There are many ways to address fine motor skills impairment, such as physical therapy. This type of therapy can include treating the underlying cause, strengthening muscles, and learning how to compensate for impaired movements.

See also Gross motor skills.

Resources

BOOKS

Bly, Lois. *Motor Skills Acquisition Checklist.* San Antonio, TX: Therapy Skill Builders, 2003.

Kurtz, Lisa A. *How to Help a Clumsy Child: Strategies for Young Children with Developmental Motor Concerns.* London, UK: Jessica Kingsley Publishing, 2003.

Liddle, Tara Losquadro, and Laura Yorke. *Why Motor Skills Matter: Improving Your Child's Physical Development to Enhance Learning and Self-Esteem.* New York: McGraw-Hill, 2003.

Smith, Jodene Lynn. *Activities for Fine Motor Skills Development.* Westminster, CA: Teacher Created Materials, 2003.

PERIODICALS

Jeansonne, Jennifer J. "Motor Skill Learning Research Looks Beyond Outcomes—Understanding the Components Needed for Skilled Performance Helps Develop Instructions and Training Methods." *Biomechanics* (June 1, 2004): 69.

Rink, Judith E. "It's Okay to Be a Beginner: Teach a Motor Skill, and the Skill May Be Learned. Teach How to Learn a Motor Skill, and Many Skills Can Be Learned—Even After a Student Leaves School." *The Journal of Physical Education, Recreation & Dance* (August 2004): 31–4.

"Should the Main Objective of Adapted Physical Education Be the Development of Motor Skills or the Development of Self-Esteem?" *The Journal of Physical Education, Recreation & Dance* 74 (November-December 2003): 10–12.

Vickers, Marcia. "Why Can't We Let Boys Be Boys?" *Business Week* (May 26, 2003): 84.

ORGANIZATIONS

American Academy of Pediatrics. 141 Northwest Point Blvd., Elk Grove Village, IL 60007. Web site: <www.aao.org>.

Developmental Research for the Effective Advancement of Memory and Motor Skills. 273 Ringwood Road, Freeville, NY 13068. Web site: <www.dreamms.org>.

WEB SITES

"How to Help Your Toddler Develop Fine Motor Skills." *BabyCenter*, 2004. Available online at <www.babycenter.com/refcap/toddler/toddlerdevelopment/11549.html> (accessed November 18, 2004).

"Movement, Coordination, and Your Newborn." *KidsHealth*, May 2001. Available online at <www.kidshealth.org/parent/growth/movement/movenewborn.html> (accessed November 18, 2004).

Ken R. Wells

Fingertip injuries

Definition

Fingertip injuries include any **wounds** to the area at tip of the finger. They range from a simple bruise or scrape to having the fingertip taken off. Fingertip injuries occur frequently in infants and children because hands are used to explore surroundings and **play**.

Description

Fingers each have three bones (phalanges); the thumb has two. The fingertip consists of the uppermost phalanx with surrounding muscle, tissue, nerves, and nail. A fingertip is a highly complex structure, with many specialized features, one of which is a rich network of sensory nerves. The fingernail is called the nail plate. Underneath the nail plate is the nail bed, the mostly pink tissue seen under the nail. The pulp is the area of skin opposite the fingernail and is usually very vulnerable to injury. Fingertip injuries are extremely common and varied. Blunt or crush injuries can cause bleeding under the nail plate (subungual hematomas), which can be very painful. Nails can also be torn off (nail avulsions), and the fingertip bone can be broken (fracture). Sharp or shearing injuries from knives and glass result in cuts (lacerations) and punctures. Occasionally, the end of the fingertip is torn off (amputated). When portions of the fingertip are missing, the injury is described as a partial amputation. When the finger is cut more than halfway through, the injury is described as a subtotal amputation. **Burns** and **frostbite** also commonly injure fingertips.

Demographics

In the United States, fingertip injuries account for approximately two-thirds of hand injuries in children. Damage to the nail bed is reported to occur in 15–24 percent of fingertip injuries. A Florida study of hand injuries in children conducted in 2002 showed that the most frequent hand injury setting was outdoors (47%). The most frequent injuries were lacerations (30%), followed by **fractures** (16%). The fingers were the most commonly injured part of the hand, particularly the thumb (19%), and fingertips were involved in 21 percent of cases. Children younger than two years suffered fingertip injuries mostly inside the home.

Causes and symptoms

In children, fingertip injuries are the result of accidents occurring at play or in the home. They involve cuts, by glass, knives, or other sharp objects; or crushing injuries, as when the fingertip gets caught in a door or window or is hit by a hammer or rock. Symptoms depend on the nature of the fingertip injury and may include some of the following:

- **pain**
- bleeding
- swelling
- tissue loss
- movement restriction
- amputation

When to call the doctor

Parents should always see a doctor right away if their child injures the tip of a finger or thumb. Fingertips contain many nerves and are extremely sensitive. Without prompt and proper care, a fingertip injury can disrupt the complex function of the hand, resulting in permanent deformity and disability. Bleeding from minor fingertip cuts often stop on its own with direct pressure applied to the wound with a clean cloth. If continuous pressure does not slow or stop the bleeding after 15 minutes, an emergency room visit is indicated.

Diagnosis

The treating physician begins a diagnosis by carefully evaluating the fingertip injury. Bones and joints are examined for motion and tenderness. Nerves are examined for sensory (feeling sensations) and motor (movement) function. As part of injury diagnosis, the treating physician also considers the following factors:

- nature of injury (crush or sharp)
- nail or nail bed involvement
- bone involvement
- viability the tip
- presence of foreign bodies

X rays may be required either to assess alignment of fingertip phalanx fractures or to detect presence of foreign bodies.

Treatment

Doctors provide individualized treatment for fingertip injuries based on the nature and extent of the injury. The treating physician usually gives an injection (digital block anesthesia) to stop pain in the affected finger. Then he or she may rinse the wound (irrigate) with a saline solution, inspect it for exposed bone, soft tissue loss, and nail or nail bed injury. Infected or dead tissue or foreign materials are also removed (debridement) to reduce risk of infection. If blood has accumulated under the nail (subungual hematoma), the doctor may drain it by piercing through the fingernail. **Antibiotics** and a **tetanus** shot may also be prescribed. The goal of treatment is a painless fingertip that has durable and feeling skin. A normal fingertip has sensation without pain, stable pulp padding, and an acceptable appearance. The hand should be able to pinch, grip, and perform other normal functions. In cases of severe injury and whenever possible, the doctor will try to maintain the fingertip's length and appearance and preserve its fingernail.

Surgery

Fingertip injuries often require surgical treatment, usually performed with local anesthesia. Fingertip repair surgery includes the following:

- Sutures: Laceration wounds are stitched (sutured) after application of a digital block.
- Nail bed surgery: If the nail bed is injured, the nail plate may be removed, the bed carefully debrided and repaired. The nail plate is then reinserted and the injury dressed. A finger splint may be applied.
- Fingertip amputation: Various methods are used for amputation injuries including simple amputation of the fingertip, full or partial skin grafts, and skin flaps.

KEY TERMS

Avulsion—The forcible separation of a piece from the entire structure.

Debridement—The surgical removal of dead tissue and/or foreign bodies from a wound or cut.

Laceration—A cut or separation of skin or other tissue by a tremendous force, producing irregular edges. Also called a tear.

Nail bed—The layer of tissue underneath the nail.

Phalanx—Plural, plananges. Any of the digital bones of the hand or foot. Humans have three phalanges to each finger and toe with the exception of the thumb and big toe which have only two each.

Sensory nerves—Sensory or afferent nerves carry impulses of sensation from the periphery or outward parts of the body to the brain and spinal cord.

Subungual hematoma—Accumulation of blood under a nail.

Tetanus—A potentially fatal infection caused by a toxin produced by the bacterium *Clostridium tetani*. The bacteria usually enter the body through a wound and the toxin they produce affects the central nervous system causing painful and often violent muscular contractions. Commonly called lockjaw.

- Reconstructive flap surgery: If a fingertip injury exposes bone, and there is not enough tissue available on the fingertip to close it, the surgeon may need to shorten the bone and transfer a piece of skin and underlying fat and blood vessels from a healthy part of the patient's body to the injury site. A bulky dressing and splint supports the hand after surgery, with uninjured fingers left free to **exercise**. A second operation may be necessary after a few weeks to detach the flap from its origin.

- Fractured phalanx: In case of fingertip bone fracture, the bone is straightened and put in a splint or cast. A temporary metal pin may also be inserted into the bone to hold it in place until bone growth occurs. If bone is partly missing, the finger may be shortened or the surgeon may use a bone graft.

Prognosis

The outcome depends on the extent of traumatic damage to the fingertip and whether surgery is required. Small wounds to a fingertip's skin and pulp usually close on their own with complete healing within three to five weeks. In 60 percent of patients with subungual hematomas that involve more than 50 percent of the nail surface, laceration is repairable. This prognosis increases to over 95 percent when an associated fracture of the phalanx is present. Nail lacerations that are not treated may cause nail deformities. The average healing time for fingertip amputation is 21–27 days. In many cases, fingertip repair surgery gives back a large degree of feeling and function. However, infection, poor healing, loss of feeling or motion, blood clots, and adverse reactions to anesthesia are all possible complications of surgery. Mild to severe pain and sensitivity to cold following treatment for a fingertip amputation sometimes occur.

Prevention

Children should at all times be supervised in their activities. Parents should not allow children to use sharp tools and knives without supervision. They should teach them to always wash and thoroughly dry any tool or knife before use. Children should also be taught how to use knives properly, to always cut away from themselves, and to cut in small, controlled strokes.

Parental concerns

Parents should be aware that recovery from a serious fingertip injury may take months and require hand therapy. This may include hand exercises to improve movement and strength, heat and **massage therapy**, electrical nerve stimulation, splinting, traction, and special wrappings to control swelling.

See also Frostbite and frostnip.

Resources

BOOKS

Ziegler, Moritz, et al. *Operative Pediatric Surgery*. New York: McGraw-Hill, 2003.

PERIODICALS

Boyd, R., and C. Libetta. "Reimplantation of the nail root in fingertip crush injuries in children." *Emergency Medical Journal* 19, no. 2 (March 2002): 341–45.

Braga-Silva, J., and M. Jaeger. "Repositioning and flap placement in fingertip injuries." *Annals of Plastic Surgery* 47, no. 1 (July 2001): 60–3.

Fetter-Zarzeka, A., and M. M. Joseph. "Hand and fingertip injuries in children." *Pediatric Emergency Care* 18, no. 5 (October 2002): 341–45.

Wang, Q. C., and B. A. Johnson. "Fingertip injuries." *American Family Physician* 63, no. 10 (May 2001): 1961–66.

ORGANIZATIONS

American Academy of Orthopaedic Surgeons (AAOS). 6300 North River Road, Rosemont, IL 60018–4262. Web site: <www.aaos.org>.

American College of Surgeons. 633 N. Saint Clair St., Chicago, IL 60611–3211. Web site: <www.facs.org>.

American Society for Surgery of the Hand (ASSH). 6300 North River Road, Suite 600, Rosemont, IL 60018. Web site: <www.assh.org>.

WEB SITES

"Fingertip Injuries/Amputations." *Your Orthopaedic Connection,* April 2001. Available online at <www.orthoinfo.org/fact/ thr_report.cfm?Thread_ID=276& topcategory=Hand> (accessed November 29, 2004).

"Fingertip Injuries." *HandWorld.* Available online at <www.eatonhand.com/hw/hw011.htm> (accessed November 29, 2004).

Vaughn, Glen. "Fingertip Injuries." *eMedicine,* November 4, 2004. Available online at <www.emedicine.com/emerg/ topic179.htm> (accessed November 29, 2004).

Monique Laberge, Ph.D.

5p minus syndrome *see* **Cri du chat syndrome**

Flu *see* **Influenza**

Flu vaccine

Definition

The flu vaccine protects a person against getting **influenza**, caused by the influenza virus. It is administered either by injection or by inhalation.

Description

There are two types of flu vaccine. Live attenuated influenza vaccine (LAIV) was first approved for use in 2003. It contains live, but weakened, influenza virus and is administered as a nasal spray. Inactivated influenza vaccine contains killed viruses and is given by intramuscular injection.

Because influenza changes from year to year, a flu shot, unlike other types of vaccinations, is required every year. Each year, the United States Centers for Communicable Disease Control predicts the strains of influenza that are likely to appear in the coming year. Vaccine manufacturers then make products to protect against these types of flu. These vaccines only protect against the type of influenza viruses from which they are made. They are usually of no value against other types of influenza virus.

There are three types of influenza virus: A, B, and C. They differ by the proteins on their outer surface. Type A viruses are found in many different animals, including ducks, chickens, pigs, whales, horses, and seals. Influenza B viruses circulate widely, but only among humans. Type C viruses, also only among humans, cause a very mild infection, and flu vaccines do not include protection against type C influenza.

General use

Influenza is a contagious illness. Every year, 10 to 20 percent of the U.S. population gets the flu, and over 100,000 people are hospitalized because of influenza. Symptoms of flu include **fever**, **headache**, extreme tiredness, dry **cough**, **sore throat**, runny or stuffy nose, and muscle aches. When children get the flu, they often complain of **nausea** and have **vomiting** and **diarrhea**, although these problems are less common in older children and adults. While influenza virus vaccines cannot give complete protection against flu, they greatly reduce the risk of flu-like infections, reduce the risk of **hospitalization**, and shorten the duration of these infections.

All healthy children between the ages of six months and 23 months should receive influenza vaccine because these young children do not yet have fully developed immune systems and are at increased risk of getting the flu and requiring hospital treatment. Children over the age of six months should also receive the vaccine if they have certain medical risk factors:

- asthma or other lung disease
- congenital heart disease with defects that require medications or surgery or other heart disease
- glomerulonephritis, kidney failure, or other kidney disease
- diabetes or other metabolic disease
- sickle cell disease or other anemia
- immune system problems or other anemia
- juvenile rheumatoid arthritis or any other disease needing aspirin therapy

KEY TERMS

Attenuated—A live but weakened microorganism that can no longer produce disease.

Guillain-Barré syndrome—Progressive and usually reversible paralysis or weakness of multiple muscles usually starting in the lower extremities and often ascending to the muscles involved in respiration. The syndrome is due to inflammation and loss of the myelin covering of the nerve fibers, often associated with an acute infection. Also called acute idiopathic polyneuritis.

Influenza—An infectious disease caused by a virus that affects the respiratory system, causing fever, congestion, muscle aches, and headaches.

Vaccine—A substance prepared from a weakened or killed microorganism which, when injected, helps the body to form antibodies that will prevent infection by the natural microorganism.

Otherwise healthy children above the age of 23 months may have a flu shot simply to reduce the risk of influenza.

Side effects

Most people have no adverse effects from a flu shot other than soreness at the injection site that lasts a few days. The greatest risk is an allergic reaction, which can be serious, but this is very rare. A low fever occasionally occurs.

Interactions

Vaccines should not be given to patients taking antibiotic drugs. While both flu vaccines may be administered at the same time as other vaccines, if two vaccines are not given at exactly the same time, they should be spaced four weeks apart.

Flu vaccine should not be given to the following groups:

- children with a severe allergic reaction to chickens or egg protein

- children who have exhibited a moderate to severe reaction after a previous influenza shot

- children who have ever been paralyzed due to Guillain-Barré syndrome

- children who are sick with anything beyond a slight cold

Parental concerns

Unlike the swine flu vaccine used in 1976, flu vaccines in the last decades of the twentieth century and early 2000s have shown no association with Guillain-Barré syndrome (GBS) in children.

Both types of influenza vaccine may be administered to **family** members of immunosuppressed patients, as long as the patients do not require a protected environment, although the killed virus vaccine is preferred for this purpose. Family members of patients who do require a protected environment, such as people who have had a stem cell transplant, should only receive the killed virus vaccine (injection).

Parents, siblings, and other people who will be in close contact with a sick child or adult should have a flu shot whether or not they need it for their own protection.

The risk of a local reaction to a flu injection increases with age. Children under the age of 13 years rarely have reactions to the flu vaccine. Over the age of 13 years, about 10 percent of children have a reaction to the shot.

Since flu season is usually in late fall or early winter, a flu shot should be given in the autumn, so that full immunity can be built up. However, it is never too late to get a flu shot.

See also Influenza; Vaccination.

Resources

BOOKS

Mcevoy, Gerald K., et al. *AHFS Drug Information 2004.* Bethesda, MD: American Society of Healthsystems Pharmacists, 2004.

Siberry, George K., and Robert Iannone, eds. *The Harriet Lane Handbook,* 15th ed. Philadelphia: Mosby, 2000.

PERIODICALS

American Academy of Pediatrics Committee on Infectious Diseases. "Recommendations for influenza immunization of children." *Journal of Pediatrics* 113, no. 5 (May 2004): 1441–47.

Harper, Scott A., et al., Centers for Disease Control and Prevention (CDC), Advisory Committee on Immunization Practices (ACIP). "Prevention and control of influenza: recommendations of the Advisory Committee on Immunization Practices (ACIP)." *MMWR Recommendations and Reports* 53, RR-6 (May 28, 2004): 1–40.

Principi, N., and S. Esposito. "Pediatric influenza prevention and control." *Emerging Infectious Diseases* 10, no. 4 (April 2004): 574–80.

Williams, Jeff, and Patricia Goodwin. "Influenza immunization in children: good for everyone or reserved for the chosen few?" *Pediatric Respiratory Reviews* 5, no. 1 (March 2004): 85–89.

WEB SITES

"Immunization Schedule, children: Influenza (Flu)." *Medicine Consumer Health.* Available online at <www.emedicinehealth.com/articles/11995-4.asp> (accessed on September 29, 2004).

"Influenza." Available online at <www.keepkidshealthy.com/welcome/infectionsguide/influenza.html> (accessed on September 29, 2004).

"Influenza (Flu)." *Centers for Disease Control.* Available online at <www.cdc.gov/flu/professionals/vaccination/> (accessed on September 29, 2004).

"Recommendations for Influenza Immunization of Children." *National Guideline Clearinghouse.* Available online at <www.guideline.gov/summary/summary.aspx?view_id=1&doc_id=4860> (accessed on September 29, 2004).

Samuel Uretsky, PharmD

Fluoridation

Definition

Fluoridation is the addition of fluoride to water supplies to help prevent **tooth decay**.

Description

The element fluorine is the seventeenth most abundant element in the earth's crust. It occurs as fluoride ion in combination with other elements such as sodium. Most water supplies naturally contain low levels of fluoride. In much of the United States, as well as in other parts of the world, fluoride is added to community water systems to bring fluoride levels up to the recommended amount for preventing teeth decay: 0.7–1.2 parts of fluoride to 1 million parts of water (parts per million or ppm). The levels of naturally occurring fluoride in fresh water range from less than 0.1 ppm to more than 13 ppm. Seawater contains about 1.5 ppm. As of 2000, about 162 million Americans—two-thirds of the population—were served by fluoridated water systems.

Mode of action

Systemic fluorides, including fluoridated water and prescription fluoride supplements supplied as tablets, drops, or lozenges, can be incorporated into the enamel of children's developing teeth. The enamel that covers the crown, the part of the tooth that is above the gum, is made of a substance called hydroxyapatite. When enough fluoride from water, supplements, food, or other sources enters the bloodstream and reaches the teeth while the enamel is forming, the fluoride can replace a piece of the hydroxyapatite molecule to form fluorapatite. Thus fluoride becomes part of the tooth enamel. Fluoride makes the tooth more resistant to acids produced by the bacteria that cause tooth decay. These acids dissolve the enamel, causing cavities. Fluoride in the enamel appears to do the following:

• make the enamel less susceptible to bacterial acids

• reduce the bacteria's ability to produce acid

• reduce the number of bacteria in plaque deposits

It is unlikely that sufficient fluoride will be incorporated into the enamel throughout the years of crown formation. With optimally fluoridated water (1 ppm) as the primary source of fluoride, a child would have to drink two quarts of water every day for 12 to 14 years to incorporate fluoride into all of the baby and adult teeth as they form. The child would be ingesting about 2 mg. of fluoride daily.

Topical fluorides are applied directly to the surfaces of fully-formed teeth. Fluoridated water acts as a topical—as well as a systemic—source of fluoride. Other topical fluorides include fluoridated toothpastes and mouthwashes and fluoride gels that are applied to children's teeth at dental examinations. Topical fluoride is the most effective mineral for renewing or remineralizing the surface layers of enamel and dentin as they wear out and are eaten away by acids from food and bacteria. Fluoride remineralization makes the tooth surface more resistant to decay and reverses early decay processes. Thus topical fluorides help prevent decay in both children and adults. Systemic fluorides also can provide topical protection because they are incorporated into the saliva that bathes the teeth.

Sources of fluoride

Fluoridated water is a major source of fluoride. Most bottled water contains only trace amounts of fluoride. Filtered water and well water vary greatly in their fluoride content. Children who drink water that is low in fluoride may be given fluoride supplements.

Fluoride occurs in many different foods and is also added to some foods. Fruits and vegetables may contain more than 0.2 mg of fluoride per serving, depending on where they were grown and whether fluoridated water was used for irrigation and processing. Most seafood is high in fluoride. The amount of fluoride in beverages depends on the amount of fluoride in the water used to make them. Many **vitamins** and medicines also contain fluoride. Most baby food is made with nonfluoridated water.

Fluoridated toothpastes and mouthwashes contain high amounts of fluoride. A tube of fluoridated toothpaste may contain as much as 1 to 2 gm of fluoride. Nonprescription mouthwashes can contain up to 120 mg of fluoride. Children between the ages of two and six swallow about 33 percent of the toothpaste they use; children between seven and 15 swallow about 20 percent. The average child using the typical amount of fluoridated toothpaste will swallow or absorb 0.5 to 1.0 mg. of fluoride per brushing. Much of this fluoride is excreted.

It is believed that fluoridated water is between 20 and 60 percent effective in preventing cavities in children and adults. Early studies suggested that water fluoridation was eliminating tooth decay in children. However, other factors are recognized in the early 2000s as having contributed to the decline in dental cavities. The widespread use of fluoridated toothpastes and mouthwashes has increased children's sources of fluoride significantly. Furthermore, both children's and adults' knowledge about dental care and dental hygiene has improved in the last quarter of the twentieth century.

General use

History

In the early twentieth century a young dentist in Colorado Springs, Colorado, named Frederick McKay, noticed that many local residents had brown stains on their permanent teeth and that their teeth were surprisingly resistant to decay. McKay eventually discovered that this "mottling"—as he called it—resulted from high levels of naturally occurring fluoride in the drinking water.

The first fluoridation of a public water system took place in Grand Rapids, Michigan, in 1945. By the 1950s and 1960s increasing numbers of communities were fluoridating their water using by-products from the phosphate fertilizer industry. The practice became mired in controversy, and it remains so in the first decade of the twenty-first century. Since the decision to fluoridate usually is made at the local level, by public officials or a vote of the people, fluoridation has become a political as well as a scientific controversy.

Proponents

Proponents of water fluoridation argue the following:

- It significantly reduces tooth decay, both before and after tooth enamel has formed.
- The fluoride levels used are completely safe.
- The children of parents who are poorly informed about dental hygiene and cavity prevention or who cannot afford dental treatment are still protected against tooth decay.

Most government agencies and scientific and professional organizations agree that water fluoridation is safe and effective in preventing tooth decay and cost-effective in that it reduces the need for expensive dental treatment. Among the organizations that endorse fluoridation of water supplies are the following:

- American Academy of Pediatric Dentistry
- American Dental Association
- American Medical Association
- National Institute of Dental and Craniofacial Research
- U.S. Centers for Disease Control and Prevention (CDC)
- U.S. Public Health Service
- World Health Organization (WHO)

Opponents

Opponents of water fluoridation often use one or more of the following arguments:

- Any fluoride above the naturally occurring (usually trace) amounts is unnecessary and possibly toxic.
- An individual dose of fluoride cannot be controlled because it depends on the amount of fluoridated water that a child ingests each day.
- Fluoridation of public water systems deprives people of freedom-of-choice as to what they ingest.
- People can choose from a variety of fluoride-containing products that are just as effective as fluoridated water.
- Where the water is not fluoridated, schools often provide fluoridation programs, and parents can choose whether their children participate.

- Although fluoride may help prevent decay, good diet, good **oral hygiene**, and regular dental cleanings can be just as effective.

- Fluoride can be toxic and even fatal at higher doses.

- The difference between the amount of fluoride that is beneficial and the amount that can cause mottling is only two to four-fold.

- People vary in their susceptibility to the effects of fluoride.

- It is impossible to determine how much fluoride a child is ingesting because of the numerous sources of fluoride in food and products; a child may regularly drink water from sources with different fluoride levels.

- Fluoride is ineffective against gum disease, the major destroyer of teeth.

Communities throughout the United States, as well as many countries, have chosen not to fluoridate their water. In the early 2000s a number of countries have discontinued fluoridation because of ongoing concerns about possible health effects.

Fluoride dosages

There is some disagreement as to whether fluoride is an essential mineral in humans. Relatively low levels of fluoride (20–80 mg) are considered toxic. Less than 1 gm of fluoride can be fatal to a small child. The Food and Nutrition Board of the Institute of Medicine of the U.S. National Institutes of Health has determined an adequate daily intake of fluoride and a maximal safe daily intake, based on a child's weight:

- infants up to six months of age or about 16 lb (7 kg): 0.01 mg is adequate and 0.7 mg is the maximum safe intake

- infants between six and 12 months or about 20 lb (9 kg): 0.5 mg and 0.9 mg

- children one to three years of age or about 29 lb (13 kg): 0.7 mg and 1.3 mg

- children aged four to seven or about 48 lb (22 kg): 1.0 mg and 2.0 mg

- children aged nine to 13 or about 88 lb (40 kg): 2.0 mg and 10 mg

- children aged 14 to 19 or about 125–166 lb (57–76 kg): 3.0 mg and 10 mg

Fluoride supplements often are prescribed for children who drink nonfluorinated water and do not use fluoride toothpaste. Fluoride supplements should not be used if the drinking water contains more than 0.6 ppm of fluoride. One ppm of fluoride is equivalent to about 1 mg per quart (or liter) of water. Fluoride supplements should not be given to babies under six months of age regardless of the fluoride content of the water. Babies get adequate fluoride from breast milk or infant formula. Powdered or concentrated infant formula should be mixed with low-fluoride or fluoride-free water.

If the water supply contains 0.0 to 0.3 ppm fluoride, the recommended daily dosage of fluoride supplement is:

- 0.25 mg for children aged six months to three years

- 0.50 mg for children aged three to six years

- 1 mg for children aged six to 16 years

If the water supply contains 0.3 to 0.6 ppm fluoride, the recommended daily dosage of fluoride supplement is:

- 0.0 mg for babies aged six months to three years

- 0.25 mg for children aged three to six years

- 0.50 mg for children aged six to 16

Fluoride supplements usually come in the form of sodium fluoride: 2.2 mg of sodium fluoride supplies 1 mg of fluoride ion.

Precautions

A child easily can swallow enough fluoridated toothpaste to exceed the recommended daily amount of fluoride by four-fold. A medium-sized toothpaste tube contains enough fluoride to make a child seriously ill or even cause death should the child eat it all. The flavorings added to toothpaste to encourage children to brush also can entice them into eating it. Toothpaste always should be stored out of the reach of children.

Side effects

As little as four to eight mg of fluoride ingested daily while the tooth enamel is forming can cause mottling—often called fluorosis—in children under age eight. Fluorosis only affects children whose teeth are still developing within the gums. Symptoms of fluorosis include:

- teeth discoloration

- white or brown chalky spots

- brown enamel

- pitting of teeth

- excessive wear on the enamel

- structural damage to the enamel

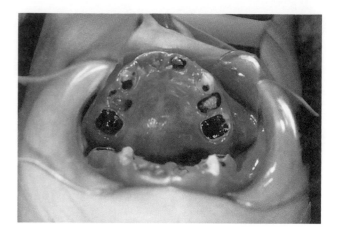

Lack of fluoridation caused this four-year old child's tooth decay. *(AP/Wide World Photos.)*

in children by 40 percent, if administered at least 150 days of every year that enamel is forming.

Topical fluoride treatments given in a dentist's office have been proven to be 40 percent or more effective in preventing decay. These treatments include fluoride gels and foams and fluoride varnishes. Advantages of fluoride varnishes include the following:

- They are more concentrated than other fluoride treatments and so are less likely to be ingested.

- They are fast and easy to apply.

- They continue to provide fluoride to the enamel for about 24 hours after application.

Varnishes may be particularly appropriate for young children and those with special needs since varnishes do not require the use of a fluoride tray.

- brittle teeth in which the enamel breaks easily

The extent of mottling depends on the following:

- when the excess fluoride is ingested

- how much is ingested

- over how long of a period it is ingested

- how much of the fluoride reaches the enamel

Most cases of fluorosis are very mild. Very mild to mild fluorosis has no effect on tooth function and may help prevent decay. Even severe fluorosis is not harmful. Fluorosis in children appears as of 2004 to be increasing; however, it is not known whether this is from water fluoridation, the excessive use of fluoride-containing products, or both.

Prevention

No type of fluoridation can replace good dental care and hygiene, which are necessary for preventing gum disease as well as tooth decay. Weekly rinsing with a fluoride mouthwash can reduce decay in children by 20–40 percent. Fluoride supplements can reduce decay

Parental concerns

It is the parents' responsibility to monitor their child's fluoride intake. Pregnant and nursing mothers should pay close attention to how much fluoride they ingest. Children should:

- be over two years of age before using a fluoridated toothpaste; younger children are likely to swallow most of their toothpaste

- use a pea-sized amount of toothpaste or less

- not use fluorinated mouthwashes until the age of six

- be prevented from swallowing fluoridated toothpaste or mouthwash

See also Dental development.

Resources

BOOKS

Bailey, K., et al. *Fluoride in Drinking Water.* London: IWA, 2002.

Bryson, Christopher. *The Fluoride Deception.* New York: Seven Stories Press, 2004.

PERIODICALS

"Anti-Fluoride Flood." *Better Nutrition* 65, no. 1 (January 2003): 30–1.

Gorman, Megan Othersen. "Got Enough Fluoride?" *Prevention* 54, no. 2 (February 2002): 48.

Mascarenhas, Ana Karina. "Risk Factors for Dental Fluorosis: A Review of the Recent Literature." *Pediatric Dentistry* 22, no. 4 (2000): 269–77.

Motavalli, Jim. "Your Health: Facing up to Fluoride." *E: the Environmental Magazine* 12, no. 1 (January/February 2001): 40–1.

Pendrys, D. G. "Risk of Enamel Fluorosis in Nonfluoridated and Optimally Fluoridated Populations: Considerations for the Dental Professional." *Journal of the American Dental Association* 131 (2000): 746–55.

Pratt, Edwin, Jr., et al. "Fluoridation at Fifty: What Have We Learned?" *The Journal of Law, Medicine, and Ethics* 30, no. 3 (Fall 2002): 117–22.

"Water Fluoridation Debate." *Journal of Environmental Health* 65, no. 3 (October 2002): 52.

ORGANIZATIONS

American Academy of Pediatric Dentistry. 211 East Chicago Avenue, Suite 700, Chicago, IL 60611–2663. Web site: <www.aapd.org>.

American Dental Association. 211 East Chicago Avenue, Chicago, IL 60611–2678. Web site: <www.ada.org>.

Fluoride Action Network. PO Box 5111, Burlington, VT 05402. Web site: <www.fluoridealert.org>.

National Center for Fluoridation Policy and Research. Department of Oral Biology, School of Dental Medicine, State University of New York at Buffalo, Buffalo, NY 14214–3008. Web site: <http://fluoride.oralhealth.org>.

WEB SITES

Connett, Paul. "The Absurdities of Water Fluoridation." *Redflagsdaily.com*, November 28, 2002. Available online at <www.redflagsweekly.com/connett/2002_nov28.html> (accessed December 27, 2004).

"Fluoride." *American Academy of Pediatric Dentistry.* Available online at <www.aapd.org/publications/brochures/content/floride.html> (accessed December 27, 2004).

"Oral Health Topics: Fluoride & Fluoridation." *American Dental Association.* Available online at <www.ada.org/public/topics/fluoride/fluoride_article01.asp> (accessed December 27, 2004).

Margaret Alic, PhD

Folate *see* **Folic acid**

Folic acid

Definition

Folic acid is a water-soluble vitamin belonging to the B-complex group of **vitamins**. These vitamins help the body break down complex carbohydrates into simple sugars to be used for energy. Excess B vitamins are excreted from the body rather than stored for later use. This is why sufficient daily intake of folic acid is necessary.

Description

Folic acid is also known as folate or folacin. It is one of the nutrients most often found to be deficient in the Western diet. There is evidence that folate deficiency is a worldwide problem. Folic acid is found in leafy green vegetables, beans, peas and lentils, liver, beets, brussel sprouts, poultry, nutritional yeast, tuna, wheat germ, mushrooms, oranges, asparagus, broccoli, spinach, bananas, strawberries, and cantaloupes. In 1998, the U.S. Food and Drug Administration (FDA) required food manufacturers to add folic acid to enriched bread and grain products to boost intake. Pregnant women whose diets are deficient in folic acid have a greater chance of having a baby with neural tube defects (NTD), such as **spina bifida**.

General use

Folic acid works together with vitamin B_{12} and vitamin C to metabolize protein in the body. It is important for the formation of red and white blood cells. It is also necessary for the proper differentiation and growth of cells in fetal development. It is also used to form the nucleic acid of DNA and RNA. It increases the appetite and stimulates the production of stomach acid for digestion, and it aids in maintaining a healthy liver. A deficiency of folic acid may lead to anemia, in which there is

KEY TERMS

Homocysteine—A sulfur-containing amino acid.

Preeclampsia—A condition that develops after the twentieth week of pregnancy and results in high blood pressure, fluid retention that doesn't go away, and large amounts of protein in the urine. Without treatment, it can progress to a dangerous condition called eclampsia, in which a woman goes into convulsions.

Recommended Dietary Allowance (RDA)—The Recommended Dietary Allowances (RDAs) are quantities of nutrients in the diet that are required to maintain good health in people. RDAs are established by the Food and Nutrition Board of the National Academy of Sciences, and may be revised every few years. A separate RDA value exists for each nutrient. The RDA values refer to the amount of nutrient expected to maintain good health in people. The actual amounts of each nutrient required to maintain good health in specific individuals differ from person to person.

Water-soluble vitamins—Vitamins that are not stored in the body and are easily excreted. They must, therefore, be consumed regularly as foods or supplements to maintain health.

decreased production of red blood cells. This situation reduces the amounts of oxygen and nutrients that are able to get to the tissues. Symptoms may include fatigue, reduced secretion of digestive acids, confusion, and forgetfulness. During pregnancy, a folic acid deficiency may lead to preeclampsia, premature birth, and increased bleeding after birth.

Pregnant women have an increased need for folic acid, both for themselves and their unborn child. Folic acid is necessary for the proper growth and development of the fetus. Adequate intake of folic acid is vital for the prevention of several types of birth defects, particularly NTDs. The neural tube of the embryo develops into the brain, spinal cord, spinal column, and the skull. If this tube forms incompletely during the first few months of pregnancy, a serious, and often fatal, defect results in spina bifida or anencephaly (formation of the head without the brain). Folic acid, taken from one year to one month before conception through the first four months of pregnancy, can reduce the risk of NTDs by 50 to 70 percent. It also helps prevent **cleft lip and palate**.

Research shows that folic acid can be used to successfully treat cervical dysplasia. This condition is considered to be a possible precursor to cervical **cancer** and is diagnosed as an abnormal Pap smear. Daily consumption of 1,000 mcg of folic acid for three or more months has resulted in improved cervical cells upon repeat Pap smears.

Precautions

Folic acid is not stable. It is easily destroyed by exposure to light, air, water, and cooking. Therefore, the supplement should be stored in a dark container in a cold, dry place, such as a refrigerator. Many medications interfere with the body's absorption and use of folic acid. This includes sulfa drugs, sleeping pills, estrogen, anticonvulsants, birth control pills, antacids, quinine, and some **antibiotics**. Using large amounts of folic acid (e.g., over 5,000 mcg per day) can mask a vitamin B_{12} deficiency and thereby risk of irreversible nerve damage.

Side effects

At levels of 5,000 mcg or less, folic acid is generally safe for use. Side effects are uncommon. However, large doses may cause **nausea**, decreased appetite, bloating, gas, decreased ability to concentrate, and insomnia. Large doses may also decrease the effects of phenytoin (Dilantin), a seizure medication.

Parental concerns

Pregnant women or those thinking of becoming pregnant should ensure that that they get the recommended amount of folic acid daily. As with all B-complex vitamins, it is best to take folic acid with the other B vitamins. Vitamin C is important to the absorption and functioning of folic acid in the body.

To correct a folic acid deficiency, supplements are taken in addition to food. Since the functioning of the B vitamins is interrelated, it is generally recommended that the appropriate dose of B-complex vitamins be taken in place of single B vitamin supplements. The Recommended Dietary Allowances (RDA) for folate is 400 mcg per day for adults, 600 mcg per day for pregnant women, and 500 mcg for nursing women. Medicinal dosages of up to 1,000–2,000 mcg per day may be prescribed. Nearly all multivitamin formulations for women include the RDA for folic acid.

Resources

BOOKS

Folic Acid: A Medical Dictionary, Bibliography, and Annotated Research Guide to Internet References. San Diego, CA: ICON Health Publications, 2004.

Heird, William C. "Nutritional Requirements." In *Nelson Textbook of Pediatrics*, 17th ed. Edited by Richard E. Behrman, et al. Philadelphia: Saunders, 2003, pp. 153–56.

Rock, Cheryl L. "Nutrition in the Prevention and Treatment of Disease." In *Cecil Textbook of Medicine*, 22nd ed. Edited by Lee Goldman, et al. Philadelphia: Saunders, 2003, pp. 1308–11.

Russell, Robert M. "Vitamin and Trace Mineral Deficiency and Excess." In *Harrison's Principles of Internal Medicine*, 15th ed. Edited by Eugene Braunwald et al. New York: McGraw Hill, 2001, pp. 461–69.

PERIODICALS

Allen, L. H. "Folate and vitamin B12 status in the Americas." *Nutrition Reviews* 62, no. 6, Pt. 2 (2004): 29–33.

Bailey, L. B. "Folate and vitamin B12 recommended intakes and status in the United States." *Nutrition Reviews* 62, no. 6, Pt. 2 (2004): S14–20.

Baro, L., et al. "The administration of a multivitamin/mineral fortified dairy product improves folate status and reduces plasma homocysteine concentration in women of reproductive age." *International Journal of Vitamin and Nutritional Research* 74, no. 3 (2004): 234–40.

Rockel, J. E., et al. "Folic acid fortified milk increases red blood cell folate concentration in women of childbearing age." *Asia Pacific Journal of Clinical Nutrition* 13, supplement (2004): S84–7.

ORGANIZATIONS

American Academy of Family Physicians. 11400 Tomahawk Creek Parkway, Leawood, KS 66211–2672. Web site: <www.aafp.org/>.

American Academy of Pediatrics. 141 Northwest Point Boulevard, Elk Grove Village, IL 60007–1098. Web site: <www.aap.org/default.htm>.

American Association of Naturopathic Physicians. 8201 Greensboro Drive, Suite 300, McLean, VA 22102. Web site: <http://naturopathic.org/>.

American Heart Association. National Center, 7272 Greenville Avenue, Dallas, Texas 75231. Web site: <www.americanheart.org/Heart_and_Stroke_A_Z_Guide/heim.html>.

American Medical Association. 515 N. State Street, Chicago, IL 60610. Web site: <www.ama-assn.org/>.

American Osteopathic Association. 142 East Ontario Street, Chicago, IL 60611. Web site:

WEB SITES

"Folate (Folacin, Folic Acid)." *Ohio State University Extension Fact Sheet.* Available online at <http://ohioline.osu.edu/hyg-fact/5000/5553.html> (accessed November 18, 2004).

"Folic Acid." *Centers for Disease Control and Prevention (CDC).* Available online at <http://www.cdc.gov/node.do/id/0900f3ec80010af9> (accessed November 18, 2004).

"Folic Acid." *March of Dimes.* Available online at <www.marchofdimes.com/pnhec/173_769.asp> (accessed November 18, 2004).

L. Fleming Fallon Jr., MD, DrPH

Food allergies and sensitivities

Definition

A food allergy or sensitivity is a person's immune system reaction to eating a particular food.

Description

The word allergy comes from two Greek words: alos, meaning "other" and argon, meaning "action." When one has an allergy, he or she has a reaction other than the one expected.

Food **allergies** and sensitivities are the body's reaction to a specific food. In a food allergy or sensitivity, when the child eats a particular food, (such as eggs, for example) usually by the time the eggs reach the stomach or the intestines, the body reads the presence of eggs as an allergen (something harmful). It sends out immunoglobulin E (IgE), an antibody, to destroy the eggs and protect the body, releasing histamines. The body remembers and produces histamines every time the food is eaten. These histamines trigger allergic symptoms that affect many areas of the body, particularly the skin, respiratory system, nervous system, and digestive system. Digestive disorders after eating specific foods are not always allergies. These reactions can be food sensitivities or intolerances. They can also be symptoms of other, more serious digestive diseases and malfunctions.

In the United states, 90 percent of all food allergies are caused by wheat, peanuts, nuts, milk, eggs, shellfish, soy, and fish. Many other foods can be at the root of food allergies or sensitivities, especially berries and other fruits, tomatoes, corn, and some meats like pork. Migraine headaches have been associated with sensitivities to chemicals contained in red wine, deli meats, aged cheeses, and the tannins in tea.

Usually, when a child is allergic to one food in a food family, he or she will most likely react to other foods in that food family. For example, if a child is sensitive to one type of fish, he or she also may be sensitive to other types of fish. This is called cross-reactivity.

Demographics

Nearly three million children in the United States have been diagnosed with food allergies. Nearly 600,000 of them have severe allergies to peanuts and possibly twice as many have severe shellfish allergies. Each year about 200 adults and children in the United States die from food-related **anaphylaxis**, an extreme reaction that causes swelling of the throat and bronchial passages, shock, and a severe drop in blood pressure. Nevertheless, food allergies tend to be under-diagnosed by doctors.

Genetics seems to play a part in food allergies. If one parent has a food allergy, the child's risk of having a food allergy is doubled. If both parents have food allergies, the risk is even higher. The child, however, may be allergic to a completely different food from the one to which the parent has demonstrated sensitivity. There also is increased risk when there are other kinds of allergy-related diseases in the family, such as hay fever or **asthma**.

Causes and symptoms

Causes

Allergies are caused by the immune system's reaction to a particular food. Usually, a child will have had a prior exposure before IgE or specific histamines are produced.

Food intolerance is often put into the same category as food allergy, even though there may be an entirely different mechanism involved. In these cases, the digestive tract reacts to a specific part of the food; for example, the protein or the sugar in a specific food. The digestive system rebels, resulting in gas, bloating, upset stomach, **diarrhea**, **nausea**, or **vomiting**. Many times, these responses are due to eating food contaminated with bacteria, rather than a true food allergy. In other cases, the child's reaction is due to an underlying digestive disorder such as **irritable bowel syndrome**, which is a chronic condition that is often triggered by specific types of food.

Gluten intolerance is not an allergy. It is a disease called **celiac disease**, or gluten-sensitive enteropathy.

The body cannot process gluten found in wheat and other grains. Though the immune system is involved, celiac disease does not behave as a true allergy. Its treatment is like many food allergies, namely avoidance of the offending substance, which in this case is gluten.

Some children may lack a specific enzyme needed to metabolize certain foods. About 10 percent of all adults and older children have **lactose intolerance**. There are two forms of lactose intolerance: inherited and acquired. The inherited form (autosomal recessive) is extremely rare and severe. The acquired type is very common, and occurs in older children (not infants) and adults. It is distressing, but not life-threatening, and occurs with increased frequency in African Americans. Sometimes infants, as well as older children and adults, have a transient lactose deficiency after an episode of diarrhea.

Children with lactose intolerance have a lactase deficiency that keeps them from processing milk and milk products. These children can often drink milk that has had this enzyme introduced into the product. Some children can drink milk that has acidophilus bacteria put into it. This bacteria breaks down the lactose, or milk sugar, in the milk so that the child can tolerate it. Some children with lactose intolerance cannot drink whole milk, but can eat cheese or drink low-fat buttermilk in small quantities. This is different from a true milk allergy where even a small amount of any dairy product will produce a reaction.

Some children may also be intolerant of food colorings, additives, and preservatives. Among these are yellow dye number 5, which can cause **hives**; and monosodium glutamate, which produces flushing, headaches, and chest **pain**. Sulfites, another additive, have been found to cause asthmatic reactions and even anaphylactoid reactions. Sulfites are preservatives used in wines, maraschino cherries, seafood, and soft drinks. They are sometimes put on fresh fruits and lettuce to maintain their fresh appearance, on red meats to prevent brown discoloration, and even in prepared deli foods like crab salad. Sulfites appear on food labels as sodium sulfite, sodium bisulfite, potassium bisulfite, sulfur dioxide, and potassium metabisulfite. The U.S. Food and Drug Administration (FDA) has banned the use of sulfites as a preservative for fruits and vegetables, but they are still in use in some foods.

Symptoms

Food allergies and sensitivities can produce a wide range of symptoms involving the skin, respiratory system, and nervous system. Children may have watery eyes, runny noses, and sneezing.

Skin **rashes** or hives can range from measles-like rashes to itchy welts. The rashes or welts can appear on a specific part of the body or can be widespread. Some children have swelling of the eyes, lips, and/or tongue.

Symptoms vary among children, even those who are sensitive to the same food. One child's specific reaction to an offending food does not mean that all children react the same. Nut allergies and shellfish, however, seem to be the most documented triggers for anaphylaxis. Nevertheless, anaphylaxis is not limited to those foods. IgE-mediated allergic reactions can progress to other allergic symptoms. For example, a child who has had hives is at risk for angioedema (swelling of the blood vessels) and anaphylaxis.

Symptoms also vary in intensity and by the amount eaten. One child may have a mild rash on the forearms when eating half a dozen strawberries. Another may be covered with a rash after eating only one. This variation is individualized and is a factor in the body's sensitivity to the target food.

Although the time between ingestion and symptoms is somewhat variable for allergic reactions (IgE-mediated), the vast majority occur within minutes. Nearly all occur within two hours. Reactions due to intolerances, like lactose, may occur somewhat later. Symptoms occurring days after a food is ingested are not likely related to the food.

When to call the doctor

Anaphylaxis is an extreme reaction to a food, usually peanuts or nuts. It causes swelling of the throat and bronchial passages, a drop in blood pressure, shock, and even death. A child with anaphylaxis should be taken to the emergency room immediately. If an emergency epinephrine pen is available, it should be administered immediately.

If a child experiences any type of allergy symptoms after eating, the child should be evaluated. Of particular concern are digestive symptoms that keep the child from eating properly or cause the child to lose weight. Equally important are neurological symptoms, especially headaches. Digestive and neurological symptoms could also be an indication of other underlying disorders. Therefore, the child should be seen by a doctor.

Diagnosis

Having a child evaluated as soon as possible will identify the offending food and allow parents to eliminate it from the child's diet. Many allergists, or doctors who specialize in allergies, will do a skin-prick test followed by a blood test. The skin-prick test is a series of pricks on the child's skin with a plastic applicator that contains a single food in concentrated form. A food allergy has been identified if the child's skin reacts by welting or becoming red. The skin-prick test for foods (not for aeroallergens) has a high incidence of false positives; that is, the test may be positive but the child is not truly allergic, or does not have symptoms from the food. This test is not used on a child with severe anaphylactic reactions or on children with widespread eczema, a skin disorder.

The allergist may also do a food challenge in the doctor's office. The child is fed the suspected food in increasing amounts to see what kind of reaction occurs.

One of the tests allergists use is called the RAST (Radio-Allergo-Sorbent Test). It measures the amount of IgE antibody in the blood that is produced for certain known food allergens. Like the skin-prick test, RAST and other antibody tests have a high rate of false positives.

Some doctors will put the child on an **elimination diet** for one week to 10 days. The basic elimination diet is a series of foods that have proven not to be allergy triggers. This diet consists of foods such as lamb, poultry, rice, vegetables, and all fruits, except citrus and berries. One new food is introduced each week. Parents record the child's reaction to each food. If the child has no reaction, the food is considered safe and can remain in the diet. If there is a reaction, it is noted and the food is removed. The child continues the elimination diet for a few more days, at which time another food is introduced. The elimination diet is often done after skin testing, so there is a logical guide for what to eliminate.

Treatment

The only treatment for IgE-mediated reactions to foods is avoidance. These reactions, as well as intolerances, are not responsive to desensitization. An epi-pen should be kept in the home for all IgE mediated food allergies and all inadvertent reactions should be treated.

It is not unusual for children to crave the very foods to which they are allergic. When the child is placed on an elimination diet, often the body will rebel at not being given the foods that cause it to react and will produce cravings for those foods.

Some doctors will prescribe **antihistamines** to help manage symptoms. These, however, are for use after an episode and not for an extended period.

Nutritional concerns

Eliminating one food or even one food family from a child's diet will not interfere with his or her nutritional

Foods such as whole-wheat flour, tuna, soy sauce, eggs, peanut butter, almonds, and milk are common causes of food allergies. (© Erik Freeland/Corbis.)

needs, nor will it keep the child from growing properly. There is enough variety in the foods available in the American diet to meet any child's needs. Some foods, however, may be difficult to find sufficient replacements for if the child wants substitutes. Wheat is particularly difficult to replace, although bread, pasta, and pastry products made with oat and rice flours are good substitutes. However, they do not taste or look exactly like risen wheat bread or regular pasta.

Prognosis

Children are known to outgrow milk allergies in most cases, but—for safety purposes—reintroduction in a medical setting is advised. Egg allergy disappearance is not as high as it is for milk allergy. Sensitivities to wheat and soy are also outgrown. Allergies to peanuts, shellfish, and other foods that can produce anaphylaxis usually remain with the child throughout life.

Prevention

If both parents have food allergies, precautions should be taken to minimize the risk of the child having a food allergy, too. Before birth and while breastfeeding, the mother can limit the baby's exposure to allergens by not bingeing on foods known to cause allergies. Breast-feeding delays the onset of allergies, but does not avoid them. The secretory IgA in breast milk fights infection but is not shown to avoid absorption of allergies.

Solid foods are slowly introduced at four to six months of age. The first solid foods should be those that have shown the potential for not producing an allergic reaction, such as fruits (except citrus fruits and berries), vegetables, and rice. Early introduction of highly allergenic foods may predispose a child to reactions, but this is controversial. It is recommended that parents avoid feeding the child highly allergenic foods until three years of age, if possible. The list of highly allergenic foods includes nuts, peanuts, fish, shellfish, and eggs. Whole cow's milk—not cow's milk formula—should be avoided during the first year. Having the child eat a variety of foods will also keep the child from too much exposure to any one particular food family.

Parents should make sure that the baby's first foods and those during the first few years of life are pure, unprocessed foods. Packaged and prepared foods (soups, stews, and toddler dinners, for example) contain many foods mixed together, along with fillers, usually wheat products, and possibly flavorings, sugar, and salt. By feeding a toddler a piece of boneless chicken, some green peas, a few cooked carrots, and a bit of potato instead of a can of chicken stew, parents can identify exactly what foods the child is eating and in what quantities. Therefore, if there is an allergic reaction, it is easier to identify what triggered it.

Parental concerns

Because children can come into contact with food allergens at school and during **extracurricular activities**, parents should meet with school officials to discuss procedures for keeping their children safe. Parents and school personnel should develop an action plan for dealing with allergens in the school and handling an emergency. Not only should the cafeteria staff be notified about the food allergy, but parents should also ask about snack time, birthdays and holiday celebrations, field trips, and arts and crafts projects. Arrangements should be made to keep medications to treat accidental exposure at the school, and personnel should be trained in their use.

Due to the seriousness of nut allergies and other allergies that can cause anaphylaxis, some school districts have created policies that forbid nuts on school premises and do not allow students to trade food at lunch. Some parents have lobbied school boards for such restrictions.

Avoiding the trigger food may be very problematic, even at home. Parents need to become proficient label readers, especially if the allergen is a nut or other food that may cause anaphylaxis. Understanding what the ingredient names mean is critical to total food avoidance. For example, dairy products can be listed as milk, casein, whey, and sodium caseinate. If a child is allergic to corn, it can be found not only as corn and corn syrup, but also cornstarch, which is a binding agent in a number of medications, including **acetaminophen** (Tylenol). Consultation with a dietitian can help parents understand food labels.

Peanut allergies in the United States doubled between 1997 and 2002. A controversial British study, reported in 2003, found a peanut/soy link, which is clinically rare. The study reported a link between early use of soy formula and peanut oil baby lotion in the later diagnosis of peanut food allergy. Soy formula may sensitize an infant to legumes, and therefore to peanuts. Peanut oil, known by doctors and nurses as arachis oil, is found in baby lotion and creams, especially those used to treat **diaper rash**, eczema, and dry skin.

Children who have severe reactions to a trigger food should wear a medical alert bracelet. Parents should also have on hand an emergency epinephrine-filled syringe like those found in bee-sting kits, or an epinephrine pen.

Parents should also notify day-care providers, Girl Scout and Boy Scout leaders, religious education teachers, **sports** coaches, and parents of their child's friends. They should explain what foods their child is allergic to, how the child reacts to the food, and how adults can help, either by making sure these foods are not served as snacks or by giving emergency care or support during an allergic reaction. In addition, parents can teach their child how to ask for help.

See also Lactose intolerance.

Resources

BOOKS

Barber, Marianne S. *The Parent's Guide to Food Allergies: Clear and Complete Advice from the Experts on Raising Your Food-Allergic Child.* NY: Owl Books, 2001.

Coss, Linda Marienhoff. *What's to Eat? The Milk-Free, Egg-Free, Nut-Free Food Allergy Cookbook.* Lake Forest, CA: Plumtree Press, 2000.

Smith, Nicole S. *Allie the Allergic Elephant: A Children's Story of Peanut Allergies.* San Francisco: Jungle Communications, Inc., 2002.

Weiner, Ellen, and Moss Freedman. *Taking Food Allergies to School.* Plainville, NY: JayJo Books, 1999.

Young, Michael C. *The Peanut Allergy Answer Book.* Gloucester, MA: Fair Winds Press, 2001.

PERIODICALS

"...And It's Easy to Misinterpret Correct Food Labels." *Child Health Alert* (Oct. 2002): 42–4.

"Origins of Peanut Allergy." *Archives of Disease in Childhood.* 88, no. 8 (August 2003): 694.

Vander Shaaf, Rachelle. "Is It a Food Allergy?" *Parenting* XVI, no. 5 (June 1, 2002): 38.

ORGANIZATIONS

Food Allergy & Anaphylaxis Network. 11781 Lee Jackson Hwy., Suite 160, Fairfax, VA 22033-3309. (800) 929-4040. Web site: </www.foodallergy.org>.

Janie Franz

Food poisoning

Definition

Food poisoning refers to illness arising from eating contaminated food. Food may be contaminated by bacteria, viruses, environmental toxins, or toxins present within the food itself, such as the poisons in some mushrooms or seafood. Symptoms of food poisoning are usually gastrointestinal, such as **nausea**, abdominal **pain**, **vomiting**, and/or **diarrhea**. Some food-borne toxins can affect the nervous system. Food poisoning is sometimes called bacterial **gastroenteritis** or infectious diarrhea and is sometimes incorrectly called ptomaine poisoning.

Description

Every year millions of people of all ages suffer from bouts of vomiting and diarrhea blamed correctly on something they ate. According to the Centers for Disease Control and Prevention (CDC), up to 33 million cases of food poisoning are reported in the United States each year. Many cases are mild and pass so rapidly that they are never diagnosed. Occasionally a severe outbreak affects many people at once, creating a newsworthy public health hazard. Although the food supply in the United States is probably one of the safest in the world, anyone can get food poisoning. Outbreaks have occurred in schools and colleges (up to 25 incidents reported annually in the United States), among restaurant clientele, in institutions such as long-term care facilities, and in other settings serving the public. Serious outbreaks are rare. When they occur, the very young, the very old, and those with weakened immune systems are subject to the most severe and life-threatening cases.

A variety of bacteria cause food poisoning, including *Salmonella*, *Staphylococcus aureus*, *Campylobacter jejuni*, *Escherichia coli*, *Shigella*, and *Clostridium botulinum*. Each type of bacteria has a different incubation period and duration, and all except the botulinum toxin cause inflammation of the intestines and diarrhea. Food and water can also be contaminated by viruses such as the Norwalk and hepatitis viruses. Environmental toxins (heavy metals) in foods or water, and poisonous substances in certain foods such mushrooms and shellfish are other causes of food poisoning.

Careless food handling between farm and table may create conditions for the growth of bacteria. Vegetables eaten raw, such as lettuce, may be contaminated by bacteria in soil, water, and dust during washing and packing. Home canned and commercially canned food may be improperly processed at too low a temperature or for too short a time to kill bacteria.

Raw meats carry many bacterial contaminants. The United States Food and Drug Administration (FDA) estimates that 60 percent or more of raw poultry sold at retail carries some disease-causing bacteria. Other raw meat products and eggs are contaminated to a lesser degree.

Although thorough cooking kills bacteria and makes the food harmless, recontamination can occur in properly cooked food if it comes into contact with cutting boards, countertops, or utensils that were used with raw meat and not cleaned and sanitized after use. Food can also become contaminated by environmental contaminants and by food handlers carrying bacteria on their hands while preparing foods for the public.

It is estimated that 50 percent of healthy people have staphylococcus organisms in their nasal passages and throats and on their skin and hair. Rubbing a runny nose and then touching food can introduce the bacteria into cooked food. Bacteria flourish at room temperature and grow rapidly in quantities capable of causing illness. To prevent this growth, food must be kept hot or cold but never just warm or at room temperature.

Travel to countries where less attention is paid to sanitation, water purification, and good food-handling practices may expose individuals to bacterial contaminants. Institutional food preparation also increases the risk of food poisoning, especially if food is allowed to stand on warming trays, under warming lights, or at room temperature before being served.

Transmission

Food poisoning is not spread from one individual to another but through direct contact with the causative bacteria, viruses, or other toxins in consumed food.

Demographics

The Centers for Disease Control and Prevention (CDC) estimates that there are from six to 33 million cases of food poisoning in the United States annually, affecting men, women, and children. Food poisoning by *E. coli* occurs in three out of every 10,000 people. One out of every 1,000 people are reported to have food poisoning caused by *Salmonella*; two-thirds are young people under age 20, and the majority are children under age nine. Although camplyobacter infections can occur in anyone, children under age five and young adults between ages 15 and 29 are more frequently infected.

Causes and symptoms

Classic food poisoning cases are caused by a variety of bacteria. The most common are the following:

- *Salmonella*
- *Staphylococcus aureus*
- *Campylobacter jejuni*
- *Escherichia coli*

- *Shigella*
- *Clostridium botulinum*

Food poisoning symptoms occur when food-borne bacteria release toxins or poisons as a byproduct of their growth in the body. These toxins (except those from *C. botulinum*) cause inflammation of the stomach lining and the small and/or large intestines, resulting in abdominal **muscle cramps**, vomiting, diarrhea, and **fever**. The severity of symptoms depends on the type of bacteria, the amount consumed, and the individual's general health and sensitivity to the toxin. **Dehydration** can result from loss of fluids through persistent vomiting and diarrhea; it is one of the most frequent and serious complications of food poisoning. When more fluids are being lost than are replaced, dehydration may occur in the very young and in the elderly, as well as in individuals who take diuretics.

Salmonella

A 2001 CDC report states that culture-confirmed cases of salmonella poisoning affected almost 50,000 people in the United States. However, it is believed that between 2 and 4 million unconfirmed cases actually occur each year. Salmonella is found in egg yolks from infected chickens, raw and undercooked poultry and other meats, dairy products, fish, shrimp, and many other foods. The CDC estimates that one of every 50 consumers is exposed to a contaminated egg yolk each year, although thorough cooking kills the bacteria, making the food harmless. Salmonella is also found in feces of pet reptiles such as turtles, lizards, and snakes. Most cases of salmonella poisoning occur in the warm months between July and October.

Symptoms of food poisoning, such as abdominal pain, diarrhea, vomiting, and fever, begin eight to 72 hours after eating food contaminated with salmonella. Symptoms generally last one to five days. Dehydration can be a complication of severe cases with persistent vomiting and/or diarrhea. People generally recover without antibiotic treatment, although they may feel tired for a week or so after the active symptoms subside.

Staphylococcus aureus

Staph organisms are found on humans and in the environment in dust, air, and sewage. The bacteria are spread primarily by food handlers using poor sanitary practices. Almost any food can be contaminated, but salad dressings, milk products, cream pastries, and any food kept at room temperature, rather than hot or cold, are likely candidates. It is difficult to estimate the number of annual cases of *Staphylococcus* food poisoning because its symptoms are so similar to those caused by

other food-borne bacteria. Many cases are mild. Victims may miss a day of school or work but never see a doctor for confirmation of food poisoning. Symptoms appear rapidly, usually one to six hours after the contaminated food is eaten. Acute symptoms of vomiting and severe abdominal cramps without fever usually last three to six hours and rarely more than 24 hours. Most people recover without medical assistance. Deaths are rare.

Escherichia coli (E. coli)

The many strains of *E. coli* are not all harmful. Non-pathogenic E. coli are, in fact, a major part of normal gut flora. The strain that causes the most severe food poisoning, however, is *E. coli O157:H7*, which affects three people in every 10,000. The food-borne organisms are found and transmitted mainly in food derived from cows, such as raw milk and raw or rare ground beef. Fruit or vegetables can also be contaminated.

Symptoms of *E. coli* poisoning are slower to appear than those caused by other food-borne bacteria. Because *E. coli* toxins are produced in the large intestine rather than higher up in the digestive system, symptoms typically occur from one to three days after eating contaminated food. Those affected have severe abdominal cramps and watery diarrhea that usually becomes bloody within 24 hours, a condition that can last from one to eight days. There is little or no fever and vomiting occurs only rarely.

Campylobacter jejuni

Campylobacter is the leading cause of bacterial diarrhea worldwide, responsible for more cases (2 million or more) of bacterial diarrhea in the United States than *Shigella* and *Salmonella* combined. *Campylobacter* is carried by healthy cattle, chickens, birds, and flies. It is also found in ponds and stream water and has been found in bottled water and on salad vegetables washed with water. Although eating chicken is a known risk factor, drinking water and eating salads have not been considered significant risks until studies of causes released in 2003 showed possible association with *Campylobacter* diarrheal infections. It is not known whether contamination occurs at the site of production or in the home or institution after contact with other contaminated foods, surfaces, or utensils. The ingestion of only a few hundred *Campylobacter* bacteria can cause food poisoning symptoms, which may begin two to five days after eating contaminated food. Symptoms will typically include fever, abdominal pain, nausea, **headache**, muscle pain, and diarrhea. The diarrhea can be watery or sticky and may contain blood. Symptoms last from seven to ten days and relapses occur in about one-fourth of infected individuals. Dehydration is a common complication. Other complications, such as arthritis-like joint pain and hemolytic-uremic syndrome (HUS), occur in rare cases.

Shigella

Shigella is a common cause of diarrhea in travelers to developing countries. It is associated with contaminated food and water, crowded living conditions, and poor sanitation. The bacterial toxins affect the small intestine. Symptoms of *Shigella* infection appear about 36–72 hours after eating contaminated food. In addition to the familiar watery diarrhea, nausea, vomiting, and abdominal cramps, the individual may also have chills, fever, and neurological symptoms. The diarrhea may be quite severe with cramping and progresses to classic dysentery. Up to 40 percent of children with severe infections show neurological symptoms. These include confusion, headache, lethargy, a stiff neck, and possible seizures. The symptoms of food poisoning by *Shigella* organisms may resemble **meningitis** and a differential diagnosis must be made by isolating the causative bacteria.

The disease runs its course usually in two to three days but may last longer. Dehydration is a common complication. Most people recover on their own, although they may feel exhausted. Children who are malnourished or have weakened immune systems may be severely affected and death can result.

Clostridium botulinum

C. botulinum causes both adult and infant **botulism** and differs significantly from other contaminants in its sources and symptoms. *C. botulinum*'s common food-borne form is an anaerobic bacterium that can only live and reproduce in the absence of oxygen. Exposure to the botulinum toxin usually occurs while eating contaminated food stored in an airless environment, as in home-canned or commercially canned or vacuum-packed food. Also, botulinum toxin is a neurotoxin that blocks the ability of motor nerves to release acetylcholine, the neurotransmitter that relays nerve signals to muscles. This neurological process can result in unresponsive muscles, a condition known as flaccid paralysis. Breathing may be severely compromised in progressive botulism because of failure of the muscles that control the airway and breathing. In infants, botulism may be caused by specific types of clostridia obtained from soil, inhaled spores, or honey containing the spores. Contamination from any of the sources results in growth of the bacteria in the infant's intestine and production of the neurotoxin.

Infant botulism is a form of botulism first recognized in 1976 that differs from food-borne botulism. Infant botulism occurs when a child younger than one year ingests the spores of *C. botulinum*. Although these spores are commonly found in soil, honey is a more frequent source of spores causing infant botulism by lodging in the baby's intestinal tract and producing the neurotoxin. Onset of symptoms is gradual. Initially, the baby is constipated, followed by poor feeding, lethargy, weakness, drooling, and a distinctive wailing cry. Eventually, the baby loses the ability to control its head muscles. From there the paralysis progresses to the rest of the body. Immediate treatment is required to avoid neurological complications and death. Infant botulism is much more likely to be fatal than other food poisoning infections. Infant botulism is a special form of food poisoning not related to the food-borne toxins that cause adult botulism.

Adult botulism outbreaks are usually associated with toxins found in home-canned food, although poisoning occasionally results from eating commercially canned or vacuum-packed foods. *C. botulinum* grows well in non-acidic, oxygen-free environments, meaning that if the cooking temperatures are too low or the cooking time too brief the bacteria in the food are not killed. Instead, bacteria may reproduce inside the can or jar, releasing the deadly neurotoxin. Heating canned food to boiling for ten minutes can render the toxin harmless. However, consuming even a very small amount of the toxin can result in serious illness or death because of lethal neurological complications.

Symptoms of adult botulism appear about 18–36 hours after the contaminated food is eaten, although times of onset have been documented ranging from four hours to eight days. Initially a person suffering from botulism feels weak and dizzy and later experiences double vision. Symptoms progress to difficulty speaking and swallowing. Paralysis moves down the body, and when the respiratory muscles are paralyzed, death can result from asphyxiation. Individuals with any signs of botulism poisoning must receive immediate emergency medical care to increase their chance of survival.

When to call the doctor

Any unexplained abdominal pain accompanied by persistent vomiting or diarrhea, whether or not a food source is suspected, should be reported to the doctor. A child having difficulty swallowing, speaking, holding the head up, or maintaining an upright posture should receive emergency medical attention. Signs of confusion, lethargy, headache, stiff neck, or seizures also require immediate medical attention.

Diagnosis

One important part of diagnosing food poisoning is the need for doctors and community health professionals to determine if a number of people have eaten the same food and show the same symptoms. If this can be proven, food poisoning is strongly suspected. The diagnosis is confirmed when the suspected bacteria is identified in the culture of a stool sample or a fecal smear from the affected individual. In some cases, the suspected bacteria, virus, or toxin can be identified in the actual food source.

Laboratory tests are used to make a definitive diagnosis, but treatment of symptoms may be started immediately without waiting for test results, which may take up to two days. Diagnostic tests focus on identifying the organism causing the illness. This process may involve performing a culture on contaminated material from the suspect food, a stool sample, or swabs of the nose or throat of the affected individual if inhaled spores are a possibility. Culture results are available from the microbiology laboratory as soon as bacteria grow in a special plate incubated at temperatures at or above body temperature. The growth of specific bacteria confirms the diagnosis. The microbiology laboratory may use samples of the bacteria grown to perform other special techniques to help identify the causative organism.

In infant botulism, the infant's stool may be cultured to isolate the organism; this test may be performed by the state health department or the Centers for Disease Control (CDC). Early diagnosis of botulism is critical so that treatment can begin in time to avoid neurological involvement. Although the definitive diagnosis comes from laboratory tests, it can usually be diagnosed by recognizing the distinctive neurological symptoms typical of contamination with *C. botulinum*.

While waiting for diagnostic test results, the doctor performs a physical examination and may ask about recently consumed food, possible open sores, recent activities and behavior, and other information that may help to rule out other disease possibilities. Imaging studies or additional diagnostic tests may be done to rule out other diseases or conditions with similar symptoms.

Many cases of food poisoning go undiagnosed, since a definite diagnosis is not necessary to effectively treat the symptoms. Because it takes time for symptoms to develop, the most recent food one has eaten may not be the cause of the symptoms.

Treatment

Treatment of food poisoning, except for botulism, focuses on preventing or correcting dehydration by replacing critical fluids and electrolytes lost through vomiting and diarrhea. Electrolytes are mineral salts that form electrically charged particles (ions) in body fluids;

they help control body fluid balance and participate in many essential body functions. Pharmacists can recommend effective, pleasant-tasting, electrolyte replacement fluids that are available without a prescription. To prevent dehydration, a doctor may decide to give fluids intravenously. In very serious cases of food poisoning, medications may be given to stop abdominal cramping and vomiting. Antidiarrheal medications are not usually given. Stopping the diarrhea actually maintains toxin levels in the body for longer periods and may prolong the infection. Severe bacterial food poisonings are sometimes treated with intravenous **antibiotics**.

Modifying the diet while recovering from food poisoning is usually recommended. During a period of active vomiting and diarrhea, solid food should be avoided and only small quantities of clear liquids should be consumed as frequently as possible. Once active symptoms stop, bland, soft, easy-to-digest foods should be consumed for two to three days. One example is the BRAT diet of bananas, rice, applesauce, and toast, all of which are easy to digest. Milk products, spicy food, and fresh fruit should be avoided for a few days, although babies should continue to breastfeed. These modifications are often the only treatment that is necessary.

Botulism is treated in an entirely different way. Older children and adults can be treated with injections of a specific antitoxin for botulism if it can be administered within 72 hours after symptoms are first observed. If given later, it provides little or no benefit. Infants, however, cannot receive this antitoxin and are usually treated instead with injections of human botulism immune globulin (BIG), an antiserum that neutralizes the botulinum toxin. This antiserum is available in the United States through the Infant Botulism Treatment and Prevention Program in Berkeley, California. Both infants and adults may require **hospitalization**, often in the intensive care unit. Mechanical ventilators may be used for those whose ability to breathe is impaired and intravenous **nutrition** may be provided until any paralysis is corrected.

Alternative treatment

Alternative practitioners offer the same advice as traditional practitioners concerning diet modification, treatment of diarrhea and vomiting, and prevention of dehydration. Charcoal tablets, *Lactobacillus acidophilus*, *Lactobacillus bulgaricus*, and citrus seed extract can be taken to help normalize the digestive system. An electrolyte replacement fluid can be made at home by adding one teaspoon of salt and four teaspoons of sugar to one quart of water. For food poisoning other than botulism, two homeopathic remedies, either *Arsenicum album* or *Nux vomica*, are recommended to help reduce symptoms.

Prognosis

Most cases of food poisoning (except botulism) clear up on their own within one week without medical assistance. As symptoms subside, the individual may continue to feel tired or weak for a few days. If dehydration has been effectively corrected or prevented, few complications can be expected. Deaths are rare and usually occur in the very young, the very old, and people whose immune systems are already weakened.

Complications of **salmonella food poisoning** may include arthritis-like symptoms that occur three to four weeks after infection. Although deaths from salmonella infection are rare, they do occur. Most deaths reported have occurred among elderly adults in long-term care.

Adults usually recover from *E. coli* poisoning without medical intervention, but many children require hospitalization for contamination with this organism. Toxins may be absorbed into the blood stream where they destroy red blood cells and platelets, tiny cells important in blood clotting. About 5 percent of victims develop hemolytic-uremic syndrome (HUS), which can result in sudden kidney failure that requires a medical procedure (dialysis) to perform the kidney's task of filtering the body's waste products.

Botulism is the deadliest of the bacterial food-borne illnesses. With prompt medical care, the death rate is less than 10 percent in children and adults.

Prevention

Food poisoning is almost entirely preventable by practicing good sanitation and good food handling techniques. These include the following measures:

• Keep hot foods hot and cold foods cold.

• Cook meat to the recommended internal temperature.

• Use a meat thermometer to check meat and cooking eggs until they are no longer runny.

• Refrigerate leftovers promptly, not letting food stand at room temperature.

• Before preparing other foods, carefully clean surfaces (cutting boards and counters, knives and other utensils) contaminated with the juices of uncooked meats.

• Do not refreeze meat once it has been thawed.

• Wash fruits and vegetables before using.

• Consume only pasteurized dairy products and fruit juices.

KEY TERMS

Antitoxin—An antibody against an exotoxin, usually derived from horse serum.

Culture—A test in which a sample of body fluid is placed on materials specially formulated to grow microorganisms. A culture is used to learn what type of bacterium is causing infection.

Diuretics—A group of drugs that helps remove excess water from the body by increasing the amount lost by urination.

Electrolytes—Salts and minerals that produce electrically charged particles (ions) in body fluids. Common human electrolytes are sodium chloride, potassium, calcium, and sodium bicarbonate. Electrolytes control the fluid balance of the body and are important in muscle contraction, energy generation, and almost all major biochemical reactions in the body.

Hemolysis—The process of breaking down red blood cells. As the cells are destroyed, hemoglobin, the component of red blood cells which carries the oxygen, is liberated.

Lactobacillus acidophilus—Commonly known as acidophilus, a bacteria found in yogurt that changes the balance of the bacteria in the intestine in a beneficial way.

Neurological—Relating to the brain and central nervous system.

Neurotoxin—A poison that acts directly on the central nervous system.

Platelet—A cell-like particle in the blood that plays an important role in blood clotting. Platelets are activated when an injury causes a blood vessel to break. They change shape from round to spiny, "sticking" to the broken vessel wall and to each other to begin the clotting process. In addition to physically plugging breaks in blood vessel walls, platelets also release chemicals that promote clotting.

Spore—A dormant form assumed by some bacteria, such as anthrax, that enable the bacterium to survive high temperatures, dryness, and lack of nourishment for long periods of time. Under proper conditions, the spore may revert to the actively multiplying form of the bacteria. Also refers to the small, thick-walled reproductive structure of a fungus.

Toxin—A poisonous substance usually produced by a microorganism or plant.

- Discard bulging or leaking cans or any food that smells spoiled.

- Wash hands well before and during food preparation and after using the bathroom.

- Sanitize food preparation surfaces regularly.

It is especially important to discard any food that seems spoiled and not to eat food that has been stored at room temperature or above for more than a few hours. Home canners must be diligent about using sterile equipment and following U.S. Department of Agriculture canning guidelines.

Infant botulism is perhaps the most difficult poisoning to prevent, because what goes into an infant's mouth is often beyond control. One important preventative measure, however, is to avoid feeding honey to infants younger than 12 months since it is a known source of botulism spores. As infants begin eating solid foods, the same food precautions should be followed as for older children and adults.

Parental concerns

Symptoms of food poisoning can appear as early as an hour after consuming the contaminated food or up to several days later. Parents may be concerned about possible contamination from unknown sources and that symptoms may occur suddenly, without warning. Practicing good sanitation and good food handling techniques is the best way parents can prevent contamination. Normal watchfulness of the parents is sufficient to notice symptoms, paying attention to any change in eating, unusual crying, increases or decreases in bowel movements, the presence of vomiting or a lack of normal responses such as turning of the head and body movements. An early report of symptoms, even if no particular food is suspected of causing illness, helps get early treatment and avoid complications.

See also Botulism; Gastroenteritis.

Resources

BOOKS

Cerexhe, Peter, et al. *Risky Food, Safer Choices: Avoiding Food Poisoning.* Boulder, Co: netLibrary, 2000.

Isle, Mick. *Everything You Need to Know about Food Poisoning.* New York: Rosen Publishing Group, 2001.

Rue, Nancy, and Anne Williams. *Quick Reference to Food Safety and Sanitation.* Boston, MA: Prentice Hall, 2002.

Trickett, Jill. *The Prevention of Food Poisoning.* Cheltenham, UK: Nelson Thornes, 2001.

ORGANIZATIONS

Centers for Disease Control and Prevention. 1600 Clifton Rd., NE, Atlanta, GA 30333. Web site: <www.cdc.gov>.

WEB SITES

"Food Safety." Available online at <www.nlm.nih.gov/medlineplus/print/foodsafety.html> (accessed November 20, 2004).

L. Lee Culvert
Suzanne M. Lutwick, MPH

Foreign objects

Definition

Foreign bodies can enter the human body by swallowing, insertion, or traumatic force, either accidentally or on purpose. The word "foreign" in this context means "originating elsewhere" or simply "outside the body."

Description

Children and adolescents may experience health problems caused by foreign objects getting stuck in their bodies. Young children in particular are naturally curious and may intentionally put such shiny objects as coins or button batteries into their mouths. They also like to stick small items in their ears and up their noses. Older children and teenagers may accidentally swallow a nonfood object or ingest a foreign body that gets stuck in the throat, like a fish bone or toothpick. Airborne particles can lodge in the eyes of people at any age. In addition, foreign bodies may be driven into the face or other parts of the body by the force of a collision or explosion.

Foreign bodies may be found in hollow organs (like swallowed batteries in the stomach) or in tissues (like bullets). They can be inert or irritating. If they irritate the surrounding tissue, they cause inflammation and scarring. Foreign objects can bring infection with them or acquire it and protect it from the body's immune defenses. They can obstruct passageways in the body either by their size or by the scarring they cause. Some foreign objects, particularly lead shot or other small objects containing lead, are toxic.

Demographics

Swallowing of foreign bodies is a fairly common pediatric emergency; about 80,000 cases involving persons 19 years old or younger are reported each year to the 67 poison control centers in the United States. In a recent survey of the parents of 1,500 children, 4 percent reported that their children had swallowed a foreign object of some kind. The highest incidence of swallowed foreign bodies is in children between the ages of six months and four years.

The type of object most frequently swallowed varies somewhat across different historical periods and cultures. A recent study comparing the Jackson collection of foreign bodies removed from children between 1920 and 1932 with data collected from North American children's hospitals between 1988 and 2000 found that coins have replaced safety pins as the objects most commonly swallowed by American children. In Asia, on the other hand, fish bones are a frequent offender because fish is a dietary staple in most countries of the Far East.

In younger children, boys are at slightly greater risk than girls (53% to 47%) of swallowing foreign objects. Among teenagers, however, males are at a much higher risk than females of swallowing foreign bodies or inserting them into the rectum.

Younger children usually swallow or insert foreign objects into their bodies accidentally, usually as a result of **play** or exploring their environment. Adolescents, however, are more likely to swallow or insert foreign bodies intentionally as a risk-taking behavior, a bid for attention, or under the influence of drugs or alcohol. Adolescent girls with eating disorders have been reported to swallow toothbrushes. A small minority of teenagers who harm themselves by swallowing or inserting foreign bodies suffer from **schizophrenia** or another psychotic disorder.

Causes and symptoms

Causes

The causes of foreign body ingestion or insertion range from traumatic accidents or casual exploration and play to intentional risk-taking, desire for sexual stimulation, an eating or personality disorder, or psychotic behavior. Cases of repeated swallowing of foreign objects by small children may indicate neglect or a dysfunctional home environment.

Symptoms

The symptoms of foreign body ingestion or insertion depend in part on the organ or part of the body affected.

EYES Dust, dirt, sand, or other airborne material can lodge in the eyes as a result of high wind or an explosion, causing minor irritation and redness. More serious damage can be caused by hard or sharp objects that penetrate the surface of the eye and become embedded in the cornea or conjunctivae (the mucous membranes lining the inner surface of the eyelids). Swelling, redness, bleeding from the surface blood vessels, sensitivity to light, and sudden vision problems are all symptoms of foreign matter in the eyes.

EARS AND NOSE Toddlers sometimes put small objects into their noses, ears, and other openings. Beans, dried peas, popcorn kernels, hearing-aid batteries, raisins, and beads are just a few of the many items that have been found in these bodily cavities. On occasion, insects may also fly into a child's ears or nose. **Pain**, hearing loss, and a feeling of fullness in the ear are symptoms of foreign bodies in the ears. A smelly or bloody discharge from one nostril is a symptom of foreign bodies in the nose.

AIRWAYS AND STOMACH At a certain age children will eat almost anything. A very partial list of items recovered from young stomachs includes the following: coins, chicken bones, fish bones, beads, pebbles, plastic **toys**, pins, keys, buckshot, round stones, marbles, nails, rings, batteries, ball bearings, screws, staples, washers, a heart pendant, a clothespin spring, and a toy soldier. Some of these items will pass right on through the digestive tract and leave the body through the feces. The progress of metal objects has been successfully followed with a metal detector or **x rays**. Other objects, like needles, broken poultry bones, or razor blades, can get stuck at various points in the digestive tract and cause trouble.

Most complications of swallowed foreign bodies occur in the esophagus at one of three points: the thoracic inlet at collarbone level (70%); the mid-esophagus (15%); and the sphincter at the lower end of the esophagus where the esophagus joins the stomach (15%). If a swallowed object passes into the stomach, it is unlikely to cause complications unless it is either sharp and pointed in shape or made of a toxic material.

Some foreign objects lodge in the airway. Although children eat small objects and stick things into their bodily openings of their own volition, they inhale them unwittingly while **choking**. Probably the most commonly inhaled item is a peanut. Items as unusual as crayons and cockroaches have also been found in children's windpipes. These items always cause symptoms (difficulty swallowing and spitting up saliva, for instance) and may elude detection for some time while the child is being treated for **asthma** or recurring **pneumonia**.

RECTUM Sometimes a foreign object will successfully pass through the throat and stomach only to get stuck at the juncture between the rectum and the anal canal. Items may also be self-introduced to enhance sexual stimulation and then get stuck in the rectum. Sudden sharp pain during elimination may signify that an object is lodged in the rectum. Other symptoms vary depending upon the size of the object, its location, how long it has been in place, and whether or not infection has set in.

When to call the doctor

The specific symptoms of foreign body ingestion vary somewhat depending on the item and its location in the body. Parents or caregivers may observe the child swallowing the object, or the child may report doing so. In general, parents should take the child to the doctor or emergency room in any of the following situations occurs:

- foreign bodies in the eyes or skin that are the result of an automobile accident, explosion, gunshot injury, or similar trauma
- foreign body appears to have caused an infection in the surrounding tissue
- foreign body is made of lead or contains corrosive chemicals (most commonly batteries)
- foreign body is pointed or has sharp edges (needles, pins, broken glass, toothpicks, razor blades, pop-off tabs from soda cans, etc.)
- child complains of pain on swallowing, pain in the chest, abdominal pain, or severe pain on defecation
- child drools heavily
- child coughs up, vomits, or defecates blood
- child loses consciousness or becomes delirious as a result of esophageal or airway blockage
- child is known to have Crohn's disease, Meckel's diverticulum, or other chronic disorder of the digestive tract (These disorders increase the risk of complications from swallowed foreign bodies.)

Diagnosis

In most cases the doctor needs only a brief history to determine what type of foreign object is involved and where it may be lodged in the child's body. Objects in the ear, nose, or eye can usually be seen on visual examination. In the case of swallowed objects, the doctor examine the inside of the child's mouth and throat to look for signs of tissue damage and bleeding. The doctor may perform a digital examination to locate objects lodged in the rectum.

In general, the doctor may use an endoscope to look for a foreign object in the body as well as to remove it. He or she may order an x ray of the neck, chest, and/or abdomen to locate a foreign body in the esophagus, airway, or

lower digestive tract. Most foreign bodies swallowed by small children are radiopaque, which means that they show up on a standard x ray. Metal detectors can successfully identify the location of soda can tops and other aluminum objects that will not show up on an x ray.

Blood tests are not usually necessary unless the doctor suspects that the foreign body has caused an infection or bleeding.

Treatment

Eyes

Small particles like sand may be removable without medical help, but if the object is not visible or cannot be retrieved, prompt emergency treatment is necessary. Trauma to the eyes can lead to loss of vision and should never be ignored. Before an adult attempts any treatment, he or she should move the child to a well-lighted area where the object can be more easily spotted. Hands should be washed and only clean, preferably sterile, materials should make contact with the eyes. If the particle is small, it can be dislodged by blinking or pulling the upper lid over the lower lid and flushing out the speck. A clean cloth can also be used to pick out the offending particle. Afterwards, the eye should be rinsed with clean, lukewarm water or an ophthalmic wash.

If the foreign object cannot be removed at home, the eye should be lightly covered with sterile gauze to discourage rubbing. A physician will use a strong light and possibly special eye drops to locate the object. Surgical tweezers can effectively remove many objects. An antibiotic sterile ointment and a patch may be prescribed. If the foreign body has penetrated the deeper layers of the eye, an eye surgeon will be consulted for emergency treatment.

Ears and nose

A number of ingenious extraction methods have been devised for removing foreign objects from the nose and ears. A bead in a nostril, for example, can be popped out by blowing into the mouth while holding the other nostril closed. Skilled practitioners have removed peas from children's ears by tiny improvised corkscrews and marbles by cotton-tipped applicators with super glue. Tweezers often work well, too. Insects can be floated out of the ear by pouring warm (not hot) mineral oil, olive oil, or baby oil into the ear canal. Metal objects can be removed from the nose or ears with the help of a magnet. Items that are lodged deep in the ear canal are more difficult to remove because of the possibility of damaging the eardrum. These require emergency treatment from a qualified physician.

Airways and stomach

Mechanical obstruction of the airways, which commonly occurs when food gets lodged in the throat, can be treated by applying the **Heimlich maneuver**. If the object is lodged lower in the airway, a bronchoscope (a special instrument to view the airway and remove obstructions) can be inserted. On other occasions, as when the object is blocking the entrance to the stomach, a fiberoptic endoscope (an illuminated instrument that views the interior of a body cavity) may be used. The physician typically administers a sedative and anesthetizes the child's throat. The foreign object then is either pulled out or pushed into the stomach, depending on whether the physician thinks it will pass through the digestive tract on its own. Objects in the digestive tract that are not irritating, sharp, or large may be followed as they continue on through. Sterile objects that are causing no symptoms may be left in place. Surgical removal of the offending object is necessary, however, if it contains a toxic substance; is likely to penetrate the stomach wall; or is longer than 2.36 inches (6 cm) or wider than 0.8 inches (2 cm).

Rectum

A rectal retractor can remove objects that a physician can feel during a digital examination of the rectum. In most cases the doctor will inject a local anesthetic before extracting the object. Surgery under general anesthesia may be required for objects deeply lodged within the body, as in the case of a 14-year-old Dutch adolescent who had inserted a soda can into his rectum.

Treatment of any health problem related to a foreign body may include a psychiatric consultation if the doctor suspects that the swallowing or insertion of the foreign body is related to **autism** or **mental retardation** (in small children) or an eating or personality disorder (in adolescents).

Prognosis

The prognosis of foreign body ingestion or insertion varies according to the nature of the object and its location in the body but is quite good in most cases. With regard to foreign bodies in the digestive tract, between 80 percent and 90 percent pass through without incident; 10–20 percent can be removed with an endoscope; and fewer than 1 percent require surgical removal.

Prevention

Using common sense and following safety precautions are the best ways to prevent foreign objects from

KEY TERMS

Bronchoscope—A lighted instrument that is inserted into the windpipe to view the bronchi and bronchioles, to remove obstructions, or to withdraw specimens for testing.

Conjunctiva—Plural, conjunctivae. The mucous membrane that covers the white part of the eyes (sclera) and lines the eyelids.

Cornea—The clear, dome-shaped outer covering of the eye that lies in front of the iris and pupil. The cornea lets light into the eye.

Crohn's disease—A chronic, inflammatory disease, primarily involving the small and large intestine, but which can affect other parts of the digestive system as well.

Endoscopy—Visual examination of an organ or body cavity using an endoscope, a thin, tubular instrument containing a camera and light source. Many endoscopes also allow the retrieval of a small sample (biopsy) of the area being examined, in order to more closely view the tissue under a microscope.

Heimlich maneuver—An emergency procedure for removing a foreign object lodged in the airway that is preventing the person from breathing. To perform the Heimlich maneuver on a conscious adult, the rescuer stands behind the victim and encircles his waist. The rescuer makes a fist with one hand and places the other hand on top, positioned below the rib cage and above the waist. The rescuer then applies pressure by a series of upward and inward thrusts to force the foreign object back up the victim's trachea.

Meckel's diverticulum—A congenital abnormality of the digestive tract consisting of a small pouch off the wall of the small bowel that was not reabsorbed before birth. A Meckel's diverticulum increases the risk that a foreign object in the digestive tract will get trapped or stuck in the small intestine and cause problems.

Radiopaque—Not penetrable by x rays. A radiopaque object will look white or light when the x-ray film is developed. Most objects that children swallow can be detected by an x-ray study because they are radiopaque.

Sphincter—A circular band of muscle that surrounds and encloses an opening to the body or to one of its hollow organs. These muscles can open or close the opening by relaxing or contracting.

entering the body. For instance, parents and grandparents should toddler-proof their homes, storing batteries in a locked cabinet and properly disposing of used batteries, so they are not in a location where curious preschoolers can retrieve them from a wastebasket. Sewing kits, razor blades, and other potentially dangerous items should also be stored in childproof locations. To minimize the chance of youngsters inhaling food, parents should not allow children to eat while walking or playing. Fish should be carefully boned before it is served to younger children. Many eye injuries can be prevented by wearing safety glasses while using tools or participating in certain **sports**.

Parental concerns

Parental concerns in younger children should be directed toward the prevention of accidental swallowing or ingestion of foreign bodies. In most cases, these accidents can be successfully treated when they do occur, and they are unlikely to cause long-term damage to the child's health. In addition, small children are not likely to repeat behaviors that result in a trip to the doctor's office or hospital emergency room.

Ingestion or insertion of foreign bodies in older children and adolescents is a matter of greater concern to parents, however, because it is much more likely to be intentional, to reflect the presence of an eating disorder or other psychiatric problem, to be a repeated behavior, and to result in serious bodily harm.

See also Heavy metal poisoning; Lead poisoning.

Resources

BOOKS

"Foreign Bodies." Section 3, Chapter 24 in *The Merck Manual of Diagnosis and Therapy*, edited by Mark H. Beers and Robert Berkow. Whitehouse Station, NJ: Merck Research Laboratories, 2002.

"Foreign Bodies in the Rectum." Section 3, Chapter 35 in *The Merck Manual of Diagnosis and Therapy*, edited by Mark H. Beers and Robert Berkow. Whitehouse Station, NJ: Merck Research Laboratories, 2002.

PERIODICALS

Cakir, B., et al. "Localization and Removal of Ferromagnetic Foreign Bodies by Magnet." *Annals of Plastic Surgery* 49 (November 2002): 541–44.

Clifton, J. C., et al. "Acute Pediatric Lead Poisoning: Combined Whole Bowel Irrigation, Succimer Therapy, and Endoscopic Removal of Ingested Lead Pellets." *Pediatric Emergency Care* 18 (June 2002): 200–02.

Douglas, S. A., et al. "Magnetic Removal of a Nasal Foreign Body." *International Journal of Pediatric Otorhinolaryngology* 62 (February 1, 2002): 165–67.

McKinney, P. E. "Acute Elevation of Blood Lead Levels Within Hours of Ingestion of Large Quantities of Lead Shot." *Journal of Toxicology: Clinical Toxicology* 38 (2000): 435–40.

Muensterer, O. J., and I. Joppich. "Identification and Topographic Localization of Metallic Foreign Bodies by Metal Detector." *Journal of Pediatric Surgery* 39 (August 2004): 1245–48.

Reilly, B. K., et al. "Foreign Body Injury in Children in the Twentieth Century: A Modern Comparison to the Jackson Collection." *International Journal of Pediatric Otorhinolaryngology* 67, Supplement 1 (December 2003): S171–S174.

Steenvoorde, P., et al. "Retained Foreign Body in a 14-Year-Old Boy." *Journal of Pediatric Surgery* 38 (October 2003): 1554–56.

ORGANIZATIONS

American Academy of Emergency Medicine (AAEM). 555 East Wells Street, Suite 1100, Milwaukee, WI 53202. Web site: <www.aaem.org>.

American Academy of Family Physicians (AAFP). 11400 Tomahawk Creek Parkway, Leawood, KS 66211–2672. Web site: <www.aafp.org>.

American Academy of Otolaryngology, Head and Neck Surgery Inc. One Prince St., Alexandria, VA 22314–3357. Web site: <www.entnet.org>.

WEB SITES

Conners, Gregory P. "Pediatrics, Foreign Body Ingestion." *eMedicine*, July 26, 2004. Available online at <www.emedicine.com/emerg/topic379.htm> (accessed November 18, 2004).

J. Ricker Polsdorfer, MD

Foster care

Definition

Foster care is full-time substitute care of children outside their own home by people other than their biological or adoptive parents or legal guardians.

Description

Children who are removed from their biological or adoptive parents, or other legal guardians, are placed in foster care in a variety of settings. They may be placed in the care of relatives other than the **family** members involved in the neglect or abuse (kin placement), non-relatives, therapeutic or treatment foster care, or in an institution or group home.

Children come to foster care for a number of reasons. In many cases, they have suffered physical or sexual abuse, or neglect at home, and are placed in a safe environment. A small percentage of children are in foster care because their parents feel unable to control them, and their behavior may have led to delinquency or **fear** of harm to others. Some children have been neglected by their parents or legal guardians, or have parents or legal guardians who are unable to take care of them because of substance abuse, incarceration, or mental health problems. These children are placed into custodial care while the parents or guardians receive treatment or counseling, or fulfill their sentences.

In all foster care cases, the child's biological or adoptive parents, or other legal guardians, temporarily give up legal custody of the child. (The guardian gives up custody, but not necessarily legal guardianship.) A child may be placed in foster care with the parents' consent. In a clear case of abuse or neglect, a court can order a child into foster care without the parents' or guardians' consent. Foster care does not necessarily mean care by strangers. If a government agency decides a child must be removed from the home, the child may be placed with relatives or with a family friend. Children may also be placed in a group home, where several foster children live together with a staff of caregivers. Therapeutic or treatment foster care can be in a group home or foster home with a specific structure and treatment focus. Foster homes are the most well-known option. The child temporarily becomes a part of another family, either with other foster children, the family's biological or adoptive children, or alone. State or county social service agencies oversee foster care decisions, although they may also work with private foundations.

Foster parents must be licensed by the agency that handles a specific region's foster care. The foster home must pass an inspection for health and **safety** and, in most states, the parents must attend training sessions covering issues of foster care and how to deal with problems. When a child is placed, the foster family takes responsibility for feeding and clothing the child, getting the child to school and to appointments, and doing any of the usual things a child's parents or legal guardians might be called to do. The foster parents might also need to meet with the foster child's therapist and will meet regularly with the child's caseworker as well. The foster parent aims to help the foster child develop normally in a safe, family environment.

Foster parents usually receive money for taking in foster children. They are expected to use the money to buy the child's food, clothing, school supplies, and other incidentals. Most of the foster parent's responsibilities toward the foster child are clearly defined in a legal contract. Foster parents do not become the guardians of foster children; legal guardianship remains with the state agency.

Foster placements may last for a single day or several weeks; some continue for years. If the parents give up their rights permanently, or their rights to their child are severed by the court, the foster family may adopt the foster child or the child may be placed for **adoption** by strangers. Foster parenting is meant to be an in-between stage, while a permanent placement for the child is settled. As such, it is stressful and uncertain, but for many families very necessary.

Federal money supports most foster care programs, and federal law governs foster care policy. The Adoption Assistance and Child Welfare Reform Act of 1980 emphasizes two aims of foster care. One is to preserve the child's family, if at all possible. Children are placed in foster care only after other options have failed, and social service agencies work with the family to resolve its problems so that children can return to their homes. The second aim of the Child Welfare Reform Act is to support the so-called "permanency planning." This means that if a child must be removed from the home, the social service agency handling the case can decide quickly whether or not the child will ever be returned. If it seems likely that parents will not be able to care for their children again, their parental rights may be terminated so that the child is free to be adopted. This policy is articulated in this law in order to prevent children from living too long in an unstable and uncertain situation.

The goal of foster care is the care of the child within the child welfare system, but also is to place all appropriate and available services at the disposal of the parents so that they can create a safe, fit home environment for their children when they are reunited. Children in the child welfare system are also overseen by a multitude of agencies. The caseworker from the state or county social services agency oversees the child's placement and makes regular reports to the court. Others involved in the child's case are private service providers (including foster homes and group homes), welfare agencies, mental health counselors, substance abuse treatment centers (for the child or the parent), and Medicaid (federal medical insurance for seniors and children at risk).

Demographics

In 1980, about 300,000 children in the United States spent some time in foster care placement. By 2001, there were nearly 800,000 children in foster care, with 540,000 children in the system at any given time. The majority of these children were the victims of abuse. The emergence of widespread homelessness, substance abuse (especially crack and methamphetamines), unemployment, increased incarceration rates, street violence, and HIV/AIDS have all impacted poor communities. Children from families with multiple problems flooded the child welfare system. Young children with physical handicaps, mental delays or mental illness, and complex medical conditions have become the fastest-growing foster care population.

The foster care population is quite young. About one-fourth of all children entering foster care for the first time are infants. Sixty percent of foster children are under four years old. Teenagers comprise one-third of the foster care population. Minority children comprise most of the foster care population, with the largest groups being African American and American Indian children.

Poor children are more likely to be in foster care than middle-class children because their families have fewer resources. Illness or loss of a job may be devastating to a poor family with no savings and no relatives who can afford to assist them. These children are also more likely to stay in foster care longer or to have been in foster care since infancy. Also, children of alcoholics or drug abusers are at high risk for neglect or abuse, and comprise 75 percent of all placements.

More than half (57 percent) of all children in foster care are returned to their original homes; however, reunification rates have declined in the 1990s and early twenty-first century. Children also spend more time in the system. The average length of stay for a child in foster care is 33 months. However, some spend a very short time in a foster home, and others are there for their entire childhoods, "aging out" at 18 when they become legal adults.

Instead of reunification, more children are being adopted from foster care. Most states doubled, and some tripled, the number of foster care adoptions since 1997. This steady increase is a response to the Adoption and Safe Families Act (ASFA) of 1997 that recommends termination of parental rights and encourages adoption if a child has been in foster care for 15 out of the previous 22 months. This can be waived by the court if the parents are making substantive progress or the caseworker believes that legal guardianship, but not adoption, is in the child's best interests.

Half of all children in foster care live with non-relative foster caregivers; about one-fourth live with relatives, and this number is growing. ASFA also recognized kinship caregivers as legitimate placements. It was customary for many poor families to take in a child informally when the child's parents or legal guardians were incarcerated, in treatment, or had died, but ASFA allowed relatives to take care of a child legally and receive financial help, and also opened the doors to a number of agencies and services the relatives could not afford.

Common problems

In most cases, children placed in foster care have been subjected to some form of abuse or neglect, and being removed from familiar surroundings is, in itself, usually highly traumatic. Children in foster care may have **nightmares**, problems sleeping or eating, and may be depressed, angry, and confused. Many young children in foster care are unable to understand why they have been taken from their parents. Even if a child is in some sense relieved to be out of a home that was dangerous, the child may still miss the parents or legal guardians, and may imagine that there is something he or she must do to get back to them. There is evidence that children from abusive and neglectful homes start to feel better in foster care; however, separation is almost always difficult for children, regardless of the circumstances.

Half of all foster children spend as much as two years in foster care and are moved from placement to placement at least three times. This leads not only to uncertainty and lack of stability in the child's life, but some of these placements may be inappropriate for the child's specific circumstances. This often is due to the lack of qualified, licensed foster caregivers, but it can also occur as a result of inexperienced or overloaded caseworkers trying to get through their caseloads.

Foster care can be difficult for foster parents as well. A child who has been neglected or abused suffers psychological damage that may make him or her withdrawn, immature, aggressive, or otherwise difficult to reach. Children with severe medical and mental problems can tax caregivers. Foster placements sometimes fail because these surrogate parents simply cannot handle the demands of a troubled foster child.

Unfortunately, the number of foster caregivers has been declining since the mid-1980s as the demand for placements has increased. States have responded by licensing responsible adults who were not married (even divorced men and women) and reaching out to seniors and children's relatives. In some areas, single mothers make up a large proportion of foster parents.

KEY TERMS

Adoption—The legal process that creates a parent and child relationship between two individuals who are not biologically related at birth.

Age out—Become a legal adult at age 18 and move out of foster care.

Medicaid—A program jointly funded by state and federal governments that reimburses hospitals and physicians for the care of individuals who cannot pay for their own medical expenses. These individuals may be in low-income households or may have chronic disabilities.

In 2002, about 405,000 children were placed in court-appointed kinship care. Caseworkers placed almost 140,000 more in the care of relatives, without court intervention. Many of these kinship caregivers are grandparents or elderly aunts and uncles. Kinship caregivers offer family support and stability, and more frequent contact with parents or legal guardians, and siblings. They also are more apt to get children to talk to them about their problems, and the presence of relatives can help ease the trauma of separation from parents.

Nevertheless, kinship caregivers, especially grandparents, face a number of challenges. Most of the formal and informal kinship caregivers experience economic hardship as they take in one or more of their relative's children. Nearly two-thirds of these placements are with financially strapped families who may not have essentials such as a car seat, crib, or **toys**. They also may not have adequate medical insurance; however, Medicaid often will cover the foster child in a formal kinship arrangement. Grandparents may not know how to raise a child in today's world, with the amount of freedoms or lack of them that children experience today. They may not be able to help their foster children with homework. Many social service agencies offer counseling, homework help, and even home tutoring for both the child and caregiver.

One other problem inherent in the child welfare system is the teenager who "ages out," or turns 18 and moves out of foster care to live independently. Many teenagers mark time within the system, without adequate preparation for the transition to adulthood. Less than one-fourth of social service agencies provide employment services for teenagers. Only 17 percent provide employment and career assessments, and 16 percent provide job-training. One-fourth offer vocational training. Without help, these teenagers often never go on to college, do not find good jobs if they find jobs at all, and become prey to bad influences on the street. If they have children of their own, these offspring fall back into the child welfare system just as they did. Adequate training, counseling, and preparation can break this cycle.

In addition, children in all types of foster care face more challenges financially, emotionally, and developmentally. A study by the Child Welfare League of America in 2004 showed that children in foster care experienced more health and developmental problems than children who had similar economic circumstances but lived with their parents or legal guardians. Foster children also have more neglect, abuse, family dysfunction, poverty, and emotional problems. This may be a direct result of the reasons for their initial placement, but these conditions continue throughout foster care. Another reason for these results may be that foster children are given more frequent and thorough medical and psychological care than their counterparts.

Parental concerns

Other foster care placements are made by families who cannot afford medical or psychological services for their children. These children may have multiple disabilities or severe social or mental disorders that have depleted the family's financial and emotional resources. Convinced by social workers that this option is the only one available to them, they give up their parental rights in order to get their children into proper treatment. According to the U.S General Accounting Office, 12,700 children were placed into the child welfare system or the juvenile justice system to receive mental health services in 2001. Despite the noble reasons for placing these children in foster care, the parents' names are placed on state registries as child abusers, and they have to petition the court and prove their fitness to get their children returned to their homes.

See also Child abuse.

Resources

BOOKS

Davies, Nancy Millichap. *Foster Care*. NY: Franklin Watts, 1994.

PERIODICALS

Bass, Sandra, et al. "Children, Families, and Foster Care: Analysis and Recommendations." *The Future of Children*. 14, no. 1 (Winter 2004): 4–30.

Hansen, Robin L., et al. "Comparing the Health Status of Low-Income Children in and out of Foster Care." *Child Welfare* 83, no. 4 (July-August 2004): 367–81.

The David and Lucile Packard Foundation. "Children, Families, and Foster Care: Analysis." (Executive Summary) *The Future of Children* 14, no. 1 (Winter 2004): S1.

ORGANIZATIONS

Foster Care Children. 507 North Sullivan Road Suite A-6. Spokane Valley, WA 99037. (509) 924-3175. Web site: <www.fostercarechildren.com>.

WEB SITES

Pew Commission on Children in Foster Care. Available online at: <http://pewfostercare.org>.

Janie Franz
A. Woodward

Fractures

Definition

A fracture is a complete or incomplete break in a bone resulting from the application of excessive force.

Description

A fracture usually results from traumatic injury to a bone, causing the continuity of bone tissues or bony cartilage to be disrupted or broken. Fracture classifications include simple or compound and incomplete or complete. Simple fractures (often called "closed") are not obvious as the skin has not been ruptured and remains intact. Compound fractures (commonly called "open") break the skin, exposing bone and causing additional soft tissue injury and possible infection. A single fracture means that one fracture has occurred, and multiple fractures refer to more than one fracture occurring in the same bone. Fractures are termed complete if the break is completely through the bone and described as incomplete or "greenstick" if the fracture occurs partly across a bone shaft. This latter type of fracture is often the result of bending or crushing forces applied to a bone.

Fractures are also named according to the specific part of the bone involved and the nature of the break. Identification of a fracture line can further classify fractures. Types include linear, oblique, transverse, longitudinal, and spiral fractures. Fractures can be further subdivided by the positions of bony fragments and are described as comminuted, non-displaced, impacted, overriding, angulated, displaced, avulsed, and segmental. Additionally, an injury may be classified as a fracture-dislocation when a fracture involves the bony structures of any joint with associated dislocation of the same joint.

Fractures line identification

Linear fractures have a break that runs parallel to the bone's main axis or in the direction of the bone's shaft. For example, a linear fracture of the arm bone could extend the entire length of the bone. Oblique and transverse fractures differ in that an oblique fracture crosses a bone at approximately a 45° angle to the bone's axis. In contrast, a transverse fracture crosses a bone's axis at a 90° angle. A longitudinal fracture is similar to a linear fracture. Its fracture line extends along the shaft but is more irregular in shape and does not run parallel to the bone's axis. Spiral fractures are described as crossing a bone at an oblique angle, creating a spiral pattern. This break usually occurs in the long bones of the body such as the upper arm bone (humerus) or the thigh bone (femur).

Bony fragment position identification

Comminuted fractures have two or more fragments broken into small pieces, in addition to the upper and lower halves of a fractured bone. Fragments of bone that maintain their normal alignment following a fracture are described as being non-displaced. An impacted fracture is characterized as a bone fragment forced into or onto another fragment resulting from a compressive force. Overriding is a term used to describe bony fragments that overlap and shorten the total length of a bone. Angulated fragments result in pieces of bone being at angles to each other. A displaced bony fragment occurs from disruption of normal bone alignment with deformity of these segments separate from one another. An avulsed fragment occurs when bone fragments are pulled from their normal position by forceful muscle contractions or resistance from ligaments. Segmental fragmented positioning occurs if fractures in two adjacent areas occur, leaving an isolated central segment. An example of segmental alignment occurs when the arm bone fractures in two separate places, with displacement of the middle section of bone.

Demographics

The exact number of fractures sustained in the United States each year is not known as many are not treated. Experts estimate the number of fractures at between 10 and 20 million. People of all ages and races experience fractures. Broken bones are slightly more common among children due to their increased level of activity and among older people due to their lack of **exercise** and inadequate intake of calcium.

Causes and symptoms

Individuals with high activity levels appear to be at greater risk for fractures. This group includes children and athletes participating in contact **sports**. Because of an increase in bone brittleness with aging, elderly persons are also included in this high-risk population. Up to the age of 50, more men suffer from fractures than women due to occupational hazards. However, after the age of 50, women are more prone to fractures than men. Specific diseases causing an increased risk for fractures include Paget's disease, rickets, **osteogenesis imperfecta**, osteoporosis, bone **cancer** and tumors, and prolonged disuse of a nonfunctional body part such as after a **stroke**.

Symptoms of fractures usually begin with **pain** that increases with attempted movement or use of the area and swelling at the involved site. The skin in the area may be pale and an obvious deformity may be present. In more severe cases, there may be a loss of pulse below the fracture site, such as in the extremities, accompanied by **numbness**, **tingling**, or paralysis below the fracture. An open or compound fracture is often accompanied by bleeding or bruising. If the lower limbs or pelvis are fractured, pain and resistance to movement usually accompany the injury causing difficulty with weight bearing.

When to call the doctor

A physician should be called when a child complains of bone pain. This is a deep pain that may be exquisitely tender to the touch.

Diagnosis

Diagnosis begins immediately with an individual's own observation of symptoms. A thorough medical history and physical exam by a physician often reveals the presence of a fracture. An x ray of the injured area is the most common test used to determine the presence of a bone fracture. Any x-ray series performed involves at least two views of the area to confirm the presence of the fracture because not all fractures are apparent on a single x ray. Some fractures are often difficult to see and may require several views at different angles to see clear fracture lines. In some cases, CT, MRI, or other imaging tests are required to demonstrate fracture. Sometimes, especially with children, the initial x ray may not show any fractures, but if it is repeated seven to 14 days later, the x ray may show changes in the bone(s) of the affected area. If a fracture is open and occurs in conjunction with

soft tissue injury, further laboratory studies are often conducted to determine if blood loss has occurred.

In the event of exercise-related stress fractures (micro-fractures due to excessive stress), a tuning fork can provide a simple, inexpensive test. The tuning fork is a metal instrument with a stem and two prongs that vibrate when struck. If an individual has increased pain when the tuning fork is placed on a bone, such as the tibia or shinbone, the likelihood of a stress fracture is high. Bone scans also are helpful in detecting stress fractures. In this diagnostic procedure, a radioactive tracer is injected into the bloodstream and images are taken of specific areas or the entire skeleton by CT or MRI.

Treatment

Treatment depends on the type of fracture, its severity, the individual's age, and the person's general health. The first priority in treating any fracture is to address the entire medical status of the patient. Medical personnel are trained not to allow a painful, deformed limb to distract them from potentially life-threatening injury elsewhere or shock. If an open fracture is accompanied by serious soft tissue injury, it may be necessary to control bleeding and the shock that can accompany loss of blood.

First aid is the appropriate initial treatment in emergency situations. It includes proper splinting, control of blood loss, and monitoring vital signs such as breathing and circulation.

Immobilization

Immobilization of a fracture site can be done internally or externally. The primary goal of immobilization is to maintain the realignment of a bone long enough for healing to start and progress. Immobilization by external fixation uses splints, casts, or braces. This may be the primary and only procedure for fracture treatment. Splinting to immobilize a fracture can be done with or without traction. In emergency situations if the injured individual must be moved by someone other than a trained medical person, splinting is a useful form of fracture management. It should be done without causing additional pain and without moving the bone segments. In a clinical environment, plaster of Paris casts are used for immobilization. Braces are useful as they often allow movement above and below a fracture site. Treatments for stress fractures include rest and decreasing or stopping any activity that causes or increases pain.

KEY TERMS

Avulsion fracture—A fracture caused by the tearing away of a fragment of bone where a strong ligament or tendon attachment forcibly pulls the fragment away from the bone tissue.

Axis—A line that passes through the center of the body or body part.

Comminuted fracture—A fracture where there are several breaks in a bone creating numerous fragments.

Compartment syndrome—A condition in which the blood supply to a muscle is cut off because the muscle swells but is constricted by the connective tissue around it.

Contrast hydrotherapy—A series of hot and cold water applications. A hot compress (as hot as an individual can tolerate) is applied for three minutes followed by an ice cold compress for 30 seconds. These applications are repeated three times each and ending with the cold compress.

Osteogenesis imperfecta—An inherited disorder of the connective tissues that involves multiple symptoms, including weakened bones that break easily.

Osteoporosis—Literally meaning "porous bones," this condition occurs when bones lose an excessive amount of their protein and mineral content, particularly calcium. Over time, bone mass and strength are reduced leading to increased risk of fractures.

Paget's disease—A chronic disorder of unknown cause usually affecting middle aged and elderly people and characterized by enlarged and deformed bones. Changes in the normal mechanism of bone formation occur in Paget's disease and can cause bones to weaken, resulting in bone pain, arthritis, deformities, and fractures. Also known as osteitis deformans.

Reduction—The restoration of a body part to its original position after displacement, such as the reduction of a fractured bone by bringing ends or fragments back into original alignment. The use of local or general anesthesia usually accompanies a fracture reduction. If performed by outside manipulation only, the reduction is described as closed; if surgery is necessary, it is described as open. Also describes a chemical reaction in which one or more electrons are added to an atom or molecule.

Rickets—A condition caused by the dietary deficiency of vitamin D, calcium, and usually phosphorus, seen primarily in infancy and childhood, and characterized by abnormal bone formation.

Traction—The process of placing a bone, limb, or group of muscles under tension by applying weights and pulleys. The goal is to realign or immobilize the part or to relieve pressure on that particular area to promote healing and restore function.

Fracture reduction

Fracture reduction is the procedure by which a fractured bone is realigned in normal position. It can be either closed or open. Closed reduction refers to realigning bones without breaking the skin. It is performed with manual manipulation and/or traction and is commonly done with some kind of anesthetic. Open reduction primarily refers to surgery that is performed to realign bones or fragments. Fractures with little or no displacement may not require any form of reduction.

Traction is used to help reposition a broken bone. It works by applying pressure to restore proper alignment. The traction device immobilizes the area and maintains realignment as the bone heals. A fractured bone is immobilized by applying opposing force at both ends of the injured area, using an equal amount of traction and countertraction. Weights provide the traction pull needed or the pull is achieved by positioning the individual's body

weight appropriately. Traction is a form of closed reduction and is sometimes used as an alternative to surgery. Since it restricts movement of the affected limb or body part, it may confine a person to bed rest for an extended period of time.

A person may need open reduction if there is an open, severe, or comminuted fracture. This procedure allows a physician to examine and surgically correct associated soft tissue damage while reducing the fracture and, if necessary, applying internal or external devices. Internal fixation involves the use of metallic devices inserted into or through bone to hold the fracture in a set position and alignment while it heals. Devices include plates, nails, screws, and rods. When healing is complete, the surgeon may or may not remove these devices. Virtually any hip fracture requires open reduction and internal fixation so that the bone will be able to support the patient's weight.

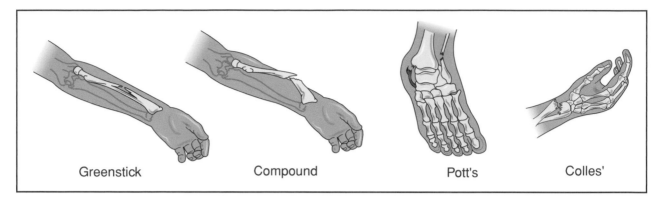

Greenstick   Compound   Pott's   Colles'

Fractures usually result from a traumatic injury to a bone where the continuity of bone tissues or bony cartilage is disrupted or broken. The illustrations above feature common sites where fractures occur. *(Illustration by Electronic Illustrators Group.)*

Alternative treatment

In addition to the importance of calcium for strong bones, many alternative treatment approaches recommend use of mineral supplements to help build and maintain a healthy, resilient skeleton. Some physical therapists use electro-stimulation over a fractured site to promote and expedite healing. Chinese traditional medicine may be helpful by working to reconnect chi (life energy) through the meridian lines along the line of a fracture. Homeopathy can enhance the body's healing process. Two particularly useful homeopathic remedies are arnica (*Arnica montana*) and symphytum (*Symphytum officinalis*). If possible, applying contrast hydrotherapy to an extremity (e.g., a hand or foot) of a fractured area can assist healing by enhancing circulation.

Prognosis

Fractures involving joint surfaces almost always lead to some degree of arthritis of the joint. Fractures can normally be cured with proper first aid and appropriate aftercare. If determined necessary by a physician, the fractured site should be manipulated, realigned, and immobilized as soon as possible. Realignment has been shown to be much more difficult after six hours. Healing time varies from person to person with the elderly generally needing more time to heal completely. A non-union fracture may result when a fracture does not heal, such as in the case of an elderly person or an individual with medical complications. Recovery is complete when there is no bone motion at the fracture site, and **x rays** indicate complete healing. Open fractures may lead to bone infections, which delay the healing process. Another possible complication is compartment syndrome, a painful condition resulting from the expansion of enclosed tissue and that may occur when a body part is immobilized in a cast.

Prevention

Fractures can be prevented if **safety** measures are taken seriously. These measures include using seat belts in cars and encouraging children to wear protective sports gear. Weight-bearing exercise also helps to strengthen bones.

Nutritional concerns

Persons who consume diets that are rich in calcium are less likely to experience a fracture than those who have diets that are deficient in calcium. Good dietary sources of calcium are milk, cheese, and other dairy products.

Parental concerns

Parents should ensure that their children drink milk to provide an adequate intake of calcium. Children should also participate in regular physical exercise.

Resources

BOOKS

Burr, David B. *Musculoskeletal Fatigue and Stress Fracture.* Boca Raton, FL: CRC Press, 2001.

Eiff, M. Patrice, et al. *Fracture Management for Primary Care*, 2nd ed. New York: Elsevier, 2002.

Jupiter, J. *Fractures and Dislocations of the Hand.* St. Louis: Mosby, 2001.

Koval, Kenneth J., and Joseph D. Zuckerman. *Handbook of Fractures*, 2nd ed. Philadelphia: Lippincott, 2001.

Moehring, H. David, and Adam Greenspan. *Fractures: Diagnosis and Treatment.* New York: McGraw Hill, 2000.

Ogden, John A. *Skeletal Injury in the Child.* New York: Springer Verlag, 2000.

PERIODICALS

Cameron, I. D. "How to manage musculoskeletal conditions: when is 'Rehabilitation'' appropriate?" *Best Practice and Research in Clinical Rheumatology* 18, no. 4 (2004): 573–86.

Lindsay, R. "Perspectives on osteoporosis prevention: How far have we come?" *Journal of Family Practice* 53, no. 8 (2004): S3–9.

Minns, J., et al. "Can flooring and underlay materials reduce hip fractures in older people?" *Nursing Older People* 16, no. 5 (2004): 16–20.

Smith-Adaline, E. A., et al. "Mechanical environment alters tissue formation patterns during fracture repair." *Journal of Orthopedic Research* 22, no. 5 (2004): 1079–85.

ORGANIZATIONS

American Academy of Emergency Medicine. 611 East Wells Street, Milwaukee, WI 53202. Web site: <www.aaem.org/>.

American Academy of Family Physicians. 11400 Tomahawk Creek Parkway, Leawood, KS 66211–2672. Web site: <www.aafp.org/>.

American Academy of Orthopedic Surgeons. 6300 North River Road, Rosemont, Illinois 60018–4262. Web site: <www.aaos.org/>.

American Academy of Pediatrics. 141 Northwest Point Boulevard, Elk Grove Village, IL 60007–1098. Web site: <www.aap.org/default.htm>.

American Academy of Physical Medicine and Rehabilitation. One IBM Plaza, Suite 2500, Chicago, IL 60611–3604. Web site: <www.aapmr.org/>.

American College of Foot and Ankle Surgeons. 515 Busse Highway, Park Ridge, Illinois 60068–3150. Web site: <www.acfas.org/index.html>.

American College of Sports Medicine. 401 W. Michigan St., Indianapolis, IN 46202–3233. Web site: <www.acsm.org/>.

American College of Surgeons. 633 North St. Clair Street, Chicago, IL 60611–32311. Web site: <www.facs.org/>.

WEB SITES

American Academy of Orthopaedic Surgeons. "Fractures." *Your Orthopedic Connection.* Available online at <http://orthoinfo.aaos.org/brochure/thr_report.cfm?Thread_ID=9&topcategory =General%20Information> (accessed November 19, 2004).

"Falls and Hip Fractures among Older Adults." *National Center for Injury Prevention and Control.* Available online at <www.cdc.gov/ncipc/factsheets/falls.htm> accessed November 19, 2004).

"Fracture Information." *About.* Available online at <http://orthopedics.about.com/cs/otherfractures/a/fracture.htm> (accessed November 19, 2004).

"Fractures." *National Library of Medicine*, October 21, 2004. Available online at <www.nlm.nih.gov/medlineplus/fractures.html> (accessed November 19, 2004).

L. Fleming Fallon, Jr., MD, DrPH

Fragile X syndrome

Definition

Fragile X syndrome, a genetic condition involving changes in the long arm of the X chromosome, is the most common form of inherited **mental retardation**. Individuals with this condition have **developmental delay**, variable levels of mental retardation, and behavioral and emotional difficulties. They may also have characteristic physical traits. Generally, males are affected with moderate mental retardation (since they only have one X chromosome) and females with mild mental retardation.

Description

Fragile X syndrome is the most common form of inherited mental retardation in the United States. Fragile X syndrome is caused by a mutation in the FMR-1 gene, located on the X chromosome. The FMR-1 gene is thought to play an important role in the development of the brain, but the exact way that the gene acts in the body is not fully understood. Language delays, behavioral problems, **autism** or autistic-like behavior (including poor eye contact and hand-flapping), enlarged genitalia (macroorchidism), large or prominent ears, hyperactivity, delayed motor development, and/or poor sensory skills are among the wide range of characteristics associated with this disorder.

Fragile X syndrome is also known as Martin-Bell syndrome, Marker X syndrome, and FRAXA syndrome.

Demographics

Fragile X syndrome affects males and females of all ethnic groups. A summary of existing research conducted by the Centers for Disease Control and Prevention in 2001 estimated that approximately one in 3,500–8,900 males is affected by the full mutation of the FMR-1 gene and that one in 1,000 males has the premutation form of the FMR-1 gene. This study also estimated that one in 250–500 females in the general population has the premutation. Another study estimated that one in 4,000 females is affected by the full mutation.

Causes and symptoms

For reasons not fully understood, the CGG sequence in the FMR-1 gene can expand through succeeding generations to contain between 54 and 230 repeats. This stage of expansion is called a premutation. People who carry a premutation do not usually have symptoms of fragile X syndrome, although there have been reports of individuals with a premutation who have subtle intellectual or behavioral symptoms. Individuals who carry a fragile X premutation are at risk for having children or grandchildren with the premutation. Female premutation carriers may also be at increased risk for earlier onset of menopause.

Premutation carriers may exist through several generations of a **family** though no symptoms of fragile X syndrome appear. However, the size of the premutation can expand over succeeding generations. When a man carries a premutation on his X chromosome, it tends to be stable and usually will not expand if he passes it on to his daughters (he passes his Y chromosome to his sons). Thus, all of his daughters will be premutation carriers like he is. When a woman carries a premutation, it is unstable and can expand as she passes it on to her children; therefore, a man's grandchildren are at greater risk of developing the syndrome. There is a 50 percent risk for a premutation carrier female for transmitting an abnormal mutation with each pregnancy. The likelihood for the premutation to expand is related to the number of repeats present; the higher the number of repeats, the greater the chance that the premutation will expand to a full mutation in the next generation. All mothers of a child with a full mutation are carriers of an FMR-1 gene expansion.

Once the size of the premutation exceeds 230 repeats, it becomes a full mutation, and the FMR-1 gene is disabled. Individuals who carry the full mutation may have fragile X syndrome. Since the FMR-1 gene is located on the X chromosome, males are more likely to develop symptoms than females. This greater inclination occurs because males have only one copy of the X chromosome. Males who inherit the full mutation are expected to have mental impairment. A female's normal X chromosome may compensate for her chromosome with the fragile X gene mutation. Females who inherit the full mutation have an approximately 30–50 percent risk of mental impairment, ranging from mild learning disability to mental retardation and behavioral problems.

Another feature of fragile X syndrome is that mosaicism is present in 15 to 20 percent of those affected by the condition. Mosaicism refers to the presence of cells of two different genetic materials in the same individual.

Individuals with fragile X syndrome appear normal at birth, but their development is delayed. Most boys with fragile X syndrome have mental impairment. The severity of mental impairment ranges from learning disabilities to severe mental retardation. Behavioral problems include attention deficit and hyperactivity at a young age. Some may show **aggressive behavior** in adulthood. Short attention span, poor eye contact, delayed and disordered speech and language, emotional instability, and unusual hand mannerisms (hand flapping or hand biting) are also seen frequently. Other behavioral characteristics include whirling, spinning, and occasionally autism or autistic-like behavior.

Characteristic physical traits appear later in childhood. These traits include a long and narrow face, prominent jaw, large ears, and enlarged testes. In females who carry a full mutation, the physical and behavioral features and mental retardation tend to be less severe. About 50 percent of females who have a full mutation are mentally retarded.

Children with fragile X syndrome often have frequent ear and sinus infections. Nearsightedness and lazy eye are also common. Many babies with fragile X syndrome may have trouble with sucking, and some experience digestive disorders that cause frequent gagging and **vomiting**. A small percentage of children with fragile X syndrome may experience seizures. Children with fragile X syndrome also tend to have loose joints, which may result in joint dislocations. Some children develop a curvature in the spine, flat feet, and a heart condition known as mitral valve prolapse.

When to call the doctor

If a child exhibits delayed development and mental impairment and has other symptoms typical of fragile X syndrome, the doctor should be consulted to determine the cause of the problems.

Diagnosis

A birth, there may be few outward signs of fragile X syndrome in the newborn infant. However, fragile X symptoms may include a large head circumference and oversized testes in males. An experienced geneticist may recognize subtle differences in facial characteristics.

However, any child with signs of developmental delay of speech, language, or motor development with

KEY TERMS

Amniocentesis—A procedure performed at 16-18 weeks of pregnancy in which a needle is inserted through a woman's abdomen into her uterus to draw out a small sample of the amniotic fluid from around the baby for analysis. Either the fluid itself or cells from the fluid can be used for a variety of tests to obtain information about genetic disorders and other medical conditions in the fetus.

CGG or CGG sequence—Shorthand for the DNA sequence: cytosine-guanine-guanine. Cytosine and guanine are two of the four molecules, called nucleic acids, that make up DNA.

Chorionic villus sampling—A procedure performed at 10 to 12 weeks of pregnancy in which a needle is inserted either through the mother's vagina or abdominal wall into the placenta to withdraw a small amount of chorionic membrane from around the early embryo. The chorionic membrane can be examined for signs of chromosome abnormalities or other genetic diseases.

Chromosome—A microscopic thread-like structure found within each cell of the human body and consisting of a complex of proteins and DNA. Humans have 46 chromosomes arranged into 23 pairs. Chromosomes contain the genetic information necessary to direct the development and functioning of all cells and systems in the body. They pass on hereditary traits from parents to child (like eye color) and determine whether the child will be male or female.

FMR-1 gene—A gene found on the X chromosome. Its exact purpose is unknown, but it is suspected that the gene plays a role in brain development.

Mitral valve prolapse—A heart defect in which the mitral valve of the heart (which normally controls blood flow from the left atrium to the left ventricle) becomes floppy. Mitral valve prolapse may be detected as a heart murmur but there are usually no symptoms.

Premutation—A change in a gene that precedes a mutation; this change does not alter the function of the gene.

X chromosome—One of the two sex chromosomes (the other is Y) that determine a person's gender. Normal males have both an X and a Y chromosome, and normal females have two X chromosomes.

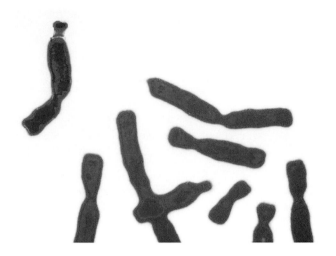

Fragile X chromosome, shaded in purple at upper left corner, is shown among other chromosomes. (© Siebert/Custom Medical Stock Photo, Inc)

no known cause should be considered for fragile X testing, especially if there is a family history of the condition. Behavioral and developmental problems may indicate fragile X syndrome, particularly if there is a family history of mental retardation. Definitive identification of the fragile X syndrome is made by means of a genetic test to assess the number of CGG sequence repeats in the FMR-1 gene. Individuals with the premutation or full mutation may be identified through genetic testing. Genetic testing for and detection of the fragile X mutation can be performed on the developing baby before birth through **amniocentesis**, chorionic villus sampling (CVS), and percutaneous umbilical blood sampling. Prenatal testing is recommended after the fragile X carrier status of the parents has been confirmed, and the couple has been counseled regarding the risks of recurrence.

Prognosis

Early diagnosis and intensive intervention offer the best prognosis for individuals with fragile X syndrome. Adults with fragile X syndrome may benefit from vocational training and may need to live in a supervised setting. About 50 percent of affected individuals develop mitral valve prolapse, a heart condition, as adults. However, life span is typically normal.

Prevention

Neither the fragile X premutation nor mutation is preventable as of 2004. Genetic counseling may help prospective parents with a family history of fragile X syndrome. Genetic testing can help determine the level of risk in the family.

Parental concerns

A child with fragile X syndrome requires many services, so parents must be prepared to invest significant time and resources to ensure the child receives the help that he or she needs.

Families may wish to seek counseling regarding the effects of the syndrome on relationships within the family. Many people respond with guilt, **fear**, or blame when a genetic disorder is diagnosed in the family, or they may overprotect the affected member. Support groups are often good sources of information about fragile X syndrome; they can offer helpful suggestions about living with it as well as emotional support.

Resources

BOOKS

Dew-Hughes, Denise. *Educating Children with Fragile X Syndrome.* New York: Falmer Press, 2004.

Fragile X Syndrome: A Medical Dictionary, Bibliography, and Annotated Research Guide to Internet Resources. San Diego, CA: Icon Health Publications, 2004.

Parker, James N., and Parker, Philip M. *The 2002 Official Patient's Sourcebook on Fragile X Syndrome.* San Diego, CA: Icon Health Publications, 2002.

Saunders, Suzanne. *Fragile X Syndrome.* New York: Taylor and Francis Group, 2001.

Weber, Jayne Dixon. *Children with Fragile X Syndrome: A Parents' Guide.* Bethesda, MD: Woodbine House, 2000.

ORGANIZATIONS

Arc of the United States (formerly Association for Retarded Citizens of the United States). 500 East Border St., Suite 300, Arlington, TX 76010. Web site: <http://thearc.org>.

FRAXA Research Foundation. 45 Pleasant Street, Newburyport, MA 01950. Web site: <www.fraxa.org>.

National Fragile X Foundation. PO Box 190488, San Francisco, CA 94119–0988. Web site: <www.FragileX.org>.

WEB SITES

"Families and Fragile X Syndrome." *National Institute of Child Health & Human Development, National Institutes of Health.* Available online at <www.nichd.nih.gov/publications/pubs/fragileX/index.htm> (accessed November 19, 2004).

Judith Sims, MS
Nada Quercia, MS, CCGC

Friedreich's ataxia

Definition

Friedreich's ataxia (FA) is an inherited, progressive nervous system disorder causing loss of balance and coordination, speech problems, and heart disease.

Description

FA is an inherited disease marked by impaired coordination that is a result of degeneration of the structures in the cerebellum and the spinal cord, which are responsible for coordination, muscle movement, and some sensory functions, including color vision and hearing. The intellect of a child with FA is normal.

FA is an autosomal recessive disease, which means that two defective gene copies, one from each parent, must be inherited to develop symptoms. A person with only one defective gene copy will not show signs of FA, but may pass along the gene to offspring. Couples with one child affected by FA have a 25 percent chance in each pregnancy of conceiving another affected child.

FA is also referred to as spinocerebellar degeneration.

Demographics

Friedreich's ataxia is the most common inherited ataxia, affecting one in 50,000 people in the United States. Females and males are affected equally.

Causes and symptoms

Causes

The gene for FA codes for a protein called frataxin. Normal frataxin is found in the cellular energy structures known as mitochondria, where it is thought to be involved in regulating the transport of iron. In FA, the frataxin gene on chromosome 9 is expanded when a particular sequence of bases in the DNA is repeated too many times. Ordinarily, there are seven to 22 repeats of the frataxin gene; in FA, this sequence may be repeated between 800 to 1,000 times. This extra DNA interferes with normal production of frataxin, thereby impairing iron transport. The triplet repeat expansion seems to interfere with the normal assembly of amino acids into proteins, significantly reducing the amount of frataxin that is made. Without a normal level of frataxin, some of the body's cells—especially those of the brain, spinal cord, and muscle—cannot handle the normal amounts of "oxidative stress," which the mitochondria produce. When excess iron in the cells (as a result of the deficiency of frataxin) reacts with oxygen, free radicals are produced. Free radicals are necessary molecules in the body's metabolism, but in excess they can also destroy cells and harm the body.

The types of symptoms and severity of FA seems to be associated with the number of repetitions. Children with more copies have more severe symptomatology, with symptoms starting at a younger age.

The nerve cells most affected by FA are those in the spinal cord involved in relaying information between muscles and the brain. Control of movement requires complex feedback between the muscles promoting a movement, those restraining it, and the brain. Without this control, movements become uncoordinated, jerky, and inappropriate to the desired action.

Symptoms

Symptoms of FA usually first appear between the ages of five and 15 years, although onset as early as 18 months or as late as age 30 years is possible. The first symptom is usually gait incoordination. A child with FA may graze doorways when passing through, for instance, or trip over low obstacles. Unsteadiness when standing still and deterioration of position sense is common. Children with FA may develop foot deformities such as **club-foot**, hammertoe, and high arches. Walking up off the heels often results from uneven muscle weakness in the legs. **Muscle spasms and cramps** may occur, especially at night. Other early symptoms include changes in speech, swallowing difficulties, loss of reflexes, and jerky eye movements (**nystagmus**).

Ataxia in the arms follows, usually within several years, leading to decreased **hand-eye coordination**. Arm weakness does not usually occur until much later. There is often a gradual loss of sensation in the extremities, which may spread to other parts of the body. In about 10 percent of children with FA, **diabetes mellitus** may develop in the later stages of the disease. Some loss of visual acuity may be noted. Hearing loss occurs in about 10 percent of children with FA, and about 20 percent develop **carbohydrate intolerance**. A side-to-side curvature of the spine (**scoliosis**) occurs in many cases, and may become severe. About 50 percent of people develop problems with control of their urge to urinate (urinary urgency), or become incontinent.

Various forms of heart disease often accompany FA, including cardiomyopathy (enlargement of the heart), myocardial fibrosis (formation of fiber-like materials in heart muscles), and cardiac failure. Symptoms of heart involvement include chest **pain**, shortness of breath, and heart palpitations. Heartbeat abnormalities such as tachycardia (rapid heart rate) and heart block (impaired conduction of the heart's cardiac impulses) are common occurrences.

When to call the doctor

Any time a child with FA reports unusual heart symptoms, such as shortness of breath on exertion, **dizziness**, fainting, chest pain or discomfort, or abnormal heart rhythms, the doctor or cardiologist should be called, or the child should be taken immediately to a hospital emergency room.

Diagnosis

Diagnosis of FA involves a careful medical history and thorough neurological exam. Laboratory tests include electromyography (a measurement of the electrical activity of muscle cells) and nerve conduction velocity tests, which measure the speed that nerves transmit impulses. An electrocardiogram and echocardiogram may be performed to diagnose heart disease. Imaging studies are conducted to provide pictures of the brain and spinal cord. A spinal tap is performed to evaluate the cerebrospinal fluid. Blood and urine samples are tested for elevated glucose levels, to determine whether the child has diabetes.

Direct DNA testing is available, allowing FA to be more easily distinguished from other types of ataxia. The same test may be used to determine the presence of the genetic defect in unaffected individuals, such as siblings.

Treatment

There is no cure for FA, nor is there any treatment that can slow its progress. Therefore, the goal of treatment is to control symptoms and maintain general health. Amantadine may provide some limited improvement in ataxic symptoms, but is not recommended in children with cardiac abnormalities. Physical therapy and activity are used to maintain range of motion in weakened muscles and to compensate for loss of coordination and strength. Some children find that using weights on the arms can help dampen the worst of the uncoordinated arm movements. Scoliosis and foot deformities can be treated with braces or surgery.

Safety is an important consideration in this disease since the child will eventually experience loss of balance and sensation. Occupational therapy is recommended to select adaptive techniques and devices such as safety railings, walkers, or other safety appliances. If the child loses feelings in various body parts, injuries can be avoided by testing bath water to prevent **burns**, inspect-

KEY TERMS

Ataxia—A condition marked by impaired muscular coordination, most frequently resulting from disorders in the brain or spinal cord.

Oxidative stress—A condition where the body is producing an excess of oxygen-free radicals.

Scoliosis—An abnormal, side-to-side curvature of the spine.

ing the body visually for injuries, and using protective shoes and helmets.

Diabetes is treated with insulin and dietary changes. Some of the heart problems can be treated with medications.

Since the disease may be associated with damage to cells caused by free radicals, antioxidants such as vitamin E and coenzyme Q10 are often prescribed for children with FA.

Prognosis

The rate of progression of FA is highly variable. Most children lose the ability to walk within 15 to 20 years after the onset of symptoms, and will require aids for walking such as scooters, walkers, or wheelchairs. In later stages of the disease, people become incapacitated.

Reduction in lifespan from FA complications is also quite variable. Average age at death is in the mid-thirties, but may be as late as the mid-sixties in persons with less severe symptoms. Many persons with FA will develop untreatable heart disease, which may shorten life expectancy.

Prevention

There is no way to prevent development of FA in a person carrying two defective gene copies. Genetic counseling and testing are recommended for prospective parents with a **family** history of FA.

Parental concerns

Coping with the challenges of raising a child with a chronic serious disease is difficult for parents and other family members. Psychological counseling and support groups are invaluable tools to help families meet the challenges and provide the child with needed support.

A child with Friedreich's ataxia is entitled to an Individual Education Plan (IEP) through the Individuals with Disabilities Education Act (IDEA). An IEP team consisting of parents, administrators, teachers, and sometimes the student and outside experts, will collaborate to develop the child's IEP.

Children with FA are considered high-risk for flu and **pneumonia**. The children and family members should receive a flu shot every year, unless there are other health considerations that would indicate that there is a reason not to receive the vaccine. The children should also periodically receive pneumococcal pneumonia shots as recommended by their doctors.

See also Movement disorders.

Resources

BOOKS

Feldman, Eva L. "Hereditary Cerebellar Ataxias and Related Disorders." In *Cecil Textbook of Medicine.* Eds. Russell L. Cecil et al. Philadelphia: W.B. Saunders Company, 2000.

Icon Health Publications. *The Parent's Guide on Friedreich's Ataxia: A Revised and Updated Directory for the Internet Age.* San Diego, CA: Icon Health Publications, 2002.

Rieffenberger, Amanda. *Through the Eyes of a Child.* Available from the author at (605) 882-2343 or at rieff1@home.com, 1996.

"Spinocerebellar Degeneration (Friedreich's Ataxia)." In *Harrison's Principles of Internal Medicine.* Eds. Kurt J. Isselbacher et al. New York: McGraw-Hill, 2001.

ORGANIZATIONS

Friedreich's Ataxia Research Alliance. 2001 Jefferson Davis Hwy, Suite 209, Arlington, VA 22202. (703)413-4468. Fax: (703) 413-4467. Web site: <www.frda.org>.

Muscular Dystrophy Association. 3300 East Sunrise Drive, Tucson, AZ 85718-3208. (520) 529-2000 or (800) 572-1717. Fax: 520-529-5300. Web site: <www.mdausa.org>.

National Ataxia Foundation. 2600 Fernbrook Lane, Suite 119, Minneapolis, MN 55447-4752. (763) 553-0020. Web site: <www.ataxia.org>.

National Organization for Rare Disorders (NORD). P.O. Box 1968, 55 Kenosia Avenue, Danbury, CT 06813-1968. (203) 744-0100 or (800) 999-6673. Fax: (203) 798-2291. Web site: <www.rarediseases.org>.

WEB SITES

Friedreich's Ataxia Fact Sheet. Available online at: <www.ninds.nih.gov/health_and_medical/pubs/friedreich_ataxia.htm>.

Friedreich's Ataxia Parents Group (FAPG). Available online at: <www.fortnet.org/fapg/>.

Judith Sims
Rosalyn Carson-DeWitt, M.D.

Frostbite and frostnip

Definition

Frostbite is damage to the skin and other tissues caused by freezing. Frostnip is a mild form of this cold injury.

Description

Skin exposed to temperatures a little below 32°F (0°C) can take hours to freeze, but very cold skin can freeze in minutes or seconds. Nevertheless, under extreme conditions, even warm skin exposed to subzero temperatures and high wind chill factors can freeze rapidly. Air temperature, wind speed, humidity, and altitude all affect how cold the skin becomes. A strong wind can lower skin temperature considerably by dispersing the thin protective layer of warm air that surrounds the body. Wet clothing readily draws heat away from the skin because water is a potent conductor of heat. The evaporation of moisture on the skin also produces cooling. For these reasons, wet skin or clothing on a windy day can lead to frostbite even if the air temperature is above freezing.

The extent of permanent injury, however, is determined not by how cold the skin and the underlying tissues become but by how long they remain frozen. When skin is exposed to freezing temperatures, three things happen. The skin begins to freeze, causing ice crystal formation, damage to capillaries (the tiny blood vessels that connect the arteries and veins), and other changes that damage and eventually kill cells. Much of this harm occurs because the ice produces pressure changes that force water (crucial for cell survival) out of the cells.

Tissue hypoxia, or oxygen deficiency, occurs next as a survival mechanism in the body kicks in, causing the blood vessels in the hands, feet, and other extremities to narrow in response to cold. Among its many tasks, blood transfers body heat to the skin, which then dissipates the heat into the environment. Blood vessel narrowing is the body's way of protecting vital internal organs at the expense of the extremities by reducing heat flow away from the center of the body. However, blood also carries life-sustaining oxygen to the skin and other tissues, and

narrowed vessels result in oxygen starvation. Narrowing also causes acidosis (an increase in tissue acidity) and increases blood viscosity (thickness). Ultimately, blood stops flowing through the capillaries) and blood clots form in the arterioles and venules (the smallest arteries and veins). Damage also occurs to the endothelial cells that line the blood vessels.

Hypoxia, blood clots, and endothelial damage lead, in turn, to the release of inflammatory mediators. These are substances that act as links in the inflammatory process, which promote further blood vessel damage, hypoxia, and cell destruction. Tissue damage is greatest when skin is exposed to freezing slowly or over a long period of time. More damage can occur when rewarming is slow or the affected area is warmed and refrozen.

Demographics

In North America, frostbite frequently occurs in Alaska, Canada, and the northern states, which have extremely cold winter temperatures. Frostbite, however, can occur almost anywhere, given the right conditions. Though there has been in the early 2000s a substantial decline in the number of frostbite cases in the United States, due to better winter clothing and footwear and greater public understanding of how to avoid cold-weather dangers, these cases are rising among the homeless who do not have adequate clothing or shelter. Frostbite has thus become an urban as well as a rural public health concern. The growing popularity of outdoor winter activities has also expanded the at-risk population.

Children are at a higher risk of experiencing frostbite and frostnip than adults because they experience heat loss from their skin more rapidly. Those children with disorders that affect circulation, such as diabetes, may be even more susceptible to frostbite and frostnip. Children who have had a recent injury, surgery, or blood loss are at risk, as well as teenagers who might be **smoking**, drinking alcohol, or taking beta-blockers for high blood pressure or a heart condition. Also, children who have had a frostbite injury in the past are more prone to having a recurrence in the same location. In addition, children from tropical climates may not be able to withstand cold temperatures as well as their cold-climate counterparts, making them more susceptible to frostbite and frostnip at higher temperatures.

Causes and symptoms

Causes

Skin damage from frostbite and frostnip occurs because of freezing, either by extremely cold weather, wet clothing in cold temperatures, or through chemical exposures, such as dry ice or highly compressed gases. Most children encounter frostbite when they participate in outdoor **sports**, camp in winter, get wet and cannot change their clothing immediately, or do not dress according to the weather conditions. Frostnip and frostbite are associated with ice crystal formation in the tissues.

Symptoms

In frostnip, no tissue destruction occurs and the ice crystals dissolve as soon as the skin is warmed. Frostnip affects areas such as the earlobes, cheeks, nose, fingers, and toes. The skin turns pale, and the person experiences **numbness** or **tingling** in the affected part until warming begins.

Frostbite, by contrast, has a range of severity. Most injuries affect the hands and feet, but about 10 percent of all frostbite cases affect the nose, cheeks, ears, and even the penis. Frostbite is classified by degree of injury (first, second, third, or fourth), or simply divided into two types, superficial (corresponding to first- or second-degree injury) and deep (corresponding to third- or fourth-degree injury). Frostnip is sometimes labeled a first-degree frostbite case.

Once frostbite sets in, the affected part begins to feel cold and, usually, numb. This condition is followed by a feeling of clumsiness. The skin turns white or yellowish. Many patients experience severe **pain** in the affected part during rewarming treatment and an intense throbbing pain that arises two or three days later and can last days or weeks. As the skin begins to thaw during treatment, edema (excess tissue fluid) often accumulates, causing swelling. In frostbite injuries of second-degree or higher, blisters appear. Third-degree cases produce deep, blood-filled blisters and a hard black eschar (scab). Fourth-degree frostbite penetrates below the skin to the muscles, tendons, nerves, and bones. Septicemia or blood poisoning and infection may also be present, as well as the possible need for amputation (the surgical removal of appendages such as fingers, toes, foot, or leg).

When to call the doctor

If a child's clothing has been wet for a long period of time or the child has been exposed to freezing temperatures, shows skin discoloration, and complains of feeling numb, the child should be seen by a doctor. In most cases, the child will be hospitalized to monitor the rewarming process and to do the necessary tests needed to determine the extent of the frostbite. Prolonged exposure to extreme temperatures can also produce hypother-

mia (lowered body temperature), which can be life threatening.

Diagnosis

Initial diagnosis is usually made based on the environmental conditions. Physical examination of the skin reveals that the skin is extremely cold and may have white, red, blue, or black areas on it. The patient may report feeling numb or a tingling sensation.

Frostbite diagnosis may also include conventional radiography (x rays), angiography (x-ray examination of the blood vessels using an injected dye to provide contrast), thermography (use of a heat-sensitive device for measuring blood flow), and other techniques for predicting the course of injury and identifying tissue that requires surgical removal. During the initial treatment period, however, a physician cannot judge how a case may progress. Diagnostic tests only become useful three to five days after rewarming, once the blood vessels have stabilized.

Treatment

Frostnip

Frostnipped fingers are helped by blowing warm air on them or holding them under one's armpits. Other frostnipped areas can be covered with warm hands. The injured areas should never be rubbed.

Frostbite

Emergency medical help should always be summoned whenever frostbite is suspected. While waiting for help to arrive, one should, if possible, remove wet or tight clothing and put on dry, loose clothing or cover with a blanket. Rubbing the area with snow or anything else is dangerous because it can cause tissue damage. The key to prehospital treatment is to avoid partial thawing and refreezing, which releases more inflammatory mediators and makes the injury substantially worse. For this reason, the affected part must be kept away from heat sources such as campfires and car heaters. Experts advise rewarming in the field only when emergency help will take more than two hours to arrive and refreezing can be prevented.

Because the outcome of a frostbite injury cannot be predicted at first, all hospital treatment follows the same routine. Treatment begins by rewarming the affected part for 15 to 30 minutes in water at a temperature of 104–108°F (40–42°C). This rapid rewarming halts ice crystal formation and dilates narrowed blood vessels. Aloe vera (which acts against inflammatory mediators) is applied

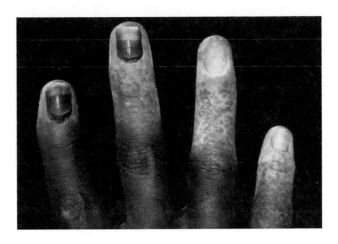

Hand with effects of frostbite. *(Photograph by SIU. National Audubon Society Collection/Photo Researchers, Inc.)*

which hydrotherapy and physical therapy are used to restore the affected part to health. Experts recommend a cautious approach to tissue removal and advise that 22 to 45 days must pass before a decision on amputation can safely be made.

Alternative treatment

Alternative practitioners suggest several kinds of treatment to speed recovery from frostbite after a person leaves the hospital. Bathing the affected part in warm water or using contrast hydrotherapy can help enhance circulation. Contrast hydrotherapy involves a series of hot and cold water applications. A hot compress (as hot as the patient can stand) is applied to the affected area for three minutes followed by an ice-cold compress for 30 seconds. These applications are repeated three times each, ending with the cold compress.

Nutritional therapy to promote tissue growth in damaged areas may also be helpful. Homeopathic and botanical therapies may also assist recovery from frostbite. Homeopathic *Hypericum* (*Hypericum perforatum*) is recommended when nerve endings are affected (especially in the fingers and toes) and *Arnica* (*Arnica montana*) is prescribed for shock. Cayenne pepper (*Capsicum frutescens*) can enhance circulation and relieve pain. Drinking hot ginger (*Zingiber officinale*) tea also aids circulation. Other possible approaches include acupuncture to avoid permanent nerve damage and oxygen therapy.

Prognosis

The rapid rewarming approach to frostbite treatment, pioneered in the 1980s, has proved to be much

to the affected part, which is then splinted, elevated, and wrapped in a dressing. Depending on the extent of injury, blisters may be debrided (cleaned by removing foreign material) or simply covered with aloe vera. A **tetanus** shot and, possibly, penicillin, are used to prevent infection, and the patient is given ibuprofen to combat inflammation. Narcotics are needed in most cases to reduce the excruciating pain that occurs as sensation returns during rewarming. Except when injury is minimal, treatment generally requires a hospital stay of several days, during more effective than older methods in preventing tissue loss and amputation. A study of 56 first-, second-, and third-degree frostbite patients treated with rapid rewarming between 1982 and 1985 found that 68 percent recovered without tissue loss, 25 percent experienced some tissue loss, and 7 percent needed amputation. In a comparison group of 98 patients, treatment using older methods resulted in a tissue loss rate of nearly 35 percent and an amputation rate of nearly 33 percent. Although the comparison group included a higher proportion of second- and third-degree cases, the difference in treatment results was determined to be statistically significant.

The extreme throbbing pain that many frostbite sufferers endure for days or weeks after rewarming is not the only prolonged symptom of frostbite. During the first weeks or months, people often experience tingling, a burning sensation, or a sensation resembling shocks from an electric current. Other possible consequences of frostbite include skin-color changes, nail deformation or loss, joint stiffness and pain, **hyperhidrosis** (excessive sweating), and heightened sensitivity to cold. For everyone, a degree of sensory loss lasting at least four years, and sometimes a lifetime, is inevitable.

Prevention

With the appropriate knowledge and precautions, frostbite can be prevented even in the coldest and most challenging environments. Appropriate clothing and footwear are essential. To prevent heat loss and keep the blood circulating properly, clothing should be worn loosely and in layers. Covering the hands, feet, and head is also crucial for preventing heat loss. Children especially should wear hats that cover their heads and ears, mittens, and coats that are wind and water resistant. Wet clothing and footwear must be removed as quickly as possible and replaced with dry clothing and shoes.

Alcohol and drugs should be avoided because of their harmful effects on judgment and reasoning. Experts also warn against alcohol use and smoking in the cold because of the circulatory changes they produce.

Parental concerns

Parents should pay close attention to weather reports before sending children out to **play** or to take part in long-exposure outdoor activities such as sledding, skiing, and winter camping. Listening to winter driving warnings and road reports is also important before taking trips in the winter or in the mountains.

In addition, parents should keep a close eye on their children when the children play outdoors in winter around lakes, streams, and other water sources. Even older children and teenagers can slip on ice or snow and fall in. The risk of hypothermia and frostbite is too great to ignore. Sometimes, even a child's getting his or her shoes wet and then continuing to play in the cold can produce serious frostbite.

See also X rays.

Resources

BOOKS

Danzl, Daniel F. "Disturbances Due to Cold." In *Conn's Current Therapy*, ed. Robert E. Rakel. Philadelphia: W. B. Saunders Co., 1996.

McCauley, Robert L., et al. "Frostbite and Other Cold-Induced Injuries." In *Wilderness Medicine: Management of Wilderness and Environmental Emergencies*, ed. Paul S. Auerbach. St. Louis: Mosby, 1995.

WEB SITES

Bjerke, H. Scott, and Amit Tevar. "Frostbite." Available online at <www.emedicine.com/med/topic2815.htm> (accessed October 25, 2004).

"Frostbite Fact Sheet." Available online at <www.mckinley.uiuc.edu/handouts/frostbit/frostbit.html> (accessed October 25, 2004).

"Frostbite." *KidsHealth for Parents.* Available online at <www.kidshealth.org/parent/firstaid_safe/ emergencies/frostbite.html> (accessed October 25, 2004).

Janie Franz
Howard Baker

Fructose intolerance *see* **Hereditary fructose intolerance**

Fugue disorder *see* **Dissociative disorders**

Fused fingers and toes *see* **Polydactyly and syndactyly**

Galactosemia

Definition

Galactosemia is an inherited disease in which the body is unable to metabolize the simple sugar galactose, which is found primarily in dairy products but is also produced by the body. If left unaddressed, galactose can increase to toxic levels in the body and may lead to damage of the liver, central nervous system, and various other body systems.

Description

Galactosemia is a rare but potentially life-threatening disease resulting from the body's inability to metabolize galactose. Galactose makes up half of lactose, the sugar that is found in milk. Persons with galactosemia either have very low levels of or are entirely lack the enzyme that assists the body in breaking down galactose. This enzyme is called galactose-1-phosphate uridyl transferase (GALT). The GALT enzyme enables the body to break down galactose into glucose for energy. The severity of the disease may vary from person to person, because some individuals with galactosemia have higher levels of this enzyme than do others.

The two main types of galactosemia are called classic and Duarte variant. Individuals with the classic type of galactosemia lack the enzyme activity necessary to metabolize galactose. Individuals with the Duarte variant have approximately 5–20 percent of the enzyme activity necessary to metabolize this sugar and often do not have signs or symptoms of galactosemia.

Transmission

Galactosemia is an hereditary disease. In order to understand this disorder, it is necessary to have a very basic knowledge of genetics. Genes, the basic components of hereditary material, contain the "blueprint" that directs the development and functioning of every cell and tissue in the human body. Genes are situated on larger structures called chromosomes that contain several thousand genes each. Genes and chromosomes exist in pairs. Every cell in the body has 23 pairs of chromosomes containing two copies of every gene. Human beings receive one copy of every gene from their mother, and another copy from their father. Most of the time, genes function normally. However, in some cases, a change or mutation in a gene can cause it to not function. These mutations can cause inherited or genetic disorders.

In galactosemia, the gene mutation which occurs is inherited in what is known as an autosomal recessive pattern. This means that a non-working copy of the gene must be inherited from both parents for a child to be affected with the disease. The parents of children are called "carriers" of the disorder, because though they themselves do not have galactosemia, they may have children who do.

Unfortunately, as of 2004, parents had no way of knowing if they carry the mutated gene that causes galactosemia until they have a child diagnosed with the disease. The chance that two parents each of whom has the defective gene will produce a child with a recessive disorder is one in four or 25 percent with each pregnancy. The chances that their child will be a carrier, like themselves, is one in two, or 50 percent, with each pregnancy.

Demographics

Galactosemia is an inherited disorder that occurs in approximately one out of 30,000 live births. The incidence for the Duarte variant type of galactosemia is estimated to be one in 16,000 live births. Although galactosemia occurs in all ethnic groups worldwide, some mutations cause a less severe type of disease and are more commonly seen in specific ethnic groups, such as African-Americans. In Japan, classic galactosemia is not diagnosed as frequently as it is in Caucasian populations in the United States.

Causes and symptoms

Galactosemia is an inherited disorder. People with the disease are unable to fully break down galactose. If an infant with galactosemia is given milk, byproducts of galactose will build up in the baby's body, causing damage to the liver, kidneys, brain, and eyes. Characteristically, a newborn with galactosemia who is fed milk products will have **jaundice**, **vomiting**, lethargy, irritability, and convulsions. Continued feeding of milk products to the infant will lead to cirrhosis, cataracts, kidney failure, and **mental retardation**.

When to call the doctor

Parents should notify their doctor if their child displays any of the symptoms of galactosemia. Couples should consult their physician if there is a **family** history of galactosemia, and they are considering having a child.

Diagnosis

As of late 2004, all 50 states had mandatory screening of newborns for galactosemia. If parents receive a call from a healthcare provider saying the screening test indicates possible galactosemia, they should promptly stop milk products and have a blood test done for galactosemia through their doctor. The physician may also perform enzyme studies on or look for the presence of "reducing substances" in the child's urine, look for ketones in the urine, and measure enzyme activity in the red blood cells.

Treatment

Galactosemia is treated by removing foods that contain galactose from the diet. Foods containing lactose and, therefore, galactose should be avoided. Because milk and milk products are the most common food source of galactose, persons with galactosemia should avoid ingesting these foods. It is recommended that persons with galactosemia avoid eating foods with galactose throughout their entire lives.

Nutritional concerns

The goal of dietary treatment is to minimize galactose intake. It is impossible to have a galactose-free diet. However, all persons with galactosemia should limit galactose intake as much as possible. The galactose-1-phosphate levels of the individual will establish the level of dietary restriction necessary. Infants can be fed soy, meat-based, or other lactose-free formulas. Abstinence from milk and milk products must continue throughout

---

KEY TERMS

Galactose—One of the two simple sugars (glucose is the other one) that makes up the protein, lactose, found in milk. Galactose can be toxic in high levels.

Recessive trait—An inherited trait or characteristic that is outwardly obvious only when two copies of the gene for that trait are present.

---

life. Parents need to find some of the many listings available that identify the galactose content in foods. Since the primary source of calcium is usually milk or milk-based foods, calcium must be supplemented. Parents of a child with galactosemia should note that lactose is often used as filler in medicines. This very frequently is not listed on the package. Parents should always check with the pharmacist before administering any new medications.

Prognosis

Approximately 75 percent of the babies with galactosemia who are not diagnosed and treated die within the first two weeks of life. By contrast, if an early diagnosis is made and if milk products are strictly avoided, most children lead a relatively normal life. With appropriate treatment, liver and kidney problems do not develop, and early mental development progresses in a normal manner. However, even with proper treatment, children with galactosemia often have a lower **intelligence** quotient (IQ) than their siblings, and they frequently have speech problems. Girls often have ovaries that do not function, and only a few are able to conceive naturally. Boys, however, have normal testicular function.

Prevention

Since galactosemia is a recessive genetic disease, it is usually first detected on a newborn screening test, as most people are not aware that they are carriers of a gene mutation causing the disease. If there is a family history of galactosemia, genetic counseling is recommended for prospective parents as they make decisions regarding pregnancy and prenatal testing. Once one child in a family is diagnosed with galactosemia, it is recommended that other members of the family receive genetic counseling as well.

Parental concerns

One of the most important things parents of a child with galactosemia can do is educate themselves thoroughly on an appropriate diet. All other caregivers or teachers involved with the child need to be notified of the child's dietary restrictions, and the potential consequences if they are not maintained.

Resources

PERIODICALS

Bosch, Annet M., et al. "Living with Classical Galactosemia: Health-Related Quality of Life Consequences." *Pediatrics* 113 (May 2004): 5.

Weese, S. Jean. "Galactose Content of Baby Food Meats: Considerations for Infants with Galactosemia." *Journal of the American Dietetic Association* (March 2003).

ORGANIZATIONS

National Newborn Screening and Genetics Resource Center. 1912 W. Anderson Lane, Suite 210, Austin, TX 78757. Web site: <http://genes-r-us.uthscsa.edu>.

"Parents of Galactosemic Children Inc." 885 Del Sol St., Sparks, NV 89436. Web site: <www.galactosemia.org>.

WEB SITES

"Galactosemia." *MedlinePlus*, January 2004. Available online at <www.nlm.nih.gov/medlineplus/ency/article/000366.htm> (accessed January 6, 2005).

"Galactosemia: An Overview." *Adult Metabolic Transition Project.* Available online at <http://depts.washington.edu/transmet/gal.html> (accessed January 6, 2005).

Deanna M. Swartout-Corbeil, RN

Gangs

Definition

Youth gangs are variously defined in the social science and criminal justice literature. They are commonly understood to be a loosely-organized association of socially excluded, alienated, or bigoted individuals acting together within a fluid structure with informal leadership. Youth gangs are bound by a common ethnicity, race, social class, or other determinant and employ distinctive symbols, including style and color of dress, hand signs, **tattoos**, and graffiti. Loyal gang members follow a gang-defined system of rules, rituals, and codes of behavior. Gangs serve some individuals as a substitute **family** structure. Membership imparts a sense of empowerment as members act together to defend territory and provide mutual protection. Youth gangs typically engage in delinquent, criminal, and violent activities, often for financial gain.

Description

Gangs have been a part of U.S. culture since the early 19th century. Immigrant youth organized themselves into street gangs, often as a means of economic survival. Social scientists have been studying and reporting on gang membership and attributes since early in the 20th century. Gangs have been seen as a normal adolescent peer activity that occurs "within a continuum of behaviors, from conventional to wild," as suggested by the classic 1927 research of Frederic Thrasher, a social scientist who studied 1,313 Chicago gangs. A more recent view by the U.S. Department of Justice in 1998 holds that "a group must be involved in a pattern of criminal acts to be considered a youth gang." This criterion is also used by the Federal Bureau of Investigation who contend that it is "participation in criminal activity" that separates a community group or social club from a gang.

Gangs are more prevalent in neighborhoods where the community network is weak, with few ties among individual residents or between residents and conventional community institutions. Among adolescent males, the best predictor of gang membership is the absence of a positive male role model. Most girls who participate in gang activity have run away from home at least once due to family problems including the drug **addiction** and/or arrest of a parent.

Gang violence has reached a crisis level in the United States. A 1998 study revealed that gang members possess significantly more guns than other at-risk youth. The ready availability of such deadly weapons has led to an increase in violence such as drive-by shootings and a loss of life among gang members and others caught in the crossfire. Research reported in 1991 found that gang access to firearms "led to lethal violence in circumstances that might otherwise have been settled with less-than lethal means." Gang culture increasingly involves its youth membership in the use of weapons, drugs, and criminal activity.

Risk factors

According to Lonnie Jackson, author of the book *Gangbusters: Strategies for Prevention and Intervention*, many factors contribute to the likelihood of youth gang involvement. Some of the factors he cites include:

- frequent exposure to crime and violence during formative years
- few positive role models, particularly of their own ethnicity
- unstable family life, with little parental control
- lack of economic opportunities conducive to lawful self-sufficiency
- inadequate constructive social and recreational activities for youths
- hopelessness engendered by minimal employment opportunity
- inadequate skills, education, or employment qualifications
- lure of power and money, particularly through the drug trade
- cultural environment that highly values immediate gratification
- unmet needs for **safety**, a sense of belonging, and secure emotional relationships
- low **self-esteem** and feelings of insignificance and powerlessness

Demographics

"Gang activity is notably prevalent in the biggest cities (over 100,000 population) in the United States," according to research reported by the National Youth Gang Center. Between 1996 and 2001, more than 90 percent of the largest U.S. cities reported gang activity. However, between 1998 and 1999, the research shows an increase in gang membership by 27 percent in suburban areas and by 29 percent in rural areas. Gang membership is no longer limited to ethnic minorities in America's inner cities, but is found in all ethnic groups, economic classes, and in rural, urban, and suburban settings.

Researchers studying gang life focused first on the behavior of male gangs. Later research, however, has revealed a growing number of girl gangs, with estimates as high as 10 percent of all youth gangs. However, the incidence of female gangs may be much higher than reports indicate. Female gang activity is less violent than that of their male counterparts and is underreported by law enforcement agencies.

Gang membership remains predominantly the province of male adolescents and young adults from 12 to 24 years of age. When young women become involved in gangs, it is usually through relationships with boyfriends or brothers, according to research by A. Campbell reviewed in the *Journal of Criminal Justice*. Girl gang members experience more long-term, harmful effects from gang membership than their male counterparts, and some research finds that "gang membership itself opened up young women to additional victimization risk."

The proportion of gang members of particular race or ethnicity reflects the demographics of the community where they live. "Nearly half (49 percent) of all gang members are Hispanic/Latino, 34 percent are African American/black, 10 percent are Caucasian/white, 6 percent are Asian, and the remainder are of some other race/ethnicity," according to respondents to the 2001 National Youth Gang Survey. The Survey estimated that "youth gangs were active in over 2,300 cities with populations over 2,500 in 2002."

Causes

Research studies throughout the 1980s and 1990s, during a period of growing gang involvement among North American youth, cite complex social problems as the root cause of the persistence and proliferation of youth gangs. Dysfunctional families, often with an absent father, low socio-economic circumstances, poor educational opportunities, unemployment, indigence, deteriorated neighborhoods with high crime rates, racism, and limited opportunities for bringing about a change in circumstances, are among the serious factors that put youth at high risk for gang involvement.

Though there is no conclusive evidence, many critics of popular media cite youth exposure to violent films and song lyrics, particularly rap music, as a negative influence glamorizing gang life and encouraging at-risk youth to join gangs or to participate in gang-related crime as a means of gaining a sense of belonging and empowerment.

When to intervene

Early intervention is the most effective means of diverting at-risk youth into pro-social activities and associations before they seek affiliation with youth gangs. Children as young as eight years old are attracted by the lure of gang membership. Parents, teachers, and concerned others should seek the help of culturally-sensitive and well-trained counselors who can intervene with information and alternatives that address unmet needs for safety, and provide a feeling of belonging, and a sense of power and purpose.

Indicators

Concerned and attentive parents and school counselors should be on the alert for indications of possible gang membership in at-risk youth. Some indicators are poor academic achievement and frequent **truancy**, anti-social and delinquent behaviors, adoption of gang dress in style and color, appearance of tattoos, use of hand signals, and other gang-related signs, preference for music with gang themes, and the presence of gang activity in the community.

Treatment

Effective treatment must be culturally sensitive, diverse, and experienced as relevant to the lives of the gang-involved youth. Treatment plans must address the myriad and serious underlying personal and social problems that lead to gang involvement. Young people need information about alternatives to street gangs that can realistically meet their needs in pro-social ways. Treatment for drug addiction, sexual abuse, and other physical and emotional traumas are a prerequisite to providing lasting help. Mental health treatment must address delayed stress issues from repeated exposure to trauma, violence, and economic hardship. Education and training in skills of nonviolent conflict resolution are also important components of a successful treatment plan. Counselors must be skilled, knowledgeable, and trustworthy and able to help the gang-involved youth to examine choices in ways that encourage clear thinking and provide a broader view of potential and possibilities outside gang life.

Prognosis

Early intervention with at-risk youth to relieve some of the personal and environmental stressors that lead to gang involvement has the best prognosis. Youth who have already joined a gang usually also have well-developed manipulative skills. They exhibit a fierce loyalty to other gang members and are highly resistant to change, even after arrest and detention for gang-related crimes.

Prevention

Community intervention at the grassroots, neighborhood level, can be an effective first step in a multi-faceted approach to prevention of gang involvement. Eliminating underlying social problems that lead to development of youth gangs and strengthening community ties can reduce the influence of gangs and deter gang crime that thrives when neighborhoods fail to work together. Parental involvement with teachers can head off many problems of truancy, and community education on gang culture will help parents and teachers to identify early signs of gang involvement. Strong after-school programs that assist working parents meet children's needs

for supervision and provide structured, pro-social activities to young children may reduce attraction to gang-related activities. Former gang members who are willing to speak about the negative side of gang life, and adults who are willing to serve as mentors and tutors can provide critical positive role models for at-risk youth, an indispensable component to a successful prevention strategy. Job skills training and meaningful employment opportunities will divert many youth from the path to gang membership.

Parental concerns

The prevalence of youth gangs throughout the United States, and the increase in violence associated with gang membership are serious issues of concern for any parent. Delinquent and antisocial behaviors in young children, particularly those who live in environments where poverty, unemployment, and drug addiction are common, are early danger signs. Seeking help from concerned and qualified school counselors, church, and community leaders can alleviate many parental concerns and provide opportunity for early intervention.

Resources

BOOKS

Branch, Curtis W. *Clinical Interventions with Gang Adolescents and Their Families.* Boulder: Westview Press., 1997.

Jackson, Lonnie *Gangbusters: Strategies for Prevention and Intervention.* Lanham, Maryland: American Correctional Association, 1998.

Wolff, Lisa *Gangs.* San Diego: Lucent Books, Inc., 2000.

PERIODICALS

Decker, Scott H. and G. David Curry. "Gangs, gang homicides, and gang loyalty: Organized crimes or disorganized criminals." *Journal of Criminal Justice* 30, no. 4 (July–August 2002): 343-352. Science Direct.

St. Cyr, Jenna L. and Scott H. Decker. "Girls, guys, and gangs: Convergence or divergence in the gendered construction of gangs and groups." *Journal of Criminal Justice* 31, no. 5 (September–October 2003): 423-433. Science Direct.

Wang, Alvin Y. "Pride and prejudice in high school gang members." *Adolescence* 29 no. 114 (Summer 1994): 279. EBSCO.

ORGANIZATIONS

Institute for Intergovernmental Research. *National Youth Gang Center.* Post Office Box 12729, Tallahassee, FL 32317; Phone:(850) 385-0600. <www.iir.com/nygc/maininfo.htm>

WEB SITES

"Chicago officials innovative in battling street gang life." *Los Angeles Daily News.* Belleville News-Democrat and wire service sources. [cited October 11, 2004]. <www.belleville.com>.

"Frequently Asked Questions Regarding Gangs." National Youth Gang Center. *Institute for Intergovernmental Research.* [Cited October 11, 2004]. <www.iir.com/nygc/faq.htm>.

"Gangs Fact Sheet." *National Youth Violence Prevention Resource Center.* [cited October 11, 2004] <www.safeyouth.org/scripts/facts/gangs.asp>.

Hagedorn, John. "Discussion of Gang Definitions." *Crime & Justice: A Review of Research.*24. (1998): 366-368. [cited September 27, 2004]. <gangresearch.net/GangResearch/Seminars/definitions/CJdef.html>.

Clare Hanrahan

Gastroenteritis

Definition

Gastroenteritis is an inflammation of the digestive tract, particularly the stomach, and large and small intestines. Viral and bacterial gastroenteritis are intestinal infections associated with symptoms of **diarrhea**, abdominal cramps, **nausea**, and **vomiting**.

Description

Gastroenteritis is an uncomfortable and inconvenient ailment, but is rarely life-threatening in the United States and other developed nations. Viral gastroenteritis is frequently referred to as the stomach or intestinal flu, although the **influenza** virus is not associated with this illness.

Demographics

Viral gastroenteritis is one of the most common acute (sudden-onset) illnesses in the United States, with millions of cases reported annually. Each year, an estimated 220,000 children younger than age five are hospitalized with gastroenteritis symptoms. Of these children, 300 die as a result of severe diarrhea and **dehydration**. In developing nations, diarrheal illnesses are a major source of mortality.

Causes and symptoms

Causes

Gastroenteritis is caused by the ingestion of viruses, certain bacteria, or parasites. Food that has spoiled may also cause illness. Young children may develop signs and symptoms of gastroenteritis as a reaction to a new food.

VIRAL INFECTION Viral infection is the most common cause of gastroenteritis. Viral gastroenteritis is highly contagious and can be spread through close contact with an infected person. Exposure also can occur through the fecal-oral route, such as by consuming foods or beverages contaminated by fecal material related to poor sanitation or poor hygiene, or by touching contaminated surfaces and then touching the mouth and ingesting the germs. The four types of viruses that cause most viral gastroenteritis include rotavirus, adenovirus, calicivirus, and astrovirus.

Typically, children ages three to 15 months are more vulnerable to rotaviruses, the most significant cause of acute watery diarrhea. Outbreaks of diarrhea caused by rotaviruses are common during the winter and early spring months, especially in child care centers. Symptoms in children last for three to eight days, and occur one to two days after exposure to the virus. Worldwide, rotaviruses are estimated to cause 800,000 deaths annually in children under five years of age. For this reason, much research has gone into developing a vaccine to protect children from this virus. Adults can be infected with rotaviruses, but these infections typically have minimal or no symptoms.

Children under age two are more susceptible to adenovirus serotypes 40 and 41. Vomiting and diarrhea symptoms occur about one week after exposure to the virus.

Caliciviruses cause infection in people of all ages. This family of viruses includes the noroviruses (such as the Norwalk virus) and the sapoviruses (such as the sapporo virus). Caliciviruses are transmitted from person-to-person contact, as well as through contaminated water or food. These viruses are the most likely to produce vomiting as a major symptom. Muscle aches also are common symptoms. The symptoms usually appear within one to three days after exposure to the virus.

Astrovirus primarily infects infants, young children, and the elderly. This virus is most active during the winter months. Symptoms of vomiting and diarrhea appear within one to three days after exposure to the virus.

BACTERIAL AND PARASITIC INFECTIONS Bacterial gastroenteritis is frequently a result of poor sanitation, the lack of safe drinking water, or contaminated food (conditions common in developing nations). Natural or man-made disasters can worsen underlying problems in sanitation and food safety.

In developed nations, including the United States, bacterial gastroenteritis may result from contaminated water supplies, improperly processed or preserved foods, or person-to-person contact in places such as child-care centers. The modern food production system potentially exposes millions of people to disease-causing bacteria through its intensive production and distribution methods. Common types of bacterial gastroenteritis can be linked to *Salmonella* and *Campylobacter bacteria*. However, *Escherichia coli (E. coli)* 0157:H7 and *Listeria monocytogenes*, bacterial causes of food borne illnesses, have caused increased concern in developed nations.

Cholera and *Shigella* remain two diseases of great concern in developing countries, and research to develop long-term vaccines against them is underway. *Shigella* bacteria are dangerous because they attack the intestinal wall and cause bleeding ulcers.

Parasitic infections that cause gastroenteritis are most commonly caused by *Giardia*, which is easily spread through contaminated water and human contact. *Cryptosporidium* is another common parasitic organism that causes the symptoms of gastroenteritis.

Symptoms

Gastroenteritis symptoms include **nausea and vomiting**, watery diarrhea, and abdominal **pain** and cramps. These symptoms are sometimes accompanied by bloating, low **fever**, chills, **headache**, and overall tiredness or weakness. Gastroenteritis symptoms typically last two to three days, but some viruses may last up to a week.

Infants, young children, the elderly, and anyone with an underlying disease are more vulnerable to complications of gastroenteritis. The greatest danger presented by gastroenteritis is dehydration. The loss of fluids through diarrhea and vomiting can upset the body's electrolyte balance, leading to potentially life-threatening problems such as heart beat abnormalities (arrhythmia). The risk of dehydration increases as symptoms become prolonged. Untreated, severe dehydration can be life threatening. Dehydration should be suspected if symptoms of a dry mouth, increased or excessive thirst, or decreased urination are experienced.

When to call the doctor

If symptoms do not resolve within one week, an infection or disorder more serious than gastroenteritis may be involved. Prompt medical attention is required if the child has any of these symptoms:

- a high fever of 102°F (38.9°C) or above
- blood or mucus in the diarrhea
- blood in the vomit
- bloody stools or black stools
- confusion
- severe abdominal pain or swelling
- inability to keep liquids down

If a child has the following symptoms, the parent should contact the child's pediatrician:

- diarrhea or vomiting that wakes the child during the night
- persistent or severe diarrhea or vomiting
- dehydration symptoms, including dry mouth, increased or excessive thirst, few or no tears when crying, decreased urination, dark yellow urine, irritability, low energy, lightheadedness or fainting, severe weakness, and sunken abdomen, eyes, and cheeks
- no improvement in symptoms after 36 hours

Diagnosis

A usual bout of gastroenteritis should not require a visit to the doctor. However, medical treatment is essential if symptoms worsen or if the child has any symptoms of dehydration.

A physician makes the diagnosis of gastroenteritis based on the presence of symptoms and after performing a medical examination. Unless there is an outbreak affecting several people or complications are encountered in a particular case, identifying the specific cause of the illness is not a priority. However, if identification of the infectious agent is required, a stool sample will be collected and analyzed for the presence of rotavirus, disease-causing (pathogenic) bacteria, or parasites.

When symptoms continue even after treatment or to rule out the presence of other illnesses with similar symptoms, the diagnostic evaluation may include blood tests, a hydrogen breath test, or an x ray of the bowel, called a barium enema. Endoscopic tests such as a colonoscopy or sigmoidoscopy may be performed. An endoscopic test is an internal examination of the colon using a flexible instrument (sigmoidoscope or colonoscope) inserted through the anus. When symptoms persist, a nutritional **assessment**, performed by a registered dietitian, may be included in the child's diagnostic evaluation.

Treatment

Gastroenteritis is a self-limiting illness that will resolve by itself. **Acetaminophen** (such as Tylenol) or ibuprofen (such as Advil or Motrin) should be used sparingly for relief of discomfort. Parents should ask the child's doctor for specific guidelines. Should pathogenic bacteria or parasites be identified in the patient's stool sample, medications such as **antibiotics** will be prescribed. Over-the-counter antidiarrheal medications such as Imodium should not be given to the child unless advised by the child's doctor, as these drugs may make it more difficult for the child's body to eliminate the virus.

An adequate intake of liquids and oral rehydrating solutions may be enough to treat mild dehydration. More severe dehydration requires medical treatment with intravenous (IV) fluids and may require **hospitalization**. IV therapy can be followed with oral rehydration as the patient's condition improves. Once normal hydration is achieved and symptoms have cleared, the patient can resume a regular diet.

Nutritional concerns

It is important for the child to stay hydrated and nourished during a bout of gastroenteritis. Formula feeding and breastfeeding should continue as normal. If dehydration is absent, drinking generous amounts of fluids, such as water or juice, is adequate. **Caffeine** should be avoided since it increases urine output and can contribute to or worsen dehydration. Dairy products, sugary beverages and foods, highly seasoned foods, and fatty or fried foods should be avoided until symptoms have cleared.

When diarrhea and vomiting symptoms have subsided, plain foods can be given. The traditional BRAT diet—bananas, rice, applesauce, and toast—is tolerated by the tender gastrointestinal system. Other foods can be gradually reintroduced into the diet once the child is symptom-free.

Minimal to moderate dehydration can be treated by giving the child generous amounts of fluids, including water, clear liquids, and oral rehydrating solutions containing glucose and electrolytes. Oral rehydrating solutions—including brands such as Pedialyte, Infalyte, Ceralyte, and Oralyte—are available at most grocery and drug stores. They are essential for replacing fluids, **minerals**, and salts lost from diarrhea or vomiting, and should be given when diarrhea or vomiting first occur.

Small sips of water, clear liquids, or ice chips are usually tolerated better than a large glass of liquid given all at once.

If the water supply is thought to be contaminated because of a recent storm or other reason, the water should be boiled or bottled water should be given.

The Centers for Disease Control and Prevention (CDC) recommends that families with infants and young children keep a supply of oral rehydration solution (two bottles or packages) at home at all times. However, it is important to make sure that the product has not expired before giving it to the child. Parents and caregivers should follow usage directions on the package.

Oral rehydrating solutions are formulated based on physiological properties. Fluids that are not based on these properties—such as cola, apple juice, broth, and sports beverages—are not recommended to treat dehydration.

Alternative treatment

Alternative and complementary therapies include approaches that are considered to be outside the mainstream of traditional health care. Symptoms of uncomplicated gastroenteritis can be relieved with adjustments in diet and homeopathy.

Probiotics, bacteria that are beneficial to a person's health, are recommended during the recovery phase of gastroenteritis. Specifically, live cultures of *Lactobacillus acidophilus* are said to be effective in soothing the digestive tract and returning the intestinal flora to normal. *L. acidophilus* is found in live-culture yogurt, as well as in capsule or powder form at health food stores. The use of probiotics has some support in the medical literature. Castor oil packs applied to the abdomen can reduce inflammation and also lessen spasms or discomfort.

Before using any alternative remedy, it is important for the parent/caregiver and child to learn about the therapy, its safety and effectiveness, and potential side effects. Although some remedies are beneficial, others may be harmful to certain patients. Dietary supplements should not be used as a substitute for medical therapies prescribed by a doctor. Parents should discuss these alternative treatments with the child's doctor to determine the techniques and remedies that may be beneficial for the child.

Prognosis

For most people, gastroenteritis is not a serious illness. It typically resolves within two to three days and there are usually no long-term effects. If dehydration occurs, recovery is extended by a few days. Gastroenteritis is not an anatomical or structural defect, nor is it an identifiable physical or chemical disorder.

KEY TERMS

Barium enema—An x ray of the bowel using a liquid called barium to enhance the image of the bowel. This test is also called a lower GI (gastrointestinal) series.

Colonoscopy—An examination of the lining of the colon performed with a colonoscope.

Constipation—Difficult bowel movements caused by the infrequent production of hard stools.

Defecation—The act of having a bowel movement or the passage of feces through the anus.

Dehydration—An excessive loss of water from the body. It may follow vomiting, prolonged diarrhea, or excessive sweating.

Diarrhea—A loose, watery stool.

Electrolytes—Salts and minerals that produce electrically charged particles (ions) in body fluids. Common human electrolytes are sodium chloride, potassium, calcium, and sodium bicarbonate. Electrolytes control the fluid balance of the body and are important in muscle contraction, energy generation, and almost all major biochemical reactions in the body.

Endoscopy—Visual examination of an organ or body cavity using an endoscope, a thin, tubular instrument containing a camera and light source. Many endoscopes also allow the retrieval of a small sample (biopsy) of the area being examined, in order to more closely view the tissue under a microscope.

Feces—The solid waste, also called stool, that is left after food is digested. Feces form in the intestines and pass out of the body through the anus.

Gastroenterologist—A physician who specializes in diseases of the digestive system.

Glucose—A simple sugar that serves as the body's main source of energy.

Hydrogen breath test—A test used to determine if a person is lactose intolerant or if abnormal bacteria are present in the colon.

Influenza—An infectious disease caused by a virus that affects the respiratory system, causing fever, congestion, muscle aches, and headaches.

Intravenous (IV) therapy—Administration of fluids or medications through a vein, usually in the hand or arm.

Lactose—A sugar found in milk and milk products.

Microflora—The bacterial population in the intestine.

Pathogenic bacteria—Bacteria that produce illness.

Probiotics—Bacteria that are beneficial to a person's health, either through protecting the body against pathogenic bacteria or assisting in recovery from an illness.

Sigmoidoscopy—A procedure in which a thin, flexible, lighted instrument, called a sigmoidoscope, is used to visually examine the lower part of the large intestine. Colonoscopy examines the entire large intestine using the same techniques.

Prevention

A few steps can be taken to avoid gastroenteritis. Thorough hand washing is the most effective way to prevent the fecal-oral transmission of certain viruses, especially rotaviruses. People should wash their hands frequently, especially after using the bathroom and before eating. Child-care providers and caregivers should wash their hands after diapering a child and before preparing, serving, or eating, food. The child's hands also should be washed after every diaper change. Separate towels or disposable paper towels should be used to dry hands. Clean bathroom surfaces, disinfected **toys**, and prompt washing of soiled clothes in hot water also help prevent the spread of infectious germs.

Ensuring that food is prepared safely well-cooked and unspoiled can prevent bacterial gastroenteritis, but may not be effective against viral gastroenteritis. All kitchen utensils, counters, or cutting boards that come in contact with raw meat, especially poultry, should be washed with hot water and a chlorine bleach-based cleaner to prevent the spread of harmful bacteria. Meats should be refrigerated as soon as possible after bringing them home from the grocery store, and cooked leftovers should be refrigerated as soon as possible after a meal to prevent spoilage.

Consuming contaminated food or water can cause gastroenteritis when traveling to other countries. To reduce the risk, travelers should use bottled water for drinking and brushing teeth, and avoid ice (it may be made with contaminated water) and raw foods, including peeled fruit, raw vegetables, and salads.

Research is underway involving vaccines that will decrease the risk of rotavirus infection, especially among infants and young children.

Parental concerns

Parents should reinforce with the child that gastroenteritis is not a serious condition and that symptoms usually subside in a few days. It is most important to prevent dehydration by following the recommendations listed previously. Parents should assure that the child gets adequate rest; the child should be kept home from school or **day care** until the symptoms have cleared. The child may be contagious before the onset of diarrhea and a few days after the diarrhea has ended. To prevent the spread of infection among family members, soiled clothing or bedding should be washed in hot water immediately, hands must be washed frequently, there should be no sharing of utensils or cups used by the child, and toys and bathroom surfaces should be cleaned with a chlorine-based cleaner.

See also Food poisoning.

Resources

PERIODICALS

DeWit, Matty A.S., et. al. "Risk Factors for Nororvirus, Sappporo-like Virus, and Group A Rotavirus Gastroenteritis." *Emerging Infectious Diseases* 9, no. 12 (December, 2003): 1563–70. Available online at: <www.cdc.gov/eid>.

ORGANIZATIONS

American College of Gastroenterology (ACG). P.O. Box 3099, Alexandria, VA 22302. (703) 820-7400. Web site: <www.acg.gi.org/patientinfo>.

American Gastroenterological Association. 4930 Del Ray Ave., Bethesda, MD 20814. (301) 654-2055. Patient Information Resources. Web site: <www.gastro.org/generalPublic.html>.

Centers for Disease Control and Prevention. 1600 Clifton Rd., Atlanta, GA 30333. (800) 311-3435 or (404) 639-3534. Web site: <www.cdc.gov>.

National Institute of Diabetes and Digestive and Kidney Diseases (NIDDK). 2 Information Way, Bethesda, MD 20892-3570. (800) 891- 5389. Web site: <www.niddk.nih.gov>.

WEB SITES

"Gastroenteritis." September 24, 2003. *Mayo Clinic.* Available online at: <www.mayoclinic.com/invoke.cfm?id=DS00085>.

"Gastrointestinal Infections and Diarrhea." *KidsHealth.* Nemours Foundation, February 2002. Available online at: <www.kidshealth.org/PageManager.jsp?dn=KidsHealth&lic=1&os=107&cat_id=13 7&article_id=22887>.

"Viral Gastroenteritis." [cited August 20, 2001]. *Centers for Disease Control.* Available online at: <www.cdc.gov/ncidod/dvrd/revb/gastro/faq.htm>.

Julia Barrett
Angela M. Costello

Gastroesophageal reflux disease

Definition

Gastroesophageal reflux disease (GERD) is a gastric disorder which causes stomach acids to back up into the esophagus, the tube leading from the mouth to the stomach. This action causes **pain**, which is often called heartburn. GERD can disrupt **sleep** and make eating difficult. It can lead to respiratory infections, ulcers, and even **cancer**.

Description

The reflux action of gastroesophageal reflux disease is a function of the weakening of the lower esophageal sphincter (LES). The LES is a muscle located at the bottom of the esophagus and acts as a doorkeeper to the stomach. When food is eaten, it passes through the esophagus and the LES and into the stomach. The LES closes after food enters the stomach and usually keeps the stomach contents from returning up the esophagus.

In an infant, the LES may not be well formed, which causes the baby to spit up or vomit. In an older child or adolescent, the LES weakens and acids from the stomach come into the esophagus, causing the characteristic burning in the middle of the chest, known as heartburn.

Everyone has experienced this reflux occasionally, and it is not a concern. It is when the reflux occurs often that the condition should be evaluated. Infants and children who do not vomit or complain of heartburn or stomachache may have this condition. When the stomach contents moves into the esophagus, there is the possibility that this material will be aspirated into the windpipe, which can cause **asthma**, **pneumonia**, and possibly suffocation or sudden death. GERD was thought to be implicated in **sudden infant death syndrome** (SIDS); however, subsequent studies concluded it was not.

Some children and adults have few episodes of heartburn over their lifetimes, but they have frequent bouts of ear infection, **sinusitis**, **bronchitis**, and even asthma. Some children and adults only experience a vague indigestion. They come to the doctor because they are having trouble eating. They feel that there is something in their throats or that their food keeps getting stuck when they eat. This may be a serious condition called dysphagia, which develops from long-term GERD. The stricture of the esophagus is caused by a thickening of the lining of the esophagus in response to acids from the stomach. Sometimes, when swallowing hurts, the condition is called odynophagia. This type of GERD is often referred to as silent reflux.

Constant irritation by stomach acids in the esophagus can cause a condition called esophagitis, in which the esophagus becomes red and irritated. Because the lining of the esophagus is thinner and not as acid-proof as the stomach or the intestines, undiagnosed GERD over many years can cause ulcers along the esophagus. These can bleed and can, in turn, result in anemia. Scar tissue can also build up.

Sometimes, the body tries to protect the esophagus by growing a thicker lining, made up of cells like those in the stomach and intestine. This is known as Barrett's esophagus and is a pre-cancerous condition that usually leads to cancer of the esophagus.

Demographics

One-third of the adult population (95 million) have GERD symptoms once a month, while 15 million have symptoms every day. Though half of people who have GERD are between the ages of 45 and 64, infants, children, and teenagers also have GERD.

GERD affects 50 percent of all healthy, full-term newborns. It is the primary reason for most **vomiting** in infants during the first four months, at which time the vomiting should stop. Less than 5 percent of infants with GERD continue the problem into adulthood. However, this figure may be revised upward as more and more young children experience GERD symptoms and are diagnosed with this condition.

Some children seem to be more at risk for having GERD than others, particularly children who have hiatal **hernia**, **cystic fibrosis**, neurological impairment or delay, or an immature esophagus and LES.

Causes and symptoms

Causes

GERD is caused by a weakened or immature LES. It can also be caused by a hiatal hernia that traps the sto-

mach contents. Having too much acid in the stomach can also weaken the LES.

Heredity plays a small part in whether a child has GERD. GERD seems to be more prone to occur in some families than others.

Other factors that seem to weaken the LES are **allergies** and neurological disorders that affect specific muscles in the body. Diabetes and rapid weight gain can also be factors in causing GERD.

Some medications also can weaken the LES. They include calcium channel blockers used to treat high blood pressure, theophyline used to treat asthma, and **antihistamines**. Nitrates in medications and foods can also trigger GERD.

In infants, it may simply be a matter of having an immature digestive system. Once the body begins to mature, the GERD goes away. For adolescents, the hormones of **puberty** seem to trigger acid reflux.

Certain foods have been known to affect the muscle tone of the LES and increase stomach acids. Chocolate, peppermint, and high fat foods can allow the LES to relax and stay open more often. Citrus foods, tomatoes, and tomato products increase acid production in the stomach.

Lifestyle habits can also trigger episodes of acid reflux. Using **caffeine** and alcohol, **smoking**, eating large meals, and having poor posture can produce GERD.

Symptoms

Though heartburn is the characteristic symptom of GERD in adolescents and adults, GERD in children and infants is not so easy to recognize. Frequent vomiting or spitting up is the usual indicator for GERD in children. However, vomiting can be a symptom of many other childhood disorders, including stomach flu, allergy, or a related symptom to almost any illness. Frequent vomiting that continues after the first four months of life or is excessive at any time usually indicates the presence of GERD. Constant crying with back arching usually accompanies the frequent vomiting.

Children with GERD who are **preschool** age and older often have gas and abdominal pain above the navel. They only have intermittent vomiting. They can also experience chest pain or true heartburn symptoms, which can last up to two hours and get worse after eating. Bending over or lying down makes the heartburn worse.

Children with GERD exhibit difference symptoms. They can either gain or lose weight. One group of children will eat more because they are uncomfortable and a full stomach seems to make them feel better temporarily. Another group of children are often very picky about what they eat, refusing specific foods. These children will only eat a few bites even though they might be very hungry. A third group of children report having trouble swallowing; they choke or gag whenever they eat, no matter what foods are served. A fourth group of children will drink liquids constantly because doing so soothes the burning feeling in their esophagus.

Respiratory symptoms are twice as likely to occur in children with GERD as those who do not have it. Children often have frequent sore throats when they wake up in the morning, sinus infections, bronchitis, and dry coughs. These children have a constantly runny nose or a hoarse, deep voice. They can also experience wheezing or other asthma symptoms. Some children aspirate the stomach contents, which can cause pneumonia or even sudden death.

Sleep is often disturbed. Children often wake up with a nighttime **cough** or choke when they lie down. Some children experience sleep apnea (interrupted breathing).

Other children have frequent ear infections or drool a lot. Some infants and toddlers will insist on being held upright and not laid down, often falling asleep over a parent's shoulder or in a parent's arms. In some extreme cases, when there is a lot of stomach acid regurgitation, the child's teeth will show enamel erosion.

Children with GERD may also have hiccups or belch a lot. They can also have bad breath and complain of having a sour taste in their mouths.

Some children with GERD have anemia. This condition usually develops because there is an ulcer in the lining of the esophagus that has begun to bleed.

When to call the doctor

It is important to call the doctor if GERD symptoms occur frequently or get worse. If symptoms disturb the child's sleep and interfere with school and **play**, a doctor should be consulted to determine a course of treatment. Also, if a child is not eating or gaining weight or has breathing difficulty, parents should seek medical advice as soon as possible. For a child of any age, if blood is present in vomit, a doctor should be called. If a child over two complains of swallowing difficulty, a serious condition could exist and a doctor should be called.

Diagnosis

In some cases, the doctor will diagnose GERD after taking a thorough medical history, listening carefully for GERD symptoms, and doing a physical exam. Many doctors will also order a series of tests to gauge the extent of damage done by GERD. Sometimes, chest **x rays** are ordered to check for pneumonia or lung damage due to aspiration of stomach contents.

The most common tests, however, are the upper GI (gastrointestinal) series and the upper GI endoscopy. The upper GI series looks at the esophagus, the stomach, and the duodenum, or the first section of the small intestine. The child is asks to drink a cup of liquid that coats the digestive track. Because this liquid has usually been barium, a metallic, chalky substance, the upper GI series is sometimes called a barium swallow.

X rays or images are then taken as the barium flows down the esophagus, into the stomach, and into the duodenum. The child may be asked to turn on his or her side so that the technician can gently massage the stomach to move the barium into the duodenum. Images are often sent to a video monitor where the doctors and technicians observe the behavior of the upper digestive tract and snap still images from the monitor.

The upper GI series is particularly important in diagnosing infants. It can tell if there are anatomical changes in the esophagus, such as a hiatal hernia, a condition where the stomach bulges above the diaphragm. It can also assess damage to the esophagus and can determine if there are stomach ulcers or ulcers in the duodenum.

The upper GI endoscopy, also called the esophagogastroduodenoscopy (EGD), by contrast, is a more sensitive test and offers a more complete picture of what is happening in the upper digestive tract. As of 2004, it was the test of choice for many gastroenterologists (doctors specializing in diseases of the digestive system).

For the endoscopy, the patient receives a mild sedative, then a small, flexible tube is inserted into the esophagus. The tube has a light and a tiny camera attached to its end. There also is a small instrument to take tissue samples if the doctor needs to do so. The camera broadcasts live images from the esophagus and stomach to a video monitor. Using these tools, the doctor can capture still images for further diagnosis and hospital records, and the doctor can examine suspicious areas more closely with the camera or by taking tissue samples.

The EGD allows the doctor to determine the extent of damage to the esophagus and to rule out serious complications like Barrett's esophagus. Mild GERD may show no damage to the esophagus at all. The GED is a good tool for determining esophagitis.

Another test the doctor may order is esophageal manometry. It measures how well the LES and motor function of the esophagus are. A thin tube is inserted through the nose and down the throat. Coupled with the 24-hour pH probe study, the test becomes the best determinant of GERD because it actually monitors how often the patient has reflux into the esophagus during a full day. One episode of acid reflux is considered having a pH of less than 4 for at least 15 to 30 seconds. This test can see if there is a correlation between episodes of acid reflux and other symptoms, such as chronic cough, wheezing, or sleep apnea.

The doctor may also order a gastric emptying study. For this test, the child is asked to drink milk mixed with a radioactive chemical. Then, the child is monitored, using a special camera. Episodes of reflux can be seen with this test.

Though esophagitis may have been found in one of these tests, the doctor will need to determine whether it was caused by GERD or by milk allergy, which does not respond to acid suppressant therapy.

Treatment

There are two main treatment methods for GERD. The first is lifestyle change. This usually means that patients should not eat within three hours of going to bed. This lets the stomach empty and the acid decrease. Lying down will cause the stomach contents to come back up. Elevating the bed about six inches will also keep the acid within the stomach. Eating smaller meals more frequently will control the amount of acid in the stomach. Patients should also avoid fatty foods, caffeine, mints and mint-flavoring, spicy foods, citrus fruits, and anything with tomatoes. Carbonated beverages can also irritate the already sensitive lining of the esophagus. Alcohol and smoking should be avoided. Improved posture, with no slumping, will reduce pressure on the stomach, as will losing excess weight.

For an infant, lifestyle changes are simple. Holding a baby upright for about a half hour after breastfeeding or bottle feeding will help keep reflux to a minimum. Feeding a baby on formula smaller portions more frequently can also help manage spitting up. Some doctors recommend thickening the baby's formula with rice cereal or using pre-thickened formulas such as Enfamil. This will decrease the amount of spit up or vomit, but it does nothing for reflux. It does fill up the child on a smaller amount of food and can also make the baby sleep and thus stop crying. Placing a baby in a semi-prone position as in an infant car seat only makes GERD worse. Babies with GERD should sleep on their backs in a crib or bed that has the head of the bed elevated to a 30 degree angle.

Medication is the second main way to treat GERD. The doctor may first recommend non-prescription medications, such as antacids and histamine-2 receptor blockers (H2 blockers). Antacids, such as Gaviscon, Maalox, Mylanta, and Tums, help neutralize acid already in the stomach or esophagus. Some have a foaming agent, which also helps prevent acid from backing up into the esophagus. Antacids can be used every day for three weeks. If taken longer, they can produce **diarrhea**, interfere with calcium absorption in the body, and build up magnesium, which can damage the kidneys. The doctor will determine if they can be taken longer. Infants are only given antacids in limited doses because of the risk of aluminum toxicity.

Common H2 blockers are nizatidine (Axid), ranitidine (Zantac), famotidine (Pepcid), and cimetidine (Tagamet). These should be taken one hour before meals. They block acid formation but have no effect on acid already present in the stomach.

If these remedies do not work or the patient's GERD is very serious, the doctor will usually move onto the more powerful proton-pump inhibitors (PPIs). These include omeprazole (Prilosec), esomeprazole (Nexium), lansoprazole (Prevacid), rabeprazole (Aciphex), and pantoprazole (Protonix). These medications block the production of an enzyme that aids in the production of acid. PPIs stop acid production better than H2 blockers.

In addition to PPIs, the doctor may prescribe coating agents, such as sucralfate (Carafe), to cover the sores and mucous membranes of the esophagus and stomach. This acts as a protective barrier to stomach acids.

Some doctors also use promotility agents to tighten the LES and promote faster emptying of the stomach. These include metoclopramide (Reglan) and bethanechol (Duvoid). However, many doctors are reluctant to use these drugs because they have serious side effects. For example, cisapride (Propulsid) was pulled from the market because of safety concerns about lethal drug interactions.

One last option that doctors have to treat GERD is surgery. Because lifestyle changes and medications work for most children and adolescents with GERD, the election of surgery is only used for a small number of people for whom all the other options did not work.

Fundoplication is a surgical procedure that puts pressure on the LES to keep acid from backing up. During the surgery, the doctor wraps a part of the stomach around the esophagus and sews it down. This produces a one-way valve. This procedure can be done laparoscopically, a less invasive surgery where the doctor makes small cuts into the abdomen to insert a camera and the surgical instruments. This surgery produces very little scarring and has a faster recovery rate. Fundoplication is not always successful and can have complications. The surgery also comes undone in about 20 percent to 30 percent of cases.

Prognosis

Many babies outgrow infantile GERD, but some keep having symptoms well into adulthood. In most cases, GERD is easily managed. For 60 percent of children and adolescents with mild to moderate GERD, lifestyle changes and H2 blockers are very effective. For those with severe symptoms, including esophagitis, PPI therapy works well. For relapses, long-term therapy or surgery may be necessary.

Prevention

GERD can be prevented by maintaining a healthy body weight, avoiding alcohol and smoking, eating smaller meals, limiting fatty foods, and eliminating trigger foods.

Parental concerns

GERD diagnosis is a recent phenomenon. Though it may have existed in the distant past, only since the 1990s have doctors begun to recognize GERD as an individual disease. Diagnosing GERD in children is sometimes controversial. Some doctors have recognized GERD as a temporary condition in infants but do not recognize GERD in children or in adolescents. Many doctors are, as of 2004, beginning to understand that GERD, like many other digestive disorders, can occur at any age. The North American Society for Pediatric Gastroenterology and Nutrition drafted guidelines for treating children and adolescents with GERD in 2001. Being educated about the disease can help parents discuss their child's GERD symptoms and treatment options with their child's doctor.

Parents should help children understand that they need to take their medications regularly and that they need to make lifestyle changes. It can be hard to explain to a child that chocolate and candy canes are off limits, but like **food allergies**, children will learn to modify their food choices because of their special sensitivities.

Parents can also help children cope emotionally with this disease. For some children, it is just a matter of eating right and taking medication once a day. For others, it is a lifelong struggle with food and their digestive tract. They will have good days and bad days. It may

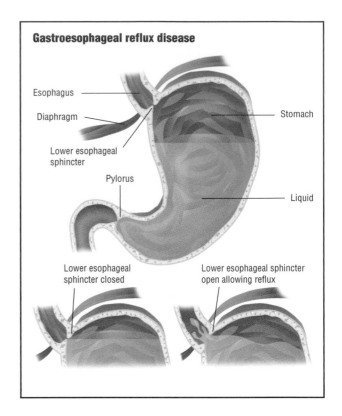

Normally, the lower esophageal sphincter keeps the stomach contents contained with the stomach (top). However, with gastroesophageal reflux disease, the sphincter opens, allowing the acidic contents to flow up the esophagus. *(Illustration by GGS Information Services.)*

be difficult for children to communicate their condition to their friends or their teachers who might not always understand that on one day they are fine and on the next they are not. Parental support will help children and teenagers cope with GERD.

Resources

BOOKS

Cheskin, Lawrence J., and Brian E. Lacy. *Healing Heartburn.* Baltimore, MD: Johns Hopkins University Press, 2002.

Shimberg, Elaine Fantie. *Coping with Chronic Heartburn: What You Need to Know about Acid Reflux and GERD.* New York: St. Martin's Press, 2001.

Sklar, Jill, and Annabel Cohen. *Eating for Acid Reflux: A Handbook and Cookbook for Those with Heartburn.* New York: Marlowe & Company, 2003.

PERIODICALS

Arguin, Amy Lynn, and Martha K. Swartz. "Gastroesophageal Reflux in Infants: A Primary Care Perspective." *Pediatric Nursing* 30, i. 1 (January-February 2004): 45–53.

"GERD and Respiratory Infections." *Pediatrics for Parents* 20, i. 2 (February 2002): 4.

KEY TERMS

Dysphagia—Difficulty in swallowing.

Esophagogastroduodenoscopy (EGD)—An imaging test that involves visually examining the lining of the esophagus, stomach, and upper duodenum with a flexible fiberoptic endoscope.

Esophagus—The muscular tube that leads from the back of the throat to the entrance of the stomach. It is coated with mucus and surrounded by muscles, and pushes food to the stomach by sequential waves of contraction. It functions to transport food from the throat to the stomach and to keep the contents of the stomach in the stomach.

Fundoplication—A surgical procedure that increases pressure on the lower esophageal sphincter by stretching and wrapping the upper part of the stomach around the sphincter.

Gastroenterologist—A physician who specializes in diseases of the digestive system.

H2RAs—Medications used to treat some GERD symptoms, for example, Tagamet, Pepcid, Axid.

Heartburn—A burning sensation in the chest that can extend to the neck, throat, and face. It is the pri-

mary symptom of gastroesophageal reflux (the movement of stomach acid into the esophagus).

Hiatal hernia—A condition in which part of the stomach protrudes through the diaphragm into the chest cavity.

Laparoscopic surgery—Minimally invasive surgery in which a camera and surgical instruments are inserted through a small incision.

Odynophagia—Pain in swallowing.

Lower esophageal sphincter (LES)—A muscle located at the base of the esophagus which keeps the stomach contents from coming back into the esophagus.

Proton pump—A structure in the body that produces and pumps acid into the stomach.

Silent reflux—An acid reflux problem that does not cause vomiting but can cause chronic, recurrent respiratory symptoms much like asthma.

Regurgitation—The flow of material back up the esophagus and into the throat or lungs. Also refers to the backward flow of blood through a partly closed heart valve.

ORGANIZATIONS

American Academy of Pediatrics. 141 Northwest Point Blvd., Elk Grove Village, IL 60007–1098. Web site: <www.aap.org>.

American College of Gastroenterology. 4900 B South 31 St. Arlington, VA 22206. Web site: <www.acg.gi.org>.

WEB SITES

"Gastroesophageal Reflux Disease." *Cincinnati Children's Hospital.* Available online at <www.cincinnatichildrens.org/health/info/abdomen/diagnose/gerd.htm> (accessed October 21, 2004).

"GERD Treatment Options in Infants and Children." *WebGERD.* Available online at <www.webgerd.com/GerdTreatmentInInfants.htm> (accessed October 21, 2004).

Janie Franz

Gastroschisis *see* **Abdominal wall defects**

Gaucher's disease *see* **Lipidoses**

Gay issues *see* **Homosexuality and bisexuality**

Gender constancy

Definition

A child's realization that gender is fixed and does not change over time.

Description

The concept of gender constancy, influenced by the **cognitive development** theory of French psychologist Jean Piaget (1896–1980), was introduced by Lawrence Kohlberg (1927–1987). In 1966, Kohlberg presented a revolutionary new view of early gender role development. Parting with previous views generally held by psychologists, Kohlberg emphasized that children actively self-construct their gender through a conceptual pattern in the mind called a schema. Gender schema models stress the roles of children's selective attention to gender and their internal motivation to conform to societal standards and stereotypes of gender roles. These cognitive-developmental models of the development of gender roles are perhaps best known, however, for the introduction of the construct of gender constancy. Gender constancy has been defined as children's understanding of the irreversibility of their sex, which develops in stages between about the ages of two and seven years. Kohlberg acknowledged that some awareness of gender roles emerges in children before full attainment of an understanding of gender constancy, although he argued that once children attain full understanding of gender constancy, they become increasingly motivated to observe, incorporate, and respect gender roles.

Addressing the formation of **gender identity** in terms of cognitive development, Kohlberg advanced the idea that the development of sex roles depends in large part on a child's understanding that gender remains constant throughout a person's lifetime. Children realize that they are male or female and are aware of the gender of others by the age of three. However, at these ages they still do not understand that people cannot change genders the way they can change their clothes, names, or behavior. Kohlberg theorized that children do not learn to behave in gender-appropriate ways until they understand that gender is permanent, which occurs at about the age of seven. At this point they start modeling the behavior of members of their own sex.

Kohlberg's idea of the prerequisite significance of an understanding of gender constancy for gender typing has been controversial, and empirical support for the notion has been mixed. Kohlberg's exact claims about the prerequisite importance of gender constancy understanding for gender-typing to take place have added to the controversy. Although it has been supported by some research studies, Kohlberg's theory has also been criticized on the grounds that children do show certain types of gender-associated behavior, such as toy and playmate selection, by the ages of two or three. This observable pattern points to the fact that there are others factors, such as parental reinforcement, that influence the adoption of sex-typed behavior. The significance of gender constancy understanding on early gender-typing remains unclear, both theoretically and empirically.

A gender constancy interview is often used by psychologists to determine a child's level of gender constancy. Although questions used in the interview can vary, the interview generally consists of 13 questions and counterquestions. Previous research indicated that, based on their responses to questions in the interview, children may reliably be assigned to one of four levels of gender constancy understanding. Children who failed to express any understanding of the 13 questions in levels two through four are classified at level one and are considered pre-gender constant. Level two has four questions and examines children's understanding of their own sex and the sex of a pictured person. Level three has two questions and verbally measures children's under-standing that sex is permanent over time despite changes in appearance, desires, or activities. Level four contains seven questions that measures children's understanding that pictured people do not change sex through changes in hair length, clothing, or both.

Infancy and toddlerhood

There is a growing amount of scientific research that suggests gender identity develops at a very early age. Several studies show that infants can discriminate between male and female faces and associate faces and voices according to gender by the time they reach one year old. However, gender-labeling tasks, such as toy identification, do not occur until about age two. Gender identity and awareness of sex differences generally emerge in the first three to four years of a child's life. However, children begin to demonstrate a preference for their own sex starting at about age two.

Gender identification is often associated with the choice and use of **toys** in this age group, according to a number of studies done in the 1970s, 1980s, and 1990s. Sex differences in toy **play** have been found in children as young as one year of age. By age two, children begin to spontaneously choose their types of toys based on gender. Several of these studies show that by age one, boys display a more assertive reaction than girls to toy disputes. By age two, the reaction of boys is more aggressive.

Between the ages of 18 and 24 months, children know whether they are boys or girls and can identify adults as males or females. However, they do not develop a sense of gender constancy for several or a few more years. This means that they do not fully understand that they will be a boy or girl for the rest of their lives. At this age, children are unsure about whether gender remains constant from childhood to adulthood.

Preschool

By age three, most children know that men have a penis and women have breasts. Also at age three, children begin to apply gender labels and stereotypes, identifying gentle, empathic characteristics with females and strong and aggressive characteristics with males. Even in the twenty-first century, most young children develop stereotypes regarding gender roles, associating nurses, teachers, and secretaries as females and police officers, firefighters, and construction workers as males.

School age

By the first or second grade (ages six or seven), children's thinking becomes more logical, and they come to realize and understand that they will either be a boy or girl for the rest of their lives. They will draw upon what they have learned and what they see in the world around them as they continue to refine their ideas about what it means to be either a girl or a boy.

Common problems

While most children follow a predictable pattern in the acquisition of gender constancy, some develop a gender identity inconsistent with their biological sex, a condition variously known as gender confusion, gender identity disorder, or transsexualism, which affects about one in 20,000 males and one in 50,000 females. Researchers have found that both early socialization and hormonal factors may play a role in the development of gender identity disorder. Children with gender identity disorder usually feel from their earliest years that they are trapped in the wrong body and begin to show signs of gender confusion between the ages of two and four. They prefer playmates of the opposite sex at an age when most children prefer to spend time in the company of same-sex peers. They also show a preference for the clothing and typical activities of the opposite sex: transsexual boys like to play house and play with dolls. Girls with gender identity disorder are bored by ordinary female pastimes and prefer the rougher types of play typically associated with boys, such as contact **sports**.

Both male and female transsexuals believe and repeatedly insist that they actually are, or will grow up to be, members of the opposite sex. Girls cut their hair short, favor boys' clothing, and have negative feelings about maturing physically as they near **adolescence**. In childhood, girls with gender identity disorder experience less overall social rejection than boys, as it is more socially acceptable for a girl to be a tomboy than for a boy to be perceived as a "sissy." About five times more boys than girls are referred to therapists for this condition. Teenagers with gender identity disorder suffer social isolation and are vulnerable to depression and **suicide**. They have difficulty developing peer relationships with members of their own sex as well as romantic relationships with the opposite sex. They may also become alienated from their parents.

Parental concerns

Children with gender identity disorder refuse to dress and act in sex-stereotypical ways. It is important to remember that many emotionally healthy children experience fantasies about being a member of the opposite sex. The distinction between these children and gender identity disordered children is that the latter experience significant interference in functioning because of their cross-gender identification. They may become severely depressed, anxious, or socially withdrawn. Most children eventually outgrow gender identity disor-

der. About 75 percent of boys with gender identity disorder develop a homosexual or bisexual orientation by late adolescence or adulthood, but without continued feelings of transsexuality. Most of the remaining 25 percent become heterosexuals (also without transsexuality). Those individuals in whom gender identity disorder persists into adulthood retain the desire to live as members of the opposite sex, sometimes manifesting this desire by cross-dressing, either privately or in public. In some cases, adult transsexuals (both male and female) have their primary and secondary sexual characteristics altered through a sex change operation, consisting of surgery followed by hormone treatments.

When to call the doctor

Gender identity disorder (GID) is generally diagnosed when children display any four of the following symptoms:

- They repeatedly state a strong desire to be, or insist that they are, of the opposite sex.

- They show a preference for cross-dressing.

- They display a strong and long-term preference for fantasies and role-play that allows them to see themselves as members of the opposite sex.

- They participate in or want to play stereotypical games of the opposite sex.

- They show a strong preference for friends and playmates of the opposite sex.

GID is typically diagnosed by a psychiatrist or psychologist, who conducts an interview with the patient and takes a detailed social history. **Family** members may also be interviewed during the **assessment** process. Most children diagnosed with GID eventually grow out of it but some psychiatrists try to speed up the process, usually using psychotherapy. This treatment itself is controversial and has received much criticism within both the psychiatric and gay, lesbian, bisexual, and transgendered communities. For children, a clear diagnosis may not be possible until the teenage years since most children grow out of GID problems. Some psychiatrists are critical of gender identity disorder being classified as a psychiatric condition at all, saying it is more a social stigma. To prove their case, some psychiatrists point to the fact that boys are up to six times more likely to be diagnosed with GID and singled out for treatment than girls. This is not because the disorder is more common in boys, but because most parents tend to worry more if a son starts wearing dresses than if their daughter starts playing with toy trucks.

See also Gender identity.

Resources

BOOKS

Abrahams, George, and Sheila Ahlbrand. *Boy v. Girl? How Gender Shapes Who We Are, What We Want, and How We Get Along.* Minneapolis, MN: Free Spirit Publishing, 2002.

Archer, John, and Barbara Lloyd. *Sex and Gender.* Cambridge, UK: Cambridge University Press, 2002.

Cohen-Kettenis, Peggy T., and Friedmann Pfafflin. *Transgenderism and Intersexuality in Childhood and Adolescence: Making Choices.* London: SAGE Publications, 2003.

PERIODICALS

Barrett, Anne E., and Helene Raskin White. "Trajectories of Gender Role Orientation in Adolescence and Early Adulthood: A Prospective Study of the Mental Health Effects of Masculinity and Femininity." *The Journal of Health and Social Behavior* 43 (December 2002): 451–68.

"Both Halves of the Sky: Gender Socialization in the Early Years." *Sexual Health Exchange* (Fall 2002): 16.

Hines, Melissa, et al. "Testosterone during Pregnancy and Gender Role Behavior of Preschool Children: A Longitudinal, Population Study." *Child Development* 73 (November-December 2002): 1678–87.

Warin, Jo. "The Attainment of Self-Consistency through Gender in Young Children." *Sex Roles: A Journal of Research* (February 2000): 209–31.

ORGANIZATIONS

Gender Identity Research & Education Society. Melverly, The Warren, Ashtead, Surrey, KT21 2SP, United Kingdom 01372–801554. Web site: <www.gires.org>.

National Academy of Child & Adolescent Psychiatry. 3615 Wisconsin Ave. NW, Washington, DC 20016. Web site: <www.aacap.org>.

Ken R. Wells

Gender identity

Definition

Gender identity is a person's sense of identification with either the male or female sex, as manifested in appearance, behavior, and other aspects of a person's life.

Description

Psychologists believe human sexual identities are made up of three separate components. The first shows the direction of a child's sexual orientation, whether he or she is heterosexual (straight), homosexual (gay), or bisexual. The second is the child's style of behavior, whether a female is a "tomboy" or homemaker-type and a male is a "macho guy" or a "sensitive boy." The third component is what psychologists call the core gender identity. According to an article in the May 12, 2001 issue of *New Scientist*, it is the most difficult to ascertain but is essentially the deep inner feeling a child has about whether he or she is a male or female.

In most people, the three components point in the same direction but in some people, the components are more mixed. For example, a gay woman (lesbian) might look and act either feminine or masculine (butch), but she still deeply feels she is a female. Scientists are uncertain about where the inner feeling of maleness or femaleness comes from. Some believe it is physical, from the body, while others believe it is mental, from the hypothalamus region of the brain. There is also debate on whether the determination is shaped by hormones, particularly testosterone and estrogen, or by genes assigned at conception.

Gender identity emerges by the age of two or three and is influenced by a combination of biological and sociological factors reinforced at **puberty**. Once established, it is generally fixed for life.

Aside from sex differences, other biological contrasts between males and females are already evident in childhood. Girls mature faster than boys, are physically healthier, and are more advanced in developing oral and written linguistic skills. Boys are generally more advanced at envisioning and manipulating objects. They are more aggressive and more physically active, preferring noisy, boisterous forms of **play** that require larger groups and more space than the play of girls the same age.

In spite of conscious attempts to reduce sex role stereotyping in the final decades of the twentieth century and in the early 2000s, boys and girls are still treated differently by adults from the time they are born. The way adults play with infants has been found to differ based on gender. Girls are treated more gently and approached more verbally than boys. As children grow older, many parents, teachers, and other authority figures still tend to encourage independence, competition, aggressiveness, and exploration more in boys and expression, nurturance, motherhood and childrearing, and obedience more in girls.

Infancy and toddlerhood

There is a growing amount of scientific research that suggests gender identity develops at a very early age.

Several studies show that infants can discriminate between male and female faces and associate faces and voices according to gender by the time they reach one year old. However, gender-labeling tasks, such as toy identification, do not occur until about age two. Gender identity and awareness of sex differences generally emerge in the first three to four years of a child's life. However, children begin to demonstrate a preference for their own sex starting at about age two.

Gender identification is often associated with the choice and use of **toys** in this age group, according to a number of studies done in the 1970s, 1980s, and 1990s. Sex differences in toy play have been found in children as young as one year old. By age two, children begin to spontaneously choose their types of toys based on gender. Several of these studies show that by age one, boys display a more assertive reaction than girls to toy disputes. By age two, the reaction of boys is more aggressive.

Most two-year-olds know whether they are boys or girls and can identify adults as males or females. By age three, most children know that men have a penis and women have breasts. Also at age three, children begin to apply gender labels and stereotypes, identifying gentle, empathic characteristics with females and strong, aggressive characteristics with males. Even in the twenty-first century, most young children develop stereotypes regarding gender roles, associating nurses, teachers, and secretaries as females and police officers, firefighters, and construction workers as males.

Preschool

Preschoolers develop an increasing sense of self-awareness about their bodies and gender differences. Fears about the body and body mutilation, especially of the genitals, are often major sources of **fear** in preschoolers. As children become more aware of gender differences, preschoolers often develop intense feelings of vulnerability and **anxiety** regarding their bodies.

School age

By the age of six years, children are spending about 11 times as much time with members of their own sex as with children of the opposite sex. This pattern begins to change as the child approaches puberty, however.

By the teenage years, most children have an established sexual orientation of heterosexual, homosexual, or bisexual. They have also established their style of behavior and core sexual identity. However, a very small fraction have not.

While most children follow a predictable pattern in the acquisition of gender identity, some develop a gender identity inconsistent with their biological sex, a condition variously known as gender confusion, gender identity disorder, or transsexualism, which affects about one in 20,000 males and one in 50,000 females. Researchers have found that both early socialization and hormonal factors may play a role in the development of gender identity disorder. Children with gender identity disorder usually feel from their earliest years that they are trapped in the wrong body and begin to show signs of gender confusion between the ages of two and four. They prefer playmates of the opposite sex at an age when most children prefer to spend time in the company of same-sex peers. They also show a preference for the clothing and typical activities of the opposite sex; transsexual boys like to play house and play with dolls. Girls with gender identity disorder are bored by ordinary female pastimes and prefer the rougher types of play typically associated with boys, such as contact **sports**.

Both male and female transsexuals believe and repeatedly insist that they actually are, or will grow up to be, members of the opposite sex. Girls cut their hair short, favor boys' clothing, and have negative feelings about maturing physically as they near **adolescence**. In childhood, girls with gender identity disorder experience less overall social rejection than boys, as it is more socially acceptable for a girl to be a tomboy than for a boy to be perceived as feminine. About five times more boys than girls are referred to therapists for this condition. Teenagers with gender identity disorder suffer social isolation and are vulnerable to depression and **suicide**. They have difficulty developing peer relationships with members of their own sex as well as romantic relationships with the opposite sex. They may also become alienated from their parents.

Common problems

The psychological diagnosis of gender identity disorder (GID), commonly called transsexualism, is used to describe a male or female who feels a strong identification with the opposite sex and experiences considerable distress because of their actual sex. Children with gender identity disorder have strong cross-gender identification. They believe that they are, or should be, the opposite sex. They are uncomfortable with their sexual role and organs and may express a desire to alter their bodies.

While not all persons with GID are labeled as transsexuals, there are those who are determined to undergo sex change procedures or have done so, and, therefore, are classified as transsexual. They often attempt to pass socially as the opposite sex. Transsexuals alter their physical appearance cosmetically and hormonally and may eventually undergo a sex-change operation.

Most children eventually outgrow gender identity disorder. About 75 percent of boys with gender identity disorder develop a homosexual or bisexual orientation by late adolescence or adulthood, but without continued feelings of transsexuality. Most of the remaining 25 percent become heterosexuals (also without transsexuality). Those individuals in whom gender identity disorder persists into adulthood retain the desire to live as members of the opposite sex, sometimes manifesting this desire by cross-dressing, either privately or in public. In some cases, adult transsexuals (both male and female) have their primary and secondary sexual characteristics altered through a sex change operation, consisting of surgery and hormone treatments.

Parental concerns

Children with gender identity disorder refuse to dress and act in sex-stereotypical ways. It is important to remember that many emotionally healthy children experience fantasies about being a member of the opposite sex. The distinction between these children and gender identity disordered children is that the latter experience significant interference in functioning because of their cross-gender identification. They may become severely depressed, anxious, or socially withdrawn.

According to an article in the January 2003 issue of *The Brown University Child and Adolescent Behavior Letter*, psychiatrists offer these suggestions for parents of children diagnosed with GID:

• Create an atmosphere of acceptance so the child feels safe within the **family** to express his or her interests. Identify and praise the child's talents.

• Use gender-neutral language in discussing romantic attachments.

• Watch television programs and movies and read books that have gay themes or characters.

• Encourage the child to find activities that respect his or her interests, yet help the child "fit in" to society.

• Insist on classroom discussions about diversity and tolerance. Ensure the child's school has anti-discrimination policies that include gender identity and that the policies are enforced.

• If indicated, take the child to a psychotherapist with expertise and tolerance for issues related to gender identity and sexual orientation.

When to call the doctor

Gender identity disorder is generally diagnosed when children display any four of the following symptoms:

KEY TERMS

Core gender identity—The deep inner feeling a child has about whether he or she is a male or female.

Estrogen—Female hormone produced mainly by the ovaries and released by the follicles as they mature. Responsible for female sexual characteristics, estrogen stimulates and triggers a response from at least 300 tissues. After menopause, the production of the hormone gradually stops.

Gender identity disorder (GID)—A strong and lasting cross-gender identification and persistent discomfort with one's biological gender (sex) role. This discomfort must cause a significant amount of distress or impairment in the functioning of the individual.

Hypothalamus—A part of the forebrain that controls heartbeat, body temperature, thirst, hunger, body temperature and pressure, blood sugar levels, and other functions.

Psychotherapy—Psychological counseling that seeks to determine the underlying causes of a patient's depression. The form of this counseling may be cognitive/behavioral, interpersonal, or psychodynamic.

Testosterone—Male hormone produced by the testes and (in small amounts) in the ovaries. Testosterone is responsible for some masculine secondary sex characteristics such as growth of body hair and deepening voice. It also is sometimes given as part of hormone replacement therapy to women whose ovaries have been removed.

Transsexualism—A term used to describe a male or female that feels a strong identification with the opposite sex and experiences considerable distress because of their actual sex. Also called gender identity disorder.

• They repeatedly state a strong desire to be, or insist that they are, of the opposite sex.

• They show a marked preference for cross-dressing.

• They display a strong and long-term preference for fantasies and role-play as members of the opposite sex.

• They participate in or want to play stereotypical games of the opposite sex.

• They show a strong preference for friends and playmates of the opposite sex.

GID is typically diagnosed by a psychiatrist or psychologist, who conducts an interview with the patient and takes a detailed social history. Family members may also be interviewed during the **assessment** process. Most children diagnosed with GID eventually grow out of it, but some psychiatrists try to speed up the process, usually using psychotherapy. This treatment itself is controversial and has received much criticism within both the psychiatric and gay, lesbian, bisexual, and transgendered communities. For children, a clear diagnosis may not be possible until the teenage years, since most children grow out of GID problems.

Some psychiatrists are critical of the psychiatric classification of gender identity disorder, saying it is more a social stigma. To prove their case, some psychiatrists point to the fact that boys are up to six times more likely to be diagnosed with GID and singled out for treatment than girls. This is not because the disorder is more common in boys, but because most parents tend to worry more if a son starts wearing dresses than if their daughter starts playing with toy trucks.

Resources

BOOKS

Abrahams, George, and Sheila Ahlbrand. *Boy v. Girl?: How Gender Shapes Who We Are, What We Want, and How We Get Along.* Minneapolis, MN: Free Spirit Publishing, 2002.

Archer, John, and Barbara Lloyd. *Sex and Gender.* Cambridge, UK: Cambridge University Press, 2002.

Cohen-Kettenis, Peggy T., and Friedmann Pfafflin. *Transgenderism and Intersexuality in Childhood and Adolescence: Making Choices.* London: SAGE Publications, 2003.

Zderic, Stephen A., et al. *Pediatric Gender Assignment: A Critical Reappraisal.* New York: Kluwer Academic/Plenum Publishers, 2002.

PERIODICALS

Barrett, James. "Disorders of Gender Identity." *The Practitioner* (June 4, 2003): 472.

Bartlett, Nancy H., et al. "Cross-sex Wishes and Gender Identity Disorder in Children: A Reply to Zucker." *Sex Roles: A Journal of Research* (August 2003): 191–92.

Franklin, Deeanna. "For Gender-variant Children, Validation Is Key: Outreach Programs for Parents." *Clinical Psychiatry News* (October 2003): 41.

Perrin, Ellen C. "Helping Parents and Children Understand Gender Identity Disorder." *The Brown University Child and Adolescent Behavior Letter* (January 2003): 1–4.

Phillips, Helen. "Boy Meets Girl." *New Scientist* (May 12, 2001): 29.

Zieman, Gayle. "Gender Identity Disorder." *Clinical Reference Systems* (Annual 2002): 1401.

ORGANIZATIONS

The Gender Identity Research & Education Society. Melverly, The Warren, Ashtead, Surrey, KT21 2SP, UK. 01372–801554. Web site: <www.gires.org>.

The Renaissance Transgender Association. 987 Old Eagle School Road, Suite 719, Wayne, PA 19087. Web site: <www.ren.org>.

WEB SITES

Gender Education and Advocacy, 2004. Available online at <www.gender.org> (accessed September 3, 2004).

Gender Identity Disorder Sanctuary. Available online at <www.mhsanctuary.com/gender> (accessed September 3, 2004).

Ken R. Wells

GERD *see* **Gastroesophageal reflux disease**

German measles *see* **Rubella**

Gingivitis *see* **Periodontal disease**

Gluten sensitive enteropathy *see* **Celiac disease**

Gonadal dysgenesis *see* **Turner syndrome**

Granular conjuctivitis *see* **Trachoma**

Grieving *see* **Death and mourning**

Gross motor skills

Definition

Gross motor skills are the abilities required in order to control the large muscles of the body for walking, running, sitting, **crawling**, and other activities.

Description

Motor skills are actions that involve the movement of muscles in the body. They are divided into two groups: gross motor skills, which are the larger movements of arms, legs, feet, or the entire body (crawling, running, and jumping); and **fine motor skills**, which are smaller actions, such as grasping an object between the thumb and a finger or using the lips and tongue to taste objects. Motor skills usually develop together since many activities depend on the coordination of gross and fine motor skills. Gross motor skills develop over a relatively short period of time. Most development occurs during childhood. However, soldiers, some athletes, and others who engage in activities requiring high degrees of endurance may spend years improving their level of muscle and body coordination and gross motor skills.

Gross motor skills development is governed by two principles that also control physical growth. Head to toe development refers to the way the upper parts of the body develop, beginning with the head, before the lower ones. The second principle of development is trunk to extremities. Head control is gained first, followed by the shoulders, upper arms, and hands. Upper body control is developed next, followed by the hips, pelvis, and legs.

Encouraging gross motor skills requires a safe, open **play** space, peers to interact with, and some adult supervision. Promoting the development of gross motor abilities is considerably less complicated than developing fine motor skills. Helping a child succeed in gross motor tasks requires patience and opportunities for a child to practice desired skills. Parents and other persons must understand the child's level of development before helping him or her master gross motor skills. Children reach developmental milestones at different rates. Pushing a child to perform a task that is impossible due to development status promotes frustration and disappointment. Children should be allowed to acquire motor skills at their own paces.

There are a number of activities parents can have children do to help develop gross motor skills. These include:

- playing hopscotch and jumping rope; activities that help children learn balance

- hitting, catching, kicking, or throwing a ball, such as a baseball, football, or soccer ball; activities that help develop hand-eye or foot-eye coordination

- kangaroo hop, in which children hold something, such as a small ball or orange, between their knees and then jump with their feet together frontward, backwards, and sideways

- playing wheelbarrow, in which someone holds the children's legs while they walk on their hands along a specific route

- walking on a narrow bar or curb, while holding a bulky object in one hand, then the other hand, and then repeating the activity walking backwards and sideways

- toss and catch, in which children toss an object, such as a baseball, in the air and then catch it, while sitting or lying down and also while using alternate hands

Infancy

The first gross motor skill infants learn usually is to lift their heads and shoulders before they can sit up, which, in turn, precedes standing and walking. Lifting the head is usually followed by head control. Although they are born with virtually no head or neck control, most infants can lift their heads to a 45-degree angle by the age of four to six weeks, and they can lift both their head and chest at an average age of eight weeks. Most infants can turn their heads to both sides within 16 to 20 weeks and lift their heads while lying on their backs within 24 to 28 weeks. By about nine to 10 months, most infants can sit up unassisted for substantial periods of time with both hands free for playing.

One of the major tasks in gross motor development is locomotion, the ability to move from one place to another. Infants progress gradually from rolling (eight to 10 weeks) to creeping on their stomachs and dragging their legs behind them (six to nine months) to actual crawling (seven to 12 months). While infants are learning these temporary means of locomotion, they are gradually becoming able to support increasing amounts of weight while in a standing position. In the second half-year of life, babies begin pulling themselves up on furniture and other stationary objects. By the ages of 28 to 54 weeks, on average, they begin navigating a room in an upright position by holding on to the furniture to keep their balance. Eventually, they are able to walk while holding on to an adult with both hands and then with only one. They usually take their first uncertain steps alone between the ages of 36 and 64 weeks and are competent walkers by the ages of 12 to 18 months.

Toddlerhood

Toddlers are usually very active physically. By the age of two years, children have begun to develop a variety of gross motor skills. They can run fairly well and negotiate stairs holding on to a banister with one hand and putting both feet on each step before going on to the next one. Most infants this age climb (some very actively) and have a rudimentary ability to kick and throw a ball. By the age of three, children walk with good posture and without watching their feet. They can also walk backwards and run with enough control for sudden stops or changes of direction. They can hop, stand on one foot, and negotiate the rungs of a jungle gym. They can walk up stairs alternating feet but usually still walk down putting both feet on each step. Other achievements include riding a tricycle and throwing a ball, although they have trouble catching it because they hold their arms out in front of their bodies no matter what direction the ball comes from.

Preschool

Four-year-olds can typically balance or hop on one foot, jump forward and backward over objects, and climb and descend stairs alternating feet. They can bounce and catch balls and throw accurately. Some four-year-olds can also skip. Children this age have gained an increased degree of self-consciousness about their motor activities that leads to increased feelings of pride and success when they master a new skill. However, it can also create feelings of inadequacy when they think they have failed. This concern with success can also lead them to try daring activities beyond their abilities, so they need to be monitored especially carefully.

School age

School-age children, who are not going through the rapid, unsettling growth spurts of early childhood or **adolescence**, are quite skilled at controlling their bodies and are generally good at a wide variety of physical activities, although the ability varies according to the level of maturation and the physique of a child. Motor skills are mostly equal in boys and girls at this stage, except that boys have more forearm strength and girls have greater flexibility. Five-year-olds can skip, jump rope, catch a bounced ball, walk on their tiptoes, balance on one foot for over eight seconds, and engage in beginning acrobatics. Many can even ride a small two-wheel bicycle. Eight- and nine-year-olds typically can ride a bicycle, swim, roller skate, ice skate, jump rope, scale fences, use a saw, hammer, and garden tools, and play a variety of **sports**. However, many of the sports prized by adults, often scaled down for play by children, require higher levels of distance judgment and **hand-eye coordination**, as well as quicker reaction times, than are reasonable for middle childhood. Games that are well suited to the motor skills of elementary school-age children include kick ball, dodge ball, and team relay races.

In adolescence, children develop increasing coordination and motor ability. They also gain greater physical strength and prolonged endurance. Adolescents are able to develop better distance judgment and hand-eye coordination than their younger counterparts. With practice, they can master the skills necessary for adult sports.

Common problems

There are a range of diseases and disorders that affect gross motor skill development and skills. Among young persons, developmental problems such as genetic disorders, **muscular dystrophy**, **cerebral palsy**, and some neurological conditions adversely impact gross motor skill development.

Gross motor skills

Age	Skill
One month	May hold up head momentarily.
Two months	Lifts head when placed on stomach. Holds up head briefly when held in a seated or standing position.
Three months	Holds head and shoulders up when placed on stomach. Puts weight on forearms.
Four months	Holds head up well in sitting position. Can lift head to a 90-degree angle when placed stomach. May start to roll over.
Five months	Has full head control. When pulled by hands to a sitting position, the head stays in line with body.
Six months	Rolls over (front to back first). Bears a large. percentage of body weight when held in a standing position.
Seven months	Can stand with support. May sit without support for short periods. Pushes upper part of body up while on stomach.
Eight months	Stands while holding onto furniture. Sits well unsupported. Gets up on hands and knees; may start to crawl backwards.
Nine months	Crawls first by pulling body forward with hands. May move around a room by rolling.
Ten months	Pulls up to standing. Is very steady while sitting; moves from sitting to crawling position and back. Crawls well.
Eleven months	"Cruises," walking while hanging onto furniture. Walks with two hands held.
Twelve months	Walks with one hand held. May walk with hands and feet. Stands unsupported for longer periods of time.
Fifteen months	Walks without help. Crawls up stairs. Gets into a standing position without support.
Eighteen months	Seldom falls while walking. Can walk and pull toy. Runs. Climbs stairs holding railing. May walk backward.
Two years	Kicks a ball. Walks up and down stairs, two feet per step.
Two and a half years	Jumps with both feet. Jumps off step. Can walk on tiptoe.
Three years	Goes upstairs one foot per step. Stands on one foot briefly. Rides tricycle. Runs well.
Four years	Skips on one foot. Throws ball well overhand. Jumps a short distance from standing position.
Five years	Hops and skips. Good balance. Can skate or ride scooter.

SOURCE: *Miller-Keane Encyclopedia and Dictionary of Medicine, Nursing, and Allied Health, 5th ed.* and Child Development Institute, http://www.childdevelopmentinfo.com.

(Table by GGS Information Services.)

Gross motor skills can become impaired in a variety of ways, including injury, illness, **stroke**, and congenital deformities. Developmental coordination disorder affects motor skills. A person with this disorder has a hard time with skills such as riding a bike, holding a

Girls using their gross motor skills, large muscle movements, to play soccer. *(Photograph by Tony Freeman. PhotoEdit.)*

pencil, and throwing a ball. People with this disorder are often called clumsy. Their movements are slow and awkward. People with developmental coordination disorder may also have a hard time completing tasks that involve movement of muscle groups in sequence. For example, such a person might be unable to do the following in order: open a closet door, get out a jacket, and put it on. It is thought that up to 6 percent of children may have developmental coordination disorder, according to the 2002 issue of the annual journal *Clinical Reference Systems.* The symptoms usually go unnoticed until the early years of elementary school; the disorder is usually diagnosed in children who are between five and 11 years old.

Children with any one or combination of developmental coordination disorder symptoms should be seen by a pediatrician who specializes in motor skills development delays. There are many ways to address gross motor skills impairment, such as physical therapy. This type of therapy can include treating the underlying cause, strengthening muscles, and teaching ways to compensate for impaired movements.

Parental concerns

Parents, teachers, and primary caregivers need to have a clear understanding of how young children develop gross motor skills and the timetable for development of the skills. The Lincoln-Oseretsky Motor Development Scale is an individually administered test that assesses the development of motor skills in children and adults. Areas covered include fine and gross motor skills, finger dexterity and speed, and hand-eye coordination. The test consists of 36 tasks arranged in order of increasing difficulty. These include walking backwards, standing on one foot, touching one's nose, jumping over a rope, throwing and catching a ball, putting coins in a box, jumping and clapping, balancing on tiptoe while opening and closing one's hands, and balancing a rod

KEY TERMS

Cerebral palsy—A nonprogressive movement disability caused by abnormal development of or damage to motor control centers of the brain.

Congenital malformation—A deformity present at birth.

Developmental coordination disorder—A disorder of motor skills.

Fine motor skill—The abilities required to control the smaller muscles of the body for writing, playing an instrument, artistic expression and craft work. The muscles required to perform fine motor skills are generally found in the hands, feet and head.

Lincoln-Oseretsky Motor Development Scale—A test that assesses the development of motor skills.

Locomotion—The ability to move from one place to another.

Muscular dystrophy—A group of inherited diseases characterized by progressive wasting of the muscles.

vertically. Norms have been established for each part of the test for children aged six to 14.

When to call the doctor

Parents, who suspect that their child has a delay in developments should follow their instincts in having that child evaluated. The earliest intervention possible offers the highest response and success rate among children with special needs. Parents should call the doctor any time they have a concern about their child's motor skill development. Parents should keep in mind that children develop at different rates and try to focus on the skills their children have mastered instead of those they may have yet to master. Still, there are certain signs that may point to a problem, and these should be discussed with a pediatrician or physician. These signs include not walking by 15 months of age, not walking maturely (heel to toe) after walking for several months, walking only on the toes, and not being able to push a toy on wheels by age two. Toddlers may begin to prefer one hand to the other, the first sign of right- or left-handedness, or to use both hands equally. This preference should be allowed to develop naturally. Parents should call a doctor if the child does not seem to use one hand at all or has a strong hand preference before he or she is one year old.

See also Fine motor skills.

Resources

BOOKS

Bly, Lois. *Motor Skills Acquisition Checklist*. San Antonio, TX: Therapy Skill Builders, 2003.

Kurtz, Lisa A. *How to Help a Clumsy Child: Strategies for Young Children with Developmental Motor Concerns*. London: Jessica Kingsley Publishing, 2003.

Liddle, Tara Losquadro, and Laura Yorke. *Why Motor Skills Matter: Improving Your Child's Physical Development to Enhance Learning and Self-Esteem*. New York: McGraw-Hill, 2003.

Smith, Jodene Lynn. *Activities for Gross Motor Skills Development*. Westminster, CA: Teacher Created Materials, 2003.

PERIODICALS

Horsch, Karen. "Clumsy Kids." *Parenting* (October 1, 2003): 246.

Jeansonne, Jennifer J. "Motor Skill Learning Research Looks Beyond Outcomes—Understanding the Components Needed for Skilled Performance Helps Develop Instructions and Training Methods." *Biomechanics* (June 1, 2004): 69.

Rink, Judith E. "It's Okay to Be a Beginner: Teach a Motor Skill, and the Skill May Be Learned. Teach How to Learn a Motor Skill, and Many Skills Can Be Learned—Even After a Student Leaves School." *The Journal of Physical Education, Recreation & Dance* 75 (August 2004): 31–4.

"Should the Main Objective of Adapted Physical Education be the Development of Motor Skills or the Development of Self-Esteem?" *The Journal of Physical Education, Recreation & Dance* (November-December 2003): 10–2.

Vickers, Marcia. "Why Can't We Let Boys Be Boys?" *Business Week* (May 26, 2003): 84.

ORGANIZATIONS

American Academy of Pediatrics. 141 Northwest Point Blvd., Elk Grove Village, IL 60007. Web site: <www.aao.org>.

Developmental Research for the Effective Advancement of Memory and Motor Skills. 273 Ringwood Road, Freeville, NY 13068. Web site: <www.dreamms.org>.

WEB SITES

"Motor Skills Disorder." *eMedicine*, January 3, 2003. Available online at <www.emedicine.com/ped/topic2640.htm> (accessed November 19, 2004).

Ken R. Wells

Growth *see* **Skeletal development**

Growth hormone tests

Definition

Growth hormone tests measure the levels of specific hormones that regulate human growth. These hormone levels are measured in blood serum samples obtained by venipuncture. To study growth hormone function under specific conditions, certain medications may be administered before blood is taken and hormone levels are measured. Human growth hormone (hGH) (somatotropin) is produced by somatotropes in the anterior pituitary gland. Its role in normal body growth and development is to stimulate protein production in muscle cells and trigger energy release from the breakdown of fats. Diagnostic tests for growth hormones include the somatotropin hormone test, somatomedin C test, growth hormone stimulation test (also known as the arginine test or insulin tolerance test), and growth hormone suppression test (glucose loading test).

Purpose

Growth hormone tests are ordered by physicians to determine whether levels of hGH and other related hormones in the blood are normal, increased, or decreased, and to help diagnose conditions that may result from abnormal hormone levels or pituitary gland dysfunction. Some of the common reasons for testing are:

- to identify growth abnormalities that may cause delayed **puberty** and small stature in adolescents

- to aid in the diagnosis of hyperpituitarism, which can cause **gigantism** or **acromegaly**

- to screen for pituitary gland dysfunction

- to assist in the diagnosis of pituitary tumors or tumors related to the hypothalamus, an area of the brain

- to monitor the effects of hGH therapy administered for certain conditions

Description

Human growth hormones play an important role in normal human growth and development. The major human growth hormone is a protein made up of 191 amino acids, the building blocks of proteins. The production of this protein is controlled by two other hormones secreted by the hypothalamus: growth hormone releasing hormone (GHRH), which controls secretion of hGH; and growth hormone-inhibiting hormone (GHIH), which inhibits secretion of hGH. All healthy individuals have measurable levels of hGH throughout life, but there are two notable growth spurts, one at birth and the other at puberty, and hGH plays a vital role at each time. The most obvious effect of hGH is on linear skeletal growth (height), but metabolic effects of hGH (the results of hGH activity in the body) on muscle, the liver, and fat cells are a critical part of its function. When any question arises about growth or development, pediatricians may investigate the levels of the major growth hormone hGH, its receptors and stimulants, the glands that produce the hormones, and the complex hormone interactions that control normal development.

Somatotropin (hGH) is secreted by somatotropes in the anterior pituitary gland. It is typically secreted during **sleep**, with peak release occurring around 10 p.m., midnight, and 2 a.m. Most of the effects of hGH are mediated by other hormones, including the somatomedins, IGH-I (somatomedin C) and IGH-II, which are insulin-like growth hormones that also influence linear growth, and the two hypothalamic hormones (GHRH and GHIH) that regulate hGH by responding to changes in the individual's blood sugar (glucose) and protein levels. When blood glucose levels fall, GHRH triggers the secretion of stored hGH. As blood glucose levels rise, hGH secretion is turned off by GHIH activity. Increases in blood protein levels trigger a similar response. This feedback loop, along with the effects of eating and **exercise**, is responsible for the fluctuating levels of hGH throughout the day. In addition, blood glucose and amino acid availability for growth is also regulated by the hormones adrenaline, glucagon, and insulin. All of these growth factors may be evaluated in order to understand hormone deficiencies or gland dysfunction when growth deficiencies are suspected.

A number of hormonal conditions can lead to excessive or diminished growth. Because of its critical role in producing hGH and other hormones, a dysfunctional pituitary gland will often lead to altered growth. **Dwarfism** (very small stature) can be due to underproduction of hGH, lack of IGH-I, or a flaw in target tissue response to either of these growth hormones. Overproduction of hGH or IGH-I, or an exaggerated response to these hormones, can lead to gigantism or acromegaly, both of which are characterized by a very large stature.

Gigantism is the result of hGH overproduction in early childhood leading to a skeletal height up to 8 feet (2.5 m) or more. Acromegaly results when hGH is overproduced after the onset of puberty. In this condition, the epiphyseal plates of the long bones of the body do not close, and they remain responsive to additional stimulated growth by hGH. This disorder is characterized by an enlarged skull, hands and feet, nose, neck, and tongue.

Somatrotropin

Somatrotropin (hGH) is measured in the clinical laboratory to identify hGH deficiency in adolescents with short stature, delayed sexual maturity, and other growth or development abnormalities. The somatotropin test also aids in documenting the excess hGH production responsible for gigantism or acromegaly, and confirms underactivity or overproduction of the pituitary gland (hypopituitarism or hyperpituitarism, respectively). However, due to variable secretion of hGH, as well as hGH production in response to stress, exercise, or other factors, random assays are not an adequate determination of hGH deficiency. To obtain more accurate readings, a blood sample can be drawn one to one-and-a-half hours after sleep (hGH levels increase during sleep), or strenuous exercise can be performed for 30 minutes before blood is drawn. (A person's hGH levels increase after exercise.) The hGH levels at the end of an exercise period are expected to be maximal.

Somatomedin C

The somatomedin C test is usually ordered to help detect pituitary abnormalities, hGH deficiency, and acromegaly. Also called insulin-like growth factor (IGF-1), somatomedin C is considered a more accurate reflection of the blood concentration of hGH because such variables as time of day, activity levels, or diet do not influence test results. Somatomedin C is part of a group of peptides, called somatomedins, through which hGH exerts its effects. Because it circulates in the bloodstream bound to long-lasting proteins, it is more stable than hGH. Levels of somatomedin C do depend on hGH levels, however, and typically somatomedin C levels will be low when hGH levels are deficient. Abnormally low levels of somatomedin C will require further investigation, so doctors may perform the hGH stimulation test to diagnose hGH deficiency. Nonpituitary causes of reduced somatomedin C include **malnutrition**, severe chronic illness, severe liver disease, **hypothyroidism**, and Laron's dwarfism.

Growth hormone stimulation test

The hGH stimulation test, also called hGH provocation test, insulin tolerance, or arginine test, is performed to test the body's ability to produce human growth hormone and to confirm suspected hGH deficiency. A normal patient can have low hGH levels, but if hGH is still low after stimulation, a more definitive diagnosis can be made. The test involves creating a condition of insulin-induced **hypoglycemia** (via intravenous injection of insulin) to stimulate production of hGH and corticotropin secretion as well. If such stimulation is unsuccessful, a malfunction of the anterior pituitary gland is likely. It may be necessary to obtain blood samples following an energetic exercise session lasting 20 minutes.

A substance called hGH-releasing factor has also been used for hGH stimulation. This approach is believed to be more accurate and specific for hGH deficiency caused by the pituitary. Growth hormone deficiency is also suspected when x-ray determination of bone age indicates retarded growth in comparison to chronological age. As of 2004, the best method to identify hGH-deficient patients was a positive stimulation test followed by a positive response to a therapeutic trial of hGH.

Growth hormone suppression test

This procedure, also called the glucose loading test, is performed to evaluate excessive baseline levels of hGH and to confirm diagnosis of gigantism in children (and acromegaly in adults). The procedure requires drawing two different blood samples, one before the child ingests 100 grams of glucose by mouth and a second sample two hours after glucose ingestion. Normally, a glucose load such as this will suppress hGH secretion. In a child with excessive hGH levels, failure of suppression indicates anterior pituitary dysfunction and confirms a diagnosis of gigantism (or acromegaly).

Precautions

Taking certain drugs such as amphetamines, dopamine, corticosteroids, and phenothiazines may increase or decrease growth hormone secretion. A pediatrician may discontinue certain medications prior to the performance of growth hormone tests. Other factors that may influence hGH secretion include stress, exercise, diet, and abnormal glucose levels. The pediatrician may make recommendations for the child's activity prior to testing. Growth hormone tests should not be done within a week after any radioactive scan such as an x ray, MRI, or CT scan.

Preparation

The hGH or somatotropin test requires that a fasting blood sample be drawn from a vein, usually in the arm. The child should have nothing to eat or drink from midnight the night before the test until after the blood sample is drawn. Since stress and exercise increase hGH levels, the child must be at complete rest for 30 minutes before the blood sample is drawn. If the physician has requested two samples, they should be drawn on consecutive days at approximately the same time, preferably between 6 a.m. and 8 a.m.

The somatomedin C test also requires a fasting blood sample. The patient should have nothing to eat or drink from midnight the night before until after the blood sample is drawn.

Growth hormone stimulation testing requires intravenous administration of arginine and/or insulin. Venous blood samples will be drawn at 0, 60, and 90 minutes after the injection.

Growth hormone suppression testing requires two fasting blood samples, one before the test and another two hours after the child is given a glucose solution by mouth. The child should have nothing to eat or drink from midnight the night before until after the blood samples are drawn, and physical activity should be limited for at least 10 to 12 hours before the test.

Aftercare

Usually there will be no effects from hormone testing and normal activities can be resumed. A bandage may be applied to keep the site of venipuncture or intravenous administration of medications clean and to stop any bleeding that may occur. Unusual bleeding or bruising of the site should be reported to the pediatrician. The child should be observed closely after the more extensive growth hormone stimulation test and growth hormone suppression test. A pediatrician may limit activities for the immediate pre-test period.

Risks

Growth hormone tests do not have significant risks. Minor discomfort may be experienced during and after the growth hormone stimulation test because of the intravenous line for delivery of insulin. A low blood sugar (hypoglycemia) will result from the insulin injected into the child's system, which may make some children lightheaded or lethargic. Some children may experience sleepiness, sweating, and/or nervousness, all of which can be corrected after the test by ingestion of juice or a glucose infusion, as recommended by the pediatrician. Severe cases of hypoglycemia may cause ketosis (excessive amounts of fatty acid byproducts in the body), acidosis (a disturbance of the body's acid-base balance), or shock. Medical personnel provide close observation during the test to help prevent or react to these unlikely reactions. Growth hormone suppression tests can cause some children to feel nauseous after the administration of glucose. Ice chips can help alleviate this symptom.

Normal results

Results are reported in nanograms per milliliter (ng/ml). Normal results may vary from laboratory to laboratory depending upon the method used for measurement, but results are usually within the following ranges.

Somatotropin (hGH):

• men: 5 ng/ml

• women: less than 10 ng/ml

• children: 0–10 ng/ml

• newborn: 10–40 ng/ml

Somatomedin C:

• adult: 42–110 ng/ml

• child: 0–8 years; girls 7–110 ng/ml; boys 4–87 ng/ml

• 9–10 years: girls 39–186 ng/ml; boys 26–98 ng/ml

• 11–13 years: girls 66–215 ng/ml; boys 44–207 ng/ml

• 14–16 years: girls 96–256 ng/ml; boys 48–255 ng/ml

Growth hormone stimulation: greater than 10 ng/ml

Regarding growth hormone suppression, normally, glucose suppresses hGH to levels ranging from undetectable to 3 ng/ml within 30 minutes to two hours. In children, rebound stimulation may occur after two to five hours.

Parental concerns

Parents may be concerned about the child's response to venipuncture or reaction to intravenous administration of medications prior to testing. The parents can play a calming role by reassuring the child and explaining the procedure beforehand. Medical personnel and the pediatrician may provide instruction before, during, and after the tests, as well as close observation to minimize any risks. Parents can be prepared for post-testing sleepiness or lightheadedness by having juice handy and ice chips to help relieve any feelings of **nausea**.

Resources

BOOKS

Czernichow, P., et al. *Growth and Metabolic Disorders in Chronic Pediatric Diseases: Cambridge December 2001*

Hormone Research. Basel, Switzerland: S. Karger AG, 2002.

DeGroot, Leslie, et al. *Hormone Action, Pituitary Growth, and Maturation, Immunology, Nutrition, Diabetes Mellitus.* Kent, UK: Elsevier—Health Science Division, 2001.

WEB SITES

"Growth Hormone." *Lab Tests Online: American Association for Clinical Chemistry, 2001–2004.* Available online at <www.labtestsonline.org/understanding/analytes/growth_hormone/test.html> (accessed October 21, 2004).

L. Lee Culvert
Janis O. Flores

Gum disease *see* **Periodontal disease**

H

Haemophilus influenzae infections *see*
Hemophilus infections

Haemophilus influenzae type B vaccine *see*
Hib vaccine

Hair loss *see* **Alopecia**

Handedness

Definition

Handedness is the preferred use of the right hand, the left hand, or one or the other depending on the task.

Description

Handedness is defined and categorized in different ways. Most people define handedness as the hand that one uses for writing. Within the scientific community some researchers define handedness as the hand that is faster and more precise for manual tasks. Others define it as the preferred hand, regardless of its abilities. Whereas some people always use their right hand or their left hand for most activities, others use one hand or the other depending on the activity. Still other people can use either hand for most functions.

Lefthanders usually prefer using their left hand for delicate tasks; however, there is no good method for predicting which hand a lefthander will choose for a specific task. Although left-handed children usually are more flexible in their hand usage than right-handers, this may be because they are forced to function in a world designed for right-handers.

There is no standard measure for determining degrees of handedness. Some scientists believe that there are only two types of handedness: right and non-right. These researchers believe that true left-handedness is rare and that most lefthanders are really mixed-handed. Others believe that ambidexterity—the equal use of both hands—is a third type of handedness, and some think that there are two types of ambidexterity. Other scientists believe that handedness should be measured on a continuum from completely right-handed to completely left-handed.

Demographics

It is commonly estimated that about 10 percent of the human population is left-handed or ambidextrous. Boys are about 1.5 times more likely than girls to be left-handed. Archeological evidence indicates that the proportion of left-handed to right-handed people was about the same 30,000 years ago as it is in the early 2000s.

In the past there were many social and cultural biases against left-handed children. In particular, left-handed children often were forced by parents or teachers to use their right hand for eating and writing. In the early 2000s the frequency of left-handedness appears to be on the increase. This may be due to the increased acceptance of children determining their own hand preferences. Left-handedness appears to be rarer in restrictive societies as compared with more permissive societies.

Basis of handedness

The physical basis of handedness is not well-understood. Through the centuries left-handedness has been attributed to numerous physical, psychological, and supernatural causes.

Each hemisphere of the brain has some specialized functions, a poorly-understood phenomenon called brain lateralization. In the late nineteenth century Paul Broca, a French neurosurgeon, identified an area of the left hemisphere that has a major role in the production of speech. Carl Wernicke, a German neurologist, identified another region in the left hemisphere that was responsible for language comprehension. Broca suggested that people's handedness was the opposite of their language-specialized hemisphere, so that a person with left-hemisphere language specialization would be right-handed. Thus until the 1960s, handedness was believed to be indicative of brain lateralization. Between 70 and 90 percent of humans have language specialization in their left hemispheres. The remainder may have right-hemisphere specialization or no real distinction between the two hemispheres in language specialization. However, among lefthanders, about 50 percent process language on both sides of their brains, 10 percent process language primarily in their right brains, and the remainder process language primarily in their left brains.

The 1987 Geschwind-Behan-Galaburda (GBG) Theory of Left-Handedness suggested that left-handedness was a result of some brain injury or trauma or chemical variations in the fetal environment, such as high levels of the male hormone testosterone.

For decades during the twentieth century scientists argued about whether there is a genetic basis for handedness. Children of left-handed parents have a 50 percent chance of being right-handed and 18 percent of identical **twins** differ in their handedness. Furthermore, right-handed twins are equally as likely as their left-handed twins to have left-handed children. A 2003 study appeared to identify a single gene that controls both handedness and the direction that hair spins on the scalp. An individual possessing at least one copy of the dominant form of this gene is both right-handed and has a clockwise hair spiral. However, when an individual has two copies of the recessive form of the gene—one copy from the mother and one copy from the father—the gene does not determine handedness. Thus 50 percent of these individuals are right-handed and 50 percent are non-right-handed. Furthermore, these individuals have a separate 50 percent likelihood of hair that spins clockwise or counterclockwise.

Handedness determines few if any lateralized behaviors other than fine finger dexterity. However, one study showed that right-handers preferred turning to their left side and non-right-handers preferred turning to their right side. Turning to the right or left is strongly correlated with turning toward the side of the brain that has less dopamine, an important brain hormone.

Infancy

In his pioneering work on child behavior, the American developmental psychologist Arnold Gesell claimed that infants as young as four weeks display signs of handedness and that right-handedness is clearly established by age one. However, it was as of 2004 commonly believed that babies are born ambidextrous. Although a hand preference may seem apparent towards the end of the first year, this is not necessarily due to right- or left-

handedness and may change several times over the subsequent few years.

Toddlerhood

Toddlers usually go through phases of using one hand for some activities and the other hand for other activities. Although many children exhibit clear left- or right-handedness from the age of two—and handedness usually is determined during the third year—it is not unusual for a child to repeatedly switch hand preferences well into their **preschool** years. Early hand preference may be due to a pathological problem (e.g. **stroke**).

Common problems

It may be hard for right-handers to appreciate the daily problems confronting non-right-handers. Although most of these difficulties are simply annoying or frustrating, others can cause physical injury or serious life-long problems. Most systems and tools are designed for right-handers and so have an intrinsic bias. Many items, such as screws and light bulbs, require a left-to-right turning that is easier for a right-hander. Items designed specifically for right-handers include:

- cooking utensils
- can openers
- scissors
- telephones
- calculators
- computer keyboards
- sports equipment
- musical instruments, especially stringed instruments

Non-right-handed children must either learn to use tools with their right hand, which can be awkward, inefficient, and frustrating, or to use tools backwards with their left hand. The latter can be dangerous for a child.

In the past left-handed children often were forced to write with their right hand. In the early 2000s, a non-right-handed child may still feel pressure to conform to a right-handed world. Most parents and teachers as of 2004 probably accept that it is wrong to attempt to suppress or change a child's handedness. Nevertheless, lefthanders may still suffer at school. A teacher may label a lefthander's writing as "sloppy" because of an unconscious reaction to handwriting that looks different. Left-handed children may hook their wrists while writing in order to see the paper. However, hand or wrist twisting can reduce legibility and writing fluency. This problem is avoidable with correct positioning of the paper for the lefthander. In art and science lefthanders may struggle with tools, instruments, and equipment designed for the right-handed majority. Some left-handed children may seem clumsy as they try to adapt to a right-handed world.

At various times in the past, left-handedness has been wrongly associated with numerous physical, mental, emotional, and behavioral disorders. However, there is some evidence that left-handed people may be more at risk for **schizophrenia**, **bipolar disorder**, or language-processing disorders, including **dyslexia** and **stuttering**.

Parental concerns

Many children repeatedly switch hand preferences until at least the age of three. This is normal unless it seems to interfere with the child's **fine motor skills**. By the age of two most children should be able to do the following:

• hold a fork and spoon well enough to feed themselves

• handle small objects well

• hold the paper in place while drawing

Once a child's handedness becomes apparent, parents or caregivers should never try to change it. Parents can assist left-handed children by the following:

• placing their table settings according to their handedness

• providing left-handed scissors

• helping them find the easiest ways to handle paper and pencil

• assuring that teachers and caregivers treat their lefthanders appropriately

• not dwelling on their child's non-right-handedness

Left-handed children can become very frustrated when they are trying to imitate a right-handed parent or sibling, particularly with activities such as shoe-tying. In these cases the parent or sibling should sit across from the child—rather than next to or behind the child—so as to be the child's mirror.

If handedness is not apparent by the time a child enters school, the teacher must determine which hand the child should learn to write with. Observing which hand the child consistently uses for various activities—or whether the child switches hands when repeating the activity—can help the teacher make this determination. Example of such activities include:

• holding a spoon

• cutting with scissors

• playing with puppets

• using a lock and key

• hammering nails

• screwing lids on jars

• throwing a ball

Teachers should help lefthanders to hold a pencil and place the paper in ways that are appropriate for left-handed writing.

When to call the doctor

A child who exhibits a strong preference for one hand at about one year of age—too early to clearly express handedness—may have a weakness or neuromuscular problem in the other arm or hand.

Resources

BOOKS

Annett, Marian. *Handedness and Brain Asymmetry: The Right Shift Theory.* New York: Taylor & Francis, 2002.

Healey, Jane M. *Lefties: How to Raise Your Left-Handed Child in a Right-Handed World.* New York: Pocket Books, 2001.

PERIODICALS

Brodie, Chris. "Head in Hand." *American Scientist* 92, no. 1 (January/February 2004): 27.

"Handed Down from Distant Generations." *New Scientist* 180, no. 2415 (October 4–10, 2003): 21.

Vlachos, F., and F. Bonoti. "Handedness and Writing Performance." *Perceptual and Motor Skills* 98, no. 3 (June 2004): 815.

ORGANIZATIONS

Handedness Research Institute. Hillcrest Psychology Research Center, 674 East Cottage Grove Avenue, Suite

222, Bloomington, IN 47408. Web site: <handedness.org>.

WEB SITES

Hackney, Clinton. "The Left-Handed Child in a Right-Handed World." *Zaner-Bloser Inc.* Available online at <www.zaner-bloser.com/html/HWsupport1.html> (accessed December 27, 2004).

Holder, M. K. *Gauche! Left-Handers in Society.* Available online at <www.indiana.edu/~primate/lspeak.html> (accessed December 27, 2004).

———. *What does Handedness have to do with Brain Lateralization (and who cares?).* Available online at <www.indiana.edu/~primate/brain.html> (accessed December 27, 2004).

Shoemaker, Carma Haley. "When Left Is Right: Left-Handed Toddlers." *Toddlers Today.* <http://toddlerstoday.com/resources/articles/lefthand.htm> (accessed December 27, 2004).

Margaret Alic, PhD

Hand-eye coordination

Definition

Hand-eye coordination is the ability of the vision system to coordinate the information received through the eyes to control, guide, and direct the hands in the accomplishment of a given task, such as handwriting or catching a ball. Hand-eye coordination uses the eyes to direct attention and the hands to execute a task.

Description

Vision is the process of understanding what is seen by the eyes. It involves more than simple visual acuity (ability to distinguish fine details). Vision also involves fixation and eye movement abilities, accommodation (focusing), convergence (eye aiming), binocularity (eye teaming), and the control of hand-eye coordination. Most hand movements require visual input to be carried out effectively. For example, when children are learning to draw, they follow the position of the hand holding the pencil visually as they make lines on the paper. Between four and 14 months of age, infants explore their world and develop hand-eye coordination, in conjunction with **fine motor skills**. Fine motor skills are involved in the control of small muscle movements, such as when an infant starts to use fingers with a purpose and in coordination with the eyes.

Infants are eager to move their eyes, their mouths, and their bodies toward the people and objects that comfort and interest them. They practice skills that let them move closer to desired objects and also move desired objects closer to themselves. By six months of age, many infants begin reaching for objects quickly, without jerkiness, and may be able to feed themselves a cracker or similar food. Infants of this age try to get objects within their reach and objects out of their reach. Many infants are also able to look from hand to object, to hold one object while looking for a second object, and to follow the movements of their hands with their eyes. At this age, most infants begin to poke at objects with their index fingers. After six months, infants are usually able to manipulate a cup and hold it by the handle. Many infants at this age also begin to reach for objects with one arm instead of both. At about eight months of age, as dexterity improves, many infants can use a pincher movement to grasp small objects, and they can also clap and wave their hands. They also begin to transfer objects from hand to hand, and bang objects together. Hand-eye coordination development milestones are as follows.

Birth to three years

Between birth and three years of age, infants can accomplish the following skills:

- start to develop vision that allows them to follow slowly moving objects with their eyes
- begin to develop basic hand-eye skills, such as reaching, grasping objects, feeding, dressing
- begin to recognize concepts of place and direction, such as up, down, in
- develop the ability to manipulate objects with fine motor skills

Three to five years

Between three and five years of age, little children develop or continue to develop the following skills:

- continue to develop hand-eye coordination skills and a preference for left or right **handedness**
- continue to understand and use concepts of place and direction, such as up, down, under, beside
- develop the ability to climb, balance, run, gallop, jump, push and pull, and take stairs one at a time
- develop eye/hand/body coordination, eye teaming, and depth perception

Five to seven years

Children between five and seven years old develop or continue to develop the following skills:

- improve fine motor skills, such as handling writing tools, using scissors
- continue to develop climbing, balancing, running, galloping, and jumping abilities
- continue to improve hand-eye coordination and handedness preference
- learn to focus vision on school work for hours every day

Common problems

Hand-eye coordination problems are usually first noted as a lack of skill in drawing or writing. Drawing shows poor orientation on the page and the child is unable to stay "within the lines" when using a coloring book. Often the child continues to depend on his or her hand for inspection and exploration of **toys** or other objects. Poor hand-eye coordination can have a wide variety of causes, but the main two conditions responsible for inadequate hand-eye coordination are vision problems and **movement disorders**.

Vision impairment

Vision impairment is a loss of vision that makes it hard or impossible to perform daily tasks without specialized adaptations. Vision impairment may be caused by a loss of visual acuity, in which the eye does not see objects as clearly as usual. It may also be caused by a loss of visual field, in which the eye cannot see as wide an area as usual without moving the eyes or turning the head. Vision impairment changes how a child understands and functions in the world. Impaired vision necessarily affects a child's hand-eye coordination, as well as cognitive, emotional, neurological, and physical development by limiting the range of experiences and the kinds of information to which the child is exposed.

Movement disorders

Movement disorders are characterized by impaired body movements. They have a variety of causes. An example is ataxia, characterized by a lack of coordination while performing voluntary movements. The problem may appear as clumsiness, inaccuracy, or instability. Movements are not smooth and may appear disjointed or jerky. Another example is hypertonia, a condition marked by an abnormal increase in muscle tension and a reduced ability of a muscle to stretch. What-

Good hand-eye coordination is needed to play baseball. *(Photograph by Henry Horenstein. Harcourt.)*

ever their origin, movement disorders almost always prevent the normal development of hand-eye coordination.

Parental concerns

When a child is between one and two years old, parents should start encouraging activities that allow the child to learn how to use hands to manipulate objects and learn how different things fit together. These activities are extremely important for the development of hand-eye coordination, which is itself crucial for the overall physical development of the child. Some toys are designed to assist hand-eye coordination development. They usually involve "fitting things together," but parents can also use simple kitchen cups or bowls. Letting children **play** with these objects teaches them how to fit objects together. Jigsaw puzzles are also good hand-eye coordination developers, as are blocks or tower toys that encourage playing and coordination. These toys help children learn what items can fit on top of each other and which ones will stack easily. By the time children reach two or three years of age, they are ready to start throwing things and wanting to catch them. These play activities are a great way to improve hand-eye coordination. Most child development professionals believe that the best thing parents can do when trying to improve hand-eye coordination in their children is simply to let them play with a variety of toys on their own.

When to call the doctor

Parents of **preschool** children should be alert for signs of abnormal visual development or coordination

KEY TERMS

Ataxia—A condition marked by impaired muscular coordination, most frequently resulting from disorders in the brain or spinal cord.

Binocular vision—Using both eyes at the same time to see an image.

Convergence—The natural movement of the eyes inward to view objects close-up.

Fine motor skill—The abilities required to control the smaller muscles of the body for writing, playing an instrument, artistic expression and craft work. The muscles required to perform fine motor skills are generally found in the hands, feet and head.

Gross motor skills—The abilities required to control the large muscles of the body for walking, running, sitting, crawling, and other activities. The muscles required to perform gross motor skills are generally found in the arms, legs, back, abdomen and torso.

Hypertonia—Having excessive muscular tone or strength.

Motor skills—Controlled movements of muscle groups. Fine motor skills involve tasks that require dexterity of small muscles, such as buttoning a shirt. Tasks such as walking or throwing a ball involve the use of gross motor skills.

Visual acuity—Sharpness or clearness of vision.

problems. If a child is reluctant to engage in activities that require hand-eye coordination (does not like Legos, tinker toys) or has very irregular handwriting with excessive erasures, they should consider having the child evaluated.

See also Bayley Scales of Infant Development.

Resources

BOOKS

Ball, Morven F. *Developmental Coordination Disorder: Hints and Tips for the Activities of Daily Living.* Philadelphia: Jessica Kingsley Publishers, 2002.

PERIODICALS

Bekkering, H., and U. Sailer. "Commentary: coordination of eye and hand in time and space." *Progress in Brain Research* 140 (2002): 365–73.

Carey, D. P. "Eye-hand coordination: eye to hand or hand to eye?" *Current Biology* 10, no. 11 (June 2000): R416–19.

Crawford, J. D., et al. "Spatial transformations for eye-hand coordination." *Journal of Neurophysiology* 92, no. 1 (July 2004): 10–9.

Fogt, N., et al. "The influence of head movement on the accuracy of a rapid pointing task." *Optometry* 73, no. 11 (November 2002): 665–73.

Henriques, D. Y., et al. "Geometric computations underlying eye-hand coordination: orientations of the two eyes and the head." *Experimental Brain Research* 152, no. 1 (September 2003): 70–8.

Johansson, R. S., et al. "Eye-hand coordination in object manipulation." *Journal of Neuroscience* 21, no. 17 (September 2001): 6917–32.

Pelz, J., et al. "The coordination of eye, head, and hand movements in a natural task." *Experimental Brain Research* 139, no. 3 (August 2001): 266–77.

Sailer, U., et al. "Spatial and temporal aspects of eye-hand coordination across different tasks." *Experimental Brain Research* 134, no. 2 (September 2000): 163–73.

Udermann, B. E., et al. "Influence of cup stacking on hand-eye coordination and reaction time of second-grade students." *Perception & Motor Skills* 98, no. 2 (April 2004): 409–14.

ORGANIZATIONS

American Academy of Pediatrics (AAP). 141 Northwest Point Boulevard, Elk Grove Village, IL 60007–1098. Web site: <www.aap.org>.

American Occupational Therapy Association (AOTA). 4720 Montgomery Lane, PO Box 31220, Bethesda, MD 20824–1220. Web site: <www.aota.org>.

American Psychological Association (APA). 750 First Street, NE, Washington, DC 20002–4242. Web site: <www.apa.org>.

Child Development Institute (CDI). 3528 E Ridgeway Road, Orange, California 92867. Web site: <www.cdipage.com>.

WEB SITES

"Activities for infants which develop hand eye and hand foot coordination." *A Fit Tot.* Available online at <www.topcondition.com/temp/Afittot/hand_eye_coordination.htm> (accessed November 29, 2004).

Monique Laberge, Ph.D.

Hand-foot-mouth disease

Definition

Hand-foot-mouth disease is an infection of young children in which characteristic fluid-filled blisters appear on the hands, feet, and inside the mouth.

Description

Coxsackie viruses belong to a family of viruses called enteroviruses. These viruses live in the gastrointestinal tract and are, therefore, present in feces. They can be spread easily from one person to another when poor hygiene allows the virus within the feces to be passed from person to person. After exposure to the virus, development of symptoms takes only four to six days. Hand-foot-mouth disease can occur year-round, although the largest number of cases are in summer and fall months.

An outbreak of hand-foot-mouth disease occurred in Singapore in 2000, with more than 1,000 diagnosed cases, all in children, resulting in four deaths. A smaller outbreak occurred in Malaysia in 2000. In 1998, a serious outbreak of enterovirus in Taiwan resulted in more than 1 million cases of hand-foot-and-mouth disease. Of these, there were 405 severe cases and 78 deaths, 71 of which were children younger than five years of age.

Hand-foot-mouth should not be confused with foot and mouth disease, which infects cattle but is extremely rare in humans. An outbreak of foot and mouth disease swept through Great Britain and into other parts of Europe and South America in 2001.

Demographics

Hand-foot-mouth disease is very common among young children and often occurs in clusters of children who are in daycare together.

Causes and symptoms

Hand-foot-mouth disease is spread when poor hand washing after a diaper change or contact with saliva allows the virus to be passed from one child to another.

Within about four to six days of acquiring the virus, an infected child may develop a relatively low-grade **fever**, ranging from 99 to 102°F (37.2–38.9°C). Other symptoms include fatigue, loss of energy, decreased appetite, and a sore sensation in the mouth that may

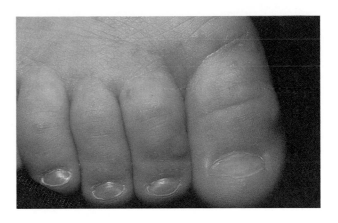

Blisters shown on the foot a child with hand-foot-mouth disease. *(Custom Medical Stock Photo, Inc.)*

interfere with feeding. After one to two days, fluid-filled bumps (vesicles) appear on the inside of the mouth, along the surface of the tongue, on the roof of the mouth, and on the insides of the cheeks. These are tiny blisters, about 3–7 mm in diameter. Eventually, they may appear on the palms of the hands and on the soles of the feet. Occasionally, these vesicles may occur in the diaper region.

The vesicles in the mouth cause the majority of discomfort, and the child may refuse to eat or drink due to **pain**. This phase usually lasts for an average of a week. As long as the bumps have clear fluid within them, the disease is at its most contagious. The fluid within the vesicles contains large quantities of the causative viruses. Extra care should be taken to avoid contact with this fluid.

Diagnosis

Diagnosis is made by most practitioners solely on the basis of the unique appearance of blisters of the mouth, hands, and feet, in a child not appearing very ill.

Treatment

As of 2004, there were no treatments available to cure or decrease the duration of the disease. Medications like **acetaminophen** or ibuprofen may be helpful for decreasing pain and helping the child to eat and drink. It is important to try to encourage the child to take in adequate amounts of fluids, in the form of ice chips or Popsicles if other foods or liquids are too uncomfortable. There is a risk of developing **dehydration**.

Prognosis

The prognosis for a child with hand-foot-mouth disease is excellent. The child is usually completely recovered within about a week of the start of the illness.

Prevention

Prevention involves careful attention to hygiene. Thorough, consistent hand-washing practices and discouraging the sharing of clothes, towels, and stuffed **toys** are all helpful. Virus continues to be passed in the feces for several weeks after infection, so good hygiene should be practiced long after all signs of infection have passed.

Prevention

Parents should be aware of the characteristic rash of hand-foot-mouth disease and monitor their children, especially if they are in a child care setting. Good hygiene practices should be strictly followed to prevent the spread of the disease.

Resources

BOOKS

Abzug, Mark J. "Nonpolio Enteroviruses." In *Nelson Textbook of Pediatrics*. Edited by Richard E. Behrman et al. Philadelphia: Saunders Company, 2004.

PERIODICALS

Hairston, B. R. "Viral diseases of the oral mucosa." *Dermatology Clinics* 21 (January 2003): 17–32.

Purdon, M. "Pediatric viral skin infections." *Clinical Family Practice* 5 (September 2003): 589.

Sy, Man-Sun, et al. "Human Prion Diseases." *Medical Clinics of North America* 5 (September 2003): 557.

Wolfrey, J. "Pediatric exanthems." *Clinical Family Practice* 86 (May 2002): 551–571.

Rosalyn Carson-DeWitt, MD
Ken R. Wells

Happy puppet syndrome *see* **Angelman's syndrome**

Harelip *see* **Cleft lip and palate**

Hashimoto's thyroiditis *see* **Hypothyroidism**

Haverhill fever *see* **Rat-bite fever**

Hay fever *see* **Allergic rhinitis**

HBF test *see* **Fetal hemoglobin test**

HBV *see* **Hepatitis B vaccine**

Head injury

Definition

Head injury is an injury to the scalp, skull, or brain. The most important consequence of head trauma is traumatic brain injury. Head injury may occur either as a closed head injury, such as the head hitting a car's windshield; or as a penetrating head injury, as when a bullet pierces the skull. Both may cause damage that ranges from mild to profound. Very severe injury can be fatal because of profound brain damage.

Description

External trauma to the head is capable of damaging the brain, even if there is no external evidence of damage. More serious injuries can cause skull fracture, blood clots between the skull and the brain, or bruising and tearing of the brain tissue itself.

Injuries to the head can be caused by traffic accidents, **sports injuries**, falls, workplace accidents, assaults, or bullets. Most people have had some type of head injury at least once in their lives, but rarely do they require a hospital visit.

Demographics

Each year about two million people suffer from a more serious head injury, and up to 750,000 of those are severe enough to require **hospitalization**. Brain injury is most likely to occur in males between ages 15 and 24, usually as a result of car and motorcycle accidents. About 70 percent of all accidental deaths are due to head injuries, as are most of the disabilities that occur after trauma. Among children and infants, head injury is the most common cause of death and disability. The most common cause of head injury in children under age two is **child abuse**.

Causes and symptoms

A head injury may cause damage both from the direct physical injury to the brain and from secondary factors, such as lack of oxygen, brain swelling, and disturbance of blood flow. Both closed and penetrating head injuries can cause swirling movements throughout the brain, tearing nerve fibers and causing widespread bleeding or a blood clot in or around the brain. Swelling may raise pressure within the skull (intracranial pressure) and may block the flow of oxygen to the brain.

Head trauma may cause a **concussion**, in which there is a brief loss of consciousness without visible structural damage to the brain. In addition to loss of consciousness, initial symptoms of brain injury may include:

- memory loss and confusion
- vomiting
- **dizziness**
- partial paralysis or numbness
- shock
- anxiety

After a head injury, there may be a period of impaired consciousness followed by a period of confusion and impaired memory with disorientation and a breakdown in the ability to store and retrieve new information. Others experience temporary amnesia following head injury that begins with memory loss over a period of weeks, months, or years before the injury (retrograde amnesia). As a person recovers, memory slowly returns. Post-traumatic amnesia refers to loss of memory for events during and after the accident.

Epilepsy occurs in 2–5 percent of those who have had a head injury; it is much more common in people who have had severe or penetrating injuries. Most cases of epilepsy appear right after the accident or within the first year and become less likely with increased time following the accident.

Closed head injury

Closed head injury refers to brain injury without any penetrating injury to the brain. It may be the result of a direct blow to the head; of the moving head being rapidly stopped, such as when a person's head hits a windshield in a car accident; or by the sudden deceleration of the head without its striking another object. The kind of injury the brain receives in a closed head injury is determined by whether the head was unrestrained upon impact and the direction, force, and velocity of the blow. If the head is resting on impact, the maximum damage will be found at the impact site. A moving head will cause a contrecoup injury where the brain damage occurs on the side opposite the point of impact, as a result of the brain slamming into that side of the skull. A closed head injury also may occur without the head being struck, such as when a person experiences whiplash. This type of injury occurs because the brain is of a different density than the skull and can be injured when delicate brain tissues hit against the rough, jagged inner surface of the skull.

Penetrating head injury

If the skull is fractured, bone fragments may be driven into the brain. Any object that penetrates the skull may implant foreign material and dirt into the brain, leading to an infection.

Skull fracture

A skull fracture is a medical emergency that must be treated promptly to prevent possible brain damage. Such an injury may be obvious if blood or bone fragments are visible, but it is possible for a fracture to have occurred without any apparent damage. A skull fracture should be suspected if there is:

- blood or clear fluid leaking from the nose or ears
- unequal pupil size
- bruises or discoloration around the eyes or behind the ears
- swelling or depression of part of the head

Intracranial hemorrhage

Bleeding (hemorrhage) inside the skull may accompany a head injury and cause additional damage to the brain. A blood clot (hematoma) may occur if a blood vessel between the skull and the brain ruptures; when the blood leaks out and forms a clot, it can press against brain tissue, causing symptoms from a few hours to a few weeks after the injury. If the clot is located between the bones of the skull and the covering of the brain (dura), it is called an epidural hematoma. If the clot is between the dura and the brain tissue itself, the condition is called a **subdural hematoma**. In other cases, bleeding may occur deeper inside the brain. This condition is called intracerebral hemorrhage or intracerebral contusion (from the word for bruising).

In any case, if the blood flow is not stopped, it can lead to unconsciousness and death. The symptoms of bleeding within the skull include:

- nausea and vomiting
- **headache**
- loss of consciousness
- unequal pupil size
- lethargy

Postconcussion syndrome

If the head injury is mild, there may be no symptoms other than a slight headache. There also may be confusion, dizziness, and blurred vision. While the head injury may seem to have been quite mild, in many cases symptoms persist for days or weeks. Up to 60 percent of persons who sustain a mild brain injury continue to experience a range of symptoms called postconcussion syndrome as long as six months or a year after the injury.

The symptoms of postconcussion syndrome can result in a puzzling interplay of behavioral, cognitive, and emotional complaints that can be difficult to diagnose, including the following:

- headache
- dizziness
- mental confusion
- behavior changes
- memory loss
- cognitive deficits
- depression
- emotional outbursts

When to call the doctor

A parent of a child who has had a head injury and who is experiencing any the following symptoms should seek medical care immediately:

- serious bleeding from the head or face
- loss of consciousness, however brief
- confusion and lethargy
- lack of pulse or breathing
- clear fluid drainage from the nose or ear

Diagnosis

The extent of damage in a severe head injury can be assessed with **computed tomography** (CT) scan, **magnetic resonance imaging** (MRI), positron emission tomography (PET) scans, electroencephalograms (EEG), and routine neurological and neuropsychological evaluations.

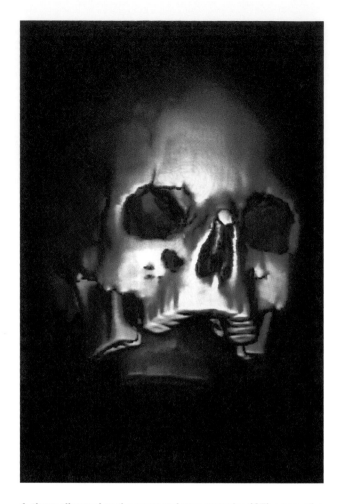

A three-dimensional computed tomography (CT) scan of a human skull showing a depressed skull fracture above the right eye. *(Custom Medical Stock Photo, Inc.)*

Doctors use the Glasgow Coma Scale to evaluate the extent of brain damage based on observing a person's ability to open his or her eyes, respond verbally, and respond to stimulation by moving (motor response). People can score from three to 15 points on this scale. People who score below eight when they are admitted usually have suffered a severe brain injury and will need rehabilitative therapy as they recover. In general, higher scores on the Glasgow Coma Scale indicate less severe brain injury and a better prognosis for recovery.

Individuals with a mild head injury who experience symptoms are advised to seek out the care of a specialist; unless a **family** physician is thoroughly familiar with medical literature in this area, experts warn that there is a good chance that people's complaints after a mild head injury will be downplayed or dismissed. In the case of mild head injury or postconcussion syndrome, CT and MRI scans, electroencephalograms (EEG), and routine neurological evaluations all may be normal because the damage is so subtle. In many cases, these tests cannot detect the microscopic damage that occurs when fibers are stretched in a mild, diffuse injury. In this type of injury, the axons lose some of their covering and become less efficient. This mild injury to the white matter reduces the quality of communication between different parts or the brain. A PET scan, which evaluates cerebral blood flow and brain metabolism, may be of help in diagnosing mild head injury.

Persons with continuing symptoms after a mild head injury should call a local chapter of a head-injury foundation that can refer people to the best nearby expert.

Treatment

If a concussion, bleeding inside the skull, or skull fracture is suspected, the person should be kept quiet in a darkened room, with head and shoulders raised slightly on pillow or blanket.

After initial emergency treatment, a team of specialists may be needed to evaluate and treat the problems that result. A penetrating wound may require surgery. Those with severe injuries or with a deteriorating level of consciousness may be kept hospitalized for observation. If there is bleeding inside the skull, the blood may need to be surgically drained; if a clot has formed, it may need to be removed. Severe skull **fractures** also require surgery. Supportive care and specific treatments may be required if the person experiences further complications. People who experience seizures, for example, may be given anticonvulsant drugs, and people who develop fluid on the brain (**hydrocephalus**) may have a shunt inserted to drain the fluid.

In the event of long-term disability as a result of head injury, there are a variety of treatment programs available, including long-term rehabilitation, coma treatment centers, transitional living programs, behavior management programs, life-long residential or day treatment programs and independent living programs.

Prognosis

Prompt, proper diagnosis and treatment can help alleviate some of the problems that may develop after a head injury. However, it usually is difficult to predict the outcome of a brain injury in the first few hours or days; a person's prognosis may not be known for many months or even years.

The outlook for someone with a minor head injury generally is good, although recovery may be delayed, and symptoms such as headache, dizziness, and cogni-

KEY TERMS

Computed tomography (CT)—An imaging technique in which cross-sectional x rays of the body are compiled to create a three-dimensional image of the body's internal structures; also called computed axial tomography.

Electroencephalogram (EEG)—A record of the tiny electrical impulses produced by the brain's activity picked up by electrodes placed on the scalp. By measuring characteristic wave patterns, the EEG can help diagnose certain conditions of the brain.

Magnetic resonance imaging (MRI)—An imaging technique that uses a large circular magnet and radio waves to generate signals from atoms in the body. These signals are used to construct detailed images of internal body structures and organs, including the brain.

Positron emission tomography (PET)—A computerized diagnostic technique that uses radioactive substances to examine structures of the body. When used to assess the brain, it produces a three-dimensional image that shows anatomy and function, including such information as blood flow, oxygen consumption, glucose metabolism, and concentrations of various molecules in brain tissue.

tive problems can persist for up to a year or longer after an accident. This can limit a person's ability to work and cause strain in personal relationships.

Serious head injuries can be devastating, producing permanent mental and physical disability. Epileptic seizures may occur after a severe head injury, especially a penetrating brain injury, a severe skull fracture, or a serious brain hemorrhage. Recovery from a severe head injury can be very slow, and it may take five years or longer to heal completely. Risk factors associated with an increased likelihood of memory problems or seizures after head injury include age, length and depth of coma, duration of post-traumatic and retrograde amnesia, presence of focal brain injuries, and initial Glasgow Coma Scale score.

As researchers learn more about the long-term effects of head injuries, they uncover links to later conditions. A 2003 report found that mild brain injury during childhood could speed up expression of **schizophrenia** in those who were already likely to get the disorder because of genetics. Those with a history of a childhood brain injury, even a minor one, were more likely to get familial schizophrenia than a sibling and to have earlier onset. Another study in 2003 found that people who had a history of a severe head injury were four times more likely to develop Parkinson's disease than the average population. Those requiring hospitalization for their head injuries were 11 times as likely. The risk did not increase for people receiving mild head injuries.

Prevention

Many severe head injuries could be prevented by wearing protective helmets during certain **sports** and when riding a bike or motorcycle. Seat belts and airbags can prevent many head injuries that result from car accidents. Appropriate protective headgear always should be worn on the job where head injuries are a possibility.

Parental concerns

Parents should insist that their children always use a seat belt when riding in a car. They should also insist that appropriate protective headgear always be worn when children engage in activities such as bicycling or rollerblading during which a head injury is possible. If a parent suspects a caregiver of abusing their child, prompt intervention is required.

Resources

BOOKS

Hergenroeder, Albert C., and Joseph N. Chorley. "Head and Neck Injuries." In *Nelson Textbook of Pediatrics*, 17th ed. Edited by Richard E. Behrman et al. Philadelphia: Saunders, 2003, pp. 2313–4.

Hodge, Charles J. "Head Injury." In *Cecil Textbook of Medicine*, 22nd ed. Edited by Lee Goldman et al. Philadelphia: Saunders, 2003, pp. 2241–2.

Ropper, Allan H. "Traumatic Injuries of the Head and Spine." In *Harrison's Principles of Internal Medicine*, 15th ed. Edited by Eugene Braunwald et al. New York: McGraw-Hill, 2001, pp. 2434–41.

Saunders, Charles E., et al. *Current Emergency Diagnosis and Treatment*. New York: McGraw-Hill, 2003.

PERIODICALS

Chamelian, L., and A. Feinstein. "Outcome after mild to moderate traumatic brain injury: The role of dizziness." *Archives of Physical Medicine and Rehabilitation* 85, no. 10 (2004): 1662–6.

Hrysomallis, C. "Impact energy attenuation of protective football headgear against a yielding surface." *Journal of Science and Medicine in Sport* 7, no. 2 (2004): 156–64.

Stern, B., et al. "Profiles of patients with a history of mild head injury." *International Journal of Neuroscience* 114, no. 9 (2004): 1223–37.

Stocchetti, N., et al. "Inaccurate early assessment of neurological severity in head injury." *Journal of Neurotrauma* 21, no. 9 (2004): 1131–40.

ORGANIZATIONS

American Academy of Emergency Medicine. 611 East Wells Street, Milwaukee, WI 53202. Web site: <www.aaem.org/>.

American Academy of Neurology. 1080 Montreal Avenue, St. Paul, MN 55116. Web site:

American Academy of Pediatrics. 141 Northwest Point Blvd., Elk Grove Village, IL 60007–1098. Web site: .

American College of Emergency Physicians. PO Box 619911, Dallas, TX 75261–9911. Web site: .

American College of Sports Medicine. 401 W. Michigan St., Indianapolis, IN 46202–3233. Web site: .

International Brain Injury Association. 1150 South Washington St., Suite 210, Alexandria, VA 22314. Web site: .

WEB SITES

Cyr, Dawna L., and Steven B. Johnson. "First Aid for Head Injuries." *University of Maine Cooperative Extension*. Available online at <www.cdc.gov/nasd/docs/d000801-d000900/d000815/d000815.html> (accessed January 6, 2005).

"Head and Brain Injuries." *MedlinePlus*. Available online at <www.nlm.nih.gov/medlineplus/headandbraininjuries.html> (accessed January 6, 2005).

"Head Injuries: What to Watch for Afterward." *American Academy of Family Physicians*. Available online at <http://familydoctor.org/x4958.xml> (accessed January 6, 2005).

"Head Injury." *Institute for Neurology and Neurosurgery*. Available online at <http://nyneurosurgery.org/head_intro.htm> (accessed January 6, 2005).

"The Management of Minor Closed Head Injury in Children (AC9858)." *American Academy of Pediatrics*. Available online at <www.aap.org/policy/ac9858.html> (accessed January 6, 2005).

L. Fleming Fallon, Jr., MD, DrPH

Head lice *see* Lice infestation

Head Start programs

Definition

Head Start is a federally funded **preschool** program that provides comprehensives services to both low-income children and their families.

Description

Head Start is a federal program for preschool children three to five years of age in low-income families. Its aim is to prepare children for success in school through an early learning program. The Head Start program is managed by local nonprofit organizations in almost every county in the country. Children who attend Head Start engage in various education activities. They also receive free medical and dental care, have healthy meals and snacks, and enjoy playing indoors and outdoors in a safe setting.

Head Start helps all children succeed, even those with disabilities. Services are also available to infants and toddlers in selected sites.

Head Start began in 1965 as part of the War on Poverty program launched by president Lyndon B. Johnson. Nearly half the nation's poor people were children under age 12, and Head Start was developed to respond as early as possible to the needs of poor children. A few privately funded preschool programs for poor children in inner cities and rural areas showed marked success in raising children's intellectual skills. Many low-income children also had unrecognized health problems and had not been immunized. Head Start was imagined as a comprehensive program that would provide health and nutritional services to poor children, while also developing their cognitive skills. The program aimed to involve parents as well. Many parents of children in the program were employed as teachers' aides so they would understand what their children were learning and help carry on that learning at home.

The program was political from its beginning. Head Start was launched with much fanfare by Lady Bird Johnson, Lyndon Johnson's wife. Measuring the program's success is not a simple matter, however. Head Start saves taxpayers' money, because children who attend Head Start are more likely to graduate high school and get a job than their peers who do not attend. While the savings long-term that result from this program cannot be estimated in dollar value, some sources have suggested that $6 are probably saved for every $1 invested in the Head Start program. Other studies merely suggest that Head Start graduates are more likely than their peers

to stay in the proper grade level for their age in elementary school.

In the early 2000s, Head Start serves nearly 700,000 children across the nation. Most programs are half-day and include lunch. The curriculum is not the same in every program, but in most programs school readiness is stressed. Children may be taught the alphabet and numbers and to recognize colors and shapes. Health care is an important part of the program, and children in Head Start are surveyed to keep them up-to-date on their immunizations, and testing is also available for hearing and vision. Most centers are accredited by the National Association for Education of Young Children (NAEYC).

What Head Start programs offer

Head Start provides children with work that helps them grow mentally, socially, emotionally, and physically. The staff in these programs recognizes parents as the first and most important teachers of their children. They welcome parental involvement in the programs and will work as partners to help both the parent and child progress.

The staff create an environment that offers the child love, acceptance, understanding, and the opportunity to learn and to experience success. Head Start children socialize with others, solve problems, and have other experiences that help them become self-confident. The children also improve their listening and speaking skills.

The children spend time in stimulating settings where they form good habits and enjoy playing with **toys** and working on tasks with classmates. Children leave Head Start programs more prepared for kindergarten, excited about learning, and ready to succeed.

Head Start routine

When the children arrive at the Head Start center, they are greeted by their teachers or student aides. They put whatever they have brought from home in a place that is their own to use every day. Classroom time includes many different tasks. Some teachers begin the day by asking the children to sit in a circle. This encourages the children to talk about an idea or experience they want to share with others. In some centers, the children plan their work. They choose among art, playing and blocks or table toys, science, dancing to music, looking at books, or pretend housekeeping. Children can switch tasks when they are ready for a change.

Each day, the children have time to work in small groups with other children and to **play** outdoors on safe playground equipment when weather allows. In bad weather indoor play is planned. At lunchtime children receive a nutritious meal and brush their teeth after eating. All children are taught to wash their hands before meals and are encouraged to develop good personal and health habits. If they come for an afternoon session, they receive a healthy snack.

Choice of programs

Several different choices are available to meet the varying needs of families:

- Five days per week with half-day preschool classrooms offer various developmental correct educational actions.

- Five days per week, extended-day classroom, are often the choice for working families.

- The combination program option (CPO) strongly focuses on involving the parent, guardian, or primary caregiver in the child's education. Children are invited to take part in a developmentally correct education classroom experience two or three days per week. A home visitor meets with every **family** in their home to provide continuing support and resources at least twice a month.

- Home-based programs provide families with one-hour home visits weekly, and children attend a classroom one day each week. In the home, parents and the visitor plan classwork together.

Family services

Head Start offers children other support services and a chance to be involved in programs designed to help the whole family. Some participating parents learn the English language; others learn to read. Head Start also offers support to parents interested in getting a high school General Equivalency Diploma (GED). If a family member has a special problem, such as drug or alcohol abuse, job loss, or other problem, the family can receive help through Head Start.

Head Start staffers refer families to medical, social welfare, or employment specialists they know in the community, and follow up to be sure the family receives help. Parents can become Head Start volunteers and learn more about child development. This experience may later qualify the volunteer for training that may lead to new employment in the childcare field. Parents also have a voice in the Head Start program by serving on various committees. Parents' experiences in Head Start have raised their own self-confidence and improved their ability to pursue a better life.

Support services for families take various forms. Family counseling advocates work with families to secure proper support to meet individual family needs. Referrals, crisis interventions, and short-term counseling provide families with the necessary tools to become self-sufficient. Health services employ at least one full-time nurse for children and other family members. Nurses screen children within 45 days of enrollment for vision and hearing problems, as well as check each child's height and weight. **Nutrition** and dental services provide students with breakfast and lunch daily. Children in an extended-day program also receive daily snacks. A registered dietitian provides individual nutrition counseling and nutrition workshops. Children learn about good eating habits through weekly nutrition education or cooking projects. A registered dental hygienist helps families find a dentist for their child if needed. Dental screenings are completed on each child within 45 days of enrollment, and hygienists work with children and families to achieve good **oral hygiene**. The program also includes a family liaison, a person who promotes parental participation in the children's education and in workshops on literacy, nutrition, budgeting, health, and other topics. Family orientations are scheduled regularly that give families an opportunity to share in an educational activity with their child. The program offers various educational programs for families such as English as a second language (ESL) and computer science. Disabilities staff serves children with special needs. Developmental screening and **assessment** are provided for the students. Some programs even offer limited bus transportation and interpreters as needed.

Common problems

School phobia and **separation anxiety** affects 3–5 percent of school-age children. The child with school phobia becomes anxious even at the thought of leaving home for school. Complaints of abdominal **pain**, **nausea**, **vomiting**, lack of appetite, and **headache** occur when it is time to go to school and resolve quickly once the child is allowed to remain home. Symptoms do not occur on weekends or holidays unless they are related to going other places, such as Sunday school. These children want to go to school and often earn good grades, but **fear** and **anxiety** prevent them from going.

School phobia in young children has been connected to separation anxiety. A child with separation anxiety is not afraid to go to school but is afraid to leave home. Sometimes children develop school phobia from bullying at school, an excessively critical teacher, and rejection by peers. Events such as marital conflict, moving to a new house, or the arrival of a new sibling can cause fear of going to school.

Peer influence—Peer approval or disapproval of the child's behavior or performance.

School phobia—Childhood anxiety about leaving home to attend school.

Separation anxiety—Childhood fear of leaving parents for any reason.

School phobia affects boys and girls equally. Almost all children with school **phobias** have average or above average **intelligence**. School phobia occurs most often at the start of school for children who are three to five years of age.

Most children who enroll in Head Start attend a half-day center-based program. This sometimes causes a problem for homebound or working parents who need to have another form of child care when the four-hour session ends. However, some communities may operate a full-day program or provide Head Start services at home. In a home-based program, a home visitor teaches parents how to provide learning experiences for their children.

Parents working or volunteering in Head Start programs must learn to work with children other than their own. Sometimes they have problems breaking the maternal attachment with their child if the child is attending the same class session. Teaching the child to be independent when their parents are present may not be difficult.

Staffing and funding Head Start programs is a common problem. Hiring qualified personnel in sufficient numbers may be a problem in schools with high enrollment. Staffing ratios and qualifications are established in federal guidelines and are checked by local boards or state department. The staffing needed may also vary with the age and mental health of the children.

Parental concerns

Parents are first concerned about finding a Head Start program in their service area. They can consult the Head Start directory (on the Head Start Bureau web site). Eligibility in Head Start is determined by the federally identified poverty line.

Parents need to communicate with teachers and stay informed about their child's progress. Visiting the classroom and attending parent-teacher conferences and school activities are important. Showing respect for the teacher and supporting the child's efforts helps the child learn.

Resources

BOOKS

Lombardi, Joan, et al. *Beacon of Hope: The Promise of Early Head Start for America's Youngest Children*. Washington, DC: Zero to Three, 2004.

Vinovskis, Maris A. *The Birth of Head Start: Preschool Education Policies in the Kennedy and Johnson Administrations*. Chicago, IL: University of Chicago Press, 2005.

Zigler, Edward, et al. *The Head Start Debates*. Baltimore, MD: Paul H. Brookes Publishing, 2004.

ORGANIZATIONS

National Head Start Association. 1651 Prince St., Alexandria, VA 22314. Web site: <www.nsha.org>.

WEB SITES

"Bush Administration Sued for Attack on 1st Amendment Rights of Head Start Instructors and Parents/Volunteers." *National Head Start Association*, January 11, 2003. Available online at <www.nhsa.org/press/index_news_061103_release.htm> (accessed December 15, 2004).

Aliene S. Linwood, RN, DPA, FACHE

Headache

Definition

A headache involves **pain** in the head that can arise from many disorders or may be a disorder in and of itself.

Description

Headaches can be categorized as primary or secondary. Primary headaches occur independently and are not the result of another medical problem. Secondary headaches are caused by illness, infection, or injury and account for less than 10 percent of all headaches.

There are many classifications of headaches, including more than 150 diagnostic headache categories identified by the International Headache Society. In general, there are three types of primary headaches, including:

- Tension headaches—muscular contraction headaches that occur periodically or daily (chronic daily headache). The typical tension-type headache is described as a tightening around the head and neck, and an accompanying dull ache. The headache may last from 30 minutes to several days. Tension headaches usually are not associated with symptoms of **nausea** or **vomiting**.

- Migraine—moderate to severe throbbing pain occurring on one or both sides of the head. Migraines are often accompanied by other symptoms such as nausea, vomiting, blurred vision, and sensitivity to light, sound, strong odors, and movement. A migraine with aura has accompanying "warning signs" that indicate a pending attack. A hemiplegic migraine is associated with weakness on one side of the face, arm, or leg. A migraine may last from two to 48 hours and usually occurs two to four times per month.

- Cluster headaches—severe headaches characterized by pain centering around one eye, and eye tearing and nasal congestion occurring on the same side. The headache lasts from 15 minutes to four hours and may recur several times in a day. Cluster headaches have a characteristic grouping of attacks, which may last from two weeks to three months.

Some chronic tension headaches may start as migraines but become daily headaches. These are called transformed migraines. Drug rebound headaches are those that occur from over-using medications for headache pain; they result from exceeding labeling instructions or a physician's directions.

Headaches that occur along with other neurological symptoms, such as balance problems and vision changes, may be a sign of a disease process in the brain. These organic causes of headache may include **hydrocephalus** (abnormal build-up of fluid in the brain), infection of the brain, tumor, or other conditions.

Demographics

Headaches are very common in children and adolescents. One study reported that 56 percent of boys and 74 percent of girls between ages 12 and 17 have at least one headache within a 30-day period. Tension headaches are the most common type of headache, affecting 15–20 percent of adolescents. The American Council for Headache Education (ACHE) estimates 4–10 percent of children have migraine headaches. Many adults with headaches report that they first began in childhood, and 20 percent report headache onset before age 10. Before **puberty**, migraines occur equally in girls and boys. After puberty, girls are three times more likely to have migraines than boys because of associated hormonal changes and **menstruation**. Headaches are a major cause of missed school days.

Causes and symptoms

Causes

Most headaches in children and adolescents are benign and not the result of an underlying disease or disorder. Rather, most headaches in children are the result of stress and muscle tension, lack of **sleep**, or the **common cold**, flu, or sinus or ear infection.

Traditional theories about headaches link tension-type headaches to muscle contraction, and migraine and cluster headaches to blood vessel dilation (swelling). Pain-sensitive structures in the head include blood vessel walls, membranous coverings of the brain, and scalp and neck muscles. Brain tissue itself has no sensitivity to pain. Therefore, headaches may result from contraction of the muscles of the scalp, face or neck; dilation of the blood vessels in the head; or brain swelling that stretches the brain's coverings. Involvement of specific nerves of the face and head may also cause characteristic headaches. Sinus inflammation is a common cause of headache.

Tension-type headaches are often brought on by emotional or mental stress, overexertion, poor posture, loud noise, and other external factors.

In post-puberty girls, a hormonal connection is likely, since headaches occur at specific points in the menstrual cycle.

Secondary headaches are caused by a wide range of conditions, including some rare diseases and other more treatable conditions. Secondary headaches may be the result of infection, **meningitis**, tumors, or localized **head injury**.

Some headaches have a genetic link; sensitivities to certain environmental triggers and migraines also have been identified in one or both parents.

HEADACHE TRIGGERS Migraines are often triggered by food and environmental factors. Known food triggers include chocolate; aged cheeses; pizza; monosodium glutamate (MSG); bananas; nuts; peanut butter; ice cream; yogurt; fatty or fried foods; processed meats containing nitrates, such as hot dogs and pepperoni; certain food dyes; artificial sweeteners such as aspartame; and **caffeine**. Environmental triggers include weather changes; **smoking**; strong odors; and bright lights. Other triggers include sudden changes in sleep patterns and changes in hormone levels. By keeping a headache diary, the child and parents can identify and then avoid the specific substances that seem to cause headache symptoms.

When to call the doctor

The parent or caregiver should call the child's pediatrician or neurologist when the child has these symptoms or conditions:

- headache pain that interrupts sleep
- early morning vomiting without an upset stomach
- worsening headache symptoms
- headaches that prevent the child from participating in usual activities
- frequent headaches, occurring three or more times per week
- headache characteristics that are completely different or new
- headache caused by strenuous activity, bending, coughing, or exertion
- headaches that become more severe and/or frequent over time
- **family** history of neurological disease
- headache pain requiring a pain reliever daily or almost every day
- headache pain requiring more than the recommended dose of over-the-counter pain relievers

The parent or caregiver should seek prompt medical attention when the child has these symptoms or conditions:

- Headache is described as the "Worst headache of my life." This may indicate an aneurysm or other neurological emergency.
- Headache accompanied by weakness, **numbness**, paralysis, visual loss, speech difficulty, loss of balance, falling, seizures, shortness of breath, mental confusion, or loss of consciousness. These symptoms could indicate a pending **stroke**.
- Sudden onset of headache, especially if accompanied by a **fever** and stiff neck. These symptoms could indicate meningitis.
- Visual changes, including blurry vision, "blind spots," or double vision.
- Headaches that persist after a head injury or accident.
- Personality changes or inappropriate or unusual behavior.
- Headaches accompanied by severe nausea or vomiting.
- A fever, rash, or stiff neck that occurs with a headache.

Diagnosis

All children who experience headaches on a relatively regular basis should be evaluated. Since headaches arise from many causes, a physical exam assesses general health and a neurological exam evaluates the possibility of neurological disease that is causing the headache. The doctor will look for signs of illness, including fever, high blood pressure, muscle weakness, difficulties with balance, or visual problems.

If the headache is the primary illness, the doctor elicits a thorough history of the headache to help classify the headache, including:

- age of onset
- duration and frequency
- types of headaches experienced
- when the headaches occur
- pain intensity and location
- accompanying symptoms or warning signs of headache onset
- possible triggers or causes of the headaches
- types of headache treatments used and their effectiveness
- presence of any prior symptoms
- impact on school and activities

The child's medical and family history help the physician determine if the child has any conditions or disorders that might contribute to or cause the headache. A family history of migraines or neurological disease might suggest a genetic predisposition to the condition.

The diagnostic evaluation for headache may include blood tests and urinalysis to rule out other medical conditions that may be causing the headaches. Neurological imaging tests such as **computed tomography** (CT) scan or **magnetic resonance imaging** (MRI) may be performed to rule out the presence of neurological diseases or disorders. Other tests may include a sinus x ray and ophthalmology examination. If a condition affecting the brain and spinal cord is suspected, a lumbar puncture or spinal tap may be performed.

A psychological **assessment** is not part of a routine headache evaluation but may be performed to identify stress triggers.

Treatment

The specific treatment prescribed will depend upon the type and frequency of the headache, its cause, and the child's age.

Headache diary

A headache diary can be used to record the characteristics of headaches, including possible triggers, such as foods, weather changes, odors, mood, stressful situations, emotions, or menstrual phases. It also can help the doctor identify the appropriate treatment.

Lifestyle changes

Making certain dietary and lifestyle changes can significantly improve the child's headache symptoms. **Exercise** is an important part of a healthy lifestyle. It aids in stress reduction and improves circulation, which may help reduce headache symptoms. Relaxation and stress management techniques may help the child cope with headache symptoms. Getting enough sleep is equally important; most children and adolescents need at least eight to 10 hours of sleep per night. Counseling can help the child identify stressful situations or events that cause the headaches. It also can teach the child various coping strategies.

Medications

Some children may find enough relief with over-the-counter pain relievers in the right dose. Other children need more aggressive treatment that includes preventive (prophylactic) medication.

Headache medications are classified as abortive, prophylactic, or symptom relief. Abortive medications treat a headache in progress, prophylactic medications prevent a headache, and symptom relief medications relieve associated headache symptoms.

Abortive medications are taken with the onset of the first sign of a migraine. Some prescribed abortive medications include the triptan drugs such as sumatriptan (Imitrex), zolmitriptan (Zomig), naratriptan (Amerge), and ergotamine tartrate and caffeine (Caffergot).

Prophylactic medications are prescribed to treat frequent tension headaches or migraines, or the combination of both headaches. These medications must be taken daily to reduce the frequency and severity of headaches, and they may take a few weeks to be fully effective. Some prophylactic treatments include **antidepressants**, **antihistamines**, nonsteroidal anti-inflammatories (NSAIDs), prednisone, beta-blockers, and calcium channel blockers.

Symptom relief medications are used to relieve symptoms associated with headaches, including headache pain or nausea. These drugs may include over-the-counter pain-relieving medications such as **acetaminophen**, ibuprofen, naproxen, or anti-nausea medications (called antiemitics). Prescribed symptom relief medications may include sedatives (to induce sleep) and muscle relaxants. If symptom relief medications are needed more than twice a week, the child should see his or her doctor, who can make adjustments to the treatment plan. When taken more than three times per week, symptom relief medications can actually cause a type of headache called a rebound headache. To treat rebound headaches, all pain-relieving medications are usually discontinued for a few weeks (as advised by the physician), then used no more than two to three times per week to relieve symptoms.

Alternative treatment

Alternative headache treatments include:

- relaxation techniques, such as meditation, deep breathing exercises, progressive muscle relaxation, guided imagery, and relaxation to music
- **yoga**
- acupuncture or acupressure
- biofeedback
- chiropractic
- homeopathic remedies chosen specifically for the individual and his or her type of headache
- hydrotherapy
- massage to reduce stress and tension and relieve tight muscles in the neck and shoulders
- essential oils such as lavender, ginger, peppermint, and wintergreen that can provide relief by simply smelling them or applying them to the temples or neck
- regular physical exercise

Biofeedback, which teaches patients how to direct mental thoughts to influence physical functions, may be helpful for some patients. For example, patients can use certain relaxation techniques to help them learn how their personal response to muscle tension is related to their headache symptoms. By practicing biofeedback, a patient may be able to stop a migraine attack before it occurs or prevent headache symptoms from becoming worse.

Follow-up care

It is important for the child to keep a regular follow-up appointment schedule so the doctor can monitor the effects of treatment and make any necessary medication adjustments.

KEY TERMS

Abortive—Referring to treatment that relieves symptoms of a disorder. Abortive headache medications are used to stop the headache process and prevent symptoms of migraines, including pain, nausea, sound and light sensitivity, and other symptoms.

Acupuncture—Based on the same traditional Chinese medical foundation as acupressure, acupuncture uses sterile needles inserted at specific points to treat certain conditions or relieve pain.

Acute—Refers to a disease or symptom that has a sudden onset and lasts a relatively short period of time.

Analgesics—A class of pain-relieving medicines, including aspirin and Tylenol.

Aneurysm—A weakened area in the wall of a blood vessel which causes an outpouching or bulge. Aneurysms may be fatal if these weak areas burst, resulting in uncontrollable bleeding.

Anti-inflammatory—A class of drugs, including nonsteroidal anti-inflammatory drugs (NSAIDs) and corticosteroids, used to relieve swelling, pain, and other symptoms of inflammation.

Antidepressant drug—A medication prescribed to relieve major depression. Classes of antidepressants include selective serotonin reuptake inhibitors (fluoxetine/Prozac, sertraline/Zoloft), tricyclics (amitriptyline/Elavil), MAOIs (phenelzine/Nardil), and heterocyclics (bupropion/Wellbutrin, trazodone/Desyrel).

Antiemetic drug—A medication that helps control nausea; also called an antinausea drug.

Antihistamine—A drug used to treat allergic conditions that blocks the effects of histamine, a substance in the body that causes itching, vascular changes, and mucus secretion when released by cells.

Aura—A subjective sensation or motor phenomenon that precedes and indicates the onset of a neurological episode, such as a migraine or an epileptic seizure. This term also is used to refer to the emanation of light from living things (plants and animals) that can be recorded by Kirlian photography.

Biofeedback—A training technique that enables an individual to gain some element of control over involuntary or automatic body functions.

Chiropractic—A method of treatment based on the interactions of the spine and the nervous system.

Chiropractors adjust or manipulate segments of the patient's spinal column in order to relieve pain.

Chronic—Refers to a disease or condition that progresses slowly but persists or recurs over time.

Cyclic vomiting—Uncontrolled vomiting that occurs repeatedly over a certain period of time.

Decongestants—A group of medications, such as pseudoephedrine, phenylephrine, and phenylpropanolamine, that shrink blood vessels and consequently mucus membranes.

Episodic—Occurring once in a while, without a regular pattern.

Homeopathy—A holistic system of treatment developed in the eighteenth century. It is based on the idea that substances that produce symptoms of sickness in healthy people will have a curative effect when given in very dilute quantities to sick people who exhibit those same symptoms. Homeopathic remedies are believed to stimulate the body's own healing processes.

Hydrotherapy—The use of water (hot, cold, steam, or ice) to relieve discomfort and promote physical well-being. Also called water therapy.

Inflammation—Pain, redness, swelling, and heat that develop in response to tissue irritation or injury. It usually is caused by the immune system's response to the body's contact with a foreign substance, such as an allergen or pathogen.

Lumbar puncture—A procedure in which the doctor inserts a small needle into the spinal cavity in the lower back to withdraw spinal fluid for testing. Also known as a spinal tap.

Magnetic resonance imaging (MRI)—An imaging technique that uses a large circular magnet and radio waves to generate signals from atoms in the body. These signals are used to construct detailed images of internal body structures and organs, including the brain.

Meningitis—An infection or inflammation of the membranes that cover the brain and spinal cord. It is usually caused by bacteria or a virus.

Nervous system—The system that transmits information, in the form of electrochemical impulses, throughout the body for the purpose of activation, coordination, and control of bodily functions. It is comprised of the brain, spinal cord, and nerves.

KEY TERMS (contd.)

Neurologist—A doctor who specializes in disorders of the nervous system, including the brain, spinal cord, and nerves.

Neurology—The study of nerves.

Nitrate—A food additive, commonly found in processed meats, that may be a headache trigger for some people.

Prophylactic—Preventing the spread or occurrence of disease or infection.

Stroke—Interruption of blood flow to a part of the brain with consequent brain damage. A stroke may be caused by a blood clot or by hemorrhage due to a burst blood vessel. Also known as a cerebrovascular accident.

Trigger—Any situation (people, places, times, events, etc.) that causes one to experience a negative emotional reaction, which is often accompanied by a display of symptoms or problematic behavior.

Prognosis

Most headaches are benign (not the result of a severe disease). Headaches are typically resolved through the use of **analgesics** and other treatments. As a child grows, the headaches may disappear.

Prevention

Some headaches may be prevented if the child avoids triggering substances and situations, or practices alternative therapies, such as yoga or biofeedback. Regular exercise and good sleep habits also can help prevent headaches.

Nutritional concerns

Since **food allergies** are often linked with headaches, especially cluster headaches and migraines, identifying and eliminating the allergy-causing food(s) from the diet can be an important preventive measure. To help control migraines, the child should eat three balanced meals at regular intervals, take a multi-vitamin supplement to maintain adequate nutrient needs, and drink four to eight glasses of non-caffeinated fluids per day. Sports drinks during exercise and during a headache can help balance sugar and sodium levels. To prevent headache symptoms associated with certain foods, parents should work with a registered dietitian to facilitate specific dietary changes. They also should carefully read food labels to identify and avoid dietary triggers.

Parental concerns

It is important for parents to reassure their child that most headaches are not caused by a serious illness. Parents can help their child create and maintain a headache diary to record headache symptoms, triggers, as well as the duration and frequency of the headaches. Parents should make sure their child drinks enough fluids, eats three well-balanced meals each day, gets plenty of sleep, and balances activities to avoid an over-crowded schedule that may cause stress and lead to a headache. When headaches occur, parents should allow the child to take a nap; a dark, quiet room is usually preferred by the child. In addition, parents can help the child learn relaxation techniques to help relieve or prevent headache symptoms. If the headaches are linked to **anxiety** or depression, the parents should ask the child's doctor for a referral to a counselor who can provide additional assistance.

Resources

BOOKS

Diamond, Seymour, M.D. *Headache and Your Child: The Complete Guide to Understanding and Treating Migraine and Other Headaches in Children and Adolescents.* New York: Fireside, 2001.

Silberstein, Stephen D., M.D., FACP, et al. *Headache in Clinical Practice.* 2nd ed. London, England: Martin Dunitz, Ltd., 2002.

Wolff, Harold G., et al. *Wolff's Headache and Other Head Pain.* New York: Oxford University Press, Inc., 2001.

ORGANIZATIONS

American Council for Headache Education (ACHE). 19 Mantua Road, Mt. Royal, NJ 08061. (856) 423-0258. Web site: <www.achenet.org>.

American Headache Society. 19 Mantua Rd., Mt Royal, NJ 08061.(856) 423-0043. Web site: <www.ahsnet.org>.

MAGNUM (Migraine Awareness Group: A National Understanding for Migraineurs). 113 South St. Asaph St., Suite 300, Alexandria, VA 22314. (703) 739-9384. Web site: <www.migraines.org>.

National Headache Foundation. 820 N. Orleans, Suite 217, Chicago, IL 60610. (888) NHF-5552. Web site: <www.headaches.org>.

National Institutes of Health (NIH). National Institute of Neurological Disorders and Stroke. NIH Neurological Institute. P.O. Box 5801, Bethesda, MD 20824. (800) 352-9424. Web site: <www.ninds.nih.gov>.

WEB SITES

Excedrin Headache Resource Center. Sponsored by Bristol-Myers Squibb Company. Available online at: <www.Excedrin.com>.

Headache Impact Test. A tool to measure the impact headaches are having on patients' lives, to track headaches over time, and to share this information with the physician. Available online at: <www.headachetest.com>.

Migraine Information Center. Sponsored by GlaxoSmithKline. Available online at: <www.migrainehelp.com>.

"When Kids Get Headaches." The Nemours Foundation. [cited October 12, 2004]. Available online at: <www.kidshealth.org/parent/general/aches/headache.html>.

Julia Barrett
Angela M. Costello

Hearing impairment

Definition

Hearing impairment is the temporary or permanent loss of some or all hearing in one or both ears.

Description

There are three types of hearing impairment that occur in young children:

- conductive hearing loss, a usually temporary interference with the reception of sound from the outer ear to the middle or inner ear
- sensorineural hearing impairment, a permanent abnormality of the cochlear hair cells of the inner ear, the auditory nerve, or the auditory center of the brain
- mixed hearing impairment, a combination of conductive and sensorineural impairments

Hearing impairments also are classified as prelingual (occurring before a child learns to speak) and postlingual (occurring after the child has acquired language).

Normal hearing in children is defined as the ability to hear sounds in the range of 0–25 decibels (dB). Hearing impairments are classified in the following degrees:

- Mild, in which a child hears sounds from 26–40 dB. Speech and conversation are usually unaffected but distant sounds may be difficult to hear.
- Moderate, in which a child hears sounds from 41–70 dB. The ability to form sounds and hear normal conversation is affected.
- Severe, in which a child hears sounds from 71–90 dB. The child requires a hearing aid to hear conversations.
- Profound, in which a child can only hear sounds above 90 dB. A hearing aid may help but the child will not be able to articulate words normally.

Demographics

Temporary and permanent hearing impairments are not uncommon among children.

Conductive hearing impairment is most often caused by **otitis media**, an infection of the middle ear. This is very common in children between the ages of six months and four years. About 20 percent of children have an episode of acute otitis media every year. It affects boys and girls equally. Otitis media is more common among children of Eskimo or Native American descent and among children whose parents smoke. The condition is less common in children over the age of eight. Chronic secretory otitis media, also called otitis media with effusion or suppurative otitis media, is the most common cause of temporary hearing impairment in children under eight. It is more common in boys and rare in children over age eight.

About 12,000 American infants annually are born with some degree of hearing impairment. Although congenital (present at birth) deafness is the rarest form of deafness, it is the most common congenital abnormality in newborns. Three out of every 1,000 children are born with significant hearing impairment. About 65 percent of these children are born deaf and an additional 12 percent become deaf before the age of three. In the United States 14.9 percent of children aged six to 19 have measurable hearing impairment in one or both ears.

Noise-induced hearing impairment is increasing in the United States. It is not uncommon for teenagers to become permanently hearing impaired in the high-frequency range above 4,000 hertz.

Causes and symptoms

Conductive hearing impairment

Children develop otitis media because the eustachian tubes that connect the middle ear with the back of the mouth and equalize air pressure and drain fluid are small and easily obstructed. Acute otitis media can result from a respiratory infection such as a cold that causes an inflammation that blocks a eustachian tube. The fluid that builds up in the middle ear is susceptible to bacterial and viral infection. If the blockage persists it causes chronic secretory otitis media, the most common cause of conductive hearing impairment in children.

A painful earache and temporary hearing impairment in one ear are common symptoms of acute otitis media. The symptoms of secretory otitis media develop gradually and fluctuate. They are usually worse in the winter. Symptoms of partial hearing loss from secretory otitis media may go unnoticed for some time and may include the following symptoms:

- immature speech
- behavioral problems resulting from frustration at not being able to hear well
- sitting close to the television or turning up the volume
- poor school performance

Otitis media sometimes runs in families, indicating that there may be a hereditary component. Second-hand smoke also is a risk factor for otitis media. Conductive hearing impairment from middle ear infections may be associated with other medical conditions including the following problems:

- asthma or allergic rhinitis
- **cleft palate**, which impairs drainage of the middle ears through the eustachian tubes (Some 30% of children with cleft palate have conductive hearing loss.)
- other head or facial abnormalities
- **Down syndrome**, which is characterized by narrow ear canals resulting in susceptibility to middle ear infections (About 80% of children with Down syndrome have some hearing impairment.)

Another cause of conductive hearing impairment is an excessive build-up of earwax that prevents sound waves from reaching the eardrum. Although earwax, produced by glands in the outer ear canal, normally works its way out of the ear, sometimes excessive amounts build-up and harden in the outer ear canal, gradually impairing hearing.

Sensorineural hearing impairment

Sensorineural hearing impairments result from abnormal development or disorders of the cochlea, the spiral cavity of the inner ear, disorders of the auditory nerve that transmits electrical impulses from the inner ear to the brain, or abnormalities of the auditory center of the brain. Such conditions have a variety of causes. For example, more than 70 known inherited disorders account for about one-half of all severe sensorineural hearing impairments; however, 90 percent of children with congenital hearing impairment are born to parents with normal hearing. In addition, the following problems are associated with sensorineural hearing impairment:

- craniofacial anomalies
- Down syndrome, in many of which cases the child has some immune deficiency that leads to frequent ear infections resulting in hearing loss
- problems during or shortly after birth that may damage the inner ear or auditory nerve
- low birth weigh, below 3.5 lb (1.6 kg)
- incubator noise affecting premature infants
- neonatal exposure to aminoglycoside **antibiotics**
- bacterial infections such as **meningitis** during infancy
- cytomegalovirus (CMV) infection during childhood
- accidents involving head injuries

High-frequency hearing impairment in teenagers most often results from exposure to loud noise such as amplified music.

While about 50 percent of congenital hearing impairments have no known cause, prenatal risk factors for congenital hearing impairment include:

- **rubella** (German **measles**) (More than 50% of children born to mothers who contracted rubella during the first ten weeks of pregnancy suffer from congenital malformations.)
- CMV, the most common viral infection in fetuses, a leading cause of congenital deafness (CMV affects 1% or 40,000 newborns annually; about 8,000 of these newborns have birth defects.)
- other infections, including **toxoplasmosis**, herpes, syphilis, or flu
- drug or alcohol consumption
- drugs that are ototoxins

Symptoms of congenital deafness in newborns include:

- lack of response to loud noises
- lack of response to voices or noise when sleeping in a quiet room
- failure to calm down at the sound of the mother's voice
- failure to make normal baby sounds including cooing by six weeks of age
- failure to look for the source of a noise by three to six months of age

- failure to **play** with noisy **toys**, such as a rattle, by four to eight months
- failure to babble by about six months of age

Symptoms that a baby or young child may have a hearing impairment include:

- lack of reaction to loud noises
- failure to imitate sounds
- lack of response to the child's name during the first year of life
- failure to vocalize (to imitate simple words, enjoy games that involve speech, or talk in two-word sentences during the second year)
- failure to understand simple directions during the third year

When to call the doctor

A physician should be consulted immediately if a parent suspects that a child has a hearing impairment.

Diagnosis

Parents are usually the first to suspect a hearing impairment in their child. Early detection of and intervention for hearing impairments are crucial for preventing or minimizing developmental and educational delays. Hearing-impaired children who are identified and receive early intervention before six months of age develop significantly better language skills than children identified after six months of age. However, in the United States, the average age of diagnosis is at two years of age, and significant hearing impairments have gone undiagnosed in children as old as six.

Newborn hearing tests often are administered only if an infant is considered at risk for congenital deafness. However, routine screening of sleeping newborns is on the increase. If a problem is detected, additional tests are used to determine the type and severity of the impairment. Tests used are as follows:

- An evoked otoacoustic emissions (OAE) test that detects an echo emitted by the inner ear in response to sound; the echo is produced only if the inner ear is healthy and functioning normally.
- An automated auditory brainstem response (ABR) test, or brainstem auditory-evoked response (BAER) test, in which brainstem responses to sounds are monitored through small electrodes taped to the child's head.

Pediatricians may examine a child's ears with a viewing instrument called an otoscope. Age-appropriate hearing tests may be performed routinely throughout childhood. Test administrators who suspect a hearing impairment may cover their mouths to prevent the child from lip reading, also called speech reading. Types of hearing tests include:

- behavioral tests that measure the quietest sound that the child can hear and the ability to understand words
- speech discrimination tests for children with simple vocabularies
- the McCormick toy discrimination test for three-year-olds, in which the child is asked to identify words that sound similar, such as tree and key
- a simple form of **audiometry** that assesses frequency perception through earphones
- tympanometry, in which a probe inserted into the ear measures sound waves bouncing off the eardrum
- acoustical impedance tests to identify middle ear problems including otitis media

Treatment

Conductive hearing impairment

Acute otitis media may be treated with antibiotics. Secretory otitis media usually disappears without treatment. However, a procedure called **myringotomy** or tympanostomy may be used for recurrent acute otitis media or secretory otitis media that persists for several months. A small plastic tube is inserted through the eardrum to drain fluid and equalize the air pressure between the middle ear and the ear canal. The tube usually falls out within six to 12 months and the hole in the eardrum closes. Myringotomy is an outpatient procedure performed under general anesthesia.

Excessive earwax usually can be removed at home, following a doctor's instructions. Special drops are used to soften the wax, and the ears are flushed with water. If necessary a doctor may remove earwax using suction or a metal probe.

Sensorineural hearing impairment

Sensorineural hearing impairment and congenital deafness are incurable. However, any residual hearing can be maximized with a hearing aid. Many types of hearing aids are available for children as young as three months. A postauricular hearing aid fits behind the ear and is connected to a plastic mold that is custom-fitted for the child's ear. These must be replaced as the child grows.

An older child with sufficient residual hearing can use an in-the-ear or in-the-canal hearing aid, in which the entire apparatus fits inside the ear. Hearing aids may be programmed to match a child's particular type of hearing loss. A transposer can change high-pitched sounds that are inaudible to many hearing-impaired children into lower-pitched sounds.

Cochlear implants may be used in children who are profoundly deaf and thus are not candidates for hearing aids. Electrodes are surgically implanted into the cochlea through a hole drilled in the mastoid bone. Cochlear implants rely on three external components: a microphone to pick up sound, a speech processor to select and arrange the sounds, and a transmitter and receiver/stimulator that converts the signals from the processor into electrical impulses. The electrodes in the cochlea collect the impulses from the stimulator and send them to the brain. Although they do not restore normal hearing, cochlear implants can provide substantial improvement in speech recognition and production, as well as the ability to hear and identify common sounds such as doorbells. Most children receive implants between the ages of two and six. As of 2002 about 10,000 American children had cochlear implants. Children with cochlear implants have been found to be at an increased risk for bacterial meningitis.

Various educational approaches are employed for children with hearing impairments:

- lip reading and sign language, particularly for children with severe hearing impairment

- a bilingual-bicultural (bi-bi) approach that considers the deaf community as a separate culture with its own language (American Sign Language [ASL])

- the auditory-oral approach, which relies on powerful hearing aids or cochlear implants, supplemented with lip reading, and uses spoken rather than sign language

- the auditory-verbal (A-V) approach, which relies on enhanced residual hearing and one-on-one teaching to develop auditory skills without lip reading or sign language

- cued speech, a simple visual phonetic-based system of eight handshapes, each representing several consonant sounds, and four positions around the mouth, each representing several vowel sounds

- the total communication approach, which uses multiple methods of communication, including hearing amplification, gestures, lip reading, finger spelling, and one of several English-based sign languages known collectively as Manually Coded English (MCE)

Prognosis

Symptoms of acute otitis media usually disappear within a few days, although a ruptured eardrum may take several weeks to heal. Sometimes hearing is affected for three months or more until all of the fluid has drained from the ear. Following a myringotomy hearing in the affected ear usually returns to normal, often within a few days. As a child grows the eustachian tubes widen and stiffen, allowing air to enter and fluid to drain from the middle ear more efficiently. However, recurrent or chronic otitis media can result in ongoing moderate hearing impairment, often at a stage in which hearing is essential for **language development**.

Children who receive early intervention for hearing impairments can develop at nearly the same rate as other children. However, even a minor hearing impairment can significantly affect a baby's ability to understand and communicate and to acquire speech and language. The effects of hearing impairment on learning depend on the following:

- the severity of the impairment
- the affected frequency range
- the age at which the impairment occurred
- how early the impairment was detected
- how early treatment was initiated

Prevention

Couples with **family** histories of congenital deafness may seek genetic counseling to assess the risks for their children. If they have not already had rubella, women should be vaccinated before becoming pregnant. During pregnancy women should take only drugs that are known to be safe for the fetus.

It is very important for the hearing-impaired to protect residual hearing from loud noise. Teenagers should be encouraged to avoid very loud music. Those at risk for hearing impairment from other loud noises should be encouraged to wear earplugs.

Parental concerns

Hearing is very important for the development of emotional relationships between a child and the family. Families of hearing-impaired children must find additional means of connecting emotionally. Support groups often are very helpful for hearing-impaired children and their families.

Because hearing impairments may delay speech and language acquisition, interfere with **cognitive development**, and disrupt progress in school, the educational decisions that parents make for their child are of special significance. About 50 percent of all children with congenital deafness attend regular schools; the other 50 percent receive some type of specialized schooling.

KEY TERMS

Audiometry—The measurement of hearing ability, usually with the an audiometer.

Auditory brainstem response (ABR)—Brainstem auditory evoked response (BAER), brainstem evoked response (BSER), auditory evoked response (AER); a hearing test that records electrical activity in the brain in response to sound via electrodes on the scalp; used for newborns, infants, and young children.

Cochlea—The hearing part of the inner ear. This snail-shaped structure contains fluid and thousands of microscopic hair cells tuned to various frequencies, in addition to the organ of Corti (the receptor for hearing).

Cochlear implantation—A surgical procedure in which a small electronic device is placed under the skin behind the ear and is attached to a wire that stimulates the inner ear, allowing people who have hearing loss to hear useful sounds.

Conductive hearing impairment—Hearing impairment associated with the outer or middle ear, often caused by infection.

Cytomegalovirus (CMV)—A common human virus causing mild or no symptoms in healthy people, but permanent damage or death to an infected fetus, a transplant patient, or a person with HIV.

Decibel—A unit of the intensity of sound or a measure of loudness. Normal speech is typically spoken in the range of about 20-50 decibels.

Eustachian tube—A thin tube between the middle ear and the pharnyx. Its purpose is to equalize pressure on either side of the ear drum.

Myringotomy—A surgical procedure in which an incision is made in the ear drum to allow fluid or pus to escape from the middle ear.

Otitis media—Inflammation or infection of the middle ear space behind the eardrum. It commonly occurs in early childhood and is characterized by ear pain, fever, and hearing problems.

Otoacoustic emission (OAE)—Sounds or echoes created by vibrations of hair cells in the cochlea in response to sound; used to screen for hearing impairment in newborns.

Otoscope—A hand-held instrument with a tiny light and a funnel-shaped attachment called an ear speculum, which is used to examine the ear canal and eardrum.

Sensorineural hearing loss—Hearing loss caused by damage to the nerves or parts of the inner ear governing the sense of hearing. Sound is conducted normally through the external and middle ear.

Tympanometry—A test where air pressure in the ear canal is varied to test the condition and movement of the ear drum. This test is useful in detecting disorders of the middle ear.

See also Cochlear implants.

Resources

BOOKS

Kurtzer-White, Ellen, and David Luterman, eds. *Early Childhood Deafness.* Washington, DC: AG Bell, 2001.

Niparko, John, et al. *Cochlear Implants: Principles and Practices.* Washington, DC: AG Bell, 2000.

Olsen, Wayne, ed. *Mayo Clinic on Hearing.* Rochester, MN: Mayo Clinic Health Information, 2003.

Roush, Jackson. *Screening for Hearing Loss and Otitis Media in Children.* Washington, DC: AG Bell, 2001.

ORGANIZATIONS

Alexander Graham Bell Association for the Deaf and Hard of Hearing (AG Bell). 3417 Volta Place, NW, Washington, DC 20007. Web site: <www.agbell.org>.

American Speech-Language-Hearing Association. 10801 Rockville Pike, Rockville, MD 20852. Web site: <http://asha.org>.

Deafness Research Foundation. 1050 17th St., NW, Suite 701, Washington, DC 20036. Web site: <www.drf.org>.

WEB SITES

"FDA Public Health Web Notification: Risk of Bacterial Meningitis in Children with Cochlear Implants." *U.S. Food and Drug Administration*, September 25, 2003. Available online at <www.fda.gov/cdrh/safety/cochlear.html> (accessed December 28, 2004).

Gordon Langbein, Amic. "Facts About Hearing Loss in Children." *Alexander Graham Bell.* Available online at <www.agbell.org/information/brochures_faq.cfm> (accessed December 28, 2004).

"So Your Child has a Hearing Loss: Next Steps for Parents." *Alexander Graham Bell.* Available online at

<www.agbell.org/information/brochures_parent_so.cfm> (accessed December 28, 2004).

Margaret Alic, PhD

Hearing test with an audiometer *see* **Audiometry**

Heart disease, congenital *see* **Congenital heart disease**

Heart murmurs

Definition

A heart murmur is an abnormal swishing or whooshing sound made by blood moving through the heart, heart valves, or blood vessels near the heart during the heartbeat cycle. It is heard through a stethoscope by a physician.

Description

When the heart beats, normally it makes two sounds, "lubb" when the valves between the atria and ventricles close, and "dupp" or "dub" when the valves between the ventricles and the major arteries close. A heart murmur is a series of vibratory sounds made by turbulent blood flow through the heart. The sounds are longer than normal heart sounds and can be heard between the normal sounds of the heartbeat.

Heart murmurs can be present at birth or develop later in life. Murmurs are common in infants and children. Nearly two-thirds of heart murmurs in children are produced by a normal, healthy heart and are harmless. This condition is called an innocent heart murmur. It also may be called functional, physiologic, or benign. Innocent heart murmurs are usually very faint, intermittent, and occur in a small area of the chest. They can disappear and reappear from one examination to the next. Most innocent murmurs disappear by adulthood, but some adults may still have them.

Less commonly, heart murmurs can result from a valve defect, narrowed blood vessel, or other cardiovascular defect. These conditions may have been present since birth (congenital) or developed as the result of another medical illness. These conditions, called pathologic heart murmurs, may indicate the presence of a serious heart defect, especially when accompanied by other signs and symptoms of a heart problem such as shortness of breath, rapid heartbeats, or fainting. They are louder, continual, and may be accompanied by a click or gallop sound. **Failure to thrive** is an accompanying symptom.

Some heart murmurs are continually present; others happen only when the heart is working harder than usual, for example during **exercise** or with certain illnesses. Heart murmurs can be diastolic, systolic, or continuous. Diastolic murmurs occur during relaxation of the heart between beats, and systolic murmurs occur during contraction of the heart muscle. Continuous murmurs occur during both the relaxation and contraction of the heart. The characteristics of the murmur may suggest specific alterations in the heart or its valves.

Demographics

Heart murmurs are most commonly discovered in children from ages two to four, although they can be diagnosed at any age. Congenital cardiovascular defects that may cause pathologic heart murmurs affect 36,000 infants (about nine of every 1,000 infants or 1 percent of live births) annually in the United States.

Causes and symptoms

Causes

Many children have heart murmurs that are heard by their doctors at some time in their lives. Innocent heart murmurs are caused by blood flowing faster than normal through the chambers and valves of the heart or the blood vessels near the heart. An increased amount of blood flowing through the heart can also cause an innocent heart murmur. Innocent murmurs may be heard in children because their hearts are very close to their chest walls. Sometimes **anxiety**, stress, **fever**, anemia, and overactive thyroid cause innocent murmurs.

Pathologic heart murmurs are caused by structural abnormalities of the heart. These include defective heart valves, hypertrophic cardiomyopathy (enlarged heart muscle), holes or abnormal openings in the walls of the heart (septal defects), aortic aneurysm, or other **congenital heart disease**.

Heart valve disease is the most common cause of pathologic heart murmurs. Valves that are narrow, tight, or stiff (valvular stenosis) do not open completely and limit the forward flow of blood through the valve. Valves that do not close properly may cause blood to leak back through the valve (called valve regurgitation). Bacterial endocarditis (an infection of the heart) or **rheumatic fever** can damage heart valves or other structures of the heart and lead to heart murmurs.

A septal defect or aortic aneurysm can cause heart murmurs. The most common types of septal defects are **atrial septal defect**, an opening between the two upper heart chambers (atria), and ventricular septal defect, an opening between the two lower heart chambers (ventricles). Some septal defects close on their own; others require surgical treatment to prevent progressive damage to the heart. An aortic aneurysm is an abnormal bulging of part of the aorta that may cause blood to leak through the aortic valve and flow the wrong direction.

Symptoms

The symptoms of heart murmurs differ, depending on the cause of the heart murmur. Innocent heart murmurs and those that do not impair the function of the heart usually do not have symptoms. Murmurs caused by severe abnormalities of a heart valve or another congenital cardiovascular defect may cause feeding problems or failure to grow normally in infants, shortness of breath, **dizziness**, fainting, chest **pain**, palpitations or rapid heartbeats, fatigue with exertion or exercise, and lung congestion.

When to call the doctor

The parent or caregiver should call the child's pediatrician if the child has these symptoms or conditions, which could be the sign of an underlying heart problem:

- feeding problems in infants
- poor weight gain
- swelling in the ankles or feet
- swollen abdomen
- poor exercise tolerance
- recurrent chest colds and respiratory infections
- abnormal blood pressure
- signs of infection including **sore throat**, general body aches or fever

The parent or caregiver should seek emergency treatment by calling 911 in most areas when the child has these symptoms or conditions:

- bluish skin tone
- bluish coloration around the lips, fingernail beds, and tongue
- breathing difficulties or rapid breathing
- dizziness or fainting
- uncontrolled coughing or coughing with blood
- irregular heart beats or palpitations (abnormal heart beats that feel like fluttering in the chest)
- chest pain (although rare in children)

Diagnosis

Heart murmurs can be heard when a physician listens to the heart through a stethoscope during a regular physical exam or check-up. While listening to the heartbeat, the physician carefully evaluates several factors, including the loudness, frequency, pitch, duration, location, and timing of the murmur with the patient's heartbeat. A systolic heart murmur may be classified according to how loud it is, based on a scale from one to six, with a grade 6 being the loudest. However, this scale is not a precise measurement, since it is based on each physician's judgment. If a suspicious heart sound is detected, the physician will evaluate how breathing, exercise, or change of body position affect the sound.

Murmurs caused by congenital cardiovascular disease are often heard at birth or during infancy.

Very loud heart murmurs and those with clicks or extra heart sounds should be evaluated further. Infants who have heart murmurs and do not thrive, eat, or breathe properly, and older children who lose consciousness suddenly or are intolerant to exercise should be evaluated. Children with these symptoms may be referred to a pediatric heart specialist, called a pediatric cardiologist. The cardiologist will perform a physical examination, review the child's personal and **family** medical history, and order tests to evaluate the source of the heart murmur.

The physical exam will be performed to identify signs of illness or physical problems. The child's blood pressure, pulse, reflexes, and height and weight are measured and recorded. Internal organs are palpated, or felt from the outside, to determine if they are enlarged.

To determine if the child has any conditions or disorders that might increase the risk of a cardiovascular defect, the physician will review the child's family medical history.

Tests may include a chest x ray, echocardiogram, or electrocardiogram. A chest x ray is used to look at the size, shape, and location of the heart and lungs. The chest x ray can indicate if the heart is enlarged and can help the doctor identify some heart and lung problems.

An echocardiogram, or echo (cardiac ultrasound) may be used to distinguish an innocent murmur from a pathologic one. On the echo, the doctor may be able to identify a structural heart or vascular problem that is causing the heart murmur. An echo uses ultrasound, or high-frequency sound waves, to create an image of the heart's internal structures. The technician applies gel to a hand-held transducer then presses it against the patient's chest. The sound waves are converted into an image that can be displayed on a monitor. Performed in a cardiology outpatient diagnostic laboratory, the test takes 30 minutes to an hour.

An electrocardiogram (ECG) shows the heart's electrical activity and may reveal muscle thickening, damage, or a lack of oxygen. Electrodes (small, sticky patches) covered with conducting jelly are placed on the patient's chest, arms, and legs. They send impulses of the heart's activity through a monitor (oscilloscope) to a recorder that traces them on a moving strip of paper. The test takes about 10 minutes and is commonly performed in a physician's office. An exercise ECG can reveal additional information.

Cardiac **magnetic resonance imaging** (MRI) is a scanning method that uses magnetic fields and radio waves to create three-dimensional images of the heart. The MRI reveals how blood flows through the heart and how the heart is working. Although not commonly used to diagnose heart murmurs, it may be used to help physicians evaluate certain congenital cardiovascular defects.

In rare cases when the chest x ray, echo, or ECG tests are not conclusive enough to confirm the presence of an underlying congenital cardiovascular defect, a more invasive diagnostic procedure such as angiography and cardiac catheterization may be performed to show the type and severity of heart disease. These procedures should be performed by a specially trained physician and diagnostic team in a well-equipped heart center.

During the catheterization, a long, slender tube called a catheter is inserted into a vein or artery and slowly directed to the heart, using x-ray guidance. To better view the heart and blood vessels, contrast material (dye) is injected through the catheter and viewed and recorded on an x-ray video as it moves through the heart. This imaging technique is called angiography.

Treatment

Innocent heart murmurs do not affect the patient's health and require no treatment. If a septal defect is causing the heart murmurs, corrective surgery may be required. If heart valve disease is causing the heart murmurs, treatment may include medications or surgery. Valve replacement or valve repair surgery are two treatment options for severely damaged or diseased valves. The pediatric cardiologist can recommend the appropriate type and timing of treatment, based on the child's age, condition, and overall health. Patients with heart disease need prophylactic antibiotic for any dental work or medical procedures they undergo.

Alternative treatment

Alternative and complementary therapies include approaches that are considered to be outside the mainstream of traditional health care. If a heart murmur requires surgical treatment, there are no alternative treatments, although there are alternative therapies that are helpful for pre- and post-surgical support of the patient, such as guided imagery for relaxation.

If the heart murmur is innocent, heart activity can be supported using the herb hawthorn (*Crataegus laevigata* or *C. oxyacantha*) or coenzyme Q10. These remedies improve heart contractility and the heart's ability to use oxygen. If the murmur is valvular in origin, herbs that act like **antibiotics** and build resistance to infection in the valve areas may be considered.

Before using any particular technique or remedy, it is important for the parent/caregiver and child to learn about the therapy, its safety and effectiveness, potential side effects, and the expertise and qualifications of the practitioner, if applicable. Although some practices are beneficial, others may be harmful to certain patients. Alternative treatments should not be used as a substitute for medical therapies prescribed by a doctor. Parents should discuss these alternative treatments with the child's doctor to determine the techniques and remedies that may be beneficial for the child.

Nutritional concerns

Children with an underlying congenital cardiovascular defect tend to gain weight slowly. An 8-ounce to 1-pound (225–450-gram) weight gain in a month may be acceptable. The physician will monitor the child's weight gain and advise the parents of the goal weight gain and any necessary dietary changes. The most common reason for poor growth among children with congenital cardiovascular defects is they are not taking in enough calories or nutrients. Some other factors that may interfere with growth are the following:

- rapid heart beat and increased breathing rate
- poor appetite
- decreased food intake due to rapid breathing and fatigue
- frequent respiratory infections
- poor absorption of nutrients from the digestive tract
- decreased oxygen in the blood

For infants with congenital cardiovascular defects, **nutrition** supplements may need to be added to regular formula or breast milk. Sometimes additional feedings are required with the aid of a nasogastric tube to provide

Anemia—A condition in which there is an abnormally low number of red blood cells in the bloodstream. It may be due to loss of blood, an increase in red blood cell destruction, or a decrease in red blood cell production. Major symptoms are paleness, shortness of breath, unusually fast or strong heart beats, and tiredness.

Artery—A blood vessel that carries blood away from the heart to the cells, tissues, and organs of the body.

Atrial—Referring to the upper chambers of the heart.

Atrial fibrillation—A type of heart arrhythmia in which the upper chamber of the heart quivers instead of pumping in an organized way. In this condition, the upper chambers (atria) of the heart do not completely empty when the heart beats, which can allow blood clots to form.

Bacterial endocarditis—An infection caused by bacteria that enter the bloodstream and settle in the heart lining, a heart valve, or a blood vessel. People with congenital cardiovascular defects have an increased risk of developing bacterial endocarditis, so preventive antibiotics are prescribed before surgery, invasive tests or procedures, and dental work to reduce this risk.

Congenital—Present at birth.

Echocardiogram—A record of the internal structures of the heart obtained from beams of ultrasonic waves directed through the wall of the chest.

Electrocardiagram (ECG, EKG)—A record of the electrical activity of the heart, with each wave being labeled as P, Q, R, S, and T waves. It is often used in the diagnosis of cases of abnormal cardiac rhythm and myocardial damage.

Hypertension—Abnormally high arterial blood pressure, which if left untreated can lead to heart disease and stroke.

Hypothyroidism—A disorder in which the thyroid gland produces too little thyroid hormone causing a decrease in the rate of metabolism with associated effects on the reproductive system. Symptoms include fatigue, difficulty swallowing, mood swings, hoarse voice, sensitivity to cold, forgetfulness, and dry/coarse skin and hair.

Pathologic—Characterized by disease or by the structural and functional changes due to disease.

Pericardium—The thin, sac-like membrane that surrounds the heart and the roots of the great vessels. It has two layers: the inner, serous (or visceral) pericardium and the outer, fibrous (or parietal) pericardium.

Phenylketonuria—A condition caused by a genetic error of the body's metabolism, characterized by the absence of phenylalanine hydroxylase (an enzyme that converts phenylalanine into tyrosine). Phenylalanine accumulates in blood and seriously impairs early neuronal development. The defect can be effectively controlled by diet.

Rheumatic fever—An illness that arises as a complication of an untreated or inadequately treated streptococcal infection of the throat. It ususally occurs among school-aged children and cause serious damage to the heart valves.

Septal—Relating to the septum, the thin muscle wall dividing the right and left sides of the heart. Holes in the septum are called septal defects.

Septum—A wall or partition. Often refers to the muscular wall dividing the left and right heart chambers or the partition in the nose that separates the two nostrils. Also refers to an abnormal fold of tissue down that center of the uterus that can cause infertility.

Stenosis—A condition in which an opening or passageway in the body is narrowed or constricted.

Ventricles—The lower pumping chambers of the heart. The ventricles push blood to the lungs and the rest of the body.

enough calories and promote weight gain. The nasogastric tube is placed in the baby's nose and passes to the stomach, and formula or breast milk is delivered through the tube. Breastfeeding may not be possible right after delivery, depending on the child's condition, so a breast pump may be used to maintain the mother's milk supply during times when the baby cannot nurse.

Babies with congenital cardiovascular defects tire quickly during feedings, so frequent feedings are necessary. Feedings should be on-demand and may need to be as frequent as every two hours in the first few months. Some babies have difficulty feeding from a regular bottle nipple, so different brands may need to be tried. If medications are prescribed, they should be given before a feeding. Medications should not be mixed in the formula or breast milk unless the doctor advises to do so.

The pediatrician will advise when solid foods can be started, usually around six months of age. Fat should not be restricted in the diet, especially in the first two years. High-calorie foods and snacks can play an important role in providing good nutrition and helping the child grow at a healthy rate.

Follow-up care

Along with routine medical care and standard immunizations, periodic heart check-ups are necessary in children who have congenital cardiovascular defects. Usually, heart check-up appointments are scheduled more frequently just after the diagnosis or after treatment. Additional immunizations, such as the **influenza** vaccine, may be recommended.

Prognosis

Most children with innocent heart murmurs grow out of them by the time they reach adulthood. Children with complex heart disease may continue to need special medical attention throughout **adolescence** and into adulthood for survival and to maintain quality of life.

Prevention

Heart murmurs cannot be prevented. However, if a child has been diagnosed with valve disease or another congenital cardiovascular defect, the American Heart Association recommends regular dental check-ups to prevent infections of the mouth as well as the preventive use of antibiotics to reduce the risk of heart infections (endocarditis). Preventive antibiotics should be taken before surgery, invasive tests or procedures, and dental work.

Parental concerns

It is reassuring to know that two-thirds of heart murmurs are produced by a normal heart and do not require treatment.

If an underlying congenital cardiovascular defect is diagnosed, there are many treatment options that allow children to be fully active and grow up to be healthy adults. If treatment is needed, there is help available to cover medical expenses. Parents can discuss financial aid with the child's doctor or hospital, and some organizations, including the Heart of a Child Foundation and Little Hearts on the Mend Fund, provide financial assistance to children in need of heart surgery. Support groups are available to help parents and caregivers cope with the challenges of providing care for a child with a congenital cardiovascular defect. It is important for parents to take care of themselves, too, by eating properly, exercising regularly, taking care of personal hygiene, keeping in contact with friends and family members for support, and managing stress by practicing relaxation techniques.

So that the proper treatment can be provided in the event of an emergency, children with congenital cardiovascular defects should wear a medical identification bracelet or necklace to alert healthcare providers of their condition.

See also Congenital heart disease.

Resources

BOOKS

Friedman, William F., and John S. Child. "Disorders of the Cardiovascular System." In *Harrison's Principles of Internal Medicine*. Edited by Dennis L. Kasper, et al. New York: McGraw Hill, 2004.

"If Your Child Has a Congenital Heart Defect." In *Heart Diseases and Disorders Sourcebook*, 2nd ed. Edited by Karen Bellenir and Peter D. Dresser. Detroit, MI: Omnigraphics, Inc., 2000.

McGoon, Michael D., and Bernard J. Gersh, eds. *Mayo Clinic Heart Book: The Ultimate Guide to Heart Health*, 2nd ed. New York: William Morrow and Co. Inc., 2000.

Parker, James N., et al. *Heart Murmur: A Medical Dictionary, Bibliography, and Annotated Research Guide to Internet References*. Boulder, CO: netLibrary, 2004.

Shelov, Stephen P., et al. "Heart Murmurs." In *Caring for Your Baby and Young Child: Birth to Age 5*, 4th ed. New York: Bantam, 2004.

Topol, Eric J. "Pediatric and Congenital Heart Diseases." In *Cleveland Clinic Heart Book: The Definitive Guide for the Entire Family from the Nation's Leading Heart Center*. New York: Hyperion, 2000.

Trout, Darrell, and Ellen Welch. *Surviving with Heart: Taking Charge of Your Heart Care*. Golden, CO: Fulcrum Publishing, 2002.

Wild, C. L., and M. J. Neary. *Heart Defects in Children: What Every Parent Should Know*. Minneapolis, MN: Chronimed Publishing, 2000.

ORGANIZATIONS

Adult Congenital Heart Association (ACHA). 1500 Sunday Dr., Suite 102, Raleigh NC 27607–5151. Web site: <www.achaheart.org>.

American College of Cardiology. Heart House, 9111 Old Georgetown Rd., Bethesda, MD 20814–1699. Web site: <www.acc.org>.

American Heart Association. 7320 Greenville Ave., Dallas, TX 75231–4596. <www.americanheart.org/children>.

Children's Heart Services. PO Box 8275, Bartlett, IL 60108–8275. Web site: <www.childrensheartservices.org>.

The Cleveland Clinic Heart Center. The Cleveland Clinic Foundation, 9500 Euclid Ave., F25, Cleveland, Ohio, 44195. Web site: <www.clevelandclinic.org/heartcenter>.

Congenital Heart Disease Information and Resources. 1561 Clark Dr., Yardley, PA 19067. Web site: <www.tchin.org>.

Heart Support of America. 4873 N. Broadway, Knoxville, TN 37918. Web site: <www.heartsupport.com>.

International Children's Heart Foundation. 1750 Madison, Suite 100, Memphis, TN 38104. Web site: <www.babyhearts.com>.

National Heart, Lung, and Blood Institute. PO Box 30105, Bethesda, MD 20824–0105. Web site: <www.nhlbi.nih.gov>.

Texas Heart Institute. Heart Information Service, PO Box 20345, Houston, TX 77225–0345. Web site: <www.tmc.edu/thi>.

WEB SITES

"The Heart: An Online Exploration." Franklin Institute Online. Available online at <http://sln2.fi.edu/biosci/heart.html> (accessed November 19, 2004).

HeartCenterOnline. Available online at <www.heartcenteronline.com> (accessed November 19, 2004).

Heart Information Network. Available online at <www.heartinfo.org> (accessed November 19, 2004).

OTHER

The Heart of a Child Foundation. Financial assistance to children in need of heart surgery. 26710 Fond Du Lac Rd., Rancho Palos Verdes, CA 90275. Web site: <www.heartofachild.org> (accessed November 19, 2004).

Little Hearts on the Mend Fund. Financial assistance to children in need of heart surgery. Available online at <www.littleheartsonthemend.org> (accessed November 19, 2004).

Mended Little Hearts. Support program for parents of children with cardiovascular defects. Available online at <www.mendedhearts.org/MLH/mlh.htm> (accessed November 19, 2004).

Lori De Milto
Angela M. Costello

Heat disorders

Definition

Heat disorders are a group of physically related illnesses caused by prolonged exposure to hot temperatures, restricted fluid intake, or failure of temperature regulating mechanisms of the body. Disorders of heat exposure include heat cramps, heat exhaustion, and heat stroke (also called sunstroke).

Description

Hyperthermia is the general name given to heat-related illnesses. The two most common forms of hyperthermia are heat exhaustion and heat stroke, the latter of which is especially dangerous and requires immediate medical attention.

The thermal regulation centers of the brain help to maintain the body's internal temperature. Regardless of extreme weather conditions, the healthy human body keeps a steady temperature of approximately 98.6°F (37°C). In hot weather or during vigorous activity, the body perspires. As perspiration evaporates from the skin, the body is cooled. The thermal regulating centers in the brain help the body adapt to high temperatures by adjusting the amount of salts (electrolytes) in the perspiration. Electrolytes help the cells in body tissues maintain water balance. In hot weather, a healthy body will lose enough water to cool the body while creating the lowest level of electrolyte imbalance. If the body loses too much salt and fluid, symptoms of **dehydration** will occur.

Heat cramps

Heat cramps are the least severe of the heat-related illnesses. This heat disorder is often the first signal that the body is having difficulty with increased temperature. Individuals exposed to excessive heat should view heat cramps as a warning sign of a potential heat-related emergency.

Heat exhaustion

Heat exhaustion is a more serious and complex condition than heat cramps. Heat exhaustion can result from prolonged exposure to hot temperatures, restricted fluid intake, or failure of temperature regulation mechanisms of the body. Heat exhaustion requires immediate attention, as it can rapidly progress to heat stroke.

Heat stroke

Heat stroke is life threatening, and because a high percentage of individuals who experience heat stroke die, immediate medical attention is critical when symptoms first appear. Heat stroke, like heat exhaustion, is also a result of prolonged exposure to hot temperatures, restricted fluid intake, or failure of temperature regulation mechanisms of the body. However, the severity of impact on the body is much greater with heat stroke.

Demographics

Heat disorders are harmful to people of all ages, but their severity is greatest in young children and the elderly. Young children are at risk because, in relation to their weight, they have a large surface area of skin through which to lose water. In addition, until about age two, children's kidneys are not able to concentrate urine and preserve body fluids as efficiently as adult kidneys. The elderly also often have reduced kidney function or underlying diseases, or take medications that make them more vulnerable to dehydration. In healthy adults, heat stroke and heat exhaustion often affect athletes, firefighters, construction workers, factory workers, and anyone who exercises heavily and/or wears heavy clothing in hot, humid weather. Obese individuals and those with poor circulation or who take medications to reduce excess body fluids (diuretics) can be at risk when conditions are hot and humid.

Causes and symptoms

Heat cramps

Heat cramps are painful **muscle spasms** caused by the excessive loss of electrolytes due to heavy perspiration. The correct balance of electrolytes is crucial to many body functions, including muscle contraction and nerve impulse transmission. Heavy exertion in extreme heat and/or restricted fluid intake may lead to heat cramps.

With heat cramps, muscle tissue becomes less flexible, causing **pain**, difficult movement, and involuntary tightness. Cramps occurs more often in the legs and abdomen than in other areas of the body.

Heat exhaustion

Heat exhaustion is caused by exposure to high heat and humidity for many hours, resulting in excessive loss of fluids and salts through heavy perspiration. The skin may appear cool, moist, and pale. The child may complain of **headache** and **nausea**, with a feeling of overall weakness and exhaustion. **Dizziness**, faintness, and mental confusion are often present, as is a rapid, weak pulse. Breathing becomes fast and shallow. Fluid loss reduces blood volume and lowers blood pressure. Intense

thirst and a highly concentrated, reduced volume of deep yellow or orange urine are signs of inadequate fluid intake.

Heat stroke

Before heat stroke occurs, an individual experiences heat exhaustion and the associated symptoms. When the body can no longer maintain a normal temperature, heat exhaustion escalates and becomes heat stroke. Heat stroke is a life-threatening medical emergency that requires immediate life-saving measures.

Heat stroke is caused by overexposure to extreme heat, resulting in a breakdown of the body's heat regulating mechanisms. Body temperature reaches a dangerous level. An individual with heat stroke has a body temperature higher than 104°F (40°C), and possibly as high as 106°F (41.1°C).

Other symptoms of heat stroke include mental confusion with possible combativeness and bizarre behavior, staggering, and faintness. The pulse becomes strong and rapid (160–180 beats per minute). The skin takes on a dry and flushed appearance. There is often very little perspiration. The individual can quickly lose consciousness or have convulsions.

When to call the doctor

The doctor should be called when the child shows any symptoms of heat exhaustion of if he or she has been exposed to heat and dehydrating conditions and has a body temperature of over 102°F (38.9°C). Emergency medical services should be called immediately if the individual has any symptoms of heat stroke or is having difficulty breathing.

Diagnosis

Diagnosis of heat cramps usually involves observation of symptoms such as muscle cramping and thirst. Diagnosis of heat exhaustion or heat stroke, however, may require a healthcare worker to review the child's medical history, document symptoms, and obtain blood pressure and temperature readings. A physician may take blood and urine samples for further laboratory testing. A test to measure the body's electrolytes can also give valuable information about chemical imbalances caused by the heat-related illness.

Treatment

Heat cramps

The care of heat cramps includes placing the child at rest in a cool environment, while giving cool water with a teaspoon of salt per quart, or a commercial sports drink (e.g. Gatorade). Usually, rest and liquids are all that is needed for the child to recover. Mild stretching and massaging of the muscles may be helpful once the condition improves. The child should not take salt tablets, because such a high concentration of salt may actually worsen the condition. When the cramps stop, the person usually can begin light activity again if there are no other signs of illness. The child needs to continue drinking fluids and should be watched carefully for further signs of heat-related illnesses.

Heat exhaustion

The child suffering from heat exhaustion should stop all physical activity and move immediately to a cool place out of the sun, preferably a cool, air-conditioned location. He or she should lay down with feet slightly elevated, remove or loosen clothing, and drink cold (but not iced), slightly salty water or a commercial sports drink. Rest and replacement of fluids and salt is usually all the treatment that is needed, and **hospitalization** is rarely required. Following rehydration, the child usually recovers rapidly.

Heat stroke

Simply moving the individual experiencing heat stroke to a cooler place is not enough to reverse internal overheating. Emergency medical assistance should be called immediately. While waiting for help to arrive, quick action to lower body temperature must take place.

Immediate treatment involves getting the child to a cool place, loosening clothing or undressing the person, and allowing air to circulate around the body. The next step is to wrap the child in wet towels or clothing, and place ice packs in areas with the greatest blood supply. These areas include the neck, under the arm and knees, and in the groin. Once the patient is under medical care, cooling treatments continue as appropriate. The child's body temperature is monitored constantly to guard against overcooling. Breathing and heart rate are monitored, and fluids and electrolytes are replaced intravenously. Anti-convulsant drugs may be given. After severe heat stroke, hospitalization may be necessary and bed rest is recommended for several days.

Prognosis

Prompt treatment for heat cramps is usually very effective, allowing the individual to return rapidly to activity. Treatment of heat exhaustion usually brings full recovery in one to two days. Heat stroke is a very serious condition and its outcome depends upon the general health and age of the individual. Due to the high body temperature resulting from heat stroke, permanent damage to the brain, kidneys, heart, and other internal organs is possible. Heat stroke can be fatal, especially for infants and toddlers.

Prevention

Because heat cramps, heat exhaustion, and heat stroke have a cascade effect, the prevention of the onset of all heat disorders is similar.

- Avoid strenuous **exercise** when it is very hot.
- Drink plenty of fluids, especially water, and avoid drinking alcoholic beverages; drink frequently, even if not thirsty.
- Wear light and loose-fitting clothing that allows the air to circulate around the body in hot weather.
- Eat lightly salted foods which can help replace salts lost through perspiration.
- Provide proper ventilation of hot areas (fan, open window, air conditioning).
- Use sunblocks and **sunscreens** with a protection factor of SPF 15 or greater when exposed to direct sunlight.
- Never leave a child locked in a hot environment such as a car, even for a minute.
- Monitor children's activity and fluid intake frequently.
- Offer infants supplemental bottles of water in hot weather.
- Soak bandanas or other clothing in water to wear while working or playing in the heat.
- Wear a hat that allows air circulation (mesh, straw) in the sun.

Parental concerns

Parents need to be especially alert to dehydration and the development of heat disorders in infants who cannot ask for something to drink. Parents need to take the initiative in encouraging children to drink frequently in hot weather. Water or sports drinks are a better choice of liquids than soft drinks.

Before the 1970s, some coaches felt it was good training to limit the amount of fluids athletes drank at practices. As a result, there were 39 documented heat-related deaths in athletes between 1964 and 1973. As the water-electrolyte balance of the body became better understood, most coaches have recognized that water should be freely available during athletic practices and events. As a result, documented heat-related deaths declined substantially in the 1980s. When children participate in athletics, parents need to be aware of the potential for heat disorders and assure that appropriate measures for prevention are taken by coaches.

See also Sunburn.

Resources

BOOKS

American Red Cross. *Standard First Aid*. St. Louis: Mosby Year Book, 1993.

Larson, David E., ed. *Mayo Clinic Family Health Book*. 3rd ed. New York: HarperResource, 2003.

Mellion, Morris B. et al. *The Team Physicians Hand Book*. Philadelphia: Hanley & Belfus, 2001.

WEB SITES

"The Life Secretariat: Heat Disorders." *United States Air Force*. Available online at" <www.mindef.gov.sg/life/heatd.htm> (accessed March 3, 2005).

Tish Davidson, A.M.
Jeffrey P. Larson, RPT

Heavy metal poisoning

Definition

Heavy metal **poisoning** is the toxic accumulation of heavy metals in the soft tissues of the body.

Description

Heavy metals are chemical elements that have a specific gravity (a measure of density) at least five times that of water. The heavy metals most often implicated in human poisoning are lead, mercury, arsenic, and cadmium. Some heavy metals, such as zinc, copper, chromium, iron, and manganese, are required by the body in small amounts, but these same elements can be toxic in larger quantities.

Heavy metals may enter the body in food, water, or air, or by absorption through the skin. Once in the body, they compete with and displace essential **minerals** such as zinc, copper, magnesium, and calcium, and interfere with organ system function. People may come in contact with heavy metals in industrial work, pharmaceutical manufacturing, and agriculture. Children may be poisoned as a result of playing in contaminated soil.

Demographics

Heavy metal poisoning is relatively uncommon. In children, lead ingestion is the major culprit of heavy metal poisoning. In 2000, an estimated one in 22 American children had high levels of lead in their blood. Children in urban areas with old lead water pipes and lead-painted homes are especially at risk. Mercury poisoning is possible from eating contaminated fish.

Causes and symptoms

Symptoms will vary, depending on the nature and the quantity of the heavy metal ingested. Affected people may complain of **nausea**, **vomiting**, **diarrhea**, stomach **pain**, **headache**, sweating, and a metallic taste in the mouth. Depending on the metal, there may be blue-black lines in the gum tissues. In severe cases, people exhibit obvious impairment of cognitive, motor, and language skills. The expression "mad as a hatter" comes from the mercury poisoning prevalent in seventeenth-century France among hat makers who soaked animal hides in a solution of mercuric nitrate to soften the hair.

When to call the doctor

A healthcare professional should be contacted whenever exposure to any heavy metal is suspected. The Centers for Disease Control and Prevention (CDC) recommends testing all children for lead exposure at 12 months of age and, if possible, again at 24 months. Testing should start at six months for children at higher risk for **lead poisoning**.

Diagnosis

Heavy metal poisoning may be detected using blood and urine tests, hair and tissue analysis, or x ray.

In childhood, blood lead levels above 80 μg/dL generally indicate lead poisoning; however, significantly lower levels (>30 μg/dL) can cause **mental retardation** and other cognitive and behavioral problems in affected children. The Centers for Disease Control and Prevention considers a blood lead level of 10 μg/dL or higher in children a cause for concern. In adults, symptoms of lead poisoning are usually seen when blood lead levels exceed 80 μg/dL for a number of weeks.

Blood levels of mercury should not exceed 3.6 μg/dL, while urine levels should not exceed 15 μg/dL. Symptoms of mercury poisoning may be seen when mercury levels exceed 20 μg/dL in blood and 60 μg/dL in urine. Mercury levels in hair may be used to gauge the severity of chronic mercury exposure.

Since arsenic is rapidly cleared from the blood, blood arsenic levels may not be very useful in diagnosis. Arsenic in the urine (measured in a 24-hour collection following 48 hours without eating seafood) may exceed 50 μg/dL in people with arsenic poisoning. If acute arsenic poisoning is suspected, an x ray may reveal ingested arsenic in the abdomen (since arsenic is opaque to **x rays**). Arsenic may also be detected in the hair and nails for months following exposure.

Cadmium toxicity is generally indicated when urine levels exceed 10 μg/dL of creatinine and blood levels exceed 5 μg/dL.

Treatment

The treatment for most heavy metal poisoning is chelation therapy. A chelating agent specific to the metal involved is given orally, intramuscularly, or intravenously. The three most common chelating agents are calcium disodium edetate, dimercaprol (BAL), and penicillamine. The chelating agent encircles and binds to the metal in the body's tissues, forming a complex; that complex is then released from the tissue to travel in the bloodstream. The complex is filtered out of the blood by the kidneys and excreted in the urine. This process may be lengthy and painful and typically requires **hospitalization**. Chelation therapy is effective in treating lead, mercury, and arsenic poisoning, but it is not useful in treating cadmium poisoning. As of 2004, no treatment had been proven effective for cadmium poisoning.

In cases of acute mercury or arsenic ingestion, vomiting may be induced. Washing out the stomach (gastric lavage) may also be useful. The affected person may also require treatment such as intravenous fluids for complications of poisoning such as shock, anemia, and kidney failure.

Prognosis

The chelation process can only halt further effects of the poisoning; it cannot reverse neurological damage already sustained.

Prevention

Because exposure to heavy metals is often an occupational hazard, protective clothing and respirators should be provided and worn on the job. Protective clothing should then be left at the work site and not worn home, where it could carry toxic dust to **family** members. Industries are urged to reduce or replace the heavy metals in their processes wherever possible. For the sake of children's health along with everyone else's, exposure to environmental sources of lead, including lead-based paints, plumbing fixtures, vehicle exhaust, and contaminated soil, should be reduced or eliminated.

Nutritional concerns

Parents should avoid preparing or serving food in containers that have lead in their glazing.

Parental concerns

Parents living in homes built prior to 1978 should be vigilant in removing flaking or peeling paint because it might contain lead. Simply repainting such surfaces will not solve the problem. Parents must monitor the environments in which their children **play** and the objects that go into their children's mouths. Cleanliness is a must if old paint is in a child's environment. Removal (stripping paint to bare metal or bare wood) of lead is the best way to prevent lead exposure in children. Areas where removal is taking place should be sealed off from the rest of the house. In addition, children should be kept away from occupational sources of other heavy metals. Parents who are concerned about their child's exposure to lead should have the child tested.

See also Lead poisoning.

Resources

BOOKS

Goto, Collin S. "Heavy Metal Intoxication." In *Nelson Textbook of Pediatrics*, 17th ed. Edited by Richard E. Behrman, et al. Philadelphia: Saunders, 2003, pp. 2355–7.

Gupta, S. K., et al. *Emergency Toxicology: Management of Common Poisons*. Boca Raton, FL: CRC Press, 2003.

Klaasen, Curtis D., and John Doull. *Casarett and Doull's Toxicology: The Basic Science of Poisons*, 6th ed. New York: McGraw Hill, 2001.

Markowitz, Morrie. "Lead Poisoning." In *Nelson Textbook of Pediatrics*, 17th ed. Edited by Richard E. Behrman, et al. Philadelphia: Saunders, 2003, pp. 2358–61.

PERIODICALS

Clark S, et al. "The influence of exterior dust and soil lead on interior dust lead levels in housing that had undergone lead-based paint hazard control." *Journal of Occupational and Environmental Hygiene* 1, no. 5 (2004): 273–82.

Counter, S. A., and L. H. Buchanan. "Mercury exposure in children: a review." *Toxicology and Applied Pharmacology* 198, no. 2 (2004): 209–30.

Dorea, J. G. "Mercury and lead during breast-feeding." *British Journal of Nutrition* 92, no. 1 (2004): 21–40.

Yassin, A. S., and J. F. Martonik. "Urinary cadmium levels in the U.S. working population, 1988–1994." *Journal of Occupational and Environmental Hygiene* 1, no. 5 (2004): 324–33.

ORGANIZATIONS

American Academy of Clinical Toxicology. 777 East Park Drive, PO Box 8820, Harrisburg, PA 17105–8820. Web site: <www.clintox.org/index.html>.

American Academy of Family Physicians. 11400 Tomahawk Creek Parkway, Leawood, KS 66211–2672. Web site: <www.aafp.org/>.

American Academy of Pediatrics. 141 Northwest Point Boulevard, Elk Grove Village, IL 60007–1098. Web site: <www.aap.org/default.htm>.

American Association of Poison Control Centers. 3201 New Mexico Avenue NW, Washington, DC 20016. Web site: <www.aapcc.org/>.

American College of Occupational and Environmental Medicine. 55 West Seegers Road, Arlington Heights, IL 60005. Web site: <www.acoem.org/>.

Multiple Sclerosis Foundation. 6350 North Andrews Ave., Fort Lauderdale, Fl 33309–2130. Web site: <www.msfacts.org/>.

National Multiple Sclerosis Society. 733 Third Avenue, New York, NY 10017. Web site: <www.nmss.org/>.

WEB SITES

"Heavy Metal Poisoning." *Med Help International.* Available online at <www.medhelp.org/HealthTopics/Heavy_Metal_Poisoning.html> (accessed November 10, 2004).

"Heavy Metals (Toxicology)." *National Multiple Sclerosis Society.* Available online at <www.nationalmssociety.org/Sourcebook-Heavy%20Metals.asp> (accessed November 10, 2004).

Hoekman, Theodore. "Heavy Metals Toxicology." Available online at <www.luminet.net/~wenonah/hydro/heavmet.htm> (accessed November 10, 2004).

"Toxicity, Heavy Metals." *eMedicine.* Available online at <www.emedicine.com/emerg/topic237.htm> (accessed November 10, 2004).

L. Fleming Fallon, Jr., MD, DrPH

Heimlich maneuver

Definition

The Heimlich maneuver is an emergency technique for removing a foreign object lodged in the airway that is preventing a child or an adult from breathing.

Purpose

The Heimlich maneuver is used when a person is **choking** on a foreign object to the extent that he/she cannot breathe. Oxygen deprivation from a foreign body airway obstruction can result in permanent brain damage or death in four minutes or less. Using the Heimlich maneuver can save a choking victim's life. The Heimlich maneuver is not performed on infants under one year of age (see below for technique for infants). Indications that a choking victim's airway is blocked include the following:

- inability to **cough**, cry, or speak
- blue or purple face color from lack of oxygen
- grabbing at throat
- weak cough and labored breathing that produces a high-pitched noise
- all of the above, followed by loss of consciousness

Each year, more than 17,000 infants and children are treated in hospital emergency departments for choking-related incidents, and more than 80 percent of these occur in children aged four years and younger. Airway obstruction death and injury are especially prevalent in children under age four due to their anatomy (small airway), natural curiosity and tendency to put objects in their mouths, and incomplete chewing. In infants, choking usually results from inhalation of small objects (e.g., coins, small **toys**, deflated balloons, buttons) that they place in their mouth.

Description

In 1974, Henry Heimlich first described an emergency technique for expelling foreign material blocking the trachea. This technique, now called the Heimlich maneuver, is simple enough that it can be performed immediately by anyone trained in the maneuver. The Heimlich maneuver is a standard part of all first-aid and **cardiopulmonary resuscitation** (CPR) courses.

The theory behind the Heimlich maneuver is that by compressing the abdomen below the level of the diaphragm with quick abdominal thrusts, an "artificial cough" is created. Air is forced out of the lungs to dislodge the obstruction in the trachea and bring the foreign object back up into the mouth.

The Heimlich maneuver can be performed on all people; however, modifications are necessary infants, children, obese individuals, and pregnant women.

Performing the Heimlich maneuver on children

To perform the Heimlich maneuver on a conscious child, the rescuer stands or kneels behind the child, who may be seated or standing. The rescuer makes a fist with one hand, and places it, thumb toward the child, below the rib cage and above the waist. The rescuer encircles the child's waist, placing his other hand on top of the fist then gives a series of five quick and distinct inward and upward thrusts. If the foreign object is not dislodged, the

cycle of five thrusts is repeated until the object is expelled or the child becomes unresponsive. As the child is deprived of oxygen, the muscles of the trachea relax slightly, and it is possible that the foreign object may be expelled on a second or third attempt.

If the victim is unconscious or becomes unconscious, the rescuer should lay him or her on the floor, bend the chin forward, make sure the tongue is not blocking the airway, and feel in the mouth for the foreign object, being careful not to push any farther into the airway. The rescuer kneels astride the child's thighs and places his fists between the bottom of the victim's breastbone and the navel. The rescuer then executes a series of five quick compressions by pushing inward and upward.

After the abdominal thrusts, the rescuer repeats the process of lifting the chin, moving the tongue, feeling for and possibly removing the foreign material. If the airway is not clear, the rescuer repeats the abdominal thrusts as often as necessary. If the foreign object has been removed, but the victim is not breathing, the rescuer starts CPR.

The technique in children over one year of age is the same as in adults, except that the amount of force used is less than that used with adults in order to avoid damaging the child's ribs, breastbone, and internal organs.

OBESE CHILDREN AND ADOLESCENTS The main difference in performing the Heimlich maneuver on an obese victim is in the placement of the fists. Instead of using abdominal thrusts, chest thrusts are used. The fists are placed against the middle of the breastbone, and the motion of the chest thrust is in and downward, rather than upward. If the victim is unconscious, the chest thrusts are similar to those used in CPR.

Foreign body obstruction in infants under age one year

The Heimlich maneuver as described above is not performed on infants under one year of age. Instead, a series of back blows and chest thrusts are used. The rescuer sits down and lays the infant along his or her forearm with the infant's face pointed toward the floor and tilted downward lower than the body. The rescuer's hand supports the infant's head, and his or her forearm rests on his or her own thigh for additional support. Using the heel of the other hand, the rescuer administers five rapid blows to the infant's back between the shoulder blades.

After administering the back blows, the rescuer sandwiches the infant between his or her arms and turns the infant over so that the infant is lying face up supported by the opposite arm. Using the free hand, the rescuer places the index and middle finger on the center of the breastbone just below the nipple line and makes gives five quick chest thrusts. This series of back blows and chest thrusts is alternated until the foreign object is expelled. If the infant becomes unconscious, CPR should be initiated.

Precautions

Any lay person can be trained to perform the Heimlich maneuver and to know how may save someone's life. Before doing the maneuver, it is important to determine if the airway is completely blocked. If the victim choking can talk or cry, the Heimlich maneuver should not be administered. If the airway is not completely blocked, the choking victim should be allowed to try to cough up the foreign object on his or her own.

Aftercare

Vomiting may occur after being treated with the Heimlich maneuver. All infants and children who experience a choking episode severe enough to require the Heimlich maneuver should be taken to the hospital emergency room to be examined for airway injuries.

Risks

Incorrectly applied, the Heimlich maneuver can break bones or damage internal organs. In infants, the rescuer should never attempt to sweep the baby's mouth without looking to remove foreign material. This is likely to push the material farther down the trachea. Following the Heimlich maneuver, dysphagia (swallowing difficulty) and obstructive pulmonary edema (fluid accumulation in the lungs) may occur.

Normal results

In many cases the foreign material is dislodged from the throat, and the choking victim suffers no permanent effects of the episode. If the foreign material is not removed, the choking victim may suffer permanent brain damage from lack of oxygen or may die.

Parental concerns

Because most choking incidents occur in the home, all parents and infant/child caregivers should be trained in the Heimlich maneuver. Training is available through the American Red Cross and American Heart Association at local schools, YMCAs, and community centers.

The likelihood of choking incidents can be reduced by closely supervising infants and children while eating and playing. Most choking incidents are associated with

---

KEY TERMS

Diaphragm—The thin layer of muscle that separates the chest cavity containing the lungs and heart from the abdominal cavity containing the intestines and digestive organs. This term is also used for a dome-shaped device used to cover the back of a woman's vagina during intercourse in order to prevent pregnancy.

Trachea—The windpipe. A tube composed of cartilage and membrane that extends from below the voice box into the chest where it splits into two branches, the bronchi, that lead to each lung.

---

food items, especially hot dogs, candies, grapes, nuts, popcorn, and carrots. Common non-food items that are choking hazards include deflated balloons, buttons, coins, small balls, small toys, and toy parts. All toys should be examined to make sure they are age-appropriate and do not have loose parts.

Resources

BOOKS

Basic Life Support for Healthcare Providers. Dallas, TX: American Heart Association, 2001.

PERIODICALS

Ringold, Sarah, et al. "Postobstructive Pulmonary Edema in Children." *Pediatric Emergency Care* 20 (June 2004): 391–95.

Vilke, Gary M., et al. "Airway Obstruction in Children Aged Less Than 5 Years: The Prehospital Experience." *Prehospital Emergency Care* 8 (2004): 196–99.

ORGANIZATIONS

American Heart Association. 7320 Greenville Ave. Dallas, TX 75231. Web site: <www.americanheart.org>.

The Heimlich Institute. 311 Straight St., Cincinnati, OH 45219–9957. Web site: <www.heimlichinstitute.org>.

WEB SITES

"Heimlich Maneuver." *American Heart Association,* 2004. Available online at <www.americanheart.org/ presenter.jhtml?identifier=4605> (accessed November 20, 2004).

"Infant First Aid for Choking and CPR: An Illustrated Guide." *BabyCenter,* 2004. Available online at <http:// www.babycenter.com/general/9298.html> (accessed November 20, 2004).

Jennifer E. Sisk, MA

Hemangiomas *see* **Birthmarks**

Hemoglobin F test *see* **Fetal hemoglobin test**

Hemophilia

Definition

Hemophilia is a coagulation disorder arising from a genetic defect of the X chromosome; the defect can either be inherited or result from spontaneous gene mutation. In each type of hemophilia (hemophilias A, B, and C), a critical coagulation protein is missing, causing individuals to bleed for long periods of time before clotting occurs. Depending on the degree of the disorder in the affected individual, uncontrolled bleeding may occur spontaneously with no known initiating event, or occur after specific events such as surgery, dental procedures, immunizations, or injury.

Description

The body's normal mechanism for blood clotting is a complex series of events (coagulation cascade) involving interaction between the injured blood vessel, blood cells called platelets, 13 specific coagulation factors (designated by Roman numerals I through XIII), and other substances that circulate in the blood.

When blood vessels are injured in a way that causes bleeding, platelets collect over the injured area, forming a temporary plug to prevent further bleeding. This temporary plug, however, is too disorganized to serve as a long-term solution, so a series of chemical events occurs that results in the formation of a more reliable plug. The final plug or clot involves tightly woven fibers of a material called fibrin. The production of fibrin requires the interaction of a series of proteins, clotting factors I through XIII, in a process called amplification to rapidly produce the proper-sized fibrin clot from the small number of molecules initially activated by the injury. In the complex coagulation process, the absence or inactivity of just one clotting factor can greatly increase bleeding time. In hemophilia, certain clotting factors are either decreased in quantity, absent altogether, or improperly formed, preventing the formation of a clot and resulting in uncontrolled bleeding.

Hemophilia A is the most common type of coagulation disorder and involves decreased activity of factor VIII. There are three levels of factor VIII deficiency: severe, moderate, and mild. This classification is based on the percentage of normal factor VIII activity present:

- Individuals with less than 1 percent of normal factor VIII activity level have severe hemophilia. Half of all people with hemophilia A fall into this category. Such individuals frequently experience spontaneous musculoskeletal bleeding into their joints, skin, and muscles. Surgery or trauma can result in life-threatening hemorrhage and must be carefully managed.

- Individuals with 1–5 percent of normal factor VIII activity level have moderate hemophilia and are at risk for heavy bleeding after seemingly minor traumatic injuries.

- Individuals with 5–40 percent of normal factor VIII activity level have mild hemophilia and must prepare carefully for any surgery or dental procedures.

In hemophilia B, or Christmas disease, the deficient clotting factor is factor IX, but the symptoms are very similar to those of hemophilia A. Factor IX is produced in the liver and is dependent on interaction with vitamin K in order to function properly. A deficiency in vitamin K can affect the clotting factor's performance as well as a deficiency in the factor itself.

Hemophilia C is rare and much milder than hemophilia A or B. It involves reduced activity of factor XI and is characterized by mild bleeding such as nosebleeds (epistaxis) or prolonged menstrual bleeding, or mild bleeding after tonsillectomies or dental extractions.

Demographics

Hemophilia A affects between one in 5,000 to one in 10,000 males in most populations. Hemophilia B occurs in one in 40,000 to 50,000. The prevalence of hemophilia is estimated to be 13.4 cases per 100,000 U.S. males (10.5 hemophilia A and 2.9 hemophilia B). By race/ethnicity, the prevalence is 13.2 cases in 100,000 among white males, 11.0 among African-American males, and 11.5 among Hispanic males. Hemophilia C occurs primarily among individuals of Jewish descent.

Causes and symptoms

Hemophilia A and B are both caused by a genetic defect present on the X chromosome. (Hemophilia C is inherited in a different fashion.) About 70 percent of all people with hemophilia A or B inherited the disease. The other 30 percent develop from a spontaneous genetic mutation.

Both factors VIII and IX are produced by a genetic defect of the X chromosome, so hemophilia A and B are both sex-linked diseases passed on from a female to male offspring. (All humans have two chromosomes determining their gender: females have XX, males have XY. Because the trait is carried only on the X chromosome, it is called sex-linked.) Because a female child always receives two X chromosomes, she will nearly always receive at least one normal X chromosome. Therefore, even if she receives one flawed X chromosome, she will still be capable of producing a sufficient quantity of factors VIII and IX to avoid the symptoms of hemophilia. Such a person who has one flawed chromosome but does not actually suffer from the disease is called a carrier. She carries the flaw that causes hemophilia and can pass it on to her offspring. If, however, she has a son who receives her flawed X chromosome, he will be unable to produce the right quantity of factors VIII or IX, and he will suffer some degree of hemophilia. (Males inherit one X and one Y chromosome and, therefore, have only one X chromosome.)

In rare cases, a hemophiliac father and a carrier mother can pass on the right combination of parental chromosomes to result in a hemophiliac female child. However, the vast majority of people with either hemophilia A or B are male.

About 30 percent of all people with hemophilia A or B are the first member of their **family** to ever have the disease. These individuals have had the unfortunate occurrence of a spontaneous mutation, meaning that in their early development, some random genetic accident affected their X chromosome, resulting in the defect that causes hemophilia A or B. Once such a spontaneous genetic mutation takes place, offspring of the affected person can inherit the newly created, flawed chromosome.

In the case of severe hemophilia, the first bleeding event usually occurs prior to 18 months of age. In some babies, hemophilia is suspected immediately when a routine **circumcision** (removal of the foreskin of the penis) results in unusually heavy bleeding. Toddlers are at particular risk because they fall frequently and may bleed into the soft tissue of their arms and legs. These small bleeds result in bruising and noticeable lumps but do not usually require treatment. As a child becomes more active, bleeding may occur into the muscles, a much more painful and debilitating situation. These muscle bleeds result in **pain** and pressure on the nerves in the area of the bleed. Damage to nerves can cause **numbness** and decreased ability to use the injured limb.

Christmas disease varies from mild to severe, but mild cases are more common. The severity depends on the degree of deficiency of factor IX. Hemophilia B symptoms are similar to those of hemophilia A, including numerous large and deep **bruises** and prolonged bleeding.

Some of the most problematic and frequent bleeds occur into the joints, particularly the knees and elbows. Repeated bleeding into joints can result in scarring within the joints and permanent deformities. Individuals may develop arthritis in joints that have suffered continued irritation from the presence of blood. Mouth injuries can result in compression of the airway, which interrupts breathing and can be life-threatening. A blow to the head, which might be totally insignificant in a normal child, can result in bleeding into the skull and brain. Because the skull has no room for expansion, the hemophiliac is at risk for brain damage due to blood taking up space and exerting pressure on the delicate brain tissue.

People with hemophilia are at very high risk of severe, heavy, uncontrollable bleeding (hemorrhage) from injuries such as motor vehicle accidents and also from surgery.

Some other rare clotting disorders such as von Willebrand's disease present similar symptoms but are not usually called hemophilia.

When to call the doctor

Hemophilia is usually discovered when an injury initiates bleeding and the bleeding will not stop. In very young children, spontaneous musculoskeletal bleeding may occur around the time the child begins to walk; these episodes may be the first sign of hemophilia. In some children, a simple surgical procedure, such as a tooth extraction or injection, may present with uncontrolled bleeding. Any signs of deep bruises or the presence of prolonged bleeding after a bump or an injury that breaks the skin should be reported to a physician or emergency service immediately. Bleeding under the skin (hematoma), which looks like a severe bruise, should also be reported and medical care sought immediately.

Diagnosis

Various diagnostic tests are available to measure, under carefully controlled conditions, the length of time it takes to produce certain components of the final fibrin clot. The activated partial thromboplastin time (APTT) is performed and will typically be prolonged while a prothrombin time (PT) will likely be normal. Factor assays, measurement methods performed by the clinical laboratory, can determine the percentage of factors VIII and IX present compared to normal percentages. This information helps to confirm a diagnosis of hemophilia and identifies the type and severity of hemophilia present.

Families with a history of hemophilia can also have tests done during a pregnancy to determine whether the fetus will have hemophilia. Chorionic villous sampling is a test that examines proteins for deficiencies or defects that are characteristic of hemophilia. The test can be performed at 10 to 14 weeks; test performance is associated with a 1 percent risk of miscarriage. **Amniocentesis** is a method of withdrawing amniotic fluid from the placenta to allow examination of fetal cell DNA shed into the amniotic fluid, helping to identify genetic mutations. Amniocentesis can be performed at 15 to 18 weeks gestation and is associated with a one in 200 risk of miscarriage.

Treatment

The treatment of hemophilia involves replacing or supplementing the deficient coagulation factors. Various preparations of factors VIII and IX are available to replace missing factors as needed. Cryoprecipitate, for example, is a single- or multiple-donor human plasma preparation rich in coagulation factors; it is made available as a frozen concentrate. Fresh frozen plasma is a single-donor preparation of factor-rich plasma; it is used primarily for replacing factor XI in individuals with hemophilia C. Concentrated factor preparations may be obtained from a single donor, by pooling the donations of as many as thousands of donors, or by laboratory creation through highly advanced genetic techniques. These preparations are administered directly into the individual's veins (intravenous administration).

The frequency of treatment with coagulation factors depends on the severity of the individual's disease. Relatively mild disease will only require treatment in the event of injury, or to prepare for scheduled surgical or dental procedures. More severe disease will require regular treatment to avoid spontaneous bleeding.

Appropriate treatment of hemophilia can decrease suffering and be lifesaving in the presence of hemorrhage. Complications associated with treatment, however, can also be quite serious. About 20 percent of all individuals with hemophilia A begin to produce antibodies in their blood against the specific factor protein; the presence of antibodies may then rapidly destroy infused factor VIII. The presence of such antibodies may greatly hamper efforts to prevent or stop a major hemorrhage.

Individuals who receive coagulation factors prepared from pooled donor blood were once at risk for serious infections that could be passed through the infusion of human blood products, such as the hepatitis virus and HIV. Concern has also been raised about the possibility

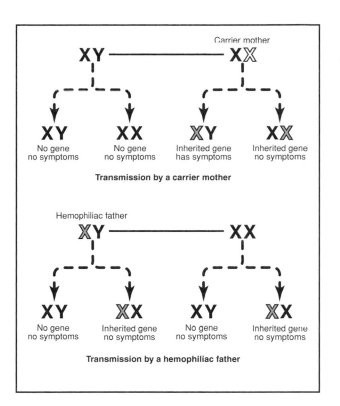

Chart showing how hemophilia is transmitted on the X chromosome. However, some 30 percent of hemophilia cases are caused by random genetic mutation. *(Illustration by Electronic Illustrators Group.)*

of hemophiliacs contracting a fatal slow virus infection of the brain (Creutzfeldt-Jakob disease) from blood products. However, more sensitive testing techniques have been developed and as of 2004 were employed by the companies producing pooled precipitates from human plasma. These improved methods of donor testing, as well as methods of inactivating viruses present in donated blood, have greatly lowered the risk of infection.

Molecular biological techniques have introduced gene therapies as new treatment possibilities for hemophilia. Gene therapy involves sophisticated methods of transferring new genes to hemophiliacs, correcting deficiencies or defects in the clotting mechanism. These methods are being researched in the early 2000s.

Prognosis

Variations in the type and severity of hemophilia makes it difficult to generalize a prognosis, however, for individuals with mild hemophilia, the prognosis is quite good. Those with more severe hemophilia can also live relatively normal lives with careful management and avoidance of injury. Many individuals achieve normal life expectancy. Without treatment of bleeding episodes,

KEY TERMS

Amplification—A process by which something is made larger. In clotting, only a very few chemicals are released by the initial injury; they trigger a cascade of chemical reactions which produces increasingly larger quantities of different chemicals, resulting in an appropriately-sized, strong fibrin clot.

Coagulation factors—Specific coagulation proteins in the blood required for clotting. Coagulation proteins are designated with roman numerals I through XIII.

Fibrin—The last step in the blood coagulation process. Fibrin forms strands that add bulk to a forming blood clot to hold it in place and help "plug" an injured blood vessel wall.

Hemorrhage—Severe, massive bleeding that is difficult to control. The bleeding may be internal or external.

Mutation—A permanent change in the genetic material that may alter a trait or characteristic of an individual, or manifest as disease. This change can be transmitted to offspring.

Platelet—A cell-like particle in the blood that plays an important role in blood clotting. Platelets are activated when an injury causes a blood vessel to break. They change shape from round to spiny, "sticking" to the broken vessel wall and to each other to begin the clotting process. In addition to physically plugging breaks in blood vessel walls, platelets also release chemicals that promote clotting.

Trauma—Serious physical injury. Also refers to a disastrous or life-threatening event that can cause severe emotional distress, including dissociative symptoms and disorders.

severe muscle and joint pain and eventually permanent damage can occur. Much depends upon the physical activity level of the individual and the possibility of accidental injuries or surgeries required for other conditions, which cannot be predicted.

Prevention

Because of its genetic origins, hemophilia cannot be prevented in those born with the inherited defects or factor deficiencies. However, individuals who have a family history of hemophilia may benefit from genetic testing and counseling before deciding to have a baby.

The most important way for individuals with hemophilia to prevent complications of the disease is to avoid activities that may lead to injury. Those individuals who require dental work or any type of surgery may need to be pre-treated with an infusion of factor VIII to avoid hemorrhage. Hemophiliacs should also avoid medications or drugs that promote bleeding; aspirin is one such medication and many prescription drugs have anticoagulant properties.

Parental concerns

When a child has an inherited coagulation disorder such as hemophilia, parents will be concerned about the possibility of trauma or injury that may lead to potentially dangerous bleeding episodes. The watchfulness of parents along with effective management of hemophilia by physicians can help the child to lead a relatively normal life. Careful avoidance of injury is essential. Counseling is available to help children handle the psychosocial aspects of living with hemophilia. Education is available from public health organizations to help parents be informed about their child's condition.

See also Coagulation disorders.

Resources

BOOKS

Britton, Beverly. *Diseases and Disorders: Hemophilia.* Farmington Hills, MI: Gale, 2003.

Khoury, Muin J., Wylie Burke, and Elizabeth J. Thomson, eds. *Genetics and Public Health in the 21st Century: Using Genetic Information to Improve Health and Prevent Disease.* New York: Oxford University Press, 2000.

McDougald, Monroe. *Hemophilia Care in the New Millennium.* Lancaster, UK: Kluwar Academic Publishers, 2001.

Rodriguez-Merchan, E. C., et al. *Inhibitors in Patients with Hemophilia.* Oxford, UK: Blackwell Publishing, 2002.

ORGANIZATIONS

National Hemophilia Foundation. 116 West 32nd St., 11th Floor, New York, NY 10001. Web site: <www.hemophilia.org>.

National Organization for Rare Disorders (NORD). PO Box 8923, New Fairfield, CT 06812–8923. Web site: <www.rarediseases.org>.

WEB SITES

"Hemostatis and Coagulation." *The Merck Manual Online,* 2003. Available online at <www.merckcom/pubs/mmanual/section11/chapter131.131c.htm> (accessed October, 22, 2004).

March of Dimes. Available online at <www.modimes.org>
(accessed October 22, 2004).

L. Lee Culvert
Jennifer F. Wilson, MS

Hemophilus infections

Definition

Hemophilus infections, most of which are due to *Haemophilus influenzae* infections, are a group of contagious diseases that are caused by a bacterium and affect only humans. Some hemophilus infections are potentially fatal.

Description

H. influenzae is a common organism worldwide; it has been found in the nasal secretions of as many as 90 percent of healthy individuals in the general population. Hemophilus infections are characterized by acute inflammation with a discharge (exudate). They may affect almost any organ system but are most common in the respiratory tract. The organism can be transmitted by person-to-person contact or by contact with nasal discharges and other body fluids. Hemophilus infections in the United States are most likely to spread in the late winter or early spring.

Demographics

The primary factor influencing the rate of infection is age; children between the ages of six months and four years are most vulnerable to *H. influenzae.* In the twentieth century, about 50 percent of children would acquire a hemophilus infection before reaching one year of age; almost all children would develop one before age three. In the United States, these figures have declined, however, as a result of the increasing use of hemophilus vaccines for children. Worldwide, however, *Haemophilus influenzae* remains a significant childhood pathogen. It is the primary cause of childhood **meningitis** and the second most common cause of childhood **pneumonia.** In developing countries, *Haemophilus influenzae* is responsible for 500,000 annual deaths in children under the age of five.

Causes and symptoms

Hemophilus infections are primarily caused by *Haemophilus influenzae,* a bacterium that is capable of spreading from the nasal tissues and upper airway, where it is usually found, to the chest, throat, or middle ear. The organism sometimes invades localized areas of tissue, producing meningitis, infectious arthritis, **conjunctivitis,** cellulitis, **epiglottitis,** or inflammation of the membrane surrounding the heart. The most serious infections are caused by a strain called *H. influenzae* b (Hib). Before routine **vaccination,** Hib was the most common cause of bacterial meningitis and responsible for most of the cases of acquired **mental retardation** in the United States.

Bacterial sepsis in the newborn

Bacterial sepsis (the presence of illness-causing microorganisms, or their poisons, in the blood) is a potentially fatal illness in newborn infants. The child may acquire the disease organism as it passes through the mother's birth canal or from the hospital environment. *H. influenzae* can also produce inflammations of the eye (conjunctivitis) in newborn children. The signs of sepsis may include **fever,** fussiness, feeding problems, breathing difficulties, pale or mottled skin, or drowsiness. Premature birth is the most significant risk factor for hemophilus infections in newborns.

Epiglottitis

Epiglottitis is a potentially fatal hemophilus infection. Although children are more likely to develop epiglottitis, it can occur in adults as well. When the epiglottis (the flap that covers the trachea during swallowing so that food odes not enter the lungs) is infected, it can swell to the point where it blocks the windpipe. The symptoms of epiglottitis include a sudden high fever, drooling, the feeling of an object stuck in the throat, and **stridor** (a high-pitched, noisy respiratory sound). The epiglottis will look swollen and bright red if the doctor examines the patient's throat with a laryngoscope (a viewing device).

Meningitis

Meningitis caused by Hib is most common in children between nine months and four years of age. The child usually develops upper respiratory symptoms followed by fever, loss of appetite, **vomiting, headache,** and a stiff or sore neck or back. In severe cases, the child may have convulsions or go into shock or coma.

Other infections

Hib is the second most common cause of middle ear infection and **sinusitis** in children. The symptoms of sinusitis include fever, **pain**, bad breath, and coughing. Children may also develop infectious arthritis from Hib. The joints most frequently affected are the large weight-bearing ones.

Diagnosis

The diagnosis is usually based on a combination of the patient's symptoms and the results of blood counts, cultures, or antigen detection tests.

Laboratory tests

Laboratory tests can be used to confirm the diagnosis of hemophilus infections. The bacterium can be grown on chocolate agar or identified by blood cultures or Gram stain of body fluids. Antigen detection tests can be used to identify hemophilus infections in children. These tests include latex agglutination and electrophoresis.

Other laboratory findings that are associated with hemophilus infections include anemia (low red blood cell count) and a drop in the number of white blood cells in children with severe infections. Adults often show an abnormally high level of white blood cells; cell counts of 15,000 to 30,000/mm^3 are not unusual.

Treatment

Because some hemophilus infections are potentially fatal, treatment is started without waiting for the results of laboratory tests.

Medications

Hemophilus infections are treated with **antibiotics**. Patients who are severely ill are given ampicillin or a third-generation cephalosporin, such as cefotaxime or ceftriaxone, intravenously. Patients with milder infections are given oral antibiotics, including amoxicillin, cefaclor, erythromycin, or trimethoprim-sulfamethoxazole. Patients who are allergic to penicillin are usually given cefaclor or trimethoprim-sulfamethoxazole.

Patients with Hib strains that are resistant to ampicillin may be given chloramphenicol. Chloramphenicol is not a first-choice drug because of its side effects, including interference with bone marrow production of blood cells.

The duration of antibiotic treatment depends on the location and severity of the hemophilus infection. Adults with respiratory tract infections, or Hib pneumonia, are usually given a 10 to 14 day course of antibiotics. Meningitis is usually treated for 10 to 14 days, but a seven-day course of treatment with ceftriaxone appears to be sufficient for infants and children. Ear infections are treated for seven to 10 days.

Supportive care

Patients with serious hemophilus infections require bed rest and a humidified environment (such as a **croup** tent) if the respiratory tract is affected. Patients with epiglottitis frequently require intubation (insertion of a breathing tube) or a tracheotomy to keep the airway open. Patients with inflammation of the heart membrane, pneumonia, or arthritis may need surgical treatment to drain infected fluid from the chest cavity or inflamed joints.

Supportive care also includes monitoring of blood cell counts for patients using chloramphenicol, ampicillin, or other drugs that may affect production of blood cells by the bone marrow.

Prognosis

The most important factors in the prognosis are the severity of the infection and promptness of treatment. Untreated hemophilus infections—particularly meningitis, sepsis, and epiglottitis—have a high mortality rate. Bacterial sepsis of the newborn has a mortality rate of 13–50 percent. The prognosis is usually good for patients with mild infections who are treated without delay. Children who develop Hib arthritis sometimes have lasting problems with joint function.

Prevention

Hemophilus vaccines

There are three different vaccines for hemophilus infections used to immunize children in the United States: PRP-D, HBOC, and PRP-OMP. PRP-D is used only in children older than 15 months. HBOC is administered to infants at two, four, and six months after birth, with a booster dose at 15 to 18 months. PRP-OMP is administered to infants at two and four months, with the third dose at the child's first birthday. All three vaccines are given by intramuscular injection. About 5 percent of children may develop fever or soreness in the area of the injection.

Other measures

Other preventive measures include isolating patients with respiratory hemophilus infections; treating appropriate contacts of infected patients with rifampin; maintaining careful standards of cleanliness in hospitals,

Henoch-Schönlein purpura *see* **Allergic purpura**

KEY TERMS

Bacteria—Singular, bacterium; tiny, one-celled forms of life that cause many diseases and infections.

Epiglottitis—Inflammation of the epiglottis, most often caused by a bacterial infection. The epiglottis is a piece of cartilage behind the tongue that closes the opening to the windpipe when a person swallows. An inflamed epiglottis can swell and close off the windpipe, thus causing the patient to suffocate. Also called supraglottitis.

Exudate—Cells, protein, fluid, or other materials that pass through cell or blood vessel walls. Exudates may accumulate in the surrounding tissue or may be discharged outside the body.

Intubation—A procedure in which a tube is inserted through the mouth and into the trachea to keep the airway open and to help a patient breathe.

Nosocomial infection—An infection acquired in a hospital setting.

Sepsis—A severe systemic infection in which bacteria have entered the bloodstream or body tissues.

Stridor—A term used to describe noisy breathing in general and to refer specifically to a high-pitched crowing sound associated with croup, respiratory infection, and airway obstruction.

Tracheotomy—An surgical procedure in which the surgeon cuts directly through the patient's neck into the windpipe below a blockage in order to keep the airway open.

including proper disposal of soiled tissues; and washing hands properly.

See also Hib vaccine.

Resources

BOOKS

Daum, Robert S. "*Haemophilus influenzae.*" In *Nelson Textbook of Pediatrics.* Edited by Richard E. Behrman et al. Philadelphia: Saunders, 2004.

St. Geme, Joseph W. "*Haemophilus influenzae.*" In *Principles and Practice of Pediatric Infectious Diseases*, 2nd ed. Oxford, UK: Church Livingston, 2002.

Rebecca J. Frey, PhD
Rosalyn Carson-DeWitt, MD

Hepatitis A

Definition

Hepatitis A is a liver disease caused by the hepatitis A virus (HAV).

Description

Hepatitis A is a form of viral hepatitis also known as infectious hepatitis, due to its ability to be spread through personal contact. Hepatitis A is a milder liver disease than **hepatitis B**, and asymptomatic infections are very common, especially in children. Hepatitis A does not cause a carrier state or chronic liver disease. Once the infection ends, there is no lasting phase of illness. However, it is not uncommon to have a second episode of symptoms about a month after the first; this is called a relapse.

Transmission

HAV is found in the stool (feces) of persons infected with hepatitis A. HAV is usually spread from person to person by putting something in the mouth that has been contaminated with the stool of a person infected with hepatitis A. This is called fecal-oral transmission. Thus, the virus spreads more easily in areas where there are poor sanitary conditions or where good personal hygiene is not observed. Most infections result from contact with a houschold member who has hepatitis A. Blood-borne infection has been documented but is rare in the United States. The common modes of transmission of hepatitis A are as follows:

- consuming food made by someone who touched infected feces
- drinking water that is contaminated by infected feces (a problem in communities with poor sewage treatment facilities)
- touching an infected person's feces, which may occur with poor hand washing
- having direct contact in large daycare centers, especially where there are children in diapers
- being a resident of states in which hepatitis A is more common
- sexual contact with an infected person

Demographics

Hepatitis A has a worldwide distribution and is endemic in most countries. However, the incidence of the disease is declining in developed countries. There is a very high incidence in developing countries and rural areas. For example, in rural areas of South Africa, the rate of infection is 100 percent.

According to the Centers for Disease Control, HAV infects up to 200,000 Americans each year with the highest rate of hepatitis A being among children five to 14 years of age. Almost 30 percent of reported cases of hepatitis A occur among children under 15 years of age, chiefly because they are frequently in close contact with other children in school and at daycare. Approximately 15 percent of reported cases of hepatitis A occur among children or employees in daycare centers. The states with the highest incidence of hepatitis A account for 50 percent of the reported cases. According to the American Academy of Pediatrics, 11 states have a rate of HAV infection that is at least twice the national average, or 20 cases per every 100,000 people. The states are: Arizona, Alaska, California, Idaho, Nevada, New Mexico, Oklahoma, Oregon, South Dakota, Utah, and Washington.

Causes and symptoms

Hepatitis A is caused by HAV, also called *Enterovirus 72*, which was identified in 1973. The virus has an incubation period of three to five weeks. It enters the body via the gut and replicates in the digestive tract and spreads to infect the liver, where it multiplies. HAV is excreted in the stools for two weeks preceding the onset of symptoms.

Persons with hepatitis A may not have signs or symptoms of the disease and older persons are more likely to have symptoms than children. If present, symptoms are non-specific and usually include **fever**, tiredness, loss of appetite, **nausea**, abdominal discomfort, dark urine, and **jaundice** (yellowing of the skin and eyes). Symptoms usually last less than two months, but some persons can be ill for as long as six months.

When to call the doctor

Parents should call the doctor immediately if any of the following occurs:

- A child has changes in symptoms, is confused, is difficult to wake up, is lethargic (sluggish), or irritable.

- A child is unable to drink fluids.
- A child's skikn is yellow in color.
- A child has signs of **dehydration** such as no urine in over eight hours or a dry mouth.
- A child starts to look very sick.

Diagnosis

Hepatitis A symptoms often go unrecognized because they are not specific to hepatitis A, thus a blood test (IgM anti-HAV) is required to diagnose HAV infection. This test detects a specific antibody, called hepatitis A IgM, that develops when HAV is present in the body.

Treatment

No specific treatment is available for hepatitis A. However, the following guidelines are often recommended:

- Fluids and diet. The best treatment is to make sure that the child drinks a lot of fluids and eats well.
- Rest. The child should rest while he or she has fever or jaundice. When fever and jaundice are gone, activity may be gradually increased as with the healthcare provider's approval.
- Medications. The body's immune system fights the HAV infection. Once the child recovers from hepatitis A, the virus leaves the body. Medications, prescription or nonprescription, should not be given without consulting the doctor.

Nutritional concerns

Parents should ensure that their infected child has a well-balanced diet. Children with advanced liver disease need to follow specific diets issued by the treating physician. However, most children are not in this category, and no special diet is currently recommended for them, except that they should avoid eating fatty foods because the body has difficulty digesting fat when the liver is not working well.

However, adequate protein intake is important to regenerate liver cells. Children without liver cirrhosis require about 2–3 grams of protein per kilogram of body weight. Children with cirrhosis need an individual **nutrition** plan from their pediatric specialist or nutritionist.

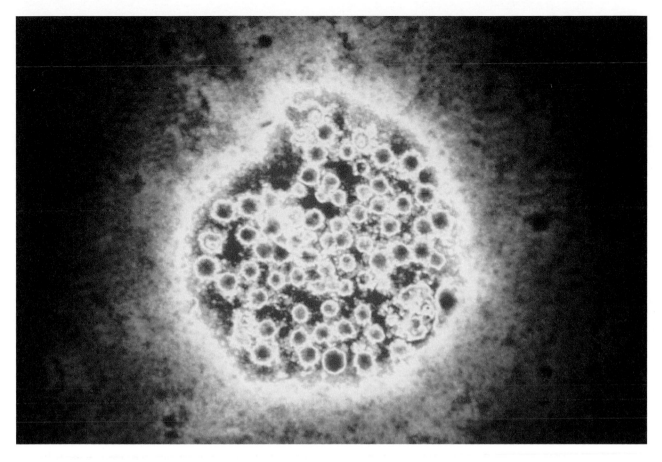

Hepatitis A virus magnified 225,000 times. *(© 1990 Custom Medical Stock Photo, Inc.)*

Prognosis

Viral hepatitis symptoms usually last three weeks to two months but may last up to six months. Children may return to daycare one week after symptoms first appear, with the doctor's permission. Most children with hepatitis get better naturally without liver problems later in life. However, some children do have subsequent liver problems. For this reason, it is important to keep in close touch with the treating physician and to keep all follow-up appointments. Chronic, or relapsing, infection does not occur with hepatitis A. In the United States, serious complications are infrequent, and deaths are very rare.

Prevention

According to the Centers for Disease Control and Prevention (CDC), routine **vaccination** of children is the most effective way to lower the incidence of hepatitis A nationwide. The CDC encourages implementation of routine hepatitis A vaccination programs for children in the 17 states which have the highest rates of hepatitis A. Hepatitis A vaccine has been licensed in the United States for use in persons two years of age and older. The vaccine is recommended (before exposure to hepatitis A virus) for persons who are more likely to get hepatitis A virus infection or are more likely to get seriously ill if they do get hepatitis A. The vaccines licensed in the United States as of 2004 were HAVRIX(r) (manufactured by Glaxo SmithKline) and VAQTA(r) (manufactured by Merck & Co., Inc).

Parents should teach their children always to wash their hands with soap and water after using the bathroom and before preparing and eating food. Travelers should avoid water and ice if unsure of their purity, or they can boil water for one minute before drinking it.

Short-term protection against hepatitis A is available from immune globulin, a preparation of antibodies that can be given before exposure for short-term protection against hepatitis A and for persons who have already been exposed to HAV. It can be given before and within two weeks after suspected contact with the virus.

KEY TERMS

Antibody—A special protein made by the body's immune system as a defense against foreign material (bacteria, viruses, etc.) that enters the body. It is uniquely designed to attack and neutralize the specific antigen that triggered the immune response.

Antigen—A substance (usually a protein) identified as foreign by the body's immune system, triggering the release of antibodies as part of the body's immune response.

Asymptomatic—Persons who carry a disease and are usually capable of transmitting the disease but who do not exhibit symptoms of the disease are said to be asymptomatic.

Endemic—Natural to or characteristic of a particular place, population, or climate.

Hepatitis A—Commonly called infectious hepatitis, caused by the hepatitis A virus (HAV). Most often spread by food and water contamination.

Immune globulin—Preparation of antibodies that can be given before exposure for short-term protection against hepatitis A and for persons who have already been exposed to hepatitis A virus. Immune globulin must be given within two weeks after exposure to hepatitis A virus for maximum protection.

Jaundice—A condition in which the skin and whites of the eyes take on a yellowish color due to an increase of bilirubin (a compound produced by the liver) in the blood. Also called icterus.

Vaccine—A substance prepared from a weakened or killed microorganism which, when injected, helps the body to form antibodies that will prevent infection by the natural microorganism.

Parental concerns

The best way to prevent exposure to HAV is good habits in washing hands. Children should wash their hands every time they go to the bathroom. Good hand washing should be enforced at home and at daycare facilities. It is also very important to keep a clean environment, such as clean toilets, bathrooms, and clothing. If a child is diagnosed with HAV, other **family** members should be treated to prevent spread of the disease. The healthcare provider can help parents to plan treatment for the entire family.

See also Hepatitis B; Vaccination.

Resources

BOOKS

Achord, James. *Understanding Hepatitis*. Jackson: University of Mississippi Press, 2002.

Berkman, Alan, and N. Bakalar. *Hepatitis A to G: The Facts You Need to Know About All the Forms of This Dangerous Disease*. Clayton, Australia: Warner Books, 2000.

PERIODICALS

Arya, G., and W. F. Balistreri. "Pediatric liver disease in the United States: Epidemiology and impact." *Journal of Gastroenterology & Hepatology* 17, no. 5 (May 2002): 521–25.

Averhoff, F. et al. "Control of Hepatitis A Through Routine Vaccination of Children." *Journal of the American Medical Association* 286, no. 23 (December 2001): 2968–73.

Ferreira, Cristina T. et al. "Immunogenicity and Safety of Hepatitis A Vaccine in Children with Chronic Liver Disease." *Journal of Pediatric Gastroenterology & Nutrition* 37, no. 3 (September 2003): 258–61.

Jenson, Hal B. "The changing picture of hepatitis A in the United States." *Current Opinion in Pediatrics* 16, no. 1 (February 2004): 89–93.

Shulman, Stanford T. "The History of Pediatric Infectious Diseases." *Pediatric Research* 55, no. 1 (January 2004): 163–176.

Murdoch, David L., et al. "Combined Hepatitis A and B Vaccines: A Review of Their Immunogenicity and Tolerability." *Drugs* 40, no. 5–6 (May-June 2004): 265–69.

ORGANIZATIONS

American Liver Foundation (ALF). 75 Maiden Lane, Suite 603, New York, NY 10038–4810. Web site: <www.liverfoundation.org>.

National Center for Infectious Diseases (NCID). Centers for Disease Control and Prevention, Mailstop C-14, 1600 Clifton Road, Atlanta, GA 30333. Web site: <www.cdc.gov/ncidod>.

Hepatitis Foundation International (HFI). 504 Blick Drive, Silver Spring, MD 20904–2901. Web site: <www.liverfoundation.org>.

WEB SITES

"Viral Hepatitis A Homepage." *NCID*. Available online at <www.cdc.gov/ncidod/diseases/hepatitis/a/index.htm> (accessed October 22, 2004.)

"What I need to know about Hepatitis A Homepage." *NIH-NDDIC*. Available online at <http://digestive.niddk.nih.gov/ddiseases/pubs/hepa_ez/> (accessed October 22, 2004).
Monique Laberge, Ph.D.

Hepatitis B

Definition

Hepatitis B is a liver disease caused by the hepatitis B virus (HBV).

Description

Hepatitis B is a form of viral hepatitis that is also known as serum hepatitis, due to its ability to be spread through body fluids and blood. HBV can cause lifelong infection, cirrhosis (scarring) of the liver, liver **cancer**, liver failure, and death. Hepatitis B is a more severe liver disease than **hepatitis A**, and asymptomatic infections occur frequently. Chronic hepatitis B infection may take one of two forms: chronic persistent hepatitis, a condition characterized by persistence of the virus but in which liver damage is minimal; and chronic active hepatitis, in which there is aggressive destruction of liver tissue and rapid progression to cirrhosis or liver failure.

Transmission

Transmission of HBV occurs through blood and body fluid exposure such as blood, semen, vaginal secretions, or saliva. Hepatitis B is not spread through food or water or by casual contact. Infants may also develop the disease if they are born to a mother who has the virus. Infected children often spread the virus to other children if there is frequent contact or a child has many scrapes or cuts. The common modes of transmission of hepatitis B are as follows:

- children born to mothers who have hepatitis B (the illness may present up to five years after the child is born)
- children who are born to mothers who have emigrated from a country where hepatitis B is widespread such as southeast Asia and China
- individuals who live in households where another member is infected with the virus
- infection through intravenous (IV) drug use and/or unprotected heterosexual or homosexual sexual contact
- infection through blood transfusions from infected donors

Demographics

Worldwide there are 450 million carriers of hepatitis B, 50 million of which are in Africa. Carriage rates vary markedly in different areas. In South Africa, infection is much more common in rural communities than in the cities.

According to the Centers for Disease Control (CDC), an estimated 78,000 persons in the United States were infected with HBV in 2001. People of all ages get hepatitis B, and about 5,000 die per year of sickness caused by HBV. An estimated 1.25 million Americans are chronically infected, of whom 20 to 30 percent acquired their infection in childhood. It is estimated that hepatitis B accounts for 20 to 25 percent of all acute viral hepatitis in children. Infected newborns rarely suffer but have 90 percent chance of becoming carriers. Twenty-five percent of all HAV positive newborns develop chronic liver disease by the third to fourth decade of life.

Causes and symptoms

Hepatitis B is caused by HBV, also called Hepadna virus. The virus has an incubation period of two to five months. It replicates in the liver, and virus particles are shed in large amounts into the blood. The blood of infected individuals is thus highly infectious.

Hepatitis B has a wide range of symptoms. It can also be mild, without symptoms. When present, the symptoms are non-specific and usually include **fever**, tiredness, loss of appetite, **nausea**, abdominal discomfort, dark urine, clay-colored bowel movements, and **jaundice** (yellowing of the skin and eyes).

When to call the doctor

Parents should call the doctor immediately if any of the following occurs:

- A child has changes in symptoms, is confused, is difficult to wake up, is lethargic (sluggish), or irritable.
- A child is unable to drink fluids.
- A child's skin becomes much more yellow in color.
- A child has signs of **dehydration** such as no urine in over eight hours or a dry mouth.
- A child starts to look very sick.

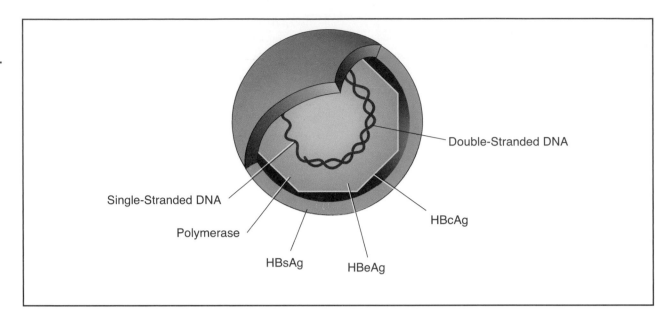

Single-Stranded DNA

Polymerase

HBsAg

HBeAg

Double-Stranded DNA

HBcAg

Hepatitis B virus (HBV) is composed of an inner protein core and an outer protein capsule. The outer capsule contains the hepatitis B surface antigen (HBsAg). The inner core contains HBV core antigen (HBcAg) and hepatitis B e-antigen (HBeAg). This cell also contains polymerase, which catalyzes the formation of the cell's DNA. HBV is the only hepatitis-causing virus that has DNA, instead of RNA. *(Illustration by Electronic Illustrators Group.)*

Diagnosis

A blood test is required to diagnose hepatitis B. The test detects one of the viral antigens called hepatitis B surface antigen (HBsAg) in the blood. Later on, HBsAg may no longer be present, in which case a test for antibodies to a different antigen, called hepatitis B core antigen, is used. If HBsAg can be detected in the blood for longer than six months, chronic hepatitis B is diagnosed.

Treatment

There is no cure for hepatitis B and no specific treatment is available. However, the following guidelines are often recommended:

- Fluids and diet. The best treatment is to ensure that the child drinks a lot of fluids and eats well.

- Rest. The child should rest while he or she has fever or jaundice. When fever and jaundice are gone, activity may be gradually increased as with the healthcare provider's approval.

- Medications. There is no medicine that gets rid of HBV or heals the liver. There are medications available to treat chronic HBV-infection. These work for some people, but experience with children is limited. Three drugs are licensed, as of 2004, for the treatment of chronic hepatitis B: Adefovir dipivoxil, alpha interferon, and lamivudine.

Nutritional concerns

Parents should ensure that their infected child has a well-balanced diet. Children with advanced liver disease need to follow specific diets issued by the treating physician. However, most children are not in this category, and no special diet is recommended for them, except that they should avoid eating fatty foods because the body has difficulty digesting fat when the liver is not working well.

However, adequate protein intake is important to regenerate liver cells. Children without liver cirrhosis require about 1–2 grams of protein per pound (2–3 grams per kilogram) of body weight. Children with cirrhosis need an individual **nutrition** plan from their pediatric specialist or nutritionist.

There is some evidence that iron can lower the response to interferon treatment in adults. Although no results have been reported for children, the issue of restricting iron intake should be discussed with the treating physician.

Prognosis

Viral hepatitis symptoms usually last three weeks to two months but may last up to six months. Children may return to daycare one week after symptoms first appear, with the doctor's permission. Most children with hepatitis get better naturally without liver problems later on in life. However, some children do have subsequent liver

KEY TERMS

Cirrhosis—A chronic degenerative disease of the liver, in which normal cells are replaced by fibrous tissue and normal liver function is disrupted. The most common symptoms are mild jaundice, fluid collection in the tissues, mental confusion, and vomiting of blood. Cirrhosis is associated with portal hypertension and is a major risk factor for the later development of liver cancer. If left untreated, cirrhosis leads to liver failure.

Hepatitis B virus (HBV)—Also called Hepadna virus, the pathogen responsible for hepatitis B infection.

Jaundice—A condition in which the skin and whites of the eyes take on a yellowish color due to an increase of bilirubin (a compound produced by the liver) in the blood. Also called icterus.

Vaccine—A substance prepared from a weakened or killed microorganism which, when injected, helps the body to form antibodies that will prevent infection by the natural microorganism.

problems. Thus, it is important to keep in close touch with the treating physician and to keep all follow-up appointments. Chronic, or relapsing, infection occurs with hepatitis B in about 5–10 percent of cases.

Prevention

A vaccine for hepatitis B is as of 2004 widely used in the United States for routine childhood immunization. Children usually receive the first vaccine between birth and two months of age, the second vaccine at one to four months, and the third vaccine at six to 18 months. The vaccine is generally required for all children born on or after January 1, 1992, before they enter school. The vaccine is available for older children who may have not been immunized before 1992 and is recommended before age 11 or 12.

Parental concerns

If mothers have HBV in their blood, they can give hepatitis B to their baby during **childbirth**. Babies who get HBV at birth may have the virus for the rest of their lives, can spread the disease, and can get cirrhosis of the liver or liver cancer. The CDC recommends that all pregnant women be tested for HBV early in their pregnancy. If the blood test is positive, the baby should receive vaccine along with hepatitis B immune globulin

(HBIG) at birth. The second dose of vaccine should be given at one to two months of age and the third dose at six months of age.

See also Hepatitis A; Hepatitis B vaccine; Vaccination.

Resources

BOOKS

Achord, James. *Understanding Hepatitis.* Jackson: University of Mississippi Press, 2002.

Berkman, Alan, and N. Bakalar. *Hepatitis A to G: The Facts You Need to Know about All the Forms of This Dangerous Disease.* Clayton, Australia: Warner Books, 2000.

Blumberg, Baruch S. *Hepatitis B: The Hunt for a Killer Virus.* Princeton, NJ: Princeton University Press, 2002.

Everson, Gregory T., et al. *Living with Hepatitis B: A Survivor's Guide.* Long Island City, NY: Hatherleigh Press, 2004.

Green, William F., and H. Conjeevaram. *The First Year— Hepatitis B: An Essential Guide for the Newly Diagnosed.* New York: Marlowe & Co., 2002.

PERIODICALS

Arya, G., and W. F. Balistreri. "Pediatric liver disease in the United States: Epidemiology and impact." *Journal of Gastroenterology & Hepatology* 17, no. 5 (May 2002): 521–25.

Helvaci, M., et al. "Efficacy of hepatitis B vaccination and interferon-[alpha]-2b combination therapy versus interferon-[alpha]-2b monotherapy in children with chronic hepatitis B." *Journal of Gastroenterology & Hepatology* 19, no. 7 (July 2004): 785–91.

Liberek, A., et al. "Tolerance of interferon-alpha therapy in children with chronic hepatitis B." *Journal of Paediatrics & Child Health* 63, no. 23 (2003): 2625–49.

Murdoch, David L. et al. "Combined Hepatitis A and B Vaccines: A Review of Their Immunogenicity and Tolerability." *Drugs* 40, no. 5–6 (May-June 2004): 265–69.

Shulman, Stanford T. "The History of Pediatric Infectious Diseases." *Pediatric Research* 55, no. 1 (January 2004): 163–176.

Sokal, Etienne. "Drug Treatment of Pediatric Chronic Hepatitis B." *Pediatric Drugs* 4, no. 6 (2002): 361–69.

ORGANIZATIONS

American Liver Foundation (ALF). 75 Maiden Lane, Suite 603, New York, NY 10038–4810. Web site: <www.liverfoundation.org>.

Hepatitis B Foundation. 700 East Butler Avenue, Doylestown, PA 18901–2697. Web site: <www.hepb.org>.

Hepatitis Foundation International (HFI). 504 Blick Drive, Silver Spring, MD 20904–2901. Web site: <www.liverfoundation.org>.

National Center for Infectious Diseases (NCID). Centers for Disease Control and Prevention, Mailstop C-14, 1600 Clifton Road, Atlanta, GA 30333. Web site: <www.cdc.gov/ncidod>.

WEB SITES

"Viral Hepatitis B Homepage." *NCID*. Available online at <www.cdc.gov/ncidod/diseases/hepatitis/b/index.htm> (accessed October 22, 2004).

"What I need to know about Hepatitis B Homepage." *NIH-NDDIC*. Available online at <http://digestive.niddk.nih.gov/ddiseases/pubs/hepb_e/> (accessed October 22, 2004).

Monique Laberge, Ph.D.

Hepatitis B vaccine

Definition

The **hepatitis B** vaccine (HBV or HepB) is an injection that protects children from contracting hepatitis B, a serious disease caused by the hepatitis B virus.

Description

The hepatitis B vaccine consists of a small protein from the surface of the hepatitis B virus called the hepatitis B surface antigen (HBsAg). After **vaccination** with HBV, the child's immune system recognizes HBsAg as foreign and produces antibodies that attach to the protein (anti-HBs). These specific antibodies remain in the blood. Later, if the child becomes infected with the hepatitis B virus, the antibodies recognize the protein and stimulate the immune system to produce large quantities of specific antibodies that attach to and destroy the virus and prevent the disease.

HBV is usually the first vaccine a child receives, most often before leaving the hospital after birth. The second and third HBV immunizations are administered by the age of 18 months, in conjunction with other routine childhood vaccinations.

Vaccine formulations

The HBsAg in HBVs is referred to as recombinant because it is genetically engineered. The gene encoding the DNA for HBsAg is introduced into common baker's yeast. The yeast is grown in vats in which large amounts of HBsAg are produced. The yeast cells are broken, and the HBsAg is isolated and purified. It is adsorbed into aluminum hydroxide.

Packaged hepatitis B vaccine contains the following:

- up to 95 percent HBsAg, with 10 to 40 micrograms of HBsAg per milliliter of vaccine
- no more than 5 percent yeast protein
- a small amount of aluminum hydroxide (0.5 mg/ml)
- very small amounts of other additives to stabilize and preserve the vaccine

Two HBVs are approved for use in the United States. Recombivax HB, manufactured by Merck & Company, is as of 2004 available as a pediatric/adolescent formulation (orange cap) and as an adult formulation (green cap). Engerix-B, made by SmithKline Beecham Biologicals, is as of 2004 available as a pediatric formulation (blue cap) and as an adult formulation (orange cap). In general these HBVs are interchangeable and either or both can be used in an individual immunization series. An HBV derived from the blood serum of people with hepatitis B was as of 2004 no longer produced in the United States.

Dosages

The immune response to HBV varies among individual children. Therefore, the HBV dose should be determined by a medical professional. In general, the recommended doses are as follows:

- Newborns: 2.5 to 20 micrograms injected into the anterolateral thigh muscle within seven days of birth or at the first visit to the physician's office, and one month and six months after the first dose, for a total of three doses.
- Newborns: 10 to 20 micrograms injected into the thigh muscle within seven days of birth and one month, two months, and 12 months after the first dose, for a total of four doses.
- Older child or adolescent: 2.5 to 20 micrograms injected into the deltoid arm muscle, with additional doses one month and six months after the first injection, for a total of three doses.

Safety

Although the vast majority of parents believe that vaccinations are important for their children, the majority of parents are also concerned about the safety of vaccines including HBV. Although controversy over the safety of HBV resulted in congressional hearings in 1999, the National Academy of Science's Institute of Medicine, as well as other authorities, considers HBV to be safe. Repeated studies have found no association between HBV and **sudden infant death syndrome** (SIDS) or other medical conditions, including neurological or immune system disorders.

Effectiveness

HBV usually is effective in protecting against hepatitis B. (HBV also protects against the related hepatitis D virus, which occurs as a co-infection with hepatitis B and usually results in more severe disease symptoms.) However, the immune response to HBV varies among children, apparently due to genetic variations in individual immune systems. In addition, the following medical conditions may cause children to benefit less from HBV:

- stomach **pain**
- cirrhosis (scarring) of the liver
- immune system impairment
- medical conditions requiring kidney dialysis

The duration of hepatitis B immunity following infant vaccination is not known. A 2004 study found that most low-risk children vaccinated at birth did not have antibodies against hepatitis B in their blood by the time they reached the age of five. Although the majority of these children responded positively to a booster HBV immunization, one-third of them did not respond. Likewise, a 2003 Israeli study found a steady decline in anti-hepatitis-B antibodies over time in children vaccinated as infants. The steepest decline in the antibodies occurred between five and eight years after vaccination.

General use

Hepatitis B in children

The U.S. Centers for Disease Control and Prevention (CDC) estimates that, prior to the launch of the infant HBV immunization program, about 33,000 American children of non-infected mothers acquired hepatitis B by the age of ten. Hepatitis B is a potentially serious disease caused by the hepatitis B virus. It may result in inflammation and damage to the liver. Hepatitis B infection may be without symptoms or with acute or short-lived symptoms that can include:

- jaundice (a yellowing of the skin and whites of the eyes)
- joint pain
- stomach pain
- itchy red **hives** on the skin

The hepatitis B virus is eventually cleared from the bodies of most infected adolescents and adults. Only about 2–6 percent of infected older children and adults develop chronic hepatitis B and can continue to transmit the virus to other people. By contrast 90 percent of infants and 30 percent of young children infected with hepatitis B develop chronic disease: the younger the child, the more likely that a hepatitis B infection will become chronic. The consequences of chronic hepatitis B infection may include:

- chronic liver disease
- cirrhosis
- liver **cancer**
- liver failure

There is no cure for hepatitis B and approximately one-fourth of chronic hepatitis B victims die of cirrhosis or liver cancer, including children who do not survive to young adulthood. Of the approximately 1.25 million Americans with chronic hepatitis B, 20–30 percent were infected as infants or children.

Risk of childhood infection

Those with the highest risk for infection are older adolescents and adults engaging in high-risk behaviors such as drug use and unprotected sex with multiple partners.

Far less common sources of childhood hepatitis B infection include:

- breast milk from an infected mother
- contact with blood, saliva, tears, or urine from an infected household member
- cuts
- blood transfusions

However, the following children are at particular risk for hepatitis B infection:

- children of immigrants and refugees or children adopted from regions where hepatitis B is endemic, including Asia, Sub-Saharan Africa, the Amazon Basin, Eastern Europe, and the Middle East
- Alaskan natives and Pacific Islanders
- children living in households with a chronically hepatitis-B-infected person
- children living in institutions
- children receiving hemodialysis
- children receiving certain blood products

Children born to infected mothers

Children of hepatitis B-infected mothers are at a 10–85 percent risk of becoming infected during birth. The CDC estimates that, prior to the infant HBV immunization program, about 12,000 American infants per year were infected by their mothers at birth. In addition, children of hepatitis B-infected mothers are at high risk of becoming infected before the age of five.

Children under the age of five who become infected with hepatitis B are at high risk for chronic infection and severe liver damage and disease later in life, even though initially they may have no symptoms. These infected children have a 90 percent risk of chronic hepatitis B infection and as many as 25 percent of them will die of chronic liver disease as adults. Mothers who have emigrated from countries with high rates of endemic hepatitis B are more likely to be infected.

Mothers with acute or chronic infectious hepatitis B can be identified by a blood test for HBsAg. Children born to mothers who have hepatitis B or whose hepatitis B status is unknown should receive their first HBV dose within 12 hours of birth. The second and third doses are given at two and six months of age. In many parts of the world, vaccine intervention before birth is required to prevent hepatitis B infection and its consequences in newborns.

It is recommended that newborns whose mothers are HBsAg-positive receive hepatitis B immune globulin (HBIG)—a preparation of serum containing high levels of antibodies to hepatitis B—as well as HBV within 12 hours of birth. About 70 percent of these newborns will be protected from chronic hepatitis B. A child's immune response to either hepatitis B infection or to HBV can be measured by a blood test for antibodies to HBsAg (anti-HBs). If a vaccinated child is exposed to hepatitis B, a measure of the anti-HBs in the blood will indicate whether another dose of HBV is required. Infants born to mothers who are HBsAg-positive should be tested for anti-HBs three to nine months following their last dose of vaccine. Their anti-HB levels should be at least 10 milli-international units per milliliter (mIU/ml), indicating that they are immune due to vaccination.

Mass immunization

HBV first became available in the United States in 1982. Between 1979 and 1989, the incidence of acute hepatitis B increased in the United States by 37 percent. There were 200,000–300,000 new infections annually between 1980 and 1991. In 1991 the CDC developed a strategy for eliminating the transmission of hepatitis B via universal childhood vaccination. The World Health Organization also declared the goal of immunizing all infants worldwide.

Nearly all states enacted laws requiring hepatitis B vaccination for enrollment in daycare, schools, and colleges. All these laws include exemptions for medical reasons and most include exemptions for religious reasons; however, only a few states allow exemptions from vaccination on philosophical grounds. Most states do not have laws mandating the screening of pregnant women for HBsAg.

By 2002, 90 percent of American children had been vaccinated against hepatitis B. The number of children carrying the virus was subsequently reduced substantially. Infant death from hepatitis B and the incidence of liver disease in children also decreased significantly. The CDC estimates that in 1998 the vaccine prevented 6,800 infections during birth and 18,700 infections in infants and children up to the age of nine. About 12,900 of these children would have developed chronic hepatitis and 3,000 of them eventually would have died of cirrhosis or liver cancer. The CDC expects the overall incidence of hepatitis B in the American population to fall throughout the early 2000s as a result of mass childhood vaccination. However, as of 2004, infants receiving HBV since 1991 had not yet reached the age when high-risk behaviors increase the likelihood of hepatitis B infection. In Pacific Island nations—where rates of hepatitis B infection are among the highest in the world—a regionally coordinated immunization program has significantly reduced the incidence of chronic infection.

Costs

HBV usually is covered by health insurance. In the United States the Vaccines for Children program covers the cost of hepatitis B vaccination for those without health insurance and for other specific groups of children, including Native Americans. The CDC estimates that infant hepatitis B vaccination saves fifty cents in direct medical costs for every dollar spent on HBV.

Precautions

Because most children are not at high risk for hepatitis B infection, and because the duration of immunity provided by HBV is not known, some parents and medical professionals question the need for and the effectiveness of childhood vaccination against hepatitis B. Some also continue to question the safety of the vaccine.

Children should not receive HBV if they are allergic to baker's yeast or thimerosal, are allergic to any other components in a combination vaccine, or have had a previous allergic reaction to HBV. A 2003 study found that

HBV was safe and effective in children with **asthma**, even those on inhaled steroid therapy.

Side effects

Although most children experience no side effects from HBV, the most common side effects are as follows:

- fatigue or irritability in up to 20 percent of children
- soreness at the point of the injection, lasting one to two days, in about one out of eleven children and adolescents
- a mild to moderate **fever** in one out of 14 children and adolescents

Other less common side effects of HBV include:

- a purple spot, hard lump, redness, swelling, pain, or **itching** at the point of injection
- unusual tiredness or weakness
- dizziness
- fever of 100°F (37.7 °C) or higher
- headache

Other rare reactions to HBV include:

- general feeling of discomfort or illness
- aches or pain in joints or muscles
- skin rash or welts that may occur days or weeks after receiving the vaccine
- blurred vision or other vision changes
- muscle weakness or **numbness** or **tingling** in the arms and legs
- back pain or stiffness or pain in the neck or shoulder
- chills
- diarrhea or stomach cramps
- nausea or vomiting
- increased sweating
- sore throat or runny nose
- itching
- decreased or lost appetite
- sudden redness of the skin
- swelling of glands in the armpit or neck
- difficulty sleeping

Although allergic reactions to HBV are rare, if they occur emergency medical help should be sought immediately. Symptoms of an allergic reaction include:

- reddening of the skin, especially around the ears
- swelling of the eyes, face, or inside of the nose
- hives
- itching, especially of the feet or hands
- sudden and severe tiredness or weakness
- difficulty breathing or swallowing

Parental concerns

Preparing a child for an injection

Most children are afraid of injections; however, there are simple methods for easing a child's **fear**. Prior to the vaccination parents should take the following steps:

- Tell children that they will be getting a shot and that it will feel like a prick; however, it will only sting for a few seconds.
- Explain to children that the shot will prevent them from becoming sick.
- Have older siblings comfort and reassure a younger child.
- Bring along the child's favorite toy or blanket.
- Never threaten children by telling them they will get a shot.
- Read the vaccination information statement and ask questions of the medical practitioner.

During the vaccination parents should take the following steps:

- Hold the child.
- Make eye contact with the child and smile.
- Talk softly and comfort the child.
- Distract the child by pointing out pictures or objects or using a hand puppet.
- Sing or tell the child a story.
- Have the child tell a story.
- Teach the child to focus on something other than the shot.
- Help the child take deep breaths.
- Allow the child to cry.
- Stay calm.

Comforting restraint

Parents may choose to use a comforting restraint method while their child is receiving an injection. These methods enable the parent to control and steady the child's arm while not holding the child down. With infants and toddlers, the following holds may be effective:

- The child is held on the parent's lap.
- The child's arm is behind the parent's back, held under the parent's arm.
- The parent's arm and hand control the child's other arm.
- The child's feet are held between the parent's thighs and steadied with the parent's other arm.

With older children, the following positions may be effective:

- The child is held on the parent's lap or stands in front of the seated parent.
- The parent's arms embrace the child.
- The child's legs are between the parent's legs.

After the injection

Following an injection parents should help in the following ways:

- Hold and caress a child or breastfeed an infant.
- Talk soothingly and reassuringly.
- Hug and praise the child for doing well.
- Review the information for possible side effects.
- Use a cool, wet cloth to reduce soreness or swelling at the injection site.
- Check the child for **rashes** over the following few days.

In addition, parents should remember the following:

- The child may eat less during the first 24 hours following a vaccination.
- The child should drink plenty of fluids.
- The medical practitioner may suggest a non-aspirin pain reliever for the child.

Resources

BOOKS

Atkinson, William, and Charles (Skip) Wolfe, eds. *Epidemiology and Prevention of Vaccine-Preventable Diseases*, 7th ed. Atlanta, GA: National Immunization Program, Centers for Disease Control and Prevention, 2003.

Blumberg, Baruch S. *Hepatitis B: The Hunt for a Killer Virus.* Princeton, NJ: Princeton University Press 2003.

Converse, Judy. *When Your Doctor Is Wrong: Hepatitis B and Autism.* Philadelphia, PA: Xlibris Corp., 2002.

KEY TERMS

Antibody—A special protein made by the body's immune system as a defense against foreign material (bacteria, viruses, etc.) that enters the body. It is uniquely designed to attack and neutralize the specific antigen that triggered the immune response.

Antigen—A substance (usually a protein) identified as foreign by the body's immune system, triggering the release of antibodies as part of the body's immune response.

Booster immunization—An additional dose of a vaccine to maintain immunity to the disease.

Cirrhosis—A chronic degenerative disease of the liver, in which normal cells are replaced by fibrous tissue and normal liver function is disrupted. The most common symptoms are mild jaundice, fluid collection in the tissues, mental confusion, and vomiting of blood. Cirrhosis is associated with portal hypertension and is a major risk factor for the later development of liver cancer. If left untreated, cirrhosis leads to liver failure.

Comvax—Hib-HepB, a combination vaccine that protects against the *Haemophilus influenzae* type B bacterium and the hepatitis B virus.

Haemophilus influenzae type B—An anaerobic bacteria associated with human respiratory infections, conjunctivitis, and meningitis.

Hepatitis B immune globulin—HBIG, a blood serum preparation containing anti-hepatitis-B antibodies (anti-HBs) that is administered along with HBV to children born to hepatitis-B-infected mothers.

Immunity—Ability to resist the effects of agents, such as bacteria and viruses, that cause disease.

Hepatitis B Vaccine: A Medical Dictionary, Bibliography, and Annotated Research Guide to Internet References. San Diego, CA: Icon Group International, 2004.

PERIODICALS

Petersen, K. M., et al. "Duration of Hepatitis B Immunity in Low Risk Children Receiving Hepatitis B Vaccinations from Birth." *The Pediatric Infectious Disease Journal* 23 (July 2004): 650–5.

Shouval, D. "Hepatitis B Vaccines." *Journal of Hepatology* 39 Suppl. 1 (2003): S70–6.

ORGANIZATIONS

Immunization Action Coalition. 1573 Selby Ave., St. Paul, MN 55104. Web site: <www.immunize.org>.

National Immunization Program. NIP Public Inquiries, Mailstop E-05, 1600 Clifton Rd. NE, Atlanta, GA 30333. Web site: <www.cdc.gov/nip>.

National Vaccine Information Center. 421-E Church St., Vienna, VA 22180. Web site: <www.909shot.com>

WEB SITES

"Hepatitis B Facts: Testing and Vaccination." *Immunization Action Coalition.* Available online at <www.immunize.org/catg.d/p2110.htm> (accessed December 22, 2004).

Margaret Alic, Ph.D.

Hereditary fructose intolerance

Definition

Hereditary fructose intolerance is a metabolic disorder in which the small intestine cannot process fructose (fruit sugar) into a source of energy because of an enzyme deficiency that prevents fructose absorption.

Description

Fructose is a simple sugar found naturally in fruits, vegetables, and honey. Synthetic fructose (in the form of corn syrup) is used as a sweetener in many foods, including baby food, and sweetened beverages. Other simple sugars include glucose (the form in which sugar circulates in the blood) and galactose (produced by the digestion of milk). Simple sugars can be absorbed by the small intestine.

Digestion of food begins in the mouth, moves to the stomach, and then into the small intestine. Along the way, specific enzymes are needed to process different types of sugars. An enzyme is a substance that acts as a catalyst to produce chemical changes without being changed itself. People with fructose intolerance do not have the enzyme 1-phosphofructaldolase (also called aldolase B enzyme and fructose 1-phosphate aldolase). This enzyme is necessary for the absorption of fructose.

When people with fructose intolerance ingest fructose or sucrose (cane or beet sugar, table sugar), complicated chemical changes occur in the body due to the absence of the enzyme needed to process these sugars. The undigested fructose accumulates in the liver, kidneys, and small intestine, progressively causing damage that can lead to liver and kidney failure. The accumulated fructose interferes with the conversion of glycogen, the body's energy storage material, into glucose. As a result, the blood sugar falls to abnormal levels (**hypoglycemia**).

An interesting feature of fructose intolerance is that children affected by the disorder develop a powerful protective aversion (feeling of intense dislike) to sweet-tasting foods and beverages. In addition, they have an exceptionally good record of dental hygiene, which is thought to be the result of diminished sugar and carbohydrate intake.

Demographics

Hereditary fructose intolerance is estimated to affect one in about 20,000 people. It is reported more frequently in the United States and northern European countries than in other parts of the world. It occurs with equal frequency in males and females.

Causes and symptoms

Causes

Fructose intolerance is an inherited disorder. Both the mother and father have the gene that causes the condition but may not have symptoms of fructose intolerance themselves. (This is called an autosomal recessive pattern of inheritance.)

Symptoms

The disorder is not apparent until the infant is fed formula, juice, fruits, or baby foods that contain fructose. Many soy-based formulas contain sucrose as a carbohydrate source. Initial symptoms include severe abdominal **pain**, **vomiting** that can lead to **dehydration**, and unexplained **fever**. Other symptoms include extreme thirst and excessive urination and sweating. There is also a loss of appetite and a failure to grow. Tremors and seizures caused by low blood sugar can occur. The liver becomes swollen, and the patient becomes jaundiced with yellowing of the eyes and skin. Left untreated, this condition can lead to coma and death.

When to call the doctor

If a child develops the following symptoms after he or she begins eating formula or solid food, the parent should contact the child's pediatrician:

- persistent or severe vomiting
- severe abdominal pain
- unexplained fever
- intolerance for fruits or avoidance of fruits/sucrose-containing foods
- extreme thirst
- excessive urination
- jaundice (yellowing of the eyes and skin)
- loss of appetite
- failure to grow
- unexplained weight loss

Early symptoms of hypoglycemia include:

- confusion
- dizziness
- feeling shaky or trembling
- hunger
- headache
- irritability
- fast heartbeat
- pale skin
- sweating
- sudden drowsiness, weakness, or fatigue

These symptoms can be treated by giving the child an oral glucose tablet, available from most pharmacies.

Symptoms of late hypoglycemia should be treated immediately. Parents should give the child a glucagon injection (a medication used in an emergency to increase blood glucose) and seek emergent treatment when the child has the following symptoms:

- inability to swallow
- numbness in mouth or tongue
- poor coordination
- poor concentration, confusion
- unconsciousness

When hypoglycemia is severe, it can lead to convulsions and coma. The child's doctor can advise the parents on how to manage the child's blood glucose levels to avoid hypoglycemic reactions as much as possible.

Diagnosis

The diagnosis includes a physical exam and evaluation of the child's **family** medical history. A family his-

tory of fructose intolerance may suggest a genetic predisposition to the disease. Several gene mutations causing hereditary fructose intolerance have been identified. Genetic testing with DNA analysis may be available to identify one of the common gene mutations that lead to this disorder. Positive results of the DNA test and the presence of clinical symptoms can serve as strong indicators of the condition. However, negative results are not a guarantee that the person does not have hereditary fructose intolerance.

Urine tests can be used to detect fructose sugar in the urine. Blood tests can also be used to detect hyperbilirubinemia and high levels of liver enzymes and uric acid in the blood. A liver biopsy may be performed to test for levels of enzymes present (aldolase assay) and to evaluate the extent of damage to the liver. A fructose tolerance test may also be used to confirm fructose intolerance. In this test, a dose of fructose is given to the patient in a well-controlled hospital or clinical setting. This test should only be performed on an asymptomatic patient. Both the biopsy and the fructose tolerance test are very risky, particularly in infants who are already sick.

Treatment

With early diagnosis, fructose intolerance can be successfully treated by eliminating fructose, sucrose, and sorbitol from the diet (less than 40 mg/kg per day). Sorbitol is an artificial sweetener found in many sugar-free products, such as sugarless gum or diet foods. Patients usually respond favorably within a few weeks and can make a complete recovery if fructose-containing foods are avoided. Early recognition and treatment of the disorder is important to avoid damage to the liver, kidneys, and small intestine.

Early symptoms of hypoglycemia can be treated with oral glucose tablets or gel, available at most pharmacies. The doctor can provide more information about how to manage a hypoglycemic reaction, as well as how to monitor the child's blood glucose levels using a blood glucose meter to prevent a hypoglycemic reaction. Severe hypoglycemia should be treated with a glucagon injection to increase the blood glucose level. In some cases, the child may need an intravenous glucose solution, given in the hospital.

Children with this condition should be managed by a medical specialist in biochemical genetics or metabolism, as well as a registered dietitian who can provide **nutrition** support and information.

Nutritional concerns

It is important for the child to avoid fructose, sucrose, and sorbitol sources and yet maintain proper nutrition. A registered dietitian can work with the parents and child to identify and avoid fructose and sucrose foods and beverages. This is very important, since many unsuspected food sources, such as potatoes when prepared a certain way, are significant sources of fructose. The dietitian can provide instructions for reading food and medication labels to detect these problem-causing substances. Regular follow-up appointments with a registered dietitian should be part of the child's overall treatment program.

Prognosis

There is no cure for hereditary fructose intolerance, since the enzyme needed to process fructose is missing at birth. The prognosis depends on how soon the diagnosis is made and how soon fructose and sucrose are eliminated from the child's diet. If the condition is not recognized and the diet is not well controlled, death can occur in infants or young children. With a well-controlled diet, the child will thrive and develop normally. In the absence of liver damage, the child's life expectancy is normal. Most of the damaging effects of the disorder can be prevented by strictly following the fructose-free diet.

Prevention

Carriers of the gene for hereditary fructose intolerance can be identified through DNA analysis. Anyone who is known to carry the disorder or who has the disorder in his or her family may benefit from genetic counseling. At-risk individuals can be assisted with family planning and reproductive decisions.

Nutritional concerns

To prevent complications from this disorder, parents should take the following steps:

- work with a registered dietitian to facilitate specific dietary changes
- carefully read food labels to identify and avoid dietary sources of fructose and sucrose
- maintain a regular follow-up schedule with the child's metabolic specialist

Parental concerns

Fructose intolerance can be a life-threatening condition if strict dietary guidelines are not followed. If the

---

KEY TERMS

Aldolase B—Also called fructose 1-phosphate aldolase, this chemical is produced in the liver, kidneys, and brain. It is needed for the breakdown of fructose, a sugar found in fruits, vegetables, honey, and other sweeteners.

Digestion—The mechanical, chemical, and enzymatic process in which food is converted into the substances suitable for use by the body.

DNA—Deoxyribonucleic acid; the genetic material in cells that holds the inherited instructions for growth, development, and cellular functioning.

Enzyme—A protein that catalyzes a biochemical reaction without changing its own structure or function.

Hyperbilirubinemia—A condition characterized by a high level of bilirubin in the blood. Bilirubin is a natural byproduct of the breakdown of red blood cells, however, a high level of bilirubin may indicate a problem with the liver.

Lactose—A sugar found in milk and milk products.

Liver biopsy—A surgical procedure where a small piece of the liver is removed for examination. A needle or narrow tube may be inserted either directly through the skin and muscle or through a small incision and passed into the liver for collection of a sample of liver tissue.

Metabolism—The sum of all chemical reactions that occur in the body resulting in growth, transformation of foodstuffs into energy, waste elimination, and other bodily functions. These include processes that break down substances to yield energy and processes that build up other substances necessary for life.

Nutrient—Substances in food that supply the body with the elements needed for metabolism. Examples of nutrients are vitamins, minerals, carbohydrates, fats, and proteins.

Sugars—Those carbohydrates having the general composition of one part carbon, two parts hydrogen, and one part oxygen.

---

diet is relaxed, the child may fail to grow normally or may develop liver or kidney complications.

Preliminary evidence suggests that parents of a child with this disorder, and other carriers of the mutant gene, may have an increased risk for gout. Gout is a form of arthritis caused by excess uric acid in the body and uric acid crystals in the joints.

Resources

BOOKS

Brostoff, Jonathon, et al. *Food Allergies and Food Intolerance: The Complete Guide to Their Identification and Treatment.* Rochester, VT: Inner Traditions International, 2000.

David, T. J. *Food and Food Additive Intolerance in Childhood.* Oxford, UK: Blackwell's Publishing, 2002.

Emerton, Victoria. *Food Allergies and Intolerance: Current Issues and Concerns.* Cambridge, UK: Royal Society of Chemistry, 2002.

Emsley, John, et al. *Was It Something You Ate? Food Intolerance: What Causes It and How to Avoid It.* Oxford, UK: Oxford University Press, 2002.

Williams, Sue Rodwell, and Eleanor Schlenker. *Essentials of Nutrition and Diet Therapy*, 8th ed. Philadelphia: Mosby, 2002.

ORGANIZATIONS

American College of Gastroenterology (ACG). PO Box 3099, Alexandria, VA 22302. Web site: <www.acg.gi.org/patientinfo>.

National Center for Biotechnology Information. U.S. National Library of Medicine, 8600 Rockville Pike, Bethesda, MD 20894. Web site: <www3.ncbi.nlm.nih.gov>.

National Institute of Diabetes and Digestive and Kidney Diseases (NIDDK). 2 Information Way, Bethesda, MD 20892–3570. Web site: <www.niddk.nih.gov>.

National Institutes of Health. National Institute of Diabetes, Digestive, and Kidney Diseases. Building 31, Room 9A04, 31 Center Drive, Bethesda, MD 20892–2560. Web site: <www.nih.gov>.

WEB SITES

"Frequently Asked Questions [about fructose intolerance]." *HFI Laboratory at Boston University.* Available online at <www.bu.edu/aldolase/HFI> (accessed November 19, 2004).

Stewart, Douglas R. "Hereditary Fructose Intolerance." *U.S. National Library of Medicine*, August 19, 2003. Available online at <www.nlm.nih.gov/medlineplus/ency/article/000359.htm> (accessed November 19, 2004).

Altha Roberts Edgren
Angela M. Costello

Hereditary hemorrhagic telangiectasia

Definition

Hereditary hemorrhagic telangiectasia is a condition characterized by abnormal blood vessels which are delicate and prone to bleeding. Hereditary hemorrhagic telangiectasia is also known as Osler-Weber-Rendu disease.

Description

The term telangiectasia refers to a spot formed, usually on the skin, by a dilated capillary or terminal artery. Telangiectasia is an arterial-venous malformation (AVM) composed of small blood vessels. In hereditary hemorrhagic telangiectasia these spots occur because the blood vessel is fragile and bleeds easily. The bleeding may appear as small, red or reddish-violet spots on the face, lips, inside the mouth and nose, or the tips of the fingers and toes. Besides the skin and mouth, telangiectasias may occur in the gastrointestinal tract (GI tract), the brain, and the lungs. Unlike **hemophilia**, where bleeding is caused by an ineffective clotting mechanism in the blood, bleeding in hereditary hemorrhagic telangiectasia is caused by fragile blood vessels. However, like hemophilia, bleeding may be extensive and can occur without warning.

Causes and symptoms

Hereditary hemorrhagic telangiectasia, an autosomal dominant disorder, occurs in one in 50,000 people. Recurrent nosebleeds are a nearly universal symptom in this condition. Usually the nosebleeds begin in childhood and become worse with age. A patient may begin to **cough** up blood or pass blood in stools. The skin changes begin at **puberty**, and the condition becomes progressively worse until about 40 years of age, when it stabilizes.

When to call the doctor

Parents should notify a doctor if a child's bleeding does not stop, or bleeding is severe, or the child has severe headaches or becomes unresponsive. Frequent nosebleeds should be followed up with the pediatrician.

Diagnosis

The physician looks for red spots on all areas of the skin, but especially on the upper half of the body and in the mouth and nose and under the tongue. Bleeding in

KEY TERMS

Autosomal dominant—A pattern of inheritance in which only one of the two copies of an autosomal gene must be abnormal for a genetic condition or disease to occur. An autosomal gene is a gene that is located on one of the autosomes or non-sex chromosomes. A person with an autosomal dominant disorder has a 50% chance of passing it to each of their offspring.

Chromosome—A microscopic thread-like structure found within each cell of the human body and consisting of a complex of proteins and DNA. Humans have 46 chromosomes arranged into 23 pairs. Chromosomes contain the genetic information necessary to direct the development and functioning of all cells and systems in the body. They pass on hereditary traits from parents to child (like eye color) and determine whether the child will be male or female.

the GI tract can cause the stool (feces) to be darker than normal.

Treatment

There is no specific treatment for hereditary hemorrhagic telangiectasia. The bleeding resulting from the condition can be stopped by applying compresses or direct pressure to the area. If necessary, a laser can be used to destroy the vessel. In severe cases, the leaking artery can be plugged or covered with a graft from normal tissue. In some cases, estrogen therapy is used to reduce bleeding episodes.

Prognosis

In most people, recurrent bleeding results in an iron deficiency. It is usually necessary to take iron supplements. Patients have a normal lifespan, and many people are not aware they are affected by the disease until a **family** is diagnosed.

Prevention

Because it is an inherited disorder, hereditary hemorrhagic telangiectasia cannot be prevented.

Parental concerns

Parents should be aware that frequent nosebleeds are a common sign of hereditary hemorrhagic telangiectasia. Genetic counseling is recommended for those who know the disease runs in their families. There are also support groups for those who are affected by the disease.

Resources

BOOKS

Sutton, Amy L. *Blood and Circulatory Disorders Sourcebook: Basic Consumer Health Information about the Blood and Circulatory System and Related Disorders.* Detroit, MI: Omnigraphics, 2005.

ORGANIZATIONS

HHT Foundation International Inc. PO Box 329, Monkton, MD 21111. Web site: <www.hht.org/web/>.

Mark A. Best
Dorothy Elinor Stonely

Hermaphroditism *see* **Intersex states**

Hernia

Definition

A hernia is the protrusion of an organ through the structure or muscle that usually contains it.

Description

There are many different types of hernias in children. The most common are direct inguinal hernias, indirect inguinal hernias, and umbilical hernias. A direct inguinal hernia occurs when a small section of bowel herniates, or protrudes, through the groin muscle. Indirect inguinal hernia occurs when part of the bowel protrudes through the muscles of the groin into a sac left over from fetal development. An umbilical hernia occurs when a portion of the bowel protrudes through a small defect in the abdominal wall muscle near where the umbilical cord attaches to the baby's abdomen. More serious defects involving herniation of abdominal contents outside the infant's body are omphalocele and gastroschisis. These are not a result of an organ protruding through weakened muscle tissue but rather are a result of a much larger defect of the muscles of the abdomen that causes the internal organs to develop outside the body.

Omphalocele and gastroschisis are considered **abdominal wall defects** and are not called hernias.

While an umbilical hernia usually resolves spontaneously as the abdominal muscles grow and requires no further treatment, in children with direct and indirect inguinal hernia, surgery is almost always required to prevent the herniated bowel from becoming incarcerated or strangulated. When an inguinal hernia is incarcerated, the bowel becomes swollen and trapped outside the body. If the hernia remains incarcerated for too long, strangulation can occur. In strangulation, the blood supply to the section of bowel that has herniated is cut off, and the tissue begins to die. When this happens, the intestines cannot function properly and are said to be obstructed. If the bowel perforates, or develops a hole in it, emergency surgery is required to repair the intestine and prevent infection.

A more severe, but less common, hernia is a diaphragmatic hernia. This occurs inside the body when the diaphragm, the large muscle that separates the abdominal cavity from the chest cavity, fails to develop fully. In children with diaphragmatic hernia, the contents of the abdomen protrude into the chest cavity. These children may have difficulty breathing. During fetal development the presence of abdominal organs in the fetal chest cavity prevents the lungs from growing normally. A diaphragmatic hernia can occur as an isolated defect or as part of a more complex syndrome. Children with diaphragmatic hernias are usually very ill and require immediate treatment after birth. Some of these children have other defects such as cardiac anomalies, chromosomal abnormalities, kidney and genital anomalies, and neural tube defects, such as **spina bifida**.

Demographics

Estimates of the true incidence of inguinal hernias vary, but they may affect 1–5 percent of all births in the United States. International rates appear to be similar. Males are more than seven times more likely to have an inguinal hernia than females, and premature infants are more likely than full term infants to have inguinal hernias and to have incarcerated hernias. While inguinal hernias seem to affect all racial groups at the same rate, umbilical hernias occur more frequently in African Americans.

Diaphragmatic hernias occur in approximately one in every 3,000 births. These hernias do not seem to affect any race or nationality more than another.

Causes and symptoms

A direct inguinal hernia is caused when the muscles of the floor of the groin area are weak and allow the bowel to press through. An indirect inguinal hernia is caused when remnants of early fetal genital development stay within the body after this development is complete. In early fetal development male and female genitalia are identical. At around the seventh week of gestation, the gonads (sex organs) begin to change, or differentiate, into the characteristic genitalia of males and females. Males develop testes, and females develop ovaries. During this process, in some fetuses, a small sac may form near the genitalia. Most often the opening to this sac, called the processus vaginalis, closes. However, in children with inguinal hernia, this sac remains patent, or open, becoming a container into which bowels may be herniated.

The main symptom of inguinal hernias (both direct and indirect) in infants is an obvious bulge in the groin in the inguinoscrotal region (near the scrotum) in boys and in the inguinolabial (near the labia) in girls. The bulge may or may not be painful. It will usually appear after straining or crying and then disappear after a period of time. If the hernia has incarcerated, the infant will be in obvious **pain**, appearing fussy, crying, and refusing to eat. The skin over the hernia may be discolored and swollen.

Umbilical hernia is caused by a small defect in the muscles of the abdominal wall. These hernias are usually small and have no symptoms other than a small protrusion near the base of the umbilical cord.

Like inguinal hernias, diaphragmatic hernias are caused early in fetal development. The structures that form the diaphragm do not properly form, allowing the contents of the lower abdomen to migrate up near the heart and lungs. The increased pressure these organs place on the lungs causes the lungs to remain small and underdeveloped. When the infant is born and must breathe air, the lungs are not able to work properly.

Children with diaphragmatic hernia have the following symptoms immediately after birth: breathing difficulty, a bluish skin color (cyanosis), rapid breathing, rapid heat rate, and asymmetrical chests—one side is not the same size as the other. These infants are often critically ill and are be placed on a ventilator—a machine to help them breath. Because the lungs have not had enough room to grow and are small, doctors must stabilize the baby's breathing before the hernia can be repaired.

When to call the doctor

If a small child, especially an infant, has a bulge in the abdominal or groin area, the child's pediatrician should be consulted. If the child is in severe pain, and the skin is discolored or swollen, medical help should be sought immediately.

Diagnosis

Umbilical and inguinal hernias are diagnosed by physical examination. For some children with inguinal hernia, a laparoscopic examination may be performed. A laparoscopy is an exploratory surgical procedure in which the doctor makes an incision and inserts a small tube connected to a camera to view the herniated area. This procedure is used most often in patients who have already had one hernia repair to see if the hernia has returned in a new location.

Diaphragmatic hernia may be diagnosed while the fetus is still in the womb using prenatal ultrasonography. After birth, physical symptoms of respiratory distress, cyanosis, and chest asymmetry can indicate the presence of a diaphragmatic hernia. In children with less severe diaphragmatic hernias, the diagnosis may be made later in childhood if the child develops **intestinal obstructions**. An x ray showing bowel loops within the chest cavity confirms the diagnosis.

Treatment

Umbilical hernia is generally a benign condition that will resolve spontaneously as the muscles of the abdomen grow. No treatment is usually required. For children in whom the umbilical hernia does not resolve, surgery is not usually performed until after the age of five. The only treatment necessary is observation of the hernia during routine physical examinations.

The standard treatment for inguinal hernias is a surgical repair called herniorrhaphy. Unlike umbilical hernias, inguinal hernias do not resolve spontaneously. Because of the risk of incarceration and strangulation, most doctors prefer to repair these hernias as soon after the initial diagnosis as possible. Herniorrhaphies are performed as an outpatient procedure in otherwise healthy full-term infants and children.

Prior to repair surgery, parents may be taught how to apply pressure to the hernia, thereby reducing it temporarily and preventing incarceration. If the hernia has already become incarcerated, the doctor will attempt to force the hernia out of the sac and back into the body manually. This process is called manual reduction. With the child on his back, the doctor will use his fingers to press the hernia back into the body. If successful, manual reduction relieves the child's pain and prevents strangulation until surgery can be scheduled. Repair surgery is usually performed within 72 hours. If an incarcerated hernia is not reducible, surgery must be performed much sooner to prevent strangulation. If strangulation occurs, emergency surgery is the only treatment.

Treatment for diaphragmatic hernia involves treatment of the other accompanying health issues. First and foremost, the infant's respiratory distress must be addressed. Most newborns with diaphragmatic hernias require intubation and ventilation. A tube is inserted through the mouth into the throat, and breathing is assisted by a ventilation machine. A feeding tube may be inserted through the nose and into the stomach to insure the infant receives sufficient **nutrition**. After the infant is stabilized, surgery to repair the hernia is performed. In diaphragmatic hernia repair surgery, the herniated abdominal organs are forced back into their proper position within the abdomen. If the bowels are injured or malrotated, this will be repaired, and the hole in the diaphragm is sewn closed and patched, if necessary, with surgical mesh.

Prognosis

If diagnosed early in childhood, the prognosis for children who have had a surgically repaired inguinal hernia is excellent. Occasionally there are complications associated with inguinal hernias including death, but these are rare, occurring most often in children who were diagnosed later in childhood or whose hernias were strangulated.

The prognosis for children with diaphragmatic hernia depends on the extent of the defects of the lungs and the impact of the treatments necessary to save their lives. Children with diaphragmatic hernias have an increased incidence of chromic lung disease. These children also have an increased risk for slow growth and development. The survival rate of these children is also related to the other anomalies these children may have. If the diaphragmatic hernia is part of a syndrome, the other birth defects may be life threatening. The survival rate after surgical repair of a diaphragmatic hernia is 60–80 percent.

Prevention

The exact cause of umbilical hernias, inguinal hernias, and diaphragmatic hernias is as of 2004 unknown. Until a cause is discovered, no prevention is available.

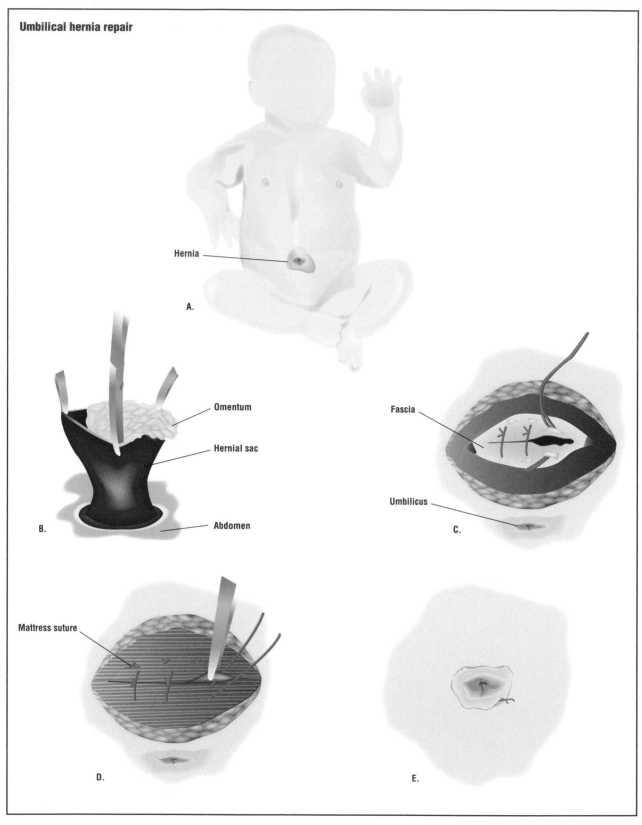

Umbilical hernia repair

Hernia

A.

Omentum

Hernial sac

Abdomen

B.

Fascia

Umbilicus

C.

Mattress suture

D.

E.

Baby with an umbilical hernia (A). To repair, the hernia is cut open (B), and the contents replaced in the abdomen. Connecting tissues, or fascia, are sutured closed (C), and the skin is repaired (D). *(Illustration by GGS Information Services.)*

KEY TERMS

Herniorrhaphy—Surgical repair of a hernia.

Incarcerated hernia—A hernia of the bowel that can not return to its normal place without manipulation or surgery.

Laparoscopy—A surgical procedure in which a small incision is made, usually in the navel, through which a viewing tube (laparoscope) is inserted. This allows the doctor to examine abdominal and pelvic organs. Other small incisions can be mad to insert instruments to perform procedures. Laparoscopy is done to diagnose conditions or to perform certain types of surgeries.

Reducible hernia—A hernia that can be gently pushed back into place or that disappears when the person lies down.

Strangulated hernia—A hernia that is so tightly incarcerated outside the abdominal wall that the intestine is blocked and the blood supply to that part of the intestine is cut off.

Ultrasonography—A medical test in which sound waves are directed against internal structures in the body. As sound waves bounce off the internal structure, they create an image on a video screen. Ultrasonography is often used to diagnose fetal abnormalities, gallstones, heart defects, and tumors. Also called ultrasound imaging.

Parental concerns

Prior to surgery, parents of a child with an inguinal hernia can be taught to apply pressure to the hernia, preventing incarceration. Parents should be aware of the circumstances under which to seek immediate medical attention for their child.

See also Abdominal wall defects.

Resources

BOOKS

Hernia Repair: Medical Dictionary, Bibliography, and Annotated Research Guide to Internet Research. San Diego, CA: Icon Group International, 2004.

LeBlanc, Karl, et al. *Laproscopic Hernia Surgery: An Operative Guide.* Oxford, UK: Oxford University Press, 2003.

Official Patient's Sourcebook on Inguinal Hernia. San Diego, CA: Icon Group International, 2002.

Parker, James, et al. *Hernia: A Medical Dictionary, Bibliography, and Annotated Research Guide to Internet Research.* Boulder, CO: netLibrary, 2003.

Rudolph, Colin D., and Abraham M. Rudolph, eds. *Rudolph's Pediatrics*, 21st ed. New York: McGraw-Hill, 2003, pp. 24–34, 36.

WEB SITES

Hebra, Audre. "Pediatric Hernias." *eMedicine*, August 2, 2004. Available online at <www.emedicine.com/ped/topic2559.htm> (accessed November 21, 2004).

Lewis, Nicola and Philip L. Glick. "Diaphragmatic Hernias." *eMedicine*, October 8, 2004. Available online at <www.emedicine.com/ped/topic2937.htm> (accessed November 21, 2004).

Deborah L. Nurmi, MS

Herpes simplex

Definition

Herpes is an infection caused by a herpes simplex virus 1 or 2, and it primarily affects the mouth or genital area.

Description

There are two strains of herpes simplex viruses. Herpes simplex virus type 1 (HSV-1) is usually associated with infections of the lips, mouth, and face. It is the most common herpes simplex virus among the general population and is usually acquired in childhood. Herpes simplex virus 2 (HSV-2) is sexually transmitted and is usually associated with genital ulcers or sores. Individuals may harbor HSV-1 and or HSV-2 and not have developed any symptoms.

Transmission

HSV-1 causes lesions inside the mouth that are often referred to as cold sores or fever blisters, and it is transmitted by contact with infected saliva. By adulthood, up to 90 percent of the population has antibodies to HSV-1. HSV-2 is sexually transmitted and not everyone develops symptoms when they have it. Up to 30 percent of adults in the United States have antibodies against HSV-2. Cross infection of type 1 and 2 viruses may occur from oral-genital contact. Herpes viruses can be transmitted to a newborn during vaginal delivery in mothers infected with herpes viruses, especially if the infection is primary (first occurrence) and is active at the time of delivery. The virus can lead to complications such as meningoencephalitis, which is an infection of the lining of the brain and the brain itself. It can also cause eye infections, in particular, of the conjunctiva and cornea.

Demographics

The prevalence of herpes simplex in the United States is as follows:

- Seventy to ninety percent of adults test seropositive (present in blood serum) for HSV-1.

- Up to 30 percent of adults test seropositive for HSV-2.

- The highest incidence of HSV-1 is in children six months to three years of age.

- The highest incidence of HSV-2 is in young adults between the age of 18 and 25 years.

- HSV-2 antibodies are present in approximately 20 percent of Caucasians and about 65 percent of African-American adults.

Causes and symptoms

A primary infection of HSV-1 typically occurs between six months and five years of age and is systemic (affecting the whole body). Transmission is generally via respiratory droplets (HSV-1) or direct contact (HSV-1 and HSV-2). The virus enters the body through mucosal surfaces, replicates in the cell nucleus, and then kills the host cell. The initial infection is self-limiting, but the immune system does not destroy the virus. The virus migrates along nerves to an area of regional ganglia (nerve centers) and then typically enters into a latent (sleeping) phase. Reactivation of the virus occurs in 50 percent of patients within five years, and it can be triggered by various factors:

- fatigue

- stress

- trauma

- immunocompromise (lack of normal immune response)

- illness, such as a cold

- fever

- sunburn

- menstruation

- sexual intercourse

The symptoms of a herpes infection can vary tremendously. Many infected individuals have few, if any, noticeable symptoms. Those who do have symptoms usually notice them from two to 20 days after being exposed to someone with HSV infection. Symptoms can last for several weeks, but the first episode of herpes is usually worse than subsequent outbreaks. The predominant symptom of herpes is the outbreak of painful, **itching** blisters filled with fluid on and around the external sexual organs or, for oral herpes, on or very near the lip. Females may have a vaginal discharge and experience flu-like symptoms with HSV2 outbreaks, including fever, **headache**, muscle aches, and fatigue. There may be painful urination, and swollen and tender lymph glands in the groin. More often than not the blisters disappear without treatment in two to 10 days, but the virus remains in the body, lying dormant among clusters of nerve cells until another outbreak is triggered.

Many people are able to anticipate an outbreak when they notice a warning sign (a **tingling** sensation, called a prodrome) of the approaching illness. It is when they feel signs that an outbreak is about to start that they are particularly contagious, even though the skin still appears normal. Most people with genital herpes have five to eight outbreaks per year, but not everyone has recurrent symptoms. In time, the number of outbreaks usually decreases. Oral herpes can recur as often as monthly or only one or two times each year. Sores typically come back near the site of the first infection, but there are fewer sores with recurrences that heal faster and are less painful.

When to call the doctor

Anyone who has a history of herpes infection and current lesions should notify the physician if the lesions do not resolve after seven to ten days or if a condition exists that weakens the immune system. Children with a herpes infection most commonly have sores in the mouth usually caused by HSV-1. This infection causes fever, irritability, **pain**, decreased appetite, and ulcers in the mouth. The most common complication is **dehydration** secondary to a refusal to drink fluids because of mouth pain and difficulty swallowing. Treatment is usually not required, and symptoms generally improve in three to five days. If, however, the child does not improve, develops a fever, and becomes lethargic, the pediatrician should be called immediately.

Herpes infections that spread throughout the body in a newborn are usually more serious, but fortunately less common than the other types of neonatal infections. They typically occur in the first week of life, with symptoms including fever, difficulty breathing, seizures, lethargy, and irritability. Since many infants in the first month of life can have a herpes infection and not have skin lesions, it takes a great deal of time and effort to diagnose and treat these infections early. Herpes should be considered in any acutely ill newborn, especially if bacterial cultures are negative and the baby is not improving after two to three days. Parents should be informed to watch the baby closely if either one of them has a history of herpes infections.

Diagnosis

Testing for neonatal herpes infections may include special smears and/or viral cultures, blood antibody levels, and polymerase chain reaction (PCR) testing of spinal fluid. Cultures are usually obtained from skin vesicles, eyes, mouth, rectum, urine, stool, and blood. For older children and adults, if there is a question as to the cause of a sore, a tissue sample or culture can be taken to determine what type of virus or other microorganism is responsible. For herpes, it is preferable to have this test done within the first 48 hours after symptoms first show up for a more accurate result.

Treatment

There are three drugs proven to treat genital herpes symptoms: acyclovir, sold under the brand name Zovirax, Famvir, and Valtrex. These are all taken in pill form. Formulas applied to the surface of the skin provide little benefit, and they are not recommended. Drug therapy is not a cure, but it can make living with the condition easier. For an initial outbreak with symptoms such as sores, a doctor should begin a brief course of antiviral therapy to relieve the symptoms or prevent them from getting worse. Seven to ten days of treatment is recommended but if the lesions do not heal, a longer period of time may be required. Following the initial outbreak there are two options to consider for further outbreaks. One is intermittent treatment, which involves the physician prescribing an antiviral drug to keep on hand in case an individual has a flare-up. The pills can be taken for three to five days as soon as sores are noticed or when an outbreak tingling sensation occurs. Sores heal and disappear on their own, but taking the drugs helps to alleviate the symptoms. For individuals who have frequent outbreaks, a suppressive treatment may work better. This treatment involves taking an antiviral drug every day. For example, someone who typically has more than six outbreaks a year, suppressive therapy reduces the number of outbreaks by 70 to 80 percent. Moreover, many who take the **antiviral drugs** daily have no outbreaks at all.

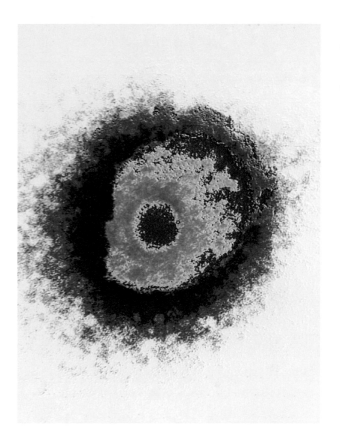

A false-color transmission electron microscopy (TEM) image of a herpes simplex virus. *(Custom Medical Stock Photo, Inc.)*

In the early 2000s herpes vaccines are being investigated, and an effective vaccine may be available in before 2010. Vaccines will only function to prevent the infection in new patients. Those who already have the simplex virus disease will probably not benefit.

Nutritional concerns

Diet is a very important factor in keeping herpes in remission. It has been found that foods high in arginine may cause herpes outbreaks. Supplementation with free-form lysine has shown to be beneficial in controlling herpes along with a diet high in lysine and low in arginine. The amount of lysine required to control herpes varies from case to case, but a typical adult dose to maintain remission is 500 mg daily, and active herpes requires 1–6 g between meals to induce healing.

Prognosis

There is no cure for herpes simplex. Once it is contracted, it is always in a person's system. However, with treatment therapies, the problems previously encountered are lessened considerably.

KEY TERMS

Conjunctiva—Plural, conjunctivae. The mucous membrane that covers the white part of the eyes (sclera) and lines the eyelids.

Cornea—The clear, dome-shaped outer covering of the eye that lies in front of the iris and pupil. The cornea lets light into the eye.

Ganglion—Plural, ganglia. A mass of nerve tissue or a group of neurons.

Latent virus—A nonactive virus that is in a dormant state within a cell. The herpes virus is latent in the nervous system.

Lesion—A disruption of the normal structure and function of a tissue by an injury or disease process. Wounds, sores, rashes, and boils are all lesions.

Meningoencephalitis—Inflammation of the brain and its membranes; also called cerebromeningitis or encephalomeningitis.

Mucosal—Refers to the mucous membrane.

Seropositive—Showing a positive reaction to a test on blood serum for a disease; exhibiting seroconversion.

Virus—A small infectious agent consisting of a core of genetic material (DNA or RNA) surrounded by a shell of protein. A virus needs a living cell to reproduce.

cularly if they have a history of genital herpes. Signs and symptoms need to be gone over, i.e., lethargy, fever, as well as the fact that there may or may not be lesions present. A newborn's own immune system begins to function around the third month, and if a mother is breast-feeding, she is passing antibodies to her baby. The primary concern is that a herpes infection does not become systemic. Thus, if the child seems to be getting sicker instead of better, parents should call the doctor immediately.

Resources

BOOKS

Ebel, Charles, and A. Wald. *Managing Herpes: How to Live and Love with a Chronic STD.* Durham, NC: American Social Health Association, 2002.

The Official Patient's Sourcebook on Genital Herpes. San Diego, CA: Icon Group International, 2002.

Spencer, Judith V., et al. *Herpes.* Langhorne, PA: Chelsea House Publishers, 2005.

Westheimer, Ruth K. *Dr. Ruth's Guide to Talking about Herpes.* New York: Grove/Atlantic Inc., 2004.

ORGANIZATIONS

American Social Health Association. PO Box 13827, Research Triangle Park, NC 27709. Web site: <www.ashastd.org/hrc/>.

Linda K. Bennington, MSN, CNS

Prevention

Whereas it is almost impossible to keep a baby or child from being exposed to herpes simplex due to its universal presence, there are conditions that can be used to prevent its transmission. Hand washing is one of the biggest factors in the transmission of all diseases, and it is especially true of herpes simplex since it is spread by respiratory droplets through mucosal membranes. In terms of genital herpes, education regarding the use of condoms is the best tool. Young adults should also be reminded that herpes simplex can be transferred from oral-genital contact. Since many teenagers do not consider oral or anal sex as sexual intercourse per se, it is imperative to spell out exactly what, when, and how these viruses can be spread.

Parental concerns

It is important that the pediatrician discusses the possibility of herpes infections with new parents, parti-

Hib vaccine

Definition

The Hib vaccine is an injection that helps protect children from contracting infections due to *Haemophilus influenzae* type B (Hib), a bacterium that is capable of causing serious illness and potential death in children under age five.

Description

H. influenzae type B (Hib) is a common organism worldwide; it is found in most healthy individuals in the general population. Small children can pick up the bacteria from people who are not aware that they are carriers. When the bacteria spread to the lungs and bloodstream, serious illness, including **pneumonia** and **meningitis**, can result. Another serious disease stemming from this pathogen is **epiglottitis**, an infection of the epiglottis that cause swelling of the airways and potential death.

Pediatricians and the Centers for Disease Control (CDC) recommend that all infants are vaccinated against Hib disease. In general, the vaccine is considered highly effective, with few side effects. Before the institution of routine infant vaccinations in the United States in the 1990s, Hib was the leading of bacterial meningitis among children younger than five years of age. Nearly 1,000 people in the United States died every year from Hib disease. As of the early 2000s, the disease has largely disappeared due to these vaccinations. In developing countries, however, Hib disease is a major cause of serious disease and death in young children.

General use

The Hib vaccine is given in three or four doses during infancy, depending on the brand used. The first dose starts at about two months of age, and the last is usually scheduled at a 12- or 15-month check-up. Children older than five years do not need **vaccination**, unless the child or adolescent has a serious health problem that lowers immunity, such as **HIV infection**, sickle cell disease, or is being treated for **cancer**.

Precautions

Infants under six weeks of age should not receive the Hib vaccine. Those babies with moderate to severe illness should wait for vaccination until they are well. If a baby has had a severe reaction to Hib vaccine, another dose should not be administered.

Side effects

Like any vaccine or medication, Hib vaccine is capable of causing an allergic reaction. However, this is extremely rare. More common side effects include inflammation at the injection site and slight **fever**, which can usually occur within 24 hours of the injection and can last two or three days.

Interactions

Interactions with medicines or food have not been reported. The Hib vaccine is routinely given at the same time as other childhood vaccines.

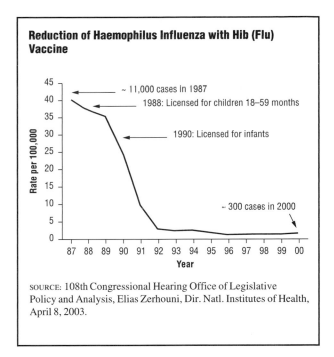

Reduction of Haemophilus Influenza with Hib (Flu) Vaccine

~ 11,000 cases in 1987
1988: Licensed for children 18–59 months
1990: Licensed for infants
~ 300 cases in 2000

SOURCE: 108th Congressional Hearing Office of Legislative Policy and Analysis, Elias Zerhouni, Dir. Natl. Institutes of Health, April 8, 2003.

This graph shows the dramatic reduction of *Haemophilus influenzae* infection with the introduction of the Hib vaccine. *(Illustration by GGS Information Services.)*

Parental concerns

Parents should be aware of the benefits this vaccine provides, as well as its overall safety and effectiveness. Any low-grade fever or soreness can be treated with ibuprofen or **acetaminophen** as recommended by the pediatrician. Serious reactions, including high fever, difficulty breathing, and fast heartbeat should receive immediate medical treatment.

See also Hemophilus infections.

Resources

BOOKS

Shelov, Steven, ed. "Immunizations." In *Caring For Your Baby and Young Child: Birth to Age 5*. American Academy of Pediatrics. New York: Bantam Books, 1998.

WEB SITES

"Hib - vaccine." *Medline Plus Medical Encyclopedia.* Available online at <www.nlm.nih.gov/medlineplus/ency/article/002023.htm> (accessed February 18, 2005).

Haemophilus Influenzae type b (Hib) vaccine. Centers for Disease Control and Prevention. Available online at <http://64.233.167.104/search?q=cache:2dwv-ZkB7ZEJ:www.cdc.gov/nip/publications/VIS/vis-hib.pdf+Hib+vaccine&hl=en> (accessed February 18, 2005).

Haemophilus Influenzae type b (Hib) vaccine. World Health Organization. Available online at <www.who.int/vaccines/en/haeflub.shtml> (accessed February 18, 2005).

Kristine Krapp

High blood pressure *see* **Hypertension**
High cholesterol *see* **Cholesterol, high**

High-risk pregnancy

Definition

Although as of 2004 there was no formal or universally accepted definition of a "high-risk" pregnancy, it is generally thought of as one in which the mother or the developing fetus has a condition that places one or both of them at a higher-than-normal-risk for complications, either during the pregnancy (antepartum), during delivery (intrapartum), or following the birth (postpartum).

Description

Certain conditions, called risk factors, make a pregnancy high risk. Maternal conditions can be identified with preconception counseling and from the maternal history. Maternal physical and social characteristics that can contribute to a high-risk pregnancy include:

- age younger than 15 years and older than 35 years
- pre-pregnancy weight under 100 lbs (45 kg) or obesity
- height under 5 ft (1.5 m)
- incompetent cervix
- uterine malformations
- small pelvis
- being a single woman
- being a smoker
- using illicit drugs
- having no access to early prenatal care
- using alcohol
- having low socioeconomic status

For women who do not have health insurance, obtaining early prenatal care is extremely difficult, and these same women are often from a socioeconomic level that prevents adequate or appropriate nutritional intake. There is a scoring system that can be used by healthcare professionals to determine the degree of risk for a pregnant woman, but it is difficult to rate risk by degrees. Nevertheless, identification of a high-risk pregnancy helps to ensure that those women who need the most care receive it.

One of the initial factors to consider when evaluating risk is the obstetrical history. If this is not the woman's first pregnancy, outcomes of her previous pregnancies are of importance in relation to the outcome of this one. An obstetrical history with any of the following conditions would be considered high risk:

- previous stillbirth
- previous neonatal death
- previous premature infant
- previous post-term (over 42 weeks) pregnancy
- fetal blood transfusion for hemolytic disease
- repeated miscarriages
- previous infant over 10 lbs (4.5 kg)
- six or more completed pregnancies
- history of preeclampsia
- history of eclampsia
- previous **cesarean section**
- history of a fetus with anomalies

Next to be considered is the medical history factor. A pregnant woman with any of the following medical conditions would be considered at risk:

- abnormal PAP test
- chronic **hypertension**
- heart disease (class II-IV, symptomatic)
- insulin-dependent diabetes
- moderate to severe kidney disease
- endocrine gland removal or ablation by autoimmune disease
- sickle cell disease
- epilepsy
- history of tuberculosis
- positive serology for syphilis
- pulmonary disease
- thyroid disease
- family history of diabetes
- HIV
- other chronic diseases
- autoimmune diseases, such as lupus

Current pregnancy risk factors would be considered as follows:

- abnormal fetal position
- mild to severe preeclampsia
- multiple pregnancy
- placenta abruption
- placenta previa
- polyhydramnios or oligiohydramnios
- gestational diabetes
- kidney infection
- Rh sensitization only
- mild (>9g/dl hemoglobin) or severe (<9g/dl hemoglobin) anemia
- vaginal spotting
- bladder infection
- emotional problems
- moderate alcohol use
- smoking more than one pack per day
- infection with parvovirus B19 (fifth disease), cytomegalovirus (CMV), **toxoplasmosis**, listeria, rubella
- exposure to damaging medications, esp., phenytoin, **folic acid** antagonists, lithium, streptomycin, tetracycline, warfarin

If prenatal testing indicates the baby has a serious congenital anomaly as a heart defect or spinal cord defect, the mother may need additional testing to determine the extent of the problem. Certain maternal or fetal problems may require the physician to deliver a baby early or to choose a surgical delivery (cesarean section) rather than a vaginal delivery.

Most women will see one healthcare provider during pregnancy, either an obstetrician, a midwife, or a nurse practitioner. Women who have a medical problem may need to see a medical specialist as well. Women diagnosed with a high-risk pregnancy should seek the care of an expert in the field of high-risk obstetrics, called a perinatologist. Perinatologists have additional training beyond the education required for an obstetrician. They care for women who have pre-existing medical problems, women who develop complications during pregnancy, and women whose fetus has problems.

Diagnosis

Labeling a woman with the diagnosis of high-risk pregnancy requires that one of the previous conditions be met. Thus, the diagnosis may be determined during history taking or if it is the fetus, during the morphological ultrasound at 16–19 weeks gestation. A woman with a high-risk pregnancy will need closer monitoring than pregnant women who are not high risk. Such monitoring may include frequent visits with the primary caregiver, tests to monitor the medical problem, blood tests to check the levels of medication, **amniocentesis**, serial ultrasound examination, and fetal monitoring. These tests are designed to follow the original condition, survey for complications, verify that the fetus is growing adequately, and make decisions regarding whether labor may need to be induced for early delivery of the fetus.

Treatment

Treatment varies widely with the type of disease, the effect that pregnancy has on the disease, and the effect that the disease has on pregnancy. If it is the fetus that has a problem, serial ultrasounds may be performed. Fetal heart rate monitoring may be necessary, or amniocentesis may be required. In addition, it may be essential to give the mother medications to act on the baby.

Prognosis

The prognosis is usually dependent on the specific medical condition. Some medical conditions make it difficult for women to get pregnant and lead to a higher risk of problems in the baby. In thyroid disease, the thyroid gland (located in the neck) may produce too much or too little thyroid hormone. Abnormal levels of this hormone can affect fertility and/or cause problems with the pregnancy and possibly affect the health of the baby. Fortunately, thyroid disease can be treated with medication. As long as the level of thyroid hormone is controlled throughout pregnancy, there should be no problems for mother or baby.

There are other medical conditions that do not interfere with pregnancy but are themselves affected by pregnancy. This group includes **asthma**, epilepsy, and ulcerative colitis. Some women with ulcerative colitis experience a worsening of their symptoms during pregnancy, while others will have no change or may get better during pregnancy. The same is true of asthma: some women notice that their asthma symptoms are better during pregnancy, some find their asthma worse, and some women notice no change in symptoms. It is not immediately apparent why this discrepancy occurs, but due to the unpredictability of diseases, all women with chronic illnesses should be monitored throughout the course of a pregnancy.

Some autoimmune diseases constitute a group of medical conditions that have a major impact on

KEY TERMS

Ablation—To remove or destroy tissue or a body part, such as by burning or cutting.

Amniocentesis—A procedure performed at 16–18 weeks of pregnancy in which a needle is inserted through a woman's abdomen into her uterus to draw out a small sample of the amniotic fluid from around the baby for analysis. Either the fluid itself or cells from the fluid can be used for a variety of tests to obtain information about genetic disorders and other medical conditions in the fetus.

Amniotic sac—The membranous sac that contains the fetus and the amniotic fluid during pregnancy.

Antepartum—The time period of the woman's pregnancy from conception and onset of labor.

Cytomegalovirus (CMV)—A common human virus causing mild or no symptoms in healthy people, but permanent damage or death to an infected fetus, a transplant patient, or a person with HIV.

Eclampsia—Coma and convulsions during or immediately after pregnancy, characterized by edema, hypertension, and proteinuria.

Endocrine—Refers to glands that secrete hormones circulated in the bloodstream or lymphatic system.

Gestational diabetes—Diabetes of pregnancy leading to increased levels of blood sugar. Unlike diabetes mellitus, gestational diabetes is caused by pregnancy and goes away when pregnancy ends. Like diabetes mellitus, gestational diabetes is treated with a special diet and insulin, if necessary.

Intrapartum—Refers to labor and delivery.

Listeria—An uncommon food-borne, life-threatening pathogen that can cause perinatal infection, which is associated with a high rate of fetal loss (including full-term stillbirths) and serious neonatal disease.

Oligohydramnios—A reduced amount of amniotic fluid. Causes include non-functioning kidneys and premature rupture of membranes. Without amniotic fluid to breathe, a baby will have underdeveloped and immature lungs.

Parvovirus B19—A virus that commonly infects humans; about 50 percent of all adults have been infected sometime during childhood or adolescence. Parvovirus B19 infects only humans. An infection in pregnancy can cause the unborn baby to have severe anemia and the woman may have a miscarriage.

Perinatal—Referring to the period of time surrounding an infant's birth, from the last two months of pregnancy through the first 28 days of life.

Phenytoin—An anti-convulsant medication used to treat seizure disorders. Sold under the brand name Dilantin.

Polyhydramnios—A condition in which there is too much fluid around the fetus in the amniotic sac.

Postpartum—After childbirth.

Preeclampsia—A condition that develops after the twentieth week of pregnancy and results in high blood pressure, fluid retention that doesn't go away, and large amounts of protein in the urine. Without treatment, it can progress to a dangerous condition called eclampsia, in which a woman goes into convulsions.

Premature labor—Labor beginning before 36 weeks of pregnancy.

Rubella—A mild, highly contagious childhood illness caused by a virus; it is also called German measles. Rubella causes severe birth defects (including heart defects, cataracts, deafness, and mental retardation) if a pregnant woman contracts it during the first three months of pregnancy.

Streptomycin—An antibiotic used to treat tuberculosis.

Tetracycline—A broad-spectrum antibiotic.

Toxoplasmosis—A parasitic infection caused by the intracellular protozoan *Toxoplasmosis gondii*. Humans are most commonly infected by swallowing the oocyte form of the parasite in soil (or kitty litter) contaminated by feces from an infected cat; or by swallowing the cyst form of the parasite in raw or undercooked meat.

Warfarin—An anticoagulant drug given to treat existing blood clots or to control the formation of new blood clots. Sold in the U.S. under the brand name Coumadin.

pregnancy. Women with lupus (a disease caused by alterations in the immune system that result in inflammation of connective tissue and organs) or kidney disease face serious risks during pregnancy. Pregnancy can cause their symptoms to worsen significantly and lead to severe complications for the mother and the baby. With systemic autoimmune diseases or vasculitis, the mother's blood circulation can be impaired and thus the ability to supply oxygen and nutrients to the baby through the placenta is affected. As a result, fetal intrauterine growth becomes restricted (IUGR). Since chronic hypertension or pregnancy-induced hypertension (preeclampsia, eclampsia) similarly affect blood circulation to the placenta, women with these problems are also at risk for IUGR. If the condition is not determined early enough to provide constant monitoring, there is increased risk of stillbirth. Other autoimmune diseases, (antiphospholipid antibody, APA; anticardiolipin antibody, ACLA) are associated with miscarriages.

Diabetes is a medical condition that is affected by pregnancy and, likewise, affects pregnancy. Diabetes can lead to miscarriages, birth defects, and stillbirths. Women with diabetes should have preconception counseling with a perinatologist. Birth defects can result from the variation in a woman's blood sugar level during the first eight to 12 weeks, which is the time period when the embryo is developing. Cardiac defects are not unusual in the babies of women with abnormal blood sugars during that time. Insulin requirements vary tremendously during pregnancy due to placenta hormones that may inhibit the action of insulin. A perinatologist who specializes in diabetes is well aware of what the pregnant woman needs in each trimester and usually recommends the use of an insulin pump for better control. Women with symptomatic cardiac disease face one of the biggest challenges in pregnancy.

Before the advent of perinatology training, women with medical problems such as chronic hypertension, diabetes, and epilepsy were advised to not get pregnant because they could die. With the advancement of technology, it is in the early 2000s possible for these women to have a baby with just a modicum of risk.

Prevention

Women who have health problems and start specific care before conception have the best chance of a healthy pregnancy. A pre-pregnancy visit with a healthcare provider is, therefore, of the utmost importance for a woman with a medical problem. Together, the perinatologist and the woman can start therapies that will improve the woman's health prior to conception. There may be medications that are safer to take during pregnancy, and the physician can discuss how other women with a specific condition fare during pregnancy. For some diseases, pregnancy can mean increased risk of health problems for mother and baby. In fact, with lupus, preconception counseling is essential to determine the optimum time period for getting pregnant, which is when the disease is in remission. The bottom line is that a woman must always weigh the risks to herself and the baby when deciding whether or not to become pregnant and she can only do this by becoming informed.

See also Amniocentesis; Cesarean section; Electronic fetal monitoring.

Resources

BOOKS

Evans, A. T., and K. R. Niswander. *Manual of Obstetrics*, 6th ed. Hagerstown, MD: Lippincott Williams & Wilkins, 2000.

Garcia-Pratts, Joseph, et al. *What to Do When Your Baby Is Premature: A Parent's Handbook for Coping with High-Risk Pregnancy and Caring for the Preterm Infant.* Westminster, MD: Crown Publishing Group, 2000.

Gilbert, Elizabeth S., et al. *Manual for High-Risk Pregnancy and Delivery*. St. Louis, MO: Mosby, 2002.

High-Risk Pregnancy: A Medical Dictionary, Bibliography, and Annotated Research Guide to Internet References. San Diego, CA: Icon Group International, 2004.

Olds, Sally, et al. *Maternal-Newborn Nursing & Women's Health Care*, 7th ed. Saddle River, NJ: Prentice Hall, 2004.

ORGANIZATIONS

American College of Obstetricians and Gynecologists. 409 12th Street, SW, PO Box 96920, Washington, DC 20090. Web site: <www.acog.org>.

Association of Women's Health, Obstetric and Neonatal Nursing. 2000 L Street, NW Suite 740, Washington, DC 20036. Web site: <www.awhonn.org.

Linda K. Bennington, MSN, CNS

Hip dysplasia, congenital *see* **Congenital hip dysplasia**

Hirschsprung's disease

Definition

Hirschsprung's disease, also known as congenital megacolon or aganglionic megacolon, is an abnormality in which certain nerve fibers are absent in segments of the bowel, resulting in severe bowel obstruction.

Description

Hirschsprung's disease is caused when certain nerve cells (called parasympathetic ganglion cells) in the wall of the large intestine (colon) do not develop before birth. Without these nerves, the affected segment of the colon lacks the ability to relax and move bowel contents along. This causes a constriction and as a result, the bowel above the constricted area dilates due to stool becoming trapped, producing megacolon (enlargement of the colon). The disease can affect varying lengths of bowel segment, most often involving the region around the rectum. In up to 10 percent of children, however, the entire colon and part of the small intestine are involved.

Demographics

Hirschsprung's disease occurs once in every 5,000 live births, and it is about four times more common in males than females. Between 4 percent and 50 percent of siblings are also afflicted. The wide range for recurrence is due to the fact that the recurrence risk depends on the gender of the affected individual in the **family** (i.e., if a female is affected, the recurrence risk is higher) and the length of the aganglionic segment of the colon (i.e., the longer the segment that is affected, the higher the recurrence risk).

Causes and symptoms

Hirschsprung's disease occurs early in fetal development when, for unknown reasons, there is either failure of nerve cell development, failure of nerve cell migration, or arrest in nerve cell development in a segment of bowel. The absence of these nerve fibers, which help control the movement of bowel contents, is what results in intestinal obstruction accompanied by other symptoms.

There is a genetic basis to Hirschsprung's disease, and it is believed that it may be caused by different genetic factors in different subsets of families. Proof that genetic factors contribute to Hirschsprung's disease is that it is known to run in families, and it has been seen in association with some chromosome abnormalities. For example, about 10 percent of children with the disease have **Down syndrome** (the most common chromosome abnormality). Molecular diagnostic techniques have identified many genes that cause susceptibility to Hirschsprung's disease. As of the early 2000s, there are a total of six genes: the RET gene, the glial cell line-derived neurotrophic factor gene, the endothelin-B receptor gene, endothelin converting enzyme, the endothelin-3 gene, and the Sry-related transcription factor SOX10. Mutations that inactivate the RET gene are the most frequent, occurring in 50 percent of familial cases (cases which run in families) and 15 to 20 percent of sporadic (non-familial) cases. Mutations in these genes do not cause the disease, but they make the chance of developing it more likely. Mutations in other genes or environmental factors are required to develop the disease, and these other factors are not understood. Also, among children with Hirschsprung's disease, some 2–5 percent have cardiac defects.

For persons with a ganglion growth beyond the sigmoid segment of the colon, the inheritance pattern is autosomal dominant with reduced penetrance (risk closer to 50 percent). For persons with smaller segments involved, the inheritance pattern is multifactorial (caused by an interaction of more than one gene and environmental factors, risk lower than 50 percent) or autosomal recessive (one disease gene inherited from each parent, risk closer to 25 percent) with low penetrance.

The initial symptom is usually severe, continuous **constipation**. A newborn may fail to pass meconium (the first stool) within 24 hours of birth, may repeatedly vomit yellow or green colored bile, and may have a distended (swollen, uncomfortable) abdomen. Occasionally, infants may have only mild or intermittent constipation, often with **diarrhea**.

While two-thirds of cases are diagnosed in the first three months of life, Hirschsprung's disease may also be diagnosed later in infancy or childhood. Occasionally, even adults are diagnosed with a variation of the disease. In older infants, symptoms and signs may include anorexia (lack of appetite or inability to eat), lack of the urge to move the bowels or empty the rectum on physical examination, distended abdomen, and a mass in the colon that can be felt by the physician during examination. It should be suspected in older children with abnormal bowel habits, especially a history of constipation dating back to infancy and ribbon-like stools.

Occasionally, the presenting symptom may be a severe intestinal infection called enterocolitis, which is life threatening. The symptoms are usually explosive, watery stools and **fever** in a very ill-appearing infant. It is important to diagnose the condition before the intestinal obstruction causes an overgrowth of bacteria that evolves into a medical emergency. Enterocolitis can lead to severe diarrhea and massive fluid loss, which can cause death from **dehydration** unless surgery is done immediately to relieve the obstruction.

Diagnosis

Hirschsprung's disease in the newborn must be distinguished from other causes of intestinal obstruction. The

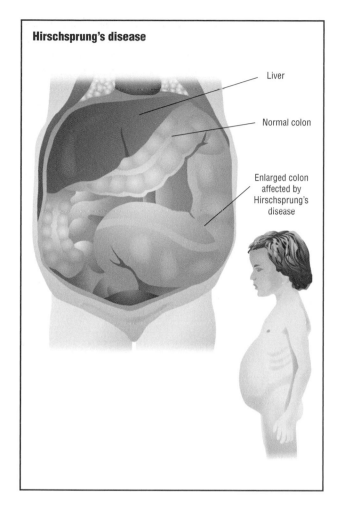

Hirschsprung's disease

Liver

Normal colon

Enlarged colon affected by Hirschsprung's disease

In Hirschsprung's disease, the flow of contents through the large intestine is halted, causing some areas to enlarge greatly. This causes many symptoms in the patient, including a distended abdomen. *(Illustration by GGS Information Services.)*

diagnosis is suspected by the child's medical history and physical examination, especially the rectal exam. The diagnosis is confirmed by a barium enema x ray, which shows a picture of the bowel. The x ray will indicate if a segment of bowel is constricted, causing dilation and obstruction. A biopsy of rectal tissue will reveal the absence of the nerve fibers. Adults may also undergo manometry, a balloon study (device used to enlarge the anus for the procedure) of internal anal sphincter pressure and relaxation.

Treatment

Hirschsprung's disease is treated surgically. The goal is to remove the diseased, nonfunctioning segment of the bowel and restore bowel function. This is often done in two stages. The first stage relieves the intestinal obstruction by

performing a colostomy. This procedure creates an opening in the abdomen (stoma) through which bowel contents can be discharged into a waste bag. When the child's weight, age, or condition is deemed appropriate, surgeons close the stoma, remove the diseased portion of bowel, and perform a pull-through procedure, which repairs the colon by connecting functional bowel to the anus. This usually establishes fairly normal bowel function.

Prognosis

Overall, prognosis is very good. Most infants with Hirschsprung's disease achieve good bowel control after surgery, but a small percentage of children may have lingering problems with soilage or constipation. These infants are also at higher risk for an overgrowth of bacteria in the intestines, including subsequent episodes of enterocolitis, and should be closely followed by a physician. Mortality from enterocolitis or surgical complications in infancy is 20 percent.

Prevention

Hirschsprung's disease is a congenital abnormality that has no known means of prevention. It is important to diagnose the condition early in order to prevent the development of enterocolitis. Genetic counseling can be offered to a couple with a previous child with the disease or to an affected individual considering pregnancy to discuss recurrence risks and treatment options. Prenatal diagnosis was not available as of 2004.

Parental concerns

Parents should understand that toilet teaching may be delayed in children who have had surgery for Hirschsprung's disease. Children who have had surgical correction of Hirschsprung's disease are also at a higher risk for constipation and dehydration. Increased fluid and fiber intake are usually sufficient to improve these problems.

Resources

BOOKS

McConnell, Elizabeth J., and John H. Pemberton. "Megacolon: congenital and acquired." In *Sleisenger and Fordtran's Gastrointestinal and Liver Disease*, 7th ed. Edited by Mark Feldman et al. St. Louis, MO: Elsevier, 2002.

Wyllie, Robert. "Motility Disorders and Hirschsprung Disease." In *Nelson Textbook of Pediatrics*. Edited by Richard E. Behrman et al. Philadelphia: Saunders, 2004.

PERIODICALS

Halter, J. "Common gastrointestinal problems and emergencies in neonates and children." *Clinical Family Practice* 6 (September 2004): 731.

Hussain, S. Z. "Motility disorders: Diagnosis and treatment for the pediatric patient." *Pediatric Clinics of North America* 49 (February 2002): 27–51.

Stewart, D. R. "The genetics of Hirschsprung disease." *Gastroenterological Clinics of North America* 32 (September 2003): 819–837.

Amy Vance, MS, CGC
Rosalyn Carson-DeWitt, MD

Histiocytosis X

Definition

Histiocytosis X is a generic term that refers to an increase in the number of histiocytes, a type of white blood cell that acts as a scavenger to remove foreign material from the blood and tissues. Research that demonstrated Langerhans cell involvement as well as histiocytes led to a proposal that the term Langerhans cell histiocytosis (LCH) be used in place of histiocytosis X. Either term refers to three separate illnesses (listed in order of increasing severity): eosinophilic granuloma, Hand-Schuller-Christian disease, and Letterer-Siwe disease.

Description

Epidermal (skin) Langerhans cells (a form of dendritic cell) accumulate with other immune cells in various parts of the body and cause damage by the release of chemicals. Normally, Langerhans cells recognize foreign material, including bacteria, and stimulate the immune system to react to them. Langerhans cells are usually found in skin, lymph nodes, lungs, and the gastrointestinal tract. Under abnormal conditions these cells affect skin, bone, and the pituitary gland as well as the lungs, intestines, liver, spleen, bone marrow, and brain. Therefore, the disease is not confined to areas where Langerhans cells are normally found. The disease is more common in children than adults and tends to be most severe in very young children.

Histiocytosis X or LCH is a family of related conditions, which are characterized by a distinct inflammatory and proliferative process but which differ from each other regarding what parts of the body are involved. The least severe of the histiocytosis X/LCH family is eosinophilic granuloma. Approximately 60 to 80 percent of all diagnosed cases are in this classification, which usually occurs in children aged five to ten years. The bones are involved 50 to 75 percent of the time, which includes the skull, or mandible, and the long bones. If the bone marrow is involved, anemia can result. With skull involvement, growths can occur behind the eyes, bulging them forward. The lungs are involved less than 10 percent of the time, and this involvement signals the worst prognosis.

Next in severity is Hand-Schuller-Christian disease, a chronic, scattered form of histiocytosis. It occurs most commonly from the age of one to three years and is a slowly progressive disease that affects the softened areas of the skull, other flat bones, the eyes, and skin. Letterer-Siwe disease is the acute form of this series of diseases. It is generally found from the time of birth to one year of age. It causes an enlarged liver, bruising and skin lesions, anemia, enlarged lymph glands, other organ involvement, and extensive skull lesions.

KEY TERMS

Anemia—A condition in which there is an abnormally low number of red blood cells in the bloodstream. It may be due to loss of blood, an increase in red blood cell destruction, or a decrease in red blood cell production. Major symptoms are paleness, shortness of breath, unusually fast or strong heart beats, and tiredness.

Biopsy—The surgical removal and microscopic examination of living tissue for diagnostic purposes or to follow the course of a disease. Most commonly the term refers to the collection and analysis of tissue from a suspected tumor to establish malignancy.

Computed tomography (CT)—An imaging technique in which cross-sectional x rays of the body are compiled to create a three-dimensional image of the body's internal structures; also called computed axial tomography.

Cytokines—Chemicals made by the cells that act on other cells to stimulate or inhibit their function. They are important controllers of immune functions.

Dendritic—Branched like a tree.

Eosinophil—A type of white blood cell containing granules that can be stained by eosin (a chemical that produces a red stain). Eosinophils increase in response to parasitic infections and allergic reactions.

Epidermal—The outermost layer of the skin.

Inflammatory—Pertaining to inflammation.

Magnetic resonance imaging (MRI)—An imaging technique that uses a large circular magnet and radio waves to generate signals from atoms in the body. These signals are used to construct detailed images of internal body structures and organs, including the brain.

Pituitary gland—The most important of the endocrine glands (glands that release hormones directly into the bloodstream), the pituitary is located at the base of the brain. Sometimes referred to as the "master gland," it regulates and controls the activities of other endocrine glands and many body processes including growth and reproductive function. Also called the hypophysis.

Prostaglandins—A group of hormone-like molecules that exert local effects on a variety of processes including fluid balance, blood flow, and gastrointestinal function. They may be responsible for the production of some types of pain and inflammation.

Serous—Pertaining to or resembling serum.

Demographics

Histiocytosis X is a rare disorder affecting only approximately one in 200,000 children or adults each year.

Causes and symptoms

Because histiocytosis X is so rare, little research has been done to determine the cause. Over time, it may lessen in its assault on the body, but there are still problems from damage to the tissues. There are no apparent inheritance patterns in these diseases with the exception of a form involving the lymphatic system.

The symptoms of histiocytosis are caused by substances called cytokines and prostaglandins, which are normally produced by histiocytes and act as messengers between cells. When these chemicals are produced in excess amounts and in the wrong places, they cause tissue swelling and abnormal growth. Thus, symptoms may include painful lumps in the skull and limbs as well as **rashes** on the skin. General symptoms may include: poor appetite, failure to gain weight, recurrent **fever**, and irritability. Symptoms from other possible sites of involvement include:

• gums: swelling, usually without significant discomfort

• ears: chronic discharge

• liver or spleen: abdominal discomfort or swelling

• pituitary gland: affected at some stage in approximately 20 percent to 30 percent of children, causing a disturbance in water balance and producing thirst and frequent urination

• eyes: behind-the-eye bulging may occur (exophthalmos)

• lungs: breathing problems

Diagnosis

The diagnosis can only be made by performing a biopsy (taking a tissue sample under anesthesia from a site in the patient thought to be involved and having it tests). Blood and urine tests, chest and other **x rays**, **magnetic resonance imaging** (MRI) and **computed tomography** scans (CT scans) (to check the extent of involvement), and possibly bone marrow or breathing tests may be required to confirm the diagnosis.

Treatment

Although this disease is not **cancer**, most patients are treated in cancer clinics. There are two reasons for this. Historically, cancer specialists treated it before the cause was known. Moreover, the treatment requires the use of drugs typically required to treat cancer.

Any cancer drugs utilized are usually given in smaller doses, which diminishes the severity of their side effects. Radiation therapy is rarely used, and special drugs may be prescribed for skin symptoms. If there is only one organ affected, steroids may be injected locally, or a drug called indomethacin may be used. Indomethacin is an anti-inflammatory medication that may achieve a similar response with less severe side effects.

Prognosis

The disease fluctuates markedly. If only one system is involved, the disease often resolves by itself. Multisystem disease usually needs treatment, although it may disappear spontaneously. The disease is not normally fatal unless organs vital to life are damaged. In general, the younger the child at diagnosis and the more organs involved, the poorer the outlook. If the condition resolves, there can still be long-term complications because of the damage done while the disease was active.

Resources

BOOKS

Ladisch, Stephan. "Histiocytosis Syndromes of Childhood." In *Nelson Textbook of Pediatrics*. Edited by Richard E. Behrman et al. Philadelphia: Saunders, 2004.

PERIODICALS

Katz, B. Z. "Treatment for multisystem Langerhans' cell histiocytosis." *Journal of Pediatrics* 86 (February 2002): 280.

Seward, J. L. "Generalized eruptive histiocytosis." *Journal of the American Academy Dermatology* 86 (January 2004): 116–20.

ORGANIZATIONS

Histiocytosis Association of America. 302 North Broadway, Pitman, NJ 08071. Web site: <www.histio.org>.

Linda K. Bennington, CNS
Rosalyn Carson-DeWitt, MD

Hitting *see* **Aggressive behavior**

HIV infection and AIDS

Definition

Human **immunodeficiency** virus (HIV) is a retrovirus that causes acquired immune deficiency syndrome (AIDS) by infecting helper T cells of the immune system. The most common serotype, HIV-1, is distributed worldwide, while HIV-2 is primarily confined to West Africa. AIDS is a severe immunological disorder caused by the retrovirus HIV, resulting in a defect in cell-mediated immune response that is manifested by increased susceptibility to opportunistic infections and to certain rare cancers, especially Kaposi's sarcoma. It is transmitted primarily by exposure to contaminated body fluids, especially blood and semen. Everybody who has AIDS also has HIV disease, but not everybody with HIV disease is classified by the United States (U.S.) government as having AIDS. The U.S. government uses CD4 cell counts (part of the immune system) to make this distinction.

Description

The earliest known case of HIV-1 came from a human blood sample collected in 1959 from a man in Kinshasa, Democratic Republic of Congo. The method by which he became infected is not known; however, genetic analysis of his blood sample suggested that HIV-1 might have stemmed from a single virus in the late 1940s or early 1950s. HIV has existed in the United States since the mid to late 1970s. During 1979 to 1981, rare types of **pneumonia**, **cancer**, and other illnesses were reported by physicians in Los Angeles and New York among a number of male patients who had sex with other men. Since it is rare to find these diseases in people with a healthy immune system, public health representatives became concerned that a new virus was emerging.

In 1982, the term AIDS was introduced to describe the occurrences of opportunistic infections, Kaposi sarcoma, and *Pneumocystis carinii* pneumonia in previously healthy persons and formal tracking of these cases in the United States began that year. The virus that causes AIDS was discovered in 1983 and named human T-cell lymphotropic virus-type III/lymphadenopathy-associated virus (HTLV-III/LAV) by an international scientific committee who later changed it to HIV. Many theories as to the origins of HIV and how it appeared in the human population have been suggested. The majority of scientists believed that HIV originated in other primates and was somehow transmitted to man. In 1999, an international group reported the discovery of the origins of HIV-1, the predominant strain of HIV in the developed world. A subspecies of chimpanzees native to west equatorial Africa were identified as the original source of the virus. The researchers believe that HIV-1 was introduced into the human population when hunters became exposed to infected blood.

Most scientists believe that HIV causes AIDS by directly inducing the death of CD4+ T cells (helper T cells in the immune system) or interfering with their normal function and by triggering other events that weaken a person's immune function. For example, the network of signaling molecules that normally regulates a person's immune response is disrupted during HIV disease, impairing a person's ability to fight other infections. The HIV-mediated destruction of the lymph nodes and related immunologic organs also plays a major role in causing the immunosuppression seen in persons with AIDS.

In the absence of antiretroviral therapy, the median time from HIV infection to the development of AIDS-related symptoms has been approximately 10 to 12 years. A wide variation in disease progression, however, has been noted. Approximately 10 percent of HIV-infected persons have progressed to AIDS within the first two to three years after infection, whereas up to 5 percent of persons have stable CD4+ T cell counts and no symptoms even after 12 or more years. Factors such as age or genetic differences among persons with HIV, the level of virulence of an individual strain of virus, and co-infection with other microbes may influence the rate and severity of disease progression. Drugs that fight the infections associated with AIDS have improved and prolonged the lives of HIV-infected persons by preventing or treating conditions such as *Journal of Infectious Diseases*. This approach is known formally as short-cycle structured intermittent antiretroviral therapy (SIT) or colloquially as the "7-7" approach. Dr. Mark Dybul, of the National Institute of Allergy and Infectious Diseases (NIAID) and the study author, noted that this approach together with high patient adherence could be a powerful and cost-effective tool in HIV treatment. This regimen uses half as much antiretroviral medication so not only are drug costs reduced but drug-related toxicities may be less in the long run. He believes that this is particularly important to countries with few resources around the world.

Nutritional concerns

Nutrition is definitely a concern for the individual who is HIV infected and even more so for the individual who has progressed to AIDS. The antiretroviral drugs have numerous side effects that make eating an adequate diet difficult and the disease itself affects nutritional intake. It is important for HIV individuals to supplement their diet with **vitamins** and **minerals** as well as protein drinks to maintain their energy. There are many supplements on the market and in health food stores that can be of benefit. The patient needs to go in search of what best suits their tastes.

Prognosis

The prognosis for individuals with AIDS in recent years has improved significantly because of new drugs and treatments, and educational and preventive efforts. Women whose HIV infections are detected early and receive appropriate treatment survive as long as infected men. There are several studies that have shown HIV-infected women to have shorter survival times than men. Women may be less likely than men to be diagnosed early, which may account for shorter survival times. In an analysis of several studies involving more than 4,500 people with HIV infection, women were one-third more likely than men to die within the study period. The investigators could not definitively identify the reasons for excess mortality among women in this study, but they speculated that poorer access to or use of health care resources among HIV-infected women as compared to men, domestic violence, homelessness, and lack of social supports for women may have been important factors.

Researchers have observed two general patterns of illness in HIV-infected children. About 20 percent of children develop serious disease in the first year of life; most of these children die by age four years. The remaining 80 percent of infected children have a slower rate of disease progression, many not developing the most serious symptoms of AIDS until school entry or even **adolescence**. A recent report from a large European registry of HIV-infected children indicated that half of the children with perinatally acquired HIV disease were alive at age nine. Another study, of 42 perinatally HIV-infected children who survived beyond nine years of age, found about one-quarter of the children to be asymptomatic with relatively intact immune systems.

Prevention

Because no vaccine for HIV is available, the only way to prevent infection by the virus is to avoid behaviors that put a person at risk of infection, such as sharing needles and having unprotected sex. Many people infected with HIV have no symptoms; therefore, there is no way of knowing with certainty whether a sexual partner is infected unless he or she has repeatedly tested negative for the virus and has not engaged in any risky behavior. Individuals should either abstain from having

KEY TERMS

B-cell lymphomas—Non-Hodgkin's lymphomas that arise from B cells.

CD4+ cells—Called helper T-cells, these cells work in cell-mediated immunity by causing a form of inflammation to wall off and destroy foreign material as with a bacterial infection.

Co-infection—Concurrent infection of a cell or organism with two microorganisms (pneumonia caused by coinfection with a cytomegalovirus and streptococcus).

Immunosuppression—Techniques used to prevent transplant graft rejection by the recipient's immune system.

Kaposi's sarcoma—A cancer characterized by bluish-red nodules on the skin, usually on the lower extremities, that often occurs in people with AIDS.

Lymphadenopathy—A disorder characterized by local or generalized enlargement of the lymph nodes or lymphatic vessels.

Perinatal—Referring to the period of time surrounding an infant's birth, from the last two months of pregnancy through the first 28 days of life.

Pneumocystis carinii—A parasite transitional between a fungus and protozoan, frequently occurring as aggregate forms existing within rounded cystlike structures. It is the causative agent of pneumocystosis.

Retrovirus—A family of RNA viruses containing a reverse transcriptase enzyme that allows the viruses' genetic information to become part of the genetic information of the host cell upon replication. Human immunodeficiency virus (HIV) is a retrovirus.

T cell—A type of white blood cell that is produced in the bone marrow and matured in the thymus gland. It helps to regulate the immune system's response to infections or malignancy.

---

sex or use male latex condoms or female polyurethane condoms, which may offer partial protection, during oral, anal, or vaginal sex. Only water-based lubricants should be used with male latex condoms. Although some laboratory evidence shows that spermicides can kill HIV, researchers have not found that these products can prevent a person from getting HIV.

The risk of HIV transmission from a pregnant woman to her baby can be significantly reduced with the use of antiretroviral drugs taken during pregnancy, labor, and delivery and administered to the baby for the first six weeks of life. In addition, the International Perinatal HIV Group reported in 1999 that elective **cesarean section** delivery could help reduce vertical transmission of HIV, although it is not without risk to certain women.

Parental concerns

Parental concerns are reflected in the status of a reproductive couple to prevent the transmission of the virus before pregnancy and if this is not possible, to obtain adequate prenatal care to prevent the transmission to the baby.

See also High-risk pregnancy.

Resources

BOOKS

Cohen, J., and W. Powderly. *Infectious Disease.* Philadelphia, PA: Mosby, 2003.

PERIODICALS

Schechter, M. "Therapy for early HIV infection: how far back should the pendulum swing?" (Editorial Commentary) *Journal of Infectious Diseases* 190, no. 6 (Sept. 2004): 1043.

Dybul, M. et al. "A proof-of-concept study of short-cycle intermittent antiretroviral therapy with a once-daily regimen of didanosine, lamivudine, and efavirenz for the treatment of chronic HIV infection." *Journal of Infectious Diseases* 189, no. 11 (June 2004): 1974–83.

ORGANIZATIONS

Center for Disease Control and Prevention, National Center for HIV, STD and TB Prevention. 1600 Clifton Rd., Atlanta, GA 30333. (800) 311-3435. Web site: <www.cdc.gov/hiv/dhap.htm>.

WEB SITES

Postive Lists, Inc. *HIV Support.* [cited March 5, 2005]. Available online at: <www.hiv-support.org/>.

AIDS/HIV Support Groups. [cited March 5, 2005]. Available online at: <http://herpes-coldsores.com/std/aids_support_groups.htm>.

Seattle Aids Support Group (SASG). [cited March 5, 2005]. Available online at: <www.sasg.org>.

Linda K. Bennington, MSN, CNS

Hives

Definition

Hives is an allergic skin reaction causing localized redness, swelling, and **itching**.

Description

Hives is a reaction of the body's immune system that causes areas of the skin to swell, itch, and become reddened (wheals). When the reaction is limited to small areas of the skin, it is called urticaria. Involvement of larger areas, such as whole sections of a limb, is called angioedema.

Demographics

Many children and adults experience hives at various times during their lives. As hives is not a reportable event, no accurate prevalence statistics are available.

Causes and symptoms

Hives is an allergic reaction. The body's immune system is normally responsible for protection from foreign invaders. When it becomes sensitized to normally harmless substances, the resulting reaction is called an allergy. An attack of hives is set off when such a substance, called an allergen, is ingested, inhaled, or otherwise contacted. It interacts with immune cells called mast cells, which reside in the skin, airways, and digestive system. When mast cells encounter an allergen, they release histamine and other chemicals, both locally and into the bloodstream. These chemicals cause blood vessels to become more porous, allowing fluid to accumulate in tissue and leading to the swollen and reddish appearance of hives. Some of the chemicals released sensitize **pain** nerve endings, causing the affected area to become itchy and sensitive.

A wide variety of substances may cause hives in sensitive people, including foods, drugs, and insect **bites** or **stings**. Common culprits include:

- nuts, especially peanuts, walnuts, and Brazil nuts
- fish, mollusks, and shellfish
- eggs
- wheat
- milk
- strawberries
- food additives and preservatives

- penicillin or other antibiotics
- flu vaccines
- tetanus toxoid vaccine
- gamma globulin
- bee, wasp, and hornet stings
- bites of mosquitoes, fleas, and scabies

Urticaria is characterized by redness, swelling, and itching of small areas of the skin. These patches usually grow and recede in less than a day but may be replaced by others in other locations. Angioedema is characterized by more diffuse swelling. Swelling of the airways may cause wheezing and respiratory distress. In severe cases, airway obstruction may occur.

When to call the doctor

A doctor or other healthcare professional should be called when hives do not spontaneously clear within a day of their appearance or when they include swelling of the throat. If the reactions are severe, as in anaphylactic reaction or shock, immediate medical care is needed.

Diagnosis

Hives are easily diagnosed by visual inspection. The cause of hives is usually apparent but may require a careful medical history in some cases.

Treatment

Mild cases of hives are treated with **antihistamines**, such as diphenhydramine (Benadryl). More severe cases may require oral corticosteroids, such as prednisone. Topical corticosteroids are not effective. Airway swelling may require emergency injection of epinephrine (adrenaline).

An alternative practitioner will try to determine what allergic substance is causing the reaction and help the person eliminate or minimize its effects. To deal with the symptoms of hives, an oatmeal bath may help to relieve itching. Chickweed (*Stellaria media*), applied as a poultice (crushed or chopped herbs applied directly to the skin) or added to bath water, may also help relieve itching. Several homeopathic remedies, including *Urtica urens* and *Apis* (*Apis mellifica*), may help relieve the itch, redness, or swelling associated with hives.

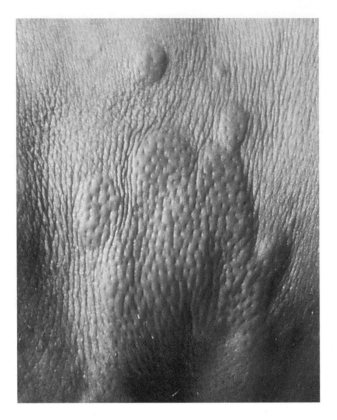

Hives on the back of a young woman's legs. The accompanying inflammation develops as an allergic reaction which ranges in size from small spots to patches measuring several inches across. (© 1994 Caliendo/Custom Medical Stock Photo, Inc.)

Prognosis

Most cases of hives clear up within one to seven days without treatment, providing the cause (allergen) is found and avoided.

Prevention

Preventing hives depends on avoiding the allergen causing them. Analysis of new items in the diet or new drugs taken may reveal the likely source of the reaction. Chronic hives may be aggravated by stress, **caffeine**, alcohol, or tobacco; avoiding these may reduce the frequency of reactions.

Nutritional concerns

Hives may be triggered or worsened by caffeine or alcohol (in adults), or specific allergenic foods, which depend entirely on the patient. Avoiding these substances may reduce the occurrence of hives.

Parental concerns

Parents should monitor their children to ensure that any attack of hives does not involve the throat area. Young children should be encouraged not to stratch their skin too vigorously. If hives are a recurrent problem, parents should keep track of the foods the child eats in an attempt to discover the allergen.

Resources

BOOKS

Duvic, Madeleine. "Urticaria, Drug Hypersensitivity Rashes, Nodules and Tumors, and Atrophic Diseases." In *Cecil Textbook of Medicine*, 22nd ed. Edited by Lee Goldman et al. Philadelphia: Saunders, 2003, pp. 2475–85.

Frank, Michael M. "Urticaria and Angioedema." In *Cecil Textbook of Medicine*, 22nd ed. Edited by Lee Goldman et al. Philadelphia: Saunders, 2003, pp. 1610–3.

Leung, Donald Y. M. "Urticaria and Angioedema (Hives)." In *Nelson Textbook of Pediatrics*, 17th ed. Edited by Richard E. Behrman et al. Philadelphia: Saunders, 2003, pp. 778–80.

Yancy, Kim B., and Thomas J. Lawley. "Immunologically Mediated Skin Disorders." In *Harrison's Principles of Internal Medicine*, 15th ed. Edited by Eugene Braunwald et al. New York: McGraw-Hill, 2001, pp. 331–5.

PERIODICALS

Beltrani, V. S. "Urticaria: reassessed." *Allergy and Asthma Proceedings* 25, no. 3 (2004): 143–9.

Clarke, P. "Urticaria." *Australian Family Physician* 33, no. 7 (2004): 501–3.

Dice, J. P. "Physical urticaria." *Immunology and Allergy Clinics of North America* 24, no. 2 (2004): 225–46.

Grattan, C. E. "Autoimmune urticaria." *Immunology and Allergy Clinics of North America* 24, no. 2 (2004): 163–81.

Lawlor, F., and A. K. Black. "Delayed pressure urticaria." *Immunology and Allergy Clinics of North America* 24, no. 2 (2004): 247–58.

Rumbyrt, J. S., and A. L. Schocket. "Chronic urticaria and thyroid disease." *Immunology and Allergy Clinics of North America* 24, no. 2 (2004): 215–23.

Sheikh, J. "Advances in the treatment of chronic urticaria." *Immunology and Allergy Clinics of North America* 24, no. 2 (2004): 317–34.

ORGANIZATIONS

American Academy of Dermatology. 930 N. Meacham Road, PO Box 4014, Schaumburg, IL 60168–4014. Web site: <www.aad.org/>.

American Academy of Pediatrics. 141 Northwest Point Blvd., Elk Grove Village, IL 60007–1098. Web site: <www.aap.org/>.

WEB SITES

"Hives." *MedlinePlus.* Available online at <www.nlm.nih.gov/medlineplus/ency/article/000845.htm> (accessed January 6, 2005).

"Hives (Urticaria)." *San Francisco State University Student Health Service.* Available online at <www.sfsu.edu/~shs/skinclinic/urticaria.htm> (accessed January 6, 2005).

"Urticaria (Hives)." *American Osteopathic College of Dermatology.* Available online at <www.aocd.org/skin/dermatologic_diseases/urticaria.html> (accessed January 6, 2005).

L. Fleming Fallon, Jr., MD, DrPH

Home schooling

Definition

Home schooling is the process of educating school-aged children at home rather than at a school. As of the early 2000s, it is perhaps one of the fastest growing trends in education in the United States. Since 1993, the practice has been legal in all 50 states. About 1.1 million students were being home-schooled in the spring of 2003, according to the National Household Education Surveys Program (NHES), which was conducted by the United States Department of Education. In addition, the percentage of the school-age population that was being home-schooled increased from 1.7 percent in 1999 to 2.2 percent in 2003. Parents choose to home-school their children for a variety of reasons, though certain factors appear to be more prevalent than others. Nearly two-thirds of the parents of home-schooled students reported that their primary reason for home schooling was either concern regarding the environment of schools or a wish to provide moral or religious instruction.

Description

Societies have practiced home schooling for centuries. In North America, home schooling was widespread until the 1870s, when compulsory school attendance laws and the development of professional educators came together to institutionalize education in the form recognized in the early 2000s as the school. Some pre-eminent historical figures who were home-schooled include several presidents, such as George Washington, John Quincy Adams, Abraham Lincoln, and Franklin Delano Roosevelt. Other home-schooling successes in American history include Thomas Edison, General Robert E. Lee, Booker T. Washington, and Mark Twain.

Although home schooling was practiced in a limited way after the 1870s, it was not until the 1960s that this practice claimed attention from a large number of parents and educators. The writings of Raymond Moore, a former U.S. Department of Education official, and John Holt, author of several books on education, gave credence and national presence to a growing home school movement. Moore began researching the institutionalization of children's education and concluded that a child's first foray into formal education should not begin until sometime between eight and 12 years of age. Holt advocated the decentralization of schools and a greater degree of parental involvement. He believed that the most civilized way to educate a child was through home schooling.

Prior to 1993, when home schooling became legal in all states, many parents who taught their children at home often faced arrest and jail time, amidst accusations of neglect and abuse. Most of that changed over the following decade. Even so, attitudes about home schooling vary widely from state to state, and there is a patchwork of regulation across the country. Some states may require a state-approved curriculum, conduct home visits periodically, and require that home-schooling parents be certified teachers. Others may not require a parent to have any contact with the state and have no minimum educational standards for the home-schooling parent.

Despite greater acceptance, home schooling has its critics, such as the National Education Association (NEA). This organization sees the **safety** of children and the economics of public schools as potential home school problems. They cite a few well-publicized incidences of abuse and state a **fear** that in states where there is no accountability of the home-schooling parents to the government, some children may be placed at higher risk for

A mother home schools her children. (© Ed Kashi/Corbis.)

abuse, neglect, and other problems. The NEA is also concerned that home schooling will eventually lead to a diversion of funding from the public schools.

Characteristics of home schoolers

In the 1960s and 1970s, most home-schooling parents were members of the counter-cultural left. By the 1980s, however, most home-schooling parents were part of what is often called the Christian Right. In the early 2000s, approximately 75 percent of American home schoolers are practicing Christians. However, not all home-schooling parents are Christians. The rise in home schooling is reaching a much broader range of families. For example, the fastest growing number of practicing home schoolers is among Muslim Americans. Some surveys show that the average home-schooling **family** has an above average income. Others indicate that the household income of home schoolers is very similar to that of non-home-schooling families. Most home-schooling families have above-average levels of education. One important factor is that home-schooling families are 97-percent two-parent families, and most home-schooling mothers do not work outside the home. The average size of a home-schooling family is three children or more.

Reasons parents choose homeschooling

The decision to home-school is not based solely on conservative religious or political views. Although parents homeschool for a variety of reasons, the primary reason is dissatisfaction with public education. Other reasons stated by home-schooling parents include the following:

- the opportunity to impart a certain set of beliefs and morals
- higher academic performance through one-on-one instruction
- the ability to develop stronger parent-child relationships
- the lack of **discipline** in public schools
- the opportunity to escape negative **peer pressure** through more controlled interactions with a student's peers
- an inability to pay private school tuition

• a physically safer environment in which to learn

Home schooling involves a tremendous commitment from the parents. At least one parent must be willing to work closely with the child, develop lesson plans, keep current with government requirements, and sometimes negotiate issues with the local school district. The most common home-schooling arrangement is for the mother to teach while the father works outside the home. There are numerous educational materials available that are geared for home-schooled children. These include correspondence courses, full curricula, and single topic books in areas such as math or phonics. There are both religious and non-religious publishers of these materials. Some parents do not use these materials and develop individualized lessons based on their children's unique learning needs.

Performance of home-schooled students

One of the questions many people have is how home-schooled children perform academically. According to the U.S. Department of Education, virtually all of the data available illustrate that home-schooled students perform at an above average level on a variety of tests, including the Scholastic Aptitude Test (SAT). Interestingly, one study found that students whose parents are certified teachers performed no better than other students and that neither parental income nor parents' educational background had a significant impact on student performance. In the late 1990s and early 2000s, home-schooled students have gained admission and scholarships to such prestigious universities as Harvard, Yale, Stanford, and MIT. In 2000, Patrick Henry College opened, a university established especially for home-schooled children.

Common problems

One disadvantage to home schooling is the loss of an income in a family, since many families make the decision to live on a single income so that one parent can devote time to educating the children. Some home-schooling families find the practice of home-schooling confining. It takes a great deal of dedication and preparation for instruction and schoolwork. One of the most often voiced concerns is that children who are home schooled are not properly socialized. However, there are numerous opportunities for home-schooled students to interact with others, including libraries, scouting, 4-H, **sports** teams, and a variety of church activities. In addition, many local communities have formed home-schooling associations in which children have many outlets for interacting with their peers.

Parental concerns

Parents interested in teaching their children at home should thoroughly research what is involved before making the decision to do so. They need to be informed regarding the laws in their state and local school district, which may affect their decision.

Resources

BOOKS

Holt, John, Patrick Farenga, and Pat Farenga. *Teach Your Own.* Boulder, CO: Perseus Publishing, 2003.

Pride, Mary. *Mary Pride's Complete Guide to Getting Started in Homeschooling.* Princeton, NJ: Harvest House Publishers, 2004.

PERIODICALS

Butler, Shery. "The 'H' Word: Home Schooling." *Gifted Child Today Magazine.* (September 2000.)

Klicka, Christopher J. "The Facts Are In: Homeschoolers Excel." *Practical Homeschooling* (January/February 2004): 12–14.

Postlewaite, Charlotte C. "The Home School Debate: States are Responding to the Increasing Number of Parents Who are Home Schooling Their Children." *State Government News* (February 2004): 18–20.

ORGANIZATIONS

Home School Legal Defense Association. PO Box 3000, Purcellville, VA 20134–9000. Web site: <www.hslda.org>.

National Home Education Research Institute. PO Box 13939, Salem, OR 97309. Web site: <www.nheri.org>.

WEB SITES

"1.1 Million Homeschooled Students in the United States in 2003." *National Center for Education Statistics*, July 2004. <http://nces.ed.gov/pubs2004/2004115.pdf> (accessed December 11, 2004).

Deanna M. Swartout-Corbeil, RN

Homosexuality and bisexuality

Definition

Homosexuality is the consistent sexual and emotional attraction, including fantasy, interest, and arousal to a person of the same sex. Bisexuality is the sexual and emotional attraction to members of both sexes.

Description

References to homosexuality and bisexuality can be found in recorded history and literature dating back thousands of years. They are part of a trio of classifications referred to collectively as sexual orientation. The third is heterosexuality, the sexual and emotional attraction to members of the opposite sex. Both male and female homosexuals are commonly referred to as gay while homosexual females are called lesbians.

The earliest documentation of homosexuality in Western civilization occurs in ancient Greece, where same-sex relationships were considered normal by society. Although there were some homosexual relationships between adult males, most were between men and boys. Although there is some disagreement among historians, a number of historical figures were believed to be gay, including Alexander the Great (356 B.C.–323 B.C.), Plato (20 B.C.–45 A.D.) Virgil (Vergil) (70 B.C.–19 B.C.), Leonardo da Vinci (1452–1519), and Michelangelo (1475–1564). Homosexuality in Asian, especially Japanese and Chinese, cultures has been documented since at least 600 B.C.

Social attitudes towards homosexuality and bisexuality have varied over the centuries, from complete rejection, or homophobia, through covert acceptance, to complete normalization, with many degrees in between. The religious response to homosexuality varies, though in the three major Western religions (Judaism, Christianity, and Islam) homosexuality and bisexuality are considered sins.

In some cultures, especially those influenced by homophobic religions, homosexuality is considered a perversion and has been outlawed; in some jurisdictions homosexual behavior is a crime punishable by death. Persecution of homosexuals in such cultures is common. In Nazi Germany, homosexuals and bisexuals were sent to concentration camps and were murdered in gas chambers along with other minority and religious groups.

The modern gay rights movement began in the late 1960s and included the development of the often activist academic treatment of sexuality in colleges and universities. This focus led to changes in social acceptance and in the media portrayal of homosexuality and bisexuality. In 1973, the American Psychiatric Association (APA) removed homosexuality from its list of mental disorders. The legalization of same-sex marriage and non-gender-specific civil unions is one of the major goals of gay rights activism. Toward the end of the 1990s and into the early 2000s, a number of jurisdictions relaxed or eliminated laws curbing homosexual behavior, including sodomy laws and laws preventing homosexuals from serving in armed forces. This trend culminated on June 26, 2003, with the landmark U.S. Supreme Court decision *Lawrence v. Texas* which overturned all sodomy laws in the United States.

In 2003, Canada legalized same-sex marriages, according the same rights to gay married couples as to heterosexual married couples. Gay marriage is also legal in The Netherlands and Belgium. In 2004, due to several local and state actions, gay marriages were legalized in San Francisco; Massachusetts; Portland, Oregon; and several other areas. They were as of 2004 all under legal challenge, and the California Supreme Court nullified the San Francisco gay marriages in mid-2004. The Defense of Marriage Act, signed by President Bill Clinton in 1996, prevents federal recognition of same-sex marriage and allows states to ignore same-sex licenses from outside their borders.

The correct term or terms to use when referring to homosexuals varies widely by location and culture. In the United States and Europe, even the use of the word homosexual can be seen as insulting. In Washington state, The Safe Schools Coalition of Washington's *Glossary for School Employees* advises that *gay* is the preferred synonym for homosexual and goes on to advise avoiding the term homosexual, because it is clinical, distancing, and archaic.

The causes of homosexuality and bisexuality are unknown, although there are many controversial theories. These include genetic, biological, psychological, and social factors, as well as conscious choice. A majority of researchers believe sexual orientation is most likely determined by a combination of factors. Since about the 1970s, researchers have tended to rule out conscious choice. The reason can be answered in a question: Why would anyone choose a lifestyle which may well bring them discrimination, hatred, and even violence?

Much research suggests sexual orientation is set in early childhood. In surveys of gay men and lesbians, most say they believe they were born that way. This awareness usually occurs during **puberty** but sometimes earlier. Many experts believe sexual orientation, whether homosexual, bisexual, or heterosexual, is determined by a complex interaction between anatomical and hormonal influences during fetal development.

There is also no definitive research on the percentage of the population that is homosexual or bisexual. Studies in the 1940s and 1950s by biologist and sex researcher Alfred C. Kinsey (1894–1956) found that 2 percent of women and 10 percent of men were exclusively homosexual and that 37 percent of men reported having at least one same-sex experience after **adoles-**

cence. The validity of this research, while often cited in scientific literature, is questionable, since most of the study subjects were over 30 years old, white, and not randomly selected.

School age

Several studies suggest that first sexual attraction, whether for homosexuals, bisexuals, or heterosexuals, begins in middle childhood at about age 10. At this time, the adrenal glands begin to produce sex steroids, which motivate sexual attraction as well as social and emotional behavior.

Development of sexual identity in middle childhood and early adolescence is a natural process but is more stressful for homosexual adolescents, according to the American School Health Association (ASHA). To avoid rejection and hostility, homosexual adolescents feel obliged to hide their sexual identities. Professionals generally agree that homosexual identity development usually occurs in stages, according to a March 2003 article in ASHA *Journal of School Health*.

The first stage is identified as "sensitization" or early awareness, where, around age 10, a child experiences same-sex attraction and feelings of being different than other children. The second stage is "identity confusion," in which simple awareness is no longer ignored. Gay male and lesbian children usually try to hide their sexual identities because society encourages heterosexuality. This stage is usually resolved by denying or hiding homosexual feelings, repressing same-sex attraction, or taking on a homosexual identity.

The next stage is "identity assumption," in which the person accepts their homosexuality but usually limits disclosure to others. The final stage is "identity consolidation," also known as "coming out," in which disclosure may be expanded and the homosexual identity may be incorporated into social activities.

After identifying themselves as homosexual or bisexual, adolescents face the often-difficult problem of deciding whom to tell that they are gay or bisexual. According to a 1999 report by Cornell University, the average coming-out age for a gay and lesbian young person in the United States is 14–15 years, significantly younger than the average age of 19–23 during the late 1970s and early 1980s, according to the advocacy group Tolerance.com. Confidence and openness about their sexual orientation at a younger age, however, almost invariably exposes young people to homophobia and abuse at an early age, the group states on its Web site (<www.tolerance.org>).

Common problems

In hiding their sexual identities, homosexual and bisexual adolescents deprive themselves and each other of positive role models. However, disclosure to **family** members may lead to pressure to change through psychological or religious "conversion" therapies, which the ASHA regards as ineffective. The ASHA and most other professional organizations say family support when an adolescent discloses that they are gay or bisexual is crucial to the child's mental and emotional health. Children and teens who reveal that they are gay or bisexual to non-supportive families are much more likely to become runaways and resort to prostitution for financial support.

Research shows inconsistencies regarding disclosure. To test how a family will react, a gay or bisexual child or teen will often first tell a sibling whom they feel they can trust and whom they believe is most likely to be supportive, most often a sister. Mothers are more often disclosed to than fathers because fathers tend to have a more negative reaction. Studies also show that parents react more negatively when a son tells them he is gay or bisexual than when a daughter reveals she is lesbian or bisexual.

Numerous studies show that gay and bisexual youth are at a higher risk of dropping out of school, of being kicked out of their homes, and becoming prostitutes, than their heterosexual peers. They also have a higher incidence of drug, alcohol, and tobacco use. Studies have also shown that gay and bisexual adolescents are two to seven times more likely to commit or attempt **suicide** compared to heterosexual children and teens. Other studies have found that 45 percent of gay males and 20 percent of lesbians were victims of verbal or physical abuse in middle and high school and were two to four times more likely to be threatened with a weapon compared to heterosexual students.

Parental concerns

Studies have shown that parents usually go through a series of stages when they learn a child is gay or bisexual. In the first stage, nearly all parents go through a grieving period after learning their child is gay or bisexual. The parents mourn the loss of what they assumes was their child's heterosexuality and "traditional" lifestyle, the lack of grandchildren and their role as potential grandparents, and the improbability of changing their child's sexual orientation.

Soon after disclosure, parents often experience **fear** and guilt and may deny their child is gay or bisexual. They may urge their child to change their sexual orientation or urge them to keep their sexuality secret. Also, parents often become angry and seek to blame someone for their child's sexual orientation, such as a gay teacher, a sexual abuser, or as often is the case with gay males, to blame the father for a lack of engaging the child in perceived masculine activities such as **sports**. During this anger stage, parents often threaten or abuse the child or try to force them to change. Any of these actions tends to drive a wedge between the parents and child and is the primary reason many gay and bisexual youth run away from home. Sometimes they are thrown out of the house by their parents and are forced to live on the streets, often turning to prostitution to survive.

The anger stage is usually followed by the bargaining stage, where parents try to get their child to change their sexual orientation, sometimes through God or religion, or through psychological intervention. In this stage, parents sometimes experience one or a combination of emotions, including shame, guilt, and depression.

The final stage is resolution, where the parents either accept or deny that their child is gay or bisexual, though studies show few fully accept it. Some families remain in denial indefinitely. Others ostracize the child through eviction from the home or family.

When to call the doctor

Gay and bisexual adolescents may need psychological help in dealing with their sexual orientation. The vast majority of experts say this counseling should be supportive and not seek to change the child's sexual orientation. Counseling that offers emotional support may be helpful for teens who are uncomfortable with their sexual orientation. Therapy may also help the adolescent adjust to personal, family, or school-related problems.

Therapy directed specifically at changing homosexual or bisexual orientation is not recommended and may be harmful for an unwilling teen, according to a behavioral health advisory issued in 2002 by the journal *Clinical Reference Systems*. It may create more confusion and **anxiety** by reinforcing negative thoughts and emotions with which the child is already struggling, the advisory states.

Signs that a child or teem may be gay or bisexual and is having problems dealing with it include social isolation, avoiding school, threats of **running away**, poorly developed dating skills, low **self-esteem**, self hatred, alcohol and/or drug abuse, harassment at school or home, feelings of inferiority, depression, threats of suicide, and eating disorders.

Advice for healthcare professionals

The American Academy of Pediatrics (AAP) has issued guidelines for pediatricians in dealing with gay and bisexual adolescents. An article in the June 2004 issue of the AAP journal *Pediatrics* states: "Pediatricians should be aware that some youths in their care may have concerns about their sexual orientation or that of siblings, friends, parents, relatives, or others. Health care professionals should provide factual, current, nonjudgmental information in a confidential manner."

The article states that pediatricians and other healthcare professionals should be attentive of various psychological difficulties, offer counseling or refer for counseling when necessary, and ensure that all sexually active youths receive a physical examination, immunizations, appropriate laboratory tests, and counseling about **sexually transmitted diseases**, and appropriate treatment if necessary.

The *Pediatrics* article also states: "Not all pediatricians may feel able to provide the type of care [necessary]. Any pediatrician who is unable to care for and counsel nonheterosexual youth should refer these patients to an appropriate colleague."

Most gay and bisexual youth seen by pediatricians and other healthcare providers will not raise the issue of sexual orientation on their own. Therefore, healthcare professionals should raise issues of sexual orientation and sexual behavior with all adolescent patients or refer them to a colleague who can these issues, according to the AAP. Pediatricians should also consider displaying posters and offering brochures that demonstrate support for gay and bisexual teens. The AAP publishes a brochure dealing with sexual orientation, "Gay, Lesbian, and Bisexual Teens: Facts for Teens and their Parents."

Advice for teachers, counselors, and other school employees

Because students who discover they are gay or bisexual often experience rejection, discrimination, isolation, and violence, it is important for teachers and administrators to be supportive and highly sensitive to the stress gay and bisexual youth feel, according to the American School Health Association. Schools are legally obligated to protect students from discrimination and harassment from other students, from teachers, and from all other school employees. In 1996, a federal appeals court ruled that school officials can be held liable under the Equal Protection Clause of the U.S. Constitution for not protecting gay and bisexual students from harassment and discrimination.

The non-profit group Parents and Friends of Lesbians and Gays (PFLAG) makes the following recommendations for all schools:

- have a harassment policy or student bill of rights that explicitly includes sexual orientation

- provide annual, mandatory training for all school employees about sexual orientation and on intervention against bullying of gay and bisexual students

- have a support group for gay, bisexual, and straight students

- have information on display and readily available in the library on gay and bisexual issues

- include gay and bisexual issues in the curriculum, including history, social studies, literature, political science, health, and arts

Resources

BOOKS

Baker, Jean M. *How Homophobia Hurts Children: Nurturing Diversity at Home, at School, and in the Community.* Binghamton, NY: Haworth Press. 2001.

Bernstein, Robert A. *Straight Parents, Gay Children: Keeping Families Together.* New York, NY: Thunder's Mouth Press, 2003.

Jennings, Kevin, and Pat Shapiro. *Always My Child: A Parent's Guide to Understanding Your Gay, Lesbian, Bisexual, Transgendered, or Questioning Son or Daughter.* Norfolk, VA: Fireside, 2002.

PERIODICALS

Frankowski, Barbara L. "Sexual Orientation and Adolescents." *Pediatrics* (June 2004): 1827–1832.

Harrison, Therese W. "Adolescent Homosexuality and Concerns Regarding Disclosure." *Journal of School Health* (March 2003): 107–112.

Rosenberg, Miriam. "Recognizing Gay, Lesbian, and Transgendered Teens in a Child and Adolescent Psychiatry Practice." *Journal of the American Academy of Child and Adolescent Psychiatry* (December 2003): 1517–1521.

Saltzburg, Susan. "Learning that an Adolescent Child Is Gay or Lesbian: The Parent Experience." *Social Work* (January 2004): 109–118.

ORGANIZATIONS

The Gay, Lesbian, Straight Education Network. 121 W. 27th St., Suite 804, New York, NY 10001. Web site: <www.glsen.org>.

Gay-Straight Alliance Network. 160 14th St., San Francisco, CA 94103. Web site: <www.gsanetwork.org>.

KEY TERMS

Adrenal glands—A pair of endocrine glands (glands that secrete hormones directly into the bloodstream) that are located on top of the kidneys. The outer tissue of the glands (cortex) produces several steroid hormones, while the inner tissue (medulla) produces the hormones epinephrine (adrenaline) and norepinephrine.

Coming out—The process by which gays and bisexuals become public or tell others about their sexual orientation.

Gay bashing—Physical or verbal violence directed against homosexuals.

Homophobia—An irrational hatred, disapproval, or fear of homosexuality and homosexuals.

Sexual orientation—The direction of somebody's sexual desire, toward people of the opposite sex (heterosexual or straight) or of the same sex (homosexual or gay), or of both sexes (bisexual).

Sodomy—Anal intercourse.

Transgender—Any person who feels their assigned gender does not completely or adequately reflect their internal gender, such as a biological male who perceives himself to be female.

The Healthy Lesbian, Gay, and Bisexual Students Project. American Psychological Association Education Directorate, 750 First St. NE, Washington, DC 20002. Web site: <www.apa.org/ed/hlgb/>.

Parents, Families, and Friends of Lesbians and Gays. 1726 M St. NW, Suite 400, Washington, DC 20036. Web site: <www.pflag.org>.

WEB SITES

"Gay and Lesbian Youth Network." *Mogenic: Inside and Out,* 2004. Available online at <www.mogenic.com> (accessed October 22, 2004).

Ken R. Wells

Hospitalization

Definition

Hospitalization is admittance to the hospital as a patient.

Purpose

Patients are admitted to the hospital for a variety of reasons, including scheduled tests, procedures, or surgery; emergency medical treatment; administration of medication; or to stabilize or monitor an existing condition.

Description

Preparation

Because no one can predict when a child may face an emergency hospital stay, it is a good idea for all parents to spend some time talking to their children about hospitals. Even though the information presented here is geared toward a planned hospitalization, the communication tips will also prove helpful to parents when their child's hospitalization is emergent.

Parents should describe and explain, as honestly and thoroughly as possible, what will happen to the child in the hospital. Parents should tell their child as much of the truth as he or she can understand. A toy doctor kit can help prepare a child for the experience. There are children's books about hospitalization, written for all age levels, that parents can read to their child before the hospital stay. Parents need to reassure young children, with their limited concept of time, that the hospital stay will be temporary. They can plan a party afterward or read a storybook part way through and mark the place where it will be resumed once the child comes home.

For **preschool** children, explanations should be simple and concrete. It will not ease the child's anxiety to try to explain that he or she will undergo a series of tests or will spend three weeks in the hospital. Instead, the parent might indicate the part or parts of the body that are to be "fixed," using a doll or stuffed animal.

By the time children reach five or six years of age, they can understand hospitalization on a more sophisticated level. They will be familiar with some medical instruments and concepts, and better able to grasp the time frame involved. Children of this age may feel they are going to the hospital because they have done something wrong, and parents need to reassure their child that hospitalization is not a punishment.

Teens should be given an honest explanation of what to expect during their hospital stay. They should be included in the discussions about their care. They also should be encouraged to ask their health care providers questions.

Overall, the best reassurance parents can give children of any age is the promise that they will be there to help them through the experience, even if they cannot be physically present during the entire ordeal. Parents should encourage their child to ask questions and talk about their feelings.

LEARNING ABOUT THE HOSPITAL Many hospitals allow parents and children to tour the pediatric facilities before the hospital stay, further reassuring the child. Children may be shown rooms similar to that in which they will stay. The tour may include a visit to the unit's playroom, a chance to meet the nursing staff, and the opportunity to become familiar with some of the hospital equipment. It is best for parents to be present during these tours, so the child can see that they approve of the facilities and trust the care providers.

Most hospitals provide information to the parents in advance of a planned hospital stay. This information may include directions to the hospital, parking information, and other services available. Parents should take advantage of the services offered during their child's hospital stay, especially support groups or educational classes that provide more information about the child's condition.

For a planned hospital stay, the parents need to contact their insurance company, if insured, to determine if the hospital is covered by their insurance plan. Once a hospitalization date is confirmed, the parents are required to notify the insurance company. If the hospital admission was emergent, the parents should notify the insurance company as soon as possible. Parents also need to review the credentials of the health care providers and hospital, gather information about the hospital, including services offered and specific policies (especially the visitation, boarding, and rooming-in policies), schedule the hospital stay, take the child to complete pre-admission testing, and receive and follow all of the appropriate pre-admission instructions. If certain medications need to be discontinued before the hospital stay, the hospital staff will notify the parents or send a complete list of medications to avoid.

MAKING SURE THE CHILD IS HEALTHY It is important for the child to be as healthy as possible before a planned hospitalization. The child should eat healthy foods, and rest and **exercise** as normal, unless given other instructions. The child needs to get extra **sleep** before the hospitalization, since his or her normal sleep patterns will likely be disrupted during the hospital stay. If the child has a **fever**, **cough**, or cold, the parents should call the child's doctor to determine if the hospitalization should be delayed.

PACKING FOR THE HOSPITAL STAY The child should help the parent pack items for the hospital stay. It is helpful to pack familiar pajamas, **toys**, games, a special **family** photo, and other belongings that will provide comfort. Personal items should be labeled with the child's name. Valuables should be left at home.

Children should not bring latex (rubber) balloons to the hospital, as they can be a serious **safety** hazard, as well as a health hazard for children with a latex allergy. Shiny, metallic balloons (Mylar) are usually permitted. Parents should check the hospital's policies before packing any electronic items, such as **video games** or hair dryers. Some items may cause interference with the hospital equipment. Also, parents should check the specific unit's policy for bringing fresh flowers or plants. In most cases, bringing food from home is not permitted since certain foods may be restricted and the child's specific dietary intake may need to be recorded.

The parents should bring a complete list of the child's medications, medical conditions, and any known **allergies**. The child's medications should remain at home; all necessary medications will be provided in the hospital.

SELECTING A FAMILY SPOKESPERSON Because of privacy regulations established by the Health Insurance Portability and Accountability Act (HIPAA), some hospitals require families to select one spokesperson to communicate with health care providers. The spokesperson helps maintain the patient's privacy and also improves communication with the health care providers. The family spokesperson should be responsible for communicating information about the child's health to outside family members. Families and friends who call the child's nursing unit will not be able to obtain information about the patient, due to privacy regulations.

Aftercare

Before the child leaves the hospital, the health care providers will review discharge instructions with the child and parents. These instructions include incision care, signs of infection or complications to watch for, information on when to call the doctor, medication guidelines, activity guidelines, dietary restrictions, information about when the child may return to work or school, a follow-up appointment schedule, and other specific instructions as applicable to the patient's condition. Follow-up appointments may be scheduled, and the necessary prescriptions will be given to the parents.

If the child weighs less than 40 lbs (18 kg) or is under four years of age, he or she is required by most state laws to ride home in a safety seat. Parents should remember to bring the car seat with them on the day of the child's hospital discharge.

If health care services will be needed at home (home care), they can be arranged by a social worker or the nursing staff.

Risks

The risks of hospitalization are related to the type of treatment or procedure the child will be having. Every procedure has risks, which the parents should discuss with the child's doctor and health care team. Parents should make sure they understand the potential risks of any procedure prior to signing the informed consent form.

Normal results

Hospital admission

For planned hospitalizations, the parents register their child at the hospital registration or admitting area. For emergency hospital admissions, the parents register their child in the emergency department. The parents are required to complete paperwork and show an insurance card, if insured. Often, a pre-registration process performed before a planned hospitalization makes the registration process on the day of admission run smoothly.

A health care provider will review an informed consent form with the parents, and they will be asked to sign it. Informed consent is an educational process between health care providers and patients or their guardians. Parents are encouraged to ask questions. Before signing the form, the parents should understand the nature and purpose of the child's hospital stay and medical treatment, the risks and benefits, and alternatives, including the option of not proceeding with the medical treatment. Signing the informed consent form indicates that the parents permit a treatment to be administered to their child.

Upon admission, an identification bracelet that includes the patient's name and doctor's name will be placed on the child's wrist. The child may wear his or her own pajamas, or a hospital gown, depending on the hospital and nursing unit's policy. A nurse usually consults with the parents to learn about the child's dietary restrictions or preferences. Daily menu choices are available.

Hospital room

Usually, the child will share a room with one or more other children, unless a private room was requested or is required for health reasons. A typical feature of children's hospitals or children's hospital units is a playroom where children can interact with others who are undergoing similar experiences.

Most non-intensive care wards allow parents to stay overnight, at least initially, either in a special nearby unit or on a cot or chair in the child's room.

Health care team

Children's units in many hospitals are staffed by at least some nurses who specialize in caring for infants and children and understand their special needs. A children's activities specialist, also called a child life specialist, is usually on staff. This specialist has a background in child development and therapeutic **play**.

A variety of physicians, specialists, nurses, and teachers may make up the child's health care team. Parents should make sure they know who is providing care for their child during the hospital stay.

Hospital routine

The child's daily hospital experience will likely vary each day. The first day may be consumed by tests to determine the proper course of treatment. The health care team will discuss with the parents the anticipated length of stay in the hospital, based on the child's diagnosis.

Some of the typical hospital routines may be as follows: the nurse checks the child's vital signs (blood pressure, temperature, and heart rate) several times throughout the day and night; the attending physician and medical team usually visit in the morning (medical rounds); medications are administered; tests are performed; and meals are provided three times a day. During the entire hospital stay, the child will be made as comfortable as possible. The health care team will provide the parents with as much information as possible about the child's condition, care, and treatment throughout the hospital stay. Parents are encouraged to ask questions.

Most hospitals have designated visiting hours. The hospital staff is usually accommodating to close family members who want to visit at other times. Each hospital has its own visitation policy that should be investigated before the child's hospitalization. Parents should inquire about sibling visitation guidelines. Usually, only the child's parent or guardian may stay in the room with the child after a certain time in the evening. In some cases, the health care team may ask visitors to wait outside the patient's room during a procedure or treatment.

Depending on the reason for the hospital stay, certain medications may be prescribed or restricted. The health care team will provide specific guidelines and provide all necessary medications during the child's hospital stay.

Many children's hospitals will assign a teacher to any child able to do some assignments. Social workers can help arrange home-schooling as needed after the child is discharged from the hospital.

Resources for families

Educational classes may be available for family members to learn more about the child's condition and what to expect during the child's recovery at home.

Most hospitals have on-site pharmacies where family members can fill the patient's prescriptions; gift shops; and a cafeteria. Usually a list of on-site and off-site dining options can be obtained from the hospital's information desk or social work department.

Parental concerns

Before they can reassure their children, parents need to deal with their own fears about the impending experience. It may be easy for parents to unintentionally communicate these fears to the child. The parents should learn all they can about their child's condition and about the hospital, the child's health care team, and available services.

Even with preparation and support, it is normal for children to experience certain fears when they are hospitalized. The most common **fear** is **separation anxiety**. The hospital is a frightening place full of unfamiliar sights, sounds, and people, and the child's primary source of security and reassurance is a parent. Many young children have never spent even a single night away from their parents, and if the parents leave for the night, especially at the beginning of a hospital stay, a child can easily fear that they will never return. Even a parent's short absence during the day can prove upsetting to a child. Once the child has become familiar with the hospital environment and personnel, the parents can encourage attachments to particular staff members or playmates to prevent the child from feeling abandoned during periods when the parents must be away.

In addition to separation anxiety, it is common for hospitalized children to fear injury or even death. Children may or may not verbalize these fears. Besides comforting their children simply by their presence, parents can also help them cope by trying as much as possible to help the child feel he or she has some control over things, such as what toys to play with, or what to eat or wear. Parents should answer their child's questions as honestly and thoroughly as possible.

Children may cope with their emotions by being withdrawn or aggressive, or they may have an unnatural

KEY TERMS

Anesthesia—Treatment with medicine that causes a loss of feeling, especially pain. Local anesthesia numbs only part of the body; general anesthesia causes loss of consciousness.

Anesthesiologist—A medical specialist who has special training and expertise in the delivery of anesthetics.

Attending physician—The doctor who is in charge of the patient's overall care and treatment in the hospital. This doctor may or may not be the child's primary physician.

Case manager—A professional who designs and monitors implementation of comprehensive care plans (i.e., services addressing medical, financial, housing, psychiatric, vocational, social needs) for individuals seeking mental health or social services.

Clinical nurse specialist—A nurse with advanced training as well as a master's degree.

Discharge planner—A health care professional who helps parents arrange for health and home care needs after their child goes home from the hospital.

Electrocardiagram (ECG, EKG)—A record of the electrical activity of the heart, with each wave being labeled as P, Q, R, S, and T waves. It is often used in the diagnosis of cases of abnormal cardiac rhythm and myocardial damage.

Financial counselor—Professional who can provide assistance with financial matters associated with the patient's hospital stay. The financial counselor can help families evaluate their insurance plan's hospitalization coverage, determine a payment plan for medical expenses that are not covered, and discuss possible sources of financial aid.

General anesthesia—Deep sleep induced by a combination of medicines that allows surgery to be performed.

Home care—Health care services provided in the patient's home. If home health services will be needed after the patient is discharged, they can be arranged by the social worker or nursing staff.

Inpatient surgery—Surgery that requires an overnight stay of one or more days in the hospital. The number of days spent in the hospital after surgery depends on the type of procedure performed.

Local anesthesia—Pain-relieving medication used to numb an area while the patient remains awake. Also see general anesthesia.

Nursing unit—The floor or section of the hospital where patient rooms are located.

Nutrition therapy—Nutrition assessment, counseling, and education, usually provided by registered dietitians.

Outpatient surgery—Also called same-day or ambulatory surgery. The patient arrives for surgery and returns home on the same day. Outpatient surgery can take place in a hospital, surgical center, or outpatient clinic.

Patient education—Instruction and information that helps patients prepare for a procedure, learn about a disease, or manage their health. Patient education may include one-on-one instruction from a health care provider, educational sessions in a group setting, or self-guided learning videos or modules. Informative and instructional handouts are usually provided to explain specific medications, tests, or procedures.

Patient rights and responsibilities—Every hospital has an established list of patient rights and responsibilities, established by the American Hospital Association. They are usually posted throughout the hospital.

Pediatric intensivist—A physician who completed a three-year residency in pediatrics after medical school and an additional subspecialty fellowship training in intensive care.

Regional anesthesia—Blocking of specific nerve pathways through the injection of an anesthetic agent into a specific area of the body.

Registered nurses—Specially trained nurses who provide care during the patient's hospital stay. Registered nurses provide health care, administer medications, monitor the patient's condition, and educate the patient.

Social worker—Health care professional available to help patients and families manage the changes that may occur as a result of the patient's hospitalization. Socials workers provide referrals to community resources and can help the family make arrangements for care in the home as necessary after the patient is discharged from the hospital.

degree of obedience stemming from the fear that if they are "bad," worse things will happen. All of these emotions are normal and generally transient reactions that do not cause any long-lasting emotional harm.

It is common for children to experience some developmental regression in response to being hospitalized, either during the experience or after they come home. Often, they temporarily lose a recent advance, such as staying dry at night or overcoming certain fears. It can be helpful for children to cope with their feelings about hospitalization once they are home by playing with dolls and other toys. A doctor kit, selected to help prepare for the hospitalization, is sometimes very helpful in replaying children's reactions once they return home.

Whether planned or on an emergency basis, hospitalization causes disruption in the life of any child. However, with the special accommodations that hospitals usually make for children and their parents, a stay in the hospital need not be a traumatic event. If children receive proper support from family members and the hospital staff, hospitalization can even make them feel proud for having successfully negotiated a challenge to their maturity, self-discipline, and courage.

Resources

BOOKS FOR CHILDREN

Bridwell, Norman. *Clifford Visits the Hospital.* For children ages four to eight years. New York: Cartwheel Books/ Scholastic, 2000.

Jennings, Sharon, et al. *Franklin Goes to the Hospital.* New York: Scholastic, 2000.

Rey, Margaret, and H.A. Rey. *Curious George Goes to the Hospital.* New York: Scholastic, 1974.

Rogers, Fred, and Jim Judkis. *Going to the Hospital.* Itasca, Illinois: Putnam Publishing Group, Reprint Edition, 1997.

BOOKS FOR PARENTS

"Planning a hospital stay." In *The Gale Encyclopedia of Surgery.* Detroit: Gale Group, 2003.

"Preoperative Care." In *Mosby's Medical, Nursing and Allied Health Dictionary.* 5 (1998): 7033.

Schaefer, Charles E., and Theresa Foy DiGeronimo. *How to Talk to Your Kids About Really Important Things: Specific Questions and Answers and Useful Things to Say.* 1st ed. Indianapolis, Indiana: Jossey-Bass, 1999.

ORGANIZATIONS

Agency for Health Care Policy and Research (AHCPR). Publications Clearinghouse P.O. Box 8547, Silver Spring, MD 20907. (800) 358-9295. Web site: <www/ahcpr.gov>.

American Hospital Association One North Franklin, Chicago, IL 60606. (312) 422-3000. Web site: <www.hospitalconnect.com>.

Association for the Care of Children's Health. 7910 Woodmont Ave., Suite 300, Bethesda, MD 20814. (301) 654-6549.

Joint Commission on Accreditation of Healthcare Organizations (JCAHO) One Renaissance Boulevard, Oakbrook Terrace, IL 60181. (630) 792-5800. Web site: <www.jcaho.org>.

WEB SITES

KidsHealth. Available online at: <www.kidshealth.org>.

Salo, David, M.D., Ph.D. "Hospital Admissions." Emedicine Consumer Health. 2003. Available online at: <www.emedicinehealth.com/fulltext/11983.htm>.

Angela M. Costello

Human bite infections

Definition

Human bite infections are potentially serious injuries that develop when a person's teeth break the skin of the hand or other body part and introduce saliva containing disease organisms below the skin surface.

Description

There are three common types of injuries caused by human **bites**:

- Closed-fist injuries: These are injuries to the hand sustained in a fight when the skin over the knuckles is broken and penetrated by the teeth in the opponent's mouth.

- Occlusional or chomping injuries: This type of injury results when a person bites down hard on another person's ear, nose, or finger.

- Avulsion injuries: Avulsion is the medical term for a ripping or tearing of the skin or body part. Human bites on the head and neck may cause avulsion injuries to the ears, nose, cheeks, or scalp.

Demographics

Exact statistics on human bite **wounds** are difficult to establish, although one figure for closed-fist bites in the United States is 11.8 per 100,000 persons per year. Bite injuries account for about 1 percent of emergency room admissions in the United States and Canada, with human bites ranked third after dog and cat bites respectively. About 70 percent of all human bite wounds reported in North America involve adolescent males or adult males below the age of 40.

Closed-fist and chomping injuries account for most human bite infections. In one study done in a California hospital, closed-fist injuries accounted for 56 percent of the human bite infections treated, with the remaining 44 percent caused by occlusional bites.

Causes and symptoms

Causes

In children, bite infections result either from accidents during **play** or from fighting. Toddlers often bite one another when they are roughhousing; however, they usually do not bite hard enough to cause serious injury. Deep bite wounds on a young child may indicate abuse by an adolescent or adult.

Most infected human bites in adolescents and adults result from fighting, and some are inflicted on police officers or institutional staff. Alcohol or drug intoxication is an additional factor in closed-fist injuries.

The structure of the human hand contributes to the frequency with which closed-fist bites are likely to become infected. When a person closes the hand to make a fist, a tendon known as the extensor tendon is stretched. When the person hits the teeth in another person's mouth hard enough to break the skin, bacteria from the saliva in the mouth get into the tendon and its overlying sheath. After the hand is opened, the extensor tendon relaxes and returns to its normal position underneath the skin, but it is now carrying bacteria with it. The bacteria can then invade tissues that are very difficult to cleanse when the person finally seeks medical help. A similar chain of events is involved in infections of chomping injuries. Like the back of the hand, the fingers also have tendons lying just below the skin. A chomping bite that is hard enough to break the skin can also introduce bacteria into the finger tendons or their sheaths.

The infection itself can be caused by a number of bacteria that live in the human mouth. These include streptococci, staphylococci, anaerobic organisms, *Prevotella melaninogenica*, *Fusobacterium nucleatum*, *Candida spp.* and *Eikenella corrodens*. Infections that begin less than 24 hours after the injury are usually produced by a mixture of organisms and can produce a necrotizing infection (causing the death of a specific area of tissue), in which tissue is rapidly destroyed.

Symptoms

The most common sign of infection from a human bite is inflammation, which usually develops within eight to 24 hours following the bite. The skin around the wound is red and feels warm, and the wound may ooze pus or a whitish discharge. Nearby lymph glands may be swollen, and there may be red streaks running up the arm or leg from the wound toward the center of the body. Complications can arise if the infection is not treated and spreads into deeper structures or into the bloodstream.

Live disease-causing bacteria within the bloodstream and tissues may cause complications far from the wound site, including transmission of **HIV infection**. Deep bites or bites near joints can damage joints and bones, causing inflammation of the bone and bone marrow, necrotizing fasciitis, or septic arthritis.

When to call the doctor

Parents should call the doctor or take the child to the emergency room for examination and treatment of any human bite severe enough to break the skin, no matter what part of the body is affected. Even wounds that appear to be minor abrasion-type injuries may prove to be deeper puncture wounds when the doctor examines them.

Diagnosis

In most cases the diagnosis is made by an emergency room doctor on the basis of the patient's history.

The medical examination involves taking the history of the injury and assessing the type of wound and damage. The child's record of **tetanus** immunization and general health status are checked. An x ray may be ordered to assess bone damage and to check for **foreign objects** in the wound. In the case of a closed-fist injury, there may be fragments of teeth present in the wound. Wound cultures are done for infected bites if the victim is at high risk for complications or if the infection does not respond to treatment. If the child was bitten severely on the head, the emergency room doctor will call in a neurologist for consultation, particularly if the eyes, ears, or neck were injured or the skull was penetrated. Young children are particularly at risk for infection of puncture wounds from bites on the head because the skin on the scalp and forehead is relatively thin and soft. The doctor may also consult a plastic surgeon if the bites are extensive, if large pieces of tissue have been lost or if the functioning or appearance of the injured part of the body is likely to be affected.

Because the human mouth contains a variety of bacteria, the doctor may order a laboratory culture in order to choose the most effective antibiotic. Cultures are most commonly done when the wound has begun to show signs of infection.

Treatment

Treatment depends on the wound type, its site, and such other risk factors for infection as the condition of the patient's immune system. All wounds from human bites are cleaned and disinfected as thoroughly as possible. The doctor will begin by injecting a local anesthetic in order to examine the wound thoroughly without causing additional **pain** to the child. The next step is to remove dead tissue, foreign matter, and blood clots, all of which can become sources of infection. This removal is called debridement. After debriding the wound, the doctor will cut away the edges of the tissue, as clean edges heal faster and are less likely to form scar tissue. The doctor will then irrigate, or flush, the wound with saline solution forced through a syringe.

Doctors do not usually suture a bite wound on the hand because the connective tissues and other structures in the hand form many small closed spaces that make it easy for infection to spread. Emergency room doctors often consult surgical specialists if a patient has a deep closed-fist injury or one that appears already infected.

Bites on the ear are also difficult to treat because the cartilage in the ear does not have a good blood supply. If the cartilage has been exposed by the bite, the doctor will administer intravenous **antibiotics** for 48 hours and delay closing the wound for 24 hours or longer following the injury.

The doctor will make sure that the patient is immunized against tetanus, which is routine procedure for any open wound. Because of risk of infection, all patients with human bite wounds should be given antibiotics. The usual choice for human bite wounds on the hand is a first-generation cephalosporin and either penicillin or amoxicillin-clavulanate (Augmentin). If the child has a weakened immune system, the doctor will prescribe either amoxicillin or erythromycin. Patients with severe closed-fist injuries may need inpatient treatment in addition to an intravenous antibiotic.

Prognosis

The prognosis depends on the location of the bite and whether it was caused by a child or an adult. Bites caused by children rarely become infected because they are usually shallow. Between 15 and 30 percent of bites caused by adults become infected, with a higher rate for closed-fist injuries.

The prognosis for restoring the function or appearance of a hand, ear, or other body part following a severe bite depends on the location of the bite, the promptness of treatment, and the availability of specialized surgical repair. Infections of the hand have a high rate of permanent scarring, tissue damage, and loss of function when treatment is delayed.

Prevention

Prevention of human bite infections depends upon prompt treatment of any bite caused by a human being, particularly a closed-fist injury. Long-term prevention, particularly in young males, requires teaching children how to resolve arguments or quarrels without resorting to violence.

Parental concerns

Biting is fairly normal behavior in toddlers and rarely reflects intentional malice. Children in this age group sometimes bite one another because they are overstimulated or tired or because they have not yet learned to use words to express their feelings. Suggestions for preventing biting in young children include scheduling naps after highly stimulating activities, giving the child a washcloth or similar object to bite, and observing the child to see whether a particular person or situation is triggering the biting behavior. As has been mentioned earlier, toddlers' bites are rarely severe enough to cause a serious infection unless the bitten child has a weakened immune system.

Parental concerns for older children and adolescents include the possibility that the child is abusing drugs or alcohol, has a **conduct disorder**, or is being bullied, as well as fears of disfigurement or lasting injury from an infected bite on the face or hand.

See also Animal bite infections.

Resources

BOOKS

"Infections Caused by Bites." Section 5, Chapter 61 in *The Merck Manual of Diagnosis and Therapy*, edited by Mark H. Beers and Robert Berkow. Whitehouse Station, NJ: Merck Research Laboratories, 2002.

KEY TERMS

Avulsion—The forcible separation of a piece from the entire structure.

Closed-fist injury—A hand wound caused when the skin of the fist is torn open by contact with teeth.

Debridement—The surgical removal of dead tissue and/or foreign bodies from a wound or cut.

Fasciitis—Inflammation of the fascia (plural, fasciae), which refers to bands or sheaths of connective tissue that cover, support, or connect the muscles and internal organs. Human bites can lead to infection of the fasciae in the hand.

Fight bite—Another name for closed-fist injury.

Irrigation—Cleansing a wound with large amounts of water and/or an antiseptic solution. Also refers to the technique of removing wax (cerumen) from the ear canal by flushing it with water.

Necrotizing—Causing the death of a specific area of tissue. Human bites frequently cause necrotizing infections.

Occlusional—Referring to a type of injury caused by the closing of the teeth on a finger or other body part. Occlusional injuries are also called chomping injuries.

PERIODICALS

Stierman, K. L., et al. "Treatment and Outcome of Human Bites in the Head and Neck." *Otolaryngology and Head and Neck Surgery* 128 (June 2003): 795–801.

Talan, D. A., et al. "Clinical Presentation and Bacteriologic Analysis of Infected Human Bites in Patients Presenting to Emergency Departments." *Clinical Infectious Diseases* 37 (December 1, 2003): 1481–89.

ORGANIZATIONS

American Academy of Emergency Medicine (AAEM). 555 East Wells Street, Suite 1100, Milwaukee, WI 53202. Web site: <www.aaem.org>.

Centers for Disease Control and Prevention. 1600 Clifton Rd., NE, Atlanta, GA 30333. Web site: <www.cdc.gov>.

WEB SITES

McNamara, Robert M. "Bites, Human." *eMedicine*, August 23, 2004. Available online at <www.emedicine.com/emerg/topic61.htm> (accessed November 10, 2004).

Rebecca Frey, PhD

Hunter's syndrome *see* **Mucopolysaccharidoses**

Hurler's syndrome *see* **Mucopolysaccharidoses**

Hyaline membrane disease *see* **Respiratory distress syndrome**

Hydrocephalus

Definition

Hydrocephalus is an abnormal expansion of cavities, called ventricles, within the brain, which is caused by an abnormally large accumulation of cerebrospinal fluid (**CSF**).

Description

Hydrocephalus is the result of an imbalance between the formation and drainage of CSF. There are four ventricles in the human brain. CSF is formed by structures within these ventricles. Once formed, CSF circulates among all the ventricles before it is absorbed and returned to the circulatory system. When the ventricles are obstructed, the CSF cannot circulate and be absorbed. An elevated level of CSF in the brain leads to pressure within the ventricles. This pressure pushes against the soft tissues of the brain, resulting in damage to these tissues.

There are three different types of hydrocephalus: communicating hydrocephalus, noncommunicating hydrocephalus, and normal pressure hydrocephalus. Communicating hydrocephalus is the most common type and exists when one or more passages connecting the ventricles become blocked. This blockage prevents the movement of CSF to its drainage sites in the subarachnoid space just inside the skull. In noncommunicating hydrocephalus, the tissue within the brain responsible for absorption of CSF is damaged. Normal pressure hydrocephalus is marked by ventricle enlargement without an apparent increase in CSF pressure. This type affects mainly the elderly and will not be discussed in this entry.

Hydrocephalus may be either congenital (present at birth) or acquired. An obstruction within the brain is the most frequent cause of congenital hydrocephalus. Acquired hydrocephalus may result from other birth defects such as **spina bifida**, conditions related to **prematurity** such as intraventricular hemorrhage (bleeding

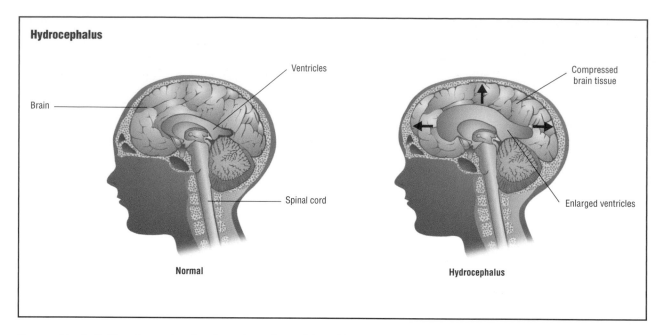

Hydrocephalus

Brain

Ventricles

Spinal cord

Normal

Compressed brain tissue

Enlarged ventricles

Hydrocephalus

A normal brain (left) and one showing the enlarged ventricles of hydrocephalus. The additional fluid in the ventricles causes increased pressure on the brain. *(Illustration by GGS Information Services.)*

within the brain), infections such as **meningitis**, or other causes such as head trauma, tumors, and cysts.

Demographics

Hydrocephalus is believed to occur in approximately one to two of every 1,000 live births. It is not more prevalent in males or females, nor in any individual racial group.

Causes and symptoms

Hydrocephalus has a variety of causes including the following:

- congenital brain defects
- hemorrhage, either into the ventricles or the subarachnoid space
- infection of the central nervous system (syphilis, herpes, meningitis, **encephalitis**, or mumps)
- tumor

Signs and symptoms of elevated-pressure hydrocephalus include the following:

- headache
- nausea and **vomiting**, especially in the morning
- lethargy
- disturbances in walking (gait)
- double vision

- subtle difficulties in learning and memory
- delay in achieving childhood developmental milestones

Irritability is the most common sign of hydrocephalus in infants. If this is not treated, it may lead to lethargy. Bulging of the fontanelles, or the soft spots between the skull bones, may also be an early sign. When hydrocephalus occurs in infants, fusion of the skull bones is prevented, which leads to abnormal expansion of the skull.

Diagnosis

Imaging studies such as x ray, **computed tomography** scan (CT scan), ultrasound, and especially **magnetic resonance imaging** (MRI) are used to assess the presence and location of obstructions, as well as changes in brain tissue that have occurred as a result of the hydrocephalus. Lumbar puncture (spinal tap) may be performed to aid in determining the cause when infection is suspected.

Treatment

The primary method of treatment for hydrocephalus is surgical installation of a shunt. A shunt is a tube connecting the ventricles of the brain to an alternative drainage site, usually the abdominal cavity. A shunt contains a one-way valve to prevent reverse flow of fluid. In some cases of non-communicating hydrocephalus, a direct connection can be made between one of the ventricles and the subarachnoid space, allowing drainage without a shunt.

Installation of a shunt requires lifelong monitoring by the recipient or **family** members for signs of recurring hydrocephalus due to obstruction or failure of the shunt. Other than monitoring, no other management activity is usually required.

Some drugs may postpone the need for surgery by inhibiting the production of CSF. These include acetazolamide and furosemide. Other drugs that are used to delay surgery are glycerol, digoxin, and isosorbide.

Prognosis

The prognosis for elevated-pressure hydrocephalus depends on a wide variety of factors, including the cause, age of onset, and the timing of surgery. Studies indicate that about half of all children who receive appropriate treatment and follow-up will develop IQs greater than 85. Those with hydrocephalus at birth do better than those with later onset due to meningitis. For individuals with normal pressure hydrocephalus, approximately half will benefit by the installation of a shunt.

Prevention

There is no known prevention of congenital hydrocephalus. Some cases of elevated pressure hydrocephalus may be avoided by preventing or treating the infectious diseases that precede them. Prenatal diagnosis of congenital brain malformation is often possible, offering the option of family planning.

Parental concerns

Parents may be concerned about the intellectual development of a child with hydrocephalus. While nearly 50 percent of all children with hydrocephalus have average **intelligence**, many do not. Early intervention programs are important to the development of children with special needs and are available in most communities. In addition to developmental issues, many children with hydrocephalus require medical care. It is important for parents to prepare children for medical treatment and surgery. A healthcare team including a pediatrician, surgeon, and social worker is a valuable asset for parents and most children's hospitals can assist parents in finding the support and resources they need.

When to call the doctor

The most common treatment for hydrocephalus is the surgical installation of a shunt. If a child with a shunt has any of the following symptoms, parents should contact the child's doctor because the shunt may not be func-

> ## KEY TERMS
>
> **Cerebrospinal fluid**—The clear, normally colorless fluid that fills the brain cavities (ventricles), the subarachnoid space around the brain, and the spinal cord and acts as a shock absorber.
>
> **Choroid plexus**—Specialized cells located in the ventricles of the brain that produce cerebrospinal fluid.
>
> **Fontanelle**—One of several "soft spots" on the skull where the developing bones of the skull have yet to fuse.
>
> **Shunt**—A passageway (or an artificially created passageway) that diverts blood flow from one main route to another. Also refers to a small tube placed in a ventricle of the brain to direct cerebrospinal fluid away from a blockage into another part of the body.
>
> **Ventricles**—Four cavities within the brain that produce and maintain the cerebrospinal fluid that cushions and protects the brain and spinal cord.

tioning properly. According to the Spina Bifida Association of America, nearly 40 percent of shunts malfunction and may need to be replaced within one year, 60 percent will require revision within five years, and 80 to 90 percent within ten years.

For this reason, parents need to be aware of the symptoms of shunt malfunction and contact their physician if they notice any of the following symptoms:

- headaches
- nausea
- vomiting
- seizures
- change in intellect or personality
- swallowing problems
- impaired muscle function, balance, or coordination

Resources

BOOKS

Cinalli, G., et al. *Hydrocephalus.* New York: Springer, 2004.

PERIODICALS

"Hydrocephalus." *Review of Optometry* 137, no. 8 (August 15, 2000): 56A.

ORGANIZATIONS

Hydrocephalus Foundation Inc. (HyFI). 910 Rear Broadway, Saugus, MA 01906. Web site: <www.hydrocephalus>.

WEB SITES

"Hydrocephalus." *American Association of Neurological Surgeons/Congress of Neurological Surgeons.* Available online at <www.neurosurgery.org/pubpages/patres/hydrobroch.html> (accessed October 22, 2004).

"Hydrocephalus." *Hyman-Newman Institute of Neurology and Neurosurgery.* Available online at <http://nyneurosurgery.org> (accessed October 22, 2004).

L. Fleming Fallon, MD, PhD, DrPH
Deborah L. Nurmi, MS

Hyperbilirubinemia *see* **Jaundice**

Hyperglycemia

Definition

Hyperglycemia is a complex metabolic condition characterized by abnormally high levels of blood sugar (blood glucose) in circulating blood, usually as a result of **diabetes mellitus** (types 1 and 2), although it can sometimes occur in **cystic fibrosis** and **near-drowning** (submersion injury).

Description

Hyperglycemia, also known as diabetic ketoacidosis, is a condition that develops over a period of a few days as the blood glucose levels of a type 1 or type 2 diabetic gradually rise. Ketoacidosis occurs when increasing glucose levels are met by a lack of sufficient or effective insulin production, starting a sequence of physiologic events as follows:

- The combination of excess glucose production and low glucose utilization in the body raises levels of blood glucose, which leads to increased urinary output (diuresis) followed quickly by a loss of fluid and essential mineral salts (electrolytes) and, ultimately, **dehydration**. The loss of fluid may finally result in dehydration. If the entire process is severe enough over several hours (serum glucose levels over 800mg/dL), swelling can occur in the brain (cerebral edema), and coma can eventually result.

- In a metabolic shift to a catabolic (breaking down) process, cells throughout the body empty their electrolytes (sodium, potassium, and phosphate) into the bloodstream. Electrolytes control the fluid balance of the body and are important in muscle contraction, energy generation, and almost all major biochemical reactions in the body. As a result of electrolyte imbalance, many functions can become impaired.

- Free fatty acids from lipid stores are increased, encouraging the production of ketoacids in the liver, leading to an over-acidic condition (metabolic acidosis) that causes even more disruption in body processes.

Without effective treatment of the hyperglycemic episode, the child can lapse into a diabetic coma, which sometimes leads to death.

In diabetes type 2, which is characterized by insulin resistance, enhanced glucose production in the liver and decreased insulin secretion can be aggravated by low physical activity and/or a high-calorie, high-fat diet. Over time as glucose production accelerates, the child develops hyperglycemia or glucotoxicity and lipotoxicity (hyperlipidemia or high fat levels in the blood) as well. It is primarily thought to be a disease affecting sedentary, obese adults over age 40, but it is found in young people as well, most of them obese at the time of diagnosis. Pediatric type 2 diabetes is increasing in the early 2000s among adolescents and has become the fastest growing form of diabetes. Therefore, hyperglycemic episodes are also noted to be increasing in frequency among young people admitted to hospitals for treatment of diabetes.

Demographics

The incidence of hyperglycemia approximately parallels the incidence of diabetes type 1 cases, which represents about 70 percent of all diabetes cases (17 million Americans diagnosed) in the United States. It occurs more in whites than blacks or Asians. About 30 percent of all new cases of diabetes are children with diabetes type 2. Diabetes type 2 occurs more often in African American youth but also in Native Americans, white Americans, and Hispanic youth between ages 10 and 19. Those with type 2 have fewer symptoms and are not treated as frequently for hyperglycemia.

Causes and symptoms

Diabetes is a chronic metabolic disorder with hyperglycemia, gradually rising levels of glucose, as its primary characteristic. As diabetes develops and symptoms increase, hyperglycemia becomes progressive but will occur only occasionally in the carefully managed diabetic patient. Hyperglycemia can be triggered by irregular self-administration of insulin, by insulin resistance or defective insulin response in the body, by stress or infection, and by the activation of certain autoimmune processes characteristic of type 1 diabetes. It occurs in 20 to 40 percent of children newly diagnosed with diabetes and in children who are not yet successfully managed. Many young type 2 diabetics do not have symptoms because their hyperglycemia is moderate compared to type 1 diabetics, and they are not taking insulin.

The first signs of hyperglycemia or ketoacidosis are frequent urination and increased thirst. The child may then show any of the following symptoms:

- flushed face
- dry skin
- dry mouth
- **headache**
- abdominal **pain**
- **nausea and vomiting**
- drowsiness and lethargy
- blurred vision
- fruity-smelling breath
- rapid heartbeat
- deep and labored breathing

When to call the doctor

The pediatrician or **family** doctor should be consulted about any sudden change in the child's urinary output, frequency of urination, or increased thirst, especially if accompanied by dry skin or mouth, flushed face, headache, abdominal pain, nausea or vomiting, unusual drowsiness and lack of movement, rapid heartbeat, or difficulty breathing. Parents should be aware of the last insulin injection if the child is on insulin therapy.

Diagnosis

Hyperglycemia can be diagnosed fairly quickly in known diabetic children. The non-fasting serum glucose will exceed 200mg/dL with classic symptoms such as increased urination, extreme thirst, dry skin or mouth, flushed face, headache, abdominal pain, nausea or vomiting, unusual drowsiness and lack of movement, rapid heartbeat, or difficulty breathing. If elevated glucose levels are present, the doctor will want to determine if ketoacidosis is also present by measuring levels of ketones in the blood serum and urine. Electrolyte levels will be measured along with carbon dioxide and pH and serum osmolality, which may indicate hypertonic dehy-

dration. Routine screening of blood glucose levels and glucose tolerance tests is not recommended in children; symptoms are believed to help confirm hyperglycemia more readily. It is also not considered necessary to test non-obese children for autoimmune antibodies, which are more apt to be found in adult type 2 diabetics.

Treatment

Treatment for hyperglycemia must be delivered carefully and with close monitoring to avoid the risk of hypokalemia (higher than normal serum levels of potassium) and subsequent cerebral edema. Treatment will take place over a period of several days, including administration of insulin, usually in combination with administration of intravenous fluids and salts to restore fluid and electrolyte balance. Fluid intake and output is carefully monitored, and serum electrolytes are tested hourly or even more frequently to make sure balance is restored to support normal metabolic activity in the body. Children must be rehydrated very gradually; this can be done orally in mild hyperglycemia and over an extended period (30 to 36 hours) of intravenous administration with severe hyperglycemia. Administration of insulin helps move glucose back into cells, reduces glucose production by the liver, and stops the release of fatty acids. Insulin injections, while helping to normalize glucose production, also increase the risk of hypokalemia and abnormally low levels of glucose in the blood (**hypoglycemia**), the opposite of the hyperglycemic condition being corrected. Glucose is sometimes infused with the insulin to help avoid hypoglycemia. The insulin infusion will be slowed once hyperglycemia has been corrected (blood glucose levels less than 250mg/dL); in children with moderate hyperglycemia, this can often be accomplished within 24 hours. It may take several days, however, to restore normal cellular levels of potassium, sodium, and phosphate. The acidosis will be reversed, reflected in a gradual increase in pH.

In severe cases of hyperglycemia in which cerebral edema occurs, mannitol is administered at the first sign of edema, such as unconsciousness, difficulty breathing, severe headache, irregular heartbeat, or seizures. Changes can occur very rapidly. Children with moderate to severe hyperglycemia may be treated in an intensive care unit for continuous monitoring and rapid response capabilities.

In rare instances, a child may have a hyperglycemic episode that is triggered by a stressful situation or a physically challenging situation such as another illness. Transient hyperglycemia can be triggered by any type of stress that overtaxes the child's mental and physical resources. Stress hyperglycemia may be reversed completely when the stressors are removed or relieved. Temporary hyperglycemia of this type will still require careful monitoring for symptoms and testing and treatment as above if any symptoms occur.

Alternative treatment

Although alternative treatment for diabetes includes taking chromium picolinate to improve the efficiency of insulin in glucose metabolism and coenzyme Q10 to improve blood circulation and stabilize blood glucose levels, hyperglycemia and diabetic ketoacidosis require immediate measures such as insulin injections and rehydration and cannot be treated by nutritional means.

Nutritional concerns

Nutritional therapy along with insulin therapy can both help avoid hyperglycemia and relieve associated symptoms. Immediate medical attention is needed, however, and parents should not undertake correction of hyperglycemia or dehydration on their own. Basic nutritional requirements for children with diabetes can be provided by the pediatrician, based on the child's age, sex, weight, activity levels, food preferences, and ethnic or cultural factors. The recommended diet for those with diabetes calls for complex carbohydrates such as whole (unrefined) whole grains, plenty of fresh vegetables and fruits, with an overall intake of foods that are low in fat and high in fiber. This diet reduces the need for insulin and lowers fat levels in the blood, all helping to stabilize glucose levels.

Prognosis

The prognosis for children with mild to moderate hyperglycemia is good; the condition can usually be corrected within 24 hours. Severe hyperglycemia (serum glucose levels in the range of 800mg/dL) may lead to cerebral edema, coma, and death if not treated immediately. Hyperglycemia in children during severe illness is a risk factor for poor outcomes in the underlying illness and has been reported as a cause of increased mortality in pediatric intensive care units. Morbidity (the incidence of other diseases) and mortality are higher in adults than in children because of long-term complications that include vascular conditions, circulatory problems, nervous system disorders, liver problems, and heart disease.

Prevention

Occurrences of hyperglycemia can be prevented by careful monitoring of blood glucose levels and insulin injections while balancing **exercise** and diet. Diabetic adolescents are especially susceptible to hyperglycemia, since hormone levels are in flux and many adolescents exhibit erratic eating and sleeping patterns. Athletic activities can be beneficial, since exercise makes use of surplus blood glucose. Obese children must be encouraged to eat properly and to avoid the fats and sugary sweets that can lead to increased weight, decreased mobility, and hyperglycemia.

Nutritional concerns

Nutrition, of course, is important in the treatment of diabetes and accordingly can play a role in preventing hyperglycemic episodes. Diabetic children must avoid sweetened and high-carbohydrate foods such as white flour and white sugar products and generally eat a high-fiber, low-fat diet consisting of whole grains, high quality protein (lean meat, eggs, low-fat dairy), fresh vegetables, and fresh fruits.

Parental concerns

Parents of a diabetic child may live with the uncertainty of possible hyperglycemic episodes but can be reassured by knowing that continuous glucose monitoring, a proper diet as advised by the pediatrician, insulin therapy if prescribed, and appropriate exercise can control the disease and help avoid extremes that lead to hyperglycemia. It is important to maintain close contact with the child's diabetes team of professionals and to learn as much as possible about the disease and the symptoms to watch for in the child that may signal hyperglycemia. The parents of school-age children should make sure that teachers also understand the warning signs of hyperglycemia so that immediate medical attention can be given when needed.

See also Diabetes mellitus.

Resources

BOOKS

American Diabetes Association Complete Guide to Diabetes: The Ultimate Home Reference from the Diabetes Experts, 3rd ed. New York: McGraw-Hill, 2002.

Becker, Gretchen. *The First Year Type 2 Diabetes*. New York: Marlowe, 2001.

Children's Hospital of Philadelphia Guide to Diabetes. New York: John Wiley & Sons, 2004.

ORGANIZATIONS

National Diabetes Education Program. One Diabetes Way, Bethesda, MD 20814–9692. Web site: <www.ndep.nih.gov>.

National Institute of Diabetes & Digestive & Kidney Diseases (NIDDK). NIH Building 31, Room 9A, 4 Center Drive,

KEY TERMS

Antibody—A special protein made by the body's immune system as a defense against foreign material (bacteria, viruses, etc.) that enters the body. It is uniquely designed to attack and neutralize the specific antigen that triggered the immune response.

Autoimmune—Pertaining to an immune response by the body against its own tissues or types of cells.

Cerebral—Pertaining to the brain.

Coma—A condition of deep unconsciousness from which the person cannot be aroused

Diabetes—A disease characterized by an inability to process sugars in the diet, due to a decrease in or total absence of insulin production.

Edema—The presence of abnormally large amounts of fluid in the intercellular tissue spaces of the body.

Electrolytes—Salts and minerals that produce electrically charged particles (ions) in body fluids. Common human electrolytes are sodium chloride, potassium, calcium, and sodium bicarbonate. Electrolytes control the fluid balance of the body and are important in muscle contraction, energy generation, and almost all major biochemical reactions in the body.

Hypertonic saline solution—Fluid that contains salt in a concentration higher than that of healthy blood.

Ketones—Poisonous acidic chemicals produced by the body when fat instead of glucose is burned for energy. Breakdown of fat occurs when not enough insulin is present to channel glucose into body cells.

Metabolic—Refers to the chemical reactions in living organisms.

Osmolality—The concentration of osmolar particles in the blood (or other solutions) that can help determine if the body is dehydrated.

Physiologic—Refers to physiology, particularly normal, healthy, physical functioning.

MSC 2560, Bethesda, MD 20892–2560. Web site: <www.niddk.nih.gov>.

WEB SITES

National Diabetes Information Clearing House (NDIC). Available online at <www.niddk.nih.gov> (accessed October 18, 2004).

L. Lee Culvert

Hyperhidrosis

Definition

Hyperhidrosis is a medical condition characterized by excessive sweating in the armpits, palms, soles of the feet, face, scalp, and/or torso.

Description

Hyperhidrosis involves sweating in excess of the amount required normally for the body's level of activity and temperature. There are two types of hyperhidrosis—primary and secondary. In primary hyperhidrosis, the cause is unknown and excessive sweating is localized in the armpits, hands, face, and/or feet. Primary hyperhidrosis begins during childhood or early **adolescence**, gets worse during **puberty**, and lasts a lifetime. In secondary hyperhidrosis, which is less common than primary hyperhidrosis, excessive sweating is caused by another medical condition and usually occurs over the entire body. Medical conditions that can cause secondary hyperhidrosis include **hyperthyroidism**, menopause, **obesity**, psychiatric disorders, and diabetes. Secondary hyperhidrosis may also be caused by use of certain medications.

In about 60 percent of cases, the hands and feet are affected, and in about 30–40 percent of cases, the armpits are affected.

Demographics

Axillary (underarm) hyperhidrosis occurs more frequently in females and in individuals of Asian or Jewish ancestry. Hyperhidrosis of the hands and feet occurs 20 times more frequently in the Japanese. Previously, it was thought that hyperhidrosis was rare, occurring in only 0.6–1 percent of adolescents and young adults; however, a national survey conducted in 2004 found that up to 2.8 percent of Americans (approximately 7.8 million individuals) may have hyperhidrosis.

Causes and symptoms

The exact cause of hyperhidrosis is as of 2004 unknown. Excessive sweating in the affected area is caused by overactivity of the nerves linked to the sweat glands. Specifically, acetylcholine, a chemical in the body that transmits nerve signals, is released from nerve endings and stimulates secretion of sweat. Genetics may also be a factor, since 25–40 percent of individuals with hyperhidrosis also have a **family** member with the condition.

In hyperhidrosis, sweating may be continuous or start suddenly. Usually, excessive sweating does not occur in response to **exercise** and does not occur during **sleep**. Emotional stress, high room/environmental temperature, and digestion of certain foods can aggravate hyperhidrosis. Symptoms of hyperhidrosis vary depending on the body area affected:

- In palmar hyperhidrosis, the palms of the hands are excessively wet or moist and also cold to the touch.

- In axillary hyperhidrosis, excessive sweating in the underarm area occurs, leaving large wet marks and staining clothes.

- In scalp/facial hyperhidrosis, excessive sweating of the face and scalp occurs, as well as moderate to severe facial blushing.

- In plantar hyperhidrosis, the soles of the feet sweat excessively. This condition is often associated with hyperhidrosis in other body areas.

- In truncal hyperhidrosis, the torso area sweats excessively. This condition is rare alone and usually occurs with hyperhidrosis in other areas.

When to call the doctor

Parents should call the doctor if their child or adolescent experiences excessive sweating unrelated to an obvious medical condition (e.g., high **fever**) or physical exertion. Usually, consultation and treatment will be given by a dermatologist.

Diagnosis

Hyperhidrosis is diagnosed by physical examination. For suspected secondary hyperhidrosis, laboratory and imaging tests may be performed to determine the underlying medical condition causing the hyperhidrosis.

Treatment

Topical agents applied to the skin in the affected area are the first course of treatment for hyperhidrosis. Topical applications include anticholinergic drugs, boric acid, tannic acid solutions, and glutaraldehyde. Drysol, an aluminum chloride solution, is the most commonly used and most effective topical application; it is applied nightly on dry skin. Systemic medications may be taken orally and include anticholinergic drugs, sedatives or tranquilizers, and calcium channel blockers. These oral drugs do have side effects, such as dry mouth and eyes, blurry vision, and **constipation**, and may not be appropriate for pediatric patients.

Iontophoresis, which involves the application of an electrical current across the skin, can be used to treat plantar and palmar hyperhidrosis but requires daily treatment for about 30 minutes, often multiple times daily.

As a last resort, surgery is used to treat palmar, plantar, and axillary hyperhidrosis. Surgical procedures involve removing portions of the nerves responsible for excessive sweating and removing sweat glands during an open or minimally invasive surgical procedure. Liposuction may be used to remove sweat glands in the underarm area.

In 2004, the U.S. Food and Drug Administration approved the use of botulinum toxin (Botox) for treatment of axillary (underarm) hyperhidrosis that resists treatment with topical drugs. Botox is commonly used for cosmetic treatment of wrinkles but is also used to treat neuromuscular problems, including migraine and cervical dystonia. In the early 2000s researchers are also investigating the use of Botox to treat hyperhidrosis of the hands, feet, and face. Although most studies of Botox for hyperhidrosis included adult patients, some physicians use Botox to treat hyperhidrosis in children with some success. Even though Botox has only been approved to treat axillary hyperhidrosis, physicians can legally use Botox "off-label" to treat other affected areas of the body. Botox is injected into the affected area, and one series of injections may last for several months. Botox is a likely treatment when topical applications fail.

In 2004, guidelines were proposed by expert physicians for treating primary hyperhidrosis. Topical treatments followed by Botox if the topical agent fails is recommended for treating axillary and facial hyperhidrosis. For palmar and plantar hyperhidrosis, topical treatment and iontophoresis, followed by Botox are recommended. Surgery is mentioned as an option only for palmar and axillary hyperhidrosis and only as a last resort.

Alternative treatment

Although no evidence has documented an effective alternative treatment for hyperhidrosis, acupuncture, homeopathy, and/or herbal preparations are used by some individuals with hyperhidrosis. A common home remedy involves soaking the affected body parts in home-brewed tea, which contains tannic acid, a natural antiperspirant. Because stress can trigger sweating, relaxation techniques such as **yoga**, massage, and meditation can help with stress reduction.

Prognosis

Hyperhidrosis is not a life-threatening condition. However, it can severely affect quality of life and comfort in social situations. Children and adolescents who receive early treatment have a better quality of life. If left untreated, hyperhidrosis can result in physical, social, and occupational impairments.

Prevention

Hyperhidrosis treatments help to prevent excessive sweating but may not entirely eliminate the condition. Hyperhidrosis can be managed by using simple daily personal hygiene methods, such as the following:

- bathing daily to reduce bacteria
- washing and changing clothes frequently
- changing socks or pantyhose at least twice daily
- airing out shoes and rotating shoes worn each day
- wearing absorbent socks, clothing shields, and natural fabrics
- using antiperspirants in the evening and gently massaging them into the skin
- using foot powders and going barefoot frequently to air out feet

Nutritional concerns

Although no foods cause hyperhidrosis, certain foods and food ingredients can stimulate sweating and should be avoided. These include **caffeine**, alcohol, and spicy foods. Hot beverages, like coffee and hot chocolate, may also increase sweating. Consuming foods with strong odors, such as those containing garlic and onions, should be avoided because it can cause a person's sweat to smell stronger.

Parental concerns

Children and adolescents with hyperhidrosis suffer extreme social embarrassment related to their condition, and hyperhidrosis can result in low **self-esteem**, difficulties in school, and difficulties in and avoidance of social situations. For example, children with palmar hyperhidrosis may have difficulties holding a pen to write, and adolescents may be reluctant to shake or hold hands with others. Children with axillary hyperhidrosis may be made fun of for excessive body odor and sweat stains. Early treatment is essential to improve children's quality of life. Joining a support group or participating in online hyperhidrosis chat groups may help individuals better manage their condition through peer support.

Resources

BOOKS

ABBE Research Division Staff. *Sweat, Sweating, Sweat Gland Problems: Index and Analysis of New Information, Research, and Clinical Results.* Washington, DC: ABBE Publishers Association of Washington, DC, 2003.

Bartone, John C., Sr. *Human Sweat and Sweating, Normal and Abnormal, including Hyperhidrosis and Bromhidrosis, with Index of New Information and Guidebook for Reference and Research.* Washington, DC: ABBE Publishers Association of Washington, DC, 2001.

PERIODICALS

Bhakta, B. B., and S. H. Roussounnis. "Treating Childhood Hyperhidrosis with Botulinum Toxin Type A." *Archives of Disease in Childhood* 86 (January 2002): 68.

Hilton, Lisette. "Stopping Sweat . . . and Soon: Botulinum Toxin Effective for Pediatric Hyperhidrosis." *Dermatology Times*, April 1, 2003.

ORGANIZATIONS

International Hyperhidrosis Society. 18 South 3rd Street Philadelphia, PA 19106. Web site: <www.ihhs.net/index.html>.

WEB SITES

Altman, Rachel. "Hyperhidrosis." *eMedicine*, August 18, 2004. Available online at <www.emedicine.com/derm/topic893.htm> (accessed November 10, 2004).

"National Survey Finds Hyperhidrosis Affects Nearly Three Times as Many People as Previously Thought." *International Hyperhidrosis Society*, August 2, 2004. Available online at <www.ihhs.net/about_hhs/press10.asp> (accessed November 10, 2004).

Jennifer E. Sisk, M.A.

Hyper-IgM syndrome

Definition

Hyper-IgM syndrome is a primary **immunodeficiency** disorder in which the child's body fails to produce certain specific types of antibodies. The term primary means that the disorder is present from birth, in contrast to secondary immunodeficiencies (such as **AIDS**), which are acquired later in life by previously healthy persons. Hyper-IgM syndrome is caused by mutations in a gene or genes in the body's T cells, which are a type of white blood cell or lymphocyte. T cells regulate the production of antibodies, which are protein molecules produced as the first line of the immune system's defense against disease-causing organisms. Hyper-IgM syndrome is also known as hypogammaglobulinemia with hyper IgM.

There are two forms of hyper-IgM syndrome, defined by their patterns of inheritance. The more common of the two, known as X-linked hyper-IgM syndrome (XHIM), is caused by an abnormal gene on the X chromosome and affects only boys. The less common form, autosomal recessive hyper-IgM syndrome (ARHIM), occurs in children who have inherited an abnormal gene from both parents. ARHIM affects girls as well as boys.

Description

Hyper-IgM syndrome appears during the first year of life when the child develops recurrent infections of the respiratory tract that do not respond to standard antibiotic treatment, along with chronic **diarrhea**. Other early symptoms may include enlarged tonsils; swelling of the liver and spleen; enlarged lymph nodes; or opportunistic infections. Children with XHIM are more likely to develop enlarged lymph nodes than children with other primary immunodeficiency disorders. Opportunistic infections are caused by organisms that do not usually cause disease in people with normally functioning immune systems. The most common opportunistic infection in children with XHIM is a lung disease known as *Pneumocystis carinii* **pneumonia** (PCP). Children with either XHIM or ARHIM who are not diagnosed early may show delays in growth and normal weight gain.

Hyper-IgM syndrome is a disorder with a high degree of morbidity, which means that patients diagnosed with it often suffer from other diseases or disorders. The most common morbid conditions associated with XHIM include the following:

- Recurrent and chronic infections of the lungs and sinuses leading to chronic dilation of the bronchi (the larger air passageways) in the lungs. This condition, called bronchiectasis, is marked by frequent attacks of coughing that bring up pus-streaked mucus.

- Chronic diarrhea leading to weight loss and **malnutrition**. The diarrhea is usually caused by opportunistic infections of the digestive tract; the most common disease agents are *Cryptosporidium parvum*, *Giardia lamblia*, *Campylobacter*, or rotaviruses.

- Frequent mouth ulcers, skin infections, and inflammation of the area around the rectum (proctitis). These complications are associated with neutropenia, a condition in which the blood has an abnormally low number of neutrophils. Neutrophils are a special type of white blood cell that ingests bacteria and other foreign substances. The connection between hyper-IgM syndrome and neutropenia was not as of 2004 yet fully understood.

- Infections of the bones and joints leading to arthritis or osteomyelitis.

- Disorders of the nervous system caused by meningoencephalitis, or inflammation of the brain and its overlying layers of protective tissue. Patients with these disorders may have problems with thinking clearly, have difficulty walking normally, or develop paralysis on one side of the body (hemiplegia).

- Liver disease. About 70 percent of patients with XHIM develop liver disease by age 30, usually as a result of recurrent *Cryptosporidium* infections.

- Malignant tumors, most commonly non-Hodgkin's lymphoma or cancers of the gall bladder and liver.

Demographics

Both XHIM and ARHIM are rare disorders. One group of researchers at Johns Hopkins University estimates the incidence of XHIM in the general North American population as one in 1,030,000 males. In the early 2000s, however, it is thought that the disorder may be underdiagnosed. The incidence of ARHIM has not been established as of 2004, but it is known to be much less common than XHIM. As of the early 2000s, researchers do not know whether these disorders are more common in some racial or ethnic groups than others or whether they are equally common in all parts of the world. The only registries of patients as of 2004 diagnosed with hyper-IgM syndrome are located in Europe and the United States. The registry that was established in the United States in 1997 contains the records of 79 patients from 60 unrelated families, while the European database contains the records of XHIM patients from 130 unrelated families.

Causes and symptoms

Causes

Hyper-IgM syndrome is caused by a mutation in a gene on the X chromosome that affects the patient's T cells. The gene has been identified at locus Xq27. Normal T cells produce a ligand (a small molecule that links to larger molecules) known as CD40. CD40 is a protein found on the surface of T cells that signals B cells to stop producing IgM, which is the antibody that is first produced in response to invading organisms and switch to producing IgG and IgA, which are more specialized antibodies. As a result, boys with XHIM have abnormally low levels of IgG and IgA in their blood, with normal or higher than normal levels of IgM. Because they lack these "second line of defense" antibodies, they are more vulnerable to infections.

About 70 percent of patients diagnosed with XHIM have inherited the disorder through their mother; about 30 percent of cases, however, are caused by new mutations. Females who carry the defective gene have a 50 percent chance of passing it on to their sons but are not affected themselves by the disorder. The daughters of carriers have a 50 percent risk of carrying the defective gene to the next generation.

Symptoms

The symptoms of hyper-IgM syndrome usually become noticeable after the baby is six months to a year old. At this point the antibodies received from the mother during pregnancy are no longer present in the baby's blood. The child develops a series of severe ear, throat, or chest infections that do not clear up with standard antibiotic treatment. Another early warning sign is recurrent or chronic diarrhea. In addition, the child may have more than one infection at the same time. The most common telltale symptom, however, is PCP; in fact, the frequency of *Pneumocystis carinii* pneumonia in children with hyper-IgM syndrome was a useful clue to geneticists searching for the mutation that causes the disorder.

When to call the doctor

The Jeffrey Modell Foundation (JMF) and the American Red Cross have drawn up a list of 10 warning signs of hyper-IgM syndrome and other primary immunodeficiency disorders:

- The child has eight or more ear infections within one year.
- The child has two or more serious sinus infections within one year.
- The child has been treated with **antibiotics** for two months or longer with little effect.
- The child has been diagnosed with pneumonia more than twice within the past year.
- If an infant, the child is not growing or gaining weight normally.
- The child has repeatedly developed deep skin abscesses.
- If older than 12 months, the child has persistent thrush.
- The child needs intravenous antibiotics to clear infections.
- The child has two or more deep-seated infections (**meningitis**, osteomyelitis, sepsis, or cellulitis).
- Other **family** members have been diagnosed with a primary immunodeficiency disorder.

Diagnosis

Most children with hyper-IgM syndrome are diagnosed before they are a year old; about 40 percent have PCP at the time of diagnosis. If the doctor has seen the child on a regular basis since birth, there will be a record of the number of infections the child has had, the length of time the child has had each infection, and the child's response to treatment. If the doctor suspects a primary immunodeficiency disorder, he or she will ask the parents about a family history of such disorders.

The next step in diagnosis is a thorough physical examination. Children with primary immunodeficiencies are often underweight or small for their age and may look pale or generally unwell. The doctor will listen for unusual sounds in the lungs when the child breathes in and out and will check the child's skin and the inside of the mouth for **rashes**, ulcers, or sores. As the doctor palpates or feels the child's abdomen, he or she will pay particular attention to the size of the spleen and liver. The doctor will also examine the child's joints and the lymph nodes in the neck for signs of swelling.

The doctor will order a blood test to screen the child for an immunodeficiency disorder. The most common tests performed to screen for hyper-IgM syndrome are a complete blood count (CBC) and a quantitative immunoglobulin test. The CBC will help to determine whether the child has neutropenia. The quantitative test measures the levels of the different types of immunoglobulins in the blood as well as the total level of all immunoglobulins. A child with hyper-IgM syndrome will be found to have abnormally low levels of IgA and IgG antibodies and a normal or elevated level of IgM.

The doctor may also order x-ray studies of the child's chest or sinuses in order to determine whether lung damage has already occurred or to make a baseline evaluation of the child's lungs.

The diagnosis of hyper-IgM syndrome can be confirmed by molecular genetics testing for the defective CD40 gene. The test involves DNA sequencing and has been available since the early 2000s.

Treatment

Intravenous immunoglobulin (IVIG) therapy

Intravenous immunoglubulin (IVIG) has been the mainstay of treatment for a number of primary immunodeficiencies since it was first approved by the Food and Drug Administration (FDA) in the early 1980s. IVIG involves the infusion of immunoglobulins derived from donated blood plasma directly into the patient's bloodstream as a protection against infection. In the case of children with XHIM, IVIG is given to replace the missing IgG antibodies and to reduce or normalize the IgM level. IVIG infusions are usually given every three to four weeks for the remainder of the patient's life. They can be given in an outpatient clinic or in the patient's home. Patients with neutropenia may be treated with G-CSF (Neupogen), a protein given by injection that stimulates the body to produce more neutrophils.

IVIG therapy is the only effective treatment for ARHIM as of the early 2000s.

Antibiotics

Boys diagnosed with XHIM are given antibiotics as a prophylactic (preventive) treatment to protect them against *Pneumocystis carinii* pneumonia. They are usually started on a regimen of trimethoprim-sulfamethoxazole (Bactrim or Septra) as soon as they are diagnosed.

Bone marrow transplantation

A subsequent treatment for XHIM is bone marrow transplantation (BMT), which is also referred to as hematopoietic stem cell transplantation (HSCT). It is considered to be a cure for primary immunodeficiency disorders. Although BMT has been performed on children with severe immunodeficiency disorders since the 1980s, it was usually restricted to those with limited life expectancy because of complications associated with transplantation. Several advances since the late 1990s, however, have made this form of treatment more feasible for boys with XHIM. These advances include better matching of potential donors and recipients through more accurate tissue typing and improved surgical techniques. As of 2004, however, doctors recommended that boys with XHIM be given BMT before significant infections or organ damage occur. This form of treatment is not recommended for patients who already have signs of liver damage.

The best source of bone marrow for transplantation is the affected child's siblings. They will be tissue-typed to determine whether their bone marrow has the same human leukocyte antigens (HLA) as the affected child. Human leukocyte antigens are genetically determined proteins that allow the body to distinguish between its own cells and those from an outside source. The closer the HLA match between a bone marrow donor and recipient, the lower the chances that the recipient's body will reject the transplanted tissue. In addition to siblings, another choice is bone marrow from one of the parents, who shares half the affected child's HLA antigens. With the expansion of bone marrow registries since the early 2000s, it is also possible to use bone marrow from an unrelated donor whose tissues closely match those of the affected child. These are called matched unrelated donor (MUD) transplants. The most successful bone marrow transplants in hyper-IgM children, however, have used marrow donated by HLA-identical siblings.

Cord blood stem cell transplantation

Another approach to transplantation as a cure for hyper-IgM syndrome is the use of stem cells from cord blood. This technique was first used for immunodeficiency disorders in 1988. Stem cells are undifferentiated precursor cells whose daughter cells can differentiate into more specialized cells. The stem cells used for transplantation are taken from blood collected from a baby's umbilical cord or the placenta (afterbirth) immediately following delivery. Cord blood from healthy siblings can be used for transplantation to treat XHIM patients. Stem cell transplants from cord blood have two advantages over bone marrow transplants: they have a lower rate of rejection in recipients, and they can be stored ahead of time. Families with a history of primary immunodeficiency disorders can save cord blood in private storage facilities for later use if needed.

Experimental and investigational treatments

Researchers have found that giving artificial CD40 ligand to specially bred immunodeficient mice improves their ability to make IgA and IgG antibodies. The National Institutes of Health (NIH) is in the early 2000s conducting studies to evaluate the effectiveness of this treatment in humans.

As of the early 2000s, researchers at the National Institutes of Health and the University of Pennsylvania are investigating the possibility of treating hyper-IgM syndrome with gene therapy. Gene therapy involves the insertion of a normal gene into a targeted cell to replace an abnormal gene by means of a vector or carrier molecule. The most common vectors are genetically altered viruses. Reports on this research published in 2004, however, indicate that gene therapy for hyper-IgM syndrome will be more complicated and take longer to develop than was originally expected.

Nutritional concerns

Nutritional concerns for children with XHIM are related to infections of the digestive tract resulting in chronic diarrhea. The primary risks with chronic diarrhea are **dehydration** and malnutrition. To prevent dehydration, the doctor may recommend a clear liquid diet for infants and toddlers during episodes of diarrhea. If the child is able to keep the clear liquids down, milk or diluted formula can be given. The child's rectal area should be coated with petroleum jelly to reduce irritation.

If the diarrhea is caused by *Cryptosporidium* or another infectious organism, the child's diapers and bed linens should be washed separately from the rest of the family's laundry, and the bathroom should be cleaned regularly with a disinfectant.

Prognosis

The prognosis for children diagnosed with XHIM is poor as of the early 2000s; morbidity and mortality for this disorder are significantly higher than for other primary immunodeficiency disorders. A study done in 2000 indicated that only 20 percent of patients with hyper-IgM syndrome survived to the age of 25. However, researchers expect the outlook to improve for children in treatment in 2004, particularly those patients who are good candidates for bone marrow transplantation. In one Japanese study, five out of seven patients who received BMT survived, with four of the five producing T cells with normal CD40 ligand without supplementary IVIG therapy. In general, children who are treated with IVIG and/or BMT as infants have a better prognosis than those who are diagnosed after the age of two years.

Prevention

As both forms of hyper-IgM syndrome are caused by genetic mutations, there is no way to prevent the disorders after the child is born. Parents who already have a child with hyper-IgM syndrome or who come from families with a history of primary immunodeficiency disorders may wish to consider genetic counseling and prenatal genetic testing with future pregnancies.

There are also some preventive measures that families can take to lower the risk of opportunistic infections and other complications in affected children. These precautions include the following:

- Practicing good hygiene, including careful washing of the hands before and after meals and after using the toilet. Antibacterial hand wipes can be packed with the child's school lunches.
- Careful cleansing of even small cuts or scrapes with an antiseptic liquid or cream.
- Proper dental care. Children with primary immunodeficiency syndromes are at increased risk of **tooth decay** and gum disorders as well as thrush and mouth ulcers.
- Avoiding the use of vaccines made from live viruses (**measles**, poliovirus, **mumps**, **rubella**). Vaccines made with killed viruses should be given regularly.
- Having the home water supply tested for possible contamination by *Cryptosporidium parvum*.
- Avoiding crowded stores, theaters, or athletic events during flu season.
- Giving the affected child his own room if possible.
- Having other family members take primary responsibility for the care of household pets. Children with hyper-IgM syndrome are highly susceptible to infection from animal bites.

Nutritional concerns

Proper **nutrition** is a lifelong concern for children with hyper-IgM syndrome because of the possibility of malnutrition caused by chronic diarrhea. A normal well-balanced diet is recommended for older children, with multivitamin supplements as prescribed by the child's primary doctor. Older children can be given a nutritional supplement (Ensure) during episodes of severe diarrhea. In extremely severe cases the child may require parenteral nutrition, which is a liquid food given intravenously. Parenteral nutrition is also known as hyperalimentation.

Parental concerns

Hyper-IgM syndrome has a major impact on the family of a child diagnosed with the disease. The following are some of the important concerns for parents:

- High financial costs. Children diagnosed with hyper-IgM syndrome require careful monitoring for liver

Antibody—A special protein made by the body's immune system as a defense against foreign material (bacteria, viruses, etc.) that enters the body. It is uniquely designed to attack and neutralize the specific antigen that triggered the immune response.

B cell—A type of white blood cell derived from bone marrow. B cells are sometimes called B lymphocytes. They secrete antibodies and have a number of other complex functions within the human immune system.

Bronchiectasis—A disorder of the bronchial tubes marked by abnormal stretching, enlargement, or destruction of the walls. Bronchiectasis is usually caused by recurrent inflammation of the airway.

Cord blood—The blood that remains in the umbilical cord and placenta after birth. Stem cells from cord blood can be used in place of bone marrow for treating primary immunodeficiency disorders.

Gene therapy—An experimental treatment for certain genetic disorders in which a abnormal gene is replaced with the normal copy. Also called somatic-cell gene therapy.

Human leuckocyte antigen (HLA)—A group of protein molecules located on bone marrow cells that can provoke an immune response. A donor's and a recipient's HLA types should match as closely as possible to prevent the recipient's immune system from attacking the donor's marrow as a foreign material that does not belong in the body.

Immunoglobulin G (IgG)—Immunoglobulin type gamma, the most common type found in the blood and tissue fluids.

Ligand—Any type of small molecule that binds to a larger molecule. Hyper-IgM syndrome is caused by a lack of a ligand known as CD40 on the surfaces of the T cells in the child's blood.

Lymphocyte—A type of white blood cell that participates in the immune response. The two main groups are the B cells that have antibody molecules on their surface and T cells that destroy antigens.

Morbidity—A disease or abnormality. In statistics it also refers to the rate at which a disease or abnormality occurs.

Neutropenia—A condition in which the number of neutrophils, a type of white blood cell (leukocyte) is abnormally low.

Opportunistic infection—An infection that is normally mild in a healthy individual, but which takes advantage of an ill person's weakened immune system to move into the body, grow, spread, and cause serious illness.

Osteomyelitis—An infection of the bone and bone marrow, usually caused by bacteria.

Primary immunodeficiency disease—A group of approximately 70 conditions that affect the normal functioning of the immune system.

Prophylactic—Preventing the spread or occurrence of disease or infection.

Stem cell—An undifferentiated cell that retains the ability to develop into any one of a variety of cell types.

T cell—A type of white blood cell that is produced in the bone marrow and matured in the thymus gland. It helps to regulate the immune system's response to infections or malignancy.

Thrush—An infection of the mouth, caused by the yeast *Candida albicans* and characterized by a whitish growth and ulcers.

---

function, lung function, nutritional status, **oral hygiene**, and normal growth patterns as well as blood antibody levels. In most cases the child will be seen every three to six months by a clinical immunologist as well as his primary care doctor. Such procedures as bone marrow or cord blood transplantation are also costly.

• Emotional wear and tear on the family. In addition to the extra time and attention required for the affected child, parents are likely to confront emotional problems in the family, ranging from resentment on the part of siblings to **anxiety** about the affected child's

survival and decisions about future pregnancies. Support groups and/or **family therapy** may be helpful.

• Genetic testing. Genetic counselors recommend having the affected child's siblings tested to see whether they are carriers of the defective gene.

• Education and future employment. Children who are receiving IVIG treatment can attend a regular school and participate in most **sports** provided that minor injuries are treated promptly. Adults with hyper-IgM syndrome can attend college or graduate school and work in most fields of employment.

- Peer pressure in **adolescence**. It is important for parents to warn children with hyper-IgM syndrome that **smoking**, alcohol consumption, and the use of recreational drugs are far more dangerous for them than for adolescents with normal immune systems.

See also Immunodeficiency; Immunoglobulin deficiency syndromes.

Resources

BOOKS

"Biology of the Immune System," sect. 12, chap. 146 in *The Merck Manual of Diagnosis and Therapy*, edited by Mark H. Beers and Robert Berkow. Whitehouse Station, NJ: Merck Research Laboratories, 2002.

IDF Patient and Family Handbook for the Primary Immune Deficiency Diseases, 3rd ed. Towson, MD: Immune Deficiency Foundation (IDF), 2001.

PERIODICALS

Chinen, G., and W. T. Shearer. "Advances in Asthma, Allergy, and Immunology Series 2004: Basic and Clinical Immunology." *Journal of Allergy and Clinical Immunology* 114 (August 2004): 398–405.

Cooper, Megan A., Thomas L. Pommering, and Katalin Koranyi. "Primary Immunodeficiencies." *American Family Physician* 68 (November 15, 2003): 2001–08.

Cron, R. N. "CD154 Transcriptional Regulation in Primary Human CD4 T Cells. *Immunologic Research* 27 (2003): 185–202.

Dimicoli, S., et al. "Complete Recovery from *Cryptosporidium parvum* Infection with Gastroenteritis and Sclerosing Cholangitis after Successful Bone Marrow Transplantation in Two Brothers with X-Linked Hyper-IgM Syndrome." *Bone Marrow Transplantation* 32 (October 2003): 733–37.

Paul, Mary E. "Diagnosis of Immunodeficiency: Clinical Clues and Diagnostic Tests." *Current Science* 2 (2002): 349–55.

Tomizawa, D., et al. "Allogeneic Hematopoietic Stem Cell Transplantation for Seven Children with X-Linked Hyper-IgM Syndrome: A Single-Center Experience." *American Journal of Hematology* 76 (May 2004): 3339.

Winkelstein, J. A., et al. "The X-Linked Hyper-IgM Syndrome: Clinical and Immunologic Features of 79 Patients." *Medicine (Baltimore)* 82 (November 2003). 373–84.

ORGANIZATIONS

American Academy of Allergy, Asthma, and Immunology (AAAAI). 611 East Wells Street, Milwaukee, WI 53202. Web site: <www.aaaai.org>.

Immune Deficiency Foundation (IDF). 40 West Chesapeake Avenue, Suite 308, Towson, MD 21204. Web site: <www.primaryimmune.org>.

Jeffrey Modell Foundation (JMF). 747 Third Avenue, New York, NY 10017. Web site: <www.jmfworld.com>.

National Institute of Allergy and Infectious Diseases (NIAID). Building 31, Room 7A50, 31 Center Drive, MSC 2520, Bethesda, MD 20892–2520. Web site: <www.niaid.nih.gov>.

National Institute of Child Health and Human Development (NICHD). 31 Center Drive, Room 2A32, Bethesda, MD 20892–2425. Web site: <www.nichd.nih.gov>.

National Organization for Rare Disorders Inc. (NORD). 55 Kenosia Avenue, Danbury, CT 06813–1968. Web site: <www.rarediseases.org>.

WEB SITES

Shigeoka, Anne O'Neill. "X-Linked Immunodeficiency with Hyper IgM." *eMedicine*, October 4, 2002. Available online at <www.emedicine.com/neuro/topic664.htm>.

OTHER

National Institute of Allergy and Infectious Diseases (NIAID). *Fact Sheet: Primary Immune Deficiency*. Bethesda, MD: NIAID, 2003.

National Institute of Child Health and Human Development (NICHD). *Primary Immunodeficiency*. NIH Publication No. 99–4149. Bethesda, MD: NICHD, 2004.

Rebecca Frey, PhD

Hypertension

Definition

Hypertension is high blood pressure. Blood pressure is the force of blood pushing against the walls of arteries. Arteries are the blood vessels that carry oxygenated blood from the heart to the body's tissues.

Description

As blood flows through arteries, it pushes against the inside of artery walls. The more pressure the blood exerts on the artery walls, the higher the blood pressure is. The size of arteries also affects the blood pressure. When the muscular walls of arteries are relaxed, or dilated, the pressure of the blood flowing through them is lower than when the artery walls narrow, or constricted.

Blood pressure is highest when the heart beats to push blood out into the arteries. When the heart relaxes to fill with blood again, the pressure is at its lowest point. Blood pressure when the heart beats is called systolic pressure. Blood pressure when the heart is at rest is called diastolic pressure. When blood pressure is measured, the systolic pressure is stated first and the diastolic pressure second. Blood pressure is measured in millimeters of mercury (mm Hg). For example, if a person's systolic pressure is 120 and diastolic pressure is 80, it is written as 120/80 mm Hg.

Blood pressure measurements

The National Heart, Lung, and Blood Institute in Bethesda, Maryland released clinical guidelines for blood pressure in 2003, lowering the standard normal readings for adults to less than 120 over less than 80.

Although there are set blood pressure ranges for adults, normal blood pressure ranges for children vary according to age, gender, and height so that different levels of growth are considered when evaluating blood pressure. In children, blood pressure normally rises during growth and maturation and varies greatly during **adolescence**.

Specific systolic and diastolic blood pressure percentiles have been established for each age, gender, and height group. In children ages six to 12, up to 125/80 mm Hg is considered normal. In youth ages 12–15, 126/78 mm Hg is normal, and for ages 16–18, 132/82 mm Hg is normal.

Children whose blood pressure is above the 95th percentile for their age/gender/height group are diagnosed with hypertension. Children whose blood pressure is between the 90th and 95th percentile are diagnosed with pre-hypertension. Adolescents whose blood pressure is greater than 120/80 also may be diagnosed with pre-hypertension.

Complications

Childhood hypertension is serious because it increases the risk of heart disease, **stroke**, and other medical problems in adulthood. Serious complications can be avoided by ensuring the child gets regular blood pressure checks and by treating hypertension as soon as it is diagnosed.

If left untreated, hypertension can lead to the following long-term complications:

- atherosclerosis, also called arteriosclerosis
- peripheral vascular disease
- heart attack
- stroke
- enlarged heart and heart failure
- kidney damage or kidney failure
- retinopathy or blindness

Atherosclerosis is hardening of the arteries. The walls of arteries have a layer of muscle and elastic tissue that makes them flexible and able to dilate and constrict as blood flows through them. High blood pressure can make the artery walls thicken and harden. When artery walls thicken, the inside of the blood vessel narrows. Cholesterol and fats are more likely to build up on the walls of damaged arteries, making them even narrower. Blood clots also can get trapped in narrowed arteries, blocking the flow of blood. When atherosclerosis occurs in the blood vessels leading to the legs and feet, it is called peripheral vascular disease. Blood flow is decreased to the legs and feet with peripheral vascular diseases and can cause poor circulation in the legs, claudication, or aneurysm.

Arteries narrowed by atherosclerosis may not deliver enough blood to organs and other tissues. Reduced or blocked blood flow to the heart can cause a heart attack. If an artery to the brain is blocked, a stroke can result.

Hypertension makes the heart work harder to pump blood through the body. The extra workload can make the heart muscle thicken and stretch. When the heart becomes enlarged it cannot pump enough blood. If the hypertension is not treated, the heart may fail.

The kidneys remove the body's wastes from the blood. If hypertension thickens the arteries to the kidneys, less waste can be filtered from the blood. As the condition worsens, the kidneys fail and wastes build up in the blood. Dialysis or a kidney transplant is needed when the kidneys fail.

Hypertension can cause damage to blood vessels in the eyes, leading to retinopathy, or damage to the retina. Retinal damage becomes severe when blood pressure levels are high and remain elevated for a prolonged period of time.

Demographics

In the United States, an estimated 5–10 percent of children have hypertension, and one in four adults (about 50 million) have hypertension. About 30 percent of those with hypertension do not know they have it. Hypertension is more common in men than women and in people over age 65 than in younger persons. It also is more frequent and severe in African-American and Mexican-American adults and children than in white Americans. The prevalence of high blood pressure among African-Americans and whites in the southeastern United States is greater, and death rates from stroke are higher than among those in other regions.

In the early 2000s, high blood pressure in children and adolescents is on the rise. A 2003 report indicated this increase is most likely due to a greater number of overweight and obese children and adolescents. The U.S. Centers for Disease Control and Prevention studied the health and **nutrition** of Americans in the National Health and Nutrition Examination Surveys for more than 40 years, and the last data were collected in 2000. Researchers found a trend of high blood pressure in children ages eight to 17 years who were overweight or obese.

Causes and symptoms

Causes

Many different actions or situations can normally raise blood pressure. Physical activity and changes in position can temporarily raise blood pressure. Stressful situations can make blood pressure go up. When the stress goes away, blood pressure usually returns to normal. Certain medications also may change blood pressure, but usually blood pressure returns to normal when the drug is discontinued. These temporary increases in blood pressure are not considered hypertension. A diagnosis of hypertension is made only when a person has at least three separate high blood pressure readings performed one to several weeks apart.

Hypertension without a known cause is called primary or essential hypertension. Although the cause of hypertension is unknown in 90–95 percent of adults, primary hypertension is uncommon in children, occurring in less than 1–2 percent of hypertensive children.

When a child has hypertension caused by another medical condition, it is called secondary hypertension. Secondary hypertension can be caused by a number of different illnesses. Kidney disease causes hypertension in 80–85 percent of childhood cases. The kidneys regulate the balance of salt and water in the body. If the kidneys cannot rid the body of excess salt and water, blood pressure goes up. Kidney infections, a narrowing of the arteries that carry blood to the kidneys, called renal artery stenosis, and other kidney disorders can disturb the salt and water balance.

As body weight increases, blood pressure rises. Being overweight or obese is the strongest predictor of hypertension in young adults. **Obesity** has steadily increased in children and adolescents over the years. An estimated 16 percent of school-age children are overweight. High blood pressure develops about 10 years after a young person becomes overweight. Obesity may

cause other cardiovascular diseases if it is not managed or treated properly.

Risk factors

Risk factors are conditions that increase the chance of developing hypertension. Some of these risk factors can be changed to reduce the risk of developing hypertension or to lower blood pressure:

- being overweight or obese
- lack of physical activity
- a diet high in fat, salt, and sugar
- heredity
- low birth weight and subsequent rapid weight gain
- male sex
- race
- congenital conditions, such as coarctation of the aorta
- diabetes
- kidney disease
- in adolescents, heavy alcohol consumption and use of oral contraceptives
- in adults, being over the age of 60

Although **smoking** is not directly related to high blood pressure in children and adolescents, those who smoke should stop to reduce their risk of developing other health problems such as coronary artery disease.

Some risk factors for hypertension can be changed, while others cannot. Some children inherit a tendency to develop hypertension, and the risk increases if both parents are hypertensive. Children who have the risk factors above can work with their doctor and **family** to manage the controllable risk factors.

Symptoms

Hypertension generally does not cause symptoms. When symptoms occur, they are usually mild and non-specific. In young children (age three and younger), symptoms may include:

- irritability
- excessive crying
- failure to gain weight
- poor feeding
- low-grade fever

In older children, symptoms may include:

- dizziness

- headaches

- vomiting

- heart palpitations

In severe and acute (sudden-onset) cases, hypertension can cause seizures, swelling throughout the body, blindness, or renal (kidney) failure. All of these symptoms require immediate medical attention and **hospitalization**.

When to call the doctor

If a child has any of the following symptoms, the parent or caregiver should call the child's doctor:

- unexplained headache

- sudden or gradual changes in vision

- dizziness or light-headedness that does not resolve with rest

- nausea associated with headache

- unexplained or uncontrollable vomiting

- heart palpitations

If a child has any of these symptoms, the parent or caregiver should immediately seek emergency medical attention:

- severe headache

- fainting

- seizures or convulsions

- swelling throughout the body

- unexplained blurred vision or vision loss

- severe chest **pain** or shortness of breath

- unexplained sudden weakness

Diagnosis

Blood pressure in children should be checked regularly: at least at every doctor's visit after age three. Early detection and treatment of hypertension improve the child's overall health and decrease the risk of future health problems associated with hypertension.

Blood pressure is measured with an instrument called a sphygmomanometer. A cloth-covered rubber cuff is wrapped around the upper arm and inflated. When the cuff is inflated, an artery in the arm is squeezed to momentarily stop the flow of blood. Then, the air is let out of the cuff while a stethoscope placed over the artery is used to detect the sound of the blood spurting back through the artery. This first sound is the systolic pressure, the pressure when the heart beats. The last sound heard as the rest of the air is released is the diastolic pressure, the pressure between heartbeats. Both sounds are recorded on the mercury gauge on the sphygmomanometer.

The arm cuff used to measure blood pressure in children must be appropriate to the child's size, or the reading may be inaccurate.

A typical physical examination to evaluate hypertension includes:

- medical and family history

- physical examination

- ophthalmoscopy: examination of the blood vessels in the eye

- blood and urine tests

The physical exam may include several blood pressure readings at different times and in different positions. For at least five minutes before the blood pressure reading is taken, the child should be seated in a chair, with feet on the floor and arms supported at heart level. For best results, the child should not eat or drink caffeinated products within the 30 minutes prior to the exam. The physician uses a stethoscope to listen to sounds made by the heart and blood flowing through the arteries.

During the physical exam, the child's pulse, reflexes, and height and weight are checked and recorded. Internal organs are palpated to determine if they are enlarged.

Because hypertension can cause damage to the blood vessels in the eyes, the eyes may be checked with a instrument called an ophthalmoscope. The physician will look for thickening, narrowing, or hemorrhages in the blood vessels.

Urine and blood tests may be done to evaluate health and to detect the presence of certain substances that may indicate an underlying condition that is causing the hypertension.

Usually blood tests and urine tests, along with the physical examination and medical history, are enough to make the diagnosis of hypertension. If necessary, to rule out other medical conditions or to assess any damage from hypertension and/or its treatment, the following tests may be performed:

- Chest x ray: To detect an enlarged heart, other vascular abnormalities, or lung disease.

- Electrocardiogram (ECG): To measure the electrical activity of the heart. It can detect if the heart muscle is enlarged and if there is damage to the heart muscle from blocked arteries.

- Echocardiogram (echo): To produce a graphic outline of the heart's movement, valves, and chambers, used to evaluate the function of the heart and valves. Echo is often combined with Doppler ultrasound and color Doppler. During the echo, an ultrasound transducer (hand-held wand placed on the skin of the chest) emits high-frequency sound waves to produce pictures of the heart's valves and chambers. An echo is used in pediatric patients diagnosed with hypertension to determine the extent of left ventricular hypertrophy, a condition in which the heart's main pumping vessel is enlarged.

Treatment

There is no cure for primary hypertension, but blood pressure can almost always be lowered with the correct treatment. The goal of treatment is to lower blood pressure to levels that will prevent heart disease and other complications of hypertension that could manifest in adulthood. In secondary hypertension, the disease that is responsible for the hypertension is treated in addition to the hypertension itself. Successful treatment of the underlying disorder may cure the secondary hypertension.

Clinicians should work with the child and the parents or caregivers to develop an individual treatment plan. Specific treatment goals vary. Treatment should be provided by a pediatric cardiologist or pediatrician with special knowledge and experience in the treatment of high blood pressure.

Lifestyle changes

Depending on the results of diagnostic tests, childhood hypertension is generally treated with lifestyle changes, including diet and **exercise**, before antihypertensive medication is prescribed. Lifestyle changes that may reduce blood pressure include:

- losing weight

- exercising regularly

- reducing fat, salt, and sugar in the diet

- managing stress and anxiety

- quitting smoking and reducing alcohol consumption, as applicable in older children

Reaching and maintaining a healthy body weight is important. Overweight children with hypertension are recommended to lose weight until they are within 15 percent of their healthy body weight. Even a small amount of weight loss can make a major difference. Physical activities should be encouraged, and sedentary activities such as watching television or playing **video games** should be limited. The recommended exercise goal is aerobic activity, such as brisk walking, at least 30 minutes per day, most days of the week.

A pediatrician can calculate a healthy range of body weight for the child, recommend dietary guidelines, and provide activity guidelines to help the child safely and effectively lose weight. A consultation with a registered dietitian also may assist the parent or caregiver in implementing dietary changes.

Nutritional concerns

Dietary guidelines are individualized, based on the child's blood pressure levels and specific needs. In children older than two years of age, the following low-fat dietary guidelines are recommended:

- Total fat intake should comprise 30 percent or less of total calories consumed per day.

- Calories consumed as saturated fat should equal no more than 8 to 10 percent of total calories consumed per day.

- Total cholesterol intake should be less than 300 mg/dl per day.

Elevated blood pressure can be reduced by an eating plan that emphasizes fruits, vegetables, and low-fat dairy foods, and which is low in saturated fat, total fat, and cholesterol. The DASH diet is recommended for patients with hypertension and includes whole grains, poultry, fish, and nuts. Fats, red meats, sodium, sweets, and sugar-sweetened beverages are limited. Sodium should also be reduced to no more than 1,500 milligrams per day.

A gradual transition to a heart-healthy diet can help decrease a child's risk of coronary artery disease and other health conditions in adulthood. Parents can replace foods high in fat with grains, vegetables, fruits, lean meat, and other foods low in fat and high in complex carbohydrates and protein. They can resist adding salt to foods while cooking and avoid highly processed foods that are usually high in sodium, such as fast foods, canned foods, boxed mixes, and frozen meals.

Alternative treatment

Alternative and complementary therapies include approaches that are considered to be outside the mainstream of traditional health care.

Techniques that induce relaxation and reduce stress, such as **yoga**, tai chi, meditation, guided imagery, and relaxation training, may be helpful in controlling blood pressure. Acupuncture and biofeedback training also may help induce relaxation. Before learning or practicing any particular technique, it is important for the parent/caregiver and child to learn about the therapy, its safety and effectiveness, potential side effects, and the expertise and qualifications of the practitioner. Although some practices are beneficial, others may be harmful to certain patients.

Dietary supplements, including garlic, fish oil (omega-3 fatty acids), L-arginine, soy, coenzyme Q10, phytosterols, and chelation therapy may be beneficial, but the exact nature of their effects on blood pressure is unknown. There is little scientific evidence that these therapies lower blood pressure or prevent the complications of high blood pressure, and most of these supplements have not been studied extensively in children and adolescents.

Vitamin E and beta carotene supplements were once thought to help prevent the development of heart disease, but subsequent studies disprove that assumption.

Medications

Medications usually are not prescribed for children as a first-line treatment for hypertension. Medications are prescribed, however, to treat hypertension when the child has significant high blood pressure or organ damage, or when diet and exercise are not adequately controlling the child's blood pressure.

Follow-up care

Follow-up care for hypertension includes home blood pressure monitoring. The parent or caregiver checks the child's blood pressure at different times of the day and records the readings. The doctor reviews this blood pressure record during the child's check-ups to evaluate the effectiveness of the child's treatment and to make any necessary adjustments.

Depending on the child's blood pressure levels and presence of other medical conditions such as diabetes, the doctor may recommend annual eye exams to detect the presence of vision changes and the development of retinopathy.

Prognosis

There is no cure for hypertension. However, it can be well controlled with the proper treatment. Therapy with a combination of lifestyle changes and sometimes antihypertensive medicines usually can manage blood pressure. For most children, early primary hypertension causes no immediate risk of serious health problems, but it does increase the risk for future organ damage. The key to avoiding serious complications of hypertension is

to detect and treat it at the earliest possible age so that preventive treatment can be initiated.

Prevention

Avoiding or eliminating known risk factors helps reduce the risk of developing hypertension. Making the same changes recommended for treating hypertension can reduce a child's risk of developing hypertension:

- losing weight if overweight or obese
- exercising regularly
- reducing salt, fat, and sugar in the diet
- reducing fat intake
- managing stress and anxiety
- quitting smoking and limiting alcohol, as applicable in older children

Parental concerns

Parents should reinforce with the child that hypertension is a serious condition that can cause more health problems later in life. Parents should work with their child to make dietary changes and increase their activity level to manage hypertension and prevent it from getting worse. Everyone can benefit when a heart-healthy lifestyle is followed, so the dietary and activity changes made for the hypertensive child will benefit the entire family.

Resources

BOOKS

McGoon, Michael D., and Bernard J. Gersh, eds. *Mayo Clinic Heart Book: The Ultimate Guide to Heart Health*, 2nd ed. New York: William Morrow and Co., Inc., 2000.

Moore, Thomas, et al. *The Dash Diet for Hypertension: Lower Your Blood Pressure in Fourteen Days without Drugs.* New York: Simon & Schuster, Inc., 2001.

Topol, Eric J. *Cleveland Clinic Heart Book: The Definitive Guide for the Entire Family from the Nation's Leading Heart Center.* New York: Hyperion, 2000.

Trout, Darrell, and Ellen Welch. *Surviving with Heart: Taking Charge of Your Heart Care.* Golden, CO: Fulcrum Publishing, 2002.

PERIODICALS

McNamara, Damian. "Obesity Behind Rise in Incidence of Primary Hypertension." *Family Practice News* (April 1, 2003): 45–51.

KEY TERMS

Aneurysm—A weakened area in the wall of a blood vessel which causes an outpouching or bulge. Aneurysms may be fatal if these weak areas burst, resulting in uncontrollable bleeding.

Aorta—The main artery located above the heart that pumps oxygenated blood out into the body. The aorta is the largest artery in the body.

Arteriosclerosis—A chronic condition characterized by thickening, loss of leasticity, and hardening of the arteries and the build-up of plaque on the arterial walls. Arteriosclerosis can slow or impair blood circulation. It includes atherosclerosis, but the two terms are often used synonymously.

Artery—A blood vessel that carries blood away from the heart to the cells, tissues, and organs of the body.

Atrial—Referring to the upper chambers of the heart.

Claudication—Cramping or pain in a leg caused by poor blood circulation. This condition is frequently caused by hardening of the arteries (atherosclerosis). Intermittent claudication occurs only at certain times, usually after exercise, and is relieved by rest.

Coarctation of the aorta—A congenital defect in which severe narrowing or constriction of the aorta obstructs the flow of blood.

Dialysis—A process of filtering and removing waste products from the bloodstream, it is used as a treatment for patients whose kidneys do not function properly. Two main types are hemodialysis and peritoneal dialysis. In hemodialysis, the blood flows out of the body into a machine that filters out the waste products and routes the cleansed blood back into the body. In peritoneal dialysis, the cleansing occurs inside the body. Dialysis fluid is injected into the peritoneal cavity and wastes are filtered through the peritoneum, the thin membrane that surrounds the abdominal organs.

Diastolic blood pressure—Diastole is the period in which the left ventricle relaxes so it can refill with blood; diastolic pressure is therefore measured during diastole.

Heart attack—Damage that occurs to the heart when one of the coronary arteries becomes narrowed or blocked.

Obesity—An abnormal accumulation of body fat, usually 20% or more over an individual's ideal body weight.

Overweight—Being 25 to 29 percent over the recommended healthy body weight for a specific age and height, as established by calculating body mass index.

Retinopathy—Any disorder of the retina.

Sphygmomanometer—An instrument used to measure blood pressure.

Stroke—Interruption of blood flow to a part of the brain with consequent brain damage. A stroke may be caused by a blood clot or by hemorrhage due to a burst blood vessel. Also known as a cerebrovascular accident.

Systolic blood pressure—Blood pressure when the heart contracts (beats).

Ventricles—The lower pumping chambers of the heart. The ventricles push blood to the lungs and the rest of the body.

———. "Trial Shows Efficacy of Lifestyle Changes for Blood Pressure: More Intensive than Typical Office Visit." *Family Practice News* (July 1, 2003): 1–2.

"New Blood Pressure Guidelines Establish Diagnosis of Pre-hypertension: Level Seeks to Identify At-risk Individuals Early." *Case Management Advisor* (July 2003): S1.

Sorof, Jonathan M., et al. "Cardiovascular risk factors and sequelae in hypertensive children identified by referral versus school-based screening." *Hypertension* 43 (2004): 214.

ORGANIZATIONS

American College of Cardiology. Heart House, 9111 Old Georgetown Rd., Bethesda, MD 20814–1699. Web site: <www.acc.org>.

American Heart Association. 7320 Greenville Ave., Dallas, TX 75231. Web site: <www.american heart.org>.

American Society of Hypertension. 148 Madison Ave., 5th Floor, New York, NY 10016. Web site: <www.ash-us.org>.

The Cleveland Clinic Heart Center. The Cleveland Clinic Foundation, 9500 Euclid Ave., F25, Cleveland, OH 44195. Web site: <www.clevelandclinic.org/heartcenter>.

Toni Rizzo
Teresa G. Odle
Angela M. Costello

Hyperthyroidism

Definition

Hyperthyroidism is the overproduction of thyroid hormones by an overactive thyroid.

Description

The term hyperthyroidism covers any disease which results in overabundance of thyroid hormone. Other names for hyperthyroidism, or specific diseases within the category, include Graves' disease, diffuse toxic goiter, Basedow's disease, Parry's disease, and thyrotoxicosis.

Located in the front of the neck, the thyroid gland produces the hormones thyroxin (T4) and triiodothyronine (T3), which regulate the body's metabolic rate by helping to form protein ribonucleic acid (RNA) and increasing oxygen absorption in every cell. In turn, the production of these hormones is controlled by thyroid-stimulating hormone (TSH) that is produced by the pituitary gland. When production of the thyroid hormones increases despite the level of TSH being produced, hyperthyroidism occurs. The excessive amount of thyroid hormones in the blood increases the body's metabolism, creating both mental and physical symptoms.

Demographics

Only about 5 percent of all individuals with hyperthyroidism are younger than 15 years of age. About five times as many girls as boys develop hyperthyroidism. Almost all cases of pediatric hyperthyroidism are the form called Graves' disease. There is a form of hyperthyroidism called neonatal Graves' disease, which occurs in infants born of mothers with Graves' disease. Children with other conditions, such as trisomy 21, Addison's disease, diabetes, systemic lupus erythematosus, rheumatoid arthritis, myasthenia gravis, vitiligo, pernicious anemia, and immune thrombocytopenic purpura are more likely to develop Graves' disease.

Causes and symptoms

Hyperthyroidism is often associated with the body's production of autoantibodies in the blood which causes the thyroid to grow and secrete excess thyroid hormone. This condition, as well as other forms of hyperthyroidism, may be inherited. Regardless of the cause, hyperthyroidism produces the same symptoms, including weight loss with increased appetite, shortness of breath and fatigue, intolerance to heat, heart palpitations, increased frequency of bowel movements, weak muscles, tremors, **anxiety**, and difficulty sleeping. Adolescent girls may also notice decreased menstrual flow and irregular menstrual cycles.

Patients with Graves' disease often have a goiter (visible enlargement of the thyroid gland), although as many as 10 percent do not. These patients may also have bulging eyes. Thyroid storm, a serious form of hyperthyroidism, may show up as sudden and acute symptoms, some of which mimic typical hyperthyroidism, as well as the addition of **fever**, substantial weakness, extreme restlessness, confusion, emotional swings or psychosis, or coma. Fortunately, such a fulminant course of Graves' disease is rare in children and adolescents.

Babies with neonatal Graves' disease may suffer from **prematurity**, airway obstruction, and heart failure. Death occurs in as many as 16 percent of these babies, and other complications from which survivors may suffer include **craniosynostosis** (early closure of the sutures of the skull, which can result in compression of the growing brain), and **developmental delay**.

When to call the doctor

Parents should contact a child's pediatrician if the child shows the following symptoms: rapid weight loss, shortness of breath, intolerance to heat, heart palpitations, increased frequency of bowel movements, weak muscles, tremors, anxiety, and difficulty sleeping. An enlarged thyroid gland, seen as a bulge in the neck, should be examined by a doctor.

Diagnosis

Physicians will look for physical signs and symptoms indicated by patient history. On inspection, the physician may note symptoms such as a goiter or eye bulging. Other symptoms or **family** history may be clues to a diagnosis of hyperthyroidism. An elevated body temperature (basal body temperature) above 98.6°F (37°C) may be an indication of a heightened metabolic rate (basal metabolic rate) and hyperthyroidism. A simple blood test can be performed to determine the amount of thyroid hormone in the patient's blood. The diagnosis is usually straightforward with this combination of clinical history, physical examination, and routine blood hormone tests. Radioimmunoassay (a test to show concentrations of thyroid hormones with the use of a radioisotope mixed with fluid samples) helps confirm the diagnosis. A thyroid scan is a nuclear medicine procedure involving injection of a radioisotope dye, which tags the thyroid and helps produce a clear image of

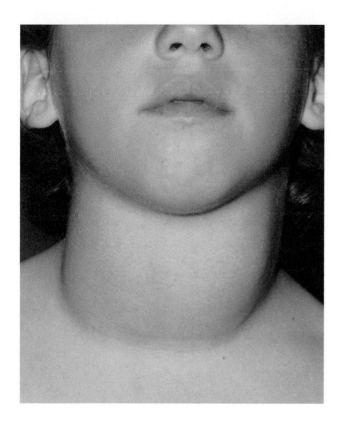

A symptom of hyperthyroidism is the enlargement of the thyroid gland, as seen in this youngster's neck. *(Photograph by Lester V. Bergman. Corbis)*

inflammation or involvement of the entire thyroid. Other tests can determine thyroid function and thyroid-stimulating hormone levels. Ultrasonography, **computed tomography** scans (CT scan), and **magnetic resonance imaging** (MRI) may provide visual confirmation of a diagnosis or help to determine the extent of involvement.

Treatment

Treatment depends on the specific disease and individual circumstances such as age, severity of disease, and other conditions affecting a patient's health.

Antithyroid drugs

Antithyroid drugs are often administered to help the patient's body cease overproduction of thyroid hormones. This medication may work for young adults, pregnant women, and others. Women who are pregnant should be treated with the lowest dose required to maintain thyroid function in order to minimize the risk of **hypothyroidism** in the infant.

Radioactive iodine

Radioactive iodine is often prescribed to damage cells that make thyroid hormone. The cells need iodine to make the hormone, so they absorb any iodine found in the body. The patient may take an iodine capsule daily for several weeks, resulting in the eventual shrinkage of the thyroid, reduced hormone production, and a return to normal blood levels. Some patients may receive a single larger oral dose of radioactive iodine to treat the disease more quickly. This should only be done for patients who are not of reproductive age or are not planning to have children, since a large amount can concentrate in the reproductive organs (gonads).

Surgery

Some patients may undergo surgery to treat hyperthyroidism. Most commonly, patients treated with thyroidectomy, in the form of partial or total removal of the thyroid, suffer from large goiter and have suffered relapses, even after repeated attempts to address the disease through drug therapy. Some patients may be candidates for surgery because they were not good candidates for iodine therapy or refused iodine administration. Patients receiving thyroidectomy or iodine therapy must be carefully monitored for years to watch for signs of hypothyroidism (insufficient production of thyroid hormones), which can occur as a complication of thyroid production suppression.

Prognosis

Hyperthyroidism is generally treatable and carries a good prognosis. Most patients lead normal lives with proper treatment. Thyroid storm, however, can be life-threatening and can lead to heart, liver, or kidney failure. Luckily, this form of fulminant hyperthyroidism is rare in children and adolescents.

Prevention

As of 2004 there are no known prevention methods for hyperthyroidism; its causes are either inherited or not completely understood. The best prevention tactic is knowledge of family history and close attention to symptoms and signs of the disease. Careful attention to prescribed therapy can prevent complications of the disease.

Parental concerns

Parents should be aware that hyperthyroidism is very rare in young children. However, once diagnosed, the condition needs short- and long-term treatment, with regular follow-up visits to the doctor.

Resources

BOOKS

"Hyperthyroidism." In *Nelson Textbook of Pediatrics.* Edited by Richard E. Behrman et al. Philadelphia: Saunders, 2004.

PERIODICALS

Hanna, C. E. "Adolescent Thyroid Disorders." *Adolescent Medicine* 13 (February 2002): 13–35.

ORGANIZATIONS

Thyroid Foundation of America. 350 Ruth Sleeper Hall, RSL 350, Parkman St., Boston, MA 02114. Web site: <www.clark.net/pub/tfa>.

Teresa Norris, RN
Rosalyn Carson-DeWitt, MD

Hypertonia *see* **Spasticity**

Hypoglycemia

Definition

Hypoglycemia is a condition characterized by low blood sugar, or abnormally low levels of glucose in the blood.

Description

Hypoglycemia (also known as a hypo, insulin shock, and a low) is brought on by abnormally low levels of glucose in the blood (i.e., 70 mg/dl or less). The condition is common among children with type 1 diabetes, but may also occur less frequently in children or teens with type 2 diabetes who are taking a sulfonylurea drug. An inade-quate diet, improperly calculated insulin dose, minor illnesses, or excessive activity without adequate sustenance can contribute to the condition. If unchecked, hypoglycemia can lead to unconsciousness. In very rare cases, the victim may suffer a seizure.

A hypoglycemic child will appear irritable, sweaty, shaky, and confused and may complain of being very hungry. In most cases, a snack of quick-acting carbohydrates (e.g., juice or hard candy) will remedy the situation. Glucose tablets or gel can also be taken. A child who has lost consciousness due to hypoglycemia may require a glucagon shot to return blood sugar levels to normal.

Newborns of women with gestational, type 1, or type 2 diabetes during pregnancy may also experience hypoglycemia at birth, particularly if the mother's blood glucose levels were not well controlled in late pregnancy. High levels of maternal glucose cause the fetus to generate equally high levels of insulin to handle the overload, and when the maternal glucose source is disconnected at birth with the cutting of the umbilical cord, all of that insulin causes the newborn's blood sugar levels to plummet. Intravenous administration of a glucose solution to the newborn can help re-establish normal blood sugar levels.

A rare type of hypoglycemia, known as reactive hypoglycemia, may occur in children and teens without diabetes. In reactive hypoglycemia, blood glucose levels drop to 70 mg/dl approximately four hours after a meal is eaten, causing the same symptoms of low blood sugars that can occur in people with diabetes.

Also rare is fasting hypoglycemia, a condition in which blood sugars are 50 mg/dl or lower after an overnight fast or between meals. Certain medications and medical conditions can cause this problem in children who do not have diabetes.

Demographics

Among children with diabetes, hypoglycemia is much more common in those with type 1 diabetes (also known as insulin-dependent diabetes or juvenile diabetes) than in those with type 2 diabetes (formerly known as adult-onset diabetes).

Causes and symptoms

Hypoglycemia in children and teens with diabetes can be triggered by too much insulin, excessive **exercise** without proper food intake, certain oral medications, skipping meals, and drinking alcoholic beverages.

Symptoms of hypoglycemia include:

- shakiness
- nervousness
- irritability
- dizziness
- sweating
- confusion
- fatigue
- hunger
- feelings of anxiety

Reactive hypoglycemia can be triggered by enzyme disorders and by gastric bypass surgery. Causes of fasting hypoglycemia in children without diabetes may include insulin-producing tumors, certain hormonal deficiencies, medications (including sulfa drugs and large doses of aspirin), and critical illnesses. Fasting hypoglycemia is more likely to occur in children under the age of 10.

When to call the doctor

Children who are experiencing frequent episodes of hypoglycemia should see their diabetes care doctor as soon as possible as they may require an insulin adjustment, medication change, or another change in their treatment regimen.

If a child or teen with diabetes starts experiencing low blood sugars without any symptoms, he or she may be developing hypoglycemic unawareness and the child's physician should be notified immediately. In hypoglycemic unawareness, the body stops sending its normal warning signs of hypoglycemia, and a child may not realize that blood glucose levels are dangerously low until he or she loses consciousness.

Diagnosis

Episodes of hypoglycemia in children and adolescents with diabetes can be confirmed with a blood test on a home blood glucose monitor. A small needle or lancet is used to prick the finger or an alternate site and a small drop of blood is collected on a test strip that is inserted into the monitor. The monitor then calculates and displays the blood glucose reading on a screen. Although individual blood glucose targets should be determined by a medical professional in light of a child's medical history, the general goal is to keep them as close to normal (i.e., 90 to 130 mg/dl or 5 to 7.2 mmol/L before meals) as possible. Glucose levels that are below 70 mg/dl (3.9 mmol/L) are typically considered hypoglycemic.

In order to diagnose reactive hypoglycemia in those without diabetes, a blood sample must be drawn while a child is experiencing symptoms. If the blood glucose levels are 70 mg/dl or lower and the symptoms subside after food or drink is provided, reactive hypoglycemia is diagnosed.

Treatment

Children with diabetes who exhibit symptoms of hypoglycemia should check their blood glucose levels on a home glucose meter immediately. If levels are 70 mg/dl (3.9 mmol/L) or lower, they should take 15 grams of a fast-acting carbohydrate (e.g., glucose tablets, Life Savers, regular cola), wait 15 minutes, and test their blood sugars again. If levels are still too low, repeating the procedure is necessary until blood glucose is within a safe range.

Giving an unconscious child or teen food or drink by mouth can be potentially dangerous due to the possibility of **choking**. A glucagon injection should be used on a child that has lost consciousness due to hypoglycemia. Glucagon is a hormone manufactured by the pancreas that triggers the release of blood glucose by the liver. The synthetic version of the hormone is used to rapidly raise blood glucose levels in people with diabetes experiencing a severe low. A glucagon injection kit contains a syringe of sterile water and a vial of powdered glucagon. The water is injected into the glucagon vial and then mixed, and the resulting solution is drawn back into the syringe for injection into any muscular area (e.g., arm, buttock, thigh). Glucagon can cause **vomiting**, so a child that is given a glucagons injection should be monitored carefully to prevent aspiration.

Episodes of reactive and fasting hypoglycemia in children without diabetes can also be treated with a fast-acting carbohydrate.

Nutritional concerns

For children with diabetes, eating or drinking large quantities of carbohydrates in an attempt to push blood glucose levels back to normal can result in **hyperglycemia**, or blood sugars that are too high. The 15 grams/15 minutes rule is important to follow to avoid dramatic blood sugar swings.

Eating small, frequent meals and spreading carbohydrate intake throughout the day may help keep blood glucose levels from bouncing too high or too low.

Prognosis

With early detection and immediate and appropriate treatment, children will recover quickly from hypoglycemia.

Prevention

The best way to prevent hypoglycemia is to check blood glucose levels frequently and treat falling blood sugars before they become dangerously low. However, even the most dedicated child or parent may be faced with situations that trigger lows, such as a delay in restaurant service after an insulin injection has been taken or a broken hotel elevator that requires one to climb 20 flights of stairs after a vigorous workout in the pool. Because hypoglycemia can be predictable, children with diabetes and their parents should always have a source of fast-acting carbohydrate on hand for treatment.

A child diagnosed with reactive hypoglycemia can alleviate the problem by consuming small, frequent meals (about every three hours) that are heavy in high-fiber, low-sugar foods. Some physicians may also recommend a high-protein, low-carbohydrate diet.

Parental concerns

Parents of children with diabetes must work with their child's teachers and school administrators to ensure that their child is able to test his or her blood sugars regularly, take insulin as needed, and have access to food or drink to treat hypoglycemia when necessary. Someone at school should also be trained in how to administer a glucagon injection, an emergency treatment for a hypoglycemic episode when a child loses consciousness. Caregivers of children with type 1 diabetes should have access to an emergency glucagon kit and be trained in its use. This should include a responsible adult at the child's school and at any **extracurricular activities** where parents are not present.

Section 504 of the Rehabilitation Act of 1973 enables parents to develop both a Section 504 plan (which describes a child's medical needs) and an individualized education plan, or IEP (which describes what special accommodations a child requires to address those needs). An IEP should cover issues surrounding hypoglycemia detection and treatment, and should outline how these episodes should be handled.

Because children who are self-conscious about their differences may not comply with their treatment routines as well as they should when their peers are around, parents should work with schools and caregivers to ensure that their child has a clean and private place to test blood glucose levels and take injections.

KEY TERMS

Fast-acting carbohydrate—A carbohydrate that causes blood sugar levels to rise quickly rather than slowly and steadily. Also called simple sugars. Examples include glucose tablets, honey, fructose, hard candy, and cake frosting.

Glucagon—A hormone produced in the pancreas that changes glycogen, a carbohydrate stored in muscles and the liver, into glucose. It can be used to relax muscles for a procedure such as duodenography. An injectable form of glucagon is sometimes used to treat insulin shock.

Hypoglycemic unawareness—A condition in which normal warning signals of a blood sugar low, such as shakiness, sweating, or rapid heartbeat, are no longer felt.

Reactive hypoglycemia—A rare condition in which blood sugars drop below normal levels approximately four hours after eating.

Sulfonylurea drug—A medication for type 2 diabetes that causes the pancreas to produce more insulin, and may trigger hypoglycemia in some people.

Teens who drive and have type 1 diabetes should always test their blood glucose levels before getting behind the wheel, and should have a snack before driving if their levels have fallen below the low range of normal (i.e., 90 mg/dl or 5 mmol/L or lower). Keeping the glove compartment stocked with a roll of glucose tablets can help in the case of an unexpected low on the road.

Because alcohol can also trigger hypoglycemia, adolescents should be informed of the risks of drinking. Parents should let their children know that alcohol is both illegal for minors and potentially dangerous to their health, but they should also ensure that teens know what to do to avoid a dangerous low if they do choose to drink. Food should always accompany alcohol, and anyone who drinks in the evening should consider setting an alarm to test blood sugar levels during the night. Many of the symptoms of hypoglycemia can mimic intoxication, so even those teens who do not drink but do attend parties where alcohol is available should always make sure they are with someone whom they can trust who knows what to do in case of hypoglycemia.

See also Diabetes mellitus.

Resources

BOOKS

Brand-Miller, Jennie Kaye Foster-Powell and Rick Mendosa. *What Makes My Blood Sugar Go Up and Down?* New York, NY: Marlowe & Company, 2003.

Ford-Martin, Paula. *The Everything Diabetes Book.* Boston, MA: Adams Media, 2004.

ORGANIZATIONS

American Diabetes Association. 1701 North Beauregard Street, Alexandria, VA 22311. (800) 342–2383. Web site: <www.diabetes.org>.

American Dietetic Association. 216 W. Jackson Blvd., Chicago, IL 60606–6995. (312) 899–0040. Web site: <www.eatright.org>.

Children With Diabetes. Diabetes 123, Inc. 5689 Chancery Place, Hamilton, OH 45011. info@diabetes123.com. Web site: <www.childrenwithdiabetes.org>.

Juvenile Diabetes Research Foundation. 120 Wall St., 19th Floor, New York, NY 10005. (800) 533–2873. Web site: <www.jdrf.org>.

National Diabetes Information Clearinghouse. 1 Information Way, Bethesda, MD 20892–3560. (800) 860–8747. Ndic@info.niddk.nih.gov. Web site: <www.niddk.nih.gov/health/diabetes/ndic.htm>.

Paula Ford-Martin

Hypogonadism

Definition

Hypogonadism is the condition in which the production of sex hormones and germ cells (sperm and eggs) is inadequate.

Description

Gonads are the organs of sexual differentiation: in the female, they are ovaries; in the male, the testes. Along with producing eggs and sperm, they produce sex hormones that generate all the differences between men and women. If they produce too little sex hormone, then either the growth of the sexual organs or their function is impaired.

The gonads are not independent in their function, however. They are closely controlled by the pituitary gland. The pituitary hormones are the same for males and females, but the gonadal hormones are different. Men produce mostly androgens, and women produce mostly estrogens and progesterone. Androgens regulate the development of the embryo, determining whether it is a male or a female (male in the presence of androgens and female in the absence of androgens). They also direct the adolescent maturation of sex organs into their adult form. Further, they sustain other sexual organs and their function throughout the reproductive years. Estrogen and testosterone help to maintain bone mass and strength and may protect the cardiovascular system.

Hormones can be inadequate during or after each stage of development—embryonic and adolescent. During each stage, inadequate hormone stimulation will prevent normal development. After each stage, a decrease in hormone stimulation will result in failed function and perhaps some shrinkage. The organs affected principally by sex hormones are the male and female genitals, both internal and external, and the female breasts. Body hair, fat deposition, bone and muscle growth, and some brain functions are also influenced.

Demographics

Hypogonadism may occur at any age; however, consequences differ according to the age at onset. If hypogonadism occurs prenatally (even if incomplete), sexual ambiguity may result. If hypogonadism occurs before **puberty**, puberty does not progress. If hypogonadism occurs after puberty, infertility and sexual dysfunction result. The demographics of hypogonadism vary depending on the cause. XYY syndrome has an incidence of one in 1,000 newborn males. However, since many males with XYY syndrome look like other males without XYY syndrome, they may never be identified.

Kallman's syndrome (KS) is the most frequent cause of hypogonadotropic hypogonadism and affects approximately one in 10,000 males and one in 50,000 females. Kallman's syndrome is found in all ethnic backgrounds. The incidence of KS in males is about five times greater than KS in females; the reason is not known. Turner's syndrome occurs in approximately one out of every 2,500 live births. However, all but 2 percent of fetuses affected by the disorder are miscarried. Of all the chromosomal abnormalities that result in spontaneous abortion or miscarriage, Turner's syndrome is the most common, accounting for about 20 percent of all miscarriages.

Causes and symptoms

There are a number of causes of hypogonadism, including stress, elevated prolactin levels, and several genetic disorders. Sex is determined at the moment of conception by sex chromosomes. Females have two X chromosomes, while males have one X and one Y chromosome. Male sperm cells contain either an X or a Y; if the sperm with the Y chromosome fertilizes an egg, the baby will be male. Genetic defects sometimes result in changes in the chromosomes. If sex chromosomes are involved, there is a change in the development of sexual characteristics. Female is the default sex of the embryo, so most of the sex organ deficits at birth occur in boys. Some, but not all, are due to inadequate androgen stimulation. The penis may be small, the testicles undescended (cryptorchidism) or various degrees of "feminization" of the genitals may be present.

After birth, sexual development does not occur until puberty. Hypogonadism most often shows up as an abnormality in boys during puberty. Again, not every defect is due to inadequate hormones. Some are due to too much of the wrong ones. Female problems in puberty are usually not caused by too little estrogen. Turner's syndrome leads to failure of puberty in some girls due to the lack of estrogen and progesterone production. Female reproductive problems are usually related to complex cycling rhythms gone wrong. The most common problems with too little hormone happen during menopause, which is normal hypogonadism.

A number of adverse events can damage the gonads and result in decreased hormone levels. The childhood disease **mumps**, if acquired after puberty, can infect and destroy the testicles—a disease called viral orchitis. Ionizing radiation and **chemotherapy**, trauma, several drugs (spironolactone, a diuretic, and ketoconazole, an antifungal agent), alcohol, marijuana, heroin, methadone, and environmental toxins can all damage testicles and decrease their hormone production. Severe diseases in the liver or kidneys, certain infections, **sickle cell anemia**, and some cancers also affect gonads. To treat some male cancers, it is necessary to remove the testicles, thereby preventing the androgens from stimulating **cancer** growth. This procedure, called castration or orchiectomy, removes androgen stimulation from the whole body.

For several reasons, the pituitary gland can fail to produce hormones. It happens rarely after pregnancy. The pituitary used to be removed to treat advanced breast or prostate cancer. Sometimes the pituitary develops a tumor that destroys it. Failure of the pituitary is called hypopituitarism and, of course, leaves the gonads with no stimulation to produce hormones. Besides the tissue changes generated by hormone stimulation, the only other symptoms relate to sexual desire and function. Libido is enhanced by testosterone, and male sexual performance requires androgens. The role of female hormones in female sexual activity is less clear, although hormones strengthen tissues and promote healthy secretions, facilitating sexual activity.

XYY syndrome

XYY syndrome is a chromosome disorder that affects males. Males with this disorder have an extra Y chromosome. The error that causes the extra Y chromosome can occur in the fertilizing sperm or in the developing embryo. There are no physical abnormalities in most males with XYY syndrome. However, some males can have one or more of the following characteristics. Males who have XYY syndrome are usually normal in length at birth but have rapid growth in childhood, typically averaging in the seventy-fifth percentile (taller than 75 percent of males their same age). Many males with XYY syndrome are not overly muscular, particularly in the chest and shoulders. Individuals with XYY syndrome often have difficulties with their coordination. As a result, they can appear to be awkward or clumsy. During their teenage years, males with XYY syndrome may develop severe **acne** that may need to be treated by a dermatologist.

Men with XYY syndrome have normal, heterosexual function, and most are fertile. However, numerous cases of men with XYY syndrome presenting with infertility have been reported. Most males with XYY syndrome have normal hormones involved in their sperm production. However, a minority of males with XYY syndrome may have increased amounts of some hormones involved in sperm production. This may result in infertility due to inadequate sperm production. The actual incidence of infertility in males with XYY syndrome is unknown.

Kallman's syndrome

Kallman's syndrome is a disorder of hypogonadotropic hypogonadism, delayed puberty, and anosmia (the inability to smell). Kallman's syndrome is a birth defect in the brain that prevents release of hormones and appears as failure of male puberty. Some boys have adequate amounts of androgen in their system but fail to respond to them, a condition known as androgen resistance. Hypogonadotropic hypogonadism (HH) occurs when the body does not produce enough of two important hormones, luteinizing hormone (LH) and follicle stimulating hormone (FSH). This results in underdeveloped gonads and often infertility. Anosmia, the inability to smell, was first described with hypogonadotropic hypogonadism in 1856, but it was not until 1944 that an instance of Kallman's reported the inheritance of the two symptoms together in three separate families. Hence, the syndrome of hypogonadotropic hypogonadism and anosmia was named Kallman's syndrome (KS). Affected people usually are detected in **adolescence** when they do not undergo puberty. The most common features are

HH and anosmia, though a wide range of features can present in an affected person. Other features of KS may include a small penis or undescended testicles in males, kidney abnormalities, **cleft lip** and/or palate, **clubfoot**, hearing problems, and central nervous system problems such as synkinesia (the performance of an unintended movement when making a voluntary one), eye movement abnormalities, and visual and hearing defects.

Diabetes mellitus

Type 1 diabetes (**diabetes mellitus**) occasionally has been associated with hypogonadism. Most cases seem to be due to the hypogonadism of **malnutrition** and respond to improved control. Some specific conditions associated with diabetes mellitus, such as hemachromatosis, and the Laurence-Moon Biedl, Alstrom, and Cushing syndromes, also typically produce hypogonadism. Normal gonadal function is required for normal male development of the genital tract and for maintenance of some elements of male sexual behavior. The most clearly androgen-dependent aspects include libido, sexual activity, and spontaneous erections. In normal, young males with hypogonadism, sexual acts, fantasies, and desire are significantly diminished. Spontaneous erections also decrease by approximately 40 percent. Replacement with testosterone prevents these changes, suggesting that an intact male gonadal system is required to maintain sexual function. However, visual and possibly tactile stimulus-bound erections are not impaired in males with hypogonadism after infancy. This implies that androgen action is not required to maintain the capacity for erection.

Turner's syndrome

Turner's syndrome is a genetic disorder caused by a missing X chromosome that occurs only in females. Women with Turner's syndrome are characterized by short stature, absence of secondary sexual characteristics, infertility, and a number of other physical abnormalities. Women with Turner's syndrome are born with underdeveloped ovaries that are eventually replaced by connective tissue. Because of the resulting lack of sex hormones, these individuals do not have menstrual periods and their breasts remain undeveloped, although they may develop underarm and pubic hair. Turner's syndrome does not affect **intelligence**, although persons with the condition have poor spatial perception and mathematical aptitude, often accompanied by learning disabilities.

In girls, hypogonadism during childhood will result in lack of **menstruation** and **breast development** and short height. If hypogonadism occurs after puberty, symptoms include loss of menstruation, low libido, hot flashes, and loss of body hair. In boys, hypogonadism in childhood results in lack of muscle and beard development and growth problems. In males the usual complaints are sexual dysfunction, decreased beard and body hair, breast enlargement, and muscle loss. If a brain tumor is present (central hypogonadism) there may be headaches or visual loss or symptoms of other hormonal deficiencies (such as **hypothyroidism**). In the case of the most common pituitary tumor, prolactinoma, there may be a milky breast discharge. People with **anorexia nervosa** (excessive dieting to the point of starvation) also may have central hypogonadism.

When to call the doctor

Parents should consult a **family** physician or pediatrician if their child has any signs or symptoms of hypogonadism. Establishing the cause of hypogonadism is an important first step to getting appropriate treatment. Children may require a consultation with an endocrinologist, a physician who specializes in the hormone-producing (endocrine) glands. If the primary care physician suspects the condition is present, he or she may refer the child to an endocrinologist. Parents may also consider taking the child directly to an endocrinologist without a referral.

Diagnosis

As of the early 2000s, there are accurate blood tests for most of the hormones in the body, including those from the pituitary and even some from the hypothalamus. Chromosomes can be analyzed, and gonads can be, but rarely are, biopsied. Tests may be done that check estrogen levels (women) and testosterone levels (men) as well as FSH levels and LH levels, the pituitary hormones that stimulate the gonads. Other tests may include a thyroid level; sperm count; prolactin level (milk hormone); blood tests for anemia, chemistries, and iron; and genetic analysis. Sometimes imaging is necessary, such as a sonogram of the ovaries. If pituitary disease is suspected, a **magnetic resonance imaging** (MRI) or computerized tomography (CT) scan of the brain may be done.

Treatment

Replacement of missing body chemicals is much easier than suppressing excesses. Estrogen is recommended only to control hot flashes and sweats after menopause but is used in young women who do not produce hormones on their own. Estrogen can be taken by mouth, injection, or skin patch. It is strongly recommended that the other female hormone, progesterone, be taken by women who have an intact uterus as well, because doing so prevents overgrowth of uterine lining and uterine cancer. Testosterone replacement is available for males who are deficient. Testosterone comes in the form of an injection, patch, or gel.

Alternative treatment

Ethinyl estradiol, an estrogen derivative, is sometimes used for the treatment of hypogonadism.

Prognosis

Many forms of hypogonadism are potentially treatable and have a good prognosis.

Prevention

People should maintain normal body weight and have healthy eating habits to prevent anorexia nervosa. Other causes may not be preventable.

Parental concerns

Adolescents with hypogonadism may have problems fitting in socially due to delayed sexual development. Testosterone replacement therapy can induce puberty, and at a slow pace in order to allow time for adjustment to body changes and new feelings. In girls with hypogonadism, complications include the social implication of failing to go through puberty with peers (if hypogonadism occurs before puberty). A supportive family that understands the diagnosis of hypogonadism is important. Adolescents may need psychological or family counseling. Support groups can help people with hypogonadism and related conditions cope with similar situations and challenges.

See also Intersex states; Turner syndrome.

Resources

BOOKS

Turner's Syndrome: A Medical Dictionary, Bibliography, and Annotated Research Guide to Internet References. San Diego, CA: Icon Health Publications, 2004.

Winters, Stephen J. *Male Hypogonadism: Basic, Clinical, and Therapeutic Principles.* Totowa, NJ: Humana Press, 2004.

PERIODICALS

Carlson, Robert H. "Panel: Here are Twenty-Five Recommendations on Hypogonadism." *Urology Times* 31 (November 2003): 22.

KEY TERMS

Biopsy—The surgical removal and microscopic examination of living tissue for diagnostic purposes or to follow the course of a disease. Most commonly the term refers to the collection and analysis of tissue from a suspected tumor to establish malignancy.

Diabetes mellitus—The clinical name for common diabetes. It is a chronic disease characterized by the inability of the body to produce or respond properly to insulin, a hormone required by the body to convert glucose to energy.

Embryo—In humans, the developing individual from the time of implantation to about the end of the second month after conception. From the third month to the point of delivery, the individual is called a fetus.

Endocrinologist—A physician who specializes in treating patients who have diseases of the thyroid, parathyroid, adrenal glands, and/or the pancreas.

Fetus—In humans, the developing organism from the end of the eighth week to the moment of birth. Until the end of the eighth week the developing organism is called an embryo.

Hypothalamus—A part of the forebrain that controls heartbeat, body temperature, thirst, hunger, body temperature and pressure, blood sugar levels, and other functions.

Ionizing radiation—Radiation that can damage living tissue by disrupting and destroying individual cells at the molecular level. All types of nuclear radiation–x rays, gamma rays, and beta rays–are potentially ionizing. Sound waves physically vibrate the material through which they pass, but do not ionize it.

Kallman's syndrome—A disorder of hypogonadotropic hypogonadism, delayed puberty, and anosmia. Kallman's syndrome is a birth defect in the brain that prevents release of hormones and appears as failure of male puberty.

Turner syndrome—A chromosome abnormality characterized by short stature and ovarian failure caused by an absent X chromosome. It occurs only in females.

Undescended testicle—A testicle that is still in the groin and has not made its way into the scrotum.

XYY syndrome—A chromosome disorder that affects males.

Godek, Brent W., and Neil S. Skolnik. "Hypogonadism in Men." *Family Practice News* 34 (May 15, 2004): 28.

Sadovsky, Richard. "Androgen Deficiency in Women: Review of the Subject." *American Family Physician* (December 15, 2001): 2000.

———. "Effect of Male Hypogonadism on Bone Architecture: Tips." *American Family Physician* (December 15, 2003): 2297.

Sullivan, Michele G. "Guidelines Take New Look at Management of Hypogonadism in Men (Testosterone Replacement Options)." *Internal Medicine News* 36 (February 1, 2003): 6.

ORGANIZATIONS

American Association of Clinical Endocrinologists. 1000 Riverside Avenue, Suite 205, Jacksonville, FL 32204. Web site: <www.aace.com>.

National Institute on Child Health and Human Development. PO Box 3006, Rockville, MD 20847. Web site: <www.nichd.nih.gov>.

WEB SITES

"Hypogonadism." *Medline Plus*, November 14, 2002. Available online at <www.nlm.nih.gov/medlineplus/ency/article/001195.htm> (accessed November 10, 2004).

"Male Hypergonadism." *Ohio Health*, 2004. Available online at <www.ohiohealth.com/healthreference/reference/E97FDCB5-E617-4C36-859B911C1A0E9257.htm> (accessed November 1o, 2004).

J. Ricker Polsdorfer
Ken R. Wells

Hypopigmentation *see* **Albinism**

Hypospadias

Definition

Hypospadias is a congenital defect of the penis in which the urinary tract opening, or urethral meatus, is abnormally located away from the tip of the penis.

Description

In males with hypospadias, the urinary opening is located on the underside of the penis. Often there is an accompanying underdevelopment of the foreskin in which the penis has a hooded appearance. Most of the foreskin is located on the top and sides of the tip of the penis. The urethral meatus may be located at any point along the penile shaft from just below the tip of the penis to closer to the body and/or near the scrotum. It may appear as a small hole in the penis or, in more severe cases, may be a longer slit-like opening. Some cases may involve chordee, a condition in which the penis bends down or away from the body during erection.

Demographics

Hypospadias is the most common anomaly of the penis affecting approximately one in 250 males born. Research has shown a doubling of the number of babies born with this anomaly. The reason for this increase is as of 2004 unknown.

Causes and symptoms

Hypospadias is a congenital anomaly resulting from incomplete closure of the tissue of the penis that forms the urethra (the tube that carries urine from the bladder to the outside of the body). The potential symptoms of hypospadias if left untreated include an abnormal direction of the urine stream, abnormal appearance of the penis, infertility if the defect is located far enough away from the tip of the penis, and an inability to have sexual intercourse in cases involving chordee.

Diagnosis

Hypospadias is diagnosed most often during the initial newborn physical examination and is classified based on where the urethral meatus is located. In rare cases infants with hypospadias occurring closer to the body and who also have undescended testicles, a karyotype or genetic screen may be performed to determine gender. Males who have hypospadias located within or near the scrotum should also have a procedure called a voiding cystogram to rule out additional urinary tract anomalies. In general, very few babies with hypospadias have other birth defects. Many males with multiple congenital anomalies, however, may also have hypospadias.

Prognosis

The prognosis for boys who have undergone hypospadias repair is excellent. Very few children experience complications. In most cases, the penis appears normal and functions normally. Less than 5 percent of children with mild hypospadias experience postoperative complications. Complications include wound infections, unexpected opening near the repair

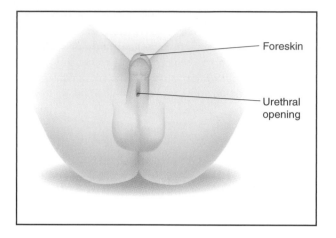

Foreskin

Urethral opening

Hypospadias, a condition in which the urethral opening is not at the tip of the penis, but rather along the penile shaft. *(Illustration by Argosy, Inc.)*

site, and rarely, meatul stenosis, a narrowing of the urinary tract opening.

Prevention

There was as of 2004 no known prevention of hypospadias.

Parental concerns

Most hypospadias cases are minor and involve few complications. Initially, parents should be sure their son is not circumcised because the foreskin is often essential in hypospadias repair surgery. Should the parents decide to allow corrective surgery, they should find a pediatric urologic surgeon with experience in performing hypospadias repairs. After surgery, care must be taken to follow all postoperative instructions and to obtain follow-up care from both the pediatrician and pediatric urologist. Parents may be concerned about the appearance and function of the penis. In most cases, following hypospadias repair surgery, the penis functions normally and is normal in appearance as well. Most males who have had a hypospadias repair are able to stand to urinate, experience normal sexual function, and normal fertility. Parents may be concerned about the physical and emotional **pain** of genital surgery. The recommended age of surgical repair is between four and 12 months. This age is ideal for many reasons including the size of the penis and the slow rate of growth of the penis at this age, the relatively low risk from anesthesia, and the fact that children at this age have not formed long-term memory and will not remember the surgery.

Resources

BOOKS

Berhman, Richard E., et al., eds. *Nelson Textbook of Pediatrics*, 16th ed. Philadelphia: Saunders, 2000.

Rudolph, Colin D., and Abraham M. Rudolph, eds. *Rudolph's Pediatrics*, 21st ed. New York: McGraw-Hill, 2003.

WEB SITES

"Hypospadias." *Children's Hospital Boston*, 2001. Available online at <www.childrenshospital.org/cfapps/A2ZtopicDisplay.cfm?Topic=Hypospadias> (accessed December 11, 2004).

"Hypospadias." *Digital Urology Journal.* Available online at <www.duj.com/hypospadias.html> (accessed December 11, 2004).

Deborah L. Nurmi, MS

Hypothyroidism

Definition

Hypothyroidism, or underactive thyroid, develops when the thyroid gland fails to produce or secrete as much thyroxine (T_4) and triiodothyonine (T_3) as the body needs. Because these thyroid hormones regulate such essential functions as heart rate, digestion, physical growth, and mental development, an insufficient supply of this hormone can slow metabolic processes, damage organs and tissues in every part of the body, and lead to life-threatening complications.

Description

Hypothyroidism is one of the most common chronic diseases in the United States. Symptoms may not appear until years after the thyroid has stopped functioning and often are mistaken for signs of other illnesses. Although this condition is believed to affect up to 11 million adults and children, as many as two out of every three people with hypothyroidism may not know they have the disease.

Nicknamed "Gland Central" because it influences almost every organ, tissue, and cell in the body, the thyroid is shaped like a butterfly and located just below the larynx, or Adam's apple, and in front of the trachea, or windpipe. The thyroid stores iodine that the body obtains from food, and uses this mineral to create the thyroid hormones. Low thyroid hormone levels can alter weight, appetite, **sleep** patterns, body temperature, and a variety of other physical, mental, and emotional characteristics.

Although hypothyroidism is most common in women who are middle-aged or older, the disease can occur at any age. In addition, an infant can be born with congenital hypothyroidism, i.e., without a functioning thyroid. In older children, the development of hypothyroidism may progress slowly and it may be several years before the disease is diagnosed.

Demographics

The most common cause of hypothyroidism in mid- to late-childhood and **adolescence** is Hashimoto's thyroiditis, which occurs in up to 1.2 percent of the school age population. Congenital hypothyroidism is less common. One out of every 4,000–5,000 infants is born without a properly functioning thyroid gland. Congenital hypothyroidism is twice as common in girls as in boys and about five times more common in whites than in blacks.

Causes and symptoms

Congenital hypothyroidism is a disorder that affects infants from birth, resulting from the loss of thyroid function due to the failure of the thyroid gland to develop correctly. Sometimes the thyroid gland is absent or is ectopic, i.e., in an abnormal location. This congenital defect means that the infant does not produce sufficient thyroid hormones, resulting in abnormal growth and development as well as slower mental function.

Hypothyroidism may also be caused by an abnormality of the immune system that results in damage and destruction of the thyroid gland (Hashimoto's thyroiditis). This process can result in either loss of thyroid tissue or enlargement of the thyroid. In most cases, there is no **pain** or tenderness associated with this disease, although sometimes persons affected complain of difficulty in swallowing, as if they had a lump in the throat.

Less often, hypothyroidism develops when the pituitary gland fails and does not release enough thyroid-stimulating hormone (TSH), which stimulates the thyroid to produce and secrete normal amounts of T_4 and T_3. TSH may be deficient for several reasons:

- disease of the pituitary gland (occurs rarely)
- disease of the hypothalamus (located about the pituitary), which stimulates the pituitary gland
- tumor, cyst, or other abnormal structure between the hypothalamus and pituitary gland that prevents the pituitary from receiving the stimulus to secrete TSH

Other causes of hypothyroidism include:

- Radiation. Radioactive iodine used to treat **hyperthyroidism** (overactive thyroid) or radiation treatments for head or neck cancers can destroy the thyroid gland.
- Surgery. Removal of the thyroid gland because of **cancer** or other thyroid disorders can result in hypothyroidism.
- Viruses and bacteria. Infections that depress thyroid hormone production usually cause permanent hypothyroidism.
- Medication. Nitroprusside, lithium, or iodides can induce hypothyroidism. Because patients who use these medications are closely monitored by their doctors, this side effect is very rare.
- Environmental contaminants. Certain man-made chemicals such as PCBs, found in the local environment at high levels, may also cause hypothyroidism.

Often babies with congenital hypothyroidism will appear normal at birth, which is why screening is vital.

However, some infants may have one of more of the following symptoms:

- large size (despite poor feeding habits) and increased birth weight
- puffy face and swollen tongue
- hoarse cry
- low muscle tone
- cold extremities
- persistent **constipation**, with distended abdomen
- lack of energy, sleeping most of the time and appearing tired when awake
- little or no growth

Children born with symptoms have a greater risk of **developmental delay** than children born without symptoms. The longer a child with hypothyroidism remains untreated, the greater is the loss of intellectual capacity, as measured by the standard **intelligence** testing (IQ). The ultimate IQ has been shown to be significantly higher in children whose hypothyroidism was detected and treated prior to six weeks of age, compared to those children whose hypothyroidism went untreated for six to 12 weeks.

Hypothyroidism that develops after birth is sometimes referred to as a silent disease because early symptoms may be so mild that no one realizes anything is wrong. Untreated symptoms become more noticeable and severe, and can lead to confusion and mental disorders, breathing difficulties, heart problems, fluctuations in body temperature, and death.

A child or adolescent who has hypothyroidism may have one or more of the following symptoms:

- fatigue
- decreased heart rate
- progressive hearing loss
- weight gain
- problems with memory and concentration
- depression
- goiter (enlarged thyroid gland)
- muscle pain or weakness
- numb, tingling hands
- dry skin
- swollen eyelids
- dryness or loss of hair
- extreme sensitivity to cold
- constipation

- delayed (common) or early (rare) onset of sexual development at adolescence
- irregular menstrual periods
- elevated cholesterol levels in the blood
- hoarse voice

Although hypothyroidism usually develops gradually, when the disease results from surgery or other treatment for hyperthyroidism, symptoms may appear suddenly and include severe **muscle cramps** in the arms, legs, neck, shoulders, and back.

People whose hypothyroidism remains undiagnosed and untreated may eventually develop myxedema. Symptoms of this rare, but potentially deadly, complication include enlarged tongue, swollen facial features, hoarseness, and physical and mental sluggishness. Myxedema coma can cause unresponsiveness; irregular, shallow breathing; low blood sugar; and drops in blood pressure and body temperature. The onset of this medical emergency can be sudden in children with undiagnosed hypothyroidism; it can be brought on by illness, injury, surgery, use of sedatives or anti-depressants, or exposure to very cold temperatures. Without immediate medical attention, myxedema coma can be fatal.

When to call the doctor

The doctor should be called if signs of hypothyroidism or myxedema are present. Every child who has a decrease in rate of growth in height during childhood and adolescence should be tested to determine if the growth problem is caused by hypothyroidism.

Diagnosis

In the United States, newborn infants between 24 and 72 hours old are tested for congenital thyroid deficiency (cretinism) using a test that measures the levels of thyroxine in the infant's blood. If the levels are low, the physician will likely repeat the blood test to confirm the diagnosis. The physician may take an x ray of the infant's legs. In an infant with hypothyroidism, the ends of the bones have an immature appearance. Treatment within the first few months of life can prevent **mental retardation** and physical abnormalities.

Older children who develop hypothyroidism may suddenly stop growing. If the child was above average height before the disease occurred, he or she may now be short compared to other children of the same age. Therefore, the most important feature of hypothyroidism in a child is a decrease in the rate of growth in height. If the disease is recognized early and adequately treated, the child will grow at an accelerated rate until reaching the same growth percentile where the child measured before the onset of hypothyroidism. Diagnosis of hypothyroidism is based on the patient's observations, medical history, physical examination, and thyroid function tests. Doctors who specialize in treating thyroid disorders (endocrinologists) are most likely to recognize subtle symptoms and physical indications of hypothyroidism. A diagnostic evaluation may include a blood test known as a thyroid-stimulating hormone (TSH) assay, thyroid nuclear medicine scan, thyroid ultrasound, or needle aspiration biopsy (which is also used to provide information on thyroid masses). All patients should be sure their doctors are aware of any recent procedures involving radioactive materials or contrast media.

The blood test is extremely accurate, but some doctors doubt its ability to detect mild hypothyroidism. They advise patients to monitor their basal (resting) body temperature for below-normal readings that could indicate the presence of hypothyroidism.

Alternative treatment

Alternative treatments are primarily aimed at strengthening the thyroid but will not eliminate the need for thyroid hormone medications. Herbal remedies to improve thyroid function and relieve symptoms of hypothyroidism include bladder wrack (*Fucus vesiculosus*), which can be taken in capsule form or as a tea. The shoulder stand **yoga** position (done at least once daily for 20 minutes) is believed to improve thyroid function.

Nutritional concerns

Because the thyroid makes T_4 from iodine in food, an iodine-deficient diet can cause hypothyroidism. Adding iodine to table salt and other common foods has eliminated iodine deficiency in the United States. Some foods, including cabbage, rutabagas, radishes, peanuts, peaches, soybeans, and spinach, can interfere with thyroid hormone production. Anyone with hypothyroidism may want to avoid these foods. A high-fiber diet along with regular **exercise** is recommended to help maintain thyroid function and prevent constipation.

Prognosis

Thyroid hormone replacement therapy generally maintains normal thyroid hormone levels unless treatment is interrupted or discontinued.

KEY TERMS

Cretinism—Severe hypothyroidism that is present at birth and characterized by severe mental retardation.

Endocrine system—A group of ductless glands and parts of glands that secrete hormones directly into the bloodstream or lymphatic system to control metabolic activity. Pituitary, thyroid, adrenals, ovaries, and testes are all part of the endocrine system.

Goiter—Chronic enlargement of the thyroid gland.

Hyperthyroidism—A condition characterized by abnormal over-functioning of the thyroid glands. Patients are hypermetabolic, lose weight, are nervous, have muscular weakness and fatigue, sweat more, and have increased urination and bowel movements. Also called thyrotoxicosis.

Hypothalamus—A part of the forebrain that controls heartbeat, body temperature, thirst, hunger, body temperature and pressure, blood sugar levels, and other functions.

Myxedema—Severe hypothyroidism, characterized by swelling of the face, hands, and feet, an enlarged tongue, horseness, and physical and mental sluggishness.

Pituitary gland—The most important of the endocrine glands (glands that release hormones directly into the bloodstream), the pituitary is located at the base of the brain. Sometimes referred to as the "master gland," it regulates and controls the activities of other endocrine glands and many body processes including growth and reproductive function. Also called the hypophysis.

Thyroid-stimulating hormone (TSH)—A hormone produce by the pituitary gland that stimulates the thyroid gland to produce the hormones that regulate metabolism. Also called thyrotropin.

Thyroxine (T_4)—The thyroid hormone that regulates many essential body processes.

Triiodothyronine (T_3)—A thyroid hormone similar to thyroxine but more powerful. Preparations of triiodothyronine are used in treating hypothyroidism.

Prevention

Hypothyroidism usually cannot be prevented, but the symptoms and effects of the disease can be controlled by prompt diagnosis and treatment.

Parental concerns

Parents must ensure that medication is taken on a routine basis by making the process a part of the family's lifestyle. Taking the medication as prescribed helps assure the child's optimal growth and development.

Resources

BOOKS

Gomez, Joan. *Thyroid Problems in Women and Children: Self-Help and Treatment.* Alameda, CA: Hunter House, 2003.

Langer, Stephen, and James F. Scheer. *Hypothyroidism: The Unsuspected Illness.* New Canaan, CT: Keats Publishing, 1995.

Pratt, Maureen. *The First Year—Hypothyroidism: An Essential Guide for the Newly Diagnosed.* New York: Marlowe and Company, 2003.

Rosenthal, M. Sara. *The Hypothyroid Sourcebook: Everything You Need to Know.* New York: McGraw Hill, 2002.

Shomon, Mary J. *Living Well with Hypothyroidism: What Your Doctor Doesn't Tell You...That You Need to Know.* New York: Harper Resource, 2000.

Wood, Lawrence C., et al. *Your Thyroid: A Home Reference.* New York: Ballantine Books, 1996.

ORGANIZATIONS

American Thyroid Association. Montefiore Medical Center, 111 E. 210th St., Bronx, NY 10467. Web site: <www.thyroid.org>.

Endocrine Society. 4350 East West Highway, Suite 500, Bethesda, MD 20814-4410. (301) 941-0200. Web site: <www.endo- society.org>.

Thyroid Foundation of America, Inc. Ruth Sleeper Hall, RSL 350, Boston, MA 02114-2968. (800) 832-8321 or (617) 726-8500. Web site: <www.tsh.org>.

Thyroid Society for Education and Research. 7515 S. Main St., Suite 545, Houston, TX 77030. (800) THYROID or (713) 799-9909. Web site: <www.the-thyroid-society.org>.

WEB SITES

Thyroid Diseases. National Institutes of Health. Available online at: <www.nlm.nih.gov/medlineplus/thyroiddiseases.html>.

Judith Sims, M.S.
Maureen Haggerty

Hypotonia

Definition

Hypotonia, or severely decreased muscle tone, is seen primarily in children. Low-toned muscles contract very slowly in response to a stimulus and cannot maintain a contraction for as long as a normal muscle. Hypotonia is a symptom that can be caused by many different conditions.

Description

Hypotonia, also called floppy infant syndrome or infantile hypotonia, is a condition of decreased muscle tone. The low muscle tone can be caused by a variety of conditions and is often indicative of the presence of an underlying central nervous system disorder, genetic disorder, or muscle disorder. Muscle tone is the amount of tension or resistance to movement in a muscle. It is not the same as muscle weakness, which is a reduction in the strength of a muscle, but it can co-exist with muscle weakness. Muscle tone indicates the ability of a muscle to respond to a stretch. For example, if the flexed arm of a child with normal tone is quickly straightened, the flexor muscle of the arm (biceps) will quickly contract in response. Once the stimulus is removed, the muscle then relaxes and returns to its normal resting state. A child with low muscle tone has muscles that are slow to start a muscle contraction. Muscles contract very slowly in response to a stimulus and cannot maintain a contraction for as long as a normal muscle. Because low-toned muscles do not fully contract before they again relax, they remain loose and very stretchy, never achieving their full potential of sustaining a muscle contraction over time.

Hypotonic infants, therefore, have a typical "floppy" appearance. They rest with their elbows and knees loosely extended, while infants with normal muscle tone tend to have flexed elbows and knees. Head control is usually poor or absent in the floppy infant with the head falling to the side, backward, or forward. Infants with normal tone can be lifted by placing hands under their armpits, but hypotonic infants tend to slip between the hands as their arms rise unresistingly upward. While most children tend to flex their elbows and knees when resting, hypotonic children hang their arms and legs limply by their sides. Infants with this condition often lag behind in reaching the fine and gross motor developmental milestones that enable infants to hold their heads up when placed on the stomach, balance themselves, or get into a sitting position and remain seated without falling over. Hypotonia is also characterized by problems with mobility and posture, lethargy, weak ligaments and joints, and poor reflexes. Since the muscles that support the bone joints are so soft, there is a tendency for hip, jaw, and neck dislocations to occur. Some hypotonic children also have trouble feeding and are unable to suck or chew for long periods. Others may also have problems with speech or exhibit shallow breathing. Hypotonia does not, however, affect intellect.

Demographics

No demographic information as of 2004 was available for hypotonia, since it is a symptom of an underlying disorder. However, a study conducted in year 2000 by the University of Illinois provides some insights. The study followed 243 infants with hypotonia for three to seven years. By the age of three, about 30 percent had minimal problems and 46 percent had significant impairments, while 24 percent of the infants were normal. Hypotonic infants who matured into children with minimal disabilities were highly likely to have poor motor coordination at age three (78%). About 25 percent had learning problems or **language delay**; 20 percent had borderline cognition or attention deficits; and 66 percent had two or more of these characteristics.

Causes and symptoms

Hypotonias are often of unknown origin. Scientists believe that they may be caused by trauma; environmental factors; or by other genetic, muscle, or central nervous system disorders. The National Institutes of Health list the following common causes of hypotonia:

- Down syndrome: a chromosome abnormality, usually due to an extra copy of the twenty-first chromosome.

- Myasthenia gravis: a neuromuscular disorder characterized by variable weakness of voluntary muscles, which often improves with rest and worsens with activity. The condition is caused by an abnormal immune response.

- Prader-Willi syndrome: a congenital disease characterized by **obesity**, severe hypotonia, and decreased mental capacity

- Kernicterus: also called Rh incompatibility, a condition that develops when there is a difference in Rh blood type between that of the mother (Rh negative) and that of the fetus (Rh positive).

- Cerebellar ataxia: a movement disorder which with its sudden onset, often following an infectious viral disease, causes hypotonia.

- Infant **botulism**: a type of botulism, in which *Clostridium botulinum* bacteria grow within an infant's digestive tract, producing a toxin which is potentially life-threatening.

- Familial dysautonomia: also called Riley-Day syndrome, an inherited disorder that affects the function of nerves throughout the body.

- Marfan syndrome: an inherited disorder of connective tissue (tissue that adds strength to the body's structures), affecting the skeletal system, cardiovascular system, eyes, and skin.

- Muscular dystrophy: a group of disorders characterized by progressive muscle weakness and loss of muscle tissue.

- Achondroplasia: a disorder of bone growth that causes the most common type of dwarfism.

- Trisomy 13: a syndrome associated with the presence of a third number 13 chromosome.

- Sepsis: a severe, life-threatening illness caused by overwhelming infection of the bloodstream by toxin-producing bacteria.

- Aicardi syndrome: a rare genetic disorder characterized by infantile spasms (jerking), absence of the corpus callosum (the connection between the two hemispheres of the brain), **mental retardation**, and lesions of the retina of the eye or optic nerve.

- Canavan disease: an inherited metabolic disorder characterized by degeneration of the white matter of the brain.

- Congenital **hypothyroidism**: a disorder that results from decreased thyroid hormone production.

- Hypervitaminosis D: a condition that appears several months after excessive doses of vitamin D are administered.

- Krabbe disease: an inherited disorder characterized by a deficiency of the enzyme galactosylcereamidase, resulting in destruction of myelin, the fatty material that surrounds and insulates many of the nerves.

- Metachromatic leukodystrophy: an inherited disease characterized by the absence of the enzyme arylsulfatase A, which causes a material called cerebroside sulfate to accumulate in cells, which is toxic to cells, especially to the cells of the nervous system.

- Methylmalonic academia: an inherited metabolic disorder, usually diagnosed in infancy, which causes the accumulation of methylmalonic acid in the body and can lead to severe metabolic disturbances.

- Rickets: a childhood disorder involving softening and weakening of the bones, primarily caused by lack of vitamin D, calcium, or phosphate.

- Spinal muscular atrophy type 1 (Werdnig-Hoffman): a group of inherited diseases causing progressive muscle degeneration and weakness, eventually leading to death.

- Tay-Sachs disease: a genetic disorder found predominantly in Ashkenazi Jewish families results in early death.

- Vaccine reaction: any injury or condition that occurs as a result of a vaccination.

The following are common symptoms associated with hypotonia. Each child may experience different symptoms, depending on the underlying cause of the hypotonia:

- decreased muscle tone; muscles feel soft and doughy

- ability to extend limb beyond its normal limit

- failure to acquire motor skill developmental milestones (such as holding head up without support from parent, rolling over, sitting up without support, walking)

- feeding problems (inability to suck or chew for prolonged periods)

- shallow breathing

- mouth hangs open with tongue protruding (underactive gag reflex)

When to call the doctor

Normally developing children tend to develop motor skills, posture control, and movement skills by a given age. Motor skills are divided into two categories. **Gross motor skills** include the ability of an infant to lift its head while lying on the stomach, to roll over from its back to its stomach. Normally, by a given age, a child develops the gross motor skills required to get into a sitting position and remain seated without falling over, crawl, walk, run, and jump. **Fine motor skills** include the ability to grasp, transfer an object from one hand to another, point out an object, follow a toy or a person with the eyes, or to feed oneself. Hypotonic children are slow to develop these skills, and parents should contact their pediatrician if they notice such delays or if their child appears to lack muscle control, especially if the child previously seemed to have normal muscle control.

Diagnosis

Hypotonia is normally discovered within the first few months of life. Since it is associated with many different underlying disorders, the doctor will accordingly seek to establish a **family** history as well as the child's medical history. A physical examination will be performed, usually including a detailed nervous system and muscle function examination. The latter may be performed with instruments, such as lights and reflex hammers, and usually does not cause any **pain** to the child. Most of the disorders associated with hypotonia also cause other symptoms that, when taken together, suggest a specific disorder and cause for the hypotonia. Specific diagnostic tests used will vary depending on the suspected cause of the hypotonia. Typical medical history questions include:

- When was the hypotonia first noticed?

- Was it present at birth?

- Did it start suddenly or gradually?

- Is the hypotonia always the same or does it seem worse at certain times?

- Is the child limp all over or only in certain areas?

- What other symptoms are present?

The following diagnostic tests may also be used:

- Blood tests.

- Creatine kinase (CK) test: elevated CK level in blood indicating muscles are damaged or degenerating.

- Computerized tomography scan (CT scan): a diagnostic imaging procedure that uses a combination of x-rays and computer technology to produce cross-sectional images. CT scans help physicians evaluate bone and muscle structures.

- Magnetic resonance imaging (MRI): a diagnostic procedure that uses a combination of large magnets, radio frequencies, and a computer to produce detailed images of organs and structures within the body.

- Electromyogram (EMG): a test used to evaluate nerve and muscle function.

- Electroencephalogram (EEG): a test that measures the electrical activity in the brain. An EEG measures brain waves through small button electrodes that are placed on the child's scalp.

- Spinal tap: also called lumbar puncture, measures the amount of pressure in the spinal canal and/or to remove a small amount of cerebral spinal fluid (**CSF**) for testing. Cerebral spinal fluid bathes the brain and spinal cord.

- Karyotype: a test that performs a chromosomal analysis from a blood test, used to determine whether the hypotonia is the result of a genetic disorder.

- Muscle biopsy: a sample of muscle tissue removed and examined under a microscope. Hypotonia can be assessed because muscle fibers have a smaller diameter than that of normal muscle.

Treatment

When hypotonia is caused by an underlying condition, that condition is treated first, followed by symptomatic and supportive therapy for the hypotonia. Physical therapy can improve fine motor control and overall body strength. Occupational and speech-language therapy can help breathing, speech, and swallowing difficulties. Therapy for infants and young children may also include sensory stimulation programs. Specific treatment for hypotonia is determined by the child's physician based on the following:

- the child's age, overall health, and medical history
- the extent of the condition
- the underlying cause of the condition
- the child's tolerance for specific medications, procedures, or therapies
- expectations for the course of the condition
- parent opinion or preference

No specific treatment is required to treat mild congenital hypotonia, but children with this problem may periodically need treatment for common conditions associated with hypotonia, such as recurrent joint dislocations. Treatment programs to help increase muscle strength and sensory stimulation programs are developed once the cause of the child's hypotonia is established. Such programs usually involve physical therapy through an early intervention or school-based program among other forms of therapy.

Hypotonic children are often treated by one or more of the following specialists:

- Developmental pediatrician: a pediatrician with specialized training in children's social, emotional, and intellectual development as well as health and physical growth. He or she may conduct a developmental **assessment** which will determine any delays the child has and to what extent the delay is present.
- Neurologist: a physician who has trained in the diagnosis and treatment of nervous system disorders, including diseases of the brain, spinal cord, nerves, and muscles. Neurologists perform neurological examinations of the nerves of the head and neck; muscle strength and movement; balance, ambulation, and reflexes; and sensation, memory, speech, language, and other cognitive abilities.
- Geneticist: a specialist in genetic disorders. He or she starts with the detailed history of the family's background, looks at the child's features and orders blood tests to look at the 46 chromosomes and possibly at specific genes on those chromosomes.
- Occupational therapist (OT): a professional who has specialized training in helping to develop mental or physical skills that help accomplish daily living activities, with careful attention to enhancing fine motor skills. In a developmental assessment, the occupational therapist assesses the child's fine motor skills, coordination, and age-appropriate self-help skills (eating with utensils, dressing, etc.).
- Physical therapist (PT): a professional trained in assessing and providing therapy to treat developmental delays using methods such as **exercise**, heat, light, and massage. In a developmental assessment, the physical therapist assesses the ability and quality of the child's use of legs, arms, and complete body by observing the display of specific gross motor skills as well as observing the child in play.
- Speech/language pathologist (SLP): a professional who is trained in assessing and treating problems in communication. Some SLPs are also trained to work with oral/motor problems, such as swallowing, and other feeding difficulties resulting from hypotonia.

Nutritional concerns

In some hypotonic infants, sucking is weak and in some cases not present at all. They do not act hungry or show interest in feeding. Special techniques and procedures are then required to provide adequate **nutrition**, such as special nipples, manipulation of mouth and jaw, and on rare occasions, insertion of a gastrostomy tube.

Prognosis

The outcome in any particular case depends largely on the nature of the underlying disease. Hypotonia can be life long, but in some cases, muscle tone improves over time. Children with mild hypotonia may not experience **developmental delay**, although some children acquire gross motor skills (sitting, walking, running, jumping) more slowly than most. Most hypotonic children eventually improve with therapy and time. By age five, they may not be the fastest child on the playground, but many will be there with their peers and will be holding their own. Some children are more severely affected, requiring walkers and wheelchairs and other adaptive and assistive equipment.

Prevention

As of 2004 there was no prevention for hypotonia. However, measures of prevention are increasingly possible in the early 2000s for several underlying disorders.

Parental concerns

Parents of an hypotonic child must follow the treating physician's orders for treatment of the underlying cause. They must exercise special care when lifting and carrying the hypotonic infant to avoid causing an injury to the child. If lifted under the armpits, the hypotonic infant's arms will raise with no resistance and easily slip between the hands.

A six-week-old baby girl is held horizontally by the trunk in a test for hypotonia, sometimes called "floppy infant syndrome." The girl is normal. *(Saturn Stills/ Science Photo Library/Photo Researchers, Inc.)*

Another source of concern that parents face is addressing the special needs of their hypotonic child. The world of typical children can be a difficult place for a hypotonic child, and it is tempting to isolate the child. It is not easy to go to a playgroup of toddlers when a child's latest milestone is getting from the floor into a sitting position while the other children are running across the room. There are resources for parents to help their child become as able and independent as he or she can possibly be, and the family physician is a good resource for advice.

See also Bayley Scales of Infant Development; Muscular dystrophy.

Resources

BOOKS

Amiel-Tison, Claudine, et al. *Neurological Development from Birth to Six Years: Guide for Examination and Evaluation.* Baltimore, MD: Johns Hopkins University Press, 2001.

Preedy, Victor R., and Timothy J. Peters. *Skeletal Muscle: Pathology, Diagnosis, and Management of Disease*, 3rd ed. Edited by Kenneth J. Ryan. Albuquerque, NM: Health Press, 2002.

PERIODICALS

Carboni, P., et al. "Congenital hypotonia with favorable outcome." *Pediatric Neurology* 26, no. 5 (May 2002): 383–86.

Heilstedt, H. A., et al. "Hypotonia, congenital hearing loss, and hypoactive labyrinths." *American Journal of Medical Genetics*3, no. 3 (August 2002): 238–42.

Richer, L. P., et al. "Diagnostic profile of neonatal hypotonia: an 11-year study." *Pediatric Neurology* 25, no. 1 (July 2001): 32–37.

Thompson, C. E. "Benign congenital hypotonia is not a diagnosis." *Developments in Medical Child Neurology* 44, no. 4 (April 2002): 283–84.

Trifiro G., et al. "Neonatal hypotonia: don't forget the Prader-Willi syndrome." *Acta Paediatrica* 92, no. 9 (September 2003): 1085–89.

Pomerance, H. H., et al. "Infant with inadequate feeding and weight gain, progressive respiratory difficulty, hypotonia, and weakness, with onset at birth." *American Journal of Medical Genetics* 94, no. 1 (September 2000): 68–74.

KEY TERMS

Ataxia—A condition marked by impaired muscular coordination, most frequently resulting from disorders in the brain or spinal cord.

Biceps—The muscle in the front of the upper arm.

Biopsy—The surgical removal and microscopic examination of living tissue for diagnostic purposes or to follow the course of a disease. Most commonly the term refers to the collection and analysis of tissue from a suspected tumor to establish malignancy.

Central nervous system—Part of the nervous system consisting of the brain, cranial nerves, and spinal cord. The brain is the center of higher processes, such as thought and emotion and is responsible for the coordination and control of bodily activities and the interpretation of information from the senses. The cranial nerves and spinal cord link the brain to the peripheral nervous system, that is the nerves present in the rest of body.

Chromosome—A microscopic thread-like structure found within each cell of the human body and consisting of a complex of proteins and DNA. Humans have 46 chromosomes arranged into 23 pairs. Chromosomes contain the genetic information necessary to direct the development and functioning of all cells and systems in the body. They pass on hereditary traits from parents to child (like eye color) and determine whether the child will be male or female.

Computed tomography (CT)—An imaging technique in which cross-sectional x rays of the body are compiled to create a three-dimensional image of the body's internal structures; also called computed axial tomography.

Fine motor skill—The abilities required to control the smaller muscles of the body for writing, playing an instrument, artistic expression and craft work. The muscles required to perform fine motor skills are generally found in the hands, feet and head.

Flexor muscle—A muscle that serves to flex or bend a part of the body.

Gene—A building block of inheritance, which contains the instructions for the production of a particular protein, and is made up of a molecular sequence found on a section of DNA. Each gene is found on a precise location on a chromosome.

Genetic disease—A disease that is (partly or completely) the result of the abnormal function or expression of a gene; a disease caused by the inheritance and expression of a genetic mutation.

Gross motor skills—The abilities required to control the large muscles of the body for walking, running, sitting, crawling, and other activities. The muscles required to perform gross motor skills are generally found in the arms, legs, back, abdomen and torso.

Immune response—A physiological response of the body controlled by the immune system that involves the production of antibodies to fight off specific foreign substances or agents (antigens).

Immune system—The system of specialized organs, lymph nodes, and blood cells throughout the body that work together to defend the body against foreign invaders (bacteria, viruses, fungi, etc.).

Magnetic resonance imaging (MRI)—An imaging technique that uses a large circular magnet and radio waves to generate signals from atoms in the body. These signals are used to construct detailed images of internal body structures and organs, including the brain.

Motor control—The control of movement and posture.

Motor neuron—A nerve cell that specifically controls and stimulates voluntary muscles.

Muscle tone—Also termed tonus; the normal state of balanced tension in the tissues of the body, especially the muscles.

Muscle weakness—Reduction in the strength of one or more muscles.

Neurons—Any of the conducting cells of the nervous system that transmit signals.

Recessive disorder—Disorder that requires two copies of the predisposing gene one from each parent for the child to have the disease.

Spinal cord—The elongated nerve bundles that lie in the spinal canal and from which the spinal nerves emerge.

Underlying condition—Disorder or disease that causes the appearance of another medical disorder or condition.

ORGANIZATIONS

Child Development Institute (CDI). 3528 E. Ridgeway Road, Orange, California 92867. Web site: <www.childdevelopmentinfo.com>.

Genetic and Rare Diseases Information Center. PO Box 8126, Gaithersburg, MD 20898–8126. Web site: <www.rarediseasesinfo.nih.gov>.

March of Dimes Birth Defects Foundation. PO Box 3006, Rockville, MD 20847. Web site: <www.marchofdimes.com>.

Muscular Dystrophy Association. 3300 East Sunrise Drive, Tucson, AZ 85718–3208. Web site: <www.mdausa.org>.

National Institute of Child Health and Human Development (NICHD). 31 Center Drive, Rm. 2A32, MSC 2425, Bethesda, MD 20892–2425. Web site: <www.nichd.nih.gov>.

National Institute of Neurological Disorders and Stroke (NINDS). PO Box 5801, Bethesda, MD 20824. Web site: <www.ninds.nih.gov>.

National Organization for Rare Disorders (NORD). PO Box 1968, 55 Kenosia Avenue, Danbury, CT 06813–1968. Web site: <www.rarediseases.org>.

WEB SITES

"Hypotonia." *Family Village*. Available online at <www.familyvillage.wisc.edu/lib_hypot.htm> (accessed October 18, 2004).

"What is Benign Congenital Hypotonia?" *Benign Congenital Hypotonia Site*. Available online at <www.lightlink.com/vulcan/benign/aboutbch.htm> (accessed October 18, 2004).

Monique Laberge, Ph.D.

IBS *see* **Irritable bowel syndrome**

Ibuprofen *see* **Nonsteroidal anti-inflammatory drugs**

Idiopathic thrombocytopenia purpura

Definition

Idiopathic thrombocytopenic purpura (ITP) is a bleeding disorder caused by an abnormally low level of blood platelets, small disc-shaped cells essential to blood clotting (coagulation). ITP describes both the cause and symptoms of the condition: idiopathic means that the disorder has no apparent cause; thrombocytopenia refers to a decreased number of blood platelets; and purpura refers to a purplish or reddish-brown skin rash caused by the leakage into the skin of blood from broken capillaries. ITP is as of 2004 often called immune thrombocytopenic purpura rather than idiopathic because studies in the early 2000s have shown the presence of autoimmune antibodies in the blood. Other names for ITP include purpura hemorrhagica and essential thrombocytopenia.

Description

Coagulation, or clotting, is a complex process in which specific proteins found in blood plasma combine with other blood components, including platelets, to form clots and prevent blood loss. Platelets are tiny colorless disc-shaped cells in the blood that collect (aggregate) in blood vessels to form a plug when a vessel is injured. The platelet plug then binds coagulation proteins to form a clot that stops bleeding. A deficiency in platelets or a disorder that affects platelet production can disrupt clotting and severely complicate blood loss from accidental injury, surgery, and specific diseases or conditions in which bleeding can occur. ITP affects the overall number of blood platelets rather than their function. The normal platelet level in adults is between 150,000 and 450,000/mm^3. Platelet counts below 50,000/mm^3 increase the risk of dangerous bleeding from trauma; counts below 20,000/mm^3 increase the risk of spontaneous bleeding.

ITP may be either acute or chronic. The acute form occurs in children between ages two and six. Although chronic ITP is most common in adult females, 10 to 20 percent of children with ITP have the chronic form.

Demographics

Acute ITP affects children of both sexes between the ages of two and six years. The chronic form, although most common in adult females between the ages of 20 and 40, is found in 10 to 20 percent of children with ITP. ITP does not appear to be related to race, lifestyle, climate, or environmental factors.

Causes and symptoms

In children, ITP is usually triggered by a virus infection, most often **rubella**, **chickenpox**, **measles**, cytomegalovirus (CMV), or Epstein-Barr virus (EBV). ITP usually begins about two or three weeks after the infection.

Acute ITP is characterized by bleeding into the skin or from the nose, mouth, digestive tract, or urinary tract. The onset is usually sudden. Bleeding into the skin takes the form of purpura or petechiae. Purpura, a purplish or reddish-brown rash or discoloration of the skin, and petechiae, small round pinpoint hemorrhages, are both caused by the leakage of blood from tiny capillaries under the skin. In addition to purpura and petechiae, spontaneous **bruises** may occur. In extreme cases, ITP may cause bleeding into the lungs, brain, or other vital organs.

Chronic ITP has a gradual onset and may have minimal or no external symptoms. The low **platelet count** may be discovered in the course of a routine blood test. Most parents consult a pediatrician or primary care doctor after noticing their child has the typical purpuric skin rash, frequent nosebleeds, or bleeding from the digestive or urinary tract.

In adults, ITP is considered an autoimmune disorder, which means that the body produces antibodies that damage some of its own products—in this case, blood platelets. Some adults with chronic ITP may have other autoimmune diseases such as lupus (systemic lupus erythematosus or SLE), rheumatoid arthritis, or scleroderma. Women with ITP may experience unusually heavy or lengthy menstrual periods. Risk factors for the development of chronic ITP in adults include being female, age over 10 years at onset of symptoms, bruising, and having another known autoimmune disease.

When to call the doctor

When a child bruises easily, has frequent nosebleeds, bloody stools, or develops a purplish or reddish-brown rash or tiny spots of hemorrhage, the symptoms should be reported to the pediatrician or **family** doctor, especially if they are noticed in the weeks following measles or chickenpox or a virus infection such as mononucleosis.

Diagnosis

ITP is usually considered a diagnosis of exclusion, which means that the doctor makes a diagnosis by ruling out other possible causes for the symptoms and physical findings. The presence of **fever**, for example, does not indicate ITP, whereas fever may occur in lupus and some other types of thrombocytopenia. Likewise, the doctor will look for an enlarged spleen by pressing on (palpating) the abdomen; if the spleen is noticeably enlarged, ITP is not absolutely ruled out but is a less likely diagnosis. If ITP is suspected, the doctor will examine the child's skin for bruises, purpuric areas, or petechiae. If nosebleeds or bleeding from the mouth or other parts of the body have been reported, the doctor will examine these areas for other possible causes of bleeding. Individuals with ITP usually look and feel healthy except for the bleeding. If the child has had a recent childhood illness (measles, chickenpox) or a virus, the risk for ITP is greater, and this fact will be considered along with diagnostic testing results.

Diagnostic tests will begin with a complete blood count (CBC), including a platelet count. A blood test for autoantibodies may be performed early in the diagnostic process as well as a test for antiplatelet antibodies. Specific diagnostic tests for autoimmune diseases and viruses (CMV, EBV, and rheumatoid factor or RF) may be performed. Coagulation tests, including clotting time, will be performed to determine the ability of the child's blood to form a clot. Platelet aggregation tests may be performed to evaluate platelet function, particularly if the platelet count is low.

KEY TERMS

Autoimmune disorder—One of a group of disorders, like rheumatoid arthritis and systemic lupus erythematosus, in which the immune system is overactive and has lost the ability to distinguish between self and non-self. The body's immune cells turn on the body, attacking various tissues and organs.

Clotting factors—Substances in the blood, also known as coagulation factors, that act in sequence to stop bleeding by triggering the formation of a clot. Each clotting factor is designated with a Roman numeral I through XIII.

Idiopathic—Refers to a disease or condition of unknown origin.

Petechia—Plural, petechiae. A tiny purple or red spot on the skin resulting from a hemorrhage under the skin's surface.

Platelet—A cell-like particle in the blood that plays an important role in blood clotting. Platelets are activated when an injury causes a blood vessel to break. They change shape from round to spiny, "sticking" to the broken vessel wall and to each other to begin the clotting process. In addition to physically plugging breaks in blood vessel walls, platelets also release chemicals that promote clotting.

Prednisone—A corticosteroid medication often used to treat inflammation.

Purpura—A group of disorders characterized by purplish or reddish brown areas of discoloration visible through the skin. These areas of discoloration are caused by bleeding from broken capillaries.

Splenectomy—Surgical removal of the spleen.

Thrombocytopenia—A persistent decrease in the number of blood platelets usually associated with hemorrhaging.

Children with ITP will usually have platelet counts below 20,000/mm^3 and a prolonged clotting time. The size and appearance of the platelets may be abnormal, which is observed microscopically. The red blood cell count (RBC) and white blood cell count (WBC) are usually normal, although about 10 percent of individuals with ITP are also anemic (have reduced RBCs and hemoglobin). The bone marrow test yields normal results. Detection of antiplatelet antibodies in the blood usually confirms a diagnosis of ITP.

Treatment

There is no specific treatment for ITP except to manage symptoms. In most cases, the disorder will resolve within two to six weeks without medications or surgery. Nosebleeds can be treated with ice packs when necessary. General care may include asking parents to watch for bruising, petechiae, or other signs of recurrence. Parents are also advised to avoid giving the child aspirin, ibuprofen, or other over-the-counter **pain** medications because these drugs are known to lengthen the clotting time of blood.

Children with acute ITP who are losing large amounts of blood or bleeding into their central nervous system require emergency treatment. This may include transfusions of platelets, intravenous immunoglobulins, or prednisone. Prednisone is a steroid medication that decreases the effects of antibodies on platelets and eventually lowers antibody production. If the child has been treated before for ITP and has not responded to prednisone or immunoglobulins, surgery may be required to remove the spleen (splenectomy), an organ that sometimes stores platelets and keeps them out of the general blood circulation. Splenectomy is usually avoided in children younger than five years because of the increased risk of a severe postoperative infection. In older children, however, splenectomy is recommended if the child has been treated for 12 months without improvement, if the ITP is very severe or is getting worse, or if the child begins to bleed into the head or brain.

Children with chronic ITP can be treated with prednisone, immune globulin, or large doses of intravenous gamma globulin. Although 90 percent of those with ITP respond to immunoglobulin treatment, it is an expensive treatment. Response to prednisone therapy is about 80 percent. Platelet transfusions are not recommended for routine treatment of ITP. If platelet levels do not improve within one to four months, or high doses of prednisone are required, splenectomy may be recommended. If the patient is an adolescent female with extremely heavy periods, splenectomy may also be recommended. Adults treated with splenectomy usually experience remission of chronic ITP. All medications for ITP are given either orally or intravenously; intramuscular injection is avoided because of the possibility of causing bleeding into the skin.

Prognosis

The prognosis for recovery from acute ITP is good; 80 percent of those affected recover without special treatment. The prognosis for chronic ITP is also good; most individuals experience long-term remission. In rare instances, however, ITP can cause life-threatening hemorrhage or bleeding into the central nervous system.

Prevention

Because as of 2004 the exact cause for ITP is unknown, no specific preventive measures are recommended. However, episodes of bleeding can be prevented in children with ITP by discouraging rough contact **sports** or other activities that increase the risk of trauma. To reduce the risk of ITP associated with other illnesses, children can be immunized against childhood diseases and kept away as much as possible from other children or adults with known or unidentified viruses.

Parental concerns

The sudden onset of ITP-like symptoms can be a concern, but the presence of a rash or bruising is not a signal for alarm because there are so many possible causes of these symptoms in childhood. Parents can be generally watchful, but not fearful. The symptoms to be alert for are frequent nosebleeds or frequent bruising with no specific cause, particularly if the child has had a recent illness or virus. It is helpful to remember that ITP, whether acute or chronic, has an excellent prognosis and may cause bleeding but not life-threatening hemorrhage in most cases. Parents can ask the pediatrician when in doubt and understand that simple blood and coagulation tests can be performed to rule out ITP.

See also Coagulation disorders; Infectious mononucleosis; TORCH test.

Resources

BOOKS

Alving, Barbara M. *Blood Components and Pharmacologic Agents in the Treatment of Congenital and Acquired Bleeding Disorders.* Basel, Switzerland: S. Karger AG, 2000.

"Blood Disorders." *The Merck Manual of Medical Information*, 2nd Home Edition. Edited by Mark H. Beers et al. White House Station, NJ: Merck & Co., 2003.

ORGANIZATIONS

National Heart, Lung, and Blood Institute (NHLBI). 6701 Rockledge Drive, PO Box 30105, Bethesda, MD 20824–0105. Web site: <www.nhlbi.nih.gov>.

L. Lee Culvert
Rebecca J. Frey, PhD

IgA deficiency *see* **Immunoglobulin deficiency syndromes**

IgG subclass deficiencies *see* **Immunoglobulin deficiency syndromes**

Ileus

Definition

Ileus is a partial or complete non-mechanical blockage of the small and/or large intestine.

Description

There are two types of **intestinal obstructions**, mechanical and non-mechanical. Mechanical obstructions occur because the bowel is physically blocked and its contents cannot pass the point of the obstruction. This happens when the bowel twists on itself (volvulus) or as the result of hernias, impacted feces, abnormal tissue growth, or the presence of foreign bodies in the intestines. By contrast, non-mechanical obstruction, called ileus, occurs because the rhythmic contractions that move material through the bowel (called peristalsis) stop.

Demographics

The total rate of bowel obstruction due both to mechanical and non-mechanical causes is one in 1,000 people. Meconium ileus accounts for 9–33 percent of bowel obstructions in newborns.

Causes and symptoms

Ileus is most often associated with an infection of the peritoneum (the membrane lining the abdomen) or other intra-abdominal infections such as **appendicitis**. It is one of the major causes of bowel obstruction in infants and children. Another common cause of ileus is a disruption or reduction of the blood supply to the abdomen. Handling the bowel during abdominal surgery can also cause peristalsis to stop, so people who have had abdominal surgery are more likely to experience ileus.

Ileus can also be caused by kidney diseases, especially when potassium levels are decreased (a condition called hypokalemia). Narcotics and certain **chemotherapy** drugs, such as vinblastine (Velban, Velsar) and vincristine (Oncovin, Vincasar PES, Vincrex) can also cause ileus. Infants with **cystic fibrosis** are more likely to experience meconium ileus (obstruction of a dark green material in the intestine in newborns).

When the bowel stops functioning, the following symptoms occur:

- abdominal cramping
- abdominal distention (**pain** often increases as distention increases)
- nausea, **vomiting**, and/or **diarrhea**
- failure to pass gas or stool

When to call the doctor

A healthcare professional should be contacted if a child experiences persistent abdominal distention, is unable to have normal bowel movements, or exhibits other symptoms of ileus. Persistent abdominal pain and chronic or prolonged **constipation** are also reasons to call the doctor.

Diagnosis

When a doctor listens with a stethoscope to the abdomen of a child suffering from ileus, there will be few or no bowel sounds, indicating that the intestine has stopped functioning. Ileus can be confirmed by **x rays** of the abdomen, **computed tomography** scans (CT scans), or ultrasound. It may be necessary to do more invasive tests, such as a barium enema or upper GI series, if the obstruction is mechanical. Blood tests may also be useful in diagnosing ileus.

Barium studies are used in cases of mechanical obstruction but may cause problems by increasing pressure or intestinal contents if used in ileus. Also, in cases of suspected mechanical obstruction involving the gastrointestinal tract (from the small intestine downward) use of barium x rays are contraindicated, since they may contribute to the obstruction. In such cases a barium enema should always be done first.

Treatment

Patients may be treated with supervised bed rest in a hospital and bowel rest, where nothing is taken by mouth, and patients are fed intravenously or through the use of a nasogastric tube, a tube inserted through the nose, down the throat, and into the stomach. A similar tube can be inserted in the intestine. The contents are then suctioned out. In some cases, especially where there is a mechanical obstruction or death (necrosis) of intestinal tissue, surgery may be necessary.

Drug therapies that promote intestinal motility (ability of the intestine to move spontaneously), such as cisapride and vasopressin (Pitressin), are sometimes prescribed.

Alternative treatment

Alternative practitioners offer few treatment suggestions but focus on prevention by keeping the bowels healthy through eating a good diet, high in fiber and low in fat. If the case is not a medical emergency, homeopaths and practitioners of traditional Chinese medicine can recommend therapies that may help to reinstate peristalsis.

Nutritional concerns

Following abdominal surgery, uncomplicated cases of ileus can be managed by minimizing the amount of food the patient consumes, ensuring adequate fluid intake, and correcting any electrolyte disturbances such as low potassium.

Prognosis

The outcome varies depending on the cause of ileus. When ileus results from abdominal surgery, the condition is usually temporary and lasts approximately 24–72 hours. The prognosis is less certain in cases in which death of intestinal tissue occurs; surgery becomes necessary to remove the necrotic tissue. In children with cystic fibrosis in which meconium ileus becomes evident soon after birth, the prognosis is linked with the primary disease; the median age of survival for cystic fibrosis patients is 30 years. However, new interventions in the treatment of CF are increasing the age span of people with CF every year.

Prevention

Most cases of ileus are not preventable. Surgery to remove a tumor or other mechanical obstruction may help to prevent a recurrence.

Nutritional concerns

In cases in which electrolyte imbalance is the cause of ileus, it is important to treat the underlying cause of the imbalance, which in many cases is related to chronic vomiting and/or diarrhea, poor fluid and/or food intake, or abuse of **laxatives** and diuretics (such as in individuals with **bulimia nervosa**).

Parental concerns

When their child is diagnosed with ileus, parents may be concerned about the necessity of surgery to correct the problem. Surgery, however, is considered only in medical emergencies and for patients for whom more conservative treatments have failed.

KEY TERMS

Bulimia nervosa—An eating disorder characterized by binge eating and inappropriate compensatory behavior, such as vomiting, misusing laxatives, or excessive exercise.

Computed tomography (CT)—An imaging technique in which cross-sectional x rays of the body are compiled to create a three-dimensional image of the body's internal structures; also called computed axial tomography.

Meconium—A greenish fecal material that forms the first bowel movement of an infant.

Peritoneum—The transparent membrane lining the abdominal and pelvic cavities (parietal peritoneum) and the membrane forming the outer layer of the stomach and interstines (visceral peritoneum). Between the visceral and parietal peritoneums is a potential space called the peritoneal cavity.

Resources

BOOKS

Turnage, Richard H., and Patricia C. Bergen. "Intestinal Obstruction." In *Sleisenger & Fordtran's Gastrointestinal and Liver Disease*, 7th ed. Edited by Mark Feldman et al. Philadelphia: Saunders, 2002.

Wyllie, Robert. "Ileus, Adhesions, Intussusception, and Closed-Loop Obstructions." In *Nelson Textbook of Pediatrics*, 17th ed. Edited by Richard E. Behrman, Robert M. Kleigman, and Hal B. Jenson. Philadelphia: Saunders, 2004.

PERIODICALS

Miedema, Brent W., and Joel O. Johnson. "Methods for Decreasing Postoperative Gut Dysmotility." *The Lancet Oncology* 4, no. 6 (June 2003): 365–72.

ORGANIZATIONS

American Gastroenterological Association. 4930 Del Ray Ave., Bethesda, MD 20814. Web site: <www.gastro.org>.

WEB SITES

Beers, Mark H. and Robert Berkow, eds. "Ileus." *The Merck Manual of Diagnosis and Therapy*, 2004. Available online at <www.merck.com/mrkshared/mmanual/section3/chapter25/25c.jsp> (accessed January 6, 2005).

Bernstein, Linda R. "Clinic and Cost Impact of Postoperative Ileus." *Medscape*, April 30, 2002. Available online at <www.medscape.com/viewarticle/429661_1> (accessed January 6, 2005).

Irish, Michael. "Surgical Aspects of Cystic Fibrosis and Meconium Ileus." *eMedicine*. October 17, 2003.

Available online at <www.emedicine.com/ped/topic2995.htm> (accessed January 6, 2005).

Tish Davidson, AM
Stephanie Dionne Sherk

Immobilization

Definition

Immobilization refers to the process of holding a joint or bone in place with a splint, cast, or brace. This is done to prevent an injured area from moving while it heals.

Purpose

Splints, casts, and braces support and protect broken bones, dislocated joints, and injured soft tissues such as tendons and ligaments. Immobilization restricts motion to allow the injured area to heal. It can help reduce **pain**, swelling, and **muscle spasms**. In some cases, splints and casts are applied after surgical procedures that repair bones, tendons, or ligaments. This allows for protection and proper alignment early in the healing process.

Description

When an arm, hand, leg, or foot requires immobilization, the cast, splint, or brace will generally extend from the joint above the injury to the joint below the injury. For example, an injury to the mid-calf requires immobilization from the knee to the ankle and foot. Injuries of the hip and upper thigh or shoulder and upper arm require a cast that encircles the body and extends down the injured leg or arm.

Casts and splints

Casts are generally used to immobilize a broken bone. Once the doctor makes sure the two broken ends of the bone are aligned, a cast is put on to keep them in place until they are rejoined through natural healing. Casts are applied by a physician, a nurse, or an assistant. They are custom-made to fit each person, and are usually made of plaster or fiberglass. Fiberglass weighs less than plaster, is more durable, and allows the skin more adequate airflow than plaster. A layer of cotton or synthetic padding is first wrapped around the skin to cover the injured area and protect the skin. The plaster or fiber-

glass is then applied over this and is then allowed to dry. It can take up to 24 hours for a cast to dry completely.

Most casts should be kept dry. However, some types of fiberglass casts use Gore-tex padding that is waterproof, allowing the cast to be completely immersed in water when taking a shower or bath. There are some circumstances when this type of cast material cannot be used.

A splint is often used to immobilize a dislocated joint while it heals. Splints are also often used for finger injuries, such as **fractures** or baseball finger. Baseball finger is an injury in which the tendon at the end of the finger is separated from the bone as a result of trauma. Splinting is also used to immobilize an injured arm or leg immediately after an injury. Before moving a child who has injured an arm or leg, some type of temporary splint should be applied to prevent further injury to the area. Splints may be made of acrylic, polyethylene foam, plaster of paris, or aluminum. In an emergency, a splint can be made from a piece of wood or rolled magazine.

Slings

Slings are often used to support the arm after a fracture or other injury. They are generally used along with a cast or splint, but are sometimes used alone as a means of immobilization. They can be used in an emergency to immobilize the arm until a doctor can see the child. A triangular bandage is placed under the injured arm and then tied around the neck.

Braces

Braces are used to support, align, or hold a body part in the correct position. Braces are sometimes used after a surgical procedure is performed on an arm or a leg. They may also be used when an injury has occurred. Since some braces can be easily taken off and put back on, they are often used when the child needs physical therapy or must **exercise** the limb during the healing process. Many braces can also be adjusted to allow for a certain amount of movement.

Either a custom-made or a ready-made brace can be used. The off-the-shelf braces are made in a variety of shapes and sizes. They generally have Velcro straps that make the brace easy to adjust and to put on and take off. Both braces and splints offer less support and protection than a cast and may not be a treatment option in all circumstances.

Collars

A collar is generally used for neck injuries. A soft collar can relieve pain by restricting movement of the

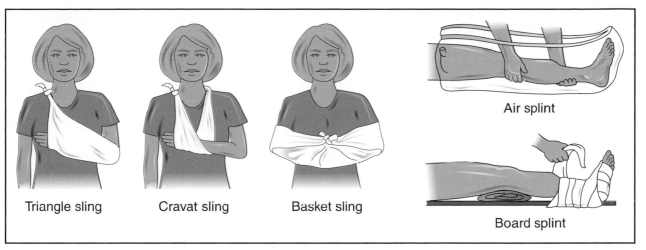

Triangle sling   Cravat sling   Basket sling

Air splint

Board splint

These illustrations feature several types of immobilization techniques, including slings and splints. *(Illustration by Electronic Illustrators Group.)*

head and neck. Collars also transfer some of the weight of the head from the neck to the chest. Stiff collars are generally used to support the neck when there has been a fracture in one of the neck bones. Cervical collars are widely used by emergency personnel at the scene of injuries when there is a potential neck or **head injury**. The collar helps to ensure that the neck and head do not move, which could make the injury worse.

Traction

Immobilization may also be secured by traction. Traction involves using a method for applying tension to correct the alignment of two structures (e.g., two bones) and hold them in the correct position. For example, if the bone in the thigh breaks, the broken ends may have a tendency to overlap. Use of traction will hold them in the correct position for healing to occur. The strongest form of traction involves inserting a stainless steel pin through a bony prominence attached by a horseshoe-shaped bow and rope to a pulley and weights suspended over the end of the patient's bed.

Traction must be balanced by countertraction. This may be obtained by tilting the bed and allowing the patient's body to act as a counterweight. Another technique involves applying weights pulling in the opposite direction.

Traction for neck injuries may be in the form of a leather or cotton cloth halter placed around the chin and lower back of the head. For very severe neck injuries that require maximum traction, tongs that resemble ice tongs are inserted into small holes drilled in the outer skull. All traction requires careful observation and adjustment by doctors and nurses to maintain proper balance and alignment of the traction with free suspension of the weights.

Immobilization can also be secured by a form of traction called skin traction. This is a combination of a splint and traction that is applied to the arms or legs by strips of adhesive tape placed over the skin of the arm or leg. Adhesive strips, moleskin, or foam rubber traction strips are applied on the skin. This method is effective only if a moderate amount of traction is required.

Precautions

It is important to ensure that the cast is not too tight, such that blood flow is cut off and swelling is not restricted.

Preparation

There are many reasons for immobilization using splints, casts, and braces. It can be helpful if the child understands why immobilization is being done, as it may help with compliance.

Aftercare

After a cast or splint has been put on, the injured arm or leg should be elevated for 24 to 72 hours. It is recommended that the child lie or sit with the injured arm or leg raised above the level of the heart. Rest, combined with elevation, will reduce pain and speed the healing process by minimizing swelling.

Fingers or toes can be exercised as much as can be tolerated after casting. This has been found to decrease swelling and prevent stiffness. If excessive swelling is noted, the application of ice to the splint or cast may be helpful.

After the cast, splint, or brace is removed, gradual exercise is usually performed to regain muscle strength

KEY TERMS

Decubitus ulcer—A pressure sore resulting from ulceration of the skin occurring in persons confined to bed for long periods of time

Ligament—A type of tough, fibrous tissue that connects bones or cartilage and provides support and strength to joints.

Pneumonia—An infection in which the lungs become inflamed. It can be caused by nearly any class of organism known to cause human infections, including bacteria, viruses, fungi, and parasites.

Tendon—A tough cord of dense white fibrous connective tissue that connects a muscle with some other part, especially a bone, and transmits the force which the muscle exerts.

and motion. The doctor may also recommend hydrotherapy, heat treatments, and other forms of physical therapy.

Risks

For some children, such as those in traction, immobilization will require long periods of bed rest. Lying in one position in bed for an extended period can result in sores on the skin (decubitus ulcers) and skin infection. Long periods of bed rest can also cause a buildup of fluid in the lungs or an infection in the lungs (**pneumonia**). Urinary infection can also be a result of extended bed rest. Occasionally, blood clots can develop in the injured area.

People who have casts, splints, or braces on their arms or legs will generally spend several weeks not using the injured arm or leg. This lack of use can result in decreased muscle tone and shrinkage of the muscle (atrophy). This loss can usually be regained, however, through rehabilitation after the injury has healed.

Immobility can also cause psychological stress. A child restricted to a bed with a traction device may become frustrated and bored, and perhaps even depressed, irritable, and withdrawn. It may be helpful to have a bed that can be moved more easily than a traditional bed, so that the child can participate in as many **family** activities (such as dinner time and movie nights) as possible.

There is the possibility of decreased circulation if the cast, splint, or brace fits too tightly. If swelling occurs

but the cast is tight enough that the swelling cannot be accommodated, serious complications can occur. Excessive pressure over a nerve can cause irritation or possible damage if not corrected. If the cast, splint, or brace breaks or malfunctions, the healing process of the bone or soft tissue can be disrupted and lead to deformity.

Parental concerns

Children can find immobilization very frustrating. Being restricted from participating in normal activities with friends because of a broken an arm or leg, or having to sit in bed for weeks if significant traction is required can be stressful. Children can be helped if parents try to provide alternate activities and engage the child in as many activities as possible with the family.

Resources

WEB SITES

"Fractures and Sprains: Reference Summary." *National Medical Library-National Institutes of Health.* 2001. Available online at: <http://www.nlm.nih.gov/medlineplus/tutorials/fracturesandsprains/op139101.pdf> (accessed October 9, 2004).

"Fractures in Children." *Cincinnati Children's Hospital Medical Center.* January 2004. Available online at: <www.cincinnatichildrens.org/health/info/orthopaedics/diagnose/fractures.htm> (accessed October 9, 2004).

"Weightlessness, Bed Rest and Immobilization." *National Institutes of Health: Osteoporosis and Related Bone Diseases-National Resource Center.* August 2001. Available online at: <www.osteo.org/newfile.asp?doc=r608i&doctype=HTML+Fact+Sheet&doctitle=Weightlessness%2C+Bed+Rest+ and+Immobilization> (accessed October 9, 2004).

Tish Davidson, A.M.
Jeffrey P. Larson, RPT

Immune system development

Definition

The child's immune system is an intricate network of interdependent cell types, substances, and organs that collectively protect the body from bacterial, parasitic, fungal, viral infections, and tumor cells.

Description

The immune system was not recognized as a functional unit of the body until the late twentieth century, probably because its parts are not directly connected to each other and are spread in different parts of the body.

Organs of the immune system

The immune system contains the following organs and cells: tonsils and adenoids; the thymus gland; lymph nodes; bone marrow; and white blood cells that leave blood vessels and migrate through tissues and lymphatic circulation. The spleen, appendix, and patches of lymphoid tissue in the intestinal tract are also parts of the immune system.

The essential job of this system is to distinguish self-cells from foreign substances and to recognize and take protective action against any materials that ought not to be in the body, including abnormal and damaged cells. The immune system can seek out and destroy disease germs, infected cells, and tumor cells. The immune system includes the following cells:

• T lymphocytes (T cells)

• B lymphocytes (B cells)

• natural killer cells (NK cells)

• dendritic cells

• phagocytic cells

• complement proteins

These cells develop from "pluripotential hematopoietic stem cells" starting from a gestational age of about five weeks. They circulate through various organs in the lymphatic system as the fetus develops. T and B lymphocytes are the only units of the immune system that have antigen-specific recognition powers; they are responsible for adaptive immunity. In other words, the T and B cells are important in the immunity that **vaccination** promotes.

How immunity works

The lymphatic system is a key participant in the body's immune actions. It is a network of vessels and nodes unified by the circulatory system. Lymph nodes occur along the course of the lymphatic vessels and filter lymph fluid before it returns to the bloodstream. The system removes tissue fluids from intercellular spaces and protects the body from bacterial invasions.

Types of immunity

Immunity is the ability of the body to resist the infecting agent. When an infectious agent enters the body, the immune system develops antibodies which can weaken or destroy the disease-producing agent or neutra-lize its toxins. If the body is re-introduced to the same agent at a later time, it is capable of developing antibodies at a much faster pace. As a result, the individual would likely not become sick, and immunity has developed.

Natural immunity is present when a person is immune to a disease despite not having either the disease itself nor any vaccination against it. Acquired immunity may be either active or passive. Active immunity comes from having the disease or by inoculation with antigens, such as dead organisms, weakened organisms, or toxins of organisms. The antigens introduced during vaccination produce antibodies that protect the body against the infecting agent, despite the fact that the person does not become sick. Passive immunity is relatively short lived and is acquired by transferring antibodies from mother to child in the uterus or by inoculation with serum that contains antibodies from immune persons or animals. Passive immunization is used to help a person who has been exposed or is already infected to fight off disease. Although various types of serums may be used to produce passive immunization, gamma globulin is the most frequently used source of human antibodies.

Development of the immune response

Normal infants have the capability to develop responses to antigens at birth. Infants also start life with some immunoglobulin antibodies acquired from the mother. These antibodies cross the placental barrier, but not all types are transmitted equally. In particular, infants start with antibodies to viruses and gram-positive organisms, but not to gram-negative organisms. Gram is the name of a stain that distinguishes broad classes of bacteria. Gram-negative organisms are responsible for many diseases, including gonorrhea, pertussis (whooping cough), salmonella poisoning, and cholera. *Escherichia coli (E. coli)* is another common gram-negative organism.

Immunoglobulin antibodies are divided into five classes. The capacity of the body to produce each immunoglobulin varies with age. Newborn babies (premature and full-term) begin to synthesize antibodies at an increased rate soon after birth in response to antigenic stimulation of their new environment. At about six days after birth the serum concentration of specific antibodies rises sharply, and this rise continues until adult levels are achieved by approximately the end of the first year. Maternal immunity gradually disappears during the first six to eight months of life. A concentrated level of antibodies is reached and maintained by seven to eight years of age.

Common problems

Persistent infections

One of the greatest strains on the immune system is an infection it cannot remove. Parents should pay attention to unexplained fevers; night sweats; or tender, swollen lymph nodes. These symptoms can signify a hidden infection or **cancer**. Infections of the mouth and gums as well as sexually transferred infections often go unnoticed while they drain the vitality of the immune system.

Indiscriminate use of antibiotics

When the immune system successfully controls an infection on its own, it becomes stronger and better able to handle future threats. **Antibiotics** are powerful medicines that should be given only when the immune system cannot contain a bacterial infection. Overuse of antibiotics may cause the body to breed new strains of antibiotic-resistant or more dangerous bacteria. In the long run, overuse of antibiotics weakens the immune system.

Misuse of immunosuppressive drugs

Immunosuppressive drugs used in cancer **chemotherapy** or to suppress rejection of organ transplants are necessary. Of greater concern is the widespread use of corticosteroids or steroid derivatives used to treat **allergies**, autoimmune diseases, and inflammatory conditions. Though sometimes necessary, these drugs cripple the immune response and are often misunderstood, abused, and over-prescribed.

Radiation and hazardous chemicals

Exposure to radiation and hazardous chemicals may also damage the immune system. Excessive radiation of diagnostic **x rays** of the neck and chest may damage the thymus gland behind the breastbone. The thymus gland is an integral part of the immune system.

Blood transfusions and injections of blood products

Blood transfusions and injections of blood products may broadcast viral diseases like hepatitis that stress the immune system by flooding it with foreign proteins. In an emergency it may not be possible to do without blood transfusions. Sources of blood and blood products are regulated and screened for infectious substances and were as of 2004 much safer.

Other factors

Certain factors have damaging effects on the immune system of infants. Excessive consumption of alcohol during pregnancy leads to depressive levels of vitamin B and zinc, which are essential to immune competence. **Alcoholism** can also reduce the uptake of several other important nutrients needed for neonatal immune systems. Prolonged stress during pregnant and in breastfeeding mothers reduces the effectiveness of the immune system as well as the quality of immunologic factors in breast milk.

Cigarette **smoking** raises the white blood cells count, activating the immune system; however, smoking causes low-grade chronic **bronchitis**, low birth weight infants, and weakened natural immunity in newborns. Infants and children constantly exposed to cigarette smoke have weakened immune systems.

Toxic points—areas of localized infections such as dental abscesses or infected tonsils—may disturb the normal neutralization and weaken the cellular defenses in pregnant mothers and in children.

Deficiencies of many nutrients, especially certain **vitamins** and **minerals**, may weaken the immune system. Excessive **exercise** may depress the immune system temporarily.

Autoimmunity

Autoimmunity occurs when the immune system mistakenly attacks the body's own tissues, resulting in disease that can be mild or severe. Common autoimmune disorders are rheumatoid arthritis, glomerulonephritis, **rheumatic fever**, and systemic lupus erythematosus (SLE). Autoimmune reactions may be set off by infection, tissue injury, or emotional trauma in people with a genetic tendency to them.

Parental concerns

Parents may be concerned that children with acute illnesses have compromised immune systems and are less likely to have a positive response to vaccines or may be more likely to develop adverse reaction to the vaccine than healthy children. Parents may also believe that children who are ill should not further burden an immune system already committed to fighting an infection.

Most pediatricians would agree that there should be a delay in vaccinations for children with severe illnesses until the symptoms of illness are gone. The reason for deferring immunization is to avoid superimposing a reaction to the vaccine on the underlying illness or attributing symptoms of the underlying illness to the vaccine by mistake. However, a low-grade **fever** or cold is not a contraindication for routine vaccinations.

KEY TERMS

Antibody—A special protein made by the body's immune system as a defense against foreign material (bacteria, viruses, etc.) that enters the body. It is uniquely designed to attack and neutralize the specific antigen that triggered the immune response.

Antigen—A substance (usually a protein) identified as foreign by the body's immune system, triggering the release of antibodies as part of the body's immune response.

Corticosteroids—A group of hormones produced naturally by the adrenal gland or manufactured synthetically. They are often used to treat inflammation. Examples include cortisone and prednisone.

Immune system—The system of specialized organs, lymph nodes, and blood cells throughout the body that work together to defend the body against foreign invaders (bacteria, viruses, fungi, etc.).

Immunization—A process or procedure that protects the body against an infectious disease by stimulating the production of antibodies. A vaccination is a type of immunization.

Lymphocyte—A type of white blood cell that participates in the immune response. The two main groups are the B cells that have antibody molecules on their surface and T cells that destroy antigens.

Phagocytosis—A process by which certain cells envelope and digest debris and microorganisms to remove them from the blood.

Parents may also be concerned that the many different vaccines that infants are given may overwhelm a child's immune system. However, infants have the capacity to respond to large numbers of antigens. Parents who worry about the increasing number of recommended vaccines may take comfort in knowing that children are exposed to fewer antigens in vaccines as of the early 2000s than in previous decades. Two reasons account for this decline: the worldwide elimination of smallpox and advances in protein chemistry in vaccines with fewer antigens.

Vaccines may cause temporary suppression of delayed-type hypersensitivity skin reactions or alter certain lymphocyte function tests. However, the short-lived immunosuppression caused by certain vaccines does not result in an increased risk of infections from other pathogens soon after vaccination.

Resources

BOOKS

Burney, Lucy. *Boost Your Child's Immune System: A Program and Recipes for Raising Strong, Healthy Kids.* New York: Newmarket Press, 2005.

Janeway, Charles. *Immunobiology: The Immune System in Health and Disease.* New York: Garland Publishing, 2004.

Parham, P. *The Immune System.* New York: Garland Publishing, 2004.

PERIODICALS

Offit, Paul A. "Addressing Parents' Concerns: Do Multiple Vaccines Overwhelm or Weaken the Infant's Immune System?" *Pediatrics* 109 (January 2002): 124.

Aliene Linwood, RN, DPA

Immunization *see* **Vaccination**

Immunodeficiency

Definition

Immunodeficiency disorders are a group of disorders in which part of the immune system is missing or defective. The body's ability to fight infections is, therefore, impaired. As a result, a child with an immunodeficiency disorder has frequent infections that are generally more severe and last longer than in a healthy child.

Description

The immune system is the body's main defense against infections. Any defect in the immune system decreases a person's ability to fight infections. A person with an immunodeficiency disorder may get more frequent infections, heal more slowly, and have a higher incidence of some cancers.

The normal immune system involves a complex interaction of certain types of cells that can recognize and attack foreign invaders, such as bacteria, viruses, and fungi. It also plays a role in fighting **cancer**. The immune system has both innate and adaptive components. Innate immunity is made up of immune protections people are born with. Adaptive immunity develops throughout life. It adapts to fight off specific invading organisms. Adaptive immunity is divided into two components: humoral immunity and cellular immunity.

The innate immune system is made up of the skin (which acts as a barrier to prevent organisms from entering the body); white blood cells called phagocytes; a system of proteins called the complement system; and chemicals called interferons. When phagocytes encounter an invading organism, they surround and engulf it in order to destroy it. The complement system also attacks bacteria. The elements in the complement system create a hole in the outer layer of the target cell, which leads to the death of the cell.

The adaptive component of the immune system is extremely complex and is as of the early 2000s still not entirely understood. Basically, it has the ability to recognize an organism or tumor cell as not being a normal part of the body and to develop a response to attempt to eliminate it.

The humoral response of adaptive immunity involves a type of cell called B lymphocytes. B lymphocytes manufacture proteins called antibodies (which are sometimes also called immunoglobulins). The terms antibody and immunoglobulin are often used interchangeably, although immunoglobulin refers to the larger classification system for antibodies. There are five types or classes of immunoglobulin that antibodies fit into, and each has a slightly different role in response against bacteria and viruses. Antibodies attach themselves to the invading foreign substance. This allows the phagocytes to begin engulfing and destroying the organism. The action of antibodies also activates the complement system. The humoral response is particularly useful for attacking bacteria.

The cellular response of adaptive immunity is useful for attacking viruses, some parasites, and possibly cancer cells. The main type of cell in the cellular response is the T lymphocyte. There are helper T lymphocytes and killer T lymphocytes. The helper T lymphocytes play a role in recognizing invading organisms, and they also help killer T lymphocytes to multiply. As the name suggests, killer T lymphocytes act to destroy the target organism.

Defects can occur in any component of the immune system or in more than one component (combined immunodeficiency). Different immunodeficiency diseases involve different components of the immune system. The defects can be inherited (congenital) or acquired.

Congenital immunodeficiency disorders

Congenital immunodeficiency is present at the time of birth and is the result of genetic defects. These immunodeficiency disorders are also called primary immunodeficiencies. Even though more than 70 different types of congenital immunodeficiency disorders have been identified, they rarely occur. Congenital immunodeficiencies may occur as a result of defects in B lymphocytes, T lymphocytes, or both. They also can occur in the innate immune system.

HUMORAL IMMUNITY DISORDERS The congenital immunodeficiency disorder, **Bruton's agammaglobulinemia**, also known as X-linked agammaglobulinemia, results in a decrease or absence of B lymphocytes and, therefore, a decreased ability to make antibodies. People with this disorder are particularly susceptible to infections of the throat, skin, middle ear, and lungs. It is seen only in males because it is caused by a genetic defect on the X chromosome. Since males have only one X chromosome, they always have the defect if the gene is present. Females can have the defective gene, but since they have two X chromosomes, there will be a normal gene on the other X chromosome to counter it. Women may pass the defective gene on to their sons.

B LYMPHOCYTE DEFICIENCIES If there is an abnormality in either the development or function of B lymphocytes, the ability to make antibodies will be impaired. This deficit makes the body susceptible to recurrent infections.

A type of B lymphocyte deficiency involves a group of disorders called selective **immunoglobulin deficiency syndromes**. The five different types of immunoglobulins are called IgA, IgG, IgM, IgD, and IgE. The most common type of immunoglobulin deficiency is selective IgA deficiency, occurring in about one in every 500 white persons. The amounts of the other antibody types are normal. Some patients with selective IgA deficiency experience no symptoms, while others have occasional lung infections and **diarrhea**. In another immunoglobulin disorder, IgG and IgA antibodies are deficient, and there is increased IgM. People with this disorder tend to get severe bacterial infections.

Common variable immunodeficiency (CVID) is another type of B lymphocyte deficiency. In this disorder, the production of one or more of the immunoglobulin types is decreased, and the antibody response to infections is impaired. It generally develops in people between the ages of ten and 20. The symptoms vary among affected people. Most people with this disorder have frequent infections, and some also experience autoimmune phenomena, such as autoimmune hemolytic anemia or rheumatoid arthritis. Persons with CVID develop cancer at a higher rate than the general population, particularly lymphomas.

T LYMPHOCYTE DEFICIENCIES Severe defects in the ability of T lymphocytes to mature result in impaired immune responses to infections with viruses, fungi, and certain types of bacteria. These infections are usually severe and can be fatal.

DiGeorge syndrome is a genetic syndrome most frequently associated with a chromosomal deletion (22q11.2). This syndrome is often associated with T lymphocyte deficiencies. Children with DiGeorge syndrome either do not have a thymus or have an underdeveloped thymus. Since the thymus is a major organ that directs the production of T lymphocytes, these patients have low numbers of T lymphocytes. If the T cell count is very low the patients are susceptible to recurrent infections. The syndrome can be associated with other physical abnormalities. For example, these individuals may have distinctive facial features such as thin upper lip and flattened nasal bridge, and they may have low calcium from hypoparathyroidism or cardiac defects. If the entire syndrome is not present (as is the usual case), the syndrome is called incomplete DiGeorge, and if all elements are present and the thymus is absent, the syndrome is called complete. Children with complete DiGeorge are particularly susceptible to viral and fungal infections.

In some cases, no treatment is required for DiGeorge syndrome because T lymphocyte production improves. Either an underdeveloped thymus begins to produce more T lymphocytes, or organ sites other than the thymus compensate by producing more T lymphocytes.

COMBINED IMMUNODEFICIENCIES Some types of immunodeficiency disorders affect both B lymphocytes and T lymphocytes. For example, **severe combined immunodeficiency** disease (SCID) is caused by the defective development or function of these two types of lymphocytes. It results in impaired humoral and cellular immune responses. SCID usually is recognized during the first year of life. It tends to cause fungal infections, including severe thrush that does not respond to usual treatment; severe diarrhea; and serious bacterial infections. If the deficiency is not treated (usually by bone marrow transplant), a person with SCID usually dies from infection before the age of two years. The most common form of SCID is X-linked, i.e. the defect is on the X chromosome and, therefore, occurs only in boys. In the early 2000s new genetic defects leading to SCID are being identified each year.

DISORDERS OF INNATE IMMUNITY Disorders of innate immunity affect phagocytes or the complement

system. These disorders also result in recurrent infections.

Acquired immunodeficiency disorders

Acquired immunodeficiency is more common than congenital immunodeficiency. It is the result of an infectious process or other disease. For example, the human immunodeficiency virus (HIV) is the virus that causes acquired immunodeficiency syndrome (**AIDS**). HIV, however, is not the most common cause of acquired immunodeficiency.

Acquired immunodeficiency often occurs as a complication of other conditions and diseases. For example, the most common causes of acquired immunodeficiency are **malnutrition**, some types of cancer, and infections. People who weigh less than 70 percent of the average weight of persons of the same age and gender are considered to be malnourished. Examples of types of infections that can lead to immunodeficiency are **chickenpox**, cytomegalovirus, German **measles** (**rubella**), measles, **tuberculosis**, **infectious mononucleosis** (Epstein-Barr virus), chronic hepatitis, lupus, and bacterial and fungal infections.

In some cases, acquired immunodeficiency is brought on by drugs used to treat another condition. For example, patients who have an organ transplant are given drugs to suppress the immune system so the body will not reject the organ. Also, some **chemotherapy** drugs that are given to treat cancer have the side effect of killing cells of the immune system. During the period of time that these drugs are being taken, the risk of infection increases. It usually returns to normal after the person stops taking the drugs.

Demographics

About 50,000 new cases of congenital immunodeficiencies are diagnosed in the United States each year. The frequency of severe combined immunodeficiency is estimated to be one out of every 50,000 to 500,000 births, and of combined variable immunodeficiency, one out of every 10,000 to 50,000 births. As of 2004 HIV is estimated to affect approximately 4.4 million children worldwide.

Causes and symptoms

Congenital immunodeficiency is caused by genetic defects that generally occur while the fetus is developing in the uterus. These defects affect the development and/or function of one or more of the components of the immune system. Acquired immunodeficiency is the result of a disease process, and it occurs later in life. The causes can be diseases, infections, or the side effects of drugs given to treat other conditions.

People with an immunodeficiency disorder tend to become infected by organisms that do not usually cause disease in healthy persons. The major symptoms of most immunodeficiency disorders are repeated infections that heal slowly. These chronic infections cause symptoms that persist for long periods of time. People with chronic infection tend to be pale and thin. They may have skin **rashes**. Their lymph nodes may be absent or larger than usual, and in some types of immune deficiency the spleen and liver may be enlarged. (The lymph nodes are small organs that house antibodies and lymphocytes.) This can result in black-and-blue marks in the skin. The person may lose hair from their head. Sometimes, a red inflammation of the lining of the eye (**conjunctivitis**) is present. They may have a crusty appearance in and on the nose from chronic nasal dripping.

When to call the doctor

In an undiagnosed child, parents should inquire about immune deficiency if there are frequent infections, prolonged infections, unusual infections, unusual complications of usual infections, or if there is a **family** history of immune deficiency. If a child is known to have an immunodeficiency disorder, a healthcare provider should be contacted if the child shows signs of having an infection, such as **fever**, **vomiting**, diarrhea, swelling of the lymph nodes, or unusual fatigue.

Diagnosis

Usually, the first sign that individuals may have an immunodeficiency disorder is that they do not improve rapidly when given **antibiotics** to treat an infection. An immunodeficiency disorder is likely to be present when rare diseases occur or the patient gets ill from organisms that do not normally cause diseases, especially if the patient gets repeatedly infected. When this happens in very young children, a genetic defect may be causing an immunodeficiency disorder. When this situation occurs in older children or young adults, their medical history may indicate that childhood diseases may have caused an immunodeficiency disorder. Other possibilities also exist, such as recently acquired infections (e.g. HIV, hepatitis, tuberculosis, etc.).

Laboratory tests are used to determine the exact nature of the immunodeficiency. Most tests are performed on blood samples. Blood contains antibodies, lymphocytes, phagocytes, and complement components, all of the major immune components that might cause immu-

nodeficiency. A blood cell count determines if the number of phagocytic cells or lymphocytes is below normal. Lower than normal counts of either of these two cell types correlates with immunodeficiency. The blood cells also are checked for their appearance. Sometimes a person may have normal cell counts, but the cells are structurally defective. If the lymphocyte cell count is low, further testing is usually done to determine whether any particular type of lymphocyte is lower than normal. A lymphocyte proliferation test is done to determine if the lymphocytes can respond to stimuli. The failure to respond to stimulants correlates with immunodeficiency. Antibody levels can be measured. Complement levels can be determined by immunodiagnostic tests.

Treatment

There is no cure for congenital immunodeficiency disorders. Therapy is aimed at controlling infections (such as with antibiotics) and, for some disorders, replacing defective or absent components.

Patients with Bruton's agammaglobulinemia must be given periodic infusions of pooled immunoglobulin from multiple donors. The product is called intravenous immunoglobulin (IVIG). The infusions are given approximately once a month for life to compensate for the patients' inability to make these proteins.

Common variable immunodeficiency also is treated with periodic infusions of IVIG throughout life. Additionally, antibiotics are given when necessary to treat infections.

Patients with selective IgA deficiency usually do not require any treatment. Antibiotics can be given for frequent infections.

In some cases, no treatment is required for DiGeorge syndrome because T lymphocyte production improves on its own. In some severe cases, a bone marrow transplant or thymus transplant can be performed to correct the problem.

For most patients with SCID, bone marrow transplantation is necessary. In this procedure, healthy bone marrow from a donor who has a similar type of tissue (usually a relative, such as a brother or sister) is removed. The bone marrow, a substance that is found in the cavity of bones, is the factory that produces blood cells, including some of the white blood cells that make up the immune system. The bone marrow of the person receiving the transplant is destroyed and is then replaced with marrow from the donor. One type of SCID called adenosine deaminase (ADA) deficiency is treated with infusion of the deficient enzyme on a regular basis, and another type of SCID due to an absence of an interleukin, a protein that is important in directing the immune response, is also treated by infusions of the missing protein.

Treatment of the **HIV infection** that causes AIDS consists of drugs called antiretrovirals. These drugs interrupt the virus replication cycle and, therefore, spare the T cells. Several of these drugs used in various combinations with one another can treat but not cure the disease. Decreasing the viral in the blood to very low levels allows the immune system to remain in tact. Other treatments for people with AIDS are aimed at the particular infections and conditions that arise as a result of the impaired immune system.

For people being treated for cancer, periodic relief from chemotherapy drugs can restore the function of the immune system. In some cases, IVIG is utilized to boost the immune system.

Alternative treatment

For some individuals, alternative treatments such as acupuncture therapy to ease infection-related symptoms or homeopathic medicines to boost immunity may be used in conjunction with traditional medicine as part of a patient's treatment plan.

Nutritional concerns

In most cases, immunodeficiency caused by malnutrition is reversible. The health of the immune system is directly linked to the nutritional status of the patient. Among the essential nutrients required by the immune system are proteins, **vitamins**, iron, and zinc.

Prognosis

The prognosis depends on the type of immunodeficiency disorder. People with Bruton's agammaglobulinemia who are given IVIG infusions generally live into their 30s or 40s. They often die from chronic infections, usually of the lung. People with selective IgA deficiency generally live normal lives. They may experience problems if given a blood transfusion, and therefore they should wear a Medic Alert bracelet or have some other way of alerting any physician who treats them that they have this disorder.

SCID is the most serious of the immunodeficiency disorders. If a bone marrow transplant is not successfully performed, the child usually may not live beyond two years of age.

People with HIV/AIDS are living longer than in the past because of the antiretroviral drugs that became available in the mid-1990s. In the early 2000s HIV is still a potentially fatal illness, but medications have changed the face of the disease for those who have access to them. If medical treatment is timely and successful, T cells do not become depleted and opportunistic infections do not occur.

Prevention

Primary or congenital immunodeficiencies are genetic and are not preventable by avoidance of exposures or by dietary measures. However, someone with a congenital immunodeficiency disorder might want to consider getting genetic counseling before having children in order to find out if there is a chance they will pass the defect on to their children.

Some of the infections associated with acquired immunodeficiency can be prevented or treated before they cause problems. For example, there are effective treatments for tuberculosis and most bacterial and fungal infections. HIV infection can be prevented by practicing safe sex (e.g. using a **condom**) and by not using illegal intravenous drugs. These are the primary routes of transmitting the virus.

Nutritional concerns

In general, people with immunodeficiency disorders should maintain a healthy diet because malnutrition can aggravate immunodeficiencies. People can prevent malnutrition by getting adequate **nutrition**. They also should avoid being near others who have colds or are sick because they can easily acquire new infections. For the same reason, they should practice good personal hygiene, especially dental care. People with immunodeficiency disorders also should avoid eating undercooked food because it might contain bacteria that could cause infection. While this food might not cause infection in others, it is a potential source of infectious organisms for someone with an immunodeficiency.

Parental concerns

If a child has been diagnosed with an immunodeficiency disorder, the parents may be instructed to refrain from having normal childhood vaccinations that contain live viruses, since even weakened versions of the virus may cause serious disease. In some cases, the immunodeficient child needs to be encouraged to wear a mask when in public or around family members who are sick in order to reduce the risk of developing an infection.

KEY TERMS

Agammaglobulinemia—The lack of gamma globulins in the blood, associated with an increased susceptibility to infection.

B lymphocytes—Specialized blood cells that manufacture proteins called antibodies that attach themselves to invading foreign substances.

Chromosome—A microscopic thread-like structure found within each cell of the human body and consisting of a complex of proteins and DNA. Humans have 46 chromosomes arranged into 23 pairs. Chromosomes contain the genetic information necessary to direct the development and functioning of all cells and systems in the body. They pass on hereditary traits from parents to child (like eye color) and determine whether the child will be male or female.

T lymphocytes—Specialized blood cells that recognize invading organisms (helper T lymphocytes) and destroy them (killer T lymphocytes).

Resources

BOOKS

Doan, Thao. *Concise Medical Immunology.* Hagerstown, MD: Lippincott Williams & Wilkins, 2005.

Fireman, Philip. *Atlas of Allergies and Clinical Immunology.* St. Louis, MO: Mosby, 2005.

Mahon, Connie. *Clinical Immunology.* Paramus, NJ: Prentice Hall PTR, 2005.

Playfair, J. H., et al. *Immunology at a Glance.* Oxford, UK: Blackwell Publishing, 2005.

PERIODICALS

Bonilla, Francisco A., and Raif S. Geha. "Primary Immunodeficiency Disorders." *Journal of Allergy and Clinical Immunology* 112, no. 2 (February 1, 2003): S571–81.

Cooper, Megan A., Thomas L. Pommering, and Katalin Koranyi. "Primary Immunodeficiencies." *American Family Physician* (November 15, 2003): 2001.

Fischer, Alain. "Have We Seen the Last Variant of Severe Combined Immunodeficiency?" *The New England Journal of Medicine* (November 6, 2003): 1789.

ORGANIZATIONS

Children Affected by AIDS Foundation. 6033 W. Century Blvd., Suite 280, Los Angeles, CA 90045. Web site: <www.caaf4kids.org>.

Immune Deficiency Foundation. 40 W. Chesapeake Ave., Suite 308, Towson, MD 21204. Web site: <www.primaryimmune.org>.

WEB SITES

Frye, Richard E., and Delia M. Rivera-Hernandez. "Human Immunodeficiency Virus Infection." *eMedicine*, December 14, 2004. Available online at <www.emedicine.com/ped/topic1027.htm> (accessed January 7, 2005).

Makhoul, Hanan, et al. "Combined B-Cell and T-Cell Disorders." *eMedicine*, June 29, 2003. Available online at <www.emedicine.com/med/topic3538.htm> (accessed January 7, 2005).

Park, C. Lucy. "Common Variable Immunodeficiency." *eMedicine.* May 26, 2004. Available online at <www.emedicine.com/ped/topic444.htm> (accessed January 7, 2005).

Trigg, Michael. "Severe Combined Immunodeficiency Syndrome." *Nemours Foundation*, August 2002. Available online at <http://kidshealth.org/parent/medical/allergies/severe_immunodeficiency.html> (accessed January 7, 2005).

Wong, Henry, and Clarissa Yang. "Severe Combined Immunodeficiency." *eMedicine*, November 12, 2002. Available online at <www.emedicine.com/derm/topic879.htm> (accessed January 7, 2005).

John T. Lohr, PhD
Teresa G. Odle
Stephanie Dionne Sherk

Immunoglobulin deficiency syndromes

Definition

Immunoglobulin deficiency syndromes are a group of disorders that involve defects of any component of the immune system or a defect of another system that affects the immune system, leading to an increased incidence or severity of infection. In these disorders, specific disease-fighting antibodies (immunoglobulins such as IgG, IgA, and IgM) are either missing or are present in reduced levels. Children who have **immunodeficiency** syndromes may be subject to infection, diseases, disorders, or allergic reactions to a greater extent than individuals with fully functioning immune systems.

Description

Immunodeficiency is a defect of any component of the immune system or a defect of another system that affects the immune system leading to an increased incidence or severity of infection. Immunoglobulin deficiencies refer to missing or reduced levels of immunoglobulin (IgG, IgA, IgM) associated with an inability to make adequate specific antibody. These antibodies are specific proteins (immunoglobulins) produced by the immune system to respond to bacteria, viruses, fungi, parasites, or toxins that invade the body. Each class of antibody binds to corresponding molecules (antigens) on the cell surfaces of certain foreign organisms or substances, attempting to protect the body against reactions or illness. When the immune system is challenged by invading organisms, the antibodies may each play a protective role:

- Immunoglobulin G (IgG) is the most abundant class of immunoglobulins, directed toward viruses, bacterial organisms, and toxins. It is found in most tissues and in plasma, the clear portion of blood.

- Immunoglobulin M (IgM) is the first antibody produced in an immune response to any invading organism or toxic substance.

- Immunoglobulin A (IgA) is activated early in response to invasion by bacteria and viruses. It is found in saliva, tears, and all other mucus secretions.

- As of the early 2000s, IgD activity is not well understood.

- Immunoglobulin E (IgE) is found in respiratory secretions and is directed toward invasion of the body by parasites and in allergic reactions such as hay fever, **atopic dermatitis**, and allergic **asthma**.

Immunoglobulins are made by white blood cells known as B cells (B lymphocytes). Any disease that harms the development or function of B cells will, therefore, affect the production of immunoglobulin antibodies. T cells, another type of white blood cell, may also be involved in immunodeficiency disorders. About 70 percent of immunoglobulin deficiencies involve B lymphocytes and 20–30 percent involve T lymphocytes. Another 10 percent may involve both B and T lymphocytes.

Many of the infections that occur in children with immunoglobulin deficiency syndromes are caused by bacterial organisms or microbes. Certain of these invasive organisms form capsules when they enter the body, a mechanism used to confuse the immune system. In a healthy body with an adequately functioning immune system, immunoglobulin antibodies bind to the capsule and overcome the bacteria's defenses. Streptococci, meningococci, and *Haemophilus influenzae*, organisms that cause diseases such as **otitis media**, **sinusitis**, **pneumonia**, **meningitis**, osteomyelitis, septic arthritis, and sepsis, all make capsules. Children with immunoglobulin deficiencies are also prone to viral infections, including echovirus, enterovirus, and **hepatitis B**. They may also develop infection after receiving live (attenuated) **polio vaccine**. This is one of the reasons that live **polio** vaccine is no longer used routinely in the United States.

There are two types of immunodeficiency diseases: primary and secondary. Immunoglobulin deficiency syndromes are primary immunodeficiency diseases. They account for 50 percent of all primary immunodeficiencies and are the largest group of immunodeficiency disorders. Some are well defined and some are not fully understood. Secondary disorders occur in normally healthy people who are suffering from an underlying disease that weakens the immune system. Successful treatment of the disease usually reverses the immunodeficiency.

Examples of well defined immunoglobulin deficiency disorders include the following:

- X-linked agammaglobulinemia is an inherited disease stemming from a defect on the X chromosome, consequently affecting more males than females. Defect results in absence or reduced numbers of B cells that do not mature and perform normal function. Mature B cells are capable of making antibodies and developing memory, a feature in which the B cell will rapidly recognize and respond to an infectious agent the next time it is encountered. All classes of immunoglobulin antibodies are decreased in agammaglobulinemia.

- Immunoglobulin heavy chain deletion, a form of agammaglobulinemia, is a genetic disorder in which part of the antibody molecule is absent. This condition results in the loss of several antibody classes and subclasses, including most IgG antibodies and all IgA and IgE antibodies. The disease occurs because part of the gene for the heavy chain has been lost.

- X-linked hypogammaglobulinemia can occur in combination with growth hormone (GH) deficiency, producing short stature and delayed **puberty**, primarily in boys but also occurring in girls.

- Transient hypogammaglobulinemia of infancy is a temporary disease of unknown cause. It is believed to be caused by a defect in the development of T helper cells (cells that recognize foreign antigens and activate T and B cells in an immune response). As the child ages, the number and condition of T helper cells improves, and this situation corrects itself.

Hypogammaglobulinemia is characterized by low levels of gammaglobulin antibodies in the blood. During the disease period, children may have decreased levels of IgG and IgA antibodies. In some infants with this disorder, laboratory tests are able to show that the antibodies present do not react properly with infectious bacteria.

- IgG subclass deficiency is a disorder associated with a poor ability to respond and make antibody against polysaccharide antigens, primarily pneumococcus.

- Selective IgA deficiency is an inherited disease characterized by a failure of B cells to switch from making IgM to IgA antibodies. The amount of IgA produced is limited in either serum or the mucosal linings of organs. This condition may result in more infections of mucosal surfaces, such as the nose, throat, lungs, and intestines. However, most persons with this abnormality are asymptomatic.

- IgM deficiency is characterized by the absence or low level of total IgM antibodies, the body's first defense against infection. This condition results in slow response to infective organisms and slow response to treatment.

- IgG deficiency with hyper-IgM is a disorder that results when B-cells fail to switch from making IgM to IgG. This condition produces an increase in the amount of IgM antibodies present and a decrease in the amount of IgG and IgA antibodies. This disorder is the result of a genetic mutation.

- **Severe combined immunodeficiency** (SVID) is not precisely an immunoglobulin deficiency, but a combined deficiency resulting from a T-cell disorder. The T-cell dysfunction can either be X-linked, affecting more males than females and characterized by the absence of T lymphocytes, or it can occur through autosomal inheritance (not sex linked), resulting in an absence of both T and B lymphocytes and a deficient thymus gland, the lymphoid organ that produces T-cell lymphocytes.

- **Common variable immunodeficiency** (CVID) is a primary immunodeficiency with onset of symptoms typically occurring in the second or third decade of life. It is never diagnosed before two years of age and is diagnosed only after drug toxicity and other primary immune deficiencies have been ruled out. IgG and IgA and/or IgM will be measured at about two standard deviations below normal. The individual will typically not make antibodies against protein or polysaccharide antigens and will not make IgM antibodies against incompatible blood group antigens (hemagluttinins). T-cell dysfunction is the variable in this disorder. Children who have this disorder are subject to recurring

infections and may not respond appropriately to immunization.

Demographics

Primary immunoglobulin deficiency syndromes occur only rarely. Those that are X-linked occur more in males than females; other immunoglobulin deficiencies occur equally in both sexes. Detection of the syndromes usually occurs in childhood. Numbers of new cases of specific syndromes are difficult to estimate because many deficiencies go undiagnosed. Among the syndromes for which incidence rates are available are IgA deficiency (one in 500–700), agammaglobulinemia (one in 50,000–100,000), severe combined immunodeficiency or SCID (one in 100,000–500,000), and common variable immunodeficiency or CVID (one in 50,000–200,000).

Causes and symptoms

Primary immunoglobulin deficiencies are primarily the result of congenital defects that affect the development and function of B lymphocytes (B cells), the white cells that fight infection and disease. Defects can occur at two main points in the development of B-cells. First, B cells can fail to develop into antibody-producing cells. X-linked agammaglobulinemia is an example of this disease. Secondly, B cells can fail to make a particular type of antibody or fail to switch classes during maturation. Initially, when B cells start making antibodies for the first time, they make IgM. As they mature and develop memory, they switch to one of the other immunoglobulin classes. Failure to switch or failure to make a subclass can lead to immunoglobulin deficiency diseases. Defects in the thymus gland that manufactures T lymphocytes or defects in the T lymphocytes themselves can also result in reduced production of immunoglobulins.

Symptoms are frequent and so are persistent infections, particularly of the respiratory system. Frequent digestive disturbances and **diarrhea** may lead to malabsorption of essential nutrients and **failure to thrive**. Children with primary immunoglobulin deficiency syndromes will exhibit some of the following characteristics:

- signs of infection in the first days or weeks of life

- a slow response to treatment

- infection suppressed by appropriate treatment but not cured

- common bacterial or viral organisms causing increasingly acute recurring infections

- uncommon bacterial or viral organisms causing infection
- multiple simultaneous infections at more than one site
- delays in growth and development
- development of unexpected complications such as **anemias** and chronic diseases

When to call the doctor

Parents should seek medical care from a pediatrician or **family** practitioner if their young child or teenager has frequent or persistent infections such as upper respiratory infections, or chronic **cough**, ear infections, sinusitis, asthma, or pneumonia. Sores that do not heal or recurring or long-lasting skin irritations may also be signs of reduced immune system functioning.

Diagnosis

An immunodeficiency disease is suspected when children become ill frequently, especially repeat illness caused by the same organisms. Diagnosis will begin with a detailed history of the child's illnesses (dates, duration, and infection site) and review of all prior medications and immunizations and results of diagnostic tests performed. Determining which immunoglobulins are present and which are absent or present in reduced amounts is critical for diagnosis. Diagnostic testing may include routine blood tests such as a complete blood count (CBC) and differential (peripheral blood smear) to evaluate overall health and determine the type and number of red cells, white cells, and platelets present in the blood. Tests or cultures may be performed to determine the type of bacteria or virus causing recurring infections. B lymphocytes and T lymphocytes may be quantified. When immunodeficiency is suspected, levels of the classes of immunoglobulins are measured in blood serum by using a clinical laboratory procedure called electrophoresis. This procedure both quantifies the amount of each antibody present and identifies the various classes and subclasses of antibodies. Deficiencies may be noted in one class or subclass or in combinations of antibodies. Genetic testing may be done to help identify the type of immunodeficiency disease.

Treatment

Immunoglobulin deficiency diseases cannot be cured, but treatment that replaces or boosts specific immunoglobulins can help support immune function in affected children. Immune serum, obtained from donated blood that contains adequate levels of IgG antibodies, may sometimes be transfused as a source of antibodies to boost the immune response, even though it may not contain all antibodies needed and may lack antibodies specific for some of the recurring infections. The preferred treatment is to give specific immunoglobulins intravenously (immunoglobulin intravenous therapy or IVIG) or subcutaneously. No replacement therapy is available for treating IgA deficiencies.

Treatment will also focus on controlling infections in immunodeficient children. Immunization against frequent infection can be achieved in some children by administering polysaccharide-protein conjugate vaccines shown to improve immune response in certain types of infection. **Antibiotics** are used routinely at the first sign of an infection to help eliminate infectious organisms. Antifungal drug therapy may be administered to treat fungus infections. Few drugs are effective against viral diseases, and each viral illness will be evaluated and treated differently, depending on the virus and the overall health of the child. Bone marrow transplantation may correct immunodefiency in some cases.

Alternative treatment

Several nutritional supplements are reported to help build the immune system. These include garlic (contains the essential trace element germanium), essential fatty acids (found in flax seed oil, evening primrose oil, and fish oils), sea vegetables such as kelp, acidophilus to supply natural bacteria in the digestive tract, and **vitamins** A and C, both powerful antioxidants that improve immune function and increase resistance to infection. Zinc is another nutrient essential to immune system functioning. Green drinks made with young barley are believed to cleanse the blood and supply chlorophyll and nutrients for tissue repair. Alcohol, certain prescription and over-the-counter drugs, and coffee and other **caffeine** drinks should be avoided. Stress is known to produce biochemicals that reduce white blood cell functioning, making it important to get sufficient **sleep** and reduce stress to help keep the immune system functioning. Therapeutic massage, **yoga**, and other types of stress reduction programs are available in most communities.

Nutritional concerns

Immune system function requires having certain essential nutrients and avoiding things that depress immunity. A diet that improves immune system functioning includes nutrients obtained as much as possible from whole foods such as fresh fruits and vegetables, whole grain breads and cereals, and brown rice and whole grain pasta for essential vitamins, **minerals**, and fiber. Such a diet also limits or eliminates refined foods.

KEY TERMS

Antibody—A special protein made by the body's immune system as a defense against foreign material (bacteria, viruses, etc.) that enters the body. It is uniquely designed to attack and neutralize the specific antigen that triggered the immune response.

Antigen—A substance (usually a protein) identified as foreign by the body's immune system, triggering the release of antibodies as part of the body's immune response.

Autosomal inheritance—Inheritance involving any of the autosomes (22 pairs) and not involving sex-linked chromosomes X and Y.

Bacteria—Singular, bacterium; tiny, one-celled forms of life that cause many diseases and infections.

Immunization—A process or procedure that protects the body against an infectious disease by stimulating the production of antibodies. A vaccination is a type of immunization.

Immunoglobulin G (IgG)—Immunoglobulin type gamma, the most common type found in the blood and tissue fluids.

Thymus gland—An endocrine gland located in the upper chest just below the neck that functions as part of the lymphatic system. It coordinates the development of the immune system.

Virus—A small infectious agent consisting of a core of genetic material (DNA or RNA) surrounded by a shell of protein. A virus needs a living cell to reproduce.

Fish, fowl, and lean meats can be consumed in moderation. Sweets should be reduced or avoided.

Prognosis

Regular medical observation, treatment of symptoms, and appropriate immune system boosting usually produces a good result in children with immunodeficiencies. Prognosis is related to the immune system's ability to produce the specific antibodies that are missing or present in reduced amounts. Individuals with immunodeficiency syndromes may have a normal life span although a variety of complications can occur, including autoimmune, gastrointestinal, granulomatous, and malignant conditions as a result of progressive immune deficiency disorders and/or repeat infections.

Prevention

Immunodeficiency cannot be prevented; however, challenges to the immune system can be reduced and infections avoided in immunodeficient individuals. Immunoglobulin deficiencies require impeccable health maintenance and care, paying particular attention to good hygiene, balanced **nutrition**, sufficient rest, regular check ups and immunizations, and optimal dental care, as well as avoiding crowds and contact with other children or relatives with bacterial or virus infections.

Nutritional concerns

A healthy immune system can be maintained by providing essential nutrients through a good diet and regular supplementation. Parents can help assure that their children and teens have three nutritious, low-fat, high-fiber, whole-food meals a day (limiting or eliminating altogether refined or prepared foods and fast foods) and healthy snacks in between, such as nuts, fresh fruit, popcorn, raw veggies, and whole grain crackers with nut butters (if no **allergies** to peanuts or other nuts), naturally sweetened jellies, and low-fat cheeses. Vitamin supplements should include vitamins A, C, and E, valuable parts of the body's defense system that help to increase production of healthy white blood cells and to fight infection.

Parental concerns

Parents with immunoglobulin deficient children and teenagers will likely be concerned that their children are in frequent contact with schoolmates and friends, the common route to infection. When infection occurs frequently, it is important to remember that the pediatrician or family practitioner will have specific criteria and diagnostic tests for evaluating the child, identifying the immunodeficiency, and determining appropriate therapy. Meanwhile, parents can help keep their children away from crowds and avoid contact with other children or relatives with bacterial or virus infections.

Resources

BOOKS

Beers, Mark H., ed. *Merck Manual of Medical Information, Second Home Edition.* Whitehouse Station, NJ: Merck Research Laboratories, 2003.

Sompayrac, Lauren. *How the Immune System Works.* Oxford, UK: Blackwell, 2003.

ORGANIZATIONS

Centers for Disease Control and Prevention. 1600 Clifton Road, Atlanta, GA 30333. Web site: <www.cdc.gov>.

WEB SITES

Chin, Terry. "IgA and IgG Subclass Deficiency." *eMedicine.* Available online at <www.emedicine.com/ped/topic190.htm> (accessed January 14, 2005).

Makhoul, Issam. "Pure B-Cell Disorders." *eMedicine.* Available online at <www.emedicine.com/med/topic216.htm> (accessed January 14, 2005).

L. Lee Culvert
Jacqueline L. Longe

Immunotherapy *see* **Allergy shots**

Impetigo

Definition

Impetigo refers to a very localized bacterial infection of the skin. There are two types, bullous and epidemic.

Description

Impetigo is a skin infection that tends primarily to afflict children. Impetigo caused by the bacterium *Staphylococcus aureus* (also known as staph) affects children of all ages. Impetigo caused by the bacteria called group A streptococci (also known as strep) are most common in children ages two to five.

The bacteria that cause impetigo are very contagious. They can be spread by a child from one part of his or her body to another by scratching or contact with a towel, clothing, or stuffed animal. These same methods can pass the bacteria on from one person to another.

Impetigo tends to develop in areas of the skin that have already been damaged through some other mechanism (a cut or scrape, burn, insect bite, or vesicle from **chickenpox**).

Demographics

About 10 percent of all skin problems in children are ultimately diagnosed as impetigo.

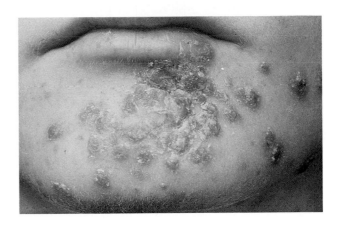

Impetigo is a contagious bacterial skin infection that has affected the area around this patient's nose and mouth. *(© NMSB/Custom Stock Medical Photo, Inc.)*

Causes and symptoms

The first sign of bullous impetigo is a large bump on the skin with a clear, fluid-filled top (a vesicle). The bump develops a scab-like, honey-colored crust. There is usually no redness or **pain**, although the area may be quite itchy. Ultimately, the skin in this area will become dry and flake away. Bullous impetigo is usually caused by staph bacteria.

Epidemic impetigo can be caused by staph or strep bacteria and (as the name implies) is very easily passed among children. Certain factors, such as heat and humidity, crowded conditions, and poor hygiene increase the chance that this type of impetigo will spread rapidly among large groups of children. This type of impetigo involves the formation of a small vesicle surrounded by a circle of reddened skin. The vesicles appear first on the face and legs. When a child has several of these vesicles close together, they may spread to one another. The skin surface may become eaten away (ulcerated), leaving irritated pits. When there are many of these deep, pitting ulcers, with pus in the center and brownish-black scabs, the condition is called ecthyma. If left untreated, the type of bacteria causing this type of impetigo has the potential to cause a serious kidney disease (glomerulonephritis). Even when impetigo is initially caused by strep bacteria, the vesicles are frequently secondarily infected with staph bacteria.

Impetigo is usually an uncomplicated skin condition. Left untreated, however, it may develop into a serious disease, including osteomyelitis (bone infection), septic arthritis (joint infection), or **pneumonia**. If large quantities of bacteria are present and begin circulating in the bloodstream, the child is in danger of developing an overwhelming systemic infection known as sepsis.

Diagnosis

Characteristic appearance of the skin is the usual method of diagnosis, although fluid from the vesicles can be cultured and then examined in an attempt to identify the causative bacteria.

Treatment

Uncomplicated impetigo is usually treated with a topical antibiotic cream called mupirocin. In more serious, widespread cases of impetigo, or when the child has a **fever** or swollen glands, **antibiotics** may be given by mouth or even through a needle placed in a vein (intravenously).

Prognosis

Prognosis for a child with impetigo is excellent. The vast majority of children recover quickly, completely, and uneventfully.

Prevention

Prevention involves good hygiene. Hand washing; never sharing towels, clothing, or stuffed animals; and keeping fingernails well-trimmed are easy precautions to take to avoid spreading the infection from one person to another.

Resources

BOOKS

"Cutaneous Bacterial Infections." In *Nelson Textbook of Pediatrics.* Edited by Richard E. Behrman et al. Philadelphia: Saunders Company, 2004.

Darmstadt, Gary L. "Cellulitis and Superficial Skin Infections." In *Principles and Practice of Pediatric Infectious Diseases*, 2nd ed. Edited by Sarah S. Long et al. St. Louis, MO: Elsevier, 2003.

PERIODICALS

Sanfilippo, A. M. "Common bacterial skin infections." *American Family Physician* 66 (July 2002): 119–24.

Stulberg, D. L. "Common pediatric and adolescent skin conditions." *American Family Physician* 16 (October 2003): 269–83.

Wolfrey, J. "Pediatric exanthems." *Clinical Family Practice* 5 (September 2003): 55–7.

Rosalyn Carson-DeWitt, MD

Impulse control disorders

Definition

Impulse control disorders are a relatively new class of **personality disorders** characterized by an ongoing inability to resist impulses to perform actions that are harmful to oneself or others. The most common of these are **intermittent explosive disorder**, kleptomania, pyromania, compulsive gambling disorder, and **trichotillomania**.

Description

Impulse control disorders include five conditions that involve a recurrent failure to resist impulsive behaviors that harm one's self or others: intermittent explosive disorder, pyromania, kleptomania, trichotillomania, and compulsive gambling disorder. Intermittent explosive disorder involves unusually aggressive and violent outbursts. Pyromania is characterized by repetitive and purposeful fire-setting. Kleptomania involves urges to steal and repetitive acts of unnecessary theft. Trichotillomania is recurrent pulling out of hair. Compulsive gambling disorder is maladaptive, repetitive gambling.

Repetitive **self-mutilation** is considered by some experts to be a type of impulse control disorder. In this condition, people cause intentional harm to themselves through burning, cutting, or scratching.

Demographics

The incidence of impulse control disorders in children and adolescents is difficult to determine. In general, intermittent explosive disorder, pyromania, and compulsive gambling disorder are more common in boys, while kleptomania is more common in girls.

Causes and symptoms

Exact causes of impulse control disorders are unknown, but may be linked to genetics, **family** environment, and/or neurological factors. Some research suggests that impulse control disorders are linked to certain hormones, abnormal nerve impulses, and variations in brain chemistry and function. Children and adolescents who have had a severe **head injury** and who have epilepsy may be at greater risk of developing these disorders. In children and adolescents, impulse control disorders often occur along with other psychological conditions, such as attention-deficit hyperactivity disorder (ADHD).

Intermittent explosive disorder is characterized by episodes of aggressive and violent outbursts and loss and lack of control of anger. Often, explosive episodes result in destruction of property, domestic violence, and physical assault, which, in turn, have legal ramifications. The degree of aggressiveness during each episode is grossly out of proportion to any stresses.

Pyromania is the repetitive, deliberate, and purposeful setting of fires. Children and adolescents with pyromania are often aroused by fire-setting, and/or feel pleasure, relief, or gratification when setting fires or witnessing the consequences of fire. In addition, pyromaniacs are fascinated and attracted to fire and related accessories (e.g., matches, lighters), and are unnaturally curious about its use and consequences. Fire-setting is not performed for any other reasons, such as for financial gain, to express anger, to conceal a criminal act, or to express sociopolitical views.

Kleptomania is an inability to resist impulses to repetitively steal objects that are not necessary for personal use or monetary value. Children and adolescents with kleptomania experience a growing sense of tension just before **stealing**, followed by pleasure, relief, or gratification during or just after stealing. Career thieves, those who steal out of need or to support substance abuse, and those who steal because they have no regard for society's laws, are not considered to have kleptomania. Individuals with kleptomania do not want to steal and feel guilty about it.

Trichotillomania is characterized by recurrent pulling out of one's hair to produce noticeable hair loss. Children and adolescents with trichotillomania experience a growing sense of tension or stress just before pulling hair out or when trying to resist hair pulling. They experience pleasure, relief, or gratification when pulling out the hair.

Compulsive gambling disorder, also called pathological gambling, is recurrent and persistent gambling behavior characterized by five or more of the following:

- having a preoccupation with gambling
- needing to gamble with increasingly larger amounts of money to achieve the same excitement
- having repeated unsuccessful efforts to control gambling
- telling lies to family members, therapists, and others to conceal extent of gambling involvement
- committing forgery, fraud, or theft to finance gambling
- being restless or irritable when trying to stop gambling
- gambling to escape problems or to relieve tension or other feelings
- jeopardizing or losing a significant job, relationship, or other opportunity due to gambling
- relying on others to provide financial support due to financial difficulties caused by gambling

When to call the doctor

Parents of children and adolescents who exhibit problems with impulse control should see a physician as soon as possible. Usually, a referral to a psychologist, psychiatrist, or therapist will be given.

Diagnosis

Impulse control disorders are diagnosed by psychological and psychiatric evaluations, interviews with family members, teachers, and caregivers, and observation and interviews with the child or adolescent. Diagnosis is based on clinical criteria defined in the American Psychiatric Association's *Diagnostic and Statistical Manual of Mental Disorders, Fourth Edition, Text Revision C (DSM-IV-TR)*.

Impulse control disorders often have characteristics in common with other psychological disorders and often occur in conjunction with other conditions, such as ADHD or **conduct disorder**. Therefore, diagnosis of impulse control disorders may be difficult, and they are usually diagnosed after exclusion of other disorders. For example, intermittent explosive disorder is diagnosed if the aggressive episodes cannot be better explained by another psychological disorder, such as **antisocial personality disorder**; a manic episode; ADHD; or by substance abuse or medical conditions such as head trauma. Pyromania is diagnosed when fire-setting is not better explained by conduct disorder, antisocial personality disorder, mental impairment, delusions or hallucinations, or intoxication. Kleptomania is diagnosed when repetitive stealing is not better explained by anger or vengeance, **peer pressure**, delusions or hallucinations, conduct disorder, a manic episode, or antisocial personality disorder. Trichotillomania is diagnosed when pulling out of hair is not better explained by another mental disorder or a dermatological or medical condition, and when this practice causes clinically significant social or occupational dysfunction or impairment. Compulsive gambling disorder is diagnosed when the behavior cannot be better explained by a manic episode, conduct disorder, or peer pressure.

Treatment

Impulse control disorders are treated with medication, psychotherapy, and behavior modification. If these disorders are occurring in conjunction with another condition, such as ADHD, medication and therapy for that condition often helps alleviate the impulse control disorder. Depression is often an underlying factor in some impulse control disorders, particularly compulsive gambling disorder and trichotillomania. Therefore, treatment with **antidepressants** may be helpful.

Long-term counseling and psychotherapy is usually necessary as well. Therapy methods to help with impulse control generally involve behavior modification, anger and stress management, and psychoanalysis. Therapy can occur in residential or day treatment facilities, or on an outpatient basis. Support groups, such as Gamblers Anonymous, may also help.

Prognosis

Prognosis depends on the severity of the disorder and the commitment of the individual to seek therapy. Impulse control disorders can affect social, academic, and occupational functioning, as well as result in legal problems. Long-term participation in individual counseling and group therapy can improve prognosis.

Prevention

Impulse control disorders cannot be prevented.

Parental concerns

Children and adolescents with impulse control disorders may have difficulties in school and at home. In some cases, impulse control disorders can result in expulsion from school. Parents should investigate **alternative school** settings that may be able to provide counseling and group therapy integrated with academics. **Family therapy** may help alleviate stressful family situa-

---

KEY TERMS

Alternative school—An educational setting designed to accommodate educational, behavioral, and/or medical needs of children and adolescents that cannot be adequately addressed in a traditional school environment.

Antisocial personality disorder—A disorder characterized by a behavior pattern that disregards for the rights of others. People with this disorder often deceive and manipulate, or their behavior might include aggression to people or animals or property destruction, for example. This disorder has also been called sociopathy or psychopathy.

Attention deficit hyperactivity disorder (ADHD)—A condition in which a person (usually a child) has an unusually high activity level and a short attention span. People with the disorder may act impulsively and may have learning and behavioral problems.

Conduct disorder—A behavioral and emotional disorder of childhood and adolescence. Children with a conduct disorder act inappropriately, infringe on the rights of others, and violate societal norms.

Manic episode—A distinct period of abnormally and persistently elevated, expansive, or irritable mood, lasting at least one week, characterized by inflated sense of self-importance, decreased need for sleep, extreme talkativeness, racing thoughts, and excessive participation in pleasure-seeking activities.

---

tions and help other family members understand the impulse control disorder.

Resources

BOOKS

Grant, J. E., and S. W. Kim. *Stop Me Because I Can't Stop Myself: Taking Control of Impulsive Behavior.* New York: McGraw-Hill, 2003.

Williams, J. *Pyromania, Kleptomania, and Other Impulse-Control Disorders.* Berkeley Heights, NJ: Enslow, 2002.

PERIODICALS

Weisbrot, D. M., and A. B. Ettinger. "Aggression and Violence in Mood Disorders." *Child and Adolescent Psychiatric Clinics of North America* 11 (2002): 649–71.

ORGANIZATIONS

American Academy of Child and Adolescent Psychiatry. 3615 Wisconsin Ave., N.W., Washington, D.C. 20016-3007.

(202) 966-7300. Fax: 202-966-2891. Web site: <www.aacap.org>.

American Psychiatric Association. 1000 Wilson Boulevard, Suite 1825, Arlington, Va. 22209-3901. (703) 907-7300 Web site: <www.psych.org>.

Gamblers Anonymous. P.O. Box 17173, Los Angeles, CA 90017. (213) 386-8789. Web site: <www.gamblersanonymous.org>.

WEB SITES

American Academy of Child and Adolescent Psychiatry. Psychotherapies for Children and Adolescents. [cited January 2003]. Available online at: <www.aacap.org/publications/factsfam/86.htm>.

*Psychology Information Online.*Impulse Control Disorders. [cited October 2004]. Available online at: <www.psychologyinfo.com/problems/impulse_control.html>.

Psychotherapy. [cited October 2004]. Available online at: <www.psyweb.com/Mdisord/impud.html>.

Reyes, A. *Impulse Control Disorders.* [cited October 2004.] Available online at: <http://health.discovery.com/encyclopedias/2885.html>.

Jennifer E. Sisk, M.A.

Inclusion conjunctivitis

Definition

Inclusion **conjunctivitis** is an inflammation of the conjunctiva, or white of the eye. In the neonate this condition is part of a larger group of eye diseases called neonatal conjunctivitis. Inclusion conjunctivitis is also called a chlamydial conjunctivitis.

Description

Chlamydiae are similar to bacteria but cannot produce their own energy and thus live in the cells of other organisms. Once inside the host cell, chlamydiae replicate and form inclusion bodies. They then replace and finally destroy the cell membrane of the host, releasing more chlamydiae to continue the infection process. The life cycle of chlamydia is 72 hours. Chlamydiae are found in parts of the body with a mucosal membrane, which are the eye, the respiratory tract, and the genitourinary tract.

Transmission

Neonatal inclusion conjunctivitis develops within five to 12 days after birth and is contracted as the child passes through the mother's cervix. Two-thirds of those females with a chlamydial infection pass the infection on to the child during **childbirth**.

Adult inclusion conjunctivitis, which can affect sexually active adolescents, is usually transmitted sexually and develops when the eye is infected by the urogenital secretions of an individual infected with chlamydia, but it can be transmitted by eye-to-eye contact. Symptoms do not always exist with chlamydial infections, and thus it is often transmitted unknowingly. Up to 80 percent of female adults and adolescents with inclusion conjunctivitis are asymptomatic, and almost half of those with adult inclusion conjunctivitis do not have a systemic infection of chlamydia.

Demographics

The exact number of individuals with adult inclusion conjunctivitis is not known. But adult inclusion conjunctivitis, which is seen only if one is infected with chlamydia, affects 3 million annually in the United States. It is seen most often in sexually active 15 to 30 years olds, and most of these infections are reported in women 15 to 19. Forty-six percent of new cases of chlamydia fall within this group. Up to 10 percent of pregnant women harbor the chlamydial parasite. Twenty-five percent of those men with chlamydia infections are not aware of their infection.

Up to 6 percent of newborns develop neonatal inclusion conjunctivitis. Forty percent of neonatal conjunctivitis is due to chlamydia. Between 35 and 50 percent of newborns infected with chlamydia develop neonatal inclusion conjunctivitis. Neonatal chlamydial or inclusion conjunctivitis is 10 times more common than neonatal gonorrheal conjunctivitis.

Causes and symptoms

Inclusion conjunctivitis is caused by an intracellular organism called *Chlamydia trachomatis.*

The signs and symptoms of adult inclusion conjunctivitis appear two to 19 days after contact with an individual who harbors the chlamydia parasite. The symptoms of adult inclusion conjunctivitis are a foreign body sensation, watery eyes, and eyelids that stick together upon awakening. Large follicles may be seen if the lower lid is pulled down. The lymph nodes near the ears, called the preauricular nodes, may be swollen. Because the symptoms of chlamydia wax and wane and because the adolescent or adult may be asymptomatic, proper diagnosis may be delayed.

The signs of neonatal inclusion conjunctivitis appear five to 14 days after birth. Since the lymphatic system of the newborn is not well developed, follicles will not usually be present, and the lymph nodes will not be enlarged, but the eye of the neonate with chlamydia will be red and inflamed. The infant will be tearing and have a purulent ocular discharge, and the eyelids will be swollen. Other accompanying symptoms in the infant include a **cough** and **rhinitis**.

When to call the doctor

Any red eye, with or without discharge, should be examined by an appropriate healthcare practitioner. There are many causes of eye problems, and appropriate treatment should be instituted as soon as possible if inclusion conjunctivitis is the cause of the ocular problem.

The children of mothers who give birth outside the traditional hospital setting should contact their healthcare provider regarding the necessity of prophylactic antibiotic drops. A healthcare provider should be informed if the mother or father of a newborn has an untreated sexually transmitted disease.

Diagnosis

The diagnosis of inclusion conjunctivitis cannot be made definitively without laboratory testing, but the signs of inclusion conjunctivitis can be seen by the eye care provider, even if a patient is not symptomatic. Follicles can seen on the inside inferior eyelids and occasionally under the superior eyelid of the patient with adult inclusion conjunctivitis, and if treatment has been delayed, scarring of the interior of the eyelids may be present as well as kerititis, an inflammation of the cornea, and neovascularization, or new blood vessel formation of the cornea. Upon questioning the individual may report a history of a genitourinary infection.

The laboratory testing for inclusion conjunctivitis begins with swabbing a sample from the inside of the eyelids to test for the presence of the characteristic inclusion bodies made only by chlamydia. The Giemsa stain is used often to diagnose neonatal inclusion conjunctivitis. This technique has a high rate of false positives for the adult with inclusion conjunctivitis. Immunofluorescence monoclonal antibody testing is very sensitive technique that gives a rapid diagnosis of inclusion conjunctivitis. Other techniques used to diagnose a chlamydial infection are enzyme immunoassays, serum antibody tests, and DNA probes.

Since inclusion conjunctivitis can mimic other diseases, it is important to rule out other types of conjunctivitis, such as those of viral etiology or allergy or those caused by gonorrhea.

Treatment

Neonatal inclusion conjunctivitis may resolve spontaneously within nine months without treatment. But the standard treatment for an infant younger than four months of age is oral erythromycin, four times a day for two weeks. The eye may be irrigated with saline to help remove the mucus discharge. The parents of the infant are treated as well.

Doxycycline, tetracycline, ocufloxacin, and erythromycin are sometimes prescribed. Tetracycline is not given to children under eight years of age, and ocufloxacin is not given to those under 18 years of age. Neither drug is given to pregnant or nursing women because of side effects. **Topical antibiotics** are not required if systemic or oral medication is prescribed, but if there is a co-existing inflammation in the eye, then topical steroids may be given. Finally, the sexual partners of individuals with inclusion conjunctivitis must also be receive antibiotic treatment.

Prognosis

Usually adult inclusion conjunctivitis resolves within two to four weeks with treatment. Rarely does inclusion conjunctivitis lead to blindness, unless it has been left untreated for months or longer. If untreated, a chlamydial infection can lead to pelvic inflammatory disease and scarring of fallopian tubes in women, causing infertility or ectopic pregnancies. In males, urethritis may result.

Ten to 20 percent of infants infected with chlamydia develop **pneumonia** during the first six months of life. In the infant, inclusion conjunctivitis may persist for several years.

Prevention

Since in the United States adult inclusion conjunctivitis is primarily a sexually transmitted disease, the incidence of inclusion conjunctivitis can be decreased either through abstinence or through the use of condoms. Pregnant women with a chlamydial infection should talk to their doctor about treatment of the infection. Antibiotic eye drops only may not be sufficient to prevent inclusion conjunctivitis in the newborn if the mother is infected with chlamydia.

KEY TERMS

Chlamydia—The most common bacterial sexually transmitted disease in the United States. It often accompanies gonorrhea and is known for its lack of evident symptoms in the majority of women.

Conjunctiva—Plural, conjunctivae. The mucous membrane that covers the white part of the eyes (sclera) and lines the eyelids.

Cornea—The clear, dome-shaped outer covering of the eye that lies in front of the iris and pupil. The cornea lets light into the eye.

Gonorrhea—A sexually transmitted disease that causes infection in the genital organs and may cause disease in other parts of the body.

Trachoma—A type of chlamydia that causes blindness.

The incidence of neonatal conjunctivitis can be reduced by applying erythromycin ointment to the newborn's eyes shortly after delivery. Silver nitrate, which may be instilled at some institutions at birth (instead of erythromycin), is not effective against chlamydia.

Parental concerns

In the newborn, inclusion conjunctivitis may resolve spontaneously, but there are chlamydial infections which can cause blindness if not treated. So, any eye problem in the newborn needs to be diagnosed properly and treated as indicated by the pediatrician or eye-care provider.

When inclusion conjunctivitis is diagnosed in an adolescent, it is almost always has been contracted through sexual activity. Sixty-five percent of adolescents have had sexual intercourse by age 16. Only 40 percent of young adults between 18 and 21 years of age used a **condom** during their most recent sexual encounter, and 45 percent of these individuals have already had more than three sexual partners. Because **peer pressure** makes it difficult to resist sex and because adolescents have difficulty understanding they are risks of contracting **sexually transmitted diseases**, including chlamydial infections, parents should be involved in helping the adolescent understand these risks.

Resources

BOOKS

Adamis, Anthony P., et al. "Chlamydia and Acanthamoeba Infections of the Eye." In *Principles and Practice of Ophthalmology*. Philadelphia: Saunders, 2000.

Dawson, Chandler R. "Inclusion Conjunctivitis." In *Current Ocular Therapy*. Philadelphia: Saunders, 2000.

Frangie, John P. "Conjunctivitis." In *Conn's Current Therapy*.Philadelphia: Elsevier Inc., 2004.

PERIODICALS

Cothran, Mary M., and Joyce P. White. "Adolescent Behavior and Sexually Transmitted Diseases: The Dilemma of Human Papillomavirus." *Health Care for Women International* 23 no. 3 (April-May 2002): 306–19.

WEB SITES

"Neonatal Conjunctivitis." *Medline Plus*.Available online at <www.nlm.nih.gov/medlineplus/print/ency/article/001606.htm> (accessed November 29, 2004).

Martha Reilly, OD

Infant massage

Definition

Infant massage is the process of rubbing an infant's muscles and stroking the infant in a manner specifically designed for them. Although there are professionally trained and certified infant massage therapists, the obvious first choice to massage the baby is the mother, father, grandparent, or guardian. Equally important are the people who care for children outside the home such as, nurses on neonatal intensive care units (NICU) that work with premature babies and those who work with the disabled. The benefits derived from massage are applicable and advantageous for all of these groups.

Purpose

Infant massage provides many benefits for the infant. A caring touch is good for everyone, but especially for infants who are new to the world and need the reassurance of someone special being there for them. However, there are some major benefits for the massage givers as well. They gain an increased awareness of the baby and his or her needs while enhancing the **bonding** process between care giver and baby. Research from experiments conducted at the Touch Research Institutes at the University of Miami School of Medicine and Nova Southeastern University has been cited for the clinical benefits massage has on infants and children. Touch therapy triggers many physiological changes that help infants and children grow and develop.

Studies have shown that infant massage alleviates the stress that newborns experience as a result of the enormous change that birth creates. They have just spent nine months in a home that fed them; kept them warm; brought them the oxygen they needed; took care of waste products; and provided a gentle rocking motion to soothe them. Now, the outside world has taken over, and things are not as simple as they were. Massage enables a smoother transition from the comfortable womb to that of humankind. The benefits of massage for the infant include:

- It helps baby learn to relax.
- It improves immune system.
- It promotes bonding and communication.
- It promotes positive body image.
- It decreases the production of stress hormones.
- It promotes sounder and longer sleep.
- It helps to regulate digestive, respiratory, and circulatory systems.
- It helps relieve discomfort from gas and **colic**, congestion, and teething.

The benefits of massage for parents include:

- It improves parent-infant communication.
- It helps parents to understand and respond appropriately to baby's nonverbal cues.
- It eases stress of parent who must be separated from child during the day.
- It promotes feelings of competence and confidence in caring for baby.
- It provides a special focused time that helps deepen bonding.
- It increases parents' ability to help child relax in times of stress.
- It is fun and relaxing for parents to massage their children.

There are additional benefits that can be derived from infant massage to elicit positive outcomes for premature infants and disadvantaged mothers. They include:

- Cross-cultural studies show that babies who are held, massaged, carried, rocked, and breast fed grow into less aggressive and violent adults who demonstrate a greater degree of compassion and cooperation.
- Recent research demonstrates benefits for premature infants, children with **asthma**, diabetes, and certain skin disorders.

- Mothers with postpartum depression have shown improvement after starting infant massage.
- Teenage mothers have shown improved bonding behavior and interactions with their infants.

Description

Origins

Infant massage is an ancient practice used primarily in Asian and Pacific Island cultures because touch in these cultures is considered healthful both physically and spiritually. For example, the inclusion of infant massage into regular bath time is typical of the Maoris and Hawaiians. With the introduction of infant massage in the West in the late 1970s, it was tested to prove or disprove its efficacy. Dr. Frederick Leboyer, a French physician who advocated natural **childbirth**, supported the interest in infant massage with the publication of his photojournalistic book on the Indian art of baby massage. He believed that touch is the child's first language and that understanding spoken language comes long after understanding touch.

Infant massage was introduced formally into the United States in 1978 when Vimala Schneider McClure, a **yoga** practitioner who served in an orphanage in Northern India, developed a training program for instructors at the request of childbirth educators. An early research study by R. Rice in 1976 had shown that premature babies who were massaged surged ahead in weight gain and neurological development over those who were not massaged. McClure's practice in India, her knowledge of Swedish massage and reflexology along with her knowledge of yoga postures, which she had already adapted for babies, served to make her the foremost authority on infant massage. The International Association of Infant Massage (IAIM) had its origins in 1980 and was incorporated in 1986 by McClure and her original seven trainers. As of 2004, there were over 30 countries that have chapters of IAIM and over 15,000 certified instructors have been trained in the United States.

Various techniques are used in infant massage, with the different strokes specific to a particular therapy. Special handling is used for treating a baby with gas and colic. Some of the strokes are known as Indian milking, which is a gentle stroking of the child's legs; and the twist and squeeze stroke, a gentle squeeze of the muscles in the thigh and calf. The light strokes often employed in regular Swedish massage are applied at the end of a massage. The procedure is not unlike certain forms of adult massage, but with extra care taken for the fragility of the infant.

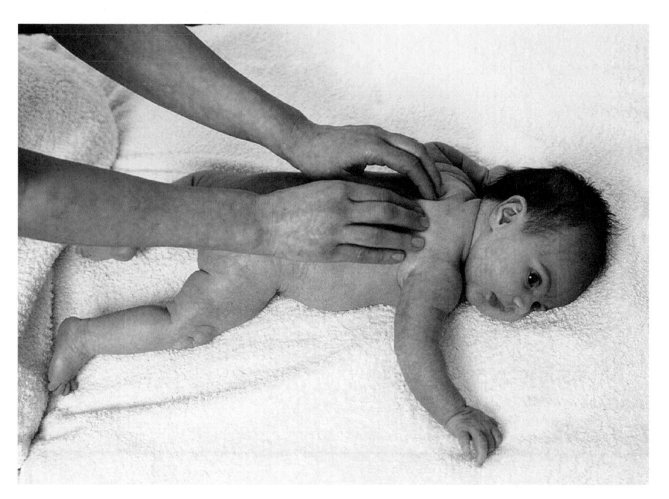

Infant receiving a massage. *(© Photo Researchers, Inc.)*

There are also specific Chinese techniques of pediatric massage, including massage of children with special needs. In China, these forms of massage can be given by medical professionals, but parents are often taught how to do the simpler forms for home treatment of their children.

Preparation

It is good to get a baby into a routine for massage. The time can be early in the morning, after a bath, or just before bedtime—the caregiver and baby know what is best and the time can be determined by the response. The room needs to be warm because the baby's clothes will be removed and infants have a difficult time regulating their body temperature. This is especially true for premature babies. It is preferable to have the room not be too bright with electrical light or sunlight shining on the baby's face. Research has shown that babies prefer to be massaged with oil such as a vegetable or plant oil. Traditional baby oils are mineral based, which are not readily absorbed. The two oils preferred by most massage therapists are grape seed oil and sweet almond oil. A caregiver can try both and see which is the most desirable. Generally, removing the diaper permits greater freedom of movement for the baby. For protection, the baby can by placed on a thick towel.

Precautions

It is necessary to use caution when performing infant massage in order not to injure the infant. Strokes are made with the greatest delicacy, and appropriate techniques are taught by licensed massage therapists to ensure that the infant is treated with accepted physical touch. Anyone who is unfamiliar with handling a baby should receive appropriate instruction before beginning infant massage.

Risks

No adverse side effects have been reported when infant massage is done properly after careful instruction, or by a licensed massage therapist who specializes in infant care.

Normal results

Many studies have been mentioned relating to the benefits of massage and there has been research published as early as 1969 relating to the topic. Hundreds of individual projects have been conducted throughout the world focusing on infant massage. Many of the studies are related to the benefits of massage and touch for premature infants and others born with such risk factors as drug dependence or **cerebral palsy**. Needless to say, the benefits are overwhelmingly positive and the research indicates that infant massage is increasingly recognized as a legitimate health care treatment.

Resources

BOOKS

Auckett, A. D. *Baby Massage: Parent-Child Bonding through Touch.* Reissue edition. New York, NY: Newmarket Press, 2004.

Cline, K., LMT. *Chinese Massage for Infants and Children: Traditional Techniques for Alleviating Colic, Teething Pain, Earache, and Other Common Childhood Conditions.* Rochester, VT: Inner Traditions International, Limited, 1999.

Ferber, S. G., M. Laudon, J. Kuint, et al. "Massage Therapy by Mothers Enhances the Adjustment of Circadian Rhythms to the Nocturnal Period in Full-Term Infants." *Journal of Developmental and Behavioral Pediatrics* 23, no. 6 (Dec. 2002).

Gordon, J., MD, and B. Adderly. *Brighter Baby: Boosting Your Child's Intelligence, Health and Happiness through Infant Therapeutic Massage.* Washington, DC: LifeLine Press, 1999.

Kluck-Ebben, M. *Hands On Baby Massage.* Philadelphia, PA: Running Press Book Publishers, 2004.

McClure, V. S. *Infant Massage—Revised Edition: A Handbook for Loving Parents.* New York: Bantam Books, 2000. Periodicals

ORGANIZATIONS

International Association of Infant Massage. IAIM Corporate Office, 1891 Goodyear Avenue, Suite 622, Ventura, CA 93003. (805)644-7699. Web site: <http://www.iaim-us.com>.

International Institute of Infant Massage. 605 Bledsoe Rd., NW, Albuquerque, NM 87107. (505)341-9381. Fax: (505)341-9386. Web site: <http:// www.infantmassage.com>.

WEB SITES

Field, Tiffany. *Infant Massage.* [cited March 5, 2005]. Available online at: <www.zerotothree.org/ massage.html>.

Infant Massage [cited March 5, 2005]. Available online at: <http://www.infantmassage.com>.

OTHER

Gentle Touch Parent-Child Program, LLC. *Gentle Touch Infant Massage Video.* Sylva, NC: Gentle Touch, Inc., 2004.

Linda K. Bennington, MSN, CNS

Infant mortality

Definition

The infant mortality rate is the number of deaths of infants under one year of age per 1,000 live births in a given population. In 2002, the United States' infant mortality rate varied widely by race of the mother from 14.3 for infants of black mothers to 5.9 for infants of Hispanic mothers to 5.8 for infants of white mothers. As can be noted, the mortality rate for black infants is more than twice that of white infants. The overall infant mortality rate in 2002 for all races was 7.0 per 1,000 live births, which was a slight increase over the previous year.

Description

Infant mortality rate is one of the key indicators of a nation's health status. When the rate increases, as it did from 2001 to 2002, the factors that precipitated this change need to be assessed and scrutinized. The U.S. infant mortality rate is of great concern because the United States has fallen to the twenty-second nd place among industrialized nations in infant mortality rankings. Therefore, healthcare professionals and the public have stressed the need for better prenatal care, coordination of health services, and the provision of comprehensive maternal-child services.

Infant mortality rates have typically been the highest for the babies of adolescent mothers and lowest for women in their late 20s and early 30s. The rates have also been high for women in their forties and older. In general, infant mortality rates decrease with increasing maternal educational levels. Similarly the infant mortality rate for unmarried mothers is often more than 83 percent higher than the mortality rate for married women. Likewise, the infant mortality rate is characteristically higher for the infants of mothers who smoke than for those of nonsmokers.

The leading cause of infant mortality is congenital malformations, deformations and chromosomal abnormalities with a rate of 20.2 percent. Disorders related to short gestation and low birth weight was the second leading cause of death for all infants at 16.4 percent of all deaths. **Sudden infant death syndrome** (SIDS) is the third leading cause of infant death. Its incidence decreased by about

9 percent, which it has been doing since 1988. The fourth leading cause of death comes under the heading of newborn affected by maternal complications of pregnancy. This rate actually increased from 2001 to 2002 from 37.2 per 100,000 live births to 42.9 per 100,000 in 2002.

An analysis of the data established that the rise in the infant mortality rate was concentrated in the neonatal period (less than 28 days) and primarily in the first week of life where more than half of all infants' deaths occur. Final birth data for 2002 made it apparent that two key predictors of infant health, the percentage of infants born preterm (less than 37 weeks gestation) and low birth weight (less than 2,500 grams) rose during this time frame. This has been a continuing long-term upward trend. The **cesarean section** rate for 2002 rose to 26.1, which is the highest ever recorded in the US. The primary cesarean rate was 7 percent higher than the previous year, and the rate of vaginal birth after cesarean (VBAC) experienced a sharp decline. The cesarean rate increase could be due to nonmedical factors as demographics, physician practice patterns, and maternal choice. Other contributing factors may be the use of continuous **electronic fetal monitoring** and inductions before 41 weeks gestation. Unnecessary interventions can contribute to a rise in cesarean rates. On the other hand, the perinatal mortality rate (the number of late fetal deaths [28 weeks or more gestation] and early neonatal deaths [less than 7 days] per 1,000 live births) remain unchanged.

Common problems

The infant mortality rate increased in the United States in 2002 for the first time since 1958, which indicates a need to examine what factors contributed to this raise. Is there a difference in mortality rates among racial groups? That is obvious—the rate for blacks is 14.2 and the rate for whites is 5.8. Experts associate this difference with the availability of prenatal care to minorities. It is expensive, and over 40 million Americans do not have health insurance. The mother's socioeconomic status is a possible contributing factor because the leading cause of death was related to congenital malformations, which in some cases can be eliminated with appropriate nutritional intake and prenatal **vitamins**. Lack of prenatal care could also contribute to the fourth largest cause

of infant death, which is maternal complications. Many other industrialized countries have a socialized system of health care, which offers universal access to prenatal care and helps lower country-wide infant mortality rates.

Parental concerns

Recent data showed good news for parents of teenagers. The teen birth rate declined by 30 percent over the past decade to a historic low and the rate for black teens was down by more than 40 percent. For young black teens (15 to 17 years) the results were even more striking—the rate was cut in half since 1991. The average age at first birth was 25.1 years in 2002, an all-time high in the United States. Birth rates for women 35–39 (41 births per 1,000 women) and 40–44 (eight per 1,000) were the highest in more than three decades. The rate for women ages 20–24 (104 births per 1,000 women) was on the decline and the rate for those 25–29 was stable, but still the highest of all age groups, at 114 per 1,000 women. In contrast, the rate for teens was 43 per 1,000. In addition, just over one in 10 women smoked during pregnancy in 2002, a decline of 42 percent since 1989.

Resources

ORGANIZATIONS

Center of Disease Control and Prevention; 1600 Clifton Rd.; Atlanta, GA 30333.(800)311-3435. Web site: <www.cdc.gov>.

U.S. Department of Health and Human Services. National Center for Health Statistics. Hyattsville, MD 20782. (301) 458-4000.

WEB SITES

Centers for Disease Control. *Infant Mortality: Fast Stats.* [cited March 6, 2005]. Available online at: <http://www.cdc.gov/nchs/fastasts/infmort.htm>.

Child Trends Databank. *Infant, Child, and Youth Mortality.* [cited March 6, 2005]. Available online at: <http://www.childtrendsdatabank.org/indicators/63ChildMortality.cfm>.

Linda K. Bennington, MSN, CNS

Infant respiratory distress syndrome *see* **Respiratory distress syndrome**

Infantile eczema *see* **Atopic dermatitis**

Infantile paralysis *see* **Polio**

Infectious hepatitis *see* **Hepatitis A**

Infectious mononucleosis

Definition

Infectious mononucleosis is a contagious illness caused by the Epstein-Barr virus that can affect the liver, lymph nodes, and oral cavity. While mononucleosis is not usually a serious disease, its primary symptoms of fatigue and lack of energy can linger for several months.

Description

Infectious mononucleosis, frequently called "mono" or the "kissing disease," is caused by the Epstein-Barr virus (EBV) found in saliva and mucus. The virus affects a type of white blood cell called the B lymphocyte, producing characteristic atypical lymphocytes that may be useful in the diagnosis of the disease.

The disease typically runs its course in four to six weeks in people with normally functioning immune systems. People with weakened or suppressed immune systems, such as **AIDS** patients or those who have had organ transplants, are particularly vulnerable to the potentially serious complications of infectious mononucleosis.

Demographics

While anyone, even young children, can develop mononucleosis, it occurs most often in young adults between the ages of 15 and 35 and is especially common in teenagers. The mononucleosis infection rate among college students who have not previously been exposed to EBV has been estimated to be about 15 percent. In younger children, the illness may not be recognized.

Causes and symptoms

The EBV that causes mononucleosis is related to a group of herpes viruses, including those that cause cold sores, **chickenpox**, and shingles. Most people are exposed to EBV at some point during their lives. Mononucleosis is most commonly spread by contact with virus-infected saliva through coughing, sneezing, kissing, or sharing drinking glasses or eating utensils.

In addition to general weakness and fatigue, symptoms of mononucleosis may include any or all of the following:

• **sore throat** and/or swollen tonsils

• fever and chills

• nausea and **vomiting**, or decreased appetite

• swollen lymph nodes in the neck and armpits

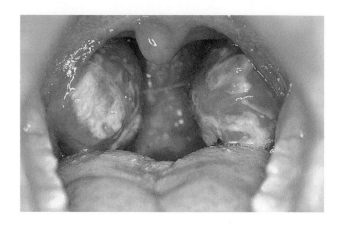

Sore throat and swollen tonsils caused by infectious mononucleosis, frequently called mono or the kissing disease. *(Photograph by Dr. P. Marazzi. Science Photo Library/Photo Researchers, Inc.)*

• headaches or joint **pain**

• enlarged spleen

• jaundice

• skin rash

Complications that can occur with mononucleosis include a temporarily enlarged spleen or inflamed liver. In rare instances, the spleen may rupture, producing sharp pain on the left side of the abdomen, a symptom that warrants immediate medical attention. Additional symptoms of a ruptured spleen include light-headedness, rapidly beating heart, and difficulty breathing. Other rare, but potentially life-threatening, complications may involve the heart or brain. The infection may also cause significant destruction of the body's red blood cells or platelets.

Symptoms do not usually appear until four to seven weeks after exposure to EBV. An infected person can be contagious during this incubation time period and for as many as five months after the disappearance of symptoms. Also, the virus will be excreted in the saliva intermittently for the rest of their lives, although the individual will experience no symptoms. Contrary to popular belief, the EBV is not highly contagious. As a result, individuals living in a household or college dormitory with someone who has mononucleosis have a very small risk of being infected unless they have direct contact with the person's saliva.

Diagnosis

If symptoms associated with a cold persist longer than two weeks, mononucleosis is a possibility; however, a variety of other conditions can produce similar symptoms. If mononucleosis is suspected, a physician will

KEY TERMS

Antibody—A special protein made by the body's immune system as a defense against foreign material (bacteria, viruses, etc.) that enters the body. It is uniquely designed to attack and neutralize the specific antigen that triggered the immune response.

Herpes virus—A family of viruses including herpes simplex types 1 and 2, and herpes zoster (also called varicella zoster). Herpes viruses cause several infections, all characterized by blisters and ulcers, including chickenpox, shingles, genital herpes, and cold sores or fever blisters.

Reye's syndrome—A serious, life-threatening illness in children, usually developing after a bout of flu or chickenpox, and often associated with the use of aspirin. Symptoms include uncontrollable vomiting, often with lethargy, memory loss, disorientation, or delirium. Swelling of the brain may cause seizures, coma, and in severe cases, death.

typically conduct a physical examination, including a "Monospot" antibody blood test that can indicate the presence of proteins or antibodies produced in response to infection with the EBV. These antibodies may not be detectable, however, until the second or third weeks of the illness. Occasionally, when this test is inconclusive, other blood tests may be conducted.

Treatment

The most effective treatment for infectious mononucleosis is rest and a gradual return to regular activities. Individuals with mild cases may not require bed rest but should limit their activities. Any strenuous activity, athletic endeavors, or heavy lifting should be avoided until the symptoms completely subside, since excessive activity may cause the spleen to rupture.

The sore throat and **dehydration** that usually accompany mononucleosis may be relieved by drinking water and fruit juices. Gargling salt water or taking throat lozenges may also relieve discomfort. In addition, taking over-the-counter medications, such as **acetaminophen** or ibuprofen, may relieve symptoms, but aspirin should be avoided because mononucleosis has been associated with **Reye's syndrome**, a serious illness aggravated by aspirin.

While **antibiotics** do not affect EBV, the sore throat accompanying mononucleosis can be complicated by a streptococcal infection, which can be treated with anti-

biotics. Cortisone anti-inflammatory medications are also occasionally prescribed for the treatment of severely swollen tonsils or throat tissues.

Prognosis

While the severity and length of illness varies, most people diagnosed with mononucleosis are able to return to their normal daily routines within two to three weeks, particularly if they rest during this time period. It may take two to three months before a person's usual energy levels return. One of the most common problems in treating mononucleosis, particularly in teenagers, is that people return to their usual activities too quickly and then experience a relapse of symptoms. Once the disease has completely run its course, the person cannot be reinfected.

Prevention

Although there is no way to avoid becoming infected with EBV, paying general attention to good hygiene and avoiding sharing beverage glasses or having close contact with people who have mononucleosis or cold symptoms can help prevent infection.

Parental concerns

The main concern for parents of children with mononucleosis is to keep the child resting until he or she fully recovers from the illness. Parents should also be aware of the symptoms of more serious complications of the liver and spleen, and should seek medical attention for a child who complains of severe abdominal pain, light-headedness, rapid heartbeat, or difficulty breathing.

Resources

BOOKS

Jensen, Hal B. "Epstein-Barr Virus." In *Nelson Textbook of Pediatrics.* Edited by Richard E. Behrman et al. Philadelphia: Saunders, 2004.

Katz, Ben Z. "Epstein-Barr Virus (Mononucleosis and Lymphoproliferative Disorders)." In *Principles and Practice of Pediatric Infectious Diseases*, 2nd ed. Edited by Sarah S. Long et al. St. Louis, MO: Elsevier, 2003.

PERIODICALS

Auwaerter, P. G. "Infectious mononucleosis: return to play." *Medical Clinics of North America* 23 (July 2004): 485–97.

ORGANIZATIONS

National Institute of Allergy and Infectious Disease. Building 31, Room 7A-50, 31 Center Drive MSC 2520, Bethesda,

MD 20892–2520. Web site: <www.niaid.nih.gov/default.htm>.

Susan J. Montgomery
Rosalyn Carson-DeWitt, MD

Influenza

Definition

Usually referred to as the flu or grippe, influenza is a highly infectious respiratory disease. The disease is caused by certain strains of the influenza virus. When the virus is inhaled, it attacks cells in the upper respiratory tract, causing typical flu symptoms such as fatigue, **fever** and chills, a hacking **cough**, and body aches. Influenza victims are also susceptible to potentially life-threatening secondary infections. Although the stomach or intestinal "flu" is commonly blamed for stomach upsets and **diarrhea**, the influenza virus rarely causes gastrointestinal symptoms. Such symptoms are most likely due to other organisms such as rotavirus, *Salmonella*, *Shigella*, or *Escherichia coli*.

Description

The flu is considerably more debilitating than the **common cold**. Influenza outbreaks occur suddenly, and infection spreads rapidly. In the 1918–19 Spanish flu pandemic, the death toll reached a staggering 20 to 40 million worldwide. Approximately 500,000 of these fatalities occurred in the United States.

Influenza outbreaks occur on a regular basis. The most serious outbreaks are pandemics, which affect millions of people worldwide and last for several months. The 1918–19 influenza outbreak serves as the primary example of an influenza pandemic. Pandemics also occurred in 1957 and 1968 with the Asian flu and Hong Kong flu, respectively. The Asian flu was responsible for 70,000 deaths in the United States, while the Hong Kong flu killed 34,000.

Epidemics are widespread regional outbreaks that occur every two to three years and affect 5–10 percent of the population. The Russian flu in the winter of 1977 is an example of an epidemic. A regional epidemic is shorter lived than a pandemic, lasting only several weeks. Finally, there are smaller outbreaks each winter that are confined to specific locales.

The earliest existing descriptions of influenza were written nearly 2,500 years ago by the ancient Greek physician Hippocrates. Historically, influenza was ascribed to a number of different agents, including "bad air" and several different bacteria. In fact, its name comes from the Italian word for "influence," because people in eighteenth-century Europe thought that the disease was caused by the influence of bad weather. It was not until 1933 that the causative agent was identified as a virus.

There are three types of influenza viruses, identified as A, B, and C. Influenza A can infect a range of animal species, including humans, pigs, horses, and birds, but only humans are infected by types B and C. Influenza A is responsible for most flu cases, while infection with types B and C virus are less common and cause a milder illness.

Demographics

The annual death toll attributable to influenza and its complications averages 20,000 in the United States alone. In the United States, 90 percent of all deaths from influenza occur among persons older than 65. Flu-related deaths have increased substantially in the United States since the 1970s, largely because of the aging of the American population. In addition, elderly persons are vulnerable because they are often reluctant to be vaccinated against flu.

Hospitalization due to complications of influenza are common in children. Among children with chronic illnesses, about 500 children per every 100,000 between the ages of birth and age four are hospitalized annually due to influenza, while about 100 children per 100,000 without chronic illnesses are hospitalized annually. Among those with underlying high-risk conditions, infants younger than six months have the highest hospitalization rates (approximately 10–40 per 100,000 population).

Causes and symptoms

Approximately one to four days after infection with the influenza virus, the victim is hit with an array of symptoms. "Hit" is an appropriate term, because symptoms are sudden, harsh, and unmistakable. Typical influenza symptoms include the abrupt onset of a **headache**, dry cough, and chills, rapidly followed by overall achiness and a fever that may run as high as 104°F (40°C). As the fever subsides, nasal congestion and a **sore throat** become noticeable. Flu victims feel extremely tired and weak and may not return to their normal energy levels for several days or even a couple of weeks.

Influenza complications usually arise from bacterial infections of the lower respiratory tract. Signs of a secondary respiratory infection often appear just as the victim seems to be recovering. These signs include high fever, intense chills, chest pains associated with breathing, and a productive cough with thick yellowish green sputum. If these symptoms appear, medical treatment is necessary. Other secondary infections, such as sinus or ear infections may also require medical intervention. Children with heart and lung problems, as well as other chronic diseases, are at higher risk for complications from influenza.

With children and teenagers, it is advisable to be alert for symptoms of **Reye's syndrome**, a rare, but serious complication. Symptoms of Reye's syndrome are **nausea and vomiting**, and more seriously, neurological problems such as confusion or delirium. The syndrome has been associated with the use of aspirin to relieve flu symptoms.

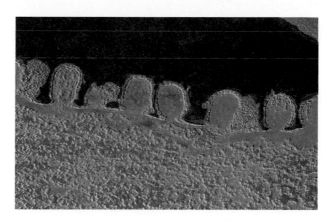

A transmission electron microscopy (TEM) image of influenza viruses budding from the surface of an infected cell. *(CNRI/Science Photo Library, National Audubon Society Collection/Photo Researchers, Inc.)*

Diagnosis

Although there are specific viral culture tests available to identify the flu virus strain from respiratory samples, results can take several days. Therefore, doctors typically rely on a set of symptoms and the presence of influenza in the community for diagnosis. Specific tests are useful to determine the type of flu in the community, but they do little for individual treatment. Doctors may administer tests, such as throat cultures, to identify secondary infections.

Several rapid (30-minute) diagnostic tests for flu have become commercially available. These tests appear to be especially useful in diagnosing flu in children, allowing doctors to make more accurate treatment decisions in less time.

Treatment

Essentially, a bout of influenza must be allowed to run its course. Symptoms can be relieved with bed rest and by keeping well hydrated. A steam vaporizer may make breathing easier, and **pain** relievers can mask the aches and pain. Food may not seem very appetizing, but an effort should be made to consume nourishing food. Recovery should not be pushed. Returning to normal activities too quickly invites a possible relapse or complications.

Drugs

Since influenza is a viral infection, **antibiotics** are useless in treating it. However, antibiotics are frequently used to treat secondary infections.

Over-the-counter medications are used to treat flu symptoms, but it is not necessary to purchase a medication marketed specifically for flu symptoms. Any medication that is designed to relieve symptoms, such as pain and coughing, will provide some relief. Medications containing alcohol, however, should be avoided because of the dehydrating effects of alcohol. The best medicine for symptoms is simply an analgesic, such as **acetaminophen** or naproxen. (Without a doctor's approval, aspirin is generally not recommended for people under 18 owing to its association with Reye's syndrome, a rare aspirin-associated complication seen in children recovering from the flu. To be on the safe side, children should receive acetaminophen or ibuprofen to treat their symptoms.)

As of 2004, there were a number of **antiviral drugs** marketed for treating influenza. To be effective, treatment should begin no later than two days after symptoms appear. These medications are useful for decreasing the severity and duration of symptoms. Antivirals may be useful in treating patients who have weakened immune systems or who are at risk for developing serious complications. They include amantadine (Symmetrel, Symadine) and rimantadine (Flumandine), which work against Type A influenza, and zanamavir (Relenza) and oseltamavir phosphate (Tamiflu), which work against both Types A and B influenza. Amantadine and rimantadine can cause side effects such as nervousness, **anxiety**, lightheadedness, and **nausea**. Severe side effects include seizures, delirium, and hallucination, but are rare and are nearly always limited to people who have kidney problems, seizure disorders, or psychiatric disorders. Zanamavir and oseltamavir phosphate can cause **dizziness**, jitters, and insomnia.

KEY TERMS

Common cold—A mild illness caused by upper respiratory viruses. Usual symptoms include nasal congestion, coughing, sneezing, throat irritation, and a low-grade fever.

Epidemic—Refers to a situation in which a particular disease rapidly spreads among many people in the same geographical region in a relatively short period of time.

Guillain-Barré syndrome—Progressive and usually reversible paralysis or weakness of multiple muscles usually starting in the lower extremities and often ascending to the muscles involved in respiration. The syndrome is due to inflammation and loss of the myelin covering of the nerve fibers, often associated with an acute infection. Also called acute idiopathic polyneuritis.

Pandemic—A disease that occurs throughout a regional group, the population of a country, or the world.

Prognosis

Following proper treatment guidelines, healthy people under the age of 65 usually suffer no long-term consequences associated with flu infection. The elderly and the chronically ill are at greater risk for secondary infection and other complications, but they can also enjoy a complete recovery.

Most people recover fully from an influenza infection, but it should not be viewed complacently. Influenza is a serious disease, and approximately one in 1,000 cases proves fatal.

Prevention

The Centers for Disease Control and Prevention recommends that people get an influenza vaccine injection each year before flu season starts. In the United States, flu season typically runs from late December to early March. Vaccines should be received two to six weeks prior to the onset of flu season to allow the body enough time to establish immunity. Adults only need one dose of the yearly vaccine, but children under nine years of age who have not previously been immunized should receive two doses with a month between each dose.

Each season's **flu vaccine** contains three virus strains that are the most likely to be encountered in the coming flu season. When there is a good match between the anticipated flu strains and the strains used in the vaccine, the vaccine is 70–90 percent effective in people under 65. Because immune response diminishes somewhat with age, people over 65 may not receive the same level of protection from the vaccine, but even if they do contract the flu, the vaccine diminishes the severity and helps prevent complications.

The virus strains used to make the vaccine are inactivated and will not cause the flu. In the second half of the twentieth century, flu symptoms were associated with vaccine preparations that were not as highly purified as modern vaccines, not to the virus itself. In 1976, there was a slightly increased risk of developing Guillain-Barré syndrome, a very rare disorder, associated with the swine flu vaccine. This association occurred only with the 1976 swine flu vaccine preparation and as of 2004 had not recurred.

Serious side effects with modern vaccines are extremely unusual. Some people experience a slight soreness at the point of injection, which resolves within a day or two. People who have never been exposed to influenza, particularly children, may experience one to two days of a slight fever, tiredness, and muscle aches. These symptoms start within six to 12 hours after the **vaccination**.

It should be noted that certain people should not receive an influenza vaccine. Infants six months and younger have immature immune systems and will not benefit from the vaccine. Since the vaccines are prepared using hen eggs, people who have severe **allergies** to eggs or other vaccine components should not receive the influenza vaccine. As an alternative, they may receive a course of amantadine or rimantadine, which are also used as a protective measure against influenza. Other people who might receive these drugs are those that have been immunized after the flu season has started or who are immunocompromised, such as people with advanced HIV disease. Amantadine and rimantadine are 70–90 percent effective in preventing influenza.

Certain groups are strongly advised to be vaccinated because they are at increased risk for influenza-related complications. These groups are:

- children under age two
- all people 65 years and older
- residents of nursing homes and chronic-care facilities, regardless of age
- adults and children who have chronic heart or lung problems, such as asthma
- adults and children who have chronic metabolic diseases, such as diabetes and renal dysfunction, as well as severe anemia or inherited hemoglobin disorders

- children and teenagers who are on long-term aspirin therapy

- women who will be in their second or third trimester during flu season or women who are nursing

- anyone who is immunocompromised, including HIV-infected persons, **cancer** patients, organ transplant recipients, and patients receiving steroids, and those receiving **chemotherapy** or radiation therapy

- anyone in contact with the above groups, such as teachers, care givers, healthcare personnel, and **family** members

- travelers to foreign countries

A person need not be in one of the at-risk categories listed above, however, to receive a flu vaccination. Anyone who wants to forego the discomfort and inconvenience of an influenza attack may receive the vaccine.

Parental concerns

Parents should make sure that their children who fall into any of the risk categories should be vaccinated against the flu. Pregnant women in the second or third trimesters should also be vaccinated. Flu vaccines are available through pediatricians or local public health departments. Parents should also make sure kids follow good hygiene practices, including regular hand washing, and covering the mouth when sneezing or coughing. Children may acquire secondary infections, such as ear infections or sinus infections, so parents should call the pediatrician if a child develops a high fever, sudden pain in the ears or sinuses, or develops a productive cough with thick yellow-green phlegm.

Resources

BOOKS

Subbarao, Kanta. "Influenza Viruses." In *Principles and Practice of Pediatric Infectious Diseases*, 2nd ed. Edited by Sarah S. Long et al. St. Louis, MO: Elsevier, 2003.

Wright, Peter. "Influenza Viruses." In *Nelson Textbook of Pediatrics*. Edited by Richard E. Behrman et al. Philadelphia: Saunders, 2004.

PERIODICALS

Larkin, M. "Will influenza be the next bioweapon?" *Lancet Infectious Disease* 138 (January 7, 2003): 53.

Nett, M. J. "ACIP Releases 2004 Guidelines on the Prevention and Control of Influenza." *Annals of Internal Medicine* 70) (July 2004): 199–204.

Stiver, G. "The treatment of influenza with antiviral drugs." *Canadian Medical Association Journal* 138 (January 2003): 49–56.

ORGANIZATIONS

Centers for Disease Control and Prevention. 1600 Clifton Rd., NE, Atlanta, GA 30333. Web site: <www.cdc.gov>.

National Institute of Allergy and Infectious Diseases (NIAID). 31 Center Drive, MSC 2520, Bethesda, MD 20892–2520. Web site: <www.niaid.nih.gov>

WEB SITES

"Flu." *Health Matters*, November 2004. Available online at <www.niaid.nih.gov/factsheets/flu.htm> (accessed December 28, 2004).

Julia Barrett
Rebecca J. Frey, PhD
Rosalyn Carson-DeWitt, MD

Influenza vaccine *see* **Flu vaccine**
Inner ear infection *see* **Labrynthitis**
Insect bites *see* **Bites and stings**

Insect sting allergy

Definition

Many children experience insect **stings** every year. For most of them, these stings only cause mild **pain** and discomfort lasting for just a period of hours. Symptoms might include swelling, **itching**, and redness at the sting site. However, some children are allergic to insect stings. When they are stung by an insect to which they are allergic, their bodies produce an antibody called immunoglobulin E (IgE), which reacts with the insect venom and triggers the release of various chemicals, including histamine, that cause the allergic reaction. Stings may be life threatening for a small number of children. These severe allergic reactions may develop quickly and can involve several body organs. This type of reaction is called **anaphylaxis** and can be fatal.

Description

The majority of insect stings in the United States are from wasps, hornets, bees, yellow jackets, and fire ants. The class of insects capable of injecting venom into a person is called Hymenoptera. With the exception of fire ants, all of these insects are found throughout the United States. Fire ants are found primarily in the southeastern region of the country but have also been noted in some western states.

Insect venom is made up of proteins and other substances that usually only cause itching, pain, and swelling in those who are stung. This local reaction is usually confined to the site of the sting. Sometimes the redness and swelling may extend from the sting site and cover a larger area of the body. These large, local, non-allergic reactions can persist for days. Occasionally the site may become infected, requiring antibiotic treatment. Although most local reactions are not serious, if they are near the face or neck, swelling can block the airway and cause serious problems.

Some children may have a venom allergy, and more serious reactions can result if they are stung. It is important to note that allergic reactions to stings normally do not occur after the initial sting. A reaction may take place after two or more stings that have happened over an extended period of time. Therefore, it is essential to be aware of the possibility for allergic symptoms in children, even if they have been stung previously and had no reaction.

Demographics

It is estimated that over 2 million Americans are allergic to stinging insects. Up to one million hospital emergency room visits occur annually because of insect stings. Between 50 and 150 Americans die each year as a result of insect sting-induced anaphylaxis. It is possible that this number may be markedly underestimated. Bee, wasp, and insect stings cause more deaths in the United States than any other kind of injection of venom. Most deaths occur in people 35 to 45 years of age. About one out of 100 children has a systemic allergic reaction from the sting of an insect. Fifty percent of deaths occur within 30 minutes of the sting.

Causes and symptoms

Allergic reactions to insect stings result from an overreaction of a child's immune system to the venom injected by the insect. After the first sting, the child's body produces an allergic substance called immunoglobulin E (IgE) antibody, which reacts with the insect venom. If the child is stung again by the same type of insect or by one from a similar species, the insect venom will interact with the IgE antibody produced in response to the previous sting. This in turn causes the release of histamine and several other chemicals that cause allergic symptoms.

The sting of an insect may only cause a local response, where pain, redness, itching, and swelling are confined to the site of the sting. This type of reaction is considered normal. The normal reaction to fire ant stings

is different. Clear blisters usually form within several hours then become cloudy within 24 hours. (The reaction usually presents in a ring or cluster, since a fire ant pivots and repeatedly stings. Also, fire ants travel in groups and a child may receive multiple stings from many ants.)

Larger allergic reactions often affect almost the entire arm, leg, foot, hand, or other area of the sting. Swelling occurs, and may last as long as seven to 10 days. The child may also experience a low-grade **fever**, fatigue, and **nausea**.

Some children experience a more severe allergic reaction. For a small percentage of these individuals, the stings may be life threatening. Severe allergic reactions can involve multiple body organs and may progress rapidly. This reaction is called anaphylaxis. Anaphylaxis is considered a medical emergency and may be fatal. The symptoms of anaphylaxis include the following:

- wheezing
- difficulty breathing
- itching and **hives** over large areas of the body
- swelling in the tongue or throat
- **dizziness**, chest pain, racing heartbeat, or fainting
- stomach cramps, nausea, or **diarrhea**

In severe cases, a rapid fall in blood pressure may result in shock and loss of consciousness. (This is less common in children than adults.) The progression of these symptoms may only take a few minutes.

When to call the doctor

For the majority of insect stings, home care is all that is necessary. However, in many cases medical attention is warranted. If any of the following are true, parents should seek professional assistance promptly.

- Symptoms progress beyond the site of the sting.
- Swelling becomes extensive and painful.
- The sting is located on the head or neck area.
- The child has had severe large reactions in the past.
- There is evidence of infection, such as increased pain, redness, warmth, and swelling at the sting site.

If a child develops hives, has difficulty breathing or swallowing, swelling of the lips or face, fainting, or dizziness, he or she should be transported to an emergency department immediately.

Diagnosis

An allergy to insect stings is determined by the doctor, who takes a thorough history from the patient and his or her parents. The history will usually show that the child has been stung previously. The doctor will also note the presence of the various symptoms common to insect sting allergic reactions. Skin testing may be performed by an allergist to determine the specific sensitivities the child may have.

Treatment

If a child has been stung by an insect that has left its stinger, it should be removed by flicking the fingers at it. Avoid squeezing the venom sac, as this can force more venom into the skin. If fire ants have stung the child, they should be carefully brushed off to prevent repeated stings.

Local treatment is normally all that is needed for small skin reactions. The affected arm or leg should be elevated and an ice pack applied to the area to reduce swelling and pain. Over-the-counter products can also be used to decrease the pain and itching. These include the following:

- products with a numbing effect, including topical anesthetics like benzocaine and phenol

- hydrocortisone products, which may decrease inflammation and swelling

- skin protectants, such as calamine lotion and zinc oxide, which have astringent, cooling, and antibacterial affects

- diphenhydramine, an antihistamine, which will help to control itching, and will counter some of the substances produced as part of the reaction

- ibuprofen or **acetaminophen** for pain relief

It is important to keep the area of the sting clean. The site should be gently cleansed with mild soap and water. Avoid breaking any blisters, as this can increase the chances of a secondary infection.

Any symptoms that progress beyond the local area of the sting require immediate attention. Allergic reactions to insect stings are considered medical emergencies. The physician will treat the child with epinephrine (adrenaline), which is usually given as an injection into the arm. An antihistamine such as diphenhydramine is usually given by mouth or injection to diminish the histamine reaction. Gluococorticoids, such as prednisone or methylprednisolone, are often given to decrease any swelling and to suppress the immune response. The phy-

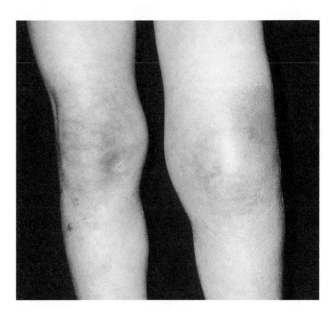

Swelling in the patient's left knee from an allergic reaction to a wasp sting. (© Dr. P. Marazzi/Photo Researchers, Inc.)

sician may write prescriptions for both **antihistamines** and steroids to take after the child leaves the hospital.

After a child has experienced a severe allergic reaction and received emergency treatment, the doctor may write a prescription for a self-injecting epinephrine device. This device should be carried by the parent or child at all times, especially when the child is out of reach of medical care, such as on an airplane or in the woods. However, sometimes epinephrine is not enough, and other treatment may be needed. Whenever children with a known severe insect sting allergy are stung, they should receive prompt medical attention, even if they have received an epinephrine injection.

Prognosis

Prompt treatment normally prevents immediate complications, but a delay in the treatment of a severe allergic reaction can result in rapid deterioration and even death. The long-term prognosis is usually good, with the rare exception of possible local infections. If a child develops anaphylaxis after an insect sting, that child is at an increased risk of developing anaphylaxis if stung again.

Prevention

Obviously the best way to avoid an allergic reaction from an insect sting is to avoid getting stung in the first

KEY TERMS

Allergy shots—Injections given by an allergy specialist to desensitize an allergic person. Also known as immunotherapy treatment.

Anaphylaxis—Also called anaphylactic shock; a severe allergic reaction characterized by airway constriction, tissue swelling, and lowered blood pressure.

place. One way to do this is to be able to identify stinging insects and where they live.

- Honeybees have a fuzzy, rounded body with dark brown coloring and yellow markings. After stinging, the honeybee normally leaves its barbed stinger in its victim, and then the bee dies. Honeybees are usually not aggressive and will only sting if provoked. However, the so-called "killer bees," or Africanized honeybees, are far more aggressive and may sting in swarms. Wild honeybees live in honeycombs or colonies in cavities of buildings or in hollow trees. Africanized honeybees may nest in old tires or holes in the ground, in house frames, or between fence posts.

- Yellow jackets are black with yellow markings. Their nests have a papier-mâché appearance and are usually located underground. However, they can also be found in woodpiles, in the walls of frame buildings, or in masonry cracks.

- Paper wasps have slender, elongated bodies and are black, red, or brown with yellow markings. Their nests are also made of a paper-like substance that opens downward, in a circular comb of cells. Their nests are often located behind shutters, in shrubs or woodpiles, or under eaves.

- Fire ants are reddish brown to black stinging insects. They build nests of dirt in the ground that may be quite tall. Fire ants attack with little warning.

A variety of precautionary measures will decrease the chances of a child getting stung.

- Avoid walking barefoot on lawns and wear closed-toe shoes. The majority of honeybee stings occur on the bottom of the foot when a child steps on the bee.

- Hire an exterminator to destroy nests and hives around the home.

- The smell of food attracts insects, so be careful when eating, drinking, or cooking outdoors. Keep food covered.

- Remain calm and quiet if flying insects are noted and move away slowly. Do not attempt to swat them.

- Avoid using highly scented perfumes, colognes, or hair sprays.

- Avoid wearing brightly colored clothing.

- Do not wear loose fitting garments that can trap insects between the material and skin.

- Keep the areas around trash containers clean and at some distance away from where children are playing.

Allergy shots

Allergy shots for insect stings, also known as venom immunotherapy, can be an effective treatment for children who experience a severe reaction to insect stings. Any child who has had a significant reaction to an insect sting should be evaluated by an allergy specialist. Not all children who have had a reaction will get allergy shots, but many should. It was once believed that most children would outgrow insect sting **allergies** and that allergy shots were not needed. However, as of 2004, it is known that about one in five will remain allergic into adulthood. Because of this pattern, it is recommended that immunotherapy should be used for the approximately 40 percent of children who experience moderate-to-severe systemic reactions to insect stings.

Venom immunotherapy is a highly effective **vaccination** program that actually prevents future sting reactions in most patients who receive them. The child is initially tested to determine their individual sensitivities. The treatment normally involves twice weekly injections of venom in dosages that are gradually increased over about 10 to 20 weeks. At this point, a maintenance dosage is administered about every one to two months. Allergy shots given in childhood can protect the child for 10 to 20 years.

Nutritional concerns

For children who have a known allergy to the venom of honeybees, parents need to use caution (and consult with a physician) before using any honeybee products.

Parental concerns

Parents should be aware of the potential risks of insect stings and should teach their children to take measures to avoid being stung. If their child does get stung, parents need to begin treatment immediately and watch the child closely for any signs of allergic reaction. If these do occur, parents should transport their child immediately to a hospital emergency department.

Resources

BOOKS

Connolly, H. *10 Things to Know about Bees and Other Stinging Insects: Bee Aware and Bee Safe.* Beaufort, NC: 2Lakes Publishing, 2002.

Welch, Michael J. *American Academy of Pediatrics Guide to Your Child's Allergies and Asthma: Breathing Easy and Bringing Up Healthy, Active Children.* Westminster, MD: Villard Books, 2000.

PERIODICALS

Jones, Stacie M. "Insect Sting Allergy with Negative Venom Skin Test Responses." *Pediatrics* 110 (August 2002): 437–39.

ORGANIZATIONS

American Academy of Allergy, Asthma, and Immunology. 555 East Wells Street, Suite 1100, Milwaukee, WI 53202–3823. Web site: <www.aaaai.org>.

American College of Allergy, Asthma, and Immunology. 85 West Algonquin Road, Suite 550, Arlington Heights, IL 60005. Web site: <allergy.mcg.edu/home.html>.

WEB SITES

Janson, Paul A., and Mary Buechler. "Insect Sting, Allergy." *eMedicine*, April 21, 2001. Available online at <www.emedicine.com/aaem/topic269.htm> (accessed October 19, 2004).

Deanna M. Swartout-Corbeil, RN

Insomnia *see* **Sleep disorders**

Insulin shock *see* **Hypoglycemia**

Intelligence

Definition

Intelligence is an abstract concept whose definition continually evolves and often depends upon current social values as much as scientific ideas. Modern definitions refer to a variety of mental capabilities, including the ability to reason, plan, solve problems, think abstractly, comprehend complex ideas, learn quickly, and learn from experience, as well as the potential to do these things.

Description

Several theories about intelligence emerged in the twentieth century and with them debate about the nature of intelligence and whether it determined by hereditary factors, the environment, or both. As methods developed to assess intelligence, experts theorized about the measurability of intelligence, its accuracy, and the field known as psychometrics, a branch of psychology dealing with the measurement of mental traits, capacities, and processes. Publication in 1994 of *The Bell Curve: Intelligence and Class Structure in American Life* by Richard J. Herrnstein and Charles Murray stirred the controversy. Their findings pointed to links between social class, race, and intelligence quotient (IQ) scores, despite questions by many about the validity of IQ tests as a measurement of intelligence or a predictor of achievement and success.

Part of the problem regarding intelligence stems from the fact that nobody has adequately defined what intelligence really means. In everyday life, people have a general understanding that some people are "smart," but when they try to define "smart" precisely, they often have difficulty because a person can be gifted in one area and average or below in another. To explain this phenomenon, some psychologists have developed theories to include multiple components of intelligence.

Since about 1970, psychologists have expanded the notion of what constitutes intelligence. Newer definitions of intelligence encompass more diverse aspects of thought and reasoning. For example, American psychologist Robert Sternberg developed a three-part theory of intelligence which states that behaviors must be viewed within the context of a particular culture; that a person's experiences impact the expression of intelligence; and that certain cognitive processes control all intelligent behavior. When all these aspects of intelligence are viewed together, the importance of how people use their intelligence becomes more important than the question of "how much" intelligence a person has. Sternberg has suggested that some intelligence tests focus too much on what a person has already learned rather than on how well a person acquires new skills or knowledge.

Another multifaceted approach to intelligence is Howard Gardner's proposal that people have eight intelligences:

- Musical: Children with musical intelligence are always singing or tapping out a beat. They are aware of sounds others miss. Musical children are discriminating listeners.

- Linguistic: Children with linguistic intelligence excel at reading, writing, telling stories, and doing crossword or other word puzzles.

- Logical-Mathematical: Children with this type of intelligence are interested in patterns, categories, and relationships. They are good at mathematic problems, science, strategy games, and experiments.

- Bodily-Kinesthetic: These children process knowledge through their senses. They usually excel at athletics and **sports**, dance, and crafts.
- Spatial: These children think in images and pictures. They are generally good at mazes and jigsaw puzzles. They often spend lots of time drawing, building (with blocks, Legos, or erector sets), and daydreaming.
- Interpersonal: This type of intelligence fosters children who are leaders among their peers, are good communicators, and understand the feelings and motives of others.
- Intrapersonal: These children are shy, very aware of their own feelings, and are self-motivated.
- Naturalist: This type of intelligence allows children to distinguish among, classify, and use features of the environment. These children are likely to make good farmers, gardeners, botanists, geologists, florists, and archaeologists. Naturalist adolescents can often name and describe the features of every make of car around them.

Intelligence tests

There are many different types of intelligence tests, and they all do not measure the same abilities. Although the tests often have aspects that are related with each other, one should not expect that scores from one intelligence test that measures a single factor will be similar to scores on another intelligence test that measures a variety of factors. Many people are under the false assumption that intelligence tests measure a person's inborn or biological intelligence. Intelligence tests are based on an individual's interaction with the environment and never exclusively measure inborn intelligence. Intelligence tests have been associated with categorizing and stereotyping people. Additionally, knowledge of one's performance on an intelligence test may affect a person's aspirations and motivation to obtain goals. Intelligence tests can be culturally biased against certain groups.

STANFORD-BINET INTELLIGENCE SCALES Consisting of questions and short tasks arranged from easy to difficult, the Stanford-Binet measures a wide variety of verbal and nonverbal skills. Its fifteen tests are divided into the following four cognitive areas: verbal reasoning (vocabulary, comprehension, absurdities, verbal relations); quantitative reasoning (math, number series, equation building); abstract/visual reasoning (pattern analysis, matrices, paper folding and cutting, copying); and short-term memory (memory for sentences, digits, and objects, and bead memory). A formula is used to arrive at the intelligence quotient, or IQ. An IQ of 100 means that the child's chronological and mental ages match. Traditionally, IQ scores of 90–109 are considered average; scores below 70 indicate **mental retardation**. Gifted children achieve scores of 140 or above. Revised in 1986, the Stanford-Binet intelligence test can be used with children starting at age two. The test is widely used to assess **cognitive development** and often to determine placement in **special education** classes.

WECHSLER INTELLIGENCE SCALES The Wechsler intelligence scales are divided into two sections: verbal and nonverbal, with separate scores for each. Verbal intelligence, the component most often associated with academic success, implies the ability to think in abstract terms using either words or mathematical symbols. Performance intelligence suggests the ability to perceive relationships and fit separate parts together logically into a whole. The inclusion of the performance section in the Wechsler scales is especially helpful in assessing the cognitive ability of children with speech and **language disorders** or whose first language is not English. The test can be of particular value to school psychologists screening for specific learning disabilities because of the number of specific subtests that make up each section.

KAUFMAN ASSESSMENT BATTERY FOR CHILDREN The Kaufman **Assessment** Battery for Children (KABC) is an intelligence and achievement test for children ages 2.5–12.5 years. It consists of 16 subtests, not all of which are used for every age group. A distinctive feature of the KABC is that it defines intelligence as problem-solving ability rather than knowledge of facts, which it considers achievement. This distinction is evident in the test's division into two parts—intelligence and achievement—which are scored separately and together. The test's strong emphasis on memory and lesser attention to verbal expression are intended to offset cultural disparities between black and white children. In addition, the test may be given to non-native speakers in their first language and to hearing impaired children using American Sign Language.

Infancy

Babies were once thought to enter the world with minds that were blank slates that developed through a lifetime of experiences. It is as of the early 2000s known that newborns have brains as sophisticated as the most powerful supercomputers, pre-wired with a large capacity for learning and knowledge. In the first few months of life, a baby's brain develops at an amazing rate. At birth, infants have the senses of sight, sound, and touch. At about three or four months, infants begin to develop memory, and it expands quickly. Modern brain imaging techniques have confirmed that children's intelligence is not just hereditary but is also affected greatly by environment. Babies' brains develop faster during their first year than at any other time. By three months, babies can follow moving objects with their eyes, are extremely interested in their surroundings, and can recognize familiar sounds, especially their parents' voices. At six months, infants begin to remember familiar objects, react to unfamiliar people or situations, and realize that objects are permanent. At seven months, babies can recognize their own name. Parents can help their infants develop their intelligence by talking and reading to them, playing with them, and encouraging them to **play** with a variety of age-appropriate **toys**.

Toddlerhood

Toddlers' lives generally revolve around experimenting with and exploring the environment around them. The primary source of learning for toddlers is their families. During their third year, toddlers should be able to sort and group similar objects by their appearance, shape, and function. They also start to understand how some things work, and their memory continues to improve rapidly. They are able to remember and seek out objects that are hidden or moved to a different location. Toddlers should be able to follow two-step instructions and understand contrasting ideas, such as large and small, inside and outside, opened and closed, and more and less. Toddlers also develop a basic understanding of time in relation to their regular activities, such as meals and bedtime.

Preschool

At age three, preschoolers can say short sentences, have a vocabulary of about 900 words, show great growth in communication, tell simple stories, use words as tools of thought, want to understand their environment, and answer questions. At age four, children can use complete sentences, have a 1,500-word vocabulary, frequently ask questions, and learn to generalize. They are highly imaginative, dramatic, and can draw recognizable simple objects. Preschoolers also should be able to understand basics concepts such as size, numbers, days of the week, and time. They should have an attention span of at least 20 minutes. Children this age are still learning the difference between reality and fantasy. Their curiosity about themselves and the world around them continues to increase.

School age

At age five, children should have a vocabulary of more than 2,000 words. They should be able to tell long

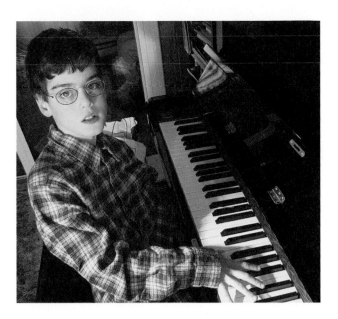

Gifted 11-year-old jazz pianist Matt Savage. Many gifted musicians have above-average intelligence. (© Rick Friedman/Corbis.)

stories, carry out directions well, read their own name, count to ten, ask the meaning of words, know colors, begin to know the difference between fact and fiction, and become interested in their surrounding environment, neighborhood, and community. Between the ages of seven and 12, children begin to reason logically and organize their thoughts coherently. However, generally, they can only think about actual physical objects; they cannot handle abstract reasoning. They also begin to lose their self-centered way of thinking. During this age range, children can master most types of conservation experiments and begin to understand that some things can be changed or undone. Early school-age children can coordinate two dimensions of an object simultaneously, arrange structures in sequence, change places or reverse the normal order of items in a series, and take something such as a story, incident, or play out of its usual setting or time and relocate it in another.

Starting at about age 12, adolescents can formulate hypotheses and systematically test them to arrive at an answer to a problem. For example, they can formulate hypotheses based on the phrase "what if." They can think abstractly and understand the form or structure of a mathematical problem. Another characteristic of the later school-age years is the ability to reason contrary to fact. That is, if they are given a statement and asked to use it as the basis of an argument, they are capable of accomplishing the task. Until they reach the age of 15 or 16, adolescents are generally not capable of reasoning as an adult. High school-age adolescents continue to gain

KEY TERMS

Autism—A developmental disability that appears early in life, in which normal brain development is disrupted and social and communication skills are retarded, sometimes severely.

Down syndrome—A chromosomal disorder caused by an extra copy or a rearrangement of chromosome 21. Children with Down syndrome have varying degrees of mental retardation and may have heart defects.

Fragile X syndrome—A genetic condition related to the X chromosome that affects mental, physical, and sensory development. It is the most common form of inherited mental retardation.

Intelligence quotient (IQ)—A measure of somebody's intelligence, obtained through a series of aptitude tests concentrating on different aspects of intellectual functioning.

Kaufman Assessment Battery for Children—An intelligence and achievement test for children ages 2.5 to 12.5 years.

Psychometrics—The development, administration, and interpretation of tests to measure mental or psychological abilities. Psychometric tests convert an individual's psychological traits and attributes into a numerical estimation or evaluation.

Stanford-Binet intelligence scales—A device designed to measure somebody's intelligence, obtained through a series of aptitude tests concentrating on different aspects of intellectual functioning. An IQ score of 100 represents "average" intelligence.

Wechsler intelligence scales—A test that measures verbal and non-verbal intelligence.

cognitive and study skills. They can adapt language to different contexts, master abstract thinking, explore and prepare for future careers and roles, set goals based on feelings of personal needs and priorities, and are likely to reject goals set by others.

Common problems

Autism

Autism is a profound mental disorder marked by an inability to communicate and interact with others. The condition's characteristics include language abnormalities, restricted and repetitive interests, and the appearance of these characteristics in early childhood. As many as two-thirds of children with autistic symptoms are mentally deficient. However, individuals with autism can also be highly intelligent. Autistic individuals typically are limited in their ability to communicate nonverbally and verbally. About half of all autistic people never learn to speak. They are likely to fail in developing social relationships with peers, have limited ability to initiate conversation if they do learn how to talk, and show a need for routine and ritual. Various abnormalities in the autistic brain have been documented. These include variations in the frontal lobes of the brain that focus on control and planning and in the limbic system, a group of structures in the brain that are linked to emotion, behavior, smell, and other functions. Autistic individuals may suffer from a limited development of the limbic system. This would explain some of the difficulties faced by autistic individuals in processing information.

Mental retardation

Mental retardation usually refers to people with an IQ below 70. According to the American Psychiatric Association, a mentally retarded person is significantly limited in at least two of the following areas: self-care, communication, home living, social-interpersonal skills, self-direction, use of community resources, functional academic skills, work, leisure, health, and **safety**. Mental retardation affects roughly 1 percent of the U.S. population. According to the U.S. Department of Education, about 11 percent of school-aged children were enrolled in special education programs for students with mental retardation. There are four categories of mental retardation: mild, moderate, severe, and profound. There are many different causes of mental retardation, both biological and environmental. In about 5 percent of cases, retardation is transmitted genetically, usually through abnormalities in chromosomes, such as **Down syndrome** or **fragile X syndrome**. Children with Down syndrome have both mental and motor retardation. Most are severely retarded, with IQs between 20 and 49. Fragile X syndrome, in which a segment of the chromosome that determines gender is abnormal, primarily affects males.

Parental concerns

Autism symptoms begins in infancy, but typically the condition is diagnosed between the ages of two to five. The symptoms of mental retardation are usually evident by a child's first or second year. In the case of Down syndrome, which involves distinctive physical characteristics, a diagnosis can usually be made shortly after birth. Mentally retarded children lag behind their peers in developmental milestones such as sitting up, smiling, walking, and talking. They often demonstrate lower than normal levels of interest in their environment and less responsiveness to others, and they are slower than other children in reacting to visual or auditory stimulation. By the time a child reaches the age of two or three, retardation can be determined using physical and **psychological tests**. Testing is important at this age if a child shows signs of possible retardation because alternate causes, such as impaired hearing, may be found and treated. There is no cure for autism or mental retardation.

When to call the doctor

Parents should consult a healthcare professional if their child's intellectual development appears to be significantly slower than their peers. Children suspected of having intelligence development problems should undergo a comprehensive evaluation to identify their difficulties as well as their strengths. Since no specialist has all the necessary skills, many professionals might be involved. General medical tests as well as tests in areas such as neurology (the nervous system), psychology, psychiatry, special education, hearing, speech and vision, and physical therapy may be needed. A pediatrician or a child and adolescent psychiatrist often coordinates these tests.

Parents should pay close attention to possible symptoms in their children. Autism is diagnosed by observing the child's behavior, **communication skills**, and social interactions. Medical tests should rule out other possible causes of autistic symptoms. Criteria that mental health experts use to diagnose autism include problems developing friendships, problems with make-believe or social play, endless repetition of words or phrases, difficulty in carrying on a conversation, obsessions with rituals or restricted patterns, and preoccupation with parts of objects. A diagnosis of mental retardation is made if an individual has an intellectual functioning level well below average and significant limitations in two or more adaptive skill areas. If mental retardation is suspected, a comprehensive physical examination and medical history should be done immediately to discover any organic cause of symptoms. If a neurological cause such as brain injury is suspected, the child may be referred to a neurologist or neuropsychologist for testing.

Resources

BOOKS

Armstrong, Thomas, and Jennifer Brannen. *You're Smarter than You Think: A Kid's Guide to Multiple Intelligences*. Minneapolis, MN: Free Spirit Publishing, 2002.

Brill, Marlene Targ. *Raising Smart Kids for Dummies*. New York: Wiley Publishing, 2003.

Deary, Ian J. *Intelligence: A Very Short Introduction*. Oxford, UK: Oxford University Press, 2001.

Georgas, James, et al. *Culture and Children's Intelligence: Cross-Cultural Analysis of the WISC-III*. Burlington, MA: Academic Press, 2003.

PERIODICALS

Bailey, Ronald. "The Battle for Your Brain: Science Is Developing Ways to Boost Intelligence, Expand Memory, and More. But Will You be Allowed to Change Your Own Mind?" *Reason* (February 2003): 25–31.

Bower, Bruce. "Essence of G: Scientists Search for the Biology of Smarts-General Factor Used to Determine Intelligence Level." *Science News* (February 8, 2003): 92–3.

Furnham, Adrian, et al. "Parents Think Their Sons Are Brighter than Their Daughters: Sex Differences in Parental Self-Estimations and Estimations of their Children's Multiple Intelligences." *Journal of Genetic Psychology* (March 2002): 24–39.

Gottfredson, Linda S. "Schools and the G Factor." *The Wilson Quarterly* (Summer 2004): 35–45.

Stanford, Pokey. "Multiple Intelligences for Every Classroom." *Intervention in School & Clinic* (November 2003): 80–85.

ORGANIZATIONS

Child Development Institute. 3528 E Ridgeway Road Orange, CA 92867. Web site: <www.cdipage.com>.

National Academy of Child & Adolescent Psychiatry. 3615 Wisconsin Ave. NW, Washington, DC 20016. Web site: <www.aacap.org>.

WEB SITES

Rosenblum, Gail. "Baby Brainpower." *Sesame Workshop*, 2004. Available online at <www.sesameworkshop.org/babyworkshop/library/article.php?contentId=860> (accessed November 10, 2004).

"The Theory of Multiple Intelligences." *Human Intelligence*, Fall 2001. Available online at <www.indiana.edu/~intell/mitheory.shtml> (accessed November 10, 2004).

Ken R. Wells

Intermittent explosive disorder

Definition

Intermittent explosive disorder (IED) is a mental disturbance that is characterized by specific episodes of violent and **aggressive behavior** that may involve harm to others or destruction of property. IED is discussed in the *Diagnostic and Statistical Manual of Mental Disorders*, fourth edition *(DSM-IV)* under the heading of "Impulse-Control Disorders Not Elsewhere Classified." As such, it is grouped together with kleptomania, pyromania, and pathological gambling.

A person must meet certain specific criteria to be diagnosed with IED:

- There must be several separate episodes of failure to restrain aggressive impulses that result in serious assaults against others or property destruction.

- The degree of aggression expressed must be out of proportion to any provocation or other stressor prior to the incidents.

- The behavior cannot be accounted for by another mental disorder, substance abuse, medication side effects, or such general medical conditions as epilepsy or head injuries.

Description

People diagnosed with IED sometimes describe strong impulses to act aggressively prior to the specific incidents reported to the doctor and/or the police. They may experience racing thoughts or a heightened energy level during the aggressive episode, with fatigue and depression developing shortly afterward. Some report various physical sensations, including tightness in the chest, **tingling** sensations, tremor, hearing echoes, or a feeling of pressure inside the head.

Many people diagnosed with IED appear to have general problems with anger or other impulsive behaviors between explosive episodes. Some are able to control aggressive impulses without acting on them while others act out in less destructive ways, such as screaming at someone rather than attacking them physically.

DSM-IV's classification of IED is not universally accepted. Many psychiatrists do not place intermittent explosive disorder into a separate clinical category but consider it a symptom of other psychiatric and mental disorders. In many cases individuals diagnosed with IED do in fact have a dual psychiatric diagnosis. IED is frequently associated with mood and **anxiety** disorders; substance abuse; eating disorders; and narcissistic, paranoid, and antisocial **personality disorders**.

One culturally specific psychiatric syndrome resembling IED is amok, which was first reported in Malaysia. As the English phrase "running amok" implies, the syndrome is characterized by sudden outbursts of indiscriminate aggression or murderous rage that are completely unprovoked or that are triggered by trivial slights.

Demographics

Although the editors of *DSM-IV* stated in 2000 that IED "is apparently rare," a group of researchers in Chicago reported in 2004 that it is more common than previously thought. They estimate that 1.4 million persons in the United States meet the criteria for IED, with a total of 10 million meeting the lifetime criteria for the disorder.

The symptoms of IED can appear at any time from late childhood through the early 20s, although the disorder is not usually diagnosed in children. The onset may be abrupt, without any warning in the form of a period of gradual change in the child or adolescent's behavior. IED appears to be more common in people from families with a history of **mood disorders** or substance abuse. The severity of the disorder appears to peak in people in their thirties and to decline rapidly in people over 50.

With regard to gender, 80 percent of individuals diagnosed with IED in the United States are adolescent and adult males; amok is a syndrome that almost always involves males. Women do experience IED, however, and have reported it as part of **premenstrual syndrome** (PMS).

Causes and symptoms

Causes

As with other impulse-control disorders, the cause of IED has not been determined. As of 2004, researchers disagreed as to whether it is learned behavior, the result of biochemical or neurological abnormalities, or a combination of factors. Some scientists have reported abnormally low levels of serotonin, a neurotransmitter that affects mood, in the cerebrospinal fluid of some anger-prone persons, but the relationship of this finding to IED is not clear. Similarly, some individuals diagnosed with IED have a medical history that includes migraine headaches, seizures, attention-deficit hyperactivity disorder, or developmental problems of various types, but it is not clear that these cause IED, as most persons with migraines, learning problems, or other neurological disorders do not develop IED.

Symptoms

Some psychiatrists who take a cognitive approach to mental disorders believe that IED results from rigid beliefs and a tendency to misinterpret other people's behavior in accordance with these beliefs. According to

Aaron Beck, a pioneer in the application of cognitive therapy to violence-prone individuals, most people diagnosed with IED believe that other people are basically hostile and untrustworthy, that physical force is the only way to obtain respect from others, and that life in general is a battlefield. Beck also identifies certain characteristic errors in thinking that go along with these beliefs:

- Personalizing: The person interprets others' behavior as directed specifically against him.

- Selective perception: The person notices only those features of situations or interactions that fit his negative view of the world rather than taking in all available information.

- Misinterpreting the motives of others: The person tends to see neutral or even friendly behavior as either malicious or manipulative.

- Denial: The person blames others for provoking his violence while denying or minimizing his own role in the fight or other outburst.

When to call the doctor

Parents should seek help for any older child or adolescent who has had more than one episode of irrationally angry or destructive behavior—if possible before the individual causes serious injury to others, has his education cut short, or gets into trouble with the law.

Diagnosis

The diagnosis of IED is basically a diagnosis of exclusion, which means that the doctor will eliminate such other possibilities as neurological disorders, mood or substance abuse disorders, anxiety syndromes, and personality disorders before deciding that the patient meets the *DSM-IV* criteria for IED. In addition to taking a history and performing a physical examination to rule out general medical conditions, the doctor may administer one or more psychiatric inventories or screening tests to determine whether the person meets the criteria for other mental disorders.

In some cases the doctor may order imaging studies or refer the person to a neurologist to rule out brain tumors, traumatic injuries of the nervous system, epilepsy, or similar physical conditions.

Treatment

Emergency room treatment

A person brought to a hospital emergency room by **family** members, police, or other emergency personnel after an explosive episode will be evaluated by a psychiatrist to see whether he can safely be released after any necessary medical treatment. If the patient appears to be a danger to self or others, he or she may be committed for further treatment. In terms of legal issues, a physician is required by law to notify the specific individuals as well as the police if the patient threatens to harm particular persons. In most states, the doctor is also required by law to report suspected abuse of children, the elderly, or other vulnerable family members.

The doctor will perform a thorough medical examination to determine whether the explosive outburst was related to substance abuse, withdrawal from drugs, head trauma, delirium, or other physical conditions. If the patient becomes violent inside the hospital, he or she may be placed in restraints or given a tranquilizer (usually either lorazepam [Ativan] or diazepam [Valium]), most often by injection. In addition to the physical examination, the doctor will obtain as detailed a history as possible from the family members or others who accompanied the patient.

Medications

Medications that have been shown to be beneficial in treating IED in nonemergency situations include lithium, carbamazepine (Tegretol), propranolol (Inderal), and such selective serotonin reuptake inhibitors as fluoxetine (Prozac) and sertraline (Zoloft). Adolescents diagnosed with IED have been reported to respond well to clozapine (Clozaril), a drug normally used to treat **schizophrenia** and other psychotic disorders.

Psychotherapy

Some persons with IED benefit from cognitive therapy in addition to medications, particularly if they are concerned about the impact of their disorder on their education, employment, or interpersonal relationships. Psychoanalytic approaches are not useful in treating IED.

Alternative treatment

Some patients diagnosed with IED have reported being helped by biofeedback, mindfulness meditation, and various forms of martial arts. Mind/body therapies appear to be helpful in gaining greater self-control, while martial arts workouts help to channel the person's physical energy or muscular tension.

Prognosis

The prognosis of IED depends on several factors that include the individual's socioeconomic status, the stability of the immediate family, the values of the

KEY TERMS

Amok—A culture-specific psychiatric syndrome first described among the Malays, in which adolescent or adult males are overcome by a sudden fit of murderous fury provoked by a perceived insult or slight. Some researchers consider amok to be a variant of intermittent explosive disorder.

Cognitive therapy—Psychological treatment aimed at changing a person's way of thinking in order to change his or her behavior and emotional state.

Delirium—Sudden confusion with a decreased or fluctuating level of consciousness.

Kleptomania—An impulse control disorder in which one steals objects that are of little or no value.

Neurotransmitter—A chemical messenger that transmits an impulse from one nerve cell to the next.

Pyromania—An impulse control disorder characterized by fire setting.

Serotonin—A widely distributed neurotransmitter that is found in blood platelets, the lining of the digestive tract, and the brain, and that works in combination with norepinephrine. It causes very powerful contractions of smooth muscle and is associated with mood, attention, emotions, and sleep. Low levels of serotonin are associated with depression.

surrounding neighborhood, and his or her motivation to change. One reason why the Chicago researchers think that IED is more common than previously thought is that most people who meet the criteria for the disorder do not seek help for the problems in their lives that result from it. The researchers found that although 88 percent of the 253 individuals with IED whom they studied were upset by the results of their explosive outbursts, only 13 percent had ever asked for treatment in dealing with it.

Prevention

Since the cause(s) of IED are not fully understood as of the early 2000s, preventive strategies should focus on treatment of young children who may be at risk for IED before they enter **adolescence**.

Parental concerns

An adolescent or young adult diagnosed with IED can cause severe disruption to family life in many different areas, ranging from the economic costs of property damage or accidents to emotional problems in other family members to serious legal penalties. It is important for the person's family to know that they do not have to tolerate violent behavior, destruction of property, harm to pets, or abuse of smaller or weaker family members. Depending on the specific situation and the pattern of previous explosive episodes, family members of adolescents or young adults may decide to leave the immediate situation, call the police or other emergency help, or take out a restraining order.

Another important dimension of IED is the damage done to the person's own life. One reason for seeking treatment for IED is to get help before the person establishes a record of school suspensions, arrests or other legal problems, hospitalizations for injuries sustained in fights or automobile accidents, or repeated firings from jobs. A history of such issues can lead to a self-fulfilling prophecy in which the person with IED continues to have episodes of uncontrolled aggression because of the belief that he or she cannot overcome the past.

Resources

BOOKS

Diagnostic and Statistical Manual of Mental Disorders, 4th edition, Text Revision. Washington, DC: American Psychiatric Association, 2000.

"Psychiatric Emergencies." Section 15, Chapter 194 in *The Merck Manual of Diagnosis and Therapy*, edited by Mark H. Beers and Robert Berkow. Whitehouse Station, NJ: Merck Research Laboratories, 2002.

PERIODICALS

Coccaro, E. F., et al. "Lifetime and 1-Month Prevalence Rates of Intermittent Explosive Disorder in a Community Sample." *Journal of Clinical Psychiatry* 65 (June 2004): 820–24.

Grant, J. E., and M. N. Potenza. "Impulse Control Disorders: Clinical Characteristics and Pharmacological Management." *Annals of Clinical Psychiatry* 16 (January-March 2004): 27–34.

Kant, R., et al. "The Off-Label Use of Clozapine in Adolescents with Bipolar Disorder, Intermittent Explosive Disorder, or Posttraumatic Stress Disorder." *Journal of Child and Adolescent Psychopharmacology* 14 (Spring 2004): 57–63.

ORGANIZATIONS

American Academy of Child and Adolescent Psychiatry. 3615 Wisconsin Avenue, NW, Washington, DC 20016–3007. Web site: <www.aacap.org>.

American Psychiatric Association. 1400 K Street, NW, Washington, DC 20005. Web site: <www.psych.org>.

National Institute of Mental Health. 6001 Executive Boulevard, Room 8184, MSC 9663, Bethesda, MD 20892–9663. Web site: <www.nimh.nih.gov>.

WEB SITES

Citrome, Leslie L., and Jan Volavka. "Aggression." *eMedicine*, February 8, 2002. Available online at <www.emedicine.com/Med/topic3005.htm> (accessed November 10, 2004).

Wilson, William H., and Kathleen A. Trott. "Psychiatric Illness Associated with Criminality." *eMedicine*, March 5, 2004. Available online at <www.emedicine.com/med/topic3485.htm> (accessed November 10, 2004).

Janie F. Franz

Intersex states

Definition

Intersex states are conditions where a newborn's sex organs (genitals) look unusual, making it impossible to identify the gender of the baby from its outward appearance.

Description

All developing babies start out with external sex organs that look female. If the baby is male, the internal sex organs mature and begin to produce the male hormone testosterone. If the hormones reach the tissues correctly, the external genitals that looked female change into the scrotum and penis. Sometimes, the genetic sex (as indicated by chromosomes) may not match the appearance of the external sex organs.

Persons with intersex states can be classified as a true hermaphrodite, a female pseudohermaphrodite, or a male pseudohermaphrodite. This is determined by examining the internal and external structures of the child.

True hermaphrodites are born with both ovaries and testicles. They also have mixed male and female external genitals. This condition is extremely rare.

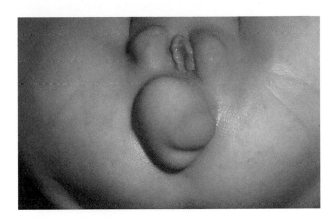

This infant was born with female and male genitalia. *(Photograph by Mike Peres. Custom Medical Stock Photo, Inc.)*

A female pseudohermaphrodite is a genetic female. However, the external sex organs have been masculinized and look like a penis. This may occur if the mother takes the hormone progesterone to prevent a miscarriage, but more often it is caused by an overproduction of certain hormones.

A male pseudohermaphrodite is a genetic male. However, the external sex organs fail to develop normally. Intersex males may have testes and a female-like vulva, or a very small penis.

Demographics

About one in every 2,000 births results in a baby whose sex organs look unusual. True hermaphrodites are extremely rare.

Any abnormality in chromosomes or sex hormones, or in the unborn baby's response to the hormones, can lead to an intersex state in a newborn. Intersex states may also be caused by a condition called **congenital adrenal hyperplasia**, which occurs in about one out of every 5,000 newborns. This disease blocks the baby's metabolism and can cause a range of symptoms, including abnormal genitals.

Common problems

When doctors are uncertain about a newborn's sex, a specialist in infant hormonal problems is consulted as soon as possible. Ultrasound can locate a uterus behind the bladder and can determine if there is a cervix or uterine canal. Blood tests can check the levels of sex hormones in the baby's blood, and chromosome analysis (called karyotyping) can determine sex. Explorative

KEY TERMS

Chromosome—A microscopic thread-like structure found within each cell of the human body and consisting of a complex of proteins and DNA. Humans have 46 chromosomes arranged into 23 pairs. Chromosomes contain the genetic information necessary to direct the development and functioning of all cells and systems in the body. They pass on hereditary traits from parents to child (like eye color) and determine whether the child will be male or female.

surgery or a biopsy of reproductive tissue may be necessary. Only after thorough testing can a correct diagnosis and determination of gender be made.

Parental concerns

Treatment of intersex states is controversial. Traditional treatment assigns sex according to test results. Most doctors believe this gives the child the potential to identify with a sex. Treatment may then include reconstructive surgery followed by hormone therapy. Babies born with congenital adrenal hyperplasia can be treated with cortisone-type drugs and sometimes surgery.

Counseling should be given to the entire **family** of an intersex newborn. Families should explore all available medical and surgical options. Counseling should also be provided to the child when he or she is old enough.

Since the mid-1950s, doctors have typically assigned a sex to an intersex infant based on how easy reconstructive surgery would be. The American Academy of Pediatrics states that children with these types of genitals can be raised successfully as members of either sex, and recommends surgery within the first 15 months of life.

Some people are critical of this approach, including intersex adults who were operated on as children. The remolded genitals do not function sexually and can be the source of lifelong **pain**. They suggest that surgery be delayed until the individual can make informed choices about surgery and intervention.

Resources

BOOKS

Dreger, Alice D. *Intersex in the Age of Ethics*. Hagerstown, MD: University Publishing Group, 1999.

New, Maria I. and Nathalie Josso. "Disorders of Sexual Differentiation." In *Cecil Textbook of Medicine*. 22nd ed. Ed. by Lee Goldman, et al. Philadelphia: Saunders, 2003, 1463-71.

Preves, Sharon E. and Susan E. Preves. *Intersex and Identity: The Contested Self*. South Brunswick, NJ: Rutgers University Press, 2003.

Wilson, Jean D. and James E. Griffin. "Disorders of Sexual Differentiation." In *Nelson Textbook of Pediatrics. Harrison's Principles of Internal Medicine. 15th ed*. Ed. by Eugene Braunwald et al., New York, McGraw Hill, 2001, 2172-83.

PERIODICALS

Akhtar, J. "Assigning gender to babies with intersex anomalies." *Journal of the College of Physicians and Surgeons in Pakistan* 14, no. 3 (2004): 127-8.

Biswas, K., et al. "Imaging in intersex disorders." *Journal of Pediatric Endocrinology and Metabolism* 17, no. 6 (2004): 841-5.

Lee, P. A. and Money, J. "Communicating with parents of the newborn with intersex: transcript of an interview." *Journal of Pediatric Endocrinology and Metabolism* 17, no. 7 (2004): 925-30.

Ronfani, L. and Bianchi, M.E. "Molecular mechanisms in male determination and germ cell differentiation." *Cellular and Molecular Life Sciences* 61, no. 15 (2004): 1907-25.

ORGANIZATIONS

American Academy of Family Physicians. 11400 Tomahawk Creek Parkway, Leawood, KS 66211-2672. (913) 906-6000. E-mail: fp@aafp.org. Web site: <http://www.aafp.org/>.

American Academy of Pediatrics. 141 Northwest Point Boulevard, Elk Grove Village, IL 60007-1098. (847) 434-4000, Fax: (847) 434-8000. E-mail: kidsdoc@aap.org. Web site: <http://www.aap.org/default.htm>.

American Board of Obstetrics and Gynecology. 2915 Vine Street Suite 300, Dallas TX. 75204. (214) 871-1619. Fax: (214) 871-1943. E-mail: info@abog.org. Web site: <http://www.abog.org>.

American College of Obstetricians and Gynecologists. 409 12th St., S.W., PO Box 96920, Washington, D.C. 20090-6920. Web site: <http://www.acog.org>.

WEB SITES

"Advocacy." *Intersex Society of North America*. Available online at: <http://www.isna.org/drupal/index.php>.

"Ambiguous Genitalia Support Network." *Genetic Alliance*. Available online at: <http://www.geneticalliance.org/diseaseinfo/displayorganization.asp?orgname=Ambiguous+Genitalia+ Support+Network>.

"Sexuality and Sexual Differentiation Syndromes." *University of Kansas College of Medicine*. Available online at: <http://www.kumc.edu/gec/support/ambig.html>.

"Support." *Intersex Support Group International*. Available online at: <http://www.xyxo.org/isgi/index.html>.

L. Fleming Fallon, Jr., MD, DrPH

Intestinal obstructions

Definition

Intestinal obstructions are a partial or complete blockage of the small or large intestine, resulting in failure of the contents of the intestine to pass through the bowel normally.

Description

Intestinal obstructions can occur in children as a result of congenital defects, with symptoms appearing any time between birth and adulthood. Abdominal **pain** and **vomiting** are the most frequent symptoms and a common cause of admission to emergency rooms. It is difficult for doctors to predict at birth which infants will suffer intestinal obstructions.

Intestinal obstructions can be mechanical or non-mechanical. Mechanical obstruction is the physical blockage of the intestine by a tumor, scar tissue, or another type of blockage that prevents intestinal contents from getting past the point of obstruction. One type of mechanical obstruction is caused by the bowel twisting on itself (volvulus) or telescoping into itself (intussusception). Mechanical obstruction can also result from hernias, fecal impaction, abnormal tissue growth, the presence of foreign bodies in the intestines, or inflammatory bowel disease (Crohn's disease). Non-mechanical obstruction occurs when the normal wavelike muscular contractions of the intestinal walls (peristalsis), which ordinarily move the waste products of digestion through the digestive tract, are disrupted (as in spastic **ileus**, dysmotility syndrome, or psuedo-obstruction) or stopped altogether as in paralysis of the bowel walls (paralytic ileus).

Mechanical obstruction in infants under one year of age can be caused by meconium ileus, volvulus, intussusception, and hernias. Meconium ileus is a disorder that occurs in newborns in which the meconium, the neonate's first fecal excretion after birth, is abnormally thick and stringy, rather than the collection of mucus and bile that is normally passed. The abnormal meconium blocks the intestines and must be removed with an enema or through surgery. This condition is due to a deficiency of the enzyme trypsin and other digestive enzymes produced in the pancreas. It can be an early clue that the infant may have **cystic fibrosis**. Intussusception commonly follows an infection that causes increased lymph node size in the gut, which acts as the point of folding for the intussusception.

Hirschsprung's disease (congenital megacolon), which may involve meconium ileus, is a motility disorder that is responsible for 25 percent of newborn non-mechanical intestinal obstructions, though symptoms may not develop until late in infancy or in childhood, delaying diagnosis. Children diagnosed with Hirschsprung's disease lack nerve cells (ganglia) in the large intestine, severely affecting the wavelike movements that propel material through the colon. In most affected infants, the first sign is failure to pass a stool (meconium) within 24 to 48 hours after birth. Between birth and age two, these children will likely develop other symptoms, such as chronic **constipation**, small watery stools, a distended abdomen, vomiting, poor appetite, slow weight gain, and **failure to thrive**. Most children will require surgery to remove the affected part of the colon. Surgery can be performed at age six months or as soon as diagnosed in an older infant or child. Symptoms can be removed in at least 90 percent of children born with Hirschsprung's disease. The disease is sometimes associated with other congenital conditions, such as **Down syndrome**.

Volvulus is the twisting of the small or large bowel around itself (malrotation). Volvulus of the large bowel is rare in infants and children; when it does occur it is usually in the sigmoid (sigmoid volvulus) in the lower colon. Duodenal volvulus occurs when the duodenum, the portion of small intestine that connects the stomach and jejunum, is twisted. Twisting of any portion of the intestines may cut off the supply of blood to a loop of bowel (strangulation), reducing the flow of oxygen to bowel tissue (ischemia) and leading to tissue death (gangrene). Strangulation occurs in about 25 percent of bowel obstruction cases and is a serious condition that can progress to gangrene within six to 12 hours.

Intussusception is a condition in which the bowel telescopes into itself like a radio antenna folding up. Intussusception is the most common cause of intestinal obstruction in children between the ages of three months and six years. Boys are twice as likely as girls to suffer intussusception.

Hernias are weaknesses in the abdominal wall that can trap a portion of intestine (incarceration) and cut off the passage of food and waste through the digestive tract. In 1–5 percent of children, a **hernia** results when a feature of fetal anatomy in the inguinal area of the groin (processus vaginalis, the space through which the testis or ovaries descend) fails to close normally after birth. These inguinal hernias easily become incarcerated, trapping the bowel and causing obstruction. They are sometimes found on both sides (bilateral hernia) and they occur nine times more often in boys than girls. Parents may see a bulge in the groin area when an inguinal hernia is present. Incarceration occurs only rarely after eight years of age. In most cases, the incarcerated hernias are corrected manually rather than surgically by pushing the incarcerated bowel back up into the abdominal cavity.

Congenital adhesions or post-surgical adhesions can also cause intestinal obstruction in children. Adhesions are bands of fibrous tissue that can bind the loops of intestine to each other or to abdominal organs, narrowing the space between the intestinal walls or pulling sections of the intestines out of place, blocking the passage of food and waste. In adults, adhesions are most often caused by repeat surgery; children who have a history of abdominal surgery can also develop adhesions that can obstruct the intestines. It is not known precisely what causes the abnormal growth of fibrous tissue in congenital adhesions.

Demographics

Each year, one in 1,000 individuals of all ages are diagnosed with intestinal obstruction. Adhesions are responsible for 50–70 percent of cases. In children, 2.4 cases of intussusception are reported among 1,000 live births annually in the United States. Inguinal hernias occur in 1–5 percent of infants, with a male to female ratio of nine to one. Volvulus occurs in older children (mean age seven years) with a male to female ratio of 3.5 to one.

Causes and symptoms

The causes of small bowel obstruction in children are most often volvulus, intussusception, adhesions, or abdominal hernia, a weakness in the abdominal wall that traps a portion of intestine. The most frequent causes of large-bowel obstruction are tumors, volvulus, or small pouches that form on the intestinal wall (diverticula) that can fill with waste and expand to block the intestines. Motility disorders such as Hirschsprung's disease and psuedo-obstruction may cause blockages by retarding peristalsis, the intestinal muscle contractions that move food and waste.

Meconium ileus in newborns is caused by increased viscosity of waste products in the intestinal tract, and is sometimes secondary to cystic fibrosis. Its primary symptom will be failure of the infant to eliminate the meconium within the first two days of life.

One of the earliest signs of mechanical intestinal obstruction is abdominal pain or cramps that come and go in waves. Infants typically pull up their legs and cry in pain, then stop crying suddenly. They may behave normally for as long as 15–30 minutes between episodes, only to start crying again when the next cramp begins. The cramping results from the inability of the muscular contractions of the bowel to push the digested food past the obstruction. A classic symptom is passage of "current jelly stool" (i.e. blood) by infants after a crying fit during intussusception. Some children with intussusception may appear lethargic or have altered mental status, believed by physicians to be related to ischemia of the bowel and a decreased level of consciousness.

Vomiting is another typical symptom of intestinal obstruction. The speed of its onset is a clue to the location of the obstruction. Vomiting follows shortly after the pain if the obstruction is in the small intestine, but is delayed if it is in the large intestine. The vomited material may be green from bile or fecal in character. If the blockage is complete, the individual will not pass any gas or feces. If the blockage is only partial, however, **diarrhea** can occur. Initially there is little or no **fever**.

When the material in the bowel cannot move past the obstruction, the body reabsorbs large amounts of fluid and the abdomen becomes sore to the touch and swollen (distended). Persistent vomiting can result in **dehydration**. Fluid imbalances upset the balance of certain important chemicals (electrolytes) in the blood, which can cause complications such as irregular heartbeat and, without correction of the electrolyte imbalance, shock. Kidney failure is a serious complication that can occur as a result of severe dehydration and/or systemic infection from perforation of the bowel.

When to call the doctor

Medical attention is needed early in intestinal obstruction and should be sought as soon as symptoms suggest abdominal distress. Symptoms may begin with abdominal pain or cramping that may cause a toddler or older child to double over in pain. Infants will periodically cry in pain and pull their legs up to their chest. Fever may or may not be present. Vomiting may occur along with pain. If pain and crying occur every 15 or 30 minutes, it is critical to see the pediatrician or go to the emergency room so that early diagnosis can be made and treatment begun.

Diagnosis

If the doctor suspects intestinal obstruction based on the child's symptoms and the physical examination, imaging studies will be ordered that may include abdominal

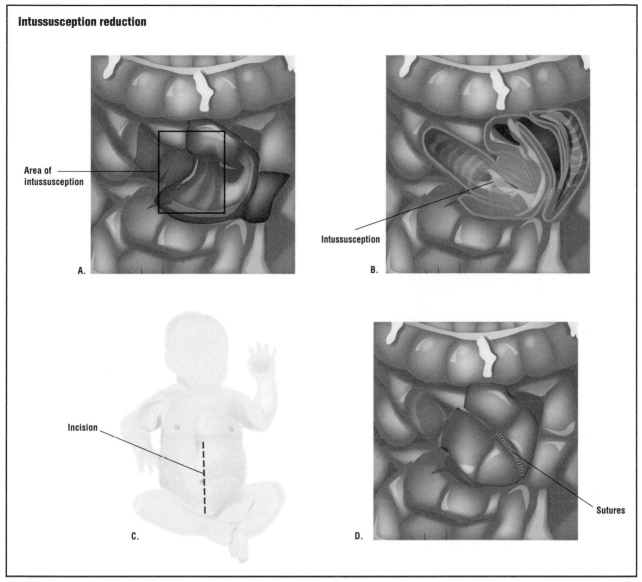

Intussusception reduction

Area of intussusception

A.

Intussusception

B.

Incision

C.

Sutures

D.

Intussusception of the bowel results in the bowel telescoping onto itself (A and B). To repair it, an incision is made in the baby's abdomen to expose the bowel (C). If the surgeon cannot manipulate the bowel into a normal shape manually, the area of intussusception will be removed and remaining bowel sutured together (D). *(Illustration by GGS Information Services.)*

x rays, **computed tomography** (CT scan), or an ultrasound evaluation of the abdomen. Abdominal ultrasound is able to effectively visualize and diagnose most obstructions. The x ray images may be enhanced by giving the child a barium enema, a form of contrast or opaque media that allows more detail to be seen in x rays and MRI or CT scans. In a barium enema, barium sulfate is infused through the rectum and the intestinal area is scanned. With contrast enhancement, the exact location of the obstruction can be pinpointed in the scans or x ray film. Sometimes a lighted, flexible fiber optic instrument (sigmoidoscope) may be inserted rectally in conjunction with a barium enema to visualize the bowel. It may not possible to determine if an obstruction is simple or strangulated on scanning, and this will only be determined by performing abdominal surgery.

Diagnostic testing will include a complete blood count (CBC), electrolytes (sodium, potassium, chloride) and other blood chemistries, blood urea nitrogen (BUN), and urinalysis. Coagulation tests may be performed if the child requires surgery.

Bowel—The intestine; a tube-like structure that extends from the stomach to the anus. Some digestive processes are carried out in the bowel before food passes out of the body as waste.

Dysmotility—Abnormally slow or fast rhythmic movement of the stomach or intestine.

Electrolytes—Salts and minerals that produce electrically charged particles (ions) in body fluids. Common human electrolytes are sodium chloride, potassium, calcium, and sodium bicarbonate. Electrolytes control the fluid balance of the body and are important in muscle contraction, energy generation, and almost all major biochemical reactions in the body.

Gangrene—Decay or death of body tissue because the blood supply is cut off. Tissues that have died in this way must be surgically removed.

Ileus—An obstruction of the intestines usually caused by the absence of peristalsis.

Intussusception—The slipping or telescoping of one part of the intestine into the section next to it.

Ischemia—A decrease in the blood supply to an area of the body caused by obstruction or constriction of blood vessels.

Meconium—A greenish fecal material that forms the first bowel movement of an infant.

Motility—The movement or capacity for movement of an organism or body organ. Indigestion is sometimes caused by abnormal patterns in the motility of the stomach.

Peristalsis—Slow, rhythmic contractions of the muscles in a tubular organ, such as the intestines, that move the contents along.

Shock—A medical emergency in which the organs and tissues of the body are not receiving an adequate flow of blood. This deprives the organs and tissues of oxygen and allows the build-up of waste products. Shock can be caused by certain diseases, serious injury, or blood loss.

Sigmoid colon—The final portion of the large intestine that empties into the rectum.

Strangulated obstruction—An obstruction in which a loop of the intestine has its blood supply cut off.

Volvulus—A twisting of the intestine that causes an obstruction.

Treatment

Children with suspected intestinal obstruction will be hospitalized after the initial diagnostic evaluation. Treatment will likely begin immediately and proceed rapidly to avoid strangulation, which can be fatal. The first step in treatment is inserting a nasogastric tube to suction out the contents of the stomach and intestines. Intravenous fluids will be infused to prevent dehydration and to correct electrolyte imbalances that may have already occurred. Surgery can be avoided in some cases. With volvulus, for example, it may be possible to guide a rectal tube into the intestines to straighten the twisted bowels. In infants, a barium enema may reverse intussusception in 50–90 percent of cases. Another newer contrast agent, gastrografin, may be used; it is believed to have therapeutic properties as well as its ability to enhance scans. An air enema is sometimes used instead of a barium or gastrografin enema. This treatment successfully relieves partial obstruction in many infants. Children usually remain hospitalized for observation for two to three days after these procedures.

Surgical treatment will be necessary if other efforts are unsuccessful in correcting or removing the blockage. Generally, complete obstructions require surgery while partial obstructions do not. Strangulated obstructions require emergency surgery. The obstructed area is removed and part of the bowel is cut away (bowel resection). If the obstruction is caused by tumors, polyps, or scar tissue, they will be surgically removed. Hernias, if present, are repaired to correct the obstruction. **Antibiotics** may be given pre- or post-operatively to avoid the threat of infection at the site of the obstruction. Fluid replacement is given intravenously as needed.

Alternative treatment

Immediate surgery is often the only means of correcting intestinal obstruction. Alternative practitioners may recommend a high fiber diet to encourage proper stool formation; however, simple constipation is not the cause of intestinal obstruction.

Prognosis

Most intestinal obstructions can be corrected with prompt treatment and the affected child will recover without complications. Untreated intestinal obstructions can be fatal, however. The bowel either strangulates or perforates, causing massive infection. Recurrence is likely in as many as 80 percent of those in whom volvulus is treated medically rather than surgically. Recurrences in infants with intussusception are most likely to happen during the first

36 hours after the blockage has been cleared. The mortality rate for unsuccessfully treated infants is 1–2 percent.

Prevention

Most cases of intestinal obstruction are not preventable. Surgery to remove tumors or polyps in the intestines helps prevent recurrences, although adhesions can form after surgery, which can be another cause of obstruction.

Nutritional concerns

Preventing certain types of intestinal problems that may lead to intestinal obstruction may include making sure that the diet includes sufficient fiber to help encourage proper stool formation and regular elimination. High-fiber foods include whole grain breads and cereals; apples and other fresh fruits; dried fruits such as prunes; pumpkin and squash; fresh raw vegetables; beans and lentils; and nuts and seeds.

Parental concerns

Diagnosis of intestinal obstruction in a child is dependent on recognizing related symptoms. Parents may be concerned about preventing intestinal problems in their children and about missing the symptoms of possible intestinal obstruction. It is important to remember that a healthy diet with plenty of whole fruits, vegetables, and grains, and drinking a sufficient amount of water each day, will help keep the intestines healthy and elimination regular. Parents should be aware of the child's bowel habits and report constipation, diarrhea, abdominal pain, and vomiting to the pediatrician when it occurs. Diagnosed early, intestinal obstruction can be corrected without complications.

Resources

BOOKS

Allan, W., M.D., et al. *Pediatric Gastrointestinal Disease: Pathophysiology, Diagnosis, Management,* 3rd ed. Boston: BC Decker, 2000.

"Intestinal Obstruction." *The Merck Manual of Medical Information, Second Home Edition* Eds. Mark H. Beers, et al. White House Station, NJ: Merck & Co., 2003.

ORGANIZATIONS

American Association of Family Physicians. 11400 Tomahawk Creek Parkway, Leawood, KS 66211-2672. (800) 274-2237. Web site: <http://www.aafp.org>.

WEB SITES

Intestinal Obstruction. National Library of Medicine, Medical Encyclopedia, 2004. [cited October 11, 2004]. Available online at: <http://www.nlm.gov./medlineplus>.

Intestinal Obstruction (Pediatric). A.D.A.M., 2002. [cited October 11, 2004]. Web site: <www.medformation.com/ac/adamsurg.nsf/page/100165>.

L. Lee Culvert
Tish Davidson, A.M.

Intrauterine growth retardation

Definition

The term intrauterine growth retardation (also known as intrauterine growth restriction)(IUGR) is generically defined as a fetus who is at or below the tenth percentile in weight for its gestational age. There are two factors necessary to define an IUGR fetus: first, the fetal weight is at or below the tenth percentile for gestational age and sex; second, there is a pathological process present that prevents expression of normal growth potential. If the baby is small given its in utero age, then it is said to be small for gestational age (SGA).

Description

There are standards or averages in weight for unborn babies according to their gestational age in weeks; however, using a fetal growth curve derived from one population and applying it to another can result in over- or underestimation of the true incidence of SGA. For example, the lowest mean birth weight has been noted in Africa (New Guinea Lumi's tribe: mean birth weight = 2,400 grams); whereas the largest mean birth weight has been noted in the Caribbean (Aguilla: mean birth weight = 3,880 g). A population of smaller individuals will have smaller babies, so the difference lies in the genetic growth potential.

The normal intrauterine growth pattern occurs in three stages. In the first stage, four to 20 weeks gestation, rapid cell division and multiplication (hyperplasia) occurs as the embryo grows into a fetus. In the second stage, 20–28 weeks gestation, cell division (hyperplasia) declines and the cells increase in size (hypertrophy). In stage three, 28–40 weeks, there is a rapid increase in cell size, rapid accumulation of fat, muscle, and connective tissue. Ninety-five percent of fetal weight gain occurs during the last 20 weeks of gestation. If the delicate process of development and weight gain is disturbed or interrupted, the baby can suffer from restricted growth.

IUGR is usually classified as symmetrical or asymmetrical. Growth inhibition during the first stage produces an undersized fetus with fewer cells, but normal cell size, causing symmetric IUGR. In symmetrical

IUGR weight, head and length are all below the tenth percentile and the baby's head and body are proportionately small. Conditions associated with symmetric IUGR include: genetic (constitutional, chromosomal and single gene defects, and deletion disorders and inborn errors of metabolism), congenital anomalies, intrauterine infections, and therapeutic irradiation. Substance abuse and cigarette **smoking**, depending on dose and timing, can cause either symmetrical or asymmetrical IUGR.

Growth inhibition during stage two and three causes a decrease of cell size and fetal weight with less effect on total cell number and fetal length and head circumference, causing asymmetric IUGR. Conditions associated with asymmetric IUGR include: uteroplacental insufficiency, which is usually caused by chronic **hypertension** or preeclampsia; chronic renal disease; cyanotic heart disease; hemoglobinopathies; placental infarcts; abruptio placenta; multiple gestation; velamentous insertion of the umbilical cord and circumvallate placenta; and high altitude. In asymmetrical IUGR, weight is below the tenth percentile, and head and length are preserved. The brain can weigh five or six times more than the liver, whereas in a normal infant, the brain weighs about three times more than the liver.

Causes and symptoms

The two types of IUGR described previously contribute to IUGR according to the development at that stage. Symmetrical IUGR may occur when the unborn baby experiences a problem during early development. Asymmetrical IUGR may occur when the unborn baby experiences a problem during later development. In general, most physicians believe that IUGR is the consequence of a disease process within one or more of the three partitions that maintain and regulate fetal growth, i.e., the maternal compartment, the placenta, or the fetus.

In consideration of risk factors uteroplacental insufficiency contributes to 80 percent of IUGR due to the following maternal causes:

• deficient supply of nutrients

• smoking

• malnutrition

• anemia

• drug abuse

• vascular diseases, i.e., high blood pressure

• chronic kidney disease

• severe diabetes

• multiple gestation

Intrauterine growth retardation (IUGR)	
Conditions associated with IUGR	
Maternal history	Alcohol use
	Cocaine use
	Smoking
	Malnutrition
	Use of prescription drugs warfarin (Coumadin, Panwarfarin) and phenytoin (Dilantin)
	Prior history of IUGR pregnancy
	Residing at altitude over 5,000 ft (1,500 m)
Medical conditions (of mother)	Chronic hypertension
	Preeclampia early in gestation
	Diabetes mellitus
	Systemic lupus erythematosus
	Chronic kidney disease
	Inflammatory bowel disease
	Severe lung disease
Infectious diseases	Syphilis
	Cytomegalovirus
	Toxoplasmosis
	Rubella
	Hepatitis B
	Herpes simplex virus 1 or 2
	HIV-1
Congenital disorders (of fetus)	Trisomy 21 (Down syndrome)
	Trisomy 18 (Edwards syndrome)
	Trisomy 13 (Patau syndrome)
	Turner's syndrome

(Table by GGS Information Services.)

• antigen/antibody reactions, i.e., lupus, antiphospholipid antibody syndrome (APA)

• primary placental causes, i.e., extensive placental infarctions, chronic placental separation, placenta previa

Primary fetal causes contribute to 20 percent of IUGR and include the following:

• exposure to an infection, i.e., **rubella** (German **measles**), cytomegalovirus, syphilis, or toxoplasmosis

• birth defects, i.e., **congenital heart disease**, genitourinary anomalies, central nervous system defects

• chromosomal abnormalities, i.e., trisomy 13, 18, or 21

• primary bone or cartilage disorder

• decreased intrinsic growth, symmetrical IUGR

Diagnosis

IUGR can be difficult to diagnose but it begins with taking an extensive maternal history. A mother with a previous IUGR is at risk of having another during a subsequent pregnancy. Maternal renal and cardiopulmonary disease and multiple gestation are factors in IUGR.

KEY TERMS

Abruptio placentae—Premature separation of the placenta from the uterine wall. It occurs late in pregnancy and results in bleeding that may or may not establish an obstetrical emergency.

Circumvallate placenta—The existence of a thick, round, white, opaque ring around the periphery of the placenta that limits the expansion of the fetal vessels.

Fundus—The inside of an organ. In the eye, fundus refers to the back area that can be seen with the ophthalmoscope.

Hemoglobinopathies—Abnormal hemoglobins in the blood, i.e., sickle cell disease, thalessemia.

Hyperplasia—A condition where cells, such as those making up the prostate gland, rapidly divide abnormally and cause the organ to become enlarged.

Hypertrophy—An increase in the size of a tissue or organ brought about by the enlargement of its cells rather than cell multiplication.

Hypoplasia—An underdeveloped or incomplete tissue or organ usually due to a decrease in the number of cells.

Placenta—The organ that provides oxygen and nutrition from the mother to the unborn baby during pregnancy. The placenta is attached to the wall of the uterus and leads to the unborn baby via the umbilical cord.

Placenta previa—A condition in which the placenta totally or partially covers the cervix, preventing vaginal delivery.

Placental infarction—An area of dead tissue in the placenta that is due to an obstruction of circulation in the area.

Preeclampsia—A condition that develops after the twentieth week of pregnancy and results in high blood pressure, fluid retention that doesn't go away, and large amounts of protein in the urine. Without treatment, it can progress to a dangerous condition called eclampsia, in which a woman goes into convulsions.

Uteroplacental insufficiency—Designates the lack of blood flow from the uterus to the placenta, resulting in decreased nourishment and oxygen to the fetus.

Velamentous insertion of the umbilical cord—The attachment of the umbilical cord close to the membranes (bag of water) or in the membranes.

A positive rollover test is predictive of IUGR and is defined as a rise in diastolic blood pressure of 20 mm Hg or more with a position change from the left lateral recumbent to supine, which is an early indication of possible pregnancy-induced hypertension. Determination of an accurate due date is essential in order for the doctor to know if development and weight gain are appropriate. Checking the mother's weight and abdominal measurements can help diagnose cases in which there are no other risk factors present. During each prenatal visit, the healthcare provider uses a tape measure to record the uterine fundal height (measured from the top of the pubic area to the top of the uterus in centimeters). As the pregnancy continues and the baby grows, the uterus stretches upward in the direction of the mother's head. Between 20 and 34 weeks gestation, the uterine fundal height, in centimeters, equals the weeks of gestation. If the uterine fundal height is more than three to four below normal, IUGR is suspected. Ultrasound is used to evaluate the growth of the baby and the ratio of the head circumference (HC) to the abdominal circumference (AC) is a good predictor of asymmetric IUGR. Decreased amniotic fluid (oligohydramnios) is associated with IUGR as the fetus may have a decreased cardiac output and thus decreased renal flow to produce less urine. The grading of the placenta indicates whether it may be inappropriately aging, but this is not as accurate as fetal measurements. Doppler flow studies of the uterine artery provide information regarding the blood flow to the uterus. Doppler studies on the umbilical cord artery and the middle cerebral artery also provide information regarding fetal growth. Biochemical tests on hormone levels of estriol and human placental lactogen provide minimal information.

Treatment

Maternal bed rest is the initial approach for the treatment of IUGR. The benefit of bed rest is that it results in increased blood flow to the uterus. Studies on the efficacy of bed rest have been inconclusive, although in the early 2000s it is still used in combination with intravenous fluid therapy and oxygen therapy. The use of baby aspirin therapy remains controversial but theoretically it serves to preserve or improve blood flow to the placenta. If the baby does not grow well in utero after conservative treatment, an obstetrician may suggest inducing labor in the mother a few weeks early, or delivering the baby by **cesarean section**.

Prognosis

Outcomes for infants with IUGR differ depending on whether the condition is symmetrical or not and whether there are other sequelae from the underlying cause of the IUGR. Outcomes include an increased risk of long-term neurologic and behavioral handicaps, possible intrauterine demise, low blood sugar (**hypoglycemia**), and low body temperature (hypothermia). These risks increase with the severity of the growth restriction. The growth that occurs after birth cannot be predicted with certainty based on the size of the baby when it is born. Infants with asymmetrical IUGR are more likely to catch up in growth after birth than are infants who suffer from prolonged symmetrical IUGR. Delayed eruption of teeth and enamel hypoplasia and an increased incidence of postnatal infections are frequently seen. Each case is unique. Some infants who have IUGR develop normally, while others have complications of the nervous system or intellectual problems such as **learning disorders**. If IUGR is related to a disease or a genetic defect, the future of the infant is related to the severity and the nature of that disorder.

Parental concerns

Pregnant women who have been diagnosed with a fetus with IUGR should talk to their obstetrician about options for treatment. If the woman is uncomfortable with options presented by the doctor, she should seek a qualified second opinion. All pregnant women are well-advised to eat properly, get enough rest, and refrain from alcohol, drugs, and tobacco use for the health of the infant. In addition, pregnant women should be especially careful to keep themselves healthy by following good hygiene practices and receiving a **flu vaccine** if one is recommended.

Resources

BOOKS

Cunningham, F. Gary, et al. *Williams Obstetrics*, 21th ed. Stamford, CT: Appleton & Lange, 2002.

Olds, Sally, et al. *Maternal-Newborn Nursing & Women's Health Care*, 7th ed. Saddle River, NJ: Prentice Hall, 2004.

ORGANIZATIONS

American College of Obstetricians and Gynecologists. 409 12th Street, SW, PO Box 96920, Washington, DC 20090. Web site: <www.acog.org>.

Association of Women's Health, Obstetric and Neonatal Nursing. 2000 L Street, NW Suite 740, Washington, DC 20036. Web site: <www.awhonn.org.

Linda K. Bennington

Intravenous rehydration

Definition

Intravenous rehydration is the process by which sterile water solutions containing small amounts of salt or sugar are injected into the body through a tube attached to a needle which is inserted into a vein.

Purpose

Intravenous rehydration is used to restore the fluid and electrolyte balance of the body due to illness, surgery, or accident. Electrolytes are salts (sodium, potassium, chloride, calcium, magnesium, phosphate, sulfate, and bicarbonate) that become ions when mixed with fluids in the body and blood and have the ability to conduct electricity. The body uses electrolytes to carry electrical impulses from cell to cell. Moderate to severe **dehydration** can interfere with the body's normal functioning. Restoration of fluids and electrolytes through intravenous means is the swiftest means to achieve fluid balance.

Description

Fever, **vomiting**, and **diarrhea** can cause a child to become dehydrated fairly quickly. Infants and children are especially vulnerable to dehydration. Athletes who have over-exerted themselves in hot weather may also require rehydration with IV (intravenous) fluids. An IV for rehydration can be in place for several hours to several days and is generally used if a patient cannot drink fluids.

Basic IV solutions are made of sterile water with small amounts of sodium (an ingredient in table salt) or dextrose (sugar) supplied in bottles or thick plastic bags that can hang on a stand mounted next to the patient's bed. Additional mineral salts such as potassium and calcium, **vitamins**, or medications can be added to the IV solution by injecting them into the bottle or bag with a needle or injected directly into the IV line.

Precautions

Patients receiving IV therapy need to be monitored to ensure that the IV solutions are providing the correct amounts of fluids and **minerals** needed. People with kidney and heart disease are at increased risk for **overhydration**, so they must be carefully monitored when receiving IV therapy.

A child receiving fluids through an intravenous (IV) bag. *(© Tom Stewart/Corbis.)*

Preparation

The doctor orders the IV solution and any additional nutrients or medications to be added to it. The doctor also specifies the rate at which the IV will dispense the solution.

The IV solutions are prepared under the supervision of a pharmaceutical company, using sanitary techniques that prevent bacterial contamination, and come prepackaged. Additions to the IV solutions are supervised by a doctor or nurse. Just like a prescription, the IV is clearly labeled to show its contents and the amounts of any additives.

The skin around the area where the needle for the IV catheter is inserted is cleaned and disinfected. Once the IV catheter is in place, it is taped to the skin to prevent it from being dislodged. The IV line is then attached to the IV catheter. Any other IV lines can be added to the IV catheter.

Aftercare

Patients need to take fluids by mouth before an IV solution is discontinued. After the IV needle is removed, the site should be inspected for any signs of bleeding or infection.

Risks

There is a small risk of infection at the injection site that is usually treated topically. It is also possible that the IV solution may not provide all of the nutrients needed, leading to a deficiency or an imbalance, which would need to be corrected.

If the needle becomes dislodged, the solution can flow into tissues around the injection site rather than into the vein. This is called extravasation, or infiltration, and occurs in about half of pediatric IVs. In most cases, the patient reports a burning or stinging sensation at the site of the needle or IV catheter, especially when new IV fluids are started or the speed of the IV drip is increased. The tissues usually swell and become discolored, looking like a bruise. Usually, the IV catheter is removed and reinserted at another site.

If an IV has been in place for a long time or the child has had a medical condition that weakens the veins, the

KEY TERMS

Dextrose—A sugar solution used in intravenous drips.

Electrolytes—Salts and minerals that produce electrically charged particles (ions) in body fluids. Common human electrolytes are sodium chloride, potassium, calcium, and sodium bicarbonate. Electrolytes control the fluid balance of the body and are important in muscle contraction, energy generation, and almost all major biochemical reactions in the body.

Extravasation—To pass from a blood vessel into the surrounding tissue.

Sodium—An element; sodium is the most common electrolyte found in animal blood serum.

Thrombosis—The formation of a blood clot in a vein or artery that may obstruct local blood flow or may dislodge, travel downstream, and obstruct blood flow at a remote location. The clot or thrombus may lead to infarction, or death of tissue, due to a blocked blood supply.

child may experience vein collapse. This occurs when the vein is not able to receive anymore intravenous fluid and forces the IV solution into the surrounding tissues. It can also occur if a thrombosis, or blood clot, forms in the vein at the IV catheter site.

A collapsed vein feels and looks much like a dislodged IV catheter. This can sometimes happen when the nurse has inserted a needle or IV catheter that is too big for the size of the vein. This isn't a misjudgement on the nurse's part. Standard sized needles are used and only rarely are extremely thin needles necessary. They may be needed in adult patients as well as children. If vein collapse occurs, the IV catheter should be removed and reinserted into a different vein, usually in another part of the body. For example, if a vein in the left arm collapses, the nurse can put a new IV catheter into the right arm.

Treatment for an extravasation or a collapsed vein are similar. A warm compress is usually applied to the injection site to reduce swelling. If there is sufficient injury at the injection site, general wound care is done to prevent infection and speed healing.

Parental concerns

Usually intravenous rehydration is very effective, allowing the child's body to return to its normal fluid equilibrium. Once the child can keep fluids down orally and urine output has returned to normal, then intravenous rehydration is discontinued. Most children don't relapse once they are home if they can continue taking fluids by mouth.

Intravenous rehydration should only be used for moderate to severe dehydration. It is not recommended for mild dehydration from stomach upset or flu. Oral products that restore fluid and electrolytes balance are better for hydrating a sick child who has been vomiting during an illness or after strenuous activity in extremely hot weather. Oral rehydration also does not require a hospital stay.

To reduce the risk of displacement of the needle when the IV catheter or needle is inserted, parents should help the child keep still. The child should also be careful when moving about so as not to dislodge the IV catheter, especially at night. Parents can also look at the injection site and report any discoloration they see. They should also encourage the child to report any burning or stinging around the IV catheter to the nursing staff.

Resources

BOOKS

Josephson, Dianne.*Intravenous Therapy for Nurses.* Albany, NY: Delmar Publishers, 1998.

"Water, Electrolyte, Mineral, and Acid-Base Metabolism." In *The Merck Manual.* 16th ed. Rahway, NJ: Merck, 1992.

PERIODICALS

Atherly-John Y. C., et al. "A Randomized Trial of Oral vs Intravenous Rehydration in a Pediatric Emergency Department."*Archives of Pediatric Adolescent Medicine.* 156 (December 2002): 1240–3.

Camp-Sorrell, D. "Developing Extravasation Protocols and Monitoring Outcomes."*Journal of Intravenous Nursing.* 21, no. 4 (1998): 232-239.

Castellani, J. W., et al. "Intravenous vs. Oral Rehydration: Effects on Subsequent Exercise-Heat Stress." *Journal of Applied Physiology* 82 (Mar. 1997): 799–806.

Montgomery, L. A., Hanrahan, K. and K. Kottman. "Guideline for IV Infiltrations in Pediatric Patients."*Pediatric Nursing* 25, no. 2 (1999): 167–180.

Janie Franz
Altha Roberts Roberts

Intussusception *see* **Intestinal obstructions**

Iron deficiency anemia

Definition

Iron deficiency anemia refers to anemia that is caused by lower than normal levels of iron. This type of anemia is caused by deficient erythropoiesis, the ongoing process of the bone marrow to produce healthy red blood cells (RBCs). It is characterized by the production of small (microcytic) RBCs. When examined under a microscope, the RBCs also appear pale or light colored from the absence of heme, the major component of hemoglobin, which is the iron-bearing protein and coloring pigment in RBCs. Anemia resulting from a deficiency of iron is also called microcytic anemia.

Description

Anemia is a blood disorder characterized by abnormally low levels of healthy RBCs or reduced levels of hemoglobin (Hgb), the iron-bearing protein in RBCs that delivers oxygen to tissues throughout the body. Blood cell volume (hematocrit) may also be reduced in some **anemias**, but not necessarily in iron deficiency anemia. The reduction of any or all of these blood parameters reduces the essential delivery of oxygen through the bloodstream to the organs of the body. Iron is a mineral found in the bloodstream that is essential for growth, enzyme development and function, a healthy immune system, energy levels, and muscle strength. It is an important component of hemoglobin and myoglobin, the type of hemoglobin in muscle tissue.

Iron deficiency anemia is the most common type of anemia throughout the world, although it occurs to a lesser extent in the United States because of the higher consumption of iron-rich red meat and the practice of food fortification (addition of iron to foods by manufacturers). In developing countries in tropical climates, the most common cause of iron deficiency anemia is infestation with hookworm.

The onset of iron deficiency anemia is gradual and may not have early symptoms. The deficiency begins when the body's store of iron is depleted and more iron is being lost through bleeding or malabsorption than is derived from food and other sources. Because depleted iron stores cannot meet the red blood cells' needs, fewer red blood cells develop. In this early stage of anemia, the red blood cells look normal, but they are reduced in number. Eventually the body tries to compensate for the iron deficiency by producing more red blood cells, which are characteristically small in size (spherocytosis). Symptoms of anemia, especially weakness and fatigue, develop at this stage.

Causes and symptoms

Iron is an essential component of the production of healthy RBCs, and iron stores must be maintained for the ongoing production of RBCs by the bone marrow. Iron deficiency anemia can develop as a result of depleted iron stores from chronic blood loss, increased demands for iron as seen in periods of growth (e.g., in infancy and **adolescence**), or malabsorption of iron even when foods or supplements are supplying adequate amounts. It is accepted that iron is hard to absorb; this, in combination with diets that may not meet daily requirements, is a common route to iron deficiency and iron deficiency anemia. Iron can also be lost through strenuous **exercise** and heavy perspiration, poor digestion, frequent consumption of antacids, long-term illness, heavy menstrual cycles, and other causes.

Infancy is a period of increased risk for iron deficiency because dietary iron may not be adequate for the rapid growth of the child in the first two years of life, an example of increased demand. The human infant is born with a built-in supply of iron, which can be tapped during periods of drinking low-iron milk or formula. Both human milk and cow milk contain rather low levels of iron (0.5–1.0 mg iron/liter). However, the iron in the mother's breast milk is about 50 percent absorbed by the infant, while the iron of cow milk is only 10 percent absorbed. During the first six months of life, growth of the infant is made possible by the milk in the diet and by the infant's built-in supply of iron. However, premature infants have a lower supply of iron and, for this reason, it is recommended that pre-term infants, beginning at two months of age, be given oral supplements of 7 mg iron/ day, as ferrous sulfate. Iron deficiency can be provoked where infants are fed formulas based on unfortified cow milk. For example, unfortified cow milk is given free of charge to mothers in Chile. This practice has the fortunate result of preventing general **malnutrition**, but the unfortunate result of allowing the development of mild iron deficiency.

Children have a great need for iron as they grow, and in most cases, the diet will provide replacement iron for the iron used in growth. Children seem to stay in balance unless a bleeding disorder of some kind exists, either hereditary (**hemophilia** or von Willebrand's) or related to hookworm infection or another illness. In adolescence, girls have an increased requirement for iron because of increased growth and the start of **menstruation**. Adolescent boys also experience a major growth spurt that demands more iron; iron stores are worn thin especially when healthy red cell function is needed for adequate oxygenation of exercising muscles and developing organs. Teenagers are also not noted for making healthy food choices; often they are losing iron stores and not replenishing iron through diet.

Iron deficiency occurs most often through chronic blood loss, more often in adults than in children, although the sources of bleeding can apply to people of all ages. Blood losses from gastrointestinal bleeding, excessive menstrual bleeding, and infection with hookworm can deplete iron and lead to iron deficiency anemia. In hookworm infection, a parasitic worm that thrives in warm climates, including in the southern United States, enters the body through the skin, such as through bare feet. The hookworm then migrates to the small intestines where it attaches itself to small sausage-shaped structures in the intestines (villi) that help with the absorption of all nutrients. The hookworm damages the villi, resulting in blood loss; they simultaneously produce anti-coagulants that promote continued bleeding. Each worm can initiate losses of up to 0.25 ml of blood per day.

Chronic blood losses through gradual bleeding in the gastrointestinal tract can be provoked by other conditions such as hemorrhoids, bleeding ulcers, anal fissures, **irritable bowel syndrome**, aspirin-induced bleeding, blood clotting disorders, and diverticulosis (a condition caused by an abnormal opening from the intestine or bladder). Several genetic diseases also lead to bleeding disorders. These include the **coagulation disorders** hemophilia A and hemophilia B, and von Willebrand's disease, a bleeding disorder caused by a deficiency in von Willebrand factor, an essential component of the coagulation system. All three genetic diseases can produce symptoms and be diagnosed in childhood.

The symptoms of iron deficiency anemia appear slowly and typically include weakness and fatigue. These symptoms result because of the reduced oxygen carrying capacity of RBCs and the reduced ability of the RBCs to carry iron to working muscles. Iron deficiency can also affect other tissues, including the tongue and fingernails. Prolonged iron deficiency can result in a smooth, shiny, and reddened tongue, a condition called glossitis. The fingernails may grow abnormally and acquire a spoon-shaped appearance.

When to call the doctor

Weakness, **dizziness**, listlessness, or fatigue may be the first signs of iron deficiency anemia. A compulsion to chew on ice cubes or to eat soil is also an indication of iron deficiency. The pediatrician should be consulted if the child is extremely pale, with little or no color in the gums, nail beds, creases of the palm, or lining of the eyelids.

Demographics

In the United States, iron deficiency anemia affects thousands of toddlers between one and two years of age and more than 3 million women of childbearing age. This condition is less common in older children and in adults over 50 and rarely occurs in teenage boys and young men.

Diagnosis

Diagnosing iron deficiency anemia begins with the pediatrician taking a careful history, including the child's age, symptoms, illnesses, general state of health, and a **family** history of anemias. Symptoms noticed in children by their parents may include fatigue, weight loss, inability to concentrate, loss of appetite, and light-headedness when standing up. The physical examination may reveal paleness, and lack of color in the creases of the palms, in gums, and in the linings of the eyelids.

Diagnostic testing starts with a complete blood count (CBC) and differential, counting RBCs, white blood cells (WBCs) and measuring hemoglobin (Hgb), hematocrit (Hct), and other factors. In iron deficiency anemia, the RBC count can be normal or elevated and hemoglobin will be abnormally low. In infants, iron deficiency anemia is defined as having a hemoglobin level below 109 mg/ml when measured in whole blood, and a hematocrit of less than 33 percent. In the microscopic examination of a stained blood smear (differential), red cells may appear smaller than normal. The mean corpuscular volume (MCV) will be measured to compare the size of RBCs with normal RBCs. A reticulocyte (young RBCs) count will help determine if anemia is caused by impaired RBC production, as in iron deficiency anemia, or increased RBC destruction as in some other types of anemia. Iron, vitamin C or vitamin B_{12}, and folate levels will be measured in blood serum to identify possible deficiencies. In addition to measuring iron itself (Fe) and total iron-binding capacity (TIBC), transferrin and transferrin saturation tests may be performed to evaluate iron metabolism. Different types of hemoglobin may be measured by a diagnostic testing method called hemoglobin electrophoresis. Protoporphyrin IX, a component of hemoglobin, may be measured to help confirm a diagnosis of iron deficiency anemia. Confirmation may also be obtained by taking a bone marrow sample (bone marrow biopsy) for microscopic examination. Kidney function tests, coagulation tests, and stool examinations for occult (hidden) blood may also be performed.

The presence of occult blood found in a stool examination may indicate gastrointestinal bleeding or other causes of bleeding such as aspirin-induced or a bleeding ulcer. The physician then needs to examine the gastrointestinal tract to determine the cause and location of bleeding. In this case, a diagnosis of iron deficiency anemia may include examination with a sigmoidoscope, a flexible, tube-like instrument with a light source that permits examination of the colon. A barium-enhanced x ray of the intestines may also be used to detect abnormalities that can cause bleeding.

The diagnosis of iron deficiency anemia may include a test for oral iron absorption, especially when evidence suggests that oral iron supplements have failed to raise hemoglobin. The oral iron absorption test is conducted by injecting 64 mg iron (325 mg ferrous sulfate) in a single dose. Blood samples are then taken after two hours and four hours. The iron content of the blood serum is then measured. The concentration of iron should rise by about 22 micromolar, when iron absorption is normal. Lesser increases in concentration mean that iron absorption is abnormal and that more effective therapy may involve injections or infusions of iron.

Treatment

The goal of treatment for iron deficiency anemia is to restore iron levels and the production of healthy RBCs and increase the essential flow of oxygen to tissues. Iron preparations may be given by injection or, in older children, as oral supplements. Taking vitamin C along with oral iron supplementation is accepted as a way to achieve better absorption of the iron. Taking iron supplements can result in **constipation**, **diarrhea**, cramps, or **vomiting** in sensitive individuals. Injections and infusions of iron can be given to individuals with poor iron absorption. Treatment of iron deficiency anemia sometimes requires more than iron supplementation. When iron deficiency is provoked by hemorrhoids or gastrointestinal bleeding, for example, surgery may be required to prevent recurrent iron deficiency anemia. When iron deficiency is provoked by bleeding due to aspirin ingestion, aspirin is discontinued. Iron deficiency caused by hookworm infection requires drug therapy to eliminate the parasite; prevention includes wearing shoes when walking in soil known to be infested with hookworms.

Alternative treatment

Vitamin C is noted for helping to absorb iron in the diet and iron supplements. Cooking in a cast iron skillet may leach small amounts of absorbable iron into the diet. Besides the iron found in eggs, fish, liver, meat, poultry, green leafy vegetables, whole grains, and enriched or whole grain breads and cereals, good food sources of iron include blackstrap molasses, brewer's yeast, and certain types of sea vegetable (e.g., hijiki, kelp, dulse).

Herbal supplements that benefit individuals who have iron deficiency anemia include alfalfa, burdock root, dandelion, dong quai, mullein, nettle, raspberry leaf, shepherd's purse, and yellow dock. Herbs are available as tinctures and teas or in capsules.

Nutritional concerns

Decreased dietary iron intake is a contributing factor in iron deficiency and iron deficiency anemia. Deciding how to add enough iron to the diet, however, depends not just on which foods contain it, but in which foods iron is most available for absorption and use by the body. Bioavailability describes the percent of dietary iron that is successfully absorbed via the gastrointestinal tract to the bloodstream. Non-absorbed iron is lost in the feces. Generally, iron bioavailability in fruits, vegetables, and grains is lower than the iron availability of meat. The availability of iron in plants ranges from only 1 to 10 percent, with some exceptions, while that in meat, fish, chicken, and liver is consistently 20–30 percent. In the following list, the iron content is given parenthetically for each food.

- cabbage (1.6 mg/kg)
- spinach (33 mg/kg)
- lima beans (15 mg/kg)
- potatoes (14 mg/kg)
- tomatoes (3 mg/kg)
- apples (1.5 mg/kg)
- peanut butter (6.0 mg/kg)
- raisins (20 mg/kg)
- whole wheat bread (43 mg/kg)
- eggs (20 mg/kg)
- canned tuna (13 mg/kg)
- chicken (11 mg/kg)
- beef (28 mg/kg)

It is easy to see that apples, tomatoes, and peanut butter are relatively low in iron, while spinach, whole wheat bread, and beef are relatively high in iron. Red meat sources reliably replace the heme component of red blood cells, raising hemoglobin levels and helping to correct iron deficiency. For infants and toddlers, the most available source of iron is human milk (50% availability).

The assessment of whether a food is low or high in iron can also be made by comparing the amount of that food eaten per day with the recommended dietary allowance (RDA) for iron. The RDA for iron for the adult male is 10 mg/day, while that for the adult woman is

KEY TERMS

Erythropoiesis—The process through which new red blood cells are created; it begins in the bone marrow.

Hematocrit—A measure of the percentage of red blood cells in the total volume of blood in the human body.

Heme—The iron-containing molecule in hemoglobin that serves as the site for oxygen binding.

Hemoglobin—An iron-containing pigment of red blood cells composed of four amino acid chains (alpha, beta, gamma, delta) that delivers oxygen from the lungs to the cells of the body and carries carbon dioxide from the cells to the lungs.

Protoporphyrin IX—A protein the measurement of which is useful for the assessment of iron status. Hemoglobin consists of a complex of a protein plus heme. Heme consists of iron plus protoporphyrin IX. Normally, during the course of red blood cell formation, protoporphyrin IX acquires iron, to generate heme, and the heme becomes incorporated into hemoglobin. However, in iron deficiency, protophoryrin IX builds up.

Recommended Dietary Allowance (RDA)—The Recommended Dietary Allowances (RDAs) are quantities of nutrients in the diet that are required to maintain good health in people. RDAs are established by the Food and Nutrition Board of the National Academy of Sciences, and may be revised every few years. A separate RDA value exists for each nutrient. The RDA values refer to the amount of nutrient expected to maintain good health in people. The actual amounts of each nutrient required to maintain good health in specific individuals differ from person to person.

15 mg/day. The RDA during pregnancy is 30 mg/day. The RDA for infants five months of age or younger is 6 mg/day, while that for infants of five months to one year of age is 10 mg/day. RDA values are based on the assumption that people eat a mixture of plant and animal foods.

Prognosis

The prognosis for treating and curing iron deficiency anemia is excellent, particularly when those affected take iron supplements as advised and are able to assimilate the iron. A number of studies have shown that iron deficiency anemia in infancy can result in reduced

intelligence, when intelligence was measured in early childhood. It is not certain if iron supplementation of children with reduced intelligence, due to iron-deficiency anemia in infancy, has any influence in allowing a "catch-up" in intellectual development.

Prevention

In the healthy population, mineral deficiencies can be prevented by the consumption of inorganic nutrients at levels defined by the RDA. Iron deficiency anemia in infants and young children can be prevented by breastfeeding, consuming good dietary sources of iron, and using fortified foods. Liquid cow milk-based infant formulas are generally supplemented with iron (12 mg/L). The iron in liquid formulas is added as ferrous sulfate or ferrous gluconate. Commercial infant cereals are also fortified with iron, adding small particles of elemental iron. The levels used are about 0.5 gram iron/kg dry cereal. This amount of iron is about 10-fold greater than that of the iron naturally present in the cereal. Iron supplementation is not recommended for all infants, and children and pediatricians should be consulted before giving supplements. Vitamin C is recommended to improve the assimilation of iron in the body, especially when iron is obtained from non-food sources.

Nutritional concerns

The average diet in the United States contains about 6 mg of iron per calorie of food, which is sufficient for maintaining iron stores. Only 1 mg of iron, however, is absorbed for every 10 mg. consumed, which mean sources of iron must be carefully chosen. The bioavailability of iron in foods varies, influencing the amounts that can be absorbed through the intestines. Absorption is best when the food contains heme, just as in human red cells. That makes meat the best choice as a source of iron and iron-rich vegetables and fruits such as spinach and apricots the next best choice. Certain other plant foods that contain fiber, such as bran, actually reduce the absorption of non-heme iron; so do antacid medications, often taken to relieve the upset stomach associated with taking oral iron supplements. Additionally, food interactions reduce bioavailability. Ascorbic acid (vitamin C) is the only food constituent known to increase the availability of non-heme iron, such as in vegetables and also in food supplements.

Parental concerns

Understanding iron metabolism and the ways to ensure that iron deficiency anemia in infants and children can be successfully treated and prevented from recurring may be concerns of parents. It is important to remember that although iron deficiency anemia is common in infants and toddlers, it is easily corrected by feeding infants mother's milk or iron-fortified formulas. In older children, the diet usually balances iron usage and replacement. In teenage years, when demands for iron increase for rapid growth and to compensate for menstruation in girls, parents will need to pay attention once again to providing adequate food sources. However, supplementation of iron should only be done with a doctor's recommendation.

Resources

BOOKS

"Blood Disorders." *The Merck Manual of Medical Information*, 2nd Home Edition. Edited by Mark H. Beers et al. White House Station, NJ: Merck & Co., 2003.

Floyd, B. A. *Anemia*. Bloomington, IN: AuthorHouse, 2002.

Lark, Susan. *Heavy Menstrual Flow and Anemia Self Help Book*. Berkeley, CA: Celestial Arts Publishing, 2004.

Ross, Allison J. *Everything You Need to Know about Anemia*. New York: Rosen Publishing Group, 2001.

ORGANIZATIONS

National Heart, Lung, and Blood Institute (NHLBI). 6701 Rockledge Drive, PO Box 30105, Bethesda, MD 20824–0105. Web site: <www.nhlbi.nih.gov>.

L. Lee Culvert
Tom Brody, PhD

Irritable bowel syndrome

Definition

Irritable bowel syndrome (IBS) is a common gastrointestinal condition characterized by abdominal **pain** and cramps; changes in bowel movements (**diarrhea, constipation**, or both); gassiness; bloating; **nausea**; and other symptoms. There is no cure for IBS; however, dietary changes, stress management, and sometimes medications are often able to eliminate or substantially reduce its symptoms.

Description

IBS is the name people use today for a condition that was once called—among other things—spastic colitis, mucous colitis, spastic colon, nervous colon, spastic bowel, and functional bowel disorder. Some of these names reflected the now outdated belief that IBS is a purely psychological disorder, a product of the patient's imagination. Although modern medicine recognizes that stress, **anxiety** and depression can trigger IBS attacks, medical specialists agree that IBS is a genuine physical disorder—or group of disorders—with specific identifiable characteristics. IBS is considered a functional disorder because it is thought to result from changes in the activity of the major part of the large intestine (the colon).

Demographics

IBS is one of the most common functional gastrointestinal disorders, affecting 10-20 percent of adults in the United States. Research has demonstrated that symptoms compatible with IBS are about as common in school-age children as in adults. IBS normally makes its first appearance during young adulthood, and symptoms usually begin at about age 20. Women with IBS represent over 70 percent of IBS sufferers. IBS is responsible for more time lost from school and work than any medical problem—other than the **common cold**. It accounts for a substantial proportion of the patients seen by specialists in diseases of the digestive system (gastroenterologists).

A community-based study of 507 middle school and high school students by Hyams, et al, found that 6-14 percent of the adolescent population had IBS symptoms. Anxiety and depression scores were significantly higher for this group. Eight percent of all the students in the study had seen a physician for abdominal pain in the previous year.

Causes and symptoms

Causes

Although the exact cause or causes of IBS are unknown, research suggests that people with IBS may have a colon that is more sensitive and reactive to certain foods and stress.

After food is digested by the stomach and small intestine, the undigested material passes in liquid form into the colon, which absorbs water, nutrients and salts. Normally, the colon is quiet during most of that period except after meals, when its muscles contract in a series of wavelike movements called peristalsis. Peristalsis helps absorption by bringing the undigested material into contact with the colon wall. It also pushes undigested material that has been converted into solid or semisolid feces toward the rectum, where it remains until a bowel movement occurs.

In IBS, however, the normal rhythm and intensity of peristalsis is disrupted. Sometimes there is too little peristalsis, which can slow the passage of undigested material through the colon and cause constipation. Sometimes there is too much, which has the opposite effect and causes diarrhea. In other cases, peristalsis can be spasmodic, causing sudden strong muscle contractions that come and go.

DIET Some foods and beverages appear to play a key role in triggering IBS attacks. Certain foods and drinks may disrupt peristalsis in IBS patients, which may explain why IBS attacks often occur shortly after meals. Some of the chief culprits include:

- chocolate
- dairy products
- **caffeine** (in coffee, tea, colas, and other drinks)
- carbonated beverages (colas, pop, soda)
- wheat
- rye
- barley
- excess alcohol

Other foods also have been identified as problems, and the pattern of what can and cannot be tolerated is different for each person.

STRESS Stress—feeling mentally or emotionally tense, troubled, angry or overwhelmed—stimulates colon spasms in people with IBS since there is a close nervous system connection between the brain and the intestines. A large network of nerves control the normal rhythmic contractions of the colon. Although researchers do not yet understand all of the links between changes in the nervous system and IBS, they point out the similarities between mild digestive upsets and IBS. Just as healthy people can feel nauseated or have an upset stomach when under stress, people with IBS react the same way, but to a greater degree.

MENSTRUATION IBS symptoms sometimes intensify during **menstruation**, suggesting female reproductive hormones may trigger the condition.

Symptoms

The symptoms of IBS tend to rise and fall in intensity, rather than grow steadily worse over time. Symptoms always include:

- abdominal pain, which may be relieved by defecation
- diarrhea
- constipation
- diarrhea alternating with constipation

Other symptoms, which vary from person to person, include:

- cramps
- gassiness
- bloating
- nausea
- passage of mucus during bowel movements
- abnormal stool frequency—defined as greater than three bowel movements per day or less than three bowel movements per week
- abnormal stool form (lumpy, hard, loose, or watery stool)
- abnormal stool passage (straining, urgency, or feeling of incomplete bowel movement)

In general, symptoms are not present all the time and do not interfere with school and other normal activities. IBS symptoms rarely occur at night and disrupt the patient's **sleep**. Moderate IBS occasionally disrupts normal activities.

When to call the doctor

If a child has the following symptoms, the parent should contact the child's pediatrician or gastroenterologist:

- abdominal pain or diarrhea that wakes the child during the night
- persistent or severe abdominal pain
- unexplained weight loss
- rectal bleeding
- fever
- **family** history of irritable bowel disease

Diagnosis

The Rome II criteria are the accepted diagnostic criteria for IBS. These criteria were developed by an international group of pediatric gastroenterologists and include:

- Continuous or recurrent abdominal discomfort or pain for at least three months that is: a) Relieved with defecation and/or b) Associated with a change in frequency and/or c) Associated with a change in appearance of stool. Two or three of these features are present with an IBS diagnosis.
- No structural or metabolic abnormalities are present that may be responsible for the IBS symptoms.

The diagnosis of IBS is further supported by the presence of the symptoms listed previously. In addition, the primary pediatrician or gastroenterologist may confirm the diagnosis of IBS after questioning the child (if old enough to provide an accurate history of symptoms) or parent about his or her physical and mental health (the medical history), performing a physical examination, and ordering laboratory tests to rule out other conditions that resemble IBS, such as Crohn's disease and ulcerative colitis.

Diagnostic tests may include stool or blood tests, hydrogen breath test, or an x ray of the bowel, called a barium enema. When symptoms continue even after treatment, endoscopic tests such as a colonoscopy or sigmoidoscopy may be performed. An endoscopic test is an internal examination of the colon using a flexible instrument (a sigmoidoscope or colonoscope) that is inserted through the anus.

A nutritional **assessment** performed by a registered dietitian may be included in the child's diagnostic evaluation. The nutritional assessment includes a review of the child's fiber intake as well as his or her usual consumption of sugars such as sorbitol and fructose—common culprits of diarrhea.

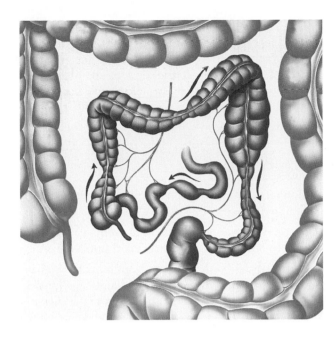

Normal and diseased (center) colons. Areas of constriction in the colon cause constipation, while areas of distention cause diarrhea. (© 1995 John Bavosi/Science Photo Library. Custom Medical Stock Photo, Inc.)

Treatment

Dietary changes and sometimes medications are considered the keys to successful treatment. Psychosocial difficulties are also addressed and treated with therapy or counseling as needed. Treatment requires a long-term commitment; six months or more may be needed before the child notices substantial improvement.

Alternative treatment

Alternative and complementary therapies include approaches that are considered to be outside the mainstream of traditional health care. Alternative and traditional approaches to IBS treatment overlap to a certain extent. Like traditional doctors, alternative practitioners advise a high-fiber diet to reduce digestive system irritation. They also suggest avoiding caffeine and fatty, gassy, or spicy foods, as well as alcohol. Recommended stress management techniques include **yoga**, meditation, guided imagery, hypnosis, biofeedback, and reflexology. Reflexology is a foot massage technique that is thought to relieve diarrhea, constipation, and other IBS symptoms.

The list of alternative treatments for IBS is quite long. It includes aromatherapy, homeopathy, hydrotherapy, juice therapy, acupuncture, chiropractic, osteopathy, naturopathic medicine, and Chinese traditional herbal medicine.

Before learning or practicing any particular technique, it is important for the parent/caregiver and child to learn about the therapy, its safety and effectiveness, potential side effects, and the expertise and qualifications of the practitioner. Although some practices are beneficial, others may be harmful to certain patients.

Relaxation techniques and dietary supplements should not be used as a substitute for medical therapies prescribed by a doctor. Parents should discuss these alternative treatments with the child's doctor to determine the techniques and remedies that may be beneficial for the child.

Nutritional concerns

Dietary changes, including a low-fat, high-fiber diet, may help decrease IBS symptoms. The addition of wheat bran or other fiber may be suggested to decrease symptoms. The formula for determining the recommended fiber intake for children, as advised by the American Dietetic Association, is to take the child's age plus five to equal the grams of dietary fiber the child should consume daily. Fiber should be added gradually to the child's diet.

The doctor may recommend a lactose-free diet for two or three weeks to determine if **lactose intolerance** is causing the symptoms. Lactose is the milk sugar found

KEY TERMS

Anus—The opening at the end of the intestine through which solid waste (stool) passes as it leaves the body.

Barium enema—An x ray of the bowel using a liquid called barium to enhance the image of the bowel. This test is also called a lower GI (gastrointestinal) series.

Colonoscopy—An examination of the lining of the colon performed with a colonoscope.

Constipation—Difficult bowel movements caused by the infrequent production of hard stools.

Crohn's disease—A chronic, inflammatory disease, primarily involving the small and large intestine, but which can affect other parts of the digestive system as well.

Defecation—The act of having a bowel movement or the passage of feces through the anus.

Diarrhea—A loose, watery stool.

Endoscopy—Visual examination of an organ or body cavity using an endoscope, a thin, tubular instrument containing a camera and light source. Many endoscopes also allow the retrieval of a small sample (biopsy) of the area being examined, in order to more closely view the tissue under a microscope.

Feces—The solid waste, also called stool, that is left after food is digested. Feces form in the intestines and pass out of the body through the anus.

Gastroenterologist—A physician who specializes in diseases of the digestive system.

Hydrogen breath test—A test used to determine if a person is lactose intolerant or if abnormal bacteria are present in the colon.

Lactose—A sugar found in milk and milk products.

Peristalsis—Slow, rhythmic contractions of the muscles in a tubular organ, such as the intestines, that move the contents along.

Sigmoidoscopy—A procedure in which a thin, flexible, lighted instrument, called a sigmoidoscope, is used to visually examine the lower part of the large intestine. Colonoscopy examines the entire large intestine using the same techniques.

Ulcerative colitis—A form of inflammatory bowel disease characterized by inflammation of the mucous lining of the colon, ulcerated areas of tissue, and bloody diarrhea.

in dairy products. Lactose intolerance is a common condition in up to 40% of patients with IBS. During the lactose-free period, the child should avoid all products containing lactose. The parent and child are asked to record the intake of all foods and beverages and note when symptoms occur after eating or drinking.

To identify other problem-causing foods or beverages, it is helpful for the parent and child to keep a diary of symptoms for two or three weeks, including daily activities, meals, symptoms and emotions. The doctor can then review the diary with the parent and child to identify possible problem areas.

In addition to lactose, known problem-causing substances include caffeine, beans, onions, cabbage, cucumbers, broccoli, fatty foods, alcohol, and certain medications. Once the specific substances that trigger symptoms are identified, they should be avoided. A registered dietitian can help the parent and child make specific dietary changes.

If lactose intolerance is a problem, the child may need to take calcium supplements or choose other foods high in calcium to meet the recommended daily requirement. If lactose intolerance is not a problem, the child can still have milk or milk products.

Medications

Medications affect each child differently, and no one medication works for every child with IBS. The child and parent will need to work with the doctor to find the best combination of medicine, diet, counseling and support to manage symptoms.

Stool softeners such as polyethelene glycol (Miralax) or an over-the-counter laxative may be recommended for constipation. Mineral oil also may be helpful. However, it is important not to use over-the-counter remedies without first consulting with the child's doctor.

Tricyclic **antidepressants** in low doses may be prescribed for pain relief. Antidepressants work by blocking pain transmission from the nervous system. Antispasmodic medications can slow bowel contractions and decrease diarrhea. Anticholinergics may help control intestinal cramping. Keep in mind that the effectiveness of these drugs to treat IBS has not been studied extensively in children.

Counseling and support

Psychological counseling or behavioral therapy may be recommended for some patients to reduce anxiety and stress and to learn to cope with the symptoms of IBS. Biofeedback, guided imagery, relaxation therapy, hypnosis, and cognitive-behavioral therapy are examples of behavioral therapy. An ongoing and supportive doctor-patient relationship is also very important. The child and family must be reassured that although IBS causes symptoms that are uncomfortable and sometimes painful, it is not a harmful condition and does indicate a serious problem.

Prognosis

IBS is not a life-threatening condition. It is not an anatomical or structural defect, nor an identifiable physical or chemical disorder. IBS does not cause intestinal bleeding or inflammation, nor does it cause other gastrointestinal diseases or **cancer**. Although IBS can last a lifetime, in up to 30% of cases the symptoms eventually disappear. Even if the symptoms cannot be eliminated, with appropriate treatment they usually can be managed enough so IBS becomes merely an occasional inconvenience.

Prevention

Nutritional concerns

To help prevent or decrease the child's symptoms, parents can:

- help the child identify and avoid problematic foods
- work with a registered dietitian to facilitate specific dietary changes
- incorporate changes in the child's diet gradually so his or her body has time to adjust
- establish set times for meals; not allowing the child to skip a meal
- encourage the child to drink at least eight 8-ounce glasses of water per day
- serve small portions during meals
- teach the child to eat slowly, to avoid swallowing too much air that can produce excess gas
- try offering smaller, more frequent meals
- keep a regular schedule for bathroom visits

Parental concerns

Parents should reinforce with the child that IBS is not a life-threatening condition and that dietary changes and stress reduction can help reduce symptoms. Remind the child that six months or more may be needed before he or she notices substantial improvement in symptoms.

Resources

BOOKS

Goldberg, Burton, John W. Anderson, and Larry Trivieri. *Alternative Medicine: The Definitive Guide, 2nd Edition.* Berkeley, CA: Ten Speed Press, 2002.

Lynn, Richard B., and Lawrence S. Friedman. "Irritable Bowel Syndrome." In *Harrison's Principles of Internal Medicine, 16th Edition.* Anthony S. Fauci, et al. New York: McGraw-Hill Professional, 2004.

Van Vorous, Heather. *Eating for IBS Diet and Cookbook.* New York, NY: Marlowe & Company, 2000.

PERIODICALS

Dalton, Christine B., and Douglas A. Drossman. "Diagnosis and Treatment of Irritable Bowel Syndrome." *American Family Physician* (Feb. 1997): 875+.

Hyams, J.S., et al. "Abdominal Pain and Irritable Syndrome in Adolescents: A Community-Based Study." *Journal of Pediatrics* (Aug. 1996): 220+.

Jarrett, Monica, et al. "Recurrent Abdominal Pain in Children: Forerunner to Adult Irritable Bowel Syndrome." *Journal for Specialists in Pediatric Nursing* (July-Sept. 2003): 81+.

ORGANIZATIONS

American College of Gastroenterology (ACG). P.O. Box 3099, Alexandria, VA 22302. (703) 820-7400. Web site: <http://www.acg.gi.org/patientinfo/cgp/cgpvol2.html>.

American Gastroenterological Association. 4930 Del Ray Ave., Bethesda, MD 20814. (301) 654-2055. Web site: <http://www.gastro.org/clinicalRes/brochures/ibs.html>.

International Foundation for Functional Gastrointestinal Disorders (IFFGD). P.O. Box 170864, Milwaukee, WI 53217-8076. (888) 964-2001. E-mail: iffgd@iffgd.org. Web site: <http://www.iffgd.org>.

Irritable Bowel Syndrome (IBS) Association. 1440 Whalley Ave., #145, New Haven, CT 06515. E-mail: ibsa@ibsassociation.org. Web site: <http://www.ibsassociation.org>.

Irritable Bowel Syndrome Self Help and Support Group. 1440 Whalley Ave., #145 New Haven, CT 06515. E-mail: ibs@ibsgroup.org. Web site: <http://www.ibsgroup.org>.

National Digestive Diseases Information Clearinghouse (NDDIC). 2 Information Way, Bethesda, MD 20892-3570. (800) 891-5389. E-mail: nddic@info.niddk.nih.gov. Web site: <http://www.niddk.nih.gov/health/digest/nddic.htm>.

WEB SITES

About IBS. Available online at <http://www.aboutibs.org.>

Howard Baker

Itching

Definition

Itching is an intense, distracting irritation or tickling sensation that may be felt all over the skin's surface or confined to just one area. The medical term for itching is pruritus.

Description

Itching instinctively leads most people to scratch the affected area. Different people can tolerate different amounts of itching, and the threshold of tolerance can change due to stress, emotions, and other factors. In general, itching is more severe if the skin is warm and if there are few distractions. This is why people tend to notice itching more at night.

Demographics

It is common for children to be itchy occasionally. Prolonged itching in a specific location and generalized itching in many different areas of the body are less common.

Causes and symptoms

The reason for the sensation of itching is not well understood. While itching is the most noticeable symptom in many skin diseases, it does not necessarily mean that a person who feels itchy has a disease.

Stress and emotional upset can make itching worse, no matter what the underlying cause. Itching is often worse at night or at times when there are no distractions. If emotional problems are the primary reason for the itch, the condition is known as psychogenic itching. Some people become convinced that their itch is caused by a parasite; this conviction is often linked to burning sensations in the tongue and may be caused by a major psychiatric disorder.

Generalized itching

Itching that occurs all over the body may indicate a medical condition such as **diabetes mellitus**, liver disease, kidney failure, **jaundice**, thyroid disorders, or rarely, **cancer**. Blood disorders such as leukemia and lymphatic conditions such as Hodgkin's disease may sometimes cause itching as well.

Some children may develop an itch without a rash when they take certain drugs such as aspirin or codeine.

Others may develop an itchy red drug rash or **hives** because of an allergy to a specific drug such as penicillin.

Itching also may be caused when any of the family of hookworm larvae penetrate the skin. This includes swimmer's itch and creeping eruption caused by cat or dog hookworm and ground itch caused by the true hookworm.

Many skin conditions cause an itchy rash. These include:

- atopic **dermatitis**
- **contact dermatitis**
- dermatitis herpetiformis (occasionally)
- eczema
- fungus infections (such as athlete's foot)
- hives (urticaria)
- insect **bites**
- lice
- lichen planus
- neurodermatitis (lichen simplex chronicus)
- psoriasis (occasionally)
- scabies

Itching all over the body can be caused by something as simple as bathing too often, which removes the skin's natural oils and may make the skin too dry.

Localized itching

Specific itchy areas may occur if a person comes in contact with soap, detergents, or wool or other rough-textured, scratchy material. Adults who have hemorrhoids, anal fissure, or persistent **diarrhea** may notice itching around the anus (called pruritus ani). When children itch in this area, the cause is most likely **pinworms**.

Intense itching in the external genitalia in women (pruritus vulvae) may be due to **candidiasis** (yeast), hormonal changes, or the use of certain spermicides or vaginal suppositories, ointments, or deodorants.

When to call the doctor

If the child is itchy all over or has a localized itch in combination with a rash, **fever**, infection, or is acting sick, the doctor should be contacted.

Diagnosis

Itching is a symptom that is obvious to its victim. Because itching can be caused by such a wide variety of triggers, a complete physical examination and medical history will help diagnose the underlying problem.

KEY TERMS

Atopic dermatitis—An intensely itchy inflammation often found on the face, in the bend of the elbow, and behind the knees of people prone to allergies. In infants and young children, this condition is called infantile eczema.

Creeping eruption—Itchy, irregular, wandering red lines on the foot made by burrowing larvae of the hookworm family and some roundworms.

Dermatitis herpetiformis—A chronic, very itchy skin disease with groups of red lesions that leave spots behind when they heal.

Eczema—A superficial type of inflammation of the skin that may be very itchy and weeping in the early stages; later, the affected skin becomes crusted, scaly, and thick.

Hodgkin's disease—One of two general types of lymphoma (cancers that arise in the the lymphatic system and can invade other organs), Hodgkin's disease is characterized by lymph node enlargement and the presence of a large polyploid cells called Reed-Sternberg cells.

Lichen planus—A noncancerous, chronic itchy skin disease that causes small, flat purple plaques on wrists, forearm, ankles.

Neurodermatitis—An itchy skin disease (also called lichen simplex chronicus) found in nervous, anxious people.

Psoriasis—A chronic, noncontagious skin disease that is marked by dry, scaly, and silvery patches of skin that appear in a variety of sizes and locations on the body.

Scabies—A contagious parasitic skin disease caused by a tiny mite and characterized by intense itching.

Swimmer's itch—An allergic skin inflammation caused by a sensitivity to flatworms that die under the skin, resulting in an itchy rash.

A variety of blood and stool tests may be needed to help the doctor to determine the cause of the itch.

Treatment

Antihistamines such as diphenhydramine (Benadryl) can help relieve itching caused by hives but will not relieve itching from other causes. Most antihista-mines also make people sleepy, which can help children **sleep** who would otherwise be awakened by the itch.

Specific treatment of itching depends on the underlying condition that causes it. In general, itchy skin should be treated very gently. While scratching may temporarily ease the itch, in the long run scratching makes the itch worse and can lead to an endless cycle in which scratching an itch makes it more itchy.

To avoid the urge to scratch, a cooling or soothing lotion or cold compress can be applied when the urge to scratch occurs. Soaps are often irritating to the skin and can make an itch worse; they should be avoided or used only when necessary.

Creams or ointments containing cortisone may help control the itch from insect bites, contact dermatitis, or eczema. Cortisone cream should not be applied to the face unless prescribed by a doctor.

Probably the most common cause of itching is dry skin. There are a number of simple things that can be done to ease the annoying itch:

• Do not wear tight clothes.

• Avoid synthetic fabrics.

• Take shorter baths.

• Wash the area in lukewarm water with a little baking soda.

• For generalized itching, take a lukewarm shower or oatmeal (or Aveeno) bath.

• Apply bath oil or lotion (without added colors or scents) right after bathing.

Children who itch as a result of mental problems or stress may benefit from seeing a mental health expert.

Prognosis

Most cases of itching resolve successfully when the underlying cause is treated.

Prevention

There are certain things people can do to avoid itchy skin. Children who tend toward itchy skin should take the following steps:

• Avoid a daily bath.

• Use only lukewarm water when bathing.

• Use only gentle soap.

• Pat dry, not rub dry, after bathing, leaving a bit of water on the skin.

- Apply a moisture-holding ointment or cream after the bath.

- Use a humidifier in the home.

Children who are allergic to certain substances, medications, or foods can avoid the resulting itch if they avoid contact with the allergen. Avoiding insect bites, bee **stings**, **poison ivy**, and similar plants can prevent the resulting itch. Treating sensitive skin carefully, avoiding overdrying of the skin, and protecting against diseases that cause itchy **rashes** are all good ways to avoid itching.

Parental concerns

Children who are itchy should have their finger nails cut short to help ensure that they do not scratch the itchy area enough to create breaks in the skin. Scratching until the skin is broken can lead to infection. Itching can be very frustrating, and, if it is severe, it can interfere with normal activities such as studying or sleeping. Itching is a symptom of many common childhood ailments such as **chickenpox** and contact with poison ivy, as well as of some more serious conditions.

Resources

BOOKS

Fleischer, Alan B., Jr. *The Clinical Management of Itching.* New York: Parthenon Publishing Group, 2000.

Yosipovitch, et al., eds. *Itch: Basic Mechanisms and Therapy.* New York: Marcel Dekker, 2004.

PERIODICALS

Moses, Scott. "Pruritus." *American Family Physician* 68 (September 15, 2003): 1135.

Yosipovitch, Gil, and Jennifer L. Hundley. "Practical Guidelines for Relief of Itch." *Dermatology Nursing* 16 (August 2004): 325–30.

Tish Davidson, A.M.
Carol A. Turkington

Jaundice

Definition

Jaundice is a yellowing of the skin and/or whites of the eyes caused by high levels of bilirubin—a dark yellow-green or orange-red pigment—in the blood.

Description

Jaundice, also called icterus or hyperbilirubinemia, is a very common condition in newborns. Newborn or **neonatal jaundice**, sometimes referred to as physiologic or physiological jaundice, affects more than half of all full-term newborns and 80 percent of premature newborns within the first few days of life. It commonly lasts for one to two weeks. Jaundice that is present at birth or that lasts more than a couple of weeks may be abnormal jaundice and a symptom of an underlying problem. Jaundice in older children or adults is a symptom of hepatitis (inflammation of the liver) or some other liver disorder.

Jaundice results from higher than normal levels of bilirubin in the blood. Bilirubin is a breakdown product of red blood cells. Red blood cells normally are removed and broken down in the spleen after about 120 days in circulation. Heme (component of hemoglobin in red blood cells that carries oxygen throughout the body) is broken down into bilirubin, which moves to the liver where it is processed and added to bile, a digestive fluid. The bile travels through the bile ducts to the intestine and is excreted in the stool.

Infants are born with excess red blood cells that are rapidly recycled by the spleen and liver, releasing bilirubin. This pigment gives a newborn's stools their yellow color. If more bilirubin is produced than can be processed by the liver, blood levels of bilirubin rise, and the excess is deposited in tissues causing the skin to appear yellow.

Demographics

Although jaundice affects the majority of newborns, it often is more severe in Asian or Native American children. It also is more common in infants who are not breastfeeding efficiently, resulting in low fluid intake.

In 2001 the U.S. Centers for Disease Control and Prevention (CDC) reported that cases of brain damage associated with hyperbilirubinemia (called neonatal encephalopathy, bilirubin-induced brain injury, or kernicterus) had been increasing since about 1990, perhaps due to shorter hospital stays following birth. One cause of hyperbilirubinemia in seemingly healthy full-term or near-term infants is **biliary atresia**, an obstruction or inflammation of the bile ducts. This condition occurs in about one in every 15,000 live births, and girls are slightly more at risk than boys.

Causes and symptoms

Neonatal jaundice

Prior to birth the mother's liver processes bilirubin for the fetus. At birth, particularly with preterm births, an infant's immature liver may not be able to process all of the bilirubin formed as red blood cells are removed from circulation. The excess bilirubin causes jaundice by the third or fourth day after birth. The jaundice usually appears first on the face and progresses downward to the chest, abdomen, legs, and feet. If newborn feeding is delayed for any reason, such as illness, a digestive tract problem, or low fluid intake due to inefficient breastfeeding; the infant produces fewer stools, resulting in critically high blood levels of bilirubin and severe jaundice.

Most full-term babies with neonatal jaundice have no other symptoms. However, if bilirubin levels continue to rise, other symptoms may include:

- sleepiness
- lethargy
- slow or reluctant feeding

Risk factors for hyperbilirubinemia include:

- birth more than two weeks before the due date
- jaundice within the first 24 hours after birth
- significant bruising or bleeding under the scalp caused by labor and delivery
- high bilirubin levels prior to hospital discharge
- difficulty breastfeeding, resulting in low fluid intake
- a parent or sibling who had high bilirubin levels at birth

Abnormal jaundice in newborns

Jaundice at birth or within the first 24 hours after birth can be a sign of abnormal jaundice. Abnormal jaundice can be dangerous, particularly in preterm or unhealthy newborns. Depending on the cause and extent of the jaundice, it also may be harmful in full-term infants.

The most common cause of abnormal jaundice is an ABO blood type incompatibility between mother and child. If the mother has O-type blood and the infant has either A or B blood type, or if the mother has A-type blood and the child has B-type or vice versa, the mother's antibodies circulating in the baby's blood attack the child's foreign blood type, causing damage to and destruction of the baby's red blood cells. This process, called hemolysis, is accompanied by the release of excess amounts of bilirubin.

In the past Rhesus (Rh) blood factor incompatibility between the mother and child was a major cause of kernicterus. An Rh-negative mother who was exposed to her fetus's Rh-positive blood during a previous pregnancy or delivery or who has accidentally received an Rh-positive blood transfusion has antibodies against Rh-positive blood cells. These antibodies can circulate in her Rh-positive newborn, initiating hemolysis and causing severe abnormal jaundice.

Rare causes of severe neonatal jaundice

Jaundice can result from a congenital (present at birth) malformation of the liver, bile ducts, or gall bladder. Jaundice resulting from a congenital defect usually does not appear until the baby is at least ten days old. Biliary atresia—the underdevelopment, inflammation, or obstruction of the bile ducts that carry bile from the liver to the gall bladder and small intestine—causes bile to build up in the liver and forces the bilirubin into the blood. The cause of biliary atresia was as of 2004 unknown, and jaundice may not appear until the infant is two to six weeks old. Other symptoms of biliary atresia include:

- itching

- dark brown urine due to excess bilirubin excreted in the urine
- light-gray or chalky-colored stools from lack of bilirubin excreted by the intestines

Jaundice that develops or persists after the second week of life also can be due to the following:

- breast milk jaundice (prolonged jaundice resulting from breastfeeding) that occurs when a chemical in the mother's breast milk interferes with the infant liver's ability to process bilirubin
- liver malfunction or damaged liver cells
- an enzyme deficiency
- an abnormality of the red blood cells such as anemia
- blood hemorrhaging
- a blood infection (sepsis)
- a liver infection such as hepatitis virus
- toxoplasmosis, an infection caused by an animal parasite and transmitted to the fetus via an infected mother (House cats can be carriers of toxoplasmosis.)
- an infection anywhere in the body that impairs the efficiency of the liver, including neonatal **herpes simplex** or salmonella

Such infections may be congenital, having been passed from the mother to the fetus, or may occur after birth.

Other causes of jaundice

There are numerous other causes of neonatal and childhood jaundice, including the following:

- liver cell damage resulting from a variety of conditions such as a viral infection, an adverse drug reaction, or drugs or other chemicals that damage the liver (Jaundice can be a late symptom of hepatitis in an older baby or child.)
- hemolytic jaundice caused by hemolytic anemia, in which red blood cells are turned over faster than usual
- Hodgkin's disease in teenagers

Symptoms accompanying jaundice caused by liver cell damage may include:

- nausea
- vomiting
- abdominal pain
- swollen abdomen

When to call the doctor

A doctor should be consulted any time a child develops jaundice. Infants who are discharged from the hospital before bilirubin levels begin to rise, about three days after birth, should have their bilirubin level tested within a few days, particularly if they were preterm infants. Infants who become lethargic or reluctant to feed should be examined immediately, because symptoms can be signs of severe hyperbilirubinemia that can cause brain damage.

Diagnosis

Newborns are examined under good light for signs of jaundice. A simple blood test, with a few drops of blood taken from the infant's heel, measures bilirubin levels in the blood. The test may be repeated frequently in a jaundiced newborn to assure that bilirubin levels are dropping. An instrument called a bilirubinometer can be held against the baby's skin to assess the level of jaundice. The Minolta/Hill-Rom Air-Shields Transcutaneous Jaundice Meter accurately measures bilirubin levels by shining lights of different colors through the skin and measuring the reflection, eliminating the need for blood tests via heel pricks.

If there is reason to believe that the newborn is suffering from an abnormal jaundice, additional tests must be performed. These include:

- blood cell counts to detect anemia
- tests for blood clotting function
- tests for excess destruction of red blood cells
- blood tests to assess liver function
- a liver biopsy, in which liver cells are removed and examined under a microscope to look for liver disease
- urine and stool samples to check for signs of bacterial or viral infection

Breast milk jaundice due to a reaction with a breast milk component is suspected when the more common causes of jaundice have been ruled out.

Biliary atresia must be detected before two months of age to prevent further liver damage. Diagnoses of biliary atresia and other liver conditions are made by imaging techniques, including the following:

- ultrasound scanning, which uses sound waves to obtain images of the liver, gallbladder, and biliary tract (Abdominal ultrasound can distinguish between jaundice caused by biliary atresia and jaundice caused by liver malfunction.)
- magnetic resonance imaging (MRI) of the liver
- computed tomography (CT) or computed axial tomography (CAT) scans, which use a thin, rotating x-ray beam to obtain an image
- endoscopic retrograde cholangiopancreatography (ERCP), in which a radiopaque dye that is visible on **x rays** is inserted into the upper portion of the small intestine so that it flows back up the biliary tract
- liver scans using radioactive dyes

Treatment

Neonatal jaundice usually requires only observation. The infant may stay in the hospital for an extra day or return within the next few days for an examination. However, jaundice in a preterm baby may require intensive care. As the infant's liver matures and the excess blood cells are removed, the jaundice disappears. The child may be given additional fluids, possibly intravenously, to help remove the bilirubin. Frequent feedings lead to more frequent stools, which reduces the reabsorption of bilirubin from the intestines into the blood. Breast milk usually is considered superior to water or formula for relieving jaundice because breast milk produces stool with every feeding, thereby excreting bilirubin. Breastfeeding should not be discontinued because of neonatal jaundice.

If an infant's bilirubin levels are quite high or rising rapidly, phototherapy can prevent complications. The child is undressed and placed in a lighted incubator to stay warm. A high-intensity, cool, blue-fluorescent light is absorbed by the bilirubin and converts it into a harmless form than can be excreted in the bile and urine. An eye shield protects the baby's eyes. The infant is removed from the incubator for feeding. Other phototherapy methods—such as a fiber optic bilirubin blanket—incorporate the light into a blanket so that the child can be breastfed during treatment or treated at home. Phototherapy is continued until bilirubin levels have returned to normal, usually within a few days.

Side effects of phototherapy may include:

- loose stools
- rash
- dehydration
- sleepiness
- disinterest in breastfeeding

If bilirubin approaches a dangerous level, an exchange blood transfusion is used to rapidly lower it. A catheter is placed into the umbilical vein at the cut surface of the umbilical cord, and the newborn's blood is replaced with an equal volume of new blood. Rh incompatibility also may be treated by exchange transfusion.

Antibiotics may be used to prevent or treat a suspected infection in jaundiced infants. Babies with very severe jaundice have their hearing tested and are monitored for several months.

Surgery for biliary atresia must be performed within the first few weeks of an infant's life to prevent fatal liver damage. About 40–50 percent of infants with biliary atresia are candidates for replacement bile ducts leading from the liver into the intestine. Called the Kasai procedure or hepatoportoenterostomy, the obstructed ducts are replaced with sections from the infant's intestines. Infants with a duct obstruction within the liver itself usually require a liver transplant by the age of two.

Prolonged breast-milk jaundice may require breastfeeding to be halted for a few days until bilirubin levels drop. The breasts should be pumped in the interim so that the mother does not stop producing milk and breastfeeding can be resumed.

Prognosis

Neonatal jaundice disappears after one to two weeks. It may last slightly longer in breastfed infants. The jaundice does not harm the infant in any way, and breastfeeding should not be discontinued.

Severe untreated jaundice leading to kernicterus may result in the following:

- mental retardation
- cerebral palsy
- deafness
- death

Untreated biliary atresia leads to biliary cirrhosis, a progressive, irreversible scarring of the liver, by about two months of age. About 50 percent of bile duct replacement surgeries are successful, and the jaundice usually disappears within several weeks. Despite this success, the liver damage often progresses on to cirrhosis.

Breast-milk jaundice, resulting from a reaction to a breast milk component, is not dangerous. The baby's liver soon adapts to the problem and the jaundice disappears.

Prevention

In 2004 the American Academy of Pediatrics issued revised guidelines for identifying and managing neonatal jaundice. They recommend:

KEY TERMS

Antibody—A special protein made by the body's immune system as a defense against foreign material (bacteria, viruses, etc.) that enters the body. It is uniquely designed to attack and neutralize the specific antigen that triggered the immune response.

Bile—A bitter yellow-green substance produced by the liver. Bile breaks down fats in the small intestine so that they can be used by the body. It is stored in the gallbladder and passes from the gallbladder through the common bile duct to the top of the small intestine (duodenum) as needed to digest fat.

Bile ducts—Tubes that carry bile, a thick yellow-green fluid that is made by the liver, stored in the gallbladder, and helps the body digest fats.

Biliary atresia—An obstruction or inflammation of a bile duct that causes bilirubin to back up into the liver.

Bilirubin—A reddish yellow pigment formed from the breakdown of red blood cells, and metabolized by the liver. When levels are abnormally high, it causes the yellowish tint to eyes and skin known as jaundice. Levels of bilirubin in the blood increase in patients with liver disease, blockage of the bile ducts, and other conditions.

Hemolysis—The process of breaking down of red blood cells. As the cells are destroyed, hemoglobin, the component of red blood cells which carries the oxygen, is liberated.

Hyperbilirubinemia—A condition characterized by a high level of bilirubin in the blood. Bilirubin is a natural byproduct of the breakdown of red blood cells, however, a high level of bilirubin may indicate a problem with the liver.

Kernicterus—A potentially lethal disease of newborns caused by excessive accumulation of the bile pigment bilirubin in tissues of the central nervous system.

Phototherapy—Another name for light therapy in mainstream medical practice.

- that all newborns be assessed for their risk of developing severe jaundice, including measuring bilirubin levels before hospital discharge
- a follow-up visit occur within three to five days after birth when bilirubin levels are likely to peak

- breastfeeding a newborn at least eight to 12 times per day, since effective breastfeeding significantly reduces the risk of hyperbilirubinemia
- that parents be provided with written and oral information about the risks of neonatal jaundice

In cases of known Rh incompatibility, the mother is given an injection of RhoGAM, an immune globulin preparation, at about 28 weeks of pregnancy and again immediately after the child's birth. This destroys any Rh-positive fetal blood cells in the mother's circulation before her immune system can produce antibodies against them.

Parental concerns

Parents should examine their infant in natural daylight and under fluorescent lighting for signs of jaundice. Jaundice may be harder to see in infants with darker skin. However, when a child's nose and forehead are pressed gently, the skin is white in healthy babies of all races, but yellowish if jaundice is present. If the skin appears yellow, the test should be repeated on the chest or abdomen. Parents also should be aware of symptoms that may accompany jaundice, including fussiness, unusual sleepiness, or difficulty feeding.

Mothers who are having difficulty breastfeeding should seek help. Although breast milk is an effective treatment for jaundice, breastfed babies may receive fewer calories than formula-fed babies during the first days of life, causing bilirubin levels to rise.

Resources

BOOKS

Maisels, M. Jeffrey, and Jon F. Watchko, eds. *Neonatal Jaundice*. Amsterdam: Harwood Academic, 2000.

PERIODICALS

Blackmon, Lillian R., et al. "Research on Prevention of Bilirubin-Induced Brain Injury and Kernicterus: National Institute of Child Health and Human Development Conference Executive Summary." *Pediatrics* 114, no. 1 (July 2004): 229.

Johnston, Carden. "Help for Newborn Jaundice." *Baby Talk* 69, no. 6 (August 2004): 18.

"Management of Hyperbilirubinemia in the Newborn Infant 35 or More Weeks of Gestation." *Pediatrics* 114 (2004): 297–316.

Obstetrics Hospitals Need to Improve Jaundice Monitoring, Commission Says. *Science Letter* (September 21, 2004): 936.

Payne, Doug. "Skin Meter Detects Jaundice." *Medical Post* (Toronto) 40, no. 32 (August 24, 2004): 35.

ORGANIZATIONS

American Academy of Pediatrics. 141 Northwest Point Boulevard, Elk Grove Village, IL 60007–1098. Web site: <www.aap.org>.

American Liver Foundation. 75 Maiden Lane, Suite 603, New York, NY 10038. Web site: <www.liverfoundation.org>.

WEB SITES

"Questions and Answers: Jaundice and Your Newborn." *American Academy of Pediatrics*, June 25, 2004. Available online at <www.aap.org/family/jaundicefaq.htm> (accessed January 11, 2005).

"What is Biliary Atresia?" *American Liver Foundation.* Available online at <www.liverfoundation.org/db/articles/1012> (accessed January 11, 2005).

Margaret Alic, PhD

Jaundice test *see* **Bilirubin test**

Jock itch *see* **Ringworm**

Juvenile arthritis

Definition

Juvenile arthritis (JA) refers to a number of different conditions, all of which strike children and all of which have joint inflammation as their major manifestation. The condition is also referred to as juvenile rheumatoid arthritis.

Description

The skeletal system of the body is made up of different types of the strong, fibrous tissue known as connective tissue. Bone, cartilage, ligaments, and tendons are all forms of connective tissue which have different compositions and different characteristics.

The joints are structures that hold two or more bones together. Some joints (synovial joints) allow for movement between the bones being joined (called articulating bones). The simplest model of a synovial joint involves two bones, separated by a slight gap called the joint cavity. The ends of each articular bone are covered by a layer of cartilage. Both articular bones and the joint cavity are surrounded by a tough tissue called the articular capsule. The articular capsule has two components: the fibrous membrane on the outside and the synovial membrane (or synovium) on the inside. The fibrous membrane may include tough bands of fibrous tissue called ligaments, which are responsible for providing support to the joints. The synovial membrane has special cells and many capillaries (tiny blood vessels). This membrane produces a supply of synovial fluid which fills the joint cavity, lubricates it, and helps the articular bones move smoothly about the joint.

In JA, the synovial membrane becomes intensely inflamed. Usually thin and delicate, the synovium becomes thick and stiff, with numerous infoldings on its surface. The membrane becomes invaded by white blood cells, which produce a variety of destructive chemicals. The cartilage along the articular surfaces of the bones may be attacked and destroyed, and the bone, articular capsule, and ligaments may begin to be worn away (eroded). These processes severely interfere with movement in the joint.

JA specifically refers to chronic arthritic conditions which affect a child under the age of 16 years and which last for a minimum of three to six months. JA is often characterized by a waxing and waning course, with flares separated by periods during which no symptoms are noted (remission). Some literature refers to JA as juvenile rheumatoid arthritis, although most types of JA differ significantly from the adult disease called rheumatoid arthritis, in terms of symptoms, progression, and prognosis.

Demographics

Between five and 18 of every 100,000 children develop juvenile rheumatoid arthritis each year; the overall prevalence is approximately 30–150 per 100,000. More than 65,000 young people in the United States develop it each year. It can affect children as young as two years of age.

Causes and symptoms

A number of different causes have been sought to explain the onset of JA. There seems to be some genetic link, based on the fact that the tendency to develop JA sometimes runs in a particular **family** and based on the fact that certain genetic markers are more frequently found in patients with JA and other related diseases. Many researchers have looked for some infectious cause for JA, but no clear connection to a particular organism had been made as of 2004. JA is considered by some to be an autoimmune disorder. Autoimmune disorders occur when the body's immune system mistakenly identifies the body's own tissue as foreign and goes about

attacking those tissues, as if trying to rid the body of an invader (such as a bacteria, virus, or fungi). While an autoimmune mechanism is strongly suspected, certain markers of such a mechanism (such as rheumatoid factor, often present in adults with such disorders) are rarely present in children with JA.

Joint symptoms of arthritis may include stiffness, **pain**, redness and warmth of the joint, and swelling. Bone in the area of an affected joint may grow too quickly or too slowly resulting in limbs which are of different lengths. When the child tries to avoid moving a painful joint, the muscle may begin to shorten from disuse. This condition is called a contracture.

Symptoms of JA depend on the particular subtype. JA is classified by the symptoms which appear within the first six months of the disorder:

- Pauciarticular JA: The most common and the least severe type of JA affects about 40–60 percent of all JA patients. This type of JA affects fewer than four joints, usually the knee, ankle, wrist, and/or elbow. Other more general (systemic) symptoms are usually absent, and the child's growth usually remains normal. Very few children (fewer than 15 percent) with pauciarticular JA end up with deformed joints. Some children with this form of JA experience painless swelling of the joint. Some children with JA have a serious inflammation of structures within the eye, which if left undiagnosed and untreated could even lead to blindness. While many children have cycles of flares and remissions, in some children the disease completely and permanently resolves within a few years of diagnosis.

- Polyarticular JA: About 40 percent of all cases of JA are of this type. More girls than boys are diagnosed with this form of JA, and it is most common in children up to age three or after the age of ten. Polyarticular JA affects five or more joints simultaneously. This type of JA usually affects the small joints of both hands and both feet, although other large joints may be affected as well. Some patients with arthritis in their knees will experience a different rate of growth in each leg. Ultimately, one leg will grow longer than the other. About half of all patients with polyarticular JA have arthritis of the spine and/or hip. Some patients with polyarticular JA will have other symptoms of a systemic illness, including anemia (low red blood cell count), decreased growth rate, low appetite, low-grade **fever**, and a slight rash. The disease is most severe in those children who are diagnosed in early **adolescence**. Some of these children test positive for a marker present in other autoimmune disorders, called rheumatoid factor (RF), which is found in adults who have rheuma-

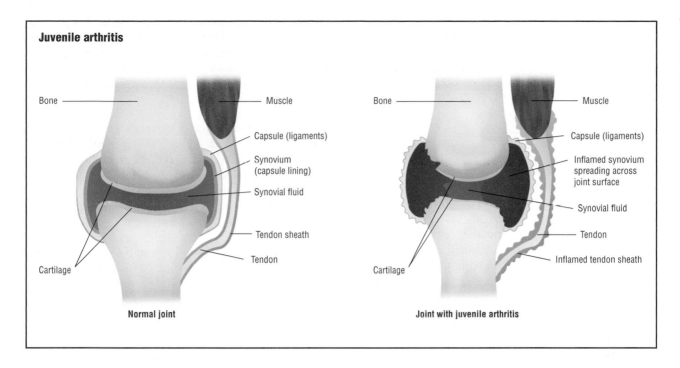

Juvenile arthritis

Normal joint

Bone — Muscle

Capsule (ligaments)

Synovium (capsule lining)

Synovial fluid

Tendon sheath

Tendon

Cartilage

Joint with juvenile arthritis

Bone — Muscle

Capsule (ligaments)

Inflamed synovium spreading across joint surface

Synovial fluid

Tendon

Inflamed tendon sheath

Cartilage

Normal knee joint (left) and one affected by juvenile arthritis, which shows damaged cartilage and inflammation of the synovial fluid and tendon sheath. *(Illustration by GGS Information Services.)*

toid arthritis. Children who are positive for RF tend to have a more severe course, with a disabling form of arthritis that destroys and deforms the joints. This type of arthritis is thought to be the adult form of rheumatoid arthritis occurring at a very early age.

- Systemic onset JA: Sometimes called Still disease (after a physician who originally described it), this type of JA occurs in about 10–20 percent off all patients with JA. Boys and girls are equally affected, and diagnosis is usually made between the ages of five and 10 years. The initial symptoms are not usually related to the joints. Instead, these children have high fevers; a rash; decreased appetite and weight loss; severe joint and muscle pain; swollen lymph nodes, spleen, and liver; and serious anemia. Some children experience other complications, including inflammation of the sac containing the heart (pericarditis); inflammation of the tissue lining the chest cavity and lungs (pleuritis); and inflammation of the heart muscle (myocarditis). The eye inflammation often seen in pauciarticular JA is uncommon in systemic onset JA. Symptoms of actual arthritis begin later in the course of systemic onset JA, and they often involve the wrists and ankles. Many of these children continue to have periodic flares of fever and systemic symptoms throughout childhood. Some children go on to develop a polyarticular type of JA.

- Spondyloarthropathy: This type of JA most commonly affects boys older than eight years of age. The arthritis occurs in the knees and ankles, moving over time to include the hips and lower spine. Inflammation of the eye may occur occasionally but usually resolves without permanent damage.

- Psoriatic JA: This type of arthritis usually shows up in fewer than four joints but goes on to include multiple joints (appearing similar to polyarticular JA). Hips, back, fingers, and toes are frequently affected. A skin condition called **psoriasis** accompanies this type of arthritis. Children with this type of JA often have pits or ridges in their fingernails. The arthritis usually progresses to become a serious, disabling problem.

When to call the doctor

A pediatrician, family physician, or other primary care doctor frequently manages the treatment of a child with JA, often with the help of other doctors. Depending on the patient's and parents' wishes and the severity of the disease, the team of doctors may include pediatric rheumatologists (doctors specializing in childhood arthritis), ophthalmologists (eye doctors), orthopaedic surgeons (bone specialists), and physiatrists (rehabilitation specialists), as well as physical and occupational therapists. The main goals of treatment are to preserve a high level of physical and social functioning and maintain a good quality of life. To achieve these goals, doctors recommend treatments to reduce swelling; maintain full movement in the affected joints; relieve pain; and identify, treat, and prevent complications. Most children with JA need medication and physical therapy to reach these goals.

Diagnosis

Diagnosis of JA is often made on the basis of the child's collection of symptoms. Laboratory tests often show normal results. Some nonspecific indicators of inflammation may be elevated, including white blood cell count, erythrocyte sedimentation rate, and a marker called C-reactive protein. As with any chronic disease, anemia may be noted. Children with an extraordinarily early onset of the adult type of rheumatoid arthritis have a positive test for rheumatoid factor.

Treatment

Treating JA involves efforts to decrease the amount of inflammation in order to preserve movement. Medications which can be used for this include nonsteroidal anti-inflammatory agents (such as ibuprofen and naproxen). Oral (by mouth) steroid medications are effective but have many serious side effects with long-term use. Injections of steroids into an affected joint can be helpful. Steroid eye drops are used to treat eye inflammation. Other drugs that have been used to treat JA include methotrexate, sulfasalazine, penicillamine, and hydroxychloroquine. Physical therapy and exercises are often recommended in order to improve joint mobility and to strengthen supporting muscles. Occasionally, splints are used to rest painful joints and to try to prevent or reduce deformities.

Alternative treatment

Alternative treatments that have been suggested for arthritis include juice therapy, which can work to detoxify the body, helping to reduce JA symptoms. Some recommended fruits and vegetables to include in the juice are carrots, celery, cabbage, potatoes, cherries, lemons, beets, cucumbers, radishes, and garlic. However, for children with osteoarthritis, citrus fruits and vegetables from the nightshade family, including potatoes, tomatoes, peppers, and eggplant, should be avoided since they can promote swelling. As an adjunct therapy, aromatherapy preparations use cypress, fennel, and lemon. Massage oils include rosemary, benzoin, chamomile, camphor, juniper, and lavender. Other types of therapy that have been used for JA include acupuncture, acupressure, and bodywork. Nutritional supplements that may be ben-

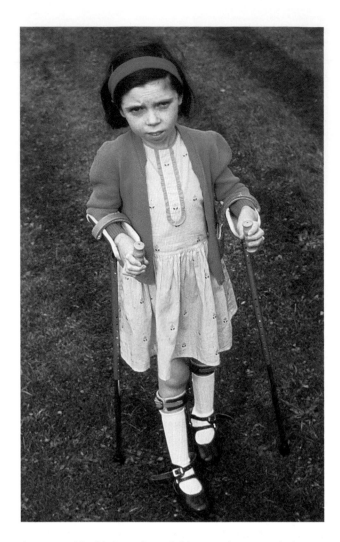

A young girl with juvenile arthritis uses braces to help rest painful joints and prevent deformities. (© John Moss/Photo Researchers, Inc.)

eficial include large amounts of antioxidants (**vitamins** C, A, E, zinc, selenium, and flavenoids), as well as B vitamins and a full complement of **minerals** (including boron, copper, and manganese). Other nutrients that assist in detoxifying the body, including methionine, cysteine, and other amino acids, may also be helpful. A number of autoimmune disorders, including JA, seem to have a relationship to **food allergies**. Identification and elimination of reactive foods may result in a decrease in JA symptoms. Constitutional homeopathy can also work to quiet the symptoms of JA and bring about balance to the whole person.

Nutritional concerns

When female patients were compared to age-matched normals, greater than one serving per week of grilled (broiled) or baked fish (other than tuna) was associated with a decreased risk of disease. This inverse association was stronger than that for omega-3 fatty acid intake alone. In another study, patients with active disease randomly received treatment with or without a diet in which the energy consumption was adjusted to normal standards for body-weight, and the intake of fish and antioxidants was increased. After six months, those following the diet demonstrated significant improvement in the duration of morning stiffness, the number of swollen joints, and pain status.

Several studies, some of which were controlled, have found beneficial effects from a vegetarian or vegan diet. In one study, for example, patients randomly received either an uncooked vegan diet or a control diet for three months. Those on the vegan diet experienced subjective relief of rheumatic stiffness and joint swellings and an improvement in general wellbeing. After returning to the meat diet, these symptoms worsened. The degree of tender joints remained unchanged in controls, but in the diet group their number decreased significantly.

Prognosis

The prognosis for pauciarticular JA is quite good, as is the prognosis for spondyloarthropathy. Polyarticular JA carries a slightly worse prognosis. RF-positive polyarticular JA carries a difficult prognosis, often with progressive, destructive arthritis and joint deformities. Systemic onset JA has a variable prognosis, depending on the organ systems affected and the progression to polyarticular JA. About 1–5 percent of all JA patients die of such complications as infection, inflammation of the heart, or kidney disease.

Prevention

Because so little is known about what causes JA, there are no recommendations available for ways to avoid developing it.

Parental concerns

JA affects the entire family who must cope with the special challenges of this disease. JA can strain a child's participation in social and after-school activities and make schoolwork more difficult. There are several things that family members can do to help the child do well physically and emotionally. These include the following:

- Ensure that the child receives appropriate medical care and follows the doctor's instructions. Many treat-

---

KEY TERMS

Articular bones—Two or more bones that are connected to each other via a joint.

Joint—The connection point where two bones meet.

Synovial joint—A fully moveable joint in which a synovial cavity is present between two articulating bones. Also called a diarthrosis.

Synovial membrane—The membrane that lines the inside of the articular capsule of a joint, and produces a lubricating fluid called synovial fluid.

---

ment options are available, and because JA is different in each child, what works for one may not work for another. If the medications that the doctor prescribes do not relieve symptoms or if they cause unpleasant side effects, patients and parents should discuss other choices with their doctor. A person with JA can be more active when symptoms are controlled.

- Encourage **exercise** and physical therapy for the child. For many young people, exercise and physical therapy play important roles in treating JA. Parents can arrange for children to participate in activities that the doctor recommends. During symptom-free periods, many doctors suggest playing team **sports** or doing other activities to help keep the joints strong and flexible and to provide play time with other children and encourage appropriate social development.

- Work closely with the school to develop a suitable lesson plan for the child and to educate the teacher and the child's classmates about JA. Some children with JA may be absent from school for prolonged periods and need to have the teacher send assignments home. Some minor changes such as an extra set of books or leaving class a few minutes early to get to the next class on time can be a great help. With proper attention, most children progress normally through school.

- Treat the child as normally as possible. Explain to the child that getting JA is nobody's fault. Some children believe that JA is a punishment for something they did. Consider joining a support group. The American Juvenile Arthritis Organization runs support groups for people with JA and their families. Support group meetings provide the chance to talk to other young people and parents of children with JA and may help a child and the family cope with the condition.

Resources

BOOKS

Gray, Susan H., and Serge Bloch. *Living with Juvenile Rheumatoid Arthritis.* Chanhassen, MN: Child's World, 2002.

The Official Patient's Sourcebook on Juvenile Rheumatoid Arthritis: A Revised and Updated Directory for the Internet Age. San Diego, CA: Icon Health Publications, 2002.

PERIODICALS

Boschert, Sherry. "Subtle Juvenile Rheumatoid Arthritis May Be More Common Than Thought." *Pediatric News* 37 (April 2003): 36.

Brunk, Doug. "When a Limp Signals Something More Serious: Make Sure to Examine the Hips." *Family Practice News* 34 (May 15, 2004): 50–51.

Labyak, Susan E., et al. "Sleep Quality in Children with Juvenile Rheumatoid Arthritis." *Holistic Nursing Practice* 17 (July-August 2003): 193–200.

ORGANIZATIONS

American Juvenile Arthritis Organization. 1330 West Peachtree St., Atlanta, GA 30309. Web site: <www.arthritis.org>.

National Institute of Arthritis and Musculoskeletal and Skin Diseases. 1 AMS Circle, Bethesda, MD 20892–3675. Web site: <www.niams.nih.gov/>.

WEB SITES

"Juvenile Rheumatoid Arthritis." *KidsHealth*, November 2001. Available online at <http://kidshealth.org/parent/medical/arthritis/jra.html> (accessed November 10, 2004).

"Types of Juvenile Arthritis." *Arthritis Foundation*, 2004. Available online at <www.arthritis.org/conditions/DiseaseCenter/typesofJA.asp> (accessed November 10, 2004).

Rosalyn S. Carson-DeWitt
Ken R. Wells

Kawasaki syndrome

Definition

Kawasaki syndrome is a potentially fatal inflammatory disease that affects several organ systems in the body, including the heart, circulatory system, mucous membranes, skin, and immune system. As of 2004 its cause was unknown.

Description

In the 1960s, Tomisaku Kawasaki noted a characteristic cluster of symptoms in Japanese schoolchildren. Ultimately named for Kawasaki, the disorder was subsequently found worldwide. Kawasaki syndrome, also called mucocutaneous lymph node syndrome (MLNS), is an inflammatory disorder with potentially fatal complications affecting the heart and its larger arteries.

Demographics

Kawasaki syndrome occurs primarily in infants and children; about 80 percent of diagnosed patients are under the age of five. On rare occasions, the disorder has been diagnosed in teenagers or adults. Nearly twice as many males are affected as females. Although persons of Asian descent are affected more frequently than either black or white individuals, there does not appear to be a distinctive geographic pattern of occurrence. Although the disease usually appears in individuals, it sometimes affects several members of the same **family** and occasionally occurs in small epidemics. About 3,000 cases are diagnosed annually in the United States.

Causes and symptoms

The specific cause of Kawasaki syndrome was as of 2004 unknown, although the disease resembles an infectious illness in many ways. It has been suggested that Kawasaki syndrome represents an allergic reaction or other unusual response to certain types of infections. Some researchers think that the syndrome may be caused by the interaction of an immune cell, called the T cell, with certain poisons (toxins) secreted by bacteria.

Kawasaki syndrome has an abrupt onset, with **fever** as high as 104°F (40°C) and a rash that spreads over the patient's chest and genital area. The fever is followed by a characteristic peeling of the skin beginning at the fingertips and toenails. In addition to the body rash, the patient's lips become very red, with the tongue developing a "strawberry" appearance. The palms, soles, and mucous membranes that line the eyelids and cover the exposed portion of the eyeball (conjuntivae) become purplish-red and swollen. The lymph nodes in the patient's neck may also become swollen. These symptoms may last from two weeks to three months, with relapses in some patients.

In addition to the major symptoms, about 30 percent of patients develop joint **pain** or arthritis, usually in the large joints of the body. Others develop **pneumonia, diarrhea**, dry or cracked lips, **jaundice**, or an inflammation of the membranes covering the brain and spinal cord (**meningitis**). A few patients develop symptoms of inflammation in the liver (hepatitis), gallbladder, lungs, or tonsils.

About 20 percent of patients with Kawasaki syndrome develop complications of the cardiovascular system. These complications include inflammation of the heart tissue (myocarditis), disturbances in heartbeat rhythm (arrhythmias), and areas of blood vessel dilation (aneurysms) in the coronary arteries. Other patients may develop inflammation of an artery (arteritis) in their arms or legs. Complications of the heart or arteries begin to develop around the tenth day after the illness begins, when the fever and rash begin to subside. A few patients may develop gangrene (the death of soft tissue) in their hands and feet. The specific causes of these complications were as of 2004 not known.

Diagnosis

Because Kawasaki syndrome is primarily a disease of infants and young children, the disease is most likely to be diagnosed by a pediatrician. The physician will first consider the possible involvement of other diseases that cause fever and skin **rashes**, including **scarlet fever**, **measles**, **Rocky Mountain spotted fever**, **toxoplasmosis** (a disease carried by cats), juvenile rheumatoid arthritis, and a blistering and inflammation of the skin caused by reactions to certain medications (Stevens-Johnson syndrome).

Once other diseases have been ruled out, the patient's symptoms will be compared with a set of diagnostic criteria. The patient must have a fever lasting five days or longer that does not respond to **antibiotics**, together with four of the following five symptoms:

- inflammation of the conjunctivae of both eyes with no discharge
- at least one of the following changes in the mucous membranes of the mouth and throat: "strawberry" tongue, cracked lips, or swollen throat tissues
- at least one of the following changes in the hands or feet: swelling caused by excess fluid in the tissues, peeling of the skin, or abnormal redness of the skin
- a skin eruption or rash associated with fever (exanthem) on the patient's trunk
- swelling of the lymph nodes in the neck to a size greater than 1.5 cm

Given the unknown cause of this syndrome, there are no laboratory tests that can confirm the diagnosis. The following test results, however, are associated with the disease:

- Blood tests show a high white blood cell count, high **platelet count**, a high level of protein in the blood serum, and mild anemia.
- A chest x ray may show enlargement of the heart (cardiomegaly).
- Urine may show the presence of pus or an abnormally high level of protein.
- An electrocardiogram may show changes in the heartbeat rhythm.

In addition to these tests, it is important to take a series of echocardiograms during the course of the illness because 20 percent of Kawasaki patients develop coronary aneurysms or arteritis that will not appear during the first examination.

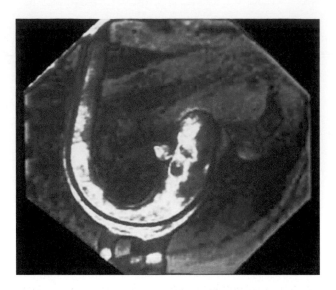

An angiogram showing abnormal coronary arteries in a child suffering from Kawasaki's disease. The coronary arteries bulge into balloon shapes, called aneurysms, along their lengths. *(Photograph by Mehau Kulyk. Photo Researchers, Inc.)*

Treatment

Kawasaki syndrome is usually treated with a combination of aspirin, to control the patient's fever and skin inflammation, and high doses of intravenous immune globulin to reduce the possibility of coronary artery complications. Some patients with heart complications may be treated with drugs that reduce blood clotting or may receive corrective surgery.

Follow-up care includes two to three months of monitoring with chest **x rays**, electrocardiography, and echocardiography. Treatment with aspirin is often continued for several months.

Prognosis

Most patients with Kawasaki syndrome will recover completely, but about 1–2 percent die as a result of blood clots forming in the coronary arteries or as a result of a heart attack. Deaths are sudden and unpredictable. Almost 95 percent of fatalities occur within six months of infection, but some have been reported as long as 10 years afterward. Long-term follow-up of patients with aneurysms indicates that about half show some healing of the aneurysm. The remaining half has a high risk of heart complications in later life.

Parental concerns

It is important that parents of children diagnosed with Kawasaki syndrome follow recommended treatments and follow-up care for the disease, because of the

KEY TERMS

Aneurysm—A weakened area in the wall of a blood vessel which causes an outpouching or bulge. Aneurysms may be fatal if these weak areas burst, resulting in uncontrollable bleeding.

Arrhythmia—Any deviation from a normal heart beat.

Arteritis—Inflammation of an artery.

Cardiomegaly—An enlarged heart.

Conjunctiva—Plural, conjunctivae. The mucous membrane that covers the white part of the eyes (sclera) and lines the eyelids.

Exanthem—A skin eruption associated with a disease, usually one accompanied by fever as in Kawasaki syndrome.

Gangrene—Decay or death of body tissue because the blood supply is cut off. Tissues that have died in this way must be surgically removed.

Hepatitis—An inflammation of the liver, with accompanying liver cell damage or cell death, caused most frequently by viral infection, but also by certain drugs, chemicals, or poisons. May be either acute (of limited duration) or chronic (contin-

uing). Symptoms include jaundice, nausea, vomiting, loss of appetite, tenderness in the right upper abdomen, aching muscles, and joint pain. In severe cases, liver failure may result.

Meningitis—An infection or inflammation of the membranes that cover the brain and spinal cord. It is usually caused by bacteria or a virus.

Mucocutaneous lymph node syndrome (MLNS)—Another name for Kawasaki syndrome. The name comes from the key symptoms of the disease, which involve the mucous membranes of the mouth and throat, the skin, and the lymph nodes. MLNS is a potentially fatal inflammatory disease of unknown cause.

Myocarditis—Inflammation of the heart muscle (myocardium).

Stevens-Johnson syndrome—A severe inflammatory skin eruption that occurs as a result of an allergic reaction or respiratory infection.

T cell—A type of white blood cell that is produced in the bone marrow and matured in the thymus gland. It helps to regulate the immune system's response to infections or malignancy.

risk of potentially serious complications. Any worsening or unexplained new symptoms should be reported to the treating pediatrician.

Resources

BOOKS

Rowland, Anne. "Bacteria: Diseases of Possible Infectious or Unknown Etiology." In *Principles and Practice of Pediatric Infectious Diseases*, 2nd ed. Edited by Sarah S. Long et al. St. Louis, MO: Elsevier, 2003.

Rowley, Anne H., and Stanford T. Shulman. "Kawasaki Disease." In *Nelson Textbook of Pediatrics*. Edited by Richard E. Behrman et al. Philadelphia: Saunders, 2004.

WEB SITES

"Kawasaki Syndrome (mucocutaneous lymph node syndrome)." *South Dakota Department of Health*, November 18, 2004. Available online at <sss.state.sd.us/doh/Pubs/Kawasaki.htm> (accessed December 29, 2004).

Rebecca J. Frey, PhD
Rosalyn Carson-DeWitt, MD

Klinefelter syndrome

Definition

Klinefelter syndrome is a chromosome disorder in males that results in **hypogonadism** (small penis and small firm testicles). People with this condition are born with at least one extra X chromosome.

Description

Klinefelter syndrome is a condition where one or more extra X-chromosomes are present in a male. Boys with this condition appear normal at birth, but the defect becomes apparent in **puberty** when secondary sexual characteristics fail to develop, or develop later. By mid-puberty, boys with Klinefelter syndrome have low levels of testosterone, resulting in small testicles and the inability to make sperm. Affected males may also have learning disabilities and behavior problems such as **shyness** and immaturity and at an increased risk for certain other health problems such as pulmonary disease, varicose veins, breast **cancer**, extragonadal germ cell tumor (a rare tumor), and osteoporosis. Some mild cases may be undetected, with no abnormalities present except infertility.

Demographics

Klinefelter syndrome is one of the most common chromosomal abnormalities. About 1 in every 500 to 800 males is born with this disorder. Approximately 3% of the infertile male population have Klinefelter syndrome.

Causes and symptoms

Normally, a person has a total of 46 chromosomes in each cell, two of which are responsible for determining that individual's sex. These two sex chromosomes are called X and Y. The combination of these two types of chromosomes determines the sex of a child. Females have two X chromosomes (the XX combination); males have one X and one Y chromosome (the XY combination).

In Klinefelter syndrome, a problem very early in fetal development results in an abnormal number of chromosomes. Most commonly, a male with Klinefelter syndrome will be born with 47 chromosomes in each cell, rather than the normal number of 46. The extra chromosome is an X chromosome. This means that rather than having the normal XY combination, the male has an XXY combination. Because people with Klinefelter syndrome have a Y chromosome, they are all male.

Approximately 1/3 of all males with Klinefelter syndrome have other chromosome changes involving an extra X chromosome. Mosaic Klinefelter syndrome occurs when some of the cells in the body have an extra X chromosome and the other have normal male chromosomes. These males can have the same or milder symptoms than those with non-mosaic Klinefelter syndrome. Males with more than one additional extra X chromosome, such as 48,XXXY, are usually more severely affected than males with 47,XXY.

Klinefelter syndrome is not considered an inherited condition. The risk of Klinefelter syndrome reoccurring in another pregnancy for a woman who had a son with Klinefelter syndrome is not increased above the risk of the general population.

The symptoms of Klinefelter syndrome are variable; not every affected person will have all of the features of the condition. Males with Klinefelter syndrome appear normal at birth and have normal male genitalia. From childhood, males with Klinefelter syndrome are taller than average with long limbs. Approximately 20–50% have a mild intention tremor, an uncontrolled shaking. Many males with Klinefelter syndrome have poor upper

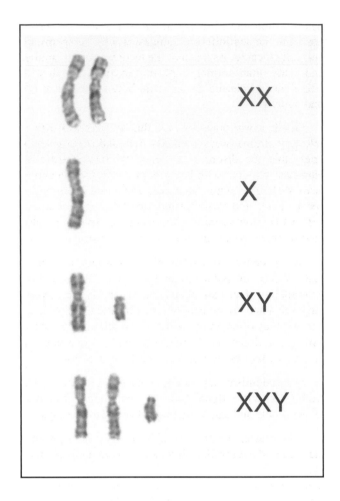

Sex chromosomes showing different phenotypes: XX–normal female; X–female with Turner syndrome; XY–normal male; and XXY–male with Klinefelter. *(Lerner & Lerner, LLC.)*

body strength and can be clumsy. Klinefelter syndrome does not cause **homosexuality**. Approximately 1/3 of males with Klinefelter syndrome have breast growth, some requiring breast reduction surgery.

Most boys enter puberty normally, though some can be delayed. The Leydig cells in the testicles usually produce testosterone. With Klinefelter syndrome, the Leydig cells fail to work properly causing the testosterone production to slow. By mid-puberty, testosterone production is decreased to approximately half of normal. This can lead to decreased facial and pubic hair growth. The decreased testosterone also causes an increase in two other hormones, follicle stimulating hormone (FSH) and luteinizing hormone (LH). Normally, FSH and LH help the immature sperm cells grown and develop. In Klinefelter syndrome, there are few or no sperm cells. The increased amount of FSH and LH cause hyalinization and fibrosis, the growth of excess fibrous tissue, in the seminiferous tubules, where the sperm are normally located. As a result, the testicles appear smaller and firmer than normal. With rare exception, men with Klinefelter syndrome are infertile because they can not make sperm.

While it was once believed that all boys with Klinefelter syndrome were mentally retarded, doctors now know that the disorder can exist without retardation. However, children with Klinefelter syndrome frequently have difficulty with language, including learning to speak, read, and write. Approximately 50% of males with Klinefelter syndrome are dyslexic. They may also have attention deficient hyperactivity disorder.

Some people with Klinefelter syndrome have difficulty with social skills and tend to be more shy, anxious, or immature than their peers. They can also have poor judgement and do not handle stressful situations well. As a result, they often do not feel comfortable in large social gatherings. Some people with Klinefelter syndrome can also have **anxiety**, nervousness and/or depression.

Taurodontism, an enlargement of the pulp of the teeth with surface thinning, is very common in Klinefelter syndrome and can be diagnosed with dental x rays.

The greater the number of X chromosomes present, the greater the disability. Boys with several extra X chromosomes have distinctive facial features, more severe retardation, deformities of bony structures, and even more disordered development of male features.

When to call the doctor

Parents should call a doctor if their son fails to develop secondary sexual characteristics at puberty.

Diagnosis

During a physical examination, a doctor will look for a simian crease (a single crease in the palm). A rectal exam may show an enlarged prostate. A single testicle may be present in the scrotum, indicating a probable undescended testicle. A semen examination will show low sperm count, while other tests will show decreased serum testosterone levels, increased levels of serum luteining and serum follicle stimulating hormones and increased serum estradiol levels (a type of estrogen).

Diagnosis of Klinefelter syndrome is confirmed by examining chromosomes for evidence of more than one X chromosome present in a male. This can be done in pregnancy with prenatal testing such as chorionic villus sampling or **amniocentesis**. Chorionic villus sampling is a procedure done early in pregnancy (approximately

10–12 weeks) to obtain a small sample of the placenta for testing. An amniocentesis is done further along in pregnancy (from approximately 16–18 weeks) to obtain a sample of fluid surrounding the baby for testing. Both procedures have a risk of miscarriage. Usually these procedures are done for a reason other than diagnosing Klinefelter syndrome. For example, a prenatal diagnostic procedure may be done on an older woman to determine if her baby has **Down syndrome**. If the diagnosis of Klinefelter syndrome is suspected in a young boy or adult male, chromosome testing can also be on a small blood or skin sample after birth.

Treatment

There is no treatment available to change chromosomal makeup. Children with Klinefelter syndrome may benefit from a speech therapist for speech problems or other educational intervention for learning disabilities. Testosterone injections started around the time of puberty and continued for life may help to produce more normal development, including more muscle mass, hair growth and increased sex drive. Testosterone supplementation will not increase testicular size, decrease breast growth or correct infertility.

Prognosis

While many men with Klinefelter syndrome live normal lives, nearly 100 percent of these men will be sterile (unable to produce a child). However, a few men with Klinefelter syndrome have been reported who have fathered a child through the use of assisted fertility services. Males with Klinefelter syndrome have an increased risk of several conditions such as osteoporosis, pulmonary disease, varicose veins, autoimmune disorders such as lupus and arthritis, diabetes, breast cancer and extragonadal germ cell tumor (a rare tumor).

Prevention

Klinefelter syndrome usually is not inherited but occurs during fetal development, so there is no means of preventing the disease. However, one risk factor for this condition is the mother giving birth at an older age; therefore, genetic counseling and testing is recommended.

Parental concerns

Families may wish to seek counseling regarding the effects of the syndrome on relationships within the **family**. Many people respond with guilt, **fear**, or

Klinefelter syndrome

KEY TERMS

Follicle-stimulating hormone (FSH)—A pituitary hormone that in females stimulates the ovary to mature egg capsules (follicles) and in males stimulates sperm production.

Luteinizing hormone—A hormone secreted by the pituitary gland that regulates the menstrual cycle and triggers ovulation in females. In males it stimulates the testes to produce testosterone.

Testosterone—Male hormone produced by the testes and (in small amounts) in the ovaries. Testosterone is responsible for some masculine secondary sex characteristics such as growth of body hair and deepening voice. It also is sometimes given as part of hormone replacement therapy to women whose ovaries have been removed.

blame when a genetic disorder is diagnosed in the family, or they may overprotect the affected member. Support groups are often good sources of information about Klinefelter syndrome; they can offer helpful suggestions about living with it as well as emotional support.

Resources

BOOKS

Bock, R. *Understanding Klinefelter's Syndrome: A Guide for XXY Males and Their Families.* Bethesda, MD: National Institutes of Health,1993.

Icon Health Publications. *Klinefelter's Syndrome: A Medical Dictionary, Bibliography, and Annotated Research Guide to Internet References.* San Diego, CA:Icon Health Publications, 2004.

Icon Health Publications. *The Official Parent's Sourcebook on Klinefelter Syndrome.* San Diego, CA:Icon Health Publications, 2002.

Probasco, Teri, and Gretchen A. Gibbs. *Klinefelter Syndrome.* Richmond, IN: Prinit Press, 1999.

ORGANIZATIONS

American Association for Klinefelter Syndrome Information and Support. 2945 West Farwell Avenue, Chicago, IL 60645-2925. (773) 761-5298, (800) 466-5747. <http://www.aaksis.org>

Klinefelter's Organisation. 234 Turton Road, Bolton, BL2 3EE, United Kingdom. <http://www.klinefelter.org.uk/>

Klinefelter Syndrome and Associates, Inc. PO Box 119, Roseville, CA 95678-0119. (916) 773-2999 or (888) 999-9428. Fax: (916) 773-1449. <http://www.genetic.org/ks>.

WEB SITES

Klinefelter Syndrome Support Group Home Page. <http://klinefeltersyndrome.org/index.html>

Judith Sims, MS
Carin Lea Beltz, MS

Kwashiorkor *see* **Protein-energy malnutrition**